ROBERT A. SCALAPINO is Robson Professor of Government and Director of the Institute of East Asian Studies at the University of California, Berkeley; he is the author of *Democracy and the Party Movement in Prewar Japan* (California, 1975) and co-author of *Communism in Korea* (California, 1973).

GEORGE T. YU is Professor of Political Science and Asian Studies at the University of Illinois; he is co-author (with Robert Scalapino) of *The Chinese Anarchist Movement* (1980) and author of *China's Africa Policy* (1975).

MODERN CHINA AND ITS REVOLUTIONARY PROCESS

Published Under the Auspices of
The Center for Chinese Studies
Institute of East Asian Studies
University of California, Berkeley

MODERN CHINA AND ITS REVOLUTIONARY PROCESS

RECURRENT CHALLENGES TO THE TRADITIONAL ORDER 1850-1920

Robert A. Scalapino
and George T. Yu

UNIVERSITY OF CALIFORNIA PRESS · BERKELEY · LOS ANGELES · LONDON

University of California Press
Berkeley and Los Angeles, California

University of California Press, Ltd.
London, England

Printed in the United States of America

1 2 3 4 5 6 7 8 9

Library of Congress Cataloging in Publication Data

Scalapino, Robert A.
Modern China and its revolutionary process.

Bibliography: p.
Includes index.
1. China—History—19th century. 2. China—History—20th century. I. Yu, George T., 1931– II. Title.
DS755.S28 1985 951'.03 84-23968
ISBN 0-520-05030-4

Robert A. Scalapino
dedicates this work to his students of the past four decades

George T. Yu
dedicates this work to his parents and Priscilla's parents

CONTENTS

MAPS

PREFACE

A lengthy work warrants a brief introduction. This study has undergone a considerable evolution since its initiation more than twenty-five years ago. At that time, we had determined to write an interpretative study of the background and development of the Chinese Communist movement. As the research progressed and our ideas began to take shape, however, it became ever more clear that only as one sought to capture the broader scene—that of China's revolutionary process in its most extensive dimensions—could one hope to achieve a thorough understanding of any particular phase of that process, including the Communist saga.

Thus, this volume deals entirely with the events that preceded the emergence of the Chinese Communists as an organized movement, ending with the years 1920–1921, on the eve of the formation of the Chinese Communist Party. We have projected a three-part study, with the second part scheduled to deal with developments between 1921 and 1949, and the final part seeking to analyze the extraordinary era since the creation of the People's Republic of China.

The present work commences with the Taiping Rebellion, which in our view was essentially traditional in nature, but was at the same time an event bearing the seeds of the future. This volume ends with the turbulent years immediately following World War I, years revealing the crisis of culture and system reflected in institutional chaos, deep cleavages within China's elites, most particularly the intelligentsia, and the electric impact of the global scene—from Washington and Wilsonian idealism to Moscow and the Bolshevik Revolution.

As will quickly be realized, we seek to deal both with structure—the political and socioeconomic systems—and with personalities, namely, the key actors who played their roles on a rapidly moving stage. In the latter connection, we have paid special attention to the flow of ideas that marked the efforts of various individuals to deal with the mounting crises. At every point, the attempt to influence minds, and thereby induce commitments, was a vital element of the scene.

We have also sought to deal with the omnipresent influence of Chinese culture upon all institutions, ideas, and actions. From the outset, China's modern rebels recognized that if they were to change the political order, they would have to challenge the social order in which it was encased. Yet this was a monumental task, especially in the absence of dynamic economic development or effective new political institutions. It is thus not surprising that most rebels, as well as the movements they represented, slipped back into traditional ways in the process of climbing the slippery slopes of power.

Two other considerations thread their way through this study—the factors of scope and time. The dimensions of China—in terms of both territory and population—constituted throughout the modern period a condition that influenced every aspect of the socioeconomic and political scene. China required very special institutions, and the prevailing Western model did not fit well. Indeed, once the evolving, carefully crafted traditional system had broken down, the effort to find a suitable substitute encountered repeated frustrations and failures, and here the very size of China played a role that must not be minimized.

In the timing of China's emergence into the modern world is also to be found a variable of major importance. Some years ago, in a study of prewar Japan by the senior author, this theme was explored in detail. In China as in Japan, timing played a crucial role in influencing the tempo of events, and their basic thrust as well. The impact of the external world upon China, both negative and positive, was of profound significance. On the one hand, external factors provided inspiration, stimulus, model (or conversely, negative example). On the other hand, external stimuli flowed from societies whose political culture and current stage of development were sufficiently different from those of China to render mechanistic borrowing or even adaptation virtually impossible. And the time was so short! Circumstances appeared to dictate that the "catching-up process" had to be telescoped into a few decades, with stages that had taken the West several generations at a minimum wholly skipped or severely abbreviated. Even within these few decades, moreover, Western developments—and the political fashions accompanying them—were undergoing an ever more rapid evolution, adding to the complexities.

As we shall note, these factors render any reductionist approach—one placing sole or primary emphasis upon a single causation—inadequate. In the final analysis, the modern Chinese revolutionary process was the product of an ever-changing interrelationship among the central variables suggested so briefly here and to be examined at various points throughout this work.

The research involved in this study could not have been completed without the assistance of many individuals who served us as Research Assistants over a number of years: Sachiyo Aoyama, Sui Chi Chan, Luke Chang, Chung-yun Cheng, I-fan Ch'eng, Tun-jen Cheng, Dai-Kwon Choi, Yuet-fong Chung, Yong-chool Ha, Robert Hsu, Kung-pei Hwang, Boris Ipatov, David Lau, Joseph T. Miller, Kōichi Mori, Philip Siu, Constance Squires, Daniel Sun, Colin Tam, Ivy Wang, Yunkun Wang, Cheong Zhung Yau, Sau-lun Yeung, and John Quan-sheng Zhao.

In our far-flung search for primary and secondary sources, and for the pictures included in this volume, we had the cooperation of many libraries, institutes, and individuals: the Centre de Recherches et de Documentation sur la Chine Contemporaine, Sorbonne University, Paris; the Asian Library of the University of Illinois; the East Asiatic Library of the University of California, Berkeley; the Hoover Institution; the Institute of International Studies, Taipei; the Institute of Oriental Studies, Moscow; the Institute of Scientific Information in the Social Sciences, Soviet Academy of Sciences, Moscow; the Keio University Library, Tokyo; the Kuomintang Archives, Taipei; the Library of Congress, Washington, D.C.; the Peking University Library, Beijing; the Revolutionary Museum, Beijing; the Sun Yat-sen Museum, Chungshan University, Canton; and the Ueno Library, Tokyo.

Nor can we express our debt adequately to those who read this manuscript in its entirety and offered valuable critiques. These include Lowell Dittmer, John K. Fairbank, Joyce Kallgren, Chalmers Johnson, Frederic Wakeman, Jr., and C. Martin Wilbur.

Our appreciation is also extended to our editor, Gene Tanke, for laboring mightily to improve the manuscript stylistically and to Gladys Castor who followed as manuscript editor, saving us from many errors in the final version; to Ann Britton for her meticulous compilation of the bibliography; to Anne Holmes for excellent proofreading; and to Leslie Scalapino for the detailed index. In addition, our gratitude also goes to a patient, efficient staff—past and present—for their varied work in preparing the study for publication: Lisa Berkson, Jane Kaneko, Catherine Lenfestey, Louise Lindquist, Kenneth Messerer, Teresa Rae, Eleanor Sanders, Sheila Saxby, Cleo Stoker, and Phoebe Wickstrom. Grant Barnes and Phyllis Killen of the University of California Press were consistently helpful.

We are also greatly indebted to the following foundations and university research units for funding in connection with this lengthy, expensive project: the Earhart Foundation; the National Endowment for the Humanities; the Henry Luce Foundation; the University of California, Berkeley, Institute of East Asian Studies and its Centers for Chinese and Japanese Studies, and the Committee on Research; the University of Illinois, Urbana, Centers for Asian and International Comparative Studies, Office of International Programs and Studies, and the Research Board of the Graduate College; in addition to the Departments of Political Science at both our universities.

To all of the above individuals, foundations, institutions, and research units, we are grateful. The use to which we have put their efforts is naturally our responsibility.

Robert A. Scalapino
George T. Yu

June 1984

1

TRADITION, CHANGE, AND THE TAIPING REBELLION

LIKE ALL GREAT transitions, the modern Chinese revolution has been an extended process. Yet measured against similar transitions in England, France, Russia, or even Japan, it has been strikingly brief. The English, taking advantage of their insularity and the early advent of economic changes, began their modern political transformation with the Glorious Revolution of 1688. Previous landmarks, such as the Magna Carta, are best treated as preparatory, "premodern" events. The French philosophers of the eighteenth century fired the mind of Western man and, aided by the elitist excesses of the age, helped to spark the Revolution of 1789, an eruption centered in France that sent shock waves across Europe, and eventually around the world. In Russia, a nation both intrigued and repelled by the West, the Decembrists of 1825 were the heralds of a long struggle for reform. Within a decade Alexander Herzen and a host of activists gave voice to growing ferment within Russian intellectual circles, and this ferment ultimately led to a series of explosive political acts that form a vital part of the history of the Russian Revolution. Meanwhile, the forceful opening of Japan in the 1850s set in motion the ever sterner challenges that brought on the Meiji Restoration of 1868 and a variety of sustained experiments in guided modernization that took the "advanced West" as their primary model.

Whereas the most recent of these developments, those in Japan and Russia, were under way by the mid-nineteenth century, China's drive toward modernization was essentially a product of the twentieth century—if we accept the fact that its opening stages occurred somewhat earlier. This assertion, of course, immediately poses a crucial question: How are we to interpret the Taiping Rebellion, that massive uprising which shook traditional China in the mid-nineteenth century? Answering that question is the main burden of this chapter. But before we take it up, we must explain our use of the concept of modernization and our understanding of the political culture of premodern China.

DEFENDING AND DEFINING THE CONCEPT OF "MODERNIZATION"

It has been argued that the concept of "modernization" embodies a narrow and parochial ethnocentrism, one that is time-bound as well as culture-specific. Its application to studies of non-Western societies is still greeted with deep suspicion by some scholars. Like any highly distilled symbol, "modernization" can indeed lend itself to distorted or erroneous judgments. One of the recurring themes of this work will be the need to recognize the dynamic interaction between "tradition" and "revolution," the continuing effect of that political culture which is the sum of a society's historical evolution on the process of change.*

This interaction will be especially intense when a society with a rich and pervasive culture—like Japan or China—makes a commitment to rapid social transformation. Deep emotionalism is released when an effort is made to wrench a people abruptly from their cultural moorings by an impatient elite using borrowed ideas and institutions, particularly when these latter forces must fight for legitimacy in an era replete with unpalatable pressures exerted by the very nations from which the borrowing is taking place. Even among "progressives," issues of self-respect and control over one's own destiny—individual and collective—were certain to color attitudes toward Western-derived "modernization" in a society like China, so proud and satisfied with its civilization and so deeply threatened by imperialist advances. These conditions affected both the timing and the character of adjustment to the global environment, although they did not dictate a uniform response on the part of such nations, as the Japanese and Chinese experiences demonstrate.

No one should minimize the importance of the greatly intensified impact of the industrial world upon the societies lagging in economic development during the past one hundred and fifty years. Yet one must also beware of fitting these societies neatly into some global order in which the only significant variable is the economic one. Immanuel Wallerstein's writings typify such an effort.[1] As these and similar works demonstrate, the charge of ahistoricism and ethnocentrism leveled against "modernization" theories might be more justly applied to certain Marxist writings, however paradoxical this seems in the light of Marxian historicism. Some scholars, including many contemporary Chinese Marxists, seek to squeeze China into the mold of Western historical experience and feel compelled to argue in ecclesiastical fashion over just when Chinese society entered and left a given universal socioeconomic and political stage.

*We use the term "political culture" in a broader sense than has been customary. The political culture of a given society is contained in the repository of political values, institutions, and behavior patterns, molded by the nature of its society *and* its unique historical experiences. Collectively, these provide perimeters, shape adaptations, and weigh upon choices at any point in its evolution, even in a "revolutionary era," thereby constituting a powerful influence upon any "new order."

A nation's political culture, however, should in no sense be viewed as a monolithic, singularly focused force. The dominant tendencies and drives attendant to a given political culture are never without challenge from countervailing, albeit subordinate forces, and even among the dominant traits the potentialities for alternative evolutionary processes exist, depending on the particular goals and adaptive skills of emerging elites.

One should be quick to insist that "modernization" need not imply a one-directional socioeconomic and political development nor an inevitable movement from "bad" to "good" in normative terms. In most if not all societies, the struggle for modernization has been exceedingly complex, with institutional or social retreats from stipulated goals occurring and new courses charted on occasion. "Inevitable, inexorable progress" was a nineteenth-century theme dominating Western intellectuals from Mill to Marx, but it can easily be challenged in the late twentieth century on the basis of accumulated experience. When it takes place, moreover, economic development exacts its price, so that new social problems and political hazards affect the citizenry at large. A normative balance sheet will never be wholly one-sided, even after undue romanticism over the old way of life has been cast aside.

A final concession to critics of "modernization" is in order. Unquestionably, the concept is time-bound. We would not pretend that the desiderata central to its goals in the nineteenth and twentieth centuries can be projected without alteration into the future. Indeed, every achievement of modernization, from the very beginning, poses new issues and problems, hence new tasks. In recent years, therefore, scholars have sometimes employed the term "postmodern societies" to signal this fact. Yet in this study, we are dealing with the nineteenth and twentieth centuries; and we can appreciate the nature of this period only if we realize that, increasingly, a majority of the people of all cultures, with their elites as vanguard, have moved toward a common set of desires encapsulated in the term "modernization." Certain values and procedures that were generally confined to the West in the eighteenth and nineteenth centuries have since acquired near universal acceptance. Overwhelmingly, national leaders, irrespective of ideological commitment or cultural tradition, have subscribed to such goals as "progress," nationalism, democracy, industrialization, and a transformation of agricultural production through scientific methods. Certainly, all of these goals have preoccupied the latest inheritors of the Chinese revolution, however they may seek to interpret, plan, and execute them.

It is appropriate to note here that "modernization" and "Westernization" are clearly not identical. Indeed, for various reasons, some of which have been indicated, most societies outside the Western historic and cultural orbit have had to develop their own interpretations of modernization, while remaining within the perimeters just sketched. Both the similarities and differences among late-developing societies are testimony to the historic, cultural, environmental, psychological, and temporal factors governing their course in the evolutionary stream.

Nevertheless, having acknowledged these facts, we believe it is both possible and necessary to speak of certain criteria for modernization in recent times which cut across cultural and temporal lines and thus enable us to offer meaningful generalizations about the political process of our era.

In the economic realm, modernization has involved the following overlapping commitments: (1) to accept, and usually to encourage, larger organizational units, and to provide economic incentives for all groups operating in the productive arena; (2) to promote increasing specialization in labor and management, greater efficiency and precision, standardization of products and lower unit costs, and better working conditions; (3) to make the maximum application of science and technology to all forms of production;

(4) to achieve increasingly mechanized production, both industrial and agricultural.

In the political sphere, modernization has underwritten these commitments: (1) to concentrate on the nation-state as the supreme object of civic loyalty and to promote the growth of centralized political power, with the state acquiring progressively greater dominance over other units of governance; (2) to eliminate religious or supernatural justifications for authority, and to make legitimacy increasingly dependent on a secular value system or ideology; (3) to replace hereditary officialdom with an increasingly differentiated civil and military bureaucracy in which the civil servants are recruited by regularized methods after higher education and the military officials are given technical training in specialized institutions, with merit playing an increasing role in selection and promotion within both groups; (4) to create a comprehensive legal system governed by a national constitution; (5) to universalize and standardize the law and legal procedures, to abolish legally privileged classes, and to move toward equal rights under the law for all citizens of the state; (6) to promote greater citizen participation in the political process, whatever the precise political patterns and institutions.[2]

To set forth these criteria is not to insist that every traditional society was totally devoid of "forces" associated with modernization. Nor is it to proclaim that all modernizing states have adhered strictly to each of these standards, or even regarded each of them in its "pure" form as a desideratum. It is to assert, however, that taken as a whole, these criteria represent the general course of nineteenth- and twentieth-century modernization, cutting broadly across a great variety of specific cultural, economic, and political systems.[3]

SALIENT ASPECTS OF CHINA'S POLITICAL CULTURE

The Chinese revolutionary movement, when it came, immediately confronted the widest possible range of issues: the family, education, literature, philosophy, language, life-style, basic values. Political controversy in modern China has always been in substantial degree a debate over alternative cultures, a debate that rejects the distinction between polity and society, trampling over the boundaries that have preoccupied most Western political scientists. This is understandable when we remember that the traditional order in China was both formidable and organic; it provided a coordinated pattern of attitudes and behavior that endured for millennia with few basic changes. The relationships within the system were such that only an all-encompassing attack could effectively challenge the old order. How could one separate the concept of a new politics from the idea of a new man, a man emancipated from old values, old priorities, and old social institutions? In China the concept of "a new socialist man" was thus preceded by the concept of "a new democratic man," and even earlier by the concept of "a new scientific man."

Naturally, the problem was more complex than simply replacing the old with the new. Although philosophically and ideologically, the assault upon tradition was total in scope, in actual practice change and tradition were by no means always in opposition. As in every society, reformers and revolutionaries in China consciously used certain aspects of their past culture and were unconsciously shaped by other aspects, even as they subjected that culture to scathing attack. Needless to say, the Communists have been no exception.

It is thus imperative that the central forces within the traditional system be understood. Only by understanding them, and the nature of the attack upon them, can we appreciate the elements of disintegration and survival that have characterized the Chinese scene in modern times. Our purpose here is not to describe every aspect of the classical system, but rather to highlight certain factors which were critical to its performance and which served as keys to the type of adaptation that would fit most naturally with China's traditions.

The concept of a balance between competing forces was deeply embedded in all aspects of Chinese culture, symbolizing at once implicit conflict and a basis for greater harmony. The coexisting opposites of yin and yang embody the essence of Chinese philosophy and the abstract personification of traditional life. They offer a cosmic explanation akin to Hegel's great conception of a dialectic. Yet Hegel's concept of motion revealed an appreciation of the explosive idea of progress which was to govern the modern West; there would be thesis, antithesis, and synthesis, *but never the same synthesis*, because the advance of the interaction itself dictated change. In contrast, the Chinese view of conflict and harmony was cyclical in character, with the ultimate surcease from the painful wheel of life coming in nonmotion and nonbeing, the completely peaceful end of a wearying repetition.

The dominant tradition within Chinese philosophy, Confucianism, held that harmony was a natural state, a product of the innate goodness of man, which predisposed him toward willing acceptance of hierarchical arrangements that were required for cosmic unity and led—without divine intercession—to the achievement of order. Man, to be sure, could be corrupted, but he could also be perfected through education. The idea that within each man lay a potential sage expressed the very essence of Confucianism.[4] The lesser philosophical tradition, Legalism, emphasized man's venality, his need for coercive law and the constraints of absolute authority. In actual political life, Legalism often prevailed, but that did not diminish the potency of Confucianism as the principal ideology and source of legitimacy.

Politics, like all other aspects of Chinese culture, reflected both political traditions. In practice as in theory, it consisted of a series of dualities containing basic paradoxes. When the two parts of a duality were in relatively balanced juxtaposition to each other, they formed a reasonably stable equilibrium. When such a relationship was not approximated, however, repression or instability resulted.

No set of forces was more central to the Chinese tradition, and no dualism in greater need of equilibrium, than that of a personalized, often arbitrary, ascriptive monarchy, on the one hand, and an impersonal, rule-applying, competitively selected bureaucracy, on the other. In its ancient, prehistoric form the Chinese monarchy must have been similar to other such institutions; and since the Japanese monarchy retained many of its original traits into modern times, we may see the ancient Chinese system mirrored in the Japanese monarchical institution of a later period. The first monarch of any Chinese dynasty reached his position through a combination of military conquest and political alliance. The symbols of legitimacy were then conferred upon him: yellow robes representative of the sun, and a host of other rituals and functions drawn from the misty past, many of them connected with homage to ancestors. Thus the ceremonial planting or reaping of grain was an act associating the emperor with the farmer, who epitomized his people and the all-important need for bountiful harvests.

From such traditions, the monarchy evolved into a major institution in historic times, far outreaching the emperor himself. Thousands of eunuchs, court functionaries, and ladies of the harem composed the imperial entourage. In essence, the politics of the Chinese court were always intensely personal; hatred, jealousy, and rivalry alternated with love, altruism, and deep commitment, to fashion a mosaic of factionalism, constant intrigue, and frequent palace upheavals. In this, Chinese politics did not differ greatly from the politics of other "absolute monarchies" of the premodern and modern era.

The pages of Chinese dynastic histories are thus replete with plots and counterplots, deeds of ignominy and debauchery, and acts of great personal heroism and sacrifice. Because these accounts were commissioned by the monarchy, we may assume exaggeration of the achievements of those whose careers were crowned with success, and undue castigation of those who failed. One can also note a strong tendency to focus on the leading characters, to the neglect of the societal setting. Yet there can be little doubt that throughout much of Chinese history the emperor was not merely the supreme symbol but the supreme authority. In his wisdom lay the potential for order, productivity, and justice. In his arbitrariness and foolishness lay the potential for violence, the wasting of lands and people, and the unnecessary sacrifices of brave ministers. Naturally, the men who occupied the throne varied greatly in ability and personality, but being mortal, they all erred at points—even those who were justly called great rulers.

In every early society, the monarch was a powerful father symbol, and that symbolism was especially strong in a Confucian society like China, where familial and political allegiances were consciously blended. The ties between monarch and subject, parent and child, husband and wife, older and younger sibling, and friend and friend were all that were necessary for any individual. It is instructive to learn from a foreign ambassador long stationed in Beijing that when Chinese citizens were asked how they felt about the death of the two leading figures of Chinese communism within months of each other, several replied that the passing of Zhou Enlai was like the death of one's mother, and that of Mao like the death of one's father.

But the passing of emperors was not always peaceful. Dynastic changes were invariably the products of conquest, sometimes at the hands of invading "barbarians" from the North. As in the collapse of the Roman Empire, however, internal fissures and weaknesses were usually the critical factors in the fall of a dynasty in China.

Although the monarchical tradition in China did not diverge greatly from its counterparts elsewhere, the traditions associated with the bureaucracy and the gentry class displayed elements of genuine uniqueness.[5] When appointment to all official positions ceased to be reserved to members of the royal family, court favorites, and scions of the nobility, and most officials began to be selected through a competitive examination system, a new pattern of politics emerged. The examination system, by strengthening the thesis that governance by the wise was the ideal, brought a heightened legitimacy to the political order as a whole. That legitimacy, moreover, was based not merely upon the supposed ability of those chosen to govern, but also upon the element of egalitarianism involved in the selection process. In reality, of course, only the sons of the privileged classes could readily afford the sort of education necessary for success in the examinations; but in theory, all were eligible to compete, and the practice of village, clan, or gentry sponsorship of truly talented youth widened the entry channels.

The examination system, together with the practice of making an equal distribution of properties among male heirs, insured a degree of mobility in the sociopolitical structure that has rarely been equaled in other traditional societies. Great families rose and fell, often with a predictable rhythm. To have a member reach the top ranks of officialdom insured a wider prosperity because here too a dualism existed. The ideal Confucian scholar-bureaucrat dispensed "righteous decisions" without fear or favor, operating as a generalist rather than a specialist. But the virtuous son repaid his obligations to parents, clan, and village, and made certain that his personal debts and responsibilities were amply met. To shirk this requirement of filial piety was at least as unethical as to fall short in applying impersonal justice in the public realm. Thus was born the great ethical-moral conflict that was to permeate the entire Confucian system, complicating the definition of terms like venality and corruption.

Collectively, the bureaucracy served as both the indispensable supporter of the monarch and his inevitable competitor. The "ideal monarch" delegated the dispensation of his power to the wisest men of the realm, and it was they who ensured that rules and customs were upheld in the process of governance. More specifically, it was they who were the prime interpreters as well as the chief executors of the Confucian system. Hence, surveillance of the monarchy itself was not wholly beyond their rightful prerogative. As is well known, the doctrine that a monarch who violated the mandate of heaven ceased to be a monarch and became instead a tyrant eligible for extinction, undoubtedly emerged first as ex post facto rationalization for dynastic change, but it was nevertheless available as the ultimate weapon of the bureaucracy against the throne. And in the course of Chinese history, a few brave censors emerged who dared to criticize a ruling monarch, taking the risks involved out of a sense of duty and as an obligation to ancestors and to posterity.

Not surprisingly, most Chinese monarchs found the bureaucracy both essential and threatening. As political institutions became more sophisticated, a system of dual or overlapping powers emerged, a system quite different from the functional specialization characteristic of Western evolution. The classical Chinese bureaucracy was not built by developing "experts" and restricting them to a limited arena; rather, it was built on competitive "generalists" who operated in a similar or identical sphere. The throne was therefore not required to rely exclusively on one individual or group. Intimately connected with the system was the censorate, one of the most famous of the traditional institutions. To appoint individuals who were to inspect and report on others, and to give them the greatest latitude, was a method of seeking to curb gross abuses. Taken together, the censorate and the system of overlapping responsibilities provided an alternative set of safeguards to those implicit in the Western system of interlocking specialists in which interdependence tends to preclude secretive, massive corruption or power-aggrandizement.

An equilibrium between monarchy and officialdom was the essence of harmony, and hence of "good government" in the great Confucian tradition. But what was equilibrium? Granting the presence of a certain scholar-official bias in the written record, it meant this: the officials accepted the throne as the source of all ultimate authority and the epitome of a unified, centrally ordered system of governance; in exchange, the monarch accepted an extensive devolution of power to his duly constituted officials, and was willing to abide by a vast body of rules, mostly customary, pertaining to his behavior as monarch, including his treatment of officials and subjects.

The ideal degree of equilibrium envisaged in this prescription was rarely reached. Monarchs, especially strong monarchs, bullied and intimidated officials, seeking to mold them into sycophants. When the monarch himself did not play this role, others from within the immediate entourage of the court might do so. Arbitrariness descending into tyranny followed. On the other hand, there were times when powerful officials scattered throughout the land, discovering weakness at the center, extended their local or regional power steadily, coming to approximate local kings and daring to operate independently of monarchical instructions, confident that the center would not learn of their actions or in any event would be powerless to act. In extreme cases, de facto separatism led to prolonged struggle and sometimes to the toppling of a dynasty.

The ceaseless search for a balance between centralization and decentralization has deep roots in Chinese history, as befits the vast, heterogeneous nature of the land and its people. But another ancient dualism served to ameliorate the conflict between these two tendencies. That dualism lay in the existence of parallel forms of governance, the public and the private.

Private government—the extensive authority of family, clan, secret society, and scholar-gentry to engage in rule-making, the adjudication of disputes, and the general ordering of life—played a crucial role in traditional China. Indeed, it was sometimes said that the authority of the state stopped at the village gate. Although this was an exaggeration, it was true that the common man could only consider the emperor a highly remote figure, and the entire apparatus of the state less important to his interests than the forms of private governance with which he was surrounded and in which he directly participated. The functions of public government were mainly limited to taxation and the recruitment of corvée labor; these exactions, though avoided when possible, were generally accepted as necessary for the preservation of order and the fulfillment of a few undertakings, such as large-scale water conservancy projects, that required major organization and financial support.

Public government, while representing the ultimate authority, was sufficiently circumscribed in its functions, and private government sufficiently organized, extensive, and stable, that even in periods of great political disorder, a surprising continuity of life and production could be maintained. In sum, with its nuclear units intact and operative, Chinese political culture could survive barbarian incursions, dynastic upheavals, and other forms of political instability with vastly less permanent change than might have occurred elsewhere. By the same token, the self-contained nature of familial and clan units provided a powerful barrier to modernization in its various forms.

In a nutshell, it was the balance between private and public governance that underwrote both the unique characteristics of Chinese politics and the elements of stability that make it so formidable. Of key importance in that balance was the gentry. The gentry were degree-holders, individuals who had passed the official examinations and were thus eligible for governmental positions. In certain periods, degrees were offered for sale, creating an "unorthodox" category of gentry. Moreover, there was a substantial difference between those who had merely passed the district examinations and those who held higher degrees. The holders of higher degrees might attain provincial or national office. The rest were not eligible for such posts, and generally took positions as local teachers and tutors or went into trade.* Scholars like Ho Ping-ti, therefore, do not believe that these "scholar-commoners" should be included in the gentry class.[6] But as Philip Kuhn has pointed out, a district scholar or even a literate non-degree-holder might exert significant influence in his local community or area.[7] Usually (although not necessarily), gentry status included some degree of affluence, thereby providing an economic as well as a social-political base for influence.**

An individual who held office was prohibited from serving in his home area, but his family—immediate or extended—might remain there. If he were retired, awaiting appointment, or without office for some other reason, he usually resided in his native place. The continuous ties of the Chinese political and economic elites to their native places, rather than to metropolitan and therefore centralized locales, was a factor powerfully influencing the character of China's traditional political culture and its proclivities for adjustment to the challenges of the modern era.

As many writers have indicated, the gentry were divided not only by rank but also according to whether they belonged to the scholar-gentry (degree-holders without official posts) or the official gentry (holders of governmental positions). At the local and district levels, members of the scholar-gentry acted as the alter ego of the magistrate, the key official at the grass roots. Their cooperation was essential to the purposes of state. Without their support, the magistrate was in deep trouble and the writ of the capital was difficult if not impossible to execute. And as we have emphasized, the Chinese familial-clan system undertook on a private basis many tasks that in other cultures would be assigned to public governance. Thus in the course of their

*In his earlier work, Chung-li Chang had divided the gentry into two strata. The lower group included those who had passed the first examinations, those who had purchased their academic title, and certain other holders of minor titles. The upper gentry was composed of the holders of higher examination degrees and those holding official titles, whether combined with higher degrees or not. Chang makes it clear that a basic difference between those two strata existed, in that the latter were the only group qualified for appointment to office; the lower gentry had either to purchase office or pass higher examinations. Status differences between the two groups were made clear in every aspect of life. See Chang, *Chinese Gentry*, pp. 6–8.

**In many respects, "gentry" is an unfortunate term. Blind to important differences among power-holders from the national to the district levels, and to the importance of some non-gentry elements who served as vital parts of the local elite, the word can easily obscure rather than clarify the nature of the traditional Chinese hierarchical structure. Yet it is now permanently imbedded in the literature, and the critical distinctions in China's premodern political elite must be determined from context. For two works, in addition to those cited, dealing with the gentry and their roles, see Chow Yung-teh, *Social Mobility in China: Status Careers Among the Gentry in a Chinese Community*, and Fei Hsiao-t'ung, *China's Gentry—Essays in Rural-Urban Relations*.

struggle for power, the Communists came to know well the source of traditional rural authority, and therefore made the gentry the central target for extermination.

At this point, it is important to mention one other dualism: the juxtaposition of military and civil power.[8] It has been commonplace for scholars to emphasize the contempt for the soldier and the long tradition of civilian control of politics and society imbedded in Chinese culture, and to discount the role of the military in Chinese history. But they ignore the fact that the rise and fall of a Chinese dynasty was usually dependent on military power. The garrison forces that guarded the frontiers at all times were sources of authority throughout vast portions of the Chinese empire, notwithstanding the many problems afflicting the Chinese military structure during much of its history. The capacity of civilians to govern the populous valleys and plains of inner China depended on the protective shield held up by the military.

At times, moreover, the public and private armies recruited from within inner China shared power in the regions of their importance, and on occasion they even challenged civil authority for supremacy. Sometimes these armies were closely connected to the secret societies. In other situations they constituted the private forces of a powerful family or clan. Not infrequently, the line between bandit groups and "military forces" was difficult to distinguish. One sure sign of dynastic disintegration, in any case, was the inability of the center to mobilize and effectively command the imperial military forces; these forces were necessary to curb lawlessness, to discourage localist elements that might challenge the center's authority, and to keep the center's own representatives in line—satisfied that they were receiving the military support they needed to enforce orders, and well aware of the center's capacity to punish deviance as well as reward loyalty.

It is from these great dualities, then, that Chinese political culture was constructed. Henceforth, whenever we refer to the traditional factor in contemporary Chinese behavior and policy, we shall be alluding to one or another of these aspects of the classical Chinese polity.

A final salient characteristic of the traditional political culture is the role of China's intellectual heritage.[9] Mankind may be said to have maintained two great intellectual traditions: that of reinterpreting revealed truth, and that of consciously engaging in the quest for originality. The Chinese followed the first tradition, but with creativity. In moments of inspiration, classical Chinese intellectuals, from Wang Mang to Kang Youwei, read into Confucianism new concepts that the master himself would scarcely have envisaged, ideas more closely attuned to prevailing conditions, some of them extraordinarily radical. Yet this was always done in the name of the sage: Confucius was repeatedly reborn. Creativity was camouflaged by the insistence that what seemed to be novel was only the *true* Confucius at last uncovered. A similar technique was pursued by later adherents of rival philosophic schools. Every philosophic discourse, every search for the eternal verities, began with the injunction "Back to the texts!" By contrast, in other cultures a premium was placed on the *further* accretion of knowledge, on the movement forward from past error or inadequacy—in this sense, on originality. If this latter intellectual tradition did not have its genesis in science, it received ever-increasing support from that quarter.

The Chinese intellectual tradition sustained the capacity to accept

Marxism-Leninism as revealed truth and at the same time, through the process of creative reinterpretation, to construct within its framework doctrines more congruent with the proclivities of Chinese society. Another intellectual tradition was of benefit in this respect, that of combining theory and practice. Almost all classical Chinese scholar-intellectuals were also practicing bureaucrats, permanently or intermittently. The essence of the scholar-bureaucracy was the wedding of the intellectual to the art of governance. To combine theory and action was deeply imbedded in Chinese tradition.

PRELUDE TO THE TAIPING

We must now return to the complex question of the immediate antecedents of the modern Chinese revolution. In the course of their rule, both Nationalists and Communists have claimed the Taiping Rebellion as a part of their heritage, while disassociating themselves from certain of its aspects.[10] Sun Yat-sen acknowledged that he had been deeply influenced at an early age by the nationalist component in the Taiping movement, and much later, he was to equate his *minshengzhuyi* (principle of people's livelihood) with the Taiping leader Hong Xiuquan's "communism."[11] Chiang Kai-shek referred approvingly to the Taiping military units as "a revolutionary army" dedicated to the overthrow of the Qing, an army possessing "an ethnic conciousness" which had "become a great monument in our history."[12]

Similarly, Marxist writers have called the Taiping leaders "revolutionary heroes" who put into practice radical policies and aroused huge masses of peasants to fight against "the feudal land system" until they were finally defeated by a combination of "reactionary landlord forces" and foreign mercenaries. In the interpretations of the 1950s and the 1960s, the Chinese Marxist position was that the Taiping Rebellion suffered defeat because Chinese society, in transition from feudalism to a semicolonial and semifeudal status, lacked a proletariat. The Taiping uprising, therefore, was a "pure peasant war." Its radical land program was defined as "utopian agrarian socialist thinking," which was doomed to failure.[13]

Recently, there have been new interpretations emanating from both non-Marxist and Marxist sources. Yet among scholars of every persuasion, a wide-ranging dispute continues as to the precise nature and meaning of the Taiping Rebellion. Was it the opening phase of China's modern, revolutionary era? Was it a revolution in the sense of mounting a fundamental challenge to the existing socioeconomic and political order? Can it be defined as a peasant rebellion? If so, was it in the tradition of the great peasant rebellions of the West? Or was it essentially the same as earlier Chinese peasant revolts? Before looking at the most recent answers to these central questions and presenting our own views, we must set forth the salient details of this massive upheaval, highlighting those factors we consider essential to a broader understanding of its role in influencing subsequent events.[14]

In certain respects, the Taiping Rebellion can be viewed as a part of that continuum of uprisings and general lawlessness that marked the decline of the Qing dynasty after the late eighteenth century. One foreigner discerned the trend at an early point. Lord George Macartney, the British diplomat in residence at the court of the Qianlong emperor in 1793–1794, kept a journal that provides fascinating insights into the current state of affairs and future possibilities. Many facets of Chinese society attracted Macartney, and he was sufficiently sophisticated to warn against facile comparisons with Europe. He was greatly impressed with the success achieved over the centuries in governing such a vast empire, and ascribed it primarily to the caliber of men who had served as emperors. Moreover, he regarded the aging Qianlong emperor as the most remarkable of his dynastic line.

Nonetheless, in the course of his travels Macartney discovered that China was "far from being easy or contented," a fact that he attributed primarily to the antagonism beween Tartar (Manchu) and Han. "There are certain mysterious societies in every province," he wrote, "who are known to be disaffected, and although narrowly watched by the government, they find means to elude its vigilance and often to hold secret assemblies, where they revive the memory of ancient glory and independence, brood over recent injuries and meditate revenge."[15] He continued: "The Chinese . . . are awakening from the political stupor they had been thrown into by the Tartar impression, and begin to feel their native energies revive. A slight collision might elicit fire from the flint, and spread flames of revolt from one extremity of China to the other." *

The secret societies to which Macartney referred were part cause and part effect of certain mounting socioeconomic and political strains. Continuous population increase, the result of a sustained period of peace and improved agricultural productivity, was putting heavy pressure on lands long cultivated; a steady migration of people to marginal regions in the west and south was under way. Such relocations frequently led to intense local friction, with the indigenous people pitted against the newcomers. Local militia groups proliferated, and private armies were maintained by those living outside the law. Governmental forces of various types had to be augmented to combat rebellion and lawlessness. Thus, in the early decades of the nineteenth century a process of militarization was under way. A society was arming against itself.[16]

Meanwhile, in the major eastern cities and towns, commerce was developing rapidly, as an increasingly affluent merchant community established new banking and credit facilities. This trend naturally produced a gap between key coastal cities and the interior, since trade and commerce expanded most swiftly where there was access to foreign business. The urban-rural gap also widened, and was made more serious by a deflationary trend that brought lower agricultural prices in the opening decades of the nineteenth century.

Although the upper reaches of officialdom did not proliferate appreciably (thereby restricting social mobility), the local bureaucracy grew, particularly at the lowest rungs. Clerks and runners multiplied like a horde of locusts, each of them demanding the highest payment the traffic would bear. The tax system, hopelessly antiquated, was ready-made for corruption. Despite sporadic efforts to reform it after the Qianlong emperor's death, no significant changes were made.

*There followed this observation: "In fact the volume of the empire is now grown too ponderous and disproportionate to be easily grasped by a single hand, be it ever so capacious and strong. It is possible, notwithstanding, that the momentum impressed on the machine by the vigour and wisdom of the present Emperor may keep it steady and entire in its orbit for a considerable time longer; but I should not be surprised if its dislocation or dismemberment were to take place before my own dissolution. Whenever such an event happens, it will probably be attended with all the horrors and atrocities from which they were delivered by the Tartar domination" (J. L. Cranmer-Byng, *An Embassy to China*, p. 239).

These various developments were most pronounced in central and southern China. The North remained somnolent, resting in the conservatism and xenophobia so compatible with its past. Climatic factors in this area made agricultural gains more difficult, and socioeconomic changes came more slowly. Regional differences were thereby exaggerated, adding to the political complexities facing the Qing.

Not unnaturally, secret societies flourished in such an environment, especially in the South. Combining economic, social, and political functions, they represented an alternate source of livelihood and authority to that furnished by the government or even by the extended-family system. Smuggling and piracy, along with gambling, were prominent among the economic pursuits of these societies, and created a need to control coastal, and later inland, waterways. Rituals and regulations bound members as tightly as in a true kinship group. Through their organizational structure and financial controls, the societies maintained an alternative government that penetrated deeply into various parts of the country. Politically, they were protonationalist associations; their pledge to overthrow the Qing and restore the Ming was directed toward the large majority of Chinese who were Han.

The most prominent of the secret societies was the Triad Society. Emerging from Taiwan, it expanded to Fujian, Guangdong, and Guangxi, and by the beginning of the nineteenth century it was also operating in the Yangtze valley. Its branches were known by various names, and it drew members from many sources: boatmen, stevedores, unemployed workers, and minor officials, and later the peasantry and even some members of the gentry.

The government could defeat but not destroy associations like the Triads because they had become a subculture, part of the very marrow of the larger society in which they operated. By the 1840s the Triads were in open revolt, attacking cities in Guangdong province. The climax came in the course of the Taiping Rebellion itself, with the so-called Red Turban revolt of 1845–1855, during which a number of district towns were seized before the Triad rebels were defeated (but not eliminated, as subsequent events were to demonstrate).

The era of large-scale revolts, however, had actually begun with the White Lotus uprising of 1796–1805. In one central respect, the White Lotus effort resembled the later Taiping Rebellion rather than the Triad Society's Red Turban revolt. Its central appeal was a religious one; Buddhism was used as the main ingredient, with many other elements added to embrace Chinese populist traditions. White Lotus influence ultimately extended from Sichuan to Shandong. When an alarmed government sought to circumscribe the movement, a full-fledged revolt occurred. Quelling the revolt took prodigious efforts, which included mobilizing local resources to the fullest. Qing military weaknesses already stood revealed.

On the eve of the Taiping Rebellion yet another event of profound importance took place, namely, the Opium War of 1839–1844. The immediate cause of the conflict was British insistence on the right to traffic with the Chinese in opium, a demand that clearly placed the Chinese on high moral ground and brought upon the British the condemnation of many, including prominent humanitarians at home. The more fundamental issue, however, and one that would tower over China's relations with the outside world in the nineteenth century, was the collision of two incompatible concepts of international relations, concepts derived from radically different global perspectives.

In any case, it was foreign barbarians who now revolted, humiliating the central government before its own people. Qing leaders had completely misjudged the power of the British, as well as the Chinese capacity to manipulate them. In defeat, they were forced to accept terms that outraged many of their staunchest supporters.

TAIPING ORIGINS

It can thus be seen that the Taiping Rebellion fitted into a broader pattern of events. Nevertheless, both in scale and in some of its essential elements, it was unique. Despite the atrocities that mark the twentieth century, the Taiping Rebellion can probably still be accounted the most destructive civil war in mankind's history. From the time when the rebellion first broke into the open in January 1851 until the bloody end of the last important battle in February 1866—a period of fifteen years—approximately twenty million people may have lost their lives amid incalculable property destruction, especially in Central and South China. The precise figures can never be known, but death and devastation reduced vast areas to virtual deserts, and recovery required several generations.

In its inception, the rebellion owed much to a single man—Hong Xiuquan. Hong was born on January 1, 1814, in a small Hakka village in Guangdong province, about thirty miles from Canton. Like many other rebels in modern China, he came from a rural family that was above "average peasant" status yet well removed from the uppermost rural elite—the sort of environment likely to nurture talented, unfulfilled individuals available for leadership in movements that challenged the existing order. Hong's ancestral tablets included the names of men who had served as officials and functioned as literati, but his father was barely a middle peasant in economic terms, possessing a few *mou* of land, one or two water buffaloes, and some chickens and pigs. The father, however, was also a man of distinction in his clan and community; he was in charge of the Hong clan collective properties and served as headman of his native village.

Young Hong was quickly recognized as a youth with talent and given the opportunity to obtain a classical education. At an early age, he passed the district examinations with the highest marks and, aided by teachers and friends, continued his studies in preparation for more advanced tests. It was Hong's fate, however, to fail repeatedly in the examinations for the *shengyuan* degree given in Canton. Despite four efforts spread over some fifteen years, he was denied the thrill of seeing his name on the list of successful candidates. His last effort came in 1843 when he was twenty-nine years of age.

Hong's experiences in Canton were to have a profound effect on his life—and on the lives of millions of his compatriots. After his second failure, at some point between 1833 and 1836, he remained in the city to attend lectures at the private academy of the renowned scholar Zhu Ciqi. While walking on the street one day, he chanced upon an American missionary, probably Edwin Stevens, and his Chinese interpreter. They were distributing tracts written by another Chinese Christian, Liang Afa, nine separate essays under the title "Good Words to Admonish the Age," comprising quotations from the Bible and simply phrased Protestant homilies. Hong took the pamphlets, glanced at them, and when he returned home, stored them away.

In 1837, after his third attempt to pass the examinations had ended in failure, Hong had a serious mental breakdown. The humiliation of failing to fulfill the early expectations placed upon him had become a burden too great to endure. In the throes of illness, his hallucinations transported him to a "beautiful and luminous place" where, according to his cousin's later account, he was first cleansed, then brought before a venerable, golden-bearded man dressed in a black robe (God).[17] Upon greeting Hong, God shed tears, lamenting that while everyone was indebted to him for their food and clothing, no one remembered or venerated him, and worshipped demons instead. He thereupon gave Hong a sword, commanding him to exterminate the demons; a seal, as symbol of authority; and yellow fruit (the imperial color) to eat.

Supposedly, the old man reproved Confucius for having failed to expound the true doctrines in his works, with Confucius "ashamed," and confessing his guilt. Later, Hong also met a middle-aged man whom he addressed as "elder brother" (Jesus). He too exhorted Hong to bring his brothers and sisters back to the path of righteousness and exterminate all evil spirits.

The illness passed, and Hong returned to his position as a village schoolteacher. Only in the spring of 1843, some six years later, did his earlier vision come into focus. A cousin found the Christian tracts among Hong's possessions and, on reading them, expressed great interest in their contents. When Hong turned to them, he quickly interpreted his earlier vision: he had been speaking to God and Jesus, and his task was now clear: to spread the Christian gospel and wipe out false gods and idols.

There is uncertainty as to precisely when Hong began to give voice to anti-Manchu sentiments. S. Y. Teng presents evidence indicating that for the next four or five years at least, Hong was essentially a religious leader, not a political rebel.* His religion, moreover, if scandalous from the standpoint of the established Chinese order, was too rudimentary and too tainted with indigenous and idiosyncratic features to be acceptable to an orthodox Christian. Nor, as later events were to demonstrate, could Hong easily be persuaded to align his beliefs more closely with the central tenets of Christianity. His creed remained an amalgam of Christian, Buddhist, and Confu-

* See Teng, *Western Powers*, pp. 41–55. Jen leaves open the issue of when Hong's religious commitments were intertwined with nationalist and reformist sentiment to form a revolutionary ideology, but cites virulently anti-Manchu sentiments which Xiuquan reportedly voiced to Rengan as early as 1845–1846. See Jen, *Revolutionary Movement*, pp. 26–28. One of these remarks is recounted to Theodore Hamberg: "God has divided the kingdoms of the world, and made the Ocean to be a boundary for them, just as a father divides his estates among his sons; every one of whom ought to reverence the will of the father, and quietly manage his own property. Why should now these Manchoos forcibly enter China, and rob their brothers of their estate?" (Hamberg, *The Visions of Hung-Siu-Tshuen*, p. 29). It must be remembered, however, that Rengan was recalling these remarks six or seven years later, in 1852.

In a recent paper entitled "Several Questions Concerning Hong Xiuquan's Thought During His Earlier Period," Shen Maoyuan argues that Hong did not bring forth his mandate from heaven until after his contacts with Roberts, possibly in 1848, using this weapon both to mobilize the people for revolution and to secure for himself the highest position in the movement. Shen also sees the fact that two other key figures, Yang Xiuqing and Xiao Chaogui, were subsequently acknowledged to be spokesmen for God and Jesus, respectively, indicates a political compromise reflective also of regional divisions (Hong and Feng Yunshan being from Guangdong, Yang and Xiao from Guangxi). Shen, incidentally, contrary to most recent scholars in the People's Republic of China, is very critical of Hong.

cianist concepts, all colored by the rural environment out of which he had emerged, and filtered through the mind of an intelligent but narrowly educated man. In its commitment to monotheism, its acceptance of Christ, and its moral code, the connection with the Christian religion was clear. But in some of its rituals and beliefs, and more importantly in the claim of Hong and others to have direct contact with God (and thus the right to interpret his word), the Society of God Worshippers (Baishangdi Hui), as Hong's flock came to be known, was clearly heretical.

Hong had discovered the God of the Old Testament, a God demanding stern punishment for those guilty of evil and idolatry. In obeying this command, Hong soon made himself a disruptive force in his village. Destroying altars and idols, he alienated many of the villagers and lost his teaching position. He and another cousin, Feng Yunshan, left the area and went to Guangxi, where there were Hakka settlements interspersed among Miao and other non-Han people. In May 1844 they reached Guixian, where Hong had relatives; here they had considerable success in proselytizing. After a few months, however, Hong returned home, where he spent the next two years as a teacher, confining his outside activities to writing religious tracts.

In early 1847 Hong made a trip to Canton to seek instruction from the American Baptist missionary Issachar J. Roberts. He stayed for about two months, and although Roberts refused to baptize him, Hong learned something about Christian worship ceremonies and received a Chinese-language Bible.* When he returned to Guangxi in the summer of 1847, he found that Feng had attracted several thousand people to the new religion and had organized the Society of God Worshippers.

During the next several years—even though Feng was imprisoned for a time, and both men returned to Guangdong at one point—the movement grew steadily, and in its initial composition and character one can see an image of similar phenomena, past and future. The central instrument remained that of religion, with believers subject to a strict moral code based on the Ten Commandments altered to include strictures against witchcraft, brawling, gambling, drinking, or smoking (both opium and tobacco). Those to be baptized had first to provide a written confession of their sins, and the subsequent ceremony included pouring a cup of water over the head, followed by drinking tea and washing the chest to symbolize the cleansing of the heart. In the absence of Hong and Feng, leadership had been assumed by Yang Xiuqing, a charcoal maker, and Xiao Chaogui, a farmer and faggot seller. These two held the movement together, partly by claiming that they had received the Word from God and Jesus while in trances.

In some of these beliefs and ceremonies, a villager could recognize similarities with past religious-political sects and with the secret societies he knew. Indeed, from an early point, the Society of God Worshippers had contacts with the anti-Manchu Triad Society. Though differences in creed and practice were sufficiently great to prevent any formal merger, Triad members joined as individuals (being required to disavow earlier commitments and accept the Society's religious tenets), and at a later point, the Taiping accepted tactical alliances with the Triads and others. Yet the Society of

*Rengan asserted that Roberts' two assistants, fearful that Xiuquan would usurp their position, persuaded him to ask Roberts for financial assistance. When he did so, Roberts, deciding that he was a "rice Christian," declined to proceed with his training (Hamberg, *Visions*, pp. 31–32).

God Worshippers was an exclusive, self-sufficient organization. Moreover, it had no scruples against using coercion when it could not prevail through persuasion. Evil could not be tolerated. Ultimately, when men and women had been remade as God had directed, China and the world would be at one in peace and prosperity. These precepts and practices foreshadowed later Chinese revolutionary creeds.

By the summer of 1849, the Society had grown to a force of over ten thousand, and a more overtly anti-Manchu note had begun to be sounded in Society propaganda and activities, largely as a result of various incidents in which local authorities opposed the Society's activities and sided with its enemies.[18] Of critical importance were the general conditions outlined earlier: widespread social and economic discontent in southern China, brought on by the combination of overpopulation, ethnic-racial tensions, economic inequities, and the existence of a corrupt, ineffective government. Given these conditions—and the long tradition of anti-Manchu sentiment in this region—it was not difficult to call for the ouster of a foreign dynasty that was faltering badly. The anti-Manchu theme could be sanctified by religious and racial doctrine: the Manchu rulers were idolaters as well as usurpers of Han rights. They had to be removed.

TAIPING RECRUITMENT PATTERNS

What was the nature of Hong's organization as it stood on the brink of open rebellion? How were members recruited? What was the character of the leadership and the rank and file? The answers to these questions are complex.

First, although the Society's appeal, especially in its religious aspects, was addressed primarily to the individual (and sometimes caused divisions within villages and even within families), recruitment generally proceeded along geographic, communal lines. Any other pattern would have been virtually impossible in rural Guangxi, given the linguistic-ethnic ties that provided identity and demarcation, the nature of relations at the village level, and the extensive network of intervillage ties based on family and clan lineages. The Society acquired some Miao and Zhuang supporters, but it first emerged as strongly Hakka in its membership, rooted in several Guangxi districts and constructed extensively on the basis of familial and clan loyalties. During its future growth, of course, the picture was to become much more complex. Individuals found a great many different reasons for affiliating with the Taiping, and many diverse groups came under its aegis, but the basic factors outlined above never wholly disappeared.

Second, despite the Society's rigorous social and religious requirements, what might be called ideological commitment often followed rather than preceded membership. Recruitment frequently resulted from highly personal or group-related considerations and had little to do with the Society's creed or purposes. The many documented cases cover a wide range of personalized actions on the part of the Society: getting a young man out of jail by bribing officials; combatting extortionists on behalf of the beleaguered scion of a well-to-do family; protecting a Hakka community from being assaulted by local Zhuang militants; befriending an individual in economic straits. Winning an individual, of course, provided an entrée to his family, clan, and village. We shall see these recruitment patterns reappearing in subsequent political movements, including those bearing revolutionary banners.

Finally, Society membership cut across class lines. Since the movement was confined to the countryside, the initial adherents came from segments of rural village society. Throughout its existence, moreover, the Taiping movement drew the great majority of its rank-and-file members and soldiers from the peasantry, although urban populations were sometimes recruited en masse—voluntarily or otherwise. The peasants, it should be remembered, provided the basis for *all* armies in China, as in other predominantly agrarian societies. They served as the mass foundation of the imperial armies that opposed the Taiping, and on occasion fought with great determination and bravery in this capacity. It is important, nonetheless, to identify the peasant as a logical recruit into the Taiping movement. It catered to his folklore and values. It was led by men who understood him because they came from the same substrata of Chinese society. It promised its own brand of utopia, on earth as well as in heaven. More important, perhaps, it provided vital assistance in times of mass disaster caused by flood or famine, and aid in the form of military power when bandits or local enemies threatened survival. And it was the only visible means of gaining revenge for the abuses of the government.

Nevertheless, to define the Taiping Rebellion as a peasant uprising oversimplifies both its goals and its constituency. The Taiping appeals were not in the first instance economic, despite certain proposed reforms. Neither Han nationalism nor the Taiping brand of Christianity was class-oriented. Nor were the personal factors that abetted recruitment limited to a single element within the society. Natural disasters, moreover, cut across class lines. It *is* important to note that the Society of God Worshippers, like many movements of its type, began its operations in a region where livelihood was precarious because of limited arable land, overpopulation, primitive communications, and widespread banditry. In such a region, poverty was the rule rather than the exception, and the distance between economic classes was both narrow and fluid. Although its foundations rested upon the poor, the Society's original members included landlords, merchants, scholars, and rich peasants as well as middle and poor peasants. From the beginning, the movement was heavily dependent upon contributions from well-to-do members.* And Taiping leaders avidly (if unsuccessfully) wooed the literati, who were respected as a class.

For one group, namely, women, the Society had a special meaning. His-

*Teng cites one example from a slightly later period. When the Taiping took the city of Yuezhou on December 13, 1852, they gathered all available people, as was their custom, outlining Taiping principles and explaining the reasons for the rebellion. After hearing Yang Xiuying speak, one listener, Tang Zhengcai, a rice and lumber merchant, was so moved that he contributed all of his boats, rice, and lumber to the cause. In return, he was appointed commander of the Taiping water force, in charge of several thousand hastily recruited boatmen (Teng, *The Taiping Rebellion*, pp. 87–88). Many similar cases can be found.

Another aspect of the complexity of the scene should be presented. In a recent monograph, James H. Cole has contributed a case study of local resistance to the Taiping through the peasant army of Shaoxing prefecture, Zhejiang, led by Bao Lisheng. In his insightful work, Cole challenges the thesis that the Taiping were generally welcomed by the peasantry, pointing out the supreme importance in Chinese history of local community security from outside invaders of whatever political stripe. See James H. Cole, *The People Versus the Taipings: Bao Lisheng's Righteous Army of Dongan*.

torically, Hakka women had worked arduously in the fields and the markets and had never engaged in such practices as foot-binding. Thus, certain egalitarian innovations in the status of women introduced by the God Worshippers were natural, even though the Society also tried to apply very strict rules concerning sexual relations. In fact, this combination of puritanism and egalitarianism with respect to male-female relations was quite possibly the most novel element in the Taiping movement, and it established commitments that would be reiterated by later radicals.

For the top leadership positions, Hong and Feng chose men from various walks of life: a charcoal maker, a faggot seller, a clerk in the district office, a young man who had aspired to be a scholar-official but had settled for managing his family's sizable estate. Most of these men came from the lower end of the socioeconomic spectrum, but each had already attracted individuals to him, and each was later to demonstrate considerable military, administrative, or political ability. Regardless of class or family background, the factors that united them were underutilized talent and the ambition to better themselves when the chance arose. It must be noted that there was not a single "pure" peasant in the early leadership group. Each of the first leaders, though intimately connected to rural China, was in the process of differentiating his life-style from that of the farmer, thereby making himself available for new pursuits.

In the beginning, of course, the great majority of the gentry, together with all active officials and all Manchu, opposed the movement. Their position, and in some cases their survival, depended on upholding the status quo. Later on, the Taiping did co-opt and utilize some gentry. Taiping leaders were not antagonistic to the gentry if they were Han, as we have noted; the hostility lay on the other side. Like its predecessors, the Qing dynasty had securely bound the literati-officials to its system. Any challenge to the existing political order, or to the Confucian principles upon which it rested, was perceived as deeply threatening by the vast majority of this group.

In sum, the Society of God Worshippers cut across various layers of Chinese society, with its initial center of gravity resting on lower socioeconomic elements, marginal men from marginal regions. It attracted individuals or groups who were discontented with their current status and with the existing power-holders. But it also acquired support of a more apolitical nature, in response to its religious appeals, its varied acts of personalized support, and in later years, indications of its invincibility. At a certain point, a seemingly victorious movement achieves momentum by attracting those who want to be on the winning side and those who see no alternative. What was unique about the Taiping, however, was the degree to which they succeeded, through intensive indoctrination, in molding disparate individuals into a cohesive movement. Success in this respect gradually wore off, but the Taiping leaders never lost their respect for the importance of ideology—and in this lay a link with political modernity.

TAIPING ORGANIZATION

In the years after 1847, Hong and his comrades proceeded to build a mass organization that was remarkable in both its military and its civil branches.[19] The military structure culminated in separate armies that could be increased in number as Taiping ranks expanded, with an overall commander-in-chief appointed when several armies were united in battle. Supreme control, moreover, was vested in the Tian Wang (Heavenly King), who combined final religious, military, and civil power in his hands.* Another feature of the military branch was a separation between the administrative and training function, which was vested in the army commander and his subordinates, and the strategic command, which was held by an army inspector (*jianjun*) whose orders were binding. The military code, which encompassed every aspect of the soldier's personal life, was exceedingly strict and prescribed severe punishment for infractions. In the opening stages of their rebellion, moreover, the Taiping formed separate male and female military units, with segregated camps. Military uniforms were fashioned in the design of the Ming era, and Taiping soldiers were required to leave their hair long, with the front part of the head unshaven—all symbols of defiance against the Manchu, and expressions of Han nationalism.

The civil structure did not take full shape until the Taiping were settled in Nanjing. Its main principles were drawn from the ancient Zhou dynasty. The administrative system was headed by a supreme ruler, the Heavenly King in the person of Hong Xiuquan, but Hong delegated administrative control to the East King (Yang Xiuqing), who was assisted by the North King (Wei Changhui) and the Assistant King (Shi Dakai)—all Guangxi veterans of the movement, survivors from the first leadership group. The top bureaucracy, whose titles were taken directly from Zhou records, served under the Heavenly Court. It was an entirely traditional structure, vulnerable to the same abuses and intrigues that had characterized Chinese palace politics over the millennia. In only one respect, the substitution of women for eunuchs in the inner court, did Hong and his followers deviate substantially from past practice. Taiping local government showed some innovations, such as the provision that local officials should be elected by the people (which appears to have happened only occasionally). Local administrative units were divided into six categories, with the smallest comprising five families and the largest numbering over thirteen thousand families.

THE COURSE OF THE REBELLION

Throughout the latter part of 1850, the Society had been secretly preparing for battle, manufacturing primitive arms and getting its military organization in order. A series of incidents involving quarrels between Hakka and indigenous peoples ensued in late 1850, with the natives supported by government troops and their own local militia. These culminated in a serious outbreak of violence between government forces and the God Worshippers on January 1, 1851, with casualties on both sides.[20] The rebellion had begun. Ten days later, on January 11, Hong formally inaugurated the new dynasty, ascending the throne in elaborate ceremonies and proclaiming a new kingdom, the Taiping Tianguo (Heavenly Kingdom of Great Peace).

In the following months, the rebels successfully defended themselves against repeated government assaults and grew in strength. They raised the siege of their original territory in the mountainous region of northern Guangxi

* At the founding of the Heavenly Kingdom, Hong had named Yang Xiujing commander in chief of the Central Army Corps, with Xiao Chaogui, Feng Yunshan, Wei Changhui, and Shi Dakai—the top figures in the original society—commanders of the other army corps. For details, see Jen, *The Taiping Revolutionary Movement*, pp. 66–67.

and began to move north. They were helped not only by the rugged terrain (and their intimate familiarity with the region) but also by the lax discipline and poor leadership prevailing in government ranks. Reports were rife of imperial officials deserting their posts without offering resistance, mistreating their own soldiers and the civilian populations, and falsely claiming victories, thereby misleading superiors. Severe famine in the region and the government's prosecution of secret society members were additional assets for the rebels.

Early on, the Taiping established clear rewards and punishments with those with whom they came into contact: rewards would be given those who surrendered to the Taiping or who furnished them with military information, contributed provisions, or aided in the transportation of ammunition; decapitation would await those who helped imperial forces, assembled units to oppose the Taiping, raped women, or molested the people.* This was another model for future revolutionaries.

The initial period, nevertheless, was one of hardship and hazard for the Taiping. Often the survival of their forces hung in the balance. Time and again, imperial armies appeared to have the rebels surrounded, but on each occasion the God Worshippers escaped, often gathering additional recruits as they went. By the autumn of 1851 the Taiping army was moving northward, and on September 25 the first walled city was captured. The movement now numbered over 40,000 persons, approximately one-half of them combatants. Procuring food presented few problems, with anti-Manchu farmers furnishing ample supplies. Taking advantage of corruption in official circles, Taiping representatives were also able to buy government equipment. Coal miners, bandits, and townspeople joined the ranks, and all were put through a program of indoctrination (which proved to be too demanding for some, especially those from bandit ranks). As the worried Guangxi governor put it in a letter to a friend, the tiger had broken out of his cage.[21]

The road ahead proved arduous for both sides. The Taiping strategy was to surround cities by investing the countryside with their forces and cooperative peasants, but the government could use the same basic tactics. Thus, by the spring of 1852 the rebels were forced out of their stronghold at Yonganzhou after a long siege during which supplies of food, salt, and ammunition grew short. But they escaped intact, and with ranks now numbering over 60,000, they moved quickly to encircle Guilin. This large city, however, had powerful fortifications, and after a month the Taiping leaders abandoned the effort to take it, moving north again. In the succeeding months, they suffered several grievous occurrences including the death of Feng Yunshan and a shocking 10,000 casualties near the Hunan border.

Yet the Taiping continued to march—and to expand. In Hunan they

*Jen, *The Taiping Revolutionary Movement*, p. 77, citing Zhong Wendian, *Taipingjun cai yongan*, p. 25. From late 1850, the God Worshippers set up military camps to which all Society members were attached. Believers were to sell all their properties and possessions and donate the proceeds to the public treasury, with the pledge that their needs would be taken care of. Teng speculates that this plan may have been suggested by a passage in one of Liang Afa's nine tracts possessed by Hong: "Jesus said unto him, if thou wilt be perfect, go and sell what thou hast, and give to the poor and thou shalt have treasure in heaven: and come follow me" (Matthew 19:21). The secret societies had also attracted members by offering free food and lodging, thus possibly suggesting a similar idea to the Taiping leaders (Jen, pp. 63–64). The separation of sexes, and the organization of both men and women into military/labor battalions, continued until 1855, after which the practices were abandoned or modified.

sought to rally the population with widely disseminated proclamations calling for the overthrow of the Manchu usurpers; these tracts cataloged Manchu crimes against the Han people and described the struggle as a war of God against demons, reiterating the unique Taiping brand of Christianity.* Their ranks soon swelled to over 100,000, but the major walled cities continued to withstand rebel assaults, as is illustrated by the unsuccessful effort to capture Changsha, the capital of Hunan. Here the Taiping, using the skill of their coal-miner recruits, planted explosives in tunnels dug under the city walls, but they were never able to penetrate the well-defended interior. Finally, at the end of November 1852, they abandoned the effort and continued north. Taiping tactics now shifted; the bulk of their forces took to the waterways in thousands of boats. For this new tactic the Taiping owed much to their early cooperation with the Guangdong-Guangxi Triad river pirates. One of the pirate leaders, Luo Dagang, who remained loyal until his death, played a particularly important role in the successful application of a naval strategy.[22] Major victories followed. By the end of 1852 the rebels had gained control of two of the three great Hubei cities, Hanyang and Hankou. The third city, Wuchang, fell on January 12, 1853, amid massive casualties, including a reported 100,000 suicides.

At this point, a critical strategic decision was taken. Should the army strike north and seek to capture Beijing, ousting the Manchu from their capital? Or should it move east, seizing Nanjing and consolidating its strength there before challenging the Qing government in its headquarters? In what many analysts have called their greatest strategic error, the Taiping leaders decided to hold to their original plan and move toward Nanjing.** By road and by river, a vast Taiping army, now numbering over 500,000 with civilian auxiliaries, moved toward its objective. Guijiang, an important city in Jiangxi, and Anjing, the capital of Anhui, were taken with ease, having been

*These excerpts will suffice to provide the flavor of the appeals: "Why should we Chinese humble ourselves to be their [Manchu] servants and slaves? China is the head; Manchus are the feet. China is the sacred land; the Manchus are demons. . . . Even by exhausting all the paper made of bamboo from the southern China mountains, we cannot finish describing their evil deeds; even using all the water taken from the Eastern Sea, we cannot wash off their filthy crimes." "A multitude of 50,000,000 Chinese is under the yoke of 100,000 Manchus; what a disgrace!" "All of you—officials, common people, husbands and wives, men and women—must do your duty and go forward swearing that you will kill all the Eight Banners. Those who arrest and bring the Hsien-feng Emperor or his head to us or who kill any Manchu chieftains, will be given high official positions. We shall always keep our promise."

"We have raised a righteous army to inflict the vengeance of God above on those who have deceived Heaven and to relieve the suffering of the Chinese people below. We urgently hope all Manchus will be wiped out. . . . He who obeys Heaven will be amply rewarded; and he who disobeys Heaven will be killed openly. This is hereby proclaimed to the empire, so that every one can hear and know it."

According to various accounts, the response to Taiping propaganda in Hunan, Hubei, and Guangdong was strongly favorable, owing in no small measure to the earlier activities of the secret societies in these provinces. (For translations of portions of several anti-Manchu declarations, see Teng, *The Taiping Rebellion*, pp. 82–85.)

**Jen argues that had the Taiping pushed ahead, they would have faced only about ten thousand poorly disciplined soldiers in Henan, defending the capital, with the Mongolian and Manchurian cavalry who were later stationed in front of Beijing not yet mustered, nor new militia like Zeng Guofan's Xiang Army yet formed. He also argues that the Taiping themselves would have seized power at the center before being corrupted, as later took place in Nanjing. For a discussion of the Taiping decision, see Jen, *The Taiping Revolutionary Movement*, pp. 107–108.

virtually abandoned. Huge stores of provisions and money were obtained, and throughout the countryside stories of Taiping invincibility created a ground swell of support.* By the time they reached the outskirts of Nanjing, in early March 1853, their total strength was approaching three-quarters of a million people. The city fell on March 20, and there followed a bloody massacre of all Manchu residents who could be found, including women and children. More than 30,000 died.

The Taiping now had a capital city and unchallengeable command of a great stretch of the Yangtze River, which gave them control over vast sections of central China. Possessing a fixed seat of government, the Taiping could now enunciate their social and political policies more fully and make efforts to implement them. Unquestionably, the Taiping aimed at making certain basic, even revolutionary, changes in their kingdom, but these changes were rationalized and defended by citing ancient Chinese practices as well as the will of God. The greatest changes probably pertained to women. Applying the premise of God-given equality, and influenced by the previous role of the Hakka farm woman, foot-binding, concubinage, prostitution, and bride payments were all proscribed.[23] The reforms, however, did not go so far as to command monogamy for the leaders. Indeed, the Heavenly King and other members of the political elite each took many wives, the only difference being that as legally married wives rather than concubines, each supposedly had equal status.

Taiping social programs included the free distribution of rice gruel to the poor, free schools, aid to refugees, and religious instruction for all citizens. Despite their commitment to the new religion, Hong and other Taiping leaders acknowledged the validity of basic Confucian doctrines, and they authorized the preparation of revised classics, expurgated so that passages in conflict with Taiping teachings were removed. In many respects, the tenets of the Heavenly Kingdom represented an amalgam of Confucian and Christian principles as set forth by Hong Xiuquan and his close associates.[24] The Taiping leaders did not alter the traditional ranking of social classes—scholar-official, farmer, artisan-worker, and merchant, in descending order. And the examination system was maintained, with changes in the questions but with the basic format left intact.

Of greatest interest was the Taiping land program. It was comprehensive in its conception, and radical despite the fact that its antecedents lay deeply buried in the Chinese past. Agricultural land was to be divided into nine grades, based on quality of soil and production records. Each adult, male and female, was to be given a specified tract of land, with individuals under sixteen years of age receiving a lesser amount.** All land taxes were to be abolished, but every farmer was to remit to the government his entire production beyond what was needed for family consumption. In exchange, the government would take care of the farmer and his family in times of dis-

*Jen, p. 111. On the other hand, many of the urban residents of towns and cities seized by the Taiping, especially the women, resisted being conscripted and forced to depart with the marching army, and even committed suicide to avoid this fate.

**On Taiping land policies, see Michael, *History and Documents*, pp. 83–88; Jen, *The Taiping Revolutionary Movement*, pp. 143–145; Teng, *The Taiping Rebellion*, pp. 104–108. Land distribution had a lengthy history in China, going back at least to the Zhou dynasty—the Taiping's principal model. In earlier times, however, women had not participated in distribution programs.

tress—drought or flood—by moving them to other sites. The projected new order was described in glowing terms: "Cultivating land in common, eating rice in common, clothing ourselves in common, and using money in common, the people of every place will share equally and there will be no one who is not fully fed and warmly dressed."[25]

In reality, this primitive communism—or communalism—was never put into effect. The Taiping had some degree of authority over huge areas of China at various times, but their control was not sufficiently continuous or complete for them to undertake a massive agrarian program. Private property continued to be the rule, and land taxes were collected, with no effort made to sequester all surplus production.* Moreover, there was a basic paradox in the Taiping leaders' philosophy as it related to the peasantry. Ren Youwen captured this well in the following passage:

> An unexpected lapse in the Taiping's idealistic projection of a society based on brotherhood and equality lay hidden in a stipulation that one of the major punishments for wicked and undutiful officials was to be "degradation to the status of peasants." The Taiping leaders, despite their own origins, despised the life of a peasant, looked upon his wretchedness as the will of Almighty God, and fought for "heaven on earth" as the new Han rulers.[26]

Less than two months after their occupation of Nanjing, Taiping leaders launched two major expeditionary armies in a bid to wrest power from the Qing by striking at their heartland. The Northern Expeditionary Army, consisting of some 20,000 to 30,000 soldiers, moved rapidly northward, traversing Anhui toward its goal, Beijing. Reverses occurred, but by the end of September 1853 Taiping forces were entering Zhili, and in late October their vanguard units reached the outskirts of Tianjin, only seventy miles from the Manchu capital. This was as far as they ever advanced. In spite of many victories against imperial forces, the Northern Army could not push through to final victory. As time passed, its failure to consolidate its rear and its extended lines of communication proved fatal. Imperial units encircled the Taiping forces, exacting heavy casualties. An enforced retreat that began in February 1854 turned into a rout as frozen, half-starved Taiping soldiers stumbled south, constantly harassed by superior imperial forces. Learning of the peril into which the Northern Expeditionary Army had fallen, Nanjing authorities sought to send reinforcements, diverting elements of the Western Expeditionary Army for this purpose. The effort failed, however, and by late spring of 1855 all but scattered remnants of the once formidable Northern Army had been wiped out, with its surviving commander, Li Kaifeng, captured, delivered to Beijing, and then put to death by slicing.

The Western Army fared somewhat better. When it set forth in mid-May of 1853 with some 50,000 troops and 1,000 ships, its goal had been to add the western provinces to the Heavenly Kingdom. Anjing was quickly recaptured, but the effort to take Nanzhang failed. In September the siege was lifted. The army had received orders to move upstream, into Hubei prov-

*Jen's research indicates that no uniform rate of taxation was ever fixed by the central government, with each unit determining the rate autonomously. His fragmentary data, however, suggests that tax rates were generally lower than under the Manchu. See Jen, p. 145.

ince. At first the campaign went well, although some battles were costly to both sides. Hankou and Hanyang, two of the three great cities dominating the Yangtze, were captured for the third time by Taiping forces in mid-February of 1854. After this, however, progress was checkered, with defeats and victories interspersed.

A youthful Chinese commander in the service of the Qing, Zeng Guofan, now emerged as a formidable Taiping opponent.[27] Zeng came from a rural family of small landowners, and like Hong he failed in his early attempts to pass the examinations.* But unlike the Taiping leader, he succeeded on the third attempt, went ultimately to the Hanlin Academy, and subsequently enjoyed rapid advances in his career. Ordered by a deeply worried central government in early 1853 to organize a local Hunan militia, Zeng proceeded to build upon units already recruited, fashioning them into a force that came to be known as the Xiang Army.**

Zeng's methods were significantly different from those regularly employed with respect to government forces. Close personal ties between officers, and between officers and their men, were encouraged. Officer candidates were rigorously screened, with a high percentage selected from the literati, and those chosen were comparatively well paid. Rank-and-file soldiers were treated decently, and strict moral standards accompanied by neo-Confucian indoctrination were imposed on officers and ordinary soldiers alike. Although the Xiang Army failed to achieve the ideal that Zeng and his supporters envisaged, and its discipline later declined, it represented a marked improvement over past imperial performance. The Taiping campaign to capture Hunan collapsed. Indeed, the Taiping were pushed onto the defensive in Hubei, and in mid-October of 1854 they were forced to abandon Hanyang and Wuchang once again. But Zeng then suffered a major defeat in the battle for Jiujiang, and the two crucial Hubei cities were reoccupied, with the imperial forces unable to dislodge the rebels despite repeated attempts.

Thus, by the beginning of 1856 the civil war appeared to be moving toward a stalemate, with the prospect that China would remain divided for a very long time. The Taiping had suffered grievously in their abortive effort to seize the Manchu capital, and North China, at least for the time being, lay outside their grasp. Moreover, in the fall of 1853, they had lost the opportunity to take Shanghai. In September of that year, the Xiaodao Hui, a branch of the Triad Society, had organized an insurrection, taking advantage of the formidable Taiping forces to the west. But the Taiping, preoccupied

*Zeng Guofan was born on November 26, 1811, in Xiang-xiang district, Hunan, to a farm family of modest means though upwardly mobile and with a strong bent toward education. Zeng's father continued his efforts to pass the examinations for the *xiucai* degree into middle age, finally succeeding on his seventeenth try in 1832, just one year before his son, Guofan, received the same degree.

**Philip Kuhn has summarized Zeng's accomplishments and the essential nature of the Xiang Army as follows: "It was Tseng Kuo-fan's achievement to bring young (locally recruited 'braves') units together into a larger organization, give them unified strategic direction, and connect them to broader sources of financial support. His unique clarity of orientation, added to his high official connections, provided a standard around which could rally the ablest of provincial elite. His deep-dyed neo-Confucianism, added to Ch'u Chi-huang's (a Ming scholar) canons of military organization, provided a framework within which personal loyalties could be reconciled with central command" (*Rebellion and Its Enemies*, p. 167).

with their commitments to the north and to the Yangtze valley, did not move to take advantage of the situation, and Shanghai was pacified. In Central China, however, the Taiping appeared more impressive than ever, and their strength was growing in South China as well.

Suddenly, in the fall of 1856, the Taiping dealt themselves a massive wound from which they never recovered. An internal struggle for power broke out in Nanjing which was to decimate the top ranks before it had ended.[28] The former charcoal maker, Yang Xiuqing, the Heavenly Kingdom's East King, had long wielded supreme power at the capital, treating other leaders, including Hong Xiuquan, contemptuously. In mid-1856 Yang and his supporters, having sent the other kings on various missions to remove them from the city, decided to make their bid for supreme power, assassinating Hong if necessary. But one of the conspirators, Hu Yihuang, defected and informed the palace of the plot. The other kings, Wei Changhui, Qin Rigang, and Shi Dakai, were immediately summoned back. Qin, previously a military commander who had been elevated to king in 1853, arrived first, awaited the return of Wei, and then with the concurrence of Hong, the two decided to move at once against Yang. Yang was stabbed to death by Qin himself in a confrontation in his palace, and then, despite an earlier agreement that only Yang and his two brothers would be slain, a general massacre in the palace and city occurred. Several thousand of Yang's relatives and supporters were killed, and battles continued in the streets for some days.

The infighting had only begun. With Yang dead, Wei and Qin moved to grasp power, and the Heavenly King realized that he was again in jeopardy. At this point, Shi Dakai returned to the capital and sought to mediate between the principals, but finding himself under suspicion by Wei and Qin, he decided to flee after less than twenty-four hours in the city. In fact, the former two kings did decide to assassinate Shi, and finding him gone, wiped out his family. In the weeks that followed, however, Wei went too far, imposing an iron rule upon Nanjing that earned him many enemies. When he, like Yang, threatened to eliminate Hong, a coalition moved against him. Shi had earlier pledged never to return to Nanjing until his enemies had been liquidated. Wei was beheaded, as was Qin, and their heads were sent to Shi, preserved in brine.

Shi returned to the capital, and a frightened, confused Heavenly King ordered him to rebuild the movement. Some 30,000 citizens had perished as a result of the inner conflict, and morale was understandably at a low ebb. Shi began the effort, but soon found himself undercut by Hong's two elder brothers, who now had the greatest access to him, as he became increasingly secluded at the top of the Taiping power structure. The Heavenly King did not break openly with Shi, but Shi decided that he could no longer remain in Nanjing. He departed at the end of May 1857, never to return.

The Taiping system had cracked at precisely its most vulnerable point, the top. Hong Xiuquan was undoubtedly a remarkable man in certain respects, combining intelligence, conviction, and charismatic qualities. But his vulnerabilities were also apparent—fragile mental health and limited interest in or capacity for administration. The self-made men who surrounded him were able, strong, and ambitious. More important, there were no safeguards in the Taiping political structure to prevent an abuse of power at the top. It was an old story, with many analogues in Chinese history, and a story that would have a future as well as a past. The principal Taiping leaders tore each other apart, leaving the movement leaderless at a point when it desperately needed firm guidance and direction.

The impact of these developments upon the military situation was rapid and dramatic. Without a central coordinating command at the capital, the various centers of Taiping power were left largely to themselves. Very soon the entire province of Hubei reverted to imperial armies, which also scored major gains in the provinces of Anhui and Jiangxi. The last city in Jiangxi to be held by the Taiping fell in September 1858. The military battles were not all lost, to be sure, and certain victories in Anhui reduced the threat to the Taiping capital, but the movement's former élan and unity were gone.

At this point, in April 1859, Hong Rengan, a cousin and early confidant of Hong Xiuquan, arrived in Nanjing. Rengan, who had pursued his studies of Christianity for many years and was regarded highly by his Western contacts, was joyously welcomed by the distraught Heavenly King and immediately elevated to the highest positions. He quickly advanced a series of reforms, intended to purge the government of nepotism and corruption, strengthen the central administrative apparatus, develop a more effective transport system, and modernize fiscal policies. Unfortunately for the Taiping cause, however, very few of the reform measures were actually implemented. At the same time, he sponsored a plan to have Taiping armies strike east, seizing Suzhou and Shanghai, thereby giving the Taiping a window to the sea—and to the West. Two young generals, Chen Yucheng and Li Xiucheng, were to play an important role in the effort to implement these plans.

By mid-1860, having taken Suzhou, the Taiping forces had surrounded Shanghai on three sides, and were ready for the assault. At this point, problems arose between the Taiping and the foreigners whose presence in Shanghai was of major importance. Earlier, Taiping troops had clashed with a small independent unit of some 200–300 men led by the American adventurer Frederick Townsend Ward.[29] Now they were to find that despite pledges of neutrality, units led by the British and French were to take an active role in the defense of the city. In truth, relations between the Taiping and the major Western powers had been troubled from the beginning. Although certain Western missionaries, journalists, and residents had expressed sympathy for the Taiping, especially in the early years, the representatives of Western governments had been antagonized by the combination of arrogance and ignorance they had met in Nanjing.[30] Beyond this, Humphrey Marshall, then American minister to China, voiced a widespread fear when he noted that if the Beijing government were toppled, China might disintegrate into chaos, its pieces becoming colonial possessions.[31] Thus, despite the fact that Great Britain and France were engaged in active hostilities with the Beijing government between 1858 and 1860 (during the so-called Arrow War), opposition to the Taiping was growing in Western quarters.

Shanghai remained under Qing rule, and in 1861 attention shifted to the struggle for Anjing, the Anhui city that held the key to Nanjing's future. Here the tide of battle surged back and forth for fourteen months. At one point, forces led by Zeng Guofan and Hong Rengan confronted each other directly, with Zeng's units scoring a major victory. After the slaughter of the

Taiping garrisons at Ling Lake in July, the fate of Anjing was sealed, and the city fell to imperial forces in early September, in some of the bloodiest carnage of the entire war.

The Taiping were still demonstrating great strength in Zhejiang, where they occupied a number of major cities and took the key port of Ningpo in April 1861. Ningpo gave the rebels access to food and military supplies, and enabled them to bring almost all of Zhejiang province, as well as a goodly portion of Jiangsu, under their control by autumn. Shanghai appeared highly vulnerable once again, but the problem of foreign reaction now loomed large. In March 1861, Sir James Hope, commander of the British squadron in Shanghai, had delivered a note to Nanjing on behalf of the British government, demanding that the Taiping not come within thirty miles of either Shanghai or Wusong, and this request had been accepted by the Heavenly King. After the capture of Ningpo, however, the Taiping asserted that they would no longer be bound by the agreement. Nevertheless, the Nanjing leaders were not united behind a decision to make a second strike at Shanghai. Some, including Hong Rengan, believed it would be a mistake to antagonize the foreign powers. But the chief commander, Li Xiucheng, felt that a quick victory, like the one at Ningpo, was possible and would neutralize foreign opposition.

The opening stages of the campaign in January 1862 went reasonably well, but by February it became clear that the British and French were prepared to cooperate actively in preventing the Taiping capture of Shanghai. In late February a series of clashes with mixed foreign-imperial units led by Ward and Hope resulted in heavy losses for the rebels, despite the fact that they vastly outnumbered the Western-led forces. These were not the Taiping soldiers of old. Young recruits, poorly trained and weakly indoctrinated, now constituted the great bulk of the Taiping armies. Most of the struggles in the spring of 1862 went against them.

The most significant form of foreign intervention was not the direct involvement of foreign troops but the training and equipment given to Chinese imperial forces by Western nations. British and French troops did play a significant role in the early defense of Shanghai, up to the late spring of 1862. But at that point, a new commander of consequence with well-disciplined troops emerged on the imperial side: Li Hongzhang, still under forty years of age, but on the brink of a long and prestigious career.[32]

Li's first major chance for distinction came in 1861, when he was put in charge of a new army formed out of units from Zeng's Xiang Army and soldiers recruited in the Huai River valley.[33] Known as the Huai Army, Li's force was shipped to Shanghai in British transports in the late spring of 1862, and Li took command of the Shanghai defense on behalf of imperial forces; at the same time he was named governor of neighboring Jiangsu province. By mid-May of 1862 the Huai Army had gone into action, operating in close conjunction with Ward's mercenary troops. In the summer the imperial units were also aided by the participation of regular British and French units. Though frequently outnumbered, this combination of forces repeatedly thwarted Taiping efforts to capture Shanghai, and by fall the Taiping challenge to the city had passed.

At this point, government forces moved to regain eastern Zhejiang and Jiangsu, provinces adjacent to China's major port. Again the foreign mercenaries played a role of some significance. Ward himself was mortally wounded in late September in a battle fought at Ningpo. His place was taken first by another American, Henry Burgevine, and then by the British major Charles Gordon, who assumed command on March 24, 1863.[34] Gordon's force, now known as the Ever Victorious Army, numbered 5,000 to 6,000 men and operated under the general command of Li Hongzhang, whose imperial troops totaled 50,000 to 60,000. By the summer of 1863 these forces had surrounded Suzhou, where approximately 40,000 Taiping troops were garrisoned. Suzhou fell at the beginning of December, and the subsequent slaughter of Taiping prisoners so sickened Gordon that he rushed to an angry confrontation with Li and afterwards relinquished his command. He resumed his post in February 1864, after Li promised to abide by the accepted principles of international law in handling prisoners of war—a pledge that was reported to be soon violated. In any case, Gordon announced the dissolution of the Ever Victorious Army on May 31, 1864. Eastern Jiangsu had been recovered for the government, and significant portions of Zhejiang as well, where the Taiping continued to suffer defeats at the hands of Li's Huai Army.

Meanwhile, the stage had earlier been set for a giant pincer operation against Nanjing. By the fall of 1862 imperial forces under the overall command of Zeng Guofan were prepared to advance on the Heavenly Capital from Anhui, Jiangsu, and Zhejiang. The first major battle between the government forces and the Taiping defenders took place in October, with Taiping armies led by General Li Xiucheng. Imperial forces were victorious in this and succeeding contests, despite the fact that the rebel forces outnumbered Zeng's units by more than twenty to one.

To relieve the new siege of Nanjing, an old Taiping strategy was revived. Expeditionary forces were dispatched with the goal of reaching Hubei, thereby forcing Zeng to disperse his troops in defense of imperial-held centers in that province. The largest of these forces—some 350,000 soldiers, more than 200,000 of them led by Li Xiucheng personally—set out at the end of February 1863. But this huge army, going by way of North Anhui, was forced to move through regions devastated by earlier campaigns, and shortages of food and supplies became increasingly critical. The effort to reach Hubei had to be abandoned, and Li returned with less than one-half of his original army.

By November 1863 the Xiang Army had completed its encirclement of Nanjing. An agreement had been reached the previous August between the Qing government and foreign ministers in Beijing to halt all shipments in foreign bottoms to the rebel capital. Naturally, this further aggravated the defenders' problem of getting food and supplies into the encircled city. By the end of the year, Li Xiucheng was advocating an evacuation of Nanjing, but the Heavenly King refused to contemplate any abandonment of his capital. As the food problem grew ever more acute, however, civilians were finally permitted to leave. Local administration broke down, and the city approached chaos in the early months of 1864. On June 1 the founder and supreme symbol of the Taiping Tianguo, Hong Xiuquan, died of an undiagnosed illness, complicated no doubt by malnutrition. Six weeks later, on July 19, Nanjing fell to imperial forces, after a massive breach in the city's walls, produced by underground explosives, enabled Zeng's troops to pour into the city. Most of the remaining Taiping leaders were captured immediately (Hong's two elder brothers) or within a few months (Li Xiucheng, Hong Rengan, and the newly appointed king, Hong's sixteen-year-old son). All were executed after being forced to write their confessions.

The war dragged on for nearly two years more because sizable Taiping armies remained in the field in Zhejiang, Jiangxi, Fujian, and Guangdong. But step by step, at an enormous cost in lives, these remaining rebel forces were eliminated. In February 1866, with the fall of Jiaying in Guangdong, organized Taiping resistance came to an end.

THE TAIPING REBELLION IN PERSPECTIVE

How has the Taiping Rebellion been interpreted in recent times? Non-Marxist scholars have generally seen it in complex terms, as a movement essentially religious in its beginnings but with early anti-Manchu manifestations and mirroring the grievances of the rural classes, especially the poorer ones. It set forth an ideology compounded of classical Chinese and recently received Christian doctrines, and in its first years built a formidable organizational structure.

The fundamental causes for its emergence are seen in a range of interrelated socioeconomic problems that collectively produced the mounting crises which characterized the late Qing era: overpopulation, social tensions between ethnic and economic groups; governmental corruption and inefficiency; the breakdown of law and order; and recurrent imperialist pressures. Its stimulus is seen as coming from the earlier values and policies of the secret societies on the one hand, and from the impact of Western ideas, most notably Protestant Christianity, on the other. Its failure is ascribed fundamentally to the inner tensions which ripped it apart in 1856, and from which the movement never truly recovered; but homage is also paid to such factors as the strategic mistakes made in the early years, the failure to cultivate the Western powers sufficiently, the gradual loss of the movement's integrity through corruption and other lapses, and fundamental weaknesses within the leadership, including the personal deficiencies of Hong Xiuquan.

Among Marxist scholars (or scholars writing in a Marxist environment), a modest revisionism has lately been under way. The early simplistic analyses are being replaced by studies containing a degree of complexity closer to that advanced by non-Marxists. The thrust is toward finding the causes for Taiping failure within the movement rather than in external forces, whether foreign or indigenous.* Thus, attention is given the military and strategic errors, including the decision to locate the capital at Nanjing.[35] Defects of leadership, both military and civilian, are also cited as being of serious consequence, and some scholars emphasize the huge cost of the fratricide of 1856, which ripped the leadership apart and ended strong centralized control.

*Our data on recent Marxist scholarship are drawn heavily from papers presented at a conference on the Taiping Rebellion held in the People's Republic of China in February 1981, all of which are cited in the bibliography. Whatever their differences, nearly every scholar attending this conference agreed in regarding the 1856 upheavals in Nanjing as a critical turning point leading to Taiping decline.

As might be expected, Marxist scholars have focused on the question of how to classify the Taiping movement. A majority argue that it began as a peasant revolution, but later underwent a process of "feudalization," because of its class foundations and also because of its timing in the context of Chinese history. The thesis is as follows: the Taiping leaders, as well as the rank and file, were drawn from the ranks of the peasantry, and made a genuine effort to topple the landowner structure and the feudal system in its critical aspects; they failed because, as peasants, they were not an independent economic class and therefore not equipped to carry out a thoroughgoing revolution. Hence, in the end, feudalism triumphed.[36]

The relationship between the Taiping and the West also gets extensive attention. Almost all Marxist scholars writing on this period accept the thesis that after the Opium War, China became a "semifeudal and semicolonial society." * For many, the primary influence of Westernism on the Taiping lay in Christianity, and most argue that this religious influence contributed to the weak ideological underpinnings of the movement and diverted the leadership from what should have been its primary economic and political goals.[37] Yet several scholars suggest that Hong used religion successfully as an instrument of mass mobilization and a source of legitimacy, and some also argue that religion enabled Hong to camouflage his revolutionary commitments in the formative stages of the rebellion.[38]

A few Marxist authors suggest that the influence of the West went beyond religion and encompassed, for the first time in China, issues of economic modernization, at least in embryonic form.[39] Homage is paid to the fact that in the military arena Western-derived tactics and equipment had a significant influence on Taiping as well as imperial armies.[40] The West is also recognized as a source of Taiping nationalism, with various writers defining the Taiping as both anti-Qing and anti-imperialist, especially in the late years of the rebellion.

Unlike their predecessors, only a few Marxist authors now assign primary responsibility for the Taiping failure to Western intervention on behalf of the Qing. As we noted, the majority of current writings see the principal cause of that failure in the ideological and organizational inadequacies of Hong and his coleaders—especially their religious and superstitious base, which accounts for the ease with which they could be drawn back into royalism, Confucianism, and feudalism.[41]

Many non-Marxist Chinese scholars now regard the Taiping as essentially a negative force, responsible not merely for enormous destruction and misery but also for weakening the Chinese society on the eve of the greatest imperialist threats to its very survival. Most Marxists, by contrast, unite in praising the Taiping Rebellion for "opening the curtain to further struggles against feudalism and imperialism," for mobilizing the peasantry against the landowner system, and for speeding the erosion of Qing authority.[42] Hong is

* For this thesis, see the papers by Huang Zhenhei and Zhen Huaxin. More traditional polemic essays were written by Huang Dianzhu and Fang Yang. Huang Dianzhu begins with the statement that Western capitalists opened the gates of China with opium, cannons, and Bibles, and adds: "Realizing that they had to use both hard and soft methods in dealing with the stubborn, corrupt Qing, they sent the missionaries as another army of aggression to China." He accuses the missionaries of "trying every trick to control, reform, and destroy the revolutionary forces of the Taiping."

generally called a great revolutionary, despite the limits imposed on his thought and action by his class and his era.*

It is appropriate at this point to present our own summary analysis of the Taiping Rebellion. We would begin by noting its substantial similarities to the sort of upheavals that had periodically marked the course of Chinese history from ancient times and that seemed to be occurring more frequently by the late eighteenth century. This upheaval began as a rural rebellion somewhere on the periphery of the empire, in a region where livelihood was precarious and social tensions due to ethnic conflicts were high. Rising population pressures, widespread banditry, and the general ineffectiveness (and corruption) of government combined to further weaken allegiance to authority and to create a society of marginal individuals.

Into this milieu came preachers of hope—sincere, intense men dispensing a set of beliefs well attuned to the psychology of their listeners, catering to their fears and hopes. In its first phases, the movement was religious, not overtly political. But the seeds of political rebellion always lay within it, because the new doctrine being set forth challenged the prevailing philosophic orthodoxies, and those orthodoxies were the foundation of the political order of the day. Thus, to destroy Confucian altars and village idols was a political as well as a religious act. And earlier movements such as the White Lotus had clearly demonstrated that for simple rural folk the shortest route to rebellion was through a millenarian faith.

The Taiping Rebellion was also closely tied with tradition in its methods of recruitment and in the composition of its membership, including its leaders. The formal appeal was to believe, and believing, to follow. The claim was upon the emotions, and upon faith, beginning with faith in the leadership. The message and its dispensers were inextricably connected. Unless one believed that the Heavenly Father himself had appeared to Hong Xiuquan in a vision, exhorting him to exterminate demons and lead the people to the one true God—and also believed in the truth of the visions of Yang Xiuqing and Xiao Chaogui—the conversion could not be genuine, the commitment could not be total. Hong was the messiah, and the premium on his charisma was very high.

Yet in reality, recruitment depended on more than charisma. It was intimately related in the first instance to earning gratitude—hence obligations—through "good works," acts of assistance and support which contributed to individual and group betterment, sometimes to survival. Such good works touched upon the social, economic, and political environment in which the Taiping and their communicants operated, but they were not necessarily related to the principles of the movement. Once bonds of loyalty with an individual had been forged, however, access to families, clans, and villages was achieved. It would of course be incorrect to think of the Taiping movement as being able to operate in organic fashion, absorbing commu-

*Rudolf Wagner has noted the shift in Marx's own attitudes regarding the Taiping Rebellion. Initially, he hailed it as an event that would hasten revolution in England, but by 1862 he was castigating the Taiping for having no aim other than that of changing dynasties, and asserted that the rebels presented "an even greater horror for the masses of people than for the old rulers. Their mission seems to be nothing else but to oppose the conservative marasma with destruction in grotesquely abominable forms, with destruction lacking any germ of a new formation" (from an article in *Die Presses*, no. 185, July 7, 1862, reproduced in *Marx-Engles Werke*, vol. 15, 514ff., quoted in Wagner).

nities and regions in their entirety; the environment was sufficiently heterogeneous and internally factionalized to prevent this. But the degree to which absorption did proceed on a communal, hence a geographic, basis should not be underestimated.

Indeed, this may have been a significant factor in the movement's ultimate demise. As the Taiping spread ever further from its original base in the subculture of South China, particularly in the rural Hakka communities of Guangdong and Guangxi, the task of creating an integral unity became vastly more complex. As diverse and only partially absorbed elements were added, the movement became more diffuse. The challenge of welding together partially or greatly disparate units, each of them centripetal in nature, became overwhelming. To the extent that social organization rests fundamentally upon lineage lines, aggregation into large-scale units of great strength and permanence becomes extremely complex.

Taiping policies strengthened the communal aspects of the movement. Once a village, district, or town had been deeply penetrated, whether by persuasion or by conquest, the Taiping could not rest until the acquisition was a total one, at least on the surface. The populace, as we have seen, was fully mobilized. Opposition in any form was not tolerated. In spite of having adopted an essentially humanist religion, the Taiping, like certain Taoist and Buddhist rebels before them, were not constrained by it in practice. Rationalizing their actions by evoking passages from the Old Testament relating to good and evil, they used threats and coercion freely. Punishments were at least as significant as rewards in keeping the faithful—and not so faithful—in line.

Despite later acquisitions, the roots of the Taiping movement lay deeply imbedded in rural China, and it was built on the peasantry, like all other movements achieving any mass following in this predominantly agrarian society. In this, too, the Taiping Rebellion was intimately connected with the past, though not with the past alone. As we have indicated, however, its leaders were not simple peasants, although all came from a rural environment and most came from the lower end of the socioeconomic spectrum of rural society. Nor did they conceive of themselves as the leaders of a peasant movement. Although their program ultimately encompassed forms of egalitarianism and primitive communalism drawn from traditional and religious doctrines, their central appeal was not based on such traditional peasant grievances as taxation or injustice suffered at the hands of government of the upper economic classes. And far from exalting the status of the peasant, they viewed his position as distinctly inferior to their own as new theocratic rulers. More important, they thought their crusade should appeal to all Chinese (non-Manchu), both because it contained religious truth and because it promised to recast society in the mold of the Zhou era, thereby recreating a Golden Age that was purely Chinese. The Taiping rebels, to be sure, found their natural opponents not only in the Manchu but in the large majority of the gentry, because the literati-officials, Han as well as Manchu, had an enormous stake in the Confucian order and the status quo. Yet the Taiping effort was to mount a religious-nationalist appeal that directed itself to all Han, cutting across socioeconomic classes.

In these respects, and particularly in the degree to which the Taiping leaders were seriously dedicated to mass mobilization on the basis of an ideology, this movement went beyond simple traditionalism and partook of modernity; it became a bridge from the past to the future. As we have noted, Taiping leaders paid careful attention to organizational matters and built a quite remarkable structure. The vaulted ceilings of this edifice were theocratic, with the divine right of a God-related Heavenly King and his similarly endowed associates challenging the legitimacy of the Qing dynasty and its supposed mandate from heaven. The foundations of the Taiping structure, however, were solidly military. Besides the fact that the key leaders—Hong Xiuquan excepted—derived their power from their armies, the citizenry was organized on the basis of military or military-related units, and the civil and military administrations were intertwined down to the local level. Thus it is legitimate to speak of Taiping government as theocratic-military rule. Various changes occurred in the course of its fifteen-year history, including ever-increasing bureaucratization, but its fundamental character did not change. Here too the shadow of the past and the portent of the future come together.

Not only was the Taiping administration cast in a theocratic-military mold; it was sustained in its militarization by the fact that it existed in a constant state of war. Throughout its brief history, it was a movement on the march. At one time or another, the Taiping held vast portions of China, but their long-term acquisitions were relatively few. In most regions, military occupation, mobilization of those citizens who remained, and indoctrination had barely been accomplished before the troops had to move out, advancing or retreating in response to decisions of the strategists. A permanent administrative structure, increasingly civilianized, with cadres developing experience and acquiring functional specialties, was impossible. There are always limits to the efficiency, appeal, and staying power of a military government on the march. In the case of the Taiping, when the army moved out it took with it whatever administrative infrastructure existed and as many citizens as it could round up; little was left behind. Meanwhile, mounting casualties were whittling down the first generation of rebels, the tough inner core that gave the Taiping movement its élan. These developments contributed to the growing fragility of the movement over the years, and to the fact that most of the reforms it envisioned could never be put into practice.

Had the Taiping aimed immediately for Beijing and succeeded in driving the Manchu from their capital, history might possibly have taken a different course. Those who hold the capital city have important psychological, political, and strategic advantages. Lacking these advantages, the Taiping challengers were confronted with the vastness of the land, the heterogeneity of its peoples, and extraordinarily primitive transport and communications. The Taiping had to settle for the existence of two Chinas; and outside Nanjing, the China they held could not yet offer stability or reasonable prospects for sustained growth. The Taiping movement thus failed in part because of a series of strategic errors in the military realm, capped by the failure to strike early for the Qing jugular.

But other factors were involved in that failure. Chief among them was the internecine warfare that cut down the key leaders in 1856 and rendered the atmosphere in Nanjing poisonous. This bloodletting occurred primarily because the Taiping failed to develop institutional safeguards against the abuse of power. In their theocracy, the Heavenly King, who theoretically held absolute power, was hobbled by serious personal limitations and disabilities; and he had delegated most of his power to a second-in-command, Yang Xiuqing, who possessed great magnetism and shrewdness but was illiterate, boundlessly ignorant of the world around him, and a victim of unbridled ambition. In hindsight, the scenario was predictable. Bizarre and extravagant rituals were instituted. Resplendent palaces were built, and thousands of courtiers attended the burgeoning elite—all in violation of the egalitarian ideals of early Taiping doctrine. Among the few who held real power, plots and counterplots proliferated and finally achieved only bloodshed. Absolute power had indeed corrupted absolutely.

Another reason for the failure was that the Taiping socioeconomic programs, though idealistic and forward-looking in certain respects, minimized or ignored a crucial factor: development. Their programs were of the sort that might be implanted in a simple, agrarian society, preferably limited in scope—precisely the type of community from which the Society of God Worshippers had emerged. There was little about them that addressed the issues of production, diversification, and development. Understandably so, one might assert, given the nature of mid-nineteenth-century China. But this meant that the Taiping were not equipped to handle the complex economic and administrative problems of managing urban centers. When economic decline ensued, idealism diminished. And when idealism deserts a utopian movement, only ruthlessness is left.

As the evidence makes clear, the Taiping sought to recruit various classes, including landowners and intellectuals, into their ranks. But they failed to attract the intellectual class in large numbers, and this became another source of weakness. In part, no doubt, this was due to the limited appeal of Taiping religion among that class. But even after a modified Confucianism was introduced, the great majority of intellectuals remained skeptical. And although Taiping leaders welcomed degree-holders, lower-ranking officials, especially in military circles, were not always friendly toward them. In the end, the bulk of the intelligentsia remained faithful to the Qing.

No doubt the gradual movement of the major Western powers away from neutrality toward opposition to the Taiping benefited the imperial side, especially in the struggle for Shanghai and vicinity. The Taiping had good reason to be irate with the leading foreign governments and their representatives in China, despite their own poor handling of foreign relations. But it is doubtful whether outside intervention did more than hasten the Taiping defeat. Men like Zeng Guofan and Li Hongzhang had already learned how to build peasant armies of their own and were a match for Taiping forces.

Another factor that ultimately did grievous damage to the cause was the Taiping willingness to expend the lives of soldiers in a profligate manner. To be sure, the imperial side often used "human wave" tactics regardless of the cost. But their use by the Taiping more sharply limited the time available for training and indoctrinating new recruits, who were hastily shoved into the front ranks. At least equally important was the loss of large numbers of Taiping officers, including a majority of those of army commander rank. Fighting capacities were drastically affected, as many campaigns of the last period were to show, and so were morale and discipline. And overall coordination of Taiping military efforts from the center had virtually ceased after the fratricide of 1856.

In the course of their defeat, however, the Taiping dragged their opponents a considerable distance down the same path, and contributed mightily to the shape of events that followed. In the economic realm, while the protracted, bloody struggle alleviated population pressures, especially in central

China, property destruction was huge, and some regions showed the scars for decades. It was during this period, moreover, that the Qing government first acquired a sizable indebtedness, creating the necessity for foreign loans. And financial transactions linking the national government to the provinces, including tax collection, were damaged, which not only reduced government revenues but prepared the ground for future problems of much wider scope.

Often overlooked is the fact that besides challenging the legitimacy of the Qing government before millions of its subjects, the Taiping caused the government to lose contact with those subjects for substantial periods of time. One might assert that this was the beginning of a divided China, even though the breach was closed for some decades in the immediate aftermath of Taiping failure. Doubts concerning the right as well as the ability of the Qing to rule had now been planted throughout South and Central China, adding to the pervasive legacy of the diehard Ming adherents. Han nationalism had been revitalized, and was now available to others who might seek to topple the Manchu.

In military terms, moreover, the seeds had been sown for yet another type of challenge to the center: the existence of locally based armies of the sort that Zeng and Li had so effectively built. In the end, these forces, together with the privately recruited militia, had been critical to imperial victory. But would they always fight on the imperial side? In any case, the extraordinary increase in the militarization of Chinese society was certain to affect the decades ahead.

It has been our thesis that the Taiping Rebellion was in its major aspects traditional in nature. In socioeconomic terms, it was a rural uprising with a peasant base, and it spoke to the villager in terms which, despite select innovations, his ancestors would have understood. At the root, moreover, the Taiping were committed to the historic paraphernalia of Chinese politics: statism, emperor-centered institutions, and a rigid hierarchy. Their theocratic-military structure was much closer in type to the institutions that prevailed during the opening decades of past dynasties than to anything that might be called modern. Their radical socioeconomic policies, lacking the all-important developmental theme, were patterned after ancient utopian models. And their military tactics and strategy were largely in line with traditional practices.

Yet it is entirely appropriate to consider the Taiping Rebellion an event that signaled the approach of China's modern era, an occurrence representing a transitional phase in China's coming quest for survival. On the one hand, it revealed the still-dominant role of classical Chinese thought, behavior, and institutions among rebels in a period when the impact of foreign stimuli was still slight. On the other hand, it was the first major movement to suggest the prodigious challenge that lay ahead—the challenge of adapting foreign values and institutions to China's existing capacities and future needs, and of meshing a new political structure with a changing socioeconomic order. To be sure, it suggested these necessities in the most embryonic form, but in its Christian borrowings it opened a path for future dissidents.

The Taiping Rebellion also sent forth another signal pertaining to the future. In its initial phases it demonstrated a vigor and an iconoclasm that seemed to threaten many of the institutions regarded as sacrosanct by a majority within Chinese society. Traditional mores, including those involving familial and sex relations, came under attack. The prevailing economic order also seemed in jeopardy. Yet in the end, the dominant forces within Chinese culture were able to reassert themselves, forcing the Taiping movement into retreat. And this retreat was propelled by the behavior and policy decisions that emanated from the Taiping leaders themselves.

Paralleling the unending struggle between two great forces—one directing China to turn outward, absorbing and adapting what other cultures had to offer, and the other urging China to turn inward, sustaining and defending its own great cultural legacy—ran another contest: a struggle between the rebels who wanted to alter Chinese culture and the elements within the culture that constantly worked to alter the rebels. These conflicts were first present in noticeable degree in the era of the Taiping, and they would grow in significance as first the Nationalists and then the Communists moved to the center of the political stage.

2

REFORM, RETREAT, AND REBELLION —CONTRAPUNTAL THEMES OF THE LATE QING ERA

If the Taiping Rebellion reflects in embryonic form the supreme challenge that was to dominate Chinese politics throughout the nineteenth and twentieth centuries, as an event it nevertheless belonged more to the past than to the future. Yet it was to shape the future mightily, leaving much of China prostrate, with its most prosperous areas grievously damaged, properties plundered or destroyed, and people reduced to a pitiable state. As the decade of the 1860s began, the Qing dynasty had never seemed more vulnerable.

At this point, however, a modest reform drive was launched under the aegis of a small group of able and perceptive officials, central and provincial. This effort, known as the Tongzhi Restoration, extended roughly from 1862 to the early 1870s, and at its high tide it suggested the possibility of an evolutionary advance toward modernization of the sort that was currently emerging in Japan.* Ultimately, the effort was stalemated, and with its momentum lost, many orthodoxies of the past were reasserted. Yet the reversion was far from complete. Certain reformers persisted in advancing the concepts and policies initiated during this era, providing some linkage between the 1860s and the 1890s. More important perhaps, the tide of events continued to challenge the old order on various fronts. For a time, however, the reformers fought a largely defensive battle, and precious years were lost.[1]

A second and more fundamental reform effort, breathtaking in its sweep and intensity, burst forth in 1898. It too was greatly influenced by Western contacts and stimulated by another humiliating military defeat, this one at

*K. C. Liu has pointed out that the term *zhongxing* in the Chinese context historically referred to "again rising" or "rising at midcourse," suggesting a period of resurgence after a time of decline (Liu, "The Ch'ing Restoration," p. 409, in Fairbank, ed., *Cambridge History of China*, vol. 10). *Zhongxing* (*ishin*) is also the ideographic combination used to designate the Meiji Restoration, and here the English word "restoration" seems appropriate, given the circumstances. The emperor Meiji, or at least the imperial court, was indeed restored to power. In the case of China, however, it would be more accurate to speak of the Tongzhi Revitalization.

the hands of Japan. Known as the One Hundred Days' Reform, the new drive—extending less than four months, from June to September of 1898—will always be associated with the names of Kang Youwei and Liang Qichao, who were to figure so prominently in the events of later years, and also with the name of the pathetic emperor Guangxu.[2]

THE REFORM-RETREAT-REVOLUTION SYNDROME

Before we analyze these two reform periods, a few words on the relation between reform, retrenchment, and revolution are in order. In the aftermath of great catastrophes like the Taiping upheaval or massive foreign incursions, when current ills and dangers are too pervasive to be ignored, the impetus for change, even for sweeping alterations, emerges naturally from within a portion of the top political elite. In traditional systems, moreover, the very weakness of the monarchy or top leadership at this point may serve as a stimulus rather than a barrier, because it enables talent from the lower echelons of the system to come forward with fresh initiatives.

Not infrequently, as in the case of the Meiji Restoration in Japan or the great reform era of early-nineteenth-century Britain, a long-term political course is set, rendering revolution progressively less necessary and less possible. But if the reform proves abortive, a combination of consequences is likely to follow: a swing of political policies and attitudes toward greater restriction, albeit with the inconsistencies and contradictions that betray a regime at bay; a corresponding increase in extremism in response, with antagonists pushed into intractable positions; the emergence of a small but dedicated revolutionary leadership, prepared to take advantage of mass lethargy and regime error; and finally, a painful and progressive fragmentation of the power-holding elite.

The movement from abortive or inconclusive reform to reaction may be repeated more than once, with the likelihood that increased tension will accompany each new cycle. At some point, a further dilemma will present itself to those in power: reform may encourage rather than forestall revolution. Regimes in grave peril may find the reforms they undertake interpreted as weakness, or rejected by a revolutionary opposition that defines all reforms as measures insidiously designed to thwart fundamental change. More important, at some stage a government may lose the inner strength to preside effectively over reform; erratic governmental behavior leads to loss of control over the very policies inaugurated by the regime itself, with the result that authority is progressively surrendered or seized, and divisions within top elites are exacerbated. Under such conditions, reform becomes a catalyst of revolution.

What we have said so far by no means exhausts the variables relating to political change and the stability or instability of regimes. Revolutions also fail, more often than is usually admitted. And a failed revolution may well generate a combination of repression and reform of the sort seen in Franco's Spain, leading to later evolutionary potentialities. In other settings, a combination of factors may be conducive to an extraordinary stasis, whereby a society, without reform or revolution, is enabled to exist in a stagnant condition for a protracted period. This stasis can continue only when there is a minimum of external intervention, but even in our times various examples can be cited.

In this typology of political scenarios, it should be clear that both Russia and China—with important internal variations—fall into the category of states involved in the reform-retreat-revolution syndrome we have outlined.

PRELUDE TO REFORM

Over the long course of Chinese history, there have been many reform drives. Generally, they aimed at replacing "evil men" with "men of virtue." Only rarely has the focus of attack broadened to encompass structural aspects of the system. Consequently, the results have usually been ephemeral. A typical instance was the campaign that got under way with the death of the Qianlong emperor in 1799.[3] After governing with vigor for many years, an aging emperor had allowed He Shen, a favorite raised up from the palace guard, to acquire enormous power and wealth. No one dared to criticize the emperor's protégé directly, although it was common knowledge that he and his clique were engaged in an endless variety of unsavory practices that influenced the conduct of officials at every level. Immediately upon the old emperor's death, however, his son, the emperor Jiaqing, ordered He Shen to commit suicide, and he purged or degraded key associates. Yet it was impossible to root out all of the officials involved in corruption; the disease was endemic. Hence most civil servants were declared honest but misled, and ordered to rectify their ways—an approach used toward profligate Chinese bureaucrats into the Maoist era and beyond.

In its essentials, the Tongzhi revitalization drive of the 1860s continued in the traditional vein. The effort was to save the system, not change it. As the decade began, the key issue was the survival of the dynasty, possibly the nation, in an era when internal rebellions were rampant and interaction with the wider world could no longer be avoided.

The twin threats of internal strife and foreign intervention led a small but strategically placed group of officials to seek both personnel changes and the introduction of Western technology, especially in the military realm. These goals were regarded as fully compatible with adherence to the neo-Confucian values that had sustained Chinese society since the Song era. The reformers were far from being "pro-Western," as their opponents charged. They were no less concerned over the prospect of Western domination than their arch-conservative critics; the issue was how best to prevent such a fate. By the late 1850s the key reformers had come to have a healthy respect for modern Western weapons as a result of their experiences during the Taiping Rebellion. That respect was heightened in the course of the conflict with the British and French known as the Arrow War, which had its origins in events transpiring in 1856. So important was this war in shaping subsequent Chinese attitudes and policies that a brief description of it is required.[4]

The initial issues were familiar ones: extraterritoriality and missionaries. In October 1856, Chinese authorities in Canton seized some Chinese crewmen aboard the *Arrow*, a British-registered lorcha (foreign hull, Chinese rig). British officials in Hong Kong protested despite the fact that they stood on very dubious legal and moral grounds. The ship's Chinese owner, living in Hong Kong, had allowed the registration to lapse; certain crew members had probably been engaged in piracy on other vessels earlier; and it is unclear whether the British flag was flying at the time the vessel was seized. Antagonized by the persistent refusal of Governor-General Ye Mingchen to open Canton to foreign intercourse earlier and his deep-seated antiforeignism, the British authorities decided to pursue a hard line. In this they received French support. The immediate French grievance concerned the "execution" in early 1856 of a French missionary charged with living in a forbidden area.

The conflict simmered without major confrontations until December 1857, more than one year later. By then British-French forces totaling nearly 6,000 men had been organized, and an ultimatum was presented to Ye requesting free access to Canton and compensation for losses incurred in earlier attacks on British property in the area. When these demands were rejected, an attack on Canton was launched and the city was quickly brought under foreign domination. Ye was transported to India as a prisoner, and an allied commission was set up to govern Canton, which it did until October 1861.

Foreign control of Canton, however, did not lead to negotiations with Beijing. After the failure of efforts to get the Chinese government to send negotiators to Shanghai to sign a treaty, the allies—with Russian and American officials accompanying them—moved north. By May 1858 a flotilla of British and French warships had assembled, and on May 20 an attack on the Dagu forts at the mouth of Beihe, the river guarding Tianjin, resulted in quick success. By May 26 foreign gunboats had reached Tianjin.

Hoping to avoid a foreign march on Beijing, reluctant Chinese authorities finally opened negotiations, beginning with the time-honored stratagem of seeking to manage the barbarians by an adroit mixture of flattery and tenacity. The British proved adamant, and Chinese negotiators finally capitulated, signing the Treaty of Tianjin with the two powers on June 26 and 27, 1858. The treaty provided for permanent residence in Beijing for a British representative (but under most-favored-nation agreements, for other nations as well); internal travel for foreigners under a Chinese-validated passport in areas beyond the unrestricted port zones; tariff duties of 5 percent ad valorem generally, and a limit on the *likin* tax (internal transit fee) for foreign goods to 2.5 percent; legalization of the opium trade; and indemnities totaling sixteen million taels.

Desperately, the conservatives headed by the emperor himself tried to modify the treaty provisions or restrict their enforcement. A new crisis soon developed. En route to Beijing in the early summer of 1859 to engage in ratification ceremonies, the British envoy, Sir Frederick Bruce, in accordance with official instructions, insisted on journeying to the capital via Dagu. Seeking to go ashore there, British forces came under fire from Chinese shore batteries, taking heavy losses. A major English-French expedition under Lord Thomas Elgin was then mounted. After futile negotiations and the seizure of both Chinese and British hostages, the expeditionary force occupied Beijing, with the emperor fleeing to Rehe (Jehol). Elgin ordered the burning of the Summer Palace as a retaliatory measure, and contemplated replacing the Manchu monarch with a Chinese emperor, but was dissuaded by the Russians and the French.

On October 24, 1860, with Prince Gong acting on behalf of the Chinese government, the Convention of Beijing was signed and the old Treaty of Tianjin ratified, maintaining and in a few respects expanding foreign rights. On November 8 allied troops left Beijing. The Russian envoy, General Nikolai Ignatiev, who had served as mediator and remained behind, took this opportunity to legalize by treaty all Russian territorial holdings east of the Ussuri River and additional commercial privileges in Xinjiang.[5]

Thus, by the end of 1860 China had been thoroughly humbled by the Western barbarians, who had demonstrated their power in an unforgettable fashion. Even more important, the major Western nations and their representatives now had legal access to the whole of China. In this sense, 1860 represented a watershed of the greatest significance. Henceforth, it would be impossible to ignore the leading Western powers or to refuse to have continuing, even intimate relations with them, unless China were strong enough to overturn existing treaties and accept the certainty of war.

THE TONGZHI REVITALIZATION EFFORTS

The Tongzhi reform efforts flowed naturally from this situation. It was also important that on the eve of the new era, the throne came under the control of two perceptive men, both Manchu—Prince Gong (Yixin) and Wenxiang. Just before the emperor Xianfeng died in August 1861, the powerful conservative Zaiyuan faction had extracted a final decree from him authorizing them to act for his five-year-old son, now ascending the throne. (This was not to be the last occasion on which death-bed decrees would figure prominently in Chinese politics.) A power struggle immediately ensued, with Prince Gong leading a palace coup, abetted by the two young empress dowagers and other partisans. The men surrounding the dead emperor at Rehe were charged with plotting to seize power illegally, deceiving Xianfeng, and giving erroneous counsel on foreign policy, thereby leading to China's humiliation. The key figures were summarily executed, forced to commit suicide, or removed from office. The throne was placed under a regency, and Prince Gong was made chief adviser.

There quickly emerged a notable group of leaders determined to save China from its gravest crisis since the founding of the Qing dynasty. At the center, the principals were Prince Gong and Wenxiang, assisted on occasion by individuals like Shen Guifen and Li Tangjie. In the provinces, Zeng Guofan and Li Hongzhang proposed innovations, with Zuo Zongtang, Hu Linyi, Luo Zenan, Liu Rong, and Luo Bingzhang among others providing support.[6]

The first task, in point of urgency, was to put down rebellion, thereby reasserting the internal authority of the government. This was no simple task. In the early 1860s four rebellions of serious proportions continued, and there were local uprisings in almost every province. The Taiping were not yet vanquished; indeed, for several years after 1858 they were in resurgence. The Nian rebels, having built a strong base in northwest Anhui, were expanding across North China.[7] In both Yunnan and the northwest, Moslem uprisings had assumed major dimensions.

In meeting these challenges, the new Tongzhi leaders relied primarily on restructured, better-led, and better-equipped military forces, of the sort epitomized by the Hunan and Anhui armies. In the course of building and leading these armies, Zeng and Li (as well as their Taiping opponents) became increasingly impressed with the effectiveness of Western weaponry, especially rifles and cannons. Western training methods were also admired. It is not surprisng, therefore, that in 1862 Zeng established the Anjing Arsenal, thereby inaugurating the effort to implant Western military technology in China. Li established the Jiangnan Arsenal three years later. By the mid-1860s, moreover, with the Taiping threat waning, both men were advocating wide-ranging military reorganization, including the reduction of troops (even in their own armies), with the savings to be applied to modern training and equipment.

These and other measures were advanced in the name of *ziqiang* (self-strengthening), a theme that first became prominent in 1861 and served in the years ahead as the reformers' principal rallying cry. If China wished to live at peace, or to be able to fend off barbarian attacks when necessary, it had to acquire the modern sources of power. This did not require fundamental alterations in traditional values, socioeconomic institutions, or the political structure, they argued. Nor did it imply that outsiders should play a primary role in reform efforts—that was a task for the Chinese themselves. In fact, one should even be wary of permitting the Westerner to gain too much knowledge about the Central Kingdom, let alone economic or political influence.* As the Meiji Restoration progressed in Japan, one of its slogans—*fukoku kyōhei* (a rich country, a strong soldiery)—struck a responsive chord among the Chinese reformers. It seemed to express the logical culmination of a successful self-strengthening movement.

Meanwhile, those who had to assume the immediate responsibility for crushing rebellion soon came to realize that victory could not come through military means alone. Experience persuaded them of the need to reform tax and fiscal policies and to curb the excesses of local officials. Some of their measures, such as the suspension or reduction of taxes in regions heavily damaged by war, were purely temporary. More meaningful reforms, however, were also projected. Chief among these were the drives to eliminate the tax advantages of well-to-do landowners and to reduce or abolish the oppressive tax surcharges being applied at the local level. To effectuate such measures, orders were given restricting the function and power of the clerks and runners, who for the ordinary subject represented the most onerous extension of government. Neglected water-conservation projects were supported, and immigration into devastated areas was encouraged—as they had been in the Yangtze provinces since the mid-1850s, at the height of the Taiping surge.

Advancing these various programs, the Tongzhi reformers were to speak repeatedly of *minsheng* (the people's livelihood) as an essential factor in restoring faith in government. Two themes, "people's livelihood" and "self-strengthening," have linked traditional Chinese monarchy, modern republicanism, and contemporary communism together.

Basic socioeconomic alterations, however, were not the order of the day in the Tongzhi era. On the commerical-industrial front, the concept of a state-centered capital-accumulation drive and a mercantilist policy encouraging both state and private industry were never seriously considered, nor were land redistribution programs of the type that would later figure prominently in Chinese reformer-revolutionary discussions. Commerce continued to be regarded with distaste. Foreign trade and industrialization failed to get support, partly because of concern over their effect on China's tradi-

*In this respect, a revealing comment was made by Shen Guifen to W. A. P. Martin: "Our true policy is to make use of foreigners, but not to let them make use of us." And toward Yung Wing, Shen revealed his animus: "I don't like him; he has married an American wife" (Martin, *Cycle of Cathay*, p. 342).

tional handicraft industries. In sum, the Tongzhi revitalization, unlike the events unfolding in early Meiji Japan, did not encompass economic modernization.

Yet the effort to stimulate agricultural production and the struggle against bureaucratic corruption were to have recurrent echoes in modern China, down to the present day. Feng Guifen succinctly expressed the reformers' antipathies when he referred to the three great evils plaguing society as the three *li*: bureaucracy, official "red tape," and profit.[8] This lament, so traditional and so modern in China, summed up the perennial problems of an intensely statist system fundamentally dedicated to collectivism, whatever its precise economic forms.

The most significant Tongzhi innovations were those pertaining to foreign relations and specialized training, two strands of the reform movement that were closely interrelated. It was recognized that foreign policy could not be left merely to the hasty improvisations of generalists, and that if the Western barbarian were to be successfully managed, a much higher degree of knowledge concerning his political values and institutions would be required. Thus the nucleus of a foreign office was set up, in the form of the Zongli Yamen. This body—which by virtue of overlapping appointments was virtually a committee of the Grand Council—evolved into an organ that handled all matters dealing with foreigners.* A training center for instruction in foreign languages was authorized, and after a brief period, select science courses were added to its curriculum.[9] The translation of Western works also began, and the results were transmitted to key officials.

The fact that the translations included not only scientific and technical works but also Wheaton's *Elements of International Law* was important, because the law treatises provided basic knowledge about the barbarians' modus operandi in the international sphere.** And from this knowledge flowed an ever stronger predilection in reformist circles to move away from policies of confrontation toward an acceptance of treaty relations of a West-

* S. M. Meng points out that when the Zongli Yamen was first established in early 1861, it was intended as a temporary office, to be dissolved as soon as military operations against the Taiping and other rebels were concluded and when foreign relations were in a more satisfactory condition. In lieu of any other organ to handle foreign affairs, however, it was retained (S. M. Meng, *The Tsungli Yamen*, p. 26). Up to 1884, when most of the members of the Zongli Yamen were also members of the Grand Council, the former body had both prestige and power. After that time, following the dismissal of six Zongli Yamen ministers including Prince Gong, the office served essentially as a secretariat for those in other offices who were actually controlling foreign policies (Meng, pp. 50–60). For another detailed and well-researched account, consult Immanuel Hsu, *China's Entrance into the Family of Nations*. See also Banno, *Origins*, pp. 219–246. Banno regards the zenith of Zongli Yamen authority to have been reached prior to the death of Wenxiang in 1876 (p. 246).

** Under the sponsorship of Lin Zexu, then Imperial Commissioner for Frontier Defense, passages from Emeric de Vattel's treatise on international law were translated as early as 1839, in an effort to get a better understanding of barbarian ways. Hao and Wang, "Changing Chinese Views," p. 147. More than twenty years later, in 1862, W. A. P. Martin commenced the translation of Henry Wheaton's *Elements of International Law*, and, encouraged by Zongli Yamen officials, continued the work aided by Chinese assistants, seeing it published in both Chinese and Japanese (Martin, *Cycle of Cathay*, pp. 221–235). Martin also reported: "With the help of my students, I have since given the Chinese translations of De Martens' 'Guide Diplomatique,' Woolsey's 'Elements of International Law,' Bluntschli's 'Volkerrecht,' and last, not least, a manual of the laws of war compiled by the European Institute of International Law," most of which were also reprinted in Japan (p. 235).

ern type. Such a major shift, involving as it did an abandonment of deeply rooted traditional Chinese practices like the tributary system, could not be accomplished in a brief period of time, and the commitment to an ultimate vanquishing of the barbarian remained attractive to most leaders. Yet the new trend must be considered radical against the background of past Chinese attitudes and behaviors.

Notwithstanding the premium on self-reliance and the almost unanimous suspicion of the foreigner, the Tongzhi reformers were forced to rely heavily on Western diplomats, officials, and missionaries in planning and executing their programs. Individuals like Ward, Gordon, and a host of other military men, both free-lancers and official representatives of their governments, were critical to the successful introduction of modern military training and technology. When the first arsenals were set up, moreover, other Western specialists were required. Western diplomats—including the Britishers Rutherford Alcock and Thomas Wade, that remarkable Irishman Robert Hart, and the American Anson Burlingame—repeatedly advanced suggestions or gave advice that was incorporated into reform policies. Western missionaries, including S. Wells Williams, John Fryer, W. A. P. Martin, and Young J. Allen, played crucial roles in introducing Western learning, and their efforts were supplemented by those of a small group of European and American teachers of secular persuasion.

By the terms of the convention signed with the British in 1860, English as well as Chinese was to be an official language in diplomatic relations. Thus, in 1862 the Zongli Yamen authorized the establishment of the Beijing Tongwen Guan (the Interpreters' College, or as Martin called it, the School of Combined Learning), with the initial purpose of the training of English-language translators and interpreters.* Instruction in the French and Russian languages was later added, and similar training centers were opened in Canton and Shanghai. Enrollees were strictly limited to those who had already completed their Chinese training, and for the most part, students were drawn from Manchu Banner families. In 1866 Hart was authorized to recruit European instructors in mathematics and astronomy, and these subjects became a part of the curriculum. Three years later, in 1869, W. A. P. Martin assumed responsibility for the school's administration and, in addition to his duties there, continued to engage in translations. He had already made a valiant but unsuccessful effort to persuade Zongli Yamen officials to adopt the telegraph.**

*Martin, whose first-hand account of the Tongwen Guan is very interesting, cites an extract from Prince Gong's memorial addressed to the throne in October 1861. In it, Gong reports that although a memorial of 1860 had resulted in a quest in Canton and Shanghai for Chinese "well acquainted with foreign letters," no suitable indigenous teachers had been found, which explained the delay in setting up a foreign-language school. The memorial concluded: "Your Majesty's servants are penetrated with the conviction that to know the state of the several nations it is necessary first to understand their language and letters. This is the sole means to protect ourselves from becoming the victims of crafty imposition. Now these nations at large expense employ natives of China to teach them our literature, and yet China has not a man who possesses a ripe knowledge of foreign languages and letters—a state of things quite incompatible with a thorough knowledge of those countries. As therefore no native candidates were sent up from Canton and Shanghai, we have no recourse but to seek among foreigners for suitable men (*Cycle of Cathay*, pp. 295–296).

**Martin had taken lessons in telegraphy while on home leave in 1862, and had brought the necessary equipment with him on returning to China. He invited Zongli Yamen repre-

At a later point, several groups of Chinese students, most of them from Guangdong province, were dispatched to the United States for education; 120 of them were abroad by 1875. This program had been initiated by Yung Wing (Rong Hong), who had graduated from Yale in 1854.

Toward the end of the 1860s, there was some reason to hope that China would make steady progress toward the type of changes that would enable not merely survival but a gradual strengthening of its position in the wider world into which it was being pushed. By mid-1867 the Nian rebellion had been crushed, ending the last serious military challenge of this era. The newly created provincial armies, whatever their defects, had succeeded in their primary assignment. A period of peace was at hand, providing the opportunity for further constructive measures. In the decade after 1860, foreign military assaults also ceased.[10]

Yet, after the mid-1870s, a retrenchment occurred. The impetus for reform was preserved by certain individuals, but the modernizers were generally held in check. Various reasons for this can be advanced. Military victory lessened the immediate threat to the dynasty, and so the urgency of reform declined. It soon became clear, moreover, that the efforts to elevate the character and efficiency of officials had scarcely reached local levels, and even among provincial officialdom quality varied greatly. The old examination system continued to operate, guaranteeing that traditional values and practices would retain their potency. Sales of titles and offices increased. The brief tenure of officials, from governors-general to *xian* magistrates, contributed to the ineffectiveness of local government and insured the power of yamen clerks, runners, and other scavengers who remained permanently in place. In short, the effort to create a government of virtuous men was floundering. Furthermore, there were no tax and fiscal reforms of the sort that had provided the basis for the far-reaching changes getting under way in Meiji Japan. The old order remained largely intact, with revenues restricted to *likin* and customs duties. The central government retained its control over these, but only a portion of the *likin* collections made by provincial authorities ever reached imperial coffers.

Thus, there was neither the will nor the means to underwrite a thoroughgoing reform program. The fact that the vast majority of the literati-officials continued to identify with the traditional order was a crucial factor inhibiting change. The limited resources of the center, a product of antiquated tax and fiscal policies, together with the weak linkage between various levels of government, provided further obstacles.

Beyond these factors, two specific developments served to slow reform: the renewal of crisis in foreign relations, and the decline, through death or lessened influence, of certain key reformers. The Tianjin massacre of 1870, which caused the always delicate relations with foreigners to deteriorate,

---

sentatives to witness an experiment at his home. Prince Gong deputed the four Chinese who were aiding him in the Wheaton translation, but they showed greater interest in the game of catching magnetic fish and geese. Undaunted, Martin requested and received permission to set his experiment up in Zongli Yamen headquarters. The officials were intrigued and participated in sending signals. The minister of finance even learned to send messages, and Wenxiang also came a second time to inspect the equipment, but although it remained at the Zongli Yamen for one year, nothing happened, so Martin removed it (*Cycle of Cathay*, pp. 299–300).

rekindled the flames of xenophobia and placed the reformers on the defensive.* Those charged with "appeasement" of the West or advocacy of "barbarian ways" were now cast into greater jeopardy. The Tianjin affair epitomized the volatile interaction between Chinese antiforeignism and forms of foreign penetration that struck at the heart of sacred and secular Chinese values. It enabled xenophobic forces, being held in check by the Meiji reformers in Japan, to reassert themselves formidably in China.

The fate of the reforms was heavily dependent upon the fate of a few key political figures. From an early point, Prince Gong was forced to struggle against the growing jealousies of the empress dowager Cixi. In 1865 she personally drew up a list of charges against him and announced his dismissal from all key positions. He was restored to his posts following an avalanche of appeals, but he never fully regained his authority. Conservatives like Woren and Prince Gong's younger brother, Prince Chun, rose in power, and Prince Gong's relations with Cixi remained troubled throughout the 1870s. Zeng Guofan, whose influence was critical to provincial reforms, died in 1872, and Wenxiang, the most influential single figure associated with the moderates at court, died in 1876. Meanwhile, in 1875 the Tongzhi emperor had died and the four-year-old son of Prince Chun and Cixi's younger sister was placed on the throne, which heightened the influence of Chun. A few modernizers like Li Hongzhang remained in important positions (in 1870 Li was appointed governor-general of Zhili), but generally speaking, staunch conservatives held power at the center.

It has been argued that the Tongzhi revitalization efforts failed fundamentally because an effective modern state could under no circumstances be grafted onto a Confucian society.[11] Although such a view contains elements of truth, it is basically unsatisfactory both as a specific answer to the question of Tongzhi failure and as an exposition of the broader issues connected with the relationship between any traditional political culture and the modernization process. Certainly, the Confucian tradition *was* incompatible with the needs and aspirations of Chinese modernizers in vital respects. But as Japan, itself deeply influenced by Confucianism, was to illustrate, a tradition can be incrementally reshaped—and even fortified, parts altered, parts

*The Tianjin massacre which took place in June 1870 followed a long period of mounting Chinese unrest over activities of the Catholics in the city. The practice of adopting foundling children, some of them in desperate physical condition and not infrequently brought in by dubious sources, and the encouragement given some young converts to become nuns led to charges of kidnapping and murder at the missions by hostile, suspicious Chinese, among them prominent members of the local gentry. Demands for a thorough search of church premises were made. In the ensuing controversy both local French and Chinese authorities became deeply involved, with errors of judgment on all sides. At the peak of the crisis a Chinese mob attacked all foreigners who could be found and destroyed foreign churches. Two French officials, including the consul, were killed, as were a number of Catholic sisters and fathers, together with seven foreign residents and many Chinese converts. The French consulate, the Catholic cathedral, and the orphanage were burned.

War was averted, but in the following months tensions remained high. Ultimately, sixteen Chinese were executed for their part in the massacre, and a mission was dispatched to France to apologize—but for both sides, the affair epitomized the gulf that existed between two radically different cultures.

For the background, see the fine study by Paul A. Cohen, *China and Christianity*; John K. Fairbank, "Patterns Behind the Tientsin Massacre." In Chinese, see Luo Yuanken, *Zhongguo jinbainian shi* and *Qingji jiaoan shiliao*, vol. 1.

eliminated, so as to serve new causes. Indeed, this was precisely what the Meiji reformers did—often being scarcely conscious of the implication of what they were doing—and it is also what certain Tongzhi reformers set out to do, again without full consciousness of their acts.

A political culture cannot be altered swiftly, whatever the intention or the method. In the process of change, the issue is what portion of the "old" culture may be subsumed under the "new," and in the long run this is determined more by fundamental structural changes on the socioeconomic and political fronts than by immediate political acts and decrees of leaders, granting an interaction between these two forces. Have not all current inheritors of the Confucian tradition acknowledged that fact, in ways not necessarily determined by their political labels? Can we not see this in such diverse polities as the People's Republic of China, the Republic of China on Taiwan, the Republic of Korea, the Democratic People's Republic of Korea, the Democratic Republic of Vietnam, and Japan? To what extent has Confucianism, in the permutations possible after interaction with external stimuli, served rather than inhibited modernization, while at the same time giving it certain unique features that cut across prevailing political typologies?

The problem of reform in mid-nineteenth-century China cannot be reduced to the fact that the reformers refused to challenge the entire Confucian legacy head on. The difficulties lay in a series of far more complex problems. In addition to those we have already outlined, there was the problem of scale—a problem that has persisted to the present, plaguing "reformers" and "revolutionaries" alike. The small and cohesive political units most susceptible to modernization—nineteenth-century states like Great Britain and Japan—were quite unlike the entity called China. Given the existing technology—in communications, armaments, and productive capacities—the governance of an empire like China (or Russia) permitted few basic political choices. The functions of the center, however all-encompassing in theory, were perforce circumscribed in reality, and the center's reach was subject to various impediments. Despite representations and labels to the contrary, power in China was shared in such a fashion as to make *national* action or *national* consciousness impossible. Moreover, socioeconomic measures on a national scale were far beyond both the economic and the technical capacities of the center.

To be effective under such conditions, a reform effort would have to be sustained and incrementally advanced over a period of many decades, during which the newly conceived and slowly evolving nation-state would be certain to face repeated challenges from both indigenous separatists and foreign sources. The odds against success would be extraordinarily high. In sum, until the technical conditions for effective political aggregation and large-scale economic planning were more favorable, the policies and attitudes under which the Chinese empire had persisted for so long were certain to prove resilient and to make partial recovery whenever reform faltered.

The Tongzhi reform effort did not collapse after the mid-1870s. A small but growing number of individuals continued to insist that Western learning was essential to China's success in coping with the imperialist challenge. The official schools established to teach foreign languages and basic sciences remained in operation and even expanded their curriculum. Translations of Western works, most of them undertaken by missionaries, continued, and were supplemented by the publication of the diaries of certain Chinese who had been able to travel in the West. Military modernization remained a recurrent drive, and after the 1870s the modernization of commerce, industry, and agriculture also became topics of discussion.

Yet conservative forces opposed to the policies of change demonstrated great power. Their arguments were varied: the aroused Chinese masses could confront the barbarians more effectively than cannons and warships; China's prosperity had never depended on learning from barbarians; the West would guard its secrets and allow China to obtain only what was obsolete. And once again, a faction advocating militant policies to combat Western inroads arose, known as the Qingliu Dang (Purist Party). Its most prominent leader was Li Hongzao, and its ranks included many younger literati-officials, including Zhang Zhidong, who only abandoned this position after 1884. Demanding confrontation with Western imperialism, the Qingliu Dang members denounced as cowardly the attitudes and policies of the *yang-wu* (Western affairs) group, headed by men like Li Hongzhang, who insisted on peaceful, moderate approaches to the foreign powers.* Antiforeignism remained strong enough to block such projects as railroad construction, telegraphs, mining, and the expansion of technical schooling. It also brought China repeatedly to the brink of war and beyond, with disastrous results.

The rhythmic swing of Chinese politics and the sustained conflict within the political arena constituted a continuous response to a single, overriding issue: survival in a new world dominated both physically and intellectually by the West. From the beginning, and down to the present day, the debate over how to meet that challenge has focused on techniques. Should China seek maximum isolation, and attempt to exclude the foreigner by whatever means necessary? Throughout most of the nineteenth century, the emotional appeal of that approach captured all but a handful of Chinese. Its potency can be seen in the events leading up to each of the wars in which China became embroiled during that century. But it did not end there. As we shall see, that emotional appeal underwrote the Boxer Rebellion; its force was exerted nearly seventy years later among the "radicals" of the Great Proletarian Cultural Revolution, and it is not wholly moribund as a sentiment today.

Invariably, however, efforts to achieve isolation failed, primarily because China lacked the power to protect policies of exclusion. After each failure, the costs and dangers of isolation prompted the adoption of another ap-

* First emerging in the late 1870s at a time of mounting tension with Russia over the Ili region, and subsequently with the French over Annam, the Qingliu Dang adherents denounced individuals like Li and Prince Gong for their alleged timidity in confronting imperialist challenges. Proclaiming that the moral qualities of the Chinese could more than compensate for the material superiority of the barbarians (men over weapons), the militants demanded that force be used in answering the West.

As in the case of the young samurai leaders of Japan after the Meiji Restoration, some Chinese shifted their position after being confronted with repeated military defeats at the hands of foreigners. Nonetheless, those representing the Qingliu Dang position remained important into the 1890s, contributing to resistance to "Westernization," on the one hand, and the weakness and ambivalence of Qing policies, on the other. See Immanuel Hsu, "Late Ch'ing Foreign Relations," pp. 97ff., and Hao and Wang, "Changing Chinese Views," pp. 180–181.

proach, that of "turning outward." With varying degrees of intensity and sincerity, the foreigner would be cultivated, his habits studied, his technology borrowed, and his institutions examined.

Here too, within a certain swing, a progression can be noted. The initial effort was to keep technology and moral values as separate as possible, using barbarian science and technology only to preserve the Confucian order. By the close of the nineteenth century, however, the quest among the small Chinese avant-garde was for a greater synthesis, or even for a wholesale Westernization that would sweep the old order away.

The zenith of this movement was reached in the early part of the twentieth century, and its spokesmen were the leaders of Chinese liberalism and certain pioneer Communists. Seen in this context, "Maoism," especially in its "pure" form, was a partial retrenchment, a reshaping of communism so that Western science and technology would once again foster values and institutions that had a unique Chinese quality, despite the Marxian quotient that had been added. Thus we can discern a clear link between the "self-strengthening" movement of Zeng Guofan and Zhang Zhidong and the recent Communist theme of "self-reliance," a linkage that speaks to the complex elements of nationalism and internationalism with which modern China has continuously had to contend.

THE POLITICAL ACTORS OF 1898

With this preface as our guide, we may begin to identify the primary trends in China on the eve of the second reform effort, the movement engineered in 1898 largely by young Cantonese enthusiasts. It is appropriate to begin this effort by describing the principal political actors, because they constitute a variable far more important than searchers after the iron laws of history have been prepared to acknowledge.

On the throne sat precariously a well-motivated but weak young man, the emperor Guangxu, whose ascension (illegal, in terms of prescribed rules) was due to the shrewd planning of his aunt, the empress dowager Cixi. By any measure, Cixi was an extraordinary woman, a fact proclaimed by her admirers and ruefully admitted by her detracters, who were legion.[12] Born in November 1835 into the prestigious Yehenala clan, she became a "guiren" rank concubine of the emperor Xianfeng, and bore him his only son. Xianfeng symbolized the often fatal weakness of an ascriptive system: the inability of any lineage to perpetuate talent indefinitely. Ultimately addicted to all available vices, he died while still a young man in 1861, bringing to the throne (after a bloody struggle for power) Cixi's son, the five-year-old emperor Tongzhi.

Since Tongzhi was a minor, the two empress dowagers, Cixi and Cian (Xianfeng's wife), were now at the summit of authority within the court. But Cian had little interest in politics, and Cixi was still young and inexperienced; consequently, key advisers like Prince Gong played the crucial roles in the first years of the reign. By the time of Tongzhi's death in January 1875, however, Cixi had grown immeasurably in influence and power. Her determination to place her nephew on the throne was opposed by many, who correctly discerned that she herself would be the real ruler; but with adroit maneuvering, her will prevailed.

Until 1889, when the emperor Guangxu reached the age of nineteen and married Cixi's niece, the empress dowager wielded full power. At that point, the formal reins of power were passed to Guangxu, and Cixi, at the age of fifty-five, retired to the Summer Palace. But having relished her power for nearly thirty years, Cixi could not conceivably divorce herself from the affairs of state. Through informants at court she was kept well briefed on important developments, and the emperor himself never failed to consult his aunt before issuing any important decree. On matters of appointment and dismissal, moreover, the empress dowager retained what amounted to a veto power. Thus the stage was set for the palace coup of September 1898.

Seldom has a ruler borne so many paradoxes within her person, a fact that may reflect the distance her society traveled between 1835 and 1908, the year of her death. Above all, Cixi was a consummate politician. Her capacity to discern and play upon personal strengths and weaknesses, her sense of timing, her willingness to take risks, but equally, her prudence when a given course seemed too hazardous, and her capacity to shift directions (and personnel) dramatically when circumstances dictated were some of the qualities that enabled her to stay in power for nearly fifty years.

Cixi could fly into a towering rage, and on occasion her cruelty could be remarkable.* She was a Manchu and never forgot that fact, protecting her people's position in China as best she could; yet she relied on Han talent extensively in both civil and military affairs. When forced to do so, she could perform as a lady of great charm and friendliness before Westerners, but she remained implacably antiforeign throughout her life, and nothing would have made her happier than to have seen the Boxers exterminate all foreigners in China and then succeed in keeping them out. She came to believe in some aspects of the "self-strengthening" movement, and was prepared to support certain reforms long before 1898. This is one reason why she could crush the movement launched that year when she perceived it (correctly) as a personal threat, and then launch her own reform movement shortly thereafter. Reform for her, as for many of her contemporaries, was a necessary means to a greater end—that of preserving the old order. And she presided over a court that was still medieval in most respects. It was replete with powerful eunuchs, like Li Lianying, whose influence over her exceeded that of all others at times; with court favorites (and rumored lovers), like the Manchu general and statesman Ronglu; and with an unending procession of relatives, retainers, and flunkies. Corruption, intrigue, and decadence were built into such a court, and they flourished despite Cixi's personal vigor.

She could banish high officials and then recall them—the custom then as now. She could condemn counsellors to death, then grant mercy by allowing them to commit suicide, or by commuting their sentences so that they could reflect upon their crimes while rusticating in some remote place. But there was one reality that Cixi and her relatives could not overcome: they were a narrow Manchu stream in a vast Han sea.

* One oft-repeated story of Cixi's cruelty took place as a harried court was preparing to flee Beijing in the wake of Boxer defeat, with foreign troops about to enter the city. The emperor's favorite, the "pearl concubine," ventured to suggest that the emperor remain in Beijing. The empress dowager, long irritated by this concubine's insubordination, immediately ordered the attending eunuchs to throw her into a palace well. Despite the emperor's protests, this was reported to have been done.

In contrast to Cixi, the emperor Guangxu seemed always to be in the shadows, even when he was on the throne. Only for a brief interval in mid-1898 did he appear to truly grasp the reins of power. Often in delicate health, trained from childhood to be subservient to his aunt, Guangxu seemed a weak reed upon which to hang the future of Chinese renovation. Some who had close contact with him, like Li Hongzhang, said that he had no mind of his own and depended wholly upon his advisers.* Kang Youwei and Liang Qichao, however, found in him the qualities that could make for constitutional monarchy, including a basic humanism and a receptivity to new ideas that went well beyond Cixi's proclivities.

In any case, there could be no doubt of the emperor's history of dependence upon the empress dowager. Relations between the two appear to have been wholly amicable until the military catastrophes of 1894–1895. Then, unwilling to see Li Hongzhang blamed for China's humiliation, Cixi reportedly complained that her advice had not been adequately sought before China embarked upon war with Japan. In the midst of failure and crisis, it is not unusual for elites to split, and for those on the sidelines to assume the role of critics in more trenchant form. But a broader division within the court and the government had long been in the making: a North-South cleavage. The Manchu dynasty had always been stronger in the "conservative" North, and protest and rebellion seemed to emanate from the "progressive" or "unruly" South. As we have remarked earlier, the cleavage line did not fall precisely between Manchu and Han. Many Han, particularly those from the North, were to be found aligned with the conservative camp, and a few Manchu espoused various reforms, while naturally remaining fiercely loyal to Qing rule. The latter group would have included Prince Gong and, for certain purposes, Ronglu. Nevertheless, ample evidence of a general political and personal fault-line running between Manchu and Han at the highest official levels (and mirroring feelings at lower levels) can easily be found in accounts of the private conversations of the period.

By 1898 political observers spoke frequently of North-South divisions within the government. Xu Tong and Li Hongzao—both Han and members of the Grand Council—were leaders of the northern faction, along with Gangyi and other venerable Manchu figures; the southern faction was headed by Weng Tonghe, a Jiangsu man and imperial tutor, who was the single most influential figure around the emperor.[13] Personal rivalries and animosities abounded at this point, reflecting not merely ethnic divisions, policy issues, and personality clashes, but also the sustained influence of regionalism. The northern and southern subcultures remained partially unreconciled, a fact that neither party ever forgot. The death of Prince Gong in

* Li's precise words as recorded by Richard were that "the Emperor had no mind of his own, but depended on every last adviser." (We are indebted to Kung-ch'uan Hsiao's work for first calling our attention to this quotation.) The old viceroy went on to speak of other matters, railing against those in power who "knew nothing about foreign matters," spoke of Western education as "devil's learning," and refused to grant posts to those qualified in Western learning. In these comments, Li reflected the internal recriminations that were currently rife at the highest political levels. He indicated that he favored drastic changes in the examination system and implied that a new curriculum based on Western subjects was necessary. Yet he was also critical of the Reform Club's organ, calling it "disgraceful" (Timothy Richard, *Forty-five Years*, p. 244). Richard was one of those missionaries who, together with men like S. Wells Williams earlier, and Dr. Young J. Allen and Dr. W. A. P. Martin, contemporaries, had a significant influence on Chinese politics, in addition to his Christian work—or as he viewed it, as an extension of that work.

early 1898 undoubtedly served to exacerbate regional and policy cleavages, because the old Manchu statesman might have served as mediator between the factions and contending forces.

The entry onto the national scene of Kang Youwei and, secondarily, Liang Qichao, must be understood in this context. Both were Guangdong men from lower-middle gentry-scholar families; both were reared in a traditional and rural environment, yet within reach of the various rebel and Western influences that were intertwined in south-central and southeastern China. Theirs was the background from which most modern Chinese reformers and revolutionaries have come. In his effort to remake China under the emperor, Kang was to consort for the most part with men of the South, a fact that quite early aroused Manchu suspicions, including those of the empress dowager. By his own account, he was recommended to the throne first by Gao Xiezeng, a Hubei man who was serving as a censor, and was subsequently supported by Weng Tonghe and by Li Duanfen, a man from Guizhou and then president of the Board of Rites.*

Kang was one of the truly remarkable men of modern China.[14] Born in 1858 into a family that had produced lower- and middle-level officials, he was a child prodigy who combined scholarship with political activism throughout his long life. As a personality, he was enormously self-confident, willing to tackle any issue, however dangerous or complex. In him were combined the qualities of brilliance and arrogance, creativity and dogmatism, conservatism and radicalism. He would not deviate from principle, even at great personal and political cost on some matters, and yet as a scholar he bent the truth to make it serve his own policies. From early youth he seemed determined to engage in politics, but he was a poor politician; he lacked the crucial qualities of realism, a sense of timing, and the capacity to build coalitions, qualities that were essential to anyone who sought to navigate successfully the treacherous shoals of Chinese politics.

Though progressive on certain fronts and radical in his utopian ideas, Kang was labeled a conservative by most contemporaries and historians because he was, above all, an incrementalist, a man who believed that China had to use its past and its present in building its future. Thus he espoused constitutionalism and democracy, but he felt strongly that a reinterpreted Confucius and an enlightened monarchy were indispensable for China if those goals were to be reached. His major disagreement with the so-called progressives and radicals lay in the fact that he was committed to remolding rather than obliterating China's classic values and institutions, and he was opposed to skipping stages in China's political development. To leap into republicanism without having lived through constitutional monarchy, he believed, was to risk anarchy or tyranny or both. And while he was committed

*Xu Zhizhong, junior vice-director of the Board of Rites, recommended Kang to the emperor because his son, Xu Renzhu, literary chancellor of Hunan, later dismissed, warmly endorsed Kang, a classmate and intimate friend. For Kang's account, see "The Crisis in China," dated October 7, Hong Kong, reprinted from the *China Mail*, *North China Herald*, October 17, 1898, pp. 738–741. In the initial period of his ascendancy, Kang did seek—and obtain—contact with the Grand Council conservatives as well as progressives. In 1888, for example, he met with Xutong as well as with Weng and Pan, but according to Hsiao, he was only able to enlist the support of Weng at this time (Hsiao, *K'ang Yu-wei*, p. 211). It should also be noted that while Gao, Weng, and Li reportedly first brought Kang to the attention of the emperor, it was Gangyi who suggested Kang's appointment as secretary-attaché in the Zongli Yamen in the spring of 1898, a position which he declined (Hsiao, p. 23).

to economic development, including the acquisition of a strong industrial component, he regarded capitalism, not socialism, as the appropriate route.

Kang championed a continuous, orderly progression, but at the end of his road was a radical utopia based on premises about issues such as human rights that were drastically different from those prevailing in China. Yet at the same time he was called "reactionary" and "archaic" for espousing monarchism long after it had passed from the Chinese scene. Indeed, it was Kang's fate never to be in the political mainstream of his society. As a reformer, he was overwhelmed first by the conservatives, then by the progressives. As a conservative, he was frequently not accepted by others to whom that label more properly applied. As a radical, he was ridiculed or ignored.

Kang's disciple Liang Qichao bridged the era from monarchy to republicanism more effectively than did his mentor, although he too fought for a succession of losing causes. Liang was another extraordinary man, certainly one of the most broadly talented intellectuals of his time and, like Kang, a political activist for the greater part of his life.[15] Born into a Guangdong gentry-scholar family in 1873, Liang was also a precocious child. He had managed to pass the provincial examinations when he was only sixteen. In the following year he failed the examinations in the capital, but the trip was a turning point in his life. En route home, he stopped in Shanghai and made the acquaintance of Kang. He immediately became a follower of the older scholar and also began to discover Western literature. After a period of teaching, he embarked upon a career as a journalist in Shanghai in 1896, editing a magazine called *Shiwu bao*, through which he sought to introduce progressive ideas to the literati. (*The China Progress* was used as the magazine's English title, but it has been translated by some Western scholars as the *Journal of Current Affairs*.)

Up to 1898 two men had a major influence on Liang's intellectual development: Kang Youwei and Yan Fu. Yan had been one of the early Chinese students sent abroad, having studied in England between 1876 and 1878. Upon his return, he began a career as interpreter and translator of the major British influences of this era: Darwin, Spencer, and Huxley, and later Adam Smith, John Stuart Mill, and the great French philosopher Montesquieu. Through essays and translations, Yan had an unequaled influence on young intellectuals in China in the 1890s.* Liang, like many others, was captivated by the scientific method, the concept of evolution, and the social implications of Darwinism as presented by Yan; he reprinted several of Yan's essays in his *Shiwu bao*, where they became a source of inspiration for a generation of reformers and revolutionaries.

*Yan was an avid exponent of Westernism in a sense far different from the advocates of Western technology. To him, the ultimate source of Western strength lay in the realm of ideas and values, particularly in the capacity of Westerners to utilize scientific methods of logic and inquiry, thus to understand and act upon the full range of phenomena governing human and natural affairs. This, together with the ability to aggregate the will and talents of free men into a collective national unity, undergirded the strength of Western civilization. Like the early Meiji liberals, Yan's attraction to liberalism was less because of its enhancement of individual rights, and more because he saw in it a weapon on behalf of state power. For a detailed analysis, see Benjamin Schwartz's insightful study, *In Search of Wealth and Power*, pp. 42ff.

Yan's importance to the reform movement lay in the fact that his essays, beginning in 1895, were widely read by the young progressive literati. Indeed, Liang Qichao republished some in his *Shiwu bao*. Thus, the concepts of liberalism, Social Darwinism, and the scientific method—so powerful in their subsequent influence upon reformers and revolutionaries alike—first emanated from this source.

Since Liang was only twenty-five years old at the time of the abortive 1898 reform, his role was that of supporter rather than leader. By imperial decree he was appointed director of a new Translation Department scheduled to publish foreign studies concerned with the natural and social sciences; needless to say, this position never materialized, since both Liang and Kang soon had to flee for their lives. Liang's role as an independent intellectual stimulus and political activist came in a later period, and will be analyzed shortly.

An actor of greater immediate significance than Liang Qichao was that preeminent representative of the new Chinese military, Yuan Shikai.[16] Born in 1859, one year after Kang Youwei, Yuan was a northerner, born into a well-to-do landowning clan of central Henan. His extended family included a prominent general and had connections with the provincial militia. While still a small boy, Yuan was adopted by his uncle, who died when he was only fourteen. As a young man, Yuan was more devoted to sports and the life of a playboy than to Confucian studies. His intelligence was high and he had the benefit of private tutors, but he failed twice to pass the civil examinations.

Yuan purchased an official title in 1880, but immediately joined the staff of General Wu Changqing of the Huai Army, and saw service in Korea beginning in 1882. There, in both military and civil roles stretching over a decade, Yuan won the confidence of many high-ranking Koreans and, more important, the respect of key political leaders in Beijing, particularly Li Hongzhang, whose protégé he temporarily became. From 1885 until 1894 he was Chinese commissioner of commerce in Korea, an important position that brought him into close contact with Korean and Japanese as well as Chinese leaders.

China's military defeat in 1894–1895 did not tarnish Yuan's career. On the contrary, having experimented with various facets of modernization in Korea, he was given the opportunity to practice his theories in China immediately after the war. With the support of such influential men as Ronglu and Li Lianying, Yuan was named commander of the Newly Created Army (*xinjian lujun*) at the end of 1895, and put in overall charge of training. Interestingly, he received this assignment despite the fact that he was known as an advocate of general reform and a man who was on friendly terms with Liang Qichao and others of the progressive group.

In the ensuing months, with the assistance of German officers, Yuan built a disciplined, well-trained military force, relatively free from corruption and equipped with modern German guns, adequate uniforms, and medical supplies. By the end of 1896 he was being credited by foreign observers with having created a military force up to Western standards. Since the troops under his control had grown to division size, numbering some 12,000, and since his army was stationed in Tianjin, in the vicinity of Beijing, Yuan was the one prospective reformer with military power—a fact that became of critical importance in the climactic days of September 1898.*

*Li Chunyi argues that while Yuan avidly adopted Western weaponry and training techniques, in his selection of key officers he clung to old practices, with some modification. Recognizing the importance of men well trained, he drew his top officers primarily from the Beiyang Military Training Academy; but by keeping appointments and dismissals strictly in his hands, Yuan bound such men closely to him, making the New Army no less "semi-personal" than others (Li, *Yuan Shikai zhuan*, pp. 57–58).

ISSUES: THE THREAT OF PARTITION

On the eve of the 1898 Reforms, the paramount problem in Chinese politics was finding a way to avoid partition at the hands of the great powers. The military defeat of 1895 had greatly exacerbated this problem in several ways. First, to pay indemnities to Japan which came to approximately three times the total annual national revenues, it was necessary for the government to borrow from foreign banking consortiums. Debts gave political leverage, as all parties were well aware. Consequently, in an effort to counteract the unhappiness of London and Berlin over the initial loans from a Franco-Russian banking consortium, subsequent loans were obtained from a British-German consortium, putting the Beijing government in debt to all of the leading European states.

The government also found itself under pressure to balance other types of concessions. The Russian government—which had taken the initiative in getting France and Germany to join in signing a three-power note pressuring Japan to withdraw from the Liaodong peninsula, as conceded in the Treaty of Shimonoseki that ended the Sino-Japanese War—had not only moved quickly to proffer a loan to China but also indicated that a direct rail line between Chita and Vladivostok was important for Chinese as well as Russian security. A number of high Chinese officials, including Li Hongzhang, had already come to the conclusion that an alliance with Russia was the best means of protecting China against the imperialism of Japan and western Europe. Consequently, an agreement was reached in 1896 whereby the Russians were permitted to construct a Chita–Vladivostok railway across portions of Chinese territory, to be controlled by an entity known as the Chinese Eastern Railway Corporation in which Russian influence would be substantial. China was guaranteed the right to redeem the railway after thirty-six years for 700 million rubles, or free of charge after eighty years. As a quid pro quo, the Russians and Chinese agreed to defend each other against any Japanese attack. This first Sino-Russian defense pact was celebrated in Moscow and Beijing.

Shortly thereafter, however, the complexities of European politics were extended to China in a new form. Germany, left behind in the course of earlier concessions, wanted a port, and when the Russian czar voiced no strong objections, the Germans took advantage of the murder of two missionaries in Shandong to seize Jiaozhou in November 1897 and to compel the Chinese government to grant them a 99-year lease.[17] This in turn prompted the Russians—who had long desired an ice-free port south of Vladivostok—to propose the establishment of Russian facilities at Port Arthur and Dalian Bay. Naturally, Moscow explained that the purpose was to protect China against the Germans and other possible predators. Thus, in March 1898, just months before the reform era began, the Russians obtained a 25-year lease on Port Arthur and Dalian. Port Arthur itself was to constitute a naval station used only by the Russians and Chinese; no Chinese military forces were to be allowed in the leased territory behind the port; and Dalian Bay was to be divided between a restricted naval station and a commercial port open to all nations.[18]

British policy had been to oppose the alienation of any Chinese territory, for like the United States, England's primary interest at this point lay in preserving an open door in China for trade. Given the moves of others, however, the British were not prepared to be left out. Hence they acquired a lease to Weihaiwei "for as long a period as Port Arthur shall remain in the possession of Russia," and then secured a 99-year lease on an additional portion of the Jiulong peninsula that came to be known as the New Territories. The French also gained a concession at Guangzhouwan.

Accompanying these acts of territorial acquisition were a series of "non-alienation" agreements designed to keep certain areas within the sphere of influence of a given power, or to prevent any threat to that power's existing colonial possessions. Thus France obtained from China in 1897 a pledge that it would never cede the island of Hainan to any third power, and in April 1898 a further promise that it would never grant another power any territory in the provinces adjoining French Indochina. Similarly, Great Britain obtained a guarantee that China would not alienate any territory in the provinces bordering the Yangtze River, where the British had extensive interests. The Japanese were given the same assurance in April 1898 with respect to Fujian, the province opposite Taiwan, an island now in their possession.

China had become a giant chessboard on which the power rivalries of Europe were represented. The historic Chinese strategy of playing off one barbarian against another no longer worked; the game continued, but under the control of the barbarians. Both foreigners and many Chinese expected that the next step would be the actual partition of the country, with various sections becoming European or Japanese colonies, followed by recurrent wars fought on Chinese soil, as each imperialist power sought to maintain or advance its gains. The situation was far more acute than in 1860, and the young intellectuals who were most conversant with the West were also the most pessimistic because they could appreciate the sources of European power and the profound nature of Chinese weakness.

COMMERCIAL-INDUSTRIAL DEVELOPMENT

To appreciate the intractability of the general problem, one must understand how two special forms of Western involvement, apart from military confrontation, interacted with nineteenth-century China. These forms were Western commercial-industrial penetration and the work of Christian missionaries. Both added complexity to an already troubled political scene.

One question has always intrigued students of comparative Asian politics and economics. Why did China and Japan respond so differently to the Western economic challenge? On balance, Japan managed to benefit from the Western intrusion, but China found it one more source of crisis, which further immobilized the nation and thrust it into quasi-colonial status.

A brief analysis of the sources of modern Japanese economic growth may enable us to see more clearly the primary inhibiting factors that governed China's response. According to Simon Kuznets, the criteria for modern economic growth are the following: the application of modern science and technology to all basic aspects of the economy; the sustained increase of real product per capita and the accelerated rise of population; high rates of transformation in the industrial structure; and an increasing involvement in international economic intercourse.[19] In the late Tokugawa era, none of these criteria were truly characteristic of the Japanese economy, and yet by the turn of the century Japan was in the process of meeting all of them. What made this possible?

The issue is still being debated, but it has been argued effectively that conditions in the late Tokugawa were far more conducive to subsequent modernization than was earlier recognized.[20] Agricultural production, the mainstay of the economy, had reached impressive levels for a traditional society, a result in part of political stability. Hence a growing agricultural surplus was available, both to the state and to portions of the citizenry. The taxes collected during the late Tokugawa era totaled approximately one-fourth of national income, with the *han* governments getting about three-fourths of these funds. Generally speaking, however, these monies were used more effectively than in most traditional societies, where they tended to be siphoned off for the personal aggrandizement of the ruling class. In part, this resulted from the propensity of the Japanese military class for modest levels of consumption. The commercialization of agriculture was another result of rising production. Although still limited, this commercialization brought with it the development of increasingly sophisticated market techniques. An entrepreneurial class was being born, a portion of it faithfully nurtured by the more progressive *han* governments as well as by the shogunate. A ready supply of labor was also available. In sum, many of the conditions necessary for an economic breakthrough were at hand.

Supportive of these developments were certain broad social and political trends. By the end of the Tokugawa period, as much as 30 percent of the adult population may have been literate, and specialized education tailored to the needs of certain classes, such as merchants, had long been available. In addition, Japanese culture as reflected among the military classes was characterized not only by modest consumption but by emphasis on the work ethic and on a disciplined response to the initiatives of superiors, whether in the public or the private sector. The acceptance of status was important, but so was the rising flexibility that marked certain class relationships, particularly the interaction between elements of the samurai and the merchant classes. By the early Meiji period, cultural borrowing and the outright fusion taking place between these two groups produced a remarkable "hybrid" type, a merchant or industrialist supported by and responsive to his government, but capable of showing great initiative in assimilating modern economic technology and adapting it to his society.

At every turn, however, the role of government was of paramount importance. Tokugawa governance has sometimes been described as "centralized feudalism," but whatever term is used, government in general—at the center and in the *han*—was relatively coordinated, efficient, and predictable. As we have noted, the income acquired by government was sufficient to lay the groundwork for a high level of public investment in the next era. Moreover, the concept of state control over the economy was well established, and equally important, that control was exercised to serve rationally planned purposes.

It would not be wise to leave the impression that Tokugawa society had already built a quasi-modern economic system. Modernity was merely feasible, not an existing reality, and therein lies the importance of the Meiji Restoration and its aftermath. Matters could have turned out differently. There was nothing inevitable about Japan's sustained march toward political centralization and economic development. After the Perry expedition of 1853, disorder was on the rise, and for more than a decade it seemed possible, even likely, that Japan would be thrown into the type of turmoil characteristic of late-nineteenth-century China. Antiforeignism was rampant; traditionalism fought a series of desperate battles, with some success; and regional and local insubordination was commonplace. The Edo government seemed increasingly incapable of coping with the rising challenges. Had Japan been plunged into protracted civil conflict in the mid-nineteenth century, its modern history would have been very different. Even after the Tokugawa were overthrown, new rulers might have pursued antiforeign, traditionalist policies, and in that case recurrent collisions with the West would most certainly have followed, as they did in the case of China.

Accident, along with certain proclivities imbedded in Japanese culture and with the events of the preceding period, made the Meiji Restoration a rolling revolution, more radical over time than most events that have borne that label. A reasonably unified government was created, especially after the Satsuma Rebellion had been quelled in 1877. Moreover, it was now a government possessing a substantial consensus on basic goals, the goals of young men prepared at last to look forward, not backward, in facing the world around them. First, the old socioeconomic order had to be changed quickly, and with it the political structure. Thus feudalism, Tokugawa-style, was dismantled. The *daimyo* (feudal lords) were pensioned off and rapidly divested of political authority. Special samurai privileges were eliminated, and the military class was provided with new purposes and a new national vision. Political centralization under the emperor was made the order of the day, and economic modernization was defined as a patriotic duty.

Policies and institutions were shaped accordingly. The creation of a modern banking system, together with various fiscal reforms beginning in the early 1870s, laid the foundations for sustained and orderly economic growth. The precedent-shattering national land tax of 1874 made possible extensive government investment in industry. Private capital accumulation continued, however, because of the propensity for frugality and saving. There were difficulties and setbacks, of course; painful mistakes were made, and periods of recession occurred. Yet by the end of the nineteenth century, Japan had turned the Western incursion to its advantage, and in so doing had recaptured economic independence. As William Lockwood has put it, out of Japanese political culture came a pragmatic instrumentalism in leadership and a resilient, cohesive response from the people, which combined to yield extraordinary results.[21]

In comparing the potential for economic development in Japan and China in the late nineteenth century, one must be careful not to overlook points of similarity. For instance, recent research by scholars like Evelyn Rawski indicates that Chinese rates of male literacy approximated those of Japan during the late nineteenth century.* The evidence also suggests that

*Rawski, surveying the available data, concludes, "Information from the mid- and late nineteenth century suggests that 30 to 45 percent of the men and from 2 to 10 percent of the women in China knew how to read and write. This group included the fully literate members of the elite and, on the opposite pole, those knowing only a few hundred characters. Thus loosely defined, there was an average of almost one literate person per family" (Evelyn

China possessed many of the prerequisites for economic modernization just sketched: commercialized agriculture, a capacity for capital accumulation and no shortage of capital, sophisticated premodern technology in select locations, and a rising urban merchant community, which despite its official status was interacting ever more closely with the gentry and officialdom.[22]

Nor were the initial stages of industrialization in Japan and China radically different. By the late 1870s the Chinese government had begun to create the *guandu shangban* system—industries under official supervision but merchant management. Mining and cotton spinning and weaving were stressed. As Albert Feuerwerker has noted, the *guandu shangban* system derived from earlier practices in connection with the salt monopoly.[23] The government had appointed official supervisors, but farmed out to various merchants the rights in connection with salt manufacture, transport, and sales. Similarly, *guandu shangban* industries partook of official supervision, had some of the characteristics of a monopoly, and were subject to bureaucratic exactions. Yet in various respects they were not dissimilar to the first industries sponsored by the Meiji government. Both societies possessed a common heritage of extensive governmental involvement in the economy.

Although an intimacy between government and private industry has remained the hallmark of modern Japan—an intimacy characterized by supervision and regulation, on the one hand, and support and encouragement, on the other—by the beginning of the twentieth century, the Meiji government had divested itself of many government enterprises and turned them over to private management. In contrast, bureaucratic capitalism was to remain a prominent feature of the modern Chinese economy in the form of overt government management and control. Yet this structural variation does not seem to account for the fundamental differences between economic development in the two nations. Rather, it is in the economic-political behavior of both the private entrepreneur and the government that basic divergencies appear. In China the only remote counterpart to the new Japanese samurai-industrialist was the compradore, whose close contact with Westerners had introduced to him a new economic technology and new managerial skills as well as equipping him with capital. But the compradores were a small group, restricted essentially to the treaty ports and often regarded as quasi-foreign. The great mass of traditional Chinese merchants were as conservative as their official counterparts, burdened with familial and clan obligations that made the development of new technology and impersonal managerial practices difficult.

One is now approaching differences of commanding importance. In contrast with Japan, the level of integration between the state and the family-clan in China was low. In certain respects, the family was always at war with the state in China, and in the struggle to obtain supreme loyalty, the family usually won. In contrast to Japan's "centralized feudalism," the traditional political order in China rested upon a social system characterized by a relatively high degree of mobility and a weak linkage between familial-kinship

---

Sakakida Rawski, *Education and Popular Literacy*, p. 140). Ronald Dore's studies of literary Japan during the Tokugawa era yield similar statistics. He estimates that 43 percent of the boys and 10 percent of the girls were receiving some form of schooling in the late Tokugawa years (Dore, *Education in Tokugawa Japan*, pp. 317–322).

units and the formal political system at comparable or higher levels.* Hence it was certain to be more difficult to appeal to the patriotism of the Chinese merchant, and equally difficult to integrate the Chinese entrepreneurial class into a coordinated national program. Moreover, the literati-official class in China remained loyal to the traditional economic and political order, whereas the lower-class ex-samurai in Japan, when suddenly thrust into national power, were willing to experiment with new routes to national salvation.

At this point, it is helpful to look more closely at the socioeconomic context of traditional Chinese politics, particularly as it has been analyzed in the works of G. William Skinner.[24] Chinese villages in the premodern era belonged to a standard market community. Allowing for major physiographic differences, such a community in the intensively cultivated areas typically consisted of approximately eighteen villages distributed over an average area of some 50 square kilometers, containing some 7,000 persons in 1,500 households.[25] The social and political life of the villager, as well as his economic activities, was largely confined to this community; lineage associations, secret societies, religious organizations, and assorted other voluntary bodies made the standard market community their organizational base.

The standard market served as the foundation of a marketing hierarchy that reached next to the intermediate market town, and from there up to the central market town. Although the peasants in outlying areas went occasionally to their nearest intermediate market town for exchange purposes, this unit was dominated by gentry and merchant classes, who served as an economic and sociopolitical transmission belt between lower and higher units. Since both peasantry and bureaucratic representatives were largely excluded from a sustained presence in this intermediate zone, political as well as economic integration at higher levels was hampered. The central market town therefore represented the highest level of the regional marketing system and, generally speaking, the lowest level of centralized political authority.

Skinner is careful to point out that although the administrative hierarchy in traditional China paralleled the market structure in some degree, it was not identical with it. The central market town, for example, might or might not be the locus of county administration, distinguished by a yamen and a wall. In any case, below the county level, the administrative system was minimal, and there was a similar scarcity of control over the marketing system below the central market.

Once again we are confronted with factors that suggest the monumental problem of integration in this vast society. Skinner estimates that as late as 1948 and the advent of Communist rule, barely 10 percent of the intermediate marketing systems of agricultural China as a whole had been converted

* For a brief exposition of this theme, see Scalapino, *Democracy and the Party Movement*, pp. 129–134. Gilbert Rozman has recently developed a similar thesis on a more elaborate scale. His basic theme is that kinship triumphed over community, with the family assuming responsibilities that in such cultures as Japan and Russia rested more with a nonkinship political entity. It is also Rozman's view that outside the family and kinship context, "alternative bases of control and coordination remained fragile," and linkage to intermediate and higher levels weak. Hence, familial freedom, on the one hand, permitted "excesses" with respect to population growth and resource consumption and, on the other hand, made social cohesion or the aggregation of extrafamilial units difficult if not impossible (Rozman, *The Modernization of China*, pp. 141–182).

into modern trading systems, and at this point approximately 58,000 standard marketing systems still operated throughout rural China, with a corresponding effect upon the peasants' social and political horizons. The existence of such a situation helps us to understand why a substantial grass-roots stability could prevail in the midst of sustained national crisis, and also why it was so hard to implement centralized economic and political policies.[26]

Skinner defines the process of modernization as that of shifting marketing activity from the standard market to higher-level markets, in the context of the development of a modern transport network within an already commercialized central marketing system which thereby removes the need for standard markets.*

One must also pay homage to another structural difference of significance. A system resting on a well-defined hierarchy can more easily produce a sense of noblesse oblige among its governors than a system resting on substantial quotients of egalitarianism and social mobility. The Japanese ruling class of the Meiji era, like the ruling class of nineteenth-century England, accepted governance as both a right and a duty; it avoided massive corruption and exhibited a self-assuredness and a spirit of national patriotism that gave strength and guidance to the citizenry. In contrast, weakness and corruption were woven into the political structure of China in the late Qing period, all the Confucian injunctions notwithstanding.

Of the taxes collected in late Qing China, not only did a sizable percentage remain in provincial and regional hands, but corruption (known popularly as "the squeeze") siphoned off sizable sums at every level. From the very beginning, moreover, there was a strong tendency for most Chinese officials to look upon industry, not as a future treasure requiring substantial investment and careful nurturing, but as an immediate source of additional revenue. Thus officials were quick to drain off profits, sometimes for personal use.

Various other explanations for the shortcomings of the Qing economy have been offered. One thesis, advanced by Mark Elvin, is that the Chinese economy was caught in a "high-level equilibrium trap," a situation in which most of the usual criteria of "backwardness" do not apply, but where technological immobility still prevails, making any sustained qualitative economic progress impossible. The argument is that the growing pressure of population on arable land progressively reduced the surplus product. Since premodern technology and practice were both at their highest possible levels, increased applications of labor, capital, and organization yielded no appreciable returns. A sufficiently high degree of integration had been achieved through premodern development to make the system politically and economically viable and preclude further centralization. The huge size of the Chinese economy constituted another aspect of the trap. Overall

*In his later work, Skinner divides China into nine physiographic regions, which, with their subregions and macroregions, served as the basis for territorially based socioeconomic systems. These influenced the political as well as the economic structure of China, but within them the county (*xian*) remained "the great constant" of society and administration. The growth of population and the necessity of expanding the number of county residents rather than increasing the number of counties (so as to keep bureaucratic costs within reason) resulted in the progressive deterioration of administrative coverage and efficiency at the local levels, he argues. See Skinner, "Introduction: Urban Development," pp. 17–23, in Skinner, ed., *The City in Late Imperial China*.

growth was held back by a combination of low farm productivity per capita and relatively high productivity per acre. In sum, technological progress under the scientific conditions then prevailing could not provide gains in production which would compensate for the costs involved, and so the incentive for change was removed.*

Whatever the validity of this thesis as a whole, several aspects of it are unquestionably germane. Certainly the dimensions of Chinese society insured massive problems for economic as well as political modernization. Japan faced the problem of integrating a society of 28 to 30 million, on a land area no greater than a single Chinese province; China faced the task of integrating and providing a coherent policy for a nation of 400 million, spread over a continent. No government of the nineteenth century had the organizational, technological, or financial capacity to handle a problem of this size, even under optimal conditions. And the conditions in China, as we have seen, were far from optimal. Civil and international conflicts were endemic, and regional autonomy was deeply entrenched. The central government had long rested on a precarious balance of power between overlapping jurisdictions, and on a fragile Manchu-Han equilibrium. Thus any fundamental innovations relating to economic modernization on a national scale would require, as a prior condition, major political alterations.

It is our central thesis that the most significant differences between Japan and China were social and political rather than economic, and that these differences, together with the critical factor of scale, shaped the capacities of each society to undertake economic modernization. We do not regard the threat posed by the West as the central determinant. It should be clear that the different capacities of Japan and China to respond to Western imperialism derived preponderantly from indigenous structural and spatial considerations. This does not mean that the timing and nature of the Western intrusion into the two societies was unimportant. It means only that it was a dependent variable, and not the crucial one.[27]

Under existing circumstances, it was natural that regional developments in China took priority. These developments were dependent upon local innovators like Zeng Guofan, Zhang Zhidong, and Li Hongzhang, or in the case of the treaty ports, upon a combination of indigenous and foreign capitalists. Since neither economic nor psychological preparations were ade-

* Elvin summarizes his basic thesis in two passages: ". . . through a number of interlocking causes, the input-output relationships of the late traditional economy had assumed a pattern that was almost incapable of change through internally-generated forces. Both in technological and investment terms, agricultural productivity per acre had nearly reached the limits of what was possible without industrial-scientific inputs, and the increase of the population had therefore steadily reduced the surplus product above what was needed for subsistence" (Elvin, *Pattern of the Chinese Past*, p. 312).

". . . In late traditional China economic forces developed in such a way as to make profitable investment more and more difficult. With a falling surplus in agriculture, and so falling per capita income and per capita demand, with cheapening labour but increasingly expensive resources and capital, with farming and transport technologies so good that no simple improvements could be made, rational strategy for peasant and merchant alike tended in the direction not so much of labour-saving machinery as of economizing on resources and fixed capital. Huge but nearly static markets created no bottlenecks in the production system that might have prompted creativity. When temporary shortages arose, mercantile versatility, based on cheap transport, was a faster and surer remedy than the contrivance of machines. This situation may be described as a 'high-level equilibrium trap'" (p. 314).

quate on the domestic front, however, many members of the elite, as well as the masses in general, identified economic modernization with foreign intrusion. To the masses, the railroad was the instrument of the foreign devil, desecrating ancestral land. Among the elite, similar beliefs prevailed, but railroads and telegraph lines were also regarded as an invasion of privacy, a foreign intrusion unsanctioned by either custom or need. Hobbled by the deeply rooted conservatism of their people, even officials who recognized the rationality of economic modernization were loathe to act.

However, these obstacles could have been surmounted by a strong government possessed of adequate determination and finances. Even if the central government lacked these qualities, could not sustained regional development have taken place under a man like Zhang Zhidong? To some extent, it did take place, as we have noted. Most regional officials, however, were transferred frequently and had to leave unfinished tasks behind; and they, too, were greatly handicapped by an insufficient economic base. At all levels of government, an antiquated and corrupt tax system and wholly inadequate financial institutions served as immediate obstacles to solid economic growth. In terms of regional development, therefore, it is not surprising that Shanghai, with its growing community of compradores and foreign enterprises, served as the front-runner. Nor should it have been unexpected that the national government would have to depend on foreign financing for such developmental programs as were approved. Consequently, Chinese economic development appeared to be harnessed to the further advances of Western and Japanese imperialism.

This was the irony of the years immediately after 1895. A consensus among high officials had finally been reached that a modernized communications and transport system was indispensable to China's progress. But this consensus inevitably made them receptive to various foreign proposals for railway construction, and led foreign governments and their financiers into a veritable stampede to obtain the new concessions.

The Russo-Chinese agreement of 1896 to extend the Trans-Siberian railway set the pattern. Between 1896 and 1899, four different agreements were made. France obtained concessions to construct rail lines in South China, including one from Tonkin (Indochina) into Yunnan. In 1898 the British received initial approval for Shanghai–Nanjing and Shanghai–Hangzhou lines. In the following year, a concession was jointly granted to British and German interests to build a railway from Tianjin to the Yangtze, with the Germans to finance and construct the northern part and the British the southern, so as to stay within their respective spheres of influence. A similar agreement respecting railway activities in each other's sphere of influence was reached between Great Britain and Russia in 1899.[28]

Even the less active nations entered the competition. On May 10, 1897, a contract was signed with the Belgians for a loan to build the Beijing-Hankou line. Shortly thereafter, a concession was granted to an American consortium to construct a railway between Hankou and Canton. In 1898 and 1899 an Anglo-Italian company received the right to develop mines and railways in Shanxi and Henan.

Since 1863 the Chinese customs office had been under a British inspector general (the forceful Irishman, Robert Hart), and in 1898 the British government demanded and received an assurance that as long as Britain's trade led that of any other nation, the post would continue to be held by a Britisher.

The French sought a similar agreement with respect to the postal service, but failed.

In sum, the most critical issues in the realm of fiscal policy, taxation, and industrial planning still lay ahead, and in order to tackle them adequately, reformers at the national level would have to reexamine the political as well as the economic structure of Chinese society. The disjointed, segmental character of government bore direct responsibility for the weak response to the appeals for private entrepreneurship, and for the backward state of the Chinese economy in both its public and its private aspects. The necessary linkage—whether in planning fiscal policies or in nurturing leadership—was lacking. We must remember, however, that neither technology nor human institutions had yet evolved to the stage at which the integration and modernization of an entire continent would be possible.

THE MISSIONARY: CHRISTIANITY AND POLITICS

On another front, Christianity was on the march. In 1889 there were about 1,300 Protestant missionaries in China, and approximately 650 Catholic priests. Shortly after the turn of the century, the Protestant missionaries numbered nearly 3,500, and the Catholic priests more than 1,000. Converts also increased rapidly during this period. In 1889 Protestant Chinese were listed as approximately 37,000, and by 1898 they numbered 80,000. In 1896 there were about 500,000 baptized Chinese Catholics, and by 1901 the number had risen to over 700,000, despite the Boxer Rebellion.

To draw a balance sheet on the missionaries and their activities is extraordinarly difficult.[29] In the first place, many different sorts of men and women went into the mission field. At one end of the scale were individuals of exceedingly limited education or culture, lacking in skills, not burdened by tolerance, fundamentalist in their beliefs, and combining an intense desire to save heathen souls with an instinctive dislike for the people among whom they worked.

At the other end were individuals whose talents—in medicine, education, and language—served both to advance the cause of a new China and to bridge in some measure the enormous gap between East and West. China's modern institutions of higher education, its hospitals and clinics, and the insights of many generations of Chinese into facets of Western life other than those of commerce and war came in no small degree from this group.

In between was a wide range of dedicated individuals, not especially gifted but deeply devoted to their cause, who over the decades had a great influence on their flocks—which were often in remote areas. Dispensing the gospel, grieving over social and political conditions, offering basic education and elementary medical aid to the extent of their abilities, these dedicated, friendly people exhibited a basic humanism that stood in dramatic contrast to the callous indifference to the "outsider" that was so deeply ingrained in Chinese society.

Whatever their character or talents, Western missionaries were revolutionaries, a fact recognized by Chinese authorities long before it dawned upon most missionaries themselves. The act of conversion—assuming that it was genuine and not the rice-Christian variety, for personal gain—took an individual or a family at least partly out of the culture into which he or they had been born. In some degree, it denationalized the communicant, made him a foreign element and an object of suspicion if not hatred among those whom he had left. The earlier religions that had penetrated China, with the notable exception of Islam, had been sufficiently eclectic to make assimilation possible, even though some—such as Buddhism—had a profound influence on the broader culture. Islam continued to be a problem, because like Christianity it was exclusivist, and tended to breed a separate community. The Moslem rebellions that followed the Taiping uprising were related to this separatism, and Chinese authorities were not unmindful of this as they sought to deal with Christianity. Groups like the Jesuits were prepared to make tactical concessions to Chinese tradition and culture, but Christianity, like Islam, was exclusivist. In demanding total commitment, at least as an ideal, it required the abandonment of certain customs attached to family, community, and sovereign which were as sacred as any article of faith and so much a part of the fabric of Chinese civilization that without them China would be unrecognizable.

But the influence of the missionary went far beyond the convert. Missionaries were in the vanguard of those promoting higher education in China. They introduced a wide range of Western literature, taught European languages, and counseled an ever-expanding number of young Chinese who were eager to learn about the outside world, among them many of the reformers and revolutionaries of the future. Given their group culture and their personal commitments, some missionaries were certain to be in the forefront of the reform movement. Thus, Timothy Richard and Dr. Gilbert Reid of the American Presbyterian mission were intimately associated with the Reform Club from its beginning in 1895.* Richard, moreover, had repeatedly presented the highest court circles in Beijing with comprehensive reform proposals, some of them closely parallel to the efforts made later during the Hundred Days.**

For the Chinese, association with Christianity, even if it did not result in conversion, was a means or a symptom of protest against the old order. Nineteenth-century Protestant evangelism in particular was a doctrine wholly incompatible with classical Chinese values and beliefs. That the individual could reach a single, omnipotent God and be heard—that both his soul and his body were sacred and worthy of cultivation and defense apart

* Richard's connections with the young Chinese reformers were of the closest nature. He indicates that when the rules for the Reform Club were drawn up by Kang Youwei and others, having borrowed heavily from earlier missionary writings, they brought these to Richard for suggestions and possible revisions. When the first meeting between Richard and Kang took place on October 17, 1895, Kang indicated a desire to cooperate closely with the missionaries in the work of regenerating China. See Richard, *Forty-Five Years*, pp. 253ff.

** Richard, for example, presented Weng Tonghe with a seven-point proposal for reform in October 1895, which included the following points: (1) two foreign advisers to the throne; (2) a cabinet of eight ministers, half to be Manchu and Han, half to be foreign officials who would know about "the progress of all the world"; (3) immediate currency reform and the establishment of sound financial policies; (4) the rapid building of railways and the opening of mines and factories; (5) the creation of a Board of Education to introduce modern schools and colleges throughout the empire; (6) the establishment of an intelligent press with experienced foreign journalists to assist Chinese editors; (7) the building of an adequate army and navy for national defense. According to Richard, Weng showed this reform program to the emperor, and it was approved (p. 256). It is doubtful whether the idea of foreign tutelage appealed to Beijing leaders, but the other proposals were in fact present in the reform decrees of 1898.

from community or state—these were iconoclastic ideas. In these beliefs, as in its unbounded humanism, the Christian creed challenged the very foundations of the old order in China. And in its combination of individualism and genuine social concern lay the route to contemporary Western radicalism which a Chinese avant-garde would subsequently follow. For example, the role of the missionaries in the education of Chinese women and in combatting such practices as foot-binding, contributed significantly to the later emergence of movements demanding greater rights and protections for women.

Naturally, this situation contained all of the ingredients required for intense conflict. Every element of Chinese society nurtured various beliefs and superstitions that were not to be transgressed with impunity. For example, like homage to one's ancestors, the commitment to *fengshui*, or geomancy—the belief that "wind and water spirits" had to be considered in the planning of events or in the construction of any man-made edifice—was nearly universal in nineteenth-century China. When churches were built in disregard of this practice—or when temples were razed to make way for the buildings of the new religion—resentment mushroomed. Attempts to save child brides, concubines, or prostitutes by taking them into the arms of the church were equally scandalizing, as were the anti-foot-binding societies sponsored by missionaries.

Certain Catholic practices aroused particular antagonism. The entry of young women into nunneries evoked the same parental response in many cases as it did among American parents whose children in the 1970s committed themselves to the Reverend Moon's Unification Church. Rumors of the most preposterous type quickly circulated as to what was *really* happening inside cathedrals, nunneries, churches, orphanages, and clinics. It was alleged, for instance, that Chinese children were being kidnapped and killed, and their vital organs used in the preparation of medicines and potions.*

*All missionary writers present graphic illustrations of the charges against Christian workers. Timothy Richard, for example, recounts one occasion in which a Chinese convert was escorting a child to the Protestant orphanage in Qingzhoufu when he was accosted by a retired district magistrate who charged him with "assisting the foreigner to kidnap children" (Richard, *Forty-five Years*, p. 85). In the same city he met with stiff resistance from the current magistrate in attempting to rent a house.

In his interview with Weng Tonghe on October 26, 1895, Richard brought with him "two bundles of books" to point out the type of false charges against missionaries which were being widely circulated with the approval of governors-general and governors and which were contributing to antiforeignism. One allegation was that Christians scooped out the eyes of Chinese, mixing them with lead to produce silver. Another charge was that missionaries dispensed medicine that caused women to become demented. The familiar assertion that missionary photographs stole the soul of those whose picture was taken was also prominently advanced. Richards followed his references to these libels by showing Weng the inscriptions of high officials in the prefaces of these works (p. 247).

At the same time, Richard recognized that apart from the deadly combination of superstition and xenophobia, some responsibility for the widespread anti-Christian movement rested with the missionaries themselves. During Richard's first year in China, a fellow missionary came to his home with the ancestral tablet of one of his converts in hand and announced that since the man had become Christian, he was going to burn the altar. Richard asked whether at the same time he intended to burn his own parents' photographs. The tablet was not destroyed (p. 146).

Another useful general discussion of missionary influence is to be found in E. R. Hughes, *The Invasion of China by the Western World*, pp. 53–103.

One grievance had merit. Certain converts used the church to uphold their interests in disputes with non-Christians or with the government. This might or might not have been justified in terms of the merits of the issue. In any case, traditional adjudication procedures were challenged and, on occasion, the authority of the state itself. Behind the missionary stood the consul, and behind him, the gunboat.*

Finally, it was usually the missionary who penetrated furthest into the interior, serving as a vanguard for all subsequent Westernization. The courage of many missionaries in pushing into remote areas among inhospitable people was truly extraordinary, and not a few paid with their lives. But it should not be assumed that the missionaries consciously paved the way for Western entrepreneurs or soldiers, who for the most part belonged to separate and often incompatible communities. A majority of treaty-port merchants saw the missionaries as a nuisance or a menace because of the antiforeignism they provoked. For their part, the missionaries were often appalled at the "godlessness" of their Western brethren and their indifference to social problems.

Yet to most Chinese, the linkages could not be denied and the similarities were sufficient to warrant lumping them all together. For the gentry class, Christianity was a barbarian superstition, commerce was the mark of a society devoid of sound values, and the Western soldier was final proof of a people lacking in culture. When this studied antipathy interacted with the xenophobic proclivities of the masses, the dilemma of the Chinese government—and the West—was portrayed in all of its complexity.

CHINA AND THE WEST: A SUMMARY OF NINETEENTH-CENTURY INTERACTION

In reflecting upon the interaction between nineteenth-century China and the West, it is difficult to avoid the conclusion that successive clashes of progressively greater scope and intensity were the most logical if not the inevitable outcome, despite the efforts of certain parties on both sides. To every state—and statesman—of the West, there could be but one model of rela-

*It should also be noted that little love was lost between Protestant and Catholic missionaries, with accusations sometimes reaching very acrimonious levels, reinforcing Chinese suspicion and antagonism. The following report from a Protestant missionary in North Jiangsu is illustrative both of the situation resented by Chinese and of the Protestant-Catholic conflict: "Another and a comparatively new source of oppression [upon the Chinese of this region] has been added in the person of the Catholic priest and his followers. It is well known that the foreign priests behave and act generally more or less in the style of native officials, and the natives know, often by sad experience, that these priests represent power."

After admitting that sometimes the priests did not know the injustices done by their Chinese followers, the writer continued, "The general principle of action seems to be, let a Chinese be but a Catholic and he shall have the protection of his foreign priests, which means foreign power. His lawsuits are taken up and put through to his advantage, and to the disadvantages of his less fortunate heathen neighbor. Thus, the helpless pagan is slowly but surely ground to dust between an upper (official) and a nether millstone. In his despair what does he do—what else can he do?—but come to the Protestant missionary, imploring his help against both his own officials and the Roman Catholic priest! The Protestant missionary is thus really in demand and sought after by the untaught idolater, not, in the majority of cases, to receive instruction, but to get his help against this two-fold oppression which is crushing out his life" (*North China Herald*, January 9, 1899, "Account from North Kiangsu," author's name omitted, p. 17).

tions between nations: the Western model, with its concepts of sovereignty, equality, and treaty obligations. Although the rules of international behavior were often broken, they remained the norms against which behavior was to be judged. Yet the Chinese did not accept this model, having other precedents to which they paid faithful allegiance. To them China was and would always be the central kingdom, with its own world order involving the tributary system, a concept of suzerainty, and the principle of cultural conformity as a standard of judging each man and society. There could be no equality between civilization and barbarism.[30]

The ensuing conflict unfolded in predictable fashion. Subordinate Chinese officials, whatever their personal leanings, were put under excruciating pressure from both sides and often found themselves in a no-win situation. Their instructions from the court were invariably to hold the line against concessions, using whatever means might be necessary. If they failed to carry out such injunctions, they usually paid with their positions, and sometimes with their lives. Western emissaries, however, did not like being put off or misled, and their negotiating stance generally stiffened with time and experience. And if negotiations broke down and conflict followed, the military inadequacies of the Chinese forces quickly made themselves manifest.

Well aware of this dilemma, Chinese officials at all levels sought to perfect strategies long employed against barbarians, strategies involving what the West labeled duplicity or cunning: procrastination, saying one thing but doing another, finding every possible means of evading the spirit if not the letter of an agreement. In memorials to the throne, officials repeatedly promised to oust the hated barbarian and spoke of him with contempt; in messages directed to these barbarians, they often exhibited great solicitude and courtesy.[31] The empress dowager herself set the standard, as one example will suggest. Soon after the coup that returned her to power, the empress dowager, needing to cover her foreign flank, held an audience with the wives of all foreign ministers resident in Beijing on the occasion of her birthday, December 13, 1898. A contemporary account of the event records that after she and the emperor had shaken hands "warmly with each guest," Cixi presented every lady with a ring set in pearls, "which she herself slipped on their fingers." Following lunch, presided over by Princess Jing, the empress entered the banquet hall "to chat affably" with her guests. Later, with the entertainment concluded, she reappeared, expressed her great pleasure over their visit and presented each lady with a scroll, a set of inlaid combs, and other gifts.[32] Scarcely six months later, Cixi was privately congratulating the Boxers on their victories and exhorting them to exterminate every foreigner.

On the Western side, emotional policy conflicts of a somewhat similar sort existed. Recurrently, Western representatives in the field or leaders at home would argue that the Chinese should be treated as equals, as men susceptible to reason (as understood by the West); patience and understanding should be shown, and conflict avoided. Then some horrendous incident would occur, and the moderates would lose ground and sometimes come to doubt their own policies. In their place would come the advocates of "firmness," insisting that Chinese ignorance, backwardness, and stubbornness could be broken effectively only by the application of force: "teach the heathens a lesson."

At the very end of the nineteenth century, a truly ironic situation prevailed. Despite the series of concessions they had wrested from China, none of the European governments wanted to see a political partition of that tottering nation, not out of altruism but for the most practical reasons. With their ports of access leased and their spheres of influence established, the costly and complex task of governing the great mass of Chinese had best be left to the Chinese themselves. For this reason, the widespread foreign desire to see Chinese reform measures succeed was entirely genuine. Almost every outside observer was convinced that without reform the Chinese empire would collapse. Partition would then follow because any region in which provincial rebellion threatened foreign lives and property was almost certain to be placed under the direct rule of one Western power, and in that case other powers would follow suit in other regions "for their own self-protection." The principle of equality established in connection with ports, railways, and spheres of influence would again be applied.

LIVELIHOOD: AN ISSUE?

There can be no question that the Western intrusion in all of its manifestations was a major issue in China on the eve of the 1898 reform drive, and that it continued to be so in the aftermath. It led, as we have noted, to a far-reaching debate that raised questions about economic, political, and social transformations. Up to this point, however, we have said little about the question of the livelihood of the people, other than to note that most reformers paid homage to *minsheng* (the people's livelihood) in a generalized fashion. Liberalism, even when championed, was seen as the ultimate weapon of state power. Economic development, likewise, was regarded as important primarily as a means of *national* survival. Was the people's livelihood really an issue, and with whom?

Reliable statistics concerning the economic situation of the average Chinese citizen have not yet been published for this period, and the differences between regions and between time-frames were probably so great as to make statistical averages of little value in any case. We are still dependent largely upon missionary accounts. One such account, written from North Jiangsu in late 1898, has this to say:

> If I were to attempt to describe the actual condition of a very large proportion—perhaps I should say the majority—of these people as it exists today by a monogram, I would write into one the two characters *chiung* and *ku*, extreme poverty and bitterness. But this monogram ought to be written so large as to cover the whole end of the province, and written not with ink, but with the life blood of thousands of poor, despairing wretches. There is not any one cause for all this wretchedness. There is a confluence of bitter streams flowing at the same time into their cup of woe.
>
> To begin with, this arid, sandy, salt-impregnated plain has a much heavier population than it can even in good seasons support comfortably, especially since so much of the land is now devoted to the growth of the poppy [opium]. Then, for at least two seasons, there has been in many places a partial failure of the crops, caused at times by lack of rain and at times by extensive floods. . . . Of course, with a not very large amount of foreign engineering, these outbreaks [breaks in the levees] could be prevented. . . .

> In the next place, the causes of these people's wretchedness are not all natural. One factor that plays a very important part in contributing to their misery is an unspeakably corrupt officialdom. The oppression of the people is aggravated just at this time, since with threatened famine the country is more than ordinarily infested with thieves and robbers, and constant depredations are being perpetrated. As a consequence, "law cases" crowd the yamens. But so slow and uncertain is even the appearance of justice that many who have cases of real grievance do not go to the official [out of] their despair of securing a just judgment and to avoid being fleeced by the underlings.[33]

Most of the missionary's account strikes a familiar note: overpopulation on marginal land; inadequate public works, especially waterworks; official corruption and incompetence; and the breakdown of law and order. It would be unfair to say that the state was totally oblivious to the misery of people living under such conditions. In this very region, subsidized grain was being rationed, with thousands lining up in front of a temple converted into a storehouse for this purpose. But the massive problems relating to transport and distribution meant that hundreds of thousands would perish of malnutrition or outright starvation before the next good harvest could be gathered.

Before assuming that such was the fate of even a majority of Chinese peasants and other "common subjects," we should take careful note of accounts like this one by Jiang Menglin, who speaks of his own Zhejiang village in the late nineteenth century:

> Although the village was small, it commanded easy communication by both land and water. Bridges spanned the canals and weeping willows grew luxuriantly on the banks. Fish, shrimps, eels, and turtles were abundant. Here and there one would find anglers taking their ease in the shade of the willows. Oxen could be seen walking in leisurely fashion round the water wheels to propel the chain of paddles which brought fresh water through a long trough to the fields. Miles of wheat fields in the spring and rice fields in summer gave one the feeling of living in a land of perpetual verdure. Swallows shuttled back and forth in the blue sky above a sea of rippling green, while eagles floated high above, circling around the village in search of little chicks.
>
> Such was the background of my childhood and the environment of my clansmen. They lived there for more than five centuries with little change in life. Nature was kind to them. The land was fertile. Floods and droughts were not frequent. Rebellions or wars in the country at large did not disturb them more than once or twice during those long centuries; they lived in peace and contentment in a world by themselves, with little distinction between the very rich and the very poor. Sufficient rice, cotton, silk, fish, meat, bamboo shoots, and vegetables kept the people warm and well fed.
>
> Morals, beliefs, and customs remained unchanged in Chinese villages through centuries of dynastic changes, in peace or war. For the villagers the world was good enough and no improvement was needed. Life alone was unstable, but consolation could be found in the transmigration of the soul. At death the soul was said to leave the body and enter that of a baby then being born. Indeed, in my own time I have seen convicts on the

way to execution who shouted to the spectators that after eighteen years they would be young men again. What a consolation![34]

It is difficult to say which picture was more typical of rural life in 1898. China as a whole presented an enormously varied picture with respect to livelihood, and any generalization must be suspect. As the population had steadily increased—in itself, a sign of productive gains—overcrowded conditions and the use of marginal land had combined to put many lives in precarious circumstances. Given the inadequacy of transport, the slightest adversity in climate, especially if repeated for a second season, wreaked havoc. Conditions could vary enormously within a relatively short distance, and much of China was noted for mercurial weather conditions.

Some provinces or districts were perpetually poor; Shaanxi was among the more notorious. But in the rich alluvial plains, supplied with ample rainfall and blessed with the most advanced premodern agricultural technology, millions lived in relative comfort and contentment, their lives disrupted only by an occasional political upheaval or a cycle of unusually bad weather. Quite possibly, the largest proportion of the peasantry should be placed somewhere between the suffering people of North Jiangsu and Jiang's Zhejiang village. But one fact is clear: when the government was lax, many more people suffered. As in the case of North Jiangsu, large-scale water conservation projects went untended, abetting floods and droughts. Official corruption flourished—and trickled down. Banditry became a way of life for additional tens of thousands. The number of marginal people in the society increased.

In any case, these problems did not preoccupy the literati reformers, and are seldom mentioned in the writings of the period. Economic suffering and other aspects of marginal life were taken for granted in a society that had known poverty from the beginning of its recorded history. For those in power and for the educated class as a whole, national weakness and the threat of the extinction of Chinese culture were the central issues of the time.

The behavior of the most distressed elements of the society, for whom political participation was impossible or of no interest, oscillated between quiet resignation and "antisocial acts," and between thievery and rebellion. Great migrations took place whenever a region was threatened with famine, and vast tracts would be deserted for a time, as if a plague had swept over the land. In their struggle to survive, people ate tree bark and sold their children; even cannibalism was not unknown. But neither these conditions nor other factors linked reformers to commoners. They had no concept of mass mobilization or political participation—except as something that might be possible in the distant future. Their first concern was to save China; when national survival was assured, there would be time to consider such issues as the people's livelihood.

FISCAL REFORM

What reforms were most essential? There was good reason to argue that the most immediate need was for a thoroughgoing fiscal reform. Only with sufficient and assured revenue could the central government establish its independence from foreign powers and initiate the other internal reforms so critically needed. It was humiliating to realize that the only honest and efficient revenue-collecting agency in the nation was the Imperial Customs Office, which was under the control of a foreigner and had a large foreign staff. Thus in an imperial decree of January 17, 1898, the emperor, acknowledging that current revenues were far from sufficient to conduct necessary reforms, called upon all generals, governors-general, and provincial governors to take measures to stop the drainage of public funds into private hands which was taking place in *likin* bureaus.[35] Less than a month later, an attempt to raise a national loan by private subscription was launched. Neither effort was successful. The central problem lay in the fact that basic fiscal reform required a complete political restructuring. As it was, the central government was dependent upon the provinces for the great bulk of its revenues. Provincial authorities did not relish the task of raising, collecting, and transmitting additional taxes, and the center did not have sufficient power to enforce such measures. Fiscal reform thus required an additional centralization of power which was certain to be contested and was beyond the reach of those currently in authority in Beijing.

MILITARY REFORM

A similar situation prevailed with respect to military reform. To understand the urgency of this problem, some background is necessary. When the Manchu invaded China and established their dynasty in 1644, they brought with them the system of Banners, military units that also had economic, social, and political functions that involved families and clans. These units were known as the Eight Banners, although in fact there came to be twenty-four of them, eight each for the Manchu, the Mongols, and the Han.[36] The Banners were concentrated in the vicinity of the capital and in certain other strategic regions, notably western and northwestern China, historic areas of barbarian trouble. Membership was hereditary and originally reserved for the Manchu. By the mid-nineteenth century the Banners probably had about 250,000 soldiers (including some 10,000 officers) and an additional 45,000 supernumeraries and retainers.

The next basic units in the imperial Chinese armies were known collectively as the Army of the Green Standard, originally created as an auxiliary Han military force to preserve order in the provinces. The officers of these units could be either Manchu or Han, but the enlisted soldiers were Han. Green Standard troops were distributed in small numbers throughout China, and by the nineteenth century they may have totaled about 660,000 in number.

Relatively firm and effective centralized control over imperial forces was established very early in the Qing era. Banner garrisons were commanded by Tartar generals, who were often relatives of the emperor, princes of royal blood. They outranked even the governors-general. The governors-general, however, were ex officio ministers of war and were therefore listed as military as well as civil officials. Their direct command extended only to their brigades, but indirectly they had control over the Green Standard troops in their region. Similarly, the provincial governors were vice-ministers of war, thereby holding joint military-civil ranks also. Naturally, the central government was not oblivious to the dangers of "mountaintopism," the excessive concentration of authority (and independence) in regional and provincial hands. Consequently, imperial commissioners, whose authority did not depend on local forces, were sometimes appointed to conduct military operations against major rebel forces.*

By the nineteenth century, however, the entire Qing military system was in serious disarray. First the Opium War and then the Taiping Rebellion revealed the profound weaknesses of both the Bannermen and the Green Standard troops.[37] Military technology had been allowed to stand still for two centuries. The Banners had grown effete and corrupt, not having been used in meaningful military roles for several generations. Opium smoking, gambling, and a total lack of discipline were prevalent. Above all, officers lacked the necessary personal or professional qualities to inspire their troops.** Morale was thus at the lowest possible ebb. These ills were equally apparent in the Green Standard forces, all units of which were grossly undermanned and overreported to central authorities, so that both civil and military officials could embezzle sizable sums.

It is not surprising that the Taiping came close to overthrowing the Qing. Indeed, survival was largely dependent upon the creation of locally recruited militia units. And among the newly created militia, as we have noted, the most effective was the Hunan Army of Zeng Guofan, first organized in 1853 and numbering some 60,000 by 1856.

In the course of the Tongzhi Restoration, Zeng and a few others attempted to extend military modernization. A new emphasis on better selection and training processes was pledged, and in 1865, using Zhili (the province surrounding Beijing) as a model, six Green Standard armies were chosen to be turned into new units known as Disciplined Forces, equipped with foreign arms and given Western-style training. In addition, an imperial edict of 1862 directed Zeng and others to select a group of officers to be given instruction from foreign officers at Shanghai and Ningpo, in an effort to train Chinese who could take over the roles played by foreigners in the Ever Victorious Army. A decade later, Li Hongzhang was to send the first

*MacKinnon challenges the emphasis on the regional character of the Beiyang and earlier Xiang and Huai armies previously advanced by various scholars. Citing Wang Ermin's study, he asserts that the latter armies, while recruited primarily from Hunan and Anhui respectively, were not stationed there, and depended on Beijing for ultimate financial and administrative control.

MacKinnon's central theses are in line with the recent general trend among certain scholars to question the argument that the progressive advent of regional power after the Taiping Rebellion rendered the center increasingly weak. We shall examine the general issue of regionalism at a later point. Suffice it to state here that MacKinnon's major points have merit, namely, that there is no straight-line progression between these early armies (and particularly the Beiyang army) and the "warlordism" of a later period, and that it is too simple to consider them regionally based, or personalized, private armies in the sense of the later "warlord armies" emerging after Yuan Shikai's demise.

Yet it seems to us that he does not give sufficient credit to the *seeds* of localism/regionalism and separatist military power implicit in the broadest military developments from the Taiping era onward. While the trends were mixed, and there were moves toward reintegration as well as toward localism, the military authority of the center *did* weaken in the late nineteenth century, part of a broader trend encompassing political, social, and economic as well as military developments.

**Speaking of the traditional military examinations from which officers were selected, Powell notes: "The literary portion of the examinations was a farce. If, as was frequently the case, a candidate was too illiterate to compose the required quotation, he could obtain assistance from a more learned aspirant. The real emphasis was placed on the tests of strength and skill. These consisted of mounted and dismounted archery, brandishing a great sword, pulling a powerful bow, and lifting a heavy stone. The Chinese suffered from the assumption that the only requirements for military leadership were brute strength and courage" (Powell, *Military Power*, pp. 18–19).

group of Chinese officers to Germany for instruction. Meanwhile, French and Germans in small numbers were hired as teachers, with the Prussian military structure becoming the model, particularly after the striking German victory in the Franco-Prussian War. Arsenals were established, the most noted of which was the Jiangnan Arsenal near Shanghai, and in 1885–1886 two military academies were established, one in Tianjin and the other near Canton, both employing German as well as Chinese instructors. After an earlier abortive attempt, the creation of a modern navy also began in the 1880s.

Taken as a whole, however, the Chinese military was still very deficient at the time of the Sino-Japanese War. Speaking of the Chinese generals who participated in that conflict, a professional British military journal of the time, after noting that they might have been adequate to deal with the border marauders or robber bands that had historically constituted China's security problems, went on to assert: "[they were] altogether unprepared by previous training or experience to cope with armies long and carefully prepared for the contingency that actually arose, and drilled, armed, and led according to the very latest of modern methods." *

Despite all efforts, both the Eight Banners and the Army of the Green Standard remained hopelessly decadent. Even the new militia forces gradually degenerated under the weight of nepotism, corruption, and the social opprobrium directed against the military profession. Military commanders and local civil authorities continued to dip deeply into funds appropriated for soldiers' pay and food. Hence conditions within the ranks were miserable. "Scrounging" was the order of the day, and truly disciplined troops were very hard to find. The following foreign-missionary account from a slightly later period faithfully depicts the situation:

> Five heads [of rebel leaders in the vicinity] were brought in a few days ago . . . but the soldiers on the march from Hankou behaved badly to the people. The rebels could not be more dreaded than the Imperial troops. From the lips of one man who came from the district, I was told that the soldiers demanded goods from shops without payment, forced tea-shop and restaurant keepers to provide food, ravished women and behaved in an extremely bad way.[38]

Charges like these, echoing down through the years, contributed heavily to the low prestige of the army, the public resentment of the government, and the continued appeal of various rebel forces.

From the government's standpoint, there were two other serious problems. First, despite rampant inefficiency, the costs of the military were a heavy burden. It has been estimated that in this general period military expenditures absorbed between one-fourth and one-half of all official revenues. Second, by the last decades of Qing rule, the signs of localism were strong enough to be worrisome. The system of financing the militia units locally through a variety of methods—including the sale of ranks, heightened taxes, and gentry contributions—continued, giving these forces a notable degree of financial independence from Beijing. Although the new im-

* Quoted from *Naval and Military Magazine*, in *North China Herald*, January 14, 1898, p. 73. Analyzing China's naval capacities, Rawlinson, in his detailed study, places extensive emphasis on deficiencies of command coordination and strategy on the part of the top Chinese naval officers. See Rawlinson, *China's Struggle for Naval Development*, pp. 167–204.

perial provincial armies (*yong-ying*) were financed by the center, in most military units a soldier's loyalty was in the first instance to his commanding officer—the man to whom he looked for food, clothing, and instruction—and normally that loyalty was not transferable. This fact encouraged the emergence of quasi-private armies, even though the ultimate loyalty was supposedly owed to the throne. Furthermore, provincial and regional authorities often held combined civil-military posts, and in the aftermath of the Taiping Rebellion it appears that a growing number of militia leaders were also appointed to high provincial offices.[39] Under these conditions the issue of central versus regional and local authority was a troubled one, notwithstanding the center's retention of the right of appointment and dismissal, and its continuing fiscal controls.

In the several years preceding the Hundred Days, the drive for military reform had accelerated. A humbling military defeat, and one generally unexpected in elitist circles, provided the impetus. Military modernization was the one issue on which a fairly broad "conservative-liberal" consensus could be achieved. Thus, in 1895 imperial approval was given to the construction of two military units on the basis of thoroughly updated organizational and technical procedures. One of these units was the Self-Strengthening Army under Zhang Zhidong, headquartered in Nanjing; the other was the Newly Created Army under Yuan Shikai, centered in Zhili. Both armies followed some of the techniques of Zeng Guofan, but placed much greater emphasis on German training and weaponry. It was Yuan's army, however, that was to set the pace, inaugurating a new era in Chinese military science and politics. No southern army would be able to match Yuan's forces for many decades. Thus was modern northern power born, and the background prepared for the militarist era that was to plague China in the future.

In this context, we may usefully recall some steps in the quest for national military reform that were taken prior to the summer of 1898. In 1896 the emperor had issued a special decree calling upon provincial authorities to disband at least one-half of the Green Standard Troops, whose rosters remained swollen with the names of individuals nonexistent or long since departed. Yet only two or three governors-general and governors made any serious effort to implement this decree, and even they ceased when they discovered that others were ignoring the order—a striking commentary on the limits of imperial power during this period. Why the resistance? First, as we have noted, the private "take" from provincial military funds was considerable; and second, to disband large numbers of officers and men without guarantees of employment risked triggering a new rebellion, as had happened in the past.

Thus, disbandment was held in abeyance, and in his decree of January 17, 1898, the emperor once again raised the issue. He pointed out that the Green Standard forces "sucked the lifeblood of the provincial treasuries to the detriment of the whole empire," and deplored the fact that the situation was as bad as before his earlier decree. Later in the same month, the emperor commended two memorials to the Grand Council and Board of War for study and report. One was from a censor, who recommended that in future military examinations the candidates be tested in sharpshooting with modern rifles rather than with the traditional bow and arrow. The second

1. *Zhang Zhidong in post of governor-general of Hubei and Guangdong* ▸

was submitted by Ronglu, then president of the Board of War, who proposed that questions on China's foreign relations be added to the examinations.

Zhang Zhidong, now governor-general of Hubei-Hunan, continued to be in the forefront of the military modernization drive. In early 1898 he proposed sending six young military officers from his region as a commission to study the Japanese military system. Even now, however, Zhang—and individuals like Ronglu and Yuan Shikai—were the exceptions to the general lethargy and resistance to change in military circles.

RELATIONS BETWEEN THE CENTER AND THE PROVINCES: THE ISSUE OF DECENTRALIZATION

The inability to conduct meaningful fiscal reforms and military modernization, as we have noted, reflected a serious imbalance in relations between levels of government—central, regional, provincial, and local. Long before Sun Yat-sen referred in despair to his countrymen as "grains of sand," foreign observers were using phrases like "a bundle of sticks, loosely tied together" to describe the Chinese polity.*

The system was a curious anomaly. The legal omnipotence of the emperor and his designated representatives was never challenged by those in regional or provincial authority. Appointments and dismissals, a seeming key to power, remained in imperial hands at all times. Yet in the realm of policy, even crucial policies of the type just discussed, the reach of the center was weak and uncertain. It is true that in theory—and until the late Qing, in practice as well—provincial-level officials came under the regular scrutiny of an inspection system, the censorate. But increasingly toward the

*The emphasis of scholars like Franz Michael on the advent of regionalism as an increasingly important factor betraying the decline of centralized power has been challenged by certain recent scholars, as we have indicated earlier. For example, in an article entitled "The Limits of Regional Power in the Late Ch'ing Period: A Reappraisal," Kwang-Ching Liu writes that the autonomous power of regional civil and military leaders, particularly the governors-general and governors in this period, has been overemphasized. He asserts first that the throne retained substantial control over local officials through its appointive powers and financial assistance. He acknowledges that after the Taiping and Nian rebellions, the role of the governors in military matters was enhanced, primarily through the new provincial armies, and also in the financial and administrative spheres, especially through control over the *likin* revenues. He argues, however, that this did not amount to truly autonomous power, particularly since the Confucian ethic, with its demand for complete loyalty to the throne, remained at the heart of the value system to which all officials subscribed.

Liu also emphasizes the restraints upon governors-general and governors which came from below, namely, from the permanent local bureaucracy, the new provincial army officers, and the *likin* collectors. Thus, he concludes, it might be more appropriate to concentrate on these phenomena and speak of the rise of "localism" rather than regionalism.

There is value in this analysis if it is kept in perspective. Unquestionably, powerful regional and provincial figures like Zhang Zhidong and Yuan Shikai—along with individuals of much less importance in such posts—remained loyal to the center, never openly challenging the ultimate authority of the imperial institution. (During the extremely critical Boxer Rebellion era, however, various southern governors ignored Beijing or pretended to understand its role in a fashion suiting their views. Even such a stalwart as Li Hongzhang, moreover, evidently toyed with the idea of an independent South.)

More important, as Liu himself makes clear, localism in a myriad of forms was making itself increasingly felt, serving as a threat both to the center and, more immediately, to the center's regional-provincial surrogates. Thus, the broadest trend after the Taiping era (acknowledging rallies of imperial power), was toward a weakening of the center.

close of the nineteenth century, the governors-general, who represented regional power, and the governors, who headed single provinces, had great latitude as long as they fulfilled two functions more or less adequately: the collection of revenue and the maintenance of order.

Even with respect to these functions, the center had long been reconciled to being duped—within limits. The authorities in Beijing knew that only a small percentage of the taxes collected reached them. They knew that when regional authorities reported the costs of maintaining territorial forces of 20,000, the actual number was probably closer to 10,000. And when great victories were reported over provincial robbers or rebels, Beijing often had good reason to be skeptical.

If the situation got completely out of hand, the principal local authorities involved could fall into deep trouble. "Contrary to your reports, the rebels have not been eliminated. They are growing stronger. You have one month to handle this matter, or severe punishment will be meted out." Such messages to governors-general and governors were not uncommon, and punishment often did follow. The official would be demoted, transferred, removed from office, sent home in disgrace, or in extreme cases imprisoned or even executed. But if he escaped death, his chances of rehabilitation were not bad. In a few months or years, he might have his rank restored—with an assignment in another region or province. To contemplate one's frailties and errors during intervals between power was sanctified by traditions as old as the interplay between Taoism and Confucianism. Furthermore, it was recognized that the basic problems were systemic, and that individual responsibility was limited. Someone had to pay, of course, but not necessarily forever. And so the system worked, down to the level of district magistrate, in a traditional way that continued to exert its influence into the Communist era.

If the relations between the center and its subunits were increasingly tenuous, so were those between region and region, province and province. As one astute foreign observer remarked in a somewhat later period, a robbery, a murder, or a rebellion that took place just outside the limits of one official's responsibility was considered no more his business than if it had occurred in the middle of the Sudan.[40] This observer went on to remark that during the Boxer uprising local magistrates sometimes persuaded the rebel leaders to cross the boundary into another county or province by offering them gifts of cash and food, whereupon they could promptly report that all rebels had been driven out of their jurisdiction (only to have them return in larger numbers shortly thereafter).

No provincial or regional leader would think of sending his military forces to another area to help put down a rebellion, or of providing economic assistance to another area during a famine, unless ordered to do so by the emperor—and even then his assistance was likely to be minimal and begrudging. A similar attitude was taken toward national crises. The young reformers of 1898 were to remark mournfully that China's defeat at the hands of Japan was regarded as a problem for the emperor, not for the people—most of whom showed a monumental lack of concern.

Needless to say, this situation could easily be used to advantage by challengers of the existing order, domestic as well as foreign. Rebel movements generally made their headquarters in border regions where jurisdictions were unclear, and when pressures became too heavy they could gain time to recuperate and recruit by moving across boundaries.

THE OFFICIALS: EDUCATION AND EXAMINATION REFORM

In the Chinese system, dependence upon the caliber of officials, subnational as well as national, was axiomatic. Yet by the late nineteenth century many were prepared to assert that in this dependency lay the true root of China's problems. Increasingly, official posts had been purchased rather than reached through the examination process, the government acquiescing in this procedure because of its need for revenue. To compensate for their inadequacies, a majority of these "ready-made" officials hired secretaries who in fact performed most of their functions. Even when office was achieved through the time-honored examination system, however, the issue of adequate training loomed ever larger. This was not a new issue, as we have seen, but events had given it new urgency. If Chinese officials were to cope with the threats confronting them, the bureaucracy would have to be revitalized, from top to bottom. This would require not only new institutions but a new type of official, one shaped by a broader and more relevant education.

Up to this point, however, educational reform and changes in the examination system had been modest. Modern education and the introduction of Western writings were still largely missionary enterprises. In fact, the role of Western missionaries in laying the foundations for the Chinese reform efforts of the 1890s is difficult to exaggerate, and a few examples are worth noting at this juncture. The Society for the Diffusion of Christian and General Knowledge (S.D.K.) was established in 1887 by Rev. Alexander Williamson, with the objective of circulating throughout China literature based on Christian principles, "written from a Chinese viewpoint, and aimed at the literati and officials." The activities of Timothy Richard, who was intimately associated with the enterprise, have already been briefly noted. In addition to contacts with key officials, Richard urged the establishment of lecture series, reading-rooms, and museums to provide useful knowledge.

In 1889 the S.D.K. began to publish a monthly magazine entitled *Wanguo gongbao* (Review of the Times), edited by Dr. Young J. Allen, who had earlier (1875–1882) put out a journal of the same name. Richard became its literary editor in 1891, and Dr. Ernst Faber, a German missionary who became associated with the enterprise, later wrote a widely read Chinese-language book entitled *Civilization*, which compared the Chinese and Christian cultures.

To facilitate communication with the young literati, the S.D.K. arranged to sell and give away its publications in provincial capitals, near places where civil service examinations were being held. In this way the society reached thousands of aspiring young students.

Richard writes that in 1892, when he asked a number of fellow missionaries to give him their views on subjects of great importance to the Chinese, they collectively provided a list of some seventy subjects, including many topics of a social, economic, and political nature. Articles on a number of the subjects suggested were subsequently published in *Wanguo gongbao*. Richard also began a translation of Robert Mackenzie's *The Nineteenth Century: A History*, which was later to be read by a sizable number of literati, young and old.[41]

Thanks to gifts of money from such individuals as Zhang Zhidong and one of the directors of the China Merchants Steamship Company, many S.D.K. publications were distributed to high Beijing officials—and others—free of charge. And in 1894 a 600-tael prize was offered for the best essay by *zhuren* examination candidates on such subjects as the advantages of a railway system; the benefits to be derived from introducing modern machinery for silk-reeling and for the processing of tea; the advantages of having had a well-run imperial maritime customs; how to stop the opium traffic; and how China's foreign relations could be improved. These were issues that went to the very heart of the later reform movement.

The central government in China had no higher educational system. In some provinces, to be sure, innovation had already begun. In Hunan, for example, materials produced by the S.D.K. had been introduced in significant quantities by late 1896, and Jiang Biao's Jiaojing Academy in Changsha became a center for "Western knowledge" and new educational experiments.[42] In September 1897 the Academy of Current Affairs (Shiwu Xuetang) was opened in the same city; from some four thousand candidates who took the entrance examinations, forty were chosen for the first class.* These developments were stimulated not only by missionary publications but also by Governor Chen Baozhen of Hunan, who was dedicated to self-strengthening through the pursuit of Western science and technology, and by a similarly minded local gentry, especially from the younger entrepreneurial set. And although this group was generally wedded to orthodox Confucianism, the more iconoclastic ideas of Kang Youwei were soon to be introduced into Hunan through various channels. One conduit was Liang Qichao, who came from Shanghai, along with a group of fellow Cantonese reformers, to teach in the new school.[43]

Earlier in Beijing, a reform club called Qiangxue Hui (National Rejuvenation Society) had been organized by Kang and others, but conservative pressures had forced its closing in the winter of 1895–1896.** The young reform leaders had established a branch in Shanghai, and after the dissolution of the Qiangxue Hui, Liang Qichao and Wang Kangnian regrouped the reformers in the somewhat freer atmosphere of that cosmopolitan city. They began publishing *Shiwu bao* (Journal of Current Affairs) in August 1896, and it eventually became a thirty-page publication issued

*The new Academy became associated with a journal, *Xiang xue bao* (Hunan Studies News), which had originally gotten under way as an organ of the society Xiangxue Hui (The Hunan Study Society), organized by Jiang Biao. By late 1897, when this journal had come under the editorship of Tan Sitong, it had veered toward the theories of Kang. See Lewis, *Prologue*, pp. 43–44, 145–146; Bays, *China Enters*, pp. 37–39.

**Members of the Qiangxue Hui were drawn from Hanlin officials, censors, and Grand Council under-secretaries, among others. According to Richard, its organ initially took the appellation *Wanguo gongbao*, the same name as that of the S.D.K. journal, and borrowed extensively from the articles of that journal, primarily to avoid official repression. The name of the society organ known to us, however, was *Zhongwai jiwen* (News from China and Abroad). Since it used the same wooden blocks employed to publish the official *Beijing Gazette*, the journal resembled China's one official organ, probably a signal advantage in attracting attention.

It was at this time that Liang Qichao became Richard's secretary for a brief period. Moreover, Richard, Reid, and Pethick, the American secretary to Li Hongzhang, were frequent guests of the Reform Club at dinners until January 1896 when the Club was forced to close. See Richard, *Forty-five Years*, pp. 254–255; also Chi-yun Chen, "Liang Ch'i-ch'ao's Missionary Education: A Case Study of Missionary Influence on the Reformers," pp. 66–125; and Bays, *China Enters*, pp. 20–22.

every ten days, with more than 10,000 copies circulating throughout China. A brief excerpt from an issue of February 1898, written by Liang Qichao, indicates its political flavor at that point:

> What is a nation? It is not merely to have rulers, officials, students, farmers, laborers, merchants and soldiers, but to have ten thousand ears with one hearing, ten thousand powers with only one purpose of life, then the nation is a nation. . . .
>
> We now in China have a population of 400 million, but there are really 400 million kingdoms. Within a few months after the humiliating war in Japan, before the indemnity had been paid or the soldiers had been disbanded, we were singing and dancing, playing and laughing as if in profound peace. . . . Officials were as greedy as ever, students composed their essays and poems in the same precious manner as ever. Where there were a few superior ones who sought real meaning, they wrangled about the relative merits of the learning of the Han and Song dynasties.*

On the eve of the 1898 effort, the Reform Club claimed some forty writers as contributors to its journal; four branches (in Hunan, Jiangxi, Sichuan, and Macao); and some 280 students pledged to aid in the drive for changes. At the outset, the Club had espoused a series of broad reform principles, which in retrospect seem remarkably moderate.[44] Essentially, they fell into three categories. First came those moral maxims that were to be advanced in training the average citizen, exhortations to do good and warnings that his actions, good or bad, would reap appropriate consequences. Confucianism was to be stoutly upheld, but with the injunction to recognize the good that existed in Taoism and Buddhism, the latter being the faith of the common people. There was no mention of Christianity. A second category related to economic development, specifically the advance of agriculture and commerce; a modern labor force, but one dedicated to peaceful production, was to be cultivated. Finally, attention was to be focused on the new learning—science and technology for practical purposes and international law for political strength. Methods of teaching the young more quickly were also to be explored.

Fundamentally, the reformers aimed at economic modernization and the application of science and technology together with the international legal norms of the Western world. The purpose was to save China from extinction. In the aftermath of the Sino-Japanese War, the mood was understandably defensive. Further disaster seemed imminent unless drastic measures were taken quickly. Yet by reinterpreting Confucianism as an instrument of reform, Kang and his supporters sought to preserve the fundamental cultural base upon which Chinese civilization rested, and in so doing to build the

*Liang Qichao, "Discussion Concerning the Reform Association of South China," *Shiwu bao*, February 11, 1898, pp. 1a–3b. A brief summary of the article in English is available in "Reform in China," *North China Herald*, April 18, 1898, pp. 676–677. It should be noted that Zhang Zhidong was able to exert considerable leverage over *Shiwu bao* as major financial supporter and on occasion objected vigorously to certain themes, such as *minquan* (people's rights), which were subsequently dropped or subdued. This was said to lead to growing differences between Wang Kangnian, who was essentially prepared to abide by Zhang's wishes, and Liang, who objected to the interference. Liang departed for Hunan in the summer of 1897, leaving Wang in charge, but continued to contribute to the journal. See Bays, *China Enters*, pp. 3–34.

maximum consensus possible within the sociopolitical elite. Belief and tactics could be happily wedded, with the reformers representing a bridge between the past and the future. Yet these tactics also served to further divide the elite, because many, including modernizers like Zhang Zhidong, could not accept Kang's radical interpretation of Confucius.

The themes being advanced by the reformers were by no means entirely novel. Various individuals had been memorializing the throne on many of these subjects for years. Indeed, Sun Yat-sen, like Kang, had entered Chinese politics in this fashion. By 1898, however, Sun had already moved out of the system to launch his revolutionary career, whereas Kang was very much involved with the system. Between 1897 and early 1898, Kang addressed no less than six memorials to the emperor, each of them dealing with the general subject of administrative reform, in ever more basic fashion.[45] He proposed promoting functional specialization, eliminating the practice of multiple assignments and overlapping responsibilities, providing adequate compensation, reducing provinces to more manageable size as administrative units, and finally, creating a new central "planning bureau" (*zhidu ju*), which would in effect be a combined planning and administrative body divided into twelve departments with functions similar to those of a national cabinet.

As might have been expected, Kang and like-minded reformers were exceedingly critical of current examination procedures and the iron rule of seniority and assignment by lot that prevailed in official appointments. They argued that although the Confucian classics should not be ignored, the old eight-legged essay (*bagu wen*), with its emphasis on ritualized memorization, was useless. Free-form essays were essential, and the subject matter should range over contemporary as well as classical subjects. Men of talent, moreover, should be sought for important offices, whatever their age and rank.

THE HUNDRED DAYS

It should not be thought that Kang Youwei single-handedly led the emperor to produce the series of decrees that began in January 1898 and culminated in the near flood of orders and directives that came from the throne between June and mid-September of that year. Several relatively senior officials close to the emperor—and many others in the provinces as well—had long regarded major reforms and resolute leadership in Beijing as essential.

Behind this development lay the gradual emergence of a vocal elite in the provinces and treaty ports, an elite increasingly alert to global trends and deeply troubled by the drift of events. Previously, it would have been inconceivable for nonofficials to express themselves publicly on the issues of the day or matters of policy. Now, however, led by a segment of the literati, discussion groups and local publications sprang up, providing an informal but indispensable support for the efforts of the reformers in Beijing.[46]

The rising pressures from below mirrored the fact that the need for change was now imperative, and those responsible for governance, whatever their personal inclinations, could no longer ignore it. The empress dowager herself, when first consulted on those matters by the emperor, gave her approval with the proviso that the Qing dynasty not be jeopardized. Nevertheless, many younger reformers looked to Kang for leadership, and with his own dogged efforts to reach the emperor and his key officials, Kang certainly played a critical role in the events of this period.

As we noted earlier, when Kang was en route to exile in Japan, he listed the names of three officials who had played primary roles in introducing him to the emperor: the censor Gao Xiezeng, the imperial tutor Weng Tonghe, and Li Duanfen, president of the Board of Rites.* Zhang Yinhuan, a trusted friend and adviser to the emperor, and Xu Zhijing have also been credited with advancing Kang's cause at court—and both were later to suffer for it.[47]

In any case, at the end of 1897 the emperor—who had not yet met Kang—ordered him to confer with the Zongli Yamen officials. According to Kang, a three-hour meeting took place on January 3, 1898, and a majority of the ministers opposed his radical ideas of administrative change. The following morning Prince Gong and Weng Tonghe reported to the emperor on the conference; the prince opposed Kang's recommendations, and Weng supported them. The emperor then ordered Kang to submit his proposals in the form of a new memorial. This was the genesis of the sixth memorial, which contained the far-reaching reorganization proposals outlined earlier.

Kang was told that the emperor was extremely pleased with the memorial and had recommended it to the Zongli Yamen, requesting a report. A majority of the ministers responded by saying that because the recommendations were so sweeping as to require virtual elimination of the current system, they did not feel it appropriate for them to make a report. At this point, Kang sent the emperor two books written by himself, one on the Meiji Restoration and one on the reforms of Peter the Great in Russia, and these works were said to have deeply influenced Guangxu.

Kang's audience with the emperor came on June 16, when he was received for two hours in the early morning.** Russia had just occupied Port Arthur and Dalian Bay, and Kang reported that the emperor looked thin and worried. He thanked Kang for his most useful books, and the scholar then

*When asked, "Who inspired the new policy in Beijing?" Kang responded, "About two years ago, two officials, Zhang Liu and Wang Mingluan, sent a memorial to the Emperor advising him to take power into his own hands, stating that the Empress Dowager was only the concubine of his uncle. . . . The result of this memorial was that the two officials were dismissed forever. . . . For the greater part of the last two years, the Emperor has been practically [a] figurehead against his own wishes. After the occupation of Kiaochou (Jiaozhou) by the Germans, the Emperor was very furious and said to the Empress-Dowager, 'Unless I have the power, I will not take my seat as Emperor; I will abdicate.' The result was that the Empress-Dowager gave in to him to a certain extent, telling him that he could do as he liked, but although she said this with her mouth, her heart was very different" (*North China Herald*, October 17, 1898, "The Crisis in China," pp. 739–740). The accuracy of the above account, and the means whereby Kang knew of it, cannot be verified, but it has a general ring of truth, and it is possible that it is the emperor's version of events.

When the question was put, "Who recommended you to the notice of the Emperor?" Kang's response was "I was recommended to the Emperor by Kao Hsi-tseng (Gao Xiezeng), one of the Censors, a native of Hupei (Hubei). Then Weng Tung-ho (Donghe), the Emperor's tutor, who is supposed to be one of the most conservative officials in China, but is not actually so, devoted some attention to me, and Li Tuan-fen (Duanfen), President of the Board of Rites. These officials wished to introduce me to the Emperor to give me some responsible office and to put me beside the emperor as his advisor" ("The Crisis in China," p. 741).

**According to Kang, Zhang did not accompany him on the June 16 audience ("The Crisis in China," p. 740).

repeated what he had written in his early memorials. Once again he drew analogies from the reforms that had taken place in France under Thiers after the Franco-Prussian War, as well as those in Russia and Japan. His emphasis continued to be on the urgent need for basic administrative changes and the replacement of the old conservatives with younger, forward-looking men. To the latter proposal the emperor reportedly replied, "I am very sorry. I have practically no power to remove any high ministers. The Empress-Dowager wants to [keep] this power in her own hands." * Kang then turned to other matters, asserting that the emperor's first act should be to revise the old examinations thoroughly and to establish an educational system based on advanced Western models. On this he obtained a promise of action.

Although Kang later sent the emperor many memorials, and was permitted to memorialize him directly, he later wrote that he did not have a second audience (various other accounts claim that he had several). Perhaps it was not necessary. The dam holding back reform measures was bursting, with imperial decrees pouring out of the court in a startling display of Guangxu's determination to make up for lost time and save China. The reform measures can be roughly divided into five categories, the most numerous group of which related to changes in the examination system and educational reform.[48] Not for eight decades would culture and education become such a major political issue again. Even before the meeting with Kang, on June 11 the emperor had directed the construction of "a major university" in the capital, which would serve as a model for the provincial capitals to copy. Work was to start immediately with officials to give their views promptly. Nine days later, the Zongli Yamen was ordered to report on how best to encourage agriculture and modern science, and the ministers were criticized for their delay in reporting on the proposed Peking University.

On July 4 agricultural schools were ordered established in each province so that modern agrarian methods could be learned and disseminated, and on the same day Sun Jianai, an ardent supporter of reform, was appointed president of Peking University. Later that month school boards were ordered established in every city of China to oversee the development of primary and secondary education. In the following month, in mid-August, schools were directed to be established overseas in conjunction with Chinese legations, so that all Chinese currently abroad could be trained to serve their nation. And on September 11 an imperial decree commanded that two additional technical schools be created, institutions specializing in tea and silk production.

Meanwhile, in a reform that shook the old order to its very marrow, the eight-legged essay was abolished as an examination requirement in an imperial decree of June 23, just one week after Kang's audience. It was to be replaced by short free-form essays, as Kang and others had recommended. Moreover, it was reiterated that a premium would be placed on questions testing knowledge in practical subjects as well as in the Confucian classics. These changes were a signal for aspiring officials throughout the land to change their study habits, and were received with a mixture of joy and consternation. **

* According to Kang, he responded, "If your Majesty has no power to remove Ministers, what you can do is to employ young and intelligent officials about you. That would be a step better than nothing" ("The Crisis in China," p. 741).

** Note the following report from a missionary in Shaanxi: "News came by telegram some

A second arena of reform pertained to military matters, which had long been of great concern. Pressures to eliminate the territorial regiments continued, and the emperor repeatedly rebuked regional officials who were slow to act. In place of the territorial regiments, an imperial decree authorized the formation of volunteer and militia corps in every city, town, and hamlet to ensure self-defense at the grass-roots level. Nor was this all. Each of these units was to engage in educational and political activities. In Hunan, where the reform program was receiving the greatest support, the units were ordered to organize a branch "club," under the parent society in Changsha, "to instruct members, high and low, and enlighten and educate them to the times so that in the future, these organizations will not be the slaves of schemers against the public peace."* Here, in embryonic form, was the nucleus of a politically indoctrinated, locally recruited, mass military-political organization. (That it should have arisen in Hunan, of all places, is fascinating, given the prominence which this native place of Mao Zedong and many other radicals was to play in later phases of the Chinese revolution.) But the time was too short, and the obstacles too great, for this idea to be developed at this point.

Meanwhile, military examination reforms continued to be pushed. On July 6 an imperial decree directed the Board of War and the Zongli Yamen to report on the proposed reforms at the earliest moment. On August 12 Ronglu, now the governor-general of Zhili (the Beijing region), and Liu Kunyi, the governor-general of Liang-Jiang stationed at Nanjing, were ordered to consult on the creation of a naval academy and the acquisition of training ships. Ronglu had already begun a series of reforms in Zhili aimed at weeding out superannuated officers and modernizing the armed forces. In Beijing administrative changes were being made in the structure governing the armed forces of all provinces. And in Hankou, Zhang Zhidong, the governor-general of Hubei-Hunan, was preparing to send fifty men from his select bodyguard to Japan for military training, the Japanese government having previously signified its willingness to pay their board and tuition. The drive to build an effective, modern Chinese military force was gaining momentum.

Unlike the Tongzhi reformers, the men of 1898 also advocated commer-

---

weeks ago that the Emperor wanted no more *wenchang* (classical essays), and today posters went up in this city (Sanyuan) intimating to all concerned that henceforth students need not burn the midnight oil any more to perfect their essays. Some are glad for even many scholars recognize the art of essay writing has been brought to a degree of unparalleled perfection and spending more time would be a waste. But many, having spent years, are bitter, as are some old teachers" (*North China Herald*, September 5, 1898, p. 436).

Various other reports indicated that Taoist and Buddhist temples were being turned into schoolrooms, and to the joy of certain missionaries, "idols are being thrown out . . . by the people themselves." See a missionary report from Jingzhoufu, Shandong, in *North China Herald*, August 22, 1898, p. 339. But this report continued, "whether the officials, who after all are the main factors in the case, will bestir themselves to give full effect to the edict is yet quite an unknown quantity. The supply of foreign teachers is also an element not immediately called into being even by the will of an Emperor. . . . One almost fears the movement has come too late."

*Quoted in *North China Herald*, August 22, 1898, p. 329. In February 1898, just a few months before the onset of the central reform edicts, the South China Society was inaugurated. Inspired by Liang Qichao, it was organized by a number of young reformers, including Tan Sitong, soon to be martyred in the aftermath of the empress dowager's coup d'etat. For details, see Lewis, *Prologue*, pp. 53–59.

cial and industrial development, a new turn in Chinese politics. One of the early decrees of the One Hundred Days period called for the enactment of patent and copyright laws, and a second decree promised special rewards for authors and inventors. A July 14 decree ordered all officials to give full support to the encouragement of trade and commerce, and on August 2 a Bureau of Mines and Railroads was established, with the objective of stimulating activity in these fields. Late in August the governors-general Liu Kunyi and Zhang Zhidong were commanded to establish commercial bureaus in Shanghai and Hankou for the promotion of trade. An era of turning outward appeared to be at hand.

In some respects, the most novel proposals had to do with broadening the political base of government, to bring both the throne and Beijing officialdom into closer contact with grass-roots sentiment. The phrases "listening to the voice of the people" and "the people's livelihood" once again came into vogue among reform-minded officials. Although the emperor took no moves to inaugurate the kind of local self-government advocated by Kang, based on a popularly elected assembly, he sought to use the press to develop and publicize new ideas. He commanded journalists to write on political subjects "for the enlightenment of authorities," and encouraged prominent citizens to set up newspapers and magazines throughout the land. By special decree he made the Reform Club's old organ, *Shiwu bao*, an official journal, with its expenses guaranteed by the Board of Revenue and copies of it to be furnished the emperor and all high officials in the capital and in the provinces.*

On September 13, in one of his last reform decrees, the emperor gave local officials the right to memorialize the throne directly, in "closed" memorials; governors-general and governors were directed not to open such communications, so that the throne could know more accurately what "the true situation" was at local levels.

Finally, some attention was paid to the problems of recruiting younger, progressive officials and promoting administrative reform, issues considered crucial by Kang and many others. On June 11 an imperial decree commanded governors-general and governors to select men they regarded as best qualified for office, men "who are not enveloped in a narrow circle of bigoted conservatism and a clinging to obsolete and impractical customs."[49] The emperor then promised to recommend such men to the Zongli Yamen regardless of their rank. Repeatedly, conservatives currently in office were chided or attacked for their stubborn resistance to the emperor's programs. For example, on June 20, Xu Yingkui, the president of the Board of Rites, was specifically asked to explain his opposition to reform. In succeeding weeks similar charges were issued against other high officials, often by name. In the same month, however, Weng Tonghe was dismissed at the de-

*Complicating this development was the continuing struggle for control of *Shiwu bao*, with the chief protagonists being Kang Youwei and Wang Kangnian, currently editor. Zhang Zhidong through Wang had exerted his influence to keep Kang's articles out of the journal. Now, by means of the emperor's edict and the involvement of Song Bolu, imperial censor, and Sun Jianai, former tutor to the emperor and newly appointed head of Peking University, not only was *Shiwu bao* made an official organ, but Kang was ordered to Shanghai to take charge. Wang resisted, supported by Zhang Zhidong, and an impasse ensued with Wang starting a new organ, and *Shiwu bao* disappearing with the collapse of the reform efforts. See Bays, *China Enters*, pp. 35–36.

mand of Cixi, which suggests the formidable power of the empress dowager and the precarious position of the reformers, including the emperor.*

September, however, was the fateful month. On September 1 six minor boards in Beijing were abolished, creating a sensation. One week later the governorships of Hubei, Guangdong, and Yunnan were eliminated as "useless expenditures," with consolidation to take place under the governors-general of the regions concerned. And on September 15, in a last major reform effort, a system of annual budgets and accounting in the Western fashion was authorized for the national government.

Even more startling, on September 4, after a furious internal struggle, Huai Tabu and Xu Yingkui, the Manchu and Chinese presidents of the Board of Rites, were ousted "for daring to disobey Our Decrees." Three days later, Li Hongzhang and Jing Xin, two of the most powerful officials of the time, were dismissed from the Zongli Yamen. Shortly thereafter, the grand secretary, Xu Yonggui, a conservative stalwart, requested permission to retire. It appeared that the emperor was now prepared to carry the battle into the very heart of the conservative camp.

By this time, however, the reformers were well aware of the risks that were being taken. The empress dowager, who had given her approval to the initial reforms, was now being pressed by the terrified conservatives en masse to "restore order" and save the dynasty. The dismissal of Li and Jing, upon whom she had long relied, may well have been a turning point for her. In any case, as the struggle reached its climactic phase, the reformers, headed by the emperor, decided to gamble their program and their personal futures on a further seizure of power. As in the case of most conspiracies, accounts concerning the events of mid-September 1898 differ on some crucial matters, but the salient factors have been established.[50] If the emperor's bold actions in dismissing the empress dowager's appointees were to be sustained, the Old Buddha herself would have to be neutralized. By early September that was presumably clear to all of Guangxu's advisers. Cixi and Ronglu were pressing the emperor to come to Tianjin in October to review the troops, and it was assumed in the reformer camp that this would set the stage for a coup to remove him from power. In order to force the empress dowager into full retirement, it would be essential to remove Ronglu, her longtime loyal supporter and the man who commanded the main military forces in Zhili.

There was only one man who could effectively oppose Ronglu: Yuan Shikai, whose Newly Created Army was the strongest of the five armies currently in the vicinity. According to some accounts, the emperor himself in-

*Tang Zhijun advances the thesis that there were four major battles between the emperor faction and the empress dowager faction during the course of the 103-day reform drive. He lists the first as the success of Cixi in forcing the resignation of Weng on June 15, and the subsequent rise of Ronglu, her confidant, immediately named governor-general of Zhili. The second was a response by the emperor in the form of the June 20 attack on Xu and other conservatives. The third was the July 8 counterattack by the empress dowager's supporters, but with the early September dismissal of key officials supporting Cixi, with this last battle leading to the final showdown.

Tang argues that one key reason why the empress dowager and her group could manifest great endurance lay in the fact that the emperor had supported the decision to go to war with Japan, thereby bearing responsibility for defeat. Lacking self-confidence, he continued to consult the empress dowager throughout the period, and on occasion, especially with respect to appointments, bowed to her will, as in the dismissal of Weng.

2. *Li Hongzhang (about 1895)*

大清國當今聖母皇太后
慈禧端佑康頤昭豫莊誠壽恭欽獻崇熙聖母皇太后

formed Yuan of the need to arrest or eliminate Ronglu in order to assure the success of his reform efforts, but the instructions may have been more subtle; he may merely have hinted at such a course by telling Yuan that he could operate independently with the emperor's full support. We do know that on September 16 Yuan had an audience with the emperor, and that immediately thereafter he was appointed vice-president of the Board of War, in full command of all military training. On the next day he returned to the emperor's chambers and, according to his own account, was informed of Guangxu's determination to carry through the reform program to the end.

Yuan claimed that it was not the emperor but Tan Sitong, one of the most ardent of the young reformers, who came to him hastily on September 18 with the news that Ronglu intended to assassinate the emperor. Tan supposedly then asserted that Yuan's task was to liquidate Ronglu and proceed with his troops to Beijing, both to guard the Forbidden City and to besiege the Summer Palace, eliminating the empress dowager as the final step. According to Yuan, Tan promised to get "a mandate in the Vermillion Pencil"—a direct imperial order—by September 20. Indeed, when pressed, Tan supposedly showed Yuan an imperial message which indicated that reform was being slowed by conservative opposition and commanded four individuals—among them Tan—to find a better approach. But no mention of assassinations was contained in this message, according to Yuan. The meeting ended with Yuan pledging to obey any imperial order. On September 20 Yuan bade farewell to the emperor and returned to Tianjin, going directly to Ronglu's quarters. He denied having told Ronglu of the plot in detail until the next morning, after the coup had already been consummated in Beijing.*

Other accounts challenge Yuan's version of events. It is probable that the emperor ordered him to carry out the plans, either directly or through a message carried by Tan. It is alleged that Yuan advised postponing a strike against Cixi and Ronglu and then sped to Tianjin, at an earlier point than he indicates in his journal, to betray the reformers by giving Ronglu the full details immediately. In any case, Ronglu went to Beijing at once, and the conservative coup, originally planned for October, was activated on September 21. Backed by loyal troops, Cixi had the emperor seized and forced

*For the full record from Yuan's journal, see Jerome Ch'en, *Yuan Shih-k'ai*, pp. 39–42. Neither Liang Qichao nor Tang Zhijun are precise regarding the role of Yuan in the crucial days of September. Liang places great emphasis upon the early development of a ploy by the empress dowager and Ronglu to isolate and defeat the emperor. With the dismissal of Weng Tonghe, Liang argues, the emperor was already lost, and the plan for an October coup was hatched at this point. Cixi began to spread rumors as early as May that the emperor was seriously ill.

The plotters were upset by the fact that the emperor decided not to go to Tianjin, being aware of the coup plans. Instead, he summoned Yuan. After Yuan's second meeting with the emperor, according to Liang, Ronglu wired Beijing that since Russia and Great Britain were engaged in hostilities at Vladivostok, it was essential that Yuan return to Tianjin. Following a third meeting, the emperor gave Yuan permission to return. Liang accepts Yuan's statement that in his meetings with the emperor there was no discussion of a removal of the empress dowager (Liang, *Wuxu zhengbianji*, pp. 64–65). The emperor himself is said to have blamed Yuan for his downfall to the end of his life and, according to some sources, on his deathbed to have urged that Yuan be punished.

In addition to Tang, a second contemporary Marxist account of the events, bitterly hostile to Yuan, is Li Chunyi, *Yuan Shikai zhuan*, p. 77.

◂3. *Empress Dowager Cixi in later life*

4. *Kang Youwei*

4, 5, 6: Prominent figures in the One Hundred Days Reform

5. *Liang Qichao*

6. *Tan Sitong*

him to sign a decree restoring her to full power. The emperor was confined as a prisoner on a small island near the Summer Palace. The leading reformers now faced execution, imprisonment, banishment, or exile.* Thus the reform era came to a dramatic end.

Why did the reformers fail? What was error, what inevitable? One certainly cannot ignore the mistakes of the emperor and his advisers. It was not merely that they tried to achieve too much too fast. More important, they showed little political skill in guarding their flanks while seeking to consolidate their gains. They made no real effort to play off one conservative faction against another, to find means of rewarding those who shifted their position in order to support reform, or to acquire the power necessary to sustain the dismissal of powerful conservatives. Above all, they challenged the empress dowager and Ronglu before they had gained secure control of the military, and they put themselves in the hands of Yuan Shikai with only slim evidence of his loyalties. The aura of amateurism hung over them.

In a broader sense, the 1898 reform effort was an elitist attempt to effect rapid, structural change from within the system at a time when the balance of power, both political and military, was still with the traditionalists at the highest levels. If the empress dowager had been out of the scene or completely neutralized, the authority of the emperor might have sufficed. But as we have noted, the capacity of the center, even in the person of the emperor, to motivate and control regional and provincial officials was limited. A few

* At the national level, thirty-eight prominent reformers were singled out for punishment. Kang Guangren, Lin Xu, Liu Guangdi, Tan Sitong, Yang Rui, and Yang Shenxiu, later to become known as the Six Gentlemen, were executed. Chang Yinhuan was exiled to Xinjiang, and Xu Zhijing was given life imprisonment; others, such as Duan Fang, were removed from office. Many arrests were also made at the local level. See Liang Qichao, "Record of the 1898 Political Reforms," in *Wuxu bianfa* 1:249–328.

of them supported the reform program, but most procrastinated despite the emperor's repeated exhortations, waiting for the outcome of the drama being played out in Beijing. Under the circumstances, survival depended on opportunism, as officials wise in the ways of the system knew so well. Quite probably, many doubted the political acumen and strength of the emperor and his new advisers.

As we have seen, the reformers made some efforts to develop an organizational base beyond officialdom. Their appeal to the merchant community and the gentry—particularly to the younger and progress-oriented gentry—was not insignificant. Given the short period of time involved, however, and the weak political linkage between the provinces and the center, there was little possibility of using these groups in the power struggle that quickly erupted. The outcome of that struggle was determined by the military-bureaucratic balance in Beijing, where the reformers were deplorably weak.

The reformers, to be sure, left a legacy—or more accurately, they supplemented one. In certain circles—primarily progressive young gentry and merchants—resentment over the fate of the reformers simply augmented the widespread antipathy toward the empress dowager and the Qing dynasty that already prevailed in the south. Rebellion was currently widespread in Guangxi and Guangdong. Hunan and Jiangxi were troubled provinces, and Shanghai, with the protection afforded by the foreign settlement, was ready-made for subversive activities. But this unrest was of limited help to Guangxu and his followers. As a later Chinese leader, in a different era, was to remark, "Political power comes out of the barrel of a gun." In the bitter showdown, the reformers did not control the guns.

THE YIHE TUAN UPRISING

The empress dowager and her supporters moved rapidly to consolidate their positions in the aftermath of their coup. An additional 10,000 troops, those of Yuan Shikai and Nie Shicheng—the best trained in the empire—were sent into Beijing, augmenting some 50,000 soldiers already there. This display of power at the capital was quite sufficient to discourage anyone bent on changing the course of events. Those who had been recently removed from office, including Cixi's Manchu clansmen, were immediately reinstated. And the drumbeat rolled against the major reforms, as one imperial decree after another ordered that they be rescinded or drastically modified. Initially, it appeared that the old order would leave scarcely a trace of the dramatic efforts of 1898 remaining.

It was natural that these developments should be accompanied by a rising tide of antiforeignism, for the menace of Western imperialism had never been greater. To meet the foreign threat, two broad options were available. The first, and the one chosen by the 1898 reformers, was to turn outward, in the manner of Meiji Japan. The second was to isolate China and exclude foreigners by force, and it also had Japanese as well as Chinese antecedents. The original theme behind the Meiji Restoration had been *sonno-joi* (revere the emperor, oust the barbarian), and it was abandoned only reluctantly when it proved untenable. Thirty years later, and under far less favorable circumstances, China appeared ready once again to pursue a strategy that had never succeeded in the past. (The oscillation between exclusion and a turning outward, to be sure, did not end with this period, as the extraordinary events of the decades between 1960 and 1980 will testify.)

Meanwhile, the empress herself displayed great political acumen. On the one hand, by providing guards outside Christian chapels in Beijing and by holding her reception for the wives of foreign diplomats, she sought to allay fears and forestall further foreign inroads. She would most certainly have rid herself of the emperor Guangxu had she not feared repercussions in the south, where anti-Manchu sentiment was rife, and in foreign circles; indeed, specific warnings were issued from the legation quarters of the major powers that liquidation of the emperor would create a major crisis. On the other hand, the empress made no secret of her bitter dislike of the foreigner, and her hatred increased after the events of 1898 because she now saw the Westerner as the prime instigator of rebellion, the chief source of treason.*

Such an appraisal was not far off the mark, although encouraging rebellion was rarely the specific intention of the Western intruder. Every important foreign government professed its desire to see China kept intact under a monarchy committed to reform, safe from revolution and partition. Given the intense rivalries between the major powers, and the prospective burdens of further conflict and direct colonial rule, there is no reason to doubt the sincerity of these sentiments. Yet in spite of itself, the West was playing a steadily accelerating revolutionary role. In part, this was a product of negative factors. Growing Western encroachment, in the form of military bases, commercial and communication concessions, and extensive loans, naturally provoked deep resentment across socioeconomic class lines. But the more formidable factors were of a positive character, and centered upon the activities of certain missionaries. Mission-supported schools and colleges, translation projects, and direct reform proposals were penetrating the youthful element within the one group that was critical to China's future, the literati. Thus Western actions operated in whiplash fashion, first serving to weaken and discredit the central government and then subverting a portion of the nation's political elite.

The conservative counterattack, paradoxically, now followed a strategy of going "to the masses," not by mobilizing them but by allowing certain "natural forces" to develop with minimal interference and sporadic encouragement. The most widespread type of mass organization throughout this period was the secret society.[51] With roots going far back into Chinese history, secret societies took various forms, distinguished by the degree of primacy accorded religion, the intensity of political commitment, and the nature of class membership. It is not always easy to assign the various secret societies a place on the continuum that runs from simple banditry to the socially conscious actions of Chinese Robin Hood bands, from spontaneous peasant rebellion to the sustained activities of covert organizations.

Generally, secret-society characteristics were these: a mixture of peasant-based folk-beliefs and superstitions, replete with paraphernalia—amulets, magic potents, and incantations; a religious base, anthropomorphic and rooted in a medley of Buddhist and Taoist traditions; some of the functions of a guild, including mutual aid and defense—which provided a reach beyond and apart from that of the official government; a nonkinship extension of the familial-clan system; and extensive political commitments of an anti-establishment character.

*The fact that Kang and Liang escaped from China with British and Japanese assistance enraged Cixi and provided clear evidence, as far as she was concerned, of foreign sympathies with the rebels.

Such organizations naturally had a strong appeal to the marginal elements in Chinese society, the dispossessed and disinherited. Thus, poorer peasants and ex-soldiers, together with such occupational categories as bearers, boatmen, and lowly monks, frequently composed the membership nucleus. Merchants, gentry, and rich peasants, however, were by no means absent from the rosters, particularly as society officeholders. The thesis that secret societies merely reflected China's common folk is inaccurate. The heterogeneity of membership and variations among individual societies make generalization difficult, but they also offer a clue to why the secret societies could play a vitally important role in the early modern Chinese revolutionary movement.*

What was the connection between the secret societies and the great rebellions of the Qing era? Some of them were perpetrated directly by such societies; the White Lotus rebellion is the foremost example, and the Boxer uprising (to be discussed shortly) is another. Yet in most cases, such as the Taiping Rebellion, secret societies served as auxiliaries rather than as leaders. Nevertheless, from the mid-nineteenth century onward, no sustained uprising was without the influence of such societies, direct or indirect. Their availability for anti-Manchu purposes, their indigenous organizational techniques, and their combined political-military skills were far too important to the cause of revolution to be overlooked. It is thus not surprising that Sun Yat-sen, along with other opponents of the Manchu, appealed directly to them for support. After Sun, moreover, the Communists made similar appeals at certain critical junctures in their long struggle for power.

Once again we are dealing with the vital relation between tradition and modernity in the course of China's evolution. On the one hand, the secret societies were not merely traditional in Chinese terms, but primitive in a primordial, universal sense. Grounded in supremely antirational practices and beliefs, they represented the innate response of all early mankind to the unknown, the dangerous, the distasteful. Yet in them also were carried the seeds of a coordinated ideological-organizational structure that with certain alterations could serve the cause of a modern revolutionary movement. In addition, they advanced the concept of political opposition on the margins of the Confucian tradition, or even outside it. Thus the spirit of revolution was abroad, among the ordinary or lower classes, and it was available for use by various elite-iconoclasts.

At the close of the nineteenth century, secret societies flourished over great stretches of China; they were particularly potent in the center and the

*Joseph Esherick, drawing upon investigations by Japanese government agents currently in China, and two Chinese scholars writing in 1962, argues that the secret societies were primarily associated with "the riverine lumpen proletariat of the commercial centers." His conclusions are that "the secret societies of central China, then, were not primarily peasant organizations engaged in some sort of 'anti-feudal' struggle. They were urban organizations of the lumpen proletariat" (Esherick, *Reform and Revolution*, p. 23). It is his basic thesis that just as the industrial revolution produced a proletariat in Europe, China's commercial revolution produced a "lumpen proletariat," epitomized by the lower socioeconomic urban classes who joined the secret societies.

In our opinion, this somewhat exaggerates the urban character of the secret societies. It is true that these societies contained a variety of such elements, with a considerable portion of them from the lower reaches of the socioeconomic ladder, but they also contained a sizable quotient of rural or "sub-urban" elements, including nearly every category of rural resident. The literature relating to the activities of the secret societies in rural areas is voluminous.

south, but they had ample representation in the north, too. One such group, which was gathering strength in Shandong, was the Yihe Quan (Righteous and Harmonious Fists), known familiarly by Westerners as the Boxers. The Yihe Quan's antecedents went back at least to the eighteenth century, to the White Lotus society and the Eight Trigrams sect. According to the hostile accounts of a censor, the Yihe Quan and similar secret societies were composed of rural people of unsavory character who engaged in gambling and fighting.

By the early nineteenth century the Yihe Quan appears to have been largely extinguished, but like most secret societies, it had a phoenix-like capacity to rise from its own ashes. Its rejuvenation in Shandong is not surprising. From the Sino-Japanese War onward, this North China province had been the target of intensive foreign intrusion. Germans, British, French, Russians, Americans, and Japanese all had representatives or concessions there. Foreign missionaries, traders, and soldiers mingled uneasily with a population that wavered between hostility and indifference. The situation was made worse by the fact that Shandong authorities, acting under imperial decree, had substantially reduced provincial military forces in 1898, creating a significant number of unemployed ex-soldiers. Poor harvests, extending from 1897 to 1899, completed the ominous picture.

The first official mention of the reappearance of the Boxers appears to have come in correspondence between the Grand Council and the governor of Shandong in May of 1898, in which they are referred to as the Yihe Tuan (Righteous and Harmonious Group).[52] From this point on, Chinese sources normally refer to them in this way (rather than as Quan), but the term Boxers remained in usage among Westerners.

The Boxers were clearly a secret society, with all of the classical attributes. Yihe Tuan membership was drawn largely from the peasantry, but Buddhist priests, Taoist monks, assorted artisans, river workers, ex-soldiers, and some gentry were also to be found. The magnet that drew these diverse elements together and caused the group to expand was now antiforeignism, with particular animus directed against Christians, foreign and indigenous.

For its own creed, Yihe Tuan drew eclectically from Taoism, Buddhism, and Confucianism, and professed a belief that the Jade emperor's spirit soldiers would arrive on earth in the year 1900 and would soon seize Beijing—an appealing millenarian message. Discipline was strict, and in matters of sex, diet, and interpersonal relations a type of puritanism pertained—in seeming contrast to the ferocity visited upon hapless Christians. The visual badge of the society was the color red—red turbans, red trousers, red flags. A young women's auxiliary known as the Hongdeng Jiao (Red Lanterns) was created for girls between the ages of twelve and eighteen, who carried red handkerchiefs and red lanterns. Groups of widows were also organized. A range of arms made up the Boxer arsenal: spears, swords, and guns of varying antiquity along with some modern weapons.

Like the peasant culture from which they sprang, the Yihe Tuan members were immersed in superstition and magic. They carried amulets to protect themselves from bullets, recited incantations to enhance their strength, and put absolute faith in the supernatural powers of their gods and leaders—despite repeated demonstrations that all humans were vulnerable to the executioner's axe and the enemy's bullet. Hierarchy, not egalitarianism, characterized the Yihe Tuan. The leaders had exalted titles in the fashion of the

Taiping. And like the Taiping, the Boxers proved highly adept at grass-roots organization. Their basic unit—called a *tuan* (group) in the rural areas and a *tan* in urban settings—had a designated head with a force of twenty-five to a hundred men, normally headquartered in the village temple, which was used for worship as well as for administrative activities.[53] Every individual under Yihe Tuan control was fully instructed in the basic goals of the society, and controls were strict. A deficiency, however, lay in the fact that organizational linkages, especially at the upper echelons, were weak.

Whether the Boxers were "revolutionaries" is a semantic issue of slight importance. It seems probable that their initial leaders were committed to an assault on the Qing dynasty as well as on the foreigner, for they identified themselves with the Ming, as did many other secret societies. But after its early leaders were executed in December 1899 (and possibly even earlier), the mainstream of the movement adopted the slogan *bao qing, mie yang* (protect the Qing, exterminate the foreigner). Dislike of the Qing may have persisted in certain Boxer quarters, but at the zenith of its power the Yihe Tuan publicly proclaimed its loyalty to Qing rule.

On the government side, ambivalence, changes of position, and deep divisions of opinion about the Boxers prevailed throughout the years of rising turmoil. Strategically placed local officials, including Yuxian, the provincial governor of Shandong prior to December 1899, were apparently sympathetic to the Boxers during the period of their initial growth—although Yuxian's co-optation of Yihe Tuan soldiers into the militia may also have represented an effort to divert their independent, anti-Manchu tendencies.* In any case, Yuxian's actions were typical of the provincial official confronted with a complex, virtually impossible task. When Beijing authorities, importuned by foreign diplomats, asked him whether resolute action was being taken against the Yihe Tuan, he always assured them that he had the situation in hand; and indeed, the three key leaders, Zhu Hongdeng, Yu Qingshui, and "the Ming Monk," were either in prison or had disappeared by the late autumn of 1899. However, local foreigners insisted that most provincial and district officials openly sympathized with the Boxers and covertly allowed them to recruit members, persecute native Christian converts, and flaunt their authority over the countryside. It was significant that pro-Qing slogans began to appear at least by the fall of 1899, and that the key leaders were not executed until after Yuan Shikai had replaced Yuxian as governor in late December.

By the end of 1899 the Yihe Tuan movement had reached alarming proportions. Scores of Chinese Christian converts had been killed, their houses burned and possessions taken. Churches were being destroyed throughout the region. The attacks spread, so that by the spring of 1900 they were taking place in Zhili (Hebei) as well as Shandong. In the initial period, however,

* Purcell presents a detailed analysis of the question whether the Yihe Tuan were initially anti-Qing, and if so, when a change took place (*The Boxer Uprising*, pp. 194–222). He concludes that when the Boxers first reappeared in May 1898, "they were not openly, and probably not actually, anti-dynastic." Nevertheless, some leadership elements *were* anti-Manchu, and Purcell accepts the likelihood that only after these elements were eliminated in the fall of 1899 did the new leadership adopt pro-Qing slogans. The White Lotus, from which the Yihe Tuan drew some of its characteristics, remained true to their antidynastic aims, and many were put to death by the Boxers for this reason in Beijing in July 1900. The role played by Yuxian and other Qing officials in shifting the Yihe Tuan toward the support of the Qing was probably substantial (pp. 265–266).

assaults on foreign missionaries, as distinct from Chinese converts, were rare indeed. Whether restrained by fear of foreign retaliation or purposefully adopting the tactic of "surrounding the missionaries," the antiforeign forces concentrated on Chinese Christians, whom they considered "traitors" to their culture and historic faith and deserving of little mercy. Since the death of the two German missionaries in 1897 no missionary had been killed in China until December 27, 1899, when a British citizen was cut down in rural Shandong. And despite the rapid growth of the Yihe Tuan from this point on, the next missionary murder did not occur until June 1, 1900, when the court's relations with foreigners were reaching a crisis. Throughout this period, however, the missionaries were being warned of Boxer intentions, and Boxer assaults on converts continued, with heavy loss of lives and property.

Once the conflict over Tianjin and Beijing broke out, the missionaries of North China were indeed in grave peril. The heaviest loss of lives occurred in Shanxi, where Yuxian had become governor after his removal from Shandong: following an order to exterminate all foreigners in the province, fifty-six adults and children were slaughtered, wiping out the entire missionary community.* Elsewhere, eleven missionaries and three children lost their lives in Baoding, in Zhili, and seven were killed in Zhuzhou, in Zhejiang.

Throughout the early months of 1900 the situation had grown steadily more complex. Cixi temporized. Consumed by a mixture of hatred and contempt for foreigners, and encouraged by recurrent reports from certain advisers that the Yihe Tuan had the strength to eradicate them, she was tempted to give the Boxers free rein. Yet grave doubts concerning their true capacities were expressed by such trusted advisers as Ronglu, and the threat of massive foreign intervention was made plausible by the increasingly insistent demands from the foreign ministers resident in Beijing that the throne adopt firm policies against Boxer depredations. When the empress resisted these demands, various ministers in Beijing urged their governments to make a show of naval force in North China waters. At the end of May, while the court was still refusing to issue an edict banning the Yihe Tuan, a decision was made by the major foreign governments to bring additional legation guards from Dagu to Beijing, and the first group arrived on June 1.

The court's policies continued to betray uncertainty and indecision. In May heavy fighting between Yihe Tuan and government soldiers had taken place in Zhili after a Boxer assault on a Christian community. But the government was also considering the possibility of incorporating Yihe Tuan soldiers into the militia and was still trying to make a distinction between "good" and "bad" elements within the movement. On June 6 a significant imperial decree was issued, urging the Yihe Tuan forces to disperse, and calling for their punishment if they did not obey.** Two days earlier, on June 4,

*A detailed description of the events in Shanxi is given in Forsyth, *China Martyrs*, pp. 30–84. The story presented is one of mounting tension, replete with the usual rumors about the foreigners' evil deeds (in one case, poisoning the water wells); the heroism and personal sacrifice of a number of Chinese Christians who stood by the missionaries and sought to save them; betrayal at the hands of "renegades," individuals who had once professed Christianity, but recanted; and the direct participation of Yuxian in the execution of missionaries in the capital of Shanxi, Taiyuan.

**For this decree, see *Yihe Tuan dangan shiliao* 1:118–119. The decree concluded with the following remark: "The Grand Councillor Zhao Shuqiao has been appointed to propa-

some twenty-four warships had arrived at Dagu, a fact that undoubtedly influenced the June 6 decree. Six days later, moreover, an allied task force of approximately 2,000 men under British Admiral E. H. Seymour set out for Beijing, only to be forced back within the week after a series of clashes with large Chinese forces, both Yihe Tuan and imperial. Although the court had reluctantly accepted the legation guard reinforcements, it was not prepared to allow a Western expeditionary force to march on the capital unchallenged.

The climax was reached in mid-June through a series of bizarre events. On the morning of June 16, after bitter debate, the Grand Council resolved upon a "compromise" course of action: envoys were to persuade the allied expeditionary force to stop its advance, and the Yihe Tuan was to be disbanded, with its better elements incorporated into the imperial army. That very afternoon, however, the empress dowager announced to the council that she had received an ultimatum from the foreign ministers in Beijing which she considered insulting and totally unacceptable. Supposedly, the ministers demanded that all revenues be collected by foreign sources, that military affairs also be placed under their control, and most important, that the emperor be restored to power. Later, it was established that this message was a forgery, perpetrated by Prince Duan, one of the prominent Yihe Tuan supporters, in an effort to turn the tide against further "appeasement" of the foreign powers.[54]

Meanwhile, ominous developments were taking place on the coast.[55] On June 15 sizable Yihe Tuan forces occupied most of Tianjin, except for the foreign settlements, and reports indicated that they were in a position to cut the railway line between Tianjin and the coast. An allied decision was immediately made to seize the Dagu forts—which guarded the mouth of the Beihe, leading inland—in order to ensure continuing contact with the forces that had been put ashore. An ultimatum given the Chinese commandant was answered with cannon fire, and after a brief but fierce struggle the forts were occupied on June 17.

In Beijing events moved toward ever greater tragedy in a seemingly uncontrollable fashion. On June 11 Sugiyama Akira, the chancellor of the Japanese legation, was killed at the main gate, the first foreign diplomat to die. Two days later a large Yihe Tuan force entered the city, and in the weeks that followed, their numbers continued to mount, reaching a total of at least 30,000, with several tens of thousands of imperial troops also in Beijing. At first, discipline was relatively good, but later law and order often broke down, and looting and assault became widespread, even against friendly officials and civilians.

On June 19, when word reached the court of the allied ultimatum against the Dagu forts, all legations were notified that the government could no longer guarantee the protection of foreigners in Beijing, and that they should leave within twenty-four hours. An escort was promised, to accompany them until they reached the coast. A general protest by the legations was immediately voiced. Evacuation in such a short time was proclaimed impossible. There was also doubt that the government was sincere in promising an escort, or at least any effective escort. These doubts were heightened

gate the imperial message to advise the Yihe Tuan to obey the decree, to disperse and live peacefully. . . . If after this proclamation, [the Yihe Tuan] should refuse to reform, Grand Secretary Ronglu should order Generals Dong Fuxiang, Song Qing, and Ma Yukun to proceed to have them exterminated."

on the next day, June 20, when the German minister, Baron Von Ketteler, was shot while attempting to reach the Zongli Yamen to discuss matters. Further efforts to negotiate were broken off, and that afternoon Chinese forces opened fire on the Legation Quarter.

Foreigners were subsequently besieged within two compounds. The first was the shrunken Legation Quarter, located outside the southeast corner of the Imperial City. Here approximately 475 dependents of foreign representatives and other civilians were defended by about 460 officers and men of various nationalities, bringing the total close to 1,000. Alongside the west wall, inside the Imperial City, the Roman Catholic North Cathedral served as the other refuge. Some 40 French and Italian military men, together with 13 French priests, 20 French nuns, and about 3,200 native converts, were congregated there.

The siege against the Legation Quarter lasted for fifty-five days, from June 20 to August 14. Until the middle of July it was marked by relatively intense and sustained Chinese attacks, although the type of mass assault that would certainly have overrun the foreigners' lines was never carried out. The final month was characterized by intermittent truces and attacks, an eerie situation where solicitude and implacable hostility emerged at unpredictable intervals.*

The seemingly irrational, inexplicable course of events mirrored faithfully the true complexity of Chinese politics during this period. A study of the imperial decrees during June and early July is most revealing. Throughout the month of June, even after hostilities had commenced in Beijing, the pronouncements of the empress dowager remained cautious, even conciliatory. No doors were completely and finally closed.[56] The decree of July 1, however, struck a harshly militant note: it demanded that all missionaries be expelled from the country, and that all Chinese Christians "awaken to their wrongdoings and repent."[57]

Two weeks later, however, on July 14, the Zongli Yamen suddenly sent a note to the besieged foreign ministers suggesting renewed negotiations; the note was accompanied by gifts of food. Until almost the end of the month, an uneasy truce prevailed, although negotiations proved abortive and the firing was subsequently reopened. What had happened to bring about this turn of events? By mid-July the court had received word that the battles around Tianjin were going badly for the Chinese. In addition to military defeats, the government now faced another problem: the southern governors-general, almost without exception, were refusing to cooperate in the war

* Marchant's edited diary of Lancelot Giles provides us with a graphic description of life and death within the legation quarters during the course of the siege. Giles was the son of Herbert Giles, longtime British Foreign Office official in China and compiler of a famous Chinese-English dictionary. Although only twenty-one years of age at the time, young Giles was knowledgeable concerning China, having been born there, though he was educated in England.

Typical of an entry is the one for June 14, a section of which follows: At 12:45 P.M. Captain Wray (Royal Marines), being on duty at the North Bridge, captured a Boxer who was calmly strolling across. He appeared in a half-dazed and mesmerized condition, and was unarmed, or else he would have been shot on the spot. He wore a yellow girdle and had a square piece of red flannel on his chest, hung from his neck. This is supposed to render all Boxers absolutely invulnerable. He was put in the cells, awaiting a decision as to his fate. Several of the Chinese servants forthwith left the Legation for good, saying that this Boxer would breathe fire and burn the place about our ears!" (p. 113). (He and another prisoner were later shot.)

against the foreigners. Deliberately misinterpreting imperial orders, they proceeded under the convenient artifice that the Yihe Tuan were acting in defiance of imperial wishes, and that the situation in the north had gotten out of control. In a narrow sense, this was true. Although the "conservatives" were currently in a strong position within the court, the lawlessness and weak coordination between various Chinese military units in Beijing reflected continuing divisions between such men as Ronglu and Prince Duan. In these circumstances, the empress dowager herself exhibited mercurial moods and uncharacteristic indecision.

The rising specter of defeat merely deepened the bitter divisions within top court circles. Late July and early August witnessed the last great "triumph" of the antiforeign forces. When five key officials, in an act of extraordinary courage and character, warned that current leadership and policies could doom China to extinction, they were quickly executed on imperial order.* At this very point, however, imperial armies, as well as Yihe Tuan forces, were being defeated on the battlefield, and their commanders were committing suicide.

Allied forces (led by Indian Rajputs) raised the legation siege on August 14, and on the next morning the empress dowager and the emperor, disguised as common folk, slipped out of Beijing with a small entourage, heading for Xian, the capital of Shaanxi. Li Hongzhang and Prince Qing, regarded as acceptable to the West and Japan, were commanded to serve as negotiators on behalf of the government. Once again China had been defeated militarily—on this occasion by a combination of all of the major powers using only a small fraction of their potential strength.

Throughout the summer of 1900 the world's attention had been drawn to China as never before. The siege of the Beijing legations, a story filled with drama and suspense, became the great media event of the era. Naturally, the accounts that filled the Western and Japanese press did nothing to enhance the international reputation of the Chinese government or the Chinese people. First came recurrent stories of the gruesome murders of missionaries and Chinese Christians.** Then the unprecedented siege of the entire diplo-

*The five officials executed were Xu Jingcheng, former minister to Russia; Yuan Chang, minister of the Zongli Yamen; Xu Yongyi, president of the War Board; Lian Yuan, subchancellor of the Grand Secretariat; and Li Shan, president of the Finance Board. Xu Jingcheng's and Yuan Chang's executions are the subject of much controversy, being associated with the "three memorials" of June and July 1900 allegedly authored by the two. The last memorial, 22 July 1900, supposedly accused Xu Tong, Gangyi, Qi Xiu, Zhao Shuqiao, Yu Lu, Yuxian, and Dong Fuxiang of bringing calamity to China and called for their execution. However, the court denied having ever received the "three memorials." The "memorials" are not found in the official history of the Qing dynasty nor in such collections as the *Yihe Tuan dangan shiliao*, cited earlier. For a discussion of the executions and the "three memorials," see Tan, *The Boxer Catastrophe*, pp. 104–109.

**The account carried in the *North China Herald* of the death of Father Victorin, a twenty-nine-year-old Belgian Catholic priest in early 1899, is one example. Victorin reportedly was captured by a mob in the course of an attack on Chinese Catholics, stripped of his clothes, tied to a board, and returned to his home. There he was bound to a tree, with pieces of flesh being cut from his thighs in a version of "the slicing death." Finally, his body was cut open from chest to abdomen, and he was disemboweled. The report asserts that some of the assassins proceeded to drink his blood, and finally his head was cut off (related by a missionary correspondent from Yichang, Hubei, entitled "A Modern Martyr," February 9, 1899, p. 255). Accounts contained in Forsyth, *The China Martyrs* are scarcely less gory in some instances.

matic community, an act totally contrary to prevailing international law, was described at length. Moreover, the threat of an even greater massacre seemed to hang over the horizon for nearly two months. The actual legation casualties were remarkably light considering the circumstances; 74 foreigners were killed and over 130 wounded during the siege on the two compounds. But China was now seen by many Westerners as a "barbarous" country where hostile natives committed atrocities against those who had come to help them.

The Westerners now exhibited their own brand of barbarism. After the fall of Beijing, vengeance was the order of the day. The fighting had been fierce up to the final hours, with the Chinese contesting every mile of the route into the city, and the victors were in no mood to be lenient. They were determined to teach the Chinese a lesson they would never forget: that attacks upon foreigners and treaty violations would be severely punished. Numerous executions, including that of the Manchu commanding general, were ordered. Looting was wholesale. Parts of the city were razed. The behavior of the allied soldiers shocked even hardened newsmen.

In distant Xian, the truncated court, gradually recovering from the trauma of defeat and exile, sought to adjust to the new situation. It sentenced several antiforeign leaders to life imprisonment or exile, partly to propitiate foreign anger and partly to save them from a worse fate. But the effort failed. Allied authorities demanded that the key figures be executed, and this end befell Yuxian among others. Some leaders conveniently committed suicide, in certain cases on request. Naturally, the Yihe Tuan and such sister societies as the Dadao Hui (Big Sword Society) were outlawed, and antiforeignism was made a crime punishable by death. Restrictions were placed on Chinese importation of arms, and certain institutional changes were made in the Beijing part of the central government. Formal apologies were demanded and obtained. Finally, a huge indemnity of 450 million taels (67.5 million pounds sterling) was assessed; paid over thirty-nine years, with interest, it would amount to 980 million taels.

Negotiations with respect to some of these matters dragged on until June 1901, and the peace protocol was finally signed on September 7. Initially, it had been assumed—and hoped—by many Chinese reformers and resident foreigners that the emperor would be restored to power and Cixi consigned to political oblivion. This did not happen, primarily because the foreign rivalries that emerged in the course of the Beijing occupation made a unified position on such a critical matter impossible. The physical absence of the emperor and doubts about his competence were additional deterrents. Thus, when Cixi finally returned to the capital on January 6, 1902, she returned with all of her previous power—but to the helm of a state weaker and less capable of dealing with its mounting problems than previously. China was now saddled with a huge additional debt; competent leadership was at an even greater premium; morale at every level had plummeted; and provincial-regional autonomy and the more important North-South cleavage were growing at an accelerated rate.

Before offering our own assessment of the Yihe Tuan uprising, it will be instructive to study other perspectives, both those of the present and recent past and those contemporary to the event. Let us turn first to Marxist accounts.

Initially, many Chinese Marxist historians interpreted the Yihe Tuan movement in a wholly favorable manner.[58] Defining the Yihe Tuan's membership as drawn from "the broad masses"—first peasants, then artisans, transport workers, peddlers, and the urban poor—various authors argued that the Yihe Tuan directed its efforts against imperialism only to be betrayed by the Qing and its functionaries. Yuxian allegedly gave recognition to the Yihe Tuan in order to deceive it, to trap and kill its leaders. When the imperialists joined together in a war against China "to suppress the people's revolution," the court treacherously prevented victory. The empress dowager's declaration of war was a hoax.* Thus, although the Yihe Tuan "fought with indomitable courage against the aggressors, the Qing government criminally undermined the movement." Ronglu, the "faithful jackal of the empress dowager," conspired in various ways to aid the imperialists, even making it possible for the legation forces to get food and ammunition. The final verdict: the Yihe Tuan movement "is the glory and pride of the Chinese people. It laid a cornerstone for the great victory of their revolution fifty years later." It caused the people to understand imperialism better; it exposed the treasonous character of the Qing government; it unmasked the real savagery of the imperialist powers; and it precipitated the subsequent growth of the revolutionary movement.[59] Such an interpretation is not totally devoid of fact, but in its utter simplicity and unrestrained passion it is an exercise more in polemics than in history.

In recent Chinese Marxist analyses of the Yihe Tuan, however, a modest revisionist trend is evident, as the papers presented at the 1980 Jinan Conference and other current writings illustrate. Many Chinese Marxist scholars now seem prepared to come to grips with greater complexity in fitting the Yihe Tuan period into a Marxian theoretical framework. It is acknowledged that the Yihe Tuan were hobbled by superstition and various self-defeating practices. As one author writes, "with burdens temporarily lifted from their backs, the masses easily became what Marx described as a 'wild, blind and undisciplined wrecking force.'"[60]

Different views on certain issues are also to be found at this point among Chinese Marxists. Some scholars deny any connection between the Boxers and the White Lotus.[61] Others find definite ties with it, both in membership and in policies. A debate continues over the degree to which the movement was "antifeudal" as well as "anti-imperialist."[62] Somewhat different analyses of the meaning of the slogan "Uphold the Qing" have been advanced, one thesis being that it was intended to encompass the Chinese nation as well as the dynasty, and should therefore be interpreted as a manifestation of nationalism.[63]

The debate over the attitude toward the Yihe Tuan taken by the Qing government—and more precisely, by the empress dowager—has also been reopened. One view is that official vacillation resulted from differing opinions within the government on the utility of using the movement to oppose foreign imperialism. It is argued that Cixi's recognition of the legitimacy of the Yihe Tuan at a crucial point was an act of self-defense: otherwise, the

* *The Yi Ho Tuan Movement of 1900* continues this account: "Owing to this Ching Government sabotage, the Yi Ho Tuan failed to take the legations, in spite of the 56-day siege, or the Pehtang Cathedral, besieged for 63 days. The Empress Dowager herself admitted: 'I imposed restraints at every point. Had I let them loose, they would undoubtedly have overrun the tiny legation quarter.' Those words amply reveal the treachery of the Ching government" (p. 83).

Boxers would have turned against the Qing. Various different interpretations of the historical role of the Yihe Tuan have also been presented, although a general consensus prevails that as a predominantly peasant-based movement, it suffered from the limitations of the peasant class.

Turning to accounts written at the time of the event, let us look first at what was said by the Kang-Liang reformers in Tokyo. In a manifesto written as the Yihe Tuan were being defeated, they struck out at Cixi and her court, charging the government with having "utterly failed to preserve the territorial integrity of China, thereby laying itself open to foreign aggression, insult, and invasion." The Yihe Tuan were largely ignored, and attention was focused upon the rulers of China. They had pursued repressive, reactionary policies; they had sought to "shut out all light" from the outside world; they had allowed themselves to become surfeited with corruption. What was the solution? The allied powers should depose "the usurper" and reinstate Emperor Guangxu so that the course of reform could be renewed. If he were dead, a provisional government should be organized until the best candidate for the emperorship could be found. Then China would advance as a constitutional monarchy, and democracy and progress patterned after the model of Great Britain would follow.[64]

The Tokyo-based reformers had no kind words for Western policies during the course of the Yihe Tuan uprising. Their relative silence on Boxer actions, however, cannot be taken as approval of Boxer methods or goals. Kang Youwei and Liang Qichao wanted to affix primary responsibility for events upon the government, and more particularly upon their old nemesis, Cixi. In this manner, they hoped to persuade the major powers to reestablish conditions that would permit a resumption of the 1898 reforms. When this did not happen, they were deeply disappointed.

Meanwhile, an interesting balance sheet on the uprising was drawn up in a debate between Chinese youth, staged at the Shanghai YMCA in the spring of 1901.[65] The topic chosen was "Will the Boxer uprising prove to be for the ultimate good of China?" Among the affirmative arguments were these: The uprising had helped to arouse the Chinese public, and at the same time had convinced the rulers of the foolishness of their exclusion policies, thereby making reform inevitable. It had demonstrated that the Chinese are patriotic, and provided the incentive for resistance to such further assaults upon Chinese sovereignty as the current Russian efforts to steal Manchuria. And finally, its failure was a blow both to superstition and to the type of conservative political dominance that had stultified progress in the past.

The arguments advanced against the long-term value of the uprising were as follows: China had lost her independence as a result of this debacle, for her external relations, the policing of her capital city, and the management of her entire financial system were now dictated by foreigners. The Boxer uprising probably foreshadowed similar upheavals, particularly since taxes had been increased to astronomical heights to pay the indemnities, and the barbarism of the allied forces would not be forgotten by the Chinese for many years. The revulsion of the world against the Chinese because of the Yihe Tuan outrages would not soon be set aside. The Russians had been given the necessary pretexts for seizing more of China's territory. North-South divisions had been exacerbated. And the missionary problem had become more rather than less complicated.

In this debate, as in real life, the negative side was given the edge. This was a performance staged under foreign auspices: some of the arguments were artificial; and the participants came from a narrow group of educated, relatively Westernized Chinese youth. Nevertheless, the themes that were raised, especially on the negative side of the ledger, unquestionably reflected the views of many of the young literati, Christian or otherwise. In their views one senses that mixture of anger, despair, and groping that was tearing the literati of all ages apart throughout this tumultuous period.

No group suffered more during the Yihe Tuan uprising than the Chinese Christians. An emotionally searing account, also filled with great insight, was written by one of them just after the uprising had been crushed.[66] It is worth considering here.

In the north, this Christian reported, the people call foreigners "great-haired" (hairy), and believers (Christians) are called "second-haired." Our countrymen, he continued, do not accept the contention that foreigners are basically good, or that Chinese Christians are loyal to their country as well as to their religion. We must not hate them, he said, but must forgive them for this attitude, because in truth the West *has* oppressed and overpowered China, treating her with severity and not benevolent mercy. Western nations have seized many parts of China, such as Annam (northern Vietnam). Other parts are under indirect Western control.

Consequently, the Chinese nonbeliever treats Westerners as enemies and thinks constantly of revenge. He also looks upon believers with suspicion because he regards them as supporters of the foreigner. In this respect, Chinese Christians have been honest and straightforward, but not wise. They have made no distinction between the truth of the Gospel and the virtues of foreign countries. Did not England bring India's opium to China? Did it not snatch Hong Kong and later Weihaiwei? Has not the United States mistreated the Chinese who have immigrated to that country? Did not Germany, after helping China to get back the Liaodong peninsula at the conclusion of the Sino-Japanese War, take Jiaozhou for herself? These are countries that believe in Jesus. How can they treat China in such a manner?

At first, Christians said that the Western countries are just, patient, and benevolent. Now it appears as if they are none of those things. Hence Christians are considered spies and are killed. Foreign missionaries have also been killed, but at least most missionaries have the money and the means to flee, and foreign soldiers will protect them, although not adequately. But Chinese Christians, having no money, cannot flee, and even those with money can find no place of refuge. More than ten thousand of them have been killed. Moreover, foreign soldiers cannot distinguish between antiforeign Chinese and believers, and so they have killed both indiscriminately. "We believers, thus meeting this suffering, do not know what great sin we have committed."

Although the Chinese views expressed just after the uprising differ in certain respects, they agree in important ways. None defended Yihe Tuan actions or found in them a solution to China's problems. Yet they shared a common anguish over the degree to which Chinese rights had been trampled upon in the course of Western intrusion, and a common despair over the Chinese political scene. Thus, in critical respects, they shared the antiforeignism of their less educated or more conservative compatriots, primarily because they shared a common resentment of Western actions and attitudes.

And what lessons were drawn from the uprising by the "old China hands," the Westerners with long experience in China? Their views differed radically, reflecting differences that went back to the earliest Western-Chinese contacts and were also to persist into the heart of the twentieth century.

The logic of one position ran as follows: The tragedy of the Boxer uprising occurred because the West had mistakenly treated the Beijing court as if it represented a unified, responsible government willing to interact with Western governments on the basis of equality, mutual understanding, and an acceptance of prevailing international law. It had failed to comprehend that the current Chinese government was weak, incompetent, reactionary, and prepared to evade its responsibilities whenever possible. This basic error on the part of the West had led to the chaos and bloodshed. The remedy was to force Beijing to do what was necessary and proper: reform its antiquated institutions, take responsibility for the actions of its people and officials, and live up to the obligations of the treaties it had signed. Until these requirements had been met, the allied forces should remain in China, serving as tutors and policemen.

A very different lesson was drawn from the past by Sir Robert Hart, who had lived and worked with the Chinese longer than almost any other Westerner at this point. Hart argued that the foreigner had terrorized China too much, threatening her sovereignty and antagonizing her people. One indigenous response to this was the rise of the Boxers, a patriotic but primitive and misguided group, who sought to redress the wrongs done to China by driving all foreigners from Chinese soil. If the Westerner were to stay in China, Hart argued, he must ultimately stay on Chinese terms, submitting to Chinese jurisdiction and trusting to the magnanimity and honor of the Chinese government. The path to Western-Chinese harmony did not lie in the direction of Western dictation and heavy-handedness.*

Still other positions were expressed during this period of widespread Western reflection. The veteran missionary-educator W. A. P. Martin insisted that only as Christian enlightenment spread across the land could China be saved from backwardness and ruin.[67] But other veterans of the China scene argued that West and East could never meet; and that the West could never successfully set rules for—let alone govern—a society like China, because

*For Robert Hart's comments, see the *North China Herald*, May 8, 1901, p. 885. The following additional remarks—extraordinarily interesting in the light of later events—are found in Hart, *These from the Land of Sinim:*

> The next few years may be quiet ones, and this eight weeks' nightmare will fade away in the past and be forgotten; but below the surface is the seed, and sooner or later will follow the crops . . . to feel the pinch of certain treaty stipulations and, when strong enough to do so, to throw off such as were originally imposed by force, is a practice for which even Christian Powers have set pagan States more than one example" (pp. 56–57).
>
> . . . "If the China of today did not hesitate on the 19th June to throw down the glove to a dozen Treaty Powers, is the China of a hundred years hence less like to do so? Of course common sense may keep China from initiating an aggressive policy and from going to extremes; but foreign dictation must some day cease and foreigners some day go, and the episode now called attention to is today's hint to the future." (P. 59)

We are indebted to C. Martin Wilbur for calling this work to our attention.

the yellow man was inherently religious, superstitious, and fatalistic, whereas the white man was quintessentially secular, rational, and aggressive.

The disparity in Western views mirrored more than differences in personality, occupation, and type of role among old China hands. It also reflected the genuine complexity of the issues at stake. Few Westerners in this era doubted the superiority of their own civilization, whatever their reservations about certain aspects of it, such as religion. And few doubted that China, despite its stubborn resistance to change, would come to accept Westernism in its essential aspects. For the nineteenth-century Westerner there was no other course for China, or for the world. Thus, among old China hands and in Western foreign offices, the issues were of a more restricted if profoundly important nature. Could and should the West serve as catalyst to modernization in a conscious, planned manner? Would some form of external tutelage be effective, and if so, what should be the mix of coercion and persuasion? And in the process of Westernization, what could be retained by China that was indigenous, and what had to be given up? And among the various Western and Japanese models for development, which was the most appropriate? In the aftermath of the Yihe Tuan uprising, both Westerners and Chinese addressed themselves to these questions with varying degrees of confidence and doubt, but with a seriousness that betokened the near-universal assumption that the old order in China could not long be sustained in its prevailing form.

3

LIANG QICHAO AND THE DEFENSE OF REFORM

In the years between the failure of the 1898 reforms and the toppling of the Qing dynasty in 1911, the momentum toward revolution in China derived from two separate but increasingly interrelated sources. The events taking place within China itself were at once catalysts of and witnesses to the progressive disintegration of the old order. Meanwhile, a "new Chinese man" was being shaped outside of China, by diverse stimuli. This new man felt the shock of being thrust into dynamic foreign environments that nurtured ideas and institutions against which the decadence of his homeland was vividly mirrored, and he faced the humiliation of being a representative of an intensely proud people who were now being called "backward."

The fortress that was China, rendered vulnerable through internal crises, rapidly confronted a challenge unique in its long history: the external threat now came from *Chinese* as well as from barbarians. Young Chinese men and women were absorbing various theories deeply subversive of many traditional values, and they were using these theories to advance reformist and revolutionary policies, even trying to construct political and military organizations abroad which could replace those in increasing disarray at home. No earlier invasion had ever taken this precise form, hence no model of defense was available to the governors from China's repository of historical experiences. And of contemporary models, only the one used by Japan seemed appropriate.

Curiously, Japan came to serve as a guide in various ways for the throne, the reformers, and the revolutionaries alike. This proved insufficient to save the Qing dynasty, of course. The Manchu rulers, and notably the empress dowager, were unable to harness the force of nationalism to their purposes, as had been possible in connection with the imperial institution in Meiji Japan. The monarchical cause, however, was not lost without a prodigious intellectual struggle, and in exploring the salient aspects of that struggle we shall be examining theories and policies that were critical to China's future.

THE TRAUMA OF THE "PROGRESSIVE" INTELLECTUAL

To an unprecedented extent, this stage of the Chinese revolutionary process was the product of youthful Chinese intellectuals fraternizing, debating, and organizing in foreign lands—France, the United States, Great Britain, Southeast Asia, and above all, Japan. Rarely if ever were external stimuli so dominant in guiding a modern revolutionary course. The British, American, and French revolutions, though clearly subject to such influences, were basically indigenous processes. The Russian revolution depended more heavily on external ideological and organizational roots, with some of the same consequences as were to apply to China. But in the remarkably compressed period of time involved and in the wide dispersal of its overseas intelligentsia, the Chinese experience can be compared only with that undergone by the Korean nationalists a decade or so later, or with the intellectual journeys of the elite in societies that began their development after 1945. (Almost all the postwar societies, however, had long-lived colonial antecedents that shaped their initial ideological-institutional proclivities, whatever the changes subsequently demanded by culture, stage of development, and external events.)

In consequence, the modern Chinese intellectual was presented with a bewildering series of alternative ideas and institutions. In the "advanced" West, political theory generally bore a close relation to the society's stage of development. Hence ideas had a logical sequence and at least some potentiality for implementation. In the case of China, it was perfectly possible for Spencer to precede Montesquieu, or Adam Smith to accompany Marx, all within an incredibly short space of time. It was difficult to create a meaningful new vocabulary, hard to divorce certain ideographs from their former connotations.* And repeatedly, the issue of relevance became paramount: Which of the new theories, if any, were applicable to China? What modifications were necessary? Or could a given theory and its accompanying institutional structure be borrowed intact?

Within scarcely more than two decades, the Chinese intellectual avant-garde had run the entire gamut of Western thought from Socrates, Plato, and Aristotle through Locke, Montesquieu, and Rousseau, on to Marx, Mill, Bentham, Kropotkin, Spencer, and Darwin, and even to John Dewey and Bertrand Russell. And there were a host of others, many of them figures of little consequence who were sometimes mistaken for giants. To separate the trivial and faddish from the truly insightful was never easy.** There was

*A notable example was the concern over the ideograph *dang*, which was adopted by both the Japanese and the Chinese to stand for "party," as in political party. Historically, *dang* had been used to indicate a political faction, gang, clique, or coterie. Because of these unfavorable connotations, writers who advocated competitive political parties and a parliamentary system were obliged to emphasize that the new political parties should not be confused with the old factions and gangs.

Countless other examples of semantic problems in the political sphere could be cited. In general, the Chinese intellectuals of this period acquired their new political terms from the Japanese, and that fact alone provided for further complications in reaching a full understanding of Western theories and institutions. For discussions of this problem, see Robert A. Scalapino, *Democracy and the Party Movement*, pp. 4–5, 71ff; Phillip C. Huang, *Liang Ch'i-ch'ao and Modern Chinese Liberalism*, pp. 68–69; Hao Chang, *Liang Ch'i-ch'ao and the Intellectual Transition in China*, pp. 146ff.; and Martin Bernal, *Chinese Socialism to 1907*, pp. 34ff, 90–91.

**In addition to the works of the philosophic and legalistic "giants," early Japanese translations enabled conversance with such individuals as Benjamin Kidd, a currently popular exponent of Social Darwinism; Richard Ely, a University of Wisconsin economist who wrote extensively on socialism; and Samuel Smiles, a popular British writer whose most successful work, *Self Help*, had been widely read in Japan. The writings of these men were closely studied and frequently cited by the Chinese intellectuals living in Japan during this period.

a certain premium, moreover, on being in the vanguard, on keeping abreast of the latest wave from the West. Thus it should not be surprising that Social Darwinism, particularly as it emanated from Japan, towered over much of the progressive Chinese intellectual literature of the first decade of the twentieth century. Nor is it strange that in a period when anarchism and anarcho-syndicalism were more stylish in Western radical circles than Marxism, men like Tolstoy, Kropotkin, and the Russian nihilists attracted greater attention among contemporary radicals than either the democratic socialists or Marx and Engels.

To be able to encompass the whole of Western thought in a veritable instant, to skip earlier stages of painful evolutionary groping, to grasp the essence and distillation of a long, quite separate tradition, and to enter the universal intellectual stream at a forward point was for the Chinese intellectual an exhilarating challenge. But there was also the pain of never being the pioneer, only the pursuer, never the leader, only the follower—and in addition, the pain of seeing one's own society incapable of encompassing in action what one had absorbed in thought, and hence of being an outcast or, at best, a marginal individual.

THE EARLY AVANT-GARDE: LIANG QICHAO AND THE REFORMERS

Kang Youwei and Liang Qichao epitomized both the trauma and the sense of purpose surrounding the Chinese intellectuals who were bent on guiding their society into the modern world. Because of his relative youth, his penchant for activism, and his extraordinary literary skills, moreover, Liang stood out as the initial inspiration for the overseas students. Up to 1905, he had an undisputed priority of influence over the small but rapidly growing body of Chinese students in Japan, which constituted the nucleus of the "progressive" movement as it then existed. Following his hasty flight into exile, Liang lost little time in establishing a journal published in Yokohama, *Qingyi bao* (Journal of Dispassionate Opinion), the first issue of which came out on December 23, 1898.[1] That journal, containing articles by Liang and various associates, survived into 1901, when a fire closed it down. Shortly thereafter, in the early part of 1902, a second journal made its debut under Liang's editorship, the fortnightly *Xinmin congbao* (The New People's Journal), which continued into 1907.[2]

Until the appearance of Sun Yat-sen's *Min bao* (People's Journal) in late 1905, Liang's journalistic competition was limited. The themes he stressed were touched on only in *Zhongguo ribao* (China Daily), founded in Hong Kong by Chen Shaobai as a revolutionary organ in 1899, and *Su bao* (Jiangsu Journal), which lasted a few short months until its radically anti-Manchu editors were arrested in Shanghai; and generally speaking, these two papers lacked the literary qualities that were to make Liang's journals so appealing to students. There were also the provincial student journals published in Japan; but Liang's journal circulated more widely, and copies of it were smuggled back into China. The ideas first set forth by Liang sparked vigorous discussion and debate wherever students and the "new literati" gathered. In these years, they were the source of both reformist and radical inspiration.

In the opening issue of *Qingyi bao*, Liang set forth four purposes of his new journal: to advance dispassionate or objective opinion (*qingyi*); to enhance the knowledge of the Chinese people; to enable communication between China and Japan, fostering a unity of views and mutual friendship; and to develop knowledge and learning in East Asia so as to preserve the essence of Asia.[3] These objectives indicate two aspects of Liang's current thinking. First, he was convinced that the salvation of China lay in education—in advancing the knowledge and hence the capabilities of the Chinese people, making them into "new men"; he believed this should be done by introducing them to the great storehouse of information and ideas from the West. Second, because the West also represented a challenge, Liang espoused a Sino-Japanese "united front" with Pan-Asian connotations to meet it. He was led to this position by several factors: his traditional Confucian education, his commitments to Kang Youwei and Kang's cosmopolitanism, his gratitude to the Japanese for saving his life and accepting him as a political exile, and his initial contacts with key Japanese Pan-Asianists.[4]

In examining the basic theses advanced by Liang and other contributors to his journals, we shall combine thematic and chronological approaches, seeking to detect the changes in viewpoint or emphasis that accompanied the tumultuous events of the period, as well as to underline the major themes that persisted through time. To convey the mood of the era and the emotions of these young intellectuals, moreover, we shall use their own words whenever possible, mainly in paraphrased form.

It is logical to begin by setting forth the immediate danger as they envisaged it. The primary threat was nothing less than the death of China and its dismemberment at the hands of the great powers. One revealing exposition of this theme is to be found in an article by Mai Menghua, published in February 1900.[5] Mai noted that throughout Chinese history, five conditions had foretold national disaster: the reign of queens, the power of eunuchs, the transgressions of mighty ministers of the court, the depredations of roving bandits, and the force of foreign aggression. Understandably, he found all of these conditions now in existence. If the empress dowager and her lackeys continued to pursue their disastrous course, China would expire, a victim of its own inner decay. At root, the crisis began with the impact of misrule upon a people who had created one of the world's great civilizations, a people possessing qualities of resourcefulness, intellectual power, and self-confidence. Having been thrust into a world not of their own making, the Chinese people at one moment looked upon Westerners as snakes and scorpions, hating their existence, and at another moment worshiped them as gods, seemingly prepared to abandon even their self-respect in order to please them.[6] A once great people had been reduced to a slavish mentality, akin to that of the people of India and other inferior societies.[7]

Yet even those writers who were deeply pessimistic could often conclude on a note of optimism: China would not die, because the Chinese people were irrepressible. "Our population is so huge and our people so perseverant," Mai asserted, that "the frontiers opened by the white people in various continents will become colonies for Chinese."[8]

A combination of despair and bravado was not untypical of student essays during this period, and stands as testimony to the complex psychology domnating the era. Indeed, Liang himself in his preface to the first issue of *Qingyi bao*, after proclaiming the extreme peril in which China found itself, quickly found hope in the "universal principle" that without disruption there could be no reconstruction, without challenge, no response. The advanced Western nations, he noted, had all gone through major travails in the course of their emergence—but after strife and catastrophe, the storms had suddenly ceased, and all had become peaceful and beautiful. The course of China in the twentieth century might well parallel that of Western Europe and Japan in the nineteenth century.[9]

The great challenge that lay ahead involved the competition between the yellow and the white races. The brown, black, and red races, being uncivilized, were doomed to one or another form of authoritarianism and could not rise to eminence.* But the Chinese race was innately superior in character and intellect. If it could shake off the supine psychology that its rulers had cultivated and the turpitude of the present government, it could survive. Otherwise, it would perish, as had so many other nations in the recent past. The loss of freedom always began *from within*, from the self-depreciation and self-destruction of a people. Above all, the Chinese had to regain their self-respect. Then other changes, including economic development, could follow.**

LIANG AND IMPERIALISM

What was the relation between the inner decay and the actions of the great powers? The penetration of China by foreign missionaries and merchants would not necessarily have been bad were it not for the pervasive weaknesses—economic, political, and moral—of the present Chinese state.[10] Under current circumstances, however, the foreign powers felt justified in imposing their own rule on China through extraterritoriality because China could not govern itself effectively. Foreign trade and investment, moreover, resulted in huge imbalances that put China into debt and paved the way for further impositions.

As we noted earlier, Liang and his supporters looked upon the Boxers as misguided primitivists whose actions were certain to bring about cruel retaliation from foreign powers. The Yihe Tuan followers were the tools, witting or not, of the empress dowager, and the southern officials were entirely

* A New Man of China (Liang), "On Government's and People's Rights and Their Limits," *Xinmin congbao* (*XMCB*), March 10, 1902, pp. 25–32. The strong strain of racism that ran through various articles in *Qingyi bao* (*QYB*), *Xinmin congbao*, and the student journals of this period illustrates the manner in which traditional instincts could be sustained and bolstered by selected strands of contemporary Western theory. In this case, the predisposition to believe in the superiority of the Chinese (and yellow) race and the classic notion that dark-skinned peoples are barbarians could be fortified by the doctrines of superiority and inferiority derived from certain expressions of Social Darwinism, such as the work of Benjamin Kidd.

** A New Man of China, "On Self-Respect," *XMCB* (July 19, 1902), pp. 1–8. The innate weakness of Korea and India, Liang wrote, stemmed from the fact that although their people had seen the wealth and power of the United States, Japan, and Europe, they lacked the necessary self-respect to give them the confidence and initiative with which to undertake their own reforms. China was in similar peril, he said. Government officials looked up to foreigners as if they were parents. Scholars, peasants, industrialists, and merchants all worked exhaustively to appease foreigners, playing the role of prostitutes. They, too, viewed China as hopeless and thought the only solution was to obtain the protection of a big power. Liang continued: blind antiforeignism is *not* self-strengthening; it will only inhibit China's development. Genuine conservatism, however, is different from the pseudo-strengthening that comes from dependence on foreign sources; it does not sap the sense of self-reliance so crucial to China's survival. Liang, incidentally, acknowledged his indebtedness to Fukuzawa Yukichi for stimulating his thoughts on these matters. Whatever the inspiration, he was raising one of the basic issues to confront emerging societies, one which was to concern Chinese of all political persuasions throughout the twentieth century.

right in seeking to resist them.[11] Briefly, after the Boxers had been defeated, Liang hoped that the intervening powers would correct the Chinese political situation: if they would only restore the emperor to power and eliminate the empress dowager, China would benefit and the citizens of foreign nations could live peacefully in an advancing society, as they now did in Japan. The emperor, Liang asserted, was learned in Western ways and admired foreign customs. Great Britain, the United States, and Japan had no desire to dismember China, and a route was now open to making China an effective nation.[12]

After the empress was allowed to retain her throne, a new tone of bitterness and despair crept into *Qingyi bao*. The terms of settlement were acknowledged to be relatively lenient, but since China was already in the palm of their hands, the major foreign powers had no need to crush the Chinese people by imposing harsh conditions.[13] Although no territory had been taken, reparations now reduced China to the status of a protectorate. Moreover, the special agreements currently being signed by regional officials, particularly in southeastern China, were tantamount to handing over the entire Yangtze valley to foreign interests, especially the British. Thus although China remained intact physically, her dismemberment was nonetheless real, and the more tragic because it was not clearly visible.[14]

As early as 1901, Liang and his associates had begun to emphasize the dangers of economic imperialism. In these warnings there was a certain note of admiration, for to Liang imperialism was a sure sign of progress, being the logical expression of a given stage of development. When a nation had created an active, participating citizenry, this combined with its dynamic economic growth to make expansion a logical, indeed an inevitable, phenomenon. Imperialism, according to Liang, was to be further understood by applying the theories of Malthus (overpopulation, hence the need for colonization) and Darwin (the survival of the fittest). Here, Social Darwinism germinated in Liang some of the same ideas that led Lenin to his analysis of imperialism.[15]

In particular, Bismarck's Germany epitomized for Liang a rapidly developing nation, and by 1902 he was chronicling in detail the reasons for its success. The first major step had been the internal consolidation of power, the creation of a genuine nationalism, uniting emperor and people. Expansion had followed, commencing in 1890, and within ten years Germany had achieved a major reputation.[16] In this recital, Liang's tone was one of admiration.

As the struggle for railroad concessions grew more intense, however, and in the aftermath of his journey to America, Liang sharpened his attacks on all forms of Western imperialism. Having listened to President Theodore Roosevelt boast of the spread of American influence in the Pacific, Liang foresaw the United States making a bid to be master of that region, and he called upon his countrymen to awake.[17] He also brooded about restrictive American immigration policies and the general treatment of his compatriots in America and elsewhere—discriminations which he ascribed to the impotence of the Chinese government.*

*Even prior to Liang's trip to the United States, *Xinmin congbao* had published articles strongly critical of American treatment of Chinese immigrants. For example, one author claimed that in early 1900, a U.S. government physician, proclaiming the threat of epidemic in San Francisco's Chinatown, had demanded that three steps be taken: encircle the area with

Thus, Liang was strongly critical of Governor Yuan Shikai for asking the Tianjin businessmen not to join Shanghai merchants in boycotting U.S. goods. Either Yuan was trying to appease the Americans, wrote Liang, or he was worried that a boycott might prejudice the current American efforts to assist in reaching a Sino-Russian agreement. There should be no worry on the latter score, argued Liang, because the strong sentiment against Chinese workers was limited to American labor and was concentrated on the Pacific coast. American capitalists wanted cheap labor, and thus the boycott would not antagonize the entire American nation.[18]

The United States, however, was not the only target. In a fascinating article published in mid-1904, occasioned by the concessions granted to the Germans regarding the Qingdao-Jinan Railway, the author remarked that cannonballs and warships would be less important than economic control in annihilating a nation.[19] Many of the great powers were now giving at least verbal support to the Open Door Policy initiated by the Americans, but would China remain intact as an entity under that policy? For ten years the major European states had tried to subjugate China with their railroad policies. Here lay the focal point of the struggle for control. Infusions of foreign capital might not do harm if China had a stable economy, but under current conditions the risks included inflation, a waste of funds due to the inefficiency of the Chinese government, and the inability to repay the loans on time.[20]

The signing of the British-Tibetan Treaty evoked the lamentation that Tibet, long a protectorate of China, had been placed within the British sphere of influence, and China was not even consulted (though since she was powerless, she could not have done anything to alter the decision).[21] And when political upheaval in Russia began in 1904, Liang made the prescient comment that since Russian imperialism differed from the imperialism practiced by Britain, America, Germany, or Japan—since it was initiated by the aristocracy rather than being an expression of a dynamic popular will—a new Russian government might relax its pressure on China for some time. "However, the Slavs are a patient and ambitious people. If we are to say that because of a change in their government, our troubles are over, we will be talking in our dreams."[22]

As the Russo-Japanese War was drawing to a close, earlier aspirations for Sino-Japanese unity against an imperialist West had already given way to grave apprehensions about Japanese intentions. *Xinmin congbao* scoffed at the belief of some that Japan would graciously hand over Manchuria to

---

a wall; burn those buildings deemed unsanitary; and inoculate the Chinese with a vaccine. After strenuous protests, according to the article, the first two demands were withdrawn, but inoculations were demanded. The vaccine, manufactured in Germany, was "highly toxic," asserted the writer, and "it could kill all the Chinese." Finally, the Chinese banded together and staged a protest strike, preventing the doctor's order from being carried out. ("Chinatown Strike in San Francisco"), *QYB*, June 17, 1900, pp. 17a–18b (6:3149–3152.) Another, less sensationalist article criticized U.S. governmental authorities for retaining Chinese immigrants in crowded, unsanitary conditions after their initial disembarkation, and alleged that although the Chinese living in the United States paid taxes to support public education, their children were not allowed to attend such schools. "American missionaries come to China to educate the Chinese," asserted the author, "yet Chinese living in America have no opportunity to be educated. Isn't this strange?" Self-Supporting Citizen, "Announcement of the Mistreatment of Chinese by the United States," *QYB* (1901), September 3, pp. 14a–14b; September 23, pp. 14a–14b; December 1, pp. 21a–22b. (11:5737–5738; 5853–5854; 12:6273–6276.)

China, calling this a dream. Rather, Japan might well seek control of the Liaodong peninsula, once denied her, now that she had defeated the Russians.[23]

Liang Qichao's generally accelerating attack on the imperialism of advanced nations in all of its forms, and on the cavalier treatment accorded the Chinese nation by foreign governments, placed him in the mainstream of intellectual protest. Indeed, it would not be an exaggeration to say that *Xinmin congbao* was the first publication to develop this issue in a sustained, comprehensive fashion, bequeathing it to those who came afterward. As in all matters, Liang was willing to acknowledge complexities. Foreign intercourse could be beneficial if the Chinese economy were strong. And extraterritoriality had not been entirely bad, because the foreign settlements within China had been a "haven of freedom of speech for the Chinese." But the need for that type of haven was ending, and extraterritoriality could no longer be defended.[24]

As the polemic struggle with Sun Yat-sen unfolded, Liang found his anti-imperialist position extremely useful. Sun was vulnerable both because of his extensive Western-Japanese connections and because of his ideas about Western economic assistance for the development of China. (These ideas were not spelled out, but they were expressed in abbreviated form during this period.) Consequently, Liang and his colleagues found it convenient to emphasize the dangers of Western economic penetration and to call for self-reliance.[25] Once again, we are glimpsing the future.

Against the call for an anti-Manchu revolution, moreover, Liang could argue that the protracted and bloody revolution required to overthrow the Qing could only heighten the danger of China's destruction. It would provide an ideal climate for direct imperialist intervention and colonization, thereby ending any hope for a restoration of national power.[26] In this manner, Liang kept his anti-imperialist credentials intact even while he wrestled with the complex question of how to make China sufficiently strong to meet the imperialist threat.

CHINA'S SALVATION: AN ENLIGHTENED PEOPLE AND A STRONG NATION

The challenge was clear. How should it be countered? In the early phases of his political crusade, Liang put the primary emphasis on the creation of thoroughly new Chinese men and women who could provide the basis for a modern Chinese nation, a state capable of competing effectively with the advanced nations that surrounded it. In effect, this was a call for a massive social revolution, although Liang gave limited attention to some aspects of it, such as economic transformation. Nevertheless, he and his associates fully recognized that if truly new individuals were to be fashioned, a radically different approach to education, politics, and culture was essential. Hence they called for a broad assault against past attitudes and practices, past thoughts and institutions—presaging later attacks on the Confucian system as a whole and the idealization of science and democracy.

It was natural, however, given his own background and China's stage of development, that Liang would be both a pioneer and a man with indissoluble links to the past. In his continuities and shifts, in his consistencies and inconsistencies, in the giant issues with which he wrestled, Liang Qichao was a near-perfect representation of the intellectual destined to be

7. *Liang Qichao as young reformer*

born into a narrow, highly traditional environment and thence to move into an ever-wider geographic and cultural arena, confronting troublesome complexities and dizzying changes at each turn. Like every serious Chinese intellectual of his generation, Liang could not avoid comparing China with this new world and attempting to draw the appropriate lessons from it. But often, as we shall see, the lessons were sufficiently obscure as to permit varied or internally contradictory conclusions; and a second or third reading of modern Western history—or current events—did not necessarily yield the same results as a first reading.

When Liang arrived in Japan in late 1898, he had already had varied experiences as student and reformer. In his early classical education, he had done brilliantly. But he was still young—only seventeen—and impressionable when Western literature and the formidable figure of Kang Youwei came into his life. The student-teacher link with Kang was never to be severed despite the strains placed on it from time to time, and it remained a substantial—albeit modified—influence. From Kang, Liang inherited a Confucianism molded into an instrument of reform; a utopian cosmopolitanism containing a concept of developmental stages for society and mankind; and on a less lofty but vitally important level, a doctrine of tutelage, the intellectual tutelage of the masses through study societies, schools, journals, and newspapers—all intellectual enterprises. In the three years prior to the abortive 1898 reform effort, moreover, Liang's work as publicist and teacher had brought him into contact both with Westerners and with China's intellectual avant-garde. Thus when he arrived in Japan at the age of twenty-five, he was already a veteran in the reform movement, and one who had more than a passing acquaintance with Western thought and institutions.[27]

Against this background, let us return to the central questions that preoccupied Liang and his associates during the years after 1898. What did it mean to create a new Chinese man? What kind of man? First, the task was to construct an educational system that would rid the Chinese of their slavish mentality and enable them to reason and to act as intelligent human beings, conscious members of a civilized community, willing participants in a self-reliant nation. The thrust was toward a new man in psychological as well as political terms, a man capable of assertiveness and pride, hence patriotism and citizenship.

The strength of a nation, Liang asserted in an early issue of *Qingyi bao*, lay in the knowledge and capacities of its people, and these were determined by the way in which they thought.[28] Under the old educational system, the premium had been upon rote memorization and ritualism, educational methods conducive only to stagnation and an unthinking acceptance of the status quo. Later, Liang was to amplify these remarks.[29] In the long history of mankind, why have only a few countries survived and become strong? The secret lay in the expanding abilities of their people. If it were to grow and prosper, the state, like the human body, demanded that various functions be properly performed, including those functions that demanded an alert, well-informed public.

If the educational level of the people was low, good rule provided no remedy, because it would sooner or later come to an end. But if the people possessed a proper education and civic consciousness, as they did in Britain or America, they did not need to rely on an able ruler in order to have a functioning system. Stability and strength came when leaders relied on their people, rather than vice versa.

Liang had come to accept nationalism as an indispensable instrument of China's survival at a very early point in his political pilgrimage. It is difficult to find any substantial commitment to Pan-Asianism or a broader universalism even in the early issues of *Qingyi bao*, despite the journal's announced goals. To be sure, many nationalist themes were advanced in a manner wholly compatible with Chinese tradition. Reference was often made to the distinction between the civilized and the barbarian, as if these constituted two distinct communities in the world.

8. *Kang Youwei at the height of his intellectual career*

We have also noted the strong tendency to think in racial terms and to believe that a decisive competition between the white and the yellow races lay ahead. One striking evidence of Liang's racial feelings is to be found in the opening essay of a series presenting biographies of great men. Liang explained that he had commenced the series with the Hungarian nationalist Louis Kossuth, a non-Chinese, because China had few heroes and he had selected someone whom he admired; but he added, "I love the yellow race more than I do the white." Moreover, he pointed with pride to the fact that Hungary was a nation "established by the yellow race on the territory of the whites" (a reference to the Hun conquest), and cited the Golden Bull of

1222, which antedated the Magna Carta, as proving that it was the yellow race that "first established a civilized polity in the world."[30]

Liang's views on these matters received extensive treatment in a serialized essay carried in the opening issues of *Xinmin congbao*, to which earlier reference has been made. From the sixteenth century onward, he wrote, European progress and global advancement were due entirely to nationalism (*minzuzhuyi*). By the end of the nineteenth century, nationalism had developed into national imperialism, which differed from traditional imperialism in being the product of the strength of the entire people. Unfortunately, China was in the direct path of this storm, Liang continued. To save the country, "we must rely upon our own nationalism. And to achieve this, we must first have 'new people.'"[31]

For this purpose, we need not abandon all of our traditions, insisted Liang. But we need to alter certain things and borrow some things we do not possess. We have had *bumin* (local-people); now we need *guomin* (nation-people). We have had the consciousness to be individuals, members of a family and clan, and even Chinese (in the sense of sharing a common culture), but not the consciousness of being nationals (*guomin*).[32] Yet the survival of the fittest is a universal law, and unless we develop that capacity, we cannot continue to exist.*

Westerners were correct, Liang stated, in asserting that the Chinese people had no sense of patriotism; national consciousness had not developed, because for thousands of years China had been the only civilized society in its region, a culture surrounded by barbarians. Hence, to its people, China was a world, not a nation. Indeed, Chinese consciousness had long ago made a leap from the family to the cosmos, so that people had no sense of being part of one nation in competition with others. Now, with other nations threatening China's survival, a national consciousness, including a sense of responsibility to the state, had to be developed.[33]

Kang's particular formulation of cosmopolitanism assisted Liang in thinking about certain universal stages through which mankind (hence China) was destined to go. Unlike some later Chinese intellectuals, he did not need the Marxian creed of economic determinism for these purposes. At the same time, his break with classic Chinese universalism was never more clearly revealed than in an article written in early 1902. He will not, he says, talk about one world or the principle of universal love. "For those, we must wait thousands of years. At present, only competition is the mother of civilization. For the individual, from his family, village, and clan to his state, there is always some competition. The largest unit of competition is the nation, without which there would be no competition, hence no civilization. The advocates of universal love are welcome to sacrifice themselves for a larger entity, but we must stop at the state as the ultimate boundary."[34]

* Among the five races of the world, Liang continued, the most powerful are the Caucasians; among them, the Teutons, and among the Teutonic people, the Anglo-Saxons—a fact that could be demonstrated by the rising number of people throughout the world who speak their languages. Why are Caucasians better? They are active, competitive, and risk-taking; other races are passive and timid. They are progressive, other races are conservative. Other races may create culture, but the Caucasians energetically spread culture, a testimony to their human energy. And among the Caucasians, the Teutonic people have greater political abilities than others, such as the Greeks and Slavs, because they have both effective state institutions at the top and a system of individual rights below ("On New People," *XMCB*, February 23, 1902, pp. 1–5).

It should be clear that Liang and others, drawing upon Social Darwinism, played strongly on the themes of challenge and response later claimed by Arnold Toynbee as a central determinant in world history. China had not faced a strong external challenge until her confrontation with Westernism, and this lack of experience had affected not only the nature of the state but the character of the Chinese people. Encased in a powerful family-clan system, they had tended to pursue private rather than public interests. Indeed, the concept of public commitment or public morality did not exist. In the political realm, an autocratic government had taught the people to pay their taxes and obey the dictates of officials, irrespective of who held power. They were thus a nation of slaves, not of citizens. It was not surprising, therefore, that they accepted outrages at the hands of foreigners, having accepted them for so long from their own rulers.[35]

Why were the Han people timid and submissive? Various writers argued that not merely government but the entire traditional culture—its religion, literature, and education—was responsible for this. Among strong nations, patriotism and a willingness to sacrifice one's life for one's country were cultivated.[36] Both in the schools and in the society, children sang patriotic songs and used textbooks that emphasized the importance of military strength. Novels and poetry glorified heroism in war, and the fruits of victory. In Japan *bushido* (the way of the warrior) was universally respected.

But what of China? Traditional religion and learning deprecated the value of military strength. Although true Confucianism stressed the importance of military preparedness, the false Confucianism that had long been propagated, which was actually Taoism in disguise, slighted militarism.[37] Chinese literature was also devoted to opposing the military on all fronts. Poems dwelt upon the hardships of military service and the tragedy of war. Novels cultivated softness and a spirit of romanticism, emphasizing as they did the supernatural, bizarre, and obscene.[38] Since these were the sources of classical education, it was not surprising that China's children had been made prematurely old by an indoctrination that encouraged effeteness, discounted physical strength and courage, and discouraged attempts to reach out beyond the narrow confines of family and clan. How could China be considered a youthful nation when it had no youth?[39]

Traditional Chinese culture had conspired to produce a well-known proverb: "A good piece of iron does not want to become a nail. A good man does not want to become a soldier." In contrast to Japan, where soldiers were respected and honored, in China able men shunned military service, and desertion did not stigmatize the soldier or his family. The prominent Japanese liberal Ozaki Yukio had remarked that China had an abundance of intellectuals but a dearth of able military men. In listing the reasons for China's weakness, he had characterized the Chinese as primarily profit-oriented, lacking in military spirit or the type of morality that emerges from such a spirit. For the Chinese, war was still conceived in theatrical terms, as a pageant of flags and drums, with scant attention paid to the necessity of modern weapons.

Liang himself was later to stress many of these same themes.[40] China had frequently been humiliated throughout its long history by various barbarians because military strength had not been cultivated. Qinshi Huangdi (the founder of the Qin dynasty and, according to legend, the father of modern China) should be admired for driving the barbarians beyond the Great Wall and assiduously cultivating a military capacity in the Chinese people.* On hearing that the Qing government had committed itself to a program of military modernization through weapons purchases and new training procedures, Liang was moved to say that this effort was likely to have only superficial results, because the primary need was for a new military spirit—one that rested on a deep emotional commitment, courage, and physical training.

Once again we are dealing with the teleology of contemporary China. Liang's comments about a military spirit bear an uncanny resemblance to those of Mao some decades later. The martial songs taught to Chinese kindergarteners, the dances with bayonets during which the nation's enemies are dispatched, the saga of Lei Feng, the model of a heroic soldier, all reflect the fact that nationalism reached unprecedented heights in China in the 1960s and 1970s, as if to make up for its belated arrival. The frustrated young intellectuals of the early 1900s also anticipated another aspect of a later scene. Like Plato and countless other reformers who had determined that their goal was to change human nature—and to transform it both rapidly and fundamentally—they were naturally brought to reconsider every activity that could affect the human personality. Literature, art, and music, as well as the social and physical sciences, had to be shaped to fit the basic goals. Religion, as well as education, had to come under scrutiny.

By early 1902 Liang's commitment to nationalism could scarcely have been more intense. In two articles published in March and June of that year, he appeared to turn his back completely on the traditional universalist doctrines so long dominant in Chinese thought.[41] Nationalism, proclaimed Liang, was a brilliant, legitimate, and just doctrine. It prohibited the encroachment of one people upon another. Simultaneously, it gave the citizenry their freedom within the nation, and nations their independence within the world.

Admittedly, one complex problem existed. At the extremity of nationalism lay a further evolutionary stage—national imperialism. Every major society, Liang wrote, passed through both stages. Like a human being, the state had to have the nutrition of nationalism to develop from an embryo into a child. And to move from nationalism to national imperialism was the necessary achievement of adulthood. Contemporary imperialism, Liang emphasized, was not the work of an individual despot but the product of a mobilized, enlightened people.

Like the early Japanese liberals, Liang and his colleagues saw representative government as a means of augmenting the power and authority of the state, not primarily as an instrument of enhancing individualism. It must be remembered that throughout the Sinic world, the traditional bias against individualism was strong. It was generally equated with selfishness, the pitting of a single ego against the community at large. Even when the Chinese reformers spoke of education, freedom, creativity, and other concepts asso-

*After expressing admiration for Qinshi Huangdi, Liang found four causes for China's subsequent failure to tend to national defense needs: early unification; the cosmopolitan, pacifist tenets contained in Confucianism; the policies of China's absolutist rulers, who feared rebellion; and the cultural traditions, including the key themes of classical Chinese literature. In this essay, Liang also pointed out that the great Roman Empire, however civilized, was toppled by the Germanic tribes, who excelled in the martial arts. He continued by praising Sparta as well as modern Germany and Japan. (Part 19 of "On New People," entitled "On the Cultivation of Military Strength," *XMCB*, June 20, 1902, pp. 1–8.)

ciated with individual rights or attributes, they almost invariably rested their ultimate defense of these attainments on the enhanced strength they would bring to the nation-state.

In this respect, Liang's discovery of the famed Swiss jurist Johann Kaspar Bluntschli, through translations of his work by Katō Hiroyuki, proved extremely useful. Katō himself was an early Japanese liberal whose interests had come to focus increasingly on making a legal and philosophic defense of the state. Like many of his generation in Japan, he was strongly influenced by German jurisprudence. It was entirely natural that Liang and Chinese nationalists of like mind would move in a similar direction, not merely because powerful Japanese intellectual currents necessarily influenced them during their exile in Japan, but because German legalism could serve their specific needs. Previously, Liang had drawn almost exclusively upon such theorists as Rousseau, Mill, Bentham, and the Social Darwinists. On balance, the thrust of these sources was to underscore the importance of libertarianism, leading to the emergence of an educated, free, and participating citizenry. Since the central objective of the reformers, however, was the salvation of China, the concepts of the national allegiance and solidarity needed a theoretical defense not easily found in the works of eighteenth-century populists or nineteenth-century libertarians. In the massively documented, carefully argued writings of Bluntschli and certain other European legalists, Liang—like many Japanese before him—found a doctrine that could unite a defense of constitutionalism, including representative government, with a defense of state. German legalism also lent itself to a defense of authoritarianism, and as we shall see, Liang was also to wrestle with this problem. At the outset, however, Bluntschli served as an authority for defining the legitimacy—and the perimeters—of the rights of citizens and the rights of the state. In cogent fashion, he established the linkage between popular rights and a cohesive, effective state for which Liang and others had been searching.*

*Despite the assertions of some scholars, Bluntschli's influence on Liang's thought and writing came before Liang's 1903 trip to the West. In his essay "The Influence of Academic Knowledge Sways the World," published in the first issue of *Xinmin congbao*, February 8, 1902, Liang wrote: "Bluntschli's doctrines of the state are in critical opposition to the theories of Rousseau. But Rousseau lived in the eighteenth century and became the progenitor of nineteenth-century thought, whereas Bluntschli lived in the nineteenth century and became the forerunner of twentieth-century thought. Only with Bluntschli do we achieve an adequate definition of the state, and come to understand its character, spirit, and function." He continued: "Before, it was said that the state was born for the people; now, we say that people are born for the state. Under this premise, nationals must take love of country as their instinctive duty . . . in the future, this will doubtless operate as the motive power of all states. How much Bluntschli has influenced the world!" (p. 74).

Among other things, Bluntschli implanted in Liang's mind an important distinction: the power of the state was unlimited, encompassing as it did the entire people, but the power of the government was limited and contingent on correct and effective rule. For Liang's elucidation of these points, see Xin Xin (Liang), "The Case of China's New Education," *XMCB*, April 8, 1902, pp. 47–55. Liang also used Bluntschli and another famous German legalist, Rudolf Von Jhering—along with Montesquieu—to stress the importance of law in the evolution of the Western state, contrasting the Western desire for a legal system that defines rights and duties with traditional China's dependence on benevolent government. Among other writings of the period, see A New Man of China, "On New People," Part 8: "On the Idea of Rights," *XMCB*, April 22, 1902, pp. 1–15; also Part 9, "On Liberty," *XMCB*, May 8, 1902, pp. 1–8.

While Liang and his associates regarded Bluntschli as an unchallengable source for de-

Liang was able to shed his early universalist views and emerge as a full-fledged nationalist with relative ease. He found it much more difficult to decide on the best means of achieving a new polity, and on what its basic political structure should be. Should the means be an anti-Manchu revolution leading to republicanism, or far-reaching but evolutionary reforms carried out under a constitutional monarchy? And of equal significance, where on the continuum between democracy and authoritarianism should the new China begin in its march toward political modernity? Since these issues were destined to have a sustained influence on twentieth-century Chinese politics in one form or another, it is essential to analyze their genesis in this period.

REVOLUTION OR REFORM—THE DILEMMA

When Liang Qichao arrived in Japan in the fall of 1898, he had narrowly escaped with his life, and the bloody finale to the reform effort had brought death to several of his closest friends. Understandably, he remained bitterly hostile toward the empress dowager and her faction, and was prepared to engage in any action that might topple her.

Indeed, Liang and other reformers supported an abortive uprising in Hankou in 1900 intended to overthrow Cixi and restore the emperor. The preparations were made in the spring and summer of that year. An earlier organization, Zhengqi Hui (Society for an Upright Spirit) was renamed Zili Hui (Independence Society), and an army was recruited under the direction of Tang Caichang. Movement leaders had communications with Kang in Singapore and Liang in Japan. As a first step, a National Assembly was convened in Shanghai in late July with widespread support from literati and the business community. Even representatives of Zhang Zhidong and Li Hongzhang were present. Meanwhile, another Kang-Liang disciple, Lin Guei, was seeking to recruit Gelao Hui members, and five military units were readied in Anhui, Hunan, and Hubei. But as the date for the uprising approached, problems had multiplied: efforts to obtain the support of Zhang Zhidong failed; the Gelao Hui chiefs seemed less than fully committed; and promised funds from abroad did not arrive. Tang postponed the August 9 date, but one of the military commanders struck when his plans were uncovered. The revolt was crushed after three days, causing mutual recriminations among the rebels.[42]

In addition to this clear-cut commitment to the use of violence to overthrow the ruling group in Beijing, Liang also indicated a willingness in 1899 to cooperate with Sun Yat-sen, and a political merger was even discussed.[43] It can thus be argued that in the years immediately following the failure of 1898, Liang and his associates had drawn no clear line between reform and revolution.[44] Further substantiation seems to come from the pages of *Qingyi bao*, which carried some articles that were strongly anti-Manchu and others that called openly for revolutionary action.*

---

fending the role and the rights of the states, they also viewed him as a "centrist" between the exponents of absolutism and the advocates of popular sovereignty. The thrust of his theories lay on the side of state power, not laissez-faireism—but it was not an unmitigated state power, without constitutional restraints. See A New Man of China, "The Theories of the Great Scholar of Jurisprudence, Montesquieu," *XMCB*, April 8, 1902, pp. 13–21.

*As examples, see Chao Zui, "On Defeat," *QYB*, August 5, 1901, pp. 1a–4b (2:5519–

Having made these points, however, it is important to note that Liang himself, even in the first years of his exile, regularly differentiated his position from that of those who called for the extinction of the Qing dynasty. At least in his published articles, he never abandoned his commitment to the restoration of Guangxu to the throne, and to the general principle of constitutional monarchy. Liang's initial arguments can be set forth as follows: China could not be saved by a revolution, because the Chinese people were not prepared to operate an open, democratic polity successfully. The only way in which China could be resurrected was for the Han and Manchu to work together to make needed political reforms.[45] Continued misrule by the empress dowager would indeed bring on revolution, warned Liang, and in that event the Manchu would have no one but themselves to blame; but if the Manchu were extinguished, the Han also would suffer because prolonged civil war and political chaos would adversely affect all of the people of China.*

Liang's arguments were buttressed by a letter to him from Kang published in the autumn of 1902.[46] In this long epistle Kang presented a rousing defense of monarchism and a sharp attack upon those who were championing an anti-Manchu revolution. Drawing analogies from Europe, Kang argued that if Bismarck and Cavour had advocated only revolution and democracy, Germany and Italy would have been divided and enslaved by France, Austria, and Russia. Instead, they saw the monarchy as a protection for the state and a means of unification. Did those who blindly argued for revolution weigh the risks of turning China into a Korea or an Egypt, or causing its provinces to emerge as eighteen separate states, paralleling the fate of modern Africa?[47]

Confucius and Mencius were the first to speak of revolution, asserted Kang, but they took the legitimate position that those who mistreated the people should be ousted, whereas those who protected the people should be supported, regardless of whether the ruler was Han or not. Indeed, who could weed out the non-Chinese at present? The distinction between Manchu and Chinese was minimal because the Manchu had followed Chinese customs closely. Moreover, some emperors had made important reforms; Kangxi, for example, had abolished corvée labor.[48]

Given the stage of China's development, it was essential to have a monarchical system within which to cultivate democracy, Kang insisted. He

---

5526); and Li Zhun, "On Bloodshed," *QYB*, August 14, 1901, pp. 1a–4b (2:5581–5588). Chao claimed: "The Manchu have done nothing creative since they won control over China, and they are decreased in numbers. Thus, the Manchu are already defeated." Li bluntly proclaimed that only bloodshed could save China, but that "Chinese are afraid of death, and are more concerned about their families than about their country." Thus, the Chinese will fight only if put in a position where they must fight or die. Liang, it should be noted, permitted essays to be published in his journal that did not necessarily reflect his own views completely, at least in this early period.

* See Liang Qichao, "On Reverence for the Emperor," *QYB*, March 22, 1899, pp. 1a–2b (2:519–522). Liang here asserts that after the Sino-Japanese War, various proposals for salvaging China had been advanced—reforms by the empress dowager, reforms by provincial governors, or a popular revolution in the fashion of the American or French revolutions—but none of them were feasible. The empress dowager was ignorant and dedicated to self-indulgence. The provincial governors had only a superficial understanding of political realities. And a popular revolution would fail because the Chinese people were not as enlightened as the Americans and the French. The only way to save China, Liang concluded, was to restore the emperor Guangxu to the throne.

himself had urged Guangxu to open politics progressively to the Chinese people—and in fact, no one could stop such a trend. Abrupt, extreme changes, however, could only end in disaster. Moreover, there was no reason to condemn all Manchu for the acts of a handful of culprits, the empress dowager and her coterie. Advanced nations did not punish an entire race for the crimes of a few.*

In the spring of 1903, Liang visited Canada and the United States, and when he returned, the debate between reformers and revolutionaries became more heated. Liang's speeches and fund-raising efforts in America had done nothing to endear him to Sun and his supporters. They now accused him of being a "running dog" of the Manchu, a man who secretly coveted official rank and was therefore willing to subvert the nationalist cause.

Liang did not deny that he had once supported violence, and he was now prepared to warn against "thoughtless destruction." As we shall see, he had returned from the United States more convinced than ever that any attempt to create instant democracy could only spell disaster for China. Liang could still call for cooperation between the reformers and the revolutionaries from time to time, but the personal animosities now rivaled the policy differences. Sarcasm, vitriol, and hyperbole were employed by both sides in the polemical battle that had erupted by early 1904, often at the expense of intellectual content.

In February 1904 Liang published a major article outlining what he called the seven evils of Chinese revolutions through past history.[49] Put briefly, these evils were as follows:

1. Revolutions in China had a private character and were led by one or two individuals, unlike Western revolutions, which were sponsored by a class, be it the aristocracy or the bourgeoisie.
2. Chinese revolutions were aimed at self-aggrandizement, for the leaders coveted personal wealth or power.

* Kang Youwei, "Mister Nanhai on Revolution," p. 67. In this period, Liang published a novel entitled *The Future of the New China* in a separate journal he was editing, *Xin xiaoshuo bao* (Journal of New Novels). In this novel, a long dialogue-debate between Huang Keqiang and his friend Li Qubing takes place, with Huang taking the reform position and Li arguing the case for an anti-Manchu revolution. Hao Chang cites this novel as one of the clearest indications of Liang's indecisiveness about revolution at this time, and says that the views of Huang and Li reflect Liang's inner debate (*Intellectual Transition*, pp. 222–224). We believe it more likely that Liang identified himself with Huang. First Huang defends himself against the charge that his views were merely reflective of the court, noting that he has no present connection with the court—exactly the defense currently being advanced by Liang. More important, Huang's arguments represented Liang's views as expressed elsewhere with remarkable precision. Thus Huang asserts at one point that if China could rise to the level of democracy in a single easy move, that would be fine, but if this is impossible, we still need a monarch. And if we develop a national assembly, political parties, and people's rights, as in England and Japan, then it does not matter who sits on the throne. At another point, Huang says that there must be a stage of state control (*ganshe zhengce*—literally "interference policy") before the stage of freedom (*ziyou zhengce*—literally "freedom policy"). In France and England, state control existed prior to freedom, when the state was becoming strong and people's knowledge was being cultivated. In the period when their knowledge and strength are not yet developed, people are like children who need their parents' control and guidance. During the period of transition between destruction and constitutionalism, the most important requirement is unity and the maintenance of public order. Without these, we can neither tear down the old nor construct the new. Both must be done by a united people, a people who have received the education of nationals. Popular rights are to be obtained, not through reading or talking, but through these necessary preparations. And when the people's charac-

3. Social revolutions in China had emanated from the lower class instead of the middle class, as in the West, and hence the motivations in China had been primarily political rather than economic in character.
4. Revolutions in the West were generally simple and engendered near-universal support, whereas in China revolutions involved complex struggles between various contenders for power; these struggles divided the Chinese people and account for the fact that they fear revolution.
5. Whereas Western revolutions were usually of short duration, Chinese revolutions had brought long years of warfare and devastation after the fall of a regime, thereby sapping the energies and resources of the country.
6. Western revolutionaries were usually able to unite, taking the government as a common enemy, but in China revolutionaries killed each other in factional disputes, sometimes turning upon close comrades.
7. In the West foreign threats were successfully countered even during the course of revolutions, but in the course of Chinese revolutions, foreigners were frequently invited to come in, or else they helped themselves—moving China toward colonialism.

One may quarrel with various aspects of Liang's analysis and see it as merely a part of his polemical struggle with Sun, but in these "seven evils" Liang was summarizing his misgivings about a contemporary revolution in China. Only if these evils could be avoided, he wrote, should the revolutionary route be supported; otherwise, a debacle would result. Do not say that your job is done, he warned Sun, after you have studied the martial arts, mobilized the secret societies, and imported weapons. You must avoid the seven evils, learn from men like Washington and Cromwell, and rally the urban merchant class to the cause. Once again, Liang was suggesting that China was not ready for a modern, bourgeois revolution of the Western type, and that the attempt to create one, whether in economic or in political form, could end only in failure.

The personal attacks included in this article reveal the level of bitterness that now existed among the disputants. The few revolutionary leaders I have met, Liang said, usually view morality and justice with contempt, and have the same penchant for power struggles that characterized the Taiping. Moreover, on the one hand they exalt nationalism, but on the other hand they follow the white man's Christianity and use their power in an effort to destroy others (reformers). Later, Liang was to remark that some extreme anti-Manchu revolutionaries took the position that even if a future Chinese constitution were as nearly perfect as that of the British or the Japanese, they would rather perish under chaotic Han than survive under capable Manchu—an attitude that testified to their irrationality.[50] Yet in this article and others, Liang continued to call for cooperation between the two exiled groups, asserting that although constitutionalism and revolution were two different means, both groups were united in their opposition to the current

---

ter, knowledge, and strength have made them ready for revolution, revolution will not be necessary. From Ding Wenjiang, *Liang Rengong xiansheng nianpu changbian chugao* 1:164–165. We shall see that these arguments were repeatedly advanced by Liang in his own name, both during this period and later, with scarcely any change in terminology.

government. And as long as they fought each other, governmental suppression would contribute only one-tenth to the weakness of the popular movement; internecine warfare would contribute the other nine-tenths.*

In the course of the next several years, Liang repeatedly returned to the subject of revolution as the debate with Sun's newly organized Tongmeng Hui (United League) mounted. Few new themes were introduced. Liang continued to deny that his position was pro-Manchu. He did not love the Manchu, he wrote in early 1906, and he was well aware of their past cruelties. If there were a way both to revenge Manchu abuses *and* to save China, he would certainly pursue it. But revenge required revolution, after which an inadequate republic would be set up, followed by chaos and the destruction of the nation. True patriots should control their emotions and move toward the goal of *political* revolution through constitutionalism. Note that Liang now sought to co-opt the term "revolution" for the reformers' cause, arguing that constitutionalism represented a political revolution that was suited to China, whereas the racial revolution advocated by Sun could only bring disaster to the nation.[51]

As the polemics against the Tongmeng Hui reached their climax, Liang was deeply engaged in the question of whether conditions in China were appropriate for a republican system, and by this time political means and ends had been fused in his arguments. A republicanism achieved through ingrained habit (a society's political culture) would be stable, he wrote, but if republicanism were artificially induced by revolution, the final product would be absolutism.** Why? Relying partly on Gustav Bornhak, Liang produced a scenario that in fact bore some resemblance to China's future. It ran as follows:

If successful, a revolution aimed at overthrowing the monarchy would draw its rulers from the lower class. Gradually, they would become extremists and would be succeeded by leaders from the propertied class. In the process, however, China would be subjected to prolonged chaos. The citizenry would come to desire order above all else. A restoration of the monarchy would be attempted, but since the dynasty had disappeared, this would prove abortive, and a "democratic absolutism" would ensue. A dictator would emerge, as had happened in modern France. Initially, he would be dependent upon the power of the army, but at some point he would au-

* Possibly as a conciliatory gesture, Liang paid some homage to revolution in this article, asserting that the process of constitutionalism could sometimes benefit from revolution, as it had in Japan and Italy, and that to deny revolution totally was to become entirely passive, a mistake even worse than that of overvaluing militarism. The recent "false reforms" of the Beijing government were provoked by concern over public discontent, and it was a pity that the people's fighting ability was not greater. Liang concluded by suggesting that the two factions stop fighting each other and recognize that both revolution and constitutionalism could be steps forward. "Today's China should be united to fight the foreign powers," insisted Liang. And "if this is not possible, at the very least, we should establish an alliance, using all of our countrymen to fight the government" (A New Man of China, "On Political Capability," *XMCB*, February 4, 1905, p. 10).

** One Who Sips Ice, "On Enlightened Absolutism," *XMCB*, February 23, 1906, pp. 1–50. Most scholars have translated the phrase *kaiming zhuanzhi* as "enlightened despotism," and that is legitimate, particularly since that term was then current in the West. However, it seems to us that a careful reading of this extended essay (spread over five issues) indicates that "enlightened absolutism" is more appropriate, especially given Liang's own definition of *zhuanzhi*. We shall soon examine this essay—which Liang himself regarded as one of his most important—in greater detail.

thorize a plebiscite in an effort to legitimize his rule. Under such circumstances, a constitution would be only a formality, a fig leaf to hide the real absolutism that had been created.

If the revolutionists would frankly admit that they wanted to emulate Liu Bang (founder of the Han dynasty) or Zhu Yuanzhang (founder of the Ming dynasty), taunted Liang, he would admire their consistency and forthrightness. But he rejected as utopian Sun's idea that after a temporary period of military government, the revolutionary leaders would voluntarily give up their military power and defer to the civilian government that was supposed to be established, first at the local and then at the national level. Few men were sufficiently idealistic to relinquish power voluntarily. Once military government was established, there would be no means of ridding China of its dominance.[52]

When he was not preoccupied with this gloomy scenario, Liang often addressed himself to the threat of foreign control that would accompany revolution. He found it easy to envisage a situation in which a revolutionary force would combine attacks on the government with antiforeign activities, thus repeating the tragedy of the Boxer uprising. A revolution in China at this time, Liang once wrote, will in fact serve as a running dog of the foreign powers and cannot benefit the nation in the slightest.*

Despite these trenchant comments, a note of ambivalence regarding the Qing never completely disappeared from the essays of Liang and other reformers. At times they regarded the court as determined to dig its own grave. This occasionally produced a "plague on both your houses" attitude. One of Liang's associates wrote that "the Chinese government, like that of Russia, is trying to crush revolutionary activities through policies of extermination." But this would never work. Why did they not recognize that the only effective measures were those of political reform, including the acceptance of the revolutionaries as an opposition party? And for their part, when would the revolutionaries place the national welfare above personal interest and show a willingness to cooperate with the government in the face of foreign threats, as had been done in Japan?[53]

DEMOCRACY VERSUS AUTHORITARIANISM—A SECOND DILEMMA

Until the 1911 Revolution, Liang Qichao remained convinced that an anti-Manchu revolution which thrust republicanism upon an unprepared China would result in unending crises and ultimate destruction. Basically, he advocated a developmental model drawn from Japanese, German, and British experience; as we shall note, the precise mix of foreign elements varied with Liang's rapidly unfolding intellectual and travel experiences and often appeared somewhat vague. To appreciate these facts, we must turn now to the second crucial issue facing all reformers and revolutionaries during this period, the issue of democracy versus authoritarianism.

In the first years of his exile, Liang and those around him approached the problem of political change—and especially the task of preparing the Chinese people for political participation—with a certain degree of optimism.

*One Who Sips Ice, "A Reply to a Certain Newspaper," *XMCB*, August 20, 1906, p. 108. Once again, in this article Liang emphatically supported what he called "a political revolution," namely, constitutionalism, as against a racial revolution, namely, an anti-Manchu upheaval.

Despite their deep concern over current trends, they argued that one need not judge the future by the past. The Chinese people and officials alike had derived their slavish mentality from the political system itself; an authoritarian government had long bred a people lacking spirit and initiative. The challenge of the moment was to undertake two assignments simultaneously: to broaden and deepen the educational system so as to create a "new Chinese man" who would prove capable of bearing the responsibilities of constitutional government; and to move at a deliberate but quickening pace toward such a government, with the first step being to have the emperor send officials abroad to survey the available constitutional models in Japan, America, and Europe.[54]

Why was a constitutional monarchy better for China than a constitutional republic? Liang answered this question in a *Qingyi bao* essay by stating that a constitutional monarchy allowed freedom for the people but did not require the severe internal competition that occurred during presidential campaigns.[55] The reformers accepted the importance of parliaments, political parties, and other accoutrements of the democratic system, but many of them, including Liang, were worried by two problems: To what extent could China tolerate the dissension and strife that accompany Western-style democracy? And to what extent could an untutored people truly assume leadership?

Within a few years these worries had become part of a general concern over the differences in political development between China and the "advanced world." Liang and his associates did not challenge the thesis that all societies, regardless of cultural variations, were destined to go through roughly similar stages of political evolution, and that this evolution would invariably lead toward a higher form of development (democracy). To their classical universalist proclivities had been added the nineteenth-century Western doctrine of progress. The question, however, was where did China currently stand in the evolutionary progression, and what were the political implications of its status?

One of the earliest clear-cut indications of concern over these matters is to be found in an essay published in the first issues of *Xinmin congbao*. It noted that although "heroes" like Gladstone and Bismarck had disappeared from the contemporary European scene, countries like England and Germany continued to thrive. Why? It was primarily because the people of these nations were now able to do the same things as the heroes of yesterday, having acquired the education, skills, and purpose previously reserved for a small elite. True civilization dawned only when the people began to rely on themselves rather than on heroes. China, however, being comparable in its development to the Europe of four hundred years earlier, *did* need a hero to lead it. Otherwise, it might remain in darkness.*

In essence, this essay, like others that were to follow, argued that although the advanced world of the West represented the apogee of political progress and sophistication, China's stage of development demanded different politi-

*A New Man of China, "The Relation Between Geography and Civilization," *XMCB*, February 8, 1902, pp. 1–12. In the same issue, in an article entitled "Mother of Public Opinion or Slave of Public Opinion?" Liang acknowledges that leaders who wish to work for the people should not work against public opinion, but then eulogizes certain heroes in history who were able to see what ordinary people could not see, and do what ordinary people could not do, citing Gladstone as an example.

cal approaches, ones similar to those pursued by European nations much earlier in their evolution. No single issue was of greater importance than this in the disputation between reformers and revolutionaries, and none provoked greater disagreement.

It would certainly be incorrect to say that Liang and his associates regarded models from the contemporary West as wholly inapplicable to China. On the contrary, in matters pertaining to education, the role of law, the nature of sovereignty, and constitutionalism, they felt that much could be learned from the West and adapted for use in China in a relatively brief period. Thus in the same issue of *Xinmin congbao* that contained the discussion of Western "heroes," Liang offered a fascinating defense of political education in the modern mold. Drawing on a variety of Western and Japanese experiences, ancient and current, he argued that it was not sufficient to cultivate expertise alone. One also had to give education a political content, a set of values that would instill in one's people the principles enabling them to form a union strong enough to survive in the competitive world. Of what use was it if one trained intellectuals who proved to be traitors to the Han?* Here we have an early expression of opinion on the "red versus expert" issue, and one that purports to be based on an evaluation of Western experience.

In this same period, Liang also urged emulation of Western respect for law and an independent legislative system. In all of China's long history, he claimed, only Wang Sushi had respected the function of legislation and sought to make the progress of lawmaking independent of the executive.[56] In fact, China had never enjoyed law in the sense of publicly enacted rules that all nationals were expected to know and obey. Moreover, instead of having the separation of political functions that characterized all advanced nations, the Chinese system had multiple overlapping jurisdictions in which officials continually checked on each other—a system that obscured responsibility and contributed to inefficiency and corruption, claimed Liang.

And in whom should legislative power be reposed? Here Liang sought to combine Bentham and Bluntschli, two influences of critical importance to him at the time. Only the people could be the judge of their own satisfaction, stated Liang. To repose legislative power in their hands therefore benefited the ruler and the state as well as the citizenry at large. As England and Japan had proved, the monarch was not adversely affected by the advent of an independent legislature. On the contrary, he drew his prestige from that of the state, and the state derived its happiness from the satisfaction of its people.** The organism as a whole was thus strengthened.

In another essay, however, Liang returned to the central problem.[57] Until the late eighteenth century, China had been an advanced nation in com-

*Liang Qichao, "Education Should Have Principles," *XMCB*, February 8, 1902, pp. 1–8. In this same article, Liang reasserted his commitment to collectivist goals. The purpose of education, he wrote, was to enable the people to group together in order to compete with other countries in the arena of survival of the fittest. It was not merely to cultivate individuals as single entities.

**A New Man of China, "On Legislative Power," *XMCB*, February 23, 1902, pp. 1–10. This article shows once again the paramount influence of Bluntschli combined with Social Darwinism. "Formerly," stated Liang, "we believed that the state was owned privately by the ruler. Then the will of the new ruler was the will of the state. . . . But now we know that the state is the public property of all its nationals, and that, under internal and external pressure, a state which is owned privately by a single individual cannot survive in this competitive world."

parison with the West. It was thus highly improper for Europeans to ridicule Asians as a people dominated by theocracy and autocracy, Liang wrote. Originally, the uncivilized West had had to borrow its religion, its culture, and such technical innovations as printing and gunpowder from Asia, especially China. But the process of evolution had moved unevenly in the two regions. Liang then proceeded to explain political evolution in cosmic terms. In mankind's earlier phase, a barbaric freedom had existed, the law of the jungle. To advance beyond this, it was necessary to organize individuals into larger, more complex social units, and this required a political system with sufficient power and authority to preserve itself and the people within its structure. The need for an authoritarian state stemmed from these requirements. China had reached this stage at a very early point, hence its capacity to share its civilization with others.

The problem lay not with the past but with the present. Whereas Europe had been able to advance to a second stage by the beginning of the nineteenth century, much of Asia, including China, continued to accept autocracy, seemingly unconcerned in the absence of any competitive challenge. Meanwhile, Europe had steadily replaced autocracy with an expanding liberalism, a system promoting freedom and stressing progress. Liang readily acknowledged that the more developed a civilization, the more extensive should be the domain of popular rights. And while he ended on a moderately optimistic note, asserting that if intellect and learning were applied to the task, China would one day achieve the second stage, he also left little doubt that a very considerable distance had to be covered before then.

As we have already suggested, the thrust of Liang's essays and those of his colleagues took no single, uniform direction during this period. When they were arguing the case for constitutionalism, they would present a more optimistic analysis of the prospects for China. Thus, within a month of his article on comparative stages of development, Liang was making the case for an early advance in popular rights and substantial limits on governmental power.[58] Nevertheless, the concepts of stages and tutelage were imbedded in his arguments. The power of government, he wrote, necessarily varied with the degree of civilization possessed by the people of any given society. The more highly developed the people, the more restricted governmental functions could be. It was like the relation between parents and children. As the children grew older and matured intellectually the parents could cease treating them like babies and allow them more freedom in making their own decisions.*

As Liang and certain other reformers explored the reaches of Western philosophy and science they became progressively more critical of Confucianism. When Liang arrived in Japan he had been deeply committed to Kang's doctrines of "the true Confucianism." Thus, in one of the early *Qingyi bao* essays, we find Kang's basic thesis reasserted in forceful terms: For thousands of years, Chinese scholars had distorted the meaning of Confucianism. A renaissance could be effected only when the true nature of Confucianism was brought forth. Confucianism stressed progressivism, not

*A New Man of China, "On Government's and People's Rights and Their Limits," *XMCB*, March 10, 1902, pp. 25–32. The strong racial prejudice characteristic of this period can be seen here. After asserting that as people advance culturally and become more able to govern themselves they have less need of governmental interference, Liang added that around the globe, all people are civilized except for the brown, black, and red races.

conservatism; equality, not dictatorship; the common good, not the individual good; strength, not weakness; cosmopolitanism, not provincialism; spirituality, not romanticism.[59]

Liang separated himself from Kang, however, over the question of whether Confucianism should be cultivated as a state religion, both to reinforce its authority within China and to combat the influence of Christianity. After what must have been considerable agonizing, Liang came out flatly against the idea.* Confucianism, he wrote, was not otherworldly, and the attempt to turn it into a religion would in fact demean it. Moreover, Christianity did not constitute a formidable threat. Like other superstitions, it was on the wane and would continue to decline as science advanced. Here Liang was manifesting his general antipathy to religion, though on occasion he was prepared to acknowledge its instrumental utility in spreading values of service to the society as a whole.**

As Liang was introduced to the major figures of Western science and philosophy he struggled to put Confucianism into a new perspective. Thus, by 1902 he was proclaiming Bacon and Descartes as the founding philosophers of modern civilization.[60] Comparing a famed Confucianist with them, he faulted Zhu Xi for failing to submit his philosophic theories to empirical testing, a flaw to which he ascribed the failure of new learning to arise in China.

In later essays Liang continued to respect Confucianism—but with reservations. The Confucian concept of benevolence, he wrote, was far less adequate than the modern concept of mankind's innate rights, since it could not prevent malicious rulers from using the people as their personal fish and meat.[61] He also criticized the Confucian refusal to take economics seriously, out of contempt for what traditionalists called "profit."[62] The rise of the West in the past 150 years, he said, was closely connected with the study of economics, a fact that the Confucianists would never realize. And although Confucianism was "basically good," it had helped prevent progress in China by being one of the forces that stifled genuine scholarly thought. He compared its role to that of Catholicism in fifteenth-century Europe, when the church held absolute power.[63] Finally, Liang held Confucianism partly to blame for "the cultivation of cowards." Confucian doctrine had preached the virtues of being educated and mild in deportment—the virtues of a

*A New Man of China, "To Preserve Confucianism as a Religion Is Not the Way to Honor Confucius," *XMCB*, February 22, 1902, pp. 59–72. But Liang did not denigrate Confucianism. On the contrary, he argued that *because* Confucianism was not a religion, it would survive while other religions died out. Liang concluded with these words: "I have exhibited an about-face regarding the protection of Confucianism. I have done this because I love truth and liberty, and since Confucius also loved truth and liberty, I feel that he would approve of what I have done in the service of truth and my people" (p. 72).

**Liang expressed antireligious sentiments in several articles written during this period. His general view was that religion was a manifestation of superstition, associated with primitive people, and destined to wither away with the advance of science. See, for example, A New Man of China, "On the General Trend Relating to Changes in Chinese Scholarly Thought," *XMCB*, March 10, 1902, pp. 41–56. Nevertheless, in "Education Should Have Principles," Liang acknowledged that certain Christian values had significance in the building of democracy, and that Christian schools were playing a powerful global role (pp. 1–8). At another point, Liang noted a paradox in the fact that although religion was a form of enslavement to superstition, it was also responsible for the type of value system conducive to order, organization, and commitment that had enabled progress in Japan and the West. See A New Man of China, "On Liberty," *XMCB*, May 8, 1902, p. 7.

gentleman. It had also emphasized the importance of endurance, outlasting travail. But the gentlemanly, patient approach—however applicable in periods of peace and prosperity—was ill suited to China's present struggle for survival. It was like preaching morality while armed robbers were breaking into the house.[64]

When Liang made his first trip to North America, between February and November of 1903, therefore, his views were in ferment. Tremendously impressed with the scope and depth of Western philosophy and science, he was in the process of posing a series of challenges to Confucianism in all of its forms. Impressed with the seeming correlation between the enlightenment of a citizenry and the strength of a state, he was arguing the case for constitutionalism, limited government, and popular rights. Yet he was also convinced that if China were to survive as an entity, beset as it was by threats at home and abroad, a strong, authoritative political system that could keep order and cultivate unity was essential. Thus his quest was to synthesize Bluntschli and Bentham, to build an enduring nation-state that could compete effectively in the struggle for survival.

Liang's American experiences produced mixed reactions, but on balance his doubts as to whether full-fledged democracy was suitable for China were substantially increased. Unquestionably, the United States was a culture shock for Liang, even though he had read about it extensively in various Japanese and Chinese works. Unable to speak or read English, he was handicapped, and now as never before the cultural gap helped to shape the intellectual response.* Nevertheless, Liang met a number of prominent Americans, including President Theodore Roosevelt and J. P. Morgan, and he traveled widely. His subsequent report expressed a blend of awe, respect, concern, and criticism.[65] The United States, as he saw it, was a young giant with a tremendous potential in productivity and power. The scale of its commerce and industry already dwarfed that of most other nations, and even threatened British hegemony in this arena. Americans had a driving energy that fitted well into a Darwinian world, and the combination of freedom and competition in politics contributed to the people's initiative and vigor. Yet many aspects of American society bothered Liang deeply. New York, the financial capital of the United States, had its dark side in the oppressive slums, the maldistribution of wealth, and the enslavement of men by machinery. Liang was also sharply critical of the extensive influence of the Jewish community. In general, he found American city politics riddled with corruption, and women's rights merely "a superficial decoration."

At one point, Liang wondered if the United States, given its limited capacity for assimilating foreigners, might not suffer the fate of the Roman Empire. Generally, he did not see America as a melting pot. Rather, he was depressed by the highly discriminatory treatment accorded various ethnic

*The tension between Liang's emotional ties to his tradition and his intellectual alienation from it is a central theme of Joseph Levenson's classic work, *Liang Ch'i-ch'ao and the Mind of Modern China*. Although in our opinion Levenson has painted this dichotomy in terms too stark and absolute, there can be little doubt that Liang—in contrast to Sun—was a man deeply attached to his culture and never completely at ease in other environments. His inability to use any Western language contributed to the unease, of course; but one suspects that even if his language facility had been greater, the Sinocentric element in Liang would have remained strong.

groups, and naturally he dwelt at length on the Chinese. Condemned to live in ghettos, forced into a few occupations, mistreated as workers, the Chinese existed in generally deplorable conditions, according to Liang. Yet they seemed unable to organize themselves into an effective pressure group. Instead, they were divided into innumerable factions and made politically impotent.

Upon his return to Japan, Liang became pessimistic in assessing the political capabilities of the Chinese and the viability of a democratic system for China. Was it only the classic absolutist political system that was responsible for the fact that the Chinese people had not demonstrated political abilities? If so, why did no one strike for freedom and self-governance, in periods between dynasties? And why were overseas Chinese so unable to create strong, effective organizations?[66] Liang now expanded the problem to include the basic social structure of China. Political absolutism had certainly played a role in shaping public capacities, but so had the family-clan system. It had created a deep consciousness of kinship, without a corresponding consciousness of class or citizenship. Indeed, the Western term "citizen" had never existed in the Chinese language. Other factors inhibiting political capacity were the general poverty of the people and the extended periods of disorder. Under these conditions, insisted Liang, to call for a destructive revolution on the grounds that it would enhance the people's political capacities would be like urging a woman to unbind her feet and immediately enter a footrace.

Even greater pessimism was expressed in a companion essay written by a member of Liang's group.[67] Under current circumstances, he asked, does it really matter whether China has absolutism or majority rule? The majority of Chinese are deeply conservative: they believe in the old examination system, foot-binding, and opium-smoking, among other things. Certain individuals, of course, argue that the answer lies in education. But if we wait until the educational process has taken effect, some foreign power will have already conquered China. If one sees the problem as urgent, therefore, one should seek one or two heroes who can grasp political power and wield it effectively so that China can regain its vitality. To dream of an enlightened society based on majority rule is impractical. What is needed is a hero like one of those from China's past—or a Napoleon, a Washington, a Peter the Great. At the time this was written, the debate with the forces of Sun Yat-sen was increasingly affecting both the style and the content of reformer literature. Still, the return in strident form to the theme of the need for a charismatic leader is noteworthy.

During this period, Liang, along with all other Chinese reformers and revolutionaries, followed developments in Russia with considerable interest. In general, he had used Russia as the prototype of the backward, autocratic state, roughly equal in political terms with China. Commenting on the activities of those whom he called Russian anarchists, Liang expressed himself as sympathetic but unconvinced.[68] He understood why they used assassination: in the presence of large governmental military forces, uprisings had repeatedly failed; little support was forthcoming from the lethargic masses; moreover, assassination was inexpensive and could be carried out in secret. The goal of abolishing all government, however, overlooked Bentham's truth that government is an evil, but it is necessary in order to prevent even greater evils. Nevertheless, assassination was a means of demanding political rights, and as such could be considered a constructive move toward a peaceful future.*

When political upheaval broke out in 1904, leading to the establishment of the Duma, various writers believed that Russia was in the throes of fundamental change and that the only question was whether the constitutional or the revolutionary route would be pursued.[69] Not infrequently, developments in Russia were interpreted by Chinese dissidents as a warning to the Qing court that revolution was inevitable if reforms were not forthcoming. Later, as repression appeared to gain the upper hand again, Liang took hope in the long-term influence of individuals like Tolstoy, and remained optimistic that by building on the heritage of local assemblies and a legal tradition, Russia would evolve toward constitutionalism. When the situation worsened, he argued that the Russo-Japanese War would be a good test of the qualities of the absolutist versus the liberal state, one that might influence China's rulers. But at the same time, he and others continued to hope that constitutionalism would carry the day in Russia, so that this message too would reach Beijing. We pray day and night, he wrote, for the success of the Russian revolution, and not merely to show our sympathy for the Russian people.

In early 1906 Liang made a major political statement in the form of a series of articles entitled "On Enlightened Absolutism."[70] He defined absolutism as a system under which the leadership could control all state organs in a monopolistic fashion and therefore operate wholly independently from those being governed. He then proceeded to establish a typology of absolutist and nonabsolutist systems. Under absolutist systems he listed monarchic, aristocratic, and democratic absolutism, according to the source of authority. Absolutism was "barbaric" or "enlightened," depending on whether it reflected the whim of a despot or a commitment to the public interest and the survival of the state. Absolutism also took two forms, complete and incomplete, depending on whether the leadership was able to wield its full power effectively. Liang admitted that incomplete absolutism might be considered a contradiction in terms, but he argued that in the real world of politics no pure absolutism was possible. China's present government was an incomplete absolutism because it held all power but was unable to exercise it effectively. The revolutionaries, whether they realized it or not, were aiming at an incomplete nonabsolutism, because a people suddenly brought to political power would not be able to wield it fully or effectively. Neither the existing system in China nor the revolutionaries' proposals were satisfactory.

Liang then advanced an intriguing case for political relativism. More than once he acknowledged that in ideal or abstract terms nonabsolutism was unquestionably better than absolutism. In actuality, however, the situation was more complex. For example, the theories of Locke, Montesquieu, and Bentham might be useful to one country but disastrous when applied to another. Even in the same country the concepts that were very effective on one occasion might be ineffective under different circumstances. "Natural

* One reason for Liang's sympathy with the Russian nihilists lay in the fact that he himself had toyed with the idea that assassinating the most reactionary Manchu functionaries could serve as a substitute for a bloody anti-Manchu revolution. For such a suggestion, see One Who Sips Ice, "A Reply to a Certain Newspaper," *XMCB*, August 20, 1906, pp. 1–8.

development" would determine whether it was time for a certain system or set of institutions. Whether a state was mature enough to have a specific political structure thus had to be decided after objective historical research. Because they based their analyses on such research, the nineteenth-century political theorists and students of jurisprudence were more reliable guides in this matter than the philosophers of the eighteenth century.

Liang then set down five historical conditions under which enlightened absolutism would be the most appropriate system:

1. When a country is first established, or when small states are federated into a single large state. In this case, unity can be assured.
2. When the aristocracy is entrenched in power and the various classes within the country are pitted against one another in strife. In this case, order can be established and a unified national sovereignty achieved.
3. When a country has long been under incomplete absolutism, resulting in the breakdown of the political system, so that the people demand indulgence, feel minimal obligations, and have an extremely marginal relation to the state. In this case, to grant the people participatory rights immediately would result in improper decisions.
4. When a country has long been under barbaric absolutism, with political freedom extremely restricted, so that the people have pursued their private interests at the expense of public morality. In this case, the tutelage of an enlightened absolutism is required.
5. When the country has been through a destructive period. In this case, it is necessary to restore order and achieve harmony.[71]

Would the period of enlightened absolutism be long or short? That depended on the precise circumstances, Liang wrote. Under three conditions, it would be lengthy: where the people's knowledge was extremely rudimentary; where the state covered a vast terrain, making national unification difficult; and where the state encompassed a multiethnic population and faced the threat of racial conflict.[72]

These conditions sounded suspiciously as if they were intended to describe China, but Liang avoided any identification. Rather, he said that they were exceptions to the norm and added that although the average country had to go through a stage of enlightened absolutism, that stage need not (and should not) be too long. And after passing through it, a country should enter the stage of constitutionalism. If there should be retrogression to barbaric absolutism, however, revolution would be required to reestablish enlightened absolutism. In sum, enlightened absolutism was the natural preparation for the constitutional state. To illustrate this theme, Liang then delved briefly into the histories of a number of modern states and found that each of them (except the United States) had passed through an absolutist stage, whether short or long.*

*One Who Sips Ice, "On Enlightened Absolutism," *XMCB*, February 8, 1906, pp. 12–14. According to Liang, England had had a very short and moderate stage of enlightened absolutism, which enabled it to become known as the fatherland of constitutionalism. France

It was now time to deal with the contention of Sun Yat-sen and the revolutionaries that a nation like China could skip stages: just as one did not have to begin with the first locomotive but could buy the most modern engine available, so one could adopt the most advanced political institutions without painfully passing through earlier systems. Indeed, Sun and his supporters were fond of pointing to Japan as an example of a nation that had skipped several decades in its drive toward modernization.

The use of the locomotive analogy, responded Liang, was misleading, because politics—which deals with human beings—must be discussed in the context of the time, the place, and the human resources.[73] To draw lessons from inanimate objects was fallacious. Now Liang began to close in on the nub of the argument. If a republic were established immediately and a national legislature were created, the nation would be greeted by a multitude of quarrelsome, factional parties, the largest of which might consist of no more than twenty or thirty members. Under such circumstances Sun's "temporary" phase of martial law would last for a very long time. On the other hand, if a decade of enlightened absolutism prepared the way for the constitutional stage, the Chinese people would not be so miserable.

Later, Liang was to say that if China wished to emulate Japan and Prussia, it would require a minimum of twenty years, but if the model were to be the United States or England, it would take considerably longer.[74] Thus, when the reader arrived at the climax of Liang's long essay he found one "enlightened absolutism" being posed against another. In effect, Liang was asking for a period of monarchical rule that would serve as a tutelage period, and he was promising that it would be a shorter stage than the type of enlightened absolutism represented by the martial law that would follow Sun's revolution.[75] In short, a guided tutelage aiming at constitutional monarchy was the most promising and least painful route for China to pursue.*

---

had had sixty to seventy years of enlightened absolutism centering on the reign of Henry IV, during which time Richelieu, Mazarin, and Colbert took charge of policies. Later, France returned to barbarian absolutism at the end of Louis XIV's reign, leading to a revolution and a decade of enlightened absolutism under Napoleon, before subsequently evolving into constitutionalism. Prussia had had one of the longest periods of enlightened absolutism, and one of the most effective in terms of enabling it to become a major power. Even under a unified Germany led by Bismarck, constitutionalism had existed in name only, and enlightened absolutism had constituted the practice. Russia had an enlightened absolutism under Peter the Great, and became the leader in Eastern Europe, but since Peter, the country had reverted to barbaric absolutism, and only in recent times had Russia moved back, gradually reentering enlightened absolutism. Liang asserted that Russia had not been able to get rid of absolutism because it had too vast a territory and too complex a racial mix, so that without absolutism, the Russian empire would dissolve (p. 13). Japan had operated under enlightened absolutism from 1867 to 1889, prior to its entry into constitutionalism, and both Italy and Austria also had a stage of enlightened absolutism in the course of their unification drives.

*In correspondence with a close friend and fellow reformer, Huang Gongdu, Liang gave his own version of the elements of change and continuity in his political views. As early as mid-1897 in Beijing, he had raised with the Japanese minister the question of whether twentieth-century China should model her polity after the European system of sharing governance between the ruler and the people. After coming to Japan, he came into contact with the Meiji popular rights movement. At first it seemed strange, but after reading Rousseau and Montesquieu, he accepted it, seeing that the era of "the great peace" (Kang's last stage of universal progression) had to depend on democracy. When he traveled to America, however, and saw the corruption, scandals, and unruliness of the political parties, he was again lost. If even a great civilized country like the United States was in this condition, what would happen to a country where the people's judgment was not well developed? He then began to study the

In concluding this section, Liang offered some advice to the revolutionaries. Stop seeking three revolutions simultaneously, he wrote. Trying to effect racial, social, and political revolutions at the same time will produce only failure. And, he added, if you aim at a racial revolution, you are really advocating absolutism rather than democracy, because you will have to enforce a long period of absolutism before democracy becomes feasible.[76]

THE DEBATE OVER SOCIALISM

Liang's reference here to a social revolution signals his quarrel with Sun Yat-sen's *minshengzhuyi* (principle of people's livelihood), and serves to introduce us to the subject of his attitude toward socialism. As early as 1899 he had spoken of the "inevitable" proletarian revolution against capitalism, and other references of a similar nature were scattered among his earlier writings, together with brief reports on happenings in the West involving socialists.[77] Indeed, on several occasions he suggested that socialism was destined to be the universal wave of the future. Despite such statements, however, Liang repeatedly made it clear that in his view Western socialist doctrines had no applicability to China, at least for the present.

The evolution of the West had followed a different course. There intensive struggles had preceded the achievement of freedom in its various forms: equality had derived from the struggle between the common people and the aristocracy; political participation had emanated from the struggle between the citizenry and the government; self-determination, including the right of colonies to establish their own government, had been attained from the struggle between the motherland and its colonies; religious freedom had been achieved by the struggle beween state and church; national independence had been gained by the struggle between the nationals of a given country and foreign aggressors; and the freedom of workers had been won through the struggle between the poor and the rich.[78] But for China, argued Liang, most of these problems did not exist. Only political participation and national independence were pressing issues at present. Unlike the West, China had no classes. With the destruction of feudalism following the Warring States period, classes had been obliterated.* The wide discrepancies be-

---

classical philosopher Mozi. After a few years, he went to England and came to believe that China should model itself partly after the British. There should be a British-style division between local and central governmental functions; elected assemblies, patterned after the Japanese system, should be established from the prefectural to the national level; and the powers of the central government should be drawn from the British, German, and American systems, with a clear-cut division of functions prevailing both within the center, and between the center and its subunits.

Liang explained his position as follows: The sovereignty (of the monarch) should be continued so that the people's knowledge can be developed, and the officials' power should be divided (with the people) so as to preserve the people's welfare (*minsheng*). In this way, the power of the ruler and the power of the people can be balanced. "This," he said, "I have always believed—without wavering" (Ding Wenjiang, *Liang Rengong xiansheng nianpu changbian chugao*, pp. 159–160). Although this explanation is too neat to accord fully with the facts as revealed in his writings, it comes close to capturing the essence of Liang's political philosophy during this period.

*A New Man of China, "On Liberty." *XMCB*, May 8, 1902, pp. 1–8, and May 22, 1902, pp. 1–8. In a slightly later essay, however, Liang made a class analysis of China based on a simple division between consumers and producers which would have startled Western economists. References were sprinkled throughout his text to Adam Smith's *Wealth of Na-*

tween rich and poor existing in advanced societies were not present in China. Since China had no colonies, the issue of self-determination was not posed. Nor was there any conflict over religious beliefs. And although the future might produce a labor problem, none now existed. What was needed, Liang implied, was not socialism but a rapid expansion of production so that the nation could take its place among modern states.

Until 1906, therefore, Liang made specific reference to socialism only occasionally—and generally in unenthusiastic or disparaging terms. At one point, presenting an account of Adam Smith, he mentioned Marx in passing, saying that Marx's *renqunzhuyi* ("massism," an attempt to capture the meaning of the English word "socialism") was specifically aimed at the protection of laborers, and owed its genesis to Smith.[79] In another essay of the same period, Liang asserted that Xu Xing's theories were close to Platonic communism (*gongchanzhuyi*) or European socialism (written in English), after which he inserted a footnote to the effect that socialism was like anarchism, although they were not exactly the same. Socialism, he continued, was excessively committed to egalitarianism and altruism (the term used was *boai*, "all-embracing love").*

As we have indicated, although Liang sometimes spoke favorably of the

---

tions, translated by Yan Fu. Among the consumers were beggars, thieves, swindlers, monks, those who had inherited their possessions, playboys, the various military types (in China the military was composed of beggars, swindlers, and playboys!), over one-half of the government officials, those fed by officials, the rich and gentry classes, over one-half of them women (since few women engaged in production outside the home, 60 to 70 percent of them should be considered consumers), the handicapped, and the prisoners. Who were the producers? They included servants, prostitutes, scholars and teachers, less than one-half of the government officials, merchants, and others engaged in commerce (although about 20 to 30 percent of these were swindlers), and those engaged in agriculture and industry. An elaborate chart followed, suggesting that about 50 percent of China's 400 million people were consumers. These came mainly from the upper and middle classes of the society, Liang asserted, and he found the current trends adverse. If we could get the other 200 million people into production, he wrote, we would be able to increase our national product by four or five fold. Moreover, of the three factors economists regarded as critical to growth—land, labor, and capital—China needed only to increase its capital, having an ample supply of land and labor. See A New Man of China, "On Production and Consumption," *XMCB*, October 2, 1902, pp. 1–17.

*A New Man of China, "On Trends in the Changes of Scholastic Thought in China," *XMCB*, April 8, 1902, p. 65. Liang argued that northern China in the pre-Qin era had espoused *ganshezhuyi* (interventionalism) or paternalism, whereas southern China had supported *fangrenzhuyi* (laissez-faireism), the same doctrines that had recently been competing in modern Europe. There was, he said, no definitive answer to which was superior. Until the eighteenth century, "interventionism" had dominated in Europe, but in the late eighteenth and early nineteenth centuries, laissez-faireism or liberalism had been emphasized. Recently, however, the trend was back toward interventionism, with Germany the prime example. Rousseau was the founder of liberalism, and Gladstone its foremost practitioner; Bluntschli was the founder of contemporary interventionism, and Bismarck had translated it most forcefully into policy.

Two points in this essay are of particular interest. First, Liang suggests that current Western controversies over the role of the state mirrored similar issues in ancient China. (Nothing is new under the sun.) Second, in addition to revealing Liang's growing attachment to German legal philosophy (Bluntschli is prominently cited), the essay displays some confusion about where to place socialism and anarchism in relation to each other and to other doctrines. At first, Liang implies that the two doctrines are closely related; later, however, he appears to equate "socialism" with the "interventionism" of Bismarckian Germany, and identifies Xu Xing's theories as "the extreme of liberalism," meaning presumably closest to anarchism, or pure nonintervention.

Russian revolutionaries and their activities, and even saw in assassination an effective means of demanding political change in China, he regarded the anarchist goal of a society totally free of government as both utopian and unwise. And he thought that even in Russia, where there were extensive economic and social injustices, socialist determination to abolish private landownership was impractical and likely "to crush the very foundation of Russia as a nation."[80]

After the creation of the Tongmeng Hui, Liang paid increasing attention to socialism, largely because of the debate with the Sun forces, although it was far from the center of his interest. Some of his attacks on Sun's doctrine of "the people's livelihood" took an extreme form. If you want socialism, he wrote, supplement Marx by creating new theories and then see whether they can be accepted by civilized societies. But if you advocate policies that would amount to the massacre of one-half of China's population and the seizure of their lands, that is indeed the behavior of bandits. At least, Western socialists take land gradually and promise compensation for owners' losses.[81]

By the fall of 1906 Liang was prepared to deal more seriously with the issue of a social revolution for China, and he sought to challenge the position of the *Min bao* writers as forcefully as possible. Let us turn first to an important article published under the general title "Miscellaneous Answers to a Certain Paper," subtitled "Is a Social Revolution Necessary in Present-Day China?"[82]

At the outset, Liang sought to distinguish between two issues: whether "the spirit of socialism" should be used by China, and whether the Chinese socioeconomic system warranted a basic revolution. Taking the second question first, Liang began with a critique of Western society that borrowed extensively from Marxian theory through indirect sources.* A picture of Europe more sinister and depressing than any ever drawn by the Sun forces—or by Liang himself—was presented. The problems of the West were not wholly of recent origin, Liang explained. Their seeds had been planted in the period before the industrial revolution. Exploitation of the peasantry by the feudal aristocracy had created a historic gulf between rich and poor that predated capitalism. It was therefore easy for those inequalities to be expanded with the industrialization process.

The accumulation of capital was possible only for the very few, although as Richard Ely had noted, during the beginnings of the industrial revolution the artisans might have banded together in cooperatives had they understood what was taking place. The new technology brought a flood of cheap manufactured goods, but the worker became separated from his product, and his surplus value went to the employer. Widening class divisions and the exploitation of the poor by the rich were thus primary products of Western modernization. Even within the capitalist class, a ruthless struggle for supremacy had taken place, and ultimately all but the largest capitalists succumbed. "Alas," remarked Liang, "the success of one person has to compensate for countless dried bones. This is what has happened to the present-day European social economy. . . . This calamity involving the tyranny of the wealthy

*Both the Sun and the Liang factions were heavily influenced by Richard T. Ely's *Outline of Economics*, which was available to them in Japanese translation. In the polemics of 1906–1907, Ely would serve as an indisputable source of Western economic history. Each side would accuse the other of misunderstanding or misusing Ely's text.

class is fiercer than floods and wild beasts, and therefore it is inevitable that the doctrine of social revolution should flourish."[83]

But Liang did not retreat from his earlier view that the situation in China was different and vastly more favorable. China had never had a powerful aristocracy who monopolized the land. At present, said Liang, there were a large number of medium-sized property owners, and unusually wealthy families were rare. Indeed, one could say that there were no classes in China, since it had been customary for men to rise from humble origins to high office and, on leaving office, to mix again with the common people. Low taxes also contributed to less exploitation; further, there was no nobility or church to oppress the peasantry. And the Chinese system of equal inheritance had been very important in equalizing wealth. Indeed, the real economic problem of China lay in the fragmentation of wealth and in the fact that capital could not be accumulated in large quantities for productive purposes.

Returning to an earlier theme, Liang asserted that the Chinese concern should be with production, not distribution. And if this problem were to be solved, mechanization had to be adopted. Still, China could avoid most of the evils of European industrialization. To obtain capital, China should adapt the joint-stock-company approach, but the stockholders ought to be drawn from the large middle class. Then there need be no curse of monopoly by the wealthy few, as in Europe. Liang's argument was that if private capitalism had the broadest possible base, including worker-financed cooperative industries, productive methods could be modernized without sacrificing a general equality of distribution.

Liang proceeded to defend his dual policy of "encouraging capital" and "protecting labor" by reiterating the threat of foreign imperialism. China had to decide whether her wealth was to be used by her own people or by foreign capitalists. Advanced capitalist societies had to look abroad for investments, and the events of the past few years proved conclusively that imperialism was advancing rapidly upon China. "Even those people who boast about *minshengzhuyi* should be able to understand this," said Liang. "We might think that Western workers have been exploited," he remarked, "but when the foreign capitalists occupy our country fully, then our four hundred million brothers will be like horses and oxen for all eternity. At that time who will be the rich and who will be the poor in China? There will be only two classes in the Chinese economic arena. One class will be those who consume the benefits of civilization; they will be the foreigners. The other class will be those who suffer the evils of civilization; they will be the Chinese." Hence the remedy for China was not socialism, admirable as that might be for the West. Why does Sun Yat-sen call for the repression of Chinese, Liang asked; does he want us to become like the people of India?

Later in the article, Liang sought to dissect the "land nationalization" program of Sun's proposed social revolution. One of his initial themes was that this land program was not really socialism—or at most it was only one part of a socialist system and could not stand alone. If one were going to accept the socialist approach to society, Liang argued, it was not sufficient merely to undertake "land nationalization" under the formula advanced by Henry George, which had many unintelligible or unworkable aspects, as Western critics had made clear. Even if land could somehow be nationalized successfully, the major part of the problem, namely, capital, would remain untouched. The rich would still grow richer as the poor grew poorer. It was grossly inaccurate for Sun to say that private ownership of land was the basic cause of social injustice in Europe. The basic cause was Western capitalism. Actually, Sun overrated agriculture and sought to promote it to the exclusion of industrialization. "Sun's socialist doctrine is nothing more than a revival of the ancient 'well-field' type of society."[84]

This criticism of Sun and the *Min bao* writers led Liang into a discussion of the forms of modern socialism. There were two broad types of socialists, he asserted. The first type was the social reformer; he accepted the contemporary social system but wished to make reforms in it. This type was represented by men like Adolf Wagner, Gustav Schmoller, and others who agreed with Bismarck's social policies. The second type was the social revolutionary; he did not accept the present social order and wished to overthrow it and build anew. This type was represented by Marx and Bebel among others. Where did Sun and his followers belong? "It is difficult for me to give a clear answer," said Liang, because they have attempted to take ideas from both schools of socialism without realizing that they are incompatible. His conclusion was brief and emphatic (the italics are his): "To put it simply, *these people have never understood what socialism is.*"[85]

As for his own views, Liang took note of *Min bao* taunts that he had once proclaimed that an economic revolution was unavoidable and had introduced socialist theory as one aspect of progress. He explained that he had been discussing the West when he had written that an economic revolution could not be avoided. As for socialism, he said: "I am absolutely sympathetic to those doctrines belonging to social reformism. I am not necessarily withholding praise from the socialist theories supportive of revolution, but I have said that these cannot be carried out, or even if it is possible, it is a matter of several hundred or a thousand years."[86] To counterattack, Liang threw in the charge that when Sun and his cohorts talked about *minshengzhuyi* gaining ground in Japan, they again revealed their failure to understand the differences between social reform and social revolution.

Liang concluded this essay by returning to the original questions. There was no reason for modern China to have a social revolution, and there were many weighty arguments against it. But if the question were put, should China adopt "the spirit of socialism" within a parliamentary framework, then he would answer "I am absolutely in support of it." The socialism he favored was social reformism. He could not discuss this concept in detail, but it should include either state or municipal ownership of utilities, regulation of monopolies, factory laws, compulsory insurance laws, progressive income taxes, an inheritance tax, and many other social measures.[87] As Liang saw it, China could accomplish these reforms easily, even if it were too late for them to be effective in most of the Western nations. What China needed, concluded Liang, was not a racial or a social revolution, but rather a political revolution (or radical change) on behalf of parliamentarism and social reform.

In his views Liang was aligning himself with the very influential school of social policy in Japan, a school comprising a number of leading Japanese intellectuals and strongly influenced by the German social policy group. Unquestionably, he had drawn most of his ideas from these sources, and in a sense the debate between Liang and Sun mirrored an older dispute that had been taking place in Japanese intellectual circles. Although the influence of

Henry George in Japan—once not insignificant—had greatly diminished by this time, it had been replaced by a complex three-cornered struggle between social policy theorists, social democrats (including, as subgroups, Christian socialists and Marxists), and anarcho-syndicalists.[88]

Xinmin congbao continued its assault on Sun's program. An article by Wu Zhongyao entitled "A Discussion of Socialism" was published in October 1906, with a preface by Liang. In his opening remarks, Liang made a caustic comment about self-centered, ambitious individuals who wanted to use socialism as a tool to incite the people, even though they are completely ignorant about the real nature of socialism and therefore only create confusion. In the text of the article, Wu spent a considerable amount of space working out various categories or divisions of the socialist movement. He presented the ideas of other authors, but the general division he himself used was between "narrow" and "broad" socialism. Narrow socialism was social-revolutionary doctrine, although communism and anarchism were to be considered separately. Broad socialism was social reform, sometimes called "the school of social policy." Wu stated his purpose at the beginning: to prove that narrow socialism could not be practiced in China under the present circumstances, but that broad socialism was indispensable for China.[89]

Wu's article was incomplete. It was to be continued in subsequent issues of the *Xinmin congbao,* but for some reason no further installments appeared. However, the main themes buttressed Liang's earlier arguments. Social revolution was the natural outcome of the excesses of Western evolution. The reasons supporting it were many and powerful. The author understood and supported them. No one could doubt that the motives and aspirations of social revolutionaries were among the highest and most advanced of mankind. However, to hope that social-revolutionary doctrine could be realized was like waiting for the millennium. Hence, broad socialism had emerged, said Wu, with the objective of correcting the excesses of individualism and avoiding the weaknesses of narrow socialism.

Liang was constantly foraging for new authorities to support his attack against *Min bao,* and many additional works were cited in a long essay that had to be spread over three issues.[90] However, heavy reliance was still placed on Adolf Wagner and others from the German social-policy group. In this essay Liang made his strongest defense of private property and a regulated capitalist system. He charged the Sun group with being basically inconsistent in trying to use the private-property system and destroy it at the same time. With respect to agricultural land, he wrote: "I say that China's future policy of managing land should not only be the retention of privately owned land in private hands, but even that land which was originally government-owned should gradually be broken up and returned to private hands." Except for forests and model farms, the state need not permanently preserve its ownership rights.[91] Perhaps municipal ownership of urban land had some merit, he added, indicating that this was as far as he would go toward his opponents' position.

In this essay Liang's defense of private enterprise and his attacks on most forms of nationalized industry also went far beyond earlier positions. Public enterprise was inferior to private enterprise, he said, partly because public administrators could not afford to be bold and take chances. If they failed, their governmental positions would be jeopardized. Thus "their intentions are not aimed at success, but at not being at fault." Ultraconservatism and inefficiency flowed from this tendency. In conclusion, Liang set forth his own choice: only when it was desirable for purposes of revenue, or to serve the cause of public justice, should the state purchase enterprises that had already been developed by private initiative. This policy, he said, had been followed in developing the successful public enterprises in Germany and the railroads in Japan.

An added hazard of the *Min bao* program was that it would lead to the rapid accumulation of great economic power by government officials. This had disadvantages even for the experienced societies of the West, but it was potentially disastrous for China: it would produce official corruption on a grand scale, and the people, with their limited experience of representative government, would be powerless to prevent this. Thus, said Liang, the unfortunate phenomenon of "democratic absolutism" would result.[92]

In his criticism of Sun's land policy, Liang added several additional charges, including the thesis that progress depended far more on industry than on agriculture. The slogan for societies like China should be not "back to the land" but "on to the factories," a point on which the Sun program was hopelessly confused. Once again Liang placed himself squarely in the ranks of the social-policy school, making clear his belief that policies of social reform could achieve society's general goals without the costs of more extreme forms of socialism.

One curious paradox emerged from Liang's writings of this period. As the debate over *minsheng* progressed, Liang moved further in the direction of supporting the private-enterprise system, and his writings began to reproduce many of the arguments that constituted classical challenges to the socialist position. To be sure, he was never quite certain whether to attack the Sun group because they were socialists or because they did not understand socialism—so he did a bit of both. At the same time, however, he did not abandon his own claim on socialism. Even as he attacked both "revolution" and "socialism" as espoused by his adversaries, he claimed to belong to the social-reform branch of socialism, and insisted that his policies outlined a true political revolution. Moreover, it is remarkable that this gradualist should have gone so far in accepting the modern socialist version of the West—its past, present, and future. One can suggest, of course, that this was one of those situations where Chinese "conservatism" could interact most easily with Western "radicalism." In any case, when it came to an analysis of the contemporary West, both the Liang and the Sun groups could claim to be in tune with socialism, and Liang might claim the more radical approach. Certainly he was closer to Marxism on this front. It was he who insisted that capital, not land, was the key to European social problems. It was he who raised the specter of Western capitalist imperialism in a fashion that would please any Marxist-Leninist. Indeed, the Sun forces felt called upon to defend the need for foreign entrepreneurship in China against Liang's fierce assaults.[93]

LIANG IN RETROSPECT

A broader analysis of the role of the reformers in the modern Chinese revolutionary movement must await the presentation of other political actors who were currently on stage. Given our extensive treatment of Liang

Qichao as the foremost representative of this group, however, a brief evaluation of the man and his contributions is in order.

Above all, Liang was possessed of a mind that would yield to contradictions, but not to simplicities. In this, of course, he was aided by the remarkably diverse experiences marking his career. Here was a man who had started as a child prodigy and pure Confucianist; he had made his own youthful revolt under the tutelage of the powerful intellect of Kang Youwei, and found himself catapulted to national fame as an ardent reformer; he had been exposed in his exile to the full impact of Japan, a nation of similar cultural background undergoing rapid transformation; and he had come to maturity with the leisure to read and travel extensively, thence sharing with his countrymen his discoveries about the Western world in its widest reaches. Who else in his time had attempted to encompass both the Chinese and the Western classics, and then to devour all available contemporary knowledge?

There were, of course, weaknesses. Liang wrote too much, too fast, and covered too many diverse subjects to be original or profound, in the usual meaning of those terms. Yet a careful reading of his major essays reveals an extraordinary ability to grasp the essence of many Western concepts with reasonable accuracy. This is all the more remarkable since these concepts were coming to Liang primarily from Japanese sources, frequently in bowdlerized form. And from Liang and a handful of colleagues, the West in its various facets was opened up to a small but growing number of students, many of whom were destined to play key roles in twentieth-century China.

An intellect capable of venturing so boldly was not likely to fear complexity, and it was this willingness to accept complexity that made Liang a gradualist. He recoiled from the simplistic, one-dimensional, invariably optimistic, intellectual framework out of which revolutionary activists so often spring. He always saw the dangers as well as the opportunities in rapid change. And like Edmund Burke, he was a "conservative" in the sense that he did not believe that the past could or should be obliterated in the course of seeking a different future.* Yet he was dedicated to the radical concept of creating a dramatically new Chinese citizen, and for this purpose he was prepared to see literature, art, and music reordered, along with philosophy, economics, and politics. In these terms, as much as any man of his generation, he presaged the revolutionary effort that lay ahead.

Liang's basic goal was to synthesize the two mighty forces that coursed through his life: the China he knew, with its great cultural traditions, its underutilized human resources, and its desperate needs; and the West he had discovered, a West that had emerged as a symbol of everything powerful, progressive, and future-oriented. Between these two cultures, he did not

*Long before his polemic battle with *Min bao* began, Liang had clearly defined his basic position with respect to change. It was as follows: Everything in the world operates on the basis of two principles, conservatism, or stability (stasis), and progress (movement). One must always use both principles simultaneously. It is not possible to adopt only one. The two will conflict, but out of conflict comes harmony. For example, we use one leg on which to stand, and the other to move forward, one hand to take, the other to hold. What we mean by "new people" is not that they should admire everything that belongs to the West and abandon all that has been ours; nor is it, as the conservatives would like to think, that the possession of several thousand years of morality, scholarship, and custom is sufficient to enable China to stand before others in the world. In this passage, we see traditional Chinese philosophy applied to a concrete, contemporary problem in such a manner as to give it the empirical quality for which Liang strove in this era.

dispense his affection equally. His love was reserved for China, and his life-style remained as Chinese as conditions would permit; the West received only respect, sometimes begrudgingly, and frequently mixed with criticism. But at an early point, Liang came to realize that his beloved China could survive only if it quickly adapted to its own use certain crucial institutions, procedures, and attitudes in which the West had pioneered. Thus, while Liang decried any revolution that would seek to overturn the existing order in a single violent stroke, he was deeply committed to the type of far-reaching change over time that was a different form of revolution—a revolutionary *process*, potentially far more profound in precisely the same sense that the transformation of modern Japan proved to be more profound than the Chinese Revolution of 1911, or even the French Revolution of 1789.

And although Liang was rarely original, he played a major role in transmitting into the mainstream of Chinese thought several concepts that were to have far-reaching repercussions. One was the idea of evolution through political stages, stages universal to human societies. As we have seen, this idea was drawn essentially from the Social Darwinists, who believed that nations, like species, had to evolve in order to survive, and that this evolution was "progressive," its apex represented by the higher forms of enlightenment, participation, and governance by the populace as a whole.

The introduction of this idea into the Chinese intellectual community of this era initiated a great debate over China's past, present, and future. Did Chinese history conform to the Western pattern? In what stage was the nation at present, and could stages be skipped or abbreviated? What were the most appropriate means of speeding up the evolutionary process, if indeed this were possible? These questions, so central to the later Chinese Communist movement, had begun to figure prominently in disputation at a time when Marxism was of scant significance to Chinese intellectuals and Leninism did not yet exist.

With the idea of developmental stages came a corollary concept, that of tutelage. Should not those who could discern the future be the ones to guide others toward the goal? And if guidance were necessary, should it not be provided through appropriate social and political institutions? From such insights also came the recognition that if people were to be motivated to work toward the goals set by the tutors, a set of appropriate values and beliefs had to be instilled in the citizenry. From this juncture, an appreciation of the importance of ideology lay only a short leap ahead.

4

SUN YAT-SEN AND THE REVOLUTIONARY MOVEMENT

IT REMAINED for Liang Qichao's lifelong rival, Sun Yat-sen, to provide an ideology for the Chinese revolution despite the fact that Sun was essentially an activist, not a theorist. In turning to the mainstream of the revolutionary movement of this period, one must first conjure with its leader, a man of both common and uncommon parts.[1]

Despite certain striking differences, Sun shared several characteristics with other leaders of modern China. He was a southerner raised in a rural village, and his father was a farmer. Born in Cuiheng, Guangdong, on November 12, 1866, Sun spent his childhood in this Pearl River delta village about halfway between Canton and Macao. It was a heavily populated, semitropical, rice-producing region, having early and sustained contacts with the West, and serving as one of the chief sources of overseas immigration. Indeed, several of Sun's uncles, as well as his eldest brother, left the village to seek their fortunes abroad, a development that was to shape Sun's life. But it was also a region that had not forgotten—nor totally forsaken—the Taiping Rebellion, and it was rife with secret societies, displaying in addition a distinctive southern subculture that was never wholly assimilated politically by the Qing.

Many sources claim that Sun came from a poor peasant background, and it is true that his father's fortunes were sometimes at low ebb. However, Sun does not appear to have known misery during his childhood, nor to have been deeply scarred by a sense of poverty. His father owned some land at this time and found occasional outside jobs, and most important, there were remittances from his brother, now living in Hawaii. Young Sun was able to go to a primary school in his village (it had been founded by an uncle), but he is said to have shown little interest in the classical education offered there.

This heritage bears comparison with that of men like Liang Qichao and Mao Zedong. They too were southern: Liang came from the same province, Guangdong, and Mao was a Hunanese. They too came from a rural, agricultural background, but one that was not cut off from urban influences. Nor were they of poor peasant status. Liang's family lived in financially comfortable circumstances and showed an appreciation for education.

Mao's father was relatively comfortable in later life, by prevailing standards. Both young men were able to pursue a higher education.

Thus, Sun, Liang, and Mao were among those individuals available for political leadership as China moved into the twentieth century, and as such, they belonged to a relatively small elite. Those who were truly outside the perimeters of the potential leadership group included youth from more remote rural environments, genuinely poor-peasant in their socioeconomic status and thereby lacking in either the motivation or the opportunity to pursue education. For them, as for countless generations of their ancestors, life ended as it began, and was passed on as a cycle to be repeated by their progeny. At most, they could lead a localized peasant revolt or a robber band. Similarly unavailable for political leadership were those from China's burgeoning, amorphous cities. Outside the mainstream of their own traditions, the urban dwellers had not been able to create a counterculture formidable enough to challenge the old order. Family-clan ties were weaker, and the urban community less cohesive. Guilds existed, but were restricted in purpose. Thus, in addition to the problem of self-identity, the urbanite could hardly engage in the type of organizational activity required to establish political leadership.*

The similarities that bound Sun, Liang, and Mao together were partly offset, to be sure, by significant differences, and these will be explored in due course. Looking only at Sun, one can see two powerful but contradictory currents that governed his career. On the one hand, there was the influence of rural Guangdong, replete with memories of Hong Xiuquan and countless other rebels against authority, including the powerful secret societies still active in the region. This current also carried with it the problems of the poorer rural classes—their thirst for land or employment, and for the right to share in the fruits of economic development. On the other hand, there was the force of the outside world, pressing relentlessly against the traditional patterns of Chinese life. This current carried with it both values and techniques: the values of progress, nationalism, and democracy; the techniques of revolution, land reform, and industrialization. All of these, together with Christianity, another Westernization, entered Sun's consciousness very early.

At the age of thirteen, Sun went to Hawaii to join his brother, and shortly thereafter he was enrolled as a boarder in the Anglican Iolani School in Honolulu. After three years he graduated and went on to Oahu College, later known as Punahou School, which was operated by American Congregationalists and catered largely to missionary children. By this time Sun had acquired a fluency in English and a commitment to Christianity. His brother, now fearful that Sun was separating himself from his Chinese heritage, angrily demanded that the youth return home to stay in 1883. It was too late. Sun went home, but after a brief and stormy period there, during which he

*We are aware that there was a rising urban component in Chinese politics from the late nineteenth century onward, manifesting itself partly in the emergence into upper political strata of Western-trained intelligentsia from urban merchant and professional families. It is also true that political leaders whose antecedents were rural gravitated by stages to China's major cities, ultimately making their headquarters in Canton, Shanghai, Beijing, and elsewhere. But these facts, we believe, do not weaken our generalization concerning the amorphous, poorly integrated character of China's major metropolitan centers and the effect of this fact on modern Chinese politics.

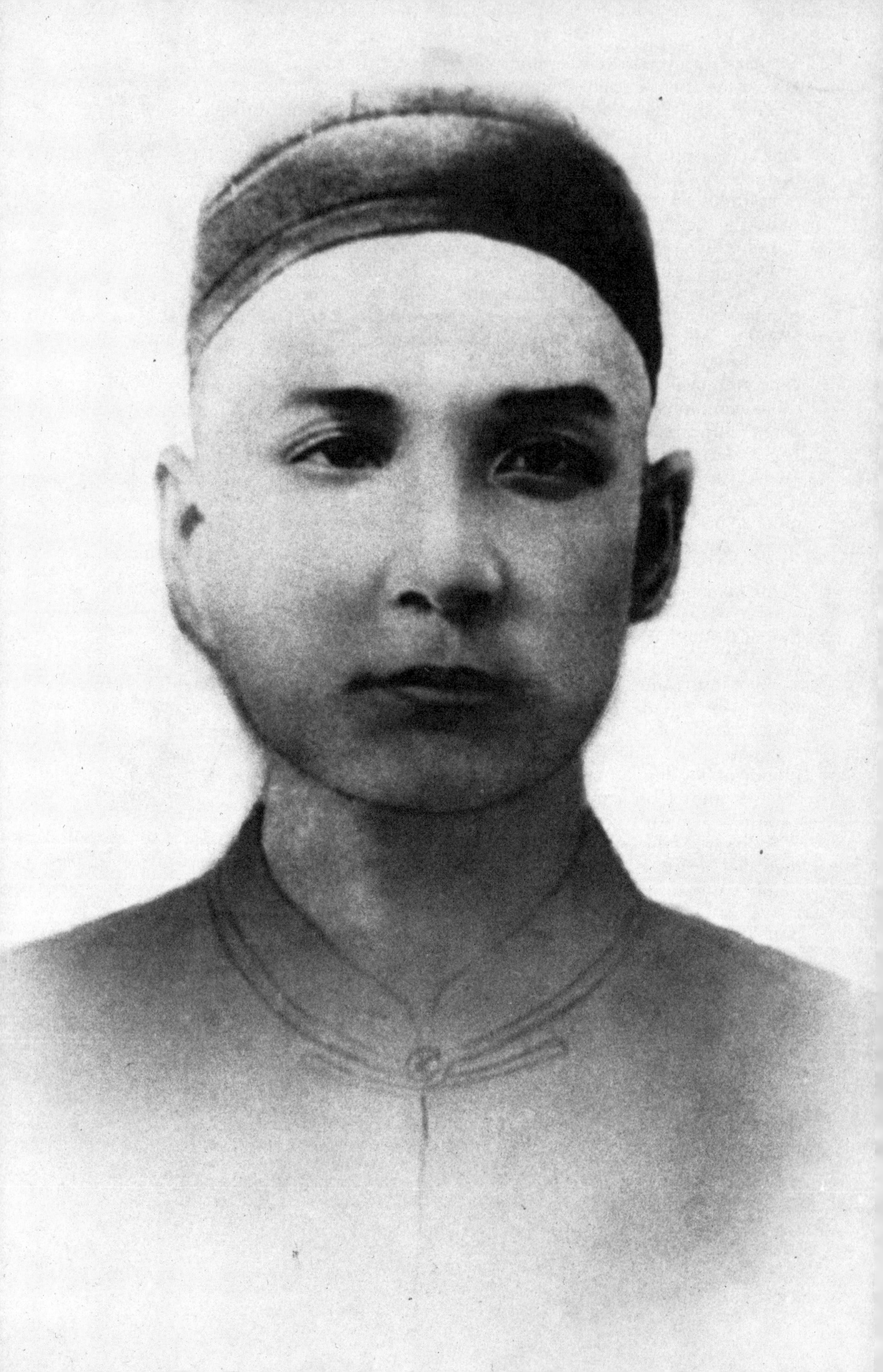

was once charged with having mutilated village idols, he departed for Canton, never to live in the countryside again.

In the years that followed, Sun continued his studies in the British colony, with a brief interlude in Hawaii during which he again strained his relations with his brother by refusing to disavow Christianity (he was now a baptized Christian) and other manifestations of Westernism. Once more, mission schools and missionaries became vital to his development.[2] As the culmination of his education, Sun undertook medical studies, first at the Canton Hospital Medical School, then at the College of Medicine for Chinese in Hong Kong, where he completed his work after five years of study between 1887 and 1892.* During this period he demonstrated an increasing concern over China's internal politics and foreign relations.[3] He engaged in many intense discussions with a small circle of intimates and dispatched reform proposals to two prominent figures known to be sympathetic to change: Zheng Zaoru, who in his long and prestigious career had been minister to both Japan and the United States, and Zheng Guanying, an influential Shanghai compradore. It was symbolic of the politics of this era that because both men were natives of Sun's home district, he had access to them across very diverse socioeconomic lines. Like the call of other reformers of this period, Sun's message was simple yet basic: only if the talents of the Chinese people were cultivated through education could the nation be made strong.[4] He also focused on the need for the advancement of agriculture. But at this point, his concern was with production, not distribution, and with the benefits to be derived from a careful study of European practices.

The results of these initial efforts were not spectacular, although Sun may have influenced Zheng Guanying's later writings pertaining to agricultural improvement. In any case, there is no hard evidence that Sun was already prepared to sacrifice a medical career for the role of full-time political activist. When he finished his training he was unable to practice as a licensed physician in Hong Kong because the College of Medicine for Chinese had not been fully accredited by the colony authorities. He set up practice in nearby Macao, combining Western medicine with a pharmaceutical business that included herbal remedies, but here too he ran into difficulties. Portuguese authorities placed restrictions on his medical practice. Before long he moved to Canton, to pursue identical lines of work.**

At this point Sun resumed his political efforts, in the same vein but on a grander scale. In late 1893 or early 1894 he drafted a letter to be presented to Li Hongzhang; and hoping to see the veteran statesman in person, he closed his medical practice and headed north, stopping first in Shanghai. The choice of Li was not quite as audacious as it might appear at first glance. Sun was well aware that Li was a staunch advocate of modernizing China through

*According to Miyazaki, Sun was enabled to go to the Guangdong medical school because of contributions made by people living in his home district, who regretted that his talents were not being fully utilized. After one year there, he transferred to the new Hong Kong school, just established. Miyazaki, *Sanjūsannen no yume*, p. 108. For this period of Sun's life, see also Luo Xinglin, *Guofu zhi daxue shidai*.

**Luo Jialun, *Guofu nianpu* 1:54–56. Miyazaki reports that at this time Sun joined an organization known as the Chinese Youth Party and became its leader (*Sanjūsannen*, pp. 108–109). No evidence for this is to be found elsewhere.

◂9. *Sun at the age of eighteen, taken in his hometown, Cuiheng, Guangdong, July 1883*

10. During Hong Kong Medical School studies. From left, seated: Yang Heling, Sun Yat-sen, Chen Shaobai, You Lie. Standing: Guan Jingliang

selective Western borrowing. He also knew that Li had brought some young Western-educated Chinese into government service. Moreover, after his wife had been successfully treated by a British medical missionary, Li had expressed special enthusiasm for Western medicine and had agreed to be a patron of the Hong Kong medical college from which Sun had graduated. Some connections thus existed.

When Sun set out on his journey with his childhood friend and fellow villager, Lu Haodong, he first consulted Zheng Guanying, the Shanghai merchant-reformer with whom he had earlier corresponded. Through Zheng he met the famous journalist-politician Wang Tao, another ardent reformer. Wang in turn provided Sun with a letter of introduction to Luo Fenglu, an official working in Li's secretariat in Tianjin. The preparations had been made as fully as conditions permitted, and a long letter outlining Sun's reformist views was sent off, but the personal interview with Li never materialized, possibly because of the imminence of the Sino-Japanese War.[5]

At the age of twenty-seven, Sun was reaching for the top of the power structure, much as Kang and Liang were doing, and at approximately the same time. The fact that Sun, a total outsider to the scholar-gentry class, could make contact with men of political significance, and could secure their aid in reaching the most influential Chinese official then living, is in itself a commentary on many facets of Chinese life: the relatively flexible nature of an extensively personalized, if hierarchical, political system; the primacy accorded birthplace as well as family-clan ties; and the degree to which a higher education of any type placed one within a very small elite. Yet it is equally important to note that a person of Sun's background—both in lineage and in education—could scarcely be accepted as a key political actor, even by the most progressive statesman of this era. Those with the classical training of Kang and Liang could speak the language of the court both literally and figuratively, and therefore had a far better chance of effecting the reforms toward which Sun aimed.

Sun's letter to Li Hongzhang had two primary purposes.* In greater part, it was a skillful appeal for Chinese economic modernization based on the model of the advanced West. But it also contained a personal request for employment under Li's patronage. At the beginning of his epistle, Sun said he had gone abroad at an early age to study Western language and science, and had been quickly impressed by the call for "a rich nation, a strong military," which expressed a governing principle of all "civilized peoples." Then, with an optimism that was to characterize his career, he said that conditions within China were ripe for a rapid thrust toward this objective. The mood of the country, he asserted, called for self-strengthening and better rule. The court, for its part, was currently seeking political stability. Thus, people and rulers could unite in support of measures that would bring China quickly abreast of the West. Already, the introduction of such Western innovations as warships, trains, the telegraph, and postal service—as well as the firearms "which Westerners have used to humiliate us"—had caused China "almost to catch up with Europe."[6]

Nevertheless, Sun continued, the root of Western wealth and power lay not so much in military strength as in the manner in which human and natural resources were cultivated. Western progress had four essential ingredients: the fullest utilization of man's talents; the advance of agricultural production; the maximum exploitation of available natural resources; and the circulation of commerce with minimal restrictions. If China were to recover its lost territories and expand its power, these goals must be pursued.

How were human talents to be developed? Sun's prescription marked him as fully in tune with the policies of the advanced capitalist world: an education tailored to the tasks at hand, followed by suitable rewards so as to encourage maximum productivity. In the West, he noted, experts were created through specialized education and extended practical experience. Civil officials were trained in institutes created for that purpose, and military officers were produced in military academies. Agricultural experts supervised advances in that field, and engineers were put in charge of construction work. China's antiquated educational system, in contrast, made it impossible even for intelligent individuals to be competent: artful words were used to cover up mistakes, and able men remained in the countryside while mediocrities thronged the corridors of power. Sun, it should be noted, placed no premium on equality. People's abilities differ, he asserted, and only through proper training could the wise be advanced and the fools halted. But there must also be adequate recompense. If scholars discover a new theory or in-

* In his *Memoirs* Sun makes no mention of this letter and asserts, "Lu Ko-Tung and I set out for the North, for Peking and Tientsin, in order to study how stable the Tai-Tsing dynasty might be, and thence we left for Wuchang to study the situation there" (p. 187). For the full text, see *Guofu quanji* 5:1–12, and Zou Lu, *Shigao* 1:224–225; for an English translation of key excerpts, see Ssu-yu Teng and John K. Fairbank et al., *China's Response to the West*, pp. 224–227.

vent a new machine, they must be rewarded as they are in the West, where people with ability are encouraged to work hard by being given appropriate incentives.

Sun's emphasis on agriculture was prophetic, signaling an issue that was to be intimately related to China's future revolutionary course. He began with a thumbnail sketch of past policies, suggesting that having reached an elementary solution to the problem of enabling the Chinese people to feed themselves, the rulers had abandoned an interest in agricultural development, with the result that recent progress had been stifled. Much land remained out of cultivation. Water conservation was not being advanced. Scientific agriculture continued to be unknown. As a result, with population increasing, food production had become precarious and natural disasters more threatening.

What was required? Soil science, together with improved seed strains, pest control, disease prevention, and scientific animal husbandry could multiply the productivity of the land several fold. Mechanization could also represent a great advance. Machines to replace oxen and horses, pumps to irrigate thousands of *mou* of paddy fields, harvesting machines to do the work of several hundred people, and mechanized implements that could dig canals and wells—all of these China should borrow from the West, with a department of agriculture to plan and supervise such developments.

Third, the appropriate exploitation of China's natural resources hinged upon a mastery of science, including the basic theories that lay behind scientific phenomena. Once this mastery had been acquired, China could be transformed. Like later reformers and revolutionaries, Sun placed enormous faith in the ability of science and technology to serve as China's national salvation; and he was quick to attack religion in its Chinese forms as the useless worship of ghosts and gods, a web of superstition that hindered the advance of truth.

As for the development of commerce and industry, the critical steps were to remove such internal barriers as the *likin* taxes and to construct a modern communications and transportation system. Beyond this, however, it was equally important for the government to support and encourage indigenous entrepreneurship. Commerce was the key to national wealth and military power, as the West had long since discovered. Thus powerful nations like Great Britain protected their businessmen, even to the extent of seizing overseas territories on their behalf, whereas China exploited commerce and industry and made it impossible to trade freely or to accumulate capital. Why was the United States now rich when it had once been poor? The answer lay in the fact that American society was managed by businessmen, and commerce and transport were protected by the state.

A more forthright defense of capitalism could not have been found. No interest in socialism, or in such concepts as the single tax on land, was in evidence here. And Sun made it clear that it would be necessary for China to enlist the aid of foreign experts if commerce and industry were to advance rapidly—a point that presaged his later position on the need for a broad range of foreign assistance, from whatever quarter.

In his letter there was no discussion of political reform. Had Sun already come to the decision that Western-style democracy was the necessary concomitant of Western-style economic modernization? If so, discretion prevailed. Far from urging a change in the system, Sun asked permission to join it. Praising Li for his many accomplishments, including the recruitment of able men into government service, Sun offered to put himself under the Grand Secretary's tutelage if a position could be found. In outlining his credentials, he pointed out that although he had a knowledge of the Chinese classics, his Western training was the most valuable asset he had to offer. Once again he invoked the rising economic crisis. Given the precarious balance between population and food, another rebellion of the Taiping type could break out unless remedies were urgently pursued. A people had to be fed before they could be taught, so the expansion of agricultural production was a matter of first priority. Yet a serious study of Western agricultural methods had not been undertaken, despite the government's extensive commitment to borrowing from the West.

Sun then related how he himself, coming from a long line of peasants, had sought to advance agriculture in his home district. Examining the soil, he had advised the peasants there to plant pineapples instead of mulberry trees for a cash crop. At the same time, he had suggested that they also grow opium poppies, asserting that as long as British-controlled opium inundated China, no control was possible, but if an indigenous supply were assured and the British monopoly broken, later elimination of the opium trade would be possible. His own experience, Sun continued, indicated that basic agriculture reform would not be difficult. First, agricultural schools should be established. After three years' training, graduates should be sent into the provinces to create an extension program that would provide the peasants with information and assistance. But of course, the experiences and knowledge of old peasants should also be sought. (Shades of Mao!)

Sun ended his letter by stating that he planned to travel to France soon, in order to study sericulture under famous experts, after which he intended to study agricultural developments throughout the world. If the Grand Secretary were interested in improving Chinese agriculture and could help him in carrying out his plans, Sun would be willing to go into the hinterland of China upon his return, to share his knowledge with the peasants.

THE FOUNDING OF THE XINGZHONG HUI

Although he failed to obtain the coveted interview with Li, Sun may have received some funds from Li's elder brother. According to J. C. Huston, an official in Li's secretariat (perhaps Luo Fenglu) reported that Sun did have an interview with Li's brother, during which Sun was offered a monthly stipend of 60 taels and was told to learn to speak Chinese (Mandarin) properly, a slight that infuriated the young reformer.* In any case, Sun now turned his

* Huston apparently had an interview with Luo, although he does not give us the name of his informant—only his office. He reported the individual's recollections as follows: "Some day, said one of the elders of the Kuomintang, they will probably tell you that Dr. Sun's revolutionary inspiration came to him upon the conclusion of his reading a life of George Washington, and that standing upon the brow of a hill back of his native village in the light of the setting sun, he then and there resolved to free China from the clutch of the Manchus and established a Republic. The facts are quite different.

"When I was in charge of the secretariat of Li Hung Chang in Tientsin, Sun Wen, a fellow provincial recently graduated from a Hongkong Medical School, came to me inquiring if it was possible to obtain an official position in the entourage of the Great Statesman. An interview was obtained with Li Hung Chang's elder brother who handled such matters. The old gentleman was unusually gruff with applicants, hoping thereby to strike fear into the heart

full attention to organizational activities. He may have obtained official approval to raise funds to establish an association for the improvement of agriculture. The precise relation between this concession and the beginning of Sun's organizational efforts in Hawaii in the fall of 1894 is not clear. Whatever the situation, during the period between November 1894 and September 1895, Sun succeeded in enlisting 112 members in the Xingzhong Hui (Association for the Regeneration of China). Recruitment was by no means easy, and Sun relied primarily on family acquaintances (he had now reconciled with his brother, who was most helpful) and fellow Cantonese.

Some mysteries still surround the purposes of the Xingzhong Hui. Was it truly an organization dedicated to revolution? Luo Jialun asserts that from its inauguration in Hawaii on November 24, 1894, the Association required each member to swear an oath, with left hand on an open Bible, that he would work to expel the Manchu, revive China, and establish a republican form of government, with God as his witness and retribution to be visited upon the unfaithful. No documentary evidence, however, has yet been found to authenticate such an oath.*

The Xingzhong Hui manifesto that does exist was harsh in its language depicting the current ills afflicting China.[7] China's weaknesses, it asserted, had two sources: at the top, the rulers were unwilling to depart from the status quo and were given to deceiving their subjects; at the bottom, childish ignorance and a lack of farsightedness among the people added to the complications. Thus, the nation had been humiliated, its soldiers defeated, and foreigners were oppressing the land. Prowling like hungry tigers, foreign aggressors were casting greedy eyes on China's minerals and products, grabbing huge pieces of territory. Only contempt was shown for Chinese culture and civilization. The needed response was clear. Taking advantage of its large population and territory, China should arise, making itself invincible before the world. Hence, the purposes of the Xingzhong Hui were to revitalize China, to defend its polity, and to support the foundations of the nation.[8]

Despite this strongly nationalist tone, the published purposes of the Asso-

---

of the neophyte. What is your name? growled the Great One. Sun Wen, replied the future savior of China in the Cantonese dialect. 'Give him sixty taels a month and teach him to speak Chinese!' Sun Wen was disgusted and greatly humiliated by this insult and returned almost immediately to the south, vowing vengeance upon the Manchus." (J. C. Huston, "Sun Yat-sen, the Kuomintang, and the Chinese-Russian Political-Economic Alliance," August 1, 1931, National Archives Microfilm Publications, pp. 4–5. This he called a "voluntary report" written during Huston's service as American consul in Canton.)

*Luo presents the oath as: "I (name), native of (X) *xian* (Y) province, swear to expel the Manchu, revive China and establish a republican government. If I am unfaithful (to these pledges), God will take notice." Given the close association of Sun and others with the Triad Society, it was not unlikely that some such oath was administered, since it was the practice of the secret societies. The inaugural meeting was held at the home of a banker, He Kuan, and several of the initial participants were businessmen. Liu Xiang, a store manager, was elected chairman, and his bookkeeper was appointed treasurer. Luo reports that by issuing "revolutionary army bonds" to yield the owner tenfold renumeration after the successful overthrow of the Manchu, the new organization obtained several hundred dollars, Sun's brother being the leading purchaser. For details on the establishment of the Xingzhong Hui, see Luo Jialun, *Guofu nianpu*, pp. 60–62; Chen Shaobai, *Xingzhong Hui*, pp. 14–17; and Chai Degeng et al., comps. *Xinhai geming* 1:1–250. See also Lin Zhangbing, ed., *Xinhai geming*, pp. 90–95.

ciation were vague enough to permit various interpretations. Presumably, Sun and the inner-core activists saw some advantages in stopping short of publicly proclaiming themselves revolutionaries; certainly that restraint would make it easier for them to operate in the open and recruit new members. There can be no doubt, however, as to their revolutionary intent. The inner group was now convinced that the Manchu must go, even though the future political structure they envisioned for China was not yet clear. At this point, Sun's movement depended heavily on secret society support, and so it may be that the possibility of a Han monarchy was not excluded.[9]

THE FIRST ASSAULT

Sun himself returned to China in early 1895. He met his close friend Chen Shaobai in Canton and then went back with him to Hong Kong, where they established Xingzhong Hui headquarters, camouflaging the organization as a business firm.[10] Plans were now laid for an uprising with its epicenter in Canton. It was scheduled to take place on October 26, the day on which Cantonese returned home to visit their ancestors' graves; the timing would enable a revolutionary force to meld with the crowds. The choice of Guangdong province, and specifically Canton, was natural. Not only were the Xingzhong Hui members and contacts almost wholly Cantonese, but the whole region was teeming with unrest. Indeed, a series of regional uprisings had taken place in Guangdong and neighboring Guangxi in recent times, some involving thousands of dissidents.

These provinces had never been totally reconciled to Qing rule; the legacy of the Taiping hung heavily over them, and they harbored numerous anti-Manchu secret societies. Now, new troubles were brewing for the government. The humiliating military defeat at the hands of the Japanese, climaxed by the signing of the Treaty of Shimonoseki in April 1895, was causing repercussions throughout China, lowering confidence in the Beijing court and stimulating nationalist as well as reformist sentiments. Thousands of demobilized soldiers, most of them unemployed, added to the problems; they were logical candidates for bandit groups, secret societies, and assorted other activities, including revolution, and there were a great many of them in Guangdong. Here also, corruption was a massive problem, capped by the involvement of Li Hanzhang, the governor-general of Guangdong-Guangxi and older brother of Li Hongzhang. If one wanted to build a coalition of secret society and military (or ex-military) elements, the Guangdong region was the ideal site. A privileged sanctuary, moreover, was available in nearby Hong Kong, where organizational and staging operations could be conducted in safety.

The plans, first discussed in March 1895 and completed in August, called for the movement of several thousand Triad Society stalwarts from Hong Kong to Canton by boat on the morning of the attack, followed by swift thrusts directed against various nerve centers of military, police, and governmental power in Canton. It was Sun's belief that if the key sources of power were immobilized, swift disintegration would follow. Guangdong and possibly Guangxi would be quickly rendered independent of Qing rule. He even hoped that a number of provincial officials would affiliate with the new government. It was assumed that once word of the successful Canton uprising spread throughout the countryside, spontaneous uprisings, led by secret societies, military dissidents, and disaffected peasants, would spring up elsewhere.

To camouflage organizational activities in Canton itself, Sun and his colleagues established an Agricultural Association several weeks prior to the scheduled coup, thereby signaling to local authorities his pursuit of the plans outlined in the letter to Li Hongzhang, plans which had been given governmental sanction. In a letter designed to recruit members and dated October 6, 1895, Sun essentially repeated some of the themes of his memorial to Li. Written to conceal any revolutionary intentions, the letter spoke of the need to unite the nation in order to avoid further defeat and humiliation, and concentrated upon explaining the purposes of the new Agricultural Association.*

Various complications of an organizational and policy nature preceded the events of late October. About two weeks before the planned uprising, a dispute over leadership developed, with a key Hong Kong organizer, Yang Chuyun, demanding the presidency of the Xingzhong Hui. After bitter words and a suggestion by one of Sun's supporters that Yang be liquidated, Sun conceded the office, convinced that if the Canton plot succeeded, his leadership would be assured.[11]

Sun, as was his custom, had gathered a very heterogeneous group under his banner. In Guangdong, in addition to the rank-and-file Triad members, a few military men had been recruited. Sun also took maximum advantage of his Christian connections, using a bookstore managed by Wang Zhifu, who served on Sunday as a Christian pastor, as a drop-point.[12] In Hong Kong he enlisted the services of his old teacher He Gai, and several British journalists also became involved. Beginning in the spring of 1895, two journalists writing in the *China Mail* and the *Hongkong Telegraph* publicized their versions of the Association's progress. They portrayed a movement that was reformist in nature, dedicated to continuing the monarchical institution under a Han family, revitalizing the bureaucracy, carrying out widespread agrarian and industrial reforms, and opening China much more widely to Western influence.[13] In reality, these ideas seem to have emanated from He Gai, whose prestige and contacts in Hong Kong were considerable. To what extent they were shared by Sun and others within the organization is diffi-

* For the full text of this letter, see *Guofu quanji* 3:11–13. In it, Sun began in traditional fashion, by asserting that a prosperous country and a happy people required "statesmanship on the part of the emperor and his ministers at the top, and learning on the part of scholars at the bottom." He went on to deplore the misfortunes that had befallen China, and said that these could not be ascribed solely to mistakes of the government. "All scholars, farmers, workers, and merchants [note the order] should confess their own mistakes." In the West, scholars and commoners were loyal to the king and loved their country; they zealously protected the public interest and contributed their skills to the government and public. Moreover, although scholars were put at the head of the four classes in China, in the West, there were various types of scholars. For farmers, there were agricultural associations, for example; for workers, trade associations, for merchants, chambers of commerce. After describing himself as "the son of a farmer, born in the countryside," Sun outlined the purposes of the new Agricultural Association as those of translating various current works on agriculture, establishing a school to train agriculture teachers, prescribing the best crops for various areas, writing special tracts for farmers, and raising capital for rural projects. The letter ended with the request that those interested send their names and addresses to a Christian Center or the Bu Chan bookstore.

cult to say, but it seems clear that both organizational and programmatic vagaries abounded on the eve of the uprising.

The long-planned Canton assault ended miserably, sabotaged by various leaks. The brother of the Xingzhong Hui's only degree-holding member learned of the plot and, fearing the retribution that would be visited upon the entire family, notified Canton authorities. Sun's camouflage almost worked, however. The current governor-general, Tan Zhonglin, at first dismissed the story, regarding Sun as a harmless crank with permission from Beijing to play with agricultural reform through his newly formed society. Meanwhile, however, other complications emerged. Yang, who was responsible for the critical Hong Kong operations, was forced to notify Sun on the morning of the twenty-sixth that "the goods" could not be sent until the next day. The Canton conspirators immediately decided to postpone the entire operation, but before word could be passed to Yang, some four hundred "soldiers" were already en route to Canton.

By now British authorities had also heard about the plot from informers, and they gave a full account to Canton officials. Thus, when the "soldiers" arrived at the Canton docks, they were met by 1,500 garrison troops headed by the district magistrate. Most of the rebels and mercenaries escaped, but several leaders and forty to fifty men were apprehended. Shortly thereafter, a raid on the plotters' Canton headquarters yielded additional prisoners and compromising materials. Sun himself barely escaped by hiding in the home of the Christian minister Wang and then fleeing to Macao.[14]

The Canton uprising bequeathed martyrs to China's revolutionary cause, but it was over before it had begun. Plagued by poor organization and overly optimistic appraisals of the ease with which a revolution could be successfully consummated, this abortive effort was symptomatic of the weaknesses that would repeatedly characterize Sun's ventures in the years ahead. The ideological threads that held the rebel coalition together were extremely thin. Nationalism was a common denominator, but the gap between the traditional nationalists (chiefly secret society members) and the modernizing nationalists (those with higher education and some overseas experience) was a substantial one. Up to this point, moreover, the numerical edge was decidedly in the traditionalists' favor. Very few college students or elements from China's upper classes were involved. Perhaps Sun had good reason to think of himself as a second Hong Xiuquan, as some of his early associates reported.

FAME AND FRUSTRATION

Following the Canton fiasco, Sun and several co-workers went first to Hong Kong, and from there to Japan. According to Chen, the time was spent wholly in reading and strolling.* Within a few days, Sun decided to go

*On arriving in Kobe, the three exiles, Sun, Chen, and Zheng Shiliang, bought a Japanese newspaper and with difficulty made out the gist of an article on "the Chinese revolutionary, Sun Yat-sen." Chen, in his account, then makes the interesting comment that up to *that* point, the conspirators thought that only those who wanted to be emperor could be called revolutionaries, and that *their* action was merely rebellious. But from this time on, the idea of being a *revolutionary* party was implanted in their minds. Chen Shaobai, *Xingzhong Hui*, pp. 22–25.

to the United States. At this point, his physical appearance underwent a major change. He had his hair cut short, Western style, and began to wear Western clothes, probably to convince American consular officials that he had been born in Hawaii, thereby enabling him to get a passport.[15] If this was the purpose, it succeeded, but it is interesting that his new look caused many Asians as well as Westerners to assume that he was Japanese.

Sun was back in Hawaii by January 1896, and he lingered there for six months, rebuilding the Xingzhong Hui and spreading the revolutionary gospel. In mid-1896 he made his way to San Francisco, and for the first time began to seek supporters among the overseas Chinese in America. At many stops between San Francisco and New York, Sun spelled out his political message: overthrow the Manchu and build a new, powerful China. The results were disappointing, and in the fall Sun decided to go to England, fulfilling a promise to visit his old friends the Cantlies (Dr. James Cantlie had been one of Sun's medical school professors in Hong Kong). He reached London on October 1.

It was in London that Sun first acquired international fame, through a bizarre episode that came to be labeled a kidnapping. In the course of his American travels, Sun had been very careless about concealing his identity. As a result, Chinese officials had been able to keep track of him easily. Thus his departure from New York was recorded, and detectives were assigned to shadow him from the moment he arrived in London. Sun, naive in such matters, appears to have been totally oblivious to the fact that his identity was fully known and all his movements watched. The Cantlies had procured a room for Sun, but he was a frequent visitor in their home, which was very close to the Chinese legation. On October 11, according to Sun, while he was en route to visit the Cantlies, a Chinese stranger struck up a friendly conversation with him and enticed him to the doorstep of a building which he presumed was this person's residence; only when he was pulled inside by two other Chinese, and the door was locked behind him, did he discover that he was a prisoner in the Chinese legation.[16]

Sun's confidant, Chen Shaobai, tells a different story. According to Chen, Sun later informed him that he had known exactly where the legation was, but having altered his appearance and name, he had decided to enter the premises and spread the revolutionary word among certain employees, among them Deng Tingjian, the "stranger" noted above, whom Sun had actually talked with on earlier occasions.[17] Chen's account appears to be accurate, and is confirmed in some measure by contemporary British reports. There can be no doubt, however, that Sun was held prisoner and that the Chinese minister intended to ship him secretly back to China as quickly as possible.

After various failures, Sun finally persuaded two British servants inside the legation to inform Cantlie of his plight. The good doctor sprang into action, bringing pressure to bear on a somewhat reluctant British Foreign Office and enlisting the aid of the press. After a series of confrontations and negotiations, Sun was finally released, having become the object of widespread public attention and sympathy. Within a few months his English-language book *Kidnapped in London* was published. Sun was now a celebrity.

During the first half of 1897, Sun remained in England, and according to various accounts he devoted himself to extensive reading and study. It was probably during these months that he came into contact—either directly or

11. Sun with Japanese friends, winter 1897. From the left, seated: Yasunaga Tonosuke, Yang Feiyang, Ping Shanzhou, Mo Yungjie, Uchida Ryōhei. Standing: Ōhara Yoshinori, Koyama Yutaro, Miyazaki Torazō, Sun, Kiyofuji Kōshichiro, Kaji Jōichi

indirectly—with the leading social theorists currently in vogue: John Stuart Mill, Herbert Spencer, Karl Marx and various other socialist writers, and the American iconoclast Henry George. Sun was later to assert that it was from this period that the genesis of his Three People's Principles stemmed.[18] In July he left England, and after a brief stop in Canada he returned to Japan, arriving in Yokohama on August 10, 1897.

For the next three years Sun lived in Japan and acquired a Japanese patina that was to remain with him throughout much of his life. Besides beginning a study of Japanese and taking a new alias that could be easily read in Japanese (Nakayama, Zhongshan in Chinese), Sun developed an intimate acquaintanceship with a group of ardent Japanese Pan-Asian nationalists, typified by Miyazaki Torazō (Tōten), who became one of his closest friends and staunchest supporters.

Miyazaki's comments on his initial meeting with Sun shortly after the young revolutionary returned from the West are revealing.[19] The meeting took place one morning at the Yokohama home of Chen Shaobai, where Sun was staying. Miyazaki's first impressions were somewhat unfavorable: Sun greeted him in his pajamas and had not bothered to brush his teeth or wash his face, thereby offending the Japanese sense of propriety. The thought flashed through Miyazaki's mind: did this man have the dignity necessary to govern a nation?

When Sun began to discourse on politics, however, Miyazaki was quickly converted. Displaying his customary eloquence and optimism, Sun insisted that republicanism had to replace Qing monarchism. Those who argued that such a political system was unsuited to China, asserted Sun, were ignorant of his country's traditions, traditions still preserved in those remote villages least subject to the suppression of the Qing. Above all, China required a sense of patriotism and a commitment to progress, and these qualities the Qing could never summon from the Chinese people. Hence a revolution was essential, but it must be a revolution quickly consummated so that China would not be plunged into protracted struggle of the type that sometimes caused hardships for innocents. This was possible if men of virtue were selected to take charge at the local levels, under the loose control of a popularly elected government at the center. And while he was a man lacking the knowledge and ability to lead the revolution, in the absence of other candidates he had volunteered to commit himself to the revolutionary cause, counting heavily on friends like Miyazaki for assistance.

Perhaps Miyazaki's most prescient remarks are contained in his analysis of Sun's charismatic qualities. Clearly, Sun mesmerized his Japanese guest. Said Miyazaki: his every word carried reason, and while he burned with a deep passion, he spoke in simple, unaffected terms. His character shone forth as a combination of rapturous music and the spirit of revolution. His personality and his words contained the power to make those who had not understood become believers. But Miyazaki also added that when he had finished with serious matters he dropped his sober mien and became like a naive country girl—as if he did not have a serious thought in his mind.

Through Miyazaki and other members of the Genyōsha (Black Ocean Society), Sun met some of the most prominent Japanese political figures of this era, including Ōkuma Shigenobu, Inukai Tsuyoshi, and Ozaki Yukio. Not all were fully sympathetic to his cause; but from some, like Inukai, a continuing interest unfolded, a development we shall examine more closely later.

Sun reciprocated. Disillusioned with the British government's refusal to let him enter Hong Kong, and disappointed over the limited support given him in the West, even from the overseas Chinese communities, Sun exhibited a powerful antagonism toward Western imperialism, as well as a warm receptivity to the idea of collaboration with Japan in the building of a new China (and a new Asia), which was extremely gratifying to his hosts. As we have seen, this position was not unique to Sun. In their initial sojourn to Japan, after the One Hundred Days fiasco, Kang and especially Liang had expressed similar sentiments. It was perhaps more striking in the case of Sun, however, because he had so recently espoused close collaboration with the West. Flexibility with respect to allies, both domestic and foreign, was to be one of the hallmarks of his long political career.

Sun's new political tack was to lead him and his Japanese friends into an ill-fated venture to aid Emilio Aguinaldo's Filipino nationalists in their resistance to American control. Their efforts to furnish the Filipino rebels with military equipment proved abortive: a first ship carrying supplies was sunk in a storm, and a second ship, scheduled to leave in early 1900, was blocked by Japanese authorities at the demand of the Americans.[20] It was nevertheless a dramatic illustration of the Pan-Asian idealism that currently united Chinese and Japanese radicals, an idealism that found its fulfillment—and its destruction—in the events of the 1930s and 1940s.

Meanwhile, the arrival of Kang and Liang in Japan had resulted in the

12. *Sun and Japanese friends, May 1899. From left to right, first row: Miyakawa Goro, Yasunaga Tonosuke; second row: Nakano Kumagoro, Sun, Uchida Ryōhei, Sakada Rinjiro; third row: Harada Bunichi, Inoue Masaji, Miyazaki Tōten, Hiraoka Kōtaro, Kiyofuji Kōshichiro*

initiation of overtures from Sun for cooperation. As we have said, these overtures came to nought despite some encouraging signs at certain points. In the end, greater estrangement and bitterness prevailed. And in this period the Kang-Liang forces were the more influential, both in overseas Chinese circles and among the small but growing body of Chinese students studying in Japan. Sun's Xingzhong Hui did not even have a newspaper until Chen Shaobai began publishing the *Zhongguo ribao* (China Daily) in Hong Kong in late 1899; this paper, moreover, had a limited circulation and slight impact.

The one promising activity undertaken by Xingzhong Hui adherents related to the cultivation of the two most powerful secret societies of South China, the Gelao Hui (Society of Brothers and Elders) and the Triad Society. With Chen playing a key role, the leaders of the two societies had agreed in late 1899 to join the Xingzhong Hui in an anti-Manchu alliance called the XingHan Hui (Association to Revive the Han), led by Sun Yat-sen.[21]

Despite the potential power of this alliance, Sun's movement was still mired in a paradox. On the one hand, its natural base of support was rural and traditionalist, rooted in the primitive nationalism of the secret societies and in the peasant unrest provoked by socioeconomic and political conditions, including foreign intrusion. (This base, it should be noted, was more potential than real, since large-scale rural mobilization was not on Sun's agenda and quite beyond the capacities of his organization.) On the other hand, Sun's goal of regaining national power for China through economic, political, and social modernization could appeal only to the educated elite and foreign supporters. Thus, although some of the secret society leaders expressed interest in Sun's "new ideas," the intellectual-political gap between the two groups remained extraordinarily wide.

It was also paradoxical that Sun should try to appeal to intellectuals, because he never really trusted the mainstream Chinese intelligentsia—and the suspicion was mutual. Most Chinese intellectuals of this era came from a gentry background; they had steeped themselves in the Chinese classics and retained some of the traditional prejudices of the long-gowned scholar toward manual labor and the lower classes, however radical they might have become from the neck up. In this respect among others, Sun and his movement resembled Mao and his movement of several decades later.

Events in connection with the Boxer Rebellion provide additional insights into Sun's place in Chinese politics. At first it seemed that the empress dowager had succeeded in harnessing a portion of the rural masses to her cause, co-opting Sun's potential base of support. Yet when the defeat of the Boxers began to seem inevitable, monarchical change became a topic of discussion even within the highest political circles. As we have seen, Kang and Liang hoped that the foreign powers would restore the emperor to the throne. But there were others who felt it more likely that all Manchu would be set aside in favor of a Han ruler. Thus, in mid-1900, when the storm clouds over China were very dark, Sun received a letter from Liu Xuexun, a Cantonese official working under Li Hongzhang, who had given Sun some support before the 1895 Canton uprising. It said that Li, now governor-general of Guangdong-Guangxi, was considering the possibility of declaring China's two southern provinces independent and wanted Sun's support, and that Sun ought to come to Canton for discussions. Sun decided to accept his offer, but being suspicious, he elected to send three Japanese associates, including Miyazaki Torazō, to meet with Liu first. After the three reached Liu's quarters, a long but indecisive discussion took place. On the very next day Li was called to Beijing by the throne. Whatever Li's earlier intentions, he now decided to put the matter of southern separation in abeyance, and in conversation with Hong Kong authorities while en route to Shanghai, he expressed no sympathy for Sun or his revolutionary movement.*

Collaboration with Li Hongzhang thus proved impossible, and since he could not land in Hong Kong, Sun sailed first to Saigon and then to Singapore, where he met with Kang Youwei in another attempt to discuss coop-

*Schiffrin, *Origins*, pp. 202–204. For a slightly different account, see Miyazaki, *Sanjūsannen*, pp. 201–202. He records that Sun summoned him one morning when he was staying aboard Sun's ship off Hong Kong and reported that a friend (Liu?) had told him of a secret conversation with the governor of Hong Kong, Sir Henry Blake. Blake wanted Li to declare Guangdong and Guangxi provinces independent, and would privately support Sun as chief administrator, working with Li. The friend had further reported that Li had agreed, but then had been ordered North. However, Blake, believing that Li might still be persuaded to remain in Canton, was proposing a secret meeting between Sun and Li. Miyazaki then added that before any such meeting could take place, word came that Li had firmly decided to go to Beijing. (One may doubt that the British governor was as fully committed to this plot as Miyazaki's account suggests, but Schiffrin uses British Foreign Office sources to document Blake's willingness to play a role in bringing Li and Sun together.) In any case, there was no meeting, and Governor-General Li soon proceeded north (a step at a time) in response to a summons.

13. *Sun at age thirty-four, Yokohama, 1899*

eration, but their talks collapsed.* Shortly thereafter, in late August, the Hankou uprising supported by the Kang-Liang reformers failed, amid mutual recriminations among those centrally involved.

It was now Sun's turn to challenge Beijing. Selecting Huizhou (Wai-

*Three of Sun's Japanese collaborators, including Miyazaki, had reached Singapore before he did and had tried to reach Kang. But in response to a rapidly spreading rumor that their real mission was to assassinate Kang, the Singapore police arrested Miyazaki and his colleague Kiyofuji Kōshichiro (Uchida Ryōhei had already departed). They were released shortly thereafter, but banned from the colony for five years. Miyazaki, *Sanjūsannen*, 232ff.

chow) prefecture in eastern Guangdong as his initial target, Sun authorized the mobilization of a small army, spearheaded by Triads and Christians. Fighting broke out in October after Guangdong authorities, alerted to the rebellion, began to mobilize against it. At first, the rebels—with substantial support from the peasantry of the region—did well. In the end, however, they were overwhelmed. Sun was in Taiwan and was unable to send them promised supplies. When he requested that the arms originally intended for the second effort on behalf of the Filipino nationalists be sent from Japan, it was discovered that certain Japanese had defrauded the revolutionaries. The arms purchased were largely unusable. A sizable amount of the money advanced, moreover, had been embezzled. Naturally, the revolutionaries were reluctant to go to the authorities, yet court action was threatened before a settlement was finally reached. By that time the Huizhou uprising was history.[22]

Sun returned to Japan, remaining there until the end of 1902 except for a brief visit to Hong Kong. He became acquainted with a young Japanese girl (by whom he later had a daughter) and lived in Yokohama with the traditional overseas Chinese community.* His contacts with the expanding Chinese student population of Tokyo appear to have been very limited. In December 1902 he embarked on another journey to raise money among the overseas Chinese, focusing this time on southeast Asia. He spent six months in Hanoi, and his emissaries canvassed other centers of Chinese population, such as Malaya. This venture met with limited success, but some useful contacts were made.

In mid-1903 Sun returned to Japan and was shattered to find that the Xingzhong Hui was little more than a memory. He made new student contacts and wrote his first article for a student journal, a sharply anti-Manchu piece playing on themes that were currently exciting the students. He also decided to organize a military academy. Each cadet would be required to take an oath pledging support to the Xingzhong Hui's three objectives—the overthrow of the Manchu, the restoration of China to the Han, and the creation of a republic—plus a new fourth goal, "the equalization of land rights."[23] Within a month after launching this venture, however, Sun had once again set sail across the Pacific to solicit support in the West. His academy fell victim to internal dissension and soon collapsed.

Sun was not to return to Japan until the middle of 1905, and the months immediately following this latest departure must have been discouraging. He left behind him in Japan neither a significant band of supporters nor an effective organization. After nearly a decade of political activism filled with hardship, peril, and crushed hopes, he had no funds and no institutional base. Wherever he went he found only ruins and remnants of the political

* Further details regarding Sun's private life during this period are now available as a result of the research of Professor Kubota Bunji of the Kobe Women's College. In 1899, Sun first became acquainted with a very young girl, Otsuki Kaoru, then living above his first-floor residence in Yokohama. Later, in 1904, when Kaoru was fifteen, a "simple marriage ceremony" reportedly was held. Sun was frequently overseas, but he wrote letters to his lover and during the summer of 1906, when he was again in Japan, Kaoru became pregnant. Their daughter, Fumiko, was adopted by another family at birth, and did not know her natural parents until much later. Otsuki Kaoru died at the age of 82, in December 1970, but after their months together in 1906, she never saw Sun again. This report has been carried in various sources, among them the *New Canadian*, a Japanese newspaper published in Toronto, September 28, 1984. We are indebted to Professor Jerome Ch'en for locating the item for us.

14. *Sun and family, Hawaii, 1903, from left. Back row: niece, brother's wife (Tan), brother's adopted son (Sun Wei), brother (Sun Dezhang), Sun, Sun's wife (Lu Muzhen), niece, servant; middle row: Sun's son (Sun Ke), mother (née Yang), daughter (Jinyan); front: daughter (Jinwan)*

structures he had so laboriously built years earlier. Without his charismatic presence, the Xingzhong Hui had evaporated. His political coalitions had been built of elements too disparate to maintain or even achieve the necessary degree of cohesion. And although some elements, like the secret societies, had deep roots in China's past and present, Sun's movement rested fundamentally on overseas bases. Could such a movement ever penetrate China sufficiently to capture power? It was possible—but only if events enfeebled the Beijing court beyond repair, and a generation of rebels that looked to the future became active. At the moment, Sun himself could be considered peripheral to the real China, a quasi-foreigner seeking to replace other quasi-foreigners, like the Manchu, or true foreigners, like the Western and Japanese intruders he had alternately praised and condemned.

While Sun was once again seeking support in Hawaii and on the American mainland, the Chinese student movement was beginning to catch fire in Japan. And since this movement was soon to be Sun's greatest source of support—and a continuous influence on the modern Chinese revolution—we must now explore in some detail the activities and writings of Chinese students in Japan.

THE STUDENT RADICALS

After 1900 the number of Chinese students coming to Japan steadily increased; by 1906 there were between ten and thirteen thousand of them.

Even when the student population was still in the hundreds, student-edited journals had begun to appear, and these were strongly political in nature. The first was probably *Guomin bao* (The Nationals' News), which appeared in mid-1901 and was edited by Qin Lishan, a Hunanese who had been a member of the Kang-Liang group but had become estranged from it after blaming Kang for the failure of the abortive 1900 Hankou revolt. Bitterly disappointed by this event, Qin took a more radical political stance, calling for the revolutionary overthrow of the Manchu.[24]

Although *Guomin bao* survived for only four issues, a host of other journals made their appearance between 1903 and 1906, most of them organs of the provincial student associations then being organized. Few of these journals lasted very long, and publication dates were irregular, as befitted the ever-shifting nature of the student population.[25] Yet taken together they constituted a new and generally more radical wave that challenged the themes now prevailing in Liang's *Xinmin congbao*. These student writers owed Liang and his pioneer group a considerable intellectual debt. Some, indeed, had initially been Liang followers. But a split between reformers and revolutionaries was beginning to emerge.

Down to 1905, the main stimulus for student radicalism came from events transpiring in China and throughout the world, funneled through the Japanese environment. Sun Yat-sen, having focused his efforts elsewhere, was not yet a significant influence. In fact, the students knew little about him, except for certain generally unflattering rumors: some said he was more barbarian than Chinese, and it was doubted whether he could even write in the Chinese language.* Thus, one finds scant reference to Sun or his movement in the early student journals.

Often without realizing it, however, the radical students were moving toward Sun politically. Before we examine their essays, a few further words about the students themselves are warranted.[26] Three types of Chinese students came to Japan: those sponsored by the central government; those provided with funds by their province; and those coming with private support, family or otherwise. The second category was the largest, and provincial identification was still very strong despite the rising nationalist movement. A significant number of students were attending military schools.

Few Chinese students were able to secure admission to the most prominent Japanese institutions of higher learning—Tokyo Imperial University, Kyoto, Waseda, or Keio. The great majority were in other institutions, including schools or programs designed specifically for Chinese. "Short courses" were offered, whereby a group of Chinese students with an interpreter received instruction in concentrated form in the Japanese language, with translation provided. There were many complaints about the quality of education, and also about discrimination at the hands of certain Japanese. Adjustment was usually difficult despite the cultural ties that existed.

For the most part, these students came from the upper and middle socioeconomic sectors of Chinese society, since only these elements could achieve

*Over fifty years later, one of Liang's faithful supporters and a student of this period who was destined to have a long and illustrious career, Carsun Chang (Zhang Junmai), reaffirmed this tendency. "Sun's key support among the Chinese students in Japan," he asserted, "came from the military students and similar types. He had limited appeal to the more serious intellectuals." (Robert A. Scalapino interview with Carsun Chang, March 2, 1957, San Francisco, California.)

the necessary educational preparation for overseas schooling. Many were the children of prominent local figures, or had some connection with such men. Any rebellion from them would thus strike close to the heart of the system.

Though every province was eventually represented, the largest number of students came from Guangdong, Hunan, Hubei, Jiangsu, Zhejiang, and Shanghai. The political and military cadres of the next generation were thus from the Yangtze valley—especially the coastal regions around Shanghai—and from the South, regions destined to dominate the political fortunes of the revolutionary movement in the decades that lay ahead.

As one leafs through the student essays of these years, one is reminded of the young age of the authors. Most were between twenty and twenty-four; a few were still teen-agers. The youthfulness shows through, in thought, style, and mood. Passion was more conspicuous than elegance or sophistication, and in many of the essays there was an interesting interplay of pessimism and hope, as in the early reformer writings. The primary source of pessimism lay, quite naturally, in the objective conditions in which China found herself: "enslavement" by the Manchu and threatened division at the hands of various Western powers and Japan; "backwardness" in every field of life and in every segment of Chinese society; and perhaps most depressing of all, the colossal indifference of the Chinese people to their fate.*

The central problem was frequently defined as essentially a moral one, and like Liang Qichao earlier, the students were drawn to the question of how to reshape the basic character of Chinese man. Possessed in the past of a great civilization, wrote one author, the Chinese people had become morally bankrupt. Now they were characterized by lethargy, a profound ignorance of the world in which they lived, and a totally self-centered attitude devoid of any sense of patriotism or public spirit. How many Chinese understood or even cared about the threat that China as a nation might become extinct in the struggle for survival? How many were prepared to make personal sacrifices for the sake of the whole society? How many had any feeling of respect for themselves, and hence any basis from which to resist enslavement at the hands of others?[27]

Brooding over such problems could sometimes lead to despair and bitterness. China is dying, proclaimed more than one young writer, and perhaps nothing can save her. Even the less pessimistic authors agreed that immediate action was necessary. The ring of urgency sounded in almost every philippic: it was the last moment to avoid destruction; there would be no more chances.[28]

But the writings that sounded an apocalyptic note usually contained a contrapuntal theme, hope for salvation: despite their present woes, there was no intrinsic reason why the Chinese people could not move from weakness to power in a very short time. They had once proven capable of developing one of the greatest civilizations known to man. Their territory was vast and

* See, for example, "The Slaughter of Fellow Countrymen," *Fu bao* (Revival News), September 25, 1906, pp. 1–8. The author opens with the words "The country is extinct; the people are enslaved." As he warms to his subject he decries the lack of initiative among the students, the lack of patriotism among the rich, and the lack of national consciousness among any of the Han. The Han are merely lower-class animals for whom no one has respect: if they are not killed by others, they will be eliminated naturally through the process of evolution, because only the strong survive in the twentieth century.

rich. Their numbers were much greater than those of any other people. With these assets, China could become a major power once her people were awakened.[29]

This basic theme, with many variations, was often advanced in sharply racial terms, following the model set in certain *Xinmin congbao* essays, with Social Darwinism underwriting such themes. The truly meaningful contest was between the white and yellow races, and among the yellow peoples the Chinese were by far superior in terms of accomplishments. It remained only to mobilize Chinese talents, to produce a national spirit so that the people could unite, and then all foreigners could be ousted and the Chinese could take over their own destiny.[30] Sometimes, as in the case of the *Xinmin congbao* writings, racial concepts were presented in more classic form—the civilized versus the barbarian—and it was acknowledged ruefully that the white race had attained a high level of civilization in recent times, largely because Western people enjoyed freedom and government under law, which enabled them to contribute to the strength of the nation and to rapid economic progress.[31] The Anglo-Saxons were dominant in the world, and a threat to China, because they governed themselves as free men.

Up to this point, there is little to distinguish the radical students from Liang and his supporters. Their themes, and even their language, were nearly interchangeable, although the decibel level was generally higher in student publications. When the radicals turned to concrete remedies, however, they invariably began by insisting that the Manchu dynasty must be overthrown in the course of a great nationalist revolution. There could be no meaning to Manchu constitutionalism, they insisted, because the Han would continue to be humiliated and enslaved by an alien, barbarian race.[32] When various young writers talked of revolution, their current frustrations seemed to be released in a flow of heroic, grandiose, and uncompromising language: the old order was totally corrupt, completely decadent. It had to be torn out by the roots, with no part left intact. One should not fear such destruction, because only when the old order had vanished could a new civilization be built—witness the enormous destruction of the French Revolution, and the resulting new era for all mankind. Conditions in China could be changed only by a war in which rivers of blood would flow. Such righteous bloodshed was the sacrifice necessary to enable subsequent generations of Chinese to be free.[33] Bold words, these—and given the emotional currents of the time, difficult if not impossible for the constitutional monarchists to counter. No doubt, some students became revolutionaries after a process of genuine soul-searching and reflection, considering alternatives and using their intellectual faculties in reaching their decision. For many, however, the espousal of revolution was a tempting means of securing emotional release. To students who were discouraged and impatient, the commitment to revolution represented a concrete, dramatic personal act through which they could dedicate themselves to a cause wholeheartedly, unselfishly, and with finality. It did not involve them in any of the intricate compromises and potential corruption that accompanied reform efforts. It was a heroic, simplistic commitment in tune with the psychological pressures of the time.

Thus *every* action of the Beijing government increased student wrath. When Beijing displayed a coolness toward the idea of organizing a student armed force in Japan to resist Russian encroachments in Manchuria, or when it became alarmed by increasing revolutionary activities and placed informers in their midst, the students naturally responded with outcries of rage and protest.[34] But the youthful radicals did not take kindly to the belated reform efforts either: these efforts, including the pledge of constitutionalism, represented a trap, they argued, an attempt to poison the minds of the Han so that they would be deflected from the revolutionary path.[35] Suppression or timid indecision, the resolution to stand firm or gestures of accommodation—whatever the mood and actions of the government, the radical student tide was not to be slowed.

Having opted for revolution, what tactics did the radicals regard as best suited for success? The influence of the Russian nihilists and the theories of anarchism were now being felt in Chinese radical circles, largely through Japanese currents. Just as the French Revolution represented to the young Chinese revolutionaries of this era the great historical model of a righteous and meaningful revolution, so the contemporary acts of the Russian revolutionaries suggested to many writers a pattern to emulate. Indeed, the equation of Russia and China, in terms of both problem and solution, was a common exercise: here were two twentieth-century dinosaurs still lumbering about in the swamps of absolutism and backwardness. Only revolution could end this anachronism. One method of striking at the decadent state was to commit a few "heroic acts." Assassination, like a clap of thunder, could arouse a whole people, and provided it reached close to the heart of the system, it might set in motion a series of reactions that would lead to massive upheaval.[36]

As we shall see, these were not idle words, an exercise in bravado. A number of youth were prepared to give their lives in emulation of the Russian terrorists. Other writers, however, saw that a modern revolution, if it were to be successful and lasting, might require methodical planning and an organization. Certainly, one immediate task was to raise both the status and the political consciousness of the military. For too long, China had depreciated the vital role of military men in defending the Chinese people at critical junctures in their history. Military heroes of the past had been deliberately obscured. It was now essential to bring them into the limelight so that the people could know the truth about the past and sense the needs of the times. The first requirement of a modern state was power, and this required a broadly based, politically aware, modern army. It required youth that were physically fit, not white-faced, short-of-breath scholars. It also required certain heroes, among whom should be the great Chinese warriors of the past and the student-warriors of the present.[37]

And after the revolution, what? On one basic theme, reformers and revolutionaries agreed. A dramatically different educational program, national in scope and aimed at the creation of a new citizenry, was essential. Some were prepared to argue that the presence or absence of such a system would be the determining factor in national survival or destruction. The fall of such nations as India, Egypt, and Poland could be traced to the backwardness or failure of their educational systems, whereas the power of the United States, Great Britain, and Japan was a testimony to the effectiveness of their educational policies.[38] The purposes of the new education should be to cultivate patriotism; to instill a new set of values based on rationality and science; to train large numbers of technicians and professionals; and to eradicate illiteracy.[39]

The writings of these youthful revolutionaries remind us once again that this was an age of enormous faith in the potentialities of the educated man, and an era in which thinking about political and social development was relatively simple and uncomplicated. The basic beliefs of many Chinese radicals were little different from those of their more mature Western contemporaries. Indeed, it was from these sources, at least indirectly, that they drew their ideas.

Apart from education, there were specific political issues to be faced. Toward what type of polity should China aim? How should individual, nation, and world be fitted together? On these and similar questions, the young revolutionaries dealt with issues we now call those of political modernization. Applying the criteria set forth at the outset of this work, one can define political modernization in the twentieth century as involving six interrelated trends: the rise of the nation-state as the primary focus of political loyalty; increased centralization of political power and a reduction of local authority, both public and private; the establishment of a government under law, capped by some type of constitutional system, and the creation thereby of equal rights under the law; the movement from an ascriptive, undifferentiated officialdom toward a technically trained, scientifically selected, specialized bureaucracy; the shift from legitimation of authority by religious or supernatural claims to legitimation by a secular ideology; and finally, the rise of mass participation in politics, with a corresponding emphasis on political organization and manipulation.

Naturally, the young Chinese rebels studying in Japan during the first decade of this century did not use our terminology, nor did they think precisely along the lines of our categories. It is striking, nevertheless, to note how closely these trends mesh with their emerging values and political goals. The first desideratum, that of nation-building, was clearly regarded as of first importance by the student writers. "Why do the foreigners treat us like dogs?" queried one author. The answer was that the Chinese people had no sense of patriotism, no willingness to sacrifice for the whole of the society, no feeling of identity as members of a single nation.[40] "We Chinese are dead," mourned another writer, "because we have no state to give our lives purpose and meaning, protection and consequence."[41]

The Chinese authors of this period—both reformers and revolutionaries—borrowed two terms from the Japanese to express the concept of nationalism. One, the term *minzuzhuyi* (Japanese, *minzokushugi*), translates literally as "racism," although to soften the opprobrium of that English word one might use the phrase "the principle of common race." Although it is a term with strong racial connotations, it was often used when the context makes it clear that the writer intended it to stand for "nationalism." The other term, *minguozhuyi* (Japanese *minkokushugi*), was at this time the standard word for nationalism, although later on the term generally used was *guojiazhuyi* (Japanese *kokkashugi*), a set of characters that omits the individual or human element in favor of the state alone. In any case, the insistence that the new China must be a Han China was well-nigh universal among student writers, who thereby infused nationalism with strong racial connotations.

Did nation-building for these students involve more than an anti-Manchu revolution followed by a broadly gauged educational program that would stress patriotism and a new civic morality? Certainly these were the two themes that received the greatest attention and emphasis. A number of writers, however, advanced other specific measures. Many felt that the first task was to break down certain old patterns of behavior and loyalty that stood as formidable barriers to the development of a modern nation-state. To a few, the chief obstacle to be frontally assaulted was the Chinese family system.[42] Perhaps these were the true avant-garde, considering the repeated attacks on this venerable and enormously powerful institution that were to follow, culminating with the Communists.

Others saw intense local and regional ties as the primary barriers to true nationalism. How could China become powerful if people refused to look beyond their own locality or province? Was it not more important to be *Chinese* than to be Hunanese or Sichuanese? These concerns, moreover, could be extended to Chinese attitudes toward the larger world, focusing on the requirements of international acceptance in the twentieth century. Thus the "isolationist, self-contented" mentality of the Chinese was attacked. It was stressed that the Chinese needed to learn to deal openly and extensively with other peoples on the basis of equality and independence, abandoning the hierarchical, Sinocentric concept of the world that had nurtured Chinese backwardness.[43] The successful creation of a Chinese nation, in sum, was inextricably connected with basic changes in mental outlook and in interpersonal-intergroup relations, ranging from new priorities for loyalty at home to a radically new approach to international relations.

Coupled with these changes, a number of students argued, basic alterations in the traditional class structure would be required. The old China had been completely dominated by the literati. Their ways and their prejudices had determined the values and the institutions of the entire society.[44] Not only had they protected a formalistic and sterile educational system; they had also exhibited contempt for military men and the entrepreneurial class. But the creation of a modern state was intimately related to the elevation of these two classes. China needed a powerful army based on universal conscription, modernized in terms of equipment and training, and strengthened in morale.[45] Similarly, it was essential to encourage the development of a spirited entrepreneurial class and to provide it with new incentives, including a new status in society.[46] A modern military establishment and modern industry were the two key pillars of a modern state.

Though these positions were not made explicit by a large number of writers, they were expressed with sufficient frequency (particularly the importance of the military) to indicate that many students were committed to a social revolution of major proportions, recognizing that the nation-building process, if it were to be successful, required drastic changes in traditional Chinese class and social relations. Only those who performed vital functions on behalf of the modern state should be recognized and rewarded. Parasites—whether traditional literati or traditional gentry—should reap neither honor nor profit (hence the initial appeal of the single-tax scheme). Certain specific economic tasks, moreover, related directly to nation-building. It was essential, for example, that railroads and other means of internal communications be developed. A sense of national identity, as well as a capacity for national action, could be achieved only when the physical barriers to contact had been removed.[47]

With respect to our second attribute of political modernization, the centralization of political power and the reduction of local authority, the students displayed a certain ambivalence. We have noted that some of them called for the abandonment of provincialism, and yet the identification with one's "homeland" often remained provincial in nature. Thus, the opening appeal in the Yunnanese journal—one of the last student organs to be created—was for Yunnanese to save Yunnan, and this was not untypical.[48] Apart from the deeply implanted localist or provincial legacy, practical considerations abetted support for an approach to nationalism that was incremental and complex. China was a vast area, greater in size and population than the whole of Europe. A strong case could be made for an initial emphasis on local self-rule as the first step in the development of national democracy. As in discussions over revolutionary tactics, to which we shall come later, one could argue that it was at the local level that the required organizational and institutional resources could be mobilized most quickly and easily, and it was here that coordinated action was most feasible.[49] The very disparate nature of the separate provincial units comprising China made an undifferentiated national approach to political change seem formidable, if not hopelessly unrealistic. The ultimate product of the revolutionary process, moreover, might well be a federal rather than a unitary political system in terms of the national polity.

It would be wrong to assume that there was any uniformity of opinion on these vital matters. A significant division was unfolding between advocates of "instant democracy" and believers in "developmental democracy." The former tended to emphasize a one-stage thrust toward modernization involving actions at the national level, uniform policies, and—by implication at least—a high degree of centralized authority. The latter stressed the importance of initiating programs of self-rule at the local and provincial levels, thereby building the foundations of a more meaningful national structure by revitalizing and strengthening political relations at the grass roots. This division, of course, was not as clearly understood as our brief statement of it might suggest. But it did exist, and it symbolized a very understandable indecision about how to approach the task of integrating a society as dispersed, and in some respects as heterogeneous, as that of China. It was a dilemma that would plague each successive wave of would-be reformers, including the Communists.

Regarding our third attribute of "modernization," government under law, legitimized by a constitution, there was little disagreement. Constitutionalism was one of the positions that commanded almost universal support. A large number of student writers attributed the weakness and backwardness of China to the inadequacies of government by absolutist decree or personal whim. They insisted that only modernized legal codes, both civil and criminal, as well as a constitution that fixed the rights and obligations of every citizen on a basis of complete equality before the law, could bring China abreast of civilized states and win it the respect of the advanced world. This was the route to ridding the nation of the iniquities of extraterritoriality, as the Japanese experience had shown. Indeed, Japanese legalism in all its aspects had a deep influence on the Chinese student writers of this period, whatever their political persuasion.[50]

In retrospect, one can discern a basic problem that the students were not likely to appreciate. In emerging societies, law (and especially constitutional law) seeks not only to fix but also to idealize rules and institutions in a period of rapid socioeconomic change. If its operational premises are too far divorced from existing realities, the new law is likely to be little more than a scrap of paper—futuristic possibly, but inoperative for the present. On the other hand, if the premises are even with or only slightly ahead of the socio-political capacities of the society, these capacities are likely to overtake the law quickly, with increasing tension developing as a result. Such a growing gap between polity and society has produced many twentieth-century upheavals.

Modern China was not to avoid the hazards of grafting constitutionalism onto an emerging society. Chinese constitutions have come and gone, generally with little permanent effect on political behavior or institutions. As the twentieth century opened, however, faith in law was at a high point among the Chinese intellectual vanguard.

On the other hand, the student writers of this period devoted limited attention to the fourth element of "modernization," namely, the recruitment, training, and values of a new bureaucracy.[51] A few general principles were usually invoked, to be sure. For example, officials in the new China should be the servants, not the masters, of the people. Occasionally, the need for technical training and selection through a civil service system was mentioned, and the old Confucian education was frequently attacked as formalistic and sterile.

Yet in this realm the students displayed hesitation, which reflected their own antecedents and the contemporary influences playing on them. Most of these students, it must be remembered, came from the upper socio-economic strata of Chinese society and were themselves the products of an early classical education. Technical or specialized training was not within their personal experience, the military students constituting an important exception. Japanese practices, moreover, offered mixed guidance. Though science and technology were being rapidly advanced, the branches of higher education that specialized in the training of officials were general rather than technical in nature, albeit extensively legalistic, and on the whole conservative. Like the British, the Japanese considered officialdom the preserve of the educated gentleman, the individuals drawn from the best schools and often the best families as well; such men were not required to undergo specialized training, for it was assumed that they could acquire any necessary expertise in connection with their specific assignments. Given their own backgrounds, the current practices to which they were witness, and the nature of their society, the Chinese students at this point were understandably more interested in encouraging a spirit of noblesse oblige toward government service than in promoting the cultivation of bureaucratic technicians.

The next element of modernization, the commitment to a secular ideology, posed no serious problem for the young Chinese revolutionaries, despite the fact that they were in a position to witness in Japan a prominent exception to the general rule: the effective use of a highly primitive religious myth for purposes of nation-building and the legitimization of authority. Their cultural heritage was different. The essentially secular character of Confucianism combined with certain unique aspects in the evolution of Chinese society to make it relatively easy for the students to dismiss religion as an appropriate base for a meaningful Chinese political ideology. Following Liang Qichao in this respect, they were willing to grant the historic importance to Western liberalism of the Judeo-Christian tradition and the church-state struggle, but they saw neither the possibility nor the need for China to follow a similar path.

It remained for Sun Yat-sen to put ideas in the service of a political movement, by taking individually held political values that were circulating among Chinese students and fashioning them into a coordinated program. Sun's central themes, to be sure, had been drawn from other sources, but they meshed well with the political currents then flowing within youthful Chinese radical circles. Unifying and articulating in simple terms both the program toward which the revolutionaries aimed and the values underlying it was Sun's primary contribution during this era. In this role, he and his followers provided the first rudimentary ideology for modern China. We say "rudimentary" because Sun's ideas were not sufficiently integrated and universal in scope to serve as tools for interpreting all social phenomena or as guides for all political action. In greater degree than any contemporaries, however, Sun and his supporters provided a basis for sustained commitment in thought and action to an ideology of liberalism, with its goals of nationalism, republican democracy, economic development, and social justice.

As we have noted, however, the Chinese students in Japan had sometimes anticipated Sun's major principles and programs, or had reached them more or less simultaneously, relying on similar sources of inspiration. This was the case with the concepts of tutelage and revolutionary stages, two themes so central to the politics of modern China. The first step in articulating these themes was that of espousing strong leadership. Reliance upon a hero had a long tradition in Chinese literature. As we noted, it was a theme picked up anew by Liang and his supporters, and it became equally prominent in the revolutionary literature of this period. Any fundamental revolution, argued various student writers, needed heroes—men who could lead their people toward new goals. One anonymous author carried the point further: China needed more than heroes; it needed the sustained guidance of a dedicated student-intellectual vanguard.[52] Another writer asserted that by right the people were sovereign, but they could assume that role and perform their legitimate function only after they had been educated and instructed in both technology and political values. This task was incumbent upon those who would hold political leadership.[53]

By mid-1905 Sun's evolving concepts of tutelage and political stages were finding their way into the student literature. The journal of the Hunanese nationalists, *Ershi shiji zhi Zhina* (Twentieth-Century China), was possibly the first to set forth his views in explicit fashion. The author of the journal's "opening statement" asserted that the guidance of the Chinese people would move through several stages, each involving a different institutional requirement. The revolution and its immediate aftermath would make necessary a period of military rule. This would be quickly followed, however, by the establishment of civilian tutelage, with an enlightened vanguard, such as members of the Tongmeng Hui, taking on the arduous task of preparing people for constitutional democracy.[54] This preparation, continued the writer, would certainly involve far more than political training, although the advancement of political thought was a factor of signal importance. Social and economic changes of major proportions were also vital: industrialization, changes in the agrarian system, tax reform, the promotion of new learning, alterations in the family system, and greater equalization of wealth and opportunity were among the policies that had to be inaugurated.

Sun Yat-sen and his student supporters in this period were setting forth in embryonic form the first concept of "guided democracy" to be enunciated in the non-Western world. Though the formulation was imprecise and incomplete, the vital issues of the future were raised: the notion of tutelage, hence the necessity of a "vanguard" or modernizing elite; the need for specific stages of development, each with different authority and institutional structures; and the simultaneous execution of political and socioeconomic reform, so that Western ills could be avoided and one revolution would suffice. A few decades later the mainstream of political thought throughout the non-Western world would be devoted to these concerns. Interestingly, in many circles Lenin would be given credit for having initiated them. But Sun and the Chinese students in Japan did not need Lenin in order to arrive at similar positions, and they deserve more credit than they have been given for anticipating the great issues of their century.

We have already introduced the sixth and last element associated with twentieth-century political modernization, namely, mass participation in politics. By definition, democracy demanded the involvement of the citizenry. Yet the old system had kept the people illiterate, poverty-stricken, and backward. Unlike Liang, however, Sun and his student followers believed that the chasm between the need for mass political participation and the inadequacies of the masses could be bridged in a relatively short time—provided that the innate capacities of the people were recognized, that good leadership was provided, and that the task of educating the people was undertaken with all of the resources that could be summoned.

In this belief, certain aspects of Chinese culture were brought forward to complement the main thrust of contemporary Western thought. As we have suggested, this was an age dominated by an almost childlike faith in the rationality of man, if only he could be freed from the shackles that bound him. Only later did a sadder and wiser generation conclude that democracy and its necessary companion, limited government, could best be defended by admitting the existence of some quotient of irrationality in all men. The Chinese revolutionaries of this period, however, were not deeply troubled by the thought of any permanent limitations existing in mankind. They were concerned only with the conditions in which *Chinese* men temporarily found themselves, conditions that had been arbitrarily imposed and could be rapidly changed.[55]

As we have seen from the writings of Liang and other *Xinmin congbao* authors, the argument for mass enlightenment and political involvement did not stem exclusively from a commitment to the values of liberalism. Even more powerful as a motivation was the belief that an educated, politically active citizenry contributed mightily to the strength of the state—and this premise was as important to the revolutionaries as to the reformers. The spirit of the Meiji Restoration had been encapsulated in one phrase, *fukoku kyōhei* ("a rich nation, a strong soldiery"), and this same phrase was unsurpassed in its appeal to all segments of the "advanced" Chinese intelligentsia of this era, since it combined the goals of nationalism and progress. Indeed, its reverberations were to be heard throughout the decades that followed, down to the present.

The political goals of the student revolutionaries, nevertheless, were basically liberal. These were young men and women thoroughly committed to Western-style parliamentarism as the best system of government known to man. Moreover, although some of the students called themselves socialists or at least considered socialism the inevitable wave of the future, none could

15. *Members of the Qingnian Hui (Youth Association) established by Chinese overseas students in Japan in 1901*

be classified as collectivists in the true sense, and as we shall see, anarchism was dismissed by the great majority as utopian. Most of them, even those who accepted Sun's program of "land equalization" (to which we shall turn shortly), fell into the category of social reformers.

Although their political values were primarily liberal, the radical students were fully prepared to use violence in overthrowing the Qing dynasty. They exhibited no tolerance toward the Manchu, and as early as 1901 organizational efforts of a revolutionary nature got under way in Japan, accompanying the literary exhortations we have been examining. In the winter of that year, a few students established the Qingnian Hui (Youth Association), with avowedly revolutionary aims.[56] Anti-Manchu sentiments were openly expressed at the New Year's party of January 29, 1903, attended by more than a thousand Chinese students in Tokyo and members of the Chinese legation, including the Chinese minister to Japan.[57] Ironically, however, it was Russia, or more precisely, Russian policies with respect to Manchuria, that triggered sustained and significant organizational activities among student radicals. Not for the last time, a foreign imperialist threat unwittingly served the Chinese revolutionary cause.

In the spring of 1903 the Russians advanced a series of demands in connection with any withdrawal of their military forces from Manchuria, forces that had come into the region in the course of foreign intervention against the Boxers. It appeared to many Chinese, and especially to the students in Japan, exposed as they were to an anti-Russian Japanese press, that yet another imperialist conquest was in the offing. A mass meeting was held in Tokyo on April 29, with some five hundred students in attendance. Spokesmen from the Youth Association—including a man who would figure prominently in later revolutionary activities, Huang Xing—urged the creation of a student corps to oppose the Russians.

Since Huang was destined to rank second only to Sun in the revolutionary movement now unfolding, a few details concerning his background are required.[58] Huang was born on October 25, 1874, in Changsha, Hunan, his given name being Huang Zhen. His father was a respected schoolteacher. His mother died when Huang, the youngest of six children, was only eight years old. The father remarried, and Huang's stepmother was relatively well educated for the times, later serving as head of a Changsha girls' school. The young boy was given the standard classical education. At eighteen years of age, he was married to the daughter of a member of the local gentry, and in the same year, 1894, he passed the district examinations, receiving the *xiucai* degree. Four years later, although he was now the father of two children, Huang was studying at the Hunan-Hubei Academy in Wuchang, preparing to follow in his father's footsteps as a teacher.

Huang was said to be deeply affected by the failure of the One Hundred Days Reform, and particularly by the martyrdom of Tan Sitong, a fellow provincial. In the summer of 1902 he was sent to Japan by the Hubei provincial government, and promptly enrolled in the Tokyo Kōbun Institute, a school established especially for Chinese students and specializing in teacher training. Huang, however, showed a keen interest in Japanese military training, foreshadowing his subsequent role as military leader. He also began to gravitate toward political activism, participating in the founding of a student magazine and the establishment of the Hunan Translation Society, an organization dedicated to the introduction of progressive ideas through translations of Japanese and Western materials.

Thus, when news of the Russian demands reached Chinese students in Japan, Huang was prepared to accept a leading role on behalf of student nationalists. A Student Army was immediately formed, and two representatives were sent to China to present student demands for resistance to Russia to Yuan Shikai, in the hope that he would rally China's military forces. The Beijing government, correctly suspecting anti-Manchu potentialities in the movement, took a dim view of these developments and requested the Japanese government to order the disbandment of the Student Army. Conditions were now fully ripe for the creation of patriotic, anti-Manchu activism, and almost immediately radical students began to set up organizations, both in Tokyo and in Shanghai. In the Japanese capital the students organized the Jun Guomin Jiaoyu Hui (Association for National Military Education) on May 11, 1903, with Huang Xing among its members.[59] This group was composed primarily of Chinese military students in Japan, and its publicly avowed purpose was the cultivation of patriotism and a martial spirit, but its secret declaration of principles made clear that its central goal was the overthrow of the Manchu and the creation of a revitalized China that could successfully repel foreign aggressors. When the Tongmeng Hui was founded some two years later, the Association immediately merged with it.[60]

At precisely the same time, returned students from Japan were radicalizing the Shanghai newspaper *Su bao* and seeking to stimulate organizational activities in China's most Westernized city. These activities, too, had their antecedents. In the spring of 1902 various young nationalist firebrands, in-

16. Huang Xing

cluding several who had recently returned from Japan, established the Chinese Educational Association, ostensibly to produce modern textbooks for students, but actually to further the revolutionary cause. Among the leaders were men who were subsequently to achieve fame in Chinese revolutionary history, such as Cai Yuanpei, Wu Zhihui, and Zhang Binglin. Later, in November, a new school, the Aiguo Xueshi (Patriotic School), was organized in Shanghai by Cai and a number of dissident students who had previously departed from Nanyang Gongxue (Southern Public School) because of a dispute over the right to discuss politics. Yet another student group came from the Nanjing Military Academy after troubles there. Cai became the

17. *Teachers and students of the Aiguo Xueshi (Patriotic School), Shanghai, 1902*

principal of the new institution, Wu the educational supervisor, and Zhang the teacher of Chinese literature.*

The Patriotic School was a natural vehicle for the student nationalist movement, and from the beginning close contact was maintained with the Tokyo student radicals. Events in south China soon combined with the Russian threat to evoke a mass meeting in Shanghai paralleling the one held earlier in Tokyo. The Guangxi governor had reportedly been negotiating with the French, who were close by in Vietnam, to assist him in suppressing the Guangxi rebels. These rebels were wreaking havoc throughout the province, and local authorities had sought aid from neighboring provincial governments in vain. (How often this scenario had paved the way for the advance of Western imperialism, in Asia and elsewhere!) Protests poured forth in Shanghai and other areas, and to combat further French involvement in China as well as the Russian menace, some twelve hundred persons of both sexes gathered in the Shanghai garden of Zhang Suhe, a wealthy merchant.

According to a contemporary account, about one-third of those attending were students, with the Patriotic School and a similar institution, the Cultivator of Talent School, most prominently represented.[61] Many others were

*The Patriotic School was reportedly subsidized by *Su bao*, and, in exchange, teachers at the school, including Wu Zhihui, were expected to contribute articles to the newspaper. See Feng Ziyou, "The Chinese Educational Association and the Patriotic School," in *Geming yishi* 1:115–119. Later, in 1904, Cai Yuanpei, Zhang Binglin, and others were to organize the Guangfu Hui (Restoration Society), most of whose members joined with Sun's group in the Tongmeng Hui when it was formed.

also present, however, including a number of Shanghai's "modernized" citizenry. The meeting opened with the adoption of rules and the singing of a patriotic song. There followed the reading of a cable from the Tokyo students, describing their demand for war with Russia and the formation of a student volunteer battalion, ending with the request for support. At this point, the males left the garden to go to a grassy plot just outside, face the northeast (in the direction of Tokyo), and pledge their unwavering support. Here too military volunteers were asked to step forward.

Instead of trying to make use of this nationalist upsurge, the government denounced the meeting and demanded the arrest of its leaders. Such ineptness courted alienation on an ever wider base. The Shanghai students, as we have noted, had received some support from merchants and other community figures. Shanghai, of course, was a logical nationalist enclave for several reasons: It had long been the most cosmopolitan city of China, the source of greatest contact with Westernism through commerce, schools, churches, and publications—all products in considerable measure of the Western trader, missionary, and journalist. It also provided a privileged sanctuary in the form of the International Settlement, into which Chinese authority could not penetrate without permission. *Su bao*, among other journals, was published there, its current owner being Chen Fan, a Hunanese associate of Huang Xing. Together with six others, they had earlier founded the Hunan Translation Society, whose publications were distributed through *Su bao* offices.

When the radicals decided they needed a journalistic outlet, they turned to *Su bao*. Chen was available. Once a Kang supporter, he had become progressively disillusioned with the prospects of the Manchu monarchy as a result of recent events. In the spring of 1903 Zhang Binglin and Wu Zhihui became regular contributors to the paper, and late in May Zhang Shizhao became its chief editorial writer, although the paper had already taken on a strongly radical cast. An examination of *Su bao* for May and June of 1903 reveals a fascinating picture of Chinese radicalism at this point and underlines the key themes we have already described.

An apocalyptic note identical to the one contained in the Tokyo student journals now ran through many of the *Su bao* essays and editorials. China would disappear within ten years, the Chinese race within one hundred years, unless drastic action were taken.[62] The Chinese had the attributes of humans—eyes, ears, and mouth—but no more knowledge than a dog or a horse because of the slavish condition in which they had been forced to live.[63] Like their contemporaries, these writers saw the remedy in popular education, and one article—quite possibly written by Wu Zhihui—discussed the possibility of students going to France for study, thus hinting at a later movement of great importance.[64]

The *Su bao* writers, however, did not rest their case with education. Revolution was essential. Manchu rule must be extinguished, and for these purposes it would be necessary to shed blood.[65] And if revolution were to succeed, it required a revolutionary army with its roots in the people. For too long the spirit of militarism had been despised, and the physical fitness necessary to make good soldiers had been ignored; this must change.* And

* *Su bao*, May 13, 1903. This article was written in connection with the creation of an athletic club, with the author asserting that given the competition between the yellow and the

18. Cai Yuanpei

to help it change, the *Su bao* radicals gave publicity to a pamphlet entitled "The Revolutionary Army" written by an eighteen-year-old Sichuanese returnee from Tokyo, Zou Rong.[66] Zou's pamphlet could hardly have been more inflammatory, calling as it did for the expulsion of all Manchu living in China, the killing of the emperor so as to end forever the absolutist mo-

white races, the development of a martial spirit was essential, and this in turn was linked to athletics. The lack of development of athletics in China was a basic reason for its current inferiority. The foundations of modern power lay in people's armies.

narchical system, and the creation of a Chinese republic modeled after that of the United States.[67]

In addition to publicizing Zou's pamphlet, *Su bao* urged all students to join the Zhongguo Xuesheng Tongmeng Hui (Chinese Student Alliance), which it announced had just been organized by Zou to serve as a single national organization that could "wage a bloody battle for China's future."[68] In the course of this exhortation, the importance of the students to the revolutionary cause was emphasized. China's life or death was in their hands. Until now their lack of organizational unity, their division into provincial groups, had rendered them relatively ineffective. But in such societies as Austria, Italy, and Russia, students had played a great role in effecting radical political change, it added. All Chinese students should accept their responsibility to lead the revolution.[69]

Throughout these months, *Su bao* carried frequent news from Russia, together with interpretative articles. Russia served the young revolutionaries as both a model and a warning. Soon there would be no absolutist system left, announced one writer; reforms were being forced upon the czar, both because of internal pressures, including those of the students, and because of the fact that since external expansion was continuing, domestic tranquility was required.[70] This was of great import to China, he added. Another writer, in a somewhat satirical vein, described absolutism as the best factory for the manufacture of nihilism and asserted that although the Chinese had not had a totally absolutist system for thousands of years (only Qinshi Huangdi could be compared with Alexander II), the nihilist tide was approaching China, with its object the expulsion of an alien race and the recovery of Han sovereignty.[71]

The nihilists, indeed, received much attention. One writer argued that by their assassinations and terrorist campaigns they were forcing the czarist regime to release political prisoners in Siberia and to grant constitutionalism.[72] Implicit in such articles was the thesis that assassination was a means of effecting rapid change which could work in China as well. Revolution is very complex, asserted one essayist: it involves the killing of a single individual, but it also demands a general uprising of all Han against the Manchu; and those officials who seek to oppose the revolution will become targets, making of themselves "dead heroes" to the cause of revolution, de facto members of the revolutionary party.[73]

The *Su bao* writers directed threats not merely against Manchu officials but also against reformers, notably Kang Youwei. One author, noting the rumor that Kang was going to be called back by the government, remarked contemptuously that he could have no influence on China's future, because this was a revolutionary era. The assassination tide was beginning, moreover, and Kang's life was "something to which the revolution would pay attention."[74]

It is not surprising that the Beijing government demanded the suppression of *Su bao* and the remanding of all those connected with it to Chinese jurisdiction for trial. After considerable indecision the latter demand was rejected, but *Su bao* was suppressed by International Settlement authorities, and several of the key figures who chose not to flee, including Zhang Binglin and Zou Rong, were put on trial before the Mixed Court in December 1903.[75] The *Su bao* case became a cause célèbre throughout the Chinese intellectual world, especially among the young radicals. Zhang received a

19. *Zou Rong*

three-year sentence, Zou a two-year term—far less severe than the certain execution that would have awaited them had the Chinese government been in charge of the proceedings.[76] But Zou died in prison in April 1905, a few weeks before he was scheduled to be released, becoming yet another martyr to the revolutionary cause.

In December 1903, just as the trial was taking place, Huang Xing and Chen Tianhua were founding yet another revolutionary organization, the Huaxing Hui (Society for the Revival of China), in Hunan. It was composed exclusively of young Hunanese literati, many of them former students in

Japan. Huang's plan was to unite military men, students, and secret society members in revolutionary activity, using Hunan as a revolutionary base in the hope that other provinces could be persuaded to join in the Manchu overthrow.[77] As can be seen, this was a plan remarkably similar to the earlier efforts of Sun Yat-sen; hence it was natural that Huang could be influential with Sun, especially on military matters.

Huaxing Hui leaders planned an uprising aimed at capturing Changsha, the Hunan capital.[78] The plot centered on the idea of planting a bomb among a gathering of dignitaries who would be assembled to celebrate the seventieth birthday of the empress dowager on November 16, 1904; this would be followed by the seizure of key installations and ultimate control of the province. The plotters counted on assistance from the leading secret society in Hunan, the Gelao Hui, and from sympathizers within the provincial army. Parties to the plot included two leaders of a Hubei offshoot of the Huaxing Hui, Hu Ying and Song Jiaoren, thereby linking revolutionaries from an adjoining province that was to figure prominently in subsequent upheavals.* The government managed to infiltrate radical ranks, however, and the plan aborted. Huang Xing was ultimately forced to flee to Japan with other comrades, and many participants, including the Gelao Hui head, Ma Fuyi, were killed in the course of the revolt or shortly thereafter. Yet another precarious scheme for ending the Qing era had gone awry.

Other plots were hatched during this period, including plans to assassinate prominent provincial and national officials, but as 1905 opened, revolution did not seem close at hand, despite the many problems faced by a perceptibly faltering regime.

SUN, THE STUDENT RADICALS, AND THE TONGMENG HUI

In the spring of 1905 Sun was in Europe, making his first contacts with Chinese students living in Belgium, Germany, and France.[79] Accounts of his meetings with student leaders in Europe indicate that initial differences of significance were either reconciled or papered over. Naturally, the students questioned Sun's exclusive reliance on the secret societies and the overseas Chinese in his efforts to construct a revolutionary movement. Past experience had made Sun ready to doubt the consistency or loyalty of students from gentry families, and he was also skeptical about the wisdom of trying to subvert the young officers of China's New Army. But after much debate and discussion, he finally indicated his acceptance of an enlarged revolutionary base, with students and the military playing enhanced roles.

On the issues of postrevolutionary programs and institutional structures, some questions were raised, especially regarding land equalization, but in general, student acceptance appears to have been obtained. Sun outlined what were to become his "three people's principles": nationalism, democracy, and people's livelihood (which at this point consisted of Henry George's single-tax system of land revenue and control). He also presented a new in-

* Huang and his colleague Liu Kuiyi had persuaded the leader of the Hunan branch of the Gelao Hui, to join in an alliance, with an agreement that the Gelao Hui would strike in the rural areas at the time of the Changsha effort. Meanwhile, Hu Ying, Song Jiaoren, and others had organized the Kexue Buxi Suo (Institute for the Diffusion of Science) in Wuchang after a visit by Huang Xing in the summer of 1903, as an affiliate of the Huaxing Hui. See Lewis, *Prologue*, pp. 163–174.

stitutional plan: an American model containing separate executive, legislative, and judicial organs, with the addition of a Chinese inheritance—an examination branch to preside over the selection of officials, and a censorate to maintain surveillance over all branches of government, guarding against corruption and inefficiency.

Initially, Sun was able to recruit about fifty students in the course of his European swing.* At a Brussels meeting, some thirty youth joined what was called the Chinese Revolutionary Party and pledged themselves to a now familiar program: the overthrow of the Manchu, the restoration of Han rule, the creation of a republican form of democracy, and the equalization of land rights. As Sun was about to leave Europe a crisis threatened to disrupt the new effort: several student defectors revealed Sun's efforts to the Chinese minister in Paris and gave the legation a list of Revolutionary Party members. As it happened, neither the Chinese minister nor the French government showed an interest in pursuing the matter, but some students, frightened by the incident, withdrew from the party. Nonetheless, when Sun left Europe he had the beginnings of a student contingent, and he was now determined to enlist the Tokyo students, by far the largest group of overseas student intellectuals. A new era for Sun had commenced.

On July 19, 1905, Sun arrived in Yokohama. Immediately, he plunged into discussions with student leaders like Huang Xing and Song Jiaoren, using the good offices of his old Japanese friend Miyazaki Torazō. Throughout these days Miyazaki and other members of the Japanese Kokuryūkai (Amur River Society) provided introductions, meeting places, and liaison, thereby playing a crucial role as midwife to the emerging revolutionary organization.

Song was to play a vital role in the early revolutionary movement, and a brief account of his early career will offer us a glimpse of the life and times of other young Chinese revolutionaries during this era.[80] Song was born on April 5, 1882, in Taoyuan, Hunan. He was attending a Wuchang middle school when the nationalist movement began to grow in his region, primarily as a result of Russian activities in Manchuria. In 1904 he joined Huang Xing's Huaxing Hui through his Wuchang Institute and quickly became an active revolutionary. He was given responsibility for organizing an uprising in Changde in coordination with the revolt planned on the occasion of the empress dowager's birthday celebration in November. Song's diary begins shortly after this abortive effort, when he had been forced to flee Changde, a man with a price on his head.

The opening pages of his diary present a vivid picture of the intimate network of young radicals scattered throughout the main centers of Hunan, and the dangerous yet relatively loose atmosphere in which they operated. Once again, one notes the active role that certain Chinese Christians were playing as revolutionaries, although Song himself was not a convert. After moving to Shanghai (and finding that most of his anticipated contacts had been arrested), Song sailed for Japan, arriving in Tokyo on December 13, 1904. Almost immediately he became deeply involved in politics, surrounded by old and new acquaintances from Hunan. By early January 1905 he was promot-

*See Wei and Wu, *Xinhai geming shi* 1:15–16. Sun met with students in Brussels, Berlin, and Paris. In May he also visited the leaders of the Second International in Brussels, and according to Wei and Wu, he requested membership for his Chinese Revolutionary Party in the Socialist International (p. 16).

20. *Song Jiaoren*

ing the idea of a journal, and found himself selected as one of the two editors and the general manager of *Ershi shiji zhi Zhina* (Twentieth-Century China).

Like most of his comrades, Song was essentially an ardent Han nationalist at this point, with few political ideas beyond that of bringing the Chinese back into control of their country. His heroes were Qinshi Huangdi, George Washington, and the Italian nationalists Garibaldi and Mazzini. His political activities continually interfered with his schooling, and he was also undecided as to his academic interests. Song—like many prominent student activists of this and later times—flitted in and out of schools and special tutorial programs, berating himself from time to time for fickleness and lack of discipline. He eventually acquired sufficient knowledge of Japanese, along with some English, to work as a translator. This, together with jobs teaching Chinese, provided an income—most of which he spent for books and magazines on subjects ranging from Confucian classics to writings on health, sex, astrology, and science. Song lists an incredible array of subjects among his purchases, and he appears to have been a voracious reader. He was also prone to neurosis, and on one occasion spent a protracted period in a Tokyo hospital—requesting and receiving sufficient payment from the Chinese government to provide him with second-class rather than third-class accommodations, even while he continued to work for Manchu overthrow.

Song met Miyazaki (whom he described as a man who regretted that he was Japanese instead of Chinese) only a short time before Sun's arrival in Japan. When he first came into contact with Sun in the company of Miyazaki on July 28, 1905, the veteran revolutionary, after listening to an account of nationalist activities in Hunan, spoke of the need for coordination and unity, warning that if China disintegrated into twenty warring states, foreign intervention was likely. According to Song, he then said that a potentially strong revolutionary base existed in Guangdong and Guangxi because of the prominence of secret societies and anti-Manchu sentiments there, and he implied that revolutionaries should focus their activities in those provinces.

On the very next day Sun met with Hunanese students at Huang Xing's house, and the issue of establishing a single revolutionary party was discussed. No agreement was reached, and it was decided that each individual could decide for himself whether to join such an association. Many Hunanese, including Song, decided to participate, however, and attended the Akasaka meeting of July 30, at which Sun spoke.[81]

At this point, meetings were being held almost daily. On July 30 it was decided to form a new association, the Zhongguo Tongmeng Hui (United League of China), with the same four-point program earlier enunciated in Europe. Sun's long association with the secret societies—and his desire to retain their support—was in evidence in the ceremonies surrounding the initiation of members, in the choice of symbols, and in the very name of the organization. But for the first time in Sun's lengthening career as a revolutionary he had become the leader of a large student movement.

Two weeks later, on August 13, Sun addressed a group of students, variously estimated at between 600 and 1,300, who crowded into the Fuji Restaurant in Tokyo to hear this thirty-eight-year-old revolutionary veteran.* He did not disappoint them. The speech opened on an optimistic note. There had been extensive worry that China might suffer the fate of Africa or Australia, Sun remarked, but given the progress currently taking place among the Chinese people, the nation need not be lost. He then undertook a brief analysis of the places he had visited in the past two years, using each to illustrate points he wished to make concerning China. Japan served to

* For a complete text of the speech, see *Guofu quanji* 3:1–6. Song, who introduced Sun, reports that there were 600 to 700 people in the hall when the guards ordered the doors closed, but finally all who were outside were admitted. Song, *Wo zhi lishi*, p. 73. Feng, writing much later from memory, says there were 1,300.

underline China's mistakes. The Japanese had imported their ancient civilization from China, Sun asserted, and the leaders of the Meiji Restoration had drawn on the concepts of "the great Chinese philosopher Wang Yangming," which united knowledge and action. This, and their esteem for the military, had served to save the nation. In contrast, China had abandoned its own culture when it accepted that of the Manchu, and the Chinese government was now responding to contemporary challenges with a futile effort to preserve the existing order.

Sun then spoke of the United States with unqualified enthusiasm. The St. Louis Exposition was testimony to the extraordinary prosperity and vitality of the new America, he reported. Yet it was Europe that provided the most basic lesson for China, for it had experienced the transition through which the Chinese must pass. The old European civilizations had failed and new forces had sprung up; those who had once been barbarians, the Teutons, had emerged as the most dynamic. Facing a new and rapidly changing Western world, China was being left behind, rendered decrepit.

Yet once again Sun's optimism triumphed. If its abundant resources and manpower were thoroughly applied to adopting Western ideas and methods, China could easily be transformed into a strong, new nation. Indeed, China could surpass the United States. Why? Because America did not have the traditions of an ancient civilization to sustain it. China's combined size and population, moreover, were greater than those of any other nation. "We are lucky to have been born in China," Sun proclaimed; "but if one keeps silent, and does not advocate nationalism or aid in the creation of a republic, it will be a great tragedy." Westerners had been able to seize such areas as Dalian and Jiulong because they believed that we Chinese were afraid of them, Sun argued, but with the revival of China, they will become afraid of us. Under the proper circumstances, the Chinese could reach their goals in twenty years, he insisted, whereas Japan had taken thirty years from the time of the Meiji Restoration.

Sun then took up the question of stages. "Some have said that the European-American style of republican politics does not suit China now. The natural order is from barbarism to absolutism, from absolutism to constitutional monarchy, and from constitutional monarchy to republicanism, and they further argue that this process should not be hastened. Hence the reform of China should take the form of a constitutional monarchy, not a republic."

"This opinion is entirely wrong," he asserted, introducing the analogy of building a railway system: one does not have to start with the most primitive engine; it is eminently logical to begin with the most advanced locomotive. Furthermore, one could not sustain the thesis that the political consciousness of the Chinese people was insufficiently high to permit the establishment of a republic. Even Hawaii, a truly uncivilized place one hundred years ago, had moved directly from barbarism to republicanism. Could one say that the consciousness of the Chinese was lower than that of the Hawaiian natives? Or beneath that of the American ex-slaves? Pursuing these shaky analogies, Sun posed a final rhetorical question: "If we are not prepared to build a republic, are we mere animals, inferior to Hawaiians and black slaves?"

Sun contradicted himself almost immediately by making out a strong case for tutelage. The future, he stated, depended on the leadership of enlightened persons, since the ordinary people of China knew nothing. We people who have the inspiration must select the best political system and leadership to serve our countrymen, he concluded.

Sun ended with a powerful appeal for revolution. China's current government was that of a foreign race. Under it, no independence of thought or action could be developed; everything was forbidden. After the shock of a change at the top, progress would ensue, and in a decade or so independence would be imprinted on the minds of the entire citizenry. Then, shifting course, he made a different point: China had been spoiled by the fact that everything had been so good for four thousand years that change had not been desired. Now the Chinese realized that they must learn from others, and this meant learning from the best and most advanced, not from the mediocre.

Sun's speech was well designed to capture an audience composed primarily of young students. It was optimistic in its tone, simple in its logic, and powerful in its emotional appeal. Analyzed closely, the talk abounded in contradictions, questionable facts, and unanswered questions. But in politics, especially the politics of revolution, these are not necessarily fatal deficiencies; they may even be assets. And in his remarks Sun did manage to raise in abbreviated form many of the issues that were at the heart of the ongoing debate with the reformers. The case for republicanism rested on three somewhat uncoordinated pillars: the time-tested civilization and superior capacities of the Chinese people; the capacity of people—and nations—to skip stages of political evolution, moving to the most advanced model; and the utility, indeed the indispensability, of elitist tutelage of the masses in abetting this process.

One important subject, that of "land equalization," does not appear to have been mentioned, at least according to the text available to us. Perhaps Sun did not want to raise a divisive issue on this occasion or to suggest a program that had not yet been fully worked out. This was soon to be remedied, as we shall see.

The Tongmeng Hui rapidly took shape during mid-1905 and the months that followed.[82] The task of uniting diverse individuals and provincial groups into a single association was extremely difficult, as the entire history of modern China was to indicate. In this instance, the attitude of Huang Xing and his Hunanese comrades was crucial, since they constituted the best organized and the strongest existing revolutionary group. Several preliminary discussions and meetings had been held in late July, prior to the Fuji Restaurant reception in mid-August. The most important of these took place on July 30 at the home of Uchida Ryōhei, a leading functionary of the Kokuryūkai. Between forty and seventy persons heard Sun and Huang speak, and then agreed to join a unified revolutionary organization. The name Zhongguo Tongmeng Hui was finally selected after various suggestions had been put forward.*

An oath drafted by Sun bound each member to adhere to the basic tenets of the League, namely, the overthrow of the Manchu, the restoration of

* Sun himself had advocated the name Chinese Revolutionary Party, which he had already used in Europe, but Huang did not favor it. One suggestion was to call the new association the Anti-Manchu League, but this was rejected on the grounds that Manchu who supported the organization's principles should be allowed to join. For a discussion of this issue, see Tian Tong, "The Establishment of the Tongmeng Hui," in *Geming wenxian* 2:2–5. See also Song, *Wo zhi lishi*, p. 70.

Han sovereignty, the creation of a republican form of government, and land equalization. A secret sign for recognition purposes was also introduced, further evidence of the pervasive influence of traditional secret society practices.

One week after the Fuji Restaurant meeting, on August 20, 1905, the Tongmeng Hui was formally inaugurated. The basic goals set forth above were approved, and party regulations were adopted. Officers were also chosen, with Sun being elected chairman and Huang made chief of the Executive Department. Other key officers included Zhang Ji and Wang Jingwei, who at the age of twenty-one was made head of the Examination Department.

Over the next eighteen months, some 963 members were officially registered at Tongmeng Hui headquarters, all but 100 of them affiliated with the Tokyo branch.[83] Whereas the Xingzhong Hui had been composed primarily of politically marginal overseas Chinese who had weak ties to China, the Tongmeng Hui was essentially a student organization, and among its youthful members were many who would later play a crucial role in China's future. The membership also clearly indicated where China's revolutionary heartland lay: nearly 60 percent of the Tokyo branch members came from the four provinces of Guangdong, Hunan, Sichuan, and Hubei.* Anti-Qing sentiment had always been strongest in the South and in south-central China, and these were the provinces that would figure prominently in all subsequent revolutionary movements.

The first overseas branches were established in the winter of 1905. Feng Ziyou went to organize branches in Hong Kong, Macao, and Canton. Cai Yuanpei was sent to Shanghai to set up a branch. Other branches were established in Vietnam and Singapore, as we shall see, and there had been the earlier branch created in Europe. Organizations in North America did not emerge until 1910, reflecting Sun's weakness there.

GOALS AND VALUES OF THE NATIONALIST REVOLUTIONARIES

To discern the central themes of the Tongmeng Hui, one must turn to its organ, *Min bao*. The first issue of this key journal came out in late November of 1905. Publication continued somewhat irregularly until the fall of 1908, when the Japanese government, under pressure from Beijing, banned the magazine.** The first editor was Zhang Ji, and Hu Hanmin played an

*According to Wei and Wu, nearly 90 percent of the early Tongmeng Hui members were students, with secret society members, soldiers, low-ranking officers of the New Army, and overseas Chinese joining at a later point. Of the 979 early members, 170 were from Guangdong, 158 from Hunan, 131 from Sichuan, and 125 from Hubei (*Xinhai geming shi* 1:63). Writing from a Marxist perspective, Wei and Wu assert that the Tongmeng Hui cannot be defined as an intellectual party, because intellectuals are not an independent class and because most members fell into the petty bourgeois category—more progressive than the weak bourgeois class but politically representative of it (pp. 64–65). In fact, a sizable number of the students came from rurally based and relatively affluent or prestigious families, who would be classified in occupation as "gentry" or "official." The problem of forcing the facts to fit a Western-derived, Marxist analysis is once again clear.

**At first, Tongmeng Hui leaders, on Huang Xing's recommendation, decided to make *Ershi shiji zhi Zhina (Twentieth-Century China)*, the publication of the Hunan Association, their organ; but the second issue of that journal was confiscated by Japanese authorities, and so a new name was chosen to avoid trouble. Many of the same individuals, however, were involved in the publication. See Song, *Wo zhi lishi*, pp. 75–87. *Min bao* publication dates present several problems. One is that traditional Chinese dates must be carefully translated to

21. *Zhang Binglin*

active role in the editorial process. Beginning with the sixth issue, Zhang Binglin, recently released from prison in Shanghai, became editor in chief, and retained this position through 1908.

The perspectives of the League's leaders were reflected not only in their writings and speeches but in the pictures printed in *Min bao*, which vividly suggest their priorities, preferences, and uncertainties. It is significant, for

conform to the Western calendar. More troublesome, the date on a journal is not necessarily the date of its actual publication—which becomes clear as one tries to relate the substance of the articles to ongoing events, and to the flow of the debate with Liang. We can only give the dates as published, but possible discrepancies should be kept in mind. The 24th issue of *Min bao*, published on October 10, 1908, was confiscated by the Japanese government, although some issues survived. Two additional issues were put out in January and February of 1910 under the editorship of Wang Jingwei; their place of publication was given as Paris to mislead the authorities, but in fact they were printed in Tokyo.

example, that the first picture in the opening issue was that of the Yellow Emperor, a legendary hero credited with fighting off the barbarians and whom the *Min bao* editors referred to as "the first great nationalist of the world."[84] Accompanying the Yellow Emperor were pictures of Jean Jacques Rousseau, "the first great advocate of human rights," George Washington, "the first founder of republican government," and Micius (Mo Zi), "the first advocate of the love and equality of mankind." Subsequent issues featured a range of radicals and revolutionary movements. The second issue, for instance, presented a picture of a scene from the French Revolution and portraits of the heroine of the Russian Narodnik movement, Sophie Perovskaya, and the Chinese martyr Chen Xingtai. In the third issue there were pictures of Mikhail Bakunin and of Wu Yue, the young radical who had tossed a bomb at the Constitutional Mission group as they sought to leave the Beijing railway station on September 24, 1905.

In later issues, victories of the Taiping rebels were depicted, along with pictures of the assassination of a Russian official, of Louis XVI en route to the guillotine, and of "three great Chinese nationalists"—the first Ming emperor, the Taiping leader Hong Xiuquan, and Sun Yat-sen. It was in character that the very last issue of *Min bao*, published on February 1, 1910, carried the picture of An Chong-kun, the Korean assassin of Itō Hirobumi, the famed Japanese statesman who was killed in Harbin, and Bal Gangadhar Tilak, the founder of the modern Indian revolutionary movement.*

The close affinity that Sun's revolutionaries felt with Russian comrades was clearly revealed by these pictures. Prominent figures in the Russian terrorist movement, episodes involving assassination, and the principal exponents of anarchism, such as Bakunin and Tolstoy, were featured. Sensing that China and Russia shared a common problem, and sometimes holding an almost mystical belief that the two countries were likely to move toward a common destiny, the Chinese radicals were excited by Russian demands for revolution and the acceptance of assassination as a meaningful tactic.[85] And yet, as we shall see, Sun and his followers dismissed anarchism as utopian, and they diverged greatly from certain Russian heroes in their championing of a racially oriented nationalism (coming close to the Slavophils in this respect).

From Sun's preface in the first issue to the final pages of the last volume, *Min bao* writers made it clear that their primary purpose was to overthrow a *foreign* as well as an oppressive regime, and to restore China to *its own people*. Sun himself argued in his first contribution to *Min bao* that in the collapse of the Roman Empire and the rise of European nationalism one could see the true path toward progress and power.[86] His article was followed by an essay by Wang Jingwei, a young author whose career was to traverse a wider political spectrum over the next four decades than that of any other political leader in modern China.

Wang, whose early name was Wang Zhaoming, was born in Canton on May 4, 1883, the youngest of ten children. His father, native to Zhejiang, had come to Guangdong to serve as legal secretary to a Qing official. Wang's early life was marked by recurrent financial difficulties for the family, and both parents died when he was a young teen-ager. Taking advantage of a classical education received under his father's tutelage and his uncle's li-

*Earlier, pictures of prominent young Chinese revolutionary martyrs such as Zou Rong had appeared, along with those of various revolutionaries from Europe and other parts of Asia.

brary, however, young Wang passed the provincial examination in 1903 and received a government scholarship for study in Japan. He pursued his studies diligently but took a different route from most Chinese students in Tokyo. He majored in constitutional law and political theory at Tokyo Law College, where he obtained a degree in 1906, the year after he joined the Tongmeng Hui.[87]

In his initial *Min bao* article, Wang first drew a distinction between race and nationality and then described four methods of molding different races into a single nationality, three of which involved coercion. In China, he argued, all races had coexisted in harmony during four thousand years of Han control, but since the fall of the Ming dynasty the Han race had been downgraded to a position of tertiary importance.[88]

As he warmed to his subject Wang's prose became harsher and more direct. The Manchu, fearing that their population of 5 million would be assimilated by the 400 million Han, had had no choice but to control the Han through diverse strategies.* The Manchu still ruled over China despite their marked inferiority because they had been able to monopolize supreme political and military power. Now that this monopoly was threatened, they sought to protect their position under the guise of constitutional monarchy.

Wang vehemently rejected the argument of the Kang-Liang forces that the Han and Manchu were basically of the same race, and that in any case one should be concerned about the quality of governance, not its racial composition. Race is not merely a matter of blood, Wang insisted, but also a matter of life-style. It is necessary to oppose both the Manchu and bad government because the two are inextricably connected: Liang may claim that the Manchu have been assimilated by the Han and that anti-Manchuism calls for narrow racial revenge, but the fact is that the Manchu really *are* wicked and cunning, and it should be the Han who govern the nature of the assimilation process, not a culturally and numerically inferior race.[89]

These arguments were to be repeated countless times. Another *Min bao* writer proclaimed bluntly that since the Manchu and the Han were mutually antagonistic, it was inconceivable that constitutional monarchy under the Manchu could produce racial cooperation. "That the Han emotionally dislike the Manchu," he continued, "is well known."[90] In many cases, hatred or contempt for the Manchu was accompanied by strong expressions of a belief in the innate superiority of the Han race, not merely in comparison with the Manchu but with reference to the white race as well.[91]

One of the ardent young nationalists around Sun was Hu Hanmin. Like Wang Jingwei, Hu was to play a prominent role during the Nationalist phase of the modern Chinese revolution. He was born in Canton on December 17, 1891.[92] In his autobiography he records that he came from a long line of peasants living in Luling *xian*, Jiangxi, but that his grandfather had moved to Guangdong to serve as private secretary to an official. His father also had a career as legal secretary to various local officials, and Hu's mother was a well-educated woman who came from a family of scholars. Despite this background, Hu's family was not affluent, and when his father died in 1895

* *Min bao*, November 26, 1905, pp. 11–12. Wang remarked that while developing their traditional skills in shooting and horseback riding so as to retain military power, the Manchu had also kept the Han subjugated by such tactics as "exhausting them in literary work" (pp. 14–15). In addition, while degrading them, the Manchu had sought to make the Han believe that racial differences between the two were nonexistent (p. 20).

23. *Hu Hanmin*

family fortunes were further affected. He could not continue his schooling at this point, but because he had received a classical education, primarily from his mother, he was able to become a tutor to earn money. From Christian sources in Canton he learned about Sun, having previously become progressively unhappy with Qing rule and stimulated by Sun's abortive Canton uprising. By 1900 Hu had decided that he wanted to study in Japan and engage in political activism, but he did not have sufficient funds. Taking the provincial examinations, he attained the *juren* degree, and with money from friends he went to Japan in 1902.

Hu soon took a leading role in opposing the policies of the Japanese government and the Qing legation toward Chinese students in Japan. Frustrated by student timidity and disunity over the issue of protest tactics, he withdrew from school and returned to China, taking a post at Wuzhou Normal School. He was soon dismissed because of his political activities. After a brief stint as a teacher in a private school, he returned to Japan in 1904. Now the time was ripe for his reentry into student politics. Bitterly critical of Liang Qichao as an "opportunist," Hu aligned himself with the revolutionaries. In his memoirs he concedes that Zhang Binglin, Zou Rong, and Chen Tianhua played a major role in spearheading the anti-Manchu movement, but he asserts that they were committed only to destruction of the old order, and that they had few constructive proposals and therefore could not convince many students.

Hu also had some interesting observations on the students as a whole. The scene was complex, he wrote: some students were interested only in the life of the bon vivant, others had quirky ideas; many concentrated wholly on their studies, particularly science, and displayed no interest in politics. Some wanted China to depend upon Japan in the future; others were unhappy with Japan, and wanted to pursue Western models. Yet despite these complications, the fundamental division was between revolutionaries and monarchists.

Hu returned briefly to Canton in 1905, but came back to Tokyo with Liao Zhongkai in late August, shortly after the founding of the Tongmeng Hui. He participated in the August 20 meeting when the League was formally inaugurated, recording that there were more than a hundred persons present, with seventeen provinces (all except Gansu) represented. At this point, Hu met Sun personally, and together with Liao and Liao's wife, they discussed Sun's ideas; they disagreed at first with the concept of land equalization, but came to accept Sun's view. Hu became secretary of the League and took charge of all confidential files. In his autobiography Hu asserts that the six principles published in the introduction to *Min bao* were written by him, as narrated by Sun, and that he served as one of the initial editors of the journal.

There can be no doubt that Hu shared the bitterly anti-Manchu views of the more militant elements within the Tongmeng Hui. In an article written to explain the six principles of the League, he proclaimed that the present government of China was bad because it was operated by a bad race who, although a small minority, wanted to assimilate the Han. The Manchu, according to Hu, were inferior even to the Mongols of the Yuan dynasty, and could easily by toppled.[93]

Sun accurately summarized the Tongmeng Hui position on nationalism in his speech commemorating the first anniversary of *Min bao* at the end of 1906, although his views were more moderately expressed than those of Wang and Hu.[94] Denying that the Han sought the destruction of the Manchu as a people, he stated that the Manchu were rejected as *rulers* because "only when we Han have power do we have our country." Although the Han were of a great cultural legacy and were larger in numbers than any other nationality, they were presently a subjugated people. The chief reason for

24. Left to right: Yu Youren, Wang Yiwen, and Zhang Dengyun

this was that the Han had lacked any organization, but this flaw was in the process of being remedied. In the coming revolution the motive would be not revenge or the liquidation of the Manchu as a race but the seizure of political power, the restoration of Han rights.

Arguments resting boldly on an appeal to race, whether couched in the restrained tones of Sun Yat-sen or the fiery rhetoric of Wang Jingwei, were enormously difficult for Kang and Liang to counter, based as they were on the deepest feelings. And this central issue naturally carried over into the debate regarding constitutional monarchy versus republicanism. Once again Sun put the Tongmeng Hui position clearly in his *Min bao* anniversary speech. A national revolution had to occur simultaneously. If a Manchu monarch were simply replaced by a Han emperor, a second political revolution could not be avoided later.[95] Sun's young followers, as we have noted, were more extreme on the subject. They saw constitutional monarchy solely as a plot through which the Manchu and their Han lackeys hoped to preserve their power. There might be new laws, but who would administer them? The same old centralized authoritarian rule under an alien race would prevail.* Thus nothing short of the creation of a new people's government based on republican principles would suffice.[96] At this point, Sun again advanced his concept of five separate and equal branches of government for the postrevolutionary era: the Western-derived executive, legislative, and judicial departments plus two indigenous institutions, the examination department and the censorate.**

Having acknowledged that the overthrow of the Manchu and the creation of a republican form of government could be brought about only by means of revolution, Sun and his group had to address the questions of the reformers about the costs and dangers of revolution. For instance, what was to stop foreign aggressors from taking advantage of the situation and seizing power for themselves as China slipped into chaos? To this, various answers were provided. Sometimes it was argued that most modern states had managed to have revolutions without external interference.[97] At other times it was also said that the major powers would be pleased if the Chinese could complete their revolution, because it would set the stage for stability and progress.[98]

It was more difficult to answer Liang's Burkean argument that revolution not only was wasteful of human and natural resources but also sowed the seeds of recurrent struggle in the future. The Sun revolutionaries responded first with the classic theme that it was necessary to destroy the old in order to build the new. In the case of China, moreover, since the Manchu obviously did not intend to depart voluntarily, there was no alternative to revolution. Yet violence and bloodshed could be minimized, particularly if the whole people, or at least the entire Han population, rallied to the cause.[99]

* In a later article, entitled "Blaming the One Who Speaks for the Manchu," Wang introduced a set of issues and a vocabulary that were remarkably similar to those used by the Communist revolutionaries two decades later. To cope with the revolutionary awakening in China, he said, the Manchu barbarians had used two methods simultaneously—suppression and "reform." Their efforts to introduce constitutionalism were merely a "reform" tactic to perpetuate their rule, and besides, the class that would benefit most from a constitutional monarchy was the gentry; the majority of the people would be forgotten. Furthermore, those who said that the people, being ignorant, needed to rely on the leadership of those who possessed knowledge had overlooked developments in Europe, including the general strikes, which had proved that workers could themselves be men of knowledge and that direct action was required to raise the people's status above that of animals. *Min bao*, January, 1910, pp. 1–19, and February, 1910, pp. 1–20.

** For an exposition of the five-power government, see Sun's speech of December 2, 1906, previously cited. Clearly eager to be original, Sun argued that whereas the United States had the best written constitution and Great Britain the best unwritten constitution, neither was ideal. The Western method of selecting officials was conducive to abuse and the rise of a spoils system. Hence the desirability of a separate examination branch. Moreover, placing the role of investigation and impeachment in the hands of the legislative branch, as in the United States, allowed the Congress to intimidate the executive, so that only strong presidents such as Lincoln, McKinley [*sic*], and Roosevelt had been able to achieve true administrative independence. Hence the desirability of a separate censorate.

Wang Jingwei also argued that having learned the lesson of the French Revolution, the Chinese revolutionaries would use the revolutionary army to prevent internal disorder while the new republic was getting under way.[100]

There remained Liang's most compelling argument: that a revolution forced upon an unready China would bring not democracy but a new absolutism. Wang Jingwei, among others, sought to respond to this challenge. He argued that Liang, by relying on the writings of Minobe Tatsukichi, Montesquieu, and the German legalists, had grossly undervalued the capacities of the Chinese people. In fact, the spirit of liberty, equality, and brotherhood had been strong in the Chinese throughout their history. With an enlightened government, and one in which they participated, their political consciousness could be quickly raised.[101]

Wang, almost alone among *Min bao* writers, was also prepared to tackle an immediate issue, that of revolutionary tactics. In one fascinating article he outlined three main strategies: attacking the capital; concentrating revolutionary power in a single region; and staging uprisings in various regions to erode the power of the central government.[102] Although the first strategy had generally prevailed in Europe, Wang noted, the situation in China was different. First, the coming revolution had to involve *all* the people, not just the urban dwellers or those in the capital. Second, with one exception, no successful revolution in Chinese history had ever been mounted on the basis of power in a single region. It was essential to establish a base area, he continued, but an uprising from a single region would not succeed, because the government could concentrate all of its power on crushing such a move. The soundest strategy was to plan for uprisings from several different regions. The danger, of course, was that these uprisings would erupt on the basis of local circumstances, without a common program or proper coordination. It was therefore essential that the revolutionary armies be indoctrinated with a common set of principles, based on nationalism, constitutionalism, and people's rights. In addition, the coordination of military actions from the various base areas had to be carefully planned.

The parallels between these themes and the later military writings and actions of the Chinese Communists are obvious. Needless to say, these parallels did not stem from Communist conversance with Wang's article, although both parties had undoubtedly read from some of the same Chinese historical sources. It was the circumstances of China that prompted the similarities. Those circumstances were bound to draw any revolutionary group into considering the same basic strategic alternatives and would probably lead them to choose the same option. Yet it is startling to find a *Min bao* writer stressing the importance of ideology as a weapon giving common purpose to revolutionary armies and speaking of the necessity of establishing coordination between revolutionary base areas.

In a second article Wang approached the question of revolutionary strategy from a political rather than a military perspective. Conceding that the Manchu would be able to put their constitution into effect, he argued that the critical issue would become whether the central government or the regional administrations would carry out the primary governing functions. The task of the Han, he submitted, was to struggle to obtain the maximum degree of regional power in all key fields, from the police force to education. The greater the degree of regional autonomy, the more opportunities for expressions of popular rights, he asserted, and the more isolated the national government. The Manchu would seek to create a system providing as much centralization as possible, and this must be combatted.[103]

It remains to explore the third major commitment of the Tongmeng Hui, a dedication to *minshengzhuyi*—the principle of people's livelihood. Having already set forth Liang's reaction to socialism generally and to the idea of "equalization of land" specifically, let us turn to the speeches and writings of Sun and his supporters and allow them to speak for themselves.

In his preface to the first issue of *Min bao*, Sun advanced one theme that would be often repeated: although China was coming to nationalism and people's rights somewhat late, the timing with respect to people's livelihood was ideal because class divisions in China were still practically nonexistent. Whereas the deep social problems of the West could now be solved only by a second revolution, China could and should carry out its national, political, and social revolutions simultaneously, thereby taking one giant step into the future.[104]

One year later, in his speech at the first anniversary of *Min bao*, Sun gave his supporters a succinct statement of his views on the specific program that would ensure people's livelihood. This section of his speech began by contrasting once again China with the West. In Europe and America the advent of capitalism had resulted in the rapid growth of wealth within the society as a whole, but also in the development of mass poverty. The rise of socialist parties and their advocacy of people's livelihood were inevitable by-products of the growing inequities between rich and poor. There were many socialist factions, Sun noted, some championing the nationalization of all capital, others advocating land redistribution to the poor. In his opinion, however, the reason Europe and America had been unable to solve their social problems was that they had not solved the land problem. Specifically, the price of land had risen rapidly in the course of industrial development.

If this situation were not anticipated by China's future leaders and controlled, great economic and social injustices would result, just as they had in the West. In China, however, capitalism had not yet been born, and the price of land had not increased greatly. Now was the time to face the issue. Then Sun remarked that among sociologists there were various theories as to how to handle the problem, but as for himself, he believed in the method of fixing land prices. For example, if a landlord owned land worth one thousand dollars, the price of that land should be fixed by the government at that amount, or at most, two thousand dollars. Later, when the development of transport and other factors had increased the value of that land to ten thousand dollars, the landlord would get his two thousand, but the eight thousand unearned profit would go to the state. In this manner, monopolies in land by a few rich individuals would be prevented, the burdens of multiple taxes on the citizenry would be avoided, and a single tax on land would produce state revenue sufficient to provide the government with ample funds. Indeed, proclaimed Sun, both the state and the people would become rich, and all economic problems could be easily handled.[105]

From these remarks it is clear that Sun was faithfully following Henry George and his concept of a single tax on land values.[106] As we noted earlier, Sun had probably become acquainted with George's theories while in London; but it may be more important that upon his return to Tokyo in 1905 he reestablished his close ties with Miyazaki Torazō and his brother Tamizō, who was a strong proponent of "land equalization" and had founded a society dedicated to this end. A study of various branches of Western radicalism by Tamizō was translated by a "Member of *Min bao*" and published in that journal in April 1906 under the title "Types of European and American Social Revolutionary Movements and a Discussion of Them." Dividing the schools of thought demanding social reformation into three broad categories—socialism, anarchism, and the equalization of land—Miyazaki proceeded to a detailed, critical discussion of each school and its subdivisions. At the end, the anonymous translator indicated his own preference for the equalization of land, but wavered over whether to support the concepts of Alfred Wallace or those of Henry George.[107]

Indeed, despite Sun's categorical endorsement of Henry George's proposal for a single tax on land values at the end of 1906, the initial months and years following the creation of the Tongmeng Hui witnessed much uncertainty and confusion among *Min bao* writers regarding the specific content of the principle of "equalization of land," and regarding the broader issue of "socialism" as well. As we have seen, Liang grasped this fact early on, and repeatedly bore down on his opponents' weaknesses and inconsistencies on this front. Except for Sun's enunciation of *minshengzhuyi* as one of the three basic principles of the Tongmeng Hui in his introduction to *Min bao*, the first two issues of that journal completely ignored the subject. A strong interest in Western socialist thought was signaled, however, by a two-part article by Zhu Zhixin presenting brief biographies of leading German social revolutionaries. Zhu, a second cousin of Wang Jingwei, made his socialist sympathies clear at the outset, and followed this with a brief, favorable biography of Marx, which included the first Chinese translation of portions of the *Communist Manifesto*, including the famous ten points.*

It was Hu Hanmin, made responsible for explicating *minshengzhuyi*, who again sought to open the subject in print. In an article published in April 1906, and almost certainly based on numerous conversations with Sun and others, Hu presented a disappointingly brief and fuzzy analysis of the Tongmeng Hui's third principle. Introducing "nationalization of land" (*tudi guoyou*) as one of the six major tasks of Chinese revolutionaries, he turned immediately to the reasons for the advent of socialism in the West, which he found in the rise of economic classes in the course of modernization. Thus, socialism has as its primary goal the equalization of economic class differences. He divided socialism into two categories—communism and state ownership, or nationalization (*guozhanzhuyi*). Nationalization could not yet be carried out in its entirety in China because of the low level

*Shi Shen (Zhu Zhixin), "Biographies of German Social Revolutionaries," *Min bao*, January 22, 1906, pp. 1–18. For a discussion of Zhu's translation and the discrepancies between it and the original, see Bernal, *Chinese Socialism*, pp. 116–118. The second part of the article, appearing in *Min bao*, April 5, 1906, pp. 1–19, was devoted to Lassalle.

Zhu Zhixin, originally named Zhu Dafu, was born in Guangdong on October 12, 1885, though his family, like that of his cousin Wang Jingwei, came from Zhejiang. Their fathers, moreover, both worked as legal secretaries in the Qing civil service. Zhu received a good classical education, and in examinations designed to select students from Guangdong province to go to Japan, he ranked first among forty-one candidates. In Japan he quickly became involved in political activities together with such comrades from Guangdong as Hu Hanmin and Wang. At the end of 1907 he returned to South China and took a post as a teacher in Canton. He later played a prominent role in the various revolutionary efforts that led to the Revolution of 1911. For details, see Boorman and Howard, eds., *Biographical Dictionary* 1:440–443.

25. *Zhu Zhixin*

of popular education, but one aspect of the policy—land nationalization—could be realized because China had the heritage of the well-field system in ancient times.[108] Hu was clearly including "land nationalization" under one branch of socialism, and there is no reference here to the key tenets of Henry George.

Two articles by Zhu Zhixin in the spring and early summer of 1906 opened up a much wider arena of discussion on the subject of socialism. In the first article, Zhu set forth the case for the nationalization of railways (and by implication, other monopolies), not primarily on the basis of revenue advantages for the state, but as a part of the welfare obligations of the government toward its citizenry and its duty to prevent exploitation.[109]

Two months later Zhu responded to a slashing attack by Liang with a major article arguing the case for a simultaneous political and social revolution designed to change the basic nature of Chinese society.[110] In this essay Zhu revealed his currently strong affinity for Marxism and at the same time managed to end up close to Sun's position with respect to *minshengzhuyi*. While rejecting "pure communism" as impractical, Zhu proclaimed that Marx and "scientific socialism" heralded a new day for socialist theory and added that the "state socialism" [*sic*] advocated by the Tongmeng Hui would be easy to put into practice.

Grasping the Marxian doctrine of economic stages, Zhu asserted that the current call for a social revolution in the West stemmed from serious flaws in an economic system based on doctrines of laissez-faire and the absolute sanctity of private property. He perceived another Marxian concept—economics as the foundation, politics as the superstructure—when he stated that a political revolution was in a sense merely part of a broader social revolution. Yet he was not consistent on this crucial aspect of Marxism; he later argued that it would not be necessary for states like France and Germany to change their political institutions in the course of carrying out a social revolution.

Zhu then undertook a detailed analysis of the conditions under which the two revolutions (political and social) could and should be conducted simultaneously, and the circumstances under which this was not feasible. In presenting his typology of revolutions, he introduced the English words "proletarian" and "bourgeois" to make the point that in a political revolution the subject was the common people (*pingmin*) and the object was the government, whereas in a social revolution the subject was the proletariat and the object was the bourgeoisie. Zhu's typology consisted of three revolutionary settings. In Europe, which was his B-1 type, the subject of the political revolution (the bourgeoisie who had challenged feudalism and monarchical absolutism) was also the object of the social revolution (to be led by the proletariat). Hence the two revolutions could not be carried out simultaneously, and western Europe was destined to have to undergo a second revolution later. Russia represented Zhu's A type. Here, the economic system was still in the feudal stage, since both economic and political power still rested in the hands of aristocrats, clergy, and landlords. The objects of both revolutions would be the same, and therefore Russia could undergo both of its revolutions at once.

China fell into type B-2, a situation in which there was no relation between the two revolutions, hence no conflict in conducting them simultaneously. Qing officials, though corrupt and covetous, did not constitute an economic class, and there was no necessary correlation between political and economic power. Nor were the bourgeoisie of China, potentially the objects of a social revolution, the subjects of the ongoing political revolution. Our Chinese revolutionary movement, he asserted, is absolutely not dependent on the bourgeoisie for its motive force. Then he lapsed into pure Marxist doctrine: the future revolution will depend not on the secret societies alone, and not on the bourgeoisie, but on the proletariat.[111]

Thus, although Russia and China fell into different categories, both were appropriate settings for simultaneous social and political revolutions, according to Zhu. He joined his comrades, moreover, in depicting China as a society in which the gap between rich and poor was small, which meant that the execution of a social revolution would be relatively easy.

At the end of his essay Zhu came to the question of land nationalization. Here, too, he felt that Chinese circumstances were conducive to the policies being advanced by the Tongmeng Hui. Throughout history Chinese politics had operated to restrict the accumulation of wealth in private hands. To extend these policies and turn them into a fundamental reform program could not be regarded as unsuited to Chinese psychology and society. Nationalization of land in essence had a long heritage. In the Tang dynasty the land tax was called rent, which meant that the government was the landlord. What was regarded as ownership of land meant only the right for individuals to till the land, and from the Tang era onward the common people knew the difference between the land tax and other taxes. Hence it would not be difficult to carry out a policy of land nationalization during a political revolution. In these passages Zhu appears to equate land nationalization with taxation policies that in effect give the state full control over changing values, thus bringing himself close to Sun and the Georgists on this question.

THE RIPENING DEBATE OVER MINSHENGZHUYI

The debate between Liang and the Tongmeng Hui spokesmen over *minshengzhuyi* and socialism reached its climax in 1907, with a volley of articles back and forth involving the *Xinmin congbao* editor and such *Min bao* stalwarts as Hu Hanmin and Zhu Zhixin. Through these articles the major points in dispute were set forth at length, often in a highly polemical manner. Liang had begun a new phase of the debate with his searing article of September 1906.[112] A response by Hu Hanmin appeared in March 1907 in an article over one hundred pages long.[113] Hu defined the content of *minshengzhuyi* as follows. "Our socialism," he wrote, is aimed at making the state "the big landlord," and by this means "the big capitalist" as well. Through the nationalization of land the state would become the sole property owner, but it would lease the land to individuals or enterprises in whatever quantities they desired and could use. In this respect it differed from the ancient well-field system: the premium was not on equality of distribution but on insuring that increasing land values benefited society as a whole instead of a few individuals. Land rent would rise as land values rose. Besides providing steadily increasing revenues for the state, this would also forestall land speculation and a widening of the gap between rich and poor. In addition, Hu argued that although any amount of land could be leased at the sum fixed by the state, there would be no tendency toward land accumulation, because the experience of the West demonstrated that large-scale, mechanized agriculture was not as productive as family-operated plots.[114]

In addition to land nationalization, Hu championed the nationalization of monopolistic sectors of the economy, such as the railroads and mines. Other sectors, however, were to be left in private hands. We do not want excessive interference by the state, he remarked, because that would end free competition and cause economic stagnation. Our aim is merely to create an economic milieu conducive to the elimination of highly unequal economic classes. There will be differences of achievement, he continued, because of differences in talent and intelligence, but that is natural. What is unnatural is the type of inequality that is a product of an unfair economic system. In concluding this section he wrote, "This is the spirit of our theory of social revolution." *

In setting forth the Tongmeng Hui position, Hu delineated what he considered to be the differences between Liang and the revolutionaries. Liang, he said, was guilty of eight errors. The most important of these were his assumption that land was a trivial problem, and capital the key issue; his belief that emphasis should be placed on production, not distribution; his willingness to sacrifice Chinese society for the sake of encouraging indigenous capitalists, and his "closed door" policy toward foreign capitalists; and finally, his relative lack of concern for an economy that would benefit society as a whole. Moreover, in rejecting the idea that a social revolution was necessary for China, Liang had carefully omitted an analysis of America; he had compared the situation in China only with conditions in Europe. But although America shared with China a legacy of no aristocracy, no primogeniture, and relatively light taxes, a closer look would show that in certain respects it was suffering from greater inequities and social problems than Europe. The United States, in sum, could not escape a social revolution, despite its many advantages. To argue that China could do so was therefore foolish.

In confronting Liang on the question of the role of foreign capital in China, Hu anticipated an issue—both theoretical and practical—that remains alive today. His basic argument was that if land were nationalized along with natural monopolies, the capacity of foreign capitalism to control the Chinese economy would be removed. In that situation, advanced Western methods could be used to national advantage, and the funds needed to develop China would quickly become available. Liang's exclusionist, protectionist policies would condemn China to economic stagnation, and his program for enhancing domestic capitalism could not produce the necessary results soon enough and would allow major abuses and inequities. Hu ended the main section of his article by asserting that Sun wanted *minshengzhuyi* translated as "demosology" rather than "socialism," because "we want to move from the ideal to the practical."

As we noted in chapter 3, Liang Qichao fired his final salvo against *minshengzhuyi* in an article spread over three issues of *Xinmin congbao* published between April and June 1907. Since this sweeping attack was the culmination of Liang's efforts to counter Sun's brand of socialism, and further clarifies certain points at issue, it deserves some further attention here.[115] Liang managed to find no less than thirty-nine reasons why the concept of *minshengzhuyi* was deficient. He divided these into three broad categories:

* Hu's position can be summarized as follows: China in the future will be a nation where land is owned by the state. Nationalization means that all land legally belongs to the state, hence the source of capital will also belong to it. We speak of land, not capital, however, because land is already in private hands, whereas Chinese capitalists have not yet been born. The reason why land must be legally owned by the state, and capital need not be, is that land is easily monopolized, whereas capital is not. After land is nationalized, it cannot be sold, but it will be leased and utilized. The state will collect rent according to the current value of the land, which will in turn depend on the development of communications and the economy in general. What we call rent the Japanese call a lease. In sum, landlord profits will be transferred to the state by making the state the landlord and various entrepreneurs the tenants. To take care of the poorest people, we can extend rental payments for up to two years, so that even if they have only a hoe and an axe, they can achieve an income. Minyi, "To Those Who Challenge *minshengzhuyi*," *Min bao*, March 6, 1907, pp. 103–119.

the financial aspects of the proposed program; its effect on the economy as a whole; and its effect on China's social problems, present and future.

Liang was on strong ground when he challenged the amount of revenue that Sun and Hu expected to be derived from the land tax, and when he queried how the government intended to raise the funds necessary to purchase all of China's land at a price to be fixed. Here he took Hu at his word, that the land would be nationalized rather than merely taxed. Servicing the national debt under such circumstances would itself be impossible, given the revenue that could be realistically expected. But he also noted that the Sunists sometimes seemed to indicate that the original owners of the land could still hold it and collect rent, paying to the state a single tax based on the value of the land (pure Georgism). If landlords can collect rent, asked Liang, how is this state ownership, and do individuals continue to have inheritance rights as well as the right to collect rent?

In general, Liang wrote under the assumption that Sun and his supporters were still basically committed to Henry George's single tax on land value, despite some confusion on their part with respect to nationalization. He thus zeroed in on George's doctrines, insisting that their impracticality had been amply demonstrated by Western scholars. One central thesis in his essay was that Sun's land program, if put into effect, would discourage increased agricultural productivity and remove incentives for agrarian modernization. Moreover, since the land policies would leave urban issues largely untouched, they could not truly alleviate China's social problems. In his desire to score a point here, Liang argued that urban land was more conducive to monopolization than rural land, so that if state ownership were to be applied, he would favor "municipalization" over "nationalization."

In the end, however, Liang moved staunchly to the defense of a free economy. It was proper in the beginning, he acknowledged, to have the state control unoccupied land, newly created land, and forests; but except for forest lands and a few model farms, the state should divest itself of such holdings at an appropriate time. State enterprise, wrote Liang, is generally inferior to private enterprise, especially in agriculture.[116]

Zhu Zhixin entered the fray with a two-piece article published in the summer and early fall of 1907.[117] Liang's savage and detailed critique of the revolutionaries' arithmetic—specifically, their estimates of expenditures and revenues in connection with land nationalization—had clearly struck home. Zhu, after admitting that Tongmeng Hui spokesmen had not yet indicated precisely how land nationalization would be carried out, outlined two possibilities: either to issue public bonds or to set land prices first and stipulate that any increase in prices would go to the state at the time of sale. In the first case, there would be no immediate repayment; the bonds would be repaid over a period of twenty years with 5 percent interest. In the interim, not only would income from land rent gradually increase, but taxes of various sorts would be applied until the nationalization process was completed. Thus, ample revenues would be available.

Seeking to avoid the impression that he was abandoning Henry George, Zhu quoted him favorably and proclaimed that by land nationalization the Sun supporters intended to allow the state to scoop away the natural increase in rent, the essence of George's program. Liang and the authorities cited by him had been mistaken, moreover, in assuming that land nationalization related primarily to agricultural land. Land-value taxes would be levied on residences, factories, warehouses, mines, and forests as well as farm lands—and special attention would be devoted to residences. When one calculated the current taxes being paid and took corruption into account, the total did not vary greatly from the figures cited earlier in *Min bao*, Zhu insisted.

He concluded on a strongly optimistic note. There was no reason why China could not become as developed as the United States within twenty or thirty years if it borrowed the most advanced programs and technology from such a society. And given China's forest and mineral riches, the state's income should reach 10 billion dollars within thirty or forty years.

The debate over land nationalization essentially ended with an article by Taiqiu published in *Min bao* in late 1907.[118] The author began by attacking Liang's desire "to help the [Chinese] capitalists squeeze the workers," and found the root of the problem in Liang's excessive fear of foreign capitalism. He then proceeded to clarify the revolutionary position on land nationalization. The policy we espouse, Taiqiu wrote, is different from the single-tax doctrine. Avoiding reference to Henry George, he assigned the latter policy to the eighteenth-century physiocrats of France. The defect in their program, he continued, was that it put the entire burden on the landlords, whereas land nationalization involving land *rent*, instead of merely a land tax, distributes responsibility over the entire society. By buying the land at fixed prices, the state avoids the single-tax system, under which no compensation is involved. Liang had really attacked physiocratic theories, not recognizing the difference between the physiocratic position and that of the *Min bao* writers. He had assumed, moreover, that the land tax alone was supposed to be the only source of state income, whereas in fact, in addition to land rent, money would be available through state enterprises, fines, and when necessary, state borrowing.

With Taiqiu's article, debate on the land question came to a close for this period, but one fascinating article by Liu Guanghan should not be ignored. Restoration of the well-field system will not be enough, Liu wrote. Only the elimination of patrician and plebian classes, and the confiscation of the land of the very wealthy in order to provide common ownership, will suffice. Even if one were to strike down all legal class distinctions between rich and poor, Liu continued, if the land remains in the hands of the wealthy, the peasants will continue to be economically dependent on them, and will therefore follow them politically. Thus elections would be meaningless, as they are in Europe, America, and Japan. Only the confiscation of the property of the wealthy could remedy this situation, and such an act had to begin with a peasant revolution (*nongmin geming*), the author concluded.[119]

From this data, it seems clear that the Tongmeng Hui principle of *minshengzhuyi* underwent a certain evolution during the two years after it was first enunciated. Elements of confusion were not wholly eliminated, and it may well be that disagreements persisted among the Sun forces. Certainly, Liang's vigorous criticisms had provoked a great deal of further thought, discussion, and debate among the revolutionaries. Sun Yat-sen himself never diverged in print from Georgism in its pure and simple form; his speech of December 1906 provides clear evidence on this score. Yet in later issues of *Min bao*, the concept of land nationalization put forth by Hu Hanmin and Zhu Zhixin was at variance in crucial respects from Henry George's single-tax doctrine. George had specifically disavowed the nationalization of land as advocated by Wallace and a host of self-proclaimed socialists. Indeed, he had come to separate himself from the socialist movement. Hu and Zhu frequently tried to reconcile their position of espousing doctrines more compatible with the prevailing socialist currents than with the American iconoclast *and* the earlier words of their own revolutionary leader, but this was not easy—as Liang was quick to point out. Finally, by the close of 1907, one *Min bao* writer was prepared forthrightly to take a different tack, rebutting Liang by asserting that one had to distinguish between "the physiocratic concept" of a single tax and "our policy of land nationalization."

Thus, as Sun was leaving in the fall of 1905 his doctrine of *minshengzhuyi*—or as he preferred to call it in English, "demosology"—was being interpreted by authoritative Tongmeng Hui spokesmen as a form of state socialism. One aspect of the program was land nationalization: state purchase of all land at a fixed price followed by a flexible system of land leases, which would enable the government to drain off the rising value of all land that would accompany general economic development. In addition, state revenues were to be augmented and social equity enforced by state ownership of "natural monopolies," such as railways and mines. Yet the revolutionaries also proclaimed themselves dedicated to promoting a vigorous private economic sector built upon competition and the free flow of incentives. Foreign capital investment, moreover, was to be encouraged—since under the above conditions, it would benefit not harm China.

Interestingly, *minshengzhuyi* was to vary greatly in emphasis and in content over the years to come. But at this point, the intellectual vigor that characterized the debates of 1905–1907 waned, and the Tongmeng Hui, like Sun's earlier revolutionary association, fell upon hard times. The Kang-Liang forces had been largely vanquished insofar as their influence among overseas students was concerned, but unforeseen events were soon to split and then enfeeble the revolutionaries.

A PLAN FOR REVOLUTIONARY GOVERNMENT

One highly significant aspect of Sun's revolutionary program remains to be set forth, namely, the specific manner in which he and his associates planned to achieve military-political control, and the successive stages through which the state would have to pass en route to parliamentarism. At the time the Tongmeng Hui was formed, an official declaration relating to these matters was prepared.[120] A "people's army" would recover the fatherland, it asserted, but this revolution would differ from that of the Ming or the Taiping: it would not stop with the ouster of the alien rulers, but would make sweeping political and social changes in the spirit of freedom, equality, and fraternity. Thus, the military government would be only the agent of the people. Its four basic objectives would be to carry out the four goals of the Tongmeng Hui, and these would be accomplished in three stages.

The first stage would be government under military rule, with the people cooperating with the local military administration, both in areas where the enemy had been defeated and in those where enemy control still existed. Military rule in any given *xian* (district) would be limited to three years, to be followed by a period of provisional constitutional rule. In this stage, which was not to last longer than six years, there would be popular election of local legislative and administrative personnel, but the military would retain overall authority. In the third and final stage, that of constitutional rule, the military would give up all control over both the civilian administration and the governance of the armed forces, and the people would elect a national president and legislature.

Against the Qing program of progressive steps toward constitutionalism which were shortly to be proposed, the revolutionaries advanced their own timetable. Within a decade, they said, China could achieve a national system of constitutional, republican governance—a tribute to Sun's optimism and to the fact that his followers were young men in a hurry. Yet in the first instance, everything hinged upon the ability of those young men to conduct a successful revolution.

ABORTIVE REVOLUTIONARY EFFORTS

Revolution partakes of little romance. Moments of high drama—heroism and sacrifice by those who truly believe—are separated by long stretches of drudgery and frustration that severely test the character and temperament of all concerned. If most revolutionaries are passionately committed individuals, a considerable quotient of impracticality—or more broadly speaking, immaturity—often exists among them. And among the most daring and most resolute, the quotient tends to be highest. Revolutionaries, moreover, are by definition impatient and therefore not generally skilled in their timing. In addition, severe depression can follow quickly on exuberance, especially if failure proves a constant companion. It must be remembered that few revolutionaries have enjoyed immediate success; many have died with their objectives unrealized, or have abandoned the cause out of disillusionment, frustration, or a conviction that only repeated defeats lie ahead. A touch of fanaticism must cling to men like Sun Yat-sen, Vladimir Lenin, Mao Zedong, and Syngman Rhee, men who fight on in utter disregard of the odds against them, doggedly fixed on a single purpose.

Sun's revolutionary movement was afflicted with all of the problems that accrue to any such enterprise. Pettiness, jealousy, duplicity, treachery, and an utter lack of realism intermingled with dedication, honesty, sacrifice, and political shrewdness. The central problems, as might have been expected, related primarily to money and revolutionary tactics. Many Tongmeng Hui members, perhaps most of them, had reservations about Sun's plan for "equalization of land," but since the dominant thrust of his movement was racial and nationalist, other political issues could be subordinated. As in most revolutionary movements, however, funding was a constant worry to Sun and his comrades, and inevitably a point of contention. Most revolutions require money. Moreover, when a movement's operations are not effectively planned or coordinated, its financial needs increase and in the absence of success become endless. Thus, funds for the many revolutionary attempts that followed 1905 had to be continuously replenished, and Sun spent much of his time in the years down to 1911 in combined organizational and fund-raising activities overseas. Old sources were tapped again and again, and a persistent foraging for new sources took place, with almost exclusive dependence on overseas Chinese communities and a few additional foreign sources.*

*A painstaking account of the fund-raising campaigns and their results may be found in Shelley Hsien Cheng, *The T'ung Meng Hui: Its Organization, Leadership and Finance, 1905–1912*. See also the extensive narrative presented by C. Martin Wilbur, *Frustrated Pa-*

Sun left Tokyo in the fall of 1905, only a few weeks after the League was founded, going first to Saigon on an organizational and money-raising campaign. Everywhere the task was similar: to bring overseas Chinese together across linguistic, regional, and class lines; induce them to accept a single political association, cause, and leader; and then urge them to contribute as generously as possible to the movement. The Tongmeng Hui, it will be remembered, was organized as a federation of diverse provincial student groups. At least the students had a generally high level of political consciousness and tended to share broad political goals at this point. This was less true of other overseas Chinese, although as partial compensation, some overseas communities, such as those in Southeast Asia, consisted of large clusters of individuals who came from the same region and spoke the same dialect. The secret societies, moreover, were often well ensconced in such communities because the immigrants were predominately composed of Chinese from the south, particularly Guangdong. Sun was able to establish a Tongmeng Hui branch in Saigon; according to some sources, he also made a quick trip to France to seek additional support, but this seems doubtful. In any case, the overall results were far from an unqualified success. Returning to Tokyo, Sun spent most of 1906 bolstering the Tongmeng Hui there, making various foreign contacts in the Japanese capital, and planning for revolution. The Chinese government was now increasingly concerned about Sun's activities, and extensive pressure was applied on the Japanese to deport him. Tokyo was reluctant, but finally proposed a "voluntary" departure, sweetened by a generous grant of money. Additional funds were donated by a sympathetic Japanese stockbroker.

Sun was perpetually careless about money, treating it with the same cavalier attitude he generally took toward organizational matters. On this occasion he presented some of the funds to *Min bao*, but he kept the bulk of the money. Zhang Binglin and other comrades subsequently charged a misappropriation of funds and demanded that Sun be replaced by Huang Xing. Although Huang declined to participate in the anti-Sun drive, a lasting cleavage was opened between the leader and some of his original supporters.*

---

triot, pp. 39–75, covering the period 1905–1912. Wilbur notes that "fund-raising clearly was a cardinal occupation during most of Dr. Sun's mature life—he was almost perpetually on the trail of cash and rather ingenious in acquiring it" (p. 39). In assessing Sun's capacity to raise money from the overseas Chinese, Wilbur places primary emphasis on Sun's appeal to their patriotism, "to their pride in being Chinese," with the message frequently being a straightforwardly racist one (p. 46). It should be noted that a good-sized portion of Sun's overseas audience consisted of Guangdong-born Chinese, who shared his native language and subculture. Wilbur concludes that despite Sun's promises and the issuance of various notes and redeemable bonds, many donors probably never expected to be repaid (p. 53).

*For details of this episode, see Hsueh, *Huang Hsing*, pp. 52–53; K. S. Liew, *Struggle for Democracy*, p. 72; Wei and Wu, *Xinhai geming shi* 1:70–74. Wei and Wu present a detailed and very useful analysis of the Tongmeng Hui's internal troubles during this period. They assert that by the spring of 1907 three issues had emerged. The first was how to respond to a new effort in January by Liang Qichao to achieve a united front with the Tongmeng Hui. This divided key party members; Song Jiaoren and Zhang Taiyan (Binglin) tended to favor cooperation but Sun opposed it (pp. 70–71). The second was a dispute in March over the question of the Tongmeng Hui flag. Huang Xing wanted a flag with the character *yi* (the well-field character), symbolizing the party's commitment to equalization of land, but Sun insisted on a blue-sky, white-sun flag. Song Jiaoren made matters worse by charging that Sun had a dictatorial personality, then resigning his post and departing for Manchuria to recruit revolutionary fighters (p. 72). The third issue, which broke in June, concerned money.

A revolutionary uprising had already taken place when this dispute arose. In early December 1906 a struggle broke out in Pingxiang district (Jiangxi) and the neighboring Liuyang-Liling districts (Hunan), involving local groups and secret societies, spearheaded by the Gelao Hui.[121] Although Sun later claimed responsibility for these uprisings, they were not planned in Tokyo, and the few Tongmeng Hui members who participated did so on their own. Indeed, Sun later acknowledged that he and others in Tokyo had not been informed of the plans in advance and consequently were unable to provide assistance.[122]

By early 1907 Sun was back in French Indochina with his chief lieutenants, and for more than a year attempts were made to establish and hold a revolutionary base in South China, taking advantage of three factors: support from French sources; the strength of the secret societies in the region; and the fissures that were developing within the New Army, which had been recently established by the Qing government.

Concerning French support, we shall have more to say later. Suffice it to note here that certain French military and intelligence officials worked closely with Sun during part of this period, enabling him and his group to have access to the Guangxi and Yunnan borders. Using Indochina as a privileged sanctuary, the revolutionaries hoped to mobilize indigenous forces. The student revolutionaries recruited in Tokyo never played a central role in the military efforts of this period, although, as individuals, a few devoted themselves to the revolutionary cause, and some sacrificed their lives. Most students, however, were unsuited by training and temperament to be transformed into soldiers. The exceptions were those students who had been sent to Japan specifically as military trainees. Many of them proved valuable, but they were far from constituting a single force, being scattered among various New Army units, north and south. Most other students returned to take up roles in their native provinces, and not a few entered provincial politics in one form or another. But as we have remarked, Sun like Mao had doubts about the tenacity and hence the reliability of the young intelligentsia.

For Sun and Huang the secret societies had much greater potential. Deeply rooted in the soil of South China, organizationally solid, with their structure resting upon familial-clan ties and traditional values, they had far greater permanency than any student group. And their anti-Manchu credentials had been repeatedly tested. Thus, although Sun had moved to incorporate students into this movement, in no sense did he break the connections with secret societies which had marked his political course from its

---

When Sun had been deported in March, he had given the *Min bao* editors 2,000 of the 15,000 yuan received, and had taken the rest with him, supposedly to finance a later uprising. When the details became known, Zhang Binglin, Song Jiaoren, Zhang Zhi, and others demanded that Sun resign in favor of Huang, but Huang refused to support this move (pp. 72–74). By 1908 these personal and factional divisions had hardened to include issues of revolutionary strategy and questions about basic principles and leadership. As one result, the old Guangfu Hui reestablished separate headquarters in Tokyo and began competitive recruiting in Southeast Asia. In addition, rebels from the Yangtze River area, dissatisfied with Tongmeng Hui inactivity there and the preoccupation of Sun and Huang with South China, organized an autonomous unit known as the Gongjin Hui (Common Advancement Society), which had strong secret society representation; although it claimed to be a Tongmeng Hui branch, the new organization paid little attention to instructions from Sun or Wang (pp. 82–88). See also Gasster, *Chinese Intellectuals*, pp. 54–56.

early days. It is now commonly acknowledged that Sun himself joined the Triad Society at one point, possibly when he was in Hawaii or Hong Kong. In this connection Huang was an ideal coconspirator, having had intimate ties with the secret society network in Hunan.

The recruitment of secret society members as activists had additional consequences: it led easily into involvement with several varieties of marginal men. One type was the rootless rural man, deprived of any steady means of livelihood, who was available for banditry or other forms of lawlessness, including the sort of military adventure passing under the name of revolution. The abortive revolts of the period 1906–1908 included such individuals, and when the Communists later began their rural recruitment they also found them available. Among this group, some were what the Burmese would call "bad hats," persons whose character had been shaped in such a fashion as to make crime a preferred way of life. Others, through indoctrination and training, could be led into a disciplined political movement. Even the Communists, who had considerably more time than Sun for the guidance of recruits, were troubled by backsliders.

A variant of this type was the successful miscreant, the leader of a local band that engaged in smuggling, highjacking, and other activities yielding an income. Such men had a considerable degree of local authority and relative affluence. Sometimes they played a Robin Hood role; not infrequently they were secret society members. Often they had virtual control over a district or area, and always their interest lay in weakening the influence of the established government. In these terms, and for certain purposes at least, they were available to the revolutionary cause. But they too were marginal men, whatever their wealth or local power.

Sun's revolutionaries now targeted another group: elements of the New Army. Once again Sun was at first skeptical about relying on men or units wearing the uniforms of the Qing government. Yet the revolutionary movement had made contact with them in Tokyo and elsewhere. Some of Sun's most enthusiastic supporters, indeed, were military students. Huang, moreover, had a keen interest in military matters and was especially eager to establish liaison with New Army sources. And despite Sun's initial skepticism, in the end dissidence within military ranks in the south proved to be the single most critical factor in making possible the Revolution of 1911, although it was not a factor wholly related to the influence of the Tongmeng Hui.

Another source of revolutionary support consisted of certain individuals within the Chinese Christian movement. Sun was a baptized Christian and had used Christian connections ever since his first revolutionary attempt in 1895. Churches often served as meeting places, since they were relatively safe from police search and seizure. Some Christian sympathizers, both foreign and Chinese, offered shelter and information, as we have noted.

Finally, a small but interesting element in the revolutionary movement of this period consisted of women, mostly young students.[123] The first organizational efforts to improve the status of women in Chinese society had developed after the Sino-Japanese War; and separate movements advocating equal educational opportunities for women and opposing foot-binding had emerged in the early years of the twentieth century, reflecting strong Western influence. Still, the relatively few women with any higher education, and the powerful traditions defining women's "proper role" in society, kept all but a tiny handful of them from involvement in political matters. To be sure, there had been famous women fighters (primarily peasants) in various historical uprisings, and this tradition would meld with an emerging political consciousness among a few avant-garde women to produce the first female revolutionary martyrs in 1900. More meaningful developments, however, awaited the growth of the Chinese student movement in Japan. Included in the rising stream of young people going to Tokyo for an education were a small number of girls. Naturally, they were influenced by the general climate of the times, including the political activities of their male companions.

In 1903 a handful of girls founded a society called the Gong Ai Hui (Mutual Love Society) in Tokyo, and in September 1906 the more important Association of Chinese Women Students in Japan (Zhongguo LiuRi Nüxuesheng Hui) was set up. Under its first leader, Li Yuan, the Association's initial purpose was to promote educational opportunities for women and at the same time to call attention to their past degradation. According to the notice announcing the founding of the organization, Chinese women constituted one-eighth of the world's population, yet they had been reduced to the status of slaves by a lack of education and organization. Fortunately, progress in global communications and transport had enabled the women of China to learn of the progress of Western women and to come to Japan to absorb a new culture. The announcement concluded with a solemn pledge to work for the right of Chinese women to end slavishness and secure their rightful position among the world's advanced people.[124] Later, such political activists as Yan Bin, Tang Qunying, Wu Yanan, and Wang Changguo—all members of this Association—were to play prominent revolutionary roles.

Paralleling developments in Japan, organizational activities got under way in Shanghai, a logical center for political movements of all types. In January 1904 the Society of Women Comrades to Oppose Russia (Dui Eguo Zhi Nü Hui) was founded by Zheng Suyi, Chen Wanyan, and others. Like the Gong Ai Hui in Tokyo, it was influenced by the patriotic mood of youthful intellectuals and the actions of male students. Shanghai also became the center of special educational institutions for women. The first school of political significance was the Aiguo (Patriotic) Girls' School, founded in conjunction with the Patriotic Society in 1902 or 1903. At first it was a small private school with only members of Society families admitted, but enrollment was later expanded.

In 1905, after her return from Japan, Qiu Jin and other returned students founded the Zhongguo Gongxue (Chinese Public School) in Shanghai; one of its principal purposes was to advance the radical nationalist cause. In the following year, moreover, she returned to her native place, Shaoxing, Zhejiang, to create two new schools. One of them, the Physical Education School, was set up to give women students military training so that they could be organized into a female army commanded by Qiu. During this period Qiu suffered a hand wound while manufacturing explosives in preparation for an assassination effort by a comrade. She later became a martyr to the cause during an abortive local uprising in 1907; executed by authorities on July 14, she was then given a prominent place in Nationalist annals.[125] Other girls' schools that bore strong political overtones were established in Canton and Hong Kong, and they later directed young women into the revolutionary cause.

Shanghai and Tokyo also brought forth feminist publications, some of a

26. *Qiu Jin*

revolutionary bent. The first woman's magazine of this type appears to have been *Nuxue bao* (Women's Educational Journal), founded by Chen Jiefen in Shanghai in 1902. It was connected with the famed *Su bao* and supported such causes as equal rights for women in politics and education, the abolition of foot-binding, and revolution on behalf of Han nationalism. It went out of existence along with *Su bao* in 1903. Three years later, the short-lived Shanghai *Zhongguo nü bao* (Chinese Women's Journal) emerged, with Qiu Jin as editor. Qiu's opening statement set forth the major themes being advanced: while the 200 million men of China were advancing into the global culture, China's 200 million women were still condemned to the darkness of hell. "Alas, my dear sisters," she wrote, "to be called a slave is something that no one in any country of the world accepts willingly. Why are my sisters accepting this humiliation so calmly?"[126]

The following year, two women students in Japan, Yan Bin and Liu Qingxia, started a monthly entitled *Zhongguo xinnü jie* (The World of the New Chinese Women), which survived for six issues.* Another feminist periodical that championed women's rights was *Tianyi bao* (Natural Justice Journal), a radical anarchist paper published in Tokyo by He Zhen and her husband, Liu Shipei (Guanghan); we shall examine it closely in the next chapter.

Sun and his close associates were always prepared to see women play an active revolutionary role. In 1905 the Tongmeng Hui set up a workshop in Yokohama to instruct revolutionaries in making and using bombs, with a Russian nihilist as instructor. A number of women attended, among them Qiu Jin, Fang Zhunying, Chen Jiefen, Lin Zongsu, Tang Chunying, Zai Hui, and Wu Mulan. Later, these and other women served the revolutionary cause in a variety of capacities: as arson squads, as couriers, as members of assassination teams, as "safe-house" operators, and as intelligence gatherers.**

It must be emphasized that in this era only a very small number of women became politically involved. For the most part, moreover, they came from educated, urban families, and many of them were drawn into political activities by the men in their families—a father, a brother, or a husband having set the pattern. Sometimes the stimulus came from school companions or from teachers. Quite naturally, the major rallying points were Tokyo and Shanghai, for these were the only places where something approaching a critical mass existed and where the issues leading to activism were intensely debated. As with male radicals, the central thrust was Han nationalism, but with strong nihilist and anarchist influences manifesting themselves, together with deep commitment to equality for women.

LATE QING REVOLUTIONARY EFFORTS

In March 1907 Sun and Hu Hanmin reached Saigon and began the task of recruiting support for the revolution from the local Chinese population and from such French citizens as they could interest. They were soon joined

*One theme in this journal was that because the female half of China was uneducated, the nation could not develop properly and would continue to be prey to imperialist pressures. The journal was suspended by Japanese police after it published an article entitled "Women Revolutionaries Should Use Assassination as Their Weapon" (Lin Wei-Hung, "Activities of Women Revolutionists," p. 251, quoting Feng Ziyou, *Zhongguo geming* in *Kaiguo wenxian*, part 1, vol. 12, p. 676).

**One of the women active on behalf of Sun's movement was He Xiangning, the wife of Liao Zhongkai. Their home was used as a meeting place and mailing address in Japan for revolutionaries, and He took care of Sun's correspondence. (He Xiangning, "My Recollections," *Xinhai geming huiyi lu* 1:13–17.) In the various revolutionary efforts preceding the 1911 Revolution, women helped to camouflage preparations by playing roles as housewives and servants, receiving messages, storing supplies, including guns and munitions, and sheltering male revolutionaries. One favorite technique was to transport guns in fake wedding processions, with the "brides" being women activists (Lin, "Activities of Women Revolutionists," pp. 273–274). Even certain Shanghai prostitutes were later enlisted in the cause, as collectors of intelligence from patrons (Lin, pp. 296–297).

27. Japanese socialists and anarchists, many of whom interacted with Chinese reformers and revolutionaries: photograph taken to commemorate a summer seminar on socialism, Tokyo, August 1907.

From the left, first row: Takeuchi Zensaku, Fukao Shō, Murata Shirō, Kōtoku Denjirō (Shūsui) (with mustache), Sakai Tameko, Sakai Magara, unknown, Tokunaga Yasunosuke (with glasses), unknown, Yamakawa Hitoshi, Nishikawa Kōjirō, Tsuihiji Nakasuke, unknown, Morichika Umpei (coat); second row: 2d, Osakabe Torahichi; 3d, Yoshikawa Morikuni (coat); 5th, Sakai Toshihiko (glasses); 6th, Katayama Sen (bearded, black kimono); 7th, Fukuda Hideko; 9th, Niimura Tadao (glasses, white coat); third row: 1st, Tazoe Tetsuji (bearded); 5th, directly in front of tree, Shibata Saburō; 10th, showing only head, Morioka Eiji; 20th, Saitō Kanejirō; 21st, Handa Ichirō (bearded).

by Huang Xing and Wang Jingwei. The next revolt—which Sun claimed to have organized—broke out on May 22, in east Guangdong, at Huanggang. Led by a local Triad chief, this revolt involved at most several hundred insurgents and was suppressed within a few days, although most of the rebels melted away and remained available for another attempt. The actual degree of Sun's involvement is unclear, but Sun himself called this attempt his "fourth revolutionary defeat."* Another small uprising occurred a short

* For a contemporary account from the scene, see "The Disturbances in South China," From Our Own Correspondent, Swatow, dated June 8, 1907, *North China Herald*, June 21, 1907, p. 714. The writer, probably a foreign missionary, reported that the rising at Huang-

time later, on June 2, near Huizhou (Waichow). It too was quickly suppressed.

While these revolts were minute in scale and primarily the product of local planning, Sun's movement now began to concern regional and national authorities deeply. In the summer of 1907, Yuan Shikai, Duanfeng, and Zhang Zhidong joined in a telegram to the throne urging Their Majesties to leave the Yihe Park Palace and reside in Beijing in order to thwart any revolutionary coup that might be attempted.[127] At approximately the same time Viceroy Zhang told the central government that he had heard that Sun was preparing to start a revolution in the Yangtze provinces at any moment. This message caused great anxiety in the capital, and orders were sent to regional officials warning them to be prepared for any emergency.[128]

In terms of the actual strength and preparations of the revolutionaries, the threat was being grossly exaggerated—which reflected in part the extensive weakness of the government at this point. The first revolt in which Sun and his comrades were directly involved was far from the Yangtze valley, in the Qingzhou district of Guangdong, near the Guangxi-Tonkin border.[129] Even in this case, the uprising began as a local dispute over increased taxes that had erupted in September 1907; the leaders had sent representatives to Hanoi to seek support from Sun. At this point, Hu Yisheng was ordered to make contact with Zhao Sheng, the commander of several battalions of New Army soldiers recently stationed in the area. Zhao had had contact with Hu and the revolutionary movement earlier, and was known to be sympathetic. Huang in turn undertook to get in touch with Zhao's superior, Guo Renzhang, who commanded several thousand Provincial Defense forces. An effort was simultaneously made to procure arms from Japan, using stores already collected there by the revolutionaries, with retired French officers recruited as military instructors.

The planned uprising, however, largely aborted. The weapons never reached the rebels, and disputes over their quality drove a further wedge between the Hanoi and Tokyo revolutionaries. Most important, the effort to enlist the support within the New Army and the Provincial Defense forces failed. Guo declined to join, and Zhao was inhibited from taking any action. Thus when Sun's forces, led by a local Triad leader with a reputation for banditry, struck on September 1, 1907, they were able to kill only a few local loyalists, including the magistrate at Fangcheng; the attack on Qing-

---

gang had been suppressed and that the insurgents had retreated into the hills. One of their rubber stamps (seals) showed a cockatoo standing on a globe and was "clearly Japanese" in origin. Their flag, the writer said, was a star of eight points, white on green, with a red background—and they also carried banners inscribed "Gemingdang" (Revolutionary Party). Once again, strong secret society influence would seem to be indicated, but Sun and the Qing government united to give Sun's movement credit for the uprising, each for separate reasons.

Wei and Wu divide the "more than ten armed uprisings" that occurred between 1906 and the Revolution of 1911 into four categories: (1) those assisted by local, spontaneous mass struggles (the Ping-Liu-Li uprising in 1906 and the Fang Cheng uprising of 1907 in Guangdong); (2) uprisings involving the mobilization of secret societies (the Huanggang uprising, the Ji-Nu-Hu uprising in Guangdong, and the Zhe-Wang uprising in Zhejiang and Anhui—all in 1907); (3) uprisings stemming from the proselytization of the New Army (the Anqing uprising of 1908 in Anhui, and the Guangzhou uprising of 1910); (4) uprisings involving the use of small commando-type bands (the Zhennan-Guan uprising of 1907, the Qingzhou Ma-Du-Shan uprising in Guangdong in 1908, the Hekou uprising in Yunnan in 1908, and the well-known Huang-Hua-Gang uprising in Guangdong in 1911). See *Xinhai geming shi*, pp. 227–228.

28. *Sun with French officials in Hanoi, circa 1908*

zhou, where Guo's troops were stationed, had to be abandoned, and by mid-September the revolt was over.*

The next effort was based on an even less promising set of circumstances. On December 1 several local leaders from backgrounds similar to that of Wang Heshun seized a frontier fortification, Zhennan Guan, in southwest Guangxi near the Indochina border. After its capture Sun came to the site with Huang Xing, Hu Hanmin, and a retired French captain. Sun stayed only three days, and was in Hanoi negotiating for additional support when his meager band was forced to retreat.

* Sun's own very brief account of this "fifth failure" ran as follows. After word of the tax revolt, he ordered Huang and Hu to visit Guo and Zhao in an effort to persuade them to come over "to the side of the revolution." Both generals declared that if "a real revolutionary army" were able to carry out a revolt effectively, they would join. Organizers were then sent to the districts involved, and several revolutionaries were dispatched to Japan to obtain weapons. Comrades were also assembled in Indochina, and demobilized French officers were recruited to train them. The hope was to seize a wide stretch of territory along the border, using some 2,000 armed men, who would quickly be joined by a force of 6,000 to be recruited from the target area. With these forces, Sun wrote, we could convince Guo to come to our side, occupy Guangdong and Guangxi, and then advance to the Yangtze, Nanjing, and Wuhan. The effort failed, according to Sun, because "troubles" within the Tokyo group prevented the arms from arriving. Even if the arms had arrived, however, it was unlikely that any major part of this ambitious but questionably planned revolt could have succeeded. Besides the fact that the arms collected were reportedly of poor quality, everything depended on Guo—and on the further disintegration of the armed forces of the Qing government. (That disintegration came later, under more persuasive pressures, in a more strategically placed locale.) Sun's revolutionaries in this episode consisted of fewer than 500 poorly trained troops.

At this point, Beijing had ample evidence of Sun's activities in Indochina and the cooperation being tendered by certain Frenchmen. His expulsion was demanded, and in March 1908 he was finally deported—after preparations for a new border uprising had been made. The "seventh revolutionary defeat" ensued, with Huang Xing leading about 600 men across the Tonkin frontier into Guangdong in late March. On this occasion the rebels had some advantages. Their ranks were well disciplined, reasonably well equipped, and were said to enjoy support from the local inhabitants. After about a month, however, they clashed with one of Guo's units, and his indifference (or ambivalence) toward the revolt ended. In the ensuing days, the revolutionaries were put under heavy attack, and their peasant allies deserted, fearing government reprisals. In early May, Huang returned to Hanoi. Another effort had failed.

The final revolutionary attempt of this period, though in certain respects the most significant in its effect, also ended in failure, becoming Sun's "eighth revolutionary defeat." Once again, a strategic border area between South China and Vietnam was chosen for assault. Hekou, a garrison post holding more than 2,500 soldiers, was in Yunnan, across the Red River from the Indochina town of Laokay. A portion of the garrison had been subverted by revolutionary propaganda prior to the attack and was prepared to revolt. The assault began on April 29, 1908, led by Huang Mingtang, the same secret society, ex-bandit leader who had replaced Wang Heshun in the Zhennan Guan attack. He commanded about 300 men, and after a midnight assault in which the regional military commander was killed, most of the garrison soldiers joined the rebels. The plan was to move along the railway line, taking Mengze and then Yunnan Fu. But Huang Mingtang and his men, dissatisfied with their meager rations, inadequate arms, and lack of pay, refused to cooperate with Huang Xing in executing this plan. And when Huang returned to Hanoi to obtain additional weapons and recruits, he was arrested and deported. At this point, the Qing government rallied, raised a sizable army, and defeated the insurgents by the end of May.*

By mid-1908 Sun's revolutionary movement was at another low ebb. Few of the efforts at revolution had come even close to success, and most Tongmeng Hui members had drifted away, unwilling to commit themselves to a hopeless cause. Among those who remained, disputes over money, supplies, and tactics had immobilized the Tokyo headquarters, which led Sun to sponsor organizational efforts elsewhere. His attention first centered upon Hong Kong, where a South China Bureau of the Tongmeng Hui was set up in the fall of 1909; Wang Jingwei, who continued to be a loyal Sun supporter, was elected secretary. Earlier, as one of the five bureaus planned, a South Seas Bureau had been established to direct party activities in Southeast Asia, and later, just prior to the Wuchang uprising, a Central China Bureau was created secretly in Shanghai; Song Jiaoren, Zhen Jimei, and others were in charge, but their lines of communication to Sun and Huang were tenuous at best.

*The earliest reports of this uprising carried in the *North China Herald* greatly exaggerated the number of revolutionaries coming from Indochina, saying they had been variously estimated at between 3,000 and 5,000. The defection of garrison soldiers was called a "cowardly surrender," though it was indicated that 2,000 Mauser magazine rifles had fallen into the hands of the revolutionaries, who proclaimed Sun as "the Supreme Head of their Society" ("Anti-Monarchist Invasion," May 16, 1908, p. 417). A later account, after total defeat was imminent, asserted that even in their "best days," the antimonarchists in Yunnan could not have exceeded 250 men (May 30, 1908, p. 578).

29. *Money-raising: Sun and members of the Chicago Tongmeng Hui, February* 1910

Sun himself was involved in almost continuous money-raising activities between mid-1908 and the Revolution of 1911. In this he was aided by Hu Hanmin and until January of 1909 by Wang Jingwei. From Singapore, where the British had reluctantly permitted him to stay after his forced departure from Hanoi, Sun set out on a fund-raising campaign in Malaya in the fall, and then planned a trip to Paris—which he had to postpone until May 1909 for lack of money. So desperate were the revolutionaries for funds that they once tried to sell classified Japanese military documents to the Russians; their messenger, Xiong Chengji, was betrayed by a friend, arrested, and executed by the Manchu government on January 10, 1910.*

By this time Sun hardly dared enter any Southeast Asian region because of opposition from the British, French, and Dutch colonial authorities. Privileged sanctuaries adjacent to China's frontiers were essentially closed to him, though not generally to his key lieutenants. Early 1910 found Sun in North America, organizing Tongmeng Hui branches in New York, Chicago, and San Francisco and raising money to support the next revolutionary effort. From this point on, fund-raising centered upon Chinese communities in Canada and the United States.

The new revolutionary plan, unlike the uprisings of 1906–1908, focused on Canton, with its chief impresarios being Huang Xing and Zhao Sheng. Zhao, having been deprived of his army rank on suspicion of prorevolutionary sympathies, had defected and come to Hong Kong, where he began working closely with Huang. Joined by another former army officer, Yi

*Hsueh, *Huang Hsing*, pp. 74–75. It might be recalled that several years earlier, in the spring of 1907, Huang Xing, with the assistance of Song Jiaoren and others in Tokyo, had plotted a revolt in Manchuria. Nothing came of it, however, and there is no evidence that foreign governments were contacted. See Song, *Wo zhi lishi*, pp. 324–331.

Yingdian, they labored to secure support within the Canton-based military forces, and were reported to have achieved significant success by the end of 1909.

With funds from a favorably disposed Hong Kong businessman and Sun's promise of additional financial aid from the United States, the uprising was scheduled for late February 1910, to coincide with the Chinese New Year. Unfortunately for the revolutionaries, it was triggered prematurely by an incident, and Yi Yingdian, leading about 1,000 soldiers, was killed at the outset. Before Huang Xing and Zhao Sheng could take command, the plans were in disarray and the uprising had been smashed. It became "the ninth defeat."

When he got word of this uprising, Sun sought to come back, but after being recognized in the port of Yokohama, and learning that the revolt had collapsed, he decided to return to Southeast Asia. After meetings with Hu Hanmin and various followers and some additional fund-raising, however, Sun was ultimately forced to return to the West, since all colonial governments strongly opposed his presence. By January 1911 he was once again in the United States, where he remained until after the Wuchang uprising.

SUN AND THE FOREIGN POWERS

One of the most enigmatic aspects of Sun's long political career was his relations with the major foreign powers. To many observers it seemed incredible that this fervent nationalist would make a series of extraordinary offers to the leading imperialist nations of this era, offers which could easily be interpreted as "country-selling" by his opponents, and which matched if not exceeded those accepted by the Qing court, Yuan Shikai, and various provincial leaders, current and future.

Sun, to be sure, always proclaimed the need for foreign assistance in the building of China, and a decade after the events we have been discussing, he outlined his most ambitious plan for such aid. Moreover, he seems to have retained a supreme confidence that if *his* revolution succeeded, a self-governing and self-confident China—responding to the political and economic concerns of the people—could turn foreign involvement to China's advantage. In this respect Sun can be compared with the Chinese Communist leaders of the late 1970s.

Nevertheless, Sun's various proposals—both before and after 1911—seem as strange today as they did to some of his contemporaries. Among his official foreign contacts, those with the greatest promise appear to have been with the Japanese and the French. Sun had various British friends, but neither the Hong Kong authorities nor the British government in London ever appears to have taken kindly to his activities. Sun had sought assistance from the Hong Kong government in mid-1900, promising that the revolutionary government would establish civil rights for all Chinese and equal opportunities for all foreigners under an Anglo-Saxon legal system.[130] He received no response. He remained persona non grata in Hong Kong, and as we have seen, London would have allowed his career to end in 1896 except for the intervention of Dr. Cantlie. In later years, authorities in British colonies in Southeast Asia were sometimes persuaded to treat Sun as a political refugee, but they did not do so willingly, and in the end he was virtually excluded from all British possessions.

Nor were Sun's contacts with the government of the United States extensive or fruitful in the years before 1911. This may seem surprising in light of Sun's oft-expressed admiration for American political institutions and historical figures. But it must be remembered that along with its official Open Door policy—equal access to China's markets and no exclusive spheres of influence for European or Japanese interests—Washington favored measures that would strengthen the Chinese government, lest in the midst of chaos and revolutionary agony it fall prey to further imperialist advances. This, indeed, had been American policy from the time of the Taiping, and official attitudes toward Sun displayed no deviation. There was, moreover, the troublesome issue of Chinese immigration, and the general anti-Oriental prejudice that enflamed politics in the western United States. It was not a time when a Chinese revolutionary could expect to win official support. Sun, however, made efforts to obtain funds from American banks. He authorized Charles B. Boothe, the Tongmeng Hui's financial agent in the United States, to borrow $2 million from banks to support revolutionary activities.[131]

The situation with respect to Japan was far more complex. As we have noted, both Chinese reformers and revolutionaries had important Japanese contacts from an early point in their periods of exile. Sun's first friendship started fittingly enough in Hawaii, when he met a Christian minister, Sugawara Den, in 1894.[132] It was three years later, however, shortly after his narrow escape in London, that Sun began his intimate acquaintance with Miyazaki Torazō and, through Miyazaki, with various other ardent Japanese nationalists. Miyazaki and Hirayama Shū, both of whom had been given Foreign Office funds to make contacts with Chinese committed to rebuilding China, took Sun to meet Inukai Tsuyoshi (Ki), one of Japan's rising young politicians, a leader of the Progressive Party and a cabinet member in the Matsukata-Ōkuma government. Inukai was to remain a friend and benefactor, and in the next decade Sun met a number of other prominent Japanese, including *genrō* (senior statesmen), party politicians, and assorted Pan-Asian nationalists dedicated to rescuing Asia from Western imperialism.

The high point in collaborative efforts during this period came in the years 1899 and 1900. We have already spoken of the abortive attempt to aid Aguinaldo, in which Sun and the Miyazaki group were so heavily involved. This was followed by the long and complicated planning for the Huizhou (Waichow) revolt. With the knowledge of governmental officials, Miyazaki and his associates worked closely with the Sun forces. Some participated in the actual fighting, and Japanese assistants, who would function during and after the revolution, were named for the key Chinese figures—a plan remarkably similar to the one later presented in more detailed form by the Japanese government and labeled the Twenty-One Demands.

As we have indicated, the Huizhou uprising failed partly because no arms were available from Japan, the purchased military supplies having proved to be unusable. With Itō Hirobumi as prime minister, the authorities in Tokyo began to pursue a tougher policy toward Sun. By this time the attention of both the Japanese government and nationalists was focused increasingly upon Korea and Manchuria, partly as a result of Russian activities in the aftermath of the Boxer Rebellion. Since Sun's efforts related primarily to South China, Tokyo's interest in his revolutionary efforts waned. Nonetheless, certain individuals—particularly those connected with the Kokuryūkai—saw a connection between supporting Sun and meeting the Russian threat. Japan, united with a new Chinese government that had succeeded in ousting the Manchu, could more effectively challenge Russian expansion. As the twentieth century comes to a close, such a doctrine has a highly contemporary ring, although the initiative is now coming from Beijing.

Sun's ties with Kokuryūkai leaders remained very close after his return to Tokyo in 1905. Miyazaki, Hirayama, and Kayano Chōchi were actually allowed to join the Tongmeng Hui, and in 1907 Miyazaki was authorized to serve as fund-raiser and arms-purchasing agent for the League. What were the common bonds between Sun, a committed republican and disciple of Western spiritual and political values, and the Japanese nationalists, whose devotion to the imperial cause was generally accompanied by a deep hatred of Westernism in all its forms? The nationalist connection was paramount, to be sure, even though it led in different directions. Beyond this, as we have seen, Sun was prepared to accept aid from almost any source, provided it contributed to victory for the cause. His concentration was wholly upon the end; contradictions or dangers in the means seldom concerned him. His lack of intellectual rigor also made it easy for him to seek allies among those of different political persuasion. It did not cause him pain to seek accommodation more or less simultaneously with men ranging from Toyama Mitsuru, the doyen of Japanese ultranationalists, to the youthful leaders of the Chinese anarchist movement.

Though Sun continued to have a wide circle of Japanese friends and supporters, the tide was turning against him at the governmental level. After the Japanese military victory over Russia in 1905, the Qing authorities in Beijing sought to model their political reforms after Meiji Japan, and Tokyo's interest in a Chinese revolution continued to decline. Moreover, skepticism about the capacities of the revolutionaries increased. It will be recalled that, under heavy Chinese pressure, the Japanese government requested that Sun leave Tokyo in early 1907. By this time, incidentally, Miyazaki was regarded as too radical by Tokyo authorities, and he no longer had easy access to top officials. Thus between 1907 and the 1911 Revolution, Sun had little success in his search for Japanese assistance.

He now turned his attention to Paris. The French interest in China, and particularly in South China, was equal to that of the British and the Japanese.[133] A separate government of South China indebted to French assistance could protect and advance French interests. It is not surprising, therefore, that certain French officials in the military, intelligence, and diplomatic sectors of the government were sympathetic to Sun's movement. Besides giving him a privileged sanctuary for his activities between 1906 and 1908, they promised him official assistance from various quarters and allowed him to recruit Frenchmen for the training of Chinese. His support came from such important individuals as a governor-general of Indochina, a minister of war in Paris, assorted Foreign Ministry officials, and prominent French *colons* residing in Indochina.

In the end, Sun failed to hold French support, despite his promises that the French would be rewarded with additional concessions when victory had been achieved. In the heyday of the collaboration, however, Frenchmen had accompanied revolutionaries on a tour of southern China to collect intelligence and assess revolutionary strength; French administrators in Indochina had taken a passive attitude toward the use of territories under their control as revolutionary staging areas; and no French officials had interfered with Sun's efforts to raise funds and secure arms—indeed, some had actively cooperated. But as in the case of Japan, Sun had his French enemies. They included the French minister to Beijing, assorted French consuls in China, elements of the army, and most important, a new premier, Georges Clemenceau, who wanted attention turned toward Germany. The failure at Hekou and an accompanying incident in June of 1908—in which Qing soldiers, in hot pursuit of rebels, shot a French officer on Indochinese soil—brought home to most French the dangers of supporting a losing revolutionary cause, and Sun's ragtag soldiers were quickly deported.

AN ASSESSMENT

As the Revolution of 1911 approached, Sun's movement seemed a complete failure. Its organization was feeble, and despite its military recruits the turnover in membership was heavy. Sun himself was now barred from entering the colonial areas adjacent to China, and it had become more difficult for him to find privileged sanctuaries anywhere, the Canton uprising of 1910 notwithstanding. Some money could still be raised, especially in North America, but the amounts were disappointingly small.

But a balance sheet would also reveal some meaningful achievements. For a select group of Chinese youth who were about to burst upon the political stage, Sun Yat-sen had provided a comprehensive political program and the beginnings of an ideology.

Since Sun's "three people's principles" constituted the ideological framework for successive stages of the Chinese revolution, and since the ideological component of both the Nationalist and Communist phases of that revolution has been of critical importance, it is necessary to make clear our own interpretation and use of the term "ideology." By ideology we mean an interrelated set of "truths" about man and society which in its organic construction and cosmic reach establishes both the basic directives and the broad perimeters for political values and actions. An ideology must encompass the whole; it can never rest with the partial. It must be universal; it can never be satisfied with the specific, even if it is intended to govern every specific thought and act in the political realm. And its application is *political*, even though its impact is felt in every aspect of individual and societal life.

We are not satisfied with past efforts to distinguish between ideologies according to instrumental ends or levels of abstraction. To us, an ideology must encompass supreme values, must operate at the highest level of abstraction, and must relate directly to man in society, hence to the political. Karl Mannheim's attempted distinction between ideologies and utopias is both factually and conceptually flawed.[134] Mannheim is seeking to separate the effort of explaining something from the effort to change it. But in our view, a true ideology must combine universally applicable explanations with clearly projected ideals. In fact, all ideologies partake extensively of a utopia, and in their relationship to that which *is*—to the present state of affairs in human society—each holds within it the potential for profound change. That potential, to be sure, may not be realized. It is likely that any given elite in power will try to make an ideology serve the status quo; yet dissidents within the society, in calling for fundamental changes, may well appeal to that same ideology.

Is it appropriate to draw a distinction between "pure" and "applied" ideology?[135] The chief defect of such a dichotomy is that it obscures the extent to which ideology must be differentiated from the political process. Instances of "applied" ideology can be multiplied at will, so that what is left of "pure" ideology is only a constantly evolving body of doctrine, scarcely distinguishable from the policies it supposedly spawns; every rationalization can claim to be an addition to the theoretical foundations on which the society supposedly rests.

We would argue that ideology must always be regarded as "pure," since it is required to represent a set of universal abstractions which dictates both the ideal social order and the generalizable principles from which all action must flow. It is the polar star from which men and societies measure their positions. Once it is applied, of course, ideology is necessarily defiled in some degree by the requirements and limitations of real people who exercise power. Political action and policies—together with the explanations accompanying them—partake of adjustment, compromise, and error. But this represents the corruption of ideology, not a different type of ideology. Any ideology can be misinterpreted, accidentally or deliberately. Any ideology can be used as a rhetorical smokescreen for actions moving in a diametrically opposite direction. Given the human personality, any ideology can and will be applied imperfectly. But ideology remains an abstract ideal of the sociopolitical order, not subject to incrementalism. Individuals may abandon one ideology and take up a new one, but ideology itself does not creep toward individuals, seeking accommodation as each new program is fashioned.

In sum, ideology should not be confused with the constant adjustments that accompany the political process. Ideologies are invariably cosmic explanations pointing to political orders that are either inevitable or feasible, and in any case also desirable. True ideologies have always been few, and they remain constant despite all changes in the policies and values justified in their name. Thus, when Lenin and Stalin talked about the need to treat Marxism as a dynamic force which needed adjustment in order to make it applicable to Russia, and when Mao interpreted "Marxism-Leninism" to suit a near-infinite variety of policies and actions, it did not mean that Marxism was "evolving" in accordance with the needs of these particular societies. It signifies instead a corruption of Marxism, made almost inevitable by the fallacies imbedded in Marxism itself and by the different characteristics of Russian and Chinese societies. In fact, a similar corruption of the liberal ideology was taking place more or less simultaneously in the industrial West. It should be clear, incidentally, that we use the term "corruption" not as a normative judgment but in order to suggest a movement away from the central tenets of the ideology. The practical application of an ideology always involves creativity, and sometimes further conceptualization; but it should be viewed as a part of the political process, not as an example of ideological development per se.

It may be objected that this deprives ideology of any evolutionary potential at all. Can an ideology spring forth fully clothed, so to speak, and thereafter defy all attempts at refinement or alteration? The answer is that the most enduring ideologies mankind has constructed have indeed rested on certain immutable abstractions about man and society. If these abstractions are successfully challenged, either conceptually or through an accumulation of empirical data, men may turn to a different ideology. But if they are merely disregarded or warped in the course of governance, no ideological transformation takes place. That will not occur until circumstances compel a new and comprehensive reconciliation between practice and theory, which produces a different ideology.

The ideology that Sun introduced to his followers was liberalism, the mainstream ideology of the contemporary West. In the effort to derive from liberalism policies and values that could be made applicable to China, Sun put into his program an element of state socialism, which he justified by appealing to both science and liberal humanism. Most of Sun's supporters accepted this ideology, though many young nationalists corrupted it by putting heavy emphasis on the role of "the free individual" in building the power of the state. In any case, for the first time, a sizable core of China's youthful elite had a political cause in which they could believe, a cause related to China's total modernization. As we have emphasized, the sweeping character of their revolutionary concerns was illustrated in the call for a new Chinese individual as well as a new Chinese nation. For both the society and its activist elements, this call was fundamentally different from that put forth by the Taiping and the Boxers. The turn from the past toward the future, from the peasant rebel to the intellectual revolutionary, was under way, and with it a new dawn.

In its practical aspects Sun's program proposed tactics which raised the primary issues that China was to wrestle with throughout the twentieth century. By advancing the concept of using an elitist tutelage of the masses under military rule to lay the foundations of civilian governance, Sun and his associates anticipated the concept of political stages that was soon to figure so prominently in debate. It is clear, of course, that Sun was not the only one to advance such ideas. From a different vantage point, his adversary Liang Qichao was publicizing similar themes. But unlike Liang, Sun was able to connect his ideas to a movement, and in the course of events to give them greater relevance to the future.

The attempt to nurture political liberalism during a period of military tutelage was an effort to skip stages and hoist a backward society into the ranks of the political avant-garde. Conceptually, it bore a close relationship to the later Soviet and Chinese Communist efforts to tie the Marxist ideology to the support of a one-party dictatorship in a preindustrial society, with the party being labeled "the proletarian vanguard." Both efforts called for a managed revolution having as its goal a greatly accelerated modernization drive. But Sun's revolution aimed at creating a liberal order, whereas the revolution advocated by the Marxist-Leninists was aimed at establishing socialism, as a prelude to "the withering away of the state."

Sun also sought in practical terms to build a united front, another concept that would have currency for China throughout the century. Sun's front was composed of all anti-Manchu elements among traditionalist secret societies, military men, and students seeking a route to modernity. In all respects except their anti-Manchu commitment, these elements were incompatible. The coalition never achieved much operative unity or discipline, and proved to be a feeble revolutionary instrument in Sun's hands. It was only one of many forces that helped bring about the collapse of the old order, and it was not strong enough to help in the building of a new one—thereby setting in motion a tragedy that would span decades.

As we shall see, events were soon to thrust Sun into an ever greater political role in his society without an organization or a coherent body of supporters. Neither in military matters nor in party-building were the necessary preparations for revolution, let alone governance, being made. Sun was an effective mobilizer but a poor institution-builder, and this deficiency was to cast an enormous shadow over China's future. Contrary to what is often assumed, moreover, it set him apart from the early Mao—though with the late Mao he had more in common on this count.

Until 1910 the Chinese revolutionary effort—at least in its explicit, organized form—was largely peripheral to China proper. Sun's movement was led by émigrés who sought to penetrate the borders of the nation with the help of indigenous forces recruited on the spot. This strategy had several weaknesses. To begin with, it depended heavily on the tolerance of the foreign powers who controlled the border lands. At first these powers often provided sanctuary or assistance to the revolutionaries; but without exception, over the years their enthusiasm waned or the balance of power turned against the officials who favored granting such aid. Furthermore, few of China's own border regions were suitable for an expanding revolutionary movement: their languages and customs were essentially foreign and caused great problems in communication. Canton, to be sure, was an exception, and given the availability of refuge in nearby British Hong Kong, it was natural to focus on Canton—a city to which the revolutionaries ultimately returned after frustrating failures elsewhere.

In a basic sense, however, even China's cities were poor recruiting grounds for a revolutionary movement at this point. As we have suggested elsewhere, they were the least integrated units in Chinese society and the most difficult to organize. The industrial labor force was still miniscule, and the family-kinship structure was much less cohesive in an urban setting. The cities tended to be disparate and amorphous breeding grounds for commercialism and its accompanying values, not logical centers for revolutionary organizations. On the other hand, Sun was not able to organize the rural peasantry either, primarily because he and his associates were unable to work safely or effectively in their native provinces. Unlike the Taiping, therefore, Sun's movement found little mass support, except within the secret societies, despite the potential strength of its appeal to Han nationalism and popular access to land.

The other route to power in rural China was through the military. Increasingly, the political future hinged upon the loyalty of China's varied armed forces. Before Mao, Sun and Huang learned the hard way that "power comes out of the barrel of a gun," and the New Army, together with various provincial forces, held those guns. Could they be penetrated? In one sense or another, the gates to influence in the army were controlled by young gentry-related men, who were increasingly Han rather than Manchu, and a rank and file of predominantly Han peasant youths. Thus, in courting the military, only an appeal to Han nationalism, similar to the one that influenced the secret societies, was likely to succeed.

It is not surprising that the third of Sun's three principles, that of the people's livelihood, receded into the background after 1907, when the intellectual debate between the Tokyo students and the reformers drew to a close. It was not to be revived until after the events of 1911. Even some of Sun's student supporters had doubts about land equalization, for reasons that are apparent when one studies their familial antecedents. The most ardent social revolutionaries in Sun's entourage, moreover, thought of socialism as a prophylactic measure, one designed to prevent *future* abuses. They did not regard economic inequity as a serious problem for China, certainly not as serious as it was for the West. It took a later generation of radicals to reverse this verdict, after a decade of political chaos.

Another paradox confronted Sun and his movement. Despite their extraordinary emphasis on nationalism, Sun and his key lieutenants were almost all southerners, and their movement drew much of its strength from a regional resentment of both the Manchu and the North, or at least a strong sense of the differences between North and South. It is not surprising that many foreign supporters believed that Sun would settle for a Republic of South China, centering on Guangdong. In any case, there had been very little penetration of the North, either ideologically or organizationally, by 1911.

The self-proclaimed revolutionaries, then, were in no position to carry through a successful national revolution, and in fact they did not do so. The revolution that came in 1911 was not of their making, although in a limited sense they inherited it. Epic events throughout China were rapidly eroding the authority and legitimacy of the imperial government. From peasant riots to the much more important generational cleavages taking place within gentry families, a widespread social disintegration was under way, and it was especially pronounced in the very classes upon whom the monarchy depended most heavily. Before turning to these developments, however, we must examine one other branch of modern China's revolutionary movement, the anarchists.

5

THE EMERGENCE OF THE ANARCHISTS

As THE POLEMICAL battles between the reformers and the anti-Manchu revolutionaries were reaching a crescendo, yet another movement made its appearance, that of the Chinese anarchists. Through meetings and journals published in Paris and Tokyo, dedicated bands of young Chinese sought to spread the doctrines of Proudhon, Bakunin, and Kropotkin, and proclaimed their allegiance to a new order based on the complete equality, freedom, and independence of all men.

Despite certain ties to Chinese traditionalism, anarchism was clearly the most radical doctrine promulgated by Chinese revolutionaries of this era. In many respects, it seemed to defy not only the main currents of the past but those of the contemporary era as well. On almost every count, the anarchists challenged the theses of Liang and Sun. Against the call for a new patriotism, a nationalist spirit supported by military power sufficient to ward off all foreign threats, the anarchists opposed both nationalism and militarism, championing the establishment of a truly international movement that would obliterate "governmental tyranny" and allegiance to the state everywhere. Against the strong racial overtones contained in both *Xinmin congbao* and *Min bao*, the anarchists insisted that all individuals had the same innate capacities and rights, regardless of sex or color. And interestingly, the anarchists were the first Chinese radicals to write and talk extensively about the exploitation of the peasant—which they did in terms highly suggestive of future revolutionary trends, despite some major differences in political tactics. They were also the first Chinese radicals to proclaim themselves communists, arguing that "scientific socialism" belonged to their branch of the socialist movement rather than to Marxism.

Chinese anarchism never attracted a large following, but its influence on the Chinese revolution was by no means negligible. Its initial effect, mixed with that of the Russian Narodniks, was to encourage an upsurge of assassination attempts and other acts of violence by young Chinese revolutionaries. Anarchism found various other modes of expression in the tumultuous years that followed the 1911 Revolution, but few young rebels of the period escaped its influence completely. In their memorable conversations of 1936, Mao Zedong remarked to Edgar Snow that he had once been much influenced by anarchist writings.* Mao was referring to the period immediately after his graduation from normal school, when he had come to Beijing from Hunan as a part of a student group that was hoping to study in France. In Beijing he had the opportunity to read translations from Kropotkin, foreign anarchist pamphlets, and the contributions of the Chinese anarchists themselves.

The stimulus Mao derived from anarchist thought was by no means unique. By this time anarchist doctrines had influenced Wang Jingwei, Cai Yuanpei, Chen Jiongming, and many other key actors on China's political and intellectual stages. Up to the point of the Bolshevik Revolution, indeed, anarchism surpassed Marxism as the foremost expression of avant-garde radicalism among China's new intelligentsia. In radical circles anarchism managed to seem the purest, the most humane, and the most futuristic of all political creeds.

THE PARIS CONVERTS

It was perhaps natural that certain young Chinese studying in Paris during this period would gravitate toward anarchism. France had a long history of anarchist activities in its intellectual and working-class communities.[1] With the aid of anarchist Elisée Reclus, Peter Kropotkin had published the journal *La Revolte*, first in Geneva, then beginning in 1885, in Paris. Succeeding *La Revolte* was *Les Temps Nouveaux*, a widely read anarchist journal that emerged in 1895 with the well-known Jean Grave as editor. Mikhail Bakunin had had a devoted band of French followers for decades, including the Reclus brothers Elie and Elisée. Elisée struck up an acquaintance with a few young Chinese students in Paris and introduced them to the sizable body of anarchist literature, particularly the writings of Kropotkin. In fact, many of Kropotkin's works were first published in Paris: *Conquest of Bread* in 1892, *Mutual Aid* in 1902, and *The State* in 1903. At the very time the Chinese anarchists were beginning their political activities in Paris, moreover, French anarchism was enjoying a new burst of energy, due primarily to the stimulus of George Sorel and his theories of anarcho-syndicalism. Sorel had little influence on the Chinese students, but his ideas created great excitement in France, especially during the period 1906–1908.

It was precisely in these years that a small group of Chinese activists launched their own anarchist movement, hoping to attract a following among overseas students throughout Europe, in Japan, and eventually among their compatriots at home. When Sun Baoqi went to France in 1902 as Chinese minister, over twenty government and private students traveled with him.[2] Included in this group were Li Shizeng and Zhang Jingjiang. Li was the son of Li Hongzao, who for some twenty-five years prior to his death in 1897 had been a powerful figure in the Manchu national administration.[3]

* Edgar Snow, *Red Star Over China*, p. 149. Mao is quoted as saying: "My interest in politics continued to increase, and my mind turned more and more radical [in 1918]. I have told you of the background for this. But just now I was still confused, looking for a road, as we say. I read some pamphlets on anarchy [*sic*], and was much influenced by them. With a student named Chu Hsun-pei, who used to visit me, I often discussed anarchism and its possibilities in China. At that time I favoured many of its proposals." In this chapter of our work, we have borrowed extensively from our earlier study, *The Chinese Anarchist Movement*. We see no need to cite passages taken from it either verbatim or in modified form.

Young Li had come to France as an attaché in the Chinese legation, but he soon gave up this position to study biology and promote anarchism. Zhang came from a wealthy Zhejiang family—his father later operated a successful business in Shanghai—and he was thus able to contribute substantial funds to the revolutionary cause. He, too, at first held a post in the Chinese legation, as a commercial attaché.* It was natural, therefore, that shortly after his arrival he founded a Chinese commercial firm, the Tongyun Company, in Paris. Between 1902 and 1906 a number of young men from Zhang's old village came to the French capital with assurances of work while they continued their studies. Some of them, such as Chu Minyi, became active in the anarchist ranks.** As an additional source of work for students, a Chinese restaurant and teahouse was also established under the auspices of Zhang's company.

Entrepreneurship, science, and politics moved in tandem in the years that followed. The first contacts between the young Chinese and the French anarchist movement cannot be dated, but by 1905 or 1906 the commitment had been made. A new figure had also arrived in the person of Wu Zhihui. Since Wu quickly assumed the intellectual leadership, and was long to play a major role in Chinese politics and intellectual life, some data on his background arc important.

Wu Zhihui was born in 1865 in Jiangsu province of well-to-do gentry parents.[4] His education was of the traditional Chinese type. He reached the *jinshi* examinations in Beijing, but failed. (Li Shizeng's father was one of the four examiners.) For a few years after 1894, Wu taught at various schools in Beijing, Tianjin, and Shanghai. At one point, he wanted to enter Hubei military academy, but lacked the funds to get there. Wu's interest in political activities began with overseas travel. He first visited Tokyo in 1901. After a brief and unhappy stay in Canton, he returned in 1902. On this occasion he became deeply involved in the student protest against the Chinese minister in Tokyo, relating to educational assistance and political activities. After being ordered to leave Japan at the request of the Chinese ministry, he jumped into a canal, intent on making a protest suicide. He was rescued by Japanese police and returned to Shanghai in May 1902.

When the Aiguo Xueshe was founded in Shanghai in November, Wu joined and moved into its headquarters. By 1903, as we have indicated, this association was secretly promoting revolution and using the newspaper *Su bao* as its organ. When the Chinese authorities struck against *Su bao* in May 1903, Wu escaped, first to Hong Kong, then to London. The next several years were spent in the British capital, with one brief trip to Paris. Zhang

*When the elder Zhang died, his son received a sizable inheritance. Though weak physically, young Zhang had strong political convictions, and began very early to think of himself as an anarchist. Some students feared that he might be a spy because of his official connections, but this was untrue. See Feng Ziyou, "The Master of *Xin shiji*, Zhang Jingjiang," *Geming yishi* 2: 227–230.

**Chu went to Japan in 1903 and studied political science and economics. He later traveled to Europe and became involved in the anarchist movement. He remained in France until shortly after the outbreak of World War I, when he returned to China. After a few years he went back to Paris to study medicine and pharmacy. In this period he participated in the establishment of the "University of Lyons," which will be discussed later. Chu's life ended in tragedy. After many years of service to the Guomindang, he threw in his lot with his old friend Wang Jingwei in 1939, and accepted the post of minister of foreign affairs in Wang's Nanjing government. After the allied victory in 1945, Chu was arrested and executed.

30. *Li Shizeng in old age*

Jingjiang visited Wu in London in 1905; Li had met him earlier in Shanghai when en route to France in 1902. Finally, in 1906, Wu moved to Paris, where he lived with Li and Chu Minyi. At this point, the group organized the Shijieshe (World Association) to undertake publishing activities; they would use a printing press Zhang had bought in Singapore during a visit home in 1906, and a Chinese printer he had also obtained there.[5] In early 1907 a Chinese pictorial entitled *Shijie* (The World) was published; ten thousand copies were widely distributed to various countries. But printing costs were high and sales income low, so the enterprise was abandoned after two issues and one supplement.

31. *Wu Zhihui at the age of thirty-six, Tokyo, 1901*

At the same time, Li, Xia Jianzhong, and several others organized the Far Eastern Biological Association, with a laboratory attached. Two years later, after various chemical experiments with beans, Li established a factory that produced assorted bean products, including traditional Chinese bean curd. As in this group's other enterprises, the idea of work-study was promoted.[6] In the evening and when not on duty, the Chinese working in the enterprise were supposed to improve their Chinese and French language ability and study such subjects as general science. Moreover, a strict moral code was enforced: among the thirty Chinese eventually employed, smoking, drinking liquor, and gambling were strictly prohibited.

These ventures had their practical aspect, of course; they were attempts to finance the education of fellow countrymen. But beneath them ran a strong current of idealism, and the ideological wellspring of that idealism lay in European anarchism.

On June 22, 1907, Wu, Li, Zhang, and Chu began to publish a weekly newspaper called *Xin shiji* (The New Century), with an additional title in Esperanto, *La Tempoj Novaj*, the same as that of Grave's journal, *Le Siècle Nouveau.*[7] For three years this paper championed the causes of anarchism and revolution and reached Chinese students and intellectuals around the world. Very few copies penetrated China proper, of course, but later on *Xin shiji*'s message began to reach the homeland through several channels.

Senior in age and experience, Wu became the acknowledged leader of the Paris anarchist group, although Li was perhaps its driving spirit. In recalling the varied influences that played upon him and his colleagues during this period, Li speaks of the Chinese classical philosophers, Darwin and the Social Darwinists, and the radical libertarians as "brought up to date" by the anarchism of Proudhon, Bakunin, and Kropotkin.[8]

The Paris students were in certain respects fervent antitraditionalists who decried any attempt to equate Lao Zi with the modern anarchists, or the ancient well-field system with modern communism. Yet almost without exception, they were young men who had received an excellent classical education. They had been exposed to a range of political ideas almost as broad as that existing in classical Western philosophy. Thus few basic anarchist concepts seemed totally alien to them, and familiarity made acceptance easier, even when the inclination was to reject traditionalism.* Yet that was only one part of the complex network of intellectual influences operating on them. This was the age of Social Darwinism, and no future-oriented Chinese intellectual could escape coming to grips with its basic themes. Li recalled how greatly he was influenced by the writings of Lamarck and Darwin, how they had opened new doors for him in history and philosophy as well as in science. Their influence was likely to be especially strong on a young man studying zoology, botany, and biology, but Li would have felt the effect of Darwinism no matter what his field. It was the *science* of Darwinism that socialists (and many nonsocialists) used as a starting point for analyzing man in society, social and political evolution, and fundamental values. One started with Darwin, regardless of where one ended. For the Chinese anarchists, the last phrase was important, however, because their hero, Peter Kropotkin, was one of the foremost critics of Social Darwinism. Against the Darwinian thesis of survival through competition and struggle, he posed a countertheme of survival through cooperation and mutual aid, drawing on scientific data from the world of animals.[9]

* To stress the influence of the classics on their anarchism, Li, in our interview on July 16, 1959, in Taibei, recalled that Wu had once painted a picture to illustrate the following ancient Chinese tale. During the Zhou dynasty, two philosophers were each asked by the emperor to be his successor. The one put his ear into some water, saying "I must clean my ear after hearing such a thing." The other said, "Do not let my oxen drink the water in which you have cleaned your ear."

It is interesting to note the bonds between the young Chinese anarchists and the sources from which they were now to draw their political inspiration. Like Bakunin and Kropotkin, they came from the rural gentry, and by birth as well as intelligence, they represented the most sensitive and concerned segment of the leisure class. From this vantage point their concern could easily extend to the peasant, since his life and theirs had been closely interwoven.* Another bond was that of science. Most of these men were committed to science, either as a profession or as a way of life. Kropotkin was an eminent geologist, Elisée Reclus a world-famous geographer, and his brother Elie an anthropologist. Li, as we have noted, was a budding biologist. Science, not Esperanto, was the true international language. And if both nature and man were to be explained rationally and universally, what was more logical than to apply science to politics, to seek a scientific theory of man in society, a cosmic explanation, predictable and therefore usable. The Marxists, it should never be forgotten, were not the only ones to make the claim that their ideological position rested on science.

There was one more significant tie between these young Chinese iconoclasts and their mentors: they emerged not merely from similar classes but also from similar political environments—from Russia and China, the two sick giants of the early twentieth century. That a resonance would be felt between the dissident intellectuals of the two societies was natural.

THE TOKYO MOVEMENT

Prior to introducing the central anarchist themes as set forth by *Xin shiji*, let us explore the background of the Chinese anarchist group in Tokyo. Among this group the central figures were Zhang Ji, Liu Shipei, and Liu's wife, He Zhen. Zhang Ji, who later became associated with his comrades in Paris, was one of the earliest Chinese students to arrive in Japan, reaching Tokyo in 1899.[10] Being from a scholar-gentry family of Hubei, Zhang had received a classical education in China, but in Japan he studied political science and economics at Waseda University. Like other Tokyo-based Chinese anarchists, he was strongly influenced by the Japanese anarchists, notably Kōtoku Shūsui and Ōsugi Sakae, with whom he established close links. Indeed, the mutuality of Japanese-Chinese intellectual relations within the anarchist movement exceeded that of most other branches of Chinese radicalism, even though Sun's ties to certain Japanese radical nationalists were very strong.**

Liu came from a long line of scholars, had received a thorough classical education, and had demonstrated remarkable intellectual ability as a youth. He was already teaching at the age of eighteen, and was awarded his *juren*

*It is quite true, as Professor Olga Lang has pointed out to us, that the appeal—and concern—of Bakunin and Kropotkin also extended to the urban working class; but in early and prolonged efforts to reach the peasants, they were set apart from Marx.

**Anarchism was on the ascendancy within the small Japanese radical community, and Kōtoku's star in particular was rising. The journals he edited and his personal writings were avidly read by the Chinese students, along with Japanese translations of Western anarchist classics. For details on trends within Japanese radicalism, in addition to the works of Kublin and Notehelfer, see George O. Totten, *The Social Democratic Movement in Prewar Japan*, and Gail Bernstein, *Japanese Marxist: A Portrait of Kawakami Hajime, 1879–1946*. Zhang Ji was later to translate some of Errico Malatesta's work on anarchism into Chinese (Zhang Ji, *Zhang Puquan xiansheng quanji*, p. 236).

degree the following year, in 1903. His conversion to the anti-Manchu cause seems to have been mainly the result of a friendship with Zhang Binglin, whose background and interests were very similar. In 1904 Liu became a member of the patriotic society Guangfu Hui, in Shanghai, having been introduced into the organization by Cai Yuanpei. Liu, it should be noted, was still in his nationalist phase at this point, but he gravitated quickly toward a radical nationalist stance; he became active in various revolutionary undertakings, including several unsuccessful assassination attempts, while he supported himself by doing some middle-school teaching.[11] Unfortunately, little is known about the background of his wife, He Zhen.

In 1907 Liu and He went to Japan. By this time, he had changed his name to Guanghan (Restore the Han), a dramatic indication of his current sympathies. His wife had also taken a new name. Initially, they lived with Zhang Binglin, and the three worked closely together, with Liu contributing a number of articles to *Min bao*, now under Zhang's editorship.[12] Within a few months, Liu and He made contact with the Japanese anarchists and were obviously much influenced by them. Kōtoku and some of his young disciples, such as Ōsugi Sakae and Yamakawa Hitoshi, were instrumental in converting their new Chinese friends to the anarchist cause. In June 1907, the same month in which the first issue of *Xin shiji* was published in Paris, Liu and He established a Society for the Study of Socialism and began to publish a journal called *Tianyi bao* (Natural Justice Journal).*

BASIC ANARCHIST THEMES

In an English-language statement on the inside cover of a surviving issue of *Tianyi bao*, the editors defined their general objectives as "Anti-imperialism, Against World Power; Anarchist Communism; the Equality of Sexes."[13] A month later these were expanded to read "to realize internationalism, abolishing all national and racial distinctions; to revolt against all the authorities of the world; to overthrow all the political systems of the present time; to realize communism; to realize absolute equality of man and [woman]."[14]

The Paris group was articulating similar goals. The basic outline of anarchist philosophy can be set forth in terms of "antis" and "pros." The *Xin shiji* and *Tianyi bao* writers were anti-government, anti-nationalist, anti-military, anti-religion, anti-traditionalist, anti-family (Chinese style), anti-elitist, anti-libertine. They were pro-freedom, pro-equality, pro-independence, pro-mutual aid through free association, pro-humanist, pro-universalist, pro-revolution, pro-violence, and pro-communist.

To understand the anarchist position more fully, these various components must be fitted together. It is entirely proper to start with the negative. The anarchists conceived their immediate task to be that of destruction. Only when the existing artificialities restraining man had been destroyed, could human freedom and equality flow. The anarchist position culminated in a frontal attack upon the state. "All governments are the enemies of free-

*The fifteenth issue of *Min bao*, published in July 1907, carried a brief news item about the new study group; it promised to send the time and place of the first meeting to anyone who forwarded their name and address (inside cover, following photos). A detailed account of the meeting, held on August 30 with about ninety people in attendance, was carried in three issues of *Xin shiji*: November 16, 1907, p. 4; December 7, 1907, pp. 3–4; and December 14, 1907, p. 4. The two major speeches were given by Liu and Kōtoku.

dom and equality," wrote Li in an early issue of his journal.[15] Two issues later, he set forth the anarchist creed more fully:

> The individual is the basic unit in society. Together with others, he forms a village, and with other villages, a country is created. Society in turn is formed through the process of bringing all countries together. The just society is that which permits free exchange between and among individuals, mutual aid, the common happiness and enjoyment of all, and the freedom from control by the force of a few. This is what anarchism seeks to realize. The governments of today are organized by the few, who in turn pass laws which are of benefit to the few. . . . In sum, what we seek is the destruction of the destroyer of the just society.[16]

Liu Guanghan expressed identical sentiments and with equal fervor. "There is no government," he asserted, "that does not oppress the people."[17] As Kropotkin had said, the state had become the God of today, and even democratic governments failed to allow for full equality. There were still the ruling and the ruled, with the capitalists oppressing the workers. Liu expanded his attack on the capitalists. They had enjoyed every right, but had accepted no responsibilities. They had seized the land, thereby deserving the label of thief which Bakunin had applied to them, and they had also controlled the means of production, leaving the workers nothing to sell except themselves. The capitalists in fact employed the state and its army to repress the workers. Today's world, Liu continued, was a world of growing extremes, with nations divided between the few rich and the many poor. Unless China achieved anarchism, it too would fall into this condition in a decade or so. Liu ended this essay with an analysis of imperialism. The expansion of state power and the desire of capitalists to expand their markets were the two central factors leading to the expansion of the white man at the expense of the red, black, and other races. In sum, the fundamental corruption emanating from government was the rule of the rich, made possible by the system of private property, and the dominance of the strong over the weak, made possible by the nation-state system.[18]

Coupled with the anarchists' central goal of bringing down all central governments was an uncompromising antinationalist and antimilitary stance. The nation-worship we call patriotism, Li insisted, brings only slavery and bloodshed. There can be no true harmony and freedom until all men are linked in free associations based on the natural social and economic ties that bring individuals together. And militarism—the existence of the police and national armies—served the state by sustaining the supremacy of the oppressor class.[19]

The anarchists, of course, were constantly made aware of the difficulty of attacking nationalism and military power in an age when Western imperialism dominated much of Asia. The nationalist supporters of Sun Yat-sen struck hard, contrasting their "realistic" view of world politics with anarchistic utopianism. For China to abandon government and the quest for military strength would result in its total conquest by various predatory powers, they insisted.[20]

China must become strong, argued the nationalists, so that no one will dare assault it. Without a military force or political unity, they insisted, even the Manchu tyranny cannot be challenged effectively, to say nothing of

Western imperialist nations. Only by developing nationalism could the Chinese people overcome Manchu rule and foreign exploitation; only then would they be able to stand as equals before the world, working for world harmony and domestic equality. The first task, in sum, was the nationalist revolution, and only after this had been achieved could a society advance to a unity of the working class, obliterating state boundaries.

The *Xin shiji* editor answered this argument by asserting that since the rich and official classes of China did not seek justice, the common people could not possibly unite with them to overthrow the Manchu. Thus long before the first Chinese Communists struggled with the problem under Comintern pressure, the anarchists faced the issue of a united front and decisively rejected it. The commoners could neither unite with nor jump over the rich oppressors within China. The only answer lay in total, complete, and simultaneous mass revolution.[21]

From his Tokyo vantage point, Liu and his colleagues were responding to similar nationalist arguments. In one of his major essays Liu proposed attacking "the domination of white powers," not through separate nationalist movements, but through a genuine international socialist effort.[22] It should be easy for the countries of East Asia to unite, he remarked, since they shared a common cultural inheritance from China, and in turn, the uniting of East and South Asia would be facilitated because of religion (an enigmatic statement that was not amplified). In their struggle against imperialism the Asian countries should cooperate with the exploited elements of the West, those for whom imperialism had produced only increasing hardship. Thus, a combination of tactics could be pursued. Inside imperialist states, socialists and anarchists with internationalist and antimilitarist commitments would urge the people not to go into military service and would persuade workers not to produce weapons. This, together with the pressures exerted by the struggle of the united Asian peoples for independence and freedom, would bring down every imperialist government.

Liu concluded by exploring the Chinese situation specifically. It had been *the government*, he noted, which had accepted the unequal treaties. Moreover, it was nonsense to assert that if no government existed, foreign powers would be free to impose their will on the Chinese people. The self-defense of people was always stronger than the self-defense of governments. And if China were temporarily not strong enough to practice anarchism, it could ask for help from like-minded parties abroad. In sum, to expel foreign capitalism from China, it would be counterproductive to pursue reformism of the type currently being advocated (by Sun and his followers). Such a course would require massive amounts of money for government, money that could only be obtained by foreign loans and result in foreign domination. The answer was that the Chinese people should join socialists and anarchists abroad in a fight against capitalism throughout the world.[23]

As in Liu's essay, Chinese anarchist attacks on nationalism and militarism usually combined general arguments drawn from Western anarchist writings with specific arguments directed toward the Chinese scene. One recurrent general argument was that the welfare of the nation and the welfare of the people are not the same. Nationalism leads to war, and in war suffering extends to the ordinary people on both sides, to winners as well as losers. Anarchist policies are called weak, but in the pursuit of righteous principles lies the ultimate strength. The opposition can be persuaded—or if necessary, assassinated. The killing of evil men is not war.[24] In fact, only when concern goes beyond one's own race or nation, when one fights against all enemies of the moral laws that govern mankind, can self-preservation be achieved.[25]

With respect to China, an effort was made to turn certain arguments advanced by Sun and his followers against them. The nationalists had called for simultaneous racial, national, and social revolutions so that a single revolution would suffice. Yet those who advocated another state to replace the present one, no matter what its type, would merely cause the postponement of the final revolution and thereby fall into the same category as the advocates of constitutional monarchy.[26] If the Han had a right to challenge Manchu control on racial grounds, moreover, did not earlier natives of Chinese soil, the Miao, have the right to challenge the Han? * As for those who implied that nationalism was a natural, even primordial sentiment, how long had the Chinese known the meaning of the term "nation," and was there any evidence that the working class of China cared about such a concept?[27]

Like the nationalists and the later Marxist-Leninists, the anarchists sometimes made use of the concept of political stages or evolution, but not necessarily in the sense of institutional change and development. They tended to view political development as being represented in an unfolding of man's grasp of higher truth and moral law. One writer explained it this way: first came individualism and self-interest; then, racial revolution and nationalism, the interest of one's people; finally, social revolution and universalism, the concern for all mankind.[28] Another wrote that man's evolution was from absolutism to anarchism.[29] Moreover, the issue of skipping stages, later to become so significant, was raised by both the anarchists and the republicans in China well before it became a Marxist-Leninist controversy. Believing that the age of nationalism was ending and, in addition, that China's heritage was different from that of the West, the Chinese anarchists argued that China could go directly to their type of socialism without having to pass through a republican-constitutional phase. This would be made easier by the fact that the revolution of the twentieth century would be a revolution encompassing the entire world, not confined to individual nation-states.

The anarchists treated nationalism and internationalism as antipodes, whereas the Marxist-Leninists were to view them as stages, and stages not wholly incompatible with each other, at least in a tactical sense. Thus, while the Chinese anarchists remained antinationalist to the core, the Marxist-Leninists began to seek a synthesis of the idealism rooted in the concept of proletarian internationalism and political tactics aimed at attaining the support of the Asian masses, or at least their politically conscious portion.

* "An Extended Discussion on the Differences and Similarities of Nationalism, Democracy, and Socialism, and Another Reply to the Letter on the Interesting Meaning of the Opening Statement of *Xin shiji*," *Xin shiji*, July 27, 1907, pp. 3–4. In an article of the same period, He and Liu set forth three major defects of "racist revolution": if the Han gained dominance, weaker races would always be suppressed in China; those filled with anti-Manchu sentiments were prepared to accept any form of government so long as it was controlled by the Han; such a situation would merely exchange one small privileged class for another—students and revolutionary activists would replace traditional officials, but the masses would undergo the same suffering as before. See He Zhen and Shen Shu (Liu), "The Relationship Between Racist Revolution and Anarchist Revolution," *Tianyi bao*, October 1907, pp. 135–144.

The Comintern was to be fashioned as the instrument of international proletarian solidarity, the symbol of commitment to the ultimate classless world of brotherhood, toward which Marxists as well as anarchists aimed. In practical terms, moreover, it was intended to link the "oppressed masses" of the industrial societies with the peoples of the backward, colonial world, just as Liu and other anarchists had urged. Yet, as we shall see, the Comintern was to find the linkage between the Western and non-Western revolutions in its support of nationalism. Thus, it defined support for Asian nationalism as essential if mobilization of the Asian masses were to be achieved in an age of imperialism and if the bourgeois-democratic revolution were to be consummated, preparatory to socialism. If the Comintern itself was essentially an instrument of Russian national interest, this was not accepted by the faithful, who in any case viewed the Soviet Union as the fatherland of the global proletariat. Thus, by uniting idealism and practicality in its programs, the international Communist movement was to fashion a formidable political weapon. In the first two decades of the twentieth century, however, there were scarcely any Chinese Marxists, and the type of pure internationalism promulgated by the anarchists confronted the strongly adverse nationalist tides.

On the issue of religion, the anarchists were on a smoother path, the beneficiaries of a heritage of Chinese secularism. For this reason, perhaps, they could look upon the European scene as detached observers, without deep emotional involvement. Their antireligious writings lacked the frenzied tone adopted by certain Western radicals. Their position, however, was unequivocal. Wu Zhihui remarked that the blind worship of religion had been one of the great historical problems of Europe, but that a significant change was taking place: the separation of church and state in France was one indication that a new, more enlightened era was at hand.[30]

The *Xin shiji* position on religion was perhaps best expressed by Wu in an exchange with a reader from Japan. The reader (presumably a Chinese student) wrote that although he was prosocialist, he felt that socialist attacks on religion were too extreme, and alienated potential supporters. Moreover, he asked, are not the moral standards of the Chinese quite as deficient as their educational standards, suggesting that they could put religion to good use? Wu responded by recommending the morality of socialism against the morality of religion. Socialist morality, he asserted, contained all of the basic ethical principles to be found in religion, without its accompanying superstitions.[31] The Tokyo anarchists wrote in a similar vein. Liu actually attributed the emergence of class to religion, noting that rulers tended to identify themselves with God, and that under this protective covering they sponsored privileged classes.*

* Shen Shu (Liu), "A View on the Equality of Anarchism," *Tianyi bao*, August 10, 1907, pp. 7–20. Later Liu equated "the superstition of the nation" with "the superstition of religion," and said that rulers, like religious spokesmen, exploited the material resources of the common people under the pretense of protecting them. Shen Shu (Liu), "The Inverse Proportions of Governmental and Popular Interests," *Heng bao* (Equity), April 28, 1908, p. 1. *Heng bao* succeeded *Tianyi bao* as the Tokyo anarchists' journal, edited by Liu. Its objectives were set forth, in Chinese and in English, in the preface of the first issue. The call was for the overthrow of governments and the practice of communism; support for disarmament and general strikes; reports on the hardships of the common people; and contacts with labor organizations and action-oriented (revolutionary) peoples throughout the world. The rising influence of anarcho-syndicalism—filtered through Kōtoku and his colleagues—is manifest in the provisions relating to general strikes and labor associations.

A more formidable obstacle than religion existed in the form of Confucianism. In the very first issue of *Xin shiji*, it was suggested that Confucius lived in an age of barbarism, and that in such an age it was not difficult for "crafty men" to make themselves into sages and be worshiped by simple folk.[32] The more basic attack on Confucianism, however, was impersonal: later generations had attempted to make Confucius into a saint and had insisted that his every word be treated as law, without regard for changed times and circumstances. (Decades later, the assault on the cult of Maoism as practiced during the Cultural Revolution was to take a similar form.)

Frequently, the attack on Confucianism was broadened to become a criticism of traditionalism in all its forms. "The Chinese seem to be the greatest lovers of things ancient," complained Chu Minyi, "so much so that their minds have been wholly bound by traditional customs and thus they have become enslaved by the ancients."[33] Even in recent decades, when it had finally been admitted that China must absorb Western learning, Chinese were still insisting that "the national character" be preserved. Chu summarized his argument in forceful manner:

> China has not been able to progress with the world, because of its emphasis on things ancient . . . and the West has progressed because of its opposite attitude. . . . We Chinese also have a tendency to treat all Western things as things that China has long experienced or possessed. For example, we say that China long ago engaged in imperialism under the Mongols . . . ; that China long ago realized nationalism under the Yellow Emperor . . . ; that Lao Zi was the founder of anarchism; that Mo Zi was the first advocate of universal love; and finally, that China long ago practiced communism under the name of the well-field system. Alas! There is reason behind the birth of the new knowledge. It comes at the appropriate time, when it has the potential of realization. One cannot take some saying from the ancients and claim in effect that all was foreseen long ago, or that all things new must be fitted into existing ancient teachings. . . . There are countless things which even modern man cannot foresee. Thus, how much can one expect of the ancients?[34]

This antitraditional position, as has been noted, placed the anarchists close to Sun Yat-sen and his followers. It symbolized the commitment to modernity, progress, and new ideas which embodied the essence of twentieth-century radicalism in Asia. And as we shall see, this attitude was soon to be voiced by Chen Duxiu and other "progressive" intellectuals writing in the influential *Xin qingnian* (New Youth) after 1915. Their searching criticisms of contemporary Chinese society were a powerful stimulus to the political events that followed. But many of these criticisms had first been advanced a decade earlier by the Chinese overseas students, and had often been expressed most sharply by the Paris and Tokyo anarchist groups.

Yet there was another side of the coin. When they were setting forth their basic position, the anarchists were antitraditionalist, but in the recesses of their minds, in the interstices of their argument, there was a bent toward the past, toward a Golden Age before man had been "brutalized and enslaved" by machines, organizations, and institutions. Rousseau's noble savage was never far away, for, as we have seen, the anarchist giants—men like Kropotkin—were often men whose passionate concern had begun with the peasantry and the land, men in whom the spirit of noblesse oblige had been translated into political activism. They were among the first to convert doubts about "progress" in its nineteenth- and early twentieth-century forms into something other than blind fury and simple destruction—into a philosophy of the future, but one with roots in the past.

How congenial this was with the intellectual environment of China and the processes of the Chinese mind! When certain writers spoke of the compatibility of China's heritage with anarchism, they were using, as well as abusing, traditionalism. At the first meeting of the Society for the Study of Socialism, Liu argued that the realization of anarchism in China should not be too difficult, because for thousands of years Chinese political life had rested upon Confucian and Taoist principles of "indifference" and "noninterference." In practice, he wrote, traditional Chinese government had not been close to the people, and they had not trusted it. Laws had been merely formal documents, and officials had held only empty positions. No individual had truly possessed power. The government had looked down on the people, treating them like plants and animals, and the people had viewed the government as repulsive and evil. This historic situation of "indifference" to government could easily be turned into a victory for anarchism, Liu submitted. Indeed, China should be the first country in the world to realize anarchism because of its unique background.[35]

He and Liu repeated these themes in subsequent essays. Confucianism and Taoism together, they wrote, had supported an ethically oriented, noninterventionist government, one that left the common people free to do largely as they pleased. It also left the masses indifferent to government because the rulers felt little responsibility toward the ruled. The traditional Chinese method of managing public affairs, continued the authors, was merely to weigh specific actions against prevailing regulations, not to consider broad social policies. Had it not been for the imposition of the Confucian-based class system, China could have realized anarchism long ago.[36]

Earlier, Liu had presented a critical discussion of Wang Mang's socialism during the Western Han dynasty, which Sun and his supporters had tried to claim as a historical antecedent for their land equalization program. Wang's desire to distribute land equally, said Liu, had good objectives, but because it did not basically challenge the class system, it enabled distinctions between the upper and lower classes to continue. And with an obvious thrust at the Tongmeng Hui, he added, "Nowadays, governments are set up which deceive people with claims of equal distribution of land and properties, similar to the practices advocated by Wang Mang."[37]

Less than a year later, Liu took a similar thesis, this time relying principally on the nature of classical Chinese society.[38] Kropotkin, he reported, had said in his *Conquest of Bread* that the movement to anarchism was actually the restoration of an ancient system. Although the peasants worked independently on their farms and in spinning, collective labor prevailed in such activities as road building and water conservation. In the present industrial sector, interdependence was at least equally pronounced, both in production and in consumption. The precedents for practicing anarchism in China were especially strong. The first emperor, Qinshi Huangdi, had supported collective ownership of property among the people, and under the well-field system everyone had his proper function: the old, a place to retire; adults, a place for their labor; the young, a place for development; and the disadvantaged, a place upon which they could depend. Thus the Confucian concept of universal harmony was not mere idealism. Moreover, in contrast to the Western emphasis on private property, any separation of property—even within the family—was regarded as immoral in China, and the rich were supposed to help the poor within the clan. Hence it should be easier for China to practice communism.

As can be seen from the essay just cited, Liu did not find the traditional family system without merit, specifically in the degree to which it represented a collective, communal unit. Nonetheless, the basic anarchist thrust was to challenge the family as an institution on several counts. First and foremost, the Chinese family system was built on hierarchy and inequality. Individual freedom had been curbed by the oppressive authority granted to elders, and above all, male supremacy had prevailed. "Confucianism," wrote He Zhen in an article demanding the liberation of women, "was cruel to females." Men were allowed to leave their spouses or to have concubines, but "the mandate of heaven" supposedly dictated a different moral code for women, keeping them subordinate to men and driving them to their deaths.*

As we have noted, the anarchists constructed a strict moral code for themselves and others—assuming that one does not blanch at the idea of assassination. They were staunchly opposed to liquor, gambling, and prostitution, and although they believed in love as the appropriate basis for sexual relations, they generally upheld the institution of marriage and also insisted on mutual fidelity. Underwriting all anarchist values, however, were the concepts of freedom and equality. In an early issue of *Tianyi bao,* Liu asserted that anarchists believed that man had three basic rights: equality, independence, and freedom. Independence was a birthright, and freedom was based on individual effort, added Liu, but the achievement of equality depended on man's collective action.[39]

The issue of equality thus became a focus of attention, especially in the writings of the Tokyo anarchists. The essence of the anarchist argument was set forth by Liu in a powerful essay of mid-1907.[40] Although equality had been the ideology of our ancient scholars, Liu asserted, differences of intelligence, strength, and class status meant that individuals had never been equal. What was required, he continued, was complete individual independence, which would flow from the abolition of all government and the establishment of a communist system under which everyone would work in accordance with his talents and age. In this fashion, artificial restraints on individuals would be removed, and an equality of rights and duties would be achieved. With independence in this form would come both freedom and equality.

The possibility that a deep and permanent contradiction existed between freedom and equality did not occur to Liu and his comrades, or if it did,

* He Zhen, "Female Revenge," *Tianyi bao,* no. 3 (1907?) pp. 7–23. This article was continued on August 10, 1907, pp. 65–70, and in later essays He and others paid special attention to the issue of justice and equality for women, for the first time in Chinese radical literature. In an article published in the fall of 1907, He connected women's liberation with anarchism, asserting that the struggle of white women for voting rights was mistaken, since the parliamentary system was the root of all evil. Only a few women from the upper class would enjoy power. Rather, liberation would come when the political power of the state was abolished, and men were thus rendered equal to women. (He Zhen, "The Problem of Women's Liberation," *Tianyi bao,* October 1907, pp. 187–192.)

they suppressed the thought. They were not oblivious to the fact that individuals differed in temperament, abilities, and culture. Nor were they uniformly optimistic about unrestrained human nature; on at least one occasion, for example, Liu admitted that by nature man was selfish and innately jealous of others. Yet the commitment to equality took precedence over all else, despite the fact that some anarchists sensed that collectivism, together with the rules necessary to enforce equality, might come perilously close to statism. To offset this threat, the anarchists advanced the collectivism of the small group as against that of the corporate state. They championed the free association of individuals based on natural economic units. Under these conditions the operative principle would be mutual aid, as was explained so eloquently by Kropotkin. The truly free individual, however, would not long tolerate equality—a problem the anarchists did not resolve and indeed refused to acknowledge.

Another interesting juxtaposition in anarchist writings was the simultaneous commitment to science and to humanism. The strength of anarchist faith in science, especially within the Paris group, was no less than that of the *Xin qingnian* generation that was to follow. In the words of Li Shizeng, "There is nothing in European civilization that does not have its origin in science."[41] To the anarchists, science was truth, knowledge, and progress. It was the only legitimate cornerstone of education, the only proper basis of values.[42] It separated the barbarian from the civilized man.*

But it is clear from their writings and speeches that the young Chinese anarchists had also acquired a deep commitment to Western humanism—a commitment that did not stem from their reverence for science, despite attempts to unite the two. The opening words of *Xin shiji* proclaimed that the journal would have as its starting point a sense of *gongli* (common rights) and *liangxin* (conscience).[43] In subsequent issues, many articles were sprinkled with words like "justice," "fairness," "human rights," and, of course, "equality" and "freedom." To the anarchists, the first and last commandment of natural law was that man should be free, and that he should substitute mutual aid (in Kropotkin's terms) for ruthless competition and sordid materialism.

The attack on constitutional government, as we have seen, derived from the moral concerns of the anarchists. They charged that if monarchy was a victory for absolutism, modern democracy was a victory for money and the wealthy class. Both were unnatural and unnecessary forms of coercion, violations of human freedom. Once again, selected aspects of Chinese traditionalism could blend easily with the Western secular humanism which these young radicals admired. Antipathy to the merchant class was writ large over their intellectual inheritance. The anarchists also made much of *datongzhuyi*, or "universalism," certainly not a novel term for those trained in the

*One article in *Xin shiji* criticized the Chinese minister to Italy for allowing the body of his wife to lie unburied for a period of time in accordance with Chinese custom. It charged that this kind of superstitious, unscientific, barbaric custom subjected the Chinese to ridicule in the eyes of Europeans. See "The Chinese in Europe," *Xin shiji*, September 28, 1907, p. 3. For still another use of science, see "The End of Imperialism," *Xin shiji*, September 5, 1908, pp. 10–12. Said the author, "I dare say that ten years from now death will come to the robber-kings of the world and universal well-being will be achieved. I hope that the youth of China will learn more science and make more bombs, each working according to his own heavenly conscience to expel the barbarians and prevent imperialism from sprouting in China."

classics. Yet anarchism was not simply a transliteration of selected elements of Chinese classical thought. Taken in its totality, it demanded from its Chinese disciples an intellectual conversion of revolutionary proportions. The exaltation of the individual over both the family and the state, and the devotion paid to science, and the concept of progress—all ran against the mainstream of Chinese thought.

The anarchists glorified revolution. They argued that mankind had moved slowly from barbarism to civilization solely because of revolution.[44] They proclaimed the twentieth century a century of global revolution, from which no nation would escape.* And they believed that violence was necessary to bring on revolution. Nationalist rivals accused them of being inconsistent in advocating both antimilitarism and violent revolution, but the anarchists refused to admit any contradiction.

> Militarism is the means by which the strong sacrifice the lives and money of others in order to preserve their own power and that of the state. Thus it is unfair and should be eliminated. Revolutionary assassination, on the other hand, is the sacrifice of the individual to eliminate an enemy of humanity, and thereby extends the common rights of the world. These two, militarism and revolutionary assassination, are as different as two things can be.[45]

To the anarchists, the bomb and the pistol were important means of advancing common rights. One author criticized the young Chinese students in Japan who were advocating suicide as a protest against Chinese government policies.

> If you fellows really see in death the answer to things, why do you not follow in the footsteps of the Russian Terrorist Party by killing one or two thieves of mankind as the price of death? Whether one plunges into the sea or is decapitated [as an assassin], both are the same death. But they are different in their impact. Whereas one has no impact and the person merely dies as a courageous man, the other has a great impact, especially upon the Chinese official class. The fear of death is one of the special characteristics of Chinese officials. In sum, in this twentieth century, if there is the possibility of eliminating even one thief of mankind and thereby decreasing a portion of dictatorial power, then the year of the great Chinese revolution will be one day closer.[46]

Assassination appealed to Chinese radicals as a revolutionary technique in large part because of the problems involved in organizing any effective mass movement in China. In the case of the anarchists, philosophical distaste for organization of any sort served as an additional incentive. Assassination was an immediately practical individual action. Other methods seemed utopian, or at best long-range, and might lend themselves to new forms of statist coercion.

* "International Revolutionary Currents" (Comments by Li Shizeng), *Xin shiji*, February 1, 1908, pp. 1–2. We are indebted to Professor Michael Gasster for pointing out that one *Xin shiji* reader argued that by advocating revolution the editors were violating the *evolutionary* principles of one of their heroes, Darwin. Wu responded by asserting that there was a difference between biology and human affairs, for human affairs were subject to control (and hence acceleration) by human action.

Still, even the anarchists agreed that a truly successful revolution had to have the support of a majority of the people. Because they were suspicious of any large-scale organization that lent itself to permanent (hence repressive) structures, they sought to stimulate spontaneous or internally generated mass action from natural socioeconomic units. To this end, they urged a campaign of propaganda and action directed against three objects: government, capitalists, and society at large. With respect to government, opposition should be concentrated on militarism, laws, and taxation. Capitalists should be combatted by an attack on the concept of private property. In society at large, religion and the family institution should be exposed. At the level of action, assassination should be used against government, strikes against capitalists, and love toward society.[47]

In another source, *La Révolution*, probably written by Li Shizeng and Chu Minyi, five means of consummating revolution were set forth: books and speeches, "so as to move people"; meetings and gatherings, "whereby the people's power may be brought together"; public resistance in the form of refusal to pay taxes; opposition to conscription, and strikes; assassination; and mass uprisings.[48]

At least one young anarchist suggested the idea of competing with Sun's revolutionaries in seeking to convert the Chinese secret societies into vehicles for revolution.[49] These societies, he argued, already had a mass base and had instilled an anti-Manchu revolutionary spirit in large numbers of common people. To be sure, the secret societies remained traditionalist and culture-bound, and were not contributing much to modern China; but it was possible that they could learn to use the new revolutionary methods of Western radicalism, such as the general strike and antimilitarism. Furthermore, if revolution were to succeed in China, unions would have to be established. But rather than building new unions, why not change the character of the secret societies? Why not cause hundreds and thousands of revolutionary comrades to join these societies and carry with them the principles of anarchist communism? Then the simple aim of overthrowing the Manchu could be broadened to include the ideas of social revolution and free federation.[50] This was perhaps the earliest proposal for radical infiltration into a "mass organization" to emanate from Chinese sources; it antedates Comintern instructions and Chinese Leninism by more than a decade.

The effect of anarcho-syndicalism on the Chinese anarchists came in 1908. Prior to that time, no extensive discussions of unionism or the use of the general strike can be found in Chinese writings, either in Paris or in Tokyo. Beginning in the spring of 1908, however, such ideas were propagated both in *Xin shiji* and in the new Tokyo anarchist journal, *Heng bao*. Besides the article just described, there were essays which advanced the thesis that the creation of trade unions was a primary duty for anarchists; other essays noted the importance of strikes, both as a means of securing workers' rights and as an instrument of union-building, and claimed that unions would play the crucial role in the politics of the future.*

* For example, see two articles in *Heng bao*, June 18, 1908, p. 1, entitled "The Victory of the Technicians' Strike in Suzhou," and "On Chinese Trade Union Associations." In the first article, the successful Suzhou strike for higher wages was described as the forerunner of a strike for political power, "the general strike which we propose, aims at social revolution." In the second article, trends in China were described as indicating an expansion of capitalist power: such formerly free rights of the common people as fishing and woodcutting were now

Even the most ardent anarchist, however, must have found it difficult to imagine the rapid emergence of an industrialized China that would support powerful labor unions. China was still a vast peasant society, and issues of the people's livelihood still revolved principally around rural conditions. Like the Tongmeng Hui leaders, the anarchists were opposed to the unrestrained private exploitation of land; but in their view, "nationalization" would simply lead to a more powerful, more centralized, more coercive state. Communal ownership should also mean communal, *local* control—the counterpart to the industrial workshop. True freedom and equality would come with the emergence of free federations of self-regulated farmers.

The anarchists did not rest with general prescriptions for rural ills. The Tokyo anarchists were the first Chinese radicals to produce empirical data on the peasantry in an effort to support their theses. In 1908 they published a series of articles describing actual conditions in various parts of rural China, with primary emphasis on the peasant, but with mention also of soldiers and urban workers. One of the most interesting of these articles dealt with peasant life in Sichuan.* In bad regions, wrote the author, food consisted of 60 percent vegetables, 30 percent potatoes, and 10 percent rice, with meat only on special days. At harvest time the peasant gained weight; gradually, as food became scarce, he became thinner. Insufficient clothing was a constant problem, and sometimes peasants were without footwear, even in winter. Peasant houses were very dirty, often unsuited to human habitation. During harvest season the peasant usually slept in the field to prevent robbery. The greatest exploitation came from moneylenders, who charged exorbitant interest rates and purchased the peasants' silk products at low prices. From such an account one receives a radically different impression than that conveyed by other Chinese writers, even by the Sun revolutionaries, who generally depicted their social reforms as necessary to prevent future abuses rather than serving as an answer to current injustices.

In advocating a socioeconomic revolution that would "liberate" the peasants and workers, the anarchists considered themselves communists, though certainly not of the Marxist type. Anarcho-communism was spelled out in a major article noted earlier, published by Liu.[51] Drawing heavily on Kropotkin, the author also turned to traditional China in making the case for freely associated socioeconomic units based on communal property. Indeed,

---

increasingly regulated by big companies; rural handicrafts were being stifled; and because of lowered incomes, farmers were abandoning their farms, coming to the cities in search of industrial work; and while the government protected capitalists, the laws pertaining to workers were harsh. Hence anarchists should concentrate on organizing labor unions to combat these conditions.

*"Peasant Life in Sichuan," *Heng bao*, June 18, 1908, p. 1. See also "The Political Exploitation of the Chinese Peasants," *Heng bao*, May 8, 1908, p. 1; "The Antagonism Between Landowners and Peasants in Zhefo," *Heng bao*, June 18, 1908, p. 1; and Shen Shu, "Three Essays on Equity," *Heng bao*, August 8, 1908, p. 1. In the latter article, after discoursing on the inequities among rich, middle, and poor peasants, Liu asserted that in ancient times, one *mou* (6.6 *mou* equals one acre) was sufficient for a family of five persons, the average production being 66 picul per mou. Even if only one-half of that amount were produced, one mou ought to suffice for eight persons, and 400 million persons would need only 50 million mou of cultivated land. Some 1,000 million mou would be left over. If one-half were reserved for future population expansion, the remaining 500 million could be divided into 100 million for housing, 100 million for the cultivation of commercial products, 100 million for pasture land, 100 million for cotton and mulberry cultivation, and 100 million in forest lands.

the author expressed unqualified approval of the ancient well-field system and Confucian "universal harmony," seeing them as traditional precedents for the anarcho-communist system currently being advanced. (There is an interesting parallel here between Liu and Kang Youwei in his idealist mood.)

Slightly later, from the vantage point of Paris, Chu Minyi presented his views on anarcho-communism with somewhat different emphases. In the *Xin shiji* issue of November 7, 1908, Chu criticized an article published in the Shanghai *Shi bao*, a progressive newspaper founded in 1904 by Ti Chuqing, a returned student from Japan; the article had been entitled "Why China Cannot Now Promote Communism (*gongchanzhuyi*)."[52] In his answer, Chu asserted that all anarchists were communists, whereas this was not necessarily true of socialists. There were many "false socialist parties" that sought to substitute the power of government (through state socialism) for the power of capitalists. Only communism, which renounced national wealth and military might and concentrated instead on the well-being of each individual in the world, could provide justice and achieve universal harmony.

The *Shi bao* article had equated communism with the well-field system, and maintained that despite attempts to effectuate communism from time to time throughout Chinese history, it could never be more than empty talk, because it ignored reality. The *Shi bao* essay had occasionally used the term *junchan* (equalization of property) instead of *gongchan* (communal property) in discussing communism. Chu consistently used the latter term, and unlike Liu, he denied that the well-field system represented modern communism. One must distinguish between various forms of collectivism, he insisted. Nationalization of property would not produce true communism. Communism was based on common property, but all authority was vested in small, natural groups, which were united only in free federation; there were no coercive instruments of control.

Chu associated himself with the view that the difference between rich and poor in China had not yet reached the extremes characteristic of the West. But communism offered the only way to avoid these extremes, and in communism there was only one basic law: "from each according to his ability; to each according to his needs." No rules were necessary, and there was no need for the higher government of a state. When the *Shi bao* writer brought Social Darwinism into play, Chu used Kropotkin's riposte: progress did not necessarily depend on competition, and competition did not always signify progress. Mutual aid was also a route to progress—and to progress with justice. In mid-1907 a chart entitled "A Comparison of the Three Principles of Nationalism, Democracy, and Socialism" was published in *Xin shiji*.[53] Chinese nationalism, according to the chart, was distinguished chiefly by its anti-Manchu and antiforeign (anti-Western) components. In a limited sense, it was antiauthority: it opposed transgressions by any foreign race on the Han people and sought to eliminate insults to them. However, it was thus drawn to support militarism as a method of opposing external dangers and strengthening the Chinese state.

Democracy was characterized by being against a monarchy and against a nobility. It was also against authority, in a limited sense: it opposed the power and coercion exercised by one person (the monarch) or by a small group (the officials), and it sought to end oppression of the people. But democracy also supported *zuguozhuyi* (fatherlandism) and its attendant militarism. Together, nationalism and democracy sought the well-being of one country or one race—at best, a decided minority of the world's people. Thus, in general terms, both nationalism and democracy were dominated by selfishness and the search for self-advantage.

Socialism, on the other hand, was dedicated to opposing all things that were against reason. Thus, it was against all authority, without reservation. It was against all political systems. It sought to eliminate every injury to human freedom and to realize certain universal moral laws. It opposed international as well as national power politics, favoring an end to warfare and the enjoyment of universal harmony. It was for the abandonment of all evil ways: the superstitions of religion (so as to eliminate falseness and reveal truth); the obligations of the family (so as to eliminate family bonds and release love among all mankind); and the customs of social intercourse (so as to eliminate artificiality and reveal naturalness). It strongly supported equality in all forms: equality in the economic system (so as to eliminate divisions between rich and poor and create common property), and equality in moral and political rules (so as to eliminate classes and special privilege). Thus the ultimate characteristic of socialism was universal harmony based on justice and a selfless love of mankind.[54]

In this article the author did not admit the existence of any brand of socialism other than the one espoused by the anarchists. Needless to say, spokesmen for the Tongmeng Hui rejected this position. At first, *Min bao* writers, like many Western radicals, treated anarchism as a generally admirable philosophy that was totally impractical under current conditions.[55] As their battle with Liang grew hot, however, some of Sun's supporters found it desirable to distinguish their position clearly from that of the anarchists. In an article published in September 1906, one *Min bao* author assailed the reformers for "slandering" the revolutionaries by equating them with the anarchists. In fact, he argued, "our two positions are completely different." "Peaceful" anarchists were prepared to await an evolutionary change in man's spirit, and "extreme" anarchists advocated destruction, collectivism, and communism; in both cases, however, the anarchist aim was to abolish politics rather than to achieve political reform, which was the goal of the revolutionaries.[56]

The anarchists, this writer maintained, made no distinction between absolutism and constitutionalism, or between monarchy and democracy, because they sought the destruction of the state in all its forms. The revolutionaries, while recognizing the evils of all government, sought to replace a bad government with a new and better one. Both socialism and anarchism were committed to the complete freedom of man, but their methods were totally different: socialism aimed at collectivizing the means of production under a democratic state, whereas anarchism had no plan other than to leave each individual free to act on his own after the destruction of the state.

THE POLITICS OF PERSONAL RELATIONS

Although the ideological differences between the anarchists in Paris and Tokyo and the mainstream Tongmeng Hui members were always clear, complex personal relations often clouded the picture. Sun's *Min bao* sometimes seemed ready to greet Russian terrorists and assorted anarchists like Perovskaya, Bakunin, and Kropotkin as kindred souls. Similarly, the anarchist journal *Tianyi bao*, though much more rigorous in adhering to its ideological position, published a translation of the *Communist Manifesto* in its January and February 1908 issues.[57] The anarchists Liu and He lived with Zhang Binglin, the editor of *Min bao*, when they first arrived in Tokyo, and Liu contributed a number of articles to that journal between May and December 1907. More important, Sun Yat-sen had developed warm personal friendships with some of the Paris-based Chinese anarchists; he had induced them to join the Tongmeng Hui and had received various types of aid from them.[58] His friendship with Wu Zhihui, for example, dated from the winter of 1905, when they were both staying in London.* How often they met is not clear, but Sun did introduce Wu to his former teacher Dr. James Cantlie.

It was also at this time that Sun and Wu met Zhang Jingjiang. Zhang promised Sun that if he ever needed money, he need only wire, and the two men worked out a code that would signify the amount required.[59] In 1906 and 1907 Sun took advantage of this offer and obtained substantial sums. Both Wu and Zhang joined the Tongmeng Hui. Wu joined in late 1905 because, it was said, he thought Sun's program was an acceptable first step and because he was convinced that all revolutionaries should work together. There can be little doubt that Sun's latitudinarian appreciation of socialist doctrine encouraged decisions of this sort. He probably praised anarchism as an "ideal," especially when he was with the Paris group. Zhang joined the Tongmeng Hui in 1907 in Hong Kong, after it had been agreed that his oath of allegiance could be modified to omit any mention of heaven—a change he had insisted upon as an anarchist.[60]

After 1907 Sun and the Paris group were brought even closer together by a mutual enemy. In the autumn of 1907 Zhang Binglin and certain other Tongmeng Hui members in Tokyo launched a movement to oust Sun as head of the revolutionary movement. Sun was in Indochina at this time, and his chief supporters were also absent from Tokyo. In October Zhang Binglin, Zhang Ji, and Tongmeng Hui members prepared a manifesto charging Sun with the misappropriation of funds, the rash sacrifice of lives in hopeless revolutionary ventures, and the use of the title *zongli* (general leader) without proper authorization.[61] The manifesto was widely circulated among Chinese overseas communities, and created great acrimony.

As we noted earlier, relations between Wu Zhihui and Zhang Binglin had been bad since the 1903 *Su bao* affair. For some reason, Zhang blamed Wu for his arrest, and a strong hostility had developed between the two men. Thus, it was easy for the Paris group, led by Wu, to defend Sun against an old enemy. By 1908 Liu and He had also split with Zhang Binglin, for different reasons. Naturally, these developments were reflected in the pages of *Min bao*, a journal Zhang was still editing. A strong attack on the anarchists was contained in an article published in late October of 1907, precisely the time when Zhang and his colleagues were striking out against Sun.[62] The author (Zhang?) asserted that any desire to eliminate a given government compelled one to assist in the creation of a new government, since every society needed direction, and relations between states were indispens-

*Yang Kailing states that Sun met Wu in Tokyo in the spring of 1901, but others insist that the London meeting was the first. See Yang, "The Father of Our Country and Mr. Wu Zhihui," *Sanminzhuzi Banyuekan* (Three People's Principles Semimonthly), May 15, 1953, pp. 28–29.

able. Thus, even if "government" were declared abandoned, it would exist in fact, whether the administrators were a social group or a tribe. The anarchists, he argued with increasing bitterness, spoke of universal harmony and refused to make distinctions between races; but since they had no power to create universal harmony, and since their position on race served to excuse the crimes of the Manchu barbarians, were they not contributing to the strengthening of the Manchu government, thereby putting themselves on the same level as other traitors?

Zhang's attacks reached a climax in early 1908, and were directed primarily against the *Xin shiji*. One article charged that the Paris-based anarchists, by advocating Esperanto, were aiming at the destruction of the indigenous Chinese language in favor of a Western-based foreign language.* In another article Zhang ridiculed anarchism as based on shallow and foolish arguments. Its promises of universal happiness, he alleged, were like the myth of a return to a Golden Era, and equally hollow. Principles should be drawn neither from the sky nor from the earth, but from actual conditions. One needed to know the background of Manchu rule and why it had to be overthrown. China needed a racially based nationalism, not anarchism.**

The *Xin shiji* leaders were not reticent in striking back. In a series of open letters, Wu denounced Zhang's conservative nationalism and challenged his credentials as a true revolutionary.[63] At this point, the exchanges had become increasingly personal and vitriolic. (Lin Youtang later described the exchanges between Zhang and Wu as excellent examples of Chinese vituperative literature.)[64]

Both Zhang Binglin and Liu Shipei have recently been classified as belonging to the "national essence" (*guosui*) school. They became committed to finding solutions for contemporary problems through a reexamination of the sources of China's historic greatness and a revitalization of the essence of Chinese culture. Both men were excellent classical scholars, and before their departure from Shanghai they had launched a journal, the *National Essence Monthly*, in February 1905. Although they joined the Tongmeng Hui because of their strong anti-Manchu feelings and, in Liu's case, affiliated temporarily with the anarchist movement owing to the influence of the Tokyo environment, their backgrounds and personalities led them to resent what they regarded as the wholesale abandonment of China's great intellec-

*Zhang Binglin, "On Striking Down the Argument Supporting China's Adoption of an International Language," *Min bao*, June 10, 1908, pp. 49–72. Zhang, an eminent young classical scholar, was incensed at the possibility of Chinese culture's being damaged. Do the anarchists, who seek to deny the validity of force, he asked, also desire to abandon learning? In this essay Zhang revealed himself as primarily committed to one goal—the overthrow of the Manchu and the restoration of Han government. He was clearly suspicious of Western-oriented radicalism, and was moving away from all branches of the Chinese revolutionary movement at this time.

**Zhang Binglin, "A Balanced Discussion of Anti-Manchuism," *Min bao*, June 10, 1908, pp. 1–12. See also Zhang, "The Taiwanese and a *Xin shiji* Correspondent," *Min bao*, July 10, 1908, pp. 31–35, in which Zhang blasted a *Xin shiji* writer, noting that in responding to a Taiwanese he spoke of "your country"—thereby suggesting that Taiwan should not be a part of China. A further attack came in "To Advise the *Xin shiji*," *Min bao*, October 10, 1908, pp. 41–65, in which Zhang challenged the scientific basis of the anarchists' philosophy and issued another blast at their advocacy of Esperanto. Earlier, Zhang had written a preface to Zhang Ji's translation of one of Errico Malatesta's writings, and this was reproduced in *Min bao*, April 25, 1908, pp. 129–130. Though not wholly unfavorable to Malatesta, Zhang treated the Italian anarchist leader in a relatively condescending manner, suggesting that his work made a good beginning but did not go far enough.

tual traditions in an indiscriminate rush toward Westernization. Retaining their anti-Manchu (and anti-imperialist) credentials, they moved separately out of the main revolutionary streams. Zhang, it should be noted, turned to Pan-Asianism. In 1908 he drafted the principles of a new Pan-Asian Society dedicated to harmony among the Asian peoples and the struggle for Asian independence from Western imperialism.[65] In succeeding decades, others would follow a similar path for similar reasons.

Meanwhile, Sun's honor was staunchly upheld in Paris while his credentials were being challenged in Tokyo. In later years Sun sought to repay his debt to old anarchist friends. He offered them positions in the Guomindang and in the government. At first most of them refused to be associated with state power, but later, as the anarchist movement faded away before the challenges of nationalism and communism, some of them accepted.

But the ideological chasm between Sun and the anarchists could never be bridged. At times, Sun seemed willing to accommodate himself to all doctrines that bore the label "socialism." And despite their early denials, anarchists like Wu, Zhang, and Li ultimately appeared willing to accept Sun's Three People's Principles as a first step in a generally correct direction. In purely ideological terms, however, there could be no meaningful compromise between Sun's one-party tutelage and the anarchists' freedom, between his concept of centralized power and their concept of free federation. Theirs was a marriage of convenience and friendship, not of logic.

In addition to defending Sun, *Xin shiji* kept up a running battle against government surveillance of overseas students. In early 1907 the Chinese government announced that it would send a supervisor to France "to assist" the students in their various activities. On June 18, 1907, the very eve of the appearance of *Xin shiji*, a meeting was convened by the Chinese students in France to discuss the matter. What percentage of the students came is not clear, but the attitude of those present toward the proposal was very clear indeed. They recommended that any supervisor should meet the following conditions: (1) he should have a good command of three languages; (2) he should be well versed in at least one science; (3) he should not be allowed to bring his family; (4) his salary should not be more than the amount paid to three students.[66] From comments in *Xin shiji*, there is good reason to believe that the anarchist group had a considerable role in framing these proposals. In the course of the meeting, some amendments were proposed. It was suggested that only those members of the official's family with bound feet be prohibited from coming, so as not to disgrace the students. The rule that Han officials should wear queues was also challenged.

The *Xin shiji* report of the meeting was written in a satirical vein. If there were a need for someone to make payments to overseas students, then an accountant should be brought, not a supervisor. Of course, the government really wanted to investigate revolutionary activities. To help the government in this respect, the writer stated that he could announce immediately that the general student sentiment was favorable to revolution; the only opposition came from those who wanted to become officials and acquire wealth. These were already serving as informers, so why waste money on a supervisor who would know so little in any case that he would have to depend on informers after his arrival. The writer made one additional offer. Henceforth, he said, we will print more news about revolutionary activities and send the paper free of charge to the supervisor; then he can stay home and still be well informed.[67] Despite this proffered "assistance," the supervisor did arrive after a considerable delay. *Xin shiji* reported his first speech, an address given on May 31, 1908.[68] It was a conciliatory talk delivered before some sixty to seventy students, but Wu took strong exception to it and sought to read amply between the lines.

Meanwhile, pressure on the revolutionary movement was everywhere on the increase. By the latter part of 1908, Chinese authorities had finally prevailed on the Japanese government to stop the publication of *Min bao* and the anarchist journal *Heng bao*. Shortly, an equally heavy blow fell. Liu and He, having broken with Zhang Binglin and being constrained in their Tokyo activities, returned to Shanghai sometime during 1908. Soon it became known that they had defected from the anarchist movement and were serving as informers for the police, working for the Manchu official Duanfang.[69] Liu reportedly told the Shanghai International Settlement police of a secret Tongmeng Hui meeting, with the result that one member was jailed. The precise pressures and circumstances that produced the defection are not clear. According to rumor, He Zhen was involved in a plot to assassinate a government official, and perhaps a deal was made to save her. In any case, this ended the revolutionary careers of two remarkable individuals and constituted a serious loss for the anarchists.*

REJECTIONISM AND RESTORATION

Liu, like Zhang Binglin, remained closer to Chinese traditionalism than most of his comrades. We have noted his extensive use of classical philosophy and history to explain, justify, and promote anarchism. The broader significance of this fact should not be lost. As long as many of China's modern revolutionaries felt a deep affinity with their past, and were consciously or unconsciously drawn to enlist Chinese tradition in the service of Western-derived radicalism, the political pendulum could swing back for them under certain conditions. The tension involved in rejecting major portions of a culture as rich and varied as that of China was always great, regardless of the background, personality, or ideological proclivities of the person concerned. And the capacity to feel truly comfortable with Westernism in any of its mysterious forms was rare indeed, even for those who were to advance furthest toward internationalism.

Thus, the line between rejectionism and restoration, a crucial line in purely theoretical terms, was often thin and wavering. Different branches of Chinese radicalism had different objectives at this point, to be sure. The goal of the nationalists was to see China politically unified, economically developed, and militarily strong. The goal of the anarchists was of a higher and broader ethical order; they proposed to deliver all men from oppression and lead them into a condition of total freedom and equality. Yet for both nationalists and anarchists, a gnawing issue remained. How far should they move away from their indigenous roots and seek to propel their society into doing likewise? From the past, what was to be rejected and what was to be "restored" through new interpretations, new techniques, and new goals?

*In later years, Liu supported Yuan Shikai. Despite Liu's political transgressions, however, Cai Yuanpei, when he became president of Peking University, appointed Liu to a professorship. Both their old personal friendship and the fact that Liu was an excellent classical scholar probably entered into this appointment. But Liu died shortly thereafter, on November 20, 1919, at the age of thirty-six. Cai Yuanpei, "A Brief Account of the Activities of Liu Shenshu," pp. 236–237.

The issue had gone far beyond the simplistic formulation "Chinese learning for values, Western learning for technology" that was prevalent in the 1890s. And as it had become more complex, it had been increasingly avoided, submerged into the subconscious, especially in radical circles. Yet the example of Japan and its "restoration" stood before every Chinese revolutionary. It was not enough to point to the very different circumstances of Japan. The issue would not go away so easily. And for the anarchists it was particularly acute. Paradoxically, among Chinese radicals they were both the most removed from the traditions of their society and the closest to them. In their denunciations of China's xenophobic, exclusivist, family-bound past, they were seeking to dig out some of the deepest roots of their political culture. Yet in their desire to confront the tides of modernity, which they saw as threatening to equality, freedom, and justice, they turned to policies and principles closely associated with certain aspects of China's past.

In their Janus-faced posture toward past and future, the anarchists epitomized the Chinese intellectual dilemma of the early twentieth century. Nationalists and Communists were to suffer the same trauma. Both sought certain modernist goals in a largely nonmodern society. With time increasingly of the essence, they were successively charged with leading a "bourgeois" revolution. Yet neither their personal backgrounds nor that of their society were conducive to the successful completion of such a task. And as failure recurrently made its appearance, a retreat into the more familiar, hence more comfortable patterns of traditional political behavior ensued. Rejection or restoration—or phrased in less absolutist terms, the quest for a complex synthesis—was not merely an anarchist challenge. It confronted, and continues to confront, every Chinese leader. The career of Mao Zedong, as we shall see, was an example par excellence of both the issue and its human environment.

ANARCHIST CURRENTS ON THE EVE OF THE REVOLUTION

The Chinese anarchists in Japan ceased to have a public voice or organization after 1908, but the Paris anarchists carried on, continuing to publish and meet until the Revolution of 1911. Some Tokyo comrades, such as Zhang Ji, joined them. The summer of 1908 found Zhang in a communal village experiment in northern France, seeking to practice what he had preached.* Another figure who moved closer to the anarchists during this period was that devoted follower of Sun Yat-sen, Wang Jingwei. Wang, it will be recalled, returned to Tokyo from Southeast Asia in 1909 and soon revived *Min bao*, serving as its editor for two final issues. While Zhang Binglin, now totally estranged from the Sun forces, bitterly denounced the journal as "a false *Min bao*," the *Xin shiji* group helped to publicize it and insisted that "party members in the East are paying no attention to Zhang's charges."** Wang, moreover, was to be the final hero of the Paris journal.

*After the 1911 Revolution, Zhang returned to China, and shortly thereafter he attempted to secure from the revolutionary government Chongming Island at the mouth of the Yangtze River "as an experimental area for world anarchism." *Minli bao* (People's Independence), Shanghai, January 26, 1912, p. 2.

**See *Xin shiji*, December 18, 1909, p. 1. In an advertisement for the new issue of *Min bao*, it was announced that one copy had been received and three hundred more were en route.

Its last issue, published on May 21, 1910, was devoted almost entirely to praise of Wang for his attempted assassination of the Manchu prince regent.

Wang was by no means the only Chinese revolutionary to be influenced by anarchist doctrines during this period. Another anarchist conquest was Liu Sifu, better known as Shifu.[70] Since he was to play an important role in the post-1911 anarchist movement, and since his political evolution faithfully reflected the basic trends of this era, a brief description of his career is warranted. He was born in 1884 near Canton, to a gentry family in Sun's home district in Guangdong. He became an excellent student of the classics, but showed radical proclivities even before leaving China. In 1904 he arrived in Japan to continue his education, and the following year he took an active part in the establishment of Sun's Tongmeng Hui. At the same time, he had begun to study the art of manufacturing explosives.*

In 1906, learning that Sun planned an uprising in Guangdong, Liu left Japan for home, along with some other students. Upon reaching Hong Kong, however, he accepted the editorship of a local journal and remained there. In 1907 it was decided that a successful revolt in Guangdong would be facilitated by the assassination of either the governor or the naval commander. The latter, Li Zhun, was chosen as the target, and Liu volunteered to serve as executioner. Because of his carelessness, however, the bomb exploded prematurely. Liu was severely wounded, and his left arm had to be amputated to the elbow. Although the police were unable to determine his precise mission, he was arrested and spent nearly three years in prison. He was released then only because his literary efforts were so admired by local officials that they petitioned higher authorities on his behalf.**

After his release from prison in 1909, Liu returned to Hong Kong. During his confinement and afterward, he had moved steadily toward anarchism, finally becoming a dedicated disciple of *Xin shiji* doctrines. In Hong Kong he and others organized an anarchist assassination group, which had no contact with the Tongmeng Hui.[71] This group tried once more to assassinate Li Zhun, and they were planning another attempt to kill the prince regent Zaiyi (Wang Jingwei's intended victim) when the Revolution of 1911 broke out. At this point, Liu and others had organized a revolutionary force known as the Chao Army, which moved into Canton along with other groups shortly after the events at Wuhan. Under the aegis of Chen Jiongming, Liu was given administrative responsibilities for uniting diverse revolutionary elements. Nevertheless, Liu soon left Canton, traveling north with a few companions, with the objective of assassinating Yuan Shikai. But Wang Jingwei, just released from prison, dissuaded Liu, asserting that a peace between the South and the North, on the brink of being achieved, could easily

* According to Mo, Shifu (Liu) developed an intimate acquaintance with Wang Jingwei at this time, and the two met a Russian nihilist living in Japan, who taught them how to make bombs. Mo goes on to assert that while they were still in Japan, they agreed on the need to assassinate key Manchu officials, with Wang accepting responsibility for the prince regent and Liu agreeing to make the Guangdong naval commander, Li Zhun, his target (Mo Jipeng, "Recalling Shifu," p. 7a. This account differs slightly from Liu's own recollection).

**According to Mo, shortly after Liu was imprisoned more than 1,000 signatures were secured for a petition asking for his release, and the signers included many of the prominent local gentry, some of whom had family ties with him. Liu remained in jail but was shifted from Canton to Xiangshan, his home district. Finally, because of local efforts and pressure from Beijing, where lobbying had taken place on his behalf, he was released ("Recalling Shifu," pp. 10a–13b).

be shattered by such an event.[72] We shall return later to Liu's subsequent activities on behalf of the anarchist cause.

THE BALANCE SHEET

On the eve of the Nationalist Revolution, the Chinese anarchists had some reason for optimism. The revolutionary movement seemed to be adopting their tactics. Assassination and other forms of "direct action" had become the order of the day. Anarchist writings had had an influence on a number of nationalists, and the leaders of the Paris group had forged close personal ties with Sun himself. Since the pro-Sun group was clearly in the ascendancy within China's revolutionary camp, the anarchists might hope to play some role in the aftermath of a successful anti-Manchu drive.

The international climate for anarchism also seemed promising. Anarchism and anarcho-syndicalism were much in vogue in European radical circles, and often forced Marxists, Christian Socialists, and other elements of the revolutionary movement into a defensive stance. Even in the United States the anarchist-oriented IWW (International Workers of the World) had created a considerable stir, and American socialism had to deal with the anarchist challenge posed by Emma Goldman and William Haywood. In Japan the anarchists had captured the commanding heights of the socialist movement, although in the aftermath of the abortive plot to assassinate the emperor Meiji in 1910, the Japanese government moved to crush anarchists and radical socialists alike. Finally, the anarchist interest in China's past was not without its benefits, as we have suggested.

Two major obstacles plagued the anarchists. First, they were running against the prevailing political tides. In an age of nationalism—when nationalist movements were only beginning to find their strength among the intelligentsia of the colonial and semicolonial world—the anarchists were proclaiming that nationalism was passé. They spoke at least a century and possibly a millennium too soon.

Beyond this, they clung stubbornly to organizational theories which guaranteed that they would never initiate or inherit the revolutions that lay ahead. In espousing "natural socioeconomic units" connected by means of free federation and dedicated to mutual aid, the anarchists were rejecting even the minimal requirements for successful revolution. Revolution has always been a precarious undertaking, and never more so than in an age when developments in technology and communications generally benefit those in power. The government, to be sure, had been gravely weakened by the progressive disintegration of Chinese society over which it presided. But even so, some military preparations and some popular mobilization were essential; at the very least, it was necessary to cultivate popular indifference to the fate of government officials so that a small revolutionary elite could operate in a neutral climate. Toward these requirements the anarchists generally responded with lofty disdain.

In retrospect, the situation in which the anarchists found themselves was ironic. As we have seen, despite their efforts to identify with the urban worker and trade unionism, the circumstances of early-twentieth-century China made this a hopeless route to power. More than other Chinese radicals, however, the anarchists remained deeply concerned about the peasant, and prepared to fight for his rights through the same natural free associations they had projected for urban life. Yet, several decades later, it was the Communists, not the anarchists, who went part of the way down this path. The Communists, to be sure, had not chosen the isolated, peasant-based, communal enclaves to which they were reduced in such areas as Jiangxi and Fujian; circumstances forced these upon them. Nor were these enclaves free associations, in any anarchist sense. Nevertheless, at a certain point in their history, the Communists were to demonstrate that with patience and luck, small associations aggregated into "mutual aid federations" could serve as building blocks for the revolution. Equally important, they were to prove that the peasantry could provide the mass base for a successful revolution, whatever class label one chose to apply to it.

As we shall see, the anarchist thread continued to be woven into the fabric of modern Chinese politics, partly because it featured the ethical side of Marxism-Leninism while rejecting its authoritarianism.

6

THE COMING OF THE 1911 REVOLUTION

In response to the political instability that has proliferated since World War II, scholars have taken renewed interest in the nature of sociopolitical upheaval. Massive changes in government structure and political systems have led them to adopt new approaches to old issues. Many of them have sought to differentiate among the various challenges that can be brought to bear on the social order by presenting typologies that set forth "pure" alternatives. Among these efforts are several recent studies of revolution that will take their place with the great classics in this field.[1]

Before we deal with the Revolution of 1911, then, we must say a few words about our own concept of revolution and how we distinguish it from other types of violence or change. Obviously, our categorization of the political and sociological processes involved in the fall of the Qing dynasty will determine in large part how we evaluate subsequent developments, including the role of the Communist movement in the evolution of modern Chinese society.

ON REVOLUTION

We shall define "political revolution" in a very specific manner, acknowledging that it is equally legitimate—indeed essential—to accept a broader concept of "social revolution," a far more complex process unlimited in time and with infinite variations.

A political revolution is a conscious set of time-specific actions that involve violence, are designed to overthrow the established political order, and are dedicated to replacing that order with a new elite, a new ideology, and a new program. Even if a political revolution succeeds in seizing power under these commitments, the broad goals may not be sufficiently realized later on to warrant calling the revolution a success. The results of a political revolution can be evaluated only over time, but the revolution itself is an act, or a series of related acts, undertaken within a reasonably limited period.

Many political revolutions fail in their initial objective, to seize power. Others that succeed in this first step eventually lose their original spirit or purpose. Indeed, to some degree this is almost always the case. What we may properly call a political revolution exists, however, if the broad goals sketched above are present and articulated by acknowledged leaders—a revolutionary elite.

What is "counterrevolution?" Counterrevolution has all of the attributes of revolution, except that the comprehensive social change being sought is the ousting of the revolutionary elite along with its ideology and program. True counterrevolutions are always attempted soon after a revolution. Even if they succeed, however, counterrevolutionaries seldom restore the prerevolutionary order unchanged. Often they do not even wish to do so. In the course of challenging the legitimacy of their opponents, they usually put forward a new combination of "orthodox" and "revisionist" values and institutions.

How does political revolution differ from two other forms of political violence, rebellion and coup d'etat? Rebellion may aim loosely at restoring an old order, real or imagined, or at purifying the current order by removing "usurpers" and evil power-holders, or by changing certain policies; but unlike revolution (or counterrevolution), it does not aim at creating a *new* order by basically altering the structure of the society. Thus the Taiping Rebellion, though it contained certain revolutionary elements, did not strike at the traditional arrangements of status and authority in China. A coup d'etat aims at seizing power from the immediate political leadership; its objective is essentially limited to changing the power-holders. A coup d'etat may sometimes move in the direction of revolution, but only if the factors relating to our definition of political revolution are present.

Our relatively narrow definition of a political revolution requires acceptance of a broader revolutionary process we have labeled "social revolution." A social revolution may or may not be accompanied by violence, including the violence of a political revolution. It may develop through a series of political changes of lesser magnitude. In any case, it cannot be completed in the course of a single action, or in a relatively short period of time. Nor does it necessarily involve self-consciously revolutionary decisions on the part of the governing elite. Indeed, it may unfold without their knowledge and consent. At some point, it is true, a social revolution will affect the fundamental structure of a given society, bringing changes in class structure, new concepts of status, and powerful challenges to the established power-holders. Unless a society's political institutions and governing elite can be continually adjusted to keep pace with social change, tensions will increase, leading first to the possibility, then the probability, and then the virtual certainty of a political revolution.

Ultimately, however, a social revolution is by its very nature evolutionary, since fundamental socioeconomic alterations can only be generated over time by the momentum of economic, social, and political change. In this connection, our era has witnessed a great paradox: many societies considered politically "conservative"—such as the United States—have in fact undergone revolutionary social change, whereas many societies commonly termed "radical" or revolutionary—such as various "people's democracies"—have been very conservative in terms of true social change. As we have noted, it has always been hard to mount a successful political revolution, and it has become more difficult as greater power can be aggregated in the hands of governing elites.* On the other hand, in the interdependent world

* Here it is also appropriate to define our use of the term "elite." An elite may be defined broadly as a group within a society or unit of that society which is differentiated from others

of our times, social change of sweeping proportions is widespread, encompassing perhaps the majority of societies. In this study, we shall have to deal continually with revolution in both senses of the term, political and social, and we shall try to make our usage clear through explicit phrasing or context.

THE EBB OF LEADERSHIP

Against this background, let us now return to an assessment of events in early-twentieth-century China. The Yihe Tuan rebellion did not extinguish the xenophobia that drove Chinese of many different ranks to oppose foreign intrusion with tactics that were at once self-sacrificing, militant, and futile. At the same time, however, the utter failure of the Boxers convinced all but a handful of diehard officials that without reform, survival was impossible. Thus conservatives now mounted a belated reform effort aimed at saving the dynasty.

Chinese politics remained highly personal, a fact rarely given sufficient emphasis by later scholars. At the apex of power was the empress dowager, whose strength appeared to wax in times of greatest peril and adversity. At one point, all seemed lost. The long march to Shaanxi, the refusal of the victorious foreign powers to accept less than capital punishment for some of her closest advisers, and the plunder of Beijing suggested that the end of her reign was in sight. Then, rivalries among the occupying forces provided a first flicker of hope. Gradually, it became apparent that the Old Buddha herself would not be punished. Her self-confidence returning, she attended the affairs of her court in exile with new vigor and prepared for the journey back to the capital, awaiting the departure of foreign troops and improvements in the roads.

If the reentry of the royal entourage into Beijing on January 6, 1902, was not precisely triumphal, it was accomplished with assurance. Cixi was clearly in command, keeping the emperor in his place, smiling graciously at foreigners, checking the lists to make certain that all of the treasures accompanying her on the train had arrived, and later making outrageously false statements about the past with total aplomb.

Most of the powerful pro-Boxer conservatives were now gone—liquidated or banished. Some had committed suicide in the course of military defeat and the occupation of Beijing. Cixi managed to save two of her favorites, Prince Duan and Duke Lan, by causing them to be permanently exiled to distant Xinjiang, but she was forced to order the decapitation of Yuxian, the former governor of Shandong and Shaanxi, and to "allow" the suicide of Prince Zhuang, Zhao Shuqiao, and Ying Nian—all advisers and friends. Gangyi, who had earlier committed suicide, was ordered posthumously decapitated, a particularly ignominious fate. Others were to fall, some in Beijing, some elsewhere.

In addition to those forcibly removed, an entire generation of elder states-

---

on the basis of the authority it commands, hence the power it can wield. An elite is a collectivity, not an individual; moreover, it is a collectivity having a separate identity, internal structure, and elevated status based on its special role in the decision-making and enforcing process of its particular constituency. Elites are to be found in every organized part of a society, including those groups labeled "revolutionary" or "counterculture." This definition closely follows the one presented in the Introduction to Robert A. Scalapino, ed., *Elites in the People's Republic of China*.

men was shortly to leave the scene. Li Hongzhang, whom the empress dowager had respected but never liked, died in November 1901, even before the government had been reestablished in Beijing. Liu Kunyi, who had helped found the Hunan Army and had worked with Zhang Zhidong to frame the related educational and military reform proposals, passed away in October 1902. And in April 1903 Ronglu expired. He had been the most powerful figure in the court, not merely because he was an old favorite of Cixi's but also because he had been correct in his evaluation of the Boxers when so many had been wrong.

Ronglu was replaced in his role by Prince Qing, a man who in ability and personal character was no match for the old Manchu warrior-statesman. At this point, Yuan Shikai appeared as the most promising light on the horizon. Only forty-three at the time of Ronglu's death, he had China's best-disciplined and best-equipped army behind him, and a record of loyalty to the empress dowager combined with a proclivity toward reform and no taint of pro-Boxer sentiments. Yuan appeared certain to have a prominent future if he could weather the onslaughts of the pro-emperor forces. One other man remained influential. Until his death in October 1909, Zhang Zhidong continued to play significant roles at the regional and national levels, throwing his weight alternately to the reform and to the moderate-conservative sides.

In 1908, however, the two figures at the top of the political structure left the scene, separated in death by a single day. The emperor Guangxu, long sickly and reportedly suffering from Bright's disease, died on November 14, 1908. There were rumors that he had been assisted in his demise by the eunuch Li Lianying and others around the empress dowager, and they certainly would not have wished to see him survive the Old Buddha; but murder may not have been necessary. In any case, Cixi rather unexpectedly died the next day, November 15. Imperial power now passed into the hands of Prince Chun, the brother of Guangxu. A few days earlier, his infant son Puyi had been named heir apparent, with the father to serve as regent until his son's maturity. A succession crisis was avoided, but almost immediately another formidable woman emerged. The new empress dowager, Longyu, Guangxu's widow (and Cixi's niece) made a sustained bid for power. On the eve of its final crisis, the throne was thus weighed down with inexperience, weakness, and factional strife.

With Prince Chun as regent, the fate of Yuan Shikai hung in the balance. It will be recalled that Guangxu had accused Yuan of "treachery" in 1898. On his deathbed, it was said, he requested his brother to punish Yuan—some say to have him executed. In any case, Prince Chun, in a decision that was to prove fateful, merely called upon Yuan to resign his offices, saying that Yuan could use the time to recover from a foot ailment! By this act, the only vigorous, younger man with a national reputation was forced to withdraw from active political life.

Collectively, these changes—and particularly those involving the throne—powerfully abetted instability. A Chinese monarch, though presented with the mandate of heaven upon his ascension, had to acquire personal authority on his own. The true legitimacy of any given monarch was measured by the degree to which his personal influence on politics and lives sustained the institutional sanctions under his control. There could be no doubt that Cixi, an object of veneration and bitter condemnation, epitomized the full-

32. *The young Emperor Puyi and his father, Prince Chun (about 1911)*

est authority of the throne. Peasant stories about the Old Buddha were legion—stories about her supposed benevolence toward the common people, her implacable hatred of "foreign devils," her decisiveness, and her wrath. Her support, as we have noted, was much stronger in the north than in the south, where rebellious sentiments had been rife since the days of the Ming, or at least the Taiping. But to supporters and opponents alike, the throne had become personalized; millions of subjects who would never lay eyes on the monarch had formed a strong mental image of her. No such personalization was possible with an infant on the throne and his little-known Manchu father serving as regent. Now, the institution alone had to sustain loyalty.

Beyond the changes that affected the throne directly were changes that affected an entire generation of seasoned political leaders in the first decade of the twentieth century. The deaths of men of the generation of Li Hongzhang, and even of the generation of Ronglu, were particularly significant because the upheavals of recent decades had made it virtually impossible to replace them from organized echelons of younger talent. Specifically, the old system of recruitment was in disarray. Higher education had been in flux, as had the examination system. Above all, the traditionalists had been steadily losing their morale and self-confidence; they were becoming nonfunctional, because the times demanded men who understood at least some facets of the modern world into which China was being dragged.

Yet the younger Japanized or Westernized intellectuals could not aspire to the upper rungs of officialdom, even when they gained access to the system. Seniority remained the dominant principle governing appointments, together with one's network of personal ties. In sum, the old was fading, but it had prevented a timely birth of the new. A hiatus in leadership thus emerged at a critical juncture in China's evolution, at a time when what the country desperately needed was a cohesive, mature, but experimentally oriented leadership that was capable of understanding and then directing events.

Could a truly iconoclastic figure like Sun Yat-sen, a man so largely outside the cultural patterns of his society, seize this occasion to acquire power and initiate a new era in radical fashion? Or would it be possible for the political "moderates," from the scholar-gentry class, to transcend the personal and ethnic problems that now surrounded the throne and build a constitutional monarchical system, with or without a Manchu at its helm?

THE FINAL REFORM EFFORTS: EDUCATION AND RECRUITMENT

The fate of the last reform efforts under the Qing must be understood partly in terms of the key actors. Even as she and her nephew were departing from Beijing in disguise, a plan for political survival must have been forming in the Old Buddha's mind. Only five days after the trek had begun, on August 20, 1900, a decree was issued in the name of the emperor, confessing to the deep remorse he felt for having contributed to the recent deplorable events and calling for immediate reforms to save the nation. There followed the fascinating imperial decree of February 13, 1901, after the court had settled in Xian. Once again, the empress dowager allowed Guangxu to assume the burden of guilt. The decree was issued in his name, and indeed fully exonerated his "august mother" who had "labored ceaselessly to instruct and train us." This document and others of its type exemplify the type of self-criticism long associated with Chinese monarchs fallen upon hard times and suggest that the Communist practice of cadre self-criticism—like the period of "reflection" associated with such undertakings as the May 7 Schools—has indigenous as well as Soviet roots.

"We can never cease to reproach ourselves; how then can we reproach others?" asserted the February 13 decree. But it did not stop there. In imprecise yet sweeping terms, a full range of reforms was commanded: corruption had to be eliminated, and honest, forward-looking officials appointed;

sound economic principles must be developed, and the tax system basically altered; a further modernization of the military structure was essential, and with it the cultivation of a sense of patriotism among the people; and friendly relations with foreign powers had to be maintained.* The reforms of 1898 were to be rehabilitated—without Kang and his colleagues.

The first serious efforts were directed at education and the examination system. In July and August 1901, while the court was still in exile, a series of imperial decrees was issued aiming at major changes, and these were followed by the far-reaching rescript of September 14, 1901. Taken together, these edicts sought to respond to a number of pressing problems. The most sweeping command, that of September, ordered the creation of a government-sponsored and controlled school system, national in scope. At its base, more primary schools were to be created so that the children of every locality would have access to basic education. Middle schools were set up in each *xian*. The provincial examination boards were to be transformed into colleges, one in each provincial capital. The educational system of Shandong province, operating under the direction of Yuan Shikai and capped by the new Jinan college, was held up in a November 1901 rescript as a model to be studied by others (in later parlance, "Learn from Shandong").

It was also made clear that the government would determine the curriculum throughout the system, and science, social science, and foreign languages were to be added to the study of the Confucian classics at various levels. For these purposes, foreign teachers were to be employed to help prepare texts and courses and to train Chinese teachers.

A second broad commitment made at this time was to the reform of the examination system, an old cause revived. The "eight-legged essay" was abolished for a second time; it was to be replaced by a three-part examination covering the classics, the government and history of China, and foreign politics and science. Each part would count equally in grading a candidate's performance. In the military examinations, moreover, the traditional tests of physical strength were once again set aside in favor of examinations requiring some knowledge of specialized military topics and world affairs.

Finally, a premium was to be put on training and recruiting a new type of scholar-official, one who would be more cosmopolitan and possess the type of "modern" knowledge so urgently required. Thus, provincial authorities were asked to devise special examinations that would secure "men of talent" for governmental service, individuals who presumably did not fit the mold of the traditional examinations. Chinese officials overseas were instructed to recruit and send back to China young Chinese who had acquired their education abroad, with the assurance that they would be given appropriate recognition after taking examinations tailored to their education. It was also

*With reference to the Boxer movement and past developments, the decree of February 13, 1901, stated that "looking back on the past, we are filled with shame and indignation" and "when the ministers and people are guilty, the blame is on the emperor." On the question of reforms, integrity and patriotism were essential. "Taxation should be restructured so that foreign indemnities can be repaid, but the poverty of the people must be kept in mind. In the recruitment of officials, good character should be considered and talented individuals encouraged." The decree continued by saying that the duty of a minister was "the abolishment of corruption and the elimination of past abuse," and that economic and military reforms were essential. See "Imperial Decree," Guangxu 26 year, 12 month, 26 day (13 February 1901), in *Yihe Tuan dangan shiliao* 2:944–947.

33. *Yuan Shikai during his tenure as governor-general of Zhili*

decreed that promising students should be sent abroad for their education, both in the military field and in all branches of civilian endeavor, with the understanding that they, too, would find employment and rank equal to their achievements.

By September 1902 the examinations at Peking University had been reshaped to produce a new type of graduate. In its first sections, short essays in English and Chinese were required. Its concluding portions contained questions on geography, history, mathematics, science, and international law.* For those aspiring to reach the top of the educational ladder in China, a classical education would no longer suffice.

Some of these reforms bearing the imperial imprimatur had been recommended by two of China's most prominent governors-general, Zhang Zhidong and Liu Kunyi. In a memorial to the throne in 1901, these two veteran administrators urged changes along three lines: the creation of institutions for advanced education within China, both in military and "literary" fields; the sending of many more promising students abroad for advanced education; and basic changes in the civil service and military examinations.

The next major step taken in educational reform came in 1904, when a revised national educational program was adopted, based on the detailed study and set of recommendations of a group headed by Zhang Zhidong and Zhang Boxi, the new chancellor of Peking University.[2] Based largely on the Japanese model, the new system called for the establishment of lower primary schools (kindergartens) in every community of one hundred families or more; higher primary schools, with a five-year program, in each *xian*, with a maximum of four hundred families per school, and the possibility of having a unified lower-higher primary educational program. There were to be middle schools in every prefecture, with four-year courses to include a foreign language, either Japanese or English, leading to a *xiucai* degree for graduates. Colleges in each provincial capital city were to offer three-year courses in one of three fields—arts, sciences, or medicine—leading to a *linsheng* degree. The Imperial University in Beijing was to provide a three-year course leading to the *zhuren* degree and a four- to five-year postgraduate course culminating in a *jinshi* degree. The University was to be divided into eight schools or faculties: classics, arts, jurisprudence, medicine, science, agronomy, civil engineering, and commerce. Provision was also made for specialized industrial, agricultural, legal, and foreign-language schools, and the creation of teacher-training schools (normal schools) throughout the nation.

With modest alterations, this system continued to represent the government's educational objectives until the end of the Qing era. The 1904 regulations provided for the progressive abandonment of the old examination system over a period of three years. In August 1905 the empress dowager

*These examinations were to be given both to the candidates for entrance and to the first-year class, with the full examination divided into nine subjects, and the student required to score at least 60 out of a possible 100 points on each of the nine subjects before he could graduate. The division was as follows: (1) a short essay on a topic to be handed out, in English; (2) a similar essay in Chinese; (3) geography—China and foreign countries; (4) history—Chinese and that of other countries; (5) sample translations from Chinese into English and vice versa; (6) algebra; (7) geometry; (8) topics in elementary international law; (9) physics and chemistry. (*North China Herald*, May 28, 1902, p. 10.)

endorsed a memorial calling for the immediate abolition of the old system, which was accomplished in 1906. In late 1905, moreover, a board of education was created in Beijing to supervise the national educational system, and to the same end commissioners of education were appointed in each province. By 1907 the minister of education had been ordered to draw up a program providing for universal primary education.*

Ironically, the government itself was now moving at an accelerated pace to create a new Chinese man—and in much lesser numbers a new woman. At the lower level, the goal was to broaden literacy and provide at least rudimentary acquaintance with those subjects like mathematics, science, and politics around which the modern world revolved. At the upper levels, the goals were equally audacious: to equip China's new political, military, and technological elites with the same type of training being given to their Japanese counterparts.

The initial results were not unimpressive. By 1911, approximately a decade after the new program had been launched, 42,444 public schools reportedly existed in the provinces, with a total of 1,284,965 enrolled students.[3] After 1902, moreover, the number of students studying abroad climbed sharply. In that year there were reportedly 274 Chinese students in Japan, 163 of whom were on governmental scholarships; smaller numbers were in various Western countries. By 1907 there were between 10,000 and 13,000 Chinese students in Japan, and from 500 to 600 in western Europe and the United States.[4] In Zhili, a center of China's major commitment to quality education at home, some 1,161 students attended various institutions of higher learning.**

If we assume that the total population of China at this time was roughly four hundred million, these figures are minuscule. Yet it could be argued that the trend was encouraging. One of the difficulties lay in the financing of the new system. Given its precarious political position and the heavy taxes already being imposed to meet reparation payments, Beijing authorities were unwilling to try to raise additional funds nationally, so responsibility for

*In 1908 the Board of Education in Beijing issued ten regulations intended to serve as a further spur to progress: (1) In every *xian*, an educational bureau should be established to encourage the gentry to open colleges and to stimulate students to attend these. (2) Every provincial capital must have at least a hundred primary schools and a minimum of 5,000 students. (3) All *fu* (prefectures) and *xian* (districts) must have at least forty schools and a minimum of 2,000 students. (4) Every village must have one primary school and a minimum of 40 students. Hamlets shall be combined to make up the classification of village. (5) Every child at the age of seven shall be compelled to attend school. (7) The parents of any child who is seven or over shall be responsible for his attending school, and shall be punished if he is not doing so. (8) Officials in charge of the *xian* educational bureaus shall be rewarded if these are successful, and reduced in rank if they fail. (9) All prefects and magistrates who fail to obtain the stipulated number of schools and students in their respective jurisdictions shall be punished. (10) The commissioner of education in each of the provinces shall make a thorough investigation on these matters and also inquire into the proficiency of the teachers, reporting on these matters. Two years shall be allowed for the completion of the task outlined above. (For details, see *North China Herald*, June 20, 1908, p. 753.) These regulations, which reveal much about traditional modes of Chinese administration, indicate how dependent the system remained upon local initiatives, both official and gentry. The difficulty in enforcing these new goals can also be imagined.

**According to a 1907 survey of enrollments at institutions of higher learning in Zhili, the number of students in seven different types of schools was as follows: law and politics (2 institutions), 346; medical, 36; technical, 211; agricultural, 117; junior college, 257; university, 194. See *Dongfang zazhi* (Eastern Miscellany), December 1907, p. 265.

funding was placed on provincial and local officials. Inevitably, financial support for the new schools varied enormously. Certain regions could not or would not raise any funds, although it was usually possible to avoid constructing new buildings by using old temples and similar structures. Many localities charged tuition, even for elementary schooling, thereby continuing the practices of the past and creating problems for the poorer segments of society.*

The other chief difficulty lay in the recruiting of qualified instructors. In late nineteenth-century China there were two distinct kinds of education. The majority of students studied with a private tutor or attended a school operated under the patronage and control of the local gentry. A much smaller but growing number of young Chinese attended missionary schools, which provided an introduction to Western learning together with instruction in Christianity. When the Qing government finally adopted the goals of modernization and universal education, the value of the classical tutor was greatly reduced, and the need for teachers familiar with Japanese or Western educational methods greatly enhanced the importance of the missionary. It is not surprising, therefore, that missionaries played a substantial role in launching the new system. Dr. W. A. P. Martin, a longtime missionary-educator in China, was a pioneer in Chinese higher education. Timothy Richard took the lead in establishing Shanxi University. In Shandong, Yuan Shikai used missionary counsel in creating his provincial educational program. Meanwhile, prominent mission schools, such as St. John's University in Shanghai, continued to train a steady stream of Chinese youth, many of them destined to play important roles in their society.

As early as 1901, however, Chinese educational leaders like Zhang Boxi argued that if an educational system appropriate to the times were to be constructed, China needed professional foreign educators rather than missionaries and retired customs officials. Whether to allow the teaching of religion in government institutions also became a troublesome controversy. A compromise was reached whereby Christianity would not be taught and worship before Confucian tablets would no longer be compulsory, but neither side was fully satisfied with this agreement. At an early point, therefore, authorities began to replace missionaries with their own personnel, particularly at the college and university level, at the same time decreeing that Chinese education should be strictly secular. The problem of acquiring trained teachers, however, especially at the primary and middle-school levels, remained acute. It was even harder to find indigenous personnel to staff the specialized vocational and technical schools that had been planned. Hence the plan for specialized schools remained largely a vision, and the transition from the older educational system proceeded far more slowly than the planners had decreed.

The government's greatest concern, however, related to politics. One of the reasons official Chinese observers were so impressed with the Japanese

*Evelyn Sakakida Rawski, in her discerning study of Qing education, has pointed out, however, that even families of very modest means were sometimes able to scrape together funds sufficient to meet elementary tuition fees for their children, especially sons. Such fees differed considerably, depending on the particular school and teacher. The government also funded certain schools for the poor. See Rawski, *Education and Popular Literacy in Ch'ing China*, pp. 81–124.

system was that it seemed to produce patriots, persons trained and motivated to serve their country in peace and in war, and supremely loyal to the system under which they lived. This impression, though not incorrect in essence, was too simple a reading of the Japanese scene. Although the graduates of Japan's primary and middle schools generally fit the patriotic pattern, the Japanese universities were creating a small but vocal radical intelligentsia—precisely the element often accused of "contaminating" many Chinese students living in Japan. The conservative nature of Japanese society combined with its high rate of economic development, however, served to isolate and contain this radicalism, so that in most cases it was a mere phase of student life, to be outgrown when the graduate obtained employment in government or industry.

In contrast, the process of radicalization engendered by providing a select number of Chinese youth with a modern higher education led much more frequently to political activism aimed squarely at the political system—indeed, at the entire social order. The Chinese government was not able to manipulate nationalist symbols or offer a range of attractive career opportunities. The modernizing student thus frequently became déclassé, estranged from government and society and prepared to express his discontent in a radical and often violent manner. In spite of itself, the government was now participating in the dismantling of the old order, including the value system upon which it rested, without being able to substitute a new ideology or system. Under such conditions, higher education bred, not patriots in the Japanese sense, but patriot-subversives similar to those being created in contemporary Russian universities, and for similar reasons. In sum, education was serving to fragment rather than unify the Chinese elite.

THE REINTRODUCTION OF MILITARY REFORMS

Military modernization was a second goal, a renewed expression of the long and painful effort to rid China of a military system that was hopelessly antiquated, corrupt, and ineffective, and to create a new military force on the Japanese-Western model. The ignominious defeat of imperial forces along with the Boxers in 1900 provided further evidence of the urgent need, if such were required. The primary thrust was in three directions: abolition of the old examination system and, with it, the senseless premium placed on brute strength; thorough modernization, with recruitment, training, equipment, and organization to be brought closer to the standards of the "advanced" world; and the creation of a truly national military force, with the political center taking over the tasks of coordination and ultimate authority.

The easiest advance was to end the old examination system, with its combination of largely irrelevant "literary" questions and tests of physical prowess. Once again, the July 1901 memorial of Zhang Zhidong and Liu Kunyi paved the way; in August of that year the traditional military examinations were eliminated.[5] New directives commanded all governors-general and governors to establish military academies. The schools created earlier by Zhang Zhidong, Liu Kunyi, and Yuan Shikai were to serve as models, and these three men were to supervise the drafting of new regulations to govern military education.

At the same time, a new organizational structure for the military was sketched out. A standing army was to be established, accompanied by reserve units that could be mobilized in the event of war; there would be a separate national police force. Personnel for the new units were to be selected from the Army of the Green Standard, provincial militia, and other existing forces, and those judged unfit were to be discharged. In this fashion, the antiquated older armies would be dissolved. Those selected for the new army and police force would be given specialized training, modern equipment and uniforms, and better pay.

These were ambitious proposals, which if realized on a national scale would have had far-reaching repercussions. Given the financial stringencies, the subsequent policies of the central government, and the indifference of many provincial governors, however, the military modernization program was at first focused primarily upon a few regions and was realized chiefly in the armies crafted by Zhang Zhidong and Yuan Shikai. In Yuan's new military force, later known as the Beiyang Army, lay the seeds of a new era for Chinese politics, one bringing politics and military power into a symbiotic relationship. But that story lies ahead.

In February 1902, aided by the empress dowager's allocation of one million taels, Yuan, currently governor-general of Zhili, began to recruit and train a force initially called the Newly Created Army (*xinjian lujun*). The funds did not permit him to proceed as rapidly as he had originally planned, but over the next four years major progress was made. As the first steps, a provincial Department of Military Administration was set up to regulate all military matters, an Officers Academy was created to train or retrain officers of the new army, 55 students were sent to Japan for advanced military education, and 14 Japanese instructors were hired to teach at the newly established Baoding Officers Academy. By 1911 about 800 officers in the Chinese army had graduated from or studied in Japanese schools, some 630 of whom had been trained in the prestigious Japanese Army Officers School.[6]

During the years 1903–1905, Yuan's Beiyang Army grew rapidly, eventually comprising six divisions with some 60,000 men, trained in accordance with the Japanese-German model, with strenuous efforts made to instill professionalism and discipline in both enlisted men and officers. Underwriting the program was a network of technical and professional military training centers.

Initially, the central government had contemplated training on a broader scale: Yuan's Zhili facilities would serve the North, and trainees from the south-central provinces would go to Hunan to learn from Zhang's German-Japanese trained units.* But in the fall of 1902 Zhang was transferred to Nanjing as acting governor-general after the death of Liu Kunyi, and he took four of his best units with him. In 1904 about 4,000 of Zhang's troops in Hubei were sent to Zhili to join Yuan's units.

Meanwhile, progress in most provinces remained slow. By the end of 1903, however, military schools existed in a number of provinces, with Japanese as well as Chinese instructors in many cases, together with a few Ger-

*Zhang, who lacked the financial resources available to Yuan, had a much smaller number of modernized troops, but some observers regarded Zhang's best troops as superior in technical training to the Beiyang Army, and they were also impressed with the facilities provided. Zhang used German instructors as the core of his foreign instruction program despite the cost, although he supplemented them with Japanese teachers and advisers. See Powell, *The Rise of Chinese Military Power*, pp. 225ff.

man teachers.* An effort was also made to extend the idea of military training into the emerging public school system. Copying the Japanese, in January 1904 the government ordered that school uniforms would be worn by children attending public institutions, and military drill would be conducted. An ever larger number of military cadets were being sent to Japan. Up to 1904, however, China's military forces remained decentralized, and in most provinces the modern element was far outweighed by the antiquated vestiges of the past. There was also a complete absence of standardization.

The only promising modern force other than Zhang Zhidong's small units, which numbered about 11,500 men by 1905, was Yuan's Beiyang Army in the North. The latter army was becoming the nucleus of a national force, largely because of policy decisions at the center. The funds being collected from provincial sources for military modernization were being allocated primarily to Yuan's army, eliciting protests from various provincial governors.[7] In December 1903, in the midst of the crisis provoked by the Russian threat in Manchuria and the impending Russo-Japanese War, the central government set up a Commission for Army Reorganization (*lianbingchu*), making Prince Qing the director, Yuan the associate director, and Tieliang, a competent Manchu military man, the assistant director. This office, actually run by Yuan, was intended to preside over the centralization of the Chinese military structure. In fact, it served to enable Yuan to channel funds to his Zhili divisions. The Beiyang Army was dependent upon the empress dowager and the center for its support, and so long as Yuan remained on top in Beijing as well as in Zhili, he could protect his interests.

In the winter of 1906–1907 factional struggles again broke out in the capital, with both personal and policy issues involved. Yuan was pitted against such influential figures as Qu Hongji and Tieliang, his former ally. A new Ministry of War with Tieliang in charge replaced the Commission for Army Reorganization, and Yuan's star appeared to fade. By the spring of 1907, however, Yuan had regained favor, and in September he was promoted to the presidency of the Ministry of Foreign Affairs and given the additional office of grand councilor in Beijing. From this position of strength he was able to protect both his military and his political interests.

Meanwhile, proposals for military reform on a national scale had continued to emanate from Beijing, and most of them reflected Yuan's ideas. The recommendations of the Commission for Army Reorganization, accepted by the throne in September 1904, provided a comprehensive plan for a national army, which was compatible with the 1901 proposals but went far beyond them. In essence, the plan called for the creation of a standing army (*lujun*) of thirty-six divisions to be set up over a period of seventeen years; for a series of military schools, capped by a general staff college, in imitation of the Japanese system of military training; and for standard equipment and training procedures to be used throughout the new army.[8]

Once again the gap between proclamation and practice proved substan-

*In an account entitled "Military Academies in China," the *North China Herald* in its January 27, 1905, issue (pp. 209–210), provided the following data on existing military academies and schools in China: Zhili had three, Hubei had two, and all but three of the remaining sixteen provinces had one, with a total enrollment of 3,344 cadets. The three provinces that lacked a military school were Guangxi (where governmental control was constantly being challenged), Gansu ("too poor"), and Henan ("where the governors have been too reactionary in the past").

tial. On the positive side, most of the provinces did make gradual if uneven progress in eliminating superannuated personnel and introducing modern training methods. By 1906, moreover, the national policies emanating from Beijing had been fleshed out. A detailed table of organization for a thirty-six-division standing army, supplemented by two classes of reserves, had been completed. Similarly, specific plans for the standardization of military-school training and government-operated arsenal production had been advanced. Provisions for provincial police were also specified.* On the negative side, the central authorities and the empress dowager knew that provincial and regional officials would strongly resist attempts to push military centralization too fast; even Zhang Zhidong and Yuan Shikai were opposed to the eradication of certain provincial controls. Given the weakened political condition of the center, and the government's perennial financial crisis, it was imperative that provincial forces not be alienated further. And so concessions to local authorities were made, contrary to current trends in Japan, from whence the model had been drawn. These concessions rendered the government unable to enforce rigorously certain provisions of the plan that it considered essential to solid progress.

Thus a number of the old ills associated with localism and the broader traditions of the society lingered on. The "squeeze," whereby everyone in the hierarchy took his cut, continued to leave those at the bottom often bereft of decent food, adequate barracks, or prompt pay. The reluctance of local authorities to dismantle the old units did not abate, despite heavy pressure from Beijing. All of the classic Qing-era units, including the Army of the Green Standard, clung to life in various provinces. And local forces remained semiprivate armies. The soldiers, locally recruited from the vast peasant pool of manpower, were tied in a very personal manner to the commanding officers, from whom they derived their livelihood and their sense of loyalty, if any. They were ill-equipped by environment or education to become "new Chinese military men."** Even among the officers who had

*A contemporary observer provides details in an article entitled "Organizing a Provincial Gendarmerie," *North China Herald*, September 7, 1906, p. 570. The plan, worked out by the Ministries of War and Public Safety, was to screen Green Standard troops, taking the intelligent, able-bodied men between the ages of twenty and forty-five for training as members of a new provincial police force under the jurisdiction of the Ministry of Public Safety. It was noted that on paper the Army of the Green Standard still numbered two million, but that if even the 250,000 possibly existing in the flesh were suddenly demobilized and thrown onto the charity of their families, the able-bodied elements would quickly turn to banditry.

**One foreign military attaché of this period estimated that about 100,000 soldiers were capable of modern wartime service, and that 60,000 of these came from the Beiyang Army, with the remainder coming from standing army units elsewhere (Powell, *The Rise of Chinese Military Power*, p. 140). An interesting article entitled "The Chinese Army" in the September 14, 1906, issue of *North China Herald* made a similar point. It asserted that despite labels, there was as yet no new Chinese army. Rather, there were two viceregal (governor-general) armies, "the pet schemes of two progressive viceroys." In addition, there were other contingents of various regional heads, "more or less useless," but no truly unified national army existed. Even concerning Yuan's forces, the writer exhibited reserve. The recent maneuvers of Yuan's forces, he wrote, had elicited foreign encomiums, but that was primarily because of the kind treatment given foreigners by Yuan. The raw material was there, and attitudes toward the military were changing among the literati; some were even joining the armed forces and were willing to become officers in a professional army. But "the fighting instinct" was still generally lacking, and "absolute integrity" in the handling of funds and supplies remained to be achieved, even in Yuan's army. The "squeeze" was taking new forms, and desertions were still "rampant," with the punishment for those caught "vindictive" (p. 667).

received modern training and possessed more than a rudimentary education, personal and provincial ties frequently outweighed the national consciousness and sense of patriotism that the government (and its revolutionary opponents) sought to cultivate.[9]

Events after 1908 sharpened the contradictions implicit in this scene. First, the center's legitimacy, hence its authority, continued to grow weaker. Not only were China's only national symbols, Cixi and Guangxu, gone from the scene, but the three men who had epitomized the quest for a new order after the Boxer debacle had all departed from the political stage by 1909—Liu Kunyi and Zhang Zhidong through death, Yuan Shikai through forced retirement. After 1909 there remained not a single individual at the center who commanded widespread respect and allegiance. Yet, in the face of that fact, the center not only pushed centralization at a more rapid pace but also moved to replace Han with Manchu in key military posts, thereby feeding the nationalist flames.

By 1910 a beleaguered government in Beijing was locked in a deepening struggle with provincial governments and their assemblies over a wide range of issues, many of them involving the issue of centralization. A conflict over the financing and control of railroads had been intermittently unfolding since 1905, and by 1909 the issues had been broadened to encompass the entire system of revenue and finance. Certainly, reform in this field, including the creation of a uniform, centrally controlled system of revenue collection and disbursement was crucial to all other reforms. But it was not a battle to be undertaken lightly, and certainly not one that a weak central government was destined to win.

Compromises continued to be half-offered, half-forced, in such fields as finance and constitutionalism, but the center made few concessions in the realm of military affairs. A demand from the national assembly for the disbandment of the Eight Banners, the traditional sinecure for Manchu supernumeraries, was rejected, although top command posts had earlier been opened to Han as well as Manchu. Efforts of the center to get rid of the Green Standard troops and other provincial forces led to renewed trouble with local officials, who argued that the *lujun* (standing army) was not sufficiently developed to warrant such a course of action. Meanwhile, Manchu generals took over most of the key regional command posts, and it was made certain that a Manchu held the post of minister of war.

After Yinchang replaced Tieliang as minister of war in March 1910, another comprehensive program of military reform was announced, and it placed an even greater premium on centralization than had previous proposals. Unfit or poorly trained officers were to be removed, following a nationally supervised inspection. A rigorous training program would be instituted, with a shift toward German guidance which reflected Yinchang's long and close relations with Germany. Suddenly, Manchu generals appeared resplendent in German-style uniforms, and drill reflected the Prussian practice. Progressively, the financial and political control exercised by provincial officials over the military, and particularly the *lujun*, was reduced. Provincial forces were ordered to reorganize as Patrol and Defense Troops, with the responsibility for maintaining local order.

This program did little to endear Yinchang and the central government to military leaders, new or old. The new minister of war brought the Beiyang Army directly under his control and pushed for the rapid expansion of the *lujun* throughout the nation. By 1910, however, the Beiyang units were among the few *lujun* divisions on whom the central government could count. Beginning in late 1908, a series of revolts or mutinies within the armed forces had erupted in Central and South China. In some places, revolutionaries had infiltrated the unit concerned; prominent among them were young officers trained in Japan. In other settings, the problems were largely traditional—inhumane treatment, poor living conditions and late pay, and favoritism based on personal or provincial ties.

Though none of the Beiyang divisions were involved, these revolts took place exclusively within the *lujun*, signaling the fact that military modernization carried with it the seeds of a major threat to the old order in Beijing. Ironically, the newly organized local Patrol and Defense Troops were usually the main force used to put down the mutinies, since they remained loyal to the government. By the beginning of 1911, therefore, the situation throughout southern China was fraught with uncertainty.

At this point, Chinese official records indicated that over one million men were in the various armed forces. The actual number appears to have been smaller.* *Lujun* forces probably totaled under 200,000; Western estimates made at the time ranged from 152,000 to 190,000. The Patrol and Defense Troops had grown rapidly and may have numbered 157,000 to 216,000. There were an additional 225,000 soldiers in the Banner armies, and the Army of the Green Standard still contained about 50,000 remnant troops. How many of these soldiers could be considered "modern," capable of holding their own with a foreign foe under contemporary battle conditions? A French observer reported that only 120,000 were truly competent, the bulk of them in the Beiyang Army. An American military attaché asserted that only one-half that number could meet currently accepted Western standards.[10]

Thus the military reforms, like their counterparts in the educational field, resulted at best in halting, uneven progress.[11] This is not surprising, given the brevity of the reform period, the dimensions of the problems, and the unique relation of the Chinese center to its parts. However, significant changes of attitude toward the military were under way. A widening circle of people within China's political, economic, and educational elites now accepted the vital importance of developing a modern and respected national

* Powell, *The Rise of Chinese Military Power*, pp. 288–289. At a slightly earlier point, in mid-1909, an interesting account of the status of the new Chinese army was given by a Japanese adviser to Zhang Zhidong, Colonel Igata, who had just returned to Tokyo and was interviewed by the *Japan Times*. Igata reported that slow progress was being made in the effort to create an army of thirty-six divisions, two in each province. Only six currently existed, the four stationed in Zhili and Shandong organized by Yuan, and the two in Nanking and Wuchang completed by Duanfang and Zhang Zhidong. In addition, there were twelve mixed brigades in various provinces. Although the Japanese system was being used in the training of these forces, the problems were numerous. In the absence of a conscription system, all Chinese troops were "hired soldiers like Indian sepoys," and their martial spirit was not high. Indeed, everything military in China was "in a state of infancy." Yet an effective conscription system would require the perfection of census and police systems (à la Japan), and this was impossible in the near future. Igata reported that the awakening of national consciousness in China was a good sign, but the "misguided notion" that the introduction of foreign capital into the country would doom it to ruin was regrettable, since this was the most promising route for the development of China's rich resources. He also noted that the Chinese navy consisted of three fleets stationed in Beiyang, made up of some twenty warships with the largest having a displacement of only 4,000 tons. The ships were good, but the Chinese did not know how to handle them effectively; hence, the old adage "treasures left to rust" was applicable. See "Colonel Igata on China," *North China Herald*, July 3, 1909, p. 35.

military force. A vision of a new military man was emerging: he should be literate, disciplined, physically and mentally fit, motivated by patriotic sentiments, and capable of handling sophisticated equipment. Reformers and revolutionaries alike shared this vision and hope.

Yet this shift in attitudes was accompanied by an equally important and potentially destructive political trend. An element long absent from Chinese politics was reappearing in new form: power was again being defined increasingly in military terms. As the old Confucian edifice crumbled, a general who commanded a partly modernized army was in the best strategic position to bid for political authority. His problem was likely to be that of extending his authority beyond the provincial or regional level. The practice of recruiting soldiers from common locales in order to minimize problems of dialect, food, and general customs made the vision of a truly national army immensely difficult to achieve. The acquisition of funds sufficient to unite provincial units into a national force posed an equally formidable obstacle. And there was the challenge of inducing from the soldier a commitment that would go beyond a desire for loot, beyond the instinct of self-preservation, or even beyond loyalty to comrades and commanders. Ideally, what was needed was a willingness to fight for a national cause, possibly even an ideology. Because these obstacles could not be removed, the phenomenon commonly known as warlordism was an eminently logical development—especially after Yuan Shikai, the one man capable of wielding military and political authority at more than a regional level, passed from the scene.

CONSTITUTIONALISM

The drive for constitutionalism represented the capstone to the reform efforts. It was an effort, however, dictated not so much by broad socioeconomic developments in Chinese society as by the increasing pressures exerted by small but influential elites upon a government *in extremis*. For this reason the promises of governmental leaders could not be translated into performance, and the process itself—far from representing the authority of the throne, as Cixi had hoped—reflected the central government's slackening grip on political life. In the end, the court had to accept every proposal thrust upon it by the National Assembly, however ill-prepared and premature. A move that had been designed to save the monarchy became one of the instruments of its destruction.

The first strong impetus for constitutionalism had come from students returning after studies abroad, particularly in Japan. As early as 1905, their exertions had led one overseas official to urge the court to grant a constitution quickly in order to forestall a rising wave of agitation that was otherwise certain to follow.[12] Undoubtedly, the empress dowager was psychologically prepared to accept such reports, since the broad commitment to reform had to encompass the granting of a constitution, the acknowledged hallmark of political modernization. Thus, in mid-1905 the throne requested Yuan Shikai, Zhang Zhidong, and Zhou Fu to investigate the feasibility of such a move. These eminent officials reported that although the people were not ready for constitutional government, each province should have a deliberative assembly composed of gentry and "other men of ability," elected by the various towns and districts, which would concern itself with such issues as public works and education. Such a body could serve as an adviser to the governor and provincial treasurer. Unless deliberative assemblies were created soon, they warned, "confusion and anarchy" might result.[13]

Implicit in this report was a dual strategy that would later be pursued by reformers and revolutionaries alike. The first commitment was to a building-block strategy: political change should begin at the local and provincial levels so that the experience gained there could provide a model to be applied in due course to the nation. As we have noted, this strategy was adopted by Sun Yat-sen early in his career, and it was later forced by events upon the Communists, who accepted it despite internal qualms. Given the vastness and heterogeneity of Chinese society, the loosely federated nature of the polity, and the relative weakness of the political center, no other strategy was feasible, a fact that all power-holders and aspirants to power in China sooner or later came to realize.

Yet the further commitment was to a strategy of progressive centralization. Nation-building in a modern world required more centralized authority than was characteristic of the traditional Chinese state. The power of the center had to be enhanced if China were to survive. It was the fate of the Qing dynasty to come to this realization and to seek to act upon it too late—at a time when it was least capable of commanding the authority necessary for success. Indeed, no single factor contributed more to the end of the dynasty. But those who followed, both Nationalists and Communists, would pursue the same objective—against the heavy odds that continued to prevail.

To the memorial of Yuan, Zhang, and Zhou, the court responded on July 16, 1905, with an edict ordering a four-man commission led by Duke Daize and Duanfang, two influential Manchus, to go abroad to examine current constitutional practices in Japan, Europe, and the United States so as to determine the best form of government for China. The empress dowager and her close advisers were now fully determined to tread the path pioneered by the Japanese court nearly two decades earlier. The commission's scheduled departure on September 24 was delayed by an act of violence symbolic of the times. At the train station where departure ceremonies were taking place, a young extremist aimed a bomb at the dignitaries, killing himself and several attendants. Although none of the leaders was seriously hurt, the trip was postponed for several months.[14]

The throne proceeded to make clear its intentions. On November 25 another imperial decree was issued, proclaiming the great benevolence of the current dynasty in its treatment of the people, and speaking in tones of concern about those "worthless persons" who were intent upon replacing the monarchy with republicanism. After reiterating the throne's commitment to political reform, the edict called for the creation of a new department to study political institutions and policies abroad, looking toward the adoption of those that suited China's needs.[15]

In mid-1906, having returned from the overseas survey, the commissioners wrote memorials to the throne which in effect urged that the Japanese constitution be used as the primary model.[16] Immediately, a royal commission headed by Prince Chun, the brother of the emperor, was appointed to consider the memorials and make recommendations. On September 1, 1906, the throne issued its most comprehensive edict on the subject of constitutionalism, a document that was enormously revealing of the hopes of the court and the tenor of the times.

The edict commenced with a frank admission of the perils in which the dynasty found itself: "At present, all nations are in free communication with each other, and in their methods of government and their laws are influenced one by another. Our political institutions, however, remain as of old, a condition of affairs which threatens danger and disaster, day by day becoming more imminent."[17]

Following earlier Japanese rationalizations closely, the court advanced one main reason for promoting constitutionalism: only through this route could the government and the people be welded into an indestructible unity and the capital and the provinces be brought closer together. These advances in turn were essential to the wealth and strength of the empire. As others would do decades later with the slogan "to the masses," the throne played upon the theme that Chinese monarchs had always listened to the people, had always called for public involvement in every issue and public participation in every decision.*

In practice, of course, "the people" would be defined to exclude "undesirable elements" and those not yet prepared for civic responsibilities. Indeed, the edict said that a period of preparation would be necessary, a time of tutelage during which the people could acquire the knowledge needed to make constitutionalism work. Thus, basic reforms had to extend to education, financial policies, the military system, police organization, and other matters that might aid "the gentry and the people to thoroughly understand political affairs."[18] And these reforms should properly start with a reorganization of the governmental structure—local, regional, and national—so as to make it more responsive to current needs.

Finally, lest there be any doubt, supreme authority was to be specifically vested in the throne. Implicit in this and similar documents was the idea that the constitution would be a gift of the benevolent monarch, an expression of his concern for the welfare of the public and state; it was not to be considered a social contract of any sort, or a response to public demands. The fact that all questions of government were to be considered by a popular assembly, moreover, did not mean that such an assembly could usurp the imperial prerogative and become a lawmaking body unto itself.

This fascinating document both draws on the past and suggests the future. The ancient concepts of monarchical benevolence and a desire to harken to the voices of the people, coupled with a firm assertion of the throne's sovereignty, were all present, if in slightly modernized form. And these would be available for later leaders, when the Nationalist or Communist Party had taken the place of the emperor. An admission of the problem, likewise, foretold the central quests that lay ahead. How, except under constitutionalism, could the people be mobilized for state loyalty and service?

*The following passage summarizes beautifully the court's perception of the central problems afflicting the state and the hopes held for constitutionalism, dreams drawn from the Japanese experience: "All are agreed that the lack of prosperity in the state is due to the separation between the officials and the people and the lack of cooperation between the capital and the provinces. The officials are ignorant of the needs of the people, and the people do not understand what is necessary to the safety of the state. The wealth and strength of other countries are due to their practice of constitutional government, in which public questions are determined by consultation with the people. The ruler and his people are as one body animated by one spirit, as a result of which comprehensive consideration is given to the general welfare, and the limits of authority are clearly defined. Even in securing and appropriating funds for public use, as well as in all political measures, there is nothing which is not made the public concern of the people" (edict of September 1, 1906, translated in *Papers Relating to the Foreign Relations of the United States*, 1906).

And how could the deplorable weakness of the central government be remedied?

Explicitly or implicitly, the imperial decree of September 1, 1906, dealt with the issues that were to concern every future political leadership: basic socioeconomic and political change, nation-building, rapid economic development, and the acquisition of military strength. The theme "toward a wealthy and strong nation," borrowed from the Meiji leaders, mirrored the supreme goal of twentieth-century China. Even the means of achieving this goal were suggested, however sketchily. For the masses to be progressively educated and mobilized for state purposes, some type of tutelage at the hands of a knowledgeable elite was necessary. In a nation as vast as China, moreover, it was essential to undertake experimentation at a local level. Thus a single district, city, or province could be used as the beginning, and its success could be offered to others as a model. Meanwhile, the process of centralization had to be encouraged so that China would become truly a nation rather than a mere congerie of federal semiautonomous provinces.

It would be a grave error to assume that each of these concepts was first enunciated in the September 1 edict, or that this document represented the perfection of a teleological process. The 1906 edict was but one step, albeit a significant one, in the dawning recognition among China's political elite—irrespective of their specific socioeconomic status, ideology, or policies—of what was required for survival and "progress." Many of the themes contained within it had been raised earlier, whether by "radicals," reformers, or the court itself. Many were to be more fully explicated in subsequent decrees, or in the writings and actions of the throne's adversaries. But the September 1 edict remains a landmark of its type, and one that despite its brevity sums up a transitional period.

Pursuant to the edict, some organizational changes at the center were ordered immediately. On September 2 a decree commanded the establishment of a small group of senior officials to consult on structural changes. It also ordered the consolidation of a number of overlapping minor departments and their corresponding boards, thereby signaling a shift toward functional specialization under a single responsible head. In addition, two national councils were established, one to consider the budget, the other to receive expressions of public opinion and deliberate on them.[19] In this fashion, sound financial policies and public involvement were acknowledged to be of transcendent importance.

The next major step came in early 1907, following a memorial prepared under the direction of Prince Qing and Grand Counselor Sun Jianai. This memorial emphasized that political reforms aimed at creating local self-government should begin at the grass-roots level. Various changes were proposed. Judicial functions should be removed from district magistrates and other local officials and placed in the hand of a separate court system. A specialization of function was also needed in such areas as finance and education. To cope with domestic troubles and such humiliations as extraterritoriality, greater professionalism was needed. Because simultaneous reform in all provinces was impossible, the government should undertake a pilot project in the three Manchurian provinces, "the homeland of the dynasty," so that the favorable results there could be emulated elsewhere.*

*The opening section of the memorial contained this interesting theme: "The vast extent of territory embraced in the twenty-two provinces of the Chinese empire and the troublesome character of the people make it impossible to compare it with the various foreign countries,

The throne accepted all of these recommendations, and in imperial edicts of April 20 and July 7 provided guidelines for the reorganization of government in Manchuria and some general revisions of the structure of provincial administration aimed at clarifying responsibilities.[20] In mid-1907, moreover, the first municipal council was elected in Tianjin, and this city—under the jurisdiction of Yuan Shikai—was declared to be a model for other municipalities. Voters were required to be twenty-five years of age, property owners, and able to write their name, age, occupation, and place of residence. Habitual opium smokers, yamen runners, Buddhist or Taoist priests, and "all leaders of a religious order" were barred from voting; also barred were those convicted of a crime, those who followed an occupation not deemed respectable, bankrupts, and the mentally defective. To be eligible for the city council, an individual had to be a male, a graduate of a district school or other higher school, or the author of an officially approved treatise, or the owner of property worth $2,000, or the trustee of funds amounting to $5,000, or a school director, or one who had managed public affairs, had held official position, or was a *xiucai* degree holder. Council members were to serve without pay for a term of two years.[21]

On September 20, 1907, an imperial edict called for the creation of a "constitutional assembly" as a preliminary step toward forming a parliament and constitutional government. At this time the court was also actively seeking to remove old Manchu privileges and equalize Han and Manchu in various respects.[22] Ten days later, another imperial edict called on the Board of Home Affairs to draw up regulations for local self-government; the governors-general and governors were to select places in which to test the operation of these regulations.[23]

The most important step was taken on October 19, when the throne, acting on earlier advice, ordered provincial authorities to establish immediately deliberative assemblies (*ziyiju*) in their respective capitals, "selecting honest and admittedly clever officials and gentry to assist in the organization thereof."[24] It was further stated that high provincial officials would be duty-bound to take the decisions of these assemblies into consideration when acting upon any matter. Assembly members, moreover, might eventually be chosen for seats in the anticipated imperial constitutional assembly.[25]

And yet, as the year 1907 drew to a close, protests and challenges to the authority of the center increased. Rebellions alternately smoldered and burst into flame in the South; assassination attempts multiplied, and one succeeded in killing the governor of Anhui; there were riots in Zhejiang. How can we account for this?

The fact is that the reforms themselves antagonized major portions of the political elites of this period. The revolutionaries were outraged at the prospect of the Qing dynasty's being able to engineer its survival through reform.

---

east or west. An examination of the system of government heretofore existing, with its higher and lower officials mutually supporting each other, shows that it is no longer entirely suited to the times." Having laid the groundwork for their proposals, the petitioners continued by arguing that because subprovincial officials were "in close touch with the people" it was "in these subdivisions of the provinces that the first efforts toward constitutional government must be made." Dealing with the provinces, the memorialists remarked that if changes were attempted throughout the empire simultaneously, they would surely result in failure, given the magnitude of the task and the paucity of funds and men of proper quality. Hence a pilot project was essential. The memorial of Prince Qing and Grand Counselor Sun Jianai is reproduced in *Papers Relating to the Foreign Relations of the United States*, 1906, pp. 181–184, taken from the *Peking Gazette*, July 10, 1907.

More important, various provincial leaders were threatened by the basic reforms, which struck at the heart of the traditional system in two critical respects. By promoting increased centralization, they attacked the provincial and regional autonomy that had enabled China to endure for millennia. And by promoting professionalism, with its specialization of functions and clear delineation of responsibility, they threatened the traditional scholar-official in the most profound manner.

It is thus not surprising that by 1907 a wave of protests had occurred over such issues as railroad loans, military reorganization, and other policies involving an increased exercise of central power. These issues blended with more traditional ones, such as food shortages, corruption, and banditry, to create a situation of rising instability, and the court in Beijing was understandably uncertain about the proper course of action.

In an imperial edict of December 24, 1907, reportedly drafted by Zhang Zhidong, one can sense the combination of concern and indignation among key officials.[26] It began by pointing out that the edict of September 1, 1906, pledging constitutional government had contained a warning that the task was one of vast magnitude and great complexity and would require thorough preparation on the part of officials and people alike. It argued (amazingly enough) that "every country constitutionally governed has relegated the ultimate authority to the throne" and asserted that in public discussions citizens are not allowed to break the law under the guise of bringing about constitutional reforms.[27] Though many among the governing classes, the merchants, the literati, and the populace at large had been performing their individual duties intelligently, there had also been many "fickle, deceitful, ignorant ones entirely lacking in insight." They had made reform a pretext for meddling in the internal and foreign affairs of the government.

Inferiors were insulting their superiors, the higher classes were becoming "unworthy," and national values were being undermined. If this were not stopped, it would lead to great confusion and could only lengthen the process of achieving constitutionalism. Very strict rules must govern the advent of parliamentarism, the operation of the constitutional assembly in Beijing, and the provincial deliberative assemblies. Persons who seek to assemble the citizens in order to seduce them with "wild fallacies" must be punished mercilessly.

Meanwhile, the efforts to bring about a rapid political transformation went forward valiantly. On December 9, 1907, the throne had proclaimed the inauguration of a new judicial system in Beijing. In the proclamation issued by the Board of Law, the following passage is particularly striking, given the Chinese tradition of playing down the law: "The essential characteristic of legal authority is that it shall be absolute in its field."[28]

Bureaucratism at the center and the inertia of most provincial governors remained formidable obstacles. Although the "immediate establishment" of provincial assemblies had been authorized in October 1907, specific instructions on their creation were not given by the throne until July 1908.[29] Membership was to range from 114 in Zhejiang to 30 in Jilin, Heilongjiang, and Xinjiang. Voting restrictions and qualifications for office were roughly similar to those outlined earlier in connection with Tianjin.[30] The functions of the deliberative assemblies, outlined broadly in the October 1907 decree, were now specified in detail. In addition to levying taxes, determining provincial administrative changes, and electing delegates to the constitutional assembly, they were to supervise local self-government, receive and consider proposals laid before them by self-governing bodies and the people, and in broad terms, to "determine the policy of the province." In connection with this policy-making, the governors were requested to prepare a list of topics to be discussed by their assemblies, and to submit the lists in advance.

Determining the precise relation of the new assemblies to the provincial governors and to the central government was a delicate matter. The July 22 regulations provided that in case of disagreement between the governor and the assembly, the governor could request a reconsideration by the assembly. If the disagreement persisted, provincial authorities were to put the matter before the constitutional assembly in Beijing. If the governor of the province "hindered" the assembly in the exercise of its lawful functions, or broke the laws, the assembly had the right to submit its complaints to the constitutional assembly. On the other hand, sovereignty remained vested in the throne and in its duly appointed officials at the provincial level. Thus the governor-general or governor could dissolve the assembly if it "transgressed the limits of its functions" or refused to obey the governor, if it took decisions of "an illegal character," or if it engaged in disorderly conduct that was impossible for its chairman to control. Specifically, any expressions of sentiments unfavorable to the throne or any acts calculated to disturb peaceful rule were grounds for dissolution.[31]

A second edict issued on the same day commanded that deliberative assemblies be convened in every province before July 22, 1909. It also requested the bureau of administrative methods and the constitutional commission to report jointly to the throne on the question of basic principles for the forthcoming constitution, as well as the methods of election to be used and powers to be given to the parliament.

Just over one month later, on August 27, 1908, the requested joint memorial on constitutional government was issued as an imperial edict.[32] This carefully drafted document accurately mirrored the political philosophy of those in authority. Constitutionalism, it said, if properly practiced, would "restore the great harmony, bringing officials and people into an indissoluble unity on behalf of the nation."[33] The vital principle to be pursued was that "above, power shall not be arbitrarily exercised, and below, there shall be no disobedience."

The constitution would stipulate that the sovereign had "absolute power, which he exercised in constitutional forms."[34] It would also specify the privileges and duties both of officials and of people beneath the monarch. The preparations would necessarily be arduous because many critical tasks had to be completed, tasks comparable to those of a person preparing for a journey. "Clothing, food, boats, and carts must be got ready, and the traveler must press on day after day without stopping for rest, and so he will reach his destination." What were the critical requirements if constitutional government were to operate successfully? First, the government's finances had to be put in order, and for these purposes a census was essential. All distinctions between Manchu and Han had to be eliminated. Laws had to be codified, and a full system of courts made functional. The duties of officials had to be carefully defined. Education had to be extended. Practice in local self-government had to be cultivated.

Given the sweeping requirements, the memorialists proposed a nine-year schedule, culminating in the extension of full constitutional government in

1917. The first year (1908) would be devoted to preparing for provincial deliberative assemblies, promulgating rules for local self-government, and publishing rules for financial reorganization; to blending the Manchu Bannermen with Han; to preparing texts so that people could learn Chinese characters more easily; to printing other "lesson books" that the people would be required to study; and to revising the criminal code and publishing various other laws and court procedures.[35]

The proposed constitution would be patterned after the Meiji constitution in its staunch defense of imperial sovereignty; the emperor would appoint all officials, possess all powers with respect to military affairs, and be able to impose laws restricting various constitutional rights in times of emergency.[36] Indeed, in some respects, the new fundamental law would go beyond the Meiji constitution in upholding imperial power and circumscribing parliament. Nevertheless, the projected Chinese constitution promised to establish a system that was more federal than unitary. Paying homage to China's traditions, the provinces were to remain significant political entities, empowered to handle "local affairs." China could not be governed like Japan, and in any case, the complex issues of centralism versus decentralization could not be resolved by fiat or simple formula.

Within a few months the court gave further evidence of being simultaneously pushed and pulled. On December 3, 1908, shortly after the deaths of Cixi and Guangxu, another imperial edict was issued to reassure the populace that there would be no change of course. Reiterating its pledge and implying that progress was slow in certain quarters, the throne used colorful language to exhort the tardy: "Let there be no reabsorption of sweat in this matter."[37] On January 18, 1909, the promised rules for local self-government, including election procedures, were promulgated.[38] Detailed regulations for the national constitutional assembly were drafted in mid-1909 and received imperial approval on October 14.[39] These provided for an assembly of two hundred members, one hundred of whom would be appointed by the throne, the other hundred to be elected by the provincial assemblies, with the proviso that their election would not be valid until approved by the provincial governor. In addition to appointing various princes, nobles, and members of the imperial clan, the throne was to appoint ten "distinguished scholars" and ten citizens "from among the highest taxpayers," in imitation of the Japanese practice with respect to its upper house.

The regulations also provided that members of the constitutional assembly must be thirty years of age and meet qualifications similar to those applying to provincial assemblymen. The assembly was to approve the national budget, enact taxes, contract loans, and create new legal codes; in other areas, proposals had to be submitted to it from the throne, after initiation by the Grand Council or the head of a board. In the event of any disagreement between the assembly and the Grand Council or board head, however, the power of final determination rested with the emperor.

Thus, by the end of 1909 the new Chinese constitutional structure was beginning to take shape. The deliberative assemblies were convened on October 14, 1909, in every province except Xinjiang. In certain provinces, such as Shandong, Shanxi, and Yunnan, considerable preparations for the elections had taken place; in other settings, almost no tutelage had been offered. Suffrage requirements kept the electorate small, and those chosen for office came from the educated and affluent class: they were mostly office-holders, scholars, gentry, and members of the business community.[40]

From the outset, the assemblies displayed a willingness to challenge provincial governors and to speak on the widest range of subjects with little restraint. Despite the limits on suffrage and candidacies, "unruly" assemblymen appeared, including some who had been overseas students only a few years earlier. In Jilin, for example, a dispute began with strong protests in the assembly against the new Manchurian Convention that the national government had signed with Japan. When the assembly sent a vigorous denunciation of this agreement to Beijing and attacked the foreign ministry for pusillanimity, the governor protested that such actions went beyond assembly prerogatives, and demanded that it end its sessions. The assembly protested to the Grand Council and the Commission on Constitutional Reforms, attacking the governor and presenting its own views; but the commission agreed with the governor and sharply censured the Jilin assembly for overstepping its authority.

Similar episodes occurred elsewhere. In Zhili another resolution protesting the Manchurian Convention was put before the assembly, but when the assistant to the governor-general asserted that it went beyond the assembly's authority, it was reluctantly withdrawn. In troubled Guangxi the new assembly almost immediately became locked in a bitter dispute with the governor over their respective rights. When the Gansu provincial assembly met, ironically, the governor-general was en route home from Beijing, having been dismissed from office for memorializing the throne that it was too early to convene an assembly in his province. In Sichuan, described by a contemporary observer as exceptionally free in its criticisms of governmental authorities, the assembly won the opening rounds of a struggle with the governor-general relating to its rights.

Generally, assembly discussions and resolutions covered subjects mirroring the immediate concerns of China's elites. In Shandong these subjects included opium prohibition, agricultural improvement, tax restructuring, trade development, and currency reform. In Zhili foreign policy and simplification of the Chinese written language were of special concern. The Zhejiang assembly took up the issues of currency reform, the census, railroad construction, wasteland reclamation, taxes, agriculture and reforestation, and the establishment of a society to promote knowledge of constitutionalism among the people. In Hubei the focus was on education, opium suppression, and agricultural-forestry development. The importance of all these issues to the future of China could scarcely be denied.

The granting of full constitutionalism was not supposed to be a topic for assembly discussion, being within the emperor's prerogative. But a few weeks after the first assemblies convened, delegates from some fifteen of them held a series of meetings in Shanghai, out of which came a petition to the government urging the speedy establishment of a national parliament. In mid-January of 1910 representatives arrived in Beijing with this petition in hand. Their demand was that "in view of the success of the provincial assemblies," a national parliament should be convened before the end of 1911.

The throne had already responded to such memorials in an edict of January 10, 1910; it had insisted that preparations were not complete and the people's knowledge was still insufficient. If a parliament were hastily opened, confusion and dissension would result, hindering the success of constitutional government in its crucial, early stages.[41] Again, on February 3, an imperial edict sharply criticized a memorial from a censor which suggested that the government was deliberately delaying the constitutional process, thereby jeopardizing the throne. The rescript insisted that the court had been "most zealous" in promoting the cause of the constitutional government, and that no changes in the timetable were contemplated.[42]

Yet the pressures, which bore little relation to the actual course of preparations, would not abate. On June 27 the regent was forced to issue another edict on the same subject as a result of a new memorial from a delegation composed of provincial assemblymen, chamber of commerce members, educational society representatives, and overseas Chinese. This time the court exhibited its irritation quite clearly. After asserting that progress was being made as rapidly as possible, the edict ended with the injunction "You people shall not memorialize us again on the matter."[43]

At this point, however, events began to move out of the control of the regent and his court. Instead of directing national policies and actions, the center could only react to the policies and actions of individuals and political groups beneath it. Defensiveness was followed by capitulation, with occasional bursts of petulance. One result was that reform became an instrument of disintegration. The political signals put out by the center's behavior were quickly transmitted to all elements of the elite. Conservatives were outraged and began to submit their resignations in growing numbers. Moderates were emboldened to become disrespectful and contemptuous. Thus, deep fissures opened between the government and its former supporters, both in Beijing and in the provinces. Opportunists and office-seekers quickly emerged from within the court itself, and some of them were prepared to support the instant-constitutionalists for their own purposes.

In this setting it was impossible to form a coalition dedicated to measured, controlled political change, as the Meiji leadership in Japan had managed to do. On the contrary, the regent and his court found themselves increasingly isolated from those on whom their survival depended. The fatal onslaught against the Qing dynasty did not come from Sun Yat-sen and his followers, nor from the constitutional monarchists inspired by Kang and Liang; it came from a loose and temporary coalition that lacked cohesive leadership and consistent policies yet encompassed a great many of the educated and affluent persons whose support was crucial: a portion of the nobility, the rising business class, and above all, a sizable element of the gentry. Students and the new intelligentsia (often of gentry background) added their weight, and in some instances served as initiators, stimulators, and catalysts. Acting alone against unified resistance, this relatively small segment of the elite could not possibly have prevailed. But such resistance could no longer be organized, because the old elite as a whole had been fragmented along a broad front. When one adds the weight of the secret societies—longtime opponents of the Manchu—and portions of the New Army, the elements in opposition were formidable indeed.

Successful politics is always coalition politics, and the greater weight of coalition now rested with forces outside the government. It was not necessary for all crucial groups to be actively antagonistic to the center; passiveness or neutrality on the part of many would suffice. And beyond a certain point, the politics of the besieged power-holders themselves began to change dramatically. As their control over the political process ebbed, they abandoned their quest for long-term approaches and began to accept any expedient that would postpone collapse. At the personal level, despite the omnipresent signs of a rapidly rising Han nationalism, Manchu were summoned to occupy an increasing number of key posts, since ethnic loyalty was assumed to be the most trustworthy.

Let us now look briefly at some events that illustrate these phenomena. As was promised, the Constituent Assembly was convened in Beijing on October 3, 1910. It was a body clearly intended to be a servant of imperial authority. Of its two hundred members, one hundred were chosen directly by the throne. The great majority of these were drawn from the nobility, in accordance with the specific rules governing the Assembly, although as we noted, provisions had been made for the appointment of ten "distinguished scholars" and ten large taxpayers. The other one hundred members were to be chosen by the provincial assemblies, with their election subject to the approval of the provincial governor. The Constituent Assembly had among its prerogatives the approval of the national budget, of taxes and loans, and of changes in the legal statutes. However, it was specifically prohibited from initiating proposals regarding constitutionalism.

Nevertheless, one of its first acts was to memorialize the throne for an early grant of a parliament, a resolution passed by acclamation and probably abetted by news of the revolution in Portugal. This time the court acquiesced. On November 4, after discussions involving a number of notables, including members of the Grand Council, the regent issued an imperial rescript announcing that the date for the opening of parliament had been advanced to 1913. Furthermore, until then a cabinet system and Privy Council would replace the prevailing administrative structure. This acceleration was the product of political pressure, not performance. The schedule of reforms set forth earlier as essential to the effective inauguration of constitutional government had not been maintained by the center. In addition, provincial results varied greatly, as the Commission on Constitutional Reform admitted in its report of late 1910. With the tide running heavily against it, however, the court could no longer resist.

Emboldened by its success, the Constituent Assembly passed various other resolutions, including one that requested an explicit imperial decree allowing all Han citizens to cut off the queue, the historical symbol of an acceptance of Manchu rule. The throne rejected this, but many "progressives" were already abandoning the queue without official sanction and were going unpunished. Permission was granted the Assembly to extend its session by ten days so as to take up questions "yet unresolved." By the end of 1910 some were referring to the Assembly—once regarded as a puppet of the throne—as the new center of power.

Meanwhile, palace politics in Beijing had become increasingly intricate. The Yehonala clansmen (from whence Cixi came) had now united with their historic rivals, the Gioro, against the regent and the House of Chun. Two women were now emerging as powerful rivals: Princess Chun, the wife of the regent and the daughter of the famous Ronglu, and the empress dowager Longyu, the widow of Guangxu and the niece of Cixi. In the waning days of the Qing, oblivious to the events around them, these women and their factions struggled for power, anticipating another woman of note who was to struggle for power in the waning days of Mao Zedong.

The new constitutional schedule called for the inauguration of a cabinet and an Advisory Council in 1911, with various civil, commercial, and criminal laws to be issued before 1913. A Privy Council would be initiated in 1912, and in the following year, after election laws had been enacted, the national parliament would be chosen and convened. An imperial decree of April 3, 1911, began the process by making the emperor the supreme commander of China's military forces, the position held by the emperor Meiji in Japan. One month later, on May 8, the ministers of the first cabinet were appointed by the regent, with an announcement that this body would "assist" him in making policies. As in Japan, heads of the military services were ordered to report directly to the throne. Rules for the Privy Council were also set forth at this time. Its members, too, were to be appointed by the throne: there would be a president and thirty-two advisory ministers, and an additional ten councilors who were to be "experienced politicians," allowed to speak but not to vote. In this structure, there were combined aspects of the Japanese Privy Council and *genrō*.

A COMPARISON WITH JAPAN AND RUSSIA

By the spring of 1911 all of the formal preparations for constitutionalism that would ever be made had been completed. They did not bear fruit, but this was not primarily because the constitutional proposals themselves were defective. To put the broader issues in perspective and emphasize the fundamental reasons for the Revolution of 1911, we can compare the efforts to establish constitutional monarchy in China with the successful Japanese drive in a similar direction which had taken place two decades earlier and with political developments that had taken place a few years previously in Russia.

It is sometimes forgotten that in the aftermath of the Meiji Restoration of 1867–1868, political stability in Japan's half-feudal, long-isolated society was far from assured. Indeed, with the expropriation of Tokugawa-bestowed properties, civil war was barely avoided, and the first pledge of representation through a national assembly was made in 1868 precisely to obtain the daimyo and samurai support that was so crucial to the survival of the imperial government. The two-house assembly (*giseikan*) functioned for only a short time, but the concept of representation at a national level had won acceptance.[44]

The most precarious years for the new government came in 1869–1870 and again in 1877–1878, but the entire decade of the 1870s was fraught with the danger that total collapse would occur, either because of disunity within the inner circle or because of a successful assault from dissidents who saw current trends as a betrayal of the original objectives of the Restoration. There was merit in the dissidents' position, for the Meiji Restoration had embraced contradictory visions of the future.

On the one hand, the Restoration envisioned a centralized state, with the emperor serving as a rallying point for a new nationalism that would enable Japan to survive in an imperialist era, when isolation was no longer possible. Implicit in this vision, moreover, was a program of economic modernization. This program aimed at mass literacy; at economic diversification, with an increasing emphasis on industrialization; and at the cultivation of science and technology, which would serve agriculture as well as industry and the military. Without such a program, the goals of national power and wealth, spelled out explicitly at the time of the Restoration, would be illusory.

On the other hand, many of the foremost exponents of ending Tokugawa rule had a different vision. They were men deeply committed to the socio-political and economic precepts of the past, members of an elite who had no intention of abandoning the privileges of their status, or the polity and economy that had sustained these. They were dedicated to a highly decentralized, fief-centered political order (based on the *han*), with an agrarian-based economy protected against the rising merchant class.

In both China and Japan, fragmentation of the rural landed elites was a prominent factor in the fall of the old order. And although economic events played a role in causing this fragmentation—especially in Japan, where a rising commercialism was challenging the traditional supremacy of the landed class—any analysis based wholly or even primarily on economic determinants distorts the complex facts. Power in all its forms was at stake, and in both societies, sizable portions of the rural gentry were moved to opposition because, above all, they resented the inability or unwillingness of the national government to preserve traditional values and institutions. The true catalyst was the Western influence in all its dimensions. Thus, in the Meiji Restoration and in the burgeoning opposition to the Qing, there was a powerful element of traditionalism, a desire to return to a mythical golden age when timeless values and institutions went unchallenged by barbarian intrusions.

There was a crucial difference, however. The new Meiji leaders were able to redirect the forces of traditionalism—blunting those that proved dangerous or useless, reshaping those that could be of service—while maintaining control of the political process. The late Qing leaders, however, having remained for the most part antagonistic to "modernization" until they were forced to accept it at a very late point, proved unable to redirect the traditionalists and curb the revolutionaries. Indeed, as we have seen, the most basic political processes slipped from under their control, and the ship of state was truly rudderless.

Of course, Japan's emergence from "centralized feudalism" was by no means easy or wholly tranquil. The first major crisis came in 1869–1870, with the decision to abolish the old *han* system in favor of a centralized system of administration, based on prefectures and metropolitan areas that gave greatly increased powers to the center. Only with great difficulty, after a combination of nationalist entreaties and economic emoluments, were a goodly portion of the old daimyo and the samurai class persuaded to accept the new order peacefully. Even so, civil war finally erupted in February 1877; but by then the center's conscript army, equipped with modern weapons, was able to defeat the localists. The death in battle of Saigo Takamori, the great feudalist leader from Satsuma, consummated the victory of the center, but the reverence with which Saigo continued to be regarded even in Tokyo was eloquent testimony to the wrenching that took place in the hearts and minds of those portions of the old aristocracy who had dedicated themselves to a new order.

Throughout this period, specific issues, such as the question of external expansion (into Korea) versus internal development, served to divide the elite and resulted in the rise of the "liberals" and the decline of the "feudalists." Yet both groups were concerned about overcentralization and the vast power now gravitating toward a small "oligarchy," and both threatened rebellion if their views and values were not heeded.

Thus, in Japan as in China, the movement toward constitutionalism was a product of many pressures, both "feudal" and "liberal." In Japan the process started as early as 1876, prior to the Satsuma Rebellion, and various draft constitutions were proposed in the late 1870s. Not until October 1881, however, at a high point in the civil rights movement (*jiyūminken undō*), did the emperor promise that a written constitution would be granted to the Japanese people. Over the next eight years the Japanese oligarchy took a series of deliberate steps to reach this goal. At the outset, a constitutional mission headed by Itō Hirobumi was sent abroad to examine various foreign systems; it confirmed the impression of the Meiji leaders that the Prussian political model would be the most serviceable. Meanwhile, the government undertook a series of administrative reforms: the establishment of a peerage, which enabled a sizable portion of the old elite to be co-opted for service in the House of Peers; the creation of a cabinet system with a prime minister directly responsible to the emperor; the initiation of a civil service based on specialized training and merit, which thereby legitimized the bureaucracy, the branch of government most critical to Japan's modernization; and the erection of a Privy Council, a body composed of trusted, veteran officials to whom was ultimately assigned the task of ratifying the new fundamental laws, including the constitution itself.

Throughout the years of preparation, the Meiji leaders jealously protected their handiwork from outside interference. The constitutional drafts—written with extensive assistance from several German scholars—were treated as secret documents. The hand of the government came down heavily whenever "popular rights" zealots threatened to disrupt the public order. Law and order was maintained, and the Meiji Constitution became in fact as well as in theory "a gift from the emperor"—a gift that provided him with some shelter from the strains of full political participation and some long-term relief from "populist" pressures (which were in fact exerted by elites). When the constitution was finally promulgated in 1889, a peaceful transition to a modern form of government roughly congruent with those in certain parts of the "advanced West" had been achieved.

Regardless of the degree to which it provided for future change and the degree to which it froze a political order, making for future tension between institutions and social development, the Meiji Constitution was the product of a masterful exercise in restraining dissidence, encouraging unity, and promoting national strength. This success can be attributed to a number of factors. The first was the political culture of Japan. The hierarchical, disciplined, and organic character of Japanese society—a product of long isolation and the modified feudalism that survived into the mid-nineteenth century—contrasted with the family-clan orientation of Chinese society, which was localist, dispersed, and partially egalitarian and antistatist in nature. To a large extent, in China society tolerated public government only because it had been able to keep governmental functions at a minimum. In Japan, on the contrary, family and clan were woven into a broader political fabric by the nonfamilial obligations imposed under Japan's "feudal" system.

Geography was a factor of equally great importance. Japan's location and relatively small size permitted centralization to be accomplished with the military, political, and economic techniques already available in the late nineteenth century. China, however, was vast, loosely organized, and readily accessible to imperialism. Its governability as a modern state awaited advances in technology beyond those possessed by any early-twentieth-century nation.

The disparity in human resources was another factor. The availability of the Japanese emperor for nationalist purposes proved to be of truly critical importance. In this era and in this setting, a politics that centered on a traditional personage like the emperor was much more likely to be a successful catalyst for nationalism and rapid economic development than any impersonal institution. This fact was recognized by many Chinese; but tragically for their cause, the Manchu dynasty, progressively discredited by its non-Han character and its active political role during a period of failure and frustration, could not serve as an effective symbol for a new nationalist China. Nor were the resources around the throne at all comparable to those in Japan. The lower samurai who were thrust into leadership by the events of the mid-nineteenth century proved sufficiently young, dissatisfied with aspects of the old order, and tentative in some of their values to adapt creatively to changing circumstances and requirements. Their society, itself the product of successive earlier adaptations from foreign models, proved able to follow their lead. In China, neither the leadership, which deteriorated with each successive crisis, nor the society at large, so amorphous and lacking in integrative forces, was able to cope with the challenges that confronted them.

Finally, there was the factor of timing, which is always critical to political outcomes. The Japanese political transition took place only two decades prior to the efforts of the Chinese court, but the lead time available to Japan was considerably longer. Furthermore, the move toward constitutionalism came at a time when Japan remained fundamentally unaltered by foreign imperialism. Despite extraterritoriality and tariff constraints, the Japanese government had not been seriously weakened by foreign territorial inroads, including various forms of de facto occupation. With its sovereignty essentially intact, the central government of Japan could use coercion, cooptation, assimilation, and above all, a gradualist approach, because neither external nor internal pressures had yet managed to undermine the authority of the state and force it into acts of desperation.

Thus, in Japan the government succeeded in controlling the constitution-making process as well as the broader political developments surrounding it. In China, on the contrary, both the timing and the symbolism of constitutionalism were increasingly governed by forces outside the control of the central government. Hence the process of seeking constitutionalism further weakened the existing government and its chief symbol, the emperor. For these reasons, commitments and processes that were similar in the two societies produced vastly different results.

In certain respects, the events in China that led to constitutionalism, and then to revolt, had their closest parallels not in Japan but in Russia.[45] In the first decade of the twentieth century, the ferment in both Russian and Chinese societies emanated from some of the same causes. In Russia the throne was occupied by a well-meaning but ineffectual monarch who found it difficult to retain able advisers. In 1905 Russia lost a war to Japan—previously regarded as a small Asian nation of little power or consequence. To be sure, Russia had fought this war in a desultory fashion, seemingly preoccupied with other matters, but the defeat had an electric effect on domestic politics.

Even many conservatives became convinced that major changes were essential. Student discontent was widespread, and various Western political models were ardently espoused. In certain circles, an avant-garde radicalism flourished, and the older commitment to peasant revolution now found competition from a Marxist-derived interest in the urban worker. Nihilism bequeathed its tradition to contemporary radicals, and assassination became a popular political weapon.

One should not exaggerate the influence of the Russian extremists. In the provinces, the Socialist Revolutionaries had some success in inciting the peasants to seize the land, but the great mass of rural dwellers remained dedicated to the church and the czar, their "little father." The opportunities for change in the urban centers seemed infinitely more promising. Truly serious political instability followed "bloody Sunday" in St. Petersburg when thousands of workers, marching with a Russian orthodox priest, Gapon, as their mentor, were fired upon by troops as they approached the Winter Palace with a petition for the czar. A general strike followed, together with other ominous signs for the throne. The grand duke Sergei, the czar's uncle and governor of Moscow, was assassinated in February 1905; a mutiny took place on the battleship *Potemkin*; and peasant uprisings were reported on an increasing scale—all signals that the Russian polity was undergoing strains scarcely less profound than those that were occurring in China.

By the summer of 1905 political parties were being organized for the first time in Russia, and the government had been forced to give the universities autonomy, which resulted in an immediate rise in radical organizational activities among students. Finally, Nicholas felt impelled to respond. In the edict that came to be known as the October Manifesto of 1905, he called for the establishment of an elected assembly (Duma) that would have the right to block (but not to initiate) legislation.

As in China, reform measures emanating from the throne split the political forces that were agitating for change. The liberals, calling themselves the Octobrist Party, rallied behind the reform measures, determined to use them to the utmost. The militants, including the Socialist Revolutionaries and the Social Democrats (who later split into Mensheviks and Bolsheviks) merely stepped up their opposition to the existing order, although they worked within the new Duma on occasion.

The elections for the first Duma went badly from the standpoint of the government, notwithstanding the limited nature of the suffrage. The Kadets and their allies, a mixed group of ardent constitutionalists, reformers, and radicals, won 179 seats; the "center" group obtained 17 seats, and parties dedicated to the czar and the status quo won only 15. There was a militant nationalist tone to the proceedings of the first Duma, heard in frequent calls for a strong Russia revitalized through far-reaching reforms. A clash with the czarist government was inevitable, and it came quickly: within two months the Duma was dissolved, ostensibly over the issue of land reform.

This situation was remarkably similar to the one that would occur a few years later in China after the election of the first provincial assemblies, and many of the same broad socioeconomic and political factors were involved. Members of the landed gentry, professionals, and a few entrepreneurs combined with an avant-garde student-intellectual force to challenge the traditional autocratic state. Participation by the "masses," particularly urban workers, was somewhat greater in Russia, reflecting its greater degree of industrialization.

After the dissolution of the first Duma, the government under Stolypin took various measures to weaken the more radical forces, but conflict continued. Finally, in 1907 the czar announced that the Duma was subversive and decreed that the next assembly would be elected under a different system, one giving much greater weight to the affluent, both urban and rural. This established greater harmony between Duma and government, but the excluded radicals and militant reformers returned to illegal and quasi-legal activities outside the assembly arena.

On the surface at least, it seemed that after repeated exercises in violence and repression during the first stages of the country's movement toward constitutionalism, the czar and his government had averted the disintegration that was threatening China by 1911, and had succeeded in establishing a politics of gradualism. The situation was fragile, however. Terrorism and repression continued to ride in tandem. Stolypin himself was assassinated in 1911, and political exiles flowed both to Siberia and to Europe.

Like China, Russia was too large to be easily modernized with the available technology, and its situation was made the more difficult by the unassimilated portions of empire it held in central Asia and to the south. The best opportunity for gradualism to prevail lay in the capacity of Russia's leaders to apply the energies of the nation to internal development, meanwhile building a political coalition—and institutions to sustain that coalition—that would move in the general direction of parliamentarism and constitutional monarchy. Russia's participation in World War I, however, made it impossible to pursue this strategy, and revealed the structural weaknesses of the government in the most appalling manner.

As we have noted, many Chinese watched the Russian experiment in political reform with keen interest. For the Chinese radicals the heroism and self-sacrifice of the Russian revolutionaries had long provided hope and a model. There can be no doubt that the use of terrorism by young Chinese revolutionaries was inspired most directly by the Russian nihilists and their successors. Even the Chinese reformers who favored constitutional monarchy often praised Russian "progressives" and observed the Russian scene carefully. When Nicholas first granted the Russian people an assembly, he was widely heralded in China as an enlightened monarch whom the Qing might well emulate; and when the experiment faltered, the "progressive" Chinese media lamented the fact and dolefully compared the backwardness of Russia and China. The court in Beijing also followed events closely, taking the actions of the Russian court as important signs of the future. Thus Cixi took Nicholas's edict of October 1905 into account in planning for China's constitutional experiment.

THE MOUNTING CRISES IN CHINA

By the spring of 1911 the authority of the center was ebbing so rapidly that imperial edicts had little effect on the course of events. Reforms, as we have noted, simply led to further demands, which often bore little relation to the realities of the situation. Standing firm—using coercion or threats—proved to be increasingly difficult, partly because of the deep fissures within the center itself. The range of protests was so broad as to defy any simple or effective set of actions in response, even if the Beijing court had been far more united, self-confident, and efficient.

Many analyses of the Revolution of 1911 have begun with a recital of economic crisis: agricultural production has been depicted as stagnant or declining, handicrafts and small-scale manufacturing are portrayed as being disrupted by the inroads of Western capitalism; and Qing efforts to increase taxes are seen as adversely affecting peasant livelihood. The cumulative effect, it is argued, was to spread agrarian unrest and to sharpen class conflicts—most notably between peasants and landlords—so that riots and rebellions began to occur throughout the empire.

Recent research raises serious questions about these assessments, at least when put in such bald form. The facts about agricultural production and peasant livelihood in the decades preceding the 1911 Revolution form a very complicated pattern. For example, it has often been asserted that per capita income in China fell steadily in the nineteenth and early twentieth centuries. Yet evidence marshalled by Dwight Perkins and his associates suggests that although there may have been short-term declines in per capita grain production because of bad weather or social violence, generally speaking, grain production kept pace with the increase in population through the early twentieth century, with only modest changes in per capita production.* They ascribe rises in grain production to increased labor power and technical progress (such as the introduction of new seed strains) within the traditional structure, on the one hand, and to an expansion of cultivated land, on the other. Perkins's data and that of Ramon Myers also suggest that over the centuries of Qing rule there was very little change in the ratio of tenant-operated to owner-operated land, which casts doubt on the thesis that tenancy was increasing rapidly.[46] In actuality, it appears that the return on investment in land was quite low for the landlord—little more than 5 percent, whereas in commerce and moneylending it was at least 10 to 20 percent. In considering these macro figures, we must keep in mind, of course, that the diversities from region to region were substantial.

Yeh-Chien Wang indicates that in the last quarter-century of the Qing era

* Perkins acknowledges that rates of production and population growth were not regular within the six centuries studied. Events like the Taiping Rebellion resulted in a sharp downward cycle, and the most seriously affected provinces did not recover during the Qing era (which also delayed a Malthusian day of reckoning by virtue of the effect on population). His central theme, however, is that traditional agriculture had not completely run out of growth potential, and that together with expanded cultivated acreage, it could match population increases averaging 1 percent per annum (pp. 23–26). Only when population growth reached and exceeded 2 percent per annum, as occurred after 1949, did new agrarian technology become imperative. See Dwight H. Perkins et al., *Agricultural Development in China—1368–1968*.

A similar view is presented by Ramon H. Myers, both in *The Chinese Peasant Economy—Agricultural Development in Hopei and Shantung—1890–1949* and in an essay prepared for the *Cambridge History of China* entitled "Trends in Agriculture: 1911–1949." See also his "Agricultural Production and Sources of Agricultural Growth in Modern China: A Preliminary Study," unpublished paper.

In broader terms, the relationship between the state and the economic system in traditional China has been dealt with in the theories of Elvin and Skinner set forth earlier, and in the well-known work of Karl Wittfogel, who seeks to link China's need for an extensive water-control system with the early development of a centralized bureaucratic state. See Karl Wittfogel, *Oriental Despotism*.

the land tax constituted only 2 to 4 percent of production in most provinces, a decline from the middle Qing era and much less than the land tax in Meiji Japan, which amounted to about 10 percent of production.[47] Almost all sources agree that land taxes and required grain deliveries during the final decades of the Qing were a very small burden on the peasantry. Wang also indicates, however, that in the three years before the 1911 Revolution, taxes in the form of temporary surcharges rose significantly in order to cover famine relief, water-control projects, modern schools, and preparations for self-government.[48] Taxation, therefore, was among the issues that surfaced at the very end of the dynasty.

Western technology, especially in the area of transport, did have an effect on the Chinese economy. It affected the patterns of grain trade and promoted the expansion of northern cities and the advance of urbanization throughout China. But as Perkins remarks, speaking of the years 1900–1910, "the burden of increased deliveries on Chinese farmers does not appear to have been very great in this period."[49] Population increases were gradual, many taking place in the northeast, where new lands were being opened for cultivation; and foreign imports of grain grew significantly in these years.

We do not mean to argue that most of the rural population of China were well-off in economic terms, or that major economic strides were being made. We do mean to point out, however, that most scholars now agree that serious agrarian crises of a systemic nature struck twentieth-century China *after* the 1911 Revolution, not prior to it. This explains, in large part, why reformers and revolutionaries alike saw no need to concentrate on the "peasant problem." Sun advocated Henry George's single tax, it will be recalled, out of a desire to prevent *future* inequities and at the same time to finance economic development on a large scale.

The evidence for a general agrarian decline in the late Qing is slim.* And in any case, one must distinguish between a general decline and temporary, regional crises caused by drought or flood. Regional crises were always present in China in some degree and may have been more acute in the period just prior to the Revolution. The years 1910–1911, for example, brought severe economic hardships to much of Central China. On the eve of the Qing overthrow, in September 1911, the *North China Herald* remarked: "Every present symptom points to the fact that the distress in Central China during the coming autumn and winter will be almost without parallel in the empire's history. . . . So large is the area affected by the floods, extending virtually from the foot of the gorges to below Jinjiang, that it has not been possible as yet to obtain even an approximately comprehensive account of the full toll of destruction."[50]

These conditions had led to the Changsha riots in April of 1910, an incident that has received extensive coverage from various scholars.[51] When the

* Perkins et al., present some composite figures taken from Li Wenzhi et al., *Zhongguo jindai nongye shi ciliao* (Historical Materials on Agriculture in Modern China) 1:755–760, which indicate relatively steady declines in farm yields between 1821 and 1911, measured against some earlier standard not specified. The data apply to nine provinces, most of them in central China. If these figures are accurate, production was comparatively poor in the last three decades of Qing rule, but Perkins argues that the Taiping Rebellion, together with other uprisings in the nineteenth century, accounted for a population decrease of as much as 50 million, affecting many of the nine provinces surveyed (Perkins et al., *Agricultural Development in China*, pp. 27–28).

husband of a poor family living in the Hunan capital returned from seeking work, he found that his wife had committed suicide in despair over rising rice prices. He then led his two children to the river, threw them in to drown, and ended his own life in the same way. A crowd gathered, including the grandparents, and blamed the government for not giving aid to the poor and for failing to reduce the price of rice. Police were summoned to control the growing throng, and fighting erupted. The crowd overwhelmed available police, and the chief of police was hanged to a tree by his queue. Then the mob surged to the governor's yamen. Negotiations failed, although officials agreed to reduce rice prices. In the ensuing violence, New Army soldiers guarding the yamen killed a number of rioters. The yamen was then burned to the ground (the governor and his staff escaped) and rice shops in the city were looted, as were government offices, foreign missions, and foreign-related buildings. The evidence strongly indicates that at this point the conservative, antiforeign gentry had seized the opportunity to direct the rioters. Only after the dispatch of 3,000 soldiers from Wuchang was order restored.

There may have been more riots of this nature in the five or six years prior to 1911 than there were in the years immediately after the Yihe Tuan uprising. Wei and Wu assert that after 1905 "spontaneous mass struggles" increased throughout the nation; there were antirent struggles, rice riots, tax riots, secret society uprisings, anti-Christian movements, and ethnic minority protests. They claim that there were more than fifty rice riots in the middle and lower Yangtze River region (a portion of the famine area) in 1910, and that tax riots mounted steadily after 1905, reaching a climax in 1910.[52]

In any case, the upheavals followed a pattern. In famine regions or areas of great scarcity, the destitute left their villages and crowded into the towns and cities, where they joined demobilized soldiers and others to form a large reservoir of unemployed. Rice prices shot up, and merchants hoarded their supplies, waiting for even higher prices. Welfare, traditionally a familial responsibility, rarely concerned the state; only after a genuine crisis had developed did the authorities take action. At the point of greatest turmoil, compromises or remedial actions were sometimes advanced. In the end, however, main force was generally the determining factor. Invariably, the designated leaders of the riots were severely punished, and usually the government officials concerned were dismissed or transferred; the situation then returned to the status quo ante.

Unquestionably, the economic blight that afflicted Central China just before the 1911 Revolution weakened the government. In the fall of 1910, reports from north Anhui and north Jiangsu spoke of vast migrations out of stricken areas and the impotence of the government to deal with the situation. Yet it would be an error to regard these events as a prime precipitating cause of the coming upheaval or as evidence of increasing class struggle. It must be remembered that in affected areas everyone suffered, and the distinctions between owner-cultivators, tenants, and even landlords were only marginally meaningful. Thus, with some exceptions, the stricken peasants did not make the landlords their target, but focused rather on officials, merchants, and sometimes foreigners.* Their objective, moreover, was simple

* In his study of Guangdong, Edward Rhoads places somewhat greater emphasis than we do on the antigentry nature of peasant riots, stating that during 1910 and early 1911 "there

and immediate: survival. Such issues as land reform or even tenant rights were rarely on the agenda.

As we have suggested, the efforts of the central government to increase taxes in the years immediately prior to 1911 did create problems, despite the low tax rates that had prevailed. The center's dilemma was acute. The need for additional revenue was desperate. China's indebtedness to foreign nations stood at 125 million pounds sterling, and some 60 million taels had to be paid annually in gold to meet foreign bondholders' dividends. The Boxer indemnities were an enormous burden, especially since the government was now at least partly committed to a program of economic development. Efforts to reform the tax structure, however, ran squarely into entrenched provincial interests. Tax reform was an aspect of centralization that was certain to be stoutly resisted, and was one of the issues on which provincial authorities could expect voluntary support from merchants and gentry.

Thus, when the national government sought to impose a stamp tax in 1909, there were loud protests from merchants, and a majority of provincial governors urged delay. Yet where could additional revenue be found? The opium suppression campaign, ironically, had made enough progress to reduce this source of revenue. To obtain a larger share of the taxes imposed on agriculture would require a frontal assault on the provinces, a campaign for which the national government had neither the will nor the strength. Foreign loans continued to be the government's crutch. In this very period, Beijing authorities were seeking a 10 million pounds sterling loan from the United States, to be used essentially for currency reform and Manchurian development, and an additional 4 million pounds sterling loan for military modernization. For the central government, it became a "no-win" situation: higher taxes in any form brought angry protests from the very groups upon which it depended, but the policy of seeking additional loans from abroad, however necessary under the circumstances, was denounced as "selling off the country."

Though economic issues brought various segments of the populace into conflict with the government, or at least into a "neutralist" position, trouble with the military posed a far greater immediate problem. As we noted ear-

---

were at least twelve serious riots against gentry self-government in widely scattered parts of Kwangtung" (*China's Republican Revolution*, p. 176). As he indicates, however, these riots were essentially directed against *government* and were related to such specific issues as tax collection, school costs, and opposition to the census (pp. 176–179). Unquestionably, certain gentry were blamed and targeted for attack because of their personal role in provincial affairs. But as Rhoads asserts, these riots posed no great threat to the government (p. 179). Nor do we regard them as evidence of class conflict.

In a recent essay entitled "The Crowd in the Revolution of 1911—The People's Armies from a Silk-Producing Region in the Canton Delta, A Case Study," Winston Hsieh has added some new data relating to the revolution in Guangdong province. He has focused on the armed forces that "swarmed over" the Canton region unresisted in the aftermath of the October uprising, defining them as "people's armies" composed of ordinary people from towns and villages—populist, antitraditionalist, and prorepublican in attitude. They reflected, Hsieh argues, the historical influence of commercialization throughout the region and, in the more immediate sense, the effect of extensive Tongmeng Hui contacts. These were community-based forces, whose members ranged from cocoon farmers, silk filature workers, and porters to storekeepers, and even opera performers. And although they were stimulated by the Tongmeng Hui's revolutionary message in some degree, these organizations rested in most cases on "personal ties, secret society bonds, and religious sanctions." Hence the task of the revolutionaries was to penetrate the existing network, winning the confidence of local leaders and indoctrinating them with radical ideas.

lier, Sun's "ninth revolutionary attempt," centering on Canton, involved approximately one thousand soldiers, recruited mainly from the First Regiment stationed in that city and led by a former low-ranking army officer turned revolutionary.[53] The government had received ample evidence of an incipient revolt from its informers, but it could not be certain about precisely when or where the revolt would occur, or what its target would be. It could only seek to transfer or demobilize potential subversives and hope that the bulk of the troops (particularly their officers) would remain loyal.

As we indicated earlier, the situation within the Chinese military had become very complex. On the one hand, the drive to modernize the army had produced efforts at stricter discipline, a more arduous training program, and the weeding out of the unfit. These efforts, together with the accelerated attempts to transfer primary authority over the military to the central government, had aroused apprehension and resentment. On the other hand, modernization had not been sufficiently successful to eliminate the traditional grievances: inhumane treatment, inadequate living conditions, and pay in arrears. The financial straits in which the Beijing government found itself had resulted in pay reductions and inadequate resources for many military units, and morale was correspondingly affected. A rich soil thus existed in which revolutionaries could work. And revolutionaries committed to Sun and his program had been manufactured in increasing numbers in Japan, as we have seen. By this time, many were back in China, installed in various units as junior officers and thoroughly committed to the overthrow of the Qing. Not only the Tongmeng Hui but also the Guangfu Hui played a significant role in subverting elements of the New Army.[54]

A significant portion of the military, however, was not prepared to support a revolution. In the North the old Beiyang armies remained largely (but not wholly) immune to revolutionary influences. One reason lay in the fact that these units were generally better financed, and therefore had fewer grievances relating to pay and rations. Nor did the North have a strong anti-Manchu legacy to infect junior officers and men in the ranks. In the South, where revolutionary penetration had been much greater, some units could be counted within the revolutionary camp, and a larger number had been rendered unsafe from the government's standpoint. Yet, except in Hubei, the revolutionaries had not scored either the propaganda victories or the organizational gains required for them to count upon sustained, dedicated support from a significant number within the existing military forces. Nor had the building of new military units by the revolutionaries progressed beyond an embryonic stage. There were, to be sure, a sizable number of military men and units sufficiently impregnated with political doubts to jump on the radical bandwagon if success appeared imminent. The younger officers were especially vulnerable. But from a military standpoint, any revolution at this point was likely to prove premature—which was small consolation to a government ever more dependent upon military men from whom it was increasingly estranged.

Meanwhile, the most fervent revolutionary spirit, as we have seen, was to be found within the student-intellectual community, and it centered primarily on a new nationalism, a determination to end China's humiliations at the hands of foreign powers and to create a strong and prosperous nation, capable of holding its own in the struggle for survival. For those so committed, there was never an absence of burning issues. In 1909 a new student protest erupted over the Manchurian Convention, an agreement signed between the Chinese government and Japan which guaranteed continued Chinese sovereignty over Manchuria but granted Japan such a range of concessions as to make that guarantee of questionable meaning. In the unending struggle to retain China's vital northeast, first against Russian encroachment and then against Japanese advances, trends were once again adverse. Echoing the pattern set in the protest against American immigration policies in 1905, thousands of students in Shenyang participated in a boycott against Japanese goods, loudly denouncing the "weak and cowardly" officials who had sold out their nation to Tokyo. It was a portentous forerunner of the May Fourth Movement a decade later.

During this period also, opposition to foreign loans continued to bubble up. The reasons were varied. Some saw the loans as a means of perpetuating Manchu rule and rejected them for the same reason they opposed reform efforts. For others, foreign loans were certain to be misused by corrupt officials. But most opponents claimed that foreign loans were an instrument of imperialist control of China. On this issue a certain unity between the new nationalists and the old provincialists was possible because many provincialists saw foreign loans as a tool for extending centralized control at the expense of their own rights and privileges.

It would be wrong, however, to assume that the students were concerned only with Beijing's impotent responses to imperialist inroads. Many internal weaknesses provoked equally grave anxieties. Even the more moderate students now demanded sweeping reforms involving the civil service, state finances, and military affairs. Such demands, moreover, drew widespread support, especially in urban centers. Merchants, literati, and journalists often provided encouragement and assistance to student "patriots," some of whom came from prestigious families.

Students possess an idealism, a purity, and a daring (or a romanticism, a naiveté, and an impracticality) that in this instance blended well with Sun Yat-sen's own personality and methods. But students are usually catalysts, not principals, in the cause of revolution. They lack the permanence of identity or organization needed to hold firm to a revolutionary course, and few have the experience or the capacity to distinguish clearly between tactics and strategy. Student generations come and go rapidly, although some continuity can be provided by longtime "professional students" who merge with a portion of the wider intellectual community.*

Sun's movement, heavily laden as it was with student members, partook of their strengths and weaknesses. Perhaps it was perfectly natural that after repeated failures with organized violence, some of Sun's adherents—those deeply influenced by the accounts of the Russian nihilists—turned to assassination as a political tactic. It did not require elaborate organization, and it could hide military weakness. Through individual heroism, it seemed, the

* In *Counterrevolution and Revolt*, Herbert Marcuse idealizes the student-led New Left, projecting it as the actual or potential articulator of a global revolution. Accepting Rudi Dutschke's strategy of a student movement that expands its base by making a "long march through the institutions," Marcuse argues that students can establish and develop a society-wide network of counter-institutions that will be decisive in the "coming revolution" (pp. 54ff). From the vantage point of the 1980s, Marcuse's view of both the student role in revolution and the New Left reveals the hazards of interpreting contemporary events in cosmic terms, yielding in the process to a romantic optimism in line with one's ideological predispositions.

linchpins of the system could be removed; terrorism could substitute for the more difficult and elaborate tasks of mass mobilization and organization. Student assassins became increasingly active after 1904, and their efforts culminated in the abortive attempt by Wang Jingwei to strike down the prince regent in April 1910. Although most of their attempts failed, a few of them succeeded. Unquestionably, officials came to fear for their lives, and an atmosphere of tension was induced. Beyond that, it is hard to see what the assassination campaign accomplished. And it did take the lives of some of the most dedicated young revolutionaries.

While treating the students alternately as an annoyance and a menace, court circles were more concerned with opposition from the provincial gentry. This group had long been the backbone of the dynasty, furnishing its sons as scholar-officials and providing an all-important layer of private government between the official governance at the top and familial-clan rule at the bottom. The role of the gentry was indispensable to the traditional political system, and without gentry support no government could long survive. But by the end of 1910 the gentry in such important provinces as Hunan, Hubei, and Sichuan were creating a storm of protest.

The immediate cause of these gentry protests was the government's decision to undertake the ownership and construction of national railroads, but this was only one of many previous "encroachments" on the power and prerogatives of provincial elites. Around this central issue a broad coalition was being constructed in the provinces, with the gentry playing prominent roles. This coalition argued for "home rule" and "opposition to foreign imperialism," thereby seizing upon two critical issues that enabled the creation of a united front of "conservatives" and "radicals."

The emerging anti-Qing coalition was loosely knit and never operated as a single entity; it cut across all socioeconomic classes and all policy-ideological lines as well. It encompassed members of both the lower classes (through the secret societies) and the upper classes (through the disaffected gentry and the student-intellectual community). It included "conservatives" who were angry because the center was departing from historic patterns, and "progressives" who were convinced that the modernization and strengthening of China demanded new leadership.

Against this background, let us look more closely at the final months of the Qing era. As the year 1911 began, the Russians—following Japan's example in Manchuria—succeeded in obtaining substantial concessions in Xinjiang, China's westernmost province, including extraterritoriality and the right to acquire land and construct buildings.[55] Once again Beijing's officials had been forced to give ground, literally as well as figuratively, in the face of heavy pressure.

In this setting, the imperial edict of April 3, 1911, in which the prince regent appointed himself head of China's military forces, had little impact. Only seven days later, the plot to assassinate the regent was uncovered, and on April 27 another rebel attempt to capture Canton was launched.

After the collapse of the February 1910 uprising led by Ni Yingdian, the members of Sun's group had occupied themselves trying to raise money in Southeast Asia and the United States while planning for yet another military effort. There were divisions of opinion among them. Some thought it would be better to concentrate on wooing soldiers from existing governmental units, and others favored building a new revolutionary army. Huang Xing continued to believe that intensive support could be gained from provincial units and New Army forces. He argued that if a revolt broke out in one province, it would quickly spread to others, and sympathizers within the armed forces would combine with secret society supporters to push the revolutionary tide forward.[56]

There is no doubt that the revolutionaries had substantial support in Central China, including support in military circles. Their plans, however, still centered on the southern province of Guangdong, and beginning in early 1911 they undertook an organizational effort more complex than any they had tried before. Revolutionary units pledged to maximum secrecy were established throughout Canton. Weapons were brought in through Hong Kong from Japan and French Indochina. Stores were set up as fronts for revolutionary activities. An intensive propaganda and organizational campaign was aimed at the soldiers of certain units stationed in the area, and a hard-core unit of some 800 revolutionaries came into being.

The plan was to carry out a four-pronged assault on key government posts in Canton and to make a simultaneous effort to win over the police and military forces. The action had to be postponed in early April because an assassination attempt led the government to impose tight security measures; but on April 27, 1911, the attack got under way. Another debacle ensued. Only one of the four planned assaults was actually executed: Huang Xing personally led some 130 men in an attack on the governor-general's office. The expected massive defections of government military forces did not occur, and within less than twenty-four hours the rebels were routed. Eighty-six of them were killed, including a number of student returnees from Japan, and Huang Xing, wounded and discouraged, fled in disguise into the countryside. When auxiliaries arrived the next morning from Hong Kong, there was no rebellion for them to assist. Inadequate planning and organization, combined with an overoptimism about the capacity of the rebels to win over the soldiers, had led to another humiliating defeat.

In May, however, problems for the government became serious on another front. A consortium loan was finally obtained from British, French, German, and American financial syndicates to build railroads from Hankou to Canton and Sichuan, a project long cherished among Beijing officials. This ran directly counter to the plans of gentry in the regions concerned, who wanted to build their own railroads with domestically procured capital. Mass meetings were held, and strenuous protests were forwarded to the capital. Disturbances were particularly acute in Sichuan and Hubei.*

As we have noted, up to this point the revolutionaries had focused their attention on Guangxi and Guangdong, primarily because of geography and the historic anti-Qing sympathies of this region. Revolutionary organizations had been formed elsewhere, however, some of them with links to the Tongmeng Hui, some connected with the Guangfu Hui, and others relatively independent. In Hubei there were two such organizations in 1911,

*For a recent analysis of the controversy over the government's railway policies in Sichuan, and the effect of Sichuan unrest on the revolution, see Liu Tai, "The Railroad Storm in Sichuan: A Study of Its Intellectual Background and Development." Liu argues that the controversy went beyond the issue of railroad nationalization to symbolize the awakening of a Chinese national consciousness and desire for constitutionalism. As we have suggested, this is one of those instances where local self-interest and nationalism, together with a defense of constitutional procedures, could be made congruent.

the Common Advancement Society (Gongjin Hui) and the Literary Society (Wenxue Hui). The former had grown out of organizations affiliated with the Tongmeng Hui.[57] The latter also had evolved from earlier organizations, and was an indigenous group with a strong military flavor.[58]

THE FINAL ASSAULT

After the failure of the Canton uprising in April 1911, Sun's forces were dispersed and discouraged. Sun himself was once again in the United States in an effort to raise funds, having arrived in New York on January 19, 1911. Meanwhile, in mid-May, an amalgamation of the two Hubei revolutionary groups was arranged, and preliminary plans for an uprising were discussed. These plans were refined in September, and a tentative date of October 6 was set, to take advantage of the mid-autumn festival.[59] Jiang Yiwu, the president and cofounder of the Literary Society, and Sun Wu, a leading member of the Common Advancement Society, were appointed provisional commander in chief and provisional chief of staff of the revolutionary forces.

The rebels counted heavily on the Hubei New Army, which had been deeply infiltrated by revolutionary elements. Instructions were transmitted to trusted individuals in various units, and specific tasks were assigned. For example, the transport and supply corps and the engineers battalion were to give the opening signal for the uprising by setting their camps on fire. This was to be followed by the artillery battalion's seizure of the key forts, while the engineers battalion was to capture the ammunition depot. Concurrently, the infantry units were to attack the viceroy's headquarters. Other units were assigned such tasks as guarding the outer city, occupying strategic roads, and seizing the Hanyang arsenal.

With an ever-widening circle of conspirators involved, it was impossible to prevent word of the impending revolt from spreading, and rumors reached imperial authorities. The situation was further complicated by an incident involving the artillery unit that threatened to expose the conspirators. It was decided to postpone the uprising for three days, and there was still some uncertainty on the assigned day until the hands of the revolutionaries were forced. On the morning of October 9, an explosion occurred in the secret quarters of the revolutionaries where bombs were being assembled. Sun Wu and several others were injured. These quarters had been set up in Hankou's Russian settlement to provide some protection from government police. Russian authorities immediately seized incriminating documents, including a membership register, and arrested all rebels they could find. Both documents and prisoners were promptly turned over to Manchu authorities, and three of the revolutionaries were executed on the morning of October 10. With their plot exposed, the Wuhan rebels had no choice. Further delay was impossible.

Thus, on the evening of October 10, they set in motion their earlier plans. The first to act were members of the Eighth Engineers Battalion of the New Army, led by Xiong Bingkun. Xiong's soldiers captured the ammunition depot against little resistance and then opened one of the city's gates, enabling an artillery unit and other rebel forces to enter. Led by General Zhang Biao, the Manchu forces tried to establish a line of defense around the viceroy's office, using loyal troops from military headquarters, the viceroy's personal bodyguard, and such other units as could be assembled. But with strong artillery support, the revolutionaries broke through the Manchu lines. Viceroy Ruizheng and General Zhang were forced to flee to Hankou, and the demoralized imperial forces scattered. At this point, the revolutionaries numbered approximately 2,000, and were pitted against Wuchang government troops numbering about 8,000 at the time of the uprising. The government forces there had totaled some 16,000 earlier, but half of them had been shifted to Sichuan and other parts of Hubei.

On October 11 the revolutionaries captured Hanyang and its arsenal, and on the next day Hankou came under their control. Thus, two days after the revolution had started, the three cities that composed Wuhan and represented the vital center of Hubei province were in rebel hands. For the first time in a long series of uprisings, antimonarchical forces had scored an immediate success, and with success the revolutionary ranks were swelled by those prepared to join a cause that had a reasonable chance of victory. The initial gains, moreover, had been accomplished virtually without top leadership. None of the key Tongmeng Hui figures were present. Chen Qimei, the most important of the local comrades, had gone to Shanghai. His deputy, Sun Wu, had been wounded. Huang Xing did not arrive in Wuhan until October 28, in disguise, with the Red Cross Medical Corps. Among the members of the small group directing the uprising, few had had military experience.

It was thus understandable that the Wuhan rebels would seek a person of some rank to serve as temporary leader. The man selected was Li Yuanhong, a brigade commander of the New Army. Li, having had no previous connection with the rebels, was at first a reluctant recruit, but he was finally persuaded to head the revolution and issue a proclamation proclaiming Manchu rule at an end.*

By the time Huang Xing arrived, however, government forces had launched a counterattack. Revolutionary losses were heavy, and Hankou finally fell to the government on November 2. Nevertheless, Huang's earlier prediction was coming true. As the news of the revolution spread, uprisings occurred in other provinces. By the end of October five provinces had joined the revolutionary column, in most cases with little bloodshed. The first was Hunan, where junior officers of the New Army once again served as the spearhead of the revolt, and "liberation" occurred on October 22. This strengthened the Wuhan revolutionaries temporarily by removing the threat of a Manchu counterattack from the south, and by making possible the dispatch of Hunan revolutionaries to aid the Wuhan fighters. Shaanxi fell to New Army revolutionaries after three days of fighting. In Yunnan, Manchu troops of-

*According to one account, when members of the Wuhan revolutionary committee, having decided upon Li, went to his home on October 11 to offer him the leadership, Li—suspecting an attempt on his life—tried desperately to hide. He was discovered by the visitors to have taken refuge under his wife's bed, a protruding heel giving him away. He then came forth, protesting his innocence and pleading for mercy. To his surprise, the head of the revolutionary group, Zhang Zhengwu, was extremely polite and said that they would be greatly honored if he and his brigade would join their ranks. Li finally agreed to accept the post of commander of the revolutionary forces and immediately issued the proclamation announcing the overthrow of the Manchu government. See T'ang Leang-Li, *Inner History of the Chinese Revolution*, pp. 77–78.

34. *Li Yuanhong, circa 1911*

fered only token resistance. A revolt of portions of the New Army in Shanxi crushed the Manchu forces and killed the provincial governor. In Jiangxi the revolutionaries triumphed easily after sporadic fighting.

The other major battle of this period, outside Wuhan, took place over Nanjing, the provincial capital of Jiangsu province. Following the Wuchang uprising, Viceroy Zhang Renjun, General Zhang Xun, General Tieliang, and other Manchu authorities disarmed the local New Army forces and set up strong defenses around and within the city. Government forces consisted of some 2,000 Manchu troops plus fourteen Chinese battalions commanded by Zhang Xun. The revolutionaries awaited reinforcements, and a major battle began on November 9, the day after these had arrived. Initially, anti-Manchu forces were repulsed outside the city by Zhang Xun's troops, and suffered extensive losses. More revolutionary troops arrived from Shanghai, Zhejiang province, and other points, and a number of battles were fought. On one occasion, revolutionary units retreating in the fog mistook their own men for the enemy, and inflicted heavy casualties on each other. Nonetheless, military pressure on government troops mounted steadily, as more revolutionary recruits arrived and the rebels attempted desperate measures, including the enlistment of suicide groups to scale the city wall. Finally, after weeks of fighting and a heavy rebel bombardment of the city, the Manchu forces surrendered on December 2.

Revolutionary victory in Nanjing came just in time. The rebel counter-offensive to retake Hankou had failed, with heavy losses, and in late November Hanyang had to be evacuated. Now Wuchang was under imperial siege. There was a certain irony in this: the rebels were losing the critical military contests in the cradle of the armed uprising. But the erosion of governmental power, long under way, now accelerated throughout other parts of China, especially in the central and southern regions. In November and December, Guizhou, Jiangsu, Zhejiang, Guangxi, Anhui, Fujian, Guangdong, Sichuan, and Shandong provinces all came under revolutionary control. Only Shandong was later regained by the Beijing government.

In some provinces the mere presence of a force proclaiming its adherence to antimonarchical banners was sufficient to cause the imperial forces, both civil and military, to capitulate without a struggle. Almost everywhere, accommodation, not extensive bloodshed, was the order of the day. As we indicated earlier, although various imperial armies fought well and showed good discipline, the New Army proved to be honeycombed with anti-Qing elements. Numerous new adherents of greatly varying political backgrounds and perspectives, moreover, appeared as the old era staggered to its end. In times of great upheaval, opportunism has more influence on events than is generally acknowledged.

None of this, however, signified that the unification of China under a new order would be easy or even possible. The task of eliminating a feeble government had been undertaken by a very loose coalition of forces: ardent young nationalists enthused over the Western concepts of republicanism and democracy; secret society members steeped in Chinese tradition as well as in the doctrine of Han supremacy; "progressive" and not so "progressive" gentry, alternately disgusted with the ineptness of the central government and alarmed by its efforts to extend its power; provincial military commanders and their soldiers, anxious not to be found on the wrong side and with varying quotients of nationalist and reformist sentiment; the merchant community, still insecure about its political role, but giving some support to developmental, nationalist goals; and not least the overseas Chinese, who compensated for their physical absence by making generous financial contributions and widely disseminating propaganda favorable to the republican cause.

Merely to list these primary adherents is to signal the essential weakness

35. *Huang Xing, about the time of the 1911 Revolution*

36. Soldiers in the Hankou Revolutionary Army

of the revolutionary cause. A revolution had been proclaimed and partially consummated without firm leadership, without effective organization, and without any broad agreement on principles, even though the thrust of the movement might be defined as a quest for political and economic modernization, with the West and Japan as models. Indeed, the initial supporters of the revolution were soon at odds with each other. In Wuchang, Li Yuanhong and veteran Tongmeng Hui members shared a mutual distrust, and with good reason. In Hunan the young secret society leader Jiao Dafeng, who had seized revolutionary authority there, was assassinated. In many regions, supporters of constitutional monarchy remained strong and struggled with revolutionaries for control. And everywhere localism was strengthened in one form or another.

It has been cogently argued that the 1911 Revolution signaled the emergence of a new urban elite committed to Western "bourgeois" values.[60] To some extent this is true. In Shanghai, Canton, and even interior cities like Changsha, certain Westernized Chinese—student-intellectuals, journalists, "enlightened" members of the gentry, and some members of the merchant community—expressed commitments to republicanism and parliamentary democracy. Yet subsequent events were to demonstrate conclusively that this new urban elite was itself too weak and fragmented to direct the course of national politics. Most of the individuals who later played important political roles in the revolution entered the urban environment at some point and sought the support of merchants, gentry, and intellectuals; but their values and their political style remained firmly rooted in traditional rural culture. Indeed, given the nature of China's socioeconomic structure, the urban elites themselves partook of similar traits.

Did the events of 1911 constitute a political revolution? According to the definition advanced at the beginning of this chapter, they did. The insurgents consciously undertook actions that involved violence, were limited in time, and were specifically designed to replace the established political order with a new elite, a new ideology, and a new program. Despite the absence of consensus among them on policy goals, Sun and his followers were a revolutionary vanguard committed to establishing a new order. In terms of its results, however, the revolution was stillborn, as we shall make clear in later chapters. Thus, it was not only a watershed in Chinese history because it brought an end to the monarchical order; it was also a further episode in the downward slide of a nation clinging precariously to existence, an existence that soon could not be contained within a single political framework.

CURRENT ANALYSES OF THE 1911 REVOLUTION

Before presenting in detail our own interpretation of the Revolution of 1911, it may be useful to examine the prevailing views of other scholars, particularly those that are now in vogue. We may begin by exploring the recent studies of Marxist scholars writing in the People's Republic of China. Fortunately, this sample is a rich one, both because the Xinhai Revolution (as it is generally called by PRC writers) has been the object of intensive study in recent years, and because the papers of the 1981 Wuhan conference held to commemorate the seventieth anniversary of that Revolution have been available to us.

At the outset, one generalization is in order. With rare exceptions, PRC Marxist scholars define the Xinhai Revolution as a "bourgeois-democratic revolution" while acknowledging that the bourgeoisie as a class played a less than dominant role in leading it.[61] The Revolution is thus defined in terms of its *goals*, which were expressed primarily by the "progressive bourgeois and petit bourgeois forces" led by Sun Yat-sen.[62] Yet it is also admitted that even these forces came from diverse classes and differed considerably in their political views.[63] In concrete terms, as most scholars attest, the spearhead of the Revolution came from three groups, each with its own centrifugal tendencies: the New Army, the secret societies, and a sizable group of students and intellectuals, most of whom had recently returned from Japan. Supplementing these organized groups were portions of the gentry (whether mobilized under localist or nationalist banners), the merchant-commercial community, and the peasantry and working class, with these latter generally finding themselves in the ranks of the revolutionary armies.

These scholars also offer an explanation of how this "bourgeois revolution" could be attempted—indeed, how it *had* to be attempted—without the leadership of the true bourgeoisie. Even though capitalism had begun to develop in China, it was advancing slowly and unevenly, and the bourgeoisie were but a tiny group in the great rural sea of a "semicolonial, semifeudal society." In the provinces where capitalist enterprises had not developed beyond a rudimentary stage, a bourgeois class was only in the first stages of being formed out of elements drawn from the local gentry and officials, elements still largely under the sway of "feudal thought."* The most advanced members of the capitalist class were to be found in Shanghai, and this strongly Westernized city provided the staunchest bourgeois support for

*See Kong Li et al., "The Overseas Chinese," p. 4. These authors make a sharp contrast between the overseas Chinese, who were influenced both positively (through Western liberalism) and negatively (through racial discrimination) by their environment, and the indigenous bourgeoisie, the upper strata of whom came mostly from "big landlords, big merchants, compradores, and officials." For a different perspective, see Zhen Youqing, "The Overseas Chinese in the United States and National Revolution: 1894–1912."

the revolutionary cause.[64] Despite the contributions of merchants and entrepreneurs in a few other cities, sustained and coordinated bourgeois support on a national scale was never possible. Thus, in the opening stages of the Revolution, a process of fragmentation began, during which various cities and provinces came under the temporary control of different elites: some were led by New Army rebels, some by secret society leaders, some by officials who had timed their move to "independent" status effectively, with support from the local gentry and merchants.

In this analysis, the reasons for the failure of the Xinhai Revolution are easily ascertained. As a class, the bourgeoisie were too weak to execute their own revolution. In the most fundamental sense, they could not be completely true to the values that should have characterized them as a class. In their obsequiousness to officials, their craving for law and order at any cost, and their willingness to shun conflict even when their own interests were at stake, they betrayed the continuing influence of feudal attitudes, which made it impossible for them to fulfill their historic role of leading the movement for bourgeois democracy. The refusal of the great majority of the bourgeoisie to support the "second revolution" that took place in 1913, when the revolutionaries led by Sun and Huang Xing sought to challenge Yuan Shikai, is cited both as proof of the ultimate failure of the Xinhai Revolution and as the best evidence of the inadequacies of the Chinese bourgeoisie.[65]

Some Chinese Marxists, however, admitting more complexity into the issues of modern history, propose additional reasons for the debacle of 1911. Thus Wei and Wu write that although the New Army, with its ample representation of petit bourgeois intellectuals, peasants, and laborers, was receptive to revolutionary ideas and proved critical to the initial success of the Revolution, it was clearly not a military force built by revolutionaries.[66] Its overall command system was in the hands of Manchu military officers, and in the end it could not be transformed into a revolutionary instrument even in the South. Since the northern Beiyang Army remained an instrument of Yuan Shikai's power, the ensuing military-political stalemate was unavoidable.

As might be expected, given the future course of the Chinese revolution, an emphasis on the role of the rural classes, and of the peasants in particular, has been sustained among Chinese Marxist historians. The basis for peasant mobilization existed, they argue. The spontaneous "mass struggles" of the years prior to 1911, though not precisely conflicts of a class nature, had contributed to the weakening of the Manchu.[67] And the instrument for peasant mobilization existed in the form of the secret societies. These societies, writes Cai Shaoqing, echoing many colleagues, were composed mainly of impoverished peasants, handicraft workers, and vagrants (lumpen proletariat).[68] In ordinary times they served as mutual-aid societies and generally had anti-Manchu sympathies.

Sun Yat-sen himself had long recognized the critical importance of the secret societies and had worked closely with them. But when the Revolution finally came, after some initial cooperation, those representing the "bourgeoisie" turned against the secret societies, suppressed peasant uprisings, killed society leaders, and abandoned policies that would benefit the poor rural classes.[69] Thus, the argument goes, the revolutionaries of 1911 separated themselves from mass support.

One can discern in these analyses a theme that became prominent in critiques of a later period, namely, the necessity for a "managed bourgeois revolution." If the Chinese bourgeoisie had neither the strength nor the convictions necessary to conduct "their revolution" successfully, that task would have to fall to another class. Needless to say, that class—given the Marxian premises—was the proletariat, soon destined to serve as the vanguard of the revolution, and commissioned to complete the managed bourgeois revolution, having first achieved victory through successfully mobilizing the peasantry.

Despite the increasing efforts of many Chinese Marxist scholars to render their analyses richer, more flexible, and closer to reality, the limitations of a reductionist, Western-derived, class-structural mold remain formidable. The assumption, for example, that a Chinese "bourgeoisie," given its historic antecedents and current requirements, could or should hold Western liberal values is but one among numerous problems that arise when one seeks to apply Marxism in its orthodox form to the Chinese scene.

Before advancing our own critique of the Revolution of 1911 and its implications, it will be useful to discuss the recent work of a Western scholar, Theda Skocpol.[70] In her study, Skocpol has outlined a sweeping comparative analysis of the French, Russian, and Chinese revolutions. She makes it clear at the outset that her objective is not to present new data but to order existing data in a new manner. Thus, an assessment of her work must hinge first on an evaluation of how she has selected her data, and then, ultimately, on a critique of her methodological and theoretical premises.

As Skocpol notes, her primary intellectual debt is to Barrington Moore, and she has also been significantly influenced by Marx and Immanuel Wallerstein—although the "unilineal Marxism" and the economic reductionism of Wallerstein's theory of world capitalism are criticized. Max Weber is yet another stimulus to be discerned, especially in the sections dealing with state-building.

Using these mentors, Skocpol approaches her subject armed with several theses: peasant revolts are the crucial insurrectionary ingredient in virtually all successful social revolutions; class conflict is central to any revolution; the prevailing international environment is important as a challenge and a catalyst; and revolutionary outcomes can best be measured through a study of subsequent political institutionalization.

Our concern will be largely confined to Skocpol's analysis of China up to 1911, yet we have already suggested certain comparisons with Japan, Russia, and France which we consider critical to a broader understanding both of China and of modern revolutions, and we shall continue in that vein, comparing some of our conclusions with those offered by Skocpol.

Skocpol's initial thesis is that the traditional societies in France, Russia, and China were essentially similar, and that "in all three Old Regimes, political crises emerged because agrarian structures impinged upon autocratic and proto-bureaucratic state organizations in ways that blocked or fettered monarchical initiatives in coping with the escalating international military competition in a world undergoing uneven transformation by capitalism."[71] Tokugawa Japan was different, according to Skocpol, chiefly because it lacked a politically powerful and landed upper class.*

The degree of similarity and difference between the three traditional so-

* Skocpol, *States and Social Revolutions*, p. 101. Skocpol's argument is that the men who led the Restoration were samurai whose access to power came from the independent resources of the outer *han* (fiefs) of Choshu and Satsuma, but since they were not landlords or closely tied to them, "nothing prevented these men from pursuing national salvation for Japan through programs of political centralization" (p. 102).

cieties under study—and more important, the implications of both similarity and difference—are clearly debatable. Certain broad structural similarities among these societies did of course exist—indeed, they existed among almost all traditional societies. But the differences, many of them of a nonstructural character, were of major consequence in determining the timing, the causes, the leadership, and the results of the various stages of the Chinese revolution, a revolution which differed from the Russian revolution in greater degree than is often appreciated, and differed from the French revolution in kind. Skocpol is correct in stressing the critical importance of the external variable—the regional and global context at any given time in relation to the internal environment. But she concentrates on the external threat—economic and political aggression on the part of capitalist-imperialist powers—and minimizes the equally important influence of positive external stimuli, as they were perceived by indigenous intellectuals seeking alternatives to the status quo.

Her assertion that "the agrarian structure" blocked Chinese monarchy's attempts to undertake domestic reforms or meet foreign challenges is not very helpful in delineating either the basic obstacles to evolutionary change or the fundamental causes of the revolution that lay ahead. As we have indicated at length, the fundamental difficulties were psychological, political, and economic. The psychological difficulty was the immense Sinocentrism imbedded in Chinese thought and culture, which affected all elites. The chief political difficulties lay in the unique degree to which members of the intelligentsia were bound to the traditional state; the absence of a countervailing political force in the form of a competitive institution like the Western church; and the problem of finding among existing Western models a workable substitute for the mix of centralized-decentralized, public-private governance that characterized the traditional order. The chief economic difficulties were posed by the high level of productivity accomplished under the traditional system of intensive agriculture, sustaining population increases in periods of protracted peace.

When one adds to these factors the highly significant problem of a Manchu monarchy that could not provide a nationalist symbolism, the overarching difficulties flowing from China's scale (both in area and in population), and the lateness at which the intellectual-official class finally came to realize that changes were essential, one has encompassed most of the underlying forces critical to an understanding of the initial revolutionary sequence through which modern China passed. Although Skocpol acknowledges some of these factors in passing, they cannot be adequately incorporated into a class-structural analysis that rests on the centrality of peasant revolt.

Our analysis of the Meiji Restoration and of the essential differences between China and Japan in the nineteenth century has been presented elsewhere. These differences did not hinge on the absence of a politically powerful landed class in Tokugawa Japan. At the time of the Meiji Restoration, whatever the inroads of wealthy commoners, most of the land was still controlled by members of the military class, even though they did not till the soil themselves, as was also the case for many of the Chinese gentry. By the adroit use of a pension system, the upper strata were divested of their feudal power, and yet, with some exceptions, interest in landownership among the ex-military classes remained intense, as the events of the early Meiji era demonstrate.

It must be remembered that the Tokugawa bequeathed a legacy of *cen-*

tralized feudalism. And the rebels, in their initial efforts to preserve that legacy and oust the barbarian, chose to rally around the imperial banner. This was a political decision, born of the circumstances of Japanese history, and it had far-reaching consequences for future developments. When some of the original leaders and supporters of the Restoration found that their movement was changing course, they rebelled on behalf of localism or "liberty," just as many of the Chinese gentry did prior to 1911. By this time, however, the chief leaders in Tokyo saw things very differently than they had when they first sought power as outer *han* rebels. The course their decisions began to follow cannot be explained simply as a result of the relationship between the political elite and landownership. The keys to their decision-making process were experience in office, an understanding of the real alternatives confronting them, and certain factors that differentiated Japan from China—such as scale, political structure, and a long heritage of cultural borrowing.

Skocpol characterizes the Revolution of 1911 as an "upper-class" revolt against the Qing. Correctly, she does not call it either a bourgeois revolution or a peasant revolt; in her analysis, peasant revolt, though a possibility from the Taiping onward, was to unfold only after 1911. Once again, however, a class analysis is less than satisfactory. The Revolution of 1911 was both more and less than an "upper-class" revolt. In class terms, the anti-Qing movement encompassed a diversity of classes and a diversity of issues. At the same time, it was also reflected in deep cleavages within all classes, most notably within the traditional elites. Indeed, cleavages *within* classes constituted a more important contribution to the 1911 Revolution than cleavages *between* classes.

One revealing result of class-structural analysis is that all events become inevitable after the fact. Thus Skocpol frequently indicates that what happened in France, Russia, and China could not have happened otherwise. There is little room for the element of accident, chance, or human decision. Yet in the course of real history, including revolutions, these elements are often of vital consequence. Indeed, one of the great challenges for the historian or the social scientist is to determine the point at which leadership decisions can make a telling difference, and to calculate the significance of accident or chance. At what point and under what circumstances does a revolution become possible, likely, highly probable, inevitable? And at what point and under what circumstances does the probability, the likelihood, or even the possibility recede?

AN INTERPRETATION

At the beginning of this chapter we advanced the thesis that social revolution is always a process, within which political revolution may or may not be a part; and that the Revolution of 1911, though it was at first more negative than positive in its consequences, was one stage in China's ongoing social revolution.

Revolution in any form has a complex gestation period and a subsequent time of maturation during which its genetic links remain clearly discernible while the opportunities for ever-more complex development progressively increase.[72] At many points, a revolution can be aborted, either by errors on the part of those promoting it or by the strengthening of the forces that seek to uphold the status quo or to sustain a slower, evolutionary pace of change.

It is also possible (or likely) that the revolutionary objectives do not lie within the capacities of the target society, at least in its current stage of development, or that the socioeconomic and political structures chosen to achieve revolutionary goals cannot serve that purpose. At various strategically important junctures, moreover, some entirely unforeseen event or accident may occur which shifts the entire course of events, even if the revolution continues to move forward. Finally, external intervention may thwart or assist the revolution.

In seeking to identify a rising revolutionary atmosphere we may look for both negative and positive signs. Among the negative signs we would list five that are particularly salient. First, acceptable procedural means of handling grievances are breaking down; the political, economic, and social institutions that have hitherto diffused conflict and provided a basis for cohesion are faltering. Second, significant groups within the society are questioning and abandoning the value system or ideological underpinnings that have previously given the state legitimacy. Third, there is growing indifference to, or outright rejection of, the leadership that personalizes authority—the monarch, the dictator, the president, or the oligarchy. Fourth, growing fissures begin to appear within the elites whose support is critically important to the prevailing order, so that the existing political structure becomes increasingly vulnerable to attack from "within" as well as from "without." Fifth, the divisions within two of the elite groups—the military-police-security forces, which are critical to the coercive arm of the state, and the intellectual community, which is vital to its propaganda-ideological arm—are especially noticeable.

Naturally, these negative occurrences are influenced by stimuli that are both internal and external to a given state or society. In the economic realm, for example, the most dangerous situation for a government often comes when a downturn follows a period of broadly diffused and sustained development, because this triggers a sense of relative deprivation or frustrated expectations. (This is a turn of events at least as likely to influence the elites, especially their lower but upwardly mobile portions, as the "masses.") In the political realm, the emergence of an attractive new model, acquired through external contacts, can provide new ideological and institutional possibilities, thereby destroying the inhibitions that spring from the feeling that however deplorable the current circumstances, no acceptable alternative exists. Indeed, a genuine revolution must always have external stimuli.

What are the positive signs of a revolutionary situation? Certainly, leadership is one variable. It may seem the pursuit of a will-o'-the-wisp to seek generalizations broad enough to cover all types of serious revolutionary leaders, since culture-specific, time-specific, and event-specific elements are often critical. Yet it is clear that some traits are shared by most revolutionary leaders. Among them are intensity and tenacity of purpose, an apparently unquenchable optimism, and the capacity to attract and hold followers with qualities usually summed up in the word "charisma"—a hold on others that partakes of an emotional, magnetic appeal going beyond rationality or intellectualism. This by no means exhausts the traits generally associated with revolutionary leaders, nor does it even touch on the idiosyncratic features that have distinguished certain individuals. It may be sufficient, however, to suggest that in analyzing revolution one cannot deal with impersonal forces alone, be they ideological or structural. Leadership can make a critical difference; and that remains true even though every leader is in some degree a "product of the times," and even though there can be periods when the advent of "great" leaders is virtually foreclosed.

Organization is another significant variable. Revolutions have rarely succeeded without long and tedious organizational efforts; these usually involve attention to both coercive and persuasive instruments, though in certain settings they have involved building primarily on common kinship, language, and geographical region. Nothing is more misguided than to believe that revolutionary organizations grow solely from the efforts of fervently committed, intellectually persuaded "true believers."[73] The "true believers" constitute an indispensable hard core, but there must be a much larger and far more diffuse soft core, bound to the movement for a great variety of reasons that range from personal loyalty to opportunism to entrapment. Indeed, even among the hard core, these motivating factors are by no means absent. The soft core, moreover, must extend outward and render a sizable segment of the society politically neutral or passive, thereby denying its support to those in power. Revolution, like all forms of politics, is coalition politics, and a revolution succeeds by constructing a coalition more powerful (though not necessarily larger) than the coalition opposing it; this coalition will almost certainly include important segments of the old elites as well as a diversity of other forces, many of whom consider themselves deprived or oppressed.

None of this is to deny a vital role for program and ideology, yet another critical variable. Leaders and groups who have not yet achieved power—and therefore are not burdened by a record of compromise and failure as well as success—have the greatest opportunity to make their appeal in terms of new policies and pure values. To pledge an end to old abuses—ineptness, corruption, lethargy—and provide a new sense of purpose, together with new institutions that will forward goals such as wealth and political participation for all, can engender support from many groups, and especially from the younger generation, whose idealism has not yet been eroded by experience.

Armed with effective leadership, careful organizational efforts, and an appealing set of principles, a revolutionary movement has its maximum potential. Nevertheless, if those in power clearly perceive the revolutionary challenge, and if they have the capacity to take effective countermeasures, either singly or with help from external forces, they may defeat even a revolutionary movement that has substantial assets.

There are other possibilities, of course. One is that a relatively feeble revolutionary effort will triumph in the immediate sense over a still more feeble government, but is stillborn, engendering either a rapid postrevolutionary retreat, prolonged chaos, or some form of new stasis.

In any case, at its climax a political revolution generally follows a predictable pattern. First, the key organs of power—the military, the police, and the executive organs of the government—are seized and reordered, giving the new leadership as close to a monopoly of power as it can achieve. Opponents or potential opponents are coerced into silence; the consequent waste of human talent, which is sometimes very great, is accepted in order to implant the new order firmly and to prevent a counterrevolution. Yet even in the most radical revolutions, a portion of the old elite has already accommodated to the new order (some of its members having played leadership roles in the revolution) or has proved willing to accommodate, thereby creating a link, rather than a complete break, between the old and the new.

Next, policies that are roughly in accordance with revolutionary pledges are enacted. Some of these will be drastically changed or even abandoned at an early stage. Others will become the foundation for the new institutions that can eventually preside over the social revolution—if it comes. With or without a political revolution, however, a social revolution may proceed, through a combination of at least three general forces. One is economic transformation. Another is indoctrination and education, stemming from both internal and external sources being consciously directed by the state and also springing "naturally" from the life experiences of the populace in their rapidly changing environment. A third is the restraints and opportunities presented by the new political system, according to its capacities for resisting or adjusting to social change.

If we apply these generalizations selectively to the Chinese Revolution of 1911, factoring into our analysis the meaningful idiosyncratic elements, we may draw several conclusions. To begin with, it is not useful to equate the 1911 Revolution with the eighteenth- and nineteenth-century revolutions in the United States and Europe, which have, with varying degrees of accuracy, been called "bourgeois revolutions." In China, some individuals from the merchant-manufacturing communities in Shanghai and other cities did participate in coalitions that demanded resistance to foreign imperialism, domestic political reform, and new approaches to social problems; but as a class the merchants and industrialists were far too weak, and for the most part too apolitical, to play a significant role in the events of this era. With some exceptions (mostly after substantial revolutionary successes), they did not even contribute their money to the effort; as we have seen, funds for the cause came primarily from overseas Chinese communities. One could argue that bourgeois values were more prominently represented in the overseas communities than among China's indigenous merchants, but it would be more accurate to say that even in the overseas setting, traditional guild and family-clan ties combined with secret society, anti-Manchu commitments to produce a political climate and set of values at least as traditional as modern.

It would be correct, however, to say that the increasing influence of Westernism, often filtered through the Japanese experience, was serving to move key elements of Chinese society toward an acceptance of liberal institutions and values *without* providing the means for quickly laying their socioeconomic foundations. In an age of growing international communications, it had become possible for a society to borrow political values and institutions that did not necessarily bear any close relation to its own socioeconomic or political conditions, nor the same relationship between values and classes as had prevailed in other societies at other times. It would be wrong, for example, to assume that the Chinese (or Japanese) "bourgeoisie"—*as a class*—in these years believed in or propagated liberalism.

These facts suggest the dilemma China was to face in the decades ahead. Curiously enough, by the end of the first decade of the twentieth century, the throne, the reformers, and the revolutionaries were agreed on at least one point: China had to move rapidly to effect constitutionalism, parliamentarism, and broadening political participation, and to modernize and industrialize the nation's economy through science and technology. These three political elites, to be sure, differed substantially not only on pragmatic questions of degree and timing but also in terms of motives and values. For the throne an acceptance of the cardinal aspects of political liberalism and economic modernization was a strategy for survival, one forced upon it, and with the process moving progressively away from its control. For the reformers—ranging from Yuan Shikai to the Kang-Liang group—it was a means of preserving much that was of value in Chinese culture, and above all of defending the integrity of the Chinese nation and people against foreign inroads. For the revolutionaries it was the beginning of a process of returning China to the Chinese and of bringing a weak, decadent nation abreast of the modern world through contact with it. In theory, these different motives and values might have been reconciled sufficiently to provide workable political coalitions, as occurred in Japan. There were potential bridges between the throne and the reformers, between the reformers and the revolutionaries, and in a pragmatic sense, even between the throne and the revolutionaries.

But no such coalition was constructed. Here, for several reasons, the key was unquestionably the throne. First, given its foreign origin, the Manchu monarchy could not easily be used on behalf of the burgeoning nationalist movement, in sharp contrast to the situation that had prevailed in Japan and in much of Western Europe. Second, the throne's long-term involvement in national politics denied it the shield that had been available to the Japanese monarchy during its political transition toward becoming a national symbol. A third significant factor was the decline of the throne in authority and effectiveness; an infant monarch and an incompetent regent could not suffice. Beyond this, events testified to the decline of the entire governing class under the chaotic events and changing recruitment patterns of the final years of the Qing era. Commanding imperial figures existed only in memory. Lower officials, unsure of the intention behind commands from the central government, baffled by its alternation between toughness and capitulation, and deeply divided among themselves on the proper course of action, gradually ceased to be an effective or cohesive force. Many traditional scholar-officials were outraged by the modernist denigration of their education and their skills. But among the new recruits to officialdom who were called upon to exhibit "modern" knowledge, the mood was at least equally rebellious. One indispensable prop of the monarchy, and of political stability in general, was thus gravely weakened.

The problems of the monarchy and the official class cannot be adequately understood without a summary of the situation of the rural classes, upon whose support monarchical authority ultimately rested. Perhaps the most important linkage here was with the gentry. As we have seen, the Chinese political system had hinged upon a delicate balance between allegiance to the center and the limitations accepted by the center on the reach and scope of its power. Indeed, the carefully preserved dualism between public and private government in the middle and lower rungs of the political structure comes close to defining the essence of the traditional system. And the class that made this dualism work was the gentry. From the gentry class came the bulk of scholar-officials who were the bearers of public authority. But prominent members of the gentry who were not public officials used their provincial and local prestige to exercise an authority over rural society which was just as strong, or stronger; they could act outside the formal political structure in far more intimate and effective ways than were possible for their official counterparts, who were limited in both their tenure and their knowledge of the region.

Events in the years before 1911 conspired to weaken the solidarity of the gentry and, more important, to strain their relations with the center. As we have indicated, the more traditional portion of this class, whether as scholar-officials or as private authorities, deeply resented "the headlong plunge" toward reform that was unfolding. They deplored the "spineless" character of the Beijing leadership and some of its regional representatives. But above all, they saw in many of the reforms a movement toward greater centralization, a shift of the balance in favor of public government. In increasing numbers, they rallied around the banners of provincialism, sometimes employing such modern slogans as "self-rule," thereby partly aligning themselves with the modernist revolutionaries.

There were other such links, as we have seen. A number of student revolutionaries bred in Japan and elsewhere came from gentry families. Sometimes, child was set against parent. In such cases political allegiance followed educational experience, not class lines. Indeed, many of the principal leaders of Sun's revolutionary movement had family antecedents that tied them to the official and the gentry classes.

What was the role of the massive peasant population, whom the monarchy had historically regarded as "our children, our wards"? If the Revolution of 1911 was not a bourgeois revolution, neither did it stem from peasant rebellion. It is true, of course, that peasant disturbances were widespread in the years immediately before 1911. But it is impossible to establish whether, as the *North China Herald* alleged, economic conditions were in fact much worse in the 1910–1911 period than they had been for many years, taking China as a whole. The available data point to a series of climatic disasters, but that was not rare. It is also possible that in the absence of large-scale wars or famines for some years previously, population was pressing more acutely upon production. Yet most peasants who suffered extreme misery either migrated to cities, where they were lost to any rural political movement, or withdrew into themselves and their families, living and dying in great silence. A survey of the three years immediately preceding October 1911 shows that most food riots or other spontaneous uprisings took place in towns and cities, not in rural areas.

This is not to say that the peasants were unavailable for political mobilization; it was merely that they had not been mobilized. The Taiping and Boxer Rebellions proved that it was possible to recruit peasants in large numbers for political movements. But how, in the years before 1911, could this be done? What were the most promising appeals? As the Taipings and the Boxers demonstrated, the peasant could be mobilized either for or against a prevailing dynasty. However, the prevalence of the secret societies, especially in South China, suggested that a form of nationalism which combined an overt appeal to ethnicity with antiforeignism had the greatest potential. No other appeal could cut across the complex class lines and network of personal loyalties (and antagonisms) that crisscrossed rural China. It fitted into the mixture of superstition and shrewdness, emotionalism and rationality that governed peasant attitudes and actions. The effectiveness of other appeals was more questionable. Peasants had a fairly clear concept of their economic rights. If these were violated by unscrupulous individuals, they might go to great lengths to seek justice or retribution. But to mobilize them against a given class or economic system would be difficult indeed, as the Communists were later to discover. Certainly it was not a promising prospect in 1911.

Peasant interests lay essentially in economic survival and, beyond that, in improvements in livelihood, measured in food, clothing, and shelter—but not at the sacrifice of the extravagances connected with weddings and other traditional ceremonies. Peasants had a strong sense of their own rights—their right of access to land and to compensation for their labor in the ways sanctioned by custom—but they also acknowledged the rights of landowners, provided these were exercised in accordance with traditional rules. In another realm, peasant interests lay in being left alone, and all intrusions—whether from government, the soldiery, immigrants, or foreigners—were resented. Outsiders of any stripe generally meant trouble.

To these basic concerns were added several others. There was a respect for elders and for the village teacher, even though formal education was considered an unattainable luxury by most. There was a deep commitment to family and clan, and also to native place—and these communal attachments were largely uncontaminated by "selfish individualism"; individual initiatives were generally justified as being exercised on behalf of one's larger social unit. There were also commitments to tending the graves of one's ancestors, to propagating children (ideally, several boys) in order to secure one's future, to expecting justice and rendering loyalty, and in general to living by the rules of hierarchy and generational propriety. These commitments formed a way of life that had flourished for centuries, and those who undertook to challenge it faced a formidable task, particularly if they were "outsiders."

Thus, when peasants rebelled during this period, one of two motivations was invariably present. Some immediate issue of survival or justice was usually central, but sometimes—especially when the secret societies were involved—broader social or political concerns existed, and these could be directed against the foreigner or against the Qing. Even when this broader influence was felt, however, it was difficult to develop the type of organization and communications that would enable an aggregation of peasant rebels to be fashioned into a regional or national movement able to sustain itself over an extended period of time. In general, the peasant was drawn into rebellion to protect his society, not to change it. He had to be taught that the socioeconomic order under which he and his ancestors had lived was evil and deserved to be uprooted. It was not a conclusion to which he was naturally drawn. And in this era, teachers with such a message were rare indeed. As we have noted, even the most revolutionary members of Sun's entourage held no such view. For them "socialism"—however they might define it—was a prophylactic to prevent Western-born social diseases, not a cure for existing Chinese ills. As in Russia, the seeming passivity and conservatism of the peasantry would break the spirit of many revolutionaries before a final mobilization occurred.

There was another side to this picture, however. When individuals, families, or villages in rural China reached a point of desperation, there remained an alternative to migration, death, or rebellion: they could enter the society of the lawless. In periods of great rural distress the numbers of marginal men expanded rapidly, and whole districts were infested with banditry, hijacking, smuggling, and various forms of "antisocial" activity. Into such areas the arm of government seldom reached. Although these regions were not necessarily havens for revolutionaries, their existence indicated the fragility, even the disintegration, of the prevailing political order.

In sum, the peasant was still available for mobilization on behalf of traditional values, but the monarchy clearly had not been able to mobilize him, except in a very limited way through the provincial armed forces. And under the prevailing conditions, peasant passivity or lawlessness offered no advantages for the authorities in Beijing.

The monarchy stood in greater jeopardy in another respect. China's new and partially modernized armed forces—intended to be the means of the nation's defense against all enemies, foreign and domestic—were developing into an instrument for the overthrow of the dynasty. New Army officers, particularly those who had received training in Japan, had been exposed to a variety of "subversive" thoughts. At least a few of them were won over by the nationalist appeals of Sun and Huang. Many others were privately disgusted with the inefficiency, confusion, and corruption that characterized military management. It is ironic that in the end the throne had to call upon the more traditional provincial forces to quell revolts among New Army units, and finally, in extremis, to recall Yuan Shikai, a man whom most court officials neither liked nor trusted, but a man who now held the balance of power between the revolutionaries and the monarchy.

Yuan's crucial role during this period symbolizes the linkage between the past and the future, for this man from Henan was both the most powerful man in the China of 1911 and an individual deeply committed to change. Although he was blamed by some—and possibly with reason—as the man who betrayed the reformers of 1898, he continued to be both a loyalist and a believer in far-reaching reforms until he was driven from office. He understood the importance of change quite as much as did Kang and Liang, men whom he privately respected and with whom he would again work. Yet Yuan did not want to see the monarchy swept away, because, like many others, he doubted that republicanism could survive in China. His dilemma, and that of men like Liang, was that despite all they could do, the monarchical cause became untenable. At that point, they could only seek to adjust to a new political order without abandoning too many of their principles. Yuan's role in these climactic years must be seen in this light.

In summary, the events of 1911 can best be understood as representing the final stage in the collapse of the Qing dynasty, when its foundations finally gave way after decades of erosion. Almost all of the negative signs foretelling revolution, which we outlined earlier, were present. Institutions were no longer operating effectively, and morale within officialdom was at a low ebb. Confusion over values had mounted; Confucianism was under increasing attack, and Han nationalism was taking precedence over traditional loyalties. The support of the intellectual class, especially its younger elements, had been largely lost. Indeed, all of the old elites were divided by doubt and dissension, and the fissures were becoming ever wider, even within the gentry. And finally, the ranks of the military had been infiltrated by revolutionaries, creating a situation so dangerous that the central government allowed a single individual—Yuan Shikai—to assume a pivotal role despite the fact that his relations with the current leadership had been less than cordial.

On the other hand, when one turns to the positive signs associated with successful revolutions, the picture is considerably different. Whatever Sun's qualities as a revolutionary leader—and there can be no doubt that he had charisma, tenacity, and optimism—he was less than adequate in several critical ways. His organizational capacities, in both the military and the political spheres, were deficient, and he did not seem able to gather around him and hold men capable of remedying these defects. As a result, the military arm of the movement was weak, coordination between the various groups that made up the potential revolutionary coalition was extremely limited, and virtually no "mass base" existed.

Beyond this, the movement's revolutionary ideology and program were vague, even in Sun's mind. The strongest cement was a simple anti-Manchu rallying cry, but this could not be expected to carry the revolution very far into the future. The student-intellectual commitment to national wealth and power through economic and political modernization, though understandable and rational, required the sort of concrete policies that had been laboriously constructed in the aftermath of the Meiji Restoration in Japan. But even as the 1911 Revolution got under way, there were signs that the strength, unity, and societal conditions necessary to fashion and advance such a program were not available.

In sum, the coalition of forces that had gradually emerged to undermine Manchu rule had a most limited potential for effective, coordinated governance after the Qing collapse. Agreement in matters of leadership, values, or policies was lacking, and given the extraordinary diversity of the forces in revolt, it could not easily be built.

With the Revolution of 1911, China reached a watershed in its history—the collapse of an institutional-ideological edifice which had endured longer than any polity ever created by man. In this sense, the events of 1911 moved China more surely toward the great social revolution that would ebb and flow over succeeding decades for the rest of the century. On all other counts, as we shall see, the Revolution failed, and in its failure propelled Chinese society into a period of mounting chaos. Yet events were to demonstrate that any restoration of old institutions would be exceedingly difficult, whatever the shortcomings and failures of the new order.

7

REPUBLICANISM —A TROUBLED BEGINNING

IN THE MONTHS that followed the uprising of October 1911, Sun Yat-sen optimistically hailed it as having achieved two of the three major goals of the Tongmeng Hui, namely, the triumph of Han nationalism and the establishment of a republican government. Only the people's livelihood, he said, remained to be secured. But Sun's optimism soon faded, and even at the time he was making these statements, they scarcely did justice to the facts. In truth, almost every issue that had arisen in the final decades of Qing rule, including the central issue of monarchism versus republicanism, remained unsolved after the 1911 Revolution. Indeed, the crisis intensified. Previously established trends of a divisive, disintegrative nature gathered momentum, and solutions proved at least as elusive as in the past.

THE TORTUOUS STEPS TOWARD A REPUBLIC

The months that followed the Wuhan uprising appeared to demonstrate conclusively that neither the revolutionaries nor the Manchu government could win a decisive, permanent military victory that encompassed the whole of China. Within less than three weeks after their Wuhan victory, the revolutionaries there were put on the military defensive and forced to give ground. In two of the three biggest battles of the Revolution, the imperial forces were the winners. The victory at Nanjing only partially balanced the scales. In contrast to the hastily gathered, poorly trained, ill-equipped revolutionary units, the government forces were professionals with superior arms, and many of their units demonstrated a willingness to fight for the dynastic cause.

By the beginning of December, shortly before the opening of negotiations between the rebels and the Beijing government now headed by Yuan Shikai, Wuchang—the last foothold within the original revolutionary center—was besieged and in chaos. Yuan was later to complain that the northern armies could have provided the coup de grâce to the revolutionary forces had he not been persuaded to enter negotiations. This may have been true, but Yuan also knew that military victories, whether in the Wuhan area or elsewhere, would not suffice to quell the revolutionary movement, which was now spreading like wildfire over Central and South China. Even as imperial troops were administering defeats to the Wuhan revolutionaries, Shanghai joined Nanjing as a "liberated" city, and by early December some fifteen provinces had declared their independence. If Beijing pursued the military route, there would not be enough fingers to catch the revolutionary fleas. In the meantime, the danger of foreign intervention would steadily mount, and a long-term separation of the border regions from China would become ever more likely.

Yet the position of the revolutionaries was equally difficult. In addition to their military liabilities, which made a military conquest of the North impossible for some time to come, new successes produced growing political divisions. Beginning with one center of power, Wuhan, the revolutionaries shortly acquired several: Canton, Shanghai, and Nanjing. Each center tended to develop its independent military force, administration, and leadership; and in the absence of Sun Yat-sen, the most likely unifier of this period, each tended to go its separate way. Li Yuanhong, having assumed leadership in Wuhan, the first site of the revolution, naturally acquired a certain preeminence, and on November 9 he sent a telegram to various provinces, requesting that delegates be sent to Wuchang to establish a provisional national government.[1] By this time, however, provinces to the east of Hubei, as well as Shanghai, had come under revolutionary control, and from this area a movement was mounted to convene a meeting of provincial delegates in Shanghai, where Chen Qimei, a close associate of Sun Yat-sen, was serving as military governor. An organizational meeting was held there in mid-November, and a Provincial Representative Council was established; but a number of the delegates agreed to recognize the Hubei military government as the central government of the Republic, and proceeded to Wuchang. Li had prevailed over the Shanghai group on this occasion.

When the delegates reached the Hubei capital in late November, however, they found the military situation extremely precarious. Hanyang had fallen, and Wuchang was jeopardized. They were forced to meet in the British Concession in Hankou, under the very shadow of imperial troops. The assembled group adopted a General Plan for the Organization of the Provisional Government on December 3. Its chief provisions were the creation of a Council of State composed of three delegates from the military government of each revolutionary province to serve as a legislative body, and the election of a provisional president by this body. As one of its final acts, the assembled group agreed to meet in Nanjing, designated as the new seat of government, and to elect a president as soon as representatives of ten provinces had gathered.

Meanwhile, however, the Shanghai group had been taking certain independent actions. After Huang Xing arrived in Shanghai (having left Wuhan earlier), the three military governors of Shanghai, Jiangsu, and Zhejiang—meeting with certain delegates who had remained in the city—decreed that Huang should be made commander in chief of the military forces and given responsibility for organizing a provisional government, with Li Yuanhong as vice-commander and military governor of Hubei. By this time, however, a military truce had relieved the pressure on the Wuhan area, and Li was prepared to challenge the Shanghai decision. By mid-December delegates from fourteen provinces had gathered in Nanjing, and the question of temporary leadership became a highly divisive issue. Looming over the meeting were two absent figures, Yuan Shikai and Sun Yat-sen. It was significant that at

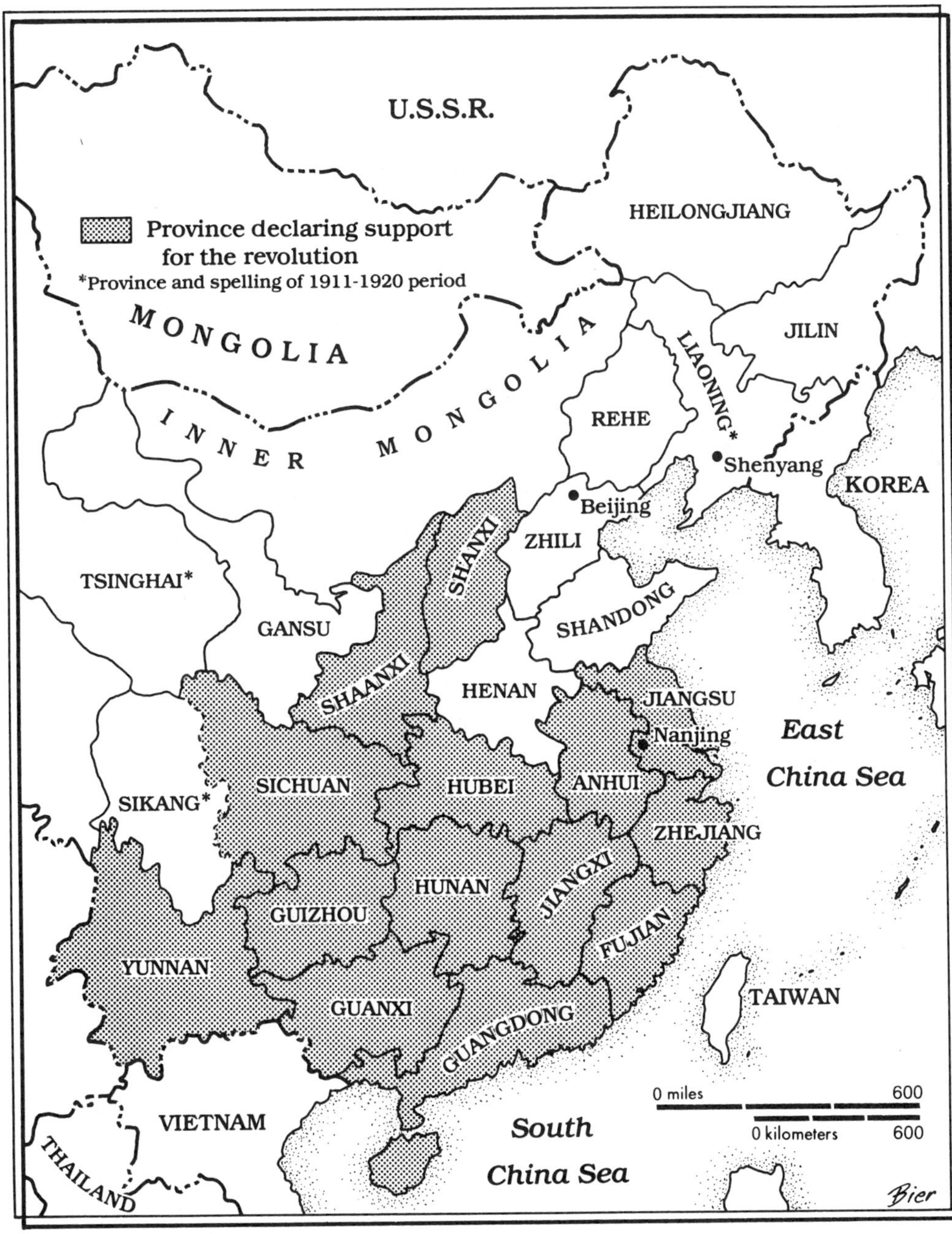

MAP 1. *China, 1911: Distribution of Revolutionary Support*

the Hankou meeting a resolution had been approved that if Yuan would support the Republic, he should be elected president. Rumors circulated in Nanjing that Yuan was prepared to take this step, which caused temporary hesitation. Sun, meanwhile, was still en route home. On November 16 he had cabled to his compatriots from Paris that Li should be elected president at this time, but that the position should later be tendered to Yuan, assuming his support for the republican cause. Already, Sun was concerned with the need for quick stabilization so that a major industrial development program could be launched.[2]

37. *Sun's arrival in Hong Kong, December 1911. His group and those welcoming him, left to right, front row: Homer Lea, Yamada Junsaburo, Hu Hanmin, Sun, three unknowns, Liao Zhongkai (2d standing), unknown; back row: Miyazaki Tōten (bearded, directly behind Sun), others unknown.*

From the outset, the revolutionaries realized that Yuan was indispensable if unity and peace were to be achieved. The essential requirement, however, was that he abandon the Qing and support the Republic, and there were persistent doubts about his willingness to take such a course. It was equally clear that the candidacy of Li Yuanhong was drawing at best a tepid response from various revolutionaries. Li was a newcomer to the cause, and there were many questions to be asked about his allegiance and his abilities. The Nanjing gathering initially reaffirmed the Shanghai decision to make Huang Xing the military commander in chief with power to serve as acting provisional president; but divisions over the issue were sharp, and when Huang declined, Li was chosen, with Huang as vice-commander. Li attempted to compromise further by designating Huang to act in his behalf, but Huang refused to accept any position under Li. Only the arrival of Sun salvaged the situation.

On November 24 Sun had sailed from Marseilles on a British mail steamer bound for Shanghai via Penang, Singapore, and Hong Kong. With him was an American, "General" Homer Lea. En route, Sun sent a telegram asking Miyazaki, who was already in China, to meet him in Hong Kong; and other Japanese associates, some of them with military experience, also joined his entourage when he arrived there. When Sun reached Shanghai on December 25, his party consisted of himself, Mr. and Mrs. Homer Lea, six Japanese, and ten Chinese.[3]

In an interview at this point, Lea identified himself as chief of the general staff of the Republican Army, a claim confirmed by Sun. Lea, a hunchback only five feet three inches tall, acknowledged that he had had no official connection with the American army, although he claimed that his military writings had been used at both West Point and Annapolis. His title, he explained, derived from the fact that he had been the commander of four divisions organized in South China eleven years earlier to "rescue the emperor Guangxu," and that later he had served as commander of Chinese troops in America. These roles have been well concealed from history, and it is likely that the *New York Times* obituary provides a more accurate background.[4] Lea reportedly joined the allied forces marching to the relief of the legations in Beijing during the Boxer uprising. Later, he helped organize the Young China Association in San Francisco and came into contact with Kang Youwei, whom he later accompanied to Europe. When Sun first visited the United States, he was supposedly impressed with Lea, and at some point after returning from Europe with Kang in 1905, Lea evidently switched his primary allegiance to Sun.[5]

In addition to his American chief of staff, Sun brought with him as his principal secretary, responsible for his appointments, a Japanese. This bizarre situation suggests Sun's tenuous ties to the great body of his fellow countrymen, his generous yet often undiscriminating relationships, and his perpetual carelessness about vital organizational matters. It was not the first time he had established intimate ties with individuals of dubious credentials or worth—nor would it be the last.*

On December 21, after his ship reached Hong Kong, Sun met with George E. Anderson, the American consul general, under arrangements made by Lea. This meeting produced a telegram, which Sun helped to draft and which he authorized to be sent to the U.S. State Department, outlining his plans.[6] It said that upon arriving in Shanghai, Sun would organize a unified provisional government with himself as president, and with a cabinet and provincial governors appointed by him. Lea, as chief of staff, would be authorized to negotiate with representatives of the Manchu government, and on the central issue at stake there would be no compromise: the Qing dynasty had to relinquish all power, but generous terms for their retirement would be granted. If necessary, Sun suggested, his government would request the president of the United States to mediate with the Manchu, although it could not authorize deviation from its central principles. Meanwhile, Sun would select the best possible administrators, drawing from sources independent of present officialdom. The provisional government would be of a military nature, but as soon as conditions permitted, a permanent government would be established in the form of a strongly centralized republican system based on a modified American model. Finally, eminent American jurists would be recruited to assist in framing the constitution.

*In an interview with Lea printed in the Chinese republican organ, *Minli bao*, on December 29, 1911, p. 4, no mention is made of any military role for Lea in the revolutionary movement. Subsequent *Minli bao* references to Lea, moreover, were brief and of little consequence, suggesting either that he was not regarded as a figure of great importance in Chinese circles or that there was no desire to feature his activities before Chinese readers. On December 31, *Minli bao* did print samples of the personal handwriting of both Sun and Lea (identified as "of the American Freedom Party"). Interestingly, Sun as well as Lea contributed his phrase in English, not Chinese, Sun writing, "'Unity' is our watchword"; Lea: "United we stand, divided we fall" (p. 1).

In his private conversation with Anderson, Sun amplified some of these themes. Regarding the revolutionary movement and his own leadership, he exuded confidence, claiming to have the same authority in the Yangtze valley and the revolutionary portions of the North as he had in South China. He acknowledged that because the revolution had begun about six months prematurely, some military units had not yet joined the cause, but he implied that the revolution was now a fait accompli. He denied that Wu Tingfang, who was currently negotiating on behalf of the revolutionaries with Tang Shaoyi, Yuan's representative in Shanghai, was authorized to represent the revolutionary movement. Wu and certain other leaders, he said, had cast their lot with the revolution only after its success had become reasonably certain. Among the jurists whom he hoped to recruit for service in drafting the constitution, Sun mentioned Philander Knox (then secretary of state) and Elihu Root. On the question of the Manchu, Sun was as adamant in private as he was in public: the revolutionaries would never cease to struggle for overthrow of the dynasty, and if funds for an effective military campaign were not available, they would carry on through guerrilla warfare.*

One of Sun's most trusted lieutenants, Hu Hanmin, has provided an analysis of the situation which provides an important supplement to Anderson's account.[7] According to Hu, the southern revolutionary group (which he describes as the "left wing") had earlier failed in their effort to persuade Sun to go from Hong Kong directly to Canton in order to build an army there that could achieve the rapid military unification of China. They feared that unless he did this, he would become the head of a powerless provisional government; Yuan's military control of the North would become stronger, and the division between Wuhan and Shanghai would grow. But Sun disagreed, arguing that his presence in Shanghai and Nanjing was critical to the unity of the revolutionary cause. With his customary optimism, he insisted that although the enemy might have military strength, he had

*Anderson's interview with Sun is recorded in *NAMP/RDSRIAC*, 893.00/1016, December 22, 1911, in a dispatch entitled "Dr. Sun Yat Sen and the Chinese Revolution," report of George E. Anderson, Consul General, Hong Kong. Anderson added his own penetrating analysis of the current political situation. The Chinese surrounding Dr. Sun, he wrote, are principally of the student class, "with little of the practical administrator about them." Hence, their interest in obtaining the services of good administrators was genuine, and while Anderson found the "dreamer" factor in the movement substantial, he also felt that a capacity existed to come to grips with problems in a concrete, practical manner.

Regarding the course of the revolution, Anderson reported that various cities and districts were coming over to the revolutionary standard one by one, sometimes as a result of the activities of the revolutionary army, but more often because local officials had decided to accommodate to the prevailing currents, and serve under revolutionary banners pending some final settlement. The weakening of the authority of provincial governments had resulted in various types of disorder in many regions, but "rural China has never been free from such troubles," Anderson noted.

Potentially troublesome was the fact that local leaders from such cities as Amoy (Xiamen) and Swatow (Shantou) resented the Cantonese domination of the revolutionary movement, and this was one reason why Sun was determined to appoint new officials diverse in background. Meanwhile, the revolutionaries also faced serious military problems. In the initial period, they had purchased arms and ammunition from any available source. Thus, when ammunition of a specific type ran out, the guns requiring that variety became useless. This had caused a delay of the movement of the Canton troops north, he wrote, and the willingness of the revolutionists to participate in the Shanghai peace discussions appeared to relate more to their lack of ammunition than to any desire to deal with the Manchu government. No compromises on their basic demands would be forthcoming, he predicted.

the support of the people. Guangdong and the South would not suffice; it was crucial to make Central China secure for the republican cause immediately. Finally, although Yuan Shikai was not to be trusted, he was more valuable than 100,000 men in the struggle to overthrow the Manchu, and it was therefore critically important to seek his cooperation.

After Sun's arrival in Shanghai, a meeting was held to discuss whether the Republic should adopt a presidential or a parliamentary form of government. Almost all of Sun's leading supporters were present, including Hu Hanmin, Wang Jingwei, Huang Xing, Chen Qimei, Song Jiaoren, Zhu Zheng, and Zhang Jingjiang. Sun favored a presidential system, but Song Jiaoren, presumably fearful of how Yuan might manipulate such a system, finally persuaded him to approve the cabinet system, and Huang Xing was tentatively chosen to head the first cabinet as premier. However, Song was later unable to persuade the Nanjing Provisional Parliament to revise the original General Plan, and so the presidential system was retained.

On December 29 Sun was elected provisional president by the delegates assembled in Nanjing. He received sixteen of the seventeen votes cast (each province being allowed one vote), and the election was then made unanimous. Sun wanted the oath of office to be administered in Nanjing just before midnight on December 31, so that the Republic of China would begin its existence on January 1, 1912. Arriving by special train from Shanghai, he rode to the old viceroy's yamen in a carriage, past countless revolutionary flags dampened by a cold drizzle. Hundreds of thousands of spectators, standing silently in the light rain, had waited for hours to catch a glimpse of the new president, a slender, dark figure dressed in a simple khaki suit of military cut, without any decorations. Only a few actually saw him, and the oath of office was taken in front of about a hundred specially selected guests, after which the chairman of the provincial delegates handed Sun the official seal of "the provisional military government of the United Provinces of China."[8]

Sun's oath of office contained an unusual commitment: the new president promised that when "the despotic government" operating from Beijing was overthrown, and when order prevailed in the nation, and the Republic had been recognized by the major powers, he would resign. The door remained open for Yuan Shikai.

In an omen of things to come, Sun immediately had difficulties with the Nanjing Provisional Assembly over appointments. Li Yuanhong was handled by making him vice-president, a largely ceremonial post; Huang Xing was given the key position of minister of war, and assigned the task of serving as liaison between the president and the Assembly. Agreement, however, stopped there. Sun at first proposed a mixture of former Qing officials and Tongmeng Hui members for cabinet posts, but the assemblymen rejected two of the Tongmeng Hui appointees, Song Jiaoren and Zhang Binglin—Song presumably because he had earlier sought to revise the General Plan. At that point, Sun delegated his power to select a cabinet to Huang Xing, who nominated Tongmeng Hui members to only three positions—army, foreign affairs, and education. As it turned out, however, none of the former Qing officials appointed to the other posts assumed office, and Tongmeng Hui vice-ministers served in their place.

In essence, the new Republic was a government of the South—and more precisely, of the Southeast. Sun's initial cabinet was composed mostly of men from Guangdong, Zhejiang, and Jiangsu. A majority favored a strongly centralized system rather than expanded local autonomy—an issue that would long divide political leaders. And yet in a military sense, China was already effectively divided, with the boundary running roughly along the Yangtze River. There were some "independent" provinces in the North, and some pockets of revolutionary authority there, but Yuan Shikai was the dominant figure in this region, and his intentions were a puzzle to foreign observers and Chinese alike. When the throne recalled Yuan, it was an act of desperation, and Yuan had used his strategic position to exact the concessions he felt essential to effective governance. Upon assuming the premiership in mid-November, therefore, he had as much authority as any official could hold in the North. Yet the problems confronting him were monumental. Northern military victories in the vicinity of Wuhan were offset by the fall of such key centers as Yantai, Amoy, and Swatow. Imperial forces were in deep trouble in Sichuan, and the peripheries of empire were rumbling with discontent.

In various areas Chinese were venting their hatred of the Manchu in bloody massacres, wiping out whole Manchu communities, down to the last man, woman, and child. These massacres were particularly savage in areas where the secret societies had played a major role in revolutionary activities. From Xianfu, Shaanxi, where the involvement of the Gelao Hui was substantial, a Catholic priest reported that "human life is not worth a chicken." Residents of the Manchu sector, he asserted, had been shot, cut to pieces, and burned alive, and there were only some women survivors from a population of 20,000 to 30,000. "Even after a month, every Manchurian man discovered is beheaded. I have seen it with my own eyes," he wrote.[9]

Reports of massacres or threats against Han by Manchu were also prevalent, especially in the period immediately after the October uprising.[10] At all times, it should be stressed, the official revolutionary position was that the Chinese nation was composed of five races or peoples—Han, Manchu, Mongolian, Tibetan, and Mohammedan—and that each should enjoy equal rights, with the aim being the unification of all races. Even the revolutionary forces in Wuhan, however, were brutal in their annihilation of the Manchu garrison when Wuchang was first captured. In retaliation, imperial troops engaged in an indiscriminate slaughter of Chinese civilians when Hankou was retaken. These events, widely reported throughout China, prompted the American chargé d'affaires in Beijing, E. T. Williams, to write, "The issue has now become more clearly defined; it is Chinese against Manchu." Williams also reported that the intensified hatred on both sides had produced panic in Beijing, so that at least a hundred thousand people had fled the capital, the Manchu fearing Chinese assailants and the Chinese fearing Manchu assassins.[11]

In this connection, it is interesting to note that a telegram from the American legation in Beijing to Washington dated November 10, 1911, revealed that the court had inquired whether the empress dowager and the emperor could seek asylum in the legation. Chargé d'affaires Williams strongly urged that asylum be granted, and Secretary Knox responded by saying that since it was in accordance with the uniform policy of the United States government to allow temporary refuge when that was necessary in order to preserve innocent human life, asylum should be granted—"assuming you and your colleagues believe that such action would not unnecessarily and greatly endanger the safety of the Legation quarters."[12] No request was made.

In most cities, order was being maintained or restored, whether the aegis was republican, imperial, or "independent." Almost everywhere, however, provincial authority had been weakened, and large political no-man's-lands appeared, particularly in the hinterland, where law and order had long depended on the type of private governance supplied by the gentry. Not surprisingly, the trends toward lawlessness and disorder that emerged in the final years of the Qing now accelerated in many parts of rural China.*

In the North, as premier of an exceedingly shaky government, Yuan's most immediate problem was that of finances. When he assumed office, the treasury held only four million taels, and if he did not pay his troops they would revolt or disband. Yet the capacity of the imperial government to collect taxes from provincial authorities was virtually nil, and the entire taxation system was in disarray. The new republican government faced the same problem. To whom could either party turn except foreign sources? We shall return to this complication later.

Meanwhile, the central issue could not be avoided: Was it possible to preserve monarchism in some form, or should Yuan ride the prevailing tides and place himself at the head of a republican structure, as many were urging? Despite his sometimes stormy relations with the Qing court, Yuan was by background and temperament a monarchist. More important, he had the gravest doubts that a republican political system would work in the China he knew. In this he was by no means alone; his doubts were shared by many Chinese and almost the whole of the foreign community. Yuan and like-minded individuals would have been happiest if a means could be found to preserve the monarchy, whether by encasing the child emperor within a changed regency and political system, or by jettisoning the Qing in favor of a new Chinese monarchy. And if a new monarchy were to be installed, who would be a more appropriate emperor than Yuan himself? Such thoughts

*An account of conditions in Canton and vicinity during this period by the resident American consul general is revealing. The city and its immediate neighborhood are normal, reported Bergholtz, but robbers are pillaging the outlying districts where revolutionary authority has not yet been established. In some instances, he continued, everyone is free to conduct his own affairs, and local officials have been chosen who refuse to vacate their offices in favor of functionaries sent out from Canton.

In Canton itself, order is in the hands of several groups, he wrote. The revolutionaries, in their haste to acquire a sizable military force, had enrolled some 35,000 "ex-brigands," under the leadership of "seven pirate chiefs," with each of the latter assigned a certain section of the city to patrol. Meanwhile, Manchu soldiers and Bannermen, numbering some 8,000, were still keeping order in the old city. But "numerous bands of brigands, pirates, or robbers, whichever you prefer to call them, fully armed, are entering the new city, which is outside the walls, wearing the uniform of volunteers and pretending to be members of the New Army." When troops are sent to dislodge them, miniature battles occur. "I am glad to say," he continued, "that these pseudo-soldiers, when captured, are promptly beheaded" (*NAMP/RDSRIAC*, 893.00/954, Bergholtz, American Consul General, Canton, to the Secretary of State, December 15, 1911, "Conditions at Canton").

For contemporary accounts of the situation in other cities, many providing explicit details regarding the relative independence of various revolutionary units, the complex factional struggles taking place at the local level, and problems of rural disorder, furthered by famine conditions in some regions, see the consular dispatches contained in vol. 5, NAMP/RDSRIAC.

did not await the events of 1915 and 1916; they were present even in the months immediately after the uprising of October 1911.*

However logical such a position was from the standpoint of the fundamental realities governing China (which would return to monarchical practices repeatedly over the years, even during the Communist era), there were countervailing short-term realities to be faced. The drive toward modernity, now manifested so powerfully in student circles, interacted with traditional anti-Manchu sentiments to create a formidable coalition, one that a feeble regime could not hope to counter.

Under these conditions, negotiations between the revolutionaries and the Beijing government got under way in mid-December of 1911, abetted by the British, who agreed to serve as intermediaries. A short-term military truce in the Wuhan region had been in effect since December 3 and was subsequently renewed. Tang Shaoyi, Yuan's emissary and a close friend since his days in Korea, arrived in Hankou on December 11. Li Yuanhong had wanted the negotiations to take place there, but Wu Tingfang, accepted by Li as a revolutionary spokesman, insisted that he would not leave Shanghai, and Li relented. Once again, the cleavage between the Wuhan and the Shanghai revolutionaries was revealed.

Both parties had special interests in seeking a political settlement at this point. As we noted, the revolutionaries had good military reasons for wanting an immediate cessation of hostilities, particularly in the Wuhan region.** Their principal hope for the negotiations, however, was that Yuan could be pried away from the Manchu—and away from Beijing. Yuan, for his part, was aware of the revolutionaries' strength in the South, but he believed—and not without reason—that factionalism would soon drive deep wedges between them, wedges that could be exploited in due time.[13]

The Shanghai negotiations were made more complex because neither of the chief negotiators could be certain of support from the forces he purported to represent. As we have noted, Sun had privately criticized Wu while he was en route to Shanghai, and at one point had designated Lea as

*See, for example, an article in the *North China Daily News*, February 1, 1912, entitled "The Outlook in China—Some Factors and a Forecast," included in *NAMP/RDSRIAC*, vol. 7, 893.00/1152. This article, signed by "Sinophilus," suggesting a foreign author, contained the following prediction: As soon as any sort of abdication decree is issued, the generals and other leaders in this area will probably declare Yuan Shikai emperor, and a wave of enthusiasm will run through the North, with troops fighting to establish him on the throne. While Sinophilus's prediction did not prove to be wholly accurate, on balance it was a prescient forecast and one that found company in other writings of this period.

Certain revolutionaries, of course, had been bitterly anti-Yuan from the earliest period of the postrevolutionary era. See, for example, an editorial in *Minli bao* dated November 18, 1911, p. 1, in which the new republic was urged to see Yuan for what he truly was, "a robber, the people's enemy and a Manchu slave." Yuan, the writer continued, was determined to destroy the revolutionary party, arresting its members and using his Northern Army to crush the Hankou uprising.

**The attraction of negotiations to those in military difficulties is understandable, as is the reluctance of those who possess the military momentum. Yuan's lament that he forsook the military route at a time when success was imminent was to be echoed later by Chiang Kai-shek in recounting American pressure on him to enter into negotiations with the Communists in the period immediately following World War II. Chiang was to insist that he could have prevented Communist expansion in this period had he not been hobbled by a cease-fire which the Communists violated. Since history cannot be replayed, the validity of this assertion can never be known. In both Yuan's and Chiang's cases, however, complex political liabilities on the domestic front, of which the two men were well aware, must be calculated.

38. *Wu Tingfang, about the time of the* 1911 *Revolution*

39. *Sun at the time he accepted the provisional presidency of the Republic, January 1912*

his negotiator with the Manchu government. This role never materialized, and about a month after Sun's inauguration Lea suffered a stroke in his Nanjing residence; he returned to the United States as soon as he was able to travel, and he died in Ocean Park, California, on November 1, 1912. Wu thus continued to represent the Nanjing government in the ongoing negotiations, and Sun became sufficiently reconciled to Wu to name him minister of justice. Yet as we shall see, Sun continued to take certain initiatives on his own. On the other side, Tang Shaoyi had greater difficulties. At an early point he had argued that republicanism would have to be accepted, and according to various accounts he sought to persuade Yuan to accept the inevitable and assume the office of the presidency. Yet down to the point of formal agreement, Yuan took pains to indicate to Americans and others that he was disappointed in Tang and could not accept a republic.[14] Indeed, Tang felt obliged to resign at the end of December, unable to cope any longer with his leader's procrastination. Whether Yuan was dissembling or adhering to conviction was a matter of strenuous debate. There could be no doubt, however, that his maneuverings served to maintain order in the North and at the same time make him the one man who was indispensable for a government of national unity.

Meanwhile, the agreements hammered out between Tang, representing the North, and Wu, speaking for the South, seemed promising. On December 29, the very day on which Sun was being elected provisional president in Nanjing, three points were accepted by the two negotiators. First, a national conference or convention was to decide by majority vote on the future form of government for China. Second, before the convention, the Qing government was not to draw on existing foreign loans or arrange new ones. And third, beginning the next day, December 30, all imperial troops were to withdraw 100 *li* from their positions, and republican forces were not to advance or occupy the areas thus evacuated, leaving control there to local police and thereby permitting a military disengagement.[15] The following day, at a fourth meeting, certain rules with respect to representation at the proposed convention were agreed upon.

However, with Yuan sufficiently mercurial in his views to bring his pro-republican representative to despair, and with both sides strongly suspicious of each other, more than six weeks of intricate moves and countermoves followed before a new political order was decreed. The creation of the Republic in Nanjing caused Yuan to angrily denounce the revolutionaries for having violated earlier agreements.[16] Inasmuch as Sun in his oath of office had pledged the eradication of the Manchu government, was he not foreclosing any role for a national convention? Wu Tingfang's response was artful: the Nanjing government was a provisional one, and the republicans had not demanded a dissolution of the Beijing government. Was not Yuan still making official appointments? Clearly, a unified governmental structure remained to be determined.*

A growing number of revolutionaries were now openly expressing the strongest suspicions about Yuan. Why was he delaying, in the face of the inevitable? Was he not seeking to divide and conquer the republicans, and to

*Yuan insisted that Wu come to Beijing to complete the negotiations regarding the time and place of the proposed national conventions, promising to guarantee his personal security. Wu in turn urged Yuan to come personally to Shanghai to undertake the final negotiations. *Minli bao*, January 7, 1912, p. 2.

further his own ambitions under some monarchical system? Members of the "radical" faction of the Tongmeng Hui—which was led by men like Hu Hanmin and had its greatest strength in Guangdong—subscribed to this view. They put increasing pressure on Sun to give up hopes of using Yuan and to mount an expedition to liberate the North by force. The Shanghai group, led by men like Song Jiaoren, adopted a more moderate position, urging further negotiations and strenuous efforts to win Yuan over, and for the time being they carried the day with the new president.

Meanwhile, despite mutual distrust and rising tension between himself and the revolutionaries, Yuan continued to maneuver the court toward abdication. A preliminary step had been taken in early December, when the prince regent was caused to resign, with Shixu and Xu Shichang replacing him as guardians to the boy emperor. The edict effecting this change, issued in the name of the empress dowager, poignantly revealed the low estate to which the royal family had fallen. It read in part: "We have dwelt in the depths of the Palace and have not been cognizant of important events, but since the commencement of trouble at Wuchang and Hankou, there have been outcries from all the provinces and calamities from military operations, and sores and ulcers have everywhere met the eye. . . . All of you, my people, should comprehend that the throne is not selfishly conserving the powers of the sovereign, but is unreservedly changing all things for the people."[17]

A much more difficult step was executed in conjunction with the December agreement when the empress dowager was caused to issue an imperial edict accepting the convocation of a national convention that would decide between constitutional monarchy and a republican system.* In effect, the fate of the dynasty was now sealed. And despite the fracas over the Nanjing Republic (and clear signals that negotiations over a national convention would break down), by mid-January Yuan had designed a formula for imperial abdication which was acceptable to most Manchu notables (and contained safeguards for his own position). It had two essential provisions. First, the emperor would turn over all powers to Yuan, thereby enabling him to negotiate with Nanjing authorities concerning China's future government. Second, satisfactory arrangements would be made for the security and livelihood of the royal family and other high Manchu dignitaries.[18]

When the republicans heard of this, however, many of them took violent exception to the first proposal. After various discussions, Sun sent a message to Yuan insisting that the Manchu must abdicate unconditionally, surrendering all sovereign power and rights; that no Manchu could participate in the provisional government of China; that the provisional capital should not be in Beijing; and that Yuan could not participate in the Republican Provi-

* For the text, see *Xuantong zhengji* 16:42:6a–6b. This imperial edict, issued December 28, 1911, was preceded by a memorial to the throne from the cabinet urging the throne to take this step and indicating the seriousness of the situation. The edict itself read in part: "We consider the problems of the adoption of a constitutional monarchy or a republic to have an important bearing upon our foreign and domestic affairs. Such a question should be resolved neither by a section of the populace nor by the throne alone. . . . There ought to be a special National Convention to which the question shall be turned over for a decision. The cabinet is ordered to telegraph this proposition to Tang Shaoyi who is to make known the same to representatives of the People's Army. . . . Heaven hears what the people hear and sees what they see. We wish and sincerely hope that our patriotic soldiers and subjects will mutually act in accordance with the principles of justice and conjointly seek the public weal."

sional Government until the major foreign powers had recognized it as the successor to the Beijing regime, and until peace prevailed.[19] Yuan responded angrily, and a rapid exchange of messages followed. Sun justified his position by saying that Yuan wanted to dissolve both the Manchu and the Republican governments, and intended to form a provisional government of his own in Beijing. Who knows whether such a government would be Republican or a constitutional monarchy, he asked, and even if it should declare itself republican, who would protect it? An assassination attempt on Yuan's life at this point, initiated by a Shanghai radical, did nothing to relieve the tension.

In the end, however, Yuan's tactics prevailed. On February 12, 1912, the final act in the drama of the Qing demise was played out. The court was caused to grant Yuan plenipotentiary powers to organize a provisional republican government and to confer with "the Republican Army" as to the methods of union.* It is noteworthy that the edict did not specifically mention abdication, although it spoke of the emperor's being able to live in retirement, and that it did not grant any form of recognition to the Republic in Nanjing. China still possessed two distinct political organizations, and in the exercise of the powers conferred upon him, Yuan immediately directed the ministers of his former cabinet to retain their portfolios for the time being.

Yet Sun took a conciliatory position at this point. Overriding radical opposition, he urged the Nanjing Assembly to elect Yuan provisional president in his place, subject to three conditions: the seat of the provisional government was to be fixed at Nanjing; Yuan was to be inaugurated there before Sun's official resignation; and the fundamental law governing the provisional government was to be maintained, thereby ensuring adherence to republicanism. On February 15 the Assembly elected Yuan, and Sun sent him a telegram of congratulations.**

The site of the capital for the Republic was a matter of great consequence to the revolutionaries. For them, Beijing had become a synonym for stupefaction, and the walls of the Forbidden City a symbol of closed, oppressive rule that could never be obliterated. Those who came under Beijing's spell, many sincerely believed, could never rid themselves of past practices and habits of thought. Nanjing was well located geographically, being approximately midway between North and South China. Accessibility to it could

*The edict is contained in *Xuantong zhengji* 16:43:32a–32b. To the end, imperial edicts retained the strong Confucian note of solicitude for the public welfare, rendering this document one of pathos. Since no settlement or peace has been reached, noted the edict, and there is evidence that in their hearts a majority of the people favor a republican form of government, "How could we then bear to oppose the will of the millions for the glory of one family." The final sentences read: "We and His Majesty the Emperor, thus enabled to live in retirement free from responsibilities and cares and passing the time in ease and comfort, shall enjoy without interruption the courteous treatment of the Nation and see with our own eyes the consummation of an illustrious government. Is not this highly admirable?"

**Yuan's messages to Nanjing during this period were most conciliatory. On February 12 he sent a telegram, the opening sentences of which read: "That the Republican form of government is the best is admitted by all the world. At one bound, the goal at which you gentlemen have been aiming by years of thoughtful labour, namely the transformation of the Imperial Government, has now been reached. This augurs blessings and happiness for the people also" (*North China Herald*, February 17, 1912, p. 442). For the text of Sun's telegram to Yuan, see *Guofu quanji* 4:182–186. In the brief message, Sun included these sentences: "A good man has been elected. My respectful congratulations and regards."

be achieved by water or by rail, yet it was far enough inland to appeal to the millions who regarded China's coastal cities as half-foreign. At the same time, it was close to China's great port and industrial city, Shanghai.

Yuan, on the other hand, had his reasons for being reluctant to move the seat of government. He was reported to feel that a movement to the South would further threaten the status of Mongolia and Manchuria as parts of China, and the situation in both of these regions was indeed precarious, as we shall soon see. Moreover, North China itself was by no means wholly reconciled to "the southern rebellion," as many called it, and Yuan's departure might trigger various revolts. But beneath these arguments undoubtedly lay another consideration of paramount importance: Yuan was naturally loathe to move from his area of historic strength and influence into "enemy territory," a region where the indigenous military forces owed no allegiance to him. Indeed, as he well knew, it was partly for this reason that republican leaders insisted he come to Nanjing: it would be a clear sign, they said, that his commitment to republicanism was firm.

Once again Yuan carried the day. The Nanjing government dispatched a small delegation to Beijing to bring Yuan the official greetings of the Assembly and to escort him south. The delegation had barely arrived in the northern capital, however, when rioting broke out there among soldiers of the Third Division and rapidly spread to other places, including Tianjin. Various causes for this outbreak were advanced. Some blamed it on the fact that in the North, as in the South, many soldiers were recent recruits, and their officers were unable to control them. Others blamed it on rumors that under the Republic there would be no place for imperial soliders, who would soon be disbanded and sent home without pay. Unquestionably, Yuan was regarded as a traitor to the imperial cause by many conservative northerners, Manchu and Chinese alike. Yet it seemed strange that the riots originated with the Third Division, because that unit had been brought to Beijing by Yuan as his special bodyguard, and it was commanded by Cao Kun, one of Yuan's most trusted associates.[20] Many revolutionaries, in fact, were convinced that Yuan had engineered or at least connived in the riots; but Sun stood by the president-elect, issuing a public statement that he had every confidence in Yuan's integrity and that the Nanjing government would assist him in restoring order by sending troops to the North. Yuan telegraphed his appreciation, but indicated that southern troops would only worsen the situation by encouraging the venting of sectional animosities.

All efforts to move Yuan were abandoned, and on March 7, after an accommodation had been reached, a telegram was sent to Yuan in the name of the National Assembly at Nanjing acknowledging that it was necessary for him to be inaugurated without delay. Yuan was asked to wire his oath of office to the Assembly, after which that body would notify the nation. He was then to place his nominees for the premiership and cabinet before the Assembly for confirmation; when these persons were confirmed, they would assume their duties in Nanjing, and Sun would retire from office.[21]

YUAN AND SUN: A STUDY IN CONTRASTS

In the stormy months that had followed October, Sun and Yuan, two men of radically different types, had greatly influenced the national political scene, despite the extensive fragmentation taking place. Contemporary estimates of them, both Chinese and foreign, varied greatly.

Yuan, now chunky and worn beyond his years by high living, was widely regarded as China's strong man. Few believed that he could be ignored in any political solution, though some radicals were prepared to seek his elimination by force. His assets were substantial. Both intelligent and shrewd (and these are not the same), what he lacked in breadth of schooling and experience in international affairs he made up for with his intimate knowledge of the Chinese scene. For decades Yuan had operated successfully in the incredibly complex labyrinth of Chinese politics. As with all successful politicians, luck played its part in Yuan's survival, but there can be no doubt that he was a powerful manipulator of men. He had a remarkable talent for taking the measure of both allies and opponents and then using their strengths and weaknesses to his advantage. What some considered his procrastination, moreover, generally proved to be clever timing as he watched circumstances turn to his advantage. In the highly personalized game of Chinese politics, Yuan had few equals. If possible, he seduced his rivals through sweet words and rewards, including ample subsidies. If it was unavoidable, he fought them—but only after he had done everything he could to divide them from others and thereby maintain his political and military superiority.

Yet doubts about Yuan accumulated, even in relatively neutral circles. Was he more than a clever politician? Could he govern? Was he capable of constructing a domestic and foreign policy for China that would be viable under the enormously difficult circumstances the nation faced? Did he have the necessary breadth of vision and knowledge? And if he did not, was he prepared to surround himself with men who could compensate for his weaknesses in these respects?

The evidence on these counts was by no means all negative. It will be recalled that Yuan had emerged in the late Qing era as a reformer, not merely in military affairs but also in such fields as education and governmental administration. Indeed, in spite of the later breach in their relations, Yuan had at first expressed great sympathy with the reform efforts of Kang and Liang. Nor was all of the evidence for Yuan's interest in reform historical. In the troubled months after the Wuchang uprising, he had appointed a number of younger, foreign-educated, technocratic leaders to his first cabinet, mixing them in with traditional official-scholars.[22] In sum, Yuan's instincts were not dissimilar from those that had motivated the young Meiji reformers of Japan. He wanted to build a strong, unified, developing China capable of achieving and maintaining equality with the major states of the world. Like all other leaders of this period, he was aware of the need for foreign assistance, but his nationalism was at least as fervent as that of Sun Yat-sen.

The real issue, therefore, was not whether Yuan had the will to be a modernizer. It was whether the broad circumstances governing Chinese politics at this time were likely to protect and nurture his "progressive" capacities, or whether, on the contrary, they were likely to stunt and subordinate these qualities and encourage him to apply even more fully his formidable talents as a practitioner of traditional politics. And there was, of course, an even broader issue. There are times when no one who aspires to effective political leadership can succeed, times when the stature of all aspirants is diminished and their baser instincts triumph because of uncontrollable events. For China, was this such a time?

The most plausible alternative to Yuan Shikai was Sun Yat-sen, who was also a man with considerable assets. Generally, Sun made a good impression on the foreigners with whom he came into contact in the first months after the revolution, and a large contingent of the foreign-trained students—China's hope for the future—were his devoted followers. His formal education was far better than Yuan's, and he knew vastly more about the contemporary world. Quiet in demeanor, he was a man who burned with patriotic passion and whose every action testified to his desire for a new, modernizing China. His courage and determination were beyond question, and in the difficult months that followed the Wuhan revolution, he repeatedly acted in a statesmanlike fashion—restraining his more radical supporters, deferring to Yuan on the matter of position while seeking to uphold his basic principles, and contributing more than his share to a political compromise that might preserve China's unity and avoid civil war. Moreover, he had an ample supply of ideas for the future, plans for far-reaching programs encompassing economic and social as well as political development.

But were his ideas practical? Or was he—as his opponents repeatedly charged—a dreamer, so hopelessly separated from the realities now governing China that to follow him would be to court failure, disillusionment, and possibly the end of China's existence as a nation? Whatever one's judgment on this score, Sun's weaknesses as a political organizer and as a judge of men could not be denied. At critical junctures, he even seemed to flee from the essential organizational tasks that lay before him. The Tongmeng Hui had neither political nor military strength in depth, but in the crucial months after October 1911, Sun paid virtually no attention to such problems and left them to his quarrelsome lieutenants. He seemed content to speak eloquently about democracy, socialism, and the opportunities for rapid development which would exist in the new China.

One of Sun's handicaps, as we have noted, was the gulf that separated him from the great body of his compatriots. By many, he was considered half-foreign, a representative of the overseas Chinese, with the accompanying attribute of being Cantonese. How could such a man attune himself to the mainstream of Chinese culture or operate in a truly Chinese manner? Furthermore, these suspicions were applicable to the whole movement of which Sun was the leader. Regionalism, always strong in China, was becoming an increasingly powerful force as the authority of the center declined. Resentment against Cantonese domination of the revolutionary movement affected even activists from other regions of the South, to say nothing of northerners. The overweening influence of the returned students within the movement, moreover, also aroused doubts. For despite the homage frequently paid them, they were often seen as impractical, impatient zealots who defied the deeply implanted laws of generational authority and political preservation through reliance on precedent.

It is not surprising, therefore, that impartial observers repeatedly asked the same questions. Could this man build a truly national foundation for himself and his movement? Could the Tongmeng Hui penetrate the deep interior of China, and could it become an effective party in the North as well as in the South? For all his charisma, could Sun convince more than a small

Westernized portion of his countrymen and those sharing his own subculture that he and his movement were offering the best path for the future?

MASSES AND ELITES—PROBLEMS OF CREATING FOUNDATIONS FOR THE REPUBLIC

It would be unfair to fault Sun for not building an effective mass organization. The masses of China were totally unprepared for political participation at this time, and they could be brought into military service on behalf of any cause if the means could be found to pay them. The American diplomat W. G. Calhoun, whose analyses of the current situation were frequently penetrating, provided a sharp commentary on the role of China's "common man." It is reported, he wrote, that while the battle for Hankou was raging, the farmers in the fields just outside the zone of fire went on with their work, unaware of or indifferent to the tragedy being enacted so close by. Whether this story was true or not, he continued, it is a fair illustration of the attitude the great toiling masses have assumed toward the revolution.[23] This seeming indifference, this passive silence, he wrote, also extended to the government.

> In the treaty ports, along the coast and throughout a large part of the Yangtze Valley, the revolutionary sentiment has seemed strong, and the enthusiasm for the republic fervent, but in the interior, among the far-off hills, in the remote valleys, the unbroken silence of the centuries still broods over the people. It is said that only twenty miles or so away from Peking, they have hardly heard of the revolution. They know in a vague way that some kind of a quarrel has been going on between Yuan Shih-k'ai and someone in the south, but as to what the quarrel was about, or how it resulted, they know nothing.
>
> There is no affirmative evidence that there is any large measure of popular support for the new government. The most that can be said is that, so far, there has been no openly expressed opposition to it. The people accept it in stolid, perhaps unsympathetic, silence.

Though they were "densely ignorant" of political matters, he wrote, the Chinese people were peacefully inclined. They had never participated in political affairs and were not disposed to do so now, and because of their passivity they were easily controlled. If peace and order were restored, if business resumed and the crops were good, the people might "go on indefinitely in their lethargic way, and remain a neutral factor in the solution of difficult political problems." Nevertheless, he warned, "it must be remembered that this great mass of unnumbered people represent an unconscious and unorganized force of tremendous power; one which can be aroused to demoniacal fury, and which cannot be safely ignored."

One can discount Calhoun's observations as the views of an outsider who could not possibly penetrate the inner thoughts of the Chinese peasantry or understand their attitudes toward the great political events of this era. Yet whatever their thoughts (which one may presume were devoted primarily to the basic issues of survival and material betterment), the data we have presented earlier suggest that the peasants' political behavior coincided with Calhoun's description. Recognizing this, all political leaders, including Sun

Yat-sen, were prone to treat the masses as the chessboard on which the political game was played rather than as players of the game itself, with the important exception of those few who were recruited as soldiers. Sun, to be sure, spoke frequently of elitist responsibilities for tutoring the people, and for the enactment of policies that would underwrite their livelihood. In all of these respects, the way was being prepared for elitist movements that would flourish later, after Western-style political egalitarianism and pluralism had apparently failed.

But could Sun or others build an effective elitist organization, if that was required as the first step in political modernization? In one sense, the most critical elite remained the gentry, for it was they who had the real links to the masses. Respect for their personages and their authority remained high, whether in local disputes, ethical standards, policies affecting the community, or more general political issues. Many of them were men of strong character, excellent classical education, and long experience in civic affairs. Yet, as we have stressed, recent events had caused fragmentation and indecision in their ranks. A growing number of them had become increasingly ambivalent and even hostile toward the Qing rulers and their policies in the final years of the dynasty. Basically, they favored maximum provincial autonomy and extensive private government. Most resented and resisted centralization in any form.

Thus, the powerful centrifugal trends that accompanied the early republican period did not displease many gentry. As the leading figures on the local scene, their roles were usually enhanced.* Whether by Beijing or the republicans, well-known gentry were often appointed to key posts. But although they were prepared to be drafted into political roles, most of them were not prepared to run for elective office, considering that unseemly. The resulting vacuum was not infrequently filled by the poorer, lower gentry—an interesting political phenomenon of the early republican period, which foreshadowed the later political involvement of young men from the middle and rich peasant classes, like Mao Zedong.

Some of the younger gentry, having had the opportunity for overseas education, enlisted in Sun's movement and returned as advocates of radical reform. A generational cleavage thus appeared. Most older members of the gentry favored constitutional monarchy, despite their unhappiness with the Qing. And although they often responded to appeals based on Han nationalism, many gentry were deeply disturbed by the disorder that accompanied the revolution, the arrogance of young revolutionary leaders, the emergence of a powerful but undisciplined soldiery, and the recurrent discussions of radical land reform. Neither Sun's background nor his policies made the gentry a logical source of support for his movement.

In any case, Sun and his associates made few systematic efforts to harness the gentry class to their cause, although volunteers were readily accepted. Overtures to the merchant class were stronger, but had mixed results. As has been emphasized, the revolutionaries depended heavily for funding on over-

*The first head of the revolutionary party in Shanghai, for example, was Li Bingshu, a member of the local gentry. In Shandong the gentry and the students each made major demands on the government, leading to the collapse of the old regime. In Sichuan the local gentry had played a critical role in bringing down the government since the railway crisis of 1910. And these are but a few examples of gentry involvement either directly or indirectly in revolutionary activities.

seas Chinese commercial-industrial sources. In the months immediately after October 1911, moreover, Hong Kong merchants played a prominent role in sustaining the Guangdong provisional government.* In a few other parts of China—Amoy and the major cities of Sichuan, for example—chambers of commerce and leading merchants often served the revolutionary cause in various ways. Yet Sun's movement had not made any deep inroads into the mainland business community prior to the revolution. The great majority of Chinese merchants simply wanted to be left alone with respect to politics, although they were often called "opportunists" because of their willingness to support any leader or government that could keep order, prevent undue extortion, and thereby enable business to proceed with minimum friction.[24] Also, it paid to be on the winner's side.

As the revolution unfolded, uneasiness rose among most merchants. Their commitment to the Qing had not been strong, and many were ready to support Han nationalism. But in those areas where revolutionary factionalism was strongest or brigandage had become a serious problem, they complained that the revolutionary movement had too many leaders, none of them able to govern effectively. Not infrequently, merchants found themselves blackmailed or harassed into making "voluntary contributions," first to one faction and then to another. Above all, they wanted a rapid restoration of law and order. Who ruled was a matter of lesser concern. Thus, as a class, they could be mobilized on behalf of the revolutionaries only if Sun and his associates could satisfy them that the republicans had the capacity to govern.

Of even greater immediate importance was a third elite—the professional military officers. Here Sun had a base in the young military cadets trained in Japan, many of whom he had recruited into the Tongmeng Hui. They played crucial roles in Wuhan and elsewhere, although they were also to be found in plentiful numbers in Yuan's camp. Within the military, however, several troublesome trends now emerged. The rank-and-file soldiers were recruited wherever they could be found, and often came from the most backward socioeconomic segments of Chinese society. They were for the most part marginal men for whom robbery, banditry, and soldiery were more or less synonymous. Their political consciousness was nil when they were recruited, and no sustained effort was made to raise it, whether they became a part of northern or revolutionary ranks. Their loyalties remained largely personal ones; they would serve the men who fed, housed, and paid them, but only for as long as those requirements were met.

*According to an American consular report from Hong Kong, the revolutionary supporters included practically all of the Chinese businessmen in the colony, working under the authority of Sun, and when the Guangdong viceroy, Zhang Mingji, departed, a group of Hong Kong entrepreneurs helped to set up the provincial government in Canton. See *NAMP/RDSRIAC*, 893.00/795, American Consul General, Hong Kong, "Hongkong Aspect of the Revolution in China," November 16, 1911.

It is not surprising, therefore, that the same source reported several months later that "the new movement (in Canton) represents the business and property holding classes of Chinese, and the remarkably small disturbance to the finances and general business conditions . . . caused by this immense revolutionary movement is itself demonstration of the conservative nature of the movement and of the ability of the conservative classes to ultimately control the situation . . . in short, to govern themselves" (*NAMP/RDSRIAC*, 893.00/1066, American Consul-General, Hong Kong to the Secretary of State, January 11, 1912). It should be noted, however, that this dispatch may have gilded the lily, since it contained a strong appeal for United States recognition of the provisional government.

The training and character of the officers in command could make a difference. Some troops were well disciplined and were taught to pay for items obtained from local sources. (The Communist guerrillas of later years did not invent such rules of conduct.) Yet far more often, looting, rape, and unrestrained indulgence in atrocities were considered fringe benefits of soldiery. Indeed, on occasion, after the capture of a given town or district, a period of time—perhaps three days—was formally given over to taking the spoils, after which some degree of order was imposed upon occupying troops by their officers. In all of these matters it was difficult to make a clear distinction between revolutionary and imperial forces. There were some good units and many bad ones on both sides.

In fact, the problems were frequently more serious on the revolutionary side. It was they who had been more often forced to enlist raw recruits hastily, wherever they could be found, and they were almost always short of funds. Their military leaders could therefore maintain their troops only through local exactions and ad hoc rules. Autonomy was a natural outgrowth of such circumstances, and sooner or later it affected even the strongest military adherents to Sun's cause.

Given the local power of military leaders, Sun's relations with men like Chen Jiongming would prove of critical importance in the years ahead. And in the immediate postrevolutionary era, the revolutionaries had to deal not merely with Yuan and his military governors in the North but also with military figures in control of critical southern regions—men like Li Yuanhong and, later, Feng Guozhang, Lu Rongting, and Li Chun, none of whom had close personal or ideological associations with the leading republicans. These were men who had no ties to the old Tongmeng Hui; in fact, many had been Qing loyalists, and some had once had close connections with Yuan Shikai. Only a handful of key military figures at the provincial level could be accounted solidly in the republican column. In a broader sense, to be sure, Yuan faced the same problem. Until military commanders and governors in the field could be brought firmly under central authority, indifference or disobedience to orders from the capital, and even political betrayal, would continue to cause problems, as the history of modern China was to demonstrate.

PARTY FORMATION

A republican system of government requires competitive political parties, and in a revolutionary era dedicated to political openness, various aspirants to power will seek to take advantage of the new opportunities. It was therefore not surprising that the October uprising spawned a plethora of parties. Yet for the Chinese few institutions were more difficult to conceptualize and put into effective operation than that of the political party. The bedrock of traditional Chinese political culture was unity under the emperor, with the familial system serving both as a model and as the main pillar of support. Disunity occurred, of course, but it was traditionally treated as an aberration, an evil to be eliminated by any means available. The legitimacy of difference and the right to opposition were concepts wholly alien to the mainstream of Chinese culture. Only if an individual retreated from society into solitary contemplation was his silent protest treated as honorable.

Thus the idea of popularly organized political bodies operating competitively and with full public legitimacy, serving as vehicles of choice and instruments of citizen participation in the political process, was extraordinarily difficult for most Chinese to grasp. With few exceptions, only those who had studied Western practices could accept it. Historically, the organizational structure of political opposition in China was epitomized by the secret society, a brotherhood of men knit together by intensely personal bonds and wedded to such techniques as blackmail and assassination. As the new Chinese political parties emerged, it was naturally impossible to separate them completely from older connotations and practices or to give them legitimacy in the eyes of traditionalists.

Indeed, the issue of whether to transform the Tongmeng Hui from a secret society into a Western-style political party, or when to do it, provoked heated debates in the months after the October uprising. Some veteran activists like Hu Hanmin argued that since the success of the revolution was still uncertain, it was too early to expose the association and its members to the dangers of open, competitive politics. In the first postrevolution meeting of the Tongmeng Hui—held on January 20, 1912, and attended by more than one thousand members—no significant organizational changes were undertaken. Wang Jingwei was chosen *zongli* (director general), but he served for less than a month before resigning. Sun, preoccupied with matters in Nanjing, did not attend and sent Hu Hanmin as his representative.[25] At a second meeting in early March, however, despite continued controversy, steps were taken to alter the association. A constitution and a nine-point program were approved, and officers were elected, with these actions being fully publicized.[26]

The new constitution restated two of Sun's original three goals—consolidation of the Republic, and measures that would promote the people's livelihood. (The overthrow of the Manchu monarchy was virtually accomplished.) The program was comprehensive, and called for changes in many areas: administrative unity and the fostering of local government (thus straddling the issue of centralization versus local autonomy); racial assimilation; state socialism; compulsory primary education; equality of the sexes; obligatory military service; financial reorganization and tax reform; international equality; and the development of wastelands through colonization. Neither the concept of elitist tutelage in a three-stage process, a prominent feature of Sun's earlier program, nor the single-tax proposal was mentioned. The call was for "republicanism now!"

Although the Tongmeng Hui became an open political party at this point, current political circumstances dictated that it would have to remain an elitist group, and this was implicit in its new membership rules. Prospective members were to be nominated by two party members and approved by an inspection department. They were required to possess "a general knowledge," presumably derived from a basic education, and were obliged to pay an entrance fee of one yuan, with annual dues of two yuan. Party headquarters were established in Nanjing, with branches projected for all provincial capitals and major cities. The principal figures on the current political stage were elected to the three top positions: Sun Yat-sen as *zongli* and Huang Xing and Li Yuanhong as associate directors, each of them to serve indefinite terms. The constitution also provided for a ten-member secre-

40. *Li Yuanhong as vice-president, circa* 1912

tariat and five administrative bureaus; the positions on these bodies were filled primarily by men from Central and South China, most of them from the "right wing" of the party.

The new Tongmeng Hui regulations provided for a powerful director general, with an unlimited term of office and the exclusive right to appoint bureau directors. But Sun had a limited interest in organizational matters, and even before the March Congress, he had resigned as provisional president and was in the process of withdrawing from active politics. Control therefore passed to the secretariat, and more particularly to the bureau chiefs. When two of the bureau chiefs, Hu Hanmin and Wang Jingwei, soon left Nanjing—Hu to assume the governorship of Guangdong, and Wang for "study" overseas—party control was assumed primarily by Song Jiaoren.

By the spring of 1912, other parties or factions had emerged, some of them offshoots of the original Tongmeng Hui. One of the first (which we shall discuss in some detail later) was the Zhongguo Shehuidang (Chinese Socialist Party), founded by Jiang Kanghu on November 5, 1911. Several other groups that appeared were essentially regional. Thus, certain Tongmeng Hui members joined with elements in Hubei to form the Minshe (People's Society); they elected Li Yuanhong as their leader and pledged themselves to republicanism, citing Rousseau's *Social Contract* as their ideological source. This development, incidentally, marked Li's permanent political split from the old Tongmeng Hui members. Another group primarily from Zhejiang, including Zhang Binglin, established the Zhonghua Minguo Lianhe Hui (Union of the Chinese Republic). Such developments were reminiscent of the provincial student associations of a decade earlier, and stemmed basically from the same strong provincial commitments.

A number of other parties emerged briefly during this period. The most prominent of these were the Gonghedang (Republican Party), the Tongyi Gonghedang (United Republican Party), and the Guomin Gongdang (Public Party of Citizens). The Gonghedang, a union of five small groups, was established on May 5, 1912, soon after the opening of the provisional parliament in Beijing. Its prominent members included Li Yuanhong, Zhao Bingzhun, Zhang Jian, and Cheng Dechuan, the latter three being former Qing officials and supporters of Yuan. In the months that followed, therefore, the party took a pro-Yuan stand on most issues.[27] The other two parties were close to the Tongmeng Hui in basic principles. The Tongyi Gonghedang was formed during the period when the provisional assembly was meeting in Nanjing. Its twelve-point policy manifesto called for administrative reorganization aiming at centralized government; fiscal reform; attention to the people's livelihood; a protective trade system; currency reform and the adoption of the gold standard; creation of a national banking system; communications and transport development; professional higher education, including advanced military training; conscription; the protection of overseas Chinese; racial assimilation within China; and the creation of a foreign policy that would protect China's rights in the international community. Party leaders included Cao E, Gu Zhongwu, and Wu Jinglian.[28] The Guomin Gongdang, a Shanghai-based party, advocated the creation of a secure republican foundation, the promotion of the national interest, and the advancement of the people's livelihood. Its leaders included Cen Chunxuan and Wu Tingfang.[29]

Whereas the first stage in postrevolutionary politics was characterized by

41. *General meeting to establish Provisional Assembly, Nanjing, January 28, 1912*

party proliferation based on a multiplicity of personal and sectional interests, the second stage—from mid-1912 to late 1913—involved efforts to build one or two national parties. Until this time even the Tongmeng Hui had been essentially a regional party, its strength drawn principally from the four provinces of Guangdong, Hunan, Anhui, and Jiangxi. The political problems between Yuan and the provisional assembly that erupted in June 1912 prompted Song Jiaoren, now the key figure in the Tongmeng Hui, to seek the creation of a truly national parliamentary party, cast in the Western mold. His efforts culminated in the basic reorganization of August, and in the emergence of the Guomindang (Nationalist Party).

It was Song's thesis that if the republican party could acquire enough strength to win the forthcoming elections and dominate parliament, it would be in a position to control policy, regardless of Yuan's actions. At this point, the provisional assembly had been transferred from Nanjing to Beijing, as had Tongmeng Hui headquarters. Almost all of the 121 assembly members had joined one of three parties. The Tongmeng Hui and the Gonghedang each claimed 40 members, with an additional 25 persons adhering to the Tongyi Gonghedang; assorted minor party supporters and independents completed the roster. The issue of a partisan versus a nonpartisan cabinet had already assumed critical importance in the debates of the period, but the Tongmeng Hui, the leading proponent of party government, lacked the parliamentary strength to enforce its position.

Song Jiaoren, serving as head of the general affairs bureau after the party's summer meeting, initiated conversations with the Tongyi Gonghedang, a political group with its primary base in the North, and shortly thereafter the Guomin Gongdang was included in the discussions. Two issues had to be resolved prior to a merger: the name of the new party, and whether to retain or abandon Sun's principle of people's livelihood (*minsheng*). Both minor parties insisted on a new name and on abandonment of Sun's third principle. At a meeting of the three groups on August 5, 1912, agreement was reached. The name Guomindang (National People's or Nationalist Party) was chosen, and a compromise was finally effected whereby the concept of *minsheng* was incorporated loosely into a five-point program. The new party pledged itself to the promotion of political unification, the development of local self-government, the encouragement of racial harmony, the adoption of policies advancing *minsheng*, and the maintenance of international peace.*

A second meeting was convened on August 11 to put party regulations and the party manifesto in final form. It was attended by two additional minor political factions that had decided to join the new venture. Song chaired the meeting, but his proposal to create a post of secretary-general to manage party affairs was rejected on the ground that it would concentrate too much power in one person. Instead, a structure involving five separate and equal departments under the director general was retained. The departments designated were those of general affairs, organization, political affairs, social affairs, and finance. The party manifesto, issued on August 12, appealed for a two-party system and a responsible cabinet-parliamentary form of government. The evils of a multiparty system were outlined, and an apolitical presidency was supported; it was proposed that the majority party should form the cabinet and, through the premier, should assume responsibility for its actions before the national parliament.[30]

None of the old parties that joined in forming the Guomindang secured the assent of all of their former members, and indeed many of those members stood in opposition to the Guomindang when the parliament was convened in April 1913. Even within the Tongmeng Hui some veteran revolutionaries were highly critical; they objected to the change of party name, or to the downgrading of *minsheng*, or to other actions, such as elimination of the pledge to promote equality of the sexes. Sun Yat-sen, however, gave the new party his full support when he arrived in Beijing on August 24, 1912, and it was formally inaugurated on the following day. Among the nine

* For details, see *Minli bao*, August 18, 1912, pp. 6–7. Party rules and regulations were not greatly dissimilar to those previously applying to the Tongmeng Hui, although they opened the party somewhat more widely: all Chinese citizens who shared the principles of the party were eligible for membership; prospective entrants were to be introduced by two current party members; a one-yuan entrance fee was assessed; members were not to belong to another party concurrently; party headquarters was to be in the national capital, with branches in various parts of the nation and in overseas areas having a Chinese population in excess of 1,000; nine directors were to be elected for a two-year term, selecting from among their group a director general; in addition, thirty counselors, elected for a two-year term, would advise on important matters; three finance officers and seven auditors were to be selected for a one-year term; secretaries were to be elected to head the five departments for a one-year term; a policy committee was to be established; and a national congress was to be held yearly at headquarters, with the possibility of emergency congresses if sanctioned by party directors.

directors elected at this time, a solid majority were former Tongmeng Hui members.*

In officiating at the birth of the new party, Sun spoke in conciliatory fashion and stressed the need to put country above party. Other political parties should be treated as brothers, he urged, because the Republic required the support of all. He suggested that the question of equality between men and women could be postponed until the stability of the Republic had been assured, and he argued that the Guomindang's new social-policy plank incorporated the spirit of the principle of people's livelihood. He forcefully denied that the party's program was intended to confiscate the wealth of the rich, referring once again to the prophylactic character of the party's social policies and the necessity of guarding against *future* exploitation. He also assured his audience that they need not fear military interference in government. The military, too, cherished the Republic and had China's national interests at heart.[31]

In this speech Sun set the tone for the Guomindang's relations with Yuan and his government in the months preceding the national elections of December 1912. The emphasis was on harmony, and Sun's personal attitude was probably best exemplified in a comment he made to his close follower Yu Youren: "Yuan is capable of doing good; do not compel him to do evil."[32] Thus, at a banquet given by Yuan in Sun's honor at the end of August, just before he departed from Beijing, Sun lavishly praised his host. It would take ten years to build a true republic, Sun remarked, and China was indeed fortunate to have in President Yuan a man rich in political experience to manage the affairs of state. He added that Yuan's skill as a military modernizer was especially valuable, and stated that he had advised Yuan to train an army of five million men in the course of his ten-year tenure in office so that China could achieve international equality. Meanwhile, Sun concluded, he would devote his own energies to the social reconstruction of the nation, beginning with an extensive railway-building program.[33]

Sun's projection of a ten-year period for the creation of a Chinese Republic coincided closely with the nine-year period of tutelage originally advanced in the Tongmeng Hui revolutionary program as a preparation for constitutional democracy. Sun apparently assigned Yuan the key role in building the military and political foundations for Chinese democracy and saw his own role as that of laying the economic groundwork. Sun's evaluation of Yuan and his capacities was not shared by everyone in the Guomindang. In particular, the old "left-wing" faction strenuously opposed all steps toward reconciliation with Yuan and his supporters. Ugly charges were hurled against Song Jiaoren and his group, to the effect that the lure of office had led them into opportunism and capitulation, and that bribery had played a part in this.

The national elections, which ended in January 1913, seemed to vindicate the moderates. Guomindang candidates captured 269 of the 596 seats in the House of Representatives and 123 of the 274 Senate seats, thereby acquiring approximately 45 percent of total parliamentary membership.

*The nine directors elected included six from the old Tongmeng Hui: Sun Yat-sen, Huang Xing, Song Jiaoren, Wang Chonghui, Wang Zhixiang, and Zhang Fenghui; Wang Renwen and Wu Jinglian of the old Tongyi Gonghedang, and a minority representative, Gongsangnuoerbu (Prince Kalaching of Inner Mongolia). For details, see *Minli bao*, August 26, 27, and 31, 1912, pp. 3 and 6.

Since Sun had resigned his position as party leader, Song Jiaoren was appointed acting director general; and it was widely believed that given its substantial margin over all other parties, the Guomindang would assume power shortly after China's first parliament convened in the spring of 1913, with Song as premier. But this was not to be. Why did events take a different course, so that political strife increased and parliamentarism was cast into increasingly greater peril? To fathom the answer, we must first examine the critical issues of institution-building that confronted the new Republic and then consider the new political elite that had come to power.

INSTITUTIONAL ISSUES AT THE BEGINNING OF THE REPUBLIC

It will be recalled that a National Assembly had convened for the first time on October 3, 1910, in the last year of the Qing era. This body continued to meet during the fall of 1911, after the revolution in October and the appointment of Yuan as premier. On November 2, 1911, it adopted a set of basic guidelines known as the Nineteen Articles, which were promulgated by the court on the following day. These were intended to establish a framework for parliamentary government under a constitutional monarchy, and as premier, Yuan operated under them until the events of December and January ended the prospects for such a government by sweeping the monarchy—and the old National Assembly—into oblivion.

Thus the Provisional National Assembly sitting in Nanjing in the spring of 1912, a product of the October uprising and later revolutionary developments, was the only national legislative body then in existence. Beginning in January 1912, it had served as the legislative arm of the fledgling Republic, and it continued in that role after Yuan Shikai assumed the provisional presidency. But its legality was derived solely from the revolution, and its representative character could easily be challenged. Of its less than forty members at the time of Yuan's inauguration as president, virtually none had been popularly elected. Some had been chosen by provincial assemblies, some had been appointed by military governors, and some were simply self-selected.

Whatever questions might be raised regarding its legitimacy the Nanjing Assembly was engaged in a significant exercise as the transition from Sun to Yuan took place. On March 10, the same day on which Yuan assumed the provisional presidency, a temporary constitution for the infant Republic was enacted by the Assembly; it was entitled the Provisional Articles for the Republic of China.[34] This document bore the strong imprint of Western constitutional experience. It guaranteed protection against illegal search, arrest, trial, and punishment; freedom of property, speech, press, movement, and religion; and the right to petition authorities, both appointive and elective. As in Japan's Meiji Constitution, however, these rights were qualified by the provision that they could be limited or modified by law, provided this was deemed necessary for the promotion of public welfare, the maintenance of public order, or by virtue of some other urgent necessity. The obligations of citizens were also specified, notably to pay taxes and to perform military service.

As might have been expected, given its auspices and the prevailing political circumstances, the provisional constitution underwrote a parliamentary rather than a presidential system. Until it was succeeded by a national par-

42. *Sun with Nanjing government officials, Office of the President, early 1912. First row from the left: Wang Jingwei, Hu Hanmin (with hat)*

liament, the *canyiyuan* (variously translated as advisory council, national council, senate, and deliberative assembly—we shall term it Assembly) was to represent the wellspring of power. It was in fact to be an extension of the Nanjing Assembly; its membership was enlarged to 121, with five members to represent each of China's twenty-one provinces, Inner Mongolia, Outer Mongolia, and Tibet, plus one member from Qinghai (Kokonor).

The new Assembly was empowered to elect the president and vice-president of the Republic (by a two-thirds vote, with three-fourths of the members in attendance), and its approval of the premier, cabinet minsters, and ambassadors was required. Similarly, for a declaration of war or the ratification of a treaty, Assembly concurrence was mandatory. All laws had to be approved by the legislature, including budgets and public loans. The powers of impeachment rested with it, and Assembly members could require cabinet ministers to come before it to answer questions.

The provisional president was empowered to operate the administrative system, introduce legislation into the Assembly, promulgate and execute laws enacted, serve as commander in chief of the armed forces, and appoint and remove civil and military officials, subject to the concurrence of the Assembly in the cases specified. Thus, although the president's powers were by no means negligible (for example, his power to appoint provincial governors and all judicial officials on his own authority placed a major weapon in his hands), the overall tilt in the provisional constitution was in the direction of the cabinet-parliamentary system, a tilt almost certain to be challenged by Yuan.

An annex to the provisional constitution contained the injunction that within ten months after its promulgation, the Assembly should establish laws providing for the organization of a national parliament and election procedures for the selection of its members. That parliament would in turn draft China's permanent constitution.

These were the legal terms on which the new democratic era was launched. In retrospect, it seems clear that a conflict between single-leader dominance and collective governance was bound to develop, regardless of the specific personalities, issues, or political systems involved; it is a conflict that has occurred in almost every twentieth-century society and with particular severity in developing states. For China, it has continued throughout the Nationalist and Communist periods, and has usually been closely related to the issue of centralization versus local autonomy.

In the second decade of the twentieth century, at least until the Russian Revolution of 1917, all "advanced" models for political institutions derived either from the West or from Japan, which had recently adapted Western constitutionalism to its own requirements. All foreign models therefore pointed in the direction of shared powers, political competition, popular participation, and a pluralistic, politically open society. The dilemma was clear, for as we have often stressed, China's political traditions stressed personalized rule, which was centralized in concept if limited in the scope of governmental functions, and placed a premium on political conformity. Moreover, as a weak society, economically backward and facing continual foreign threats, China's need for unity was obvious. As in developing societies of a later period, concerns over national integration and economic development naturally took priority over questions of political freedom, except among a handful of intellectuals who embraced Western values. These priorities encouraged the creation of a political system that blended a clear chain of command and uninhibited authority at the top with the type of personalized rule that could enlist popular attention and respect at the regional and local levels. Could any Western model meet these basic requirements? The answer has been contested but never resolved in a long struggle in modern China, a struggle between those prepared to accept institutions that support the unchallenged power of a president or a party leadership, whether exercised through an elite or based on popular sovereignty, and those who want to see power vested in parliaments, national and provincial, in order to guard against dictatorship. Yuan and his opponents had highly personal reasons for distrusting each other, reasons embedded in recent history, and this was a powerful factor in their struggle; but in a larger sense they were actors in only one brief scene of an epic drama that is still unfolding.

Political unity in this period hinged upon coalition, but the coalition between Yuan and the Tongmeng Hui was fragile from the beginning. One of Yuan's first acts as president was to appoint Tang Shaoyi as premier. In many respects, this seemed to be an ideal appointment. Tang had been a friend of Yuan's since their days in Korea together, and had worked with him in a variety of capacities. At the same time, he had shown strong sympathies for the republican cause, and in the spring of 1912 he had joined the Tongmeng Hui, after being sponsored by no less a personage than Sun Yat-sen. If anyone could serve successfully as a bridge between Yuan and the revolutionaries, Tang was the man. Despite some sentiment in favor of trying to persuade Sun to become premier, therefore, Tang was quickly approved by the Assembly on March 13, and immediately assumed office.

Securing approval for Tang's cabinet, however, proved much more difficult. On March 24, the new premier came to Nanjing from Beijing to argue his case. Yuan was prepared to accept four veteran Tongmeng Hui members in the cabinet, but he wanted to reserve the most sensitive and important positions for those with whom he had greater rapport. His choice for minister of the army was General Duan Qirui, a trusted lieutenant; for minister of the navy he nominated Liu Guanxiong; for minister of the interior he proposed Zhao Bingzhun, a member of the newly formed Gonghedang; and for minister of finance he nominated Xiong Xiling, a brilliant scholar and once an associate of Liang Qichao's in the reformist movement. For the Ministries of Foreign Affairs and Communications, respectively, he named two professional diplomats, Lu Zhengxiang and Shi Zhaoji (also known as Alfred Sze). The posts he offered to the Tongmeng Hui were the Ministries of Education (Cai Yuanpei), Justice (Wang Chonghui), Agriculture and Forestry (Song Jiaoren), and Commerce and Industry (Chen Qimei).

THE NEW POLITICAL ELITE

The composition of the Republic's first full-fledged cabinet deserves detailed analysis at this point because most of its members were to play significant roles in the future and because such an analysis can help illuminate many areas of contemporary Chinese politics.[35] First, let us look briefly at the background of the appointees who were not members of the Tongmeng Hui.

Tang Shaoyi, the new premier, was born in 1860 in Xiangshan, Guangdong. His uncle was a well-known compradore for Jardine, Matheson and Company, and later served as director of the China Merchants' Steam Navigation Company. Young Tang went to an English school in Hong Kong, and was then sent to the United States in the fall of 1874, as one of a small contingent of the Chinese youth assigned to study in Hartford, Connecticut. He continued his education at Columbia University and New York University and returned to China in 1881. On entering government service, Tang held several minor positions before being sent to Korea as assistant to the customs inspector in 1882. It was here that he came into contact with Yuan Shikai, who was serving as Chinese garrison commander, and having greatly impressed Yuan, he became a member of his personal staff and his deputy by 1885. Tang remained in Korea until 1896, his last post being Chinese consul general. Upon returning to China, he became Yuan's secretary at the headquarters of the Newly Created Army, and then followed him in 1899 to Shandong and Zhili, where he held key positions. He was later appointed special commissioner for Tibetan affairs, and dealt with the thorny Tibetan issue (and the British) until the April 27, 1906 agreement that acknowledged China's suzerainty (not sovereignty) over Tibet. He then assumed important positions in the maritime customs and railway system and supported the idea of soliciting loans from abroad for developmental purposes. This view caused heavy pressure to be brought against him, and he resigned in 1907 to assume the governorship of Fengdian. With Yuan's decline, however, Tang also suffered. He went into retirement until August 1910, when he was called back to serve on the Board of Communications. He was unemployed again when the 1911 Revolution broke out, but with Yuan's return his star immediately rose. He was named president of the Board of Communications, then Yuan's negotiator at Shanghai, and from this latter position, premier.[36]

Duan Qirui, the new minister of the army, was born on March 6, 1865, and came from an Anhui family distinguished in military pursuits. At the age of nineteen, he entered the new Beiyang Military Academy, and graduated first in his class in 1887. He was selected to study abroad, went to Germany in the spring of 1889, and returned to China in 1890. His contacts with Yuan Shikai began in 1895, when he was transferred to a camp near Tianjin where Yuan was organizing the new force that became known as the Beiyang Army. From this point on, his rise followed Yuan's. As commander of the New Army's artillery battalion, he accompanied Yuan to Shandong in 1899 and headed the garrison at Jinan, the provincial capital; and when Yuan moved to Zhili as governor-general, Duan went with him, in the civil rank of expectant prefect. When Yuan began his reorganization of the armed forces in 1902, Duan was given a series of important roles, and beginning in 1904 he served both as the commander of various army divisions and as the administrator of key army schools. When the Wuchang uprising occurred, he was in command of the Jiangbei region in Jiangsu, but with Yuan's restoration, he was made commander of the Second Army and then took command of the First Army. He served concurrently as acting governor-general of Hubei and Hunan, with full military authority in the crucial Wuhan area, which pitted him militarily against Li Yuanhong and Huang Xing. His political commitments do not appear to have been strong, and his loyalties were attached more to Yuan than to the Qing.[37]

Liu Guanxiong, the new minister of the navy, was born in 1858 in Fujian. He was educated at the Royal Navy College, Greenwich, United Kingdom. Commissioned in the Chinese navy following his return to China, he fought in the Battle of the Yalu in the Chinese-Japanese War of 1894–1895. When Liu was appointed to the first republican cabinet, he had already attained the rank of admiral. During the early years of the Republic, he was also to hold other high government positions, including acting minister of communications, acting minister of education, and acting military governor of Fujian. Liu remained a loyal supporter of Yuan Shikai, and held the navy in line up to Yuan's death in 1916.[38]

Zhao Bingzhun, the new minister of the interior, was born in 1865 in

43. *Yuan with his generals after the ceremony of becoming president, March 10, 1912*

Henan. A protégé of Yuan's, he had first caught Yuan's attention when he was police inspector-general at Tianjin. In 1905 he was appointed acting junior vice-president of the Board of Interior; he was commanded to retire from office when Yuan was dismissed in 1909, but was recalled to office as minister of the interior when Yuan formed his cabinet in 1911. After the 1911 Revolution he was elected minister of the interior in the Nanjing government. He later served as acting premier (1912) and as premier (1913) under Yuan, while retaining the position of minister of the interior.[39]

Xiong Xiling, the new minister of finance, was born in 1870 in Fenghuang *xian*, Hunan, the son of a military officer. He was a brilliant student and achieved the coveted *jinshi* degree at the age of twenty-four. In 1894 he received a three-year appointment to the Beijing Hanlin Academy, and during this period he became deeply involved in the reform movement, working with Tan Sitong and Liang Qichao among others, both in the capital and in his native Hunan. After the collapse of the One Hundred Days' Reform in 1898, Xiong was declared permanently barred from holding office, but soon thereafter his talents were called to the attention of Duanfang, and he was given an appointment in Jiangsu. In 1905 Xiong went with Duanfang to the United States and Europe to study Western systems of government. On his return, with the support of another powerful Manchu, Daize, he was appointed finance superintendent, and later, salt commissioner in Manchuria. Having managed to retain ties with both the imperial and the reform camps, he survived the events of 1911 without damage.[40]

Lu Zhengxiang, the new minister of foreign affairs, was born in 1871 in Shanghai, the son of one of China's early Christians. After his preliminary schooling, he specialized in the French language. He entered the Chinese foreign service in 1892 as an interpreter and was sent to the Chinese legation in St. Petersburg, where he continued to pursue Western studies. In 1899, while still abroad, he married the daughter of a Belgian general. After fourteen years of service in Russia, Lu was appointed Chinese minister to the Netherlands in 1906, and in this capacity he participated in the Hague Conference. He returned to China in 1908 and became acquainted with Yuan, who was then serving as head of the Board of Foreign Affairs. A few months before the Revolution of 1911, he had been appointed minister to Russia, and he was still in St. Petersburg when he was named to Yuan's cabinet.[41]

Shi Zhaoji, known in the West as Alfred Sze, was the new minister of communications. He was born on April 10, 1877, in Chunxiaoli, Jiangsu, the son of a merchant who held a *juren* degree. Sze began his higher education at St. John's Academy in Shanghai, then spent two years at the Academy of Chinese Literature. His proficiency in English led to his appointment as an interpreter at the Chinese legation in Washington, D.C., in 1893. He resigned after a brief period to resume his schooling at Cornell University; he also spent a short time in Russia, where he served as an interpreter at the request of his patron, Minister Yangru. Returning to China in 1902, Sze became English secretary to the Manchu official Duanfang, and in the ensuing years he made several trips to the West as part of visiting student groups. In 1905 he was selected to accompany the five-man mission to the West of which Xiong Xiling was a part. In the fall of that year he married the niece of Tang Shaoyi. After this Tang lent his support to Sze and helped him obtain several positions within the Chinese railway system. At the time of the 1911 Revolution, however, Sze had returned to the foreign service; he occupied the position of senior counsellor in the Board of Foreign Affairs in Beijing, and had just been appointed minister to the United States, Mexico, Cuba, and Peru. The revolution blocked his assumption of this post, so he was available for a position in the Tang cabinet.[42]

Let us now turn to the four Tongmeng Hui cabinet members. Cai Yuanpei, the minister of education, was born in January 1868 in Shanyin, Zhejiang, of a merchant-banker family whose fortunes declined after the death of Cai's father. Young Cai was given a classical education, however; he achieved the *jinshi* degree at an early age, and received the additional honor of being selected as a scholar of the Hanlin Academy. He began his career by serving as principal of a Sino-Western school, and he later taught in a Shanghai academy where he met Wu Zhihui among others. He became deeply involved in the nationalistic, anti-Manchu activities then concentrated in Shanghai, and served as the first president of the China Education Society. In 1905 he was appointed head of the Shanghai branch of the Tongmeng Hui. After 1905 he traveled to Germany. He studied German in Berlin for a year and then enrolled in the University of Leipzig, where he pursued studies in several fields between 1908 and 1911. He returned to China in November 1911, and when Sun formed his provisional government in January 1912, he named Cai minister of education. His appointment in the Tang cabinet thus represented a continuation of position.[43]

Wang Chonghui, the new minister of justice, was born in 1881 in Hong Kong, where his father, a native of Guangdong, was serving as a Protestant minister in the British Colony. His parents were well acquainted with Sun Yat-sen, who was a frequent guest in their home. Young Wang attended St. Paul's College and Queens College in Hong Kong, and also studied classical Chinese with a tutor. He continued his education at Tianjin's Beiyang University and graduated from its law school in 1900. After a brief period of teaching in Shanghai, he went to Japan, where he became involved in anti-

Manchu activities; in late 1902 he went to the United States, where he enrolled first at the University of California and then at Yale. During his American sojourn, Wang met Sun again, and was reported to have helped him draft his first public statement on the aims of the Chinese revolution. He continued his legal education in Europe, and in 1907 was admitted to the London bar. Shortly thereafter, he was appointed an aide to Lu Zhengxiang at the Second Hague Conference. Soon after his return to China in the fall of 1911, Wang became an adviser to Chen Qimei, then military governor of Shanghai. In Sun's provisional government, Wang was appointed minister of foreign affairs, just prior to being named minister of justice in the Tang cabinet.[44]

Song Jiaoren, the new minister of agriculture and forestry, was born on April 5, 1882, in Taoyuan, Hunan. His father died when he was young, and the family was supported by an older brother. At an early age he participated in the political activities of the Hua xing Hui (Restore China Society), organized by Huang Xing, and he was one of the young revolutionaries who helped plan the abortive uprisings in Hunan scheduled for November 1904 (he was to lead the assault on Changde). When the conspiracy was uncovered, Song fled to Japan. There he enrolled in the Kobun Institute, but much of his time was occupied in founding the journal *Ershi shiyi zhi Zhina* (Twentieth-Century China). After the founding of the Tongmeng Hui, Song became one of its leading figures; he also went secretly to Manchuria in a bizarre effort to enlist support for the revolutionary cause from Laodong bandits. In late 1910 he left Japan for Shanghai, and at the invitation of Yu Youren, he became the chief editor of Yu's newspaper, *Minli bao*. His journalistic activities were interrupted when he went to Hong Kong at Huang's request to participate in the unsuccessful Canton revolt of April 1911. After the October uprising, he accompanied Huang to Wuchang and later took an active role in the new revolutionary government established there. He was appointed head of the legal codification bureau in January 1912, and as we have seen, became deeply involved in discussions over the appropriate system of government for the new republic.[45]

Chen Qimei, the new minister of commerce and industry, was born in 1876 in Wuxing, Zhejiang. His father was a businessman, and after a modest education young Chen was apprenticed to a pawnbroker and later worked in a Shanghai silk company. In Shanghai he began to participate in anti-Manchu activities, and in 1906 he went to Japan, where he enrolled in a military school and joined the Tongmeng Hui. He became acquainted with Chiang Kai-shek and brought Chiang into the League; the two remained close from this point on. After two or three years he returned to China and played a leading role in revolutionary activities—soliciting recruits, establishing a secret headquarters in the Shanghai International Settlement, and engaging personally in several of the abortive uprisings between 1909 and 1911. When the Wuchang revolution began, Chen led the takeover of Shanghai in November 1911, became the first military governor, and organized the military force that seized Nanjing. Politically, Chen was strongly anti-Yuan and opposed concessions to the northern government.[46]

As these sketches indicate, the cabinet members were relatively young. The oldest member was Premier Tang, who was fifty-one, and the youngest was Song, who was only twenty-nine; the average age was in the early forties. Most of them had an urban (and urbane) background and an extensive education, which often included some Western training. Several of them had had previous governmental experience in the imperial era. Despite Yuan's affiliation with the North, almost all the appointees came from Central and South China. A surprisingly large number were from merchant families. Their educational achievements were generally very high, and with a few exceptions, personal ties were of supreme importance: each had had close relations either with Yuan or Tang, or with Sun or Huang and the Tongmeng Hui.

There were some interesting differences betwen the two groups: Yuan's selections were on the average somewhat older and better educated, and had more previous governmental experience; the Tongmeng Hui nominees, quite naturally products of the revolutionary activities of the previous decade, tended to have been involved in education or journalism or had devoted themselves to being professional revolutionaries. On balance, however, both groups were closely related branches of a new elite, largely urban and strongly concerned with modernizing China through a reliance on Western models—political, social, and economic.

Despite this fact, the Tongmeng Hui leaders were initially unhappy with the cabinet selections, and Tang was put on the defensive as soon as he arrived in Nanjing. The revolutionaries had especially wanted to have Huang Xing named minister of the army, although it could hardly be expected that Yuan would entrust the army to an opponent. To conciliate Huang's supporters, Yuan appointed him *liushou*, or resident-general of Nanjing, with authority to command all military forces in the South. The title *liushou* was an ancient one given to an official in charge of civil and military affairs during the emperor's absence from the capital. There were some 50,000 troops stationed in and around Nanjing—a formidable force should relations between Yuan and the Tongmeng Hui deteriorate. But Huang, because he had problems in paying his troops—and also, according to his biographer Chun-Tu Hsueh, because he wanted to show good faith toward the Beijing government—repeatedly asked to be relieved of his command. When that request was finally granted by Yuan in June, Huang disbanded many of his troops—setting a precedent that was rarely to be followed in the future.[47] Privately, however, Huang grew progressively bitter toward Yuan.*

There were other complaints, but after certain concessions and compromises—and a grant of funds to Sun to enable him to pay outstanding governmental expenses, including salaries—Tang's cabinet was approved by the assembly at the end of March. The Assembly did assert its authority by re-

*From his post in Nanjing, the American consul, Charles D. Tenney, reported in April 1912 that the city was under military government and that Huang's functions as head of the military structure were more important than his role as civil administrator. Huang had told him that there were some 50,000 troops in Nanjing, but Tenney believed that not over 30,000 of these were armed and equipped, the rest being new recruits, uniformed but not yet possessing weapons or trained. They came from various provinces, and Huang admitted to Tenney that a great deal of jealousy existed among them, with Huang having to play off the troops of one province against those of another in order to maintain order. He was also apprehensive about the activities of General Zhang Xun, former imperialist general of Nanjing, several of whose emissaries had been arrested for subversive activities. Zhang Xun, Huang asserted, with about 8,000 soldiers in south Shandong, was refusing to obey the orders of the republican government (NAMP/RDSRIAC, 893.00/322, April 20, 1912).

By July, Huang was in Shanghai, and exhibiting very bitter feelings against Yuan, according to reports reaching the Nanking consulate. See *NAMP/RDSRIAC*, 893.00/1410, July 8, 1912, Tenney to Calhoun.

44. After Tang Shaoyi arrived in Nanjing to assume post of prime minister, March 25, 1912. First row, from left: Hu Hanmin, Tang, Sun, Huang Xing, Wang Jingwei

jecting one initial nominee, Li Youhao, necessitating his replacement as communications minister by Alfred Sze. As a part of the compromises hammered out, moreover, Tang agreed to support the Nanjing candidates for the Zhili and Shandong military governorships. But the funds he turned over to Sun for the payment of staff salaries had in fact come from a Belgian bank loan, an act for which he was to be severely criticized both by the Western consortium and by republican sources.[48]

CENTRAL ISSUES IN THE NEW REPUBLIC

Thus did the new government get under way. It was agreed that when the Assembly reconvened, it would meet in Beijing to facilitate coordination between executive and legislature. The issue of a permanent capital was left open. Many assemblymen still had substantial reservations about Yuan and the new government as they journeyed north. When the Assembly adjourned, it had only 34 members and the Tongmeng Hui was in full control. Since the temporary constitution adopted in Nanjing called for a legislative body of 121, Yuan proceeded to order the provincial assemblies to select additional members. Many of the provincial bodies were outside Tongmeng Hui control; consequently, when the new assembly met in Beijing, it had a much more heterogenous membership. At the opening session, 72 assemblymen were present, and with additional arrivals later, membership gradually mounted to a peak of 126.*

The tasks confronting the new coalition government in Beijing were staggering, and if they were to be tackled with any hope of success, cooperation and trust between the executive and the fledgling legislative body were essential. Certain dimensions of the challenge were outlined by Li Yuanhong in a long, gloomy telegram circulated to various officials in mid-April, prior to the reconvening of the assembly in Beijing.[49] In setting forth what he called the "ten weak points and three dangerous facts" confronting the Republic, Li—himself a professional military man—concentrated on two basic ills: the overweening power of the military in provincial and local governance, and the inability of the central government to control or regulate provincial affairs.

The management of civil affairs and the exercise of military responsibilities, asserted Li, should be two separate and distinct matters. But since the revolution the military men had usurped all power and regarded both civil and military administration as their inherent right, even though few of them were qualified to assume such dual roles. The fact that certain literati and professional civil servants had been drawn into the service of the military, thereby strengthening their hold on provincial governance, he regarded as deplorable.

By what means had this come about? In the course of the revolution, Li recounted, large armies usually recruited on a local or regional basis had been added to the standing armies that already existed. The ranks of these armies, and the new ones in particular, were filled with the lowest elements of Chinese society. They were men who lacked discipline or any motivation beyond that of plunder, and yet they served as the backbone of militarist power. Meanwhile, the nation was bleeding itself white to sustain useless, even dangerous military forces; and with all finances in disarray, resort was had to unjust taxes, blackmail, and extortion. Nor was there any clear remedy for the multiple evils and injustices taking place. Under the cloak of martial law, the military dominated the judiciary, making it a tool of those in power. Legitimate grievances were answered by dispatching military contingents to restore order, a process which brought further ravages upon the hapless populace. And naturally, there was a growing interaction between the deterioration of economic and social conditions and the popular movement toward lawlessness.

Provincial military rule had produced a highly personalized system, Li explained, whereby the *dudu* (military governor) brought into office literally thousands of his relatives, fellow provincials, and longtime followers. Thus, when he was transferred or removed, his underlings followed him in a wholesale migration, and a fresh group was brought in by a new military ruler. In this situation, jealousies and personal rivalries, both between provinces and within them, were leading to incessant bloodshed and instability.

*According to one account, political distribution in the new assembly shortly after its inauguration was as follows: Gonghedang and Minzhudang, 28; Tongmeng Hui, 26; Tongyidang, 16; Construction and Debating Society, 1; and 11 without party affiliation, making a total of 82 (*North China Herald*, May 11, 1912, p. 413). As we have noted, three of these parties, namely, the Gonghedang, the Minzhudang, and the Tongyidang, were to amalgamate into the Jinbudang, thereby creating a central opponent of the Guomindang and the chief reliance of the Yuan government. See Li Shougong, *Minchu zhi guohui*, p. 43.

And yet the central government was powerless to control events, lacking the requisite finances and unity. The president's orders were regularly ignored or disobeyed, even in matters of appointment or dismissal. The provincial military leaders went their own way, contemptuous of all except those who could bring superior force to bear against them.

In his message, Li captured the essence of a problem that threatened the existence of the Chinese Republic, or indeed of any national government that might be created. In the years that were to follow, China often appeared poised on the knife-edge of disintegration, ready to enter a new age of warring kingdoms. In large measure, we have already described the factors that contributed to that predicament, including the manner in which the revolution itself had unfolded. By the end of 1911 the Beijing government had firm control (in the sense of being able to collect revenue and control local administration) of only two provinces within China proper—Zhili and Henan. Of course, it could legitimately claim partial authority in several other provinces, including the outlying territories of East Turkestan and Manchuria; yet its position was constantly being challenged in most regions, despite the superiority of its military forces. And the longer it failed to exercise its power and authority, the more difficult it would become to reimpose its governance. The revolutionaries, as we have seen, held an expanding number of enclaves, most of them southern urban centers. But vast stretches of the country, both north and south, were a political and military no-man's-land between the contesting forces, administered either by traditional private government or by those who had somehow acquired military power.

Military power ran the gamut from armies to armed bands, and those in command represented a similarly wide range of sociopolitical types. Pure robbers, kidnappers, and smugglers abounded, many of them utterly lacking in social conscience but smart enough to discover who had money and who did not. A few of them assiduously cultivated Robin Hood tactics in order to win local support and find protective cover. Some went further, investing themselves with political labels (deserved or otherwise) and joining either the revolutionary or the imperial cause. Among these, the men who survived were occasionally rewarded with office and publicly proclaimed exemplary citizens.* The restricted economy, the scarcity of opportunities for tal-

*General Xu Baoshan, popularly known as "Tiger Xu," typified those individuals who were later to be called warlords. In the prerevolutionary period, he had been a prominent salt smuggler. Taking advantage of the revolution, Xu gathered an army of 20,000 men around him and entrenched himself in the northern part of Jiangsu province. Supposedly committed to the republican cause, he actually ignored all external authority, collecting and retaining the taxes in the area he controlled. It was reported that he was strongly supported by the people of his district because he provided complete security, assessed taxes fairly, and permitted no corruption. He also favored foreign missionaries, and finally became a Christian, afterwards compelling his soldiers to attend services every Sunday.

Xu was sent to heaven on May 24, 1913, as the result of a diabolical plot. An avid collector of fine porcelain, he was informed of a rare piece in Shanghai, whereupon he dispatched a trusted messenger to pick it up. When the sealed package was opened by Xu, he was blown to shreds.

Another type of "new soldier" was exemplified by the rag-tag band of 300 who entered Amoy in early December 1911 and, after some robbery and extortion, proceeded to the governor's residence, with the leader demanding recognition and pay for himself and his men as revolutionary soldiers. He was given one thousand taels, with the promise that if he would come again that evening alone, he would receive two thousand taels for his personal use. When he arrived, he was summarily shot.

Yet men who had been thrust up as provincial officials were sometimes indistinguishable

ented people, and the fluidity of the sociopolitical situation combined to create new political rules.

Thus the military forces aligned with Yuan and with the revolutionaries not only battled each other but also struggled to hold themselves together and to wrest power from (or coalesce with) a host of independent military entrepreneurs. Recruitment and demobilization—or desertion—were constantly taking place. For these reasons, we can make only the roughest estimate of the numbers of Chinese soldiers who were bona fide members of either the revolutionary or the imperial armies.

Shortly before Sun resigned as provisional president, he stated that the republican armies had 250,000 men under arms, but whether that figure can be considered accurate even for mid-February is uncertain.[50] In January Yuan had lamented that he had only 60,000 troops, but the forces that were fighting under imperial banners were considerably larger. Later, in mid-1912, Yuan spoke of the need to reduce a military force of one million (including southern armies). Most foreign observers regarded this as an exaggeration, advanced in order to secure enough money to buy off certain military leaders as well as to pay for demobilization; but even if one assumes that the total number of soldiers in officially recognized military units was between 400,000 and 600,000, the military establishment was an enormous burden, and most leaders agreed that its reduction, reorganization, and modernization were essential to the political as well as the fiscal health of the nation.

Quite apart from the political obstacles involved in demobilization, however, the financial difficulties were acute. In many units, soldiers' pay was months in arrears. To disband a unit was fraught with peril unless the troops could be given back pay, severance pay, and enough money to return to their native places.*

---

from such individuals. In Shaanxi, for example, a missionary reported in 1913 that the two men who possessed total authority in the province, the governor and the military commander, were equally corrupt, oppressive, and arbitrary. In two years the governor had risen from being a poor man to becoming one of the wealthiest men in the city, but he was so unpopular that he seldom appeared in public for fear of being assassinated. The military commander, a beggar before the revolution and totally illiterate, was now the possessor of great wealth also, and while he was more popular, he remained extremely cruel, performing many executions with his own hands. See *NAMP/RDSRIAC*, 893.00/1990, C. L. Williams to E. T. Williams, October 1, 1913.

* Terms of military recruitment, monthly pay, and conditions of discharge varied considerably from region to region and time to time. For example, it was reported from Swatow in June 1912 that the local military commander was offering six taels to those who enlisted, with the pledge that they could return to their occupations until such time as they were called upon for service. Nearby, the commander of a small unit of 500 men dismissed one-fifth of his group, paying them each ten taels as severance pay. See *NAMP/RDSRIAC*, 893.00/1404, June 24, 1912, Williams to American Legation, Beijing.

Soldiers being demobilized in Hunan in the autumn of 1912 apparently did considerably better. They were reported to be paid 4.9 taels per month, and upon discharge, to receive severance pay equal to three months' wages plus a declining sum in three six-month installments, to enable them to return home and seek employment (Ibid., 893.00/1478, October 1, 1912, Green to the Secretary of State).

In some other cases, however, troops were kept in service for long periods without pay (meals and housing—of varying quality—being furnished) and discharged without compensation. It was perhaps natural that under such circumstances, soldiers terrorized the communities in which they were stationed, demanding food and other items from merchants, looting private residences, issuing ultimatums that if pay were not forthcoming by a given period, they would ravage the district.

Finding funds for military expenditures, including large-scale demobilization as the end of the conflict came into sight, was obviously not the government's only urgent requirement. The mere routine operations of such a government, spread over a vast terrain and counting "four hundred million people" as its subjects, were not inexpensive. Both the revolutionaries and Yuan himself, moreover, were pledged to a host of reforms and developmental programs in transport, communications, and industry, many of which had gotten under way at the close of the Qing era.

Thus the quest for monies could not await the arrival of peace. As we indicated earlier, in the midst of heightened expenditures due to the southern rebellion, the Beijing government found itself cut off from most of its normal sources of revenue. Could it raise money from abroad? That proved to be exceedingly difficult. The four powers who held the great bulk of Western assets—Great Britain, France, Germany, and the United States—had earlier supported the creation of a Four-Power Consortium consisting of the major banks within their jurisdiction which were interested in China loans. This consortium had first been active in connection with the funding of the central Chinese railways in 1909, and it remained in existence. After the outbreak of the 1911 Revolution, the four governments, with the United States playing a leading role, had agreed to maintain "strict neutrality" and a united front with respect to China. They had also persuaded Russia and Japan to accept this policy and, later, to join the consortium—although both countries insisted on the right to protect their "special interests" in Mongolia and Manchuria.

None of the governments involved claimed the right to prevent their private nationals from making loans on their own, but there was a general understanding that such activities would be discouraged, and in most cases governmental discouragement could be quite effective. Consequently, in the critical months after the Wuchang uprising, when the contest remained in some doubt, Yuan was unable to raise the foreign financial support which he insisted was essential to the Beijing government's survival. Some of the ministers stationed in Beijing were sympathetic, but the governments concerned generally maintained the "strict neutrality" position.[51]

Revolutionary efforts to raise money in the South were only slightly more effective. Whether because of a popular tradition that on a change of dynasty taxes were forgiven for two years, or because they wanted to achieve broad public support, the revolutionaries in Canton abolished certain taxes and reduced others, thereby cutting the revenues available. They then turned to a time-honored source of support by seeking to raise some two million dollars in gold from the overseas Chinese in the United States, the Straits Settlements, and Hong Kong. In various regions under revolutionary control, meanwhile, merchants and gentry were "encouraged" to make "voluntary contributions." The revolutionaries also tried printing paper money through a hastily established banking system.

Arms, ammunition, and all of the other expenses of running both a revolution and a new government constituted a heavy burden, however, and by January 1912 the revolutionaries were in desperate straits. They mortgaged the Hanyebing Iron Works for a private Japanese loan of 2.5 million taels. They also tried to force the China Merchants Steamship Navigation Company to put up its properties in exchange for a 10 million tael loan, but in the face of stiff opposition this attempt was abandoned. The republican strategy was to secure Japanese bank loans to such companies, which made them "private" loans in character, and then have the companies advance the money to the government, thereby circumventing the consortium's ban on foreign assistance to either belligerent.

In fact, however, the republicans did receive some direct aid, both money and weapons, from private British and Japanese sources. In a dispatch to J. P. Morgan for the American consortium group, W. D. Straight reported that after conversations with various leaders in Shanghai—including Dr. Zhen Jindao, the republican minister of finance—he found British and Japanese neutrality "peculiar" in its form. Zhen informed him that the British Hong Kong and Shanghai Bank had advanced a loan of 1.5 million taels, of which 200,000 taels went directly to republican officials. From Japanese sources, 200,000 rifles for the revolutionaries had been landed in Shanghai.[52] Cantonese sources reported that two Japanese steamers had delivered 50,000 rifles and two million rounds of ammunition during the same period, and indicated that the Bank of Taiwan was prepared to loan the Nanjing government funds. Surprisingly enough, confirmation of certain Japanese activities came in the course of sessions of the Japanese Diet: on February 1, the minister of the army told the lower house that some three million yen had been collected from the sale of discarded arms and ammunition to the Chinese revolutionaries.[53]

In this connection, Sun's efforts to play his Japanese card with the Americans were extremely interesting. As we have noted at length, Sun's ties with certain Japanese, including men of prominence such as Inukai Tsuyoshi, were extremely close. At first glance, therefore, it is astonishing to find Sun confiding to American officials in early February that the Japanese were pressing the Nanjing Republic for a military alliance, promising in return to assist it in organizing its armed forces; and further, arguing that Japan would get China completely under its power, through loans and military assistance, if other nations did not quickly recognize the new Republic and come to the assistance of its government. The purpose of these revelations, of course, was all too apparent; yet Sun on occasion seemed genuinely alarmed at Japanese expansionism.*

*The first indication of this theme from Sun actually came indirectly, through Homer Lea, while Sun and his party were en route to China in December. At Penang, Lea was quoted in the press as stating that a weak China would represent a danger for Great Britain. When Japan became a major power, the political equilibrium in the Orient would be destroyed, and in order to restore it, it would be necessary either to break Japan or to strengthen and consolidate China so that the latter could become a great military power, thus stopping Russian expansion. (So was it ever!) It seems difficult to believe that Lea would have made such statements if they conflicted strongly with Sun's privately expressed views. For details, see a newspaper clipping from the *Penang Gazette*, dated December 14, 1911, in *NAMP/RDSRIAC*, 893.00/984.

Sun's remarks were first made in the course of a discussion on February 7 with consular official Frederick McCormick. They came in response to statement McCormick had been instructed to relay to Sun, namely, that Secretary Knox had received assurances from the Japanese that they were acting in harmony with the American government in an effort to preserve the integrity of China and prevent foreign interference in Chinese affairs. Sun replied that Knox was evidently not fully informed as to the designs of the Japanese, and then he proceeded to indicate the pressure being exerted from Tokyo, with the request that his remarks be transmitted to Knox.

Tenney was instructed to pursue the matter further, and on February 10 a second interview with Sun took place. Sun then indicated to Tenney that the proposal for an alliance came not through official ministry channels but through the *genrō* circuit. Thus, the Japanese govern-

With the advent of coalition government, the barrier against loans by the consortium, currently known as the Quadrilateral Group, was removed, and serious negotiations for a large loan immediately got under way. On February 29, 1912, two million taels were advanced by the Group to cover immediate needs, and another 1.1 million taels were authorized on March 10, both amounts to be accounted part of the comprehensive loan when terms had been fixed. In mid-March, however, a serious controversy erupted. It was revealed that on March 14, only one day after he had been nominated premier, Tang Shaoyi had signed an agreement with a group of British, Russian, and Belgian financiers, known as the Anglo-Belgian syndicate, for a loan of one million pounds sterling. The Quadrilateral Group, backed by the ministers representing the four Western powers in Beijing, immediately launched a protest. They insisted that there had been an agreement that the Chinese government would give the consortium a prior option on any large loan, and that the initial funds had been advanced on that basis. Therefore, the secret negotiations and the consummation of an agreement with the Anglo-Belgian syndicate constituted a breach of faith.

This controversy raised issues that have characterized relations between developing and advanced societies throughout the twentieth century. The consortium, with the full backing of its members' governments, insisted on two conditions: preference with respect to major loans, and foreign supervision of loan disbursement. The reasons for insisting on preferential treatment were clear enough. The banks involved wished to protect their initial investment and to make further profits, if possible. Their agreement to cooperate in the first place had been based on a desire to pool their resources through a common effort and, more important, to insure that adequate safeguards could be enforced so that the Chinese government would not be able to play off one syndicate against another. Some financiers—and some governments—feared that in a highly competitive environment, Beijing would manipulate all other parties, use its limited collateral more than once, misappropriate its funds, pile up a colossal debt, and then renounce its international obligations. There were similar reasons for insisting on foreign supervision of loan disbursement. There was already ample evidence that loans supposedly sought for developmental purposes were being used to pay past obligations or were being thrown into the seemingly bottomless coffers of the military. Corruption and mismanagement, moreover, were rampant at every level. Without adequate supervision, consortium members insisted, any loan would be frittered away, and there would be requests for larger amounts in the near future. At some point this could lead to a confrontation involving governments as well as private institutions.

However logical and reasonable such contentions seemed from the vantage point of London, Paris, and New York (as well as the foreign business and diplomatic communities in China), it is easy to understand why consortium demands triggered violent opposition from many quarters in China. Had not the Qing rulers been overthrown, Chinese critics argued, partly because of their supine and ineffective resistance to Western imperialism? Was not foreign supervision, already operating with respect to the Maritime Cus-

ment would be in a position to deny that any negotiations had taken place. See *NAMP/RDSRIAC*, 893.00/1040 telegram, February 8, 1912, Calhoun to the Secretary of State; 893.00/1187, February 8, 1912, Tenney to Calhoun; and 893.00/1211, February 10, 1912, Tenney to Calhoun.

toms, at once a derogation of Chinese sovereignty and an insult to Chinese sensitivities? There were more than enough young Chinese trained abroad who were capable of serving as supervisors and auditors, they insisted. Even more conservative Chinese resented the idea that a few major powers should acquire a near monopoly over the financing of the New China and thus prevent the Chinese government from obtaining the most favorable terms possible.

Those who opposed the consortium's demands had additional motives, of course. Just as neither party in China had wanted the other to obtain foreign assistance during the military conflict because of its potential effect on the balance of power, so opponents of the Yuan government, notably the Tongmeng Hui stalwarts, were reluctant to see any development that might strengthen a man they distrusted and feared. Provincial leaders were fighting another battle, that of local autonomy versus centralization. They believed that large loans to the Beijing government would strengthen the center and enable it to establish dominance. They seemed to see no inconsistency in constantly beseeching the central government for funds and yet strongly opposing its acquisition of foreign loans. Finally, the Ministry of Finance announced that it was not in a position to help the provinces and that they should raise their own monies. Although this position was doubtless inescapable, the ministry's blunt statement of it was probably unwise because it was certain to reduce the provincial revenues being sent to Beijing and also to encourage separatist tendencies.

A few leaders suggested that China should avoid foreign loans altogether and depend on its own resources. The theme of self-reliance to be voiced recurrently in the future, had strong elements of logic and emotion on its side, but there was a chicken-and-egg problem. Were not foreign resources essential, at least in some degree, if China were to reach a capacity to be more self-reliant? And if the central goal was *rapid* economic development, could this be accomplished without foreign assistance? Here echoes of the old Liang-Sun debate—and portents of the future Mao-Deng division—were to be found.

The loan controversy that continued through the first years of the Republic must be seen in this context. Premier Tang immediately came under sharp attack from elements within his own party for the uses to which he had put those portions of the Anglo-Belgian loan that had been paid. Opposition, moreover, to foreign supervision of any loan mounted both in the Assembly and in the provinces, and on this issue the premier concurred. Tang was thus caught in a crossfire. Sniping at him from within the Assembly—even by members of his own party, the Tongmeng Hui—was frequent. Yet it was also widely proclaimed that he had lost the confidence of the major powers, on whom China still depended for recognition and financial aid. Loan negotiations with the consortium, now known as the Sextuple Group, were stalled, but by mid-April the British government had disavowed any support for the British nationals involved in the Anglo-Belgian syndicate, and it became apparent that this syndicate, facing strong international disapproval, could not raise sufficient money. Thus Tang was forced to submit a statement to the consortium on April 24 taking responsibility for his earlier actions and virtually agreeing to a cancellation of the Anglo-Belgian loan.

By this time it was apparent that the premier and the president had differences of opinion on the loan issue, especially regarding the question of foreign supervision. When negotiations with the consortium reopened around

May 1, Tang withdrew, and his place as negotiator was taken by the minister of finance, Xiong Xiling. Small interim loans to China were resumed by the consortium, but the negotiations dragged on without agreement, the issue of foreign supervision continuing to be the critical obstacle.[54]

From the opening session of the new Assembly on April 29, meanwhile, relations between the legislative and the executive branches of government had been marked by discord and rancor. The old issues of parliamentary versus presidential supremacy, centralization versus provincial autonomy, and—some believed—republicanism versus monarchism lay beneath almost every question, whether of personnel or of policy. A coalition government was getting under way without consensus. On the first day of the new session, many members of the old Assembly, considering themselves popularly selected (a dubious assumption), argued that the new members, being appointees in one form or another, should not participate in the organization of the legislative body. The argument was lost, but it indicated the political atmosphere.

Tang and his cabinet were frequently caught in the middle of the controversies that ensued. The premier proved unable to deliver on certain provincial appointments promised as a part of the compromise with the Nanjing Assembly, including the military governorship of Zhili, because Yuan naturally wanted to fill such key posts with men whose loyalty he could count on. In the matter of loans, Tang was accused by Assembly critics of extravagance in expenditures, and by executive critics of intransigence in negotiations with the consortium. It is perhaps not surprising, therefore, that on May 20 Tang and his colleagues submitted their resignations. The president refused to accept these, but in mid-June, after various crises, Tang abruptly left Beijing for Tianjin without even bidding farewell to Yuan. Emissaries were sent to persuade him to return, but he was adamant, saying he had lost the confidence of his own party and of foreigners as well. Shortly thereafter, the Tongmeng Hui members of the cabinet also tendered their resignations. The coalition era was over—after less than four months.

With the resignation of Tang, the Tongmeng Hui moved more decisively into the opposition. All of its cabinet members went out with Tang, and in the ensuing weeks tensions rose steadily. The Assembly approved Yuan's nomination of Lu Zhengxiang as Tang's successor, but the Tongmeng Hui opposed all of Lu's nominees, and a cabinet acceptable to a majority could not be formed. The Tongmeng Hui members now opposed a coalition cabinet, favoring a one-party government in line with their commitment to parliamentarism. Yuan, on the other hand, argued that he should appoint "the most able men available, irrespective of party." It was a classic issue, one that had figured prominently in the politics of Meiji Japan.

Yuan had a good political reason for wanting to keep some Tongmeng Hui members in any cabinet: he wanted to conciliate or neutralize his most troublesome opponents. But Song Jiaoren, now the Tongmeng Hui's leader in parliament, effectively stymied Yuan by threatening to dismiss any party members who accepted such posts. Yuan's repeated calls for unity, which expressed his own ideological convictions, were cast in strongly Confucian terms. In a presidential decree of July 12, for example, he urged that officials and people should work in harmony, "forgetting their animosities and giving up anger."[55] This decree, directed primarily at provincial assemblies but with implications for the national scene as well, revealed Yuan's deep worries about party politics. "How can the lives of the people be secure," he

45. Welcome party for Li Yuanhong in the governor's mansion, Nanjing, 1912. First row, from left: unknown, Sun Ke, Wang Jingwei, Li, Sun, Hu Hanmin, Li Xiaosheng, Zhang Shizhao, Chen Zhenpan

queried, "if the members of the provincial assemblies attack each other's errors whenever they have the least opportunity? The brains of able men will be exhausted in such useless discussions and the affairs of the country will suffer."

On July 19, however, the assembly rejected all six nominees for the cabinet placed before it by Lu, and the premier—a gentle man who could not stomach political turmoil—announced his determination to resign and soon thereafter entered a hospital. Two days later, on July 21, Yuan gave a banquet to which all Assembly members were invited, and there he made a strong appeal for support, citing the grave problems, domestic and foreign, that confronted the nation. But despite some pledges of aid after the government had presented a concrete program, opposition leaders made no compromises on the basic issues.

Like the early Meiji leaders of Japan, Yuan had made the decision not to organize a political party personally, and to seek instead a "national" image as a man above partisanship. Given China's political culture and his own proclivities, it was a natural decision, but one that made it more difficult for him to control or influence the legislative branch, despite the governmental encouragement given to parties like the Gonghedang. Neither personal appeals nor the rewards he was now beginning to dispense were proving sufficient. At this point, therefore, Yuan turned to another source of support, the military. In late July telegrams and messages poured into Beijing from provincial military governors and commanders, demanding that the Assembly back the president and approve a cabinet. Some messages carried a threatening tone, indicating that the Assembly should be dismissed or its "troublemakers" eliminated if it continued to prove recalcitrant. In Beijing itself posters and anonymous letters threatened assemblymen with dire consequences if they continued to "destroy the nation."

An informal alliance between Yuan and the military was being effected to offset the Assembly's intransigence—and it was an alliance certain to influence Yuan's future attitudes and actions. No doubt he was aware that one danger of such a union could be stronger provincialism, to which he was adamantly opposed. He tried hard, within the financial and military limits imposed on him, to exercise greater control over provincial appointments and policies. But he was not prepared to consider the alternative being offered to him, that of leading the Guomindang or some other party and fighting under the rules of the parliamentary game.

The new tactic worked. Though many members complained of the pressures being exerted upon them, the Assembly approved cabinet nominees. Meanwhile, to strengthen the professional side of his administration in preparation for constitutionalism and other types of modernization, and to win approval from the major powers, Yuan appointed various foreign advisers, beginning with G. E. Morrison, previously correspondent of the London *Times* in China, and Professor Ariga Nagao, a specialist in international law. Jeremiah Jenks from Cornell University was engaged to organize a public relations bureau in New York, but Yuan's key American adviser became Professor Frank Goodnow of Columbia University. Foreign military advisers attached to the Chinese army were also solicited from France, Germany, and Russia.

While these developments were taking place, a new political crisis erupted in mid-August. After the most perfunctory military hearings, Yuan summarily executed two political opponents of Li Yuanhong, which created an uproar among republican assemblymen and in the opposition press. Critics charged that proper procedures had not been followed, that the evidence against the men was flimsy, and that a miscarriage of justice had been condoned merely to oblige a political ally.* An impeachment motion was

*This bizarre case revealed the high quotient of personalism and arbitrariness that continued to operate in Chinese politics. Zhang Zhengwu, about thirty-five years of age, educated in Japan and prorevolution, had been teaching school in Wuchang at the outbreak of the revolt. Through a series of events, he became vice-chief of military affairs under Li. After the establishment of the Republic, however, he did not receive the type of post he desired. He then became increasingly critical of Li, and was on his second trip to Beijing to seek higher office when he was seized. On August 13 Li had sent Yuan a telegram alleging that Zhang was guilty of misappropriation of funds, the attempted instigation of revolt and assorted other misdeeds. Li asked Yuan to arrest and execute both Zhang and his associate, Fang Wei, promising that if this were done, he would attend Zhang's funeral in Wuchang and provide for his family as recognition of his earlier contributions to the revolution!

On the eve of his death, Zhang was entertaining political friends from both the Tongmeng Hui and the Gonghedang at one of Beijing's fashionable hotels. As his carriage left the party he was arrested and taken immediately before a hastily convened tribunal. Li's telegram was the only evidence produced, and despite Zhang's demand for a court martial or some type of trial, he was promptly shot. Fang and thirteen others were arrested the same night, and Fang was killed, with the others being released. Subsequently, as the protests poured in, the president got both Li and several other sources, including the Hankou Chamber of Commerce, to detail the alleged crimes of Zhang and his associate. For details, see *NAMP/RSDRIAC*, 893.00/624, August 31, 1912, Calhoun to the Secretary of State.

drafted, first including the president as well as the premier and the cabinet, but later limited to the premier. This action was dropped, but Yuan came under savage attack, with terms like "bloody butchery," "despotism," and "dictatorship" advanced in the Shanghai and Canton press.

At this point, however, the visit of Sun and other revolutionary leaders to Beijing provided some relief. Sun had said earlier that he wanted to meet with Yuan to discuss both political and developmental issues, and he did not allow the mid-August crisis to interfere with his trip. Arriving in Beijing on August 24, 1912, after a three-day stop in Tianjin, Sun was in an optimistic mood. As we have noted, in a speech at the inauguration of the Guomindang and in remarks elsewhere, he continued to give strong support to Yuan while at the same time heralding the Guomindang as a party motivated by patriotism and capable of extending its influence nationally, hence serving as a dynamic force for unity.

Sun had several extended meetings with Yuan, and the two men pronounced themselves in substantial agreement on a wide range of issues, even on land reform. On September 25 Yuan's office made public a statement in which Sun and the president agreed on eight points. These included support for a centralized government; temporary reduction in the military forces, but modernization of the army and navy; the importation of foreign capital for developmental purposes; government aid for agricultural, industrial, and financial reforms; and political harmony together with the maintenance of order so as to obtain recognition from the major nations.[56]

Yuan agreed to appoint Sun to the position of director of railways; he was to head an office with a budget of 30,000 taels monthly, charged with promoting an extraordinarily ambitious program of railway expansion to be financed through both foreign and domestic loans. Sun outlined the program on September 15 at a meeting attended by about fifty Assembly members. His aim was to build 200,000 *li* (over 70,000 miles) of railways within ten years. The nation would be divided into twenty districts for this purpose, with each district having its own administration and some 10,000 workers under its control. Work would begin simultaneously in every district. Funding would be based on several different formulas: direct loans, both domestic and foreign; the establishment of Chinese-foreign joint-stock companies; and the granting of rights to private entities to build railways with their own capital, with certain understandings, such as the government's right to repurchase. Under this program, Sun argued, China would have acquired a railway system spanning the entire nation, debt-free after forty years.[57]

Sun promptly resigned his Guomindang position, saying that he wanted to concentrate on the development programs, which could affect the fate of the nation so decisively in the years ahead. Immediately after he departed, Huang Xing arrived, and he too was given royal treatment by Yuan, despite the fact that he had bitterly denounced the recent executions.

Thus the fall and winter of 1912 were marked by a general lessening of political tension. Only the Mongolian issue (with which we shall soon deal) and the problem of foreign loans gave rise to disputation. Sun's strong support for Yuan quieted the militants and enabled Song Jiaoren to steer the new Guomindang toward a more moderate course than that which had characterized the Tongmeng Hui. Huang Xing actively cooperated in helping Yuan form a new government in which Zhao Bingzhun, a trusted associate of the president's, was to be premier.

In spite of the strong show of unity, however, certain key issues remained wholly unresolved. The most important of these was the role of the president versus the parliament. Guomindang leaders, now holding a majority in the Assembly and looking forward to winning the national parliamentary elections scheduled to begin in December 1912, held firmly to the principle of parliamentarism, including one-party cabinets responsible to the Assembly. Indeed, Huang Xing had worked hard to get Zhao's cabinet to join the Guomindang after their appointment, establishing a single-party government by this route, and the premier and a majority of the cabinet obliged. Yuan, however, continued to decline party leadership, insisting that a strong, independent presidency was essential to the political stability of the nation.

As we have seen, the national elections which ended in January 1913 resulted in a significant Guomindang victory, and that party prepared to take power. For the most part, the elections had been smoothly conducted. Strict suffrage requirements limited the electorate to a relatively small number of citizens, and an indirect system of election for the members of the House of Representatives placed the final decision in yet fewer hands. The members of the new upper house, the Senate, were elected by the provincial assemblies. It had been thought that the election laws gave the president an advantage because of his influence among the more affluent and prestigious citizens and in the provincial assemblies. However, the Guomindang had been aggressive and well-organized in its provincial work, with a result that surprised Yuan and his associates.

Countermeasures were undertaken even before the new parliament met. Liang Shiyi, Yuan's secretary, went south shortly after the elections had been concluded, and it was widely reported that one of his purposes was to induce defections from the Guomindang. Whatever his role, some fifty members of the Guomindang who had belonged to the Tongyidang prior to the merger withdrew to reestablish their old party; and other desertions were reported in March, allegedly encouraged by generous infusions of money.

Meanwhile, in late January, the Guomindang governing committee had voted overwhelmingly to support Yuan's election as president, but to recommend for premier either Song Jiaoren or Huang Xing, and to demand that all cabinets be chosen from their party. Despite the endorsement of Yuan, moreover, Guomindang opposition to his policies sharpened as the date for the opening of the new parliament approached. At a Shanghai conference of Guomindang parliamentary members, an agreement was secured on basic constitutional issues which was certain to displease Yuan. According to Zou Lu, who was present, despite disagreements on the strategy to be employed in the coming parliamentary session, the conference reached a consensus on three points. First, the provincial assemblies should serve as the bodies through which the president would be elected. Second, the national government should be organized as a parliamentary system under a premier elected by the House of Representatives and appointed by the president; the premier in turn would appoint his cabinet members, who would require presidential approval. Third, the provincial system should be maintained, with provincial governors being elected by the provincial assemblies.[58] These provisions, together with the political program drafted by Song, reduced the role of the presidency and underwrote parliamentary supremacy.[59] At this point, Song had been selected as the party's parliamentary leader.

46. Li Yuanhong and Sun in Wuchang, April 1912

Other issues emerged as the new parliament was about to convene. Yuan's nominee for minister of education was defeated in a straight partisan vote in the Assembly, the Guomindang being pitted against the progovernment Gonghedang. Guomindang spokesmen also made it clear that they did not approve of a government bill to establish a committee to draft the new constitution. Since the provisional constitution provided that a permanent

47. Sun, members of Nanjing Provisional Parliament at last meeting, April 1912. From the left, first row: 3d, Huang Zhongying; 4th, Huang Xing; 5th, Tang Shaoyi; 6th, Sun; 7th, Wang Chonghui; 8th, Cai Yuanpei; 9th, Lu Zhiyi; 10th, Wei Chenzu; 11th, Huang Dawei. Second row: 2d, Hu Hanmin; 5th, Lin Sen

constitution was to be adopted by the new National Assembly, opponents of the president's bill argued that his plan contravened this position. Yuan insisted that the appointment of a committee to draft a constitution would not violate the law, because its draft would be submitted to the new Assembly for approval before enactment, and that it had the advantage of enabling more rapid progress toward a permanent governmental structure.

Not without reason, Yuan's opponents suspected ulterior motives. What Yuan called "a committee" they saw as a constitutional convention. Of its proposed eighty members, only eight would be appointed by the Assembly; of the rest, six would be appointed by the cabinet, and sixty-six would come from provincial appointments—two from each governor and one from each provincial assembly. Since the military governors of the twenty-two provinces were in theory subject to appointment and removal by the president, the opponents of the measure charged that this would give Yuan control over at least fifty of the eighty members. In fact, of course, most southern military governors were not Yuan appointees, having come to office either through their own military efforts or by appointment from the revolutionaries. Yet Yuan had shrewdly kept them in office and played them off against the provincial assemblies. It is not surprising that nineteen of the twenty-two provincial military governors telegraphed the Assembly on March 7, urging passage of the measure. Once again the military coalition between Beijing and the provinces was operating. Meanwhile, it was announced that Professor Frank Goodnow had been engaged as constitutional adviser and would be en route to China shortly.

The dispute over constitution-making expressed the continuing division over fundamental issues and the growing suspicion that Yuan had a very limited commitment to republicanism. The president sought to reassure his opponents by issuing a long decree in March denouncing a Hubei group that had petitioned him to establish a constitutional monarchy, thus bringing up an old issue that had continued to lurk in the background. In this document, Yuan could not have been more unequivocal in his defense of republicanism. He began with the words "A republic is the best form of government and the highest emblem of political peace" and continued by praising the revolutionaries: "The rising of the patriotic army at once received response all around and achieved a success which will add lustre to our history and which commands respect throughout the world." He then offered a pledge: "I, the president, having accepted the weighty trust of the people, took the solemn oath upon my assumption of office that I am willing to devote my best ability to propagate the spirit of republicanism, to extirpate the dirt and corruption of the absolute oligarchy, and to permit no possible reappearance of the monarchical system in China."[60] After condemning the petitioners, he ordered them punished in accordance with the law. Yet these words did not put to rest the doubts of Yuan's opponents.*

THE RETREAT FROM REPUBLICANISM

In the midst of these developments, a thunderbolt struck the political scene. On March 20 Song was assassinated in the Shanghai railway station. The actual murderer, one Wu Shiying, was captured three days after the event. In confessing to the crime, he stated that he had been hired by Ying Guixing, a man of dubious reputation who had once consorted both with leading revolutionaries and with the Beijing government. Before the assassination Ying had been asked by the Yuan administration to get data linking Song with fraud during his sojourn in Japan, and the evidence clearly points to Yuan's direct involvement at this point. Whether the president was involved in or knew about the assassination plot remains unclear, but the court hearings indisputably implicated Zhang Shaozeng, a military adviser to the president, and Zhao Bingzhun, the premier. Two code-books had been given to Ying so that he could send and receive secret messages from

*In a March 1913 dispatch, E. T. Williams of the American legation provided a vignette of Yuan worthy of note: "Yuan is an old-fashioned politician; he knows no language but his own, and is not particularly well educated in that. He is not polished, nor a man of refined tastes. He is amiable, patient, of few words, and of untiring energy. He has no confidants; he trusts nobody entirely. But he is a strong personality; he attracts men to himself and wins their affection. He is courageous and not overscrupulous, and when occasion requires, he can strike swiftly and mercilessly, as in the case of Zhang Zhengwu last summer, not to refer to earlier illustrations. . . . He is believed by many to be aiming at a military dictatorship and, perhaps, at an imperial crown" (*NAMP/RSDRIAC*, 893.00/1595, March 11, 1913).

One of those so believing was Huang Xing, who on March 2 told the American consul, Hadley, in Shanghai that Yuan was seeking to become an emperor, and his followers were corrupt and inefficient, making it necessary for the Guomindang to assume "a political dictatorship" in the region. See *NAMP/RDSRIAC*, 893.00/1611, March 4, 1913, Hadley to Williams. During this period, there were even discussions of a possible amalgamation between the Guomindang and the Gonghedang, with Li Yuanhong as president, so as to pose a frontal challenge to Yuan. Li's lack of interest ended this possibility.

48. Reconvening of Provisional Parliament, Beijing, April 27, 1912. Yuan in center of front row

Beijing, and some of these messages went directly to Zhao. The contact man was Hong Shuzu, a confidential secretary to the cabinet. Armed with a letter of introduction from Zhang Shaozeng, Hong had gone to Shanghai to meet Ying and give him his instructions. In early March he issued an order for Song's assassination, promising a suitable monetary reward. It was never proved that any of the top Beijing leaders initiated this order, but the evidence against Zhao (who managed to avoid testifying) was deeply incriminating, and the Guomindang leaders never forgave Yuan for what they believed to be his personal involvement in the murder.[61]

The political atmosphere had been poisoned. When the new parliament opened on April 8, Yuan did not attend. According to some accounts, he feared assassination because parliamentary leaders had refused a governmental request to hold the initial meetings in the Forbidden City. Such a fear would have been justified. Assassination had become so common in Chinese politics that almost all prominent figures, of whatever faction, had to consider it a constant danger, and many took elaborate security precautions. For example, friends had urged Sun and Huang Xing not to travel to Beijing together in August 1912, in case an effort were made to kill them both in a single attack.

Other reports, however, argued that Yuan refused to come to the opening of parliament because some Guomindang members wanted him present only as a spectator. In any case, the president's message intended to be delivered to the opening session of the Assembly went unread; it was placed on a platform table in the form of a scroll by his secretary, Liang Shiyi. Significantly, it was rumored that Yuan had conferred with his generals, asking them whether his policy toward the parliament should continue to be conciliatory or whether the time had come "to act," and that the generals answered with a resounding vote in favor of the latter course.[62] Meanwhile, newspapers supportive of the Guomindang published a series of violent attacks on the Beijing government and on Yuan personally.

As the parliamentary sessions got under way, the Guomindang managed to secure the election of its nominees to the two top Senate posts, but it failed to win leadership in the House of Representatives, where the speakership went to Tang Hualong, a member of the Minzhudang (Democratic Party), which had been organized by Sun's historic rival, Liang Qichao.* Yuan, moreover, now began to use all the persuasive instruments at his command in an effort to reduce Guomindang power. Parliamentary members were wined and dined, and Yuan took pains to cater to their egos and their requests. Less savory techniques were also employed. Non-Guomindang members of parliament were given a monthly allowance of two hundred yuan, and money was advanced to "friendly" parties for organizational expenses. Gifts of money, moreover, were made to Guomindang members who agreed to withdraw from the party.** In some cases, Guomindang members were paid to work as an internal opposition within the party. Votes or abstentions on critical issues were purchased, and even nonattendance at parliamentary sessions was sometimes rewarded.

This massive corruption rapidly weakened the Guomindang, although a surprisingly large number of members remained loyal to party principles. Meanwhile, in May—scarcely a month after the parliament opened—a second major party emerged. It was the Jinbudang (Progressive Party), a product of the merger of the Minzhudang, the Gonghedang, and the Tongyidang. One of its leaders was Liang Qichao.[63]

In theory, one of the goals toward which the Guomindang had striven, that of a two-party system, had been achieved. In fact, however, China's first

*The prominent Guomindang member Zhang Ji was elected Senate president, with another Guomindang member, Wang Zhenting, elected vice-president. In the House, the vice-presidency went to Chen Guoxiang of the Gonghedang, foreshadowing the merger between the Minzhudang and the Gonghedang that was to take place shortly.

The initial composition of China's first parliament was as follows:

PARTY	HOUSE OF REPRESENTATIVES	SENATE
Guomindang	269	123
Gonghedang	120	55
Tongyidang	18	6
Minzhudang	16	8
Independent	26	44
Members belonging to more than one party	147	38
Totals	596	274

See Zou Lu, *Zhongguo Guomindang shigao* 1:144; Yang Youzhun, *Zhongguo zhengdang shi*, p. 61; and Xie Bin, *Minguo zhendang shi*, pp. 51–52.

**Zou Lu, one of those who remained loyal to the Guomindang, records that he rejected an offer of 400,000 yuan from the government to organize a new party. Many others succumbed, and before long, half a dozen "parties" composed of former Guomindang members had emerged, ranging in size from 20 to 70 members. See Yang Youzhun, *Zhongguo zhengdang shi*, pp. 69–70.

49. *Song Jiaoren, shortly before his assassination*

experiment in Western-style parliamentary government was already moving into deep trouble. The developments in the spring of 1913 naturally affected trends within the Guomindang. By early May the balance between moderates and militants in the party was shifting in favor of the militants, and plans were being laid for a "second revolution," which would overthrow Yuan and secure power by force. One key to this shift was Sun Yat-sen. Sun, as we have seen, had resolutely supported Yuan in the past, even in periods of bitter division, despite persistent inner doubts. By late April, however, he was in the process of changing his views. The Song assassination was a key factor, but nearly as important was Yuan's decision to ignore parliament in consummating the consortium loan, along with other signs that he intended to make the presidency the fountainhead of state power.

On May 1 Sun engaged in a most revealing conversation with Bishop J. W. Bashford, an American Methodist missionary and one of the most influential foreigners in China. Sun's hostility to Yuan was now uncompromising. He charged that Song's assassination was the direct work of Yuan, and that the president was determined to crush all opposition by any means necessary. When Bashford urged Sun to throw his weight against the development of another conflict because of the frightful consequences that would ensue for China, Sun replied that the fighting could be over in six weeks because the revolutionaries could put 300,000 men in the field immediately. In his usual optimistic frame of mind, Sun discounted the damage that would result. When it was suggested that another civil war might enable Russia and Japan to complete their seizures of Mongolia and Manchuria, he seemed willing to write off these regions. He is reported to have said that they were not "the true China," and in conversations with others he remarked that, in any case, they had already been lost, and China could regain them only when it was strong and had adequate transportation and communications facilities.

Bashford suggested that if the outer regions were seized, an imperialist struggle over China proper might follow, whereupon Sun responded by saying that in that case China would fight and would be aided by Japan. When asked why he did not challenge Yuan through peaceful, competitive elections, Sun replied that in such a contest he could not win, because Yuan would use unlimited funds for bribery and any other activities necessary to defeat him.[64]

The American consul general in Shanghai, Amos Wilder, provided his own evaluation of Sun's mood and probable actions. On occasion, Wilder wrote, Sun seems obsessed with the idea of assassinating Yuan, but not out of selfish ambition; he really believes that Yuan has betrayed the country. Being an idealist, he wants to see a reformed nation at once, with railways built tomorrow, honesty prevailing, and modern-minded Chinese in charge of government. The danger, Wilder continued, is that Sun may be urged on by his friends and the domestic press to believe that it is his duty to begin a new revolution; and if he does this, the disciplined forces of Yuan Shikai will crush Sun's partisans in a bloody debacle. He concluded by saying that Sun was depending greatly on Japan, and had in fact "thrown himself absolutely into the hands of that country," thinking that if he accepts their territorial demands, they will help him conduct a new revolution.[65]

When Wilder visited him the next day, however, Sun vigorously denied that he was contemplating another revolution. All he meant, he said, was that he had once given Yuan his hearty support, but now he had withdrawn that support.[66] The question of precisely when Sun really decided to give his assent to a new revolt remains unclear. He had been in Japan at the time of Song's death and had returned to Shanghai on March 25, 1913. Many years later, in a speech at Canton on November 25, 1923, Sun gave the impression that he had immediately opted for revolution; he declared that when party comrades had sought his advice on the course of action to be taken, he had urged immediate armed revolt because he did not believe the issue could be resolved legally.[67] Yet in a discussion with his former secretary, Ma Sou, three days after his return, Sun made no mention of the Song case, and spoke primarily about the need for establishing cordial relations between China and Japan.[68] *Minli bao*, moreover, in reporting Sun's visit to Huang Xing, stated that Sun favored a legal solution to the Song case.[69]

It may well be that in the first days after his return, Sun did not realize how deeply involved in the murder the Beijing government really was. He soon learned the facts, possibly embroidered. Dr. James Cantlie, Sun's long-time friend, sent the London *Times* a translation of a telegram which Sun had sent to Yuan on July 2, presumably having received the copy from Sun himself. In this telegram, Sun asserted, "my mind [about you] had not been altered until evidence relating to the murder of Song Jiaoren was published." Sun went on to criticize Yuan for having approved the consortium loan unconstitutionally "for the sinews of war and mobilized troops." When I supported you, Sun continued, "I was accused of trying to please the northern military." Now, he continued, you should leave the presidency, and if you do so, I will persuade the soldiers and people in the south and east to lay down their arms; but if you do not, I shall adopt the same measures toward you that we used against the monarchy.[70]

By the end of April, it should be noted, when more facts about the Song case had been revealed, Sun and Huang were demanding that a thorough investigation be conducted and the guilty parties punished.[71] And in June, after the interviews with Americans noted above, and depressed over the fact that his daughter was dying of Bright's disease, Sun told a *Central China Post* reporter that he was "finished with politics," but went on to comment on the Song affair. "The idea that the government should be implicated in the murder has outraged my sense of justice. I do not say that the president is himself concerned in it, but it was his premier, his own secretary, and he must have known something about it. . . . The whole thing has disgusted me and made me sick at heart."[72]

The issue of foreign loans deepened the hostility between Yuan and his opponents. On April 26, 1913, exactly one day after Sun and Huang Xing had joined in putting out a circular telegram demanding that the true culprits in the Song assassination be brought to justice, the consortium loan contract was signed in Beijing, and many Guomindang leaders were convinced that some of the funds would be used to destroy them.[73] A strongly worded manifesto signed by Sun attacking the loan as unconstitutional was issued on May 6.* At some point in this period, Huang Xing approached a German firm in Shanghai to purchase arms and ammunition, but this was blocked by the central government, which found out about the plan.[74] Shanghai-Nanjing railway authorities were approached by the dissidents

*This manifesto was addressed to "the governments and people of the foreign powers," and urged that the bankers be prevented from providing the Beijing government with funds which would undoubtedly be used to make war on its opponents. Since Sun was seeking to put the onus for conflict on Yuan, it is understandable that he would not want to be on record as favoring a resort to arms at this point. Thus, in the manifesto it was stated that war would "inevitably inflict terrible misery and suffering upon the people," and if the Beijing government could be kept without funds, there was a prospect for compromise between it and the people—but a liberal supply of money would probably precipitate a conflict. For the manifesto, see "Declaration of Incontrovertible Evidence on the Unconstitutional Nature of the Loan of the Yuan Government," in *Geming wenxian* 42–43:342–344.

with regard to troop transport facilities. It was also reported that the Russian and Japanese consuls general in Wuhan had sought unsuccessfully to persuade Li Yuanhong to run against Yuan for the presidency, and throughout May and June various Japanese met with Sun and Huang in Shanghai, and there were indications that in some cases at least, aid was being solicited or offered.[75]

None of these developments escaped the notice of Yuan's government, which began to prepare for a confrontation. Throughout April Yuan gave every indication that he did not intend to bow to his opponents, in parliament or outside, on such matters as foreign loans, the Song case, or the recalcitrance of provincial governors. The effort to seduce Guomindang members of parliament was stepped up and was showing results by late April. On May 3, just as the most damaging evidence against Zhao and other Beijing authorities was coming out of the Shanghai Mixed Court hearings on the Song murder, Yuan issued a tough executive order asserting that a Shanghai group was conspiring to launch a second revolution, seeking funds from merchants and attempting to make arrangements for troop movements; he concluded by promising that the government would not permit "these traitors" to destroy the Republic.

Talk of rebellion became increasingly voluble, however, despite the fact that on May 2 the United States recognized the Beijing government, an action we shall discuss later. On that same day, Yuan appointed Duan Qirui, the minister of war, to act as premier pro tem, and Duan later blocked all attempts to get his predecessor, Zhao Bingzhun, and other principals to testify in the Shanghai court proceedings. Military preparations in the North had been under way for some time, and in early June Yuan began to move against certain provincial officials whom he had reason to distrust. For months he had been in conflict with Li Liejun, the military governor of Jiangxi. Li, a Guomindang supporter, had openly defied Yuan in the spring of 1913 by refusing to accept his appointee for civil governor; and arms and ammunition intended for Li had been seized by naval ships operating under Beijing's orders. On June 9 Yuan dismissed Li, appointing Li Yuanhong to act as military governor in his place. One week later Hu Hanmin, a Guomindang stalwart, was removed as military governor of Guangdong, and shortly thereafter a third opponent, Bo Wenwei, the military governor of Anhui, was ousted.

Even at this late date, Yuan's enemies remained divided over tactics. Many of them felt that a resort to arms would end in utter failure, but the militants finally carried the day, abetted by Yuan's decision in early July to send northern troops into Jiangxi to end Li Liezhun's military control. After several false starts, the "second revolution" got under way in mid-July. Its chief leaders were Huang Xing, Li Liezhun, Bo Wenwei, and a veteran Qing official, Cen Chunxuan, who had once been close to Yuan but had fallen under suspicion because of his actions as Fujian pacification commissioner.* Sun Yat-sen himself did not take an active role in the conflict, although he supported the decision to rebel and had been fully involved in the consultations that led to it.

*The final decision to commence military operations against Beijing government forces was taken after meetings in Shanghai attended by the top revolutionary leaders. Previous efforts appear to have been directed toward assassination. In early June a small group of radicals, reported to be members of a secret assassination society and labeled anarchists by the press, had been arrested in Beijing, charged with a plot to kill Yuan and other high officials.

As had been widely predicted, the "second revolution" failed utterly. The revolutionaries lacked trained troops and military equipment. Their funds were meager, reflecting the opposition of the merchant community to more property destruction and bloodletting. Their planning was hopelessly inadequate, and coordination between various revolutionary centers was poor. Between mid-July and early August seven provinces, all of them in South and Central China, declared their "independence" from Beijing. But some of these declarations were forced by the revolutionary commanders on the scene, and by no means represented a wholehearted commitment, either by provincial officials or by the people. Moreover, they did not come simultaneously. Jiangxi and several other provinces, for example, had withdrawn their support and returned to the government fold before the Sichuan declaration was issued; and in any case, the Sichuan declaration was made in Zhongqing, but was strongly opposed by the authorities in Chengdu, the capital.

The revolution was over by September 2, when Nanjing, the last rebel stronghold, surrendered to the forces of Zhang Xun. Its reverberations continued in many provinces for years, however, and in the course of the conflict additional strains were put on relations between the Beijing government and Japan. There was ample evidence that various Japanese, probably without official sanction, had assisted the revolutionaries by providing arms, serving as military advisers, and helping to transport key leaders. Li Yuanhong was especially bitter, charging that the Japanese had at one time harbored assassins in their quarters and had later involved themselves directly in the conflict. The Japanese consul general in Hankou was forced to issue an order proclaiming Japan's neutrality and prohibiting Japanese citizens from participating on either side.* This action, however, by no means quelled

---

The government asserted that Huang Xing had given the plotters 40,000 yuan as expense money. Huang vigorously denied the charge, and no proof was ever offered. There is little doubt, however, that even if the accusation against Huang in this instance was false, various Guomindang leaders were giving serious thought to assassination as a weapon during this period, including Sun. In late June a more extensive plot of the same type was uncovered in Wuchang, involving a secret organization with the colorful name of "The Blood and Iron Thief-exterminating Society." The "thieves" were Yuan and Li Yuanhong, and some of the conspirators reportedly made use of the Japanese concession in the city. When the plot was discovered, Li struck harshly, and some fifty-five individuals were executed, although none of the key leaders appear to have been caught.

*Prior to official Japanese action, Li Yuanhong had been very blunt in speaking with a Western reporter of the *China Press* as the revolt commenced. "The present disturbances," he asserted, "are the work of the Guomindang, and the motive powers are Sun Yat-sen and Huang Xing. They are backed by Japanese influences. Whether the Japanese government is at the bottom of it, I cannot state positively." Li went on to assert that Japanese had been abetting the revolutionary cause for months, and that only a few days earlier, two Japanese military advisers to Li Liezhun had been taken to Jujiang by a Japanese steamer, with Japanese ships earlier landing arms, men, and silver in Shanghai to help the rebel cause. For the interview, see *NAMP/RDSRIAC*, 893.00/1837, July 16, 1913, Greene to Williams. A week later, Consul General Yoshizawa in Hankou wrote a letter to the *Central China Post* and the Chinese-language press which included a message addressed to Japanese citizens. Yoshizawa stated that although some Japanese "adventurers" had joined the struggle, their action was "far from the desire of the Japanese government." Because his government wished to make its position "clearer than ever," an official order was being issued. That order, which followed, stated that the policy of the Japanese government was one of "impartiality and fairness, in letter and spirit," prohibited all Japanese subjects from taking part in the civil war, and subjected violators to legal prosecution. For the clipping, see *NAMP/RDSRIAC*, 893.00/1843, July 23, 1913.

Chinese suspicions. Thus, when several Japanese citizens were killed by Zhang Xun's soldiers during the seizure of Nanjing, the government offered no immediate expressions of regret. The Japanese responded with heavy pressure, including the dispatch of a small military contingent, and Zhang Xun was finally ordered to go to the Japanese consulate personally to deliver an apology.

The abortive "second revolution" had a dramatic effect on the immediate course of Chinese politics, although it can be argued that the basic trends had already been fixed, and that the new upheaval influenced only matters of timing and intensity. Whatever its justification, the Guomindang leaders' recourse to arms presented Yuan with a stunning victory. Unquestionably, it prompted him to move more rapidly away from the republican path and toward authoritarian rule. For one thing, it dramatically increased his dependence upon provincial military governors. Indeed, in the years ahead China was to be governed essentially by military men, who relied in varying degrees on civilian technocrats. The failure of the uprising also produced deep divisions within the Guomindang and the republican forces in general, which Yuan was naturally quick to exploit.

On the eve of the revolt, the Guomindang members of parliament had once again been discussing the possibility of impeaching the government and moving toward a one-party cabinet. With respect to impeachment, they had reason to hope for the support of other parties, since there was an unprecedented degree of opposition to the Zhao administration within the parliament.* The president and his government were on the defensive, beleaguered and frustrated. When the rebellion broke out, however, Yuan regained the initiative. The more militant Guomindang members of parliament, wholly sympathetic to the revolutionary cause and sometimes directly involved in it, left Beijing for the South, fearing for their lives. A majority of Guomindang representatives remained, however, and many continued to offer surprisingly stout resistance to various governmental proposals. Nevertheless, Yuan was now able to get approval of Xiong Xiling as premier at the end of July, a sign that parliamentary obstructionism was on the wane.

In early August Yuan moved onto the political offensive, now convinced that he would score an early and decisive military victory in the South. In a presidential decree he declared that since all the leaders of the rebellion were influential members of the Guomindang, the question of whether they were acting privately or on behalf of the party had to be determined. All party members were to report for questioning before designated military authorities; and if the party had no connection with the rebellion, it was to expel all rebels from membership within three days.[76] Confronted with this ultimatum, a committee of the Guomindang in Beijing wrote to the government on August 3 that the party had no connection with the conflict, and

*Zhao had earlier appeared before the assembly after adamant demands that he answer questions, and admitted that he had paid Ying Guixing 50,000 yuan, supposedly in exchange for Ying's disbandment of his gangster-type group. Another damaging admission was that he had given Ying a copy of the secret telegraph codes. Zhao was never to testify before the Shanghai court. On May 1 he resigned as premier and immediately accepted the position of military governor of Zhili, headquartered in Tianjin. Less than a year later, he died of natural causes. One month earlier, on January 19, 1914, Ying Guixing was shot by two detectives on the Beijing-Tianjin train. Hong Zhuzu disappeared, but in May 1919 he was recognized by Song Jiaoren's son in Shanghai, arrested, tried for murder and executed. For details, see Jerome Ch'en, *Yuan Shih-k'ai*, pp. 130–131.

announced that it had expelled Huang Xing, Chen Qimei, Bo Wenwei, Li Liejun, and Chen Jiongming.[77] Interestingly, Sun was not on this list, nor did the government demand his expulsion. A few days later, however, it was announced that Sun's appointment as director of railways had been withdrawn. Huang Xing's title of General of the Army, which Yuan had conferred on him during his Beijing visit, had been revoked much earlier.

The Guomindang was now virtually leaderless and sharply divided over the issues surrounding the revolt. Sun himself had fled to Japan in early August, and Huang had followed soon after. Several hundred Guomindang rebels went into exile, and Japan again became the center of Chinese revolutionary activity.* At this point Sun regarded the Guomindang as a complete failure and described party shortcomings with considerable bitterness. Later, when he committed himself to the establishment of a new party, he would emphasize centralized power and discipline.

Meanwhile, with the second revolution suppressed, Yuan and his associates moved in two broad directions. On the one hand, they made an effort to recruit "individuals of talent"—preferably modernizers of moderate to conservative political leanings—into a strong central government that would undertake far-reaching reforms based on a firm ideological foundation. On the other hand, they moved more rapidly away from Western-style parliamentarism, convinced that liberalism when applied to China could lead only to disaster.

By early September Premier Xiong had built a cabinet that was widely regarded as the most promising yet created in the republican era. Yuan and Xiong had drawn from their very considerable pool of acquaintances to bring forth a mix of experienced literati-officials, successful entrepreneurs, professional diplomats, and military men.** All of them except Liang Qichao were at the time members of the Gonghedang, which gave the cabinet and the government a one-party character, but by this time party identification as such had become much less important. Philosophically, their predominant commitment was to social reform, with a revitalized Confucianism as the ideological underpinning. Indeed, many had participated in the reform efforts of the late imperial era. But most of them now shared Yuan's conviction that successful reform could only come through political unity, not through the divisive politics of Western-style liberalism.

One of the first reforms they discussed concerned administration in its broadest dimensions: how should China, with its vast territory and massive population, be divided in terms of administrative units for increased central control and greater efficiency? This matter was particularly urgent because

* Feng Ziyou was to write that "several thousand" Guomindang supporters went to Japan at this time. See Luo Jialun, ed., *Geming wenxian* 5:59. This is certainly an exaggeration. In April 1914, Sun claimed only 400 to 500 followers and complained of the small number who had come to Japan. See Sun's letter to Deng Zeru, *Geming wenxian* 5:579–580.

** The strong figures in the cabinet in addition to Xiong included Liang Qichao, minister of justice; Zhang Jian, a renowned scholar-entrepreneur and social reformer, as minister of agriculture and commerce; Sun Baoqi, whose career had spanned both business and diplomacy, as minister of foreign affairs; and Duan Qirui, who remained in his post as minister of war, together with Liu Guanxiong, who continued as minister of the navy. It is of more than passing interest to note that this was a cabinet in which the entrepreneurial quotient was relatively high. Like their Japanese counterparts, however, the Chinese business-industrial leaders of this period, while committed to modernization and to a strong state, were not necessarily advocates of Western liberalism, as we earlier pointed out. Their inclinations were toward mercantilism and its political concomitants.

the authority of the central government had been steadily eroding under pressure from the provincial military governors. On August 27, even before the "second revolution" had been completely quashed, Premier Xiong announced that the government had decided to divide the nation into five or six large military regions, each to be headed by a commander responsible directly to the center—a system much like the one put into effect by the Communists immediately after their victory in 1949. The provinces, Xiong continued, would be retained, but the military governorships would be abolished and civil governors would take charge of all activities at this level, including military affairs.[78]

Changes were made in this plan during the fall of 1913. In September it was announced that the cabinet had approved nine military districts, and the division of provinces into these nine units showed a marked resemblance to the old viceroy units of the late Qing era. The concept of making the military commanders directly responsible to the Ministry of War was retained, and when the names of the prospective new commanders were released in late September, almost all of them were men with strong personal ties to Yuan. Meanwhile, the government continued to assert that the provincial military governorships would be abolished, and in November a further step was taken when Liang Qichao presented a package of far-reaching reform proposals, which was eventually endorsed in slightly amended form by Premier Xiong. The basic administrative unit would be not the province but the *dao* (circuit or district) and *xian* (county). In Liang's plan, China would be divided into sixty civil districts; as ultimately recommended by Xiong, there would be eighty-two. These districts would bear the basic responsibility for all administrative functions within their jurisdiction and would be answerable directly to the central government; the *xian* beneath them would be charged with local governance.[79] This concept both recalled the past and foreshadowed the future: variants of it had been advanced since the 1898 reform period, and it sprang from motives like those that led to the experiment with the commune as an administrative unit, which began in 1957.

These proposals for basic structural reform were accompanied by attempted innovations in fiscal policy, agriculture, industry, and education. Noting that 95 percent of the tax revenues of the central government in 1912 had come from two sources, the salt gabelle and customs duties, the Xiong government advanced a comprehensive program of tax and fiscal reform. It involved increases in import duties, the imposition of a land tax, and reform of the salt gabelle, along with the abolition of the restrictive *likin* tax. The aim was to increase central revenues by over 30 percent, thereby eliminating dependence on foreign loans except for sound developmental purposes. The success of any such program naturally hinged on the ability of the Beijing government to control both the revenues and the broader fiscal policies of the provinces. To this end, it was proposed that all old provincial bank notes be recalled and replaced by national notes based on silver, and that firm restraints be placed on independent monetary or financial operations at the provincial level. A uniform system of auditing and financial reporting for all political units was also advocated.

The United States was to be the model for new agricultural policies. Agricultural credit was to be expanded through the policies of rural banks. Technology and science were to be applied to agriculture as rapidly as possible, and major attention was to be given to water conservation. The communications and transportation system was to be developed in order to provide closer links between rural and urban China; in this effort, primary emphasis was to be placed on railway construction. With respect to industry, an "open door" policy regarding foreign trade and investment was to be pursued. Foreign capital was to be especially encouraged in the mining industry, from which 60 percent of the profits were to be retained by China. Finally, compulsory primary education was to be enforced, with Confucian principles serving as the foundation for the ethical training of China's youth.

This emphasis on Confucian principles deserves some comment. By the fall and winter of 1913, the president and his key advisers in Beijing were committed to revitalizing Confucianism as a weapon against what they regarded as a serious breakdown in morality, affecting the whole social order. Like their various successors, they had come to believe that China could not exist without an ideology. Convinced that liberalism was a philosophy of selfishness and divisiveness and that anarchism and socialism led to violence and social disorder, they became increasingly committed to restoring Confucianism as an official political creed—and possibly even a religious one. Thus, when the Confucian Society of Beijing met on September 3, some three hundred dignitaries were present; Yuan sent Liang Shiyi as his representative, and both Yan Fu and Liang Qichao were speakers.[80] In the months that followed, organizational activities on behalf of Confucianism mushroomed in various provinces, many of them officially sponsored. In late November Yuan issued a presidential decree encouraging these activities. He directed the Ministry of Education to make a careful investigation of how to promote Confucian studies and then propose a specific program for discussion and adoption.[81] The long-frustrated hopes of Kang and Liang now seemed on the point of fruition, and when Kang himself returned to Canton after years of exile abroad, he was accorded lavish official honors and protection.[82]

The movement to revive Confucianism was accompanied by a purification campaign of substantial proportions. Xiong, contending that official corruption had become a cancer that had to be curbed, announced that severe penalties would henceforth be applied against persons who offered or accepted bribes. To this end also, the old practice of appointing as provincial officials individuals native to other areas was reestablished; Yuan proclaimed that this practice—largely abandoned after the revolution—would reduce the pressures for special favors from relatives and friends. Popular vices were also brought under the spotlight. Ordinances prohibiting gambling were passed, and a campaign against urban crime was launched. The government also promised that it would take more vigorous action in an effort to rid the countryside of the robber bands that infested so many areas.

In concept, these reform proposals could hardly be faulted, at least in terms of their broad goals. If their scope was sweeping, that was in line with past reform efforts and did not exceed the bounds of necessity. Overnight miracles were not to be expected, but it was hoped that some real progress could be made on the main proposals. Unfortunately, the program was stillborn. Many reasons can be found for this fact, but one occurrence that blocked immediate action was the controversy between Yuan and the parliament, which erupted once again in the fall and winter of 1913. In this struggle, Yuan was forced—somewhat against his will—to enlist further support from the provincial military leaders, and as the battle reached a climax he made the decision to eliminate first the Guomindang and then the parliament itself in an effort to gain unimpeded political authority. Although these acts were justified in executive circles as necessary preliminary steps toward thoroughgoing reform, they made the inauguration of most reforms impossible, at least temporarily; and this was especially true of reforms relating to structural reorganization and control over provincial military leaders.

Let us examine the most salient developments in this struggle between Yuan and parliament. It will be recalled that the provisional constitution enacted by the Nanjing assembly in 1912 assigned to parliament, once elected, the power to draft a permanent constitution. Yuan, with the backing of various military governors, sought to establish a special constitutional conference "to speed up the process," but this was rejected by the legislature. Pursuing its charge, the new parliament picked from within its ranks a constitutional committee of sixty, thirty from each house. Yuan's fears regarding this body were well justified from his standpoint. Dominated by Guomindang members, the constitutional committee proceeded to work toward a system that guaranteed parliamentary supremacy and provided for a relatively weak presidency. Despite the outbreak of conflict in mid-1913, moreover, and the disappearance of some Guomindang members, the committee continued its labors without veering from its original commitments.

Meanwhile, Yuan had commissioned his own draft constitution, relying heavily on two foreign experts, Ariga Nagao and Frank Goodnow. In vain, signals were hoisted that the president would not accept a constitution that made the presidency heavily dependent on the legislative branch of government. As the parliamentary committee was nearing the end of its work, Yuan sought to send representatives to it to discuss differences, but to the astonishment of many, the committee refused to meet with his emissaries. In mid-October the committee unveiled what came to be known as the Temple of Heaven Constitution, and Yuan immediately indicated that certain changes in it would have to be made.[83] It gave parliament clear supremacy over the executive, requiring legislative approval for all major officials, civil and military alike, as well as for all domestic laws, declarations of war and peace, and treaties.

On October 25 Yuan asked for five important amendments that would provide for greater presidential authority over appointments, over decisions concerning war and peace, and over interim legislation (including financial measures) when the parliament was in recess.* Significantly, Yuan addressed this appeal to provincial military governors, charging that Guomindang influence on the constitutional committee had produced a threat of parliamentary dictatorship and an emasculated presidency. Their immediate response was to condemn the new constitution and, in many cases, to demand the dissolution of the parliament, the Guomindang, or both.

*The issue between Yuan and the committee centered upon a simple matter of power. With the earlier problems which he had faced with the legislature no doubt in mind, Yuan wanted a maximum degree of independence from the parliament with respect to key appointments and foreign policy decisions, and he demanded the right to promulgate interim legislation, including emergency financial measures, while parliament was out of session, subject to legislative approval within ten days after a new session had opened. The draft constitution, on the other hand, provided for a permanent parliamentary committee composed of members of both houses, which would function between sessions specifically to monitor and keep control over governmental policies. Yuan naturally took strong exception to this provision. For Yuan's requests, see *Zhengfu gongbao* (Government Gazette), Beijing, October 25, 1913, pp. 1–2.

Later on, both of Yuan's foreign advisers were critical of certain key sections of the Temple of Heaven Constitution. Ariga in particular attacked the draft, asserting that the committee had openly disregarded the principle of the independence of the three branches of government and had aimed at subordinating the executive branch to the other two. Under Articles 43 and 83, he maintained, the president was ordered to carry out his policies through the cabinet; but since he was not given the unrestricted right to select the premier, the key individual in shaping administrative policies, the cabinet would be forced to follow parliament, not the president. He also objected to the concept of a permanent parliamentary watchdog committee, and to the fact that the president had not been allowed a voice in creating the constitution. He argued, interestingly enough, that Yuan had inherited sovereign rights from the emperor for the nation.[84]

In November Goodnow's draft constitution was made public. Leaning heavily upon the U.S. model, with some provisions drawn from the French constitution, Goodnow had aimed at a balance of powers, making the president, the legislature, and the judiciary roughly coequal—though he did not propose that the judiciary be given the power to determine the constitutionality of legislation. The president was to be elected by the two houses of parliament, but he was to have a fixed term of office, the prerogative to initiate legislation, sweeping appointment powers, the right to remove or suspend all officials except judges, and authority as commander in chief of the armed forces.[85] Although Yuan praised the Goodnow draft, he did not specifically endorse it or seek its enactment.* By this time the tide of events was moving in a very different direction.

Several months earlier, nineteen military governors headed by Li Yuanhong had urged that in the interest of stability, rules governing the election of the president and vice-president be approved by the parliament before the completion of the constitution. Working under the shadow of a civil conflict, parliament acquiesced, and the election of a permanent president and vice-president took place on October 6. With 703 out of a total of 868 members of both houses present, Yuan was elected president on the third ballot with 507 votes, and the next day Li Yuanhong was chosen vice-president, receiving 611 votes from the 719 members present.[86]

In his inaugural address Yuan stressed that "law and morality" were the twin pillars of a successful constitutional republic. Thus, a legal system for China—by which was meant a constitution—had to be clearly defined, and public order had to be established and maintained. In promising to introduce reforms "one by one," he indicated that he preferred a conservative rather than an "extreme radical" course. He concluded by asserting that it was essential for China to cultivate science, advance education, and introduce both the civilization and the capital of foreign countries in order to promote agriculture and industry. Following such a path, while making improvements in national defense, would ultimately make China strong and

*In an interview with the American minister, Paul S. Reinsch, in late November, Yuan stated that he had seen a translation of Dr. Goodnow's draft and was much impressed with its adaptability to the requirements of China. But these polite remarks were not followed by public support. In truth, the Goodnow constitution was probably too liberal for Yuan at this point, though in many respects it met the president's objections to the Temple of Heaven draft. For the interview, see *NAMP/RDSRIAC*, 893.00/2049, November 24, 1913.

self-reliant. It was to advance these concepts, he said, that Confucius had spoken of universalization.

Yuan's address contained that striking blend of political conservatism and economic modernization—drawing on China's own political culture for stability and unity, and on foreign nations for science and technology—which was to be advocated by many generations of Chinese leaders, from Zhang Zhidong to Deng Xiaoping. His interpretation of republicanism was revealing. He said, in effect, I have consulted with learned scholars of France, the United States, and other nations, and I have found that republicanism means the gathering together of the opinions of the whole citizenry to form a complete system of law meant to be strictly observed by everyone; liberty or freedom outside the law is to be forsaken by all. Our citizens, he continued, are mild and obedient, but they have not yet become accustomed to the habit of abiding strictly by the law.[87]

In the name of maintaining order, the Beijing government now took on many of the attributes of a police state. Thousands of informers and secret police were recruited to operate in the major cities. Hundreds of people were arrested on political charges, and the newspapers carried daily accounts of executions. Critics spoke of a reign of terror, and for Yuan's more militant opponents, such a description was not inaccurate. In this setting, assassination appeared to be the only feasible weapon of counterattack, and various purported plots were uncovered, including one involving the head of the Beijing mounted police.

Within the parliament, however, a surprising firmness of will remained. New parties or parliamentary groups were constantly being formed and reformed, but the majority of members remained committed to a constitution that guaranteed parliamentary supremacy.* When Yuan, now fortified by his position as the legally elected president, finally realized that fact, he struck back with a telling blow. On November 4, three presidential orders were issued. The first announced the immediate dissolution of the Guomindang. The second declared all Guomindang members expelled from parliament and called for new candidates from the affected districts to be recruited to take their seats. The third presented "documentary proof" that the Guomindang as a party had been deeply involved in subversive activities.[88] Within the cabinet, both the premier and the minister of home affairs, among others, had opposed these orders, but once issued they were enforced in dramatic fashion. Guomindang headquarters in Beijing was occupied and searched by police, and the seventeen party members discovered there were detained.** Railway stations in the city were guarded so that no party

*In the fall of 1913, several new parties emerged: the Dazhongdang (Great China Party), the product of the amalgamation of five small parties, supporting the principles of unity and patriotism; the Minxiandang (People's Constitutional party), composed chiefly of old Guomindang and Jinbudang members, with its objective that of "fighting evil and corruption in politics," but regarded by the government as a means of carrying on the Guomindang causes; and the Daode Hui (Party of Morality), the members of which to be eligible had to place morality above money or influence. A leading member was Zhao Bingzhun!

**The party members found at headquarters were detained for two days while records of the party and the correspondence of its officers were carefully examined. Not only those individuals who were currently Guomindang members, but all who had been members after the outbreak of the summer revolt, had to deliver their badges and certificate of membership to authorities and allow their private papers to be examined.

members could escape. More than 200 members of parliament were affected, along with countless provincial assemblymen and local officeholders.

This action paralyzed the parliament, for it was now unable to achieve a quorum. The injunction to fill the seats with new candidates was not enforced, primarily because most provincial governors were strongly in favor of dissolving parliament. Only if Yuan were willing to recertify some 150 members of parliament could a legal quorum be attained; but word from the executive branch indicated that he was prepared to reinstate only about 20 members.

The rump parliament continued to demonstrate remarkable tenacity. On December 1 some 300 members of both houses attended an informal meeting. A letter from the president was read, expressing the hope that parliament could resume its sessions, with substitutes filling the vacant seats. Yuan was taking this position in public largely because the major powers had expressed strong apprehensions over recent events, and he did not want to lose their support. Realizing this, various members of parliament openly challenged the government in the question period that followed the reading of Yuan's letter, insisting that the unseating of members was illegal unless they had been proved guilty of rebellion. Almost all the members present then signed letters, in the name of each house, which charged that the government was crippling parliament and was afraid to crush it completely only because such an act would be unpopular at home and abroad; they asked the government to clarify its position within three days.

By this time, however, Yuan and his supporters had no interest in seeing parliament revived.* They had fashioned a new instrument of political control—the Political Council (*zhengzhi huiyi*), a body of some 70 members appointed by the president, the cabinet, and the provinces, which had only advisory powers. It held its first meeting on December 15, with 69 members present, and it soon became clear that Yuan's government intended it to replace the old parliament, and to appoint a new committee to draft a constitution. On January 9, 1914, after requests from nearly all of the provincial military governors, the Council recommended that the parliament be disbanded, and Yuan immediately complied. Seven weeks later the Council recommended that the provincial assemblies be dissolved, and on the following day, February 28, this too was ordered. For the time being at least, parliamentarism was a dead letter in China, and its failure left a legacy of pessimism even among staunch adherents to the liberal cause. The nation had entered a period of "strong-man" rule with its primary goals being unity

*Throughout the final months of 1913, Yuan had been making disparaging remarks about parliament in private and in interviews with foreigners. In the Reinsch interview cited earlier, Yuan stated that China was like a sick child, and many physicians—the government's foreign advisers—had suggested remedies, but some of these, he regretted to state, were poisons, and certain of these poisons had been introduced through the parliament. He was a staunch believer in representative institutions, Yuan insisted, but the members of the present legislative body had not been true representatives of their constituents, and many had obtained their offices through the purchase of votes. In its seven-months' session, the present parliament had done nothing of value, he concluded.

Later, in an interview with a Reuters correspondent, Yuan insisted that parliament would be maintained, but that while he recognized the earnest, patriotic intentions of many Chinese politicians who had failed to support the central government, they were prone to believe that republicanism was a panacea, without taking into account the difficulties. The Republic baby could not be fed adult food. See *North China Herald*, December 20, 1913, p. 888.

and stability—which naturally had great appeal to a people weary of strife and unimpressed with the results of parliamentary government. To his supporters Yuan as a benevolent dictator represented the only hope for peace and modernization. To his opponents he was a bloodthirsty, deceitful tyrant. In reality he was something of both.

THE FATE OF THE CHINESE EMPIRE

The rising threat to the Chinese empire was another factor that led to the collapse of republicanism and to the growing insistence on the sort of unity that only an authoritarian government could provide. In the decade before 1911, in the debate over the relative merits of constitutional monarchy versus republicanism, Liang Qichao had argued that in the chaos that would follow a toppling of the monarchy, foreign powers might well intervene, causing a general disintegration of the Chinese nation. If the events that followed the revolution apparently justified Liang's apprehensions to a considerable extent, they did so primarily with respect to territories on the peripheries of China proper, regions that could legitimately be considered part of a loosely conceived Chinese empire. Neither Liang nor others of his persuasion, moreover, cared to emphasize the fact that most people living in the border regions—Mongols, Turkish-speaking peoples, and Tibetans, among others—did not relish Chinese rule, and under favorable conditions they would be eager to assert their independence, with whatever foreign assistance they could obtain. Here was the nub of China's problem in holding its empire.

Mongolia

In the premodern era, Chinese "rule," if we can call it that, rested lightly on the Mongolians; Chinese authority was exercised primarily through native princes and lamas, who were allowed considerable autonomy. But as the Qing dynasty neared its end, grievances among Mongolian political and religious leaders accumulated. They were particularly resentful about Chinese practices in regard to religion and colonization. The secularly minded Chinese were prone to challenge or ignore the powers and prerogatives of the lamas, thereby opposing the theocracy indigenous to the region. Equally serious from a Mongolian standpoint, Chinese merchants and settlers had followed—and sometimes preceded—Chinese authority, so that Urga (now Ulanbator), the capital of Outer Mongolia, was dominated by Chinese shopkeepers and artisans. More serious for the Mongols, who were themselves a nomadic pastoral people, Chinese peasants had moved into Mongolia, especially Inner Mongolia, by the thousands, and were farming some of the richest valley lands.

Historically, there were significant political differences between Outer and Inner Mongolia, and these led to different political attitudes. Outer Mongolia, fronting on Siberia, had very little land suitable for intensive cultivation, and its Chinese farm population was small. Indeed, the settlements that dotted the northern sector of Outer Mongolia were those of Russian peasants who had come as homesteaders. Thus, the Russians had long regarded northern Mongolia, like northern Manchuria, as a region of economic and strategic interest. Inner Mongolia, with greater opportunities for agricultural cultivation, had always been more closely connected with China, in both economic and political terms. Its sizable Chinese population contrasted with the relatively sparse number of Chinese settlers to the north.

Even before the events of October 1911, the political situation in Mongolia had become exceedingly tense. As the reforms undertaken in the final years of the Qing penetrated the territory, resistance mounted. In August 1911 the Russian minister in Beijing was instructed to inform Chinese authorities that various Mongol princes and lamas had appealed to Russia for intervention because the Chinese commissioner in Urga had refused to rescind certain reform measures relating to military training, education, and land reclamation.[89] He was instructed to demand the suspension of these measures and to warn that if this were not done, Russia would be forced to take steps to protect its interests. Early in October a small contingent of Russian troops moved into Urga, supposedly to protect resident Russian diplomats there. On October 30, with the revolution under way in China, the Hutukhtu (the head of the Buddhist hierarchy) informed the imperial commissioner in Urga by note that Mongolia would govern itself and that he was assuming political leadership. As the revolution advanced, the Mongol elite, encouraged by certain Russian mentors, were emboldened to move further.

On New Year's Day, 1912, the Hutukhtu formally proclaimed a Mongolian independence movement. The Russians insisted to Western diplomats that when the Mongols had appealed to them to back this cause, they had counseled moderation and negotiations with Beijing. At the same time, however, they complained vigorously that the Chinese government had long been indifferent to Mongolian and Russian remonstrances, and asserted that an agreement satisfactory to all parties would now have to be reached. Pursuing this line, in early January 1912 the Russian government requested Beijing to acknowledge the full autonomy of Outer Mongolia in internal matters, allowing Russian assistance to the Mongols and limiting Chinese involvement to foreign policy. They also demanded permission to construct a railway between Kiakhta and Urga, and an agreement that China would not maintain military forces in Outer Mongolia or seek to colonize the region with Chinese settlers.

In St. Petersburg, moreover, a Russian official concerned with Asian affairs offered scant encouragement to China. In an interview with an American diplomat, he said that Russia had no desire to interfere in the disturbances then rocking China and had no aggressive intentions toward Mongolia, but that given its extensive economic interests throughout the region, and the damage to these interests that a Sino-Mongolian war could cause, it was impelled to intervene. Moreover, if Mongolia should sever its political ties with China, the Russian government would be forced to enter into economic relations with an independent Mongolian government. But he also added that Russia did not favor Mongolian independence, because the Mongolians, like the people of Afghanistan, could not govern themselves, and because when China was strong again it would seek to reimpose its will on them.[90]

Whatever ambivalence existed in St. Petersburg, and whether officials there were fully aware of developments or not, Russian authorities in the region were giving military assistance to the Mongols; and thus fortified,

Outer Mongolian forces engaged in forays into Manchuria and Inner Mongolia in an effort to bolster their position and gain additional support. Realizing the seriousness of the situation, Yuan began efforts in late March to placate the Mongols (and Tibetans). In his proclamation of March 25, he ignored the Mongolian declaration of independence and acknowledged the religious authority of the Hutukhtu in Mongolia and the Dalai Lama in Tibet. In effect, he also recognized the autonomy of the two regions, without spelling out the precise terms on which autonomy might rest.

Yuan's overture, however, drew a negative response. On April 9 the Hutukhtu announced that the people of Mongolia had proclaimed their independence in order to maintain the inviolability of their religion and their territory, and said that they urged China to respect their borders and help Mongolia consolidate its administration and strengthen its friendly relations with neighboring states. It was further suggested that Yuan submit the Mongolian question to interested powers—which presumably meant Russia and Japan.

Meanwhile, the authorities in Urga, with Russian assistance, were attempting sweeping changes: Chinese civil servants were being replaced from top to bottom by Mongolians; with Russian assistance, a more modern armed force was being trained, and there were rumors that the Russians had moved sizable numbers of troops close to the Mongolian border in case large-scale intervention became necessary; and in the economic sphere, the Urga leaders were proclaiming an "open door" policy and expressing interest in attracting substantial amounts of foreign capital.[91]

Beijing's efforts to claim Chinese control over Mongolia had almost no effect. Russian diplomats continued to assert that Mongolia should be an autonomous province under Chinese suzerainty, but they now wanted Chinese acceptance of all treaties recently concluded between Russia and Mongolia. Among other things, these treaties gave Russia control over the funding of Mongolia's internal development programs and guaranteed freedom of movement in Mongolia for Russian subjects.

When Russia and Japan joined the Western consortium, they stipulated that consortium loans not be expended for the development of Mongolia or Manchuria, for they feared a repetition of the earlier American efforts to "neutralize" the region. Russia advanced another proposition, which was later withdrawn, that consortium loans not be allowed for military purposes, thereby openly indicating its fear that a strong Chinese military force could threaten Russian interests in northeast Asia.

Russian involvement in Outer Mongolia gave rise to conflicting speculations. Some sources, claiming that Russian military assistance consisted of selling obsolete weapons that had been used in the Russo-Japanese War, were gloomy over the prospect of a Russo-Chinese conflict on Mongolian soil. There were others, however, including some Russians, who felt that the coming conflict over Mongolia would be between Russia and Japan. Complicating the situation here as well as in Manchuria was the widespread antipathy among princes and lamas to the establishment of a republic in China, since a monarchy was strongly preferred by all of the Mongol elites.

The concern with Japan's response was by no means ill-founded. Indeed, the Urga Mongol authorities had actively cultivated a Japanese connection, hoping thereby to remove eastern Mongolia—the region of principal interest to the Japanese—from Chinese control. The belief was that if an independent state were to emerge in eastern Mongolia under Japanese patronage, a later union with the Urga government could be effected. All of the Mongolians recognized that they would be powerless to operate independently for any length of time unless foreign support were sustained.

In mid-July of 1912, despite the crisis in Beijing, Yuan convened a cabinet meeting to discuss "the Mongolian question." According to one account, it was decided that China should first fortify its relations with Inner Mongolia and then maneuver the Inner Mongolians to fight Outer Mongolia, at the same time lodging a strong protest with the Russians against their current politics.[92]

Yet the Russians stood firmly by their earlier demands, and the Mongols continued to purchase arms from the Russians with the avowed intention of "freeing" all Mongolia from Chinese dominance. By September, after once again consulting the military governors, the Chinese government was sufficiently worried to consider an appeal to the Hague International Tribunal about Russian moves in Mongolia and British actions in Tibet. The Russians now became bolder, asserting that if a Chinese expeditionary force were sent to suppress the Mongols, Russia would send aid to the latter. The land issue had also come to the fore, with the Mongol princes from eastern Mongolia demanding that all Chinese-held land revert to Mongolian control. As Chinese forces moved to protect their precarious position in Inner Mongolia, with troops being sent from Mukden and Jilin, the Russians took a further step. On October 19, at a colorful ceremony in Urga, the Hutukhtu and a man named Korostovetz, a special envoy from St. Petersburg, signed a convention that came close to recognizing the independence of Outer Mongolia; an accompanying protocol, unannounced at the time, gave Russia extensive rights. Protests erupted throughout China, heated debates took place in the parliament, and on November 15, 1912, Foreign Minister Liang Ruhao was forced to resign after only two months in office.

Despite demands for war by militants, those in responsible positions knew that China was in no position to fight against Russia. The course adopted was the one planned earlier. A conference of Inner Mongolian princes and high Chinese officials was convened in Zhangzhun on October 25. Although they made certain concessions, the Chinese emerged from these sessions with their authority reaffirmed by those Mongols in attendance (some important figures were absent, however). There followed a series of rewards to princes who were deemed loyal: higher rank, increased pensions, and a promise to inquire into the settler problem in eastern Mongolia. A move also got under way to reorganize the entire northern region administratively and to arrive at a clear demarcation between Inner and Outer Mongolia.

Although these actions helped keep Inner Mongolia within the fold, they did little to alleviate the tension with Russia or to regain the Chinese position in Urga. In truth, the Russian attitude toward Mongolia was based on certain fundamental considerations. St. Petersburg, contemplating a vast Chinese migration northward in the years ahead, wanted a buffer state in Outer Mongolia as protection for its own territories. Russian authorities were convinced that Inner Mongolia would gradually become Sinicized, with Chinese settlers overwhelming Mongols, and they did not want to confront the same situation on the frontiers of their underpopulated Siberian lands. Their attitude toward northern Manchuria was shaped by the same factors—a fear of Chinese inundation, and security considerations. The

Russian lifeline to the Maritime Province lay in the Siberian railway, and that railway ran very close to Mongolia. Should it be severed at any point, Russian control of its vast eastern empire would be jeopardized. Nothing short of a Chinese withdrawal could meet these concerns.

Thus, in the fall of 1912 the issue of Mongolia remained unresolved, and anti-Russian sentiment among Chinese nationalists ran high. The Russians took the position that Beijing should accept the Urga Convention, fix its northern boundaries in a precise manner, and reach a firm agreement with the Inner Mongolians. If these steps were taken, they said, relations with Outer Mongolia could be stabilized, and more harmonious relations with Russia and Japan in the region could also be achieved. By this time, however, the Russians were complaining with increasing frequency about lawlessness in northern Manchuria, claiming that the lack of Chinese control jeopardized the lives of Russian citizens there. They also initiated threatening troop movements along the Siberian-Manchurian border.

In late November the Chinese came up with an eight-point proposal on Mongolia aimed at restoring their position, but the Russian minister in Beijing showed little interest. The effort to shore up Chinese support in Inner Mongolia continued, but the Urga leaders, now strengthened by Russian assistance, continued to challenge the Chinese position. Nothing short of a Chinese capacity to apply military force effectively seemed likely to suffice. And in December, in yet another move to fortify the status quo, the Russian government agreed to accept a high-ranking Mongol mission. When the delegates reached St. Petersburg, they were given full honors, with their request for an exchange of legations and additional military assistance receiving a favorable hearing from Sassonoff, the Russian foreign minister. At this point the Russian government gave every indication that it regarded the future of Outer Mongolia as settled.

In March 1913, with internal confrontation momentarily reduced, Yuan launched the second phase of the Chinese plan. At a conference of Inner Mongolian princes, it was resolved to "annul" the authority of the Urga Hutukhtu and to prepare a military expedition against Outer Mongolia. The scheme was to use Mongols to fight Mongols, and neither the Urga Convention nor any subsequent Russian-Mongolian agreement was to be recognized. Unfortunately for Beijing, the tides of battle were currently moving in an opposite direction. Russian-trained Mongolian troops affiliated with the Urga government were threatening various communities in Inner Mongolia and Manchuria.*

Under these conditions, with the Russians holding most of the trump cards, negotiations between the two governments over the Mongolian question got under way in Beijing, and by late May a tentative agreement had been reached. In essence, the agreement accepted the status quo, and by mid-June both the Guomindang and the Gonghedang had made it em-

*A report on military developments as of mid-February 1913 by the Beijing War Office indicated that the Mongols had begun attacks on Chinese frontier settlements, having obtained the allegiance of all Outer Mongolia tribes from Kobdo to Manchuria. It further revealed that a portion of Manchuria itself had been seized. Reportedly, forty-five Russian officers were training Mongol troops in Urga, but were advising guerrilla-type attacks only. Arms and ammunition were being imported into Urga by the Russians, and some of these were being transported from there to Tibet to assist the Tibetan rebels (*NAMP/RDSRIAC*, 893.00/1612, March 18, 1913, Beijing, Williams to the Secretary of State).

phatically clear during parliamentary debates that without major amendments the agreement was unacceptable to them. In early July, Duan Qirui, the acting premier, argued before parliament that if the Urga Convention were rejected, the Russian position would stiffen. But with another revolution in sight, opposition political forces were in no mood to make concessions to the government, particularly concessions that ran against nationalist sentiments.

Only on November 5, the day after the Guomindang was outlawed, did the Yuan government decide that it could sign and publicly proclaim a Russian-Chinese covenant on Mongolia. Under its terms Chinese suzerainty was formally recognized, but Beijing agreed to accept the full autonomy of Outer Mongolia, to refrain from stationing civil officials or military troops in the territory, and to abstain from colonization. The Russian government took similar pledges, but although later negotiations were to determine the extent of Russian and Chinese interests in Outer Mongolia, Russian primacy was implicit both in the terms of the agreement and in prevailing conditions. Russia also agreed to provide its "good offices" in fostering a new relationship between China and Outer Mongolia, and it was stipulated that the three parties would participate in future discussions to establish such a relationship, in conformity with the Urga Convention and the November 5 covenant.[93]

Notwithstanding the repressive political environment that now prevailed in China, press attacks on the agreement were vitriolic. In Canton, Shanghai, and even Beijing, editorials deplored China's "loss of Outer Mongolia" and castigated the "poor diplomacy" that had been exhibited. Outer Mongolia had become a Russian province, some writers said, and the future of Manchuria and Tibet had been made more precarious than ever. The basic reason for China's retreat was not so much "poor diplomacy" as it was internal weakness, but the result was the same: the separation of Outer Mongolia from the Chinese empire appeared virtually complete as 1913 drew to a close.

Manchuria

More important to China was the fate of Manchuria, a region rich in arable land and natural resources. Like other peripheral regions, Manchuria had been only loosely connected with China proper throughout much of its history. In fact, even though the Manchu occupied the Chinese throne, Chinese migration into Manchuria had been prohibited until the late nineteenth century, and a Russian challenge in the north had been gathering momentum over several centuries. Pushing slowly across the vast Siberian hinterland, in 1643 the Russians reached the Amur River (which the Manchu considered to be deep within their territory), thereby making contact with the Manchu tribes even before they became the rulers of China. Some three decades later, the Manchu, concerned about Cossack forts on the Amur, mounted a series of attacks. By the famous Treaty of Nerchinsk (1687), the Russians withdrew from the immediate vicinity, but established themselves permanently in the region.

By the time of the 1911 Revolution, Manchuria was roughly divided into Russian and Japanese spheres of influence, as determined by the Russo-Japanese War of 1904–1905 and a series of Chinese concessions dating from the 1890s. The chief monument to Russian influence was the Chinese Eastern Railway, a Russian-financed and -operated line that served as the main artery to various mining and timber concessions in the north. Thousands of Russians lived in Harbin, the major city of the northern region, and other Russian enclaves dotted the north Manchurian countryside. In southern Manchuria, as in eastern Mongolia, the position of Japan was paramount, having been achieved through military victory and economic expansion. Here too a railway served as the fountainhead of Japanese authority. The South Manchurian Railway was built with Japanese capital, operated by Japanese authorities, and guarded by Japanese troops. Wherever the railway reached, Japanese investors and merchants were to be found. There were also important military installations at Port Arthur and Dalian, impressive testimony to the Japanese victory over Russia.

In various respects, Russo-Japanese rivalry intensified in the aftermath of the 1911 Revolution. As the internal weaknesses of China were progressively revealed, both nations pursued a policy of "protective expansionism." * Japan's actions, however, were generally both more subtle and more comprehensive. In this period as in others, the Japanese were more deeply involved in the Chinese revolution than any other nation. Yet Japanese actions toward China, official and unofficial alike, clearly revealed deep divisions of opinion—a situation that would continue for many decades. As the 1911 Revolution got under way, some Japanese in Manchuria and North China proclaimed themselves in favor of the monarchy, even as other Japanese in the South were aiding the revolutionary cause. ** It is not surprising that many Chinese and most Western observers reached the conclusion that the Japanese government secretly wanted a divided China, with a monarchical North and a republican South—and in fact, certain Japanese did see this as a desirable solution. In some degree, these differences reflected military-civilian cleavages in Japan, but complex factional and individual alignments were also involved.

* A fascinating article presenting a Russian emigré viewpoint on the current situation appeared in the Harbin Russian-language newspaper, *Novaya zhizn* (New Life). The American consulate in Harbin described the paper as "relatively extremist," though "fairly portraying the views of a majority of the Russian population of North Manchuria and of the Russian military leadership." Angrily denouncing St. Petersburg authorities for allowing the Russian colony in Manchuria to "die out," the writer asserted that if the Japanese annexed South Manchuria, "we must keep step." He continued, "The Chinese will never forgive us for assisting Mongolian independence, and sooner or later, this account must be paid; if we seriously undertake to guarantee the independence of Mongolia, and prevent China from sending an expedition there, we should have plenty of troops in Manchuria to back our words with strong arguments. Only by having a strong Russian Manchuria, can we isolate Mongolia from China." For a translation, see *NAMP/RDSRIAC*, 893.00/1558, "Political Conditions in North Manchuria," Maynard to the Secretary of State.

** Reliable reports indicated that certain Japanese in Manchuria were agitating against Yuan from an early point, and some were rendering support to those Manchu princes who were calling for an independent Manchuria under an imperial system. One high-level discussion reflective of these views was reported through intelligence circles in March 1912. Colonel Koyama Akizaka, former chief of the Japanese civil administration in Mukden, was quoted as having urged Viceroy Zhao Erxun to oppose the emperor's abdication when visiting him in early 1912, telling him that the Japanese government regretted that it had not prevented this deplorable event by providing military assistance at the outbreak of the revolution. He further asserted that the republic would end in failure and implored the viceroy to remain loyal to the throne. Zhao reportedly told Koyama that it was too late. See *NAMP/RDSRIAC*, 893.00/1244, March 15, 1912, Beijing, Calhoun to the Secretary of State.

In Manchuria, Japan's economic involvement expanded steadily after the Wuchang uprising, largely through private sources. For example, in the fall of 1911 Mitsui loaned the Manchurian government $1.5 million (Mexican silver dollars), and negotiations were under way for an additional loan of 5 million taels from three Japanese firms. Throughout 1912 economic activity was somewhat constrained by unsettled conditions and the activities of the consortium. But in the fall of 1913, after the Wilson administration had expressed a lack of interest in further American involvement in the consortium, Japan secured a release from the earlier six-power agreement banning industrial and railway loans, and quickly pushed for a number of railway concessions in southern Manchuria and eastern Mongolia. The Chinese then agreed to obtain railway loans in these regions exclusively from Japan.

Even before these developments, American diplomats in Beijing had reached much the same assessment of the future of Manchuria as that held by Sun Yat-sen. One dispatch reported: "It is generally believed here that the loss of Manchuria is only a question of time. Manchuria is like a ripe apple, ready to fall into the hands of Russia and Japan whenever they shake the tree. Ahead of China is a long period of disorder; in some stage of it, when the world is tired of its strife and struggle, Japan may lay her mailed hand on South Manchuria and Russia will do likewise for North Manchuria; no other nation will interpose an objection or offer any resistance."[94] This assessment, it turned out, was not far off the mark, although Chinese sovereignty over Manchuria was not frontally challenged until later, and then in several stages.

Tibet

The case of Tibet was more similar to that of Outer Mongolia. Once again, the roots of the postrevolutionary crisis were deeply imbedded in an earlier era. As the twentieth century opened, Chinese suzerainty over Tibet was universally recognized, but in practice Beijing exerted only minimal control over this remote region. Moreover, it was convenient for the Chinese to disclaim responsibility for Tibetan actions in the face of any external pressure. Thus, British authorities in India, and most particularly the viceroy of India, Lord Curzon, became enormously frustrated by the unwillingness of Tibet officials to negotiate or even communicate with them on trade and border issues, and by the seeming inability of the Chinese to influence Tibetan attitudes or actions.[95]

There can be no doubt, however, that British officials in India found this situation very convenient in rationalizing policies based primarily on other, broader considerations. Tibet was approximately a thousand miles from the borders of the Russian empire, but British authorities in London and New Delhi worried, not without reason, that Russia might try to extend its influence into Persia, Afghanistan, and Tibet.[96] This concern motivated leaders like Curzon to support policies of "defensive expansionism," which gave a high priority to extending British influence to Tibet. As Curzon saw it, this policy was all the more essential because China had become impotent and was on the verge of disintegration, hence Chinese suzerainty over Tibet was no more than a fiction.

Pursuing his "forward" policy, Curzon dispatched an armed mission under Colonel Francis Younghusband into Tibet in mid-1903, with instructions to negotiate with the Tibetans and Chinese at Shampa Dzong, across the border from northern Sikkim. When the Tibetans insisted that negotiations could not take place within their territory and stonewalled for five months, Younghusband was ordered to advance to Gyangtse, over the protests of both the Russians and the Chinese. A much larger military force under General Macdonald, moreover, was sent into Tibet in case Younghusband needed assistance. By April 1904, after several bloody encounters in which the Tibetans were routed with heavy casualties, the mission had reached Gyangtse, and it was then determined that negotiations would have to take place in Lhasa. On September 7, 1904, an Anglo-Tibetan Convention was signed in the Tibetan capital. By its terms, trade markets were to be opened at Gyangtse and Gartok in western Tibet, an agreement was reached on the Sikkim-Tibet border, other foreign powers were to be excluded from influence in Tibet, and a large indemnity was assessed against the Tibetans.*

The Chinese resident had assisted Younghusband during the negotiations and was present at the signing of the agreement, but did not himself sign. Since the convention contained no reference to Chinese suzerainty, and in itself indicated that the Tibetans had the authority to handle their own foreign relations, it could easily be argued that the British had replaced the Chinese in the role of the suzerain power. Younghusband, however, was instructed to obtain the Chinese resident's signature to a separate treaty of concurrence, which would also indicate British acceptance of a Chinese role in Tibet. But he could not accomplish this, and it was not until April 27, 1906, that an Anglo-Chinese Convention on Tibet was approved. It was followed by a further agreement relating to Tibet in the form of the Anglo-Russian Convention of 1907.[97] Through these agreements (in which the Tibetans did not participate) the British acknowledged Chinese rights in the region and agreed not to negotiate with Tibet except through China and not to station a representative in Lhasa.

Meanwhile, the Chinese had moved on their own to reestablish their authority. In 1905 they sent the Manchu general Zhao Erfeng to eastern Tibet, where he quickly set in motion a series of sweeping reforms, including the reorganization of the administrative structure and the appointment of new officials, the setting of limits on the powers of the monasteries, and expansion of the educational system, and the modernization of military training. Many of these reforms, though designed to facilitate Chinese control, could be regarded as progressive measures and were said to be popular with a sizable portion of the Tibetan people. But Zhao treated opponents with Draconian severity, and the combined opposition of the landed-official class and the lamas made conflict a chronic condition.

After some five years, with eastern Tibet only partly pacified, the Chinese decided to challenge the authority of the Dalai Lama, whom they regarded as the fountainhead of opposition to Chinese rule. Just eight months before the Wuchang uprising, an imperial Chinese army marched from Chamdo

*The 1904 Convention is summarized in Tieh-Tseng Li, *Tibet: Today and Yesterday*, p. 95, and the full text is presented in H. E. Richardson, *A Short History of Tibet*, Appendix, pp. 253–256. Li argues that neither the Chinese resident nor the Tibetan representative had full power to enter into a treaty with Younghusband. The Dalai Lama, the supreme authority in Tibet, had fled north as the Younghusband expedition neared Lhasa. Asserts Li: "The British Commissioner brought back with him a 'Convention' signed only by a miscellaneous assortment of all the officials and ecclesiastics he could lay hands on in Lhasa" (p. 107).

to the Tibetan capital of Lhasa and established power there. The Dalai Lama, who had returned from China at the end of 1909, fled once more, this time to India. There, in a discussion with Lord Minto, the British viceroy in India, he appealed for support in ousting Chinese troops from Lhasa and restoring Tibet's right to deal directly with the British. Citing treaty obligations in China and Russia, however, the British demurred, and also rejected the Dalai Lama's request that he be allowed to travel to London to put his case personally before the government. He then turned to Russia for support, but the authorities held firmly to cooperation with the British on the issue of Tibet.

Fundamentally, Britain's interest in Tibet was the same as Russia's interest in Outer Mongolia. The British wanted Tibet to be a buffer state, sufficiently independent of China and dependent on Great Britain to protect their imperial interests. Of course, there were differences of opinion on this matter within the London government, the Foreign Office, and the Indian Civil Service, differences at least as great as those within comparable bodies in Russia and Japan. Curzon, for example, was infuriated on more than one occasion by what he regarded as the cowardice of home authorities. But it is doubtful whether even Curzon wanted a fully independent Tibet or a Tibet that was incorporated completely into the British empire. The costs and the risks of either development would be too great. Thus, when the Dalai Lama and the Tibetan Assembly declared their independence from China, in an act paralleling that of the Outer Mongolians, British authorities ignored the gesture and hewed to the line established by the accords of 1904 and 1906.

After the outbreak of the 1911 Revolution, however, the tide of events turned against China. News of the revolution took several months to reach the Tibetan capital, but when it came, many Chinese soldiers, long dissatisfied with their living conditions, mutinied. They disarmed and robbed their officers and demanded to be sent home immediately. They also began looting Tibetan homes and monasteries, which soon provoked organized resistance from Tibetans. Once again, religious differences and the desire for independence combined to drive one of China's border regions into widespread revolt. By early 1912 Chinese and Tibetans were engaging in full-scale battles. In Lhasa about one thousand Chinese troops, greatly outnumbered, were cornered in a suburb and forced to negotiate for their surrender. The Chinese then lost Shigatse, and in early April the Chinese garrison in Gyangtse surrendered, agreeing to leave Tibet by way of India. In late June the Dalai Lama, informed that Lhasa was safely in Tibetan hands, left his Indian exile in Kalimpong to return to his homeland; he was delayed, however, and did not reach the Tibetan capital until January 1913.

The Chinese, having failed with the stick, now tried the carrot. On March 25 and April 12 of 1912, Yuan Shikai issued proclamations declaring that Tibet, Mongolia, and Xinjiang would henceforth be treated on an equal footing with the provinces of China proper, as integral elements of the Republic; he also pledged to protect the Tibetan religion and to recognize the Dalai Lama in all of his ecclesiastical roles. At the same time, however, he dispatched an expedition from Sichuan to relieve the besieged garrison in Lhasa. This force, plagued by inadequate leadership and low morale, bogged down quickly; and by August, with Nepali officials serving as intermediaries, the Chinese soldiers in Lhasa agreed to put their weapons in storage and depart for India under a safe-passage agreement, leaving behind only the Chinese resident with a small bodyguard and staff.

The British now found the time opportune to protest Chinese policies. On August 16 Sir John Jordan held a meeting with Yuan, and on the following day the British issued a memorandum objecting to the dispatch of a Chinese military force into Tibet as a violation of the terms of the 1906 Convention. After noting the Chinese declaration that Tibet would become an integral part of the Chinese Republic, it reiterated that Tibet should be allowed to manage its own internal affairs free from Chinese interference.[98] The memorandum concluded by recommending that Great Britain and China reach a new agreement on Tibet, one that would preserve the status quo.

Two weeks later, Yuan retreated. He ordered the Tibetan expedition halted, and at the end of October he restored all previous titles to the Dalai Lama, again futilely seeking to placate Tibetan rulers.* Meanwhile, the British continued to insist upon a reply to their memorandum of August 17. On December 23, 1912, a reply finally came. In effect, it affirmed the autonomy of Tibet while artfully defending the dispatch of troops as a part of China's commitment to preserve peace and order in Tibet, as expressed in the 1906 Convention. But China had no intention of stationing unlimited numbers of troops in Tibet, the memorandum asserted, and since the issues had now been clarified, there was no need for a new Sino-British agreement on the subject.[99]

At this point, word came that a Buriat Mongol, Dorjieff, acting on behalf of the Dalai Lama, had signed a treaty in Urga binding Tibet and Mongolia in a joint declaration of independence and pledging them to protect their common religion. When Jordan threatened to negotiate with Tibet alone, the Chinese reluctantly agreed to participate in a tripartite conference at Simla, India. Zhen Yifan (Ivan) was sent as the Chinese representative, and when the meetings were convened on October 13, 1913, Sir Henry McMahon presided as the British representative. The Tibetans were represented by Lonchen Shatra, a close personal friend of Sir Charles Bell, one of Britain's leading authorities on Tibet and an adviser to McMahon. The Tibetans submitted six demands, which included conditions the Chinese found exceedingly harsh, such as complete independence, indemnities, and an extension of Tibetan territory. The Chinese counterproposals reasserted

*For an insight into Chinese attitudes and policies toward Tibet that comes far closer to the mark than official proclamations, note the following communication from Vice-President Li to President Yuan: "The independence of Tibet was declared by the living Buddha several months ago. . . . Although we have been victorious in battle, it will take a long time to suppress the rebellious Tibetans. If we allow the fighting to go on, our soldiers will be worn out. . . . Tibet being mountainous and rugged, one person occupying an important place can resist thousands. . . . Though the Tibetans are stupid and ignorant, I am sure they can be educated. It is probable they will finally welcome our troops. . . .

"Once the assistance of the [foreign] power [Great Britain] is withdrawn, the living Buddha will become helpless. . . . At that time, we must send eloquent men well versed in the Tibetan language to induce the adherents of the living Buddha to persuade him to do homage to the Republic and to promise him his old privileges, except the right to interfere in politics and government. . . . Since the time of Guangxu of the old regime, the living Buddha has been in discord with the lamas. Now though they follow him in his rebellion, they were incited thereto by trickery. The sending of eloquent speakers to cast seeds of dissension among them will have the effect of separating them. They can be induced to fight each other by promising the lamas high honors after peace is restored. By these means, the Tibetan rebellion may be quelled within two months" (*NAMP/RDSRIAC*, 893.00/1484, translated from *Dahan bao* [Greater Han News], September 15, 1912, in a dispatch on Tibetan Affairs, Hankou, September 20, 1912, Jameson to Calhoun).

traditional themes: an autonomous Tibet, but one considered an integral part of China; Chinese rights to station small contingents of troops in Lhasa and elsewhere; Chinese control of Tibetan foreign and military affairs, with no independent Tibetan contacts with any foreign country permitted except through China (contacts with British trade agents being exempt); and a Tibetan-Chinese boundary fixed at roughly the line of Zhao Erfeng's furthest military penetration.

The gulf between the two positions was unbridgeable, and the negotiations remained stalemated. On February 17, 1914, quite possibly taking a signal from the Russo-Chinese Agreement signed the previous November, the British representative, Sir Henry McMahon, proposed a division of the region into an Inner and an Outer Tibet. Prolonged debate then ensued over the precise boundaries of the two areas, but finally, on July 3, all three representatives signed the Simla Convention Draft.[100] The Chinese government, however, immediately repudiated the Convention on the grounds that the boundary settlement was unacceptable.

In March 1914, in the course of the Simla negotiations, the British and Tibetan representatives reached an agreement on the issue of the frontier between Tibet and India. This border came to be known as the McMahon line, and was to figure prominently in the regional controversy of nearly a half-century later. Shortly after the Simla Convention was being signed and then rejected by Beijing, World War I opened, and for the British as well as other major states, issues like Tibet faded into the background. Events were now to be controlled not by legal covenants but by the de facto situation. The Chinese and Tibetans continued to fight an "undeclared and desultory war," in which the British supplied the Tibetans with some arms and military training while counseling both sides to end hostilities.[101] The Chinese, weakened by the fullest range of problems, were effectively excluded from "Outer Tibet" and a goodly portion of "Inner Tibet" as well.

RELATIONS WITH THE MAJOR POWERS

Thus, as Europe moved into its first twentieth-century civil war, the Chinese empire suffered serious reverses. Outer Mongolia and Tibet became virtually independent political entities, each serving as a buffer state and in some degree a protectorate (of Russia and Great Britain, respectively), and Manchuria was moving toward the status of a joint condominium of Russia and Japan. Furthermore, on its Western frontier, in Xinjiang and neighboring provinces, there were ominous rumblings among the Moslem population. Yuan called for drastic measures against foreign interlopers and domestic "traitors," but to no effect. Unless China could develop some inner strength, the status of the empire would remain precarious.

Even to secure recognition of the Republic itself from the major powers proved far more difficult than was initially imagined. After the 1911 Revolution began, the United States urged that all of the interested powers work together, through joint policies based on "strict neutrality," in an effort to prevent extended conflict and political anarchy. With certain caveats set forth earlier, the major powers agreed. Yet within each legation and home government, sharp divisions of opinion with respect to policies emerged, and political preferences made themselves manifest. Generally speaking, the heads of legations in Beijing leaned toward Yuan and favored efforts to stabilize the situation by upholding the status quo. But various consuls and representatives from the foreign community, especially those living in republican territory, often took a different tack, as did an unusually large assortment of "free-lancers"—assorted adventurers, ideologues, and mercenaries. Among the free-lancers, some—especially the Japanese—had strong ties to political factions at home; others, such as Homer Lea, were strictly on their own; both types, however, provided useful information for American diplomats.

Almost as soon as the revolution began, certain citizens and interest groups strongly urged their governments to recognize the new Chinese Republic, and nowhere was that pressure greater than upon Washington. Most American missionaries, especially those living in Central and South China, were sympathetic to the republican cause, and Bishop J. W. Bashford of the Methodist Church, a close friend of Sun Yat-sen's, was an ardent proponent of United States recognition of the new government. In the postrevolutionary period, it might be noted, Sun often gave political addresses in Christian churches and before Christian congregations. The missionaries were joined by some members of the American business community, both in China and at home, who argued that a vast China trade awaited American entrepreneurs.[102]

Republican leaders were adept at cultivating such sentiments. In a letter addressed to "Our Foreign Friends" on November 14, 1911, Dr. Wu Tingfang and Mr. Wen Zongyao wrote: "The foreign powers individually and collectively have stood hammering at the door of China for centuries pleading for the diffusion of knowledge, a reformation of national services, the adoption of Western sciences and industrial processes, a jettisoning of the crude, out-of-date and ignoble concepts which have multiplied to keep the nation without [a] place [in] the great family constituting the civilized world."[103] After promising that the Republic would offer full protection for the Manchu, and would safeguard foreign religious, educational, and commercial operations, Wu and Wen ended their appeal with this exhortation: "We are fighting for what Britons fought [for] in days of old; we are fighting for what every nation that is now worthy of the name has fought [for] in its day."[104]

Nevertheless, the Taft administration withheld recognition throughout its tenure in office, arguing that even the Beijing government defined itself as a provisional government and did not claim to be a fully established republic. In the first months after the revolution, as we have seen, Washington appeared to approve of loans to Yuan, provided such action was supported by other major states. And it also agreed to certain urgent requests from American officials in the field for small troop contingents, to act in concert with those of other powers to protect American citizens and properties. There was no surge of official support for Sun and the southern government.

With the Chinese Republic temporarily unified under Yuan, however, the pressures for early American recognition mounted. In the summer of 1912, the U.S. government privately requested its embassies abroad to inquire about the attitude of the governments of the major powers on the matter of recognition. Without exception, the responses were negative. Various reasons were given, but in the main, the argument was that until a permanent political structure had been created and greater stability achieved, diplomatic recognition would be premature.[105] With the advent of the

Wilson administration, however, the United States decided to confer recognition independently at the point when the organization of the newly elected parliament was formally completed. This occurred on May 2, 1913, and coupled with the American decision to withdraw from the consortium, it served to turn American policy back toward unilateralism, away from collective action with Europe and Japan.

Once again, the great dilemma confronting American policy-makers stood revealed. Since the early nineteenth century, they had oscillated between aloofness from the major European states and cooperation with them. From the standpoint of perceived national interest, the advantages of each position were considerable. Aloofness permitted an appeal based on American support for China's integrity and the relative altruism of the American position. It made possible a low level of involvement, with minimal costs and risks, and it did not preclude sharing the gains scored by those pursuing more "forward" policies—as critics were wont to point out. Yet its effectiveness could be questioned; its impact on the Chinese and its influence on Japanese and European policies might be minimal. On occasion, cooperation had served to sustain policies more closely attuned to American interests and values, and to provide quicker and more effective results. In any case, the pendulum now swung back toward independent action, reflecting the strong moralistic streak that ran through the Wilsonian era.

Supporting the new U.S. policy was an American enthusiasm about the "New China" that provoked "old China hands," especially those of British nationality, to expressions of amusement, condescension, and annoyance. One such response to the current American mood is illustrative. Speaking with light sarcasm, the writer took note of those Americans who, "when in China evidenced conservatism in their enthusiasm, but when placed on a platform in America, blossom out beautifully."[106] Continuing, he wrote, "Perhaps it is a bit unkind, but it cannot escape an 'old China hand' that the most inspiring bursts of enthusiasm invariably occur when the role of prophecy is assumed. One hears so much of what is going to happen to China in the next ten years that he feels anxious to get back and see the start of it all."

There are two explanations, this anonymous writer continued, for the ecstasy with which China is viewed—the enchantment of distance and the magic of the term "republic." (It would have been equally appropriate to have emphasized other factors: awe at the scale and grandeur of this society and its culture; a deep affection for the Chinese people; and a compatibility between certain facets of the American and the Chinese personality.) In any case, he said, Americans are eager to portray China as engaged in a "heroic struggle to nurture its infant democracy," whereas they are inclined to describe similar situations elsewhere as "Mexican dog-fights." He concluded, "Solemn editorials appear on the stern [Chinese] determination to stamp out opium even to the point of executing a woman smoker. . . . One wonders whether the newspaper fraternity is not having a little joke, agreeing among themselves to 'play it up' for a while."[107]

American romanticism about China—though overwhelmed at times by a rapid swing of the pendulum toward an emphasis on the backward, the threatening, and the sinister in Chinese society—was to continue throughout the twentieth century, leading to recurrent shocks and hasty reevaluations. Meanwhile, although U.S. policies of this period generally won the gratitude of Yuan, and on occasion the gratitude of Sun Yat-sen and his colleagues, there were two persistent Chinese reservations about the United States.

The first reservation had to do with consistency and predictability. American policies appeared mercurial and without clear goals, hence subject to unexpected fluctuations. In considerable part, this problem reflected the uneasy mix involved in American attitudes and actions between "morality" and "national interest," between the desire to satisfy values or ideology and the need to protect the perceived interests of an emerging world power. It was a problem that would later be faced by China itself.

The second Chinese reservation lay in the conviction that Washington had neither a sufficient interest in China nor sufficient available power to influence the course of events in a decisive fashion. Hence China's attention had to be focused primarily on Great Britain, Russia, and Japan, states that had the will and the usable power to affect developments decisively. This conviction, it might be noted, was held by both the Beijing government and the revolutionaries. Periodically, Sun Yat-sen and his colleagues would seek American assistance in various forms; but in the end, it was with certain Japanese that Sun established his closest ties and from whom he received his greatest foreign assistance during this era. For its part, Yuan's government was forced to fend off imperialist thrusts from Britain, Russia, and Japan, and yet it turned to these same nations for financial and military support.

That Yuan's situation could exist also reflected the complex and sometimes contradictory stances of the other major powers, as expressed by their representatives and nationals. For example, the British minister to Beijing, Sir John Jordan, became almost a personal friend of Yuan's and strongly championed his cause; but to the south, British representatives increasingly felt that their interests in the Yangtze valley could only be protected by reaching an understanding with the revolutionaries, and their policies were fashioned accordingly. The British position on recognition of the Republic, however, was considerably more hard-nosed than that of the Americans. Britain insisted that China would have to live up to its treaty obligations regarding Tibet, as interpreted by London, before recognition could be granted. Ultimately, the decisive test of Whitehall's China policies was whether they served existing British interests, although agreement was frequently lacking as to how those interests might best be served.

Russia, as we have noted, sought to apply similar critical criteria, and had moved swiftly to protect and expand its interests in Mongolia and northern Manchuria. As in the case of Great Britain, the strategy was to protect the empire by creating buffer zones; the tactic was "defensive expansion," making use of the grievances of ethnic groups that resented and feared Han domination.

Japanese aims and techniques were somewhat different. Japan, to be sure, had extensive security interests in Manchuria, a region that bordered on the Japanese empire and provided a meeting ground for Japanese and Russian interests. But its heavy economic involvement there made the Japanese position unique, with its stake in Manchuria greater by far than that of any other outside nation. For Japan, indeed, economics took priority over the strategic and security considerations that dominated British and Russian policies in China's border regions.

This fact also colored Japan's attitudes and policies toward China proper. The Japanese believed they understood China in a sense impossible for any

Westerner. In addition, a few of them had a growing sense of mission—that of unifying and liberating the yellow race from white dominance. Even many Japanese who rejected the appeal to race saw a great opportunity for Japan in serving as the engine for China's modernization. Yet many diverse streams ran through the Japanese consciousness, leading to great diversity of attitude and action. There were those who saw the emergence of a powerful China as a threat. Others regarded China in its current size and form as ungovernable. For these reasons, a strong sentiment existed in favor of a divided China, with a monarchical North and a republican South. It would be easy to argue that those who favored this development saw it as a way of making China more susceptible to manipulation and control. That was true in some cases, but there was also a genuine feeling in Japan that China's diversity had to be acknowledged politically. And as we have noted, a majority of foreigners professionally concerned with China always had grave doubts about whether republicanism could survive there, or at least outside its natural political base in the South.

In the end, Japanese policies toward China in the first years after the 1911 Revolution revealed a set of priorities—economic, political, and strategic—that surmounted diversities of opinion and served to propel Japan toward progressively greater involvement in China. No one could foresee where that involvement would end, but even contemporary observers could see the rising Japanese role clearly, and they speculated that a collision with either Russian or American interests—and with the still largely latent forces of Chinese nationalism—might lie ahead.

8

THE THREAT OF DISINTEGRATION

By early 1914 all of the basic forces that were to shape Chinese politics in the decade ahead had come into play. Yuan Shikai and his closest associates were committed to an authoritarian, centralized, reformist government—one dedicated to modernizing rapidly at home, to acquiring from abroad the science, technology, and economic experience of the era's advanced nations, and to protecting the Chinese empire against threatened imperialist depredations.

To achieve these ends, ultimate power had been increasingly concentrated in the presidency, making Yuan a virtual dictator; the parliamentary process had been effectively scuttled in favor of the Political Council, an appointive, advisory body incapable of independent action. Yet even Yuan remained heavily dependent on the military—more specifically, on the quasi-independent provincial military governors who commanded armies answering only to their orders. Hence Yuan's aim at this point was to reduce provincial autonomy, subordinating the military governors to centralized authority and regaining the provincial revenues that had historically gone into Beijing's coffers. To provide the ideological foundations for the new order and to check "moral decay," Confucianism was to be revitalized. In its broadest dimensions, this was a program that would be put forth many times during China's twentieth-century travails.

The government recognized that in order to achieve greater legitimacy, it had to prove itself capable of carrying out two tasks: providing stability, which in simple terms meant law and order, and promoting economic development—or at least solvency for the government and subsistence with the hope of something better for the citizenry at large.

Accomplishing the first task was a necessary precondition of undertaking the second, yet it represented an extraordinary challenge. The earlier demise of central authority, the intense factionalism and frequent changes that characterized provincial administrations, and the primitive transport and communications that prevailed over much of the country combined to render many districts prey to various types of lawlessness. Sometimes the local people themselves, in desperate economic straits and largely ungoverned from above, were responsible. In other cases, bandit armies—often led by ex-soldiers—fastened themselves upon a district. As we have noted, such bands sometimes proclaimed a social or political cause, since many of their members had been born into the peasantry and had suffered recurrent socioeconomic injustices. And sometimes in the regions under their control they imposed a rough-and-ready governance, a new law-and-order under special rules and procedures. Thus, the lines between banditry and political protest and between an imposed tyranny and acceptable governance were often blurred—which made the problem of exerting provincial control all the more intractable for Beijing.

The exploits of the guerrilla chieftain White Wolf and his followers during 1913 and 1914 illustrate the prevailing pattern.[1] The White Wolf was a native of Henan, and apparently had a military background; some said he had been a sergeant in Yuan Shikai's army, and others claimed he was a military academy graduate from a prominent family in East Henan. He was described as open and moderate in behavior, with a bent toward egalitarianism. His men referred to him as Big Brother.

From his base in Henan, the White Wolf conducted increasingly ambitious forays, accumulating supporters and arms after each success. By the fall of 1913 it was reported that there were 3,000 men (and some women) in his band. By the spring of 1914, when certain accounts claimed that his soldiery numbered 10,000 (though only a much smaller number were well equipped militarily), he was making stabs into Shaanxi and Gansu. Eventually, sizable government troops drove the White Wolf back to the Henan-Hubei and Henan-Anhui border regions; in the process his followers finally dispersed, and it is said that he himself died of battle wounds in mid-1914.

During his period of success the White Wolf proved to be a shrewd tactician. He retreated into rugged terrain when necessary, cultivated the peasantry wherever he went, surrounded his urban targets and infiltrated them with disguised followers before an assault, and used kidnapping for ransom as a means of acquiring funds and weapons. Not infrequently, his efforts were abetted by government troops; these soldiers, often unpaid for months and poorly disciplined, alienated the local people by pillage and other acts of vandalism, making them unwilling to give vital intelligence to local military leaders. From the beginning, the White Wolf took political positions. He proclaimed himself a champion of the Han people, a benefactor of the poor, and an opponent of the "criminal" government of Yuan Shikai. The authorities in Beijing insisted that he had received encouragement from both Huang Xing and Sun Yat-sen, but this connection appears to have been a tenuous one. In his political stance as in his military tactics, the White Wolf recalled the Taiping and foreshadowed the post-1927 Communists.*

*The White Wolf band shared many traits with other Chinese guerrilla forces, including the later Chu-Mao Communists. They had extraordinary mobility (they could march thirteen miles in a day when necessary); they avoided combat unless they had superior numbers; they recruited local people for corvée labor, usually releasing them after a day's march; and they cultivated espionage as a fine art, usually knowing the movements of their enemy fully. They could be ruthless, as is suggested by an account of their attack on Guangzhou, a city of 100,000. When the assault was launched outside the city walls, infiltrators already inside the city began firing, which so confused the militia and police that they mistakenly killed many of their own. As members of the main band led by White Wolf entered the city, they shouted, "Old White Wolf is here. He is going to kill the rich and save the poor. All keep indoors and you will be safe." Women and girls hid under beds, fearing rape; wealthy and middle-class citizens dressed themselves in ragged clothes to conceal their status, and some hid in the houses of the poor. The guerrillas had been instructed to shoot anyone who fired on them or carried a weapon, even a club; anyone wearing fur garments; anyone who locked his door; and anyone who looked like a soldier. The wealthy were stripped of possessions. Merchants were required to write how much they were prepared to contribute in "traveling expenses" for the guerrillas, with the figure written on a piece of paper hung over the counter. Often local

50. *Meeting, Gemingdang, Tokyo, September 27, 1913. From left, front row: Deng Jian, Zheng Henian, Xu Chongzhi, Chen Qimei, Sun, Hu Hanmin, Ju Zheng, Liao Zhongkai, Tian Tong; middle row: 6th, Xu Shaozhen; 7th, Jing Yaoyue*

By late 1914, with the elimination of the White Wolf and the steady eradication of many other dissidents, including Guomindang remnants, Yuan and his supporters could claim that China had entered a period more tranquil than any since the onset of the 1911 Revolution. Meanwhile, Yuan was pressing forward with his program for political and economic reform. A revised provisional constitution was announced at the end of April 1914. It legitimized the extensive powers which Yuan had in fact already assumed, and proclaimed that the president was responsible only to "the citizens of the Republic." Provision was made for the later establishment of a National Assembly (Lifayuan) with limited legislative powers, to be convened and dissolved at the will of the president. The cabinet was remodeled to resemble the pre-1911 Grand Secretariat, and a new Administrative Council (Canzhengyuan) was created.

"ruffians," some of them mere boys, directed them to the homes of the power-holders and participated in the looting. When a man who claimed to be a schoolteacher was discovered to have the seal of office in his possession, he was hacked to pieces. (See *North China Herald*, March 21, 1914, "White Wolf's Trail," p. 845.) According to an earlier account relying on Chinese informants, the White Wolf had drawn up the following scale of payments: for merchants, 25 rifles and 2,500 rounds of ammunition; for missionaries, 10 rifles and 1,000 rounds; for railway engineers, 5 rifles and 500 rounds (November 15, 1913, p. 533). However, a son of a missionary teacher at a girls' school was released after the payment of 350 taels (November 1, 1913, p. 332). Most accounts indicate that the White Wolf had instructed his troops not to molest foreigners.

A detailed plan for the enactment of a permanent constitution was also set forth in this document. A special constitutional committee was to be elected by the Administrative Council, consisting of ten of its members, charged with responsibility for drafting the final document. When completed, the constitution would be submitted to a specially summoned citizens' convention, whose members would be determined by the committee. Once again the quest for a permanent institutional structure was under way. In July Yuan appointed W. W. Willoughby, professor of political science at Johns Hopkins University, to replace Professor Frank J. Goodnow of Columbia as adviser on the constitution.

In early April the government had also begun the effort to provide itself with an adequate financial base from indigenous resources. The provinces were assessed fixed sums to be sent to the capital from their revenues, with the amounts based on the figures of the late imperial era. Five provinces—Guangxi, Yunnan, Guizhou, Gansu, and Xinjiang—were made exempt because of their poverty.*

On July 30 a presidential order set forth a program for provincial governance that sought to tackle the main problem. The provincial military governorships were abolished and replaced by generals (*jiangjun*) of two grades. Provincial military authority was placed in their hands, but they were put under the control of the central military administration in Beijing, which in turn reported to the Ministry of War. Civil authority, now separated from military command, was vested in administrators appointed by the president. These measures, it was hoped, would enable the central government to recapture sufficient power and authority to bring an end to local and regional insubordination.

WORLD WAR I AND ITS REPERCUSSIONS

In August 1914, when the Yuan administration was seeking to rebuild a centralized political structure, World War I broke out in Europe, and international events became a crucial factor in domestic politics.

The leaders of China immediately recognized that Japan was very likely to use this opportunity to replace Germany on the Shandong peninsula. They quickly proclaimed China's neutrality and requested both the United States and Japan to guarantee the nation's territorial integrity. The war vessels of all belligerents in Chinese waters were declared subject to being disarmed, and negotiations were opened with Germany for the immediate return of the Jiaozhou territory it had leased from China.

These efforts were to no avail. On August 15, with British support, the Japanese government delivered an ultimatum to Germany demanding that all German naval warships be withdrawn from Japanese and Chinese waters or disarmed, and that the Jiaozhou leased territory be handed over to Japan

*Although the sums assessed were relatively light, most provincial authorities immediately insisted that they could not pay them. (See *North China Herald*, April 10, 1914, pp. 229–230.) By 1914 the salt gabelle and customs duties—the two taxes under foreign control—were providing more revenue than in the past and enabling the government to meet its minimum obligations. But land tax collection had been discontinued in many regions; the records had been destroyed and the people were naturally hostile to the idea of having taxation resumed. Furthermore, the *likin* tax (internal customs) was being retained for provincial use. The central government was not receiving more than 5 percent of the prerevolutionary income from these two sources, which made dependence on foreign loans inevitable.

51. *Sun visiting Genyōsha members' graves, Fukuoka, 1913. From left: 3d, Miyazaki Torazō; 5th, Fujii Tanetaro, Sun, He Tianjiong, Dai Tianchou (Jitao)*

not later than September 15, with the understanding that it would eventually be restored to China. Five days later the Chinese proposed that Germany's Shandong possessions be given to the United States for immediate transfer to China, and Beijing continued its own negotiations with German representatives. The United States, however, wanted no involvement, and Tokyo was determined to move. On August 23 Japan declared war. On September 2, after a blockade of the Jiaozhou area, Japanese troops landed at Longzhou, on the Shandong peninsula. Heavy rains slowed their progress, but on November 7 they captured Qingdao and took complete control of the German leased territories.

Japanese authorities continued to insist that Japan had no desire for territorial aggrandizement, and that when the war was over the former German possessions would be restored to China. But the Chinese press reported deep apprehension in Chinese political circles. To know the fate of Shandong, one report claimed, one has only to look at present conditions in Manchuria and Liaodong.[2]

Japanese actions in Shandong underwrote the concern being voiced. Despite Japanese pledges to the people of the area, peasant carts were commandeered, Japanese military notes were made a compulsory medium of exchange, and in some areas crops and properties were damaged without compensation. And as Japanese control expanded, issues like those that had arisen earlier in Manchuria emerged. Japanese authorities demanded control of the key railroads leading into Qingdao, including a portion that lay outside the old leased territory.

As these developments were occurring, the Yuan government, taking a calculated risk, sought to quiet controversy rather than to encourage Chinese nationalism, a force of tremendous potential lying just beneath the surface. It made efforts to suppress the flood of anti-Japanese literature circulating in Beijing and elsewhere, cognizant of the danger of a widespread anti-Japanese campaign. Yuan was far from being pro-Japanese, but he recognized that China, politically and militarily weak, could not hope to prevail against Japan on the battlefield, at least until unity had been achieved. It was essential, he and his advisers believed, to buy time and concentrate on removing domestic weaknesses—a decision virtually identical to that made later by Chiang Kai-shek.

Thus the effort at self-strengthening continued, especially in the political realm. In late 1914 the final steps were taken to create what was supposed to be the permanent institutional structure for the national government. On October 30, in a lengthy presidential order, Yuan announced the rules and regulations for the National Assembly, scheduled to begin its first session on September 1, 1915. And in December a new presidential election law was promulgated. This law, like all other actions of the period, made it clear that Yuan was trying to construct a strongly centralized political system.*

However, the means of achieving centralization—and legitimation—continued to be widely debated. One crucial issue was whether Yuan should work through a political party and, in a broader sense, whether political parties should be allowed. In considering this question, Chinese politicians were well aware of developments in Japan. There, after a period of aloofness, or in some cases active hostility, an increasing number of key Japanese military and bureaucratic leaders had begun to organize and lead parties. This served to partially "bureaucratize" the parties, and to produce a working relation between officialdom and the parties which has survived in some respects until the present day. It also helped move Japan toward a competitive party system, albeit a system restricted by the prerogatives of the throne, the presence of the *genrō*, and a certain independence of the military. Nonetheless, in accordance with its own political culture and perceived national needs, Japan was combining democratic procedures and institutions borrowed from the West with a continued emphasis on unity under the emperor and the supremacy of the executive. The purpose, of course, was to insure stability through centralized governance.

Yuan, however, chose to stand aloof from parties, while at the same time seeking to control the decision-making process more firmly. He not only refused to create his own party, he appeared to support a recommendation by the Censorate that no member of a political party be permitted to become a

*The new provisions for the presidential election were truly unique. Only candidates who were at least forty years old and had lived in China for thirty years were eligible for election—which excluded Sun Yat-sen and almost all persons educated abroad. The nomination system was as follows. The president, "representing the people," was empowered to nominate three candidates. He would write their names on a golden tablet, which would be locked in a gold casket and placed in a stone safe-box, the keys to which would be held by the president, the secretary of state, and the chairman of the Administrative Council. When the time came, the three candidates' names would be submitted to an electoral college consisting of fifty members of the Administrative Council and fifty members of the National Assembly. The candidate who secured two-thirds of the votes cast was declared elected. Although the term of the presidency was to be ten years, the Administrative Council was empowered to extend the term if it deemed this necessary.

member of the new National Assembly. Meanwhile, he ordered Professor Willoughby to investigate the practices of other countries.

To downgrade the role of the new parties, however, was not to eliminate factions. Indeed, Beijing politics came to resemble court politics of the past, when rival factions continually maneuvered for the support of the monarch. The Progressive Party members who had cast their lot with Yuan, epitomized by Liang Qichao, declined in influence, and most of them resigned from government. The struggle for power under Yuan came to be waged increasingly by two groups: the Anhui faction, supported by the Beiyang administration and led by Duan Qirui, currently minister of war, among others; and the civil bureaucratic faction led by Liang Shiyi, a veteran adviser to Yuan. This division reflected the rising influence of military men in Chinese politics. But it also had strong regional connotations because the Anhui faction was composed largely of northern military men, whereas Cantonese were prominently represented in the civil bureaucratic faction.

The other political group with potential power—the Guomindang—was largely in exile or underground. Sun and his remaining associates were living in Japan, trying to organize yet a third revolution. The Guomindang supporters still in China were reduced once again to inactivity or sporadic acts of terrorism. Many lesser rebels, incidentally, had accepted the amnesty offered by the government in early 1914.

As 1914 drew to a close the Cantonese faction was losing ground, and Liang Shiyi was relegated to a post of secondary importance. As we noted earlier, Yuan could not resolve a central dilemma: he wanted to curb the authority of the provincial and regional military men, but he had to depend on them because they alone possessed real power in the form of semi-personal armies. Laws laid down in Beijing would not suffice to rein them in unless they were backed up by some sort of institutional strength. But such strength could not be mustered by creating another army; the burdens of militarism were already crushing. Yet Yuan had made it clear that he was not prepared to challenge provincial military power by seeking to mobilize the citizenry, using a political party as his vehicle. And the civil bureaucrats on whom he sought to rely had neither the prestige nor the resources to sustain the president's power. Thus Yuan the "dictator" was never strong enough to dictate to his generals; consequently, he had to resort to the age-old practice of playing off one military man against another.

The first months of 1915 were dominated by the crisis over Japan's Twenty-One Demands, a crisis having profound and long-lasting repercussions on Chinese politics. As soon as it secured the Shandong possessions, the Japanese government began drafting a set of proposals, which were finally presented to Beijing on January 18, 1915. Labeled the Twenty-One Demands, these proposals were set forth in five categories. The first group pertained to the Shandong territories. While it was stipulated that Japan intended to restore the old leasehold to China, various conditions were laid down which in effect perpetuated for Japan (and to a more limited extent, for other foreign nations) the rights possessed by the Germans. The second group of demands related to South Manchuria and Inner Mongolia; in addition to extending Japanese leases to ninety-nine years, they served to confirm and advance Japanese economic and political predominance in these regions. The third group centered on the Hanyeping mining company in which Japanese investors had a heavy interest, and made Japanese consent

52. *Wedding picture, Soong Chingling and Sun, Tokyo, October 25, 1914*

mandatory with respect to any changes. The fourth group prohibited the Chinese from making concessions of coastal facilities to any third party. The fifth group of demands was the most comprehensive; it guaranteed the Japanese priority with respect to capital investment in China, and provided for Japanese advisers within the key sectors of Chinese government.[3]

Exhorted by the press and the informed public, the Yuan government bargained stubbornly while slowly giving ground. As usual, China was forced to negotiate from weakness, not only because it was internally divided and militarily backward, but also because the concessions of earlier years had placed the Japanese in a strong position to advance their new claims. The text of the demands was at first kept secret, but numerous leaks were permitted, often through official Beijing sources, in the hope that an aroused citizenry and world opinion would serve to give the Japanese pause.

The immediate effect of Japanese pressure was to enhance Yuan's authority and prestige. The great majority of politically conscious Chinese wanted to present Japan with a unified nationalist front. Thus, most of Yuan's domestic opponents rallied to the cause, closing ranks in order to defend China's national honor. Telegrams and letters poured into the capital, some of them from old enemies of Yuan, demanding that the government stand firm and pledging support. Anti-Japanese publications proliferated, and mini-boycotts erupted.

The Japanese became annoyed by these developments and by Chinese procrastination in the negotiations. The Japanese minister to China, Hioki Eki, warned on March 8 that unless China moved more quickly, Japan might be forced to take (unspecified) action. In the days that followed, additional Japanese troops poured into China, arriving in Mukden, Dairen, and Jinanfu. In response, thousands of Chinese gathered in Zhang Suhe's garden in Shanghai on March 18 to discuss the Japanese demands and advocate a boycott of Japanese goods, and boycotts did get under way in certain areas despite the opposition of Chinese authorities.* The discussions dragged on through April and reached a crisis on May 7, when Minister Hioki presented the Chinese with an ultimatum giving them two days in which to accept the demands, without the fifth group. On May 9 the demands—slightly amended in the course of the negotiations—were accepted, followed by major Chinese protests in various quarters. Press accounts referred to May 7 as a day of shame that should be forever remembered by all patriotic Chinese, and this was the origin of what came to be called the National Day of Humiliation.

MONARCHISM AND THE END OF THE YUAN ERA

It is not surprising that in the midst of the major threat produced by Japanese pressure, the desire for strong leadership and a unified China mush-

* Reports from Mukden to Canton indicate several efforts to mount a boycott, all of them spearheaded by students. How deep the resentment went may be gauged by the remark of the civil governor of Liaoning, speaking to the American consul: "If anyone wants my tea cup, pen and ink, he may have them, but if he wants my wife, I certainly object and will not let her go without a struggle." But he also acknowledged that China could not win in a military confrontation, because the Japanese had made extensive preparations and had facilities in the port of Dairen and the South Manchurian Railroad which would enable them to transport a large body of troops. (See *NAMP/RDSDIAC*, 893.00/2278, Mukden, May 4, 1915, Heintzleman to Reinsch.)

roomed. Unquestionably, it abetted the movement for a restoration of the monarchy, with Yuan as the candidate in mind. The president himself continued to insist that he had no intention of becoming emperor and, indeed, that such an act would be a betrayal of trust. Yet the campaign spread, and evidence accumulated that it was being nurtured from within the presidential palace.

In August the Peace Preservation Society (Chouan Hui) was established in Beijing, with the specific purpose of advancing the monarchical cause. Among its leading members were three individuals from the Administrative Council: Sun Youyun, a former military governor of Anhui and a former Guomindang member; Yang Du, a Japanese-educated student of law and chief of the National Historical Bureau; and Dr. Yan Fu, the English-educated student of naval science who had gained fame as a translator and author. Among other prominent members was Liu Shipei, the former anarchist.

The basic thesis of the Peace Preservation Society was that republicanism represented a foreign importation ill-suited to Chinese culture and society. Promonarchists argued that the peasantry of China were incapable of loyalty to impersonal institutions of government such as legislative assemblies or even the presidency. They needed the type of continuity and personalization embodied in the monarchy, with which they had always identified. Republicanism in contemporary China had produced indifference among the masses, corruption and disunity among the elite. If the venal factionalism that accompanied the parliamentary process continued, China would disintegrate.

As they were organizing, the monarchists recruited a supporter in the person of Professor Frank Goodnow, who had returned to China for a brief visit. Goodnow expressed the view that under certain conditions constitutional monarchy would be the best system for China at present. His views were translated and widely disseminated, sometimes without the qualifications he had attached. But monarchism also lost a former adherent, Liang Qichao. Liang, convinced that it was now too late to resurrect the monarchy and increasingly unhappy with Yuan and his policies, resigned from the Constitutional Commission, stating that he had been appointed to draw up a republican constitution, not a monarchical one.

Yet Liang appeared to be in the minority. By the fall of 1915 the monarchical movement was gathering strength everywhere, and Yuan's resistance to it—always difficult to measure—was fading. Indeed, there were now indications that the movement had firm official backing—a situation that would be impossible without Yuan's acquiescence, if not his active support. Military approval seemed virtually unanimous, and messages also poured in from civilian provincial officials, urging that eligible voters be allowed to determine the form of government China should have. By mid-October Yuan was saying that he would follow the will of the majority, and on November 1 a directive was issued requesting that people's representatives from each province vote on the issue. The Administrative Council hastened to join the parade, reversing its earlier position. Only certain important ministers from foreign nations, notably the representatives of Great Britain, Japan, and Russia—and later the French and Italian ministers—voiced doubts. On December 10, 1915, electors met and unanimously voted in favor of monarchy. In mid-December, after several ritualistic refusals, "the will of the people" was finally accepted by Yuan, and plans were launched for a spectacular coronation in February.[4]

Yet trouble came quickly. Within a week after Yuan's acceptance, word of revolt in Yunnan, led by General Cai Ao, reached Beijing. Cai had been a supporter of greater centralization, but he now joined in signing a long manifesto that accused Yuan of "utter disregard for the welfare of the nation," charging that he had eliminated those who opposed him, bought the support of his followers, neglected the nation's defenses against foreign aggression, and become a traitor to the Republic. The Yunnan "patriots' army" took an oath to protect the republican form of government, to advance provincial autonomy, to establish a constitutional government both in spirit and in letter, and to consolidate friendly relations with foreign powers.[5] Among these four goals, two warrant special note. First, the issue of provincial autonomy versus centralization was intertwined with that of republicanism, reflecting both the deeply entrenched regionalism that prevailed and the unhappiness with which provincial leaders viewed efforts to reduce their power. Second, Cai and other antimonarchist rebels recognized that their action might tempt Japan into new adventures in China, and so they sought to put on the record their desire for "friendly relations" with all nations.

The new rebellion was not spearheaded by Sun or the Guomindang. Indeed, although Sun and his supporters took advantage of it to return to China, its eruption took them by surprise, as had been the case in 1911. Cai, its leader, was a follower of Liang Qichao. It is interesting to note, however, that the Yunnan revolt was in line with Sun's original plan for the Xinhai revolution, a plan rendered abortive by the Wuhan uprising.

At first neither the Yuan government nor foreign observers took the Yunnan rebellion too seriously. It was generally assumed that Yuan could keep the large majority of provincial military leaders in his camp, and that the rebellion would be confined to a single region, where it would gradually sputter to a halt. But it soon became clear that the supposedly unanimous support for monarchism was fictitious. The masses, as usual, were not involved. The politically articulate and the provincial power-holders had not been disposed to challenge what they had previously regarded as inevitable, but once opposition arose, many of them were prepared to desert Yuan's ship, including a number who had urged him to mount the throne. Oddly, Yuan himself did nothing to aid his cause at this point. Betraying uncharacteristic indecision, he dallied for weeks, apparently unable to make up his mind about the appropriate course of action, and receiving wholly contradictory advice. In retrospect, it is apparent that he was now an ill man, and that his physical ailments were being made worse by the strain of events.

Finally, on January 21, 1916, the foreign office notified the ministers of the allied powers in Beijing that the monarchical investiture ceremony scheduled for early February had been postponed. The revolt, meanwhile, was spreading. Guizhou joined Yunnan in declaring independence, Hunan was again in turmoil, and Yunnanese forces were battling in south Sichuan. On February 23, with no resolution of the revolt in sight, Yuan issued an order postponing his ascendancy to the throne, asserting that the issue had given rise to "quarrels"; but no final decision was made. Spokesmen favoring a monarchy tried to persuade Yuan that there was no need for compromise, since northern troops could easily crush the rebels. But Yuan realized that he desperately needed the support of certain key military men, notably Duan Qirui and Feng Guozhang, who were now firmly set against the monarchical movement. On March 23 Yuan finally issued an order canceling the monarchy, accepting personal responsibility for this failure in a manner quite as pathetic as that shown in the final rescript issued in the name of the infant emperor a few years earlier. Yuan's action amazed and in some cases outraged his supporters, who had been certain that he would fight for power. But it was too little and too late to please many of his opponents, most of whom were now determined to oust him from office completely.

Shortly after the order of March 23 was issued, the government and the rebels agreed on an armistice, and informal peace negotiations began. The rebels insisted on the restoration of parliament within two months, a reversion to the original provisional constitution, pardons for all political opponents, the stationing of some southern troops in Beijing, and the recall of certain northern troops from the South. Southern spokesmen at first expressed willingness to see Yuan remain as president, but this quickly became a controversial issue within their ranks. The Beijing government asked for cancellation of the provincial declarations of independence, the withdrawal of all insurgents to their original locations, the disbandment of all newly enlisted rebel troops, the maintenance of "order" in the rebellious provinces, and the dispatch of delegates from these provinces to Beijing to discuss the settlement of outstanding issues.

The political tides were now rolling against Yuan. In April, Guangdong and Zhejiang declared their independence, and Fujian and Anhui were teetering in the balance. Once again most of the South was detaching itself from the government in Beijing. Many Chinese observers now decided that Yuan was finished, having lost face so badly that he could no longer command respect. Desperately, the president moved to propitiate his opponents. He announced the restoration of cabinet government and named General Duan Qirui premier. By late April it was agreed that all executive orders would be signed by Duan, with the president affixing his seal. Nothing could have symbolized more clearly Yuan's fading authority.

At this point, four political groups were contending for power on the national scene. The first and weakest group consisted of the monarchists, now repudiated and in retreat; one result of their decline was to seal the fate of the Cantonese civil-bureaucratic faction around Yuan, since it had played a key role in advancing the monarchical cause. The second group, now gaining power and influence, consisted of the northern military leaders, most of whom had come to oppose monarchism but continued to support Yuan as president. Because they commanded the bulk of China's armies, they seemed certain to figure prominently in the political future, now that efforts to enforce centralization and civilian governance had failed. Thus, their unity or division would be critical to the fate of the nation. The third group consisted of the southern "moderates," led by civilian and military figures like Liang Qichao and Cai Ao, who had once supported Yuan but were now alienated from him and sympathetic to republicanism. The fourth group comprised the "radical republicans"—Sun, Huang, and the old Guomindang members—who were now reemerging from the political wilderness, but with uncertain unity and strength.

These factional divisions were based not merely—or in some cases, not essentially—on policy or ideological differences. Regional, personal, and

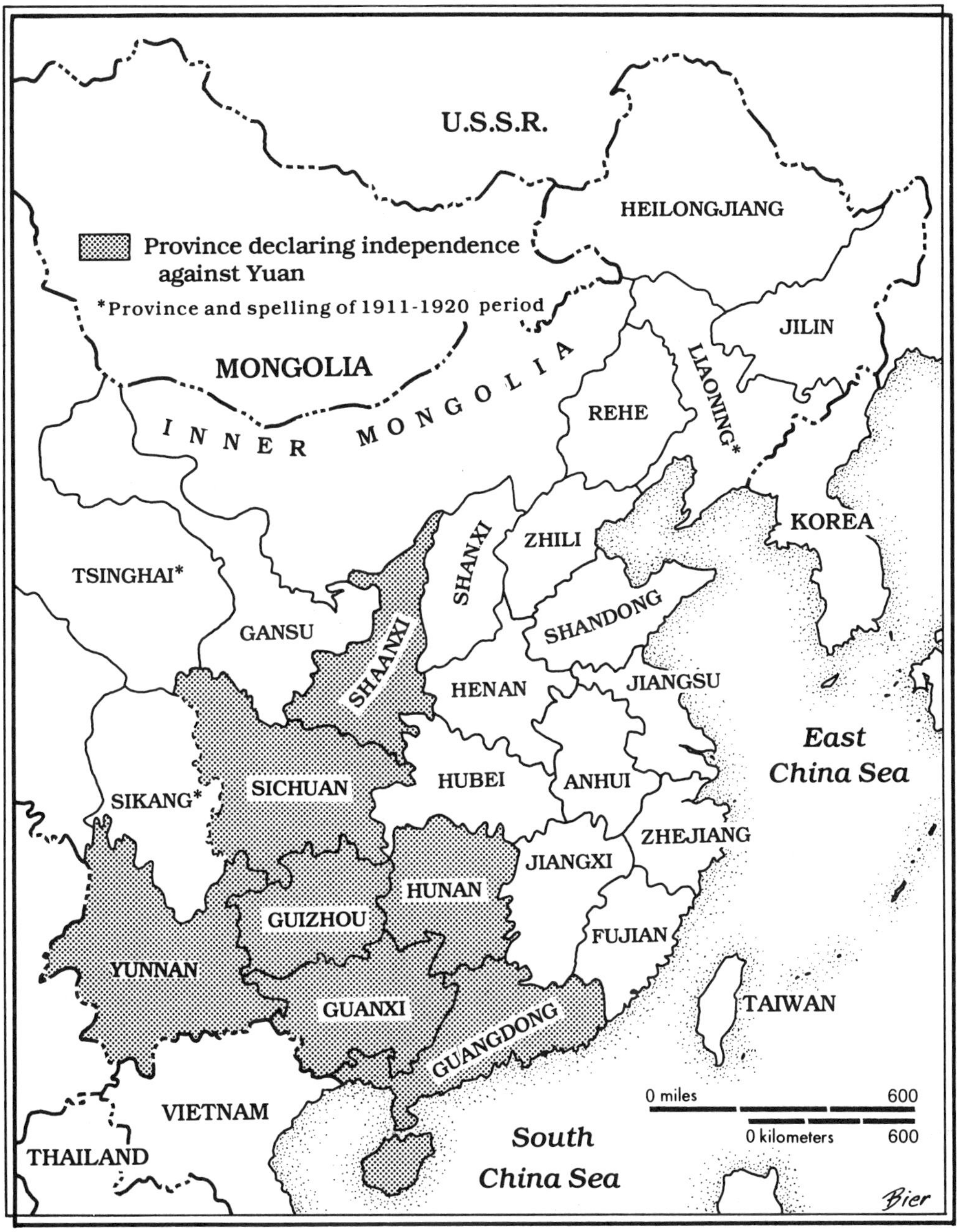

MAP 2. *China, 1916: Provinces Declaring Independence Against Yuan*

historical factors also figured prominently in them. In any case, the key question in this era was whether the second and third groups—the northern military leaders and the southern "moderates"—could form a workable coalition. Given all of the elements on the political scene, no other combination could possibly bring peace and stability.

It quickly became apparent that such a coalition would not be easily achieved. Even among the northern military leaders, numerous differences existed. In May, General Feng Guozhang called a conference in Nanjing, to which he initially invited representatives of the seventeen provinces that had not declared independence. Later, the five "independent" provinces were also invited to send delegates, but they declined, stipulating that they could participate only if Yuan's abdication from the presidency had been agreed upon in advance. Even so, the Nanjing conferees failed to reach a consensus on the same crucial question; delegates from five provinces still insisted that Yuan had to go.

By early June, Chinese politics were mired in a military and a political stalemate. Suddenly, on July 6, 1916, Yuan died, a victim of nephritis at the age of fifty-six. On his deathbed the president issued his last order, a statement that vice-president Li Yuanhong was a man with a kind heart and great wisdom who would prove himself equal to the task of overcoming the present difficulties.

An era had ended. From the time of the 1911 Revolution and even before, Chinese politics had revolved to an extraordinary degree around Yuan Shikai. A surrogate emperor even though the formal title was denied him, he had made an effort to bridge the past and the future. Autocrat, traditionalist, patriot, modernizer, Yuan tried to adjust to parliamentary politics; but neither he nor China was comfortable with Western-style republicanism, and he naturally turned to the political institutions and behavior patterns he understood. But just as he could not move China into a workable republicanism, he could not take it back to monarchism and restore the unity the throne had once provided. He died a broken man, deserted by most of his friends and bewildered by his fate.

REVOLUTIONARIES IN EXILE

Ironically, political failure bred a movement toward authoritarianism even within revolutionary circles. After the collapse of the "second revolution" in the summer of 1913, Sun and his close associates had fled to Japan. Disillusioned with the weaknesses of a Western-style party, and blaming defeat on the factionalism, corruption, and lack of discipline within the Guomindang, Sun now committed himself to creating a tightly organized, absolutely obedient revolutionary movement, drawing once again on the model of the secret society.[6]

In September 1913, only a month after he had reached Japan, Sun began to recruit followers for his new party. Each member was required to swear an oath—and to affix his fingerprint to make his commitment binding—that he was prepared to sacrifice his life and freedom for the cause of saving China and rescuing the people; that he would "obediently follow Mr. Sun Zhongshan" (Sun Yat-sen); that he would raise the banner of revolution again; and that he would always defend the principles of democracy and people's livelihood and work to establish the five-power constitution.[7]

This oath immediately produced dissension in revolutionary ranks. A group including Huang Xing, Zhang Ji, and Li Liejun protested the provision that members of the new revolutionary organization should swear to obey a single individual, asserting that this turned the movement into a personal revolution, which was contrary to the spirit of republicanism and democracy. They also argued that the fingerprint requirement was degrading, a procedure suitable only for criminals. Sun, however, insisted that past expe-

53. *Sun and wife with friends in Tokyo, 1914 or 1915. In back row, second from left, Liao Zhongkai. In front of Sun, Liao's son, Liao Chengzhi*

rience had proved that a successful revolutionary movement required an iron discipline and strict adherence to the commands of the leader.

With Sun standing firm, recruitment continued. By the spring of 1914, Sun claimed that some four to five hundred persons had taken the oath and that a political training center and a military school had been established.[8] The movement also had a new organ, *Minguo* (The Republic). Once again, moreover, Sun turned to the overseas Chinese for financial support. The split that had opened up among revolutionary leaders in 1913 over the oath had widened, however, and in mid-1914 Huang Xing, Zhang Ji, Li Liejun, and others openly broke with Sun. Huang went to the United States, Zhang and Li to France.[9]

Thus the official inauguration of Sun's new party was long delayed. A preliminary meeting was held in Tokyo on June 22, 1914, but it was not until July 8 that the party was formally established, under the name Zhonghua Gemingdang (The Chinese Revolutionary Party). The party manifesto, issued on September 1, made it clear that the new organization was to be a secret revolutionary body, different in character from a regular political party. Only those who took the oath could be members, and absolute obedience to the leader's orders was required. The revolution had to be renewed, and the first step was to eradicate the corruption that had eroded the Guomindang, by eliminating from participation all "bureaucrats and false members."[10]

The Gemingdang constitution was a fascinating document. In modified form, it reiterated the postrevolution plan for a three-stage progression first advanced in the Tongmeng Hui manifesto of 1905: a period of military government, to liquidate the old order and lay new foundations; a period of tutelage, during which the people would be trained for democracy through participation in local government; and a final stage of full-fledged constitutionalism, during which parliamentary democracy would take effect on a national scale. It was now stipulated, however, that during the first and second stages all military and political affairs would be in the hands of Zhonghua Gemingdang members only. And whereas the Tongmeng Hui manifesto had provided for nine years to reach the third stage, the Gemingdang provisions indicated no time period.*

These provisions, advanced at the outset of World War I and three years before the Bolshevik Revolution, bore a striking resemblance to certain later Communist themes and practices. Sun was now committed to a "guided democracy" under a one-party dictatorship until such time as the Chinese people had been trained to operate a constitutional democracy. Until then, a party elite with monopolistic powers would govern in the name of the people. The final objective of Sun's tutelage, to be sure, was totally dissimilar to that of the Communists, who envisioned a different utopia—a proletarian dictatorship that would lead to a classless society and the withering away of the state. Yet the means that both advocated were remarkably similar; and if one believed that the means invariably affect the end, and that power in its monopolistic form is seldom relinquished voluntarily, it was legitimate to question whether either Sun's goal or that of the Communists could ever be realized.

There was another striking similarity in the two revolutionary movements: both claimed to be pursuing the goals of socialism, although Sun leaned toward state socialism, whereas the Communists aimed at a more radical form of stateless socialism. At Sun's insistence, *minshengzhuyi*—the principle of the people's livelihood—was reinserted as a part of the Gemingdang program. Since this remained a somewhat vague concept, it would permit identification with other types of socialists whenever that seemed tactically wise.

In founding the Gemingdang, Sun made certain that he had untrammeled organizational as well as ideological powers. Taking the title of *zongli* (director general) again, he insisted on having complete authority to organize party headquarters, which would simultaneously serve as the high com-

*The standards for Gemingdang membership were rigorous. Besides the oath, there was an entrance fee of ten yuan and yearly dues of one yuan; if a member violated party regulations, both he and his sponsor were to be punished. Moreover, there were to be three categories of members: founding members, who had joined the party before the Revolution; associate members, who had joined during the period of military action but before the establishment of the revolutionary government; and general members, who had joined after the revolutionary government had become operative. During the revolutionary period, founding members could participate in both the legislative and executive branches of government, associate members could vote and hold certain offices, and general members only had the right to vote. One other startling provision was contained in the constitution. Nonmembers of the Gemingdang were to be excluded from citizenship during the first and second stages of the revolution; only with the advent of constitutional government would they be granted equal political rights with Gemingdang members. The text of the constitution is contained in Zou Lu, *Zhongguo Guomindang shigao* 1:161–167.

54. *Chen Qimei shortly before his death in May 1916*

mand of the revolutionary army. The *zongli* was authorized to appoint all bureau heads, and five bureaus were created: general affairs, party affairs, finance, military, and political. These posts were filled initially by Chen Qimei, Zhu Zheng, Liao Zhongkai, Xu Chongzhi, and Hu Hanmin, respectively. Besides these bureaus, which were treated as an embryonic executive branch of government, Sun created four councils—legislative, judicial, control, and examination—in preparation for the realization of the five-power constitution. There was provision also for an associate *zongli*, but the post was never filled, because, it was said, Huang Xing declined it and the decision was made to leave it open for his possible return to the fold.

It was during this period, as the Gemingdang was being organized, that Sun wrote a letter to his longtime acquaintance, Count Ōkuma Shigenobu, currently prime minister of Japan, requesting Japanese assistance for China, through Sun's party and movement.[11] The letter, dated May 11, 1914, was leaked to Chinese authorities in Beijing by a disillusioned follower of Sun's, who regarded the proposed concessions to Japan as outrageous. The letter, indeed, had some amazing passages. If Japan would assist in China's reform efforts, Sun promised, China would be willing "to throw open her whole country to Japanese industrial and commercial enterprises," which would allow Japan to move to the forefront of the world's great powers while enabling China "to preserve her integrity, develop her latent resources, and become a rich country on the continent of Asia."

Sun argued that if Japan were to assist his party in the course of its revolution, the struggle would be brief, and foreign entanglements (presumably European) could be removed. During the ensuing period of construction, "when the reform of administration, the training of the army, the encouragement of education, and the development of industries are all taken in hand, talents must be borrowed from more advanced countries," and "considering that Japan and China are nations of the same race and same literature . . . there are weighty reasons for the revolutionists to look for help from Japan."

He continued: "After Japan has assisted China to reorganize her administration and religion [*sic*] and to develop her potential resources, the governments and peoples of the two countries will be on much more intimate terms than [would exist] between other countries. China will throw open all the trade centers in the country to Japanese labor and merchants and enable Japan to monopolize the commercial field in China." Sun added that when China was ready to free itself from the unfair restrictions and unequal treaties imposed upon it by the major powers, it would need Japan's support, including advice on reform in the Chinese legal, judicial, and penal systems. Japan, moreover, could help in the abolition of extraterritoriality by giving its consent first. When China regained control over its customs, a commercial alliance with Japan could be consummated whereby a duty-free exchange of manufactured items and raw materials could begin.

Sun concluded the letter by castigating Yuan and insisting that China could never achieve peace unless government were in the hands of Sun's party. The Chinese, he said, were divided roughly into three classes—the official class, his party, and the masses. The masses took no active part in politics, and the official class sought merely to protect their personal interests. Only his party (which he referred to as the People's Party) strove fearlessly for national objectives.

Many of the proposals that Sun made to Ōkuma were shortly incorporated into Japan's Twenty-One Demands—but without the quid pro quos. Some were to seem relevant more than six decades later, when another generation of revolutionaries turned to Japan for economic and technical assistance. At the time, however, the disclosure of Sun's letter created a sensation and led many people—including some longtime supporters—to condemn him as a traitor to Chinese national interests, a man willing to sell his country in exchange for Japanese support of his faction.

Such charges were for the most part unfair. Despite some extravagant passages, the letter makes it clear that Sun wanted Japanese support in building a strong and independent China, though a China cast according to his own political mold. As we have seen, Sun had long harbored Pan-Asian sentiments, and he had often looked to Japan—or at least to certain Japanese—for support in his revolutionary undertakings. Yet Sun could be charged with political naïveté, and his letter to Ōkuma was an excellent example. The unrealistic exuberance for which he was so well known was also given ample play in that communication.

Nothing came of Sun's appeal to Ōkuma, and once again he and his followers were soon soliciting support among the overseas Chinese in the United States and Southeast Asia. Between mid-1914 and the time of Yuan's death in 1916, Sun's emissaries were reported to have raised money in the United States amounting to 1.2 million yen, most of which was duly advanced to Sun in Tokyo.[12] However, the split in the Guomindang created certain problems. Huang, who had refused to join the Gemingdang and had then broken with Sun, arrived in San Francisco on July 15, 1914, and was warmly welcomed as a leader by the local Chinese community. Sun's forces did not attempt to scrap the American Guomindang, preferring to put their men in key positions within the existing organization.* And rather than risk a bruising intraparty struggle, they allowed Huang's faction to have a share of the funds collected in the United States.[13]

In Southeast Asia the factional conflicts were more serious. Sun had authorized Deng Zeru to reorganize the party in this area, and in October of 1914 Deng was made head of the Gemingdang's finance bureau, charged with fund-raising in the British and Dutch colonies in the region. But Sun gave a similar authorization to Lu Wenhui, and so Deng and Lu were soon engaged in a jurisdictional dispute. In addition, a group of former Guomindang-affiliated governors—including Chen Jiongming, Bo Wenwei, and Li Liejun—objected to abandoning the old party label and moved to challenge Sun's leadership. They formed their own group, the Shuili Gongsi (Conservancy Company), and conducted separate organizational and financial drives in Southeast Asia.

Relations among the overseas anti-Yuan forces became more complex in 1915 as a result of the Japanese pressure on China. A sizable group of old Guomindang members felt that in this hour of peril political differences should be set aside, and that all patriotic Chinese should rally around the besieged Beijing government. Thus, in Japan such exiles as Li Genyuan, Zang Xinyan, and Niu Yongjian—all followers of Huang Xing—formed the Oushi Yanjiu (Association for the Discussion of European Affairs) and

* When Xie Yingpai and Lin Shen passed through Japan toward the end of 1913 and took Sun's prescribed oath, they were appointed to reorganize the Guomindang in Hawaii and in the United States. Later Wu Tiecheng, Feng Ziyou, Sun Fo (Sun's son), and others were designated representatives of the Zhonghua Gemingdang on their departure for the Western Hemisphere. Xie was elected head of the Guomindang (known as the Chinese Nationalist League) in the Americas when he arrived at party headquarters in San Francisco, but he soon resigned in favor of Feng. In the winter of 1914, at a general meeting of the American Guomindang, Lin was elected chairman and Feng became vice-chairman (Feng Ziyou, *Geming wenxian* 5:60–62).

issued an appeal for national unity. The movement spread. From their various exile posts, Bo Wenwei, Chen Jiongming, Niu Yongjian, and Huang Xing himself circulated a jointly signed telegram expressing their willingness to cease revolutionary activities and join in a common front against Japan.[14] Even within the Gemingdang some support for such a move emerged, led by men like Lin Shen and Xie Yingpai, top Gemingdang leaders in America.

But Sun remained unwilling to countenance any rapprochement with Yuan Shikai. The exact nature of Sun's relations with Japanese authorities during this period remains in dispute. Earlier, in examining Japanese Foreign Ministry files after World War II, scholars discovered an eleven-point "sample treaty" supposedly submitted by Sun to the Japanese Foreign Office, dated March 14, 1915. The document pledged that in exchange for assistance in overthrowing Yuan, Sun would rely on Japan to equip and train China's armed forces, use Japanese political advisers, seek Japanese capital to develop transportation and industry, and help create a Sino-Japanese bank to facilitate economic cooperation. But the authenticity of this document has been challenged, and certainly Sun's signature on the "treaty" appears to be a forgery.*

It is clear, however, that Sun's activities in Japan during this period alarmed and angered many of his followers. For example, certain party members in San Francisco wired the national government in Beijing, asserting their adamant opposition to the Twenty-One Demands and accusing the Gemingdang leadership of aiding the Japanese. Party members in Southeast Asia and Japan also unfurled banners of revolt. Feng Ziyou, one of Sun's most trusted lieutenants, was dispatched from the United States to Tokyo in an effort to rebuild party unity through conversations with Sun. As his earlier career had demonstrated, however, Sun Yat-sen was a stubborn man, and he refused to abandon the campaign to oust Yuan—a campaign to be carried out with whatever allies he could find, including his Japanese friends. Thus by sticking to his long-held Pan-Asian views, Sun deliberately separated himself from the rapidly mounting nationalist tide. By mid-1915 he and his movement were at a low ebb, denounced even by many old associates. Once again history seemed to have passed him by.**

*The gist of the document is set forth in Jansen, *The Japanese and Sun Yat-sen*, pp. 192–193, and also in Wilbur, *Sun Yat-sen*, pp. 83–84, but in a review of Wilbur's study, Chiang Yung-ching reproduces a portion of the document, including the signature, together with a genuine Sun signature, and a striking difference is revealed. See Chiang Yung-ching (Jiang Yongjing), "Book Reviews: Sun Yat-sen: Frustrated Patriot, by C. Martin Wilbur," *China Forum* 5:1 (January 1978); in English, pp. 221–223; in Chinese, pp. 155–186 (the comparison of signatures is to be found on p. 169). We are much indebted to Professor Wilbur for calling this review to our attention. He now suspects that the document may not have been written by Sun.

**Dr. H. H. Kung, Sun's brother-in-law (Soong Ching-ling's brother), wrote a letter to G. E. Morrison on April 3, 1915, in which he expresses the sort of concern over Sun's relations with the Japanese that was widespread during this period, even among veteran revolutionaries. Kung reported that he had had various discussions with Sun, both in Shanghai (prior to the second revolution, in which he was "dissuaded from taking any active part"), and later in Tokyo. He wrote that Sun "truly desires the good of his country," but that "because of some mistaken ideas he can easily be 'worked' by the Japanese." (See Lo, Hui-min, ed., *The Correspondence of* G. E. *Morrison* 1:388–391.) This letter came to our notice in an article by Albert A. Altman and Harold Z. Schiffrin, "Sun Yat-sen and the Japanese: 1914–16." They in turn express appreciation to Professor Ernest P. Young for sending them a copy of the letter, which is now available in the work edited by Lo.

55. *Yuan Shikai at the end of his life, 1916*

But at this point Yuan made a major blunder: his disastrous venture into monarchism opened the way for Sun's return to the political arena in China. After nearly three years of exile, Sun and a small band of dedicated followers returned to Shanghai on March 27, 1916. Shortly thereafter, Sun issued a declaration recounting Yuan's "crimes," citing these as a vindication of his own strong stand against Yuan. After demanding that "the traitor" be brought to justice, Sun said that he was seeking to learn "the real motives" and "principles" of the leaders of the ongoing anti-Yuan movement, and that although he was not their personal friend, he was willing to make common cause with anyone dedicated to removing Yuan. Unity was essential at this juncture, he continued, and all issues could be settled in accordance with the republican constitution.[15]

Although Sun claimed to have attracted many adherents to the Gemingdang within China, "even in the interior," it is difficult to find the evidence. He did put two small military units into operation, one in Guangdong, led by Zhu Zhixin, and another in Shandong under Zhu Zheng; but control of these units was essentially in hands other than his. Sun reentered the Chinese political arena with a small power base, military and political. Undoubtedly, this is the reason why the elaborate program and revolutionary schedule of the Gemingdang were completely set aside at this point, and why Sun began the arduous task of seeking alliances, as he had done before. His basic requirements were adherence to the original provisional constitution and to the reconvening of the parliament dissolved by Li Yuanhong, a parliament in which the Guomindang had enjoyed a substantial majority. And after Yuan's death, as we shall see, Sun and his supporters again tried to make Western-style parliamentary processes work, despite their recent doubts about China's capacity to achieve instant democracy. The seeds of a one-party dictatorship had been planted, but they were not to sprout in this season. A nationally effective dictatorship in any form was impossible, given the current realities of China.

POLITICAL TRENDS AT THE CENTER

In the first few months after Yuan's death on June 6, 1916, political activity accelerated, both in Beijing and in the provinces. Li Yuanhong immediately assumed the presidency, and one of his first acts was to summon representatives of various factions, including men from Central and South China, to the capital for discussions. It was announced that the provisional constitution of 1912 had been restored, and that the parliament of 1913 would be reconvened on August 1. Li also requested Duan Qirui to continue as premier and to build a cabinet that would promote national unity.

In many respects, Duan was the logical person for this task. The most able of all Yuan's protégés, a central figure in the so-called Beiyang faction of military men, and a powerful minister of war for three years, Duan had as much prestige and as many connections within military circles as anyone on the scene—and needless to say, military support for the government was indispensable at this time. He had opposed the monarchical movement at an early stage, and was also considered honest and capable of sympathetic communication with many civilian republicans, particularly those of Progressive Party lineage. Finally, although he was a native of Anhui and the acknowledged leader of the Anhui faction, his base of power lay near the capital, and

56. *Li Yuanhong as president of upper chamber of National Assembly*

he had an intimate knowledge of Beijing politics—not unimportant assets, given the uncertain attitudes of many northern military figures toward the new era.*

*Duan had become minister of war on March 20, 1912, and with a few interruptions had held that position for three years, besides serving briefly in May and June of 1913 as acting premier. He quit office at the end of May 1915, after an accumulation of differences with Yuan: Yuan's desire to create a new elite army unit in Beijing headed by nonprofessionals; the problem of the Twenty-One Demands (Duan favored rejecting the Japanese ultimatum); and Duan's opposition to monarchism. (See Ernest Young, *The Presidency of Yuan Shih-k'ai*, pp. 224–225.)

Yet it was only a matter of weeks before Duan, like his predecessors, found himself in difficulty. His efforts to get leading Guomindang politicians to join his cabinet failed. He made offers to three of them—Tang Shaoyi (foreign affairs), Zhang Yaozeng (justice), and Sun Hongyi (education)—but all three refused, offering various excuses: some cabinet members had been affiliated with the monarchist movement; Duan had not consulted the southern military council about cabinet appointments; and the government had been negligent in not removing General Long Jiguang, the military governor of Guangdong, who had committed numerous depredations in his three-year rule there.

Whether succeeding events would have been very different had the more prominent Guomindang members come north immediately and participated actively in shaping the executive branch of government can be doubted, but in any case, the foundations had been laid for an executive-legislative split of the type now familiar in Chinese parliamentary experiments. The Guomindang was the majority party in the 1913 parliament, and unless it cooperated with Duan, another impasse was virtually inevitable.

Even before parliament reconvened, the traditional Liang-Sun feud reasserted itself in a growing estrangement between Jinbudang and Guomindang partisans, for reasons that went beyond old animosities. Liang and the Jinbudang leaders, intent on increasing their substantial hold on provincial governorships, were cultivating both the president and the premier. With the support of these officials, they could enter the next parliamentary elections with confidence. Naturally, Guomindang stalwarts were determined to block this effort. With the leading civilian politicians at odds, military leaders could afford to watch and wait, convinced that republicanism and democracy would once again fail.

Nevertheless, the Beijing government took several conciliatory steps in an effort to demonstrate that the two military men who were now leading it were themselves dedicated to the republican cause. The old order was legally dismantled. All legislation relating to the National Assembly and to the special citizens' convention that was to approve the Yuan constitution was canceled. The Administrative Council was abolished, as was the censorate attached to it. And a number of prominent monarchists were arrested and ordered to be put on trial, although Duan pointed out that since virtually every official of any significance had been associated with that movement at some stage, it was not feasible to go too far.

Yet much was lacking if a stable government under republican leadership was to be achieved. Just as the Guomindang spokesmen appeared to demand absolute adherence to their positions, refusing to compromise and exhibiting an understandable wariness toward the new leadership, so Duan indicated at an early point that he planned to pursue Yuan's strategy of standing aloof from all political parties, governing from above in the name of national unity. This strategy foreclosed his direct leadership of the legislative branch and made executive dependence on shifting coalitions inevitable. Real power, moreover, would continue to rest with forces outside the parliament, primarily with the regional and provincial military commanders.

Neither Li nor Duan—nor any other figure on China's political horizon at this time—had the prestige of Yuan Shikai at his peak. Consequently, the centrifugal tendencies that speeded Yuan's decline could not be arrested. Al-

57. *Duan Qirui*

though the new government met their chief demands, most of the rebellious provinces of the South did not formally rescind their declarations of independence or resume political and financial allegiance to the center. Throughout the summer of 1916, the provinces of Yunnan, Sichuan, Guangdong, Guangxi, and Hunan were more or less out of control, and their governments and military forces, often rife with internal conflict, ignored or resisted Beijing's orders. Fighting, moreover, was taking place in various parts of Sichuan and Guangdong. In Guangdong republican forces commanded by General Li Liejun were seeking to oust General Long Jiguang. Beijing had finally ordered that Long be replaced as military governor of Guangdong by General Lu Rongting, but Lu was in Guangxi and had no intention of coming to Canton.

When the two houses of parliament met in Beijing on August 1, 138 senators and 318 representatives were in attendance, a strong showing for a body chosen four years earlier. In preparation, on July 25, Sun had in effect disbanded the Gemingdang, stating in a circular notice that the word "revolutionary" was no longer appropriate.* The way was thus paved for the Guomindang to reemerge as the more or less unified vehicle for Sun's movement. At first, the Guomindang-dominated parliament cooperated with the government. In late August Duan was confirmed as premier by an overwhelming vote in both houses. By early October, however, the old issues had surfaced again. Tang continued to refuse to come to Beijing and assume the post of foreign minister, complaining that General Zhang Xun was usurping parliamentary authority in Jiangsu and that a "true patriot," General Li Liejun, was being ignored in Guangdong. When Duan put forth another nominee for the post of military governor of Guangdong, Lu Zhengxiang, he was rejected, as was a third Duan candidate, Wang Daxie. Once again, the Guomindang was agitating for a party cabinet—but at the same time, some Guomindang members, like Gu Zhongxiu and Zhang Yaozeng, were deserting the party to become followers of Duan. The immediate crisis was surmounted when Duan accepted Wu Tingfang, the veteran Guomindang leader, as foreign minister; but in this whole process, Duan's prestige suffered a severe blow, a fact that did not go unnoticed in both military and Guomindang circles.

General Feng Guozhang, the key figure in the Yangtze valley, with his headquarters in Nanjing, was chosen vice-president. Thus the three top executive positions were held by professional military men. It should not be assumed, however, that their relationships were harmonious; clashes were recurrent. The president and the premier were both personally and politically incompatible, and the vice-president, holding strong ambitions of his own, sought to stake out a third position.

Division at the top was mirrored by division throughout the political system. The forces making for cohesion were few and fragile; those auguring conflict were powerful and growing. It was not the absence of a will for unity. Men like Duan, Feng Guozhang, Liang Qichao, and Sun Yat-sen all desired unity. The main cause of division lay in the absence of a common set of values or patterns of political behavior within the relatively small elite that sought to govern the nation. The primary fault-line lay in the relative strength of "traditional" versus "modern" traits and goals, a mix that existed in each leader. An accompanying problem lay in the challenge of unifying a vast continental society that labored under conditions of economic and technological backwardness and thus required very special political institutions. Institutions imported from the West, and the ideology that accom-

*The circular said that the primary objective of the Gemingdang had been to overthrow Yuan's dictatorship and reestablish the republic. With Yuan's death, the reconvening of parliament, and "the termination of military activities," the necessary work of destruction had concluded and the task of construction had begun. With Yuan gone, the term "revolutionary" was thus no longer appropriate, and all current party activities should come to an end. Members would be solicited regarding the future reorganization of the party (*Guofu nianpu* 2:652).

58. *Li Liejun*

59. *Feng Guozhang*

panied them, did not readily fit the contours of Chinese society at the beginning of the twentieth century. Ironically, the traditional system—personalized by the monarch and delicately balanced between centralism on one hand and local autonomy, aristocracy, and limited government on the other—fitted better, hence the recurrent efforts to return to monarchism outfitted in constitutional garb and thus "modernized."

By the end of 1916 an acute hostility had developed between the revitalized Guomindang and the forces grouped under the label "Beiyang party."[16] The Beiyang party had as its nucleus a number of military leaders, most of whom were products of Yuan's earlier military modernization program, epitomized by the Beiyang Military Academy. Relations between the various leaders in the Beiyang party were constructed on a familiar patron-client basis, but the party had by this time split into two regionally oriented groups, the Anhui and Zhili factions. The Anhui faction, led by Duan, was currently in power; the Zhili group, represented by men like Cao Kun and Wang Shizhen, was gradually growing in strength. Taken together, the northern military leaders enlisted in these two factions had approximately 200,000 troops at their command. Quite naturally, civilian politicians could only aspire to power by joining coalitions with the men who controlled the guns. The Jinbudang, whose opposition to the Guomindang was virtually an automatic reflex, had drawn close to the Beiyang party, as had the old Cantonese faction led by Liang Shiyi, which had previously supported Yuan.

Thus four political clusters had now emerged in or near the parliament. The Constitutional Government Discussion Society was essentially a Guomindang instrument, and under it were a number of factions, each with its own leader. The Constitution Research Society was the voice of the Jinbudang and was led by Tang Hualong and Liang Qichao. The Constitution Deliberation Society was composed of individuals who had left one of the two major parties at an earlier point. Finally, the Constitution Mutual Discussion Society was essentially a regional group—consisting of men from the northern provinces of Shandong and Zhili, along with others from Mongolia and Tibet—strongly conservative in its political orientation.

That each one of these groups, so similarly named, avoided the term "party" is evidence of the widespread uneasiness about that historically burdened term; that each one instead used the term "society" suggests continued preference for the traditional form of political group—the exclusive and quasi-private association. On the other hand, each insisted on adopting the term "constitution," which suggests that the quest for an institutional framework was central to the political concerns of the period.

The issues that had emerged by the end of 1916 were familiar ones. On the political front the perennial questions about a permanent constitution, the role of parliament, new elections, and provincial autonomy were still current. Throughout this period the provisional constitution of 1912 had remained in effect, primarily because the cohesion needed to launch a renewed constitution-drafting process was lacking. Attention was therefore focused on other matters. Debate over the role of the parliament was particularly contentious. Sources close to President Li Yuanhong claimed that his idea had always been that the old parliament should be recalled to undertake four specific functions only: the enactment of a new constitution; the establishment of laws relating to a new—and smaller—parliament; the confirmation of the cabinet; and the election of a vice-president. The last two actions were accomplished, but the reconvened parliament began to act increasingly like a full-fledged legislature. The Jinbudang, however, whose influence in provincial assemblies (important in the old system of indirect elections) was considerably greater than its hold on the eligible voters, was reluctant to see a shift to the direct election of members of parliament. For the same reason, it favored appointment of provincial governors by the president rather than election by the people, the position supported by the Guomindang.*

*The struggle over provincial governance between the Jinbudang and the Guomindang was a carryover from 1913. Then, a majority of the Guomindang members in Parliament had supported specific provisions defining the scope and role of provincial governments, which the Jinbudang had opposed. In 1916, when the constitution was being drafted, this issue once again became a major parliamentary dispute between the two parties. A subordinate issue was whether provincial governors should be directly elected by the people. For a discus-

60. *Cao Kun*

The issue of foreign loans had also reemerged, precipitating further acrimony. The old consortium of financial donors had been dissolved, and it was not to be reestablished until 1920. Elements within the Japanese private sector, released from most restraints and enjoying unprecedented prosperity as a result of wartime opportunities, were eager to lend. Confident of their government's support, they were prepared to take risks in order to make

sion of the constitutional battle (first published in 1935), see Yang Youzhun, *Jindai Zhongguo lifa shi*, pp. 226–238.

handsome profits and secure long-term investments. On the other side, a Chinese government burdened by unending military costs and a wholly inadequate set of fiscal-economic policies and institutions naturally continued to turn outward for aid, and although it took loans from European and American sources, its primary reliance was on the Japanese.[17]

Thus, in the fall of 1916 the Duan government negotiated loans first with some American firms and then with Japanese concerns. Various revolutionaries, including Sun and Li Liejun, demanded sizable sums from the American loan, insisting that they had an obligation to pay back money borrowed to conduct the "third revolution," but their requests were denied. The loan negotiated with a private Japanese group was for $80 million and guaranteed the Japanese the right to purchase a one-half ownership in silver mines in Hunan and copper mines in Anhui. A preliminary agreement was reached without parliamentary approval. This produced strong objections to the lack of consultation, but behind them lay a deep hostility toward the Japanese and a suspicion that Tokyo intended to subvert China, using certain Chinese officials in the process. Duan's appointment of Cao Rulin as special ambassador to Japan therefore met with vehement opposition, for Cao was considered both pro-Japanese and an ardent monarchist. The battle over Cao signaled events of much larger scope that were soon to come.

By November 1916 there were no less than four bills of impeachment against Duan being prepared for submission to parliament, and the political atmosphere in the capital was reminiscent of the days three years earlier when the dispute between Yuan and the Guomindang was building. Ties between the center and the provinces were also weakening. At least three provinces—Guangdong, Hunan, and Sichuan—continued to pursue their own paths, amid complex internal struggles for power, largely ignoring the authority of Beijing.

The successive political crises of 1917 stemmed from unresolved issues of foreign and domestic policy. On January 20, despite considerable opposition, a loan agreement between the Bank of Communications and three Japanese institutions for five million yen was signed. The pro-Japanese group within the Duan government was now steadily gaining influence, partly because the Japanese asked few questions and demanded no supervision of expenditures. As usual, most of the money obtained from loans was going into military expenditures rather than basic reform, and official corruption was reaching new heights. In the southern provinces, where revolutionary sentiments were again growing, Sun and Tang Shaoyi were also seeking Japanese support by playing Pan-Asian themes, as was their custom. Yet from diverse quarters, anti-Japanese sentiment was also on the rise, with nationalist banners being unfurled once more.

Another issue now gathering momentum was that of China's involvement in World War I. Although the Beijing government quickly declared its neutrality and sought unsuccessfully to prevent the war from involving Chinese territory, the question of China's involvement was soon being argued within the government and elsewhere. Some favored a declaration of war against the Central Powers, largely because they anticipated an Allied victory and they wanted China to be on the victorious side so that it would have a voice in postwar settlements. Others wanted neutrality and noninvolvement, either because they anticipated a German victory or because they saw the war as extraneous to China's primary concerns; and the Guomindang stalwarts opposed China's alignment with the Allies because they believed it would strengthen the Beijing regime. The issue of parliamentary approval of any declaration of war produced an additional controversy.

The matter came to a head in 1917, in connection with the growing estrangement and ultimate conflict between the United States and Germany. In many respects, the prestige of the United States attained a new high-point during these years. The younger generation in China, intent upon political as well as economic "modernization," saw in the American republic the apogee of Western achievement. Wilsonian idealism, moreover, meshed well with the values of China's "progressives." The thorny problems of Asian immigration to the United States and recurrent reports of racial prejudice cast some shadows on an otherwise positive image; but generally speaking, China's literate class found America attractive. This view was fortified by the relatively strong stand taken by the United States government in regard to Japan's Twenty-One Demands. Secretary of State William Jennings Bryan had expressed concern about the course of the Sino-Japanese negotiations on March 13, 1915; and on May 11 the State Department notified both China and Japan that the United States could not recognize any agreement between the two nations which impaired the treaty rights of the United States or its citizens, impugned the territorial integrity of China, or violated the Open Door policy.[18] On this note, the concept of nonrecognition was launched in modern American diplomacy.

Thus, in the spring of 1917, when Minister Reinsch of the United States solicited Chinese support for the Allies, the Beijing government, sensing an allied victory, declared war on Germany on March 16, some three weeks before the United States did the same (April 6). But many individuals in China, including Sun Yat-sen, remained wholly unreconciled to these decisions. Sun argued that although he understood and supported the defense of Western civilization being undertaken by the Allies, China's declaration of war was unconstitutional.* Wu Tingfang joined Sun in insisting that the Beijing declaration of war had been taken merely to serve the aims of the ruling clique.** China never participated actively in the war, but the declaration enabled Duan to form a War Participation Army with Japanese funds, thus confirming Guomindang suspicions.

POLITICS IN A DIVIDED CHINA

By mid-1917 the growing North-South cleavage in China was manifest. In May the military governors of Anhui, Henan, Shandong, and Manchuria voiced their determination to cut ties with the center unless parlia-

*On June 8 Sun Yat-sen addressed a letter to President Wilson explaining why he could not support China's declaration of war. "A band of traitors," he wrote, who pretend that "declaring war [is] for the benefit of China's interests but whose real purpose is the restoration of the monarchy, are endeavoring to enlist the sympathies and support of the Entente Allies and to obtain from them loans, nominally by joining them as faithful allies, but actually for attaining their own selfish ends. The people, knowing the real motive for their sinister action, bitterly oppose China's entering the war, with the result that militarism, the very evil that is now being fought in Europe, is employed to subjugate the people and abolish our parliament." Sun concluded that Wilson should cooperate in preventing China from being dragged into the war, thereby enabling the Chinese to destroy "militarism and anarchism." (See *NAMP/RDSRIAC*, 893.00/2631, Shanghai, June 8, 1917, Sun to Wilson.)

**A letter from Wu to Secretary of State Lansing dated August 5, 1918, contains essentially the same charges as those made by Sun. (See *NAMP/RDSRIAC*, August 6, 1918, MacMurray to the Secretary.)

ment were dissolved. The provincial military leaders were already playing a more significant role in policy-making than was the parliament, and Duan's authority as premier was extremely shaky. President Li Yuanhong decided at this point that Duan must go and dismissed him as premier.* Difficulties ensued, however, in finding an acceptable successor. Xu Shichang and Wang Shizhen both declined. Finally, Li Jingxi, the son of the famous Li Hongzhang, was nominated and approved by both houses of parliament; he took office on June 2. But the Duan supporters threatened revolt, and President Li summoned Zhang Xun to the capital to help settle the dispute.

Zhang, one of the most conservative of the northern military leaders and an unreconstructed monarchist, was a poor choice as a mediator. After first persuading Li to dissolve the parliament, at 2 A.M. on July 1 he conducted a coup, demanding Li's resignation as president and proclaiming the restoration of the Xuantong emperor with himself as premier. Once again, in the chaos and despair over the impasse between de jure parliamentarism and de facto military governance, monarchism had been resurrected.**

Like Yuan Shikai, Zhang Xun was a victim of self-delusion and the betrayal of former comrades. He was confident that most of the key military leaders would support him (men like Feng Guozhang had earlier indicated that a monarchist restoration was the only solution), but in the actual event their support evaporated. The restoration effort began to collapse only a few days after its onset, and by July 12 it was all over. Zhang took refuge in the Netherlands legation, and one of monarchy's strongest supporters, Kang Youwei, sought asylum at the home of the American minister.† Duan reentered Beijing on July 13, and the status quo ante was restored.

The abortive monarchist coup of mid-1917, however, served as the catalyst for a further division of North and South. As the monarchist coup was being quashed, Sun Yat-sen and a group of southern republicans, including Zhang Binglin, arrived at Whampoa, near Canton, from Swatow. Sun's

*Minister Reinsch reported that on May 22 President Li invited him to lunch, together with Dr. W. W. Willoughby, and made it plain that he had made up his mind to dismiss General Duan, asking Willoughby's advice on the legalities involved. The order dismissing Duan was issued the next day. (See *NAMP/RDSRIAC*, 893.00/2675, Reinsch to the Secretary, Beijing, June 14, 1917.)

**The maneuvers leading up to the coup were highly complex. Duan left for Tianjin on the night of May 23. On May 26 General Ni Sicheng, a Duan supporter and the military governor of Anhui, declared Duan's dismissal illegal and announced that Anhui would henceforth act independently of the central government. President Li, instead of moving resolutely, sent a conciliatory note to Ni. This consolidated Ni's power with others of similar mind, and a succession of military leaders declared the independence of their provinces—Henan, Shaanxi, Fujian, Shandong, and Fengdian. Meetings were held in Tianjin, and a provisional government was set up there, headed by General Lei Zhenchun. The pro-Japanese element was much in evidence during these developments. At this point, President Li invited General Zhang Xun to come to Beijing as an arbitrator. Zhang arrived in Tianjin on June 7, exuding confidence. On June 11 he persuaded Li to dissolve parliament, although Dr. Wu Tingfang, the acting premier, refused to countersign the papers and then resigned. Wu was replaced by General Jiang Chaozong, the commander of the Beijing gendarmerie, and on June 13 the dissolution was made official. Most members of parliament had already left Beijing. For a complete account of the Zhang Xun restoration effort, first published in 1917, see Zhang Zhonghe, "Fubi xiangzhi."

†Kang had arrived in Beijing on June 29 and had helped Zhang draw up the imperial edicts. He had advised Zhang that China's salvation lay in the restoration of the imperial family, and that this would be supported by the military leaders, who were all monarchists at heart. On July 8, with the effort in ruins, Kang sought refuge in Reinsch's residence. (See *NAMP/RDSRIAC*, 893.00/2703, Beijing, August 9, 1917, Reinsch to the Secretary.)

group held that only if constitutionalism in its original form were upheld—the old parliament recalled and Li reinstated as president, or his successor legally elected—could China again become a united nation. In fact, Sun wanted all military figures removed from government, especially Duan, whom he now deeply distrusted. And if these conditions were not met, the Guomindang leaders said, they were prepared to convene a parliamentary session in Canton and establish a rival government.*

The ideas of the northern military leaders were considerably different. President Li had supposedly indicated his unwillingness to resume office. But in fact, the political coexistence of Li and Duan had become virtually impossible, and Duan was again in power. Duan persuaded Feng Guozhang to come back to the capital from Nanjing and assume the presidential office. Both men, insisting that it would be impossible to reconvene the old parliament, moved toward a policy previously adopted by Yuan—the creation of a National Council charged with drafting a new constitution, which would be accompanied by the election of a new parliament.

Thus, in the fall of 1917 two political movements proceeded along parallel but separate tracks. On August 25 an extraordinary session of the rump parliament was opened in Canton, with some seventy members in attendance. It approved the establishment of a military government with one generalissimo, Sun Yat-sen, and two "commanders in chief," General Lu Rongting and General Tang Jiyao. By September 1, when these men were formally elected, some ninety-one members of the old parliament were present. The plan was that Li would remain the nominal head of government, but that until he could resume his duties the generalissimo would assume the president's functions. Under the generalissimo and the two commanders, various departments equivalent to ministries were established,

*On July 31, in an interview published in the *Canton Press*, Sun said that when parliament was convened once again a foreign loan would be necessary, but until then the government could operate on the funds contributed by patriotic citizens, both in China and abroad. He also said that although a separation of the North and the South would be deplorable, it might, like amputation, be a good thing: "The North and the South, each having the form of government it desires, may both become strong nations. Japan is only as large as the Liang-Guang region (Guangxu-Guangdong) and is now a factor in Asia." The real division, however, was not between the North and the South but between monarchists and republicans. The northern military leaders had shown an utter disregard for the constitution. Feng was a monarchist, and had displayed pusillanimous conduct during the recent crisis, and Duan was the most dangerous enemy existing in the Republic. (Soon, Sun's views on Duan would change.) Ten thousand republican troops, supported by the navy, could take over Beijing, Nanjing, and Hankou (*Canton Press*, July 1, p. 1).

In a private conversation with the American consul, Heintzleman, on the afternoon of August 11, Sun expressed many of the same views. He was in an optimistic mood as usual, indicating that there was "complete unity of purpose" among the members of parliament assembling, and throughout south and central China except for Fujian. He saw no problems with the southern military leaders, since the Guangdong and Yunnan troops were "devoted to republicanism" and the naval units would remain loyal. (No mention was made of General Lu and his Guangxi units, however.)

In concluding, Sun noted that while everyone feared the consequences of a divided China, the republicans had compromised twice in the past, but to no avail, and they were now resolved not to abandon their commitments merely to preserve unity. Thus, if the monarchists would not bend, it would be necessary to settle the issue by force of arms. He added that Japan was working for a monarchy in the North and a republic in the South; and Great Britain was once again on the wrong side, supporting the monarchist movement. (For the full discussion with Heintzleman, see NAMP/RDSRIAC, 893.00/2709, Canton, August 14, 1917, Heintzleman to Reinsch.)

their heads elected by parliament. When constitutionalism was restored, military government was to be dissolved. In some respects, this was the Gemingdang program, greatly modified.

Yet from the very beginning, the key to developments in the South lay less with Sun and his close associates then with the military leaders of the region, particularly General Lu Rongting. Lu, the military inspector general of the Guangxi-Guangdong region, was clearly the most powerful military man in South China.* Some 15,000 of his Guangxi troops were in Canton, but military authority was divided there, because the city also harbored approximately 20,000 regular Guangdong soldiers and about 8,000 Yunnan men under the command of the Guomindang supporter, Li Liejun. General Lu was not interested in a complete break with Beijing, and he had serious doubts about Sun and his military government. Indeed, he refrained from accepting the post offered him by the Canton rump parliament and spoke in rather firm tones to parliament members about the necessity of moderation. General Tang, the military governor of Yunnan, was more sympathetic to Sun's ideas, but he too held off from joining the military government at the outset. Only Admiral Cheng Bikuang, the commander of the First Squadron of the navy, who had led his unit to defect and who was personally in Canton, appeared ready to cooperate fully with the civilian politicians of the newly established government. Even the military governor of Guangdong, General Chen Bingkun, demonstrated the cleavage between the old Guomindang elements and the military; he blocked the appointment of Hu Hanmin as civil governor after his nomination had been approved by the provincial assembly, and nominated his own man instead.

Indeed, General Lu and his associates were conducting separate negotiations with the North—and apparently without having consulted Sun. Their initial proposals did include two of the Guomindang's demands—the reinstatement of President Li and the restoration of the parliament. But it was understood at the time that only their third demand—cancellation of the appointment of General Fu Liangzuo as the new military governor of Hunan—was truly critical. Lu felt threatened by Fu because northern control of Hunan would jeopardize his military and political position. The North probably could have settled with Lu, and possibly even with Tang, had they been willing to grant this demand. Together, these two generals held military control of the four southern provinces. They could not, however, afford to ignore the fact that Sun and his followers had substantial and growing support, especially from the student-intellectual and merchant communities, in such places as Canton.

In any case, the northern government did not accede to Lu's demands. Duan and Feng were divided over how to deal with the South, and they

*Lu Rongting, born in Guangxi in 1856, began his career by leading an outlaw band of several hundred men in a rural area of French Indochina near the border with Guangxi. Later, Lu and his band were absorbed into the government forces in Guangxi. By 1907 he had achieved the rank of lieutenant colonel, and he defeated the revolutionary invasion led by Huang Xing and Sun that year. After the 1911 Revolution, Lu joined with others in declaring Guangxi independent and became the deputy military governor of the province. Lu supported Yuan Shikai in 1913, then broke with him in 1916, after which he established a military government for Guangxi and Guangdong, with headquarters near Canton. Following Yuan's death, Lu was appointed inspector general for the two provinces. He cooperated with Sun in the 1917 movement to protect the constitution, and he was made one of two commanders in chief under Sun in the newly established military government in Canton.

pursued tactics that were guaranteed to fail. Feng favored a settlement by negotiations, whereas Duan opted generally for a military approach. On September 30 an order was issued for the arrest of Sun and his key associates; but as might have been expected, it went unenforced. In early October, Lu—joined by Chen Bingkun, Tan Haoming, and Cheng Bikuang—sent another telegram to Feng. It offered no objections to northern organizational efforts and made several conditional promises: the Canton military government would be disbanded, the "autonomy" of Guangdong and Guangxi would be canceled, and the naval squadron's allegiance to Beijing would be renewed. As conditions, they demanded that the northern government rescind the arrest order, admit southern leaders to the national government "on an equal footing," make no personnel changes in the leadership of naval squadrons or the officials in charge of Guangxi-Guangdong for a minimum of three years (thereby protecting the signatories among others), and finally, that it restore Tan Yankai as military governor of Hunan. Beijing's answer was couched in conciliatory tones, but it did not meet the demands. On the issue of Hunan, it claimed that Fu could not be removed immediately, because he had already assumed his post, but that he would be transferred when an opportunity presented itself.

Meanwhile, the Beijing leaders sought to implement their organizational plans. In mid-November the National Council was inaugurated; only Guangdong and Yunnan were unrepresented, with the Guangxi quota being filled by provincials residing in the capital. A prominent Anfu leader, Wang Yitang, was elected speaker, and deliberations began. But within days a full-fledged crisis occurred: on November 23, Duan's resignation as premier was accepted, amidst speculation that civil war within the North itself would soon break out. Behind Duan's resignation lay a series of mounting military, political, and economic crises.

First and foremost, Duan's military solution for the "southern problem" was not working. The northern army, plagued by high-ranking defections and the hostility of the populace, now faced bitter defeat in Hunan. Meanwhile, the authority of the central government was being defied throughout the South. An order dismissing the military governors of Guangdong and Guangxi in early November, for example, was totally ignored. In the North itself, moreover, political and economic problems abounded. Two key figures in Duan's government—Cao Rulin, the minister of communications, and Xu Shizeng, the vice-minister of war—were accused of attempting to bring the government completely under Japanese control. Beginning in the fall of 1917 and extending into 1918, a new series of loans known as the Nishihara loans were arranged, with Cao Rulin playing a key role. Nishihara had close ties with the Japanese military, and the loans, totaling 145 million yen, went in considerable measure for Chinese military expenditures, after a sizable drainage of funds into private coffers. Economic conditions were also contributing to the growing crisis. Floods had ravaged many sections of the north, and food shortages were widespread.

For all of these reasons, the Jinbudang cabinet members, including Liang Qichao, announced their intention to resign. More important, a number of military governors from northern and central China, supporters of President Feng, were threatening to declare the independence of their provinces unless Duan stepped down. The technique of threatening to act independently was now increasingly in vogue. Duan's supporters, such as Generals Zhang Zuolin (Manchuria), Ni Shichong (Anhui), and Chen Shufan (Shaanxi), demanded that Duan stand firm, using military power if necessary, and hinted that if Duan were ousted they might either sever ties with Beijing or take military action themselves.

In general, the Jinbudang was now aligned with the Zhili group, and the second prominent civilian faction, the Jiaotung Club, stood with the Anhui group. The issues ran the gamut from personal jealousies (and loyalties) to the division between Feng and Duan on how to handle the South. Military-civilian coalitions, however, were now at the heart of the political system, and the military party to each coalition was almost invariably dominant, a testimony to the key role being played by the new generation of officers. Finally, Duan stepped down. With Duan out, Feng appointed Wang Daxi acting premier, but the political situation at the center was in serious disarray as 1917 came to an end.

Like the North, the South was also plagued by disunity. In October, in an effort to give Sun's military government greater strength, an Executive Council of seven was formed, with the civilian and military elements balanced. Generals Lu and Tang together with Sun were to have charge of military affairs; Admiral Cheng, Tang Shaoyi, Cen Chunxuan, and Wu Tingfang completed the council membership. Yet Lu, whose support was crucial to any unity or success, remained essentially aloof. Suddenly, in mid-November, Sun attempted a coup. Finding the military and civil governors absent from Canton, he decided to launch a surprise military attack in the hope of overcoming Lu's Guangxi troops in the city. He tried to enlist the support of Admiral Cheng and General Li Fulin, who was in charge of the constabulary, but both men refused, probably sensing the hopelessness of the operation. The effort ended in a fiasco, which naturally widened the gap between Sun and Lu and also raised new questions about Sun's judgment.

Canton at this point hosted four separate military groups. The first was the Guangxi faction, with the absent General Lu as its head; it was the most powerful group militarily, and its leader's political sympathies were directed more toward President Feng Guozhang than toward Sun Yat-sen. The second was the constabulary, which was associated with the civil governor, Li Yaohan, and was relatively independent. The third, the Yunnan forces led by General Li Liejun, was pro-Sun. The fourth, the naval squadron under Admiral Cheng, was generally regarded as pro-Sun but showed some evidence of independence.

In January 1918, in an effort to reduce Sun's role and unify the South by concentrating authority in men who actually held military power, a plan was unveiled at Canton for a Federation of Constitutionalist Provinces in the southwest. This plan, which was promoted by the military leaders of Guangxi and Yunnan, centered on the six provinces of Guangdong, Guangxi, Yunnan, Guizhou, Hunan, and Sichuan. In terms of key personnel, the effort was to bring the principal military figures—Lu Rongting, Tang Jiyao, and Cheng Bikuang—into a working relationship with the Guomindang leaders Wu Tingfang, Tang Shaoyi, and Cen Chunxuan.*

*The Federation of Constitutionalist Provinces in the Southwest was established on January 20, 1918, at Canton. Its founders appointed Chen Bikuang, Lu Rongting, and Tang Jiyao as military representatives, Wu Tingfang as foreign affairs representative, and Tang Shaoyi as financial representative. One of the objectives of Lu and Tang in founding the Federation was to replace Sun and the Canton military government. This was achieved when Sun was formally replaced by a seven-man directorate in May of 1918. For one account of the politics of the Federation, see Tao Juyin, *Beiyang junfa tongzhi shuqi shihua* 4:88–123.

Sun himself did not participate in the discussions and soon expressed his opposition to the concept, asserting that it ignored the old parliament and his military government.

Meanwhile, negotiations between North and South continued sporadically, but without success. At the end of January, Feng was pushed toward a bellicose stance by a cluster of northern military leaders who feared that he and his Yangtze valley supporters might compromise with southern leaders. This incident illustrated the fact that Feng had very limited authority, and that provincial autonomy under military rule was the norm for both North and South. The phenomenon known as "warlordism" was now coming into full flower.

In some respects, "warlordism" is an unfortunate term, suggesting as it does both a uniform personal style and a thoroughgoing medievalism. In fact, the "warlords" themselves varied considerably in background, personality, political values, and degree of "modernity." Zhang Xun, the northern military leader who had led the abortive monarchical restoration effort of 1917, still wore his long queue, the symbol of allegiance to the Qing, and treated his soldiers as feudal retainers, mixing solicitude with firm discipline. In contrast, Li Chun, the military governor of Nanjing and a protégé of President Feng, sought to run a modern administrative state, and remained convinced that a united China could only be achieved by North-South negotiations and a common commitment to republican principles. The distance between Zhang Zuolin and Chen Jiongming was even greater in most respects. Zhang maintained his Manchurian enclave as a quasi-independent kingdom. He was the quintessential military man. Making no claim to knowledge of modern political theories and surrounding himself with men of similar type, he focused almost exclusively on one objective: to protect and enhance his regional power against all encroachments, domestic and foreign. Thus he was primarily concerned with men, not ideas—and his fluctuating alliances were fashioned accordingly. Chen, on the other hand, was fascinated by ideas, and became deeply attracted to some of the radical political currents that were now flowing from the West.*

In every case, however, the power of these men rested on armies that had to be fed, housed, and equipped. If the military commanders towered over their civil counterparts in authority, it was because they alone had the power to coerce—and this was the supreme power in a setting where political institutions scarcely existed and values of all types were disputed and challenged. Under such circumstances, civilian authority could not hope to prevail, for it could not draw upon any firm sources of legitimacy other than

*Chen Jiongming was born in Haifeng, Guangdong, in 1878, and was graduated from the College of Law and Government in Canton in 1908. In 1909 he joined the Tongmeng Hui and helped in planning the abortive revolt of April 27, 1911, after which he engaged in anti-Manchu activities in Hong Kong. When the 1911 Revolution began, he returned to Haifeng, where he organized a revolutionary army. In November 1911 he was chosen deputy governor of Guangdong, and served under Hu Hanmin; in 1913, after serving as the military commissioner of Guangdong, he was appointed governor of the province by Yuan Shikai. But when Yuan moved against the Guomindang, beginning in July 1913, Chen was removed from office. Along with other Guomindang members, he fled overseas and remained in Malaya until the outbreak of rebellion against Yuan in 1916, when he returned to China and organized a military force. After Yuan's death he ceased military operations and went to Beijing; in 1917 he joined Sun's movement to protect the constitution and returned with Sun to Canton to establish the military government. Through Sun's efforts Chen was given command of a force of twenty battalions, the foundation of his subsequent power.

61. *Zhang Xun*

those relating to military power. The concept of self-imposed limitations on power, and the acceptance of boundaries for the political contest beyond which contestants would not go, simply did not exist. Thus, Chinese politics during this era was both complex and simple. It was complex because, in this era of supremely personalized rule, governance was constantly in flux, subject to shifting coalitions, with power balances continually being altered and power-holders often changing abruptly. It was simple because the basic issues, whether immediate or fundamental, remained essentially constant.

By 1918 the authority of the central government appeared to carry no further than the walls of Beijing. The insubordination of provincial military commanders, moreover, was imitated by lesser officers. Thus, General Wu Peifu, a key lieutenant of Cao Kun's, refused to move forward on the Hunan front, and he was joined in this refusal by another young northern general, Feng Yuxiang, who found numerous excuses for avoiding further attacks on the South.* These men associated themselves with the military governors of the three Yangtze valley provinces—Jiangsu, Jiangxi, and Hubei—in favoring mediation with the South. In general terms, this put them in alignment with President Feng. Feng, however, was not able to carry the key northern generals with him, and naturally, the very weakness of the northern government made successful negotiations difficult.

After mid-February a newly appointed acting premier, the Beiyang veteran Wang Shizhen, repeatedly sought to step down, fully aware of his impotence. Finally, under strong pressure, especially from Zhang Zuolin, Feng could find no alternative except to restore Duan Qirui to power.[19] Duan reassumed the premiership on March 23, 1918, and with him returned the old issues: whether a military solution to the problem of southern secession was possible, and how close China's ties to Japan should be. Duan resumed his policies of toughness against the southern dissidents, employing Zhang Zuolin's troops in Hunan. Initially, the military policy showed signs of success, as southern forces were forced to retreat. Meanwhile, the two key ministries in the new Duan cabinet from the standpoint of the economy—the Ministries of Finance and Communications—came under the control of Cao Rulin, an outspoken advocate of a pro-Japanese policy.

At the same time, however, the northern effort to rebuild political institutions in conformity with "modern principles" continued. On February 17

*For an excellent study of Feng Yuxiang in English, see James E. Sheridan, *Chinese Warlord: The Career of Feng Yu-hsiang*. Feng was born in Zhili in 1882. His family was from Anhui, and his father served as a member of the Anhui Army, which Feng entered as a full-fledged soldier in 1896 at age fifteen. In 1902 he joined a unit of Yuan Shikai's New Army, and by 1907 he had risen to the rank of company commander. At the time of the 1911 Revolution Feng was serving in Manchuria. He was forced to resign in late 1911, for his part in an abortive revolt against the Beijing government, but he was soon reinstated, chiefly through the efforts of his friend and relative Lu Jianzhang. In 1912 Yuan had ordered Lu to recruit, organize, and train five battalions. Lu appointed Feng commander of the vanguard battalion, a force of 500 men, and this became the core of Feng's personal army. In 1914, after two years of training, Feng's men had their first taste of battle pursuing the White Wolf. By the fall of 1914, the year in which Feng became a Christian, his forces totaled some 6,000 men, organized as the 16th Mixed Brigade and stationed in southern Shaanxi. Feng was to command this brigade for the next seven years. In 1915 Feng's forces were transferred to Sichuan, where he first opposed and later joined the antimonarchical movement. After Yuan's death in 1916 Feng and his forces were stationed at Langfang, a town halfway between Beijing and Tianjin. He lost command of the 16th Mixed Brigade in the spring of 1917, then regained control in the summer after participating in the defeat of the Zhang Xun forces. Between 1918 and 1920 he stayed at Changde, Hunan, where he had his first solid experience in civil administration, and where he built the well-disciplined army that was to make him a leading figure in Chinese politics in the years ahead.

From an early point, Feng revealed himself to be a forceful, independent-minded, and colorful personality. Commanding the 16th Mixed Brigade, he had halted at Wuxi in early 1918 instead of proceeding to Hubei as ordered. When his advance was demanded, he telegraphed to Beijing saying that his ships were all stuck in the mud (although other boats were proceeding up river without difficulty). This was followed by a wire asking for leave because of "a sudden brain attack due to an enlargement." Both messages contained philosophical discussions of politics in general and events in China in particular. (See *North China Herald*, "Feng Yu-hsiang, the Funny," March 2, 1918, p. 491.)

the National Council, which had first been convened in November 1917, promulgated both a parliamentary charter and new election laws. Under the new legislation, the size of the two houses was somewhat reduced, and the local electorates rather than the provincial assemblies were authorized to elect senators except for certain special categories.* The actual elections, conducted in two stages, ended in mid-June, amidst charges of widespread corruption. Extensive vote-purchasing and pressures applied by local military leaders clouded the legitimacy of the new parliament. In contrast to the earlier elections, local administrators, and particularly the military governors, were heavily involved in efforts to shape the results. The fact that these governors now had few obligations to the center, expected to have indefinite tenure in office, and were often in conflict with other local officials, the resident gentry, or commercial interests, enhanced the temptation for them to intervene.[20]

The 1918 parliament was composed largely of new faces because few old republicans were permitted to run; all of those who had participated in the rump Canton parliament were specifically excluded. Duan and his supporters—the majority of the northern military governors—therefore reaped the gains. Of the seventeen provinces participating, thirteen were headed by military governors aligned with Duan, and eleven of these sent parliamentary delegations that were virtually unanimous in their support for the Duan government, joining en bloc its political arm, the Anfu Club, which had been organized in March.[21] Altogether, Anfu Club members constituted 330 of the 470 newly elected legislators. The Constitution Research Society, the successor to the Jinbudang, gained a disappointing 20 seats, and the old Communications faction, now known as the Qiaoyuan group, won approximately three times that number. The remaining members were classified as independents.[22]

Since the Communications faction was allied with the Anfu Club, Duan faced very limited organizational opposition from within the new parliament. His close friend Wang Yitang was elected speaker by an overwhelming vote when the lower house held its first regular session on August 20. The real opposition to Duan now lay outside parliament. In addition to the persistent southern rebellion, there were the three military governors of the Yangtze region, whose allegiance remained with Feng, and the old Jinbudang leaders, most of whom were similarly disposed. Duan continued to believe that China could be unified only by force of arms. He acknowledged that foreign loans were "regrettable," but argued that the resort to military measures made them necessary. Once unified, he insisted, China could reform its entire financial system.**

*A well-researched study of the legislation relating to the new parliament and elections, as well as the election results, is contained in Nathan, *Peking Politics*, pp. 92–105. Actually, the central government had somewhat greater influence in the new Senate. In the old Senate there had been 10 elected representatives from each of the 22 provinces, and 54 centrally controlled representatives. In the new Senate the directly elected provincial representatives were reduced to 5 for each province, and 54 members were centrally controlled (27 from Mongolia, 10 from Tibet, 3 from Qinghai, 8 from the Ministry of Education, and 6 representing the overseas Chinese). The Senate size had been reduced from 274 to 168 members, the House from 596 to 378. (In Chinese, see Luo Zhiyuan, *Zhongguo xianfa shi*, pp. 161–164.)

**Duan expressed these views in a private conversation with Minister Paul Reinsch on June 27, 1918. When Reinsch asked him whether it was wise to rely heavily on one country

Both of China's "strong men" faced a standoff by the summer of 1918. Feng could not be elected president under the new system, given the power of the Anfu faction, and Duan was rendered vulnerable by the combination of forces outside parliament which were antagonistic to him. At this point, Xu Shichang, a veteran Qing scholar-bureaucrat, was advanced as a compromise presidential candidate, primarily by Duan. Gentle in disposition and without a party or an army of his own, Xu was not a threat, and to induce Feng's support, Duan promised that if Xu were supported, he would resign as premier. Although some military men called for a postponement, the election was held as scheduled on September 4, and Xu received 425 of the 436 parliamentary votes cast. The election of a vice-president proved more difficult. At the last moment the Communications faction led by Liang Shiyi refused to support Cao Kun, the candidate accepted by the Anfu Club, and a parliamentary quorum could not be obtained on three successive occasions in October. Finally, the effort was abandoned, and Liang himself left the north for Hong Kong, where he sought to serve as a mediator in North-South relations.[23]

While these developments were unfolding in Beijing, southern politics were also in flux. On February 26, 1918, Admiral Cheng was gunned down by unknown assailants on a Canton street. Despite this blow, southern fortunes were on the rise in purely military terms. By the spring, southern armies, which already controlled the southern and southwestern provinces and most of Sichuan, were threatening Hubei and had parts of Anhui, Shaanxi, and Hunan under their influence.

The financial situation in the South, as in the North, was far from satisfactory. Although the revenues from the salt gabelle and customs had never been higher (in this respect, the war was a bonanza for China), they were collected and allocated by foreign authorities. Chinese tax collection remained generally disorganized, and expenditures, particularly in the military realm, continued to mount. To meet the need, both Beijing and Canton ardently solicited foreign assistance. Japan showed a strong interest, as we have noted, and its aid went to Beijing. The efforts of Sun and others to tap the overseas Chinese resulted in reasonably good returns, serving to provide about 50 percent of their government's total revenues.* In March the Canton government suddenly took control of the administration of the salt

---

(Japan), Duan responded that only one country stood ready to help at the time of China's greatest need; China could not wait for the formation of another consortium of powers, however desirable that might be. Duan also acknowledged the misconduct of certain northern troops, but said that one had to use whatever soldiers were available; when China was united, he said, he planned to improve military personnel and to reduce the power of military leaders. (See *NAMP/RDSRIAC* 893.00/2866, Beijing, June 27, 1918, Reinsch to the Secretary.)

*The overseas Chinese remained an important source of financial support for the Canton military government. For example, during the month of January 1918, fifteen of the twenty revenue entries recorded by the military government showed funds raised from overseas Chinese, totaling 45,932 yuan out of a total revenue of 91,432 yuan, or about half of the recorded revenue for the month. Funds came from overseas Chinese living in the United States, Canada, Cuba, Burma, Hong Kong, Malaya, the Philippines, and South Africa. Expenditures for January 1918 totaled only 49,806 yuan, with the largest allocations going to support Sun's office (10,038 yuan), the military (18,627 yuan), and Shanghai Guomindang activities (10,021 yuan). These and other figures are provided in a report by Liao Zhongkai, finance minister of the Canton military government, detailing the revenue and expenditures of the government from September 1917 through June 1918. (See *Geming wenxian* 42–43:301–323.)

revenues in Guangdong and Guangxi, despite foreign protests. These and other fund-raising activities scarcely sufficed, however, and finances continued to be a most serious problem.

On the political front, unity among the diverse southern factions remained elusive. The Guomindang leaders who had earlier advanced the federation concept now sought to bring Sun into the fold. At first, in a borrowing from the Japanese institution of the *genrō*, the selection of three "senior statesmen" was proposed; Sun, Wu Tingfang, and Cen Chunxian were to serve in this capacity. Relations between the principals remained precarious, but in mid-May a new political structure for the South appeared to be taking shape. A "constitutional government" was to be headed by an Administrative Council consisting of seven administrative directors elected by the Canton parliament, with one of the directors to serve as chairman. The Council would run affairs, but each "constitutional province" and army recognized by the government could send one deputy to attend Council meetings. The directors were elected on May 20 by the old rump parliament with 122 members present. Earlier, Sun had agreed to end "military government" in favor of the new system, and it was provided that when the parliament and the president could exercise their functions normally, this temporary structure would be set aside.* Yet Sun was clearly unhappy, and together with several close friends, including Tang Shaoyi and Hu Hanmin, he left Canton for Shanghai by way of Taiwan. Thus, when the new Administrative Council held its opening meeting on August 19, Generals Lu and Tang were present, but Sun was absent, having sent a polite letter pleading illness. The southern divisions had not been bridged.

Cen Chunxian assumed the chairmanship of the new southern government. It had been hoped in some quarters that with Duan and Feng having removed themselves from the key political posts, the southern leaders would accept Xu Shichang, and the process of reunification could get under way. Southern spokesmen, however, soon made it clear that although they did not object to Xu personally, his election by an "illegal parliament" precluded their support. Yet by August active fighting in the North-South civil war had virtually ended, and despite its unwillingness to recognize Xu, the Canton government showed an increasing interest in negotiations. As the winter of 1918 approached, a powerful new incentive appeared. With World War I finally coming to a close, it became clear that only a unified China could hope to gain anything at the Paris peace conference. Both southern and northern leaders recognized this fact. Moreover, the Beijing government was urged by ministers of the major powers to open discussions with the South. But time had served to deepen rather than to remove the divisions within the nation, and peaceful reunification appeared a truly formidable task.

* Sun continued to have deep reservations about the projected new structure; at one point he had even informed others that "we should never agree to the reorganization." In the end, however, he conceded, resigning from the position of generalissimo in the military government to make way for the new government. In his letter of resignation to the Canton parliament, dated May 4, 1918, he stated that he was putting national survival above personal considerations and that he was bowing to the forces of the people and the demands of the provinces for the governmental restructuring. (For Sun's letter of resignation and other correspondence pertaining to the reorganization, see *Guofu quanji* 4:337–359.)

HUNAN—A PROVINCIAL VIGNETTE

Although no single province was wholly "typical" in its experience of the major problems of this era, Hunan provides an example of some of the difficulties in their more acute form. As we have noted, Hunan figured prominently in the North-South controversy. It was strategically located, and it had a relatively large and articulate elite, which despite continuous divisions had figured prominently in various reform movements.

A most interesting investigation of land tenure conditions in Hunan was undertaken in 1915. It was carried out by an American consular official approximately a dozen years before Mao's noted study of Hunan agrarian conditions, and was submitted to Minister Reinsch in early 1916.[24] The author found that absentee landlordism was the general rule in the province. As much as 75 percent of all cultivated land was leased to small farmers, who were sometimes poorer members of the owner's clan. It is asserted, wrote the author, that "as soon as a family has enough to eat, it would rather rent its land to another than farm it itself"—an interesting statement, which reflects the fact that large landlords were the exception rather than the rule. Such wealthy gentry as did exist obtained their income in the form of tenant fees normally paid in unhulled rice. The rents were high—from 50 to 60 percent of the harvested crop—and were due one to two months after the harvest had been completed. Yet the lessees had important rights. Leases were for an indefinite period and gave the lessee a certain prescriptive right to the land he occupied. Indeed, a son would usually inherit the leasehold, and the land would remain in the hands of the lessee's family for several generations. It was most difficult to remove such families, wrote the author, and if the land were sold, it was often necessary to pay them a sum of money as compensation before they could be forced to leave. Irrigation in Hunan was widespread, and lease agreements covering rice land provided detailed descriptions of the water rights of the lessee.

The report concluded that the Hunanese rural population lived in fairly comfortable conditions. Most economic intercourse was carried on through barter, there being very little coin in circulation. Transportation throughout much of the region was primarily by water, and nearly all the rivers and small waterways connecting them were navigable by small boats. The inner countryside was self-sufficient and greatly isolated from the economic and political currents that flowed through the major urban centers.

With certain variations, this account of rural Hunan would apply to major parts of other central and southern provinces. And when we discuss political trends, the shifting balance of military power, and the fiscal woes of the Chinese government, we must never forget that for vast numbers of Chinese these things were like shadows on a distant wall; only occasionally were their lives directly affected by them. Thus, when we speak of political or economic chaos, we risk conveying a false image. It is worth noting that long after the People's Republic of China had been created, the people—and ultimately the nation—could survive an extended period of chaos known as the Cultural Revolution because vast sections of rural China retained some degree of "normalcy," and were affected only peripherally or sporadically by the momentous political events taking place.

Yet in the Hunan of 1915–1918, as at later times, "self-containment" and "normalcy" were available to only a part of the rural districts, and hardly at all to the towns and cities. Changsha, the provincial capital, was often described as a hotbed of political activity, with students generally playing a leading role. When a boycott of Japanese goods was initiated in response to the Twenty-One Demands in early 1915, Changsha's student and merchant classes gave it considerable support. Guomindang strength in Changsha was always substantial, partly because many veterans of the movement, like Huang Xing, were Hunanese. A commitment to nationalism, however, had to coexist with a deeply entrenched provincialism ("Hunan for the Hunanese") and a suspicion of all outsiders, both Chinese and foreign. This combination can be observed both in events and in key political personalities (including, later on, Mao Zedong).

After the collapse of Yuan's monarchist movement (which evoked little interest or enthuasism in Hunan), sizable parts of the province were seized by revolutionaries, through locally recruited troops that were sympathetic to or connected with the old Guomindang. By mid-1916 at least four conflicting forces struggled for control: the local military governor, the Beijing-affiliated northern troops, the Guomindang-related revolutionary soldiery, and the semiprivate army of Guo Baosheng, a prominent representative of the gentry class. The gentry, it should be emphasized, continued to play a major role in the economic and political life of this province, a fact of significance for the future.

Hunan, together with Sichuan, had declared its independence in May 1916, and in the months that followed, the crisis had grown steadily more intense, with Guomindang and northern military forces the primary contestants for power. On July 20 Tan Yankai, a Guomindang leader, arrived in Changsha, and some order was restored by autumn. This condition was fleeting, however, because Beijing's authority was soon reasserted by a new military governor, General Fu Liangzuo, who had close connections with Duan Qirui. Taking advantage of the fact that Fu was bitterly opposed by the local people and also by General Lu Rongting, who regarded him as a threat to his own position, the southern military government authorized the "liberation" of Hunan and gradually moved northward. Aided by key defections from the northern ranks and widespread support from the Hunanese people, the first contingents of southern armies entered Changsha on November 20, 1917, amid great celebration.

Earlier that year, on May 9, the students of Changsha Higher Normal School had demonstrated their nationalist sentiments by participating actively in China's Day of National Humiliation, commemorating the day on which the Yuan government had "capitulated" to Japanese demands in 1915. Big-character posters were plastered on the walls of the city, describing the failings of China's political leaders and the menace of Japanese imperialism.* Mao was a student at the school during this period and probably took part in these events.

Although southern armies had occupied Hunan's capital by late 1917,

*N. T. Johnson, the American consul in Changsha, witnessed events on May 9 and sent a translation of the proclamation, presumably written by students, that was posted on the wall of the Changsha Normal School. Entitled "The Latest Outline of Disgraces Which Have Been Suffered by the Country," it listed the imperialist attacks on China, starting with the Allied occupation of Beijing after the Boxer defeat. Asserting that "protection by sea has been destroyed and our debts to foreign countries have increased, so that it is impossible to call us a nation," the proclamation then called the transfer of German rights in Shandong to Japan "the worst disgrace that we have suffered." (See NAMP/RDSRIAC, 893.00/2676, Changsha, May 29, 1917, Johnson to Reinsch.) Later, the events of May 9 were celebrated on May 7, the date the Japanese ultimatum was presented.

northern forces still held the upper portion of the province. Moreover, at the beginning of 1918, the Beijing government, having determined upon a policy of unification by force, appointed Cao Kun, Zhang Huaizhi, and Zhang Jingyao commanders of an expeditionary force with orders to proceed south. Cao was also made Pacification Commissioner of Hunan and Hebei, and his forces were assigned to the Hunan front.

Cao's Third Division, under the command of his follower General Wu Peifu, crushed the southern forces and drove them out of Youzhou and Changsha in a disorderly retreat. However, a rift soon developed between Duan Qirui and Cao over issues of alliance and appointments. Furthermore, Wu was deeply antagonized by Duan's choice of Zhang Jingyao instead of himself as military governor of Hunan. Zhang, who had played no role in the campaign, proceeded to make himself thoroughly obnoxious to the Hunanese by his viciousness and corruption, which was especially felt in the northern sector where he was ensconced. Wu, meanwhile, acquired a reputation for personal honesty, enforced discipline among his troops, and aligned himself with various "progressive" elements in the province.

As early as April 1918, Cao and Wu decided that under the circumstances no further military operations in Hunan should be pursued and requested that the Third Division be allowed to withdraw. The request was denied, but Cao returned on his own to Zhili. Duan then made Wu commander in chief of the northern expeditionary forces, hoping that this appointment would separate him from Cao. Wu, however, remained loyal, and in August, together with other military commanders, he joined Cao in issuing a circular telegram urging an immediate cease-fire in the civil war and negotiations leading to reunification. In September the key military men of both north and south in Hunan agreed on a joint statement that was similar in content. Through these and other actions, Wu made himself a hero to many Hunanese, including a sizable portion of the student-intellectual community.[25]

Nevertheless, the appeals went unheeded in Beijing, and Wu was to remain in Hunan until mid-1920. With the Anfu clique in power in the capital, all money made available to Hunan went to Zhang Jingyao, who was an Anfu man. During his last ten months in the province, Wu received no funds from Beijing to pay his troops. Disgusted with Zhang's actions and the attitude of the Beijing authorities, Wu showed increasing sympathy with the growing Hunanese movement for self-government. Finally, he obtained permission from his chief, Cao Kun, to withdraw his troops. It also appears that he reached a private agreement with Tan Yankai, a former governor and now a leader of the southern forces, that if he withdrew he would be given enough money to cover the back pay owed to his troops. Wu finally began his withdrawal in late May of 1920, and Tan soon attacked Zhang's forces from the south. By the end of June, Zhang's troops had fled from Hunan, and Zhang himself had taken refuge in the Hankou foreign concession.*

*In a long report on the downfall of the Anfu faction in Beijing provided by the American legation, there is an excellent account of military developments in Hunan between early 1918 and mid-1920. When Wu began his withdrawal on May 25, 1920, he stationed his troops at strategic points along the Beijing–Hankou rail line, thereby making it impossible for Zhang to obtain assistance from the north. Thus, when Tan attacked immediately after Wu's departure, Zhang's forces—said to be greatly inflated in numbers to pad the payroll—could expect no reinforcements. In traditional fashion, the Beijing authorities sternly ordered Zhang to defend the province, and as punishment for the initial reverses, stripped him of the

Despite the fact that the northern troops under Wu's personal command were generally well disciplined, protracted warfare in Hunan during these years took a heavy toll. Stories of pillage, rape, and extortion in many towns and rural areas near the main arteries were commonplace. Small groups of disbanded soldiers, or even officially enrolled military men carrying no equipment or provisions with them except guns and ammunition, lived wholly off the countryside, demanding housing and food. Uniformed soldiers swaggered through the streets, intimidating all who came in their path. Retreating armies, whether from the North or the South, looted as they ran.

Naturally, economic conditions were seriously affected by continuous low-level warfare, and many towns lay in ashes. From all accounts—missionary, consular, and Chinese—the years between 1918 and 1920 were characterized by widespread misery and disillusionment. Even after some degree of governmental authority was reestablished by the northern occupation, getting rid of the ex-soldier "bandits" was not easy. When troops were sent after them by provincial authorities, the bandits melted into the populace for a while as farmers and workers, then resumed their raids after the coast was clear. As one source put it, either the rural residents are their friends, or they are terrorized into helping them conceal their identity.[26] This remark was pregnant with implications for the future, when bands of Communist insurgents operated under similar circumstances.

PRELUDE TO THE MAY FOURTH MOVEMENT

The miseries afflicting Hunan were in varying degree the miseries that afflicted China as a whole in the last months of World War I. At the national level, however, issues of foreign policy—and foreign intrusion—brought additional complications. By the end of 1918 China's relations with the major powers were again in a confused and potentially dangerous condition.

On balance, the United States was regarded with the greatest hope, at least by the younger generation. This was partly because it was seen as a vigorous and dynamic nation, symbolizing the values of modernization to which most of the young intellectuals subscribed. Wilsonian idealism was an added attraction, since it appeared to support Chinese nationalism.[27] Even those Chinese who did not admire the United States often regarded it as the least threatening of the major powers.

On the other hand, Chinese leaders, whether conservative or revolutionary, had repeatedly come to the conclusion that American policies toward China lacked consistency, and beyond this, betrayed an interest so small as to preclude meaningful commitments. American policy stopped with moral suasion—futile attempts to preserve Chinese sovereignty by getting nations to agree in principle, on paper. American economic and military assistance, whether governmental or private, had been minimal, and it had been made clear much earlier that the United States was not prepared to run serious risks or jeopardize its broader international interests on behalf of a weak and divided China.

The Lansing-Ishii agreement symbolized American policy of the period. On November 2, 1917, Secretary of State Robert Lansing and Ambassador

---

titles military governor and acting civil governor while authorizing him to remain in command of his troops. By the end of June, however, Zhang had fled. (See NAMP/ RDSRIAC, 893.00/3787, Ruddock to the Secretary, Beijing, Jan. 26, 1921.)

Ishii Kikujiro exchanged notes in which the United States recognized that Japan had "special interests" in China, especially in those areas (Manchuria) that were contiguous to its possessions, but both parties pledged themselves to preserve the independence and territorial integrity of China and to maintain the Open Door policy. As it had done when it introduced the policy of nonrecognition in response to the Twenty-One Demands, Washington was seeking to bind Japan to a code of good conduct toward China by moral suasion.

But would the Japanese government be bound? By the close of World War I, Japan had established a position of greater influence in China than any other power. In addition to the sizable Japanese loans advanced to a hard-pressed Chinese government in 1917–1918, an additional Sino-Japanese tie had developed. When the new Russian Soviet government and Germany concluded a separate peace after the Bolshevik Revolution, the Japanese government initiated negotiations with China directed toward "cooperative military action" in northern Manchuria and Siberia, to contain what were described as Bolshevik and German threats.

An exchange of notes took place early in March, and secret negotiations followed. Shortly afterward, incidentally, Sun Yat-sen again approached American authorities in the hope of securing United States recognition and support, and in the course of his conversation he painted an extremely dark picture of Japanese designs. The treaty that Japan was pressing on China, Sun reported, would make his nation a second Korea.*

The agreements signed in mid-May by Beijing authorities did not go that far, but they did give the Japanese extensive military rights. To combat "the enemy menace," the Japanese were given permission to bring troops into China and to use Chinese transport and supplies. It was stipulated that each country could lend military experts to the other (though the direction of the flow was never in doubt). The intelligence agencies of the two countries were to exchange information, and common secret passwords would be used. Although the agreements provided that Japanese troops would be withdrawn when the threat had ceased, their terms paralleled some of the demands made in the fifth group of the Twenty-One Demands, at least as they pertained to the Manchurian region.**

*On April 17, 1918, Sun signed a document requesting the major powers to recognize the southern government. On the previous day, one of Sun's representatives had called on the American consul, Heintzleman, in Canton. He informed him that Sun had once sought Japanese assistance in the development of China, but had felt it necessary to change his position after learning that Prime Minister Katsura had concluded a secret treaty with Germany. According to Sun's agent, the Japanese government was returning to a Katsura policy, believing that an alliance with Germany would be more advantageous than the present Anglo-Japanese alliance. Moreover, the Japanese government was pressing China to negotiate a treaty that would make China virtually a second Korea. (Sun had sent a copy of the proposed treaty to Heintzleman). If the United States did not recognize and support his military government, Sun's representative continued, it would be useless for Dr. Sun to continue the struggle. But with American assistance he could frustrate Japanese plans, save China further humiliation, and also help the United States—since without China, Japan would not dare contemplate war with America. Heintzleman took a dim view of Sun's proposal, noting that despite Sun's categorical denials, there was strong evidence that Sun had earlier accepted money from German sources. (*NAMP/RDSRIAC*, 893.00/ 2842, Canton, April 30, 1918, Heintzleman to Reinsch.)

** After outlining the provisions contained within the two agreements, Reinsch stated that the Chinese government believed that the agreements dealt adequately with the situation

Japan's rapidly increasing involvement on the Asian continent, and more particularly in China, was the product of many factors: past advances which had led to the possession of an empire that had to be protected; European preoccupation with conflict at home; the relatively low priority given to Asia by the United States; and Japan's own rapid internal growth. Combining militant threats and peaceful penetration, Japan advanced on all fronts—cultural, economic, political, and strategic. It was inevitable that these advances should come into conflict with Chinese nationalism, and yet one must not minimize the complexity of the situation. Sino-Japanese relations during this period, as in the decades ahead, were marked by many currents. No outside nation had managed as skillfully as Japan to cultivate opposing forces on the Chinese political stage. As we have seen, Japan was able to maintain contact, simultaneously, with military leaders, diehard monarchists, and southern revolutionaries; conversely, individuals from every Chinese group solicited Japanese assistance.

Such a situation was possible in the first place because many groups in Japan, both inside and outside government, had the will as well as the means to involve themselves and their nation in Chinese affairs. Unlike their counterparts in the United States, they considered developments in China vital to Japanese national interests. But in addition, the Japanese appeal could be broadly distributed because there were many Japans—the Japan of the military, of the foreign office, of the civilian Pan-Asianists and revolutionaries, of the bankers and industrialists. Within these groups, moreover, there were often significant subdivisions. In its major tradition Japan was a homogeneous, centralized, bureaucratic state, but in its minor tradition it was a society composed of competitive, relatively closed units. These groups frequently acted in concert, but they could also take independent and contradictory initiatives, as the 1930s were to demonstrate so dramatically.

Thus, there was never a uniform Japanese attitude or set of policies pertaining to China. At one end of the spectrum were the "hard-liners" who supported what came to be known as a "forward policy," insisting that Chinese political instability represented a serious threat to Japan's national interests, and that only Japan had the capacity to influence internal events in China by applying military power when other means failed. At the other end were those who argued that military intervention was certain to be counterproductive; they championed a "diplomatic policy" of economic, cultural, and political interaction aimed at creating bonds of friendship and mutual trust. Divisions within Japan over China policy did not await the 1920s and 1930s.

Japanese governments, to be sure, had their "favorite" and "nonfavorite" Chinese. Yuan Shikai, for example, was regarded by most Japanese officials with suspicion or dislike, and when his monarchical movement began to roll forward, Japanese spokesmen expressed their reservations in unmistak-

---

which had arisen on the Siberian front and did not contain anything prejudicial to Chinese sovereignty. But he added that criticism had centered on the complete secrecy with which negotiations had been conducted, the exclusion of other Allies from participation, and the possibility that under these agreements Japan would eventually make far-reaching claims involving intervention in China's internal affairs and control of its resources. (For details, see *NAMP/RDSRIAC*, 893.00/ 2868, Beijing, June 29, 1918, Reinsch to the Secretary.)

able terms. Yet many observers were firmly convinced that the Japanese government privately favored monarchy in the North (under a more suitable figure than Yuan) and republicanism in the South—a two-Chinas policy that would render both Chinas amenable to Japanese influence and control. In truth, many Japanese (and not a few other foreigners) did favor such a solution, arguing that it was the only realistic approach to a China that was in fact divided, both politically and culturally.

While most well-informed Chinese recognized Japan and the United States as the rising Pacific powers, the continuing presence of the major European states in Asia had also to be taken into account. Resentment against Great Britain was strong, especially within republican circles. Although the British and other major powers had warned against Yuan's monarchical plans, the Anglo-Japanese alliance was widely regarded as strengthening Japan's hand in the Pacific-Asian region, enabling Tokyo to expand with at least implicit British approval. Moreover, while London wanted to see China's sovereignty upheld (and actually played a role in restraining Japan as the Twenty-One Demands were being negotiated), the British had such a large stake in the Yangtze valley that they were determined to maintain their sphere of influence if other powers insisted on maintaining theirs.

Chinese concerns about European and Japanese imperialism were scarcely new; they had fed the fires of the nationalist movement in its many forms for several decades. But now there was a new development on the international horizon: the collapse of czarist Russia and the Bolshevik assumption of power. After the initial Russian revolution, Beijing—following Washington's lead—recognized the new Kerensky government in early April of 1917. With the events of October, however, the picture changed. Before the year had ended, reports reached Beijing that "anarchists" and "Bolsheviks" were active in Harbin and the Russian-controlled zone encasing the Chinese Eastern Railway, some of them having come from America and other points of earlier exile.

Under the weight of these developments and the critical importance of Chinese unity at the coming international peace conference, President Xu of the Beijing government ordered an armistice in the North-South fighting on November 17, 1918—less than a week after the armistice in Europe—and indicated a willingness on the part of the North to participate in peace talks.[28] On December 29 a northern delegation left for Nanjing, although the South was insisting that the negotiations be conducted in Shanghai. From then on, developments moved at a glacial pace. Discussions were finally opened on February 20, 1919, in the Shanghai German Club, but they were suspended on March 1 because of a dispute over northern military operations in Shaanxi. When they were resumed on April 10 the Shaanxi issue was still in dispute, but a wide range of questions about Sino-Japanese relations now came to the fore. Southern delegates demanded that the Beijing government release certain secret documents pertaining to past Sino-Japanese agreements, especially the military agreements of 1918 about anti-Bolshevik operations in Manchuria and Siberia. The perennial problem of military reorganization was also raised during the negotiations.

In this connection, the Beijing government advanced a proposal after making public some basic data. On April 11 it announced that China—North and South—had a total of 1,290,657 troops, costing $208,971,080 annually, which meant that 80 percent of China's total revenue was being used for military purposes.[29] A plan was proposed whereby the troops would be cut back to fifty divisions, the number existing in 1916; thirty of them would be placed in various provinces to help the police maintain order, ten would be sent to the border provinces (including Xinjiang, Mongolia, and Tibet), and the remaining ten would be placed in metropolitan areas and fortified sites. Disbandment was to be accomplished over twelve to eighteen months, and employment for ex-soldiers was pledged in the form of agricultural work, railroad building, canal construction, and police work. It was a beautiful plan—with no chance of success.*

As North-South negotiations languished, the news from Paris grew increasingly grim. The Versailles Peace Conference had opened on January 18, amid high hopes on the part of some Chinese that German rights and holdings in the Shandong peninsula would revert to China. But shortly after the Paris meetings opened, it became known that in February 1917, Great Britain, France, and Italy (and the czarist government of Russia) had signed secret agreements pledging support for Japan's claim on German concessions in Shandong. More damaging was a later revelation that in the fall of 1918 the Chinese government had agreed to a seven-point Japanese memorandum on Shandong; this memorandum, the quid pro quo for a secret loan for railroad construction, basically conceded to Japan the same privileges held previously by the Germans. Although the Chinese delegation in Paris presented two memoranda calling for abrogation of the May 1915 Sino-Japanese agreements and requesting a general reduction of foreign influence, these proposals were rejected, and against the background of its government's past concessions, China's case with regard to Shandong now appeared weak.**

Nevertheless, heavy pressure was brought to bear on the delegation from

* In an anonymous article entitled "China's Only Hope," appearing in the *Peking Leader*, May 10, 1919, it was asserted that although the military leaders were claiming some 1,400,000 men, there could not be more than 500,000 men actually under arms in the northern and southern forces, and probably not more than 200,000 trained troops. Thus, if they received money to disband the number of troops they claimed, they would in fact be able to share several hundred million dollars among themselves. The American military attaché estimated that at the end of February 1919 the southern troops affiliated with Sun numbered 130,000; those with Tang Jiyao, 70,000; Lu Rongting, 42,000; Cen Chunxian, 29,000; and uncertain, 33,000, for a total of 304,000. With respect to the northern troops, he reported that there were 212,000 affiliated with Duan Qirui; 20,000 with Feng Guozheng; 114,000 with "anti-Duan forces"; and 190,000 with "neutral forces," for a total of 536,000. The grand total of these figures came to 840,000. (See *NAMP/RDSRIAC*, 893.000/3180, Beijing, June 6, 1919, "Quarterly Report of Political and Economic Conditions.")

** Well before the opening of the Versailles Conference, Dr. Wellington Koo had held meetings with President Wilson, Secretary of State Robert Lansing, and Colonel Edward House in Washington. His record of the meeting with Wilson on November 26, 1918, signaled the main problem. The president said that he had always felt sympathy for the Chinese and regarded the Far East as a region where the future peace was more likely to be endangered than in any other part of the world. The ideals of China and the United States went along the same lines, moreover, and he would gladly do his best to support China at the Peace Conference. However, he added, there was one difficulty. Many secret agreements had been signed between the Chinese government and other powers, agreements injurious to China. If it had been required that they be published, they would never have been concluded. Secret diplomacy should be banned in the future. In subsequent meetings with Lansing and House, the issue of prior agreements was raised in an even more direct manner, with an indication that in a conflict between the sanctity of official agreements and "justice," the United States might feel compelled to support the former. See the collected papers of Dr. V. K. Wellington Koo in Butler Library, Columbia University.

various quarters. Chinese students and laborers who had gone to France during the war were available to contact the delegates in person.* The Canton government took up the nationalist cause with renewed vigor, finding it a useful weapon against Beijing. And in the capital itself an increasingly assertive press published exposés and rumors that aroused anti-Japanese sentiments to a new pitch, especially among the large student population.

MAY FOURTH—THE EVENT AND THE SYMBOL

It was against this background that the May Fourth Movement emerged. As in the case of other events that have been immortalized as great historical turning points, a certain romanticism surrounds many accounts of this movement. The specific incidents that occurred on May 4 partook of the accidental, and the date itself was not the result of long-term planning. Yet there can be little doubt that the happenings of May 4, 1919, and the months that followed were a forceful expression of trends that had been accumulating for years—and were, in that sense, inevitable. In the background lay the gradual emergence of a new Chinese elite, educated or at least semieducated to yearn for nationalism, development, and democracy. There was also the growing importance of an urban commercial class, now more prosperous and assertive as a result of the European war, and increasingly disgusted with the inanities and socioeconomic costs of Chinese politics. And most important, there was the constant pressure exerted on China by Japan, as the Japanese government and private sector strove to fill the vacuum left by a battered Europe, thereby capitalizing on its investments of earlier years. Thus the May Fourth Movement warrants our careful attention, less for its details—which have been set forth voluminously elsewhere—than for its significance. Let us begin, however, by briefly recounting its most salient events.[30]

In late April it gradually became clear that China's claims, including those relating to Shandong, would be rejected at Paris. The press in Beijing and other major cities began to publish stories of intrigue, corruption, and treason which implicated the Beijing government—past and present—in the humiliating defeat.** Three men in high positions were singled out for special attack: Cao Rulin, the minister of communications and managing

*In early 1916 a company was formed in Canton to recruit workers for various tasks in wartime France, including labor on farms and in factories. According to an American consulate report, the workers were promised that they would not be involved in the war itself; they would be paid in accordance with the skill required, ranging from 2 francs per day for an ordinary laborer to 2 francs 80 centimes for a carpenter or blacksmith; they would work a maximum of ten hours per day, with Sunday free; and they would receive travel expenses to and from France, with free board and lodging for a five-year contract. (See NAMP/RDSRIAC, Canton, March 17, 1916, Josselyn to Reinsch.) Other sources indicate that the first group of Chinese workers going to France numbered about 8,000 by the winter of 1916, and that two years later their number had reached 140,000, including some 28,000 who were literate. Most were from north China. And while they were not used at the front lines, they did perform services for the French, British, and American armed forces as well as in the private sector of the French economy. For an account of contacts between the Chinese delegation to the peace conference and Chinese in the area, see Wunsz King, *China at the Paris Peace Conference in 1919*. King served as secretary of the Chinese delegation.

**Some of the rumors, as might have been expected, turned out to be entirely fictitious. For example, it was reported that Wellington Koo had become engaged to Cao Rulin's daughter and was deserting to the pro-Japanese camp. This was quickly and emphatically denied.

director of the Bank of Communications, Japanese-educated and a longtime leader of the "pro-Japanese" group; Zhang Zongxiang, the Chinese minister to Japan, also Japanese-educated and active in the loan negotiations of recent years, as well as being responsible for the signing of the 1918 agreement on Shandong; and Lu Zongyu, the director general of the Currency Reform Bureau, chairman of the Bank of Communications, director of the Chinese-Japanese Exchange Bank, and Chinese minister to Japan when the May 1915 treaty was signed.

On the evening of May 3, some one thousand students attended a meeting at Peking University Law School convened by a group of student activists, most of whom were associated with the New Tide Society and the Citizens Magazine Society, groups that represented the vanguard of the young intellectuals dedicated to modernization and reform.[31] Other informal meetings were held on the same evening at different schools. After a series of emotional speeches, it was decided to demand that the Chinese delegation in Paris not sign any treaty; to request all Chinese to participate in parades on May 7, designated as the day of National Humiliation; and to meet on the next day, May 4, in Tiananmen, Beijing's central square, for a massive demonstration and parade.

These developments, of course, had substantial antecedents. Throughout 1918, to look only at the very recent past, there had been many student protests against Japan and Sino-Japanese agreements, some of them significant in scale.* The events of May 4, however, had repercussions of a far-reaching nature. The day began with a morning meeting of student representatives of some thirteen colleges and universities at Peking College of Law and Political Science to plan the afternoon's events. It was decided that after gathering at Tiananmen the students would march through the legation quarters and from there to the business district. It was also agreed that telegrams should be sent to other cities, urging similar demonstrations against the Shandong settlement approved in Paris and urging that a permanent student organization should be created to uphold student demands and serve as a liaison with other groups.

In the early afternoon over three thousand students gathered at Tiananmen, and a printed leaflet entitled "A Manifesto of All Beijing Students" was distributed. It was written by Luo Jialun and ended with these stirring words: "This is the crucial moment for China in her life and death struggle. Today we swear two solemn oaths with all our fellow countrymen: (1) China's territory may be conquered, but it will not be given away; (2) the Chinese people may be massacred, but they will not surrender. Our country is about to be annihilated. Arise, brethren!"**

*In late May of 1918, after the Sino-Japanese Military Mutual Assistance Agreements had been concluded, despite the secrecy of the negotiations, several thousand students in Beijing conducted protest rallies against them, and there were demonstrations in other cities as well. Opposition to new Japanese loans also increased in intensity in 1918, with boycotts organized and protest rallies carried out.

**Translated from Luo Jialun, *Heixue baoyu dao mingxia*, p. 1, a collection of essays first published in 1943. According to Kuang Husheng, a participant in the Tiananmen rally, students from thirteen colleges met at Tiananmen at about one o'clock. The police were also present, although they did not anticipate violence. Kuang states that the majority of the students did not expect violence either, but all believed that they should march on the legation quarters as a demonstration of Chinese public opinion. (Kuang, "Record of the May Fourth Movement," in *Wusi aiguo yundong* 1:489–502.)

Both before and during the Tiananmen rally, authorities tried to persuade the students to disband and, instead of marching, to send a few representatives to discuss matters with the government and foreign legations. This request was rejected, and at about two o'clock the march toward the legations began. Some spectators later commented on the striking contrast between the appearance of the students—some no more than thirteen or fourteen years old, generally mild in manner and led by a small, bespectacled marshal—and the vehemence of the slogans emblazoned on their banners.*

When the procession reached the legation quarters, entrance was refused by police, but four representatives were allowed to visit the key legations. They found none of the ministers in residence, and left statements. A two-hour dispute then ensued as to whether the students could march through the quarters, and when this was denied, an increasingly angry mass of young people pushed toward the Chinese Foreign Ministry. Late in the afternoon they reached Cao's residence, which was near the ministry. When Cao did not make an appearance, the demonstrators, enflamed by disputes with police and exhortations from their own militants, milled around the house. A few students scaled the walls, entered the residence, and threw open the gates. An unruly mob then rushed into the premises. Cao himself escaped through a window, but the students found Zhang Zongxiang, who happened to be visiting, and beat him severely. Cao's aged father was also manhandled, and the residence was set on fire after furniture had been smashed and windows broken.

The police present at the scene assumed a passive attitude at first, but on urgent orders from their superiors, they finally intervened. Struggles broke out, and thirty-two students were later arrested, none of them top leaders. The immediate incident ended in the early evening, when the students dispersed and the fires were put out.**

In the days that followed, two broad developments unfolded. First, student organizational efforts got under way in many urban areas, and demonstrations involving thousands of students took place in a number of cities. Second, substantial support was given to the students by China's commercial community, the press, the Canton government, leading intellectuals, and even certain military governors not affiliated with Canton—so that the Beijing government was confronted with a formidable range of opponents.

Spearheading the organization of their peers, the Beijing students lost no time in pressing their cause. On May 5 several meetings took place, and thousands of students ratified resolutions calling for the restoration of the Shandong territories to China, the punishment of traitors, and a united front of patriotic organizations throughout China. It was further resolved that Beijing students should not attend classes until the arrested students had been released. The possibility of a boycott of Japanese goods was also discussed. On May 7, National Humiliation Day, 30,000 students attended a

*Among the slogans written on the banners were "Cancel the Twenty-One Demands," "Boycott Japanese Goods," "Return Our Qingdao," and "Traitor Cao" (Kuang, "Record of the May Fourth Movement").

**By six o'clock in the evening the violence had subsided and most students had left the scene. It was then that the troops arrived; together with the police, who had been "polite" during the disturbances, the military arrested thirty-two students, nineteen of whom were from Peking University. (See *Wusi aiguo yundong* 1:456–460, 494–498.)

meeting in Jinanfu to uphold China's rights; 5,000 marched in a patriotic rally in Nanjing; 4,000 attended a demonstration in Hangzhou; and in many other cities similar activities took place.[32] Never before had student political activities achieved this scale and scope, although the rural areas, as usual, were unaffected. Student unions were now created in many major cities, with every indication that they were intended to be permanent vehicles for student action. Taking advantage of their status in a society that had long revered learning and where those who acquired higher education were a tiny minority, many students in China were once again preparing for a sustained political effort. This time, however, the effort would take place primarily at home.

The support rendered by significant representatives of the commercial and journalistic communities was of major importance. The Shanghai Commercial Federation immediately telegraphed its approval of student actions. The Beijing Chamber of Commerce expressed its willingness to coordinate a boycott of Japanese goods. In some instances, merchants joined in the subsequent demonstrations, or hung banners in front of their stores, echoing student demands. The press also indicated sympathy in many instances. Editorials criticizing the government, demanding that China's rights be upheld, and urging release of the incarcerated students were commonplace.*

As was to be expected, the Canton government quickly came to the students' defense. Its statement, issued in the name of the seven administrative directors and reportedly initiated by Sun from Shanghai, was relatively moderate, but it urged leniency on the part of the government and attention to the basic issues of principle.** A telegram sent by the Canton parliament to all provincial governments was much stronger in tone: it called for a severe punishment of "the traitors," who served as "running dogs of a foreign country," and demanded that the northern government apologize for its treatment of the students.[33]

Another voice speaking on behalf of the students was that of Kang Youwei; although he was at odds with the modernist trends, he hailed the students' action as one of the few promising events of the republican era. Support came also from Wu Peifu and from the military governors of Hunan and Jiangxi.[34]

In the face of these events, the government oscillated between moderation and toughness in a manner characteristic of doomed power-holders. At first Premier Qian Nengxun's administration adopted a hard line, overruling the counsel of Fu Zengxiang, the minister of education. The resignations of Cao and Lu were refused; orders were given to restrict student activities and to punish those responsible for the attack on Cao's residence. Security in the city of Beijing was strengthened, and communications were censored.

*Other events included a meeting of Beijing merchants, a mass rally in Shanghai, student demonstrations in Changsha and Taiyuan, and Chinese student rallies in Tokyo and Osaka. The *Shanghai Times* (pro-Japanese) reported that some 10,000 students from practically all of the Shanghai schools marched on May 7, gathering signatures on a petition demanding that the Chinese delegates not sign the Peace Treaty and that all Shandong territories be restored to China (May 8, 1919).

**In a private meeting with the consul, Sammons, in Shanghai on May 5, however, Sun gave a harsh judgment of the Beijing government. The northern militarists, he said, had betrayed the country to Japan for personal benefit and because they had lost confidence in China's ability to protect itself. (See *NAMP/RDSRIAC*, 893.00/3119, Shanghai, May 6, 1919, Sammons to Reinsch.)

Schools were ordered closed, but Fu refused to countersign this order. On May 7, however, in an effort to defuse the student demonstrations taking place, the government ordered the arrested students released on bail, which temporarily brought to an end the student boycott of classes. Nevertheless, the government repeated that it intended to prosecute the students and to keep a tight reign on political demonstrations. The chancellor of Peking University, Cai Yuanpei, moreover, under mounting pressure, resigned on May 9 and left Beijing.

The trial of the arrested students opened on May 10, and student arrests for political activities continued. On May 12 Fu, the education minister, finally left his post after many attempts to resign. On May 19 a general student strike commenced. All Beijing students attending institutions of higher education were involved, and middle-school students joined the next day. By the end of the month the strike had spread to other major Chinese cities. The Student Union presented six demands to President Xu: the government should refuse to sign the Paris treaty; the "traitors" Cao, Zhang, and Lu should be punished; Fu should be reinstated as minister of education and Cai restored as chancellor of Peking University; repressive measures against the students should be stopped; the Chinese students persecuted in Japan on May 7 should be released, and those responsible punished; and the Shanghai peace negotiations with the South should be resumed.[35] At the same time, an appeal for the boycott of Japanese goods was issued, and by the end of May the boycott was proving effective in many cities, with substantial cooperation from merchants and the general public.

The Qian government answered the students on May 21 with a statement that showed some desire for compromise but failed to meet the major student demands. Efforts to get the students back into the classrooms failed, and on June 1 martial law was declared in Beijing, provoking a new series of student-police confrontations and mass arrests. Indeed, so many students were rounded up that certain buildings on the Peking University campus had to be used as places of detention. Once again the government had veered back toward the tough line. Such actions quickly proved counterproductive. Defiantly, the students continued their street lectures, and support from the citizenry at large appeared to increase, particularly in Shanghai. In that city merchants were persuaded to close their shops in a sympathy strike, and the strike spread to include some factory workers.[36]

By June 6 the government was moving again toward compromise and retreat. The acting minister of education, Yuan Xitao, insisted on resigning and was replaced by Fu Yuefen; at the same time, Hu Renyuan, a former dean of the Engineering School, was named temporary chancellor of Peking University, suggesting that Cai might be allowed to resume his post later on. Fu Yuefen immediately made two proposals: that all soldiers and police be withdrawn from campuses, and that the students return to classes with the government's promise that such security forces would not participate in subsequent negotiations. The imprisoned students, now sensing that the momentum was moving in their direction, refused to leave their temporary places of detention unless the three "traitors" were dismissed, a guarantee of freedom of speech was given, permission to parade through the Beijing streets upon release was granted, and the government issued a public apology. Government officials were now reduced to pleading with the students to go home, and after official apologies, they and a large number of sympathizers left their quarters on June 8, triumphant despite the fact that most of their demands remained unmet.

The government's retreat continued. On June 10 the resignations of Cao, Zhang, and Lu were accepted, and three days later Premier Qian also stepped down; the minister of finance, Gong Xinzhan, was appointed acting premier. On June 24 Beijing instructed the Chinese delegation in Paris to sign the peace treaty if its protests were unavailing, but under massive pressure President Xu reversed these instructions on the following day. The second message did not reach the delegation in time, but on June 28, the day for the signing, Chinese students and workers in Paris surrounded the delegates' quarters and prevented them from attending the ceremony. Thus, in the end, the Treaty of Versailles came into effect without Chinese acceptance. A month later, the final issue of immediate consequence was settled when Cai agreed to return to the chancellorship of Peking University.

Within the realm of the possible, the victory of the students had been well-nigh complete. Although it resolved none of the fundamental problems confronting the nation, the May Fourth Movement grew in significance with the passage of time, primarily because it was used by writers and political figures to symbolize various trends—a rebirth of Chinese nationalism, the advent of mass participation in Chinese politics, and the emergence of Marxism-Leninism in China. There is an element of truth in each of these claims, and also an element of exaggeration or distortion.

It is surely correct to emphasize the degree to which this movement symbolized a new flowering of nationalism. In ever-growing numbers, China's students—now removed by more than a decade from the confines of a strictly classical education—were cognizant of the world around them, however naively and imperfectly. They watched in despair as China, with its senseless political divisions and thwarted economic development, was pitted against the dynamism of neighboring Japan. When the Europeans had turned to the task of killing each other, moreover, China had become an easy target for this dynamism. The Twenty-One Demands, the Nishihara loans, and the tightening of controls in Manchuria in the name of anti-Bolshevik measures had produced mounting frustration among the young nationalists. Need and threat, in varying combinations—these two considerations dominated Chinese thought and action regarding Japan. For the students at least, the threat loomed larger than the need. The dam finally burst with the bitter news from Paris.

Yet China was still a long way from being able to translate the nationalist emotions of its youth into a greater unity. Provincial sentiments remained powerful, and China's weak political institutions abetted them. The May Fourth Movement stirred many a heart, but it did not bring North and South together. On the contrary, shortly after its conclusion, further splits occurred in both regions. It would take a long time, and many setbacks, before the nationalist aspirations of these young people were even partly realized. And by then they would be old men, and deeply divided over fundamental political issues.

As for the advent of mass participation in politics, there can be no doubt that the May Fourth Movement witnessed a greater political involvement of the most articulate portions of the Chinese citizenry than had ever occurred before. The masses had been rallied for combat earlier—in the Taiping Rebellion, in the Boxer uprising, and to a much smaller degree in the Revolution of 1911—but never had so many individuals been mobilized for a sustained effort to affect policies without resort to large-scale violence. To be sure, the participants did not include peasants, as did the Taiping and Boxer instances; and when the peasantry did return to political action, they would do so in a largely traditional manner, as we shall see.

This was not the first wholly urban movement in China led by the student-intellectual community. Sun Yat-sen's movement, after 1905, has that distinction. But on this occasion that community was not restricted to a few thousand overseas students. Now there were tens of thousands, standing and marching to be counted, in almost every city and town in central and eastern China, with sparser numbers in the west. They were joined, moreover, by assorted clerks, shopkeepers, merchants, journalists, and professionals—some because of coercion, but many out of strong conviction.

It is tempting to do as some Chinese writers have done and call the May Fourth Movement a milestone in the Chinese bourgeois-democratic revolution and an event signaling the imminent arrival of Chinese Marxism-Leninism.* But such an interpretation is too neat. It is true, of course, that the movement was influenced by a vast outpouring of new literature after 1911, much of it impregnated with Western liberal and socialist ideas. Periodicals and newspapers proliferated rapidly from 1915 onward, expressing political views that created a climate for intensive political discussion and the dissemination of ideas supportive of a new culture and a new politics. At the same time, however, the combination of a strong nationalist upsurge and an ambivalence toward the West soon created a neo-conservative movement. The political currents, in short, did not flow in a single direction.

Concepts like liberty, justice, and progress, along with ideas relating to nationalism and imperialism, had acquired a meaning for hundreds of thousands of youth and some of their elders. But politically, the May Fourth Movement came at a time of growing disillusionment with the parliamentary process, and in economic terms Western liberalism was still largely foreign even to the class that in theory was supposed to champion it. Like their Japanese counterparts of this era, the Chinese merchants and entrepreneurs were far closer to mercantilism than to liberalism; and given their relatively low status, they might aspire to aid and influence power-holders, but it rarely occurred to them to seek power themselves or on behalf of their class.

Finally, the May Fourth Movement did initiate many Chinese youth into political action, with profound implications for their future lives, and some of them did become early Communist activists. Yet the basic thrust of the movement itself was neither pro-Soviet nor prosocialist.** Indeed, although

*Liu Yue, for example, asserts that the May Fourth Movement was the culmination of the bourgeois-democratic revolution, bringing to fruition the development of Chinese capitalism, which in turn made possible the development of the Chinese proletarian class. The May Fourth Movement was thus the beginning of China's new democratic revolution. (See Liu Yue, "Several Issues Regarding Research on Modern Chinese History."

**Unquestionably, some young radicals or individuals who were to become radical participated in it. Zhang Guotao, who was to take part in the first organizational activities of the Communist movement a few months later, claims to have played a leading role. He says that events really began on the evening of May 2 at a meeting of the *National Magazine* editorial staff, of which he was a member. At this meeting, according to Zhang, he proposed that all Beijing students should participate in a demonstration protesting Japanese imperialism. (Chang Kuo-t'ao, *The Rise of the Chinese Communist Party, 1921–1927*, vol. 1 of *The Autobiography of Chang Kuo-t'ao*, pp. 53–69.)

they became increasingly unhappy with American policies in the years that followed, the youthful leaders of the May Fourth Movement saw the United States as their principal champion. Thus Student Union leaders in Shanghai urged members to pay a visit to the American delegation and various consulates on the Fourth of July, to express gratitude to "our friends." *

It can be argued that disillusionment with parliamentary democracy and fierce resentment of Japan, combined with the seeming indifference or impotence of the liberal West, stimulated an interest in the new socialist republic in the north—thereby planting the first seeds of Chinese radicalism. There is much truth in this. But in itself, the May Fourth Movement rested on nationalism, not internationalism; on political justice, not social or economic equalization; and on the rights of the state, not class rights.

CONTINUED DISUNITY

As we have seen, the May Fourth Movement did not serve to bring North and South China together, despite the outpouring of patriotism it engendered. Emboldened by the Beijing government's problems, Tang Shaoyi put forth eight demands at the Shanghai peace talks on May 13, including the requirement that the presidential directive of June 13, 1917, dissolving parliament be declared invalid.** When Zhu Qiqian, the northern delegation leader, refused to accept these demands, both men resigned and the conference was suspended. After pressure was applied by the Allied ministers in Beijing, discussions resumed on June 5, but Zhu refused to continue, and it took more than a month to replace him with Wang Yitang. Wang's appointment was anathema to the South, since he was a principal Anfu Club leader. Tang refused to meet with him, and the negotiations were stalemated. Not until mid-1920 were discussions reopened, and shortly thereafter Tang was dismissed, and General Lu Rongting appointed an associate, Wen Zongyao, as chief southern negotiator. North and South thus remained divided.

Within both regions, moreover, weakness and division prevailed. In the North, President Xu's influence had been seriously reduced by events, and Duan Qirui was again emerging as a man with whom to reckon. Although out of office, Duan had a power base in his independent War Participation Army (later known as the Border Defense Army), a military unit created for

*Just prior to July 4, the Student Union headquarters sent a telegram to branches in Beijing, Tianjin, and Hankou. It read as follows: "July 4 being the American independence commemoration day, and as America is our country's excellent friend, having given us much sympathetic help during our patriotic demonstrations, we should all express our friendly feelings to that country. Please request all classes at your ports to hoist flags and send deputations to the American consulates and American Chambers of Commerce to tender them our heartiest congratulations and good wishes" (*North China Herald*, July 5, 1919, p. 17).

**The other seven demands were as follows: rejection of the proposed settlement of the Shandong issue; invalidation of all covenants, pacts, and other agreements secretly entered into between China and Japan, and severe punishment of those responsible; immediate disbandment of the War Participation Army; removal of military and civilian governors whose maladministration had become obnoxious to the people; the establishment of a provisional Administrative Council to enforce the decisions of the peace conference until a unified parliament could be convened; settlement of all questions brought before the peace conference; and recognition of Xu Shichang as provisional president of the Republic until the formal election of a permanent successor. (*Yirui nian nanbei yihe ziliao*, pp. 260–264. In English, see *NAMP/RDSRIAC*, 893.00/31331, Beijing, May 17, 1919, Reinsch to the Secretary.)

the ostensible purpose of fulfilling China's commitment to participate in World War I. By the fall of 1919 a power struggle had begun to unfold between Duan and two former allies, Zhang Zuolin and Cao Kun. Both parties had their surrogates. Duan was now supporting General Xu Shuzheng, known as Little Xu, and his bid for control of Mongolia, thereby threatening Zhang's position in Manchuria. Zhang and Cao threw their support to Jin Yunpeng, who became premier in late September when Gong Xinzhan resigned. General Jin had been an ally of Duan's in the past and wanted to retain his support, but almost immediately he came into conflict with the Anfu faction in parliament over cabinet appointments. Duan's intervention resulted in a compromise that permitted the formation of a cabinet, but by the spring of 1920 northern politics were in a state of complete disarray. The Anfu Club was under heavy attack for its pro-Japanese tendencies, and was becoming estranged from President Xu. The tensions among the military leaders, moreover, showed no signs of abating. On the contrary, in March a League of Eight Provinces was formed, proclaiming itself dedicated to the restoration of peace and stable government; it was composed wholly of military governors, and its primary object was to topple the Anfu group and Duan. Since these governors represented Zhili, Henan, the three Manchurian provinces, and the three Yangtze valley provinces, they held military power in the heartland of north and central China.

By mid-1920 full-fledged civil war had erupted. Wu Peifu, one of the North's most able and progressive generals, and long associated with Cao Kun, announced that he was going to break the Japanese influence in Beijing and liquidate its primary instrument, the Anfu Club. He said he intended to end government by military cliques, and was prepared to give his whole support to the students, merchants, and other classes who stood for true democracy. Events reached a climax in July. Jin resigned as premier, and the Anfu group pressed its nominee upon Xu. He resisted, and on July 13 Duan presented him with an ultimatum: Wu had to be dismissed from his posts and Cao deprived of rank, or Duan's troops would enter the capital and seize power. The anti-Duan forces now struck militarily, and after a few battles Duan admitted defeat. Wu arrived in Beijing on August 6 in triumph. The Anfu Club was proscribed, Duan's army disbanded, and Marshal Duan himself permitted to go into retirement to pursue Buddhist studies. (He would return to politics four years later.)

General Jin Yunpeng was reinstated as premier by President Xu, a man now wholly bereft of independent authority. A cabinet composed primarily of Zhili adherents came into office on August 11. The new Beijing government depended on an alliance between two key figures and their respective supporters: Zhang Zuolin, the inspector general of the three Manchurian provinces, and Cao Kun, who held the same position in the three northern provinces of Zhili, Shandong, and Henan.

To understand the power structure of China in the months that followed, one has to fathom relations between the regional, provincial, and local power-holders of this period. The clearest picture was presented by Manchuria. There, and in parts of Mongolia, authority was firmly exercised by Zhang Zuolin. Indeed, all of China north of the Great Wall in Chinese hands had come under his control. By this time Zhang had virtually eliminated military and political rivals in his realm. He could count on 100,000 regular troops and an additional 50,000 militia, and since some 70 percent of his budget went for military expenditures, his troops received their pay regularly and discontent was minimal.[37] Despite the heavy military costs, moreover, his general financial situation was good. A surplus existed in the treasury, and all outstanding loans had been repaid.

As we noted earlier, Zhang was a "pure" military man, with little interest in social and political reform. His strategic position, however, made it easy for him to intervene in national politics. His control of the Mukden–Beijing railway meant that he could move troops to the capital quickly. And the relative effectiveness of his rule contrasted sharply with the growing chaos within China proper. It is not surprising, therefore, that Zhang appears to have toyed with yet another monarchical restoration during this period, with himself as the centerpiece. He cultivated, among others, Zhang Xun—still an unreconstructed monarchist. And perhaps coincidentally, it was discovered in the fall of 1920 that Prince Duan, exiled "forever" to Xinjiang by the terms of the International Protocol of 1900 after the Boxer uprising, was living in Beijing. Duan's commitments to the monarchy, like those of Zhang Xun, had remained firm. When rumors of the monarchical restoration movement circulated in the press, Zhang Zuolin vigorously denied involvement, but many believed that he had tested the waters and found them chilly.

Zhang's principal problems during this period lay less with Chinese rivals than with the Japanese and various Russian factions operating in his territory. In matters of foreign relations, Zhang shared the sentiments of many Chinese in being strongly opposed to Japanese expansion, but circumstances forced him to be circumspect in his dealings with Tokyo's representatives. At the same time, he was prepared to push his authority against Russians of any faction whenever the opportunity permitted, and he was most hostile to the Bolsheviks.

By the spring of 1921 it was clear that relations between Zhang and Cao Kun were fragile. Once again the dominant military figure on the scene, in seeking to expand his turf, was raising the suspicions of others. Cao's domain was crucial strategically, covering the three provinces closest to the capital on the south and east. Shandong, of course, presented special problems because of the presence of the Japanese there. In Zhili, Cao operated with maximum authority. In Henan, he had to contend with the power and popularity of one of his chief lieutenants, Wu Peifu. Wu and another young allied general, Feng Yuxiang, had precisely the qualities that the older traditional military men lacked, and Cao came to realize that although Feng and Wu were nominally under his command, they were in fact becoming powers in their own right, especially Wu. Zhang Zuolin, sensing this situation, urged Cao to eliminate Wu—but that would not have been easy to do, even if Cao had been amenable.

Despite various pressures, the loose alliance between the two regional power-holders of the North remained intact through late 1920 and the spring of 1921. Their combined authority, moreover, was symbolized by a conference held first at Tianjin and then in Beijing in April and May of 1921.[38] Zhang journeyed south to meet with Cao, and in late April they were joined by Wang Zhanyuan, the military governor of Hubei. Wang, a candidate for the post of inspector general of Hubei and Hunan, had prepared for the Tianjin conference—which some called "the conference of super-duzhuns" (military governors)—by convening his own meeting in Hankou in late

March. Present were representatives of six central and southern provinces that were only nominally supportive of Beijing or had proclaimed themselves independent. Wang's plan was to unite them in support of the Beijing government, thereby elevating himself to a level of power roughly equal to that of Zhang and Cao.

Had Wang succeeded, China would have been divided roughly into four regional power centers: Manchuria and Mongolia; northern China; south-central China; and the southern government headquartered in Canton. Shortly after Wang returned to Hubei, however, he was in deep trouble, and it soon became apparent that neither he nor anyone else could unify south-central China. Meanwhile, the Beijing government was wrestling with a familiar range of problems concerning finances and troop disbandment, which were closely related. Estimates of the number of soldiers in the country ranged between 1.5 and 1.7 million. Despite the fact that at least 50 percent of the budget went to military costs, most troop payments were in arrears, equipment was generally antiquated, and training was hopelessly inadequate.

The tenure of any minister of finance depended on his ability to raise funds, and on this score the current occupant, Zhou Ziqi, reported to be "pro-American," was doing badly. The foreign consortium, with the United States once again participating, proved unwilling to consider further loans at this time. This left a variety of Japanese sources as the only alternative, and cabinet adjustments to this fact were made in the late spring of 1921, despite the protests of nationalists. Meanwhile, the government had so little money for education that in Beijing teachers from all levels, including Peking University, had gone on strike, demanding adequate support. Undoubtedly, this problem contributed to the growth of intellectual radicalism.

If the Beijing government clung to life during these troubles, it was because Zhang and Cao, the king-makers of the period, remained in precarious agreement, and because no serious challenge from the South could be mounted. Let us examine first the so-called pro-Beijing provinces, most of which were in fact largely autonomous.[39] In the north, Shanxi province, governed by General Yan Xishan, had remained essentially aloof from national alignment for many years, although its allegiance was nominally pledged to Beijing. Yan, known as a "model governor," had some 60,000 troops, a sizable burden for his people. Yet his economic and social policies were comparatively enlightened, modernization on various fronts was one of his goals, and the Shanxi provincial assembly still operated with some authority.

The adjacent province to the west, Shaanxi, was currently split. The northern portion was more or less aligned with Beijing, and the mediocre provincial governor was affiliated with Zhang Zuolin. The southern portion was occupied by "people's armies," the most important of which was led by Yu Youren, a longtime associate of Sun. Because it was desperately poor, this province was in no position to strengthen the authority of any regional confederation.

Further to the west, the province of Gansu, with a strong Moslem population, was restive. Beijing's appointment of Lu Hongdao as military governor was being strongly resisted on grounds that he had an anti-Moslem record. In distant Xinjiang the military government had remained unchanged for some years, but this region played a very limited role in national politics.

62. *Yan Xishan*

With its large Turkic population, Xinjiang was a part of the Chinese empire loosely held.

In the truly vital provinces of Hubei and Sichuan in central and southwestern China, Beijing was losing ground. In Hubei the northern government had counted heavily on Wang Zhanyuan, but Wang was unpopular with the people there, and his star was clearly waning after the Tianjin-Beijing conferences. Sichuan had long been the scene of conflicts involving local and regional military figures. By the spring of 1921, General Liu Xiang, the "pacification commissioner" at Chongqing, was the commanding figure, and under his hand Sichuan had proclaimed its independence from both Beijing and Canton. This was also the position of Yunnan to the south after the ouster of General Tang Jiyao, a Sun supporter, in early February 1921. The new military ruler, General Gu Pingzhen, once a trusted lieutenant of Tang's, had opted for independence from any external alignment despite Sun's overtures.

In the southeast the three provinces of Jiangsu, Anhui, and Zhejiang maneuvered in the fashion of small states sandwiched between stronger powers. In Jiangsu the acting military governor, General Qi Xieyuan, a member of the Zhili faction, was outwardly loyal to the Beijing government, but was regarded as strongly ambitious and opportunistic. In the northern part of the province, moreover, two quasi-independent generals were aligned with Zhang Xun, and hence with the Zhang Zuolin faction of the north. This was also the position of the Anhui military governor, Zhang Wenseng, but he was careful not to act boldly, given the pressures upon him. General Lu Rongxiang, the military governor of Zhejiang and a former Anfu leader, while remaining friendly with Beijing, proclaimed his independence from both northern and southern governments and strongly championed the cause of local autonomy.

To the south, the military governor of Fujian, Li Houji, an old Duan ally and a former member of the Anfu group, performed a difficult balancing act. Although he had earlier assisted General Chen Jiongming and maintained a tacit understanding with him, Li also retained ties with Beijing. In order to avoid making a commitment, he found it convenient to play on the theme of provincial independence. Like Zhejiang, Fujian was garrisoned with northern soldiers, and as in other provinces, localism was strong, making Li's control weak in many districts. Charges of mistreatment of civilians were rife, and the line between soldiers and bandits was difficult to draw.*

Three other southern provinces—Jiangxi, Hunan, and Guizhou—were also promoting their independence with varying degrees of intensity. In

*In an article entitled "Banditry—A New Profession," published in the March 6, 1921, issue of *China Press*, Richard Montgomery described the state of banditry in the South Fujian region, which he had recently visited. Beginning in a satirical vein, he asserted that in the new style of diplomacy, the Chinese government commissioned bandits to collect their revenue for them, in exchange for their pledge to serve the government faithfully. This made everyone happy except the common people. Unfortunately, certain bandits of the old school refused to cooperate, so an army of northern soldiers had to be brought in to persuade them that independent banditry was passé. Under the old system, the average bandit chief was something of a gentleman; that is to say, he taxed everyone fairly, killed only those who caused him trouble, and stole only from the rich and prosperous. But the soldier was no respecter of persons—except bandits—and he robbed all of the locals equally. Montgomery then described a personal experience. Coming upon a group engaged in heated argument, he surmised that a "big, sluggish, pork-eyed brute who looked capable of killing his grandmother" was the key bandit, but he was told that this man—known as "the Buzzard"—was only the "number-one coolie" who collected the "squeeze." The bandit chief was the slim gentleman in the silk coat with a fan, talking to one of the teachers. He had been given a commission and had official status with the government.

There was another side to the coin, however, unreported by Montgomery. Missionaries in the area wrote that many individuals had turned to banditry out of desperation, being unable to cope with governmental indifference and military brutality. On occasion, they were willing to return to the legal fold; but sometimes officials tricked them into surrendering by promising amnesty and then executed them, which sowed further seeds of distrust throughout the community at large.

63. *Zhang Zuolin*

64. *Wu Peifu*

Jiangxi the military governor, Chen Guangyuan, fearing an attack from Guangdong forces, sought external allies, but counted little on Beijing. Hunan's military governor, Zhao Hengti, proclaimed Hunan's autonomy, but in fact he had scant power beyond Changsha, the capital; real authority rested with the commanders of the twelve military districts into which the province had been divided. Guizhou's military governor, Lu Tao, sought funds from Beijing to counter the Canton government's influence, but the province was increasingly subject to Canton pressure even though it sought to practice self-government.

Thus, the Yangtze valley provinces and those to the immediate south were gravitating toward nonalignment, or at most toward a weak attachment to the center. But neither appeals from the Canton government nor efforts to achieve a federation within the region were notably successful. Meanwhile, in late 1920 two figures long prominent in the politics of central China passed from the scene. On October 12 Li Shun, the military governor of Jiangsu, committed suicide, and on December 27 former President Feng Guozhang, once a key leader in the region, died in Beijing. Generally speaking, the provinces of central China now had weak governors. In any case, a standoff currently existed between these provinces and the northern government. With the exception of Zhang Zuolin, Cao Kun, and Wu Peifu, no provincial leader was strong enough to influence, let alone topple, the center. But Beijing was equally unable to impose its will on most of the provinces, even those nominally under its control.

Within the southern government located in Canton, the situation also remained fluid. Sun Yat-sen, having withdrawn from active involvement in the Canton government in May 1918, was living in Shanghai.* He was spending most of his time writing a treatise on China's economic development, outlining a truly massive program involving hundreds of millions of dollars.

Sun, who referred to his proposal as a program "to make capitalism create socialism in China," advanced six major projects: the construction of harbors in northern, central, and southern China; the development of 100,000 miles of railroads and 1 million miles of macadam roads; mineral and agricultural development; water conservation and irrigation work; the development of cement, iron, and steel works; and colonization in northeast China, Mongolia, Xinjiang, Kokonor, and Tibet. The projects would be financed with international capital provided jointly by the industrial nations, and China's industries would be made into a "great trust owned by the Chinese people." It was a program hopelessly ahead of its time.[40]

In the fall of 1919, Sun and Duan Qirui established contact and even arrived at a paper alliance, to the surprise of partisans on both sides. It was one of Sun's many efforts to wed his ideas to someone else's military power, but it was a mismatch and badly timed as well. Duan was driven from power in the summer of 1920 and did not resume a strong role in politics for four years—and when he did, it was not as an ally of Sun.

Real power in the Canton government continued for the moment to rest with General Lu Rongting and his Guangxi forces, although Cen Chunxuan and Wen Zhongyao now had charge of the administration. The Can-

* Sun's letter of resignation dated May 4 was published in the *Peking Leader*, May 26, 1918. In it he described China's greatest danger as the struggle of the militarists for supremacy. "This danger," he added "is not confined to either the North or the South. Many of the officials of the so-called constitutionalist provinces have not been wholly willing to submit to law and public opinion, and most of the officials-elect of the Military Government have not seen fit to assume their offices. They have not shown the desired respect and obedience to the National Assembly in extraordinary session as they should. The lack of wholehearted internal cooperation has rendered outside recognition impossible." In conclusion he said: "Laboring almost alone, without men or arms, I have not been able to do much, but I do not feel it necessary to apologize, and I shall continue to do my duty as an individual citizen" (*Guofu quanji* 4:357–358). Whatever questions one may have about Sun's political judgment and organizational capacities, his faithfulness to liberal principles during this period cannot be faulted.

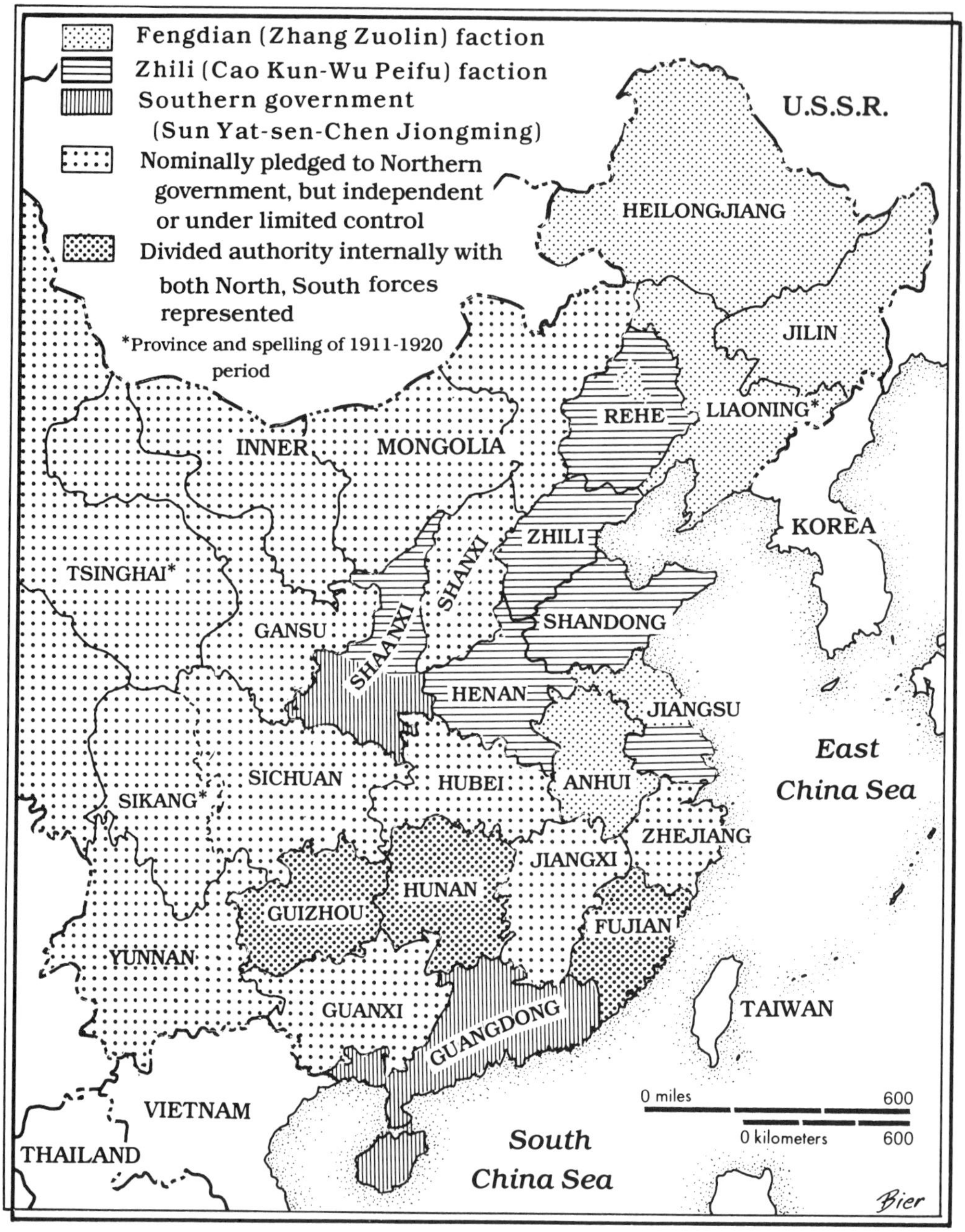

MAP 3. China, December 1920: Distribution of Political-Military Power

ton parliament was riddled with factionalism, and the Administrative Council set up earlier was so divided as to be inoperative. By the spring of 1920 both Wu Tingfang and Tang Shaoyi had defected to join Sun in Shanghai. They counted General Tang Jiyao on their side, which left the Council without a quorum.

Late in 1920 the situation in Guangdong changed dramatically. In September the military forces of General Chen Jiongming, the Cantonese reformer-revolutionary previously based in Fujian and allied with Sun,

65. *Feng Yuxiang, circa 1913*

struck against the Guangdong government. Chen demanded the resignation of General Mo Rongxin and the ouster of Guangxi forces from the province. After political negotiations (concerning funds for Mo to pay his troops) and military successes, Chen's soldiers occupied Canton at the end of October. On November 25 Sun and his key supporters left Shanghai and triumphantly returned to Canton, prepared to assume power once again.

As their government was collapsing, the Guangxi leaders—notably Mo, Cen Chunxuan, General Lu Rongting, and Admiral Lin Baoyi—had cancelled Guandong's earlier declaration of independence and announced their allegiance to Beijing. Naturally, Sun and his allies denounced this move. Progress toward unity between North and South might have been possible, however, if Sun's forces had been prepared to work with Wu Peifu. Despite Sun's earlier overtures to Duan, such an alliance would have been eminently logical in terms of the principles for which Sun and Wu stood. But Sun disliked Wu and may have seen him as a serious rival. Thus, the new southern government remained hostile to Beijing.

Despite its success in Guangdong, the Canton government made no significant progress in rallying other provinces to its side. Indeed, some developments were adverse to the South's cause. The defeat of Tang Jiyao's troops in Sichuan and their withdrawal to Yunnan and Guizhou, and the subsequent ouster of Tang as military governor of Yunnan, cost Canton the support of this region. Guangxi was hostile, of course, until the Guangxi-Guangdong war later in 1921 resulted in a victory for Canton. Fujian, having been the locus of Chen's power, had many sympathizers with the Canton government, but with northern soldiers in occupation, full allegiance was impossible. Hunan, which was critical to the fortunes of both North and South, seesawed back and forth, increasingly divided into various areas of control. The earlier Federation of Constitutionalist Provinces could not be reconstructed, at least in the short term.

By early 1921, moreover, it had become clear that the Guangdong government itself was in trouble. Finances had been a problem from the beginning. The new government had come into office promising a series of reforms, including a reduction of military forces, improvement of the tax system, the abolition of gambling, and administrative reorganization. But most of these measures would cost money, and the new government had few sources of revenue, despite appeals to the districts and the overseas Chinese. Sun again worked hard to obtain support from the U.S. government, but to no avail.* In the spring of 1921 a hard line with the foreign powers was attempted, with a demand that the customs revenues of Guangdong province, together with the accumulated surplus, be delivered to the government in Canton. Since all foreign nations recognized only the Beijing government, this was rejected, with the United States playing a crucial role in the

*Sun made himself available to various Americans in the area during the winter of 1920–1921. For example, the naval attaché of the U.S. legation visiting Canton had dinner with Sun and his advisers in February. His appraisal was generally unfavorable: "He is a clever and ambitious man, and willing to sacrifice anything or anybody to attain his ends." He also said he got the impression that he was talking to "foreign-educated Chinese," who could never hope to obtain recognition from "such real Chinese provinces as Kansu, Shansi, Honan, Hunan, Hupeh, and Szechuan" (NAMP/RDSRIAC, 893.00/3845, March 16, 1921, Crane to the Secretary). The American vice-consul in Canton, Ernest B. Price, was one of the few Americans who did not give a negative appraisal of Sun, and he complained in one report that his views were not taken seriously by the Beijing legation.

In addition to sending a cablegram to all major governments upon assuming office on May 5, Sun sent a personal, handwritten letter to President Harding. Praising the United States as "the Mother of Democracy and the champion of liberalism and righteousness," he argued that China was at a critical moment in its history, and that the decision of America would determine whether democracy in China would triumph or fail. He said that the civil war was not a war between North and South, but a national struggle between militarism and democracy, between treason and patriotism. Unless the United States, China's traditional friend and supporter, could lend a helping hand, China would be compelled to submit to Japan. Praising the John Hay Doctrine (the Open Door declaration), as providing China with the basis of its existence at present, Sun urged that Washington apply that doctrine by extending immediate recognition to his government. This letter received no response, and later, when Mr. Ma Soo, a representative of Sun, sought an interview in Washington with George B. Christian, a member of Harding's White House staff, the State Department advised Christian to decline, since the United States, like other major powers, recognized only the Beijing government. (See *NAMP/RDSRIAC*, 893.00/3998, July 27, 1921.)

decision. Rather than risk a confrontation, the Canton government backed down.

Meanwhile, two issues had emerged by the late spring of 1921 which suggested the possibility of a serious rift between Sun and his key military supporter, General Chen. One related to Sun's election as president. On April 7 remnants of the "old parliament" of 1915 gathered in Canton and elected Sun president, giving him 216 votes out of the 222 cast. But Chen and others were reported to have reservations about this action, partly because a quorum had not been mustered, which cast some doubt on the legitimacy of the act, and partly because it seemed to enhance Sun's power more than Chen and his supporters might have wished. Sun's inauguration took place on May 5.[41] The other issue concerned Guangxi. For some time Sun had favored a campaign against Guangxi, both to remove any threat to Guangdong from the west and to strengthen the Canton government's appeal to such provinces as Yunnan, Hunan, and Guizhou.* Chen, on the other hand, was cool toward such a plan, and favored efforts to develop an effective, progressive government in Guangdong. The dispute continued until the summer of 1921, when the Guangxi troops attacked.

Thus, the southern government was no stronger, no more unified, and no less problem-ridden than the northern government in the spring of 1921. After 1911 Chinese political life seemed to demean and vulgarize most men who were associated with it. Yuan Shikai, Sun Yat-sen, Liang Qichao, Duan Qirui, Tang Shaoyi—the ideals and the reputations of all had suffered.

The students had retained a certain purity, but this was because they were far from power, despite their victories in 1919, and they did not have to operate the defective institutions of government with which the nation was saddled. The student movement remained reasonably vigorous throughout 1919 and into 1920. Student-directed boycotts of Japanese goods had some effect, though not for long. Student rhetoric, perhaps as compensation, became increasingly shrill, as various manifestos were issued denouncing Beijing's leaders as traitorous and corrupt. Repression followed, and by the spring of 1920 students were again being arrested and their organizations banned.

The student vanguard was becoming more radical, and in response to the government's assaults, its tactics were changing. Mass demonstrations increasingly gave way to small-scale or individual actions of an urban-guerrilla type. Certain Bolshevik ideas were now reaching student leaders, but their new tactics were more strongly influenced by the actions of the Korean nationalists. The Korean "March First" uprising against the Japanese in 1919 had been carefully observed by a number of Chinese youth, and since their chief enemy was also Japan, they found Korean nationalist activities both instructive and stimulating.

As a segment of the student movement became more radical, however, the ranks began to split. By the end of 1920, as student strikes and boycotts were showing clear signs of becoming less effective, some students who had

*The vice-consul of the Canton consulate, Ernest B. Price, reported that Sun had personally informed him that the Guangxi expedition was necessary for two reasons. The first was "self-protection." The second was that with Guangxi "freed from its military overlords" and back in the fold of the constitutionalists, Yunnan, Hunan, and Guizhou would be more fully allied with Guangdong. (NAMP/RDSRIAC, 893.00/3864, April 6, 1921, Price to the Secretary.)

66. *Chen Jiongming*

previously been active began to question the militants' timing, tactics, and organizational methods. Disagreements cropped up between National Student Union branches in Beijing, Shanghai, Wuhan, and Canton—and within these units as well. More moderate students challenged the thesis that they should engage in union organizing among laborers or pledge themselves to a socialist revolution. Many of them wanted to concentrate on an educational campaign—to emphasize literacy programs, night-school courses, and other means of training the people for citizenship in a democratic society. Others grew indifferent to activism, feeling that events had outrun the ability of any individual or small group to influence them, so that one had better look after one's own interests. Still others looked to foreign countries to provide solutions. Disunity and defeatism were spreading.

Trends within the mature intellectual and merchant communities were not dissimilar. Even the conservative intellectuals and merchants recognized that something was profoundly wrong when soldiers and bandits plundered innocent people, trade and communications were widely disrupted, and politics were synonymous with corruption. Yet solutions were not at hand, and political involvement often brought serious trouble on one's head, with no appreciable gains. In these circles too, a certain withdrawal from politics ensued, amid a great diversity of private thoughts.

Among the masses of ordinary people there were rumblings of discontent. From such widely dispersed regions as Jiangsu, Henan, Fujian, and Sichuan came reports of peasant-based armed uprisings, directed primarily against marauding soldiers, but sometimes bearing revolutionary connotations.*

ISSUES OF EMPIRE

In any period of domestic turmoil, protecting the Chinese empire was bound to be difficult, and in these years the difficulties were increased by dramatic developments on the international stage, some of which affected China's border regions. After the overthrow of the czarist government and the victory of the Bolsheviks in Russia, it became clear that northern Manchuria and Mongolia could not escape involvement in the unfolding Russian civil war and the ensuing Allied intervention. We shall present a detailed analysis of the situation in Manchuria later in this study.[42] At this point, it is important to note that events offered the Chinese an opportunity to reassert their sovereignty over northern Manchuria, a region long dominated by the Russians, but that these same events greatly increased the threat of Japanese control.

One critical issue was control of the Chinese Eastern Railway (CER). In 1896 the Qing government had approved construction of this line through Manchuria by a company that was nominally private but in fact under the complete control of the Russian Ministry of Finance. The agreement provided for Chinese participation in management and gave the Chinese government a right to repurchase the line, but in practice Chinese involvement had been minimal and the Russians had always treated the railway as a Russian institution, the zone surrounding it as Russian territory.

After the collapse of the czarist government, Beijing feared that Japan would seek to take over control of the railway from Russia. Thus, when the

* As one example, in north Jiangsu and east Henan, two societies emerged in the summer of 1920 with the names Red Spear Society and White Spear Society. They resembled the Boxers in that their members believed that by means of certain incantations they could render themselves invulnerable. Their attacks, however, were directed against invading soldiers, not foreigners. (See *NAMP/RDSRIAC*, 893.00/3967, May 28, 1921, Davis to the Secretary.) In southwest Hubei, missionaries reported that a peasant band calling itself the Divine Army had taken up arms and issued proclamations calling for the expulsion of invading troops. A British report stated that some 5,000 followers, armed with knives on bamboo poles and made invulnerable to death by a potion provided by a priest, waved little red flags in front of them to divert bullets and frontally attacked a body of soldiers. They had been badly defeated, and their leaders had been killed. They attacked because they hated soldiers, and were tired of being robbed by them. (See *NAMP/RDSRIAC*, 893.00/3870, Hankow, April 5, 1921, Huston to the Secretary.)

Kerensky government asked the United States to operate the CER for it, Chinese authorities were pleased, seeing this arrangement as a means of preserving their rights. A commission headed by an American, Colonel John F. Stevens, was assigned the task, with the Russian Railway Service Corps serving under it. The Japanese, predictably, objected. In the meantime, the old czarist administrators continued to operate the line, but from time to time there were attempted interventions from anti-czarist factions in Harbin. On February 10, 1919, the United States accepted an earlier Japanese proposal that Stevens should remain head of the technical management of both the CER and the Trans-Siberian railway, to the extent the latter was not in Bolshevik hands, with an inter-allied force serving as railway guards; Americans were to patrol the eastern portion of the Trans-Siberian line and Japanese were to guard the CER. Friction between the Americans and the Japanese, however, rendered this arrangement less than satisfactory, and the Bolsheviks were opposed to it, even as it pertained to the CER. The stage was set for the appearance of future problems.

The Mongolian situation was no less complex. By 1914, with Russian assistance, Outer Mongolia had shed Chinese control and was seeking international recognition as an independent state. Proclaiming the Hutukhtu their supreme religious and secular ruler and Urga the capital of their sovereign nation, the Outer Mongolians were making every effort to exclude the Chinese now and for the future.

A certain retreat from this position became necessary the following year. International recognition had not been forthcoming, and considerable friction with the Russians had developed. By the spring of 1915, moreover, the Yuan government appeared stronger and more stable. After prolonged negotiations, the Kiakhta Agreement of June 7 was signed by China, Russia, and Mongolia. Under its terms, Outer Mongolia was recognized as an autonomous state under Chinese suzerainty. Urga authorities abandoned their claim to complete independence, and in exchange China agreed to allow the Outer Mongolians to manage their internal affairs without interference, and to enter into commercial treaties with other nations. The Chinese and Russian presence within Outer Mongolia was to be restricted. The Chinese were allowed to have a resident in Urga with a bodyguard of 200 troops; the Russians would have a representative with a bodyguard of 150 troops. Both nations could have consulates in three other places, each with 50 soldiers for protection. Outer Mongolia would not enter into any political or territorial treaty with another power, and in diplomatic matters it would be represented by China.[43]

This agreement remained basically intact until the Russian Revolution. In fact, however, Russian influence was predominant. A few minor controversies between Beijing and St. Petersburg arose. In mid-1916 the Russians protested the appointment of a new Chinese resident, asserting that he was unacceptable to the Mongols. They also objected to the representation of Outer Mongolia in the Chinese parliament, contending that this was improper because it was recognized as an autonomous state. On the Chinese side, certain members of parliament called for cancellation of the Russo-Chinese treaty of 1913, charging that it had never been ratified by parliament. Basically, however, the status quo was maintained without major changes.

Life in the region moved at a leisurely pace, consistent with the character of the Mongol people. The Hutukhtu became blind and in fragile health. According to one Western observer who had spent time in Urga, he was also "a devotee of the wine-bottle." An initial loan of four million rubles was spent partially on arms purchases, but also in the acquisition of 10,000 bronze Buddhas. However, governmental expenses were not great. Outer Mongolia was without public works, a parliament, or even a local police force.[44]

With the Russian Revolution, changes were set afoot. Ataman Gregorii Semenov, a Transbaikal Cossack and anti-Bolshevik leader operating in Siberia, sought to interest the Outer Mongolians in joining an independent Pan-Mongol Union that would encompass certain sections of Russian-held territory, would include Mongolia, and would unite Buriats and Mongols. The Japanese supported Semenov and his idea, and by 1919 Japanese military officers were active in the region, although a majority of Mongol princes, officials, and lamas rejected the Pan-Mongol concept at a conference held on April 1, 1919. In that same month the Beijing government sent Chinese troops to Urga, in contravention of the earlier agreements, claiming that the Russians were not able to maintain order on the Russo-Chinese borders and that Bolshevism represented a threat. General Xu Shuzheng (Little Xu), the defense commissioner for the northwest frontier, established headquarters in Suiyuan, Inner Mongolia, and directed operations in Outer Mongolia, giving every indication of intending to reclaim the region for China.

Outer Mongolia no longer had an external protector, and the Chinese regarded the Kiakhta Agreement as having been imposed on them. Before the end of 1919 Beijing moved decisively. The president—acting on a joint memorial supposedly received from the Outer Mongolian officials, princes, and lamas, and on another memorial from General Xu—canceled Mongolian autonomy. In reality, Xu had troops in the area and had given the Hutukhtu and his government a forty-eight-hour ultimatum in mid-November to request abolition of autonomous status or face the consequences.

The Russian minister in Beijing, still representing the old government, protested these actions, noting that the cancellation of earlier treaties required Russian consent. But at this point neither he nor the Soviet government in Moscow had the means to press their views. More significant, the Japanese showed greatly increased interest in the region. Japanese agents were present in ever greater numbers, and Tokyo insisted that both Mongolia and Manchuria be excluded from the concerns of the new financial consortium that was being established, signaling its desire to see these regions treated as being of "special interest" to Japan. And although Semenov's efforts to create a Pan-Mongolian nation had failed, he himself was still supported by the Japanese, and he had about 2,000 soldiers operating in the borderlands.

By late 1920 conditions in Outer Mongolia were confusing and far from tranquil. Chinese soldiers remained in Urga, and Mongol separatism had been repressed, but various anti-Bolshevik bands operated under Semenov and Baron Ungern-Sternberg, and clashes between them and Chinese forces were taking place. Deserters from various armies roamed the region at will, creating serious problems. The condition of the Russian residents in the region was pitiful, and in general both the economic and the political order were crumbling. Then, in early February 1921, Urga was captured by a mixed band of Cossacks, Tartars, Buryats, and Mongols under Ungern's command. Chinese soldiers were slaughtered along with Jews and suspected Bolsheviks. The Hutukhtu was released from prison and immediately proclaimed himself ruler of an independent Mongolia once again.[45]

In the months that followed, Chinese leaders held several meetings to plan the restoration of Chinese rule in Outer Mongolia, but without result. They lacked the amount of money that Zhang Zuolin insisted was necessary to launch the campaign; and it must be added that Zhang worried about moving Manchurian troops far away from Beijing when the political situation at the capital and elsewhere in China was fluid. The Chita government, now operating under the name of the Far Eastern Republic and clearly affiliated with Moscow, offered to assist in the "liberation" of Urga, but this was rejected. Meanwhile, the Hutukhtu sent a representative to Beijing with a proposal for an agreement similar to the one concluded in 1915, whereby Outer Mongolia would be recognized as a part of China, but no troops of the Chinese central government would be stationed there, and complete autonomy over internal matters would be guaranteed. This proposal also was rejected. Then, just as plans for a Chinese expedition were supposedly set, it was learned that troops of the Far Eastern Republic had routed the forces under Ungern in early June of 1921 and had shortly thereafter occupied Urga. For the first time Bolshevik power was established in a region historically claimed by China, raising profound issues for the future.

In Tibet developments were equally worrisome from a Chinese perspective. For more than three years after the Simla Conference of 1913 the status quo prevailed, and two of the three principal parties were preoccupied with other problems—China with ever graver internal difficulties, and Great Britain with its war effort in Europe. Thus Tibetan authorities in Lhasa governed all of western Tibet and large portions of eastern Tibet without external interference. The Chinese had never accepted such a condition as permanent, however, and in any case the current boundary dividing Chinese and Tibetan jurisdiction remained in dispute. In 1917 serious fighting broke out between the two forces, and the Tibetans scored a series of military successes. They captured Chamdo (Changdu) on the upper Mekong river, pushed the Chinese back with heavy losses, and even threatened Dajianlu.*

The British, who were once again furnishing the Tibetans with some arms, sent Eric Teichman of the China Consular Service to the frontier to negotiate a truce.** Finally, applying pressure to the Tibetans, he got them to retire to Derge (Dege), with the Chinese agreeing not to advance beyond

*Not all victories went to the Tibetans. In the spring of 1917, the brother of the Dalai Lama had started a revolt in western Sichuan, proclaiming himself king. After a series of skirmishes, the Chinese captured him. He was sent to Chengdu for trial and was subsequently executed along with his chief military adviser after they had first been paraded through the streets as a warning to others. (See *NAMP/RDSRIAC*, 893.00/2790, Chongqing, January 18, 1918, Hanson to the Secretary.)

**The British government had embargoed arms to Tibet from India in 1916, and had also prevented the Tibetan government from getting munitions from Japan. When the more or less independent governor of Sichuan, General Peng Risheng, struck out against the Tibetans in 1917, however, the British agreed to furnish some arms, and, at the same time, dispatched Teichman. With the Tibetans scoring military victories, Teichman's efforts were directed at securing a Tibetan withdrawal, and to enforce this, British arms supplies were again shut off. The truce lines ultimately established went roughly along the upper Yangtze River, almost the same frontier as had existed in the Manchu period. (See Richardson, *A Short History of Tibet*, pp. 119–120.)

Ganzi, thereby creating a no-man's-land between the Tibetan border and Chinese-controlled Sichuan. A one-year truce began in October 1918.

When the armistice expired the following October, no changes in the situation had occurred. Belated discussions got under way in the late spring of 1919, but agreement proved impossible. The Tibetans, dealing from strength, insisted that the Chinese had to accept the 1914 Convention. The Beijing government, on the defensive because of the Shandong problem and the May Fourth Movement, refused to make any such concessions and demanded that the British remove themselves from involvement in the negotiations. As of early 1921, an uneasy armistice continued to prevail despite the fact that the truce agreement had lapsed. Chinese administration extended to a portion of eastern Tibet, up to and including Ganzi on the north and Batang on the south. Beyond this, the Lhasa Tibetans held sway, governing the greater portion of Tibet as an independent nation. Even in Chinese-administered frontier areas, official control was tenuous.

Another area of China in which a sizable population of non-Han people lived was eastern Jilin province. This region, fronting on Korea, contained a large number of Koreans, many of whom harbored a deep hatred for the Japanese rulers of their native land. Korean guerrilla groups had been formed, and some had established links with Bolshevik forces in Siberia. To counter these developments and strike against those defined as "outlaws," the Japanese in September 1920 had moved troops into the Jiandao district of Jilin province, where the Korean population was especially heavy. These forces were later withdrawn, but Japanese authorities replaced them with several hundred Japanese police charged with protecting Japanese interests and keeping Korean residents under control. Chinese sovereignty over yet another part of the empire was in jeopardy.

Thus, as the decade of the 1920s got under way, Chinese authority was either challenged or precariously held in the vast borderlands that Beijing had long regarded as vital to the security of inner China and a legitimate part of Greater China. Under different circumstances, the weakening of Russia through revolution might have enabled the central government to reassert its full sovereignty over the northern territories; it might even have been possible for the Chinese to have staked out a claim to Siberian areas incorporated into the Russian empire, for the land and the people there had been regarded by many Chinese as rightfully a part of their domain. But these actions would have required a strong and unified China, capable of enforcing its claims with military power. And so, given the many weaknesses that existed within the nation, it was not China but Japan that filled the vacuum created by the Russian civil war. By the beginning of 1920 Japan had consolidated and advanced its positions in Mongolia and Manchuria and had also implanted itself in Siberia, from which it was not to withdraw fully until 1925.

The confusion that reigned in Russia had enabled China to regain its authority in Outer Mongolia for a brief period, as we have noted, but this could not be sustained. Moreover, Red and White Russian forces (with some of the Whites being supported by the Japanese) continued their sporadic struggles throughout Mongolia and Manchuria, and some of these clashes involved the Chinese. For various White bands these regions served as a sanctuary, hence a potential target for the Reds. Unless the Chinese could win the allegiance of the Mongolians living in the area or summon the military power to oust outsiders and bring the region under their full control, the future of Outer Mongolia was likely to remain uncertain.

Even in China proper, as we have seen, the end of the German enclave at Qingdao and vicinity merely provided an additional opportunity for Japan. Indeed, the signs of Japanese advance were visible at every turn—in the Twenty-One Demands, the increasing financial inroads, the commanding position assumed north of the Great Wall, and the pressures newly applied to Fujian, a province directly across the straits of Taiwan. Thus, even as European imperialism had apparently passed its zenith and was now beginning its slow and uneven decline, China was challenged by Japanese interventionism. Furthermore, in many respects Japan was more formidable, given the diversity of forces that composed its vanguard and the variety of techniques that were brought into play. Geographic and cultural proximity combined to give Japan additional advantages, as did the fact that tens of thousands of Chinese students, including a sizable number of military cadets, had received some higher education in Japan.

The evidence presented thus far should have discredited the thesis that Chinese nationalism was a solid phalanx marching to battle against Japan. Nor was this a simple drama of "traitors," who sold their country to the enemy, versus "noble patriots," who were prepared to block Japanese entrance with their bodies if necessary. Venality, to be sure, was not lacking among various Chinese power-holders; members of the Japanese government and private sector alike found that bribes often smoothed the path to accommodation. Yet one cannot overlook the effect of a considerable network of personal friendships based on school ties, business connections, and political interests. Many prominent Chinese had closer ties to their Japanese friends than to any other foreigners, ties that were strengthened by shared cultural legacies.

As we have emphasized, the primary concerns of Chinese leadership were conducive to Sino-Japanese interaction. If one were dedicated to reform and modernization (and most Chinese leaders of this era accepted these goals), what nation was a better model for China than Japan? Conservatives found much to admire in a society that had retained many of its traditions despite its commitment to rapid changes; progressives admired Japanese successes in establishing an effective, modern state based on rapid economic growth. What people had shown more convincingly that it was possible to preserve one's cultural identity while engaging in massive borrowing from the advanced West and promoting dramatic change? Many Chinese military men hoped to pattern their armies after the efficiently trained and disciplined Japanese military forces. Finally, the Japanese political and economic elite always exhibited an intense interest in China, at a time when Western leaders were often indifferent or preoccupied with other matters. As we have seen, Japanese resources—financial, technological, and human—were offered when those of other nations were withheld.

It is not surprising, therefore, that a significant number of Chinese in positions of authority—civil and military, government and opposition, conservative and revolutionary—hoped and worked for some pattern of Japanese assistance that would answer China's needs as they saw them. In sum, Chinese attitudes toward Japan were not simple but complex, a mixture of desire and suspicion, admiration and resentment, friendship and hostility.

Japan had an extraordinary opportunity at this point to tilt national sentiments in a favorable direction and to establish a harmonious and mutually advantageous relationship. Or so it appeared in abstract logic. The problem lay in the developmental differences between the two societies, and in the psychological and political behavioral traits that governed them. There could be no equality in relations between a Japan that was dynamic, increasingly confident, and militarily powerful, and a China that was confused, chaotic, weak, and increasingly bitter. Nor was equality in relationships a part of the cultural heritage of either society; the dominant party was likely to exhibit the traits of the superior. Many decades would pass before upheavals in both societies made possible a less threatening interaction.

THE FORMIDABLE CHALLENGES

As China entered the 1920s there seemed little reason for optimism. The old political structure was irrevocably lost: every attempt to resurrect it had failed. Yet since 1911 all efforts to build a new political system had also failed. The attempted transplant of Western-style parliamentary democracy into the Chinese body politic had been rejected. In this period, representative government based on doctrines of liberalism was the only model accepted by those who were committed to modernizing China. Yet the political culture and socioeconomic conditions of China did not fit that model. Western-style democracy, after all, was the most fragile political system yet devised by man. To be even minimally effective, it required special conditions of culture and development—conditions not present in much of the West itself, and scarcely at all in China.

Thus the quest for an appropriate political structure was destined to continue for decades. At a later point, variants of the old order would be reintroduced: a personalized authority and symbol of unity in the form of a supreme leader, an emperor in fact if not in law; an ideologically motivated and supremely powerful bureaucracy, which could often thwart the wishes of the supreme leader himself; and a new centralization, though one that bowed reluctantly to the considerable measure of autonomy that was inevitable in this vast, heterogeneous society.

Indeed, the resurgence of authoritarian rule backed by military power, a system with ample precedent in Chinese history, began shortly after the Revolution of 1911. Yet circumstances conspired to render the center weak, especially after the demise of Yuan Shikai. No effective substitute for the emperor as supreme source of authority was found. The attempt to legitimate a new governing elite through competitive elections rather than through examinations and imperial investiture failed, partly because the electoral process was tainted, but primarily because such a system was, at the least, premature for China, as the various advocates of political tutelage had repeatedly insisted. Possibly, it would never be appropriate. In the course of this experiment, legitimacy and power became increasingly separated. Although an effort was being made to relate legitimacy to constitutionalism and to the legal rights and obligations flowing from it, power gravitated naturally toward those with the guns. The rise of military men to the apex of power, where they stood as supreme arbiters of political events, was the most striking departure from the preceding era.

Had China been the size of France or Germany, one of the new military leaders might well have been able to consolidate his power and thus provide a period of law and order that permitted economic growth. As it was, the aggregation of power could not advance beyond a certain point, given the cultural diversities, economic weaknesses, and available mobilization techniques. Thus, in these years China became not so much a diverse nation as a loose federation of states. In addition to the overall North-South cleavage, a series of de facto states emerged, particularly in the central and southern regions. The separate or quasi-separate political orders sustained traditional and partly autarchic economic orders, which slowed the momentum for further unification. On the other hand, in the absence of sustained or full sovereignty for such "states," neither the political nor the economic instruments for development were available. Yet, as we have seen, provincial or "state" nationalism vied with Chinese nationalism in seeking to attract the loyalties of the articulate citizenry.

In this setting, power was generally maintained by "mixed" military-civilian coalitions. Politics always rests on coalitions, and a country's political structure and socioeconomic foundations determine what is required to make a coalition successful. In the case of China after 1911, the civilian elite—whether of the scholar-literati, gentry, merchant-entrepreneur, or "revolutionary" type—had to coalesce with those who could enforce their authority by military means. Some strange alliances resulted, as we have seen, but all observed this fundamental necessity. The most powerful alliances, however, had to be based on coalitions among the military leaders themselves, because only in this manner could power be aggregated as existing territorial holdings were combined. In almost all cases, moreover, the military held the dominant position within mixed coalitions.

It would be incorrect to assume that these coalitions were based solely upon considerations of personal power. The code governing patron-client relations remained as important as ever in Chinese history. Loyalty and obligation were often taken seriously, even when the hazards of supporting a given individual were recognized. The other side of the coin, of course, was the frequent resort to that innate pragmatism or opportunism that dictates the abandonment of a sinking ship. Ideological or policy affinities also played a role in supporting certain coalitions. Despite the bewildering shifts in alliances that made many observers cynical, genuine and deeply held beliefs did exist among various political and military leaders.

Whatever their basis, however, the coalitions formed during this era were invariably short-lived. Fundamentally, the problem was structural. The new system, involving a weak center and quasi-autonomous regional government, loosely federated through coalitions of varying duration, was inherently unstable. Jurisdictions were repeatedly challenged, not merely by the center but by rival regional and local coalitions. This was possible because the center itself was too weak to exercise its authority over the realm known as China, and aggregation of power at the regional level was also inhibited by economic, cultural, and political barriers. Even provincial authority declined in the face of local challenges. Without a meaningful political structure in which to encase power, and without the strong economic foundations needed to support power, truly national coalitions could not be built, and local and regional coalitions repeatedly fell apart.

As we have indicated, the international environment contributed to these difficulties, although on balance, foreign intrusions—particularly from Japan—offered the possibility of creating a powerful new nationalism that could surmount the various barriers to internal unification. Indeed, as the era closed, it seemed clear that Han nationalism was the only possible force conducive to greater unity. On matters of ideology and policy, the divisions were growing deeper.

Meanwhile, the Chinese empire remained in jeopardy, as was always the case when the central government was weak. Even parts of China below the Great Wall were threatened. If World War I had provided a certain relief from European pressures, it had also opened up new opportunities for China's dynamic island neighbor to the east. And another new force flying internationalist banners, but already exhibiting nationalist traits, was emerging to the north and the west. Chinese idealists were bitterly disappointed in the outcome of the Versailles Peace Treaty. They had hoped that, somehow, the major powers, and particularly the United States, would solve the imperialist problem for them. Realists knew that the results at Versailles bore a direct relation to Beijing's past concessions and current weaknesses.

Unrest was bubbling up in many parts of the country. Unpaid soldiers were looting and living off the land, and would occasionally mutiny against officials who had swindled them. Many of these soldiers, incidentally, had been recruited from the ranks of the unemployed, in both rural and urban areas. Farmers from drought-stricken regions migrated to the nearest places that might offer some possibility of food and shelter; the alternative, quite often, was death through starvation or disease. Such migrations, together with the sustained growth in population, added to all other social tensions. Students, aroused by Japanese pressures, used boycotts and demonstrations in an effort to rally other urban dwellers, including the merchant and professional classes, to the nationalist cause. Taking advantage of the situation, various minorities—from the Mongols in the north to the Uighurs and Hui in the west and the Tibetans in the southwest—sought independence from Han rule.

It was in this context that a new movement first made its appearance in China, a movement derived from the Russian Revolution. It was also in this context that the old revolutionaries, still led by Sun Yat-sen, began to reexamine their organizational structure and their political tactics.

9

LIBERALISM, SOCIALISM, AND THE INTELLIGENTSIA—RESPONSES ACROSS THE SPECTRUM

In the decade that followed the 1911 Revolution, political activity among the Chinese intelligentsia reached new heights. In assessing the effect of this activity, one must first take account of certain sociological factors unique to Chinese society. In premodern China, the intellectual had enjoyed extraordinarily high status, for he combined the roles of power-holder in the state bureaucracy and conservator of China's great cultural legacy. Nor did these roles disappear as China's political landscape changed. As we have seen, most cabinets after 1911 contained many men who possessed both a classical education and some overseas training. The "new intellectual" remained the keeper of the old as well as the bearer of the new. Skill in calligraphy, poetry, painting, and knowledge of the great Chinese literary classics remained the mark of the educated man. Even the great majority of those who went farthest in attacking Confucianism and urging the use of the vernacular language remained within the intellectual traditions of their society. For the few like Sun Yat-sen whose background lay largely outside those traditions, the struggle for acceptability among China's mainstream intelligentsia was arduous and never completely won.

Like all intellectuals in the premodern world, the educated man in China was a generalist. He was not uncomfortable in traversing many fields—indeed, to do less was to be incomplete—and therein lay his capacity for political theorizing. Being a generalist, he did not hesitate to tackle cosmic issues, and he addressed the widest range of socioeconomic and political concerns. Political activism is usually not the meat of the specialist—unless in the quest for emotional fulfillment he sets his specialty aside and enters the political arena as an ardent amateur. But the issue of political involvement was not posed in these terms to the Chinese intellectual during the opening decades of this century. He had no fear of grappling with the widest range of public concerns.

By the same token, the nature of Chinese intellectualism made for a certain porousness within the class structure: anyone with higher education could aspire to partake of intellectual pursuits. The image of the "warlord" as an uncouth barbarian is largely inaccurate. There were such individuals, but most members of the military elite who rose to political power in the late Qing and early republican years had great respect for learning. Among them were students of literature and men who spent their leisure hours composing poems or perfecting their calligraphy.

When, in addition to exhibiting traditional reverence for learning, military rulers acknowledged the need to acquire science and technology to make China prosperous and powerful, they had good reasons to cultivate intellectuals. Many paid close attention to the views of conservative and moderate literati like Kang Youwei and Liang Qichao, and in the chaotic decade after 1911 even a number of "socialists" received a respectful hearing from men like Yuan Shikai, Li Yuanhong, and Wu Peifu, as well as from more sympathetic types such as Chen Jiongming. To be sure, the relationship between the military and the intelligentsia in modern China was always fragile and subject to rapid change. Jealousy, suspicion, arrogance, and feelings of inferiority were omnipresent; receptivity was often followed by repression. And when the military and the intellectual—or at least the aspiring intellectual—were combined in one man, as in the case of Mao Zedong, inner contradictions were certain to abound.

The interplay between openness and repression was well exemplified in the years after the 1911 Revolution. The advent of republicanism ushered in a brief period of extensive freedom for the expression of political ideas and the creation of political organizations. Naturally, this freedom was greater in the South, the stronghold of the revolutionaries. After the compromise with Yuan, however, even in the North political advocacy was permitted in ways never previously tolerated. Concepts once confined to journals smuggled in from abroad were now openly discussed in newspapers and journals, and ideas that returned students once shared only with intimates were now advocated in public meetings.

Canton and Shanghai, cosmopolitan coastal cities which had long felt the impact of Westernism, were logical centers for such free expression. But Nanjing, Wuhan, and Changsha had their share of returned students and other representatives of the new China, so the full range of political ideas from the external world was flowing into urban centers in the interior. As organizational efforts got under way in progressive circles, many parties and groups established their own organs. With few exceptions, these publications were short-lived and catered to a small circle of the converted, or those highly susceptible to conversion. A few journals of national status, however, circulated widely within intellectual circles and began to interest themselves in such concepts as liberalism and socialism. One such journal was *Dongfang zazhi* (Eastern Miscellany), which had already been operating for a number of years. Even before the events of 1911, it had published articles setting forth the essentials of Japanese and Western political institutions and values, most of them expressing a bias in favor of constitutional government and the primacy of law.[1] In these articles certain Western sources were cited, but the dependence upon Japanese writings remained high, particularly in materials relating to socialism. Thus, in mid-1912 a translation of excerpts from Kōtoku Shūsui's *Shakaishugi shinzui* (The Quintessence of Socialism) was published over several issues.[2] This work, it should be noted, first appeared in Japan in 1903, before Kōtoku's conversion from democratic socialism to anarchism, and offered a broad exposition of basic socialist doctrines.*

In the same period, *Dongfang zazhi* also published an interesting essay simply entitled "Socialism," in which the anonymous author described the evolution of modern socialism and set forth the basic distinctions between socialism, communism, and anarchism.[3] The author's exposition was clear and concise, and showed an acquaintance with a wide range of Western theorists. One of his significant theses was that only with Marx did socialism become scientific and systematic, and he presented a brief explanation of the Marxist theory of surplus value, together with its implications for concepts of ownership. Marx and a number of others were categorized as belonging to the more "extreme" branch of socialism. They were described by the author as adherents to "republican socialism," presumably to distinguish them from the Bismarckians, who advocated national socialism or "social reformism," doctrines "supporting state intervention on behalf of the poor to challenge capitalist monopoly." In essence, he argued, state socialists would nationalize segments of the economy that were susceptible to monopolization, and would sponsor factory laws and legislation to protect women and children. He also noted the existence of "Christian socialism," which, although it is "beautifully phrased" and "appeals to our conscience," does not satisfy economists.

In delineating the basic differences between socialism and communism, the author said that whereas socialism nationalizes only the instruments of production, communism seeks to nationalize the product as well. Under the communist system, government becomes one large family or clan, with the governors serving as father, and the people as sons. Socialism seeks to eliminate class distinctions based on wealth. Anarchism wants to do the same thing, but also wants to eradicate the differences between officials and the people; it aims at uprooting the state, law, and religion, so that everyone can operate on the basis of free will, without any external controls. In essence, socialism emphasizes the omnipotence of the state, whereas anarchism emphasizes the omnipotence of the individual. Socialism intervenes, anarchism indulges. The spirit of socialism lies in absolutism, and the spirit of anarchism lies in freedom. One is the enemy and the other the friend of individualism.[4] The author's sympathies would seem to lie with anarchism, although he stated no preference specifically.

Another journal that disseminated information about socialism, and was closely connected with the republican movement, was *Minli bao* (People's Independence), edited by Yu Youren. From its first issue on October 11, 1910, one year before the Wuhan uprising, it carried stories on political trends around the world and gave special attention to international socialist activities, particularly in Japan.** At this point, Japanese socialism was in

*As F. G. Notehelfer points out, this work remained the most important Japanese exposition of socialism prior to World War I. Although Kōtoku cited Marx and Engels, he had not yet read their works, and his inspiration came primarily from three lesser socialist figures, Albert E. Schaffle, Richard T. Ely, and Thomas Kirkup—all individuals whose writings had been introduced to Asian socialists through Japanese translations. (For an excellent discussion of Kōtoku's work, see Notehelfer, *Kōtoku Shūsui*, pp. 76ff.)

**The opening issue of *Minli bao* carried an account of the eighth meeting of the World Socialist Congress in Copenhagen beginning on August 28, 1910 (October 11, 1910, p. 3).

trauma. Kōtoku and other anarchists were being tried for high treason, having been charged with plotting to assassinate the emperor Meiji. Kōtoku was executed on January 24, 1911, and a period of severe repression for all socialists in Japan began. Although *Minli bao* carried a brief biography of Kōtoku and published a list of socialist books proscribed by the Japanese government, it was not proanarchist, but leaned toward national socialism, since its editor was affiliated with Sun and the Guomindang.

Minli bao also paid close attention to the "negative lesson" of Korea and developments in Russia, always an intriguing subject to the activist segment of the young Chinese intelligentsia. In one essay, the subjugation of Korea was attributed not to Japan's superior military power but to its deeper understanding of the global situation. To survive and to protect the existence of one's own country, it was written, one had to be in some respects a citizen of the world.[5] In this same essay, harsh words were employed in evaluating the policies of the Russian government, it being alleged that they were based largely on military force; the Russians, the writer remarked, have a great desire to invade other countries.[6] But, he continued, a change lay ahead: within five years the Russian Socialist Party would be able to eliminate the present government and would have power to spare—a comment that proved prescient indeed.*

Most definitions of socialism carried in *Minli bao* were simple and moralistic, related to the values of equality, concern for others, and avoidance of class divisions.[7] When they observed the West, *Minli bao* writers tended to be pessimistic about relations between capital and labor, at least as seen from the workingman's standpoint: most strikes, they argued, failed not only because of governmental repression but because the workers would starve if they remained out of work, whereas capitalists were affected very little. Yet when writing about such subjects, they saw no relevance to current Chinese conditions. Since China was precapitalist, socialism was necessary only as a prophylactic, not as a cure. In Europe, however, where the situation was already desperate, socialism was the wave of the future.**

The Chinese writings on socialism during these years suggest several conclusions. First, an understanding of Western-style socialism had developed which was on a somewhat more mature level than what could be observed in the earlier student journals, although all the essays were basically derivative, with Japanese writers serving as the primary transmission belt for Western works. Second, Marx was now widely acknowledged to be a leader of "scientific socialism," but he was not singled out as the one supreme figure, and there was some confusion about whether he belonged to the "extrem-

*On October 21, a *Minli bao* reader responded to the editorial with a short essay entitled "The Socialist Party and Russia," the main thesis of which was that socialist-inspired antiwar propaganda had contributed mightily to Russia's defeat in the war against Japan, a fact recounted in a work by a Russian general. Propaganda had rendered the people indifferent to the war and the soldiers lacking in the will to fight. The Socialists had wanted Russia defeated, seeing this as a means of greatly advancing their cause.

**Quoting a foreign journal, *Minli bao* announced that of a total population of 300 million, Europe had 8 million adherents to socialism, with no less than 3 million of them "pure socialists." Although these 3 million were unable to control affairs, their power was not insignificant. Prospects for socialism were less promising in the United States, it reported, since capitalism there had not matured sufficiently, and ethnic-racial divisions made labor solidarity difficult. In Great Britain also, while industrialization was far advanced, "a conservative temperament" retarded socialist growth (December 14, 1919, p. 1).

ists" or the "moderates." Finally, the influence of anarchism was strong, presaging a series of battles in the period immediately ahead.

JIANG KANGHU AND THE CHINESE SOCIALIST PARTY

Intellectual involvement in the socialist cause was not limited to publications. In a new revolutionary atmosphere, political organizations sprouted quickly. The most rapidly developing socialist movement within China at this time was the Chinese Socialist Party under the leadership of Jiang Kanghu. Jiang, like many fellow radicals of this era, was born into a landed, affluent family of Jiangxi province, some of whose members had achieved official positions.[8] His early education was of the classical type, but immediately after the Boxer uprising in 1900, when he was only seventeen, he went to Japan to study. In the following year he returned to China, having been requested by Yuan—then governor-general of Zhili—to head the Beiyang Editing and Translation Bureau (Beiyang Bienyiju), which was charged with preparing primary and secondary texts for the five northern provinces. Later he served as secretary to the Board of Justice, and in 1904 he became a teacher of Japanese at Jingshi Daxuetang (Capital Teachers' College). Aided by Yuan and others, Jiang also established four women's schools in Beijing during this period, primarily for teacher-training purposes.

Jiang returned to Japan in 1907, and it was during this period that he made acquaintance with Japanese socialists, Kōtoku included. In 1909, during a trip to Europe, he visited the headquarters of the Second International in Brussels and came into close contact with two young Chinese anarchists in Paris, Wu Zhihui and Li Shizeng. Writing under a pen name, Jiang produced several articles for *Xin shiji* (New Century) attacking marriage and the family.

When Jiang returned to China after the death of his father, on December 5, 1910, he was a self-professed socialist, but he found it difficult to identify himself with a single branch of the movement. On the one hand, he had been deeply influenced by anarchist thought, and that influence was to remain. On the other hand, he also claimed to be a disciple of Henry George. Shortly after his return to China, with the aid of a Canadian missionary, he sought to convince the governor of Jiangsu, a friend of the Jiang family, that if he were permitted to set up an experiment, he could test Georgist theories.

By the summer of 1911 Jiang had become the first individual inside China to write and speak openly about socialism, and an episode at Hangzhou brought him considerable fame. In the text of a speech he wrote for delivery at several girls' schools, he commented on both women's rights and socialism, and when the text was circulated in advance to certain parties, it aroused a storm of controversy. It was demanded that some passages be altered or removed, and it would appear that Jiang actually did not deliver the speech, scheduled for June 1. Very shortly thereafter, however, it was published in *Minli bao.**

In extraordinarily bold language, Jiang lashed out at a system that bound women to the family and the home, preventing all but a few from becoming

*The address was published in several issues of *Minli bao*, beginning on June 5 and running to June 12, 1911 (p. 1). At an earlier point, during his second trip to Japan in 1907, Jiang had remained aloof from the Tongmeng Hui, and claimed to have advanced three "anti principles" in juxtaposition to Sun's three principles. These were antistate, antifamily, and antireligion—pure anarchist themes.

scholars or entrepreneurs. The best time for women to study, he said, was before marriage, and for this reason socialists had recently proposed free love and coeducational schooling. Even after marriage, he continued, when the children had reached the appropriate age, they should be sent to school so that the mother could continue her studies and the children could learn independence. Only through freedom from the "three obediences" could a woman become a complete individual.

Here Jiang was striking at the most sacred element of Chinese traditionalism. He argued that the strong dependence of children on their parents—and for girls, their absolute dependence, including arranged marriages—bred slothfulness in youth and at the same time made parents the slaves of their offspring. The wife's dependence on the husband had extremely unhealthy consequences, making the woman's role akin to that of a prostitute; and the dependence of the older woman on her son perpetuated a subordinate relationship. Taking care of the old as well as the young should be the responsibility of the state. The key to freedom for women, he concluded, was to equip them to obtain and hold a position.

In addition to these amazingly modern remarks (and one can imagine the shock they produced among the conservative gentry), Jiang spoke of the future of society in broader terms, further revealing the strong anarchist currents beneath his ideas. In the West, he remarked, technological innovation and functional differentiation had led to reductions in work load and very large, essentially self-contained factories. In the future, there would be no government, as well as no family—only syndicates composed of work groups. Already, certain large Western factories operated as if they were independent countries. Here he was expressing anarcho-syndicalist concepts in their purest form.

Jiang did not rest with speeches alone. Focusing his organizational efforts on Shanghai, where both recruits and security were most promising, he convened a meeting of what he called the Socialist Study Society on July 10, 1911. Some two hundred people attended, Jiang and several others gave short speeches, and a publication entitled the *Shehuizhuyi mingxing bao* (Star of Socialism) was launched. Continuing his public lectures, Jiang advanced the thesis that China needed a system of social education that would combat selfishness, militarism, and nationalism. Again, his anarchist bent was prominently displayed.

On November 7, just three days after Shanghai fell to the revolutionaries, Jiang, under the aegis of the Socialist Study Society, announced the organization of the Chinese Socialist Party (CSP) and set forth an eight-point program. Despite his earlier pronouncements, the program was a curious amalgam of republican, Georgist, and socialist principles. Republicanism, the integration of the races, and respect for the individual under law were combined with proposals for returning inheritances to the state, the strengthening of industries and greater rewards for labor, the expansion of public education, the abolition of all taxes except the land tax, and arms limitations.*

* For the program, see *Minli bao*, November 8, 1911, p. 3. The December 1 issue carried an advertisement saying that Chinese Socialist Party headquarters was ready to receive members, with applicants to call on Sundays, 10 A.M. to 12 noon. Regular meetings were to be held on the first Sunday of every month, colloquia to be held on the second and fourth Sundays. Members were required to sign an oath of support and also to pay monthly dues, which undoubtedly accounted for the fact that many more people attended meetings than were party members.

In a sense, the new party had something for everyone of a liberal or radical bent, and it is not surprising that it attracted a heterogeneous membership.

The Chinese Socialist Party's approach to economic equalization was an application of Henry George's principles, rather substantially modified. First, by passing inheritances to the state, land ownership would be removed from private hands within one generation, presumably to become state rental property. (Later on, this provision was greatly watered down when Jiang indicated that the donation of one's possessions would be voluntary, at least initially.) Second, by eliminating all taxes except the land tax, revenues would be provided immediately from a single source, as George advocated. In this case, the proposal was to conduct a yearly appraisal of property, with the tax assessed at one-twentieth of its declared value.*

Always keen on educational activities, Jiang encouraged the party to establish schools, and he justified this by arguing that the purpose of the Socialist Party was not to enter politics and seek governmental power but to make fundamental alterations in Chinese society. In this, one can discern the effort to attract the anarchists, who were antigovernment and antiparty, as well as socialists of various types who wanted basic social changes. By mid-December 1911 Jiang reported that classes had started in a Commoners School in Nanjing, with 5,000 people attending. It was also reported that party membership exceeded 200 after two months, and that many persons outside Shanghai were writing to discuss the possibility of establishing branches.

During this period Jiang further elucidated the plank regarding inheritances. He proposed the creation of a vanguard group that would exemplify socialist principles by agreeing that upon their death their property would belong to the Socialist Party, and in exchange the party would be responsible for the education of their children.

On New Year's Day, 1912, Jiang and Sun Yat-sen met to discuss their respective positions and the prospects for the Chinese Socialist Party. Jiang reportedly told Sun that he had accepted equalization of land as one of the party's basic principles. Sun answered, "I am a full socialist, and land equalization is only the first step—there are many other policies that are necessary, and I need to discuss this with your party."**

By early 1912 the Chinese Socialist Party was growing with amazing speed. A party branch was formally organized in Nanjing—the capital of the

* For a contemporary Chinese Marxist critique of the party program, see Xia Liangzai, "A Preliminary Discussion of the Chinese Socialist Party During the Early Republic Years." Xia criticizes the economic aspects of the party program as falling short of "scientific socialism," since these did not deal with the issue of ownership of the means of production and regarded property as the "most basic requirement" of a social revolution. Such a notion, asserts Xia, was derived from a combination of anarchism and Saint-Simonism, with the addition of "the American capitalist economist, Henry George." Xia then proceeds to quote Marx and Lenin on George. Georgian ideas, said Marx, were "the last attempt to rescue capitalism," and Lenin added, "It was a product of the capitalist era, and basically counterrevolutionary." Despite this critique of Henry George, Xia seeks to protect Sun to some extent, noting that Sun's espousal of Georgism earlier was considered "quite advanced for the times," since it could clear the way for capitalism. Jiang's concepts, however, "were aimed at improving and preserving the semicolonial and semifeudalist status quo."

** Sun also told Jiang that on his latest trip to the West he had purchased a number of the most recent books on socialism, and he hoped that they could be translated by some party members who understood socialist doctrines, so that they would be available for propaganda work.

Republic—on January 6, with 1,700 persons present. Three days later, 500 members and an additional 1,000 persons attended a meeting, and it was announced that a party organ, *Ren bao* (People's News), would be published beginning in February. A massive welcome for Wu Zhihui, just returned after many years in Paris and still an ardent anarchist, was one of the main events of the new year.

In his speech at the founding of the Nanjing branch, Jiang confined himself to broad moralisms to which few could take exception, carefully avoiding the thorny issues that divided socialists and anarchists.[9] The religiously inclined, he said, felt that people could reach a true, beautiful, and benevolent life only after death; socialists believed that it was possible during one's lifetime. Moreover, socialism for China was feasible because socialist values were compatible not only with heritage and culture but also with the current revolution, and were respected by its leader, Sun Yat-sen. Sun could not play an active role in the party, Jiang reported, because he had to represent all Chinese, but through its activities the Socialist Party could shape public opinion, thereby strengthening the cause. Only through socialism could the republican goals of liberty, equality, and fraternity be realized.

In the days and weeks that followed, CSP branches were set up in Changsha, Suzhou, and various other cities. It was reported that some 3,000 persons attended one meeting in Yangzhou, and an advertisement in *Minli bao* at the end of January announced that after only three months the party had more than thirty branches and some 5,000 members.*

Letters to the *Minli bao* editor made it clear that not all readers were convinced of the validity of the socialists' arguments. Although socialism might be necessary in the West because of the wide gap there between rich and poor, one correspondent wrote, what applicability did it have in China, where the people in general were poor, commerce and industry were weak, and no trust existed between individuals, so that there was no basis for accepting public ownership?[10]

In an interesting response to this letter, the editor revealed his own political predilections. Although he favored socialism, he could not approve of the principles of the Chinese Socialist Party. Equality in education, for example, was not feasible, because teachers could not help the stupid become intelligent. Moreover, the son of a barbarian in the mountains could have no education at all, so how could one speak of educational equality in such a case? Any effort to carry out that program would merely result in a leveling process, reducing the more intelligent to mediocrity.[11] (This was a debate, as we now know, that would persist in socialist China, with one major climax coming during the Great Proletarian Cultural Revolution.)

As for the nationalization of property, the editor wrote, there were two factions within socialism, the anarchists and the communists. The anarchists wanted to destroy the current system, to eliminate human bondage and return to nature. This was a negative form of socialism. The commu-

* The eclectic quality of the Chinese Socialist Party is illustrated by a vignette published in the March 7, 1912, *Minli bao* regarding a meeting of the Haian party branch. At five o'clock, just as the meeting was adjourning, one Zui Xuhe happened to pass by, and was persuaded by a friend to join the organization; the article went on to identify Zui as one of the "big capitalists" of the area. In Chengdu, Sichuan, a branch of the famed secret society Gelao Hui (Elder Brother Society), having been ordered disbanded, transformed itself into a Chinese Socialist Party unit (*Minli bao*, March 31, 1912, p. 2).

nists wanted to destroy the system of private property so that all would belong to society in common; but within their group there were broad and narrow types. The narrow faction recognized no difference between mental and physical labor and would distribute everything equally. The broad type would allocate goods or money in accordance with one's contribution. Neither anarchism nor narrow communism was suitable to China, but socialism of a broad type had possibilities.

The editor, however, took his stand with social reform or national socialism. Any revolution that created a great upheaval, he argued, would result in decades of instability and was to be avoided. The basic need was for a program encompassing nationalization of forests, mines, and railroads, a system of progressive taxation, and provisions for equal inheritance. Such policies would prevent the emergence of a wealthy class. On the positive side, the creation of a rural credit system, governmental assistance to medium-sized businesses, broadened educational opportunities, and factory legislation to protect workers were necessary. Then came a familiar theme: it would be easier to implement such measures in China than in the United States or Europe, where rigid class barriers already existed. He concluded with the remark that although communism might be the best doctrine in principle, it was totally impractical.*

As socialists of various persuasions debated among themselves, the movement faced a challenge from several provincial governments. Suppression was first threatened, curiously enough, in Hunan, where the governor, Tan Yankai, a Guomindang supporter, ordered party activities halted.** Later, in mid-1912, the governor of Hubei also demanded disbandment of the party, accepting criticisms of party activities from the local military command. To check such threats, Jiang made a trip in Beijing in July 1912, hoping to see Yuan Shikai and win his support. In a letter to Yuan, published on July 30, Jiang outlined his views of socialism in a manner calculated to appeal to the president. He recalled that Yuan had earlier helped him create the girls' schools in Beijing, and expressed the hope that he would look on his new endeavor with favor. Equality in education and inheritance, Jiang wrote, was entirely consistent with China's heritage, being implicit in the ancient well-field system. The Chinese Socialist Party, he added, was not a political party. It did not seek to interfere with government or demean the national leadership. Rather, it was a movement aimed at reforming society. At a time when there were no large landowners or capitalists in the nation, Jiang continued, the party could lead the struggle to reward labor properly, to promote business and thereby cure the laziness that infected the nation. He closed by

*The next day, the editor noted that since the Chinese Socialist Party favored only the nationalization of inherited properties, his criticisms were not directed at them on this score (*Minli bao*, March 31, 1912, p. 2).

***Minli bao*, June 10, 1912, p. 8. In a letter addressed to Governor Tan, a Socialist Party representative protested the closure of the party branch and school vigorously, pointing out that President Sun had gone "all over the nation advocating socialism." The suspension thus signified that President Sun was the original criminal, he added (June 13, 1912, p. 8). Later, it was admitted that the facts were complicated. The military and certain local individuals had "misunderstood" the party program, but also some party members had been swindlers, taking money for personal use. Tan apologized after consultations, saying the arrests were committed by ignorant soldiers, and it was he who had ordered the five party representatives moved to the provincial court from military jurisdiction. Earlier, their execution had been threatened. They were subsequently released.

noting that former President Sun and Premier Tang both approved of the endeavor, and that although some people were prejudiced and had deliberately distorted the movement's position, "You are so intelligent and wise that I hope you can sympathize with us." *

By coincidence, the party soon ran into difficulties with the center. In August the Ministry of Interior issued an order denying the request of a party branch for registration as a legal party, on the grounds that one of the planks in its platform violated the constitutional provision that people had the right to own property. The party's plan to make inheritances revert to the state ran counter to the private property system, the order asserted, and this would undermine society and damage the national heritage.[12] Jiang had been unaware of the action taken by this branch, and he recognized that any request for legalization as a political party would cause trouble with the anarchist faction. Consequently, in his protest to the ministry, he vigorously denied that legal authorization had been sought, although he admitted that the party now had many branches and no less than 100,000 members. To the charge that the party program violated the national constitution, he replied that the provision relating to inheritance had not been carried out, and that if it were put into effect, it would be done on a voluntary basis.

This episode ended favorably for the party, although it planted the seeds of a party split that would soon take place. The minister of the interior had a talk with Jiang, and afterwards the negative evaluation of the party which accompanied the order denying registration was rescinded. En route home from Beijing in August, however, Jiang was arrested and jailed in Hankou. After vigorous protests from various quarters he was released, and Vice-President Li Yuanhong apologized, but the incident illustrated the precarious status of the movement.

The party's real problems, however, were now internal. The controversy over registration brought anarchist-socialist differences to the surface. Any steps in the direction of transforming the Chinese Socialist Party into a party seeking political office, operating within the parliamentary arena, were in flagrant violation of anarchist precepts. On October 25 a conference to commemorate the founding of the party was held. It was announced that some four hundred branches were now in operation, with approximately 200,000 members. The strength of the anarchists was indicated by the fact that a resolution was passed at this meeting to the effect that the party advocated "pure socialism" *within the bounds of the law.* ** Efforts to compromise by uniting anarchism with legal activities did not suffice, however, and immediately thereafter the anarchists split off to form a separate group called simply the Socialist Party. In their solicitation of members, they announced that

* "A Letter to President Yuan from Jiang Kanghu," *Minli bao,* July 30, 1912, p. 8. It should be noted that Yuan had once expressed agreement with George's single-tax concept and promised to carry it out.

** Fifty-eight to sixty-one delegates attended at various times, with Jiang serving as chairman. Among the other resolutions to be sent to the national parliament were those concerned with the removal of restrictions on suffrage; general and equal education for boys and girls; a single tax on land; a heavy inheritance tax; abolition of the death penalty; armaments limitations; protective labor legislation; abolition of concubinage; and limits on prostitution. As can be seen, most of these proposals had a socialist instead of an anarchist thrust, despite the statement supporting "pure socialism." It was also agreed to join the Second International and to translate party regulations into Esperanto and forward them to all foreign socialist parties. (See "Report on the 2nd Joint Meeting," *Minli bao,* October 30, 1912, p. 8.)

the Chinese Socialist Party was "neither horse nor ass," and urged those who had been "fooled or confused" by that party to join a group subscribing to "pure socialism."*

Jiang was now forced to acknowledge that both anarchists and national socialists were bolting his party, but he defended his position with vigor. Our party, he asserted, is not prepared to seek the destruction of government, as the anarchists are, but neither is it prepared to make the state the primary base for socialism, as are the national socialists. Socialism should be rooted in the individual, at one end, and related to the world in its widest dimensions, at the other. As he advanced his position, however, Jiang appeared to be making an uneasy compromise between anarchist and state socialist themes. The party is prepared to work within the system, he asserted, and is ready to compromise in order to achieve concrete results (and to avoid suppression). Law has its defects as the ultimate source of harmony in politics, but so long as the state exists, law is inevitable. Ideally, taxes and duties of all types should be abolished, but since governmental finances require them, the party favors concentrating on a single tax, the land tax. Ideally, armaments should be totally eliminated, but in practice all the party can do is make its position on this issue clear, and since there are basic disagreements, it can only advocate arms limitation. The party, Jiang argued, takes no position that challenges the existence of the state.[13]

In November 1912, in an effort to bring about more cohesion, Jiang issued a lengthy statement spelling out the commitments and obligations of CSP members.[14] Like Sun later, Jiang sought to remedy internal divisions with a measure of authoritarianism and tighter discipline. He insisted that the program set forth by the party had attracted a huge membership and that every member had an obligation to obey the party platform faithfully. Regulations could be changed, but to criticize basic principles was to declare war on oneself and one's fellow members. Since the party was a unit, moreover, the minority had to obey the majority, and everyone had the obligation to report occurrences affecting party welfare to the appropriate officers. Recalcitrant members were to be ousted if necessary.

Propaganda, Jiang argued, was vital. Since the party's immediate goal was not to seize executive or legislative power but rather to influence and change Chinese society, massive educational and propaganda efforts would be required.

Socialism, Jiang continued, was based on the principle of collective leadership, and the Chinese Socialist Party was still in an experimental stage.

*For the new party's announcement and program, see *Minli bao*, November 12, 1912, p. 12. Its pledge was to wipe out classes, abolishing poverty and riches ("carrying out communism"), nobility and slavery ("respecting the individual"), and intelligence and ignorance ("equal education"). It also called for the abolition of nation, family, and religion, thereby removing the bonds of territory, relatives, and superstition. Finally, it proposed three types of activities: *advocating* (propagandizing in magazines, books, and newspapers); *destroying* (eliminating power-holders and preparing for world revolution); and *constructing* (nurseries, schools, hospitals, parks, and homes for the poor). Rules for members included not holding political office or joining political parties; not being soldiers or policemen; not believing in religion; not using a family name; and not marrying (those who were already married should divorce by mutual agreement). A communications bureau (the hated word "headquarters" was not used) was to be located in Shanghai, with branches elsewhere, and anyone was eligible to serve as the chairman or organizational worker of any branch.

Everyone should cooperate in study and mutual affection, uniting with those who had more knowledge and teaching those who had less. Since the party found its roots in the individual, it did not recognize the family, but instead advocated freedom in love, equality in education, and "public rights" with regard to inheritance. By these three means, the traditional family system could be destroyed. But this would take time, and one had to begin by building effective public institutions, since without these it would be impossible to move away from the old family priorities. Negatively, said Jiang, we must discourage marriage—then families will disappear naturally. But he added that so long as the family institution existed, parents had an obligation to rear their children properly, and children ought to obey their parents. Freedom in love, moreover, should not be used to advance evil motivations such as jealousy or financial greed.[15]

In the final section of his statement, Jiang contrasted the socialist endeavor with other political and religious movements. Jesus, he noted, had preached for thirty years and acquired only twelve disciples; it was after he had been nailed to the cross that he became famous. Confucius guided 3,000 students by means of seventy-two good assistants, and after he died his principles lived forever. But socialism, in contrast, was not the thought of an individual prophet or teacher. It was the thought of the common people. Thus, after only one year the Chinese Socialist Party had four hundred branches and 300,000 members. We are not fighting against society, he concluded, but we have the magnetic power to attract people, and sooner or later we shall succeed.[16]

When Yuan suppressed the anarchists in December 1912, Jiang wrote the president a letter of protest.[17] The anarchists did indeed claim to be preparing for revolution, he admitted, but they had not taken actions that disturbed the social order, and so their rhetoric should be ignored. Many individuals in Europe and America freely advocated anarchism and communism, Jiang continued, and in China "I was the first to do so." Yet he himself had come to the conclusion that although it had lofty purposes and superior theoretical premises, anarchism probably could not be realized. On such an issue, however, research was necessary and government should not restrict freedom of speech and the press. Jiang ended with a challenge that was soon to be taken up: "If you really want to trace the origins of the 'pure socialist movement,' then I am the one, and I would be willing to sacrifice myself in place of that party."[18]

Shortly thereafter, Jiang, who had been having eye trouble, announced that he was leaving for the north and that party affairs would be left in the hands of Bai Binzhou. Throughout early 1913, problems were reported, both intraparty quarrels and assaults from outside. The Song Jiaoren assassination proved to be a watershed. Immediately after the murder, a special party meeting was held in Shanghai, and telegrams were sent to Yuan demanding that he order the court to disclose all of the evidence, and also that he resign. Additional messages were sent in the name of the party, calling on parliament to impeach the government.[19]

On May 1, 1913, the Chinese Socialist Party observed international labor day in Shanghai, and about 3,000 people attended a symposium. Jiang, who was present for the occasion, spoke on the origins and meaning of labor day and reiterated CSP policies. A representative of the Labor Party, Shen

Zhouyou, also spoke, as did a British socialist, whose remarks were translated.* Others made short speeches, and Jiang closed the meeting with a sharp denunciation of the Yuan government, terming it "illegal" and calling for socialists to find "a suitable solution" to the present political malaise.[20]

A few days later, on May 5, the party addressed a message to Vice-President Li, urging action to stem prevailing trends. The Song affair, foreign loans, and the rising militarism practiced by the government, it said, were producing sentiment in many provinces for separatism and revolution. A resort to force would be disastrous for China, but it could be prevented only if resolute measures were taken. Calling Li "a hero of the Republic and one in possession of an important post," the statement exhorted him to remain neutral and work to avoid conflict.[21]

Meanwhile, one party member, Li Zhaohuan, currently in New York, promised to report on the place and time of the Socialist International meeting, and forwarded many Western socialist publications to party headquarters, most of which "favored Marx."[22] Subsequently, a letter from the British socialist who had addressed the May Day rally indicated that the Chinese Socialist Party would secure recognition from the Second International and invited the party to send delegates to the meeting in the fall of 1914. Katayama Sen also wrote, saying that as a correspondent of the international socialist movement, he was eager to know more about the party and Mr. Jiang.[23]

After the Song affair, however, and the strong anti-Yuan stand taken by the party, the government showed little tolerance for CSP activities. The governor of Zhejiang ordered party branches in that province dissolved, charging that the fourth and seventh provisions of the party program called for the carrying out of communism.** And with the advent of the "second revolution" in mid-1913, the final blow was struck. The Chinese Socialist Party was banned, along with the Guomindang.† Jiang had been treated as a radical since May, and he was now accused of being in contact with "Russian anarchists" and of jeopardizing world peace.

In fact, the Chinese Socialist Party had always been in contact with foreign socialists. Some had spoken at party meetings, a few had even joined

* Some information on the Labor Party is given in an article written by a foreign socialist who had studied this and similar groups in China. According to him, the party was organized by a man named Wen, a mechanic employed in the Shanghai government arsenal. The party program was directed wholly at improvements in worker education and employment conditions, with no mention of an ideological position. He asserted that Wen was called the "general commander" of the party and that under him were "captains," one male and one female for each trade. The party reportedly helped in the strike of Shanghai silversmiths in late 1912, but afterward Wen was persuaded by "one of the political spies of the government" to espouse a plan for an arsenal workers' revolt. When the attack took place, he was apprehended, sent to Beijing for trial, and executed, ending the Chinese Labor Party. (See "Ajax," "Reaction in China," *International Socialist Review*, December 1913, pp. 346–349.)

** Once again, party spokesmen insisted that the commitment of the party was to conduct a propaganda campaign, not to engage in political action, and that therefore it was not a threat; but that in any case, all proposals were advanced either on the basis of voluntary contributions (inheritance) or legislation to be passed by the parliament (the single tax). The party was not seeking to overthrow the government, nor to deny its right of existence. (*Minli bao*, June 20, 1913, p. 10.)

† For the presidential order for the dissolution of the CSP on the grounds that it was connected with foreign socialists and anarchists and had tried to foment disturbances in the north, see *North China Herald*, August 16, 1913, p. 530.

the party as members, and the movement was seeking to widen its foreign contacts by early 1913, as we have seen. Jiang, moreover, had earlier interested himself in the issue of China's "frontier regions." In an article written in January 1913, after the Mongolian dispute between China and Russia had erupted, Jiang had advocated internal autonomy within the Chinese Republic for such regions as Xinjiang, Tibet, and Mongolia; these areas, he believed, should be recognized by all foreign nations as "neutral zones," and socialists should be allowed to experiment with their programs there.* This drew sharp criticism, and Jiang was accused of trying to use a national emergency for his own political purposes. Other members of the party, moreover, had opted for participation in the "second revolution." Among them was the head of the Beijing branch, Zhen Jilong, who was executed in August.**

Jiang left China immediately after the dissolution order and went to the United States.† For a time he taught in the Oriental Languages Department of the University of California, Berkeley; he was later employed in the Oriental Department of the Library of Congress in Washington, D.C. He was not to return to China until 1920. Under prevailing conditions, the Chinese Socialist Party, like other antigovernment parties, quickly disappeared as an organization.

Although Jiang Kanghu was to modify his political views several times before his death (which is perhaps why he has been either ignored or castigated by scholars of Chinese socialism), he and his movement were of great importance to the status of Chinese socialism on the eve of World War I.‡ Jiang was one of the first persons in China to lecture on socialism publicly, and he was also one of the pioneers in seeking to connect the cultural movement to emancipate the Chinese woman and bring sexual equality to education with a political movement in China. His radical approach to issues concerning the Chinese family was akin to that taken by the earlier anarchists, and also by Kang Youwei, but in linking it to a public movement that espoused socialism, he anticipated the Communists by a decade. Like many who sought the modernization of China, Jiang and his associates saw the key problem in Chinese culture and society rather than in the Chinese state

* Eight years later, when he visited Lenin in Moscow in 1921, Jiang was to make roughly the same proposal with regard to Outer Mongolia. For details, see Wu Xiangxiang, "Jiang Kanghu and the Chinese Socialist Party," in Wu Xiangxiang (ed.), *Zhongguo xiandai shi congkan*, pp. 51–55, 60–62.

** "Ajax," who indicates that he and another foreign socialist had been invited to speak at Chinese Socialist Party meetings, wrote that Zhen Jilong was a youth of twenty-eight years, quiet and well-spoken, and that the charges against him were that he was a member of the Chinese Socialist Party, which had objectives the same as the Nihilist Party of Russia, and that he had been in communication with foreign anarchists ("Reaction in China," p. 347).

† "Ajax," who regarded the Chinese Socialist Party as gravely lacking in certain fundamental socialist principles, asserted that there was suspicion that Jiang Kanghu had for some reason received government money prior to his departure, since it was "well known" that he had no money—but he added that it was not known whether such a suspicion was well founded ("Reaction in China," p. 348).

‡ Both Nationalist and Communist scholars have dealt harshly with Jiang. Xia defines Jiang's approach as a mixture of reactionary socialism and anarchism, which served as "a tool to maintain the semicolonial and semifeudal state" (Xia, "Preliminary Discussion," pp. 42–43). Wu Xiangxiang, the Nationalist historian, asserts that Jiang totally failed to understand the real meaning of socialism and communism, and yet became an early propagandist for the Communist movement in China (Wu, *Zhongguo xiandai* 2:67).

as such. Their primary targets for change, therefore, had to be such basic institutions as the family, education, and land policies. In this, they epitomized the essence of Chinese radicalism and served as a link between the students of an earlier era and the Communists of later times.

Yet the Chinese Socialist Party did not disavow the necessity of government and the state. On this issue—and many related ones—Jiang and his party seemed to stand somewhere between the anarchists and the national or state socialists, but there was considerable confusion about their exact position on various issues. In part, the confusion stemmed from a conscious effort to encompass all branches of socialism. The original party program was an effort to bridge the differences between anarchists, Marxian socialists, and social democrats, whether of the national socialist or some other variety. The decision not to engage in overt political activities, such as campaigning for election or seeking administrative power, while at the same time not disavowing the need for government, was one example. Another was the attempt to use Georgism to resolve the issues of taxes and equitable land policies, but to add the concept of public acquisition of inheritances.

The problem with these broad compromises was that they tried to resolve an ambivalence toward power which was deeply rooted in Chinese culture, and particularly within the intelligentsia. Pulling in one direction was the Confucian tradition. It dealt with man in society, and hence the uses of political power; it saw the social order in terms of a hierarchy of status and talent, and emphasized the need for the lower orders to be tutored (and disciplined) by the higher ones within an essentially collectivist system. Pulling in the other direction was Taoism (along with certain other traditional values). It legitimated a deep distrust of power, especially power too concentrated and held too long in the same hands; and it was concerned with the individual man, outside society and in some respects liberated from it. It was the extreme traditional reaction to the hierarchical, bureaucratic, and confining edifice of the Confucian state. Given these opposing forces within China's heritage—forces newly brought to life by the nation's urgent domestic problems and by the stimuli of Western socialism—it was not easy for the Chinese socialists to choose an existing model or construct a new one. The Chinese Socialist Party mirrored the problem, and if it failed to control or bring together these mighty streams, its efforts were a faithful reflection of the times.

SUN'S CONTINUING QUEST FOR IDEOLOGICAL IDENTITY

While the Chinese Socialist Party was enjoying a brief period of explosive growth and extensive publicity, Sun Yat-sen remained the dominant figure in reformist-revolutionary circles, and his political views continued to reach a wide audience. No matter how far it might veer away from Sun at times, the Chinese revolutionary movement always seemed to gravitate back toward him at crucial junctures. No man in modern China had as many political deaths and rebirths, and no man swung so far, in public esteem, between contempt and veneration.

Toward the Chinese Socialist Party, Sun was supportive but aloof. No doubt this was partly because he had no intention of subordinating himself or his followers to a separate movement. But like many others, Sun regarded the CSP program as confused and defective in some respects, especially in its anarchist leanings. Yet he gave active encouragement to Jiang, and in so doing, insisted that he was a thoroughgoing socialist, not prepared to rest merely with Henry George's single tax. To emphasize this point, Sun maintained active connections with the international socialist movement, and considered himself affiliated with the Second International.

During the first months after the 1911 Revolution, Sun's thoughts were taken up with the formation of the new government, and he further elucidated his views on basic principles only after he resigned as provisional president, in a speech before the Tongmeng Hui on April 1, 1912.[24] In this talk he announced that the two principles of nationalism and democracy had been attained. (In this connection, he claimed that the Taiping rebels were the first representatives of the national revolution.) Only the principle of the people's livelihood remained to be secured—and henceforth that would be the goal. It was not enough, as some Chinese believed, merely to make China a strong nation, capable of standing alongside the European states and America. It had to be borne in mind that although the United Kingdom and the United States were the richest and strongest nations in the world, and France was the most civilized, in each of them the gap between rich and poor was very great, and revolutionary activities were therefore widespread. In those countries, a few capitalists enjoyed a luxurious standard of living while the mass of workers suffered. China had to heed this lesson and move toward socialism.

At this point Sun advanced a familiar thesis: it was wrong to believe that the social revolution, being very difficult, must wait. Such a revolution was certainly going to be traumatic for the West, where it would be resisted by an entrenched capitalist class; but in China the state was bankrupt, and a capitalist class had not yet emerged, hence a social revolution would be relatively painless.[25] Force, necessary to effect social change in the West, would not be required in China. Unfortunately, because China lacked a capitalist class, no one thought a social revolution necessary; yet if the opportunities of the present were lost, it would be a great tragedy for future generations.

The Tongmeng Hui, Sun continued, had included among its principles the equalization of land rights, and if this could be achieved, 70 to 80 percent of the social revolution would thereby be accomplished. Such equalization, moreover, could be effected by the very simple act of basing land taxes on assessed value rather than on the traditional categories now used. Some who sought equalization advocated the nationalization of land, he said, but the state did not have the resources to carry out a land-purchase program. The program should therefore be accomplished through taxation, with the state making it clear that when it needed the land, it had the right to purchase it at the assessed value. In these remarks Sun had returned to virtually pure Georgism.

In addressing the state's need for capital, Sun made a straightforward defense of foreign borrowing—but for productive purposes only, such as financing China's industrialization. All modern nations have benefited from foreign loans, he insisted, but to prevent inequities and abuses by capitalists, China must adopt national socialism, as Germany had done; major industries, railroads, and waterways should be nationalized. China's railway system should be extended by 200,000 *li*, and with the revenue that would be obtained, the system could be wholly owned national property within thirty years.[26] At this point the government would no longer be poor, and a massive program of free public education could be enacted, together with pensions for those unable to work.

Sun's exposition made it clear that his socialism was now a combination of the doctrines of Henry George and the concepts of national socialism as advanced by the Japanese school of social reformers, who had in turn been deeply influenced by the socioeconomic policies of Bismarck's Germany. During the next several months Sun made a number of speeches in South and Central China, spelling out the same basic themes.* In the fall of 1912 he was invited by Jiang to speak to Chinese Socialist Party members in Shanghai, and during October 14–16 he delivered three three-hour lectures attended by very large audiences (1,500 on the first day, 2,000 on the second, and 3,000 on the third, according to *Minli bao*). We have two versions of his remarks, one published from notes in *Minli bao* immediately afterwards, and the other contained in his collected works as published in Taibei in 1957.[27] There are a few differences in the two transcriptions, but the basic themes carried in both versions are the same.

Sun began by stating that he had long embraced socialism, and he appreciated the invitation to speak before party members. He then added that the CSP platform did not capture the essence of socialism in its complete form, and this was understandable because socialism was very complex. The earliest forms of socialism, he said, appeared thousands of years ago, and were based on the concept of an equal division of property. The equalization of property continued to be a goal of many and was expressed in the CSP platform on inheritance, but it was not the essence of socialism. The first doctrines of modern socialism, initiated by the Englishman Robert Owen, understood the existence of class divisions in emerging industrial societies, but provided no means of creating greater harmony between classes. Then, after some thirty years of research, the German sociologist Marx exposed the origins, nature, and results of capitalism. Socialism had a rebirth, and those who study society today look to *Das Kapital* as Christians look to the Bible.**

*In a speech entitled "On Social Revolution," given at a meeting of thirteen Wuchang organizations on April 10, 1912 (*Guofu quanji* 3:28–29), Sun asserted that China's revolution is a revolution to ensure the people's livelihood, which is in fact socialism. Though even absolute monarchs dared not openly oppress the people, such oppression is inherent in the capitalist role. European and American workers often go on strike, but after two or three months of hunger, they are forced to return to work. This is what happens when socialism has not been realized (p. 29). In a speech entitled "Equalization of Land Rights," given before a newspaper group in Canton, May 4, 1912 (*Guofu quanji* 3:37–40), Sun insisted that land equalization was not a return to the well-field system of ancient times but was required by the coming industrialization of China: great inequities and rampant speculation in land could be prevented only by an effective land tax, which would permit a degree of land nationalization.

Two other talks have been recorded. "Further Comments on the Equalization of Land Rights" was a discussion with the chairman of the newspaper association on May 13, 1912 (*Guofu quanji* 3:40–41). Here, Sun explained that he favored allowing the landowner himself to set the value of his property because the right of state nationalization would discourage him from setting the value too low—one of George's basic concepts. Finally, in "Resolving the Question of the People's Livelihood," a speech delivered to the founding meeting of the Guomindang in Beijing, August 25, 1913 (*Guofu quanji* 3:45–46), Sun elaborated on previous themes and painted a grim picture of developments in the West. In the United States, Britain, and similar countries, he said, oil, steel, and other essentials were controlled by capitalists, and this fact spread calamity throughout the nations and the world.

***Minli bao*, October 15, 1912, p. 2. The *Guofu quanji* version does not contain this passage, but does have the following: "Later, Marx appeared, studying the question of capital for some thirty years, writing the work *Das Kapital*, developing the truth, and turning an unsystematic teaching into a systematic theory" (vol. 6, pp. 12–13).

Sun then proceeded to identify various strands within contemporary socialism. Those who advocated the equalization of property were only one faction within the global movement, he reported. And even now, socialist thought had not become a complete science, like mathematics or astronomy. Moreover, cultural differences were important. The distinction between British socialists, whose doctrines were rooted in individualism, and German scientists, who took the state as the basic unit, was a significant one. In China the existence of the well-field system thousands of years ago represented the beginning of the principle of property equalization and communism, indicating that the Chinese people had long possessed the spirit of socialism.[28]

Sun forthrightly criticized the Chinese Socialist Party's decision to avoid active politics. Since socialism aimed to change the nature of society, he said, it must necessarily seek political power; the party's decision to separate itself from politics and oppose all government was not compatible with socialist principles. The Chinese Socialist Party had to become a major political party under China's republican system.[29] Here, Sun's challenge to the anarchist faction was unmistakable.

He then proceeded to discuss and challenge Social Darwinism. Those who accepted progress, he said, also stressed evolution, and socialism acknowledged the importance of man's evolving in the social order, with the superior succeeding and the inferior failing. Unfortunately, this doctrine could be used to justify the victory of the rich over the poor, thus allowing social injustice to prevail, and it had led some scholars to the unacceptable belief that power was the sole value in the world. The process of evolutionary selection, Sun argued, is the progress of things barbarian, whereas justice is achieved only through progress in civilized morality. Evolution may impose certain limits on social organization, but man has a vital role in molding society. In essence, socialism depended upon human beings to overcome the defects of evolution.[30]

Sun then stressed that socialism had to seek a lasting elimination of class differences by peaceful means. This could not be achieved merely by an equal division of all property, since that would amount only to a temporary leveling of everyone, human talents and interests differing. He went on to distinguish between four types of socialism: communist, collectivist, nationalist, and anarchist. In England and Germany, he added, two additional variants were to be found, namely, religious socialism and universalist socialism. Having set forth these categories, Sun stated that from his standpoint there were only two basic forms of socialism, the collectivist and the communist. National socialism belonged to the collectivist form, and anarchism to the communist form. Collectivism, Sun continued, means state ownership of various industries—railways, utilities, and land. Communism means that each shall contribute according to his abilities and receive according to his needs, and that government—as its services become unnecessary—will slowly fade away.

When one compared these two branches of socialism, Sun said, communism would at first seem better, but at present the moral standards of most citizens did not meet the preconditions necessary for its success. Differences in the moral character of men and in their evaluations of happiness or pain had to be recognized. We cannot plan for conditions that may exist two thousand years from now, as the "pure socialists" would like. We have a responsibility for today, and for today only collectivist socialism or national socialism is practical. We must nationalize land and national facilities like the railways, thereby overcoming the deficiencies of evolution and resolving in a peaceful manner the war between the poor and the rich.[31] The present campaign, Sun argued, was a continuation of this struggle for equality. By means of the national revolution, the oppression of the Han majority by the Manchu minority had been ended; now it was essential to prevent the oppression of the common people by a few capitalists and to do this before capitalism took root in China.

In his second lecture, Sun began with a moral appeal. Socialism, he proclaimed, was the voice of humanism, a call for the realization of equality, love, and freedom. These three values, indeed, constituted the essence of socialism, and they had roots in ancient China, in the writings of sages like Mo Di. But the sages were not capable of extending their values to mankind in general. Socialism, unlike the philosophies of the ancients, was a universal creed, which could be extended to all men. And since socialist thought was fundamentally concerned with the welfare of all, it had to begin with a study of economics—a field that had recently become a science. Sun then outlined the basic economic principles relating to land, labor, and capital and described the course of the industrial revolution, giving emphasis to the experience in Great Britain. He cited the Englishmen Adam Smith and Robert Owen and the Frenchmen Fourier and Blanqui, along with Malthus and—inevitably—Henry George.

The teachings of Henry George, Sun argued, coincided very closely with socialist doctrines on public ownership of land. In England, where the land belonged to the nobility and where industrial development had displaced the peasantry, the number of persons engaged in farming had decreased and food production had become insufficient to provide for the population, so that it became necessary to depend on imports. It was under these conditions that concepts of the single tax and public ownership of land had emerged. The teachings of George and Marx seemed to differ on the surface, he said, because George emphasized land and Marx stressed capital, but "both seek the well-being of a majority in society."[32]

Contemporary economists, Sun continued, were divided into two groups, the old Adam Smith faction and the new Karl Marx faction. The Smith faction tended to support capitalism of the sort that oppressed the workers, whereas the new Marxist economics taught "the truth" about the distribution of goods. Unfortunately, most Chinese students who had studied abroad had come under the sway of the old economics. Socialists, however, advocated the teachings of Marx and George and sought the well-being of all workers.[33]

Throughout his lectures Sun contrasted China with the West in a manner now familiar to us. China's landlords and capitalists, he claimed, were extremely shallow and conservative, lacking in entrepreneurial spirit. The implication was clear that they could not serve as economic or political leaders. On the other hand, it was still possible in China for the poor to become wealthy. Mechanization lay ahead, and class lines had not yet been frozen, as in the West. Changing his position from earlier writings, Sun now suggested that the great social revolution in the West would take place first in the United States, where the capitalists held massive power and treated farmers and workers "like cows and horses."[34] Sensing the catastrophe that was approaching, various socialist scholars in the West were now advocating the

Marxist approach, calling for a peaceful solution to the question of equal distribution so as to avoid the radical approach of equalization of property.

Sun concluded his speech by returning to Georgism. Using the changes in land values in Shanghai and New York as illustrations, he insisted that the solution to the problems created by the prices, the use, and the distribution of land now constituted "the essence of socialism."[35] In his final words, having painted a rosy picture of state income derived from nationalized property and the land tax, Sun pledged that under socialism China could reap many benefits: free public educational facilities for all, after which graduates would be sent to various places to serve in accordance with their abilities; support for the aged; free public hospitals; and recreational facilities for everyone. With class distinctions eliminated and everyone working according to his ability, genuine equality would be achieved and a world of *datong* (great harmony) reached.

These lectures provide an excellent summary of Sun's political views at the opening of the republican era. As we have noted, the ideological roots of Sun's program now lay in a combination of Henry George's single-tax doctrine and the policies of the Japanese school of social reform, borrowed from Germany, which generally prescribed social legislation and select nationalization. It is interesting, however, that Sun was now treating Marx very seriously, as the founder of sociology, the head of the "correct" school of economists, and the man principally responsible for systematizing socialist doctrine and rendering it scientific. Indeed, he was now prepared to rank Marx with his old idol Henry George and to minimize the differences between them.

As we have seen, Sun chose to identify Marx with collectivist socialism rather than with communist socialism, a category he reserved for the anarchists. As a result, he considered Marxism a moderate rather than an "extremist" doctrine and argued that Georgist-Marxist approaches to the issues of distribution and equity could enable the problems of social injustice to be handled peacefully, without widespread violence—at least in China. The exception Sun made for China was important. When he talked about socialism, he always invoked the West as a powerful negative example: revolution was inevitable in the West because there social ills had gone untended for too long. This view—amazing as it now seems—was shared by many Chinese radicals during this period. In effect, they argued that China was much better off—at least in a social sense—than the industrial societies of Europe and America. With rare exceptions, therefore, they did not come to embrace socialism out of a sense of injustice in their own society, at least in class terms. Rather, they saw socialism as a means of preventing the spread of Western social ills as China embarked on the path to modernization.

Finally, Sun made clear his opposition to the anarchists, though he seldom mentioned them by name. Their idealistic doctrines, he firmly believed, outran the capacities of contemporary society and were hopelessly utopian (a charge often leveled against Sun himself, as we have seen). Moreover, the anarchists were prone to take a negative and destructive outlook that was wholly incompatible with Sun's own strongly optimistic view of the possibilities for social and political development.

After the failure of the "second revolution," Sun was preoccupied with efforts to rebuild his party in exile, and when he returned to South China in 1916 after Yuan's demise, he plunged into the unrewarding task of creating a "military government," then coping with its impotence and divisions. In the course of the next few years he spent little time on philosophical speculation; and during a period of enforced leisure in Shanghai after his resignation from the Canton government, he devoted himself to creating an industrial plan for China. Until 1920, therefore, his remarks on the subject of socialism were casual and in line with his previous statements. But despite the fact that Sun broke no new ground in the decade after 1912, it could be argued that his attitudes and preconceptions about Marx—first revealed in his lectures to the Chinese Socialist Party—provided a compatible background for his later political dalliance with the Communists.

THE ANARCHIST APPEAL

Sun Yat-sen had ample reason to be concerned with the influence of anarchism on the Chinese intelligentsia in the years after 1911. From then until 1920, no doctrines had a greater influence on young Chinese radicals than those of Proudhon, Bakunin, and above all Kropotkin. The activities of contemporary anarchists, such as Kōtoku and Ōsugi Sakae in Japan, Emma Goldman and William Haywood in the United States, and Errico Malatesta in Italy, were a further inspiration to them.

We have discussed the growing strength of the Chinese anarchists in the years immediately prior to the Wuchang uprising, when they were centered in Paris and in Tokyo. We have also described the influence of anarchist ideas within the Chinese Socialist Party and in the views of its founder, Jiang Kanghu. Before we examine the principal anarchist societies that sprang up in the postrevolutionary period, it is important to emphasize that anarchist precepts found ready acceptance among a great many restless young people who did not play leading roles in the organizational efforts of this era but who later figured prominently in the political and intellectual life of modern China. In addition to such hard-core believers as Wu Zhihui, Li Shizeng, and Zhang Jingjiang, there were those individuals who became temporary believers or who found in anarchism the initial stimulus that led them into political activism. Among such individuals were Wang Jingwei, Cai Yuanpei, Yang Zilie (Madame Zhang Guotao), and Mao Zedong.

We have already speculated about the principal reasons for the anarchist appeal. Its values had a close affinity with one prominent strand of the Chinese philosophic tradition and, beyond this, with Chinese intellectual behavior patterns. The opposite side of Confucianism was Taoism; the opposite side of the official was the man retreating from office into detachment and contemplation. This dualism represented one of the great heritages of the past.

It should also be recognized, however, that during the opening years of the twentieth century, Western radicalism was gravitating toward anarchism and anarcho-syndicalism. The accelerated pace of industrialization and the advent of larger, more powerful trade unions combined with the growing sense of alienation felt by many as they were transplanted into a cold, impersonal, and specialized urban environment. Concepts of workshop governance and personal freedom from the restraints of society could only flourish in such an atmosphere. And as we have repeatedly emphasized, these concepts came to China through Japan. The sizable influence of Japanese socialism upon "Young China" meant that as the Japanese radicals under the leadership of Kōtoku moved toward anarchism, a corresponding effect would be felt in Chinese intellectual centers like Shanghai. After all, it was supremely important to be avant-garde.

The most vital component of the Chinese anarchist movement had been the Paris group and their publication, *Xin shiji* (The New Century). Most of the members of this group returned to China shortly after the 1911 Revolution and became active in several urban centers. The chief monument to their efforts was the creation of the Jinde Hui (Society to Advance Morality), founded by Wu Zhihui, Li Shizeng, Zhang Ji, and Wang Jingwei in January 1912.[36] The Jinde Hui leaders argued that the Qing regime had collapsed because of the corruption of Chinese society, and that no new order was possible so long as vices like prostitution, gambling, and concubinage prevailed. Once these evils had been eliminated, however, the need for coercive governance would cease. Thus, China had to seek a new morality in order to forge a new society.

As befitted an anarchist-inspired movement, the Jinde Hui had no president or other officers, no organizational structure, no dues or fines. New members were simply introduced by old ones and had their names recorded on a membership roll. If a member was discovered to have violated the covenant of the Society, other members were merely supposed to "raise their hats," thereby indicating their unhappiness, and "respectfully implore in silence."[37] The full Jinde Hui regulations were very complicated. There were five types of membership, with increasingly rigorous requirements at each level. "Supporting members," the lowest level, agreed not to visit prostitutes and not to gamble. "General members" agreed in addition not to take concubines. Beyond this, however, there was a separate covenant that established three special membership categories. Special A Division members accepted the above restrictions, and in addition agreed not to become government officials. "Someone has to watch over officials," noted the covenant.[38] Special B Division members added to the above prohibitions the agreement not to become members of parliament and not to smoke. "Legislators watch over officials but someone has to watch over the legislators."[39] Finally, Special C Division members accepted all previous stipulations and also promised not to drink liquor or eat meat.* The Paris rules, refined, had been brought home.

A number of organizations similar to the Jinde Hui sprang up. One of them was the Huiming xueshe (Society of Cocks Crowing in the Dark), founded by Liu Sifu and his followers in Canton. Liu, who later used the name Shifu, had come to anarchism in Tokyo, and together with Wang Jingwei and Chen Jiongming had been active in various assassination plots prior to the 1911 Revolution.[40] Even after that revolution, Shifu and a group of followers had resolved to go north and kill Yuan Shikai, but they had been dissuaded by Wang Jingwei, who, newly released from prison, felt that such an act would throw China into chaos. With the assassination plan set aside,

*From time to time, lists of members were given in *Minli bao*. General members included Cai Yuanpei, Zhang Xingyan, and according to a new list of March 1, 1912, Hu Hanmin. Special A Division members included Zhang Ji, Zhang Jingjiang, and Dai Jitao. B Division members included Wang Jingwei and Chu Minyi, and the C Division included Wu Zhihui and Li Shizeng.

Shifu returned to Canton, and in the fall of 1912 he founded the Huiming xueshe, with the goal of moving from "destructive" to "constructive" work by inculcating anarchist principles at the mass level.

Anarchist materials were printed and disseminated through this organization, and a year later a new society emerged, the Xinshe (Heart Society). It was sponsored by Shifu and another anarchist named Boan and was joined for the most part by assorted intellectuals and professionals in the Canton region. The Xinshe had twelve conditions for membership: no eating of meat; no drinking of liquor; no smoking; no use of servants; no marriage; no use of a family name (thus Liu changed his name to Shifu); no acceptance of government office; no riding in sedan chairs or rickshas; no acceptance of parliamentary seats; no joining of political parties; no participation in an army or a navy; and no acceptance of religion.*

Xinshe leaders were able to coexist with the government reasonably well in the months after the society was created, and they were planning to set up an experimental anarchist village when the "second revolution" broke out. With the defeat of the southern armies and the entry of Long Jiguang into Canton, however, anarchist activities were proscribed. Shifu, whose arrest had been ordered by Yuan Shikai, moved his operations to Macao. But as Beijing put increasingly heavy pressures on Portuguese officials to suppress the anarchists, the headquarters was transferred to the International Settlement in Shanghai, the great privileged sanctuary for Chinese radicalism.

Meanwhile, other anarchist activities abounded. It will be remembered that when the anarchist element split away from the Chinese Socialist Party, they formed the Socialist Party, headed by Luowu and Fenfen. Anarchist societies emerged in Nanjing, Shanghai, and other eastern cities. Many were offshoots of the Jinde Hui, the Huiming xueshe, or the Xinshe. For example, Cai Yuanpei established the Liubu Hui (Six No's Society), whose members swore to give up prostitutes, gambling, and concubines; abstinence from meat, liquor, and smoking was encouraged but optional.[41]

There is some indication that the widespread effect of anarchist thought served to limit the political leadership available in the new revolutionary era. For instance, according to *Minli bao*, both Sun and Yuan Shikai were willing to accept Wang Jingwei as premier at one point, but since he was a Special B Division member of the Jinde Hui, he declined.[42] Another example is provided by a letter from a comrade in Fujian province which was published in *Minli bao*. Conditions in his province were very difficult, he reported, and one Wang Ziyuan was needed to take over the educational system there. However, Wang, being a Special C Division member of the Jinde Hui, refused to serve. Would it be permissible, the writer asked, to change Wang's membership temporarily to the general category, and then, when his task was finished, restore it to Special C status?[43] Wu Zhihui, in

* *Shifu wencun*; see also Feng Ziyou, *Zhonghua·minguo* 2:207–211. One of the young men who came into contact with Shifu's movement at this time was Wang Zhunsang. Wang, already committed to socialism, had come to Canton, having joined a student revolutionary army recruited in Hong Kong shortly after the Wuchang uprising. In Canton he learned of a school teaching Esperanto and through it discovered the Xinshe, which he joined. He became close to Shifu, and followed him to Macao. Wang later went to Malaya, but he continued to write for *Min sheng* (in Esperanto, *La Voco de La Popolo*) and to translate Kropotkin's works. (Robert A. Scalapino interview with Wang Zhunsang, Macao, September 9, 1961.)

his answer, flatly refused to consider any such request. He did say, however, that if Wang wanted to aid the Fujian educational program, he could serve as the head of an educational society, or act as an adviser. In these capacities a few anarchists began to assist the Nationalist government, but there can be little doubt that many refused to play the kind of political role that was so desperately needed in a period when trained personnel were extremely scarce. In at least a minor degree, therefore, the anarchists must share the responsibility for the rapid collapse of Nationalist aspirations after 1911.

In certain respects, anarchist-communist doctrines prepared the way for Chinese intellectual receptivity to Marxism-Leninism, even though in the most essential respects the two creeds were deeply antithetical. To explore the articles in *Huiminglu* (Voice of the Crowing Cock) and *Min sheng* (Voice of the People), two important anarchist organs, is to find all of the basic theories of Western anarchism set forth passionately. *Huiminglu* opened with the declaration that it would be the voice of the people, serving as their organ against those who would oppress them.[44] Having staked out his constituency, Shifu then proclaimed that the evil nature of social organization was responsible for public misery, and that only by carrying out a thorough global revolution, destroying all present authority in society, could the people attain true freedom and happiness. "Our principles are communism, antimilitarism, syndicalism, antireligion, antifamily, vegetarianism, an international language, and universal harmony. We also support all of the new scientific discoveries which advance man's livelihood."[45] The anarchist-communist creed could not have been put more succinctly.

In his first major article, Shifu attempted a brief exposition of anarchism, drawing upon *Xin shiji* and such Western sources as Kropotkin.[46] By the abolition of government and the institution of communism, classes would be equalized and the struggle for money would cease. Then life would be free, and the society of contention would be converted into one of mutual love. If we could eliminate lust and the struggle over possessions by wiping out the institutions of marriage and private property, argued Shifu, 80 to 90 percent of all killings could be eliminated. Evil and immorality were products of society, not of man. Only through anarcho-communism, he continued, could the discoveries of science be properly used for the benefit of all. If education could be available to all without patriotic and militaristic indoctrination, then every man could have a knowledge of science and it would no longer be a monopoly of the few, to be used by capitalists for material gain.[47]

Another significant article seeking to define anarcho-communism was written by Shifu in April of 1914.[48] Since the terms "anarchism" and "communism" were new to the Chinese language, he said, many misunderstandings had resulted. Anarchism advocated complete freedom; mankind should be set free from all controls, and all leaders and organs of power should be eliminated: "The great teacher of anarchism, Kropotkin, put it simply: 'Anarchism means no authority.'" Furthermore, because the most dangerous authority in modern society is capitalism, anarchists must also be socialists: "Socialism believes that the means of production and all products must belong to society." According to Shifu, there were two major socialist factions: communists and collectivists. Communists advocated the common ownership of production and products, with each person working according to his ability and taking according to his needs. Collectivists advocated the public or state ownership of production, and private ownership of the basic essentials of livelihood. Shifu aligned himself with communism.[49]

The anarcho-communist utopia was described more fully by Shifu in one of his last major articles.[50] It would be a classless society where all would work. There would be no government, no armies, no police, and no jails. There would be no laws or regulations, only freely organized groups to adjust jobs and production in order to supply the people with their needs. There would be no institution of marriage. Women bearing children would be taken care of in public hospitals. All children from the age of six to the age of twenty or twenty-five would receive free education. Upon graduation, they would work until the age of forty-five or fifty, and then be taken care of through public old-age homes. Religion of all types would be abolished, and in its place "the natural morality of mutual aid" would be allowed to develop fully. Each person would work between three and four hours daily. Education would be given in Esperanto. "Native languages" would be slowly eliminated.

How was this utopia to be achieved? First, newspapers, books, speeches, and schools had to be used to spread these ideas to the people. During the period of propaganda and education, strikes, resistance to taxes and military conscription, and assassination were also to be employed. When the time was ripe, a popular revolution would erupt spontaneously and overthrow the government and the capitalist system. This popular revolution would start in Europe, in such countries as France, Germany, England, Spain, Italy, and Russia, where the ideas of anarchism were already widely advanced. Then it would spread to South America and North America, and finally to Asia. China had to hurry to catch up, lest she become a drag on world progress.

A great many of these ideas were later adopted by the Chinese Communist movement, despite the tremendous gulf that existed between anarchist theory and Communist practice. Even in theory, of course, certain differences were crucial, especially those relating to the role of the state in the postrevolutionary era. The fierce battle that took place between these two movements were still eight or nine years away, but the anarchists of this period did not lack targets—or enemies.

Shifu first tackled the problem of backsliders. He was shocked by the fact that Zhang Ji had allowed himself to be elected to parliament and had even accepted the office of parliamentary president under the Republic in 1913. Zhang had violated the Jinde Hui agreement, Shifu wrote to Wu Zhihui.[51] Wu defended Zhang Ji by asserting that he was already a member of parliament at the time the Jinde Hui was organized, and that because he was only a Special A Division member of the society he had not broken any rule.[52] This did not satisfy Shifu, who insisted that a true anarchist could not legitimately accept any public office.[53]

Shifu's main battle, however, was against Sun Yat-sen and Jiang Kanghu.[54] He admitted that most people believed that these two men were the leading socialists of China, and he pronounced himself touched that they had found the courage to speak out. But he denied that either was a true socialist. Sun was principally a political revolutionist, and the study of socialism was not his specialty.[55] "His heart is drunk with the teachings of Henry George, and he wants to put the single tax into practice in China."[56] Georgism, after all, was social reform, not socialism. Shifu acknowledged

67. *Jiang Kanghu*

that Sun claimed to advocate collectivist socialism, and that at a meeting of the Chinese Socialist Party he had paid homage to Marx's *Das Kapital* and called the German theorist the father of collectivism. But his assertion that the theories of Marx and George were compatible, Shifu said, was erroneous. Sun was confusing social reformism with socialism.

Jiang Kanghu, according to Shifu, was also a social reformer rather than a socialist. Although Jiang had written some words of praise about communism, his program called merely for legal reforms, arms limitations, the land tax, and equal education; it did not call for public ownership of the

68. Shifu

means of production. In fact, Shifu argued, Jiang was closer to Saint-Simon. He also regarded him as hopelessly confused, and sprang to the attack repeatedly.[57] Nor was Luowu's Socialist Party acceptable: although its constitution advocated anarcho-communism, the very fact that it acted as a conventional party barred it from orthodoxy. "We have no work except that of overthrowing the present authority," Shifu stated. "We are not like political parties which have plans and policies. Following the overthrow of governments and the attainment of anarchism, there will be no anarchist party."[58]

Never strong physically and given to a Bohemian life-style, Shifu died prematurely in 1914, a victim of tuberculosis. With his death, Chinese anarchism lost one of its most articulate and influential spokesmen. Wu Zhihui was later to write: "Since the death of Shifu, the Anarchist Party of China has been scattered and indifferent. It seems as if Shifu's death from tuberculosis has caused the Chinese Anarchist Party to suffer from the same disease."[59] Yet anarchist organizational efforts went forward, with societies operating in Beijing, Nanjing, Shanghai, and elsewhere. More important, anarchist thought spread to many parts of the political spectrum. Thus student journals such as *Jinhua* (Evolution), *Xinchao* (New Currents), and *Guomin* (The Citizen) helped carry an admixture of anarchist, socialist, and liberal ideas into China. The very individuals whom Shifu had criticized—Sun excepted—showed a strong receptivity to anarchist thought, and it had more than a negligible influence on many who were later to identify themselves as Marxists. Indeed, most Chinese radicals at first thought that the Bolshevik Revolution had succeeded in liberating men from the chains of government and the old society, goals that were central to the anarchist cause.

As World War I came to an end, anarchism in many respects played the avant-garde role in the various socialist study groups, reading circles, and intellectual journals that operated in Beijing, Canton, Shanghai, and elsewhere. Thus, when the Bolsheviks made their first overtures to Chinese intellectuals, it was inevitable that they should make intimate contact with the anarchists in China, just as they did in Japan. The fierce battles between anarchists and Communists, epitomized by the prolonged literary duel between Chen Duxiu and Ou Shengbei, and the decline of the anarchists, still lay ahead. Until the early 1920s, anarchism was a force which those Chinese committed to fundamental change had to reckon with.

THE WORK-STUDY MOVEMENT

In the years immediately after the Revolution of 1911, the anarchists who had been together in Paris developed a project for combining work and study that would enable young Chinese to study abroad, principally in France. Through this project, which was only peripherally related to the Chinese anarchist movement, the Francophile anarchists unconsciously helped lay the foundations for a French-based Chinese Communist movement that exercised considerable influence within the Chinese Communist Party until 1927.

As we have seen, after 1905 some members of the Paris anarchist group, notably Zhang Jingjiang and Li Shizeng, used family funds to launch a few business enterprises in which they could employ comrades from home, who could then simultaneously acquire an education. And when Zhang, Li, Wu Zhihui, and other anarchists returned home to China shortly after the outbreak of the Revolution, they came as ardent enthusiasts for France in addition to being anarchists. They continued to harbor the hope that as many Chinese students as possible could have the educational opportunities available in France. Their arguments as to why France was an ideal area for overseas education were interesting.[60] French education, they said, had long been separated from the superstitions of monarchy and religion. Monarchy had vanished with the French Revolution, which was a monument to human liberty; the compulsory study of religion had been abolished in 1886, and a further separation of church and state had been initiated in 1907.[61] The French were famous for the wide range and originality of their scholarship. The preeminence of French science was illustrated by the nearly universal use of French measurements and the long roster of famous French scientists; but French achievements were equally noteworthy in the humanities—where else could one find men like Montesquieu and Rousseau?[62] Finally, the French people were considerate and generous to foreigners, and a French education was relatively cheap.

In 1912, when Wu Zhihui, Wang Jingwei, Li Shizeng, Zhang Jingjiang, Chu Minyi, Zhang Ji, and Ji Zhushan founded the Liu-Fa jianxue Hui (Society for Frugal Study in France), the second phase of the overseas work-study movement began. According to Wu Zhihui, this organization was inspired by similar societies in England and France.[63] The purpose of the Society was to promote simple living and low costs for students, thus enabling them to find the means to go to France and remain there for the time necessary to complete their studies. Students were not required to work, incidentally, if they had the necessary funds. The Society also undertook to provide some advance language training and orientation for life and study abroad.[64] Frugal Study Societies were also established for study in Japan and England. The English project, which sponsored some twenty students, was initiated by Zhang Jingjiang and managed by Wu Zhihui in London during part of this period.*

It was the Society's program for study in France, however, that achieved the greatest momentum. A preparatory school was established in Beijing, with Ji Zhushan in charge and one Frenchman as an instructor. Fortunately, Cai Yuanpei, himself a returned student from France and an anarchist sympathizer, was currently serving as minister of education in the Beijing government, and he was able to provide the school with quarters. To join the Society or participate in the school, one had to be over fourteen years of age or accompanied by parents. In good anarchist fashion, the Society had no officers. Instead, a few "workers" were selected by the members to carry out specific functions. There were no dues other than the necessary educational costs, and required expenses were supposed to be met through the "mutual aid" of all comrades. In some respects, this was another scheme for putting anarchism into action.

Students were scheduled to travel to France on the Siberian railway, although, as we shall see, some took a sea route. The railway trip took fifteen to eighteen days and cost approximately two hundred yuan, on second or third class.** In France, food and lodging were to be arranged either by the

*In outlining the purposes of the Frugal Study Society, Wu reported that in order to qualify as a student for Japan under the auspices of the society, an individual needed only 20 yuan transportation money and 200 yuan schooling expenses. The latter sum, moreover, need not be advanced in one lump sum, but could be mailed in installments. School expenses were to be negotiated directly between the person and the educational institution involved. (Wu Zhihui, "Writing My Thoughts on the Frugal Study Society in the East, July 13, 1913," in *Wu Zhihui xiansheng quanji* 2:199–200.)

**See Wu Zhihui, "On Self-Supporting Students Going Abroad, November 24, 1912," *Wu Zhihui xiansheng quanji* 2:276–278. The first group of ten students who went to France under this program left in the summer of 1912. A second group of 42 left in late November, and more students went during the first part of 1913. One of the 1913 arrivals was Liu He,

school or by representatives of the Society, with the student to begin work as soon as possible to repay advances and meet ongoing costs. Yearly expenses were estimated at 600 yuan. Students were expected to commit themselves to at least three years of foreign schooling, and the type of education they were to undertake was to be determined by the number of years they agreed to spend abroad. The emphasis, however, was intended to be upon agriculture, engineering, mining, and commerce—all considered "scientific subjects." Students were to agree not to visit prostitutes and not to smoke, drink, or gamble. The regulations were said to be aimed at creating scholars who would be frugal in their living habits, pure in character, and possessed of skills to match their intelligence.[65] The anarchist themes shone through these rules quite clearly.

The Beijing preparatory school opened in the spring of 1912. The curriculum consisted of French, Chinese, and mathematics. Various comrades (notably the Paris veterans) were invited to speak before the school. The term was fixed at six months, with an examination at the conclusion. Those who passed were to be sent to France under the auspices of the Society, with the initial expenses met, if necessary, by the sponsors. The tuition for the school was determined by the number of students enrolled each term.

As might have been expected, French proved a difficult language for the students to master, and many became discouraged. However, almost one hundred students were sent to France before political changes in 1913 forced Cai out as minister of education and caused the school to be closed.[66] With the outbreak of the war in Europe, the Society's organized activities in China were largely abandoned, although Li and some others continued to propagate the cause. As the war dragged on, however, France began to face an acute manpower shortage, and the French government negotiated with the Chinese government for workers. Tens of thousands of laborers were sent, and Li and his friends saw this as another opportunity to recruit individuals who were willing to work in order to study abroad. The hope was that for each year's work a Chinese student would be able to afford two years of study.*

---

who studied agriculture, transferred to the University of Paris, and became closely associated with the operations of the Frugal Study Society in France. When the "Sino-French University" was set up in Lyons, he served as secretary and was responsible for assisting newly arrived students, particularly those who had come without adequate funds. Liu recounts that Chen Yi and Deng Xiaoping were each provided with three francs daily (Robert A. Scalapino interview with Liu He, Taibei, August 28, 1976). Liu was to battle the Communist faction within the Chinese student group, and his recollections of individuals like Zhou Enlai will be presented later.

*According to He Jianggong, Li Shizeng argued before French officials that it would be a mistake for them to send labor recruiters to China. They would be able to collect only persons of low character, who would not be good workers and who would have a bad influence on the community in which they were placed. It would be better to allow Li and others to select reliable persons (mostly from southwest China), send them to preparatory schools in China, and then bring them to France. But this plan was not followed, and labor recruitment went forward. Each man who agreed to a contract was supposed to receive a set of clothes and 300 yuan to support his family, in exchange for a stipulated period of work in France, where he was to be paid wages amounting to about 50 percent of the rate paid to Frenchmen. According to He, the Chinese labor contractors lowered the family allowance to 100 yuan, presumably pocketing the balance. He's 1958 memoir, *Qingong jianxue shenghuo huiyi*, is a most interesting account by a work-study student who went to France in 1920. Though he assaults Li Shizeng and Wu Zhihui in a polemical manner, and is careful to pay homage to Mao in accordance with the dictates of the time in which he wrote, he presents many useful factual details.

In June 1915 the Paris group and their supporters organized a new society, the Qingong jianxue Hui (Association for Diligent Work and Frugal Study).[67] The new society was specifically geared to a work-study program, but other categories of students did go to France, some through private means and a few under government scholarships. Once again, preparatory schools were opened in Beijing and elsewhere. The Association for Diligent Work and Frugal Study itself established branches in various Chinese cities. In addition, certain French citizens cooperated with the old Paris group to found the Sino-French Educational Association. Cai was made the head, and Li the secretary. In its French branches, this Association was to make arrangements for the students and help them with their problems. In China, it was to aid in recruitment and general cultural relations. Headquarters were established in Beijing, with branches in Canton, Shanghai, and other areas.

By 1917 the work-study movement had spread to several Chinese provinces and had widespread intellectual support. Moreover, prospective students were thrilled by the possibility of overseas study and were willing to do almost anything to get this opportunity. He Jianggong's account of his own experiences during these years is fascinating.[68] In the winter of 1917, he was one term away from graduating from a technical school in Changsha and was worrying about his future. Suddenly, his elementary-school teacher and friend, Luo Xiwen, returned from Canton, having made contact there with the work-study branch office and Huang Qiang, a local official who was operating it. One could work and study in France, he reported, and get a loan for transportation. Huang had given him a pamphlet on the Association and letters of introduction to Cai Yuanpei and Li Shizeng.

He wrote to the Association and they responded by saying that first a French class should be opened in Changsha, and if the provincial ministry of education approved, they would send an instructor. Delays ensued, and under pressure from other students, Luo went directly to Beijing. After a long silence, he wrote He and others to come to the capital. It was now the summer of 1918, and six or seven students from Hunan made the trip. Luo and others were currently studying French in Peking University. Indeed, some forty to fifty students from Hunan were already involved in the program—including Mao Zedong, who had heard about it from his former teacher (and later father-in-law) Yang Changji.*

The number of students seeking to enter the Beijing preparatory school quickly became so large, according to He, that three separate classes had to be established, one in Beijing and the others in Baoding and Changxindian. Mao was briefly in the Beijing class; Liu Shaoqi and Li Wuhan were among some sixty Hunanese at Baoding. Young He spent one year at Changxindian, with a schedule that called for factory work in the mornings, school in the afternoons, and study in the evenings.

His major problem lay in getting the money for his transportation to France. Originally, according to He, provincial authorities had promised to use funds from the rice and salt revenues to aid Hunanese students, but as the period of preparatory schooling approached its end, they reneged. When

* He says that he had very close contact with Mao after reaching Beijing, and for a time had daily discussions with him about training and funding. Mao argued that the work-study program should be started in Beijing, without waiting to get to France. He describes the Mao Zedong of this period as "looking like an advanced degree-holder, with his long hair and padded cotton jacket" (pp. 35–36).

a student delegation went back to Hunan to seek funds, they fell into an argument with the authorities and were incarcerated for a time. Finally, however, a payment of four hundred yuan per Hunan student was arranged. For various reasons, by no means all of the students who enrolled in the original program completed their study and made the trip to France; neither Mao nor Liu Shaoqi, for example, were among those who went abroad.*

When He and his group arrived in France early in 1920, after a two-month sea voyage, there were already about three hundred work-study students in the country. He recalls that there were several types of work-study arrangements. Some students worked part time and studied part time; others would work for three or six months and then study until their savings were exhausted; some brought a small amount of money with them, studied until it was gone, and then sought a job. He's arrival coincided with the flood-tide of students; and at one point, shortly thereafter, they were arriving at the rate of one hundred per month. We shall have occasion later to note the substantial influence which the students in France were to have on Chinese radical politics in the early 1920s, and the long-term influence which the concept of work-study would have on certain Communist veterans, including Mao, after 1949.

*He and his immediate group went to Shanghai to await a ship for France. While there, they lived in the French quarter, attended lectures (Sun Yat-sen gave a special lecture for students scheduled to go abroad), studied Esperanto, and prepared for their overseas experience. He and seven classmates bought two Western-style suits, and he recounts how they practiced putting them on, tying Western-style ties, and then "walking with good posture" on the street. This experience so exhausted them that they came home and went directly to bed (pp. 44–46).

10

LIBERALISM, SOCIALISM, AND THE INTELLIGENTSIA—THE INTELLECTUAL MAINSTREAM AND ITS OPPONENTS

THE CHINESE Socialist Party, as we have seen, achieved a formidable if heterogeneous following for a brief period; Sun Yat-sen's continuing commitments to republicanism and national socialism made their mark upon Guomindang adherents and others; and the anarchists had an influence far beyond their actual numbers. Yet none of these movements came as close to representing the range of thought within the new China as did the journal *Xin qingnian* (New Youth) and the men who were associated with it. Although it began modestly enough, *New Youth* came to represent a set of concerns shared by the mainstream of "progressive" youthful Chinese intellectuals, men and women who considered it their duty to remove old barriers and accelerate the development of China as a "modern, civilized nation, fully equipped to survive and flourish in the contemporary world."

When *New Youth* first appeared in the fall of 1915, the crisis over Japan's Twenty-One Demands had barely subsided, and the issues of monarchism and a restoration of Confucianism were animating domestic politics.* Among the many authors and translators who came to be connected with *New Youth*, three individuals—Chen Duxiu, Li Dazhao, and Hu Shi—were of particular importance to China's political and intellectual future. Through their changing views, as expressed in *New Youth* and elsewhere, we can discern the larger political currents that were flowing through China at this time. Before we examine the writings of these men, it will be useful to summarize their backgrounds.

Chen Duxiu was born in 1879 in Huaining, Anhui, the youngest child of

*The first issue was published in Shanghai on September 15, 1915, under the title *Qingnian zazhi* (Youth Magazine). In September 1916 it was renamed *Xin qingnian* (New Youth), and the full run of the journal is generally known by that title. From the beginning, Chen used the subtitle *La Jeunesse*. Its early issues contained articles of limited depth or sophistication, but by 1917 it had become the principal organ for the dissemination of new ideas in China. (See Grieder, *Intellectuals and the State in Modern China*, pp. 222–226.) We shall refer to it in the text simply as *New Youth*.

a well-to-do family.[1] After receiving a classical education he came under the influence of the Kang-Liang reform movement, and studied French, English, and naval architecture at the Qiushi Academy in Hangzhou. Between 1900 and 1903 he studied in Japan and became involved in political activities there. In 1903, with Zhang Ji and others, he helped establish a revolutionary newspaper, the *Guomin riri bao* (National Daily News), in Shanghai; he was later associated with a vernacular publication in Anhui. After returning briefly to Japan in 1906, Chen held a series of educational posts in Anhui.* Although he had been in contact with the Tongmeng Hui in Japan, it is said that he objected to its narrow Han-nationalist bias and did not join. After the Revolution, however, he became head of the education department in Anhui under the revolutionary governor Bo Wenwei—until Bo was ousted by Yuan in 1913, following the outbreak of the "second revolution." Chen then fled with Bo and others to Japan, where he engaged in antimonarchical activities until his return to Shanghai's International Settlement in the summer of 1915, to take up the task of publishing *New Youth*.

Li Dazhao was born in 1888 in a village of Luoding district, Hubei, of very young farmer parents.[2] His father died when Li was two years old, and his mother shortly thereafter, so he was raised by grandparents. The family was not poor, since his grandfather had engaged in commerce, invested his capital in land, and become a small landlord. Li received a classical education as a child, and then went to a middle school where some training in Western subjects was available. From 1907 until 1913 he studied Japanese, English, and political economy at the Beiyang College of Law and Political Science in Tianjin. He began to write as a journalist and to translate Japanese works, but his political views were still the orthodox ones of his generation of educated, "progressive" Chinese: a mixture of nationalism (admiration for Japan's commitment to a "rich country, strong military"), republicanism (constitutionalism and popular rule constituted the most advanced political system for civilized nations), and certain traditional Chinese values (a special concern for ethics and morality).

Because Beiyang College was closely associated with Yuan Shikai, it was natural that Li should initially support Yuan, and by 1913 his political affiliations were with the Jinbudang. Indeed, one of the Jinbudang leaders, Tang Hualong, assisted Li during his final two years as a student in Tianjin and helped him go to Japan for study in the fall of 1913. While in Japan Li enrolled in Waseda University and took up the study of English again, but he spent much of his time in political activities and became affiliated with Sun's Gemingdang. In 1914 and early 1915, just prior to the first issues of *Youth Magazine*, Li was writing angry attacks on foreigners like Frank Goodnow (for their superficial knowledge of China) and generally criticizing all foreign intrusions into Chinese affairs. His nationalist and somewhat xenophobic appeals, combined with his laments about the decline of China and the threatened loss of its nationhood, marked him as very much in line with the earlier student sentiment we have described.

Hu Shi, the youngest of the three men, was born in 1891 in Shanghai, although his family, like Chen's, came from Anhui; the family homestead was in the village of Shangzhuang, Huizhou prefecture, near the Zhejiang

* Some scholars have said that Chen visited France for a brief period before his return to China, but the current evidence suggests that this is not correct.

border.[3] Hu's father, a scholar and minor official whose final posts were in Shanghai and Taiwan, died when Hu was less than four years old. Left in the care of his mother and paternal uncles, young Hu attended the family school in Anhui from 1895 to 1904, where he received a classical education.

In 1904 Hu left home in the company of an elder brother and—not yet thirteen—began his education in the first of three avant-garde schools in Shanghai, where he was to study for the next four years. The last of these schools was the China National Institute (CNI), founded in 1906 by Chinese students returned from Japan, among whom were a goodly number of radical nationalists. Young Hu studied English, mathematics, the natural sciences, and other "modern subjects." During this period he also came into contact with the writings of Liang Qichao and the translations of Yan Fu, and with such subversive literature as Zou Rong's *The Revolutionary Army*. Reportedly, Hu's first interest in language reform emerged during this period. He was actively involved in student politics at CNI, and ultimately served as editor of the student newspaper, *Jingei xunbao* (The Struggle).

The CNI split in 1908, and many students left to form a new school. Hu left CNI but did not enroll in the new institution. At this point, his family was going through a financial crisis, and according to his own account, he began to keep company with "the wrong crowd," drinking, gambling, and visiting houses of prostitution. By 1910, however, he had decided to reform, and in July of that year he passed the examinations to qualify as a Boxer indemnity scholar, being one of seventy successful applicants. In August he sailed for the United States and proceeded to Ithaca, New York, where he enrolled in Cornell University. Majoring first in agriculture, he shifted later to philosophy. He was elected to Phi Beta Kappa in 1913 and received his B.A. degree in 1914. After an additional year of study in Cornell, he entered Columbia University in 1915, having spent that summer reading the works of John Dewey, whose student and foremost Chinese disciple he now became. At Columbia he submitted his doctoral dissertation, "The Development of the Logical Method in Ancient China," in 1917, with John Dewey as chairman of his committee.

Earlier, at a Chinese student conference held at Cornell University in the summer of 1915, Hu had expressed many of the ideas on literary reform which he was later to set forth in China. The subject continued to preoccupy him, and when he returned home in mid-1917 he was already a celebrity (and to conservative critics, anathema) because of two articles published a few months earlier in *New Youth*. The first, carried in the January issue, was entitled "Tentative Proposals for Literary Reform"; the second, which appeared in May, was entitled "On the Genetic Concept of Literature." Although the idea of language reform had been broached by others, Hu, with the support of Chen Duxiu, came to be regarded as the father of the "literary revolution" that followed. Increasingly, publications shifted from classical Mandarin to the vernacular, thus bringing the spoken and written languages into greater conformity and making written materials available to a much wider audience.

Yet Hu returned to China not as a revolutionary but as a pragmatist, a convert to Dewey's experimentalist philosophy. In political terms, he was a liberal. He was convinced that most complex problems could be resolved only through patient incremental efforts, and he already had doubts about whether intellectuals should preoccupy themselves with political causes.* Meanwhile, before his twenty-sixth birthday, he assumed a professorship in philosophy at prestigious Peking University, joining a small but vigorous group of "new thinkers" who had been brought there by its chancellor, Cai Yuanpei.

CHEN DUXIU—THE TROUBLED JOURNEY FROM LIBERALISM TO MARXISM

Since Chen Duxiu played the dominant role in the operations of *New Youth*, we may begin by outlining the key themes he advanced there, noting the various changes that took place in his views. Before we do so, however, it should be said that the most noteworthy fact about the articles in the early issues of *New Youth* was not the originality but rather the familiarity of the ideas they advanced. In most cases, the essays could have come from *Xinmin congbao*, *Min bao*, or one of the Japan-based student journals of the period 1901–1909—though it might be argued that *New Youth*'s range and level of sophistication were greater. There were, to be sure, individual idiosyncrasies exhibited by Chen and others. But in general, *New Youth* began by purveying theses that had been the hallmark of the young radicals, particularly the overseas students, since the turn of the century. Chen, Li, and certain others did not turn to Marxism until well after the Bolshevik Revolution, as we shall see.

Chen's essays in the first issues of *New Youth* dealt repeatedly with the hotly debated issue of whether to revitalize Confucianism and elevate it to the status of a state religion. In fact, he was never to leave this issue, because it was related to a broader concern—finding an appropriate foundation for modern Chinese ethics. Like most of his contemporaries, Chen firmly believed that in dealing with politics or any other aspect of society, one had to begin with issues of ethics and morality, for these were the determining factors in the construction of human character. In this respect he was a traditionalist, however much he might decry Confucianism.

As a Chinese intellectual, Chen found no difficulty in equating religion with superstition and fantasy.[4] The myths of a Golden Age and of a life after death no longer had any value, he argued.[5] Indeed, it was precisely because religion had been unable to answer the most basic philosophical or ethical questions regarding the origins of man's existence and the meaning of life that it had failed to satisfy man's quest for truth.

If religion could not fulfill these needs, was there something else that could do so? Chen firmly believed a viable alternative existed. Science, he proclaimed in an early essay, provided the answer to every one of modern man's needs.[6] Science presented an objective picture of all matters, and

*In 1915, when the Twenty-One Demands were arousing overseas Chinese students in the United States as elsewhere, Hu took the unpopular position that these students, instead of expending their time in senseless talk about fighting, should prepare to uplift the fatherland by devoting themselves to study. And in his diary a few months later, Hu expressed dismay that his mentor, Professor John Dewey, had participated in a woman's suffrage rally. (See Grieder, *Renaissance*, pp. 54 and 61–62.) It was a supreme paradox that Hu, who was destined to be involved in politics throughout his life, always sought to separate the role of the intellectual from that of the activist.

69. *Chen Duxiu*

truth could come only from scientific knowledge. Darwin, for example, had shattered previously held religious beliefs.[7] Science provided objective answers to the questions to which religion had failed to respond. Scientists had discovered that man was only one kind of matter in the universe, and that human life was governed by certain natural laws regulating the cosmos. At the same time, what man did in this life was important, both to himself and to succeeding generations. There was no life after death, but the actions of human beings lived on, being transmitted through their society to those who came later. In this sense, a sort of immortality did exist: man as an individual would die, but so long as society continued, man in society lived, and a collective memory or consciousness was transmitted.[8]

Chen defined science as the discovery and systemization of natural law, which gave it the qualities of universality, permanence (yet growth), and essentialness. Religion consisted of rules made by man, which were therefore particularistic, ephemeral, and inculcated through indoctrination.[9] Although modern man had a long way to travel before science had unfolded all of its truths, and one should not limit oneself to knowledge of the present, religion was a false path. It merely deceived people. Doubts could be resolved only as scientific exploration advanced.

One of Chen's greatest objections to religion lay in the fact that it rested with inflexible doctrines, ideas, and values that could not grow to keep up with the evolution of society. Thus, it inhibited progress and stultified man's intellect. This was particularly true of Confucianism, he argued. In the first place, it was absurd to try to revive Confucianism and elevate it to religious status, because China—unlike India or the worldwide Jewish community—was not a religious society. No major figures of the religious world had been born in China, and one could not artificially create homage to religion among a people lacking a religious tradition.[10] And indeed, Confucianism was not a religion but an ethical system, and one based on unilateral obligations, inequality, and hierarchy.[11]

In fact, Chen insisted, Confucianism was a morality born in feudal times and suited only to a bygone era. If the Chinese had not come into contact with Western theories of human rights, which included independence and freedom, no one in China would be criticizing Confucianism; but having discovered modern Western political theories and having chosen to pursue republicanism in politics, how could the Chinese seek to retain an antiquated moral-ethical foundation for the new political order?[12]

In later writings, Chen made certain comparisons between Confucianism and other religions and sought to analyze the influence that various religions had had in molding the Chinese character.[13] Religions and idols were basically useless in modern civilization, he repeated, but there were distinctions to be made. Buddhism had a strict discipline and relatively sophisticated doctrines. Christianity acknowledged a single deity and advanced clear, easily comprehensible theses; the vows of poverty which its clerics took, moreover, protected virtue. Both of these religions were superior to Confucianism. Yet every religion had operated in China in such a manner as to contribute to the nation's decay. Buddhism treated the world as an illusion and regarded emptiness as a supreme value, thereby cultivating passiveness and resignation. Taoism preached retreat and withdrawal from social life, and although it sought to justify its tenets by speaking of man's communion with his inner self, the result was intellectual atrophy and social neglect. Confucianism, besides serving as a prop for the ruler and the aristocracy, focused on gentlemanly conduct, ignoring the need to defend one's rights when they were challenged.

As a result, the Chinese people were a "peace-loving, rest-venerating, self-respecting, tranquil, gentle, graceful, subordinate people," easily conquered by others.[14] Westerners took war as a normal course of events. Not a single word in Europe's entire modern history had been written except in fresh blood: religious wars, political wars, and commercial wars had shaped the nature of European civilization as it presently existed. Whereas Westerners hated insults more than death, the Chinese revered peace and leisure. Thus the old saying: "The Chinese rest on earth, the Jews in heaven, and the Indians in Nirvana."

Another signal difference between West and East, asserted Chen, lay in the fact that in the West the basic unit was the individual, whereas in the East it was the family or clan. Whether in ethics, politics, law, the state, or society, the goals in the West were for the individual's maximum freedom, rights, and happiness. But under the feudal morality of the traditional patriarchal Chinese society, loyalty and filial piety became supreme values, inducing a lack of personal independence and self-respect, suffocating the individual's freedom to make choices, robbing him of his right of equality before the law, and building up qualities of dependence that destroyed individual creativity. We must move from familialism to individualism, insisted Chen.[15]

In these passages Chen was relating ethics directly to politics, and individual character to national behavior. It is thus appropriate at this point to consider the evolution of Chen's more strictly political views during these tumultuous years. In his first essay in *New Youth*, Chen expressed a strong commitment to the cardinal values of Western liberalism: maximum freedom for the individual; progress based on science and technology; internationalism rather than isolation and self-sufficiency; and the acceptance of the utilitarian creed that the greatest happiness for the greatest number of people was the measure of success in governance. In these views he drew on the ideas of Rousseau, Locke, Montesquieu, Bentham, and John Stuart Mill, along with those of Darwin and a host of modern scientists.

As a Francophile, Chen found all of these virtues in France.[16] France had led the way to converting old patterns of life into a new civilization. Modern human rights stemmed from the French Revolution, Chen insisted, and Darwin's theories regarding evolution were based on Lamarck's doctrines, first advanced at the beginning of the nineteenth century. In advancing socialism—a necessity if repression by the capitalists was to be overcome and social equality attained—France had also led the way. The Germans Lassalle and Marx had only developed theories learned from the French, notably Babeuf.[17] It is interesting to note, incidentally, that in this first reference to socialism, Chen accepted it as both necessary and desirable, at least for Europe, but did not place any particular emphasis on it, nor allow it to interfere with his commitments to key liberal doctrines.

The immediate battle to be fought in China was on behalf of republicanism and against monarchism, and here Chen's allegiance was never in any doubt. His attacks on Kang Youwei and Yan Fu were rigorous. He held Yan in greater contempt because he had encouraged Yuan to institute religious rites at the Temple of Heaven, but had then opposed Yuan's assumption of the throne; Kang at least had the virtue of consistency. In attacking monarchist arguments, however, Chen was forced to admit that a majority of the Chinese citizenry "had not been moved by republicanism."[18] How could the chances for successful republican constitutionalism in China be enhanced? Chen pinned his hopes on a final "great awakening," a process whereby a majority would become self-aware participants in politics. The burdens could not be shouldered by "great men" and "rich men" alone, although they were welcome to participate in the constitutional process. Nor could constitutionalism be effectively realized if the popular attitude was that of the slave hoping for the lord's benevolence. It demanded voluntary commitment and active involvement on the part of the people themselves.

In the course of musing about this requirement, Chen introduced two themes that later proved influential in the evolution of his political thought. The first theme was that of tutelage. Like Liang and Sun before him, Chen now reasoned that although the majority might not be ready for republicanism, "a minority could certainly act as the vanguard."[19] It was an eminently logical argument, given the condition of Chinese politics. The second theme was that a global progression in politics was universal and inevitable. The course of world history, Chen argued, was from absolutism to liberalism, from individualist politics to nationalist politics, and from bureaucratic controls to self-government—all trends that were being advanced by constitutionalism. China could neither isolate itself nor escape from this global pattern. Indeed, it was in this doctrine of inevitability that Chen found the chief basis for optimism: however inadequate Chinese republicanism might be at present, it was the wave of the future. His argument showed no hint of dialectical materialism, nor of the basic Marxian thesis about the correlation between economic system and political superstructure. On one or two occasions, Chen casually mentioned the importance of economics, but like most Chinese "progressives" of this era, he came to his political views from a humanist approach, not an economic one. Yet in the doctrines of tutelage and of China's involvement in an inevitable universal progression lay the potential for Chen's ultimate conversion to Marxism-Leninism.

Like Li Dazhao and others, Chen saw the tutors as logically coming from China's youth. But it must be a new youth, not an old youth. The time of pale-faced bookworms, buried in mounds of ancient classics, had passed. China needed modern youth—physically strong, mentally adventurous—prepared to explore the world around them and wrest from it whatever would benefit the nation.[20] Here again Chen emphasized individual character as the key to China's future. My patriotism, he wrote, lies in diligence, frugality, honesty, cleanliness, sincerity, and faithfulness. If these virtues could be inculcated in great numbers of citizens, China could be saved.[21]

These political values, which Chen held until 1917, kept him within the mainstream of his generation of young intellectuals. Between 1917 and 1920, however, events in China and in the world challenged the cohesion of this mainstream and began to lead some of its members in different directions.

In an article published in March 1917, Chen gave rather startling evidence of his strong nationalist bent, bearing the anti-imperialist overtones typical of the times.[22] Arguing that China should join the Allied powers in the war against Germany, he said that the white race had treated the Chinese like dogs and horses, and that the narrowly patriotic Germans were the worst proponents of white supremacism. If the fields of Europe were to be stained with the blood of "yellow slaves" fighting for the principles of freedom, it might awaken both the whites and the Chinese to the worth of the Chinese people. In surprisingly bellicose language, Chen proceeded to praise conflict. War, he claimed, was to a country what exercise was to a man's health. Without war, stagnation ensued. For China, the most ominous words were "to maintain the status quo." Change—any change—would be better than to go on as at present. Then he grew more practical: by joining the Allies,

China would obtain the financial support it needed to undertake economic development, and involvement in the war might also unite China's antagonistic factions. This view, it should be noted, was strongly opposed by Sun Yat-sen, who believed that many who advocated China's entry into the war were simply seeking to fortify the power of the Beijing government.

In the following month, Chen turned his attention to the Russian Revolution, now in its first phases. In an article written shortly after the February uprising and published in April, he said that the European war was essentially a struggle between monarchism and democracy, between aggression and humanitarianism.[23] A victory for Germany would mean that there was no way out for the weak; they would not be able to survive. Thus the Russian Revolution was a progressive event in history. Its significance lay not only in its overthrow of the Russian monarchy but in the encouragement it gave to the overthrow of monarchism and aggression around the world. "I wish it success," Chen wrote.

He did not believe that Russia would seek a separate peace with Germany, but even if it did, he argued, the antimonarchy and antiaggression spirit of the new Russia would permeate Germany and Austria and therefore change the international situation. Such a development, Chen remarked, would be more beneficial to China than if a monarchist, expansionist Russia had defeated Germany militarily. He then repeated his call for Chinese participation in the defeat of Germany.

In May, Chen first exhibited some serious doubts about Western-style individualism, a cause he had long championed.[24] In speaking to an audience at a Beijing Higher Normal School, he argued that it was a great mistake to think that morality was disappearing from human society as a result of the rise of science: any community of two individuals or more had to have a moral code. The real contest, therefore—which posed the basic choice to be considered—was between two branches of moral theory in the contemporary West: the individualist school based on self-interest, and the socialist school based on altruism. The Confucian morality based on the three bonds and the five relations, he warned, was rooted neither in self-interest nor in altruism, and was no more than a slave's morality that served the clan system of feudal times.

Chen was now deeply troubled by the dilemma posed by the Western philosophic-political debate. Self-interest, he admitted, was clearly a powerful motivation force for progress, as Western advances had shown. Moreover, it was a reality in every societal situation. Yet in describing the origins and growth of the individualist and socialist schools, Chen showed a clear preference for the socialist school, although he disguised it by calling for further study. Individualism, he said, had originated in the Greco-Roman world and had been advanced in the past century by such great scholars as Darwin and Nietzsche. Modern Germany, with its highly refined nationalism and militarism, was the individualist society pushed to its ultimate. Socialism had come originally from Christian civilization, but it had also prospered in modern times under various conditions. Chen chose to illustrate the growth of socialist doctrine by citing Tolstoy and the concept of mutual aid.

The more civilization advanced, Chen continued, the more the individual needed the group. What we use and eat today comes from mutual aid within society, because individual self-interest expands to encompass the self-interest of the state, of the society, and ultimately of all mankind. By means of this Tolstoyan logic (which revealed an anarchist influence), Chen was straying from liberalism and utilitarianism and groping toward an acceptance of social collectivism.

During the next confusing years, however, Chen and his generation in China were unable to abandon liberalism completely. By mid-1917 Chen found it difficult to contain his pessimism about developments in Chinese politics.[25] Though the spirit of republicanism in politics and the spirit of science in scholarship were the two great treasures of modern civilization, republican politics in China had not been "firmly established." The Guomindang was "incompetent," and the Jinbudang, despite the presence of able men, depended too much on established centers of power. Seeing no attractive organizational affiliations, Chen now appeared to advocate a loosely connected federal system for China rather than the centralized system being attempted. A centralized system, he believed, was impossible given the deep philosophic and policy differences between the northern and southern leaders: the northern leaders looked upon themselves as "Prussians" and advocated power politics based on militarism, whereas the southern leaders, dominated by the Guomindang, supported liberalism and populist politics.

After surveying China's leaders past and present, Chen passed judgment on five of the most famous figures of recent years: Zeng Guofan, Li Hongzhang, Yuan Shikai, Kang Youwei, and Sun Yat-sen. Yuan had committed the greatest crimes. Zeng and Li had done very little. Kang was "hopeless." It was too early to form a definite evaluation of Sun. Among their modern leaders, therefore, the Chinese people could not find a single man to revere and follow.[26] The issue, Chen concluded, was not only whether republicanism could survive, but whether the nation could survive.

Yet some months later, in the spring of 1918, Chen sought to refute Kang Youwei's devastating critique of the failure of republicanism in China.[27] After outlining Kang's recital of current ills, Chen admitted that it was "problematic" whether China could operate a republican system effectively, given the citizens' level of preparedness, but argued that even under monarchism the militarists would dominate Chinese politics at present. Thus the task was to prepare the citizenry, and in this cause Kang was not helping. But Chen's specific responses to Kang's analysis were weak, and he ultimately rested his case on one central assertion: republicanism would triumph because it was the present stage of a global historical process.

By the summer of 1918 Chen seemed to be floundering, cut adrift from many old beliefs but unprepared to espouse new ones. In an attempt to solve the problem of militarism, he argued that single-party rule had to be given up in favor of coalition government, so that civilian control of politics could be reasserted.[28] If China continued on its chaotic course, he insisted, foreign intervention was likely to occur. In September he again undertook the task of defending utilitarianism, by way of seeking to refute an article in *Eastern Miscellany*.* This time, however, his defense was couched in different terms. All noble behavior, he asserted, was aimed at achieving merit for the state

*Chen Duxiu, "Questioning the Journalist of the Eastern Miscellany," *Xin qingnian* 5 (September 15, 1918): 206–212. In an article published a month earlier, however, Chen had indicated the continuing influence of anarchism on his current thinking. Speaking of the need to destroy idols, he wrote: "The state is also an idol. The state is created by one or several types of people who occupy a given territory. . . . The reason why people still want to keep this idol is that it can protect the rights of the nobles and the wealthy people internally, and can encourage the invasion of small and weak states externally." See "Iconoclasm," *Xin qingnian* 5 (August 15, 1918): 89–91.

and benefitting the masses. The *Eastern Miscellany* author had claimed that utilitarianism reduced everything to the single naked purpose of attaining material satisfaction—food and clothing. But did not all institutions, Chen asked, ultimately aim at giving the individual the means to eat and clothe himself? Is it greed to struggle to maintain one's own life? In this response, there was no glorification of individualism.

During this period Chen also began to reduce his emphasis on republicanism by using the broader term "democracy." The choice for China was between democracy and science, on the one hand, and superstition, deism, and absolutism, on the other.[29] In an essay published in January 1919 he introduced his famous personages Mr. Democracy and Mr. Science, terms that became his hallmark. We attack things traditional—Confucianism, ancient literature, and similar relics of the past—proclaimed Chen, and we support democracy and science, the forces that have saved Western nations from darkness and could save China from darkness, too.[30]

In the spring of 1919, however, Chen was still searching for a philosophic base. An article he published in April of that year clearly reveals the continuing influence of Tolstoy and his doctrine of mutual aid, an influence congenial to Chen's preoccupation with human morality and the interaction between social organization and individual character.[31] Struggling to retain his usual optimism, he insisted that love, mutual aid, and the ability to distinguish good from evil were natural instincts of man. Thus, if individuals avoided accommodation or surrender and fought for basic social reforms, then domination by the great powers, political evils, the darkness of war, the injustices of private ownership and class inequities, and many other unreasonable forces in law and morality could be overcome. It all depended on how hard one was prepared to struggle.

In the next month, May 1919, *New Youth* devoted its entire issue to an exploration of Marx and his theories, with translations of articles by Angelo S. Rappoport and Kawakami Hajime, together with original essays by Chen, Gu Mengyu, Ling Shuang, and Li Dazhao. Chen's contribution was an article entitled "The Problem of Virtue and Marx's Materialist Concept of History." Dealing essentially with inequality in relations between the sexes as a product of the economic system, it was a slight piece, wholly unimpressive and with very little Marxist content.[32]

It will be noted that the publication date of this issue coincided with the May Fourth Movement, although the articles had obviously been prepared earlier. The student activities of this period stirred Chen deeply, and he sprang quickly to their defense. Indeed, as we shall see, he was to begin his career as a political activist a few weeks after May 4. Yet even at the end of 1919, despite his growing involvement in practical politics, Chen's political views remained somewhat indistinct. In a critique of Professor John Dewey's recent lectures in China, he asserted that the Chinese people did not want democracy merely in the political sense. Constitutionalism and such political rights as freedom of speech, of the press, and of residence were not sufficient. Our true goal, he continued, was "to better our social existence."[33] Politics, morality, and economics were merely tools to achieve that goal. But this required that social and economic policies occupy a major role in politics, because until the problems in these fields were solved, politics would remain backward. Society and the economy were the foundations of politics. Thus, Dewey's interpretation of political democracy, though good so far as it went, was not sufficient. We want constitutionalism and representative government, Chen said, so that political power will be in the hands of the people, but even after these objectives have been attained, there will still be certain kinds of freedom in the hands of others. Our goal should be to break the barrier between ruling and ruled in all senses, effecting a "spontaneous people's autonomy." China had had some foundation for autonomous democracy in its clans, local militia, guilds, and village schools. Although industry and commerce remained undeveloped, as did the concept of the nation-state, producing economic backwardness and political disunity, still China did not suffer from the domination of the bourgeoisie and the militarism which characterized contemporary Europe, and such traditional ideals as "the ruler and the people working side by side" and the well-field system showed that there were elements of democracy in the Chinese national character.

Once again Chen insisted that he was not pessimistic, despite the crisis at hand. We have not been seeking to establish democracy for very long, he wrote, and we had done too little propaganda work among the people before the revolution. Moreover, the military was controlled by professional soldiers rather than the citizenry at large, and the Guomindang had not understood the true meaning of democracy, believing that government should be omnipotent, ignoring the fact that the foundations of democracy must be in local, self-governing units. It is interesting that on the eve of helping to establish China's first Communist movement, Chen was arguing the case for a strongly decentralized, locally controlled political system in conformity with China's traditional structure, except for the broadening of the popular base so that all citizens would be included. It is important, of course, to remember that these concepts were also in conformity with early Bolshevik pledges, as we shall indicate more fully later.

At this point, Chen had accepted the critical importance of socioeconomic policies and, by implication at least, the necessity of a socialist system to advance them. One searches in vain, however, for a thoroughgoing Marxist analysis that would support his political and economic prescriptions. At root, Chen remained a humanist; his Marxism was a somewhat tentative graft.

A lingering ambivalence on the doctrinal front, however, did not prevent Chen from moving rapidly into the role of activist. Disputes over whether *New Youth* should be involved in political disputation, which we shall discuss later, caused Chen, Li Dazhao, and several others to establish a companion publication, *Meizhou pinglun* (Weekly Review) which was specifically for the purpose of airing their political views. And despite his opposition to the politicization of *New Youth*, Hu Shi served as editor of the new journal after Chen's political difficulties. Like *New Youth*, the *Weekly Review* reflected at various points the views of all three of the men with whom we are currently concerned, especially Chen and Li, and its central themes thus deserve a brief analysis at this point.

The *Weekly Review* made its debut on December 22, 1918, and continued until it was suppressed by the government the following September.[34] In those nine months, no source more fully revealed the changes and uncertainties characterizing the "progressive" intellectual movement during this period, and few journals had a greater influence on younger politicized intellectuals like Mao Zedong. The *Weekly Review* made its debut as a supporter of liberal democracy, particularly the values and policies of President Woodrow Wilson, and was generally sympathetic to the United States (though it was critical of American "capitalists"). It was fervently antimilitarist and antiwar, Chen's earlier praise of war notwithstanding. On balance, however, its authors were nationalists, especially on an issue like Shandong, but they tried to unite nationalism and internationalism. Finally, its first articles on the Russian Revolution showed an ambivalence between approval and disapproval, though in time the trend was toward a favorable appraisal. On each of these issues, to be sure, certain variations were to be found, depending on the given author.

Let us now examine these themes in somewhat greater detail. The first issue of the journal set the tone with respect to the United States and Wilson. The American president was praised for his intelligent, broadly gauged speeches and was described as "the very best man in the world today."[35] Two principles were identified with Wilson: opposition to the aggression by any nation against the equality and freedom of another people; and opposition to the interference by any government in its own people's equality and freedom. Our journal, the writer asserted, also has as its purpose support for justice and opposition to brute force.

Praise for Americans was not reserved for Wilson alone. When former President Theodore Roosevelt died, he was hailed as a great leader despite his vigorous support for the recent war. And in the issue published on May 4, 1919—a day destined to become historic—an article appeared complimenting the United States for its treatment of the Philippines, pointing out that it had permitted a legal nationalist movement there, and had long indicated that its policies were directed toward the eventual independence of the Filipino people.[36] In the next issue, moreover, a detailed review of the May 4 demonstrations reported that when the students stood in front of the American legation quarters, they shouted "Long life to the great United States! Long life to President Wilson!"[37] And when the journal came under Hu Shi's editorship, several issues carried detailed accounts of John Dewey's current lectures, together with pictures of the famed American educator-philosopher and his wife.[38]

The themes of democracy and human rights exemplified by Wilson were naturally advanced with respect to China. The journal's opening editorial championed the concept of having China's ordinary citizens create economic and political organizations, which would then coalesce into federations up to the province level so that the common man could participate in the management of his own affairs.[39] This was a proposal that the young Mao Zedong was to adopt with virtually no alterations in his Hunan newssheet, *Xiang jiang pinglun* (Xiang River Review), a few months later. In articles by Cai Yuanpei, Li, and others, the worth of labor and the Chinese worker was also emphasized—but not, it should be noted, from a Marxist or class-analysis standpoint. Rather, those who worked and contributed to the common good were distinguished from those who were shiftless and idle. Workers included farmers, intellectuals, businessmen, and even government officials, provided they sought diligently to advance the welfare of the community.[40] Nonetheless, attention was focused on the plight of certain workers, such as the Tangshan coal miners, and a plea was made for worker education, so that culture could be available not merely to capitalists but also to laborers.[41]

From the outset, the *Weekly Review* voiced sharp antimilitary sentiments. An opening editorial asserted that war had no value at all, although the recent conflict may have had two unintended benefits: the rise of socialist revolutions in Germany and Russia, and the possible establishment of a League of Nations and a League for Peace. But whether any of these ventures would be successful, the writer continued, could not yet be predicted.[42] At a later point, an author was to assert: We appreciate nations that loan us money to reduce our armies, and we oppose those who loan us money to expand them.[43] Many articles criticized the various "warlord" armies as useless and destructive and urged disbanding or drastically reducing China's military forces.

On the eve of the May 4 incident, criticism of Japan mounted steadily in the journal, and the Shandong issue was brought to the fore. At the same time, however, several authors—and particularly Li Dazhao—insisted that nationalism and internationalism were entirely compatible. Love for one's country and an insistence upon justice and equality, they argued, were principles that could apply globally, in the form of love for humanity and a demand for justice for all peoples.

Finally, the writers of the *Weekly Review* took a cautious and ambivalent view of the Russian Revolution. Thus, in an article published in early January 1919, one writer said, "We do not know whether the people support the radicals or not, but they control the food, so the people have to follow them to survive."[44] He also said, however, that workers and peasants who had had a painful life generally welcomed the promises of the radical government, but added that if the radicals were to win popular support, they would have to end the chaos and bring order to the new Russia. In the next issues, moreover, criticism was leveled against both the Whites and the Reds—against "the opposition" (the Whites) for suppressing and killing the working class, and against "the radicals" for using the workers to keep down the middle class and kill aristocrats and other opponents.[45] In a later issue, another writer stated that he had heard of imperial or aristocratic dictatorships, but never of a people's dictatorship.[46] Not infrequently, the *Weekly Review* carried articles that deplored the plight of the Chinese peasant and analyzed the phenomenon of banditry in China, but none of these writings were cast in class terms.

It was not Marxism but a rising disillusionment with the West and Japan in the context of Versailles and the Shandong issue that moved some *Weekly Review* authors toward greater sympathy for the Russian Revolution. Nowhere was this more clearly revealed than in an article by "Ruo Yu" in late February of 1919. It reported that the new Third International, in its organizational meeting in Moscow in late January, had agreed to organize an international socialist party that would oppose capitalism and its military forces, pursue policies directed toward the freedom and happiness of the majority of the people, and resist the tyranny of the powerful. Since China suffered not only from internal oppression by militarists but also from brute force applied by foreign powers, the author concluded, the Chinese socialist parties should unite with the international socialist parties to overthrow their aggressors, thereby creating an international revolution.[47]

Beginning in March 1919, moreover, the *Weekly Review* began to publish translations of Marxist works, with generally favorable commentaries.[48] The new Constitution of the U.S.S.R. was set forth on June 19, 1919, and later issues presented the land law and the new rules regarding marriage, among other items. At the same time, however, most editorials and essays remained at variance with key Marxist themes. In an editorial of April 27, 1919, for example, the writer said that in China it was not the rich factory owners who exploited workers, but the corrupt civil and military officials.[49] In a May 4 editorial entitled "The Crimes of the Chinese Literati and Officials" the author supported a "bourgeois revolution" for China; but it was to be led by the workers and peasants, not the bourgeoisie, and its targets were to be the aristocrats and *shidafu* (literati and officials), who were the real rulers of China—a fact not changed by the 1911 Revolution, which had merely removed the emperor. If everyone became involved in politics, if universal suffrage were the goal and moderate means were applied, a political revolution could take place. Then, later on, a social revolution could unfold, but it would be less destructive than in Russia because China did not have big capitalists.[50]

But by mid-1919 Chen was no longer content with words. Increasingly, he was determined to tap the political potential that lay within the events of May 4 in order to challenge the status quo. On June 11 he was arrested for passing out handbills that accused the government of mistreating students. At this point, it should be noted, he was still more nearly a liberal than a Marxist. He was released in September with the aid of Hu Shi and others, but he remained in Beijing for only a few months and took up residence in Shanghai in early 1920.* By the spring of that year, he was finally prepared to announce his conversion to Marxism-Leninism and was deeply involved in the activities of the fledgling Chinese Communist movement. However, problems in this conversion—numerous problems—remained.

LI DAZHAO—ANOTHER HUMANIST'S QUEST FOR ANSWERS

In many respects, Li Dazhao's conversion to Marxism was even more difficult to anticipate than that of Chen. Neither Li's earlier career nor his intellectual proclivities seemed to prepare him for such a development, and indeed, as we shall see, the transformation came in stages with certain paradoxes remaining until the end. As we noted earlier, Li had gone to Japan in late 1913. He studied political economy there, became acquainted with various political and philosophic currents then in vogue by reading Japanese and English works, and later participated in the anti-Yuan movement. In May 1916, as the crisis over Yuan's monarchical quest was reaching its zenith, he was induced to return to China. He then worked with the Jinbudang in Shanghai, becoming secretary to Tang Hualong, one of its leaders and his earlier benefactor. When Tang went to Beijing, Li followed and served briefly as editor of the Jinbudang organ, *Chenzhong bao* (Morning

* According to Hu Shi's recollection, he, Chen, and Gao Yihan met in a popular Chinese teahouse on the day of Chen's arrest, but when Chen began distributing handbills attacking the government, the other two left. (Grieder, *Renaissance*, p. 181, n. 15. For another version, see Meisner, *Li Ta-chao*, p. 103.) Chen was paroled from prison in September, through the intervention of his Anhui compatriots, according to Hu Shi. When he went to Wuhan in January 1920 to substitute for Hu Shi in a speaking engagement, he broke parole, since he was not supposed to leave Beijing without permission. Soon after he returned to the capital, he and Li Dazhao, in whose house he had been staying, were forced to flee. At this point, his salary as a Peking University Professor ended, and it was therefore agreed that he would be the sole editor of *New Youth* and would draw a salary for this activity. (Grieder's interview with Hu Shi, July 1960, reported in *Renaissance*, p. 184, n. 23.)

70. *Li Dazhao*

Bell News), later the *Chen bao* (Morning News). He also joined the Research Clique, a group composed of followers of Tang and Liang Qichao.*

Like Chen, Li's basic dedication during this period was to republicanism.

* For details, in English, see Meisner, *Li Ta-chao*, pp. 15–21; in Chinese, see *Li Dazhao zhuan*, pp. 20–22. According to the latter account, Li resigned as the editor of *Chenzhong bao* after twenty-two days because of a dispute with Tang (although the account does not mention Tang by name or identify him as Li's earlier benefactor). No mention is made of Li's affiliation with the Gemingdang in Japan, but much attention is devoted to his activities in opposing the Twenty-One Demands and the monarchist movement.

That his intellectual concerns were different from those of Chen, however, is clearly revealed in an article entitled "Youthful Spring," published in *New Youth* in September of 1916.[51] In this essay and an earlier one, he drew heavily on the thought of Henri Bergson and Ralph Waldo Emerson.* At first glance, this would suggest that Li, like Chen, had reached a phase in his intellectual development in which individualism assumed central importance. But this was only partly the case. Li made it clear that he was interested in the individual primarily as a motive force for change. By exercising his free will and striving to look beyond the past and the present, man could alter his destiny and that of the world.** It should not be overlooked, moreover, that Emerson in particular could be rendered as compatible with classical Chinese philosophy as any Western writer known to the Chinese. And in this essay Li revealed himself very much in harmony with the classical mode of thought. Writing in sweeping, metaphysical terms, he sketched the universe in which man found himself as being composed of two opposing elements, expressed variously as emptiness and existence, the absolute and the relative, or being and nothingness. Life, Li asserted, was only one point on the continuum between death and rebirth—a central Buddhist teaching and a vision to which Emerson had paid homage in his own fashion.

In truth, Li was deeply torn between his traditional turn of mind and the modern substance of his ideas. In his commitment to progress and his preoccupation with youth, he was moving sharply away from the classical mold. Rejecting the traditional belief that release from the painful wheel of life came only through the ascent into nothingness, Li had grasped the Western idea of progress. He joined Chen in praising science and disparaging religion. Science was the torch that would lead mankind toward the future. And rather than trusting in God, he wrote, we should place our trust in man and in the unlimited capacity of youth to revitalize society.

Despite Li's very considerable knowledge of Western philosophy and politics, one senses a certain reserve in his attitude toward Western culture, a deep affinity for a different style of life. Only in his fierce determination to move China out of weakness and stagnation was Li drawn to the light that shone from the West. The new always defeats the old, he said; China has been in decline since the Zhou dynasty, so it is not surprising that the nation is threatened. The solution lies, not in seeking to prevent the death of the old, white-haired China, but in encouraging youth to impregnate the society so that a new China could be born. The past was closed. It was the future—waiting to be written on the *tabula rasa* of time—that should attract the youth of China. They could write the first chapter of a new era.

* Both Bergson and Emerson were widely read during this era, in English and in Japanese translations. Bergson's metaphysical writings in particular influenced Liang Qichao (who was to meet the philosopher in 1919), Zhang Junmai, Zhang Dongsun, and Liang Souming—each of whom supported many traditional Chinese values. Bergson rejected both the scientific method (as it was being advanced by his contemporaries) and general theories or universal systems in favor of apprehending the true nature of things by intuition. He advanced concepts of motion and change as replacements for static concepts, and in his major work, *Time and Free Will* (1910), he opposed a spatial concept of time seeking to resolve the problem of free will. Emerson dwelt repeatedly on the liberating force of nature and attacked the concept of a deterministic universe, believing strongly that the self-reliant individual could decisively affect his environment, and that change in general was beneficial.

** In one passage Li asserted, "The path of no return is the path of no worry. It is the path to youth, and on this path, our youth, summoning reason and effort, will advance the civilization of the world and create happiness for mankind" ("Youthful Spring," p. 11).

Shifting his metaphor, Li then counseled that the appearance of new buds and the flowering of spring could not be taken for granted; it depended on careful cultivation of the soil, and this was the supreme task that confronted the young people of the country. It was imperative that their energies not be consumed in a search for wealth and power. They should cast off fear of the future and be determined to live and die youthful. In my youth, Li concluded (he was then twenty-seven), I can create a youthful family, a youthful nation, a youthful human race, a youthful earth, a youthful universe.[52] Thus by drawing on various sources, including a recent article by Chen Duxiu, Li turned certain classical concepts to drastically new purposes, but without leaving the traditional mode of thought with which he was most comfortable.

Less than a year later, in the spring of 1917, Li wrote again on the topic of youth, in a somewhat different vein but with the same goal in mind.[53] Modern society, he asserted, was the product of harmony: the union of aristocracy and commoners, capitalists and workers, landlords and tenants, youth and the elderly. The progress of civilization and happiness in society stemmed from such unions. For example, the elderly were careful and conservative, whereas the young were given to excesses and radicalism. The function of government should be to serve as the mediator between the two so as to insure progress. Unfortunately, the old people of China were weak both physically and intellectually because they had not cultivated their capacities during youth. We can only feed them, Li lamented, without receiving anything in exchange.* Although this essay was published in April of 1917, shortly after the overthrow of the czar in Russia, it expressed no interest in Marxism, or indeed in socialism of any sort. On the contrary, many of its themes—such as the idea of progress based on harmony between classes and generations—were antithetical to the most fundamental tenets of Marxism and wholly in tune with traditional Chinese values.

The same can be said of two essays published in April and May of 1918, half a year after the Bolshevik Revolution. In the first, entitled "Now," Li's central thesis was that the present is a precious possession and should be fully utilized in building for the future. One should not be hobbled by the past, although it was essential to realize that mistakes made today would affect the events of tomorrow.[54] Again, one theme stood out: the critical importance and the inevitability of progress. The water-flow of the great reality, Li asserted, always moves forward. Life continues and develops, following the direction of this great reality. Therefore, we should try our best to achieve great merit for the world, and for later generations, so that the "me" of eternity will be able to enjoy peace. I am the universe and the universe is me, he concluded, wrapping his belief in progress in a Buddhist invocation.** Just as Kang Youwei had reinterpreted Confucianism so that it could

* "Youthful Spring," p. 3. In an editor's note to this article, Chen took a somewhat different tack. Of course, youth should not despise old people, he wrote, but our society has had too much conservatism, and we must make a choice. At present, age is in reverse proportion to intellect in China. If we use intellect as the standard, he continued, the old people in our country should respect the young. In January 1918 Li was appointed director of the library at Peking University, and he was reported to have spent half of his salary in assistance to poor students. In June he set up an association called "Young China" and became editor of a monthly by that name. The association was dedicated to the dissemination and application of new ideas that would regenerate the nation.

** Both the term *dagongde* (great merit) and the reference to the relationship between the individual and the universe go to the heart of Buddhist thought.

serve the purposes of reform, Li put certain aspects of Buddhist and Taoist thought, supported by Western references, to a similar task, although in his case the act was certainly a less conscious one.

In the essay published in May (entitled "New! Old!"), Li continued to stress the tasks of youth. He emphasized the critical importance of striking out on a new path, not merely in politics, but also in society, literature, and the entire realm of ideas.* Like many other Chinese intellectuals, Li would settle for nothing less than a cosmic approach to China's problems, hence his implicit radicalism. But as to the design of the new order and the means of attaining it, he remained exceedingly vague. His call for youth to take command at once flattered and consoled students who were facing the future in a period of rising political chaos. But what, specifically were they to do? In concrete terms, how was China to be saved? As yet, Li had no satisfying answers.**

This is probably why the Bolshevik Revolution soon made a deep impression on him. It seemed to offer not only a new and potentially effective mode of political organization but also a practical application of the universalist outlook he had long favored. Thus, in a relatively brief article called "The Triumph of Bolshevism," published in the October 1918 issue of *New Youth*, Li emerged as China's first enthusiast for the latest phase of the Russian Revolution.[55] The defeat of German militarism, he wrote, represents the fall of the Hohenzollerns, not the failure of the German nation, and credit for the victory over militarism and autocracy belongs not to Wilson but to Lenin, Trotsky, and Koliontai, to Liebknecht and Scheideman, and to Marx. We should celebrate, he continued, not the victory of one state or several, but the new light of democracy and socialism that dawns on mankind.

The purpose of Bolshevism, according to Li, was to break state boundaries and at the same time destroy the monopolistic capitalist system of production, following the prescriptions of Marx. The war now being concluded had also been fought to smash state boundaries, he said, but for the purpose of abetting capitalist expansion: the states made strong by the war intended to benefit their bourgeoisie rather than promote the development of humanitarian, rational, and productive organizations; in fact, they sought to advance from being strong states to becoming global empires. But the Bolsheviks had uncovered this plot. They had told the Russian people the truth: that the war was for the czar and the kaiser, for kings and emperors; it was not their war. Their war was a class war, the worldwide war of the proletariat against the capitalists.

The Bolsheviks opposed war, Li continued, but they were not afraid of it. They believed that every man and woman should engage in labor, and be organized into *lianhe* (councils, or soviets). Each council would govern it-

*Li Dazhao, "New! Old!" *Xin qingnian* 4 (May 15, 1918): 307–310. At the very outset of this article, Li vividly displayed his mixed use of old and new concepts, and the gradual progression from a static toward a dynamic philosophy that was taking place in his thought. "The axis of the universe's evolution is turned by two kinds of spirits, the new and the old," he wrote. "But the direction of these spirits must be forward, not stationary (dynamic, not static); it must be whole, not divided."

**The absence of Marxist themes in Li's writings of this period cannot be attributed to a lack of conversance with them. Li had studied the works of Kawakami Hajime, the famed Japanese Marxist, during his sojourn in Japan and was certainly familiar with the central Marxist beliefs. See Meisner, *Li Ta-chao*, p. 56.

self, and through council representatives, all governments throughout the world would be organized. There would be no president or premier, no cabinet and no congress or parliament; there would be no rulers. All decisions would be made by the councils (soviets). All property would belong to the people who worked with it; there would be no other right of ownership. Finally, the worker-peasant councils would unite with the proletariat of the world to create free homelands, beginning with a United States of Europe as the foundation for a world federation of proletarian societies. This was Bolshevik doctrine, Li announced, and it offered a new creed for global revolution in the twentieth century.

Like Chen Duxiu, Li was greatly attracted to the concept of locally constructed councils of workers and peasants, self-governing and autonomous in nature, and federated into larger units to constitute national and international bodies. This idea, so clearly associated with anarcho-syndicalism, was indeed a prominent aspect of early Bolshevik policy, as was the frontal assault on the state contained in Lenin's classic *State and Revolution*, written in August and September of 1917.*

It is interesting, given his personal attraction to Bolshevism as he understood it, that in this article Li quoted a Western analysis of the Russian Revolution which was by no means wholly favorable. He cited Harold Williams, a London Times correspondent, to the effect that Bolshevism was a mass movement with certain affinities to Christianity: it promised the establishment of God's kingdom on earth, and during one's own lifetime; its manipulative and authoritarian ideas were hidden in childlike, irrational doctrines; and even embarrassing statements by its leaders were accepted as religious pronouncements. Li was content to add that the impact of Bolshevism had been felt not only by the Russian masses but by people throughout the world, in fulfillment of Trotsky's pledge to make Russia the fuse that would ignite a worldwide revolution.

Li ended this essay by asserting that because the Bolshevist movement was a genuine mobilization of the masses, it was truly an irresistible social force, capable of sweeping away all old elements—emperors, nobles, warlords, bureaucrats, and capitalists—"like the dried yellow leaves meeting the autumn wind." Here Li revealed his latest thoughts: an individual's future was related to the future of mankind. The Russian Revolution signaled major psychological changes in twentieth-century man. The victory of Bolshevism was the triumph of a new spirit, the awakening of individual humans everywhere to a great collective upsurge.[56]

A careful reading of this essay offers some clues to the reasons for Li's enthusiasm. He was still willing to quote foreign skeptics, but for him, that which was "new" and "young," that which represented the future—and was capable of wiping out the past—had been discovered. Li's knowledge of Western liberal thought may have been deeper than Chen's, but his commitment to it had been less firm, at least after 1915. His ties with tradi-

* For the early antistatist pronouncements of Lenin, see Stephen F. Cohen, *Bukharin and the Bolshevik Revolution*, pp. 47–48, 54, and 89. It was in his famous April Theses, issued upon his return to Russia in 1917, that Lenin first made the attack upon the state the foundation of the Bolshevik program. He called for the elimination of the police, the army, and the bureaucracy, and their replacement by a government of soviets, a "commune state." "Down with the Provisional Government! All power to the Soviets!" became the Bolshevik rallying cry against the Kerensky administration at the climax of this campaign.

tionalism had never been broken, and this made it easier to accept a collectivist doctrine, one he conceived to be based on humanism and universality. It made it easier for him, like others, to see in Bolshevism an antipathy to the state and a reliance on governance through small, natural groups, worker-peasant councils. And it helped him to believe that the imperialist danger could be removed by the mobilized masses, freely governing themselves and subverting other states, liberating fellow workers around the world. This route, of course, was an alternative to the goal of centralization pursued by the current Chinese power-holders and their faltering efforts to ward off Japanese expansion by appeals to the Western powers.

Bolshevism also advanced a doctrine wholly attuned to Li's optimism by preaching the inevitability of progress—progress rolling ahead in a mighty torrent, sooner or later encompassing China and sweeping it forward along with the Western world. Despite his earlier nationalism—and the elements of xenophobia attached to it—Li's traditionalist bent made him at heart a universalist; his ultimate dream was that of bringing mankind into harmony in a global order. Like Chen, he came to Marxism-Leninism, not by passing through the dismal corridors of economics (although he was soon to explore them), but by pursuing a humanistic vision buried in China's past.

In the same issue of *New Youth*, Li presented another essay exploring the same themes.[57] The real reason for the war, he asserted, lay in the development of capitalism. The productive force of capitalism could not be contained within the boundaries of the state, so the capitalist governments wanted to break state boundaries through war in order to build empires, thereby creating economic structures that would work for the profit of the capitalist class. Here, consciously or otherwise, Li was advancing a simple version of the Hobson-Lenin doctrine of imperialism. But capitalists, continued Li, who held their properties as a result of inheritance or monopoly, were in the minority; everyone shared in the capacity for labor. Hence the victory of labor was the victory of the common people. In the new era, the price of development would be struggle, but no one should be afraid. Nor should the currents of the time be resisted. As the French Revolution was to the eighteenth century, so the Russian Revolution was to the twentieth century—the precursor of a global revolution. Li ended by asserting that in the new era robbers would not be tolerated. Who were the robbers? They were those who did not work. With the entire world turned into a giant factory, there would be no room for shirkers. The Chinese had been lazy. Now everyone should rush to work.

Li, unlike Chen, had never sanctioned war in general or World War I in particular, a fact that was illuminated in his essay on women after the war, published in February 1919.[58] That essay began with a sympathetic treatment of Jeanette Rankin, the congresswoman from Montana, who had voted against United States entry into the war. But its main theme was that the basic problem of women in the contemporary world related to their class, not their sex. The suffrage movement was essentially a movement of middleclass women, said Li, repeating the standard socialist position. These women wanted to govern themselves, whereas women of the proletarian class wanted to rescue themselves from poverty. The interests of the two classes were thus completely different. The fundamental issue was an economic one. If a woman was arrested for prostitution, it did not matter whether she was questioned by a man or a woman police officer; the critical issue was the socioeconomic structure that had forced her into this trade. Thus, the quest of middle-class women for the vote could not be regarded as being in the interests of all women. To solve the women's problem in its largest dimensions, it was necessary to break the old social system.

In the same month Li published a series of four articles in the Beijing *Chen bao* under the title "Youth and the Rural Villages."[59] One of his major themes was that young Chinese intellectuals had to integrate themselves with the working people of the nation if civilization were to be brought back to society at large and enabled to take root. In China, of course, the great majority of the working people were peasants, and unless they were liberated, the nation could not be liberated. Their suffering was the nation's suffering; their ignorance, their joys, and their woes were a mirror to the politics of the country at large. It was thus imperative to enlighten them about their own interests, to alleviate their ignorance and their burdens so that they could plan effectively for their own livelihood. And if the young intellectuals did not help the peasant, who would? Here, Li found a model for such assistance in the services rendered by young Russian intellectuals in earlier decades. Giving up their comfortable surroundings, many of them had gone to the countryside, preaching humanism and socialism, talking and working with the Russian peasants. And by awakening the peasant, these pioneers had laid the groundwork for the current Russian Revolution.

Striking a new note, Li proceeded to define economic and social conditions in rural China as miserable. Corrupt officials and evil landlords exploited the peasants, who were too ignorant to know how to defend themselves or organize for mutual aid. Indeed, while the landlords were always cruel and miserly toward their tenants and hired laborers, the latter sometimes informed on each other instead of cooperating sympathetically. Educational facilities in the countryside, moreover, were wholly inadequate, and there were virtually no opportunities for adult education. The peasants' free time was therefore wasted. Even when associations to promote village welfare were established, they were dominated by the local gentry or leaders.

The cause of this deplorable situation, argued Li, was that China's educated young people preferred to stay in the city, hoping for careers as officials. Most urban youth simply drifted along, going from bad to worse in their idleness. Meanwhile, the countryside, where life should be fresh and clean, decayed for lack of intellectual stimulus. All constitutional states were advancing toward universal suffrage, but whether China chose selective or universal suffrage in the future, the peasants must be enlightened and rendered capable of making free and meaningful choices. Because they had had no past guidance from educated youth, and elections had been controlled by unsavory elements from the cities, they had been twisted into something unrecognizable. Effective constitutionalism in China depended on a renovation of the countryside.

As he concluded, Li softened his earlier harsh judgment of rural life. He suggested that young people drifting into the cities should substitute the openness, the humane qualities, and the fresh air of the countryside for the gloomy and polluted atmosphere of urban life. It would be far better for you to return to the rural village as soon as possible, he urged, and lead a simple life—teaching in primary schools, growing vegetables, or tilling the soil to produce grain. As young intellectuals joined the labor union movement and went into the countryside Chinese society would prosper, and the exploiters of workers and peasants would disappear.*

Li's words have a familiar ring today, for similar ideas have influenced the lives of millions of young people since the success of the Communist revolution. Yet Li acquired few followers for this particular crusade. From the late Qing era on, student radicals were reasonably familiar with the Russian Narodniki and their efforts to arouse the Russian peasantry, but most of them were more attracted by the heroism involved in their assassination attempts. Perhaps this was partly because they saw little evidence of success in the intellectual's attempts to enter the Russian *mir*. They preceded Li, of course, in accepting the idea that they should act as tutors who would train the people for their ultimate political role, and in this respect the idea of going to the commoners wherever they lived was implicit in their thought. But the vast majority of politically active young intellectuals, then as now, preferred to practice their radicalism in Shanghai, Beijing, or Canton. As the events following May 4, 1919, illustrated, the student was prepared to speak to workers in the cities and even to visit villages to solicit support for the resist-Japan movement. But Li's proposal that students return to rural China permanently, to share their culture and their lives with the villagers, produced few genuine volunteers.

Within a few months Li set forth in great detail his current views on Marxism. He served as editor for the special May 1919 number of *New Youth* that commemorated the one-hundredth anniversary of Marx's birth, and contributed a long article that was continued in the next issue.[60] To put Li's views in context, it is important here to consider the more important of the companion pieces.

The most significant article, apart from Li's, was written by Gu Zhaoxiong, better known as Gu Mengyu, and entitled "The Theory of Marxism."[61] Essentially, it was an effort to provide a factual analysis of the sources of Marxist ideas, especially historical materialism. While recognizing the importance of this doctrine to modern social science, Gu remarked that it also suffered from several defects. He insisted that the legal institutions of a society provided the basis for the economic order. Hence, law and politics were the foundation and economics the superstructure, not vice versa, as Marx would have it. He also discussed Marx's theory of surplus value and his analysis of capitalism, particularly the thesis that capitalism led to an ever greater concentration of productive control and wealth. He then noted the revisionist attacks on Marx, concluding with his own evaluation: "Though the teachings of Marx include many errors, the significance of his work cannot be disputed."

Marx's merit, Gu continued, lay in his criticisms of the current economic system, including his exposure of its corruption. He had motivated both the

* *Li Dazhao xuanji*, p. 150. Li ended with this appeal: "Youth, go to the countryside quickly! Go to work at sunrise and rest after sunset. Eat the food you have produced and drink the water from the well you have dug. The older men and women who work in the fields throughout the year will be comrades-in-arms. You will live in the place where you belong, where smoke comes up from your home as you return from work at dusk, with a hoe on your shoulders, amidst chickens and dogs." Li was to repeat this call at later points, as in "The Youth Movement of Young China," *Xin Zhongguo* 1 (September 15, 1919), in *Li Dazhao xuanji*, pp. 235–238.

social sciences and the social movement to consider means of renovating the present order. But Marx's dogmatism had not been supported by other scientists, and his theory of surplus value was forced and full of basic contradictions. Gu ended by asserting that his own views in general coincided with those of the revisionists. The thrust of economic development was toward socialism, but this did not mean that there was a single concrete social plan for society. Rather, the trend was in a general sense toward mutual aid and collective assistance (*lianhe huzhu*). Finally, "one cannot use an ideal theory to predict socialism's advance or detail its stages."[62]

Gu's analysis was hardly a ringing endorsement of Marxist theory, despite the homage he paid to Marx's influence and importance, and the same tone characterized most of the other articles in this issue. Gu was followed by Ling Shuang, who offered "A Critique of Marxism."[63] Ling drew on certain critics of Marx, such as W. H. Mallock, to charge that in his economic determinism Marx was guilty of reductionism and of letting "imagination ruin science."[64] Ling also cited anarchist critics, referring to Kropotkin's article on anarchism in the *Encyclopaedia Brittanica*. He defined the anarchists, symbolized by Bakunin, as the chief opponents of the Marxists, because they advocated people's free associations instead of a state organization and sought to establish the doctrine "to each according to his need."

Next came a translation of Angelo S. Rappoport's article "The Foundations of Russian Revolutionary Philosophy," which according to the translator had been written two years earlier.[65] Rappoport also paid considerable attention to the division between anarchists and Marxists. He defined Bakunin as a "true humanitarian" who wanted all oppressed people in the world to be liberated, in contradistinction to such radical nationalists as Lassalle, Mazzini, and Blanqui. Bakunin was more emotional than Marx, he wrote, and more generous, for Marx concentrated his affection on one class.[66] Marx was a rational machine, a "scientific agitator" imbued with the spirit of democratic dictatorship.

An article by Chen Duxiu, which we have already described, was followed by an essay written by Kawakami Hajime and translated by "Yuan Quan." Entitled "The Embattled Career of Marx," it was a sympathetic account of Marx's life during the period when he wrote *Das Kapital*, and said that Marx was determined to give himself (through his work) to save the world.[67]

Li's article was the most substantial of the group, but its general tone was in harmony with the others, especially the one written by Gu, which suggests that mutual consultations and discussions had taken place.* In finally coming to grips with Marxist economics in a detailed manner, Li revealed himself as a serious scholar, but his categories were a reflection of the continuing traditional influence upon him. There were three branches of economics, he said: individualist, socialist, and humanitarian. The individualist branch, also called capitalist, was based on the philosophy of laissez-faire, or letting individuals take care of themselves. It accepted the correctness of the present economic structure and of all individual endeavors based on self-interest. Socialist economics opposed the doctrine of laissez-

*Interest in Marxism during this period was by no means confined to the *New Youth* group. Dai Jitao and Hu Hanmin, for example, were also propagating Marxist concepts, and one may presume that intellectual discussions of Marxism were not uncommon.

faire, and humanitarian economics opposed actions based strictly on self-interest. Socialist economists believed that the root of all evil lay in the capitalist economic system, and that to change morality one had to change that system. Humanitarian economists believed that unless human nature was changed, individuals would always be greedy, and society would remain unable to cope with the resulting conflicts.

Russia and Germany had given the world a vision of fundamental reforms that might be carried out, Li continued, and Marx, the mentor of these radical reformers, belonged to the socialist school of economists. He alone had scientifically demonstrated the inevitability of socialist economic organization. Li then identified the three critical themes of Marxian socialism: its theory of historical materialism; its economic theories; and its concept of the socialist movement. The class struggle, he said, was the central principle that united these three. In the exposition that followed, Li accepted the primacy of the economic system in determining other facets of the social order, and in so doing indicated that he had grasped the essentials of Marxian dialectical materialism, depending upon Kawakami Hajime's translations. But he expressed some reservations about the thesis that ownership of the means of production was the sole factor in the shaping of a social order. He could not dismiss critics who insisted on giving some independent role to human endeavor—economic and political—and who questioned the apparent contradiction between Marx's thesis of the inevitability of economic and political stages and his insistence on the necessity of the class struggle. Marx had attempted to answer this, Li said, by including class interactions in his analysis of natural economic development. "I still feel it is a little forced," he wrote, echoing Gu's sentiments.[68] Yet he continued, "When a theory is first set forth, it is frequently exaggerated. Marx has already made a great contribution to sociology, combining economics, law, and history into one body."

In the next section Li sought to reconcile his humanist leanings with Marxism. He suggested that Marx never ignored the noble wishes of individuals, but believed that when such moral principles were expressed in general ethical terms they could not affect the collective behavior of men, which was bound to be based on class interest. Values such as mutual aid and philanthropy did not disappear; they simply could not be put into practice during the continued disturbances brought about by the class struggle. Man's destiny—mutual aid in the absence of class struggle—would begin when the competitive mode of production had ended.

Li then came to his own position. There was a new idealism in modern philosophy, he asserted, which could revise Marx's materialism. It saw the world as moving from a period in which ethical ideas were frequently destroyed by economic struggle, into a period in which ethical ideas could be realized. We should work to make such ideas effective, he said, and promote humanitarian movements in order to eradicate man's "evil habits." For this purpose, we cannot rely wholly on changes in the material realm, he added. "This is where Marxist theory should be revised. I believe that man's spirit should be reformed through humanitarianism, and the economic structure reformed through socialism. Neither reform alone will suffice. I believe that reform must apply both to matter and to mind and seek a consistency between the spirit and the flesh."[69]

Li concluded this first section of his two-part analysis by noting that Marxism, like other theories, was a product of its age—an age marked by the decline of religious and political power and the rise of economic power, hence, Marx's historical materialism. Marx himself forgot to view his theory as a product of his own age, Li noted. And although we cannot ignore its value for our times, it cannot be used to explain all history or even everything about our present society. This was hardly the unqualified endorsement one might expect from an enthusiast for the Bolshevik cause.

In the second section of his critique, published in the November 1919 issue, Li began with an extended discussion of Marxist economics, indicating that it had two major components—the theory of surplus value and the propensity for capital accumulation.[70] The former related to the problem of exchange value, the latter to economic evolution. Although the theory of surplus value had been introduced by predecessors of Marx, it was Marx who had brought it to scientific completeness, by stressing its economic principles and systemic underpinnings rather than the injustices it had fostered. But Li ended this discussion with a serious reservation. The actual price of a product and its value as defined by Marx were two separate things. Prices were influenced by supply and demand, and by competition, and so the theory of labor's surplus value became shaky; and if its foundations were unsteady, Marxism in its entirety could not help but suffer repercussions, he asserted, once again echoing Gu's doubts. Later, however, Li professed indignation that although the theories of capital advanced by Marx and Adam Smith agreed in their essentials, Smith was universally accepted and Marx had been severely attacked. As for capital concentration, the advent of modern trusts and cartels supported Marx's theory, though he had not lived to see this proof emerge.

In the final section of his essay, Li appeared to accept Marx's concept of the means by which socialism would emerge as the universal force of the coming era. Outlining the process by which the proletarian class, although a product of capitalism, would eventually destroy the system that produced it, Li faithfully depicted the Marxian evolution: industrialization, urbanization, and the impoverishment of the working masses through extreme social inequities. The breakdown of capitalism, he asserted, would represent the breakdown of private ownership. Because private property was acquired through capitalism rather than through one's own labor, it must be abolished. Moreover, the extensive division of labor that would have taken place would preclude the possibility of returning to a system of private ownership. Thus, the means of production must be seized by the workers and given to the whole of society—to the collectivity—instead of to individuals. Then everyone who participated in production would receive a share according to his labor. Excess labor and its surplus value would disappear with the end of capitalism.

These articles clearly indicate the limits of Li's adherence to Marxism. In expressing doubts and reservations about certain aspects of Marxist theory, he relied heavily on Western critics—from those who challenged fundamental socialist precepts to those who espoused socialism but insisted that Marxism must be revised. His receptivity to some of their arguments, however, stemmed from certain deeply held inner principles of his own. To this very Chinese intellectual, material changes alone would not suffice to restructure and ennoble human character. Values of an ethical and moral nature had an existence at least partly independent of socioeconomic structure and could be induced or influenced by a humanistic philosophy.

Li the activist and Li the philosopher were not yet wholly reconciled. Li the activist accepted the Bolshevik Revolution as pointing the way for China, a China desperately in need of new inspiration. He found its anti-militarist, anti-imperialist, universalist creed—and its insistence on governance through worker-based soviets—deeply appealing. He was attracted also to its energy, its call for a mobilization of the masses, which he hoped might awaken the Chinese masses from their lethargy. And he was stirred by the claim that socialism was inevitable, with its promise that China could join in the great world revolution and eventually catch up with the advanced nations, even if this took many years. For those who viewed China from within during these troubled years, such hopes kept alive a stubborn optimism.

But to support the Bolshevik Revolution as a harbinger of change in the twentieth century and to support socialism as the wave of the future—as necessary, desirable, and inevitable—did not require one to accept Marxism without reservations, at least for now. The philosopher in Li could not make the leap to Marxism in one massive effort. His classical, humanistic values, buttressed by more technical reservations drawn from others, made it impossible. That Marx was a great scholar, and the inspiration for the Bolshevik Revolution, Li readily acknowledged, but in his current view, Marx was neither infallible nor wholly serviceable for the present age. He believed that one could and should express doubts about particular aspects of Marxist theory without challenging its forecast of a revolution that would soon sweep the world. That revolution had now begun in Russia, and this was what interested Li most of all. Thus, although he could be defined as a revisionist at this point, Li was also prepared to work with the Bolshevik leaders in any plans they might advance for the coming global revolution.

It is interesting to note that perhaps the best in-depth studies of Marxism produced in China during this period were written by two intellectual-political figures who later played leading roles as anti-Communists, namely Hu Hanmin and Dai Jitao. Hu's article, entitled "A Materialist Study of the History of Chinese Philosophy," which appeared in the journal *Jianshe* (Construction) in October of 1919, demonstrated a reasonably thorough understanding of basic Marxist principles. Hu was also to challenge Li's criticism of Marxist materialism in a major article entitled "A Criticism of the Criticism of Historical Materialism," published in the same journal in December.[71] Meanwhile, Dai Jitao had translated a considerable portion of Karl Kautsky's *The Economic Doctrine of Karl Marx* (from a Japanese version) under the Chinese title "Introduction to Marx's *Capital*," which was published in the November 1919 issue of *Construction.**

In Li's own writings published in 1919, however, he continued to demonstrate an uncertainty about his general political and philosophic course. On some points, such as the issue of political freedom, his position was akin to

*The first translations and commentaries relating to Marx's work since Zhu Zhixin's 1906 translation of the *Communist Manifesto* appeared in 1919. Excerpts from the *Manifesto* were published in *Meizhou pinglun* in its issue of April 6, 1919. A translation of *Wage Labor and Capital* appeared in *Chen bao* from May 9 to June 1. A student monthly, *Guomin* (The Citizen), presented the first section of the *Communist Manifesto* in its November 1, 1919, issue, and on October 1, 1920, it printed a translation of Marx's preface to *Capital.* The *Manifesto* was finally published in full translation by Chen Wangdao in April 1920. For some details, see Chow, *The May Fourth Movement*, pp. 298–299, and nn. 46–48 on p. 445.

that of the ardent liberal. "There is nothing dangerous about thought itself," he asserted; "the truly dangerous things are ignorance, falsehood, and the forbidding of thought."[72] A sense of terror and ignorance are tightly bound together, he continued. "When a blind man is riding a horse toward a deep lake at midnight, it is dangerous indeed." The individual who cries "Heresy!" should at least understand the doctrines he is seeking to ban, lest he be guilty of the crime of burying the truth. In the final analysis, ideas have an overriding power; they can surmount punishment, prison, suffering, poverty, even death. It is therefore futile to try to restrict them, because in the end they will survive and spread anyway.

In broader terms, the influence of philosophic anarchism, particularly the work of Kropotkin, was apparent in many of Li's writings. Thus, he compared modern life to a life in jail; the nation, the society, and the family were all prisons, and to abolish them would be to release individuals from confinement and allow them to found a free world.[73] And in another piece he said that not only class and clan divisions but also the nation had to be removed if freedom and love were to flourish.[74] But it was a separate article written at this time that revealed most clearly the competitive pulls of Marx and Kropotkin for Li's heart and mind.[75] He began with quotations from Ruskin and William Morris in opposition to Social Darwinism and in support of mutual aid, and then he defined the underlying principle of socialism as "purely ethical," supporting a system that would foster cooperation and friendship, the most elemental principles of human social life. And he insisted that whether the form of socialism was "utopian" or "scientific," its roots lay in the spirit of friendship, mutual aid, and love for all—the drive to expand kinship to the whole world, to all of human life. Li then quoted Kropotkin's answer to Social Darwinism, in which he spoke of the need to move from struggle and individualism to cooperation and equality, from war to a peaceful world, with both society and human nature remolded.

At this point, Li undertook to reconcile Marx and Kropotkin. Marx, he said, had connected the reform of social institutions with economic change and the need for a class struggle. But Marx was convinced that the first page of real human history would begin with economic institutions of mutual aid. Given the present deplorable conditions, class struggle was inevitable, but at a later stage, fundamental reform of social institutions enlisting the cooperation of all citizens would ensue. Meanwhile, the doctrine of mutual aid was needed to reconstruct the human spirit. I am in favor of both institutional and psychological reform, Li proclaimed, "reform of the body and the soul." Class competition would die out soon, and the light of mutual aid was just around the corner.

A month later, however, in the course of a friendly debate with Hu Shi, Li appeared to accept the Marxist concepts of dialectical materialism and class struggle without qualification.[76] Hu, following Dewey, had chided certain Chinese intellectuals for flirting with abstract theories borrowed from abroad and demanding "complete solutions," instead of studying concrete problems and accepting the need for further research and step-by-step approaches to complex issues. Li, defending himself, insisted that solutions to concrete problems depended upon mobilizing public interest and support, and that this in turn required stimulating the people by giving them a vision, a broadly gauged ideal—in short, an ideology. To study problems alone or in a laboratory, isolated from the people, was in itself unrealistic. He admitted that discussions of "isms" (ideologies) could be only empty talk, and he acknowledged that in the past he had been mainly engaged in making statements on paper; but he promised to change this, thereby committing himself by implication to a more activist position. He also admitted, "I like to talk of Bolshevism," insisting that Bolshevism represented a great change of global culture and should therefore be studied by Chinese.

Li reopened the issue of Marxism in taking up Hu's criticism of those who sought "complete solutions." Marx's historical materialist approach, he argued, provided a complete solution because, according to this theory, law, politics, and ethics were all a part of the superstructure, and the economic system was their base. Hence if the issue of economic relations were solved, all other matters would fall into place. But, he added, the historical materialist viewpoint had to be combined with the theory of the class struggle in order to bring about economic change. This is why we must have a trade union movement, he asserted. Many socialists of the Marxist persuasion had failed because they had not made suitable preparations for the system of collectivized production. When the time came, he concluded, it might be necessary to have a fundamental solution (meaning a revolution), but before that, there had to be preparations.

By the end of 1919 Li had consolidated this position. In a major article published on December 1, entitled "Material Change and Moral Change," he seemed to have resolved his earlier doubts wholly in favor of Marx.[77] Posing several questions—the most important of which were "How does morality come about?" and "How does morality change, over time and place?"—he flatly stated that the answers to them had been set forth by two great scholars, Darwin and Marx. Darwin, in his studies on the origin and evolution of species, had proved that morality was not supernatural or bestowed by God, but was a social instinct of all animals, the same as the instinct of self-preservation, the breeding of one's own kind, sexual desire, and motherly love. It had emerged as an adaptation to a life of competition and survival. Surprisingly, Li then assigned to Darwin a position that Kropotkin had taken in his quarrel with the Social Darwinists: out of the need to combat hostile elements and conquer nature, mankind had developed a spirit of mutual aid and a willingness to sacrifice the individual for the society as a whole. Darwin's theory, Li concluded, elaborated very clearly the substance of morality.

As for changes in morality, only Marxist historical materialism provided a satisfactory answer. All philosophy, religion, morality, and law rested on economic foundations. Li then reviewed mankind's various stages of development up to the present, "when we know more and more about natural laws, and the mysteries connected with the supernatural have disappeared." Scientific knowledge was bringing light to everything, ushering in modern times. The interrelation between material and spiritual or moral change was absolute, Li argued, and he proceeded to outline three stages in the growth of capitalism, giving Great Britain as an example. In the first stage, aggressiveness was accompanied by the creation of a national culture; in the second stage, a golden age, internal development was paramount and was accompanied by liberalism; in the final stage, imperialism flourished, but with a world community in the offing. Material change always moved forward, and so it was with morality. It was impossible to go back to the old morality of God, class, and private ownership. What was needed was a new morality based on the community at large, in which mutual aid and human creativity were harnessed to the common good.

Two essays published in January 1920 more or less completed Li's formal conversion to Marxism. The first, published on January 1, related Marxian materialist theory to Chinese history and China's current needs.[78] The clan structure, argued Li, was the expression of China's agricultural system, and everything else—including Confucianism, the feudal ethical code, and the legal system—was a part of the superstructure. The traditional system had remained intact for two thousand years, until the industrial economy of the West had begun to oppress and erode the Chinese agricultural economy. Change did not come rapidly, although the Chinese gradually became aware of the severe pressures that were affecting their lives. The Yihe Tuan (Boxer) Rebellion, Li wrote, was "an expression of anti-Western sentiment that went to the extreme of obliterating anything made in the West." As the European capitalist system developed, Chinese handicrafts were destroyed and the life of the Chinese worker became much worse than that of his counterpart in capitalist countries.

What had been the result so far? The agricultural economy of China had been shaken, and with it the political-ethical superstructure, including the clan system. Paternalism, monarchy, and Confucian doctrines had felt the impact of the collision between Western capitalism and Chinese agrarianism, and since liberalism would follow the economic impact of the West, the downfall of the old clan system was inevitable. All sorts of liberation movements would follow—for women, for youth, for labor. The new ethic was that of "sacred labor," with the working people becoming conscious of their worth and role. Short of eliminating Europe's evolving materialistic civilization altogether and restoring China's ancient static system, there was no way these new ideas could be stopped.

Several weeks later, in an article entitled "From a Vertical to a Horizontal Structure," Li argued that the traditional social structure, which was vertical in character and built by force, was being replaced by a horizontal structure based on love, in which all the people united to overthrow the bureaucracy, provincial and local governments united to resist the central government, and the proletariat united to fight the rich capitalist class.[79] Clearly, Li's current ideal, like that of Chen Duxiu, was local autonomy, the development of unions of self-governing participants, based on occupational categories, with these aggregated into federated units reaching to the top of the sociopolitical structure. And as we have noted, it was precisely in these respects that anarcho-syndicalism (still highly influential in radical Chinese circles) and early Bolshevism came together.

In one crucial respect, Li's march at this point was not only toward Marxism but also toward Marxism-Leninism. Addressing his fellow intellectuals in late January, he asserted that since the May 4 and June 3 movements the intellectual class had scored repeated victories, and then added: "We earnestly hope that the intellectual class will serve as a vanguard for the masses, and that the masses will always support them. The significance of the intellectuals as a class is that they are a group of people loyal to the masses and are pioneers of the mass movement."[80] Theories of tutelage had been advanced in China before, as we have noted, but Li's call clearly pointed to a concrete political effort in which he himself was already engaged.

Li's espousal of Marxism continued with another major article published at the close of 1920.* It could be argued, therefore, that Li Dazhao—rather than Chen Duxiu or any other Chinese intellectual of major status—was China's first true Marxist, in the sense of one who understood as well as endorsed basic Marxist theory. And yet the old struggle between humanism and Marxism persisted in his thought. Kropotkin may have been pushed under the rug, but Kropotkinism as revealed in that telling phrase "mutual aid" lingered on. In almost every essay, Li placed his greatest emphasis on love, respect for the human personality, and good will and sympathy for one's fellow men.** Intellectually, he seemed thoroughly converted to Marxist "science," including its rigorous, impersonal application of materialist criteria to social change and its insistence on the necessity of the class struggle. But emotionally, he found Kropotkin far more compatible than Marx because, although he could become angry over injustice, he found it difficult to hate. In this respect, Chen Duxiu—a far more combative man—was better suited for the Communist movement.

Moreover, when Li, like most other Chinese radicals, railed against capitalism, he seemed to be looking into the distance. It was, after all, difficult to define Chinese capitalists in Marxist terms, or even to identify Chinese capitalism at this point. As we have noted, Li did break with custom in considering rural China the site of massive injustice and in pinpointing an ample number of villains. But it was easy for him to define the whole of China as a proletarian society and thereby place the national issue ahead of the class issue in priority.[81] These tendencies did not fade away after 1920. Indeed, they continued to influence Li's thought and action until his untimely death in 1927.

The struggle between Marxism and Kropotkinism within Li's mind proved to be more difficult to resolve than the seeming contradiction between nationalism and internationalism with which he was confronted. As we have noted, in earlier years Li had exhibited the same fervent spirit of nationalism that was characteristic of his generation of educated Chinese youth; indeed, he could be xenophobic on occasion, as was compatible with his strong traditionalist commitments. Yet by early 1919, with the help of the Bolshevik message from abroad, he had gone far toward reconciling the rising nationalist tide with a vision of an international community. In an article entitled "Greater Pan-Asianism and the New Pan-Asianism," he asserted that the answer to the Japanese threat was for all other nations of Asia, exercising the right of self-determination, to liberate themselves and undertake radical re-

* Li Dazhao, "The Value of the Materialist Interpretation of History in Modern Historical Science," *Xin qingnian* 8 (December 1, 1920). In this essay Li stressed the theme that historical materialism provided an incentive for the common man to better his lot. Under the old elite-oriented, theological treatment of history, he argued, men were led to believe that whatever befell them was determined by fate, and so apathy prevailed. The historical materialist interpretation of history, however, saw the common man as a driving force for the improvement of social conditions. He expressed concern that some people mistakenly believed that historical materialism made social progress depend entirely upon changes in the economic structure of society and left no role for human activity—which would induce the same fatalism promoted by previous theories. "Nothing could be further from the truth," he claimed, but without explaining why.

** See "Material Change and Moral Change" and "From a Vertical to a Horizontal Structure" (cited in nn. 77, 79). In the second work, the final passage read, "It is our highest ideal that all human relations be rid of force, resting instead on pure love, so that love, rather than rivalry, will govern human life."

forms, then form a federation, ultimately joining with similar federations in Europe and America to create a world confederation.[82] The parallelism with current Leninist doctrine is too striking to be missed, the only surprise being the speed with which the doctrine had traveled east.

In the months ahead, it was difficult to avoid being swept up in the great wave of nationalism being pushed forward by the students, yet Li managed to display some skepticism. In March he warned that although the terms "militarism" and "imperialism" had disappeared along with the German warlords as a result of Allied victory in the war, those who had admired the Germans were now propounding a "doctrine of national strength," and such a concept was certain to wreck the chances for world peace.[83] Nationalism, he wrote a few weeks later, was now very popular in Japan, but it was attached to concepts like militarism and monarchism.*

It is not clear precisely what part Li took in the events of May 4. His recent biographers claim that he was "one of the most active leaders," but no details are given.[84] In an article published two weeks later, however, Li skillfully combined nationalist and internationalist themes.[85] Condemning the Versailles agreement on Shandong in the sharpest possible terms, he asserted that the Chinese had opposed the division of spoils arranged at the conference, not out of "narrow patriotism" but in order to resist aggression and thievery throughout the world. Despite our hopes, he continued, the Paris Conference contained not the slightest shadow of humanity, justice, reconciliation, or light—its resolutions were only a betrayal of freedom and the rights of the weak at the hands of the major powers, who were simply robbers. President Wilson, with his plans and ideals, had been a voice crying in the wilderness, a man to be pitied.[86]

In foreign affairs, Li continued, the Chinese had always said "Let the foreign devils fight each other," and in domestic matters they had said "Rely on the existing order." Both mottos were fundamentally wrong, and revealed the nation's weakness, laziness, craftiness, and baseness. "We dream every day about how to get assistance from other nations," he added, but "the loss of one's independence is worse than the loss of some territory" (thereby coming down strongly on the side of self-reliance). Then he cast the Shandong issue in universal terms. It was not just a handful of Beijing leaders who were traitors, or the Japanese alone who were guilty of aggression. "All robber powers and all acts of thievery under the cover of secret diplomacy are our enemies," he proclaimed. The slogans for China had to be these: reform the robber's world; disavow secret diplomacy; and put the self-determination of peoples into practice. Li was clearly seeking to broaden the nationalistic

*Chang (Li), "False Labels," *Meizhou pinglun*, April 6, 1919, p. 4. In this same issue, incidentally, excerpts from the *Communist Manifesto* were published with a brief interpretation that emphasized ten points, including the following: in the communism of Marx and Engels private landownership was to be abolished and land rent would belong to the public; hereditary rights to property were to be abolished; state funds were to be used to create a national bank so that all enterprises could be nationalized; control and planning would be centralized; all citizens would have the obligation to work, including men in the armed forces, who should aid in agricultural production; peasants and workers would be united, and the differences between rural and urban areas gradually abolished; and a liberal educational system that enabled all children to go to school would be established. This interpretation ended with the comment that if all of the provisions of the *Manifesto* were realized, the class system would be abolished naturally, and a people's state, free from political corruption, would emerge (p. 3).

May Fourth movement to include global goals, which in this instance were compatible with both Wilsonian democracy and the new internationalism proclaimed by the Bolsheviks.

This did not prevent Li from standing in the front ranks of the current nationalist upsurge on occasion. A week after the article outlined above, he wrote a brief and bitter condemnation of Japan's "overlord government." "You dare to interfere in our freedom of speech," he asserted, "using words like 'warning,' 'forbidding,' and 'demanding a reply.'" * In the months that followed, moreover, Li renewed his plea that China mobilize its own strength rather than beg for help or mercy from outside authorities.[87] In October he once again advanced an "internationalist" interpretation of the May Fourth Movement. The movement, he said, is opposed to Greater Asianism, which is a euphemism for national aggression, and to all of those who use force in opposing justice, be they Japanese or non-Japanese. It is more than an expression of patriotism; it is in fact a part of the human liberation movement, and if we proceed from this point of view, the entire world will benefit.[88]

At the end of 1919, prompted by criticism from Gao Chengyuan, Li returned to his proposal for a "new Asianism."[89] He denied that his effort was to separate Asians from other peoples, or that such a regional federation would be based on principles of antiforeignism or would constitute a closed society. He insisted that the first task of the weak peoples of Asia—such as the Chinese and the Koreans—and even of the enlightened Japanese was to unite in breaking down Japan's Greater Asianism. The Sino-Japanese joint defense agreement (against the Bolsheviks), the Japanese-sponsored Asian Student Union, the proposal for Mongolian autonomy—all stemmed from Greater Asianism. The principle of self-determination should be everywhere applied. Then there would need to be no fear either of Japanese militarism and capitalism, or of world militarism and capitalism. The ultimate goal was a world federation based on brotherhood and the spirit of democracy.

In early 1920 Li outlined briefly his ideas concerning cooperation between China and Japan.[90] In both countries, he noted, the conflict between new and old ideas was present. In both, students did battle with police. And in both, the militarists, financiers, and bureaucrats worked hand in hand. When would "the simple-minded old peasants," the workers, and the students join together instead of opposing their natural brothers and serving as slaves of the militarists and some bookworm people? When would they awake?

A few months later, Li professed to see great hope in the various youth movements that were then under way in northeastern Asia.[91] In China there was the anti-imperialist movement, in Japan there were the universal suffrage and labor movements, in Korea there was the independence movement, and all were gaining strength. Although these movements were different in form and might come into conflict in some instances, Li acknowledged, they were being carried out in essentially the same spirit and were going in the same general direction. The need was to break down national boundaries, to do away with jealousies and misunderstandings so as to enable consultation and the planning of a common strategy. In this spirit China's youth

*Chang (Li), "An Overlord Government," *Meizhou pinglun*, May 26, 1919, p. 3. The brief article closed with this statement: "Ah, it is your habit to issue ultimatums. Ah, now I am aware that you act as an overlord government."

should unite with all Asian youth to form a great federation, taking the initiative in the launching of a giant pan-Asian reform government. In such an endeavor there would be no racial barriers. Whether their skins were yellow or white, all were welcome. (Interestingly, Li does not mention brown skin, which suggests that Southeast Asia was being omitted, at least for the present.) And who were the white-skinned individuals in Asia? Li supplies the answer: Even Russian youth in the Far East, he asserted, are included in Asian youth.

The immediate goal had to be to get rid of Japanese militarism and capitalism. The Japanese say that the Chinese youth movement is anti-Japanese. The Chinese say that their movement is patriotic. Both are wrong. We love the Japanese laboring class and the common people, Li said, and we feel that killing and robbing people in the name of patriotism is always inhumane and irrational. The Chinese student movement is against any effort to conquer or rule by force, he announced.

Li ended by noting that the labor and peasant government in Russia had announced that all rights taken from China in the past by the Romanov dynasty would be returned to China. He hailed this as an indication of a spirit of humanism, adding that if Japan would recognize Korea's right to independence, "our joy and admiration would be ten times greater than it is over the Russian action." All men are, or should be, brothers.*

As can be seen, Li felt completely comfortable at this point with the mixture of nationalism and internationalism being put forth by the new Bolshevik movement as he understood it. It satisfied his need to see justice done for the wrongs being perpetrated on China and at the same time provided concrete steps in the direction of a universal, harmonious brotherhood of man—a dream that he, like others nurtured within Chinese culture, could easily accept. And when he surveyed the international horizon, he found cause for optimism.

His view of the home front was quite different. In the several years after World War I, Li often gave way to gloom or despair when he considered current developments in China. The Chinese people, he wrote in early 1919, have no sense of the future; they live only for the present, and when it comes to showing regard for human life, the present is also meaningless. Militarists will do anything to get rich, and when they succeed, they build castles for their heirs. Traitorous bureaucrats are busy colluding with foreigners, making enough money to last them the rest of their lives. The politicians now in power are doing the same thing, and they fawn over the military and the bureaucrats in the hope of remaining in office.[92] On another occasion, Li remarked that Japanese politics had been described as the politics of the zoo, in which the people, surrounded by a high fence, were thrown chunks of meat by their rulers.** By comparison, he said, Chinese

*Here Li was obviously referring to the pledges contained in the First Karakhan Manifesto. The Manifesto, discussed in detail in chapter 11, had been drafted in mid-1919 but did not become known in China until the spring of 1920. Once revealed, however, it was widely heralded because of the Soviet pledge that czarist privileges wrested from China illegally and by force would be given up. For example, in its May issue, *New Youth* had praised the Soviet offer as an evidence of true internationalism.

**Chang (Li), "Butchery Politics," *Meizhou pinglun*, April 20, 1919, p. 4. Actually, the phrase "politics of the zoo" was used in Japan to describe certain antics within the Japanese Diet, including melees in which members threw inkwells and other objects at each other.

politics was the politics of the slaughterhouse, in which the people were butchered like hogs, and their blood and bones were thrown to civil and military wolves.

He professed to see little difference between civil and military rule. Sarcastically, he remarked in the fall of 1919 that the two greatest events under civil rule thus far had been the Confucian rites held in the autumn and the cancellation of the military parade on National Day, adding that the second action was probably as far as civil authorities could go.[93] Moreover, the current government was both autocratic and hopelessly corrupt. People were being denied the basic civil liberties, and offices were being openly bought and sold.[94] The officials claimed they were acting to put down the threat to security, but the real threat came from the officials themselves, who denied the people the minimal security of food and clothing.[95]

On occasion, there were streaks of militancy in Li's often fiery rhetoric. What if the workers refused to be slaves of the rich, he asked, or the soldiers refused to obey their officers? Who then would possess strength?[96] And in the summer of 1920 he urged the masses to demand the convening of a national assembly that would draw up rules and hand them to the governments of both the North and the South for implementation.[97] His personal suggestions, moreover, had an unmistakable origin. Every occupational group, he urged, should organize itself into a union or council, and these could become the basis for a permanent people's assembly.

By this time, as we shall later note, Li was in contact with Bolshevik representatives, had encouraged Marxist student and labor groups, and was preparing to assist in the organization of China's first Communist Party. His activities in the fall and winter of 1920, moreover, coincided with the spread of a massive famine in North China. In the great French Revolution, he remarked, hunger was an important factor, as it was in the Russian Revolution. Now, he continued, as a great famine unfolds in North China, "the militarists, financiers, and politicians are sitting in idleness or going about their usual activities. I fear that a great change is in the making."[98] Li's interpretation of the role of hunger in causing the French and Russian revolutions might be challenged, and his prediction about its effect in China proved to be incorrect or at least premature, but it expressed the sentiment of a growing number of his fellow intellectuals. A widespread estrangement from the prevailing politics was occurring, not merely among the intellectuals but among most articulate persons in Chinese society. It was this estrangement, rather than any mobilization of the masses, that promised a stormy future, and Li Dazhao was clearly in the vanguard of the estranged.

HU SHI: UPHOLDING THE LIBERAL CAUSE

When Hu Shi returned to China in July 1917, after an absence of nearly seven years, he was already at the center of a national controversy, and in the eyes of many he was a greater iconoclast than either Chen Duxiu or Li Dazhao. Like all ideas whose time had come, the literary revolution, as it came to be called, was gathering its own momentum, despite the protests of certain venerable literati. By general acknowledgment, the catalyst of the movement was Hu, a young man of twenty-six who, aided by Chen's promotional activities, had created a storm with the two articles he had pub-

71. *Hu Shi*

lished earlier in 1917 urging the adoption of the vernacular and the application of a new realism in literary writings.

Hu had returned from the United States strongly committed to the philosophy of John Dewey; he was determined to put this new creed into practice in structuring his own career, as well as to disseminate it among his Peking University students and the wider intellectual community. Dewey's philosophy, compounded of scientific experimentation and pragmatic humanism, was well tailored to the needs of the United States—a society beginning to set the pace in the twentieth-century scientific revolution, imbued with a strong egalitarian and humanistic ethic, and moving toward secularism, especially in intellectual circles.[99] Dewey was very much a part of the United States, though he stood outside its popular culture. It would be wrong to assume that no links whatever could be found between Deweyism and certain familiar themes in Chinese traditional thought: Hu accepted the humanistic and secular qualities of Dewey's philosophy as comfortable landmarks. Yet when taken as a whole, Dewey's thought represented a radical challenge to the greater traditions within Chinese intellectual life. In the notion of development itself, Dewey's ideas, although wholly in line with the main thrust of contemporary Western thought, departed sharply from the historic Chinese view. Dewey's insistence on making the individual the unit of supreme importance and the fulcrum for all social change, moreover, differed dramatically from the primary emphasis in Chinese thought. But perhaps the broadest and most radical separation between Dewey's philosophy and the mainstream of Chinese intellectualism lay in the areas of epistemology and method. In the Chinese intellectual tradition, truth in its widest reaches had already been discovered and revealed; it was cosmic and permanent. The central intellectual task was to make certain that this truth was properly interpreted and applied. If new ideas or new policies emerged, they did so through a reinterpretation of revealed truths.

For Dewey, truth was relative to time, place, and circumstance. It was always in a process of change. Therefore, it was to be discovered and applied in any given setting through a rigorous application of the scientific method, by investigating in a rational and dispassionate manner the detailed data pertaining to the issue. Experimentation was a necessary concomitant of study, since one learned and grew through experience. Life itself was a process of becoming. The end of the path, the final solution, would never be reached—because there was no end, either to life or to solutions. The legacy of the individual was passed on to posterity through society, and while a person lived his growth was the essential ingredient in the larger growth of his community. A dynamic, developing society came about only when the individuals constituting it were themselves independent and creative units, for they provided the primary stimulus for the growth of the whole. Furthermore, fundamental progress or change was always incremental, taking full account of the complexities and idiosyncrasies of each unit and each situation.

Whatever one's estimate of Dewey's philosophy, it was a more radical departure from traditional Chinese intellectual methods than anything else being offered at the time. The Chinese intellectual might accept or reject another body of revealed truth, such as Marxism, without challenging his intellectual traditions. He could pore over its classic texts, interpreting and reinterpreting them. He could operate at a high level of generality or abstraction, and fit the facts to suit the theory with only minimal strain. Of course, this would not be fair to Marx, who had undertaken long and arduous research, and who could claim with reason to have pursued a scientific method that elevated his findings above any that rested on mere normative judgments. Nevertheless, despite its scientific roots, Marxism could be approached in the same way as Confucianism. Deweyism simply could not.

It is doubtful whether Hu Shi realized the full dimensions of the challenge that lay before him when he took up his post at Peking University in the fall of 1917. He was a self-confident young man, fresh from a student career in the United States which had been marked by repeated triumphs. His superb command of English made it possible for him to understand Western ideas and to communicate with Americans in far greater depth than was possible for all but a handful of other overseas Chinese students. During his years in the United States, moreover, he had participated in a great variety of activities, some connected with the international student movement, others in the immediate political arena. It was in America that the basis for Hu's lifelong inner conflict between scholarship and activism was established. He believed that the proper role of the intellectual was to prepare his society for basic social progress through research in the study and the laboratory, but he found himself all too frequently drawn into political activities.*

Hu had earned the enmity of many emotionally aroused Chinese students in 1915 when he argued that demands for military action against the Japanese were senseless, insisting that the proper role for the student was to continue his studies in a calm and rational manner so that he could make his contribution to the uplifting of China in the future.[100] At the same time, however, he himself was playing an active role in student politics through the Cornell Cosmopolitan Club, the Fédération Internationale des Étudiants, and the Chinese Students' Alliance. For a time, moreover, he was strongly attracted to the pacifist movement and to a brand of internationalism that led him to question repeatedly the "narrow nationalism" he saw exhibited by so many of his fellow Chinese students.[101] When Hu returned to China he brought these sympathies with him, although his pacifism had been somewhat modified.

Since the campaign for literary reform was directly related to the broader question of transforming Chinese culture—an issue of concern to every "progressive"—we must now look more closely at the specific issues it raised. Hu had fired his first salvo in a letter to Chen Duxiu in October 1916, in which he commended Chen's response to a *New Youth* reader on the status and direction of Chinese literature.** Chen had said that "Chinese literature remains in the stage of classicism and romanticism; henceforth, it will tend toward realism."[102] Hu not only agreed but expressed his own views on the problems confronting Chinese literature. The chief reason for the decay of Chinese literature, he argued, was the emphasis placed on style at the expense of substance. The result was a lack of vitality and real-

* Early in his American sojourn, he had worn a Bull Moose button, a symbol of his enthusiasm for the vigorous reformer Theodore Roosevelt. Later, antagonized by Roosevelt's militance on the international front, he had shifted his allegiance to Wilson, in whom he saw the qualities of idealism and humanism.

** This letter is contained in *Hu Shi wencun*, 1:1–4. It was written on May 10, 1916. Actually, Hu's diary indicates clearly that he had been giving the issue of literary reform serious thought since at least the summer of 1915. (See *Hu Shi liuxue riji* 3:667–734, and Grieder, *Renaissance*, pp. 79–81.)

ism. Chinese writings had form, but they lacked meaningful content. Satisfied to imitate ancient works, Chinese authors created literary pieces that bore a superficial resemblance to past masterpieces but were characterized by excessive vagueness. To the maxim, attributed to ancient sages, that "if writings lack an elegant style, they will not spread afar," Hu replied, "If writings lack substance (fail to reflect reality), what is the use of a literary style?"

In his letter to Chen, Hu proceeded to advance eight principles that should govern future literature, and he divided them into two groups. The first group was concerned with what Hu called "the revolution in form" and included these five proposals:

1. Avoid the use of classical allusions.
2. Avoid the use of stale, time-worn literary phrases.
3. Discard sentences based on parallel construction.
4. Do not shy away from the use of vernacular words.
5. Move straight ahead, writing clearly.

Hu's second group of principles related to a "revolution in content":

6. Do not write false things—that you are ill, for example, when you are not.
7. Do not imitate the writings of the ancients; one's writing should reflect one's own personality.
8. Writing must contain substance.

These eight principles formed the basis for Hu's January 1917 article entitled "Tentative Proposals for Literary Reform," noted earlier.[103] When published, however, the principles had been unified into a single group, and "Writing must contain substance" was placed at the head of the list. Moreover, whereas in his letter Hu had called for a literary revolution, the more moderate phrase "literary reform" was substituted in the *New Youth* article. Thus, it was Chen who first used the term "literary revolution" publicly, in an article published the next month in the same journal, in which he fully supported Hu's proposals.[104]

In April 1918, Hu reformulated his position in an article entitled "A Constructive View of the Literary Revolution."[105] Writing in the vernacular, Hu restated his eight principles and advanced four more propositions, which concerned both substance and form. In essence, Hu urged authors to put forth their views in their own contemporary language, express themselves succinctly, and write only when they had something of a substantive nature to say.[106] He called Chinese literature of the past two thousand years a "dead literature" and placed the blame on linguistic practices. A dead language, he insisted, cannot produce a living literature. Although he asserted that his sole interest was in promoting "a literature in the national language and a national-language literature," Hu was in fact raising issues that extended into the furthest reaches of Chinese culture and thought.

Having proclaimed that "our instrument is the vernacular language," Hu soon moved directly into the political arena in the course of suggesting criteria for a new "literary methodology."[107] Until now, he asserted, Chinese authors had been preoccupied in their writings with either the lowest, most corrupt stratum of society or with the lives of officials. Literature, he continued, should be based on facts observed during field work and personal experience, and should deal with real social conditions and issues. The suffering of poor factory workers and peasants, the status of women, and educational issues, for example, were all proper subjects. The greater use of "imagination" should also be encouraged so as to bring literature alive and give it vitality and a broader appeal. The focus, however, should be on specific, concrete facts and issues drawn from contemporary society.

Hu went on to assert that since no models for such a literary method existed in Chinese experience, authors should emulate Western literature, drawing their inspiration from the widest range of Western writers, from Plato to Shakespeare and even nineteenth- and twentieth-century writers. To expand Chinese acquaintance with Western works, a massive translation project should be undertaken. It should bring before Chinese authors the full sweep of Western literary endeavors, including the body of social literature that was such a vital part of the Western tradition.

It is not difficult to see the influence of Dewey's experimentalism in Hu's suggestions. Another influence was Henrik Ibsen, the great Norwegian playwright. Hu's interest in Ibsen and his messages had arisen in the United States and was to grow stronger with the passage of time. In June 1918 a special Ibsen issue of *New Youth* was published, almost certainly at Hu's urging.[108] He and Luo Jialun, a Beida student who was to play a leading role in the May Fourth Movement, contributed a translation of *A Doll's House*, with a long introductory essay by Hu. In the essay Hu stressed several themes of critical importance. He applauded Ibsen's capacity to "speak frankly" against social abuses. The underlying sickness of mankind lay in the unwillingness of men to open their eyes to the real conditions existing in the world. If one wanted to improve society, one had first to recognize that the society included thieves and prostitutes. If one sought good government, one had first to admit that political conditions were bad. It was not that Ibsen enjoyed pointing out political and social ills, wrote Hu, but that as an individual concerned about his society, he felt it his responsibility to speak frankly.

At this point, Hu was drawn into a more extensive discussion of the relationship between the individual and society. The individual had to be liberated from society, he proclaimed, because society permitted abuses of authority and oppressed the spirit of individual freedom. Ibsen had put it thus: If one waited until individualism was destroyed and the spirit of freedom and independence extinguished, society itself would be lifeless, and social progress impossible.[109] In short, reform could advance only when individual freedom, hence creativity, was safeguarded and, beyond this, only when individuals were prepared to use that freedom to recognize the existence of social ills and to change their own attitudes and actions. Reformed individuals were the foundation on which a reformed society had to be built.

Societies and nations were constantly changing, Hu said, and there was no single best method for saving them. What might have been an appropriate solution even a decade earlier might no longer work. The Japanese answer might not be suitable for China, and the German approach might not be logical for the United States. At this point, Hu expressed his contempt for Kang Youwei, charging that he was still trying to apply the policies of the One Hundred Days Reform era to the current problems of China. Yet his basic theme in this section was that Ibsen (he could have said Dewey) did not provide a cure for society, but that he did suggest a method for insuring society's health.

More than a decade later, in 1930, reflecting again on Ibsen, Hu restated his faith in the individual as follows: "Presently there are some who say to you, 'Sacrifice your individual freedom for the country's freedom.' I say to you, 'To struggle for your individual freedom is to struggle for the country's freedom, and to struggle for your own personality is to struggle for the country's personality. A free and equal nation cannot be created by slaves!'"[110] And to revolutionary youth who rejected the utility of nineteenth-century "Ibsenism" to twentieth-century China, Hu had this response: "Young friends, do not laugh at this as the corrupt and stale thought of the Victorian age! We are still far from reaching the Victorian age."[111]

Within a year after returning from the United States, Hu had sketched in broad outline the philosophic and political views that were to remain with him until his death some forty-four years later. One problem, however, remained a perpetual dilemma. On the one hand, Hu firmly believed that political activism was not the proper role of the intellectual. He saw activists as individuals who operated on the basis of emotional positions, bolstered only by their adherence to an ideology. Thus they advanced grandiose, immediate "solutions" to problems without having done the necessary research or experimentation to see whether their answers had any validity. Hu, following Dewey, felt strongly that the intellectual had to be committed to the scientific method of experimentalism: initial skepticism, followed by a definition of the concrete problem, the setting forth of hypothetical solutions, the testing of each hypothesis through actual experimentation, a determination of the most efficacious approach, and finally an evaluation of the actual results once that approach had been applied. Implicit in this methodology was a commitment to gradualism (although not necessarily a rejection of radical approaches).

On the other hand, from the moment of his return to China—and indeed during his stay in the United States—Hu was never far from intense political controversy, and not infrequently he was drawn into the very vortex of a political movement, as in the case of the literary revolution. He might argue, and with considerable justice, that he was offering no solutions, only a method of approaching problems. Yet when he spoke on behalf of individualism, or challenged the traditional Chinese method of thought, he was himself expressing positions that had ideological as well as methodological underpinnings. In all fairness, it should be pointed out that Hu's type of political activism differed very significantly from that of the individuals who drafted fiery manifestos or battled police in the streets. His was an activism that emanated from the study, in the form of literary critiques or scholarly lectures. In reality, it owed much to traditional Chinese intellectualism, a fact that Hu was loathe to recognize.

Hu was an exponent of liberalism and, when he chose to be, an extraordinarily persuasive one. If pressed, he could have argued that he had come to this position after extensive study and investigation, after exploring various alternatives along the way. Whether he could legitimately claim to have followed each of the steps involved in the scientific methods he expounded, including that of defining the concrete problem in such a manner as to take into account the environmental circumstances or testing hypotheses through actual experimentation, was much more questionable. But whether Hu transgressed or not, the issue of an appropriate methodology for tackling China's problems remained no less germane.

The central issue came into sharp focus in mid-1919, in the exchange between Hu and Li Dazhao that we mentioned earlier. In June, following Chen's arrest, Hu assumed the editorship of *Meizhou pinglun*, a journal established specifically to raise political issues, and soon he launched a frontal attack on what he described as the current trend of seeking a "fundamental solution" based on an abstract "ism."[112]

Hu began by criticizing "opinion-makers" who engaged in "empty talk," whether they were supporters of Confucianism or advocates of anarchism.[113] Such individuals neither understood contemporary social needs nor carried out their primary responsibility, which was to undertake detailed investigations of actual social conditions. There were three lessons to be learned from the situation, Hu remarked. First, empty talk about an "ism" required no effort; anyone could do it. Second, it was pointless to engage in debate over various imported "isms." Like all theories, they were intended to resolve the needs of a specific society at a specific time, and their abstract beauties did not make them serviceable elsewhere. It was essential that the Chinese study in depth their own particular social problems and then fashion specific answers to them. Third, and finally, empty talk about "isms" was dangerous, not merely because it distracted attention from the real tasks at hand, but also because it was a tactic available to any unscrupulous power-seeker, militarists included. This was especially true of theories that promised everything.

Hu then defined "isms": they were abstractions, incapable of embracing all of the concrete ideas of any person or group, not to mention providing solutions to the many complex problems confronting a particular society. But this did not prevent people from using them, either on their behalf or to oppose rivals. Socialism was an excellent example. There was a basic difference between the socialism of Marx and that of Wang Yitang, an Anfu Club member. Yet supporters of each called themselves "socialists," often hoping thereby to advance their own personal political fortunes by co-opting a term that was widely approved in the abstract. "Radicalism," currently having a negative connotation, had suffered an opposite fate; one applied it as an epithet, and the government had even banned its use.

There were many social and political problems to be solved in China, Hu remarked. How were ricksha drivers to survive? How should women's liberation be handled? What should be the limitations on presidential power? How could one begin to resolve the tangled problem of North-South relations? China's anarchists and socialists avoided thorough investigations of these problems, preferring instead to advocate "fundamental solutions." This situation proved the bankruptcy of the Chinese intelligentsia, and amounted to a death wish on the part of the social reform movement.

Why were most intellectuals so fond of discussing "isms," and so few of them willing to investigate problems? Hu's answer was simple and direct: laziness. The investigation of a problem involved the collection of data, personal field work to ascertain actual conditions, and other burdensome tasks. Empty talk about "isms" required only reference to a few Western books. Having stated their case, the exponents of a given "ism" became complacent, satisfied that they had found a cure-all which made it unnecessary to search for ways of handling concrete problems.*

* *Hu Shi wencun*, p. 1. The degree to which Hu's thesis on "isms" had been shaped by Dewey is suggested by the following passage in Dewey's lecture "Science and Social Philosophy," one of the series delivered in China: "Here in China a number of people have asked me:

Hu had thrown down the gauntlet, and from Li's response (outlined earlier) we can detect that some of Hu's points struck home. Li's most impressive counterargument was that the scholar who worked in his study—engaged in research that was too partial or too complex to touch the public, and wholly separated from the common man—could not hope to affect his society. If social reform were to be brought about, the people had first to be made aware of the issues and then mobilized to support the necessary solutions. This required a generalized set of goals and values—in short, an "ism"—around which they could rally. But Li, it will be recalled, acknowledged that he himself had been mainly engaged in paper exercises and, turning Hu's proposals on their head, announced that he would become more actively involved in the pursuit of concrete programs. The chief effect of the debate seemed to be that it hastened Li's debut as a political activist on behalf of Marxism.

Toward the end of 1919 Hu set forth a clear statement of his liberal, gradualist approach to China's political and social problems in an essay of major importance entitled "The Meaning of the New Thought Tide."[114] He defined the "new thought" succinctly as a critical attitude. With reference to traditional institutions and values, those imbued with a new way of thinking asked three basic questions: Did the existing structure possess sufficient value for it to exist? Were the teachings being propagated at present correct? Were the ideas universally accepted actually valid? In asking these questions, Hu asserted, those in the vanguard of the new movement were asking why they should follow the path of others merely to conform to past practice. They were asking whether there were not more rational, beneficial methods than those presently employed.

Once again Hu attacked "isms," selecting Chen's Mr. Democracy and Mr. Science as targets. These were oversimplified, all-embracing generalizations, he wrote. What should be supported and what should be opposed within democracy and science could only be determined after a critical investigation of the specifics. He then turned to answer Li's main counterthrust of some months earlier. Was it necessary to mount an ideological movement in order to attract attention? Let us look at two different cases, he wrote. The literary movement in China had become a major problem involving a large number of people. Yet no ways to resolve the issue had been proposed. Then someone (Hu) had critically studied the problem and proposed specific methods of correcting existing defects on the basis of an examination of the concrete situation. At that point, interest in the issue mushroomed. Of course, substantial opposition to the reforms also emerged, but that in itself indicated the intensity of interest and concern. On the other hand, despite prolonged discussions of it, had Marx's theory of surplus value excited equal attention and opposition? Except for a few specialists, no one in Chinese society took an interest in this abstraction; its impact on popular attitudes or social reform in the concrete sense had been negligible. Only proposals based on a detailed study of the existing situation and offering

---

'Where should we start reforming our society?' My answer is that we must start by reforming the component institutions of the society. Families, schools, local governments, the central government—all these must be reformed, but they must be reformed by the people who constitute them, working as individuals in collaboration with other individuals. . . . If we approach our problems one by one, and seek to solve them individually, rather than by rule, we will still make mistakes, but we will not make nearly so many, nor such serious ones" (*John Dewey: Lectures in China, 1919–1920*, ed. and trans. Clapton and Ou, pp. 62–63).

practical approaches to specific problems could arouse public attention. Only in this way could the consciousness of the people be awakened to the need for reform. Thus Hu sought to turn Li's own argument against him.

At the same time, Hu indicated that he favored the importation of foreign theories into China, not because new ideas were lacking in the country nor because it was easier to translate existing studies than to conduct concrete research at home, but because foreign theories could suggest new methods or ways of looking at China's existing problems. This was, of course, a straightforward defense of Hu's own importation of Deweyism. At the same moment, as we shall see, John Dewey himself was lecturing in China.

At the end of the November article, Hu set forth his basic philosophic and political beliefs in a simple yet forceful fashion that can stand as a summary of the position he was to hold for the rest of his life:

> A civilization is not created in an all-embracing, general manner, but is created bit by bit, drop by drop. Progress is not achieved in an all-embracing, general manner, but is achieved bit by bit, drop by drop. At present, people are fond of discussing "liberation and reconstruction," but they must realize that liberation does not mean total and general liberation and reconstruction does not mean total and general reconstruction. Liberation means liberation from this or that institution, from this or that belief and for this or that individual, each to be attained bit by bit, drop by drop. And reconstruction means the reconstruction of this or that institution, of this or that idea, and of this or that individual, each of these reached bit by bit, drop by drop. The task of reconstructing a civilization requires the study of this or that problem. And progress in the reconstruction of a civilization comes in the resolution of this or that problem.[115]

The causes for which Hu and like-minded intellectuals fought were temporarily advanced by the presence of John Dewey in China. Dewey and his wife arrived in Shanghai on April 30, 1919, after delivering a series of lectures in Japan over a period of two and one-half months.[116] While in Tokyo, he had been approached by former Chinese students who proposed that he accept a visiting professorship in China for the coming academic year. As events turned out, Dewey was to spend over two years in China, departing in July 1921. Throughout the period, Hu and another prominent former student, Jiang Menglin, kept in close contact with their former teacher. Hu not only took charge of making most of the arrangements for his lectures and travel, but also, along with Jiang and several others, served as his interpreter.

Dewey's reception was extraordinarily warm, indicating the respect in which a prominent intellectual was held in China, the prestige of the United States (Versailles notwithstanding), and the sizable number of American-educated students holding educational, governmental, and professional positions. From eager youth, a few of whom actually followed him from place to place, to the Shanxi governor, Yan Xishan, a military man with commitments to reform, Dewey received a cordial reception that sometimes bordered on reverence. In the course of his sojourn, moreover, he was to reach a vast audience. He spoke in some seventy-eight different places, in seven coastal and six interior provinces, and often gave not one but a series of lectures in a single place.[117] Magazines and newspapers frequently printed his lectures in whole or in digest form. Of the principal lectures given in Beijing, translated and published in book form, nearly 100,000 copies were disseminated. No foreign scholar had ever had such an impact on the Chinese student-intellectual community, or indeed upon the entire articulate portion of Chinese society.[118]

Dewey's lectures encompassed philosophy, education, and politics, traversing the sixty-year-old educator's views as set forth over many years.[119] His experimentalism provided the critical link between topics. The Western scientific revolution, he said, had opened a new era for mankind. The scientific method, in essence, rested upon a series of steps involving the establishment and testing of hypotheses. First advanced in the natural sciences by such pioneers as Newton, it had been brought into the social sciences by Darwin, and now held sway over the entire realm of human life.

Science had changed the nature of truth and opened up new vistas in education and politics. Truth was no longer a permanent body of esoteric knowledge accessible only to an elite group. Truth was relative to a given environment and could be determined by a method universally applicable and available to all. The implication for education was obvious. The teacher could not dispense eternal verities and expect the student to accept them without question. The purpose of education, indeed, should be to create in the individual a capacity for independent critical thought, by which he could question and test every statement—and every institution.[120] Understood in this way, education was a more appropriate means for effecting social change than politics, both because it operated on the individual during his formative years and because it was through the development of critically aware individuals that a society able to reform itself was created.

Science had also opened the door to political democracy because it had enabled the common people to exercise judgment as well as to acquire knowledge. Politics could be defined as a means of diagnosing and curing social disorders.* Neither "radicals" nor "conservatives" could provide satisfactory answers to such disorders, Dewey argued. Radicals believed that only complete liberation would suffice, and so they ended up by rejecting all existing institutions. Conservatives, accepting the existing order, advocated restoring institutions to their original purposes, but this also was unrealistic. Only those who relied on a study of the current situation and sought solutions based on existing realities would find answers for a society's problems.**

*Clapton and Ou, *John Dewey: Lectures*, p. 47. "The parallels with society and politics are obvious," asserted Dewey. "When social life becomes disordered, we cannot but make the attempt to find out what causes the trouble. And, thinking of the art of medicine as restoration of the body to its former condition of well-being, we seek methods by which we hope that we may similarly restore society to the wholeness or health which our memories attribute to its earlier stages. The body of theory which we evolve and formulate as we conduct this search constitutes our social and political philosophy."

***John Dewey: Lectures*, pp. 51–53. Dewey summarized these points as follows: "From time immemorial mankind has been subject to two errors, deficiency and excess. In times of crisis men have tended to be either too radical or too conservative. They have fallen into the trap of either-or, tending to regard everything they see around them as either good or bad. Yet our common sense and our everyday observation tell us that the problems of human life cannot be solved either by completely discarding our habits, customs, and institutions, or by doggedly hanging on to them and resisting all efforts to modify and reconstruct them. What mankind needs most is the ability to recognize and pass judgment on facts. We need to develop the ability (and the disposition) to look for particular kinds of solutions by particular methods for particular problems which arise on particular occasions. In other words, we must deal with concrete problems by concrete methods when and as these problems present themselves in our experience. This is the gist of what we call the third philosophy."

In the course of his lectures, Dewey also expressed his personal views on what were the most desirable political principles. Besides being an outspoken proponent of democracy, he thought of himself as a social democrat. Interestingly, he feared that in reacting to military government and statism China might swing too far toward laissez-faire policies. (In his views concerning China, he may have been influenced by Hu.) Thus, he warned against policies that would enable capitalists to exploit workers, which would lead to grave inequalities and further social disorder.* He was careful, however, to distance himself from Marxism, which he said was erroneous in its specific evaluations of contemporary society and inimical to individual growth. In one lecture, after outlining very briefly four central Marxist theses, Dewey asserted that since the war the popularity of Marxism had waned primarily because most of Marx's predictions had not proved accurate. Not only were workers better off than ever before in terms of their living standards, but socialism had come to Russia, the least industrialized nation of Europe, instead of to Germany or the United States, as Marx had forecast. "If he could be so completely wrong about this," Dewey concluded, "people wonder if he may have been equally mistaken in other regards. It is small wonder that socialistically minded people are reconsidering the moral and ethical socialism which preceded Marx's."[121] Guild socialism, according to Dewey, had some applicability to China, and might provide a middle way economically. Indeed, Dewey sketched out a system of guild management of railroads and natural resources, along with guild representation in government, that bore some resemblance to the ideas of both the national socialists and the anarcho-syndicalists—ideas already current in China, as we have seen.** It is possible that a certain similarity of political views encouraged the mutual respect that Sun Yat-sen and Dewey displayed toward each other.[122]

Dewey could not be a revolutionary, however. His experimentalist philosophy depended upon a calm and judicious atmosphere, a willingness to consider all hypotheses, and especially a belief in incrementalism—an insistence that basic social problems could only be worked out over time and by means of changes that brought individual enlightenment. By 1920, no doubt following the views of Hu and Jiang, Dewey was voicing concern over the continued student activism and violence in China. The student movement, he said, had accomplished many things, including raising the level of public concern about vital issues, but its emotionalism and violence had become counterproductive.

As his stay in China neared its end, Dewey found himself frequently pessimistic about China's future. His experimentalism, especially with respect

* See his lecture entitled "Classical Individualism and Free Enterprise," *John Dewey: Lectures*, pp. 107–116. Noting that society in China had suffered from extensive interference from the state and family elders, Dewey acknowledged that laissez-faireism might logically have a strong appeal to Chinese, but he urged that attention be given to the social issues associated with industrialization before ills had grown to such huge proportions that control would require extreme and costly measures.

** *John Dewey: Lectures*, pp. 122–124. Like others, however, Dewey at this point seemed to feel that the new Russia might be moving in the direction he favored. Note the following passage: "At this point we need to look at another school of socialism which we can examine under two subheadings, guild socialism and syndicalism. Russia's new constitution seems to draw heavily on these two types of socialism. A fundamental characteristic here is reluctance to organize on a truly nationwide scale, and a general distrust of the efficiency of a highly centralized government" (pp. 122–123).

to socioeconomic problems, required an environment closely approximating that of a liberal society. This was necessary if the scientist or social scientist were to have full access to data and be able to carry out experiments free from external controls. And it was essential if the results of such experiments were to have any chance of being translated into policy, especially if they challenged prevailing beliefs or current power-holders.

Unfortunately, perhaps, the thesis that an enlightened mass movement would gradually arise to exert an increasing pressure for change—an idea that had enthralled certain Chinese intellectuals since the early twentieth century and was to remain a political shibboleth to "moderates" and "radicals" alike—was only a potent myth. Power in China, as in all developing societies, ultimately rested in the hands of small elites, and in this case those elites were tied directly or indirectly to the military. The gamble involved in pursuing any strategy derived from Deweyan philosophy was considerable: that by staying within the perimeters of legally permissible activities, an educational-cultural movement could not only attract an ever-increasing number of participants but also demonstrate sufficient strength and practicality of policy to influence the attitudes and actions of decision-makers.

Dewey recognized, as Hu sometimes did not, that to make this gamble was to involve oneself in politics, though it was politics of a very special type. Moreover, given the domestic and international situation, the chances of success in China were not great. One could count upon the impetuousness and intolerance of certain student leaders, armed with a moral cause and intoxicated with success. And equally, one could count on the stupidity and intransigence of certain military-political men in authority. Between these two stones, the liberal and evolutionary approach was likely to be ground to death. As the interaction between "direct action" and repression mounted, moreover, the issue was certain to become one of seizing or retaining political power.*

Nonetheless, Dewey had a very substantial influence over the intellectual community during his stay in China, especially during his first year. One example of this was the support given him even by Chen Duxiu. As we have noted earlier, that support was qualified, for Chen insisted that Dewey's ideas did not go far enough in the direction of social and economic democracy. Yet in general, he endorsed the American philosopher's views in a manner which indicated that his conversion to Marxism was not yet complete.[123] Another example was that Dewey's presence and prestige almost certainly helped Hu win a battle over the future direction of *New Youth*. In December 1919 a manifesto was published in the journal, signed by Hu, Chen, Li, and others, reiterating the magazine's identification with cultural change and stipulating that social progress depended upon the advancement of natural science and an experimentalist philosophy. While acknowledging that politics was an important aspect of society, the manifesto specifically refused to grant it primacy.[124] Behind this statement lay an ongoing struggle between Hu and the Chen-Li group about the extent of political involve-

* Keenan argues persuasively that the greatest flaw in Dewey's philosophy in the Chinese context was that it offered no strategy his followers could use to gain political power, given the militarist domination of the cultural and social as well as the political environment (Keenan, *Dewey Experiment*, p. 161). We are inclined to believe, however, that although the odds were decidedly unfavorable, the effort to develop pressure groups without provoking suppression through confrontational tactics was not without potential, especially when leadership passed to men like Wu Peifu.

ment permissible for the journal, and despite minor compromises, Hu had clearly won this round. In the same issue of *New Youth*, there appeared the opening portion of a translation of Dewey's recent lectures.[125]

Within months, as we shall see, the liberals and the Marxists were to drift apart. But before we examine that development, it is important to note the challenges presented to Hu and like-minded "liberals" by those who have been labeled, somewhat imprecisely, "conservatives" or "neo-traditionalists."[126] As is widely recognized, Chinese intellectuals and politicians throughout the twentieth century have struggled to find or create a model for China's developmental needs. This effort has gone far beyond a search for an appropriate institutional framework, although it has certainly encompassed that; it has also involved questions of philosophy, ethics, and life-style.

Inevitably, in the course of China's increasing contact with Japan and the West, the weight of opinion has tended to swing like a pendulum. After moving as far as possible in the direction of preserving Chinese culture and institutions, it has swung back toward the center, toward some type of compartmentalized division of labor that involves the retention of old values combined with the borrowing of new tools. From there it has continued to move further, toward a more complete synthesis of "Westernism" and Chinese culture and, in extreme cases, toward discarding all things Chinese in favor of the values and institutions of advanced Western culture. Just as inevitably, after an "avant-garde" has pushed as far as it can go in this direction, a counterattack has been launched, various aspects of Westernism have been subjected to searching criticism, and a call has gone out for the pursuit of a reinvigorated Chinese way.

This sort of dialectic is by no means uniquely Chinese. A similar pattern can be observed in Japan and many other societies. Unquestionably, the intellectual divisions have reflected complex and highly personal factors as well as "rational" intellectual processes. What path, we must ask, has the personal life of a given individual taken, and how has he responded to the trauma that has been a part of every Chinese intellectual's experience during this century? In more general terms, how has he related his own experience to that of his culture and the culture of other societies?

It would be misleading to try to locate each actor on China's intellectual-political stage along a Western political spectrum, to identify each one as "reactionary," "conservative," "liberal," or "radical." Many of those who denounced Westernism and defended Chinese traditions most vigorously were "conservative" only in a certain limited sense. Most of them—like Kang Youwei and countless others before him—were reinterpreting tradition in an effort to render it compatible with current needs as they saw them. Consciously or unconsciously, they were investing the past with the present, and the present included concepts borrowed from the West.

Conversely, as we have seen, many who appeared to go the furthest in rejecting their past culture and espousing Western-derived ideas had privately walked over various bridges that linked Chinese traditional thought with contemporary Western "radicalism," and in the process had rejected much that was at the heart of contemporary Western civilization. Many of the leading iconoclasts, moreover, argued that the real issue was not Westernism versus Chinese culture, but modernism versus the past, thereby defining their values and goals as universal in character.

The complexity of the issues involved, combined with the inevitable idiosyncrasies of personal experience, made it virtually impossible for any two individuals to stand in precisely the same position. In a very loose sense, one could say there was a "cultural revolution" group, which was subdivided between those who proclaimed the need for a more refined synthesis of Western and Chinese tradition and those who defined their goal as a purified Chinese culture, true to its original purposes. Yet even these broad divisions can be challenged, both with respect to their implications and with regard to their completeness.

With these caveats in mind, let us consider the challenges posed by the "neo-traditionalists." In many respects, Liang Qichao was the individual best equipped to lead the attack on the "Westernizers." He himself had been a powerful force for reform at the turn of the century, and had inspired several generations of young Chinese intellectuals. Yet Liang had never believed that reform required the abandonment of integral parts of Chinese culture and character. He was a synthesizer, though a much more sophisticated one than can be found in the generation of Zhang Zhidong. Moreover, his first trip to the West had fortified his Chineseness. He had made numerous criticisms of the United States, and later made many attacks on imperialism.[127] Liang had suffered grievously after 1898. His warnings against the dangers of revolution unheeded, he lived to see China plunged into a political morass from which there appeared to be no escape. In the eyes of many fellow intellectuals, he had tarnished his reputation by participating in the Yuan and post-Yuan governments. Yet, in his eyes and those of his supporters, he had maintained an independence of judgment and position; unlike Kang Youwei, for example, he had deserted monarchism after concluding that for better or worse, its time had passed.

Liang had come to France at the beginning of 1919 with the group of "advisers" to the official Chinese peace conference delegation, and after a tour of Europe he spent the winter of 1919–1920 with them in a Parisian suburb. While there, he wrote down his impressions of Europe and drew for his readers a picture of physical and moral exhaustion. Europe had spent itself in a militarist orgy that had left it bankrupt economically and spiritually. Everywhere, he reported, Europeans were concerned about the problems of daily livelihood, but beyond this there seemed to be no value system that could sustain hope in the future. How had this come about? In the course of their earlier struggle against autocracy and the power of the church, the Europeans had cast aside all of their traditional values. Everything had been sacrificed on the altar of individual freedom. As a result, there remained no cohesive force, no unifying structure, and social revolution was inevitable.[128]

These somber words led Liang to reflect on the role that the worship of science had played in the downfall of Western man. Man, looking to science to solve all human problems, had capitulated to materialism. Values that could not be deterministically derived no longer existed. There was no room for religion or for any philosophy that did not fit into a materialistic framework. Under such conditions, independence of will and freedom of the human spirit could not be sustained.

Liang then turned the experimentalists' words against them. The problem with science, he argued, was that it could provide no permanent truths to replace the ones it had destroyed. All truth was said to be relative, shifting, uncertain. Hence the legitimacy of any authority was always open to question, and doubts abut the future were omnipresent. It was not surprising, he said, that in reaction to those profoundly disturbing trends, certain European intellectuals had challenged materialism: Kropotkin had taken the offensive against Social Darwinism; Rudolf Eucken and more notably Henri Bergson had sought to restore a spiritual element to social existence. But such individuals needed help from outside, and Liang saw a mission for China in saving the West as its materialistic civilization collapsed.

With his usual respect for complexity, Liang avoided extremism. He said it was foolish to believe that the values and institutions connected with Western evolution had nothing to offer to the world, or that the worthwhile aspects of Westernism were all to be found in classical Chinese culture as well. If Western materialism was bankrupt, so were certain aspects of Confucianism. Chinese tradition had to be reexamined, and it was entirely proper to do so by applying exacting, scientific methods. But the need was clearly for a new culture that would mix the appropriate elements from both the Chinese and the Western experience, a culture that could offer a framework within which all humanity could live.

In and of itself, the concept of a universal culture based on a synthesis of Western and Eastern traditions was not unique. Indeed, it was an idea to which many individuals, Chinese and Western, were paying homage at this time. But in his sharp attack on Western materialism, and especially by insisting that the root of the problem lay in the exaltation of science as the supreme value, Liang was striking close to the heart of the position taken by the *New Youth* group—Hu, Chen, and Li.

Before 1920 had ended, Liang had been joined in his defense of Chinese culture by a magnetic and forceful, if somewhat confused young eccentric, Liang Shuming, who was currently delivering lectures on Eastern and Western cultures in Beijing and Tianjin.[129] Neither Liang Shuming's analyses nor his proposed solutions were in conformity with those of Liang Qichao, and indeed the young lecturer specifically attacked Liang Qichao's ideas about a synthesis. Yet in certain basic respects they concurred. Liang Shuming's central theme was that Chinese culture, although its potential remained unrealized, contained a level of spirituality that was wholly lacking in the West; as a consequence, the modern Western nations—now confronted by an unparalleled crisis—would find the key to their salvation in a revitalized Chinese culture.

These conclusions were not reached without some confusion and contradiction. At certain points, Liang Shuming insisted that the type of synthesis advocated by Liang Qichao was impossible, because a culture was the national essence of a society and this essence could never be diluted; yet at other points he urged China to accept key elements in Western culture, after that culture had been purged of its errors. And while he insisted that Chinese culture contained the road to the future, he acknowledged that China was poor and helpless before the onslaughts of Western power, and he accepted the need for both science and democracy to remedy these deficiencies.

Despite such inconsistencies in his thought, Liang Shuming had emerged as a defender of a purified (modernized) Confucianism, and in his insistence that China's mission was to spread this gospel to the world, he was providing an antidote to the now deeply rooted feelings of inferiority that were irritating the Chinese intelligentsia and thereby nurturing the rise of nationalist sentiment. In this man, moreover, could be found the same basic conflict that was to cause great inner turmoil in men as seemingly diverse as Liang Qichao and Mao Zedong. Each of them recognized that without an industrial revolution of sweeping proportions, China could never hope to achieve the degree of wealth and power needed to bring the nation equality and respect in the world. Yet each of them also harbored a deep distaste for the modern, urban, industrial culture that such a revolution had created in the West.

The two Liangs were to be joined a few years later by another young intellectual destined to have a long public career—Zhang Junmei, better known in the West as Carsun Chang.[130] Zhang had studied at Waseda University in Tokyo and then pursued postgraduate work, first in England and then in Germany, where he had been a student of Rudolf Eucken's. Like his "neo-traditionalist" colleagues, Zhang compared the spiritual qualities of Chinese culture favorably with what he regarded as the excesses of Western materialism, epitomized by the aggressive, profit-seeking behavior bred out of the triumph of science and industrialization. China could only avoid this fate if its own economic modernization took a socialist form, not Marxist in character but modeled after China's historic traditions. In taking this view, incidentally, Zhang was keeping company with Liang Shuming and, to some extent, with Liang Qichao as well.

These three men—Liang Qichao, Liang Shuming, and Zhang Junmei—each as diverse in ideas as in personality, nevertheless stood on common ground in their defense of Chinese culture (in whole or in part, as it was or as it should be). Each raised fundamental, searching questions about the contemporary West in an effort to dispel the notion that everything emanating from Chen's science and democracy or Hu's experimentalism was "progressive" or conducive to a wholesome, satisfying life. The West, they agreed, was in crisis, and only truly revolutionary measures would now suffice to relieve its agonies. Each in his own way also agreed that Chinese culture could not avoid the penetration of certain elements of Westernism. Yet each emphasized the need for a synthesis that did minimal damage to the superior humanistic and spiritual aspects of Chinese culture. And it must be understood that these men by no means stood alone. In the China just after World War I, when disenchantment with the West was deep and fear of a rapidly modernizing Japan was running high, their messages fell upon fertile ground. Had not the West failed China in more ways than one?

Hu's answer to his "neo-traditionalist" critics, like the answers of others within the "new culture" group, was trenchant and unyielding. He offered no apology for his materialism. On the contrary, he made it emphatically clear that he was just as much a materialist as any Marxist. Further, he argued that the dichotomy between spiritualism and materialism being set forth by the "neo-traditionalists" was a false one. The two were inextricably intertwined in a common experience, and spirituality in its true sense was dependent on material progress. How could the West be accused of being oblivious of spiritual values when it had elevated the livelihood of its ordinary citizen far above that of the starving societies that some people called "richly spiritual?"

And why was China lagging far behind in the capacity to provide for the welfare of its own people, or to protect itself against external aggression? The answer lay partly in the very qualities of Chinese traditionalism that some critics considered virtues—a blind adoration of permanent "truths" that were in reality not true, and a rejection of rational, scientific methods that were the only guides not only to progress but also to genuine truth. Hu did not condemn Chinese tradition root and branch. He acknowledged that certain aspects of that tradition fitted very well into the new thrust that he and others were seeking to support. Nor did he wish to see the issue as "China versus the West." The issue as he saw it was how to find a way for the Chinese—along with all other humans—to partake of the prosperity, stability, and growth that could be a part of the modern era. Naturally, some synthesis of China's past and the West's present was required, but the basic goal was to find what was truly serviceable for modern life.[131]

Even as Hu and his fellow "liberals" were speaking and writing in these terms—and their influence was just as great as that of the "neo-traditionalists"—they could see the split between themselves and the Marxists widening. Li Dazhao, as we have noted, had completed his personal conversion to Marxism-Leninism by early 1920. His personal relations with Hu, as with most other old friends in the intellectual community, remained remarkably good, considering the difference in their viewpoints, and later on he was even to participate with Hu in a few joint ventures. But the old consensus could not be rebuilt.

The break between Hu and Chen was more complete. Chen, it will be recalled, had moved to Shanghai in early 1920, and from this point on, divorced from teaching and protected by the relative freedom of the Shanghai environs (including its International Settlement), he immersed himself in political activities on behalf of the fledgling Communist movement. The debate between the Beijing "liberals" and Chen over the policies of *New Youth* heated up again. Near the end of 1920, when Chen announced that he was leaving for Canton and that the journal would henceforth be edited by Chen Wangdao, a devoted Marxist, Hu and his fellow "liberals" protested vigorously. They wanted the journal returned to Beijing, and Hu continued to insist that the terms of the journal's December 1919 manifesto be respected. Neither of these demands were met, and the breach became impossible to mend.

Thus, as 1920 came to a close, the Chinese intellectual community—for whom the vanguard role had been frequently forecast or prescribed—was deeply divided over fundamental issues, paralleling the broader political divisions within the nation. On one matter only was there a semblance of agreement. With few exceptions, all were pessimists in varying degree. The nation was fragmented politically, and no unity was in sight. The economy, having benefited from World War I, was again subject to multiple strains, including the massive drought in the north. And a new generation of restless Chinese youth was emerging on the scene with no heroes to emulate, no models to follow. Or so it seemed to all except the stalwart liberals, for whom the advanced West still offered the best hope, and a handful of Marxists, who believed they had discovered a more equitable and more appropriate model for China.

11

BOLSHEVISM AND CHINA —INITIAL INTERACTIONS

VLADIMIR ILICH LENIN'S initial interest in China, not surprisingly, was an offshoot of his commitment to revolution in Russia. As early as 1900, he was attacking Allied (and particulary Russian) military operations against the Boxers, and seeking to defend the Chinese people against charges of racism by insisting that it was not "the European people" they hated but "the European capitalists and their subservient governments.[1]

LENIN'S EVALUATION OF THE 1911 REVOLUTION AND SUN YAT-SEN

It was therefore natural for Lenin to take a great interest in the 1911 Revolution because he saw it as a challenge to the domination of Asia by the European bourgeoisie, a challenge that could advance the revolutionary cause in the West as well as liberate a vastly important region of the world.[2] His analysis of Sun Yat-sen in a 1912 article entitled "Democracy and Narodism in China" is especially interesting. Lenin saw the political path being pursued by China, and more specifically Sun's revolutionary movement, as virtually identical to earlier trends in Russia. Calling Sun "a progressive Chinese democrat," he said that although Sun had no knowledge of Russia, he argued "exactly like a Russian" and could be considered a Chinese Narodnik. From this he drew a broader conclusion: democracy and Narodism would be closely related in Asia's modern bourgeois revolutions, just as had been the case in Russia, which was itself "a profoundly Asian country."[3]

By Narodism, Lenin meant a coalition of the peasants and the emerging bourgeoisie. The Chinese peasant, he wrote, was capable of fighting together with the Asian bourgeoisie for revolutionary democracy, in opposition to such potentially treacherous leaders as Yuan Shikai. And Sun's program, "pervaded by a militant and sincere spirit of democracy," illustrated the fact that the East was taking the Western path. Unlike the Western bourgeoisie, which had now reached the stage of decay and was being confronted by the proletariat, the Asian bourgeoisie was approaching its hour of destiny and was capable of championing real democracy.

There was, however, a problem. The Chinese Narodnik, like his Russian counterpart, combined a democratic ideology with an unrealistic dream: he hoped to avoid the capitalist stage of development altogether and undertake radical agrarian reforms immediately. This had come about because China, like Russia, had been a backward, agricultural, semifeudal society in which the peasant was exploited by "feudal lords." Sun's Narodism stemmed from these conditions, and his doctrines combined a militant program of bourgeois-democratic agrarian reform with quasi-socialist theory. "The belief, however, that capitalism could be 'prevented' in China, that China's backwardness offered greater opportunities for a 'social revolution'—this type of view is 'altogether reactionary.'"[4]

In summing up his analysis of Sun and his colleagues, Lenin wrote: "While sincerely in sympathy with socialism in Europe, the Chinese democrats have transformed it into a reactionary theory, and *on the basis* of this reactionary theory of 'preventing' capitalism advocate a *purely* capitalist, a maximum capitalist, agrarian programme!" Lenin identified Sun completely with Henry George and then quoted Marx in an effort to define George's policies as "ideally perfect capitalism." He concluded by praising Sun's efforts to regenerate China by drawing as much strength as possible from the peasant masses in implementing his political and agrarian reforms. Gradually, as the number of cities like Shanghai increased, the Chinese proletariat would grow. The workers would ultimately form a labor party, which although it would criticize "the petty-bourgeois utopias and reactionary views of Sun Yat-sen, will certainly carefully single out, defend, and develop the revolutionary-democratic core of his political and agrarian programme."[5]

In addition to making it emphatically clear that he considered the peasant the key mass element at this point in China's stage of development, and the indispensable ally of the revolutionary bourgeoisie, Lenin balanced his praise and criticism of Sun in roughly equal measure, in the course of which he not only had identified Sun with the Narodniks but, in more general terms, had defined Russia and China as roughly similar societies, Russian political evolution being somewhat more advanced.

Over the next several years, Lenin continued to follow developments in China with considerable interest. At first he was optimistic. In an article published on November 8, 1912, he announced that "one quarter of the world's population had passed from torpor to enlightenment, movement, and struggle."[6] And since China had no proletariat of significance, the peasant masses were "the mainstay of the National Party," whose leaders were intellectuals educated abroad. His conclusion: "China's freedom was won by an alliance of peasant democrats and the liberal bourgeoisie." But he added a word of warning: "Whether the peasants, who are not led by a proletarian party, will be able to retain their democratic positions *against* the liberals, who are only waiting for an opportunity to shift to the right, will be seen in the near future." In these comments, Lenin was interpreting the Chinese Revolution in the light of his understanding of earlier developments in Russia.

By the spring of 1913 Lenin was beginning to feel apprehensive about trends in China. Yuan, he wrote, had united all of the reactionary parties, had won over or neutralized a part of the nationalist contingent, and was now binding China to the most reactionary European bourgeois forces through loans. And Sun's party, in attempting to meet this threat, was vulnerable: it had "*not sufficiently* drawn the *broad masses* of the Chinese people into the revolution." Lenin then proceeded to reiterate his standard thesis, but with less hope for a strong contribution by the peasantry. Because China had a very small industrial labor force, no advanced class could fight vigorously for the completion of the democratic revolution. "Not having a leader in the person of the working class, the peasants are terribly downtrodden, passive, ignorant, and indifferent to politics." But he ended on a positive note: despite the "major shortcomings" of the revolutionary leader, Sun Yat-sen—"dreaminess and irresolution born of the lack of proletarian support"—his party's advocacy of revolutionary democracy in China had done much to awaken the people, secure freedom for them, and promote democratic institutions.[7]

THE BOLSHEVIK REVOLUTION AND THE EAST

With the advent of World War I and the extraordinary opportunities—and issues—it presented to the Bolsheviks, Lenin turned away from China temporarily to concentrate on matters closer to home. Then came successive revolutions in Russia, climaxed by the Bolshevik seizure of power. At the point when the Bolshevik faction overthrew the weak liberal and social democratic government headed by Alexander Kerensky in October 1917, it confronted monumental problems. Militarily defeated and with orderly government having broken down in many regions, Russia faced the prospect of having much of its empire, west and east, either wrested from it or declaring independence. The Russian people themselves, released from the restraints of earlier times, were in varying degrees of revolt, taking both property and authority into their own hands. Even within the Bolshevik party, a considerable diversity of views existed, and some of the differences concerned fundamental issues.[8]

In Lenin, however, the Bolsheviks possessed a dynamic, resourceful leader, prepared to take the risks that most others shunned, and blessed in his daring by a combination of factors—from the indecisiveness of the Kerensky administration and the unbridgeable chasms separating Bolshevik opponents to the radical momentum of the popular uprising that had followed the overthrow of the czar in February. It was Lenin who planned and executed the October Revolution, standing firmly against doubters in his own group. Until he returned in the spring, it had been assumed that the "bourgeois" government headed by Kerensky would have a long tenure in power, with the Bolshevik role being that of a loyal opposition. In his famous April Theses, Lenin challenged this view head on. He insisted that no support be given to the provisional government and buttressed this position with a theoretical justification, arguing that the Russian Revolution was quickly advancing from its bourgeois phase toward a second stage in which power had to gravitate to the proletariat and poor peasants.[9]

This analysis may have been faulty, but Lenin's optimism abut the Bolshevik opportunity proved to be warranted, and in the life of a revolutionary it is the result and not the theory that counts. Even so, the trend of events was extraordinary. A small band of leaders, most of whom had been in exile or in prison only a few months before, heading a party of no more than 25,000 in early 1917, suddenly held power—at least in Moscow, Petrograd, and certain other areas. It is not surprising, therefore, that for Lenin and the

Bolshevik Party, practice and theory continued to evolve, and in some cases to undergo drastic change. The task of holding and expanding the Communist power base now took priority over everything else.

Early Bolshevik theory, as we have already noted, was strongly antistatist. Though Lenin and others insisted that a revolutionary state was essential in the transitional period, they also argued that it should be so constructed that it could be speedily eliminated when its tasks had been completed. It was to be replaced by self-governing worker-peasant soviets, federated to provide the minimal infrastructure necessary for growth and security. We have seen that Chinese intellectuals sympathetic to the Bolshevik Revolution were championing similar policies of decentralization, governance by councils, and federation—and that they continued to do so even after there were clear signs that the Communist party in Russia was centralizing and creating an increasingly powerful state apparatus under its aegis. New messages sometimes get transmitted slowly; and besides, there was still much confusion in China (and elsewhere) about the relationship between Bolshevism and anarchism—which is understandable, given the thrust of Lenin's early treatises. Did not Lenin himself state that their ultimate goals were the same?[10]

The original theories of the state held by the Russian radicals led naturally to support for the doctrine of self-determination. Initial Bolshevik pronouncements upheld the right of any people to form an independent political unit if they chose not to remain part of an existing state. This principle, later heralded as the right of secession, was a particularly bold one, given the recent vintage and multinational character of much of the Russian empire. Soon after coming to power, however, the Bolsheviks surrounded the doctrine of self-determination with several critically important caveats. The first was that self-determination (nationalism) could not be allowed to hamper the achievement of socialist internationalism, should the two forces threaten to come into conflict. Self-determination was generally legitimate as a bourgeois expression in a colonial setting. Indeed, Lenin and his associates firmly believed that supporting bourgeois nationalist movements in Asia and elsewhere in the colonial world was an essential tactic in defeating capitalism and insuring a global socialist victory, especially after the prospects for an early triumph in the West began to dim. In the first years of the Bolshevik era, Lenin continued to insist that socialism could not survive in the Soviet Union alone, and that it was therefore essential to keep up the global revolutionary momentum by striking at the soft underbelly of the capitalist-imperialist world. But support for bourgeois nationalism was only a tactic, an interim measure, and it should never be used in situations where the proletariat had already seized power or had a good opportunity to do so.

Beyond this, the doctrine of self-determination was used by the Bolsheviks in a desperate effort to save the empire they had inherited. That empire was under siege from within and without, and national defense required whatever measures offered any hope. Some situations, moreover, were at least temporarily beyond the control of Moscow. Thus, in an effort to secure the Western borderlands, the Bolsheviks aided in the establishment of five supposedly independent soviet republics: in the Ukraine, Byelorussia, Latvia, Estonia, and Lithuania. In May 1918 three independent non-Bolshevik republics emerged in Georgia, Armenia, and Azerbaijan without Moscow's assistance. Later, the Far Eastern Republic was created in Siberia under Soviet sponsorship to serve as a buffer state that might thwart a Japanese advance. In none of these cases, however, did the Bolsheviks intend that independence should be genuine or sustained. Already, the defense of the fatherland and the advance of a global proletarian revolution were being treated as links in an unbreakable chain. Russian nationalism and socialist internationalism were in the process of being fused.

An early illustration of this trend is to be found in Stalin's remarks on the mutual dependence of Central Russia and the Russian borderlands, delivered in October 1920. Said Stalin:

> The three years of revolution and civil war in Russia have shown that victory for the revolution is impossible without mutual assistance between Central Russia and its borderlands, just as it is impossible without such assistance to liberate Russia from the clutches of imperialism. Central Russia, which is the center of the world revolution, cannot hold on for a long time without assistance from the borderlands, which are rich in raw materials, fuel, and food supplies. . . .
>
> If it is true that the more developed proletarian West cannot put an end to the world bourgeoisie without the support of the peasant East (which is less developed, but is rich in raw materials and fuel), it is equally true that the more developed Central Russia cannot bring the revolution to its final goal without the support of the less developed borderlands of Russia, which are rich in natural resources. . . . Owing to the growing mortal struggle between proletarian Russia and the imperialist Entente, the borderlands have only two choices: *Either* with Russia, which means the liberation of the toiling masses of the borderlands from the imperialist yoke. *Or* with the Entente, which means the inevitable imperialist yoke. There is no third way. The so-called independence of the so-called independent Georgia, Armenia, Poland, Finland, and so forth, is only a facade which conceals the complete dependence of these so-called states on one or the other imperialist group.*

The struggle for survival was a desperate one. As a result of international developments, control was lost over the three Baltic states, which made the Bolshevik leaders all the more determined to regain the Transcaucasian region. Recognizing the deep fissures that existed between ethnic and religious groups, the Communists established a People's Commissariat of Nationalities in Moscow, with sections extending to the individual republics and with both federal and republic commissariats under the discipline of the appropriate Communist Party. Since the party itself was operating under "democratic centralism," policies on nationality issues could be controlled at the center. Thus, a coordinated set of policies extended not only to regions under Moscow's jurisdiction but also to the independent republics it sought to control. Moscow did everything possible to insure that the politi-

* Stalin continued, "Of course, the borderlands of Russia, the nations and tribes inhabiting these borderlands, just as any other nation, have the absolute right to separate from Russia, and if some of these nations should press a demand by the majority of the population to separate from Russia, as Finland did in 1917, Russia probably would have to accept and sanction the separation. . . . [But] the interests of the masses indicate that in the present stage of the revolution, the demand for separation of the borderlands is deeply counterrevolutionary." (See Eudin and North, *Soviet Russia and the East*, pp. 50–53. The documents and introductory essays in Eudin and North are an extremely valuable source, which we have often consulted.)

cal activities of the Communist Party were protected in these areas.* When such activities had succeeded in softening a region and providing an internal structure of support, "the aroused masses" could call for assistance from the Red Army. All of the Transcaucasian republics eventually fell to a combination of internal party activities and external military force. The Azerbaijan Republic was the first to go, in April 1920, when the Red Army entered Baku and deposed the "bourgeois government." The Armenian Republic was overthrown at the end of November, again with the cooperation of local Communists and external Red Army units. Georgia, governed by the Mensheviks, was the last to fall, in February 1921.

Given the importance of Transcaucasia, and the presence of large numbers of Central Asian Moslems in other parts of the Russian empire—many of them having little cultural identification with, or political loyalty to, the Russian state—it is understandable that the fledgling Soviet Union should place its initial emphasis on wooing the Moslem community. As early as January 1918, a Moslem unit had been created in the Commissariat of Nationalities to enlist the support of Moslems in Russia, and in November the First Congress of Moslem Communists was convened in Moscow. Among those who addressed the gathering was Joseph Stalin, who made it clear in his speech that there were factors beyond domestic considerations that warranted placing a high priority on the Moslem world. With Moslem support, Communism could penetrate Persia, India, Afghanistan, and China, he reported, thereby liberating vast numbers of people currently under the imperialist yoke.[11] Most of these border states, moreover, were dominated by Great Britain, a country the Bolsheviks regarded not only as the world's foremost imperialist power but also as a state ripe for an internal revolution.

THE FORMATION OF THE COMINTERN AND POLICIES DIRECTED TOWARD THE NON-WESTERN WORLD

Throughout 1919 further organizational activities directed toward the Moslem community were undertaken, notably in Soviet Turkestan, which was described as "a revolutionary school for the whole East."** In November the Second Moslem Congress was held in Moscow, with both Lenin and Stalin participating. In his address Lenin noted that the masses in the East were peasants, and so the struggle there would be waged against "feudal remnants," not against capitalism.[12] Among the resolutions passed by the Second Moslem Congress was one calling for the formation of Communist parties in the countries of the East as sections of the Third International.

*On May 7, 1920, the Soviet government had signed a peace treaty with the Georgian Republic promising that Russia would refrain from interference in Georgia's internal affairs. In exchange, Georgia pledged that it would not serve as host to groups or organizations seeking to overthrow the government of Russia. There was also a secret supplement to the treaty, however, which bound the Georgian government to permit without interference the activity of communist organizations, thereby opening the door to Soviet political activities. (See Eudin and North, *Soviet Russia and the East*, p. 24.)

**Writing in the fall of 1919, S. M. Dimanshtein, a Soviet specialist on the East, stated: "Our temporary loss of the Ukraine has been offset by an advance in the southeast and by a penetration of the ring of hostile forces which surround us. Our frontiers now touch Khiva, Bukhara, and Afghanistan. From Afghanistan the road leads to Hindustan, the possible key to world revolution, for it is from India that Britain draws a great deal of her strength" (*Zhizn natsionalnostei* 36, Sept. 21, 1919, p. 1; presented as Document No. 25c in Eudin and North, *Soviet Russia and the East*, p. 161).

The Third International had been envisaged by Lenin as early as 1915, when he had become convinced of the bankruptcy of the Second International, then deeply split over both doctrinal matters and the issue of the war. Nikolai Bukharin, later to play such an important role in China policy, had been assigned the task of preparing what became the charter manifesto of the new organization at its inauguration in Moscow on March 4, 1919.* From the outset, the Communist International—or Comintern, as it came to be known—was an impressive instrument of Soviet policy. Grigorii Zinoviev served as chairman of the "small bureau," its Executive Committee, and together with Bukharin, the deputy chairman, managed its operations; Lenin and others made certain that Comintern and Soviet policies meshed.

The First Comintern Congress dealt only in a peripheral way with national and colonial issues, but these questions were central to the work of the Second Congress, convened between July 19 and August 7, 1920.[13] In a specially appointed Commission on National and Colonial Questions, and in several plenary sessions of the Congress itself, fundamental policies were debated. The results were set forth in a document entitled Theses on the National and Colonial Questions, which essentially embodied the views of Lenin, modified on some points by the ideas of M. N. Roy, a brilliant young Indian radical, who like Bukharin was destined to play an important role in the Chinese Communist movement.[14]

The document opened with an overview of the global situation, and was bitterly critical of both nationalism and internationalism in their "bourgeois" manifestations. To the bourgeoisie, it proclaimed, national boundaries were no more than market commodities, and the League of Nations was only "an insurance policy to mutually guarantee the victors their prey." Although the reunion of certain artificially divided nationalities in the postwar settlement corresponded in some degree to their interests, "real national freedom and unity can be achieved by the proletariat only through revolutionary struggle and the overthrow of the bourgeoisie." That overthrow was the principal goal of the Comintern, and to accomplish it, the closest union had to be forged between Soviet Russia and all of the national and colonial liberation movements. The precise nature of that union in each case would depend on the stage of development of both the Communist and the "revolutionary liberation" movements in the "backward" country or nationality.

In countries where "feudal" or "patriarchal and patriarchal-peasant relations" prevailed, it was essential that the Communist parties give active support to "revolutionary liberation movements" and to struggle against the clergy and Christian missions there. It was also important to mobilize not only against European and American imperialism but also against Pan-Islamic and Pan-Asian movements that aimed to replace Western imperialism with Turkish and Japanese power or sought to bolster the control of the indigenous nobility, landowners, and clergy. In every backward country it

*Cohen, *Bukharin and the Bolshevik Revolution*, p. 82. For documents in connection with the First Congress, see Jane Degras, *The Communist International: Documents, 1919–1943*, vol. 1, 1919–1922, pp. 1–47. The First Congress, held in Moscow, March 2–6, 1919, was called hastily in an effort to compete with the call for a reformation of the Second International which had come a short time earlier. It had been scheduled to open on February 15, but travel difficulties forced a postponement. Some thirty-five delegates with voting rights attended, and there were an additional nineteen nonvoting delegates. Most of the delegates were selected by the Russian Central Committee and represented regions formerly within the Russian empire, Western Europe, and the United States.

was vital to support the peasant movement against landlords and all "feudal survivals" and to give that movement the most revolutionary character possible by organizing the peasants and other exploited elements into soviets. In this manner the closest union could be achieved between the Communist parties of the West and the revolutionary peasant movements of the East.

It was likewise necessary to fight against revolutionary liberation movements wearing Communist garb but which were not truly Communist. The Communist International should combine all potentially proletarian groups and then persuade them of the need to fight against the bourgeois-democratic tendencies within their respective nationalities. At the same time, the International should be ready to establish temporary relationships, and even alliances, with the bourgeois democrats of the colonies and backward countries. It should not, however, amalgamate with the bourgeoisie; the independent character of the proletarian movement should be maintained, even where its movement was in an embryonic stage.[15]

The Theses on the National and Colonial Questions, as approved by the Congress, actually represented a compromise between the views of Lenin and those of Roy and certain other non-Russian delegates. Roy and others had objected to what they regarded as Lenin's unqualified support for bourgeois-democratic movements in dependent countries. In the course of the Congress, Roy (encouraged by Lenin) drafted his Supplementary Thesis, parts of which figured in the final draft.[16] Roy focused on two points: the critical importance of the Asian colonial system to European capitalism, and the gap between the "bourgeois-democratic national movement" and the mass liberation struggle in dependent countries.* Concerning the struggle in dependent countries, he wrote in part:

> 7. Two distinct movements which grow further apart every day are to be found in the dependent countries. One is the bourgeois-democratic national movement, with a program of political independence under the bourgeois order. The other is the mass struggle of the poor and ignorant peasants and workers for their liberation from various forms of exploitation. The former endeavor to control the latter, and often succeed to a certain extent. But the Communist International and the constituent parties must struggle against such control, and help develop the class-consciousness of the working masses in the colonies. In order to overthrow foreign capitalism, which is the first step toward a revolution in the colonies, it would be profitable to make use of the cooperation of the bourgeois national-revolutionary elements.
>
> But the foremost and immediate task is to form communist parties which will organize the peasants and workers and lead

* Roy asserted that "without control of the extensive markets and vast areas for exploitation in the colonies, the capitalist powers of Europe would not be able to exist even for a short time." He further argued that "by enslaving the hundreds of millions of inhabitants of Asia and Africa, English imperialism has succeeded in keeping the British proletariat under the domination of the bourgeoisie." It would not be easy, he continued, to overthrow capitalism until it had been deprived of its colonial super-profits, especially since these were used to make repeated concessions to the "labor aristocracy" at home. Thus, coordination of the colonial and Western revolutionary forces was imperative for the final success of the global revolution. (Degras, *The Communist International*, vol. 1, p. 66.) Lenin and several others argued that Roy had overstated the dependence of the Western proletarian revolution upon the victory of revolution in the East.

them to the revolution and to the establishment of soviet republics. Thus the masses in the backward countries may reach communism, not through capitalist development, but through the leadership of the class-conscious proletariat of the advanced capitalist countries.

8. The revolutionary strength of the liberation movements in the colonies is no longer confined to the narrow circle of bourgeois-democratic nationalists. In most of the colonies there already exist organized revolutionary parties which try to keep in close contact with the working masses.
9. In its first stage, the revolution in the colonies is not going to be a communist revolution. But if, from the outset, the leadership is in the hands of a communist vanguard, the revolutionary masses will be on the right road toward their goal, and they will gradually achieve revolutionary experience. Indeed, in many of the eastern countries, it would be extremely unwise to try to solve the agrarian problem according to pure communist principles. In its first stages, the revolution in the colonies must be carried on under a program which will include many petty bourgeois reforms, such as the division of land, etc. But from this it does not in the least follow that the leadership of the revolution will have to be surrendered to the bourgeois democrats. On the contrary, the proletarian parties must carry on vigorous and systematic propaganda for the idea of soviets, and must organize peasants' and workers' soviets as soon as possible. In cooperation with the soviet republics established in the advanced capitalist countries, these soviets will work for the coming final overthrow of the capitalist order throughout the world.[17]

Lenin, in his remarks before the Congress on July 26, explained something about the nature of the debate that had taken place. We argued, he reported, over whether it was theoretically proper to declare that the International and the Communist parties were bound to support the bourgeois-democratic movements in backward countries, and we came to the unanimous conclusion that one should speak of national-revolutionary, not bourgeois-democratic, movements. Of course, every national movement had to be a bourgeois-democratic movement, because the great masses in the backward countries were peasants, "who represent bourgeois-capitalist relations," and it would be utopian to believe that proletarian parties in such countries could pursue Communist tactics and policies without supporting the peasant movement. "But to use the phrase 'bourgeois-democratic movement' might cause us to lose the sense of difference between the reformist and revolutionary movements," Lenin said, "and to take note of that difference, we agreed to substitute the term 'national-revolutionary.'"[18]

Then came the critical point: "The meaning of the above change is that we, as Communists, should support the bourgeois movements of liberation in the colonies only if these are really revolutionary, when those who represent these movements would not oppose us in our efforts to educate and organize the peasantry and the masses of exploited people in general, in the revolutionary spirit. When this is impossible, the Communists must oppose the reformist bourgeoisie, to which, likewise, belong the 'heroes' of the Second International. There are already such reformist parties in the colonial countries, and sometimes they call themselves Social Democratic or Socialist."[19]

At this point Lenin turned to the question of peasant soviets. The Russian Communists, he said, who had by now gained experience in such former czarist colonies as Turkestan, had already faced the question of how to apply Communist tactics and policies in precapitalist settings. In such regions there could be no purely proletarian movement, because there was no industrial proletariat. Nevertheless, the Communists had been "compelled to assume leadership." What was discovered, he said, was that the peasants in a state of "semifeudal dependence" could easily comprehend the idea of soviet organization, since it was a simple one. Thus, the concept of peasant soviets was applicable not only to capitalist countries but to precapitalist countries as well, and it was the duty of Communist parties to propagate this program.

Finally, Lenin reported that after considerable debate it had been agreed that it was not inevitable that all backward nationalities would have to pass through a capitalist stage of development, provided "the revolutionary victorious proletariat carry on systematic propaganda among these people, and if the soviet governments come to their assistance with every means at their disposal." Indeed, he continued, "it has been firmly established that all toiling masses, including those of the remotest nationalities, are close to the idea of soviets, and that these soviet organizations must be adapted to precapitalist relationships, and the work of the Communist parties must start at once in this direction all over the world."

Many times in the past, Lenin had expressed the view that a "bourgeois-democratic revolution" was the necessary precursor to a "proletarian revolution," the orthodox Marxist position. A subtle shift in his concept of what constituted a bourgeois revolution, however, had begun at an early point. In his treatise "Two Tactics of the Social Democrats in the Democratic Revolution," published in 1905 in Geneva, while insisting that the upheaval that had just taken place in Russia could only be a bourgeois revolution, Lenin asserted that the Social Democrats (Bolsheviks) should participate vigorously, since the sooner and more complete the victory of the bourgeois revolution, the sooner would be the advent of the proletarian revolution. Arguing that the bourgeois revolution was absolutely necessary to the proletariat, Lenin went on to say that Marx had urged the latter to play an active role so as not to allow the leadership of such a revolution to be assumed by the bourgeoisie. He continued: "We cannot jump out of the bourgeois-democratic boundaries of the Russian revolution, but we can enormously extend those boundaries, and within those boundaries, we can and must fight for the interests of the proletariat, for its immediate needs and for the prerequisites for training its forces for the complete victory that is to come."*

From these speeches and documents it is possible to discern the basic

*Lenin, *Selected Works* 3:75–77, quoted in Eudin and North, *Soviet Russia and the East, 1920–1927*, p. 37. This is a strong early expression of the idea of a two-stage revolution, but with a continuity envisaged, especially if the first stage could reflect a *managed* bourgeois revolution, namely, one in which the "proletariat" took the leadership from the bourgeoisie so as to insure that their immediate purposes were served and preparations for the future were undertaken. This was, of course, a major distortion of the original Marxist concept of given economic stages producing given political leaders and institutions, but it was to have great influence in the later history of Chinese Communism.

We have already noted Lenin's criticism of Sun in 1912 for suggesting that capitalism could be bypassed in China. The compromises effected at the Second Comintern Congress, moreover, did not basically change Lenin's views. Despite his apparent acceptance of the thesis that under certain conditions "backward countries" might skip the capitalist stage, the tactics he subsequently advanced with respect to China continued to reflect his earlier position.

Communist policies toward the colonial and dependent world of 1920—a world of which China was regarded as a vital part. Four central themes were enunciated. First, it was essential to support bourgeois nationalist movements (now called revolutionary liberation movements) if they were "truly revolutionary" (did not oppose Communist activities). This support could take the form of temporary relationships or even alliances, but there must be no amalgamation, and the proletarian movement (Communist Party) must maintain its independence. Second, the proletariat must not only work with the peasant movement but also propagate the idea of peasant soviets, since these were as applicable to backward countries in a precapitalist stage as to capitalist nations. Third, it was not necessary for all backward states to pass through capitalism before reaching socialism *if* they received external assistance from the "victorious proletariat" elsewhere, and from Soviet governments. Fourth (a theme inspired by Roy), the immediate revolutions in backward countries would not be Communist, but if they were in the hands of a revolutionary vanguard dedicated to Communist goals from the beginning, their progress would be quicker and without unnecessary detours.

These principles were to cast a long shadow over Chinese revolutionary activities in the decades ahead, even though they were formulated without Chinese assistance and at a time when the first Chinese Communist groups were only beginning to be organized in Shanghai, Beijing, and Canton. There were no official delegates from China at either the First or the Second Comintern Congresses—although two leaders of the Federation of Chinese Workers in Russia, Liu Shaozhou and Chang Yingbi, were present at the first Congress.[20] Liu was also in attendance at the Second Comintern Congress, and appears to have spoken briefly during one of the plenary sessions.* He was never to play a prominent role in the Chinese Communist movement.

Less than a month after the Second Congress ended, the First Congress of the Peoples of the East was opened in Baku, the capital of Azerbaijan, a region recently "liberated" from its status as an independent republic separate from Soviet control. Plans had been under way for such a Congress since late June. At that time a meeting was held in Moscow between the Executive Committee of the Communist International (ECCI) and a number of delegates arriving for the Second Congress. The conferees agreed to hold a Congress of the Peoples of the East, opening on September 1, and the ECCI thereupon issued an "Appeal to the Enslaved Masses of Persia, Armenia, and Turkey." The goal of the Congress, it was proclaimed, would be to unite the struggle of the workers and peasants of the West with that being waged by the peoples of the East.[21] Although the three countries listed would be the center of attention, representatives from India and other countries of the East would be welcome.

Among the planners appointed by the ECCI were E. D. Stasova, G. K.

*Liu wrote that he did not speak at the Second Congress, but wrote a brief article for *Izvestiia* (Justice). (See Liu Zeying, "A Memoir," in n. 20.) Xiang, however, notes that the Second Congress records contain a speech by Liu on July 28, 1920. (Xiang Qing, "The Comintern and the Chinese Revolution During the Period of the Founding of the Chinese Communist Party.") The published remarks deal with the May Fourth Movement and praise Wu Peifu as a dedicated revolutionary, a position currently being taken by Comintern and Bolshevik spokesmen concerned with the China scene, as we shall see. Xiang's article, incidentally, is well researched, and contains some novel observations, pointing to new perspectives on Comintern-CCP relations in the earliest period.

Ordzhonikidze, and A. I. Mikoyan, who was destined to have a long career in Soviet politics and Asian affairs.* In the course of its meetings, the planning committee decided to expand greatly the countries and regions to be covered, concentrating on areas that the Bolsheviks hoped to incorporate soon into the new Soviet Union, many of which were late additions to the old Russian empire. When the solicitations were made, some 3,280 delegates were anticipated, but the documents of the Congress indicate that between 1,891 and 1,926 persons attended, a majority of them Communist Party members or sympathizers but a significant minority being non-Communists.[22] The overwhelming number were from Central Asia, the Middle East, and South Asia, but seven delegates from China were listed, all of them apparently Chinese living in the Soviet Union.[23] Among the delegates, 576 were registered as "workers," 495 as "peasants," and 437 as "intelligentsia." Another 542 did not indicate their occupation, and most of these were probably "bourgeoisie" or "petty bourgeoisie," according to Sorkin.[24]

The Congress, held between September 1 and 8, opened with a greeting by Nariman Narimanov, a veteran Azerbaijani radical, currently serving as chief of the Moslem Near East Department of the People's Commissariat of Foreign Affairs. He was followed by various Comintern and Russian Communist Party dignitaries; the most important initial speeches were delivered by Zinoviev and Karl Radek, who was later to serve as rector of the Communist University for the Toilers of the East.[25] As might have been expected, the key themes voiced by these speakers and others were the same ones that had been set forth earlier at the Second Comintern Congress. Yet because of the greater diversity of the delegates, there were some issues on which "no resolution was possible," and a few sharp exchanges evidently occurred when nationalist representatives criticized Communist actions in their region and Russians denounced certain views as "narrow nationalism."[26]

Zinoviev, as the most authoritative figure present, set the tone. Announcing that many delegates were not affiliated with the Communist Party, he spoke of the Communist International's desire "to establish a fraternal union with all the peoples of the East, with all oppressed people." Historical development had bound the toilers of the East and the workers of the West together in a common fate. "We must conquer or perish together," he exclaimed. The first task of the Congress was "to awaken the millions of peasants," explaining to them that if they did not work together with the world's organized workers, they could not escape victimization at the hands of the English and French imperialists. A "true agrarian revolution" was required, one that would do away with "landlords, slavery, taxes, debts, and all other clever tricks invented by the rich"; it would put land into the hands of the tillers, and soviets would be organized to represent the peasant masses.

Turning to the nationalist movement, Zinoviev sought to delineate the areas of agreement and disagreement, of cooperation and struggle, insofar as the Communists were concerned. The task of the national movement, he said, is to rid the East of English imperialism, but we also have our own

*Elena Stasova was a veteran Russian revolutionary; Grigorii K. Ordzhonikidze, Stalin's lieutenant in Georgia, soon played a key role in the Bolshevik campaigns to overthrow the independent governments of Armenia and Georgia; Anastas I. Mikoyan, of course, was an Armenian who later served Stalin and the Communist Party of the Soviet Union in a great variety of capacities, including that of troubleshooter with respect to China and Korea.

sacred task—to help the toilers of the East in their struggle against the rich, to help them build communist organizations.[27] And then, invoking a Moslem phrase, he called for a "holy war" against all robbers and oppressors, beginning with the Anglo-French capitalists.*

Radek, in an equally emotional speech, echoed Zinoviev's primary theme and made several references to China:

> While the capitalists of the West portray the arising of 300 million Indian and 400 million Chinese peasants as a dire threat to the survival of culture and civilization, and regard the Communist call for a struggle of the peoples of the East . . . as an attempt to invoke the memory of the conquests of Genghis Khan and the great caliphs of Islam, we are convinced that when you unsheathed your swords and raised your guns yesterday, it was not for the purpose of conquest nor for the sake of turning Europe into a cemetery. You raised your swords to create jointly with the workers of the world a new culture, a culture of free toilers.
>
> Therefore, when the capitalists of Europe say that a new wave of barbarian invasions is threatening, a new invasion of the Huns, we answer: "Long live the Red East, which, together with the workers of Europe, will create a new culture under the banner of communism!" [Stormy applause][28]

Strident and emotional appeals to nationalism were made throughout the Congress. But the leading Bolshevik representatives made it clear that simple nationalism was not enough and, indeed, that in the hands of native "reactionaries" it could pose a dire threat. The function of nationalism was to serve as a weapon in the struggle for a proletarian revolution and a genuine socialist internationalism.

Among the other speeches dealing with imperialism and the peasant question, the most significant were given by Mikhail Pavlovich (M. L. Veltman), a prominent representative of the Russian Communist Party, and Bela Kun, the well-known Hungarian Communist and Comintern member.[29] After a long discussion of trends in postwar international politics and the role of the new Soviet state, Pavlovich turned to the question of the East. Only by relying upon the Western proletariat, now organized into the Third International, he insisted, could the masses of the East achieve victory in their social struggle. Acknowledging that the industrial revolution had not yet arrived there, he nevertheless asserted that "the spirit of the masses in the East is essentially revolutionary, its fervor sparked by the successes of the

*Zinoviev's final remarks are worth quoting here. "Comrades! Much has been said in the last few years about a holy war. The capitalists, while conducting their accursed imperialist war, tried to represent that slaughter as a holy war, and they made many people believe it. When, in 1914–16, the words 'holy war' were spoken they were a monstrous lie. But now, comrades, you, who have gathered for the first time in history in a congress of the peoples of the East, you must proclaim a true holy war against the robbers, against the Anglo-French capitalists. Now we must announce that the hour has struck, and that the workers of the world have awakened and will now arouse tens and hundreds of millions of peasants, will create a Red Army in the East, will arm it, will start a revolt in the rear of the British. . . . Comrades! Brothers! The time has now come when you should begin to organize a true people's holy war against the robbers and the oppressors. The Communist International appeals today to the peoples of the East and tells them: 'Brothers, we call you to a holy war to be directed first of all against British imperialism!'" (Eudin and North, *Soviet Russia and the East*, p. 167.)

Russian Revolution." The prerequisites for a social revolution were present, he added, because the peasantry, "the only productive class in these countries," was exploited by the gentry, the bureaucracy, and the bourgeoisie, and could improve its lot only through a social revolution. For Pavlovich as for many others, the peasant was the key to the revolution in the non-Western world.

On tactics and strategy, Pavlovich closely followed the line of the Second Comintern Congress, with emphasis on M. N. Roy's formulations. The Eastern peasantry should be organized into soviets of the Russian model, he stated, but it was obvious that revolutions in the colonies could not begin as Communist revolutions. Indeed, it would be completely erroneous to apply Communist principles to the agrarian question at the beginning. In the first stage, the revolution in the colonies had to be based on a program of "purely petty-bourgeois reformist policies," such as land distribution to the peasants. Nevertheless, if a Communist vanguard stood at the head of the revolution from the outset, the revolutionary masses of backward areas could be led to the correct path while they garnered revolutionary experience.

Bela Kun opened his remarks with a similar thesis. The bribery of the Western proletariat by their bourgeois-imperialist leaders, together with the collaboration of "sultans, emirs, and money-lenders" with the foreign rulers, made imperialism difficult to dislodge. But through the medium of actual proletarian states like Soviet Russia, the workers and peasants of East and West could now develop a union without intermediaries. As for the agrarian issue, the revolution could not stop until land had been transferred to the toilers, and all exploitation had ended. The creation of peasant soviets was also stressed.[30]

The Theses adopted by the Baku Congress on September 6 were in line with these basic themes. "Bourgeois democracy" was subjected to heavy attack. "The introduction of parliamentary methods of government in Turkey and in Persia and the reorganization of Georgia into a democratic republic under the leadership of the Mensheviks, of Armenia under the leadership of the Dashnaktsutiun Party, and of Azerbaijan under the Musavat Party, have been conducted under the slogans of liberty and equality. However, these reorganizations have failed to create even the appearance of popular government. Unbelievable poverty still exists among the masses, side by side with the luxury of the agents of foreign imperialism; the land, as before, belongs to the old owners; the old system of taxation, extremely detrimental to the toilers, is retained." Clearly, there was no reason to believe that the Communists were prepared to coexist with a "bourgeois-democratic" or parliamentary government longer than was absolutely necessary.

The September 6 Theses continued with the assertion that even after the authority of the foreign imperialists had been destroyed, the revolution of the toilers of the East would continue. Like the Russian peasantry, the Eastern peasantry would develop a great agrarian revolution, with land passing to the tillers after they had obtained the support of the revolutionary workers of the West, of the Communist International, and of present and future Soviet states. What was called democratic self-government (bourgeois democracy) was administered by privileged elements and made it impossible for the masses to control their own affairs, in contrast to the situation in Soviet Russia, in the Bashkir and the Kirghiz Republics, and in Turkestan. Moreover, even after the proletarian victory in the West, economic relations with the

East would continue to benefit only the few capitalists unless all nontoiling groups had been removed along with foreign colonial elements, and the poor had been organized into soviets.[31]

A separate thesis devoted specifically to the agrarian question was adopted on the same day, and it also closely paralleled the doctrines of the Second Comintern Congress.[32] Mere independence cannot liberate the peasants of the East from oppression, exploitation, and poverty, it was stated. Although the peasants are marching hand in hand with their own democratic bourgeoisie in an effort to win independence from Western imperialism, they must remember that they have their own special tasks to perform. True liberation demands the overthrow of local landlords and bourgeoisie, and the creation of a peasants' and workers' government. Thus, the peasants must struggle not only against foreign imperialism but also against their own despots, and that struggle must continue until complete victory over the global bourgeoisie is achieved.

We have presented a relatively detailed account of the policies presented and adopted by the two Congresses held in 1920 because these policies were to have a dramatic impact on the Chinese revolutionary movement and, indeed, on all aspects of Chinese politics in the years ahead. Although various debates were to ensue within future Chinese Communist and Nationalist circles about the validity, feasibility, and implications of the basic policies put forward at these two gatherings (and formulated by a handful of Bolshevik leaders), there can be no doubt that they were of critical importance in Nationalist-Communist relations in China throughout the 1920s and beyond. And as we have already noted, it is ironic that these were policies developed wholly without Chinese participation. There is no evidence, for example, that the seven Chinese delegates attending the Baku Congress played any significant role, and as we shall see, the ties between the Bolsheviks and their Chinese sympathizers were just in the process of being created during this period.

The last act of the Baku Congress was to set up a Council for Propaganda and Action of the Peoples of the East, as an auxiliary of the ECCI. It was to function between meetings of future Congresses, publish pamphlets and a magazine, initiate a "University of the Social Sciences" for students from the East, and support as well as help to unify Eastern "liberation movements." The Council was to meet not less than once every three months, and to consist of forty-eight members, including a Presidium of seven, two of whom would be appointed by the ECCI.[33]

This project did not last long. The journal *Peoples of the East* began publication in Russian, Turkish, Persian, and Arabic; and in November 1920, courses for Eastern students were organized in Baku, and fifty graduated in mid-January 1921.[34] But the Council was formally abolished early in 1922, and most of its activities had ceased well before that time. A Council report blamed the problems on the lack of good cadres and the frequent changes in leadership of the programs, but according to Sorkin and others, the chief difficulty lay in the impossibility of directing a great diversity of movements, at varying stages of development, from a single center. Indeed, a proposal had been made to Moscow in October 1920 that three councils be organized, with headquarters in Baku (for the Near East), Tashkent (for Central Asia, including India and Afghanistan), and Irkutsk (for the Far East, including China, Korea, Mongolia, Manchuria, Siberia, and Japan).[35]

Although this particular proposal was not acted upon, the fact was that activities relating to East Asia were already being developed from a Siberian base. At first the Regional Bureau of the Russian Communist Party in Siberia took responsibility, organizing in Irkutsk a Section for Eastern Peoples, later known as the Asian Bureau. In 1920, when the region had been generally secured by the Bolsheviks, a Special Department of the Far Eastern Secretariat of the Comintern was also established there.[36]

THE BOLSHEVIK STRUGGLE TO REGAIN SIBERIA

Communist Party contacts with the Chinese came primarily through these agencies in Irkutsk, but Soviet government efforts to secure recognition from the Beijing authorities were made in other ways. To understand early Soviet contacts, both party and government, however, it is essential to refer briefly to the civil and international conflict in which Russia found itself engulfed from early 1918 to 1920. Fortunately, there are many excellent studies of the civil war and allied intervention, and it will be necessary here only to suggest the bare essentials of these enormously complex events.[37]

In the months immediately after they seized power in October 1917, the Bolsheviks gradually came into armed conflict with various forces. Certain monarchist groups began to challenge the Leninist forces as early as November, but most groups belonging to the "center" and "left" opposition held back. One of them, the Social Revolutionaries, for example, had won a striking victory in the last open elections held in Soviet Russia, shortly after the Bolsheviks' seizure of authority, and many SR adherents still hoped to take the parliamentary road to power.[38] By the beginning of 1918, however, Lenin's government was under piecemeal military attack from several quarters.

Bolshevik control over Siberia had not come quickly. This was a vast area, and both communications and transport were rudimentary. Moreover, on the eve of the Bolshevik seizure of power, almost the entire region had been in the hands of Social Revolutionaries. Nevertheless, by various means, the Bolsheviks had taken control of most of the key regional centers by the spring of 1918. Chita had fallen first, and Ataman Grigorii Semenov had been driven toward the Mongolian border. Vladivostok and Khabarovsk had acknowledged Bolshevik authority in December, and, finally, the Red Army expelled the Buryats from the Ulan Ude area in February 1918. Thus, the new government was gradually extending its control in the eastern reaches of the old Russian empire, despite heavy German pressure on the Western front, which ended only after the Soviet government agreed to the humiliating Treaty of Brest-Litovsk on March 3.[39]

In May 1918, however, a new series of events began to unfold. During that month, about 15,000 members of the Czechoslovakian League—the vanguard of some forty to fifty thousand Czech and Slovak soldiers who had earlier broken away from German control and aligned themselves with the Allies—had reached Vladivostok, from whence they intended to be transported to Western Europe. These advance units revolted against the Bolsheviks after a series of incidents that had led Soviet forces to try to disarm them.

The Czech revolt was a catalyst to Allied intervention in Siberia. Initially, the Americans and the Japanese were to send no more than 7,000 men each, and they were to be confined to Vladivostok while the Czechs sought to "rescue" their compatriots who were still west of Irkutsk.[40] From the time of the October Revolution, however, the British and French had actively considered various means of keeping Russia in the war, or at least minimizing the effect of its departure. Recurrent rumors of Russo-German collaboration, including the arming of German prisoners of war, heightened their anxieties. Through the winter of 1917–1918, a few British and French authorities thought it might be possible to work with the Bolsheviks and prevent a separate Russo-German peace agreement. But a majority envisioned intervening in Soviet Russia in collaboration with some anti-Bolshevik force in an attempt to contain the damage to the war effort.

Meanwhile, in Japan the Terauchi cabinet viewed the Bolshevik victory with unconcealed dismay, seeing in it a threat to Japan's position in Manchuria and East Mongolia. Among all of the Allies, therefore, the Japanese were the most eager for an interventionist policy. They hoped that a non-Bolshevik state could be established in Siberia as a buffer zone to protect their continental interests.

As early as November 1917, the Terauchi cabinet adopted two new policies: it set up a Siberian Planning Committee and prepared to send troops to the Amur basin; and it planned to seek an agreement from the Beijing government which would allow Japanese troops to move freely through Chinese territory. Shortly thereafter, Tokyo began to give assistance to Semenov, to the Ussuri Cossak leader, Ivan Kalmykov, and to General Dmitrii Horvath.* In China at this time, the Duan Qirui government had returned to office. President Feng Guozhang, as a member of the Zhili group, was at loggerheads with Duan and the Anfu clique. But Duan had staged his political comeback in March 1918 with Japanese funds and a treaty with Japan in May—against U.S. advice and after considerable Japanese pressure.

The Wilson administration was at first extremely reluctant to contemplate involvement in Siberia, but it was strongly opposed to unilateral Japanese action there, and after May it became possible to justify American intervention as necessary to save the Czechs as well as to forestall Japanese expansion. Thus, the American General William S. Graves led an allied expeditionary force that landed in Archangel on August 2, 1918, and less than three weeks later, on August 19, one American division came ashore at Vladivostok, along with British, French, and Japanese units. Soon, however, Japanese forces vastly outnumbered other allied troops in the region. Their numbers reached 70,000 by November.[41]

The effect of these developments on the internal distribution of power in Russia was very great. In most areas of Siberia, the Bolsheviks were forced into retreat, with the major centers coming under the control of "center" and "rightist" forces. Beginning in the summer of 1918, an effort was made

* Horvath's plans, and his connections with other anti-Bolshevik Russians and with foreigners, are detailed in his memoirs. Although his efforts to set up an anti-Bolshevik government based in Vladivostok and Harbin in the spring of 1918 were thwarted, Horvath makes it clear that he intended to use the money budgeted for Chinese Eastern Railway guards "to organize an anti-Bolshevik movement and to form a detachment to expel the Bolsheviks from the Far East." (See *The Memoirs of Lt. General Dmitrii L. Horvath*, archives of the Hoover Institution, Stanford University, especially chapters X and XI. See also Kennan, *The Decision to Intervene*, pp. 62–71, for an appraisal of the roles of Horvath and Semenov during this period. A general analysis of Japanese activities is provided in Morley, *The Japanese Thrust into Siberia*, pp. 161–212.)

by the anti-Bolshevik forces to form an all-Russian government. A conference first scheduled for July 15 at Chelyabinsk was postponed to enable Siberian and Far Eastern representatives to attend, and was finally convened in Ufa on September 1.[42] Some two hundred delegates, ranging from monarchists and ethnic nationalists to Social Revolutionaries and Mensheviks, agreed to set up an All-Russian Directorate; but unity and power eluded this organization. In November a coup replaced the initial leadership with Admiral A. V. Kolchak, who was proclaimed the supreme ruler of Russia, with headquarters at Omsk.

Over the next year the Kolchak administration proved inept both politically and militarily. Conflicts within Russian ranks and with the Czech contingents rendered the government impotent, and by the end of 1919, with the Red Army moving ever closer, the anti-Bolshevik regime faced disaster. In January 1920 a coalition of anti-Kolchak Social Revolutionaries and Bolsheviks seized Irkutsk. Kolchak was handed over to this group by the Czechs as a part of the bargain struck with the new administration, and he was immediately executed on February 7. Before his capture Kolchak bestowed his authority upon a former enemy, Semenov, thus initiating a struggle for power between Semenov and General Horvath, Kolchak's plenipotentiary in Vladivostok.

Disillusioned by the lack of unity among the Allies, and by the hopeless incompetence and deep divisions among the anti-Bolsheviks, the United States announced on January 9 that it would withdraw its forces, an action completed in April. A few days later the British and French made similar announcements. The Japanese, however, reinforced their expeditionary army at this point, signaling that they were far from ready to abandon Siberia, which they regarded as critical to their interests in Manchuria, Mongolia, and Korea. At the end of January, however, a coalition of Social Revolutionaries and Bolsheviks established a provisional government at Vladivostok, and other Siberian centers (except for Chita) also came under revolutionary (although not wholly Bolshevik) control.

Thus, by early 1920 the Bolsheviks had good cause to be optimistic about their chances for survival, and even about their ability to reclaim much of the territory that had been incorporated into the old Russian empire in the East. Yet the Japanese remained a serious threat, as all Bolshevik leaders, including Lenin, realized. An incident that occurred in March increased the danger: some six hundred Japanese were massacred by Red partisans at Nikolaevsk, and in the major Japanese retaliation that followed, many Vladivostok radicals, including the Bolshevik Lazo, were rounded up and executed, either by the Japanese or by remaining White troops.[43] To confront the Japanese militarily was unthinkable for the Bolsheviks because all available men and equipment were needed on the Western front; the White General Deniken was operating in South Russia, and the Poles were scoring military successes in their battle against Soviet forces. Consequently, in an effort to thwart further Japanese advances, Lenin and his colleagues conceived the plan of creating their own buffer state, an artificial entity that could be abolished when its task was finished, but one that could pretend to be a separate, democratic republic until that time.[44]

The first step in the plan was taken when the Moscow government cooperated in the creation of three "self-governing" entities in the Amur, the Transbaikal, and the Maritime Province, with each government proclaiming itself independent from the Soviet Republic. The Amur government, less immediately threatened by Japan, became openly Bolshevik. In Vladivostok, the capital of the Maritime Province, a coalition government headed by A. S. Medvedev, a Right Social Revolutionary, was established. And at Verkhne Udinsk, the capital of the Transbaikal Republic, a Center-Bolshevik administration, led by the Bolshevik A. M. Krasnoshchokov, was created. Actually, this administration controlled only the west Transbaikal region, the eastern part being under the control of the Semenov government at Chita.

The next step—to unite the three provincial administrations in a single, nominally democratic government—proved difficult, for numerous rivalries and ideological differences erupted. But the Nikolaevsk massacre in March served to hasten the process by greatly increasing the possibility of further Japanese expansion and strong Japanese support for Semenov. Thus, on April 6, 1920, the establishment of the Far East Republic was announced, although full unity was not achieved until the end of the year. That the Far East Republic was neither independent nor a "bourgeois-democratic" republic was transparent; nevertheless, the fiction temporarily sufficed to serve Soviet purposes.

THE FIRST BOLSHEVIK-CHINESE CONTACTS

Against this background, let us note the opening contacts between Soviet representatives, official or otherwise, and Chinese authorities. The Chinese legation remained in operation in Petrograd for some months after the October Revolution, until late February 1918. Discussions took place in January and February between various Soviet officials and Li Shizhong, the legation secretary. The Lenin government wanted to obtain the ouster of czarist officials from their posts in China, recognition of the new soviet administration, and a settlement of the disputes that had arisen over the Chinese Eastern Railway (CER)—most urgently, so that food shipments could be resumed from Manchuria to Vladivostok.[45] Thus, on January 18 a representative of Narkomindel (the People's Commissariat of Foreign Affairs) informed Li that neither Prince Kudashev (the Russian minister in Beijing) nor General Dmitrii Horvath (the CER administrator) were acceptable to the new government, and on the following day A. N. Voznesenskii, the head of the Far Eastern Department of Narkomindel, informed Li that he had been appointed Soviet representative to China. Voznesenskii promised that if he were accepted, the Soviet government would abandon its concessions in Hankou and Tianjin as well as renounce extraterritoriality. It appears that there were also discussions about the dispatch of Chinese troops to Harbin and why they were blocking food shipments on the CER to Siberia. Although the responses of the Chinese mission were couched in friendly language, Chinese actions in the Harbin area were defended as a legitimate expression of Chinese sovereign rights and as conforming to the 1896 agreement charging China with responsibility for maintaining order in the CER zone.*

*See "From the Chinese Mission in Petrograd," *Pravda*, February 3, 1918, p. 3. After reporting the Chinese mission's statement, *Pravda* noted that the ongoing negotiations related to "orderly arrangements" to manage the CER and food shipments from Manchuria to Siberia; it added that insinuations by "the bourgeois press" of a conflict with China were

In the months that followed, with the legation in Petrograd having returned to China and with a major civil war in Russia unfolding, contacts between representatives of the central governments ceased. However, this did not prevent interactions at certain regional levels. In chapter eight we sketched developments pertaining to Mongolia. Now we must turn to trends in North Manchuria and Xinjiang, two other regions abutting Russian territory. Each had a long history of Russian involvement, and at this time neither was under the full control of the Beijing government.

Events in North Manchuria centered upon Harbin and the Chinese Eastern Railway zone, for which it served as headquarters.[46] Harbin in 1916 was a city of 90,000, of whom approximately one-half were non-Chinese. Among the latter, the Russians were predominant, numbering about 34,000, ranging from well-to-do merchants, officials, and military officers to railway workers and ordinary soldiers. Chinese control within the city was minimal, with autonomous foreign-operated administrative organs governing. After the onset of the Russian Revolution, both the Chinese and the Russian populations of the city doubled.[47]

In the aftermath of the February Revolution in Russia, a group of Harbin Russians had organized an Executive Committee committed to alignment with the Provisional Government in Petrograd. At the same time, the Russian workers of the CER had established a league with social democratic (Menshevik) proclivities, to which most Harbin workers paid allegiance. A Soviet (Council) of Workers and Soldiers had been formed on March 28, 1917, and further consolidated on June 22; its members were divided between Menshevik and Bolshevik sympathizers. Thus virtually every faction within the current Russian political spectrum was represented in this foreign enclave.

Even before the October Revolution there had been a struggle over control of the CER administration. The newly organized Executive Committee, dominated by Social Revolutionaries (moderates), sought first to oust Horvath and then to share power with him. An administrative dualism, precariously structured, ultimately came into being. Meanwhile, the effort of the Bolsheviks to seize power within the Soviet of Workers and Soldiers and in the CER zone had failed. The Russian community in North Manchuria was deeply divided on the eve of the Bolshevik advent to power at home.

During October and November of 1917 events in Moscow had an increasing effect on the Harbin scene. On October 7 the first Social Democratic Party convention was held in the city. Two slogans, "All Power to the Soviets" and "Peace with Germany," testified to Bolshevik dominance. On October 20 a Worker-Soldier Soviet convention was held in Harbin. On this occasion the proposal for peace with Germany received support, but the demand by the local Bolshevik leader Riutin that Horvath be ousted and power turned over to the Soviet failed to pass. A modified resolution was approved, calling for the establishment of a provisional revolutionary committee com-

---

"pure fabrications." On February 8 another statement from the Chinese mission indicated that the Beijing government had decided to lift the ban on food shipments to Siberia immediately. But on February 19 *Pravda* stated that despite the mission's assurances, the ban was still in effect, and CER traffic between Manchuria and Vladivostok had been halted. Two days later *Pravda* indicated that the problem had been solved, but on March 1 an article entitled "The Misunderstanding Over Food Supplies in Manchuria" stated that the Vladivostok Soviet reported that 170 carloads of flour were being detained.

posed of representatives from all groups. This proposal was accepted at an extraordinary session of the Harbin Executive Committee, and Horvath, fortified by the threat of foreign intervention if order broke down, remained in office. In the weeks that followed, however, doubts concerning Horvath's ability to control the situation mounted, and various foreign consuls expressed their support for an international police force.*

An election among Russians for delegates from the CER zone to the newly proposed constituent committee, meanwhile, was revealing. Four candidates presented themselves: Horvath was nominated by the Constitutional Democrats and the Cadet Party, Volfovich by the Social Revolutionary Party, Riutin by the Bolsheviks, and Strelkov by the Railway League and the Mensheviks. About 60 percent of the people entitled to vote went to the polls, and Strelkov was elected.[48]

With the Bolsheviks in power in Petrograd, however, a crisis of major proportions had arisen by December. The Bolshevik faction in Harbin had requested policy guidelines and instructions from the newly established Council of People's Commissars in the Soviet capital. The response came on December 4, with instructions issued by Lenin personally to take power in the name of the proletariat and the government, "liberating" the region bordering on Manchouli and Khabarovsk. By this command the Soviet government was clearly seeking to extend its control not only over the CER but also over the some 200,000 Russians living in North Manchuria.** The foreign consular corps responded by unanimously refusing to recognize Soviet authority and calling for the dispatch of foreign troops. This impasse led the Harbin Bolshevik leaders to send another telegram to Petrograd on December 8, 1917, in which they reported the problems and asked for further advice. When a reply came, it merely reiterated the command given earlier. Even before receiving that response, however, the Bolshevik faction had decided to act. On December 12 it announced that it had assumed power over railway administration, the Executive Committee, and the municipal governments of the vicinity.

This move paved the way for Chinese "intervention" in a region long beyond the reach of Chinese authority. During the previous month, in negotiations between the representatives of the major powers in Beijing, Japan had made it clear that it did not want any type of international force to be introduced, fearing that such a development would challenge the special Japanese interests in the region as a whole. The alternative was to use Chinese troops, and this was supported by Prince Kudashev, the czarist minister

* For details, see Seki, *Gendai higashi Ajia*, pp. 47–69. Horvath took the position that he should have control over all police and militia forces rather than some international or foreign body, and threatened to resign if this were not accepted. Among the Russians, it was finally decided to give supervisory power over the police to the CER civil affairs committee, composed of members of the Railway League, the Worker-Soldier Soviet, and the Executive Committee. In fact, however, Horvath had to concur in decisions to enable their enforcement. Meanwhile, various consuls in Harbin continued to press for foreign soldiers, fearing a major outbreak of violence.

** According to Seki, after Lenin's telegram was received, Riutin visited Horvath, indicating that while the Bolsheviks recognized that Horvath held power firmly, they wanted to send an inspector from the Soviet to function in his office. Horvath's response was supposedly equivocal, and Riutin chose to interpret his words as recognition of the Worker-Soldier Soviet as a state organ, a view vigorously denied by Horvath and undoubtedly contrary to his intent. (Seki, *Gendai higashi Ajia*, p. 75.)

to Beijing, who was still recognized as the legitimate representative of the Russian government. The Duan Qirui government also approved, seeing the dispatch of troops as an opportunity to reassert Chinese sovereignty. Thus, on December 15 it was determined that General Meng Enyuan would deploy troops along the railway to protect the CER administration. Horvath would remain in office, but a Chinese president would be appointed to the CER board of directors. The Bolshevik thrust would be suppressed, and political activities by Russian nationals in the CER zone would be proscribed. Some 4,000 troops were mobilized for these purposes.

During this same period, renewed conflict between the Bolsheviks and Horvath was building up. Horvath was taking steps to disband some 600 soldiers allegedly under Bolshevik control, and the Bolshevik leaders declared that Horvath and other principal railway officials had been dismissed. On December 19 the Bolsheviks declared the Harbin Executive Committee abolished, seeking to carry out their earlier instructions to seize power. Chinese troops entered the city, and after complex maneuvering on all sides, the Bolshevik leaders fled. On December 27 the soldiers aligned with the Bolsheviks and, when confronted with a Chinese ultimatum, gave up their arms after a brief fight.[49]

The Bolshevik bid for power in the CER zone had failed. In the ensuing months, though Horvath's administrative powers were temporarily restored, Russian guards were replaced by Chinese troops, and in other respects as well, the Chinese government undertook efforts to reassert its sovereign rights in the region. Meanwhile, in the place of the pro-Soviet soldiers, two small anti-Bolshevik Russian units emerged. One was under Horvath's control. The other was led by Semenov, who became Japan's primary candidate to oppose Bolshevik rule in at least a portion of Siberia.

In the course of the next two years, however, it became increasingly clear that no anti-Bolshevik military force or government could sustain itself, even with foreign support. By early 1920 the Chinese, realizing the situation, moved more resolutely to replace Russian authority in the CER zone. Horvath attempted to resist what he called "Chinese aggression," but in mid-March the military governor of Kirin issued a proclamation calling upon Horvath to resign, and at the same time Chinese police occupied Russian military headquarters and police stations in Harbin and elsewhere. In succeeding months foreigners, and particularly Russians, complained bitterly that under the weight of corruption and inefficiency law and order were breaking down. But by the end of 1920 Russian political and military authority had almost completely disappeared from the CER zone. In the autumn, at a Beijing meeting of stockholders, Horvath was eliminated as CER manager; he was relegated to the post of "adviser to the Chinese government on railway affairs" and was required to reside in the capital. His place was taken by a Russian railway engineer, Mr. Ostroumoff, and although other Russians remained in key posts, many subordinate positions were given to Chinese. At the same time, the Inter-Allied Technical Board, headed by an American, John F. Stevens, increased its authority over the CER, thus checking Chinese control in some degree. But the earlier Soviet proposal that a joint Soviet-Chinese committee be created to resolve the issue of railway administration, advanced in the course of the Narkomindel–Li Shizhong talks of January and February of 1918, received no response from Beijing. On the contrary, as 1921 opened, the Chinese had high hopes of permanently eliminating Russian control of North Manchuria, including the CER zone, and implanting their own authority. The central government, however, had to contend with two rising forces—Zhang Zuolin and the Japanese.

Meanwhile, Bolshevik contacts with Chinese administrators had opened on another front—in distant Xinjiang.[50] Soviet authority in Central Asia was at first largely limited to Tashkent, but by early 1918 a much more extensive area had been encompassed. On March 3, 1918, the Bolsheviks organized a government in Vernyi, known today as Alma Ata, which was the administrative center of the Semirechye region, close to the Xinjiang border. Shortly thereafter, a special Soviet trade mission left for Xinjiang to buy grain and other badly needed items. The Xinjiang provincial government was headed at that time by Yang Zengxin. Although Yang had very considerable autonomy, he was careful to consult with Beijing on matters concerning Russia. Xinjiang, however, being out of the mainstream of major power involvement, represented an ideal arena for localized Bolshevik-Chinese contacts.

The primary obstacles were posed by the czarist officials still in Xinjiang, including the consul and the director of the provincial branch of the Russo-Asian bank. A second Soviet delegation, however, came to China in April, led by a commissar of civil affairs and a commissar of food. But at this point, anti-Bolshevik Kazakhs moved into control of key border areas, disrupting contacts until mid-June. In late June, however, arrangements were made by the governor of Ili for Xinjiang merchants to sell desperately needed supplies to Semirechye, and on August 17 a special agency manned by Bolshevik representatives appointed by the Semirechye Executive Committee was established in Kuldja to handle trade matters, approximating a consulate in its function.

In September, moreover, a new representative from Soviet Turkestan was sent to Xinjiang with the title of commercial agent, seeking recognition. While this was denied pending the sanction of Beijing, he was allowed to operate without interference. The historic economic ties between Russia and China in Central Asia had been reestablished notwithstanding the political obstacles.

By the autumn of 1918, however, the civil war in Central Asia was going badly for the Red Armies, and shortly thereafter, the Turkestan Soviet Republic was cut off both from the central regions of Soviet Russia and from Xinjiang. Indeed, anti-Bolshevik military forces were now using Xinjiang as a base from which to attack the Bolsheviks from the east. Not until the beginning of 1920 did the Reds regain the military initiative. At this point, negotiations between Bolshevik officials and Xinjiang authorities resumed. One key issue was the presence of White Guards in Xinjiang; Chinese authorities agreed that they would seek to prevent the Whites from entering Soviet territory from the Ili region, and promised to make an effort to disarm them. In April, Xinjiang authorities invited Soviet representatives to Kuldja to discuss various issues, including the refugee problem. On May 27, 1920, an agreement known as the Ili Protocol was concluded, signed by a representative of the Commissariat of Foreign Affairs of Turkestan and the governor of Ili. In the document, the Russians renounced extraterritoriality and accepted the right of Chinese authorities to levy customs duties on Russian products coming into Xinjiang, a right previously denied. It was also agreed that refugees would be returned to the Soviet side, and later on, the issue of economic losses, caused by the civil war, to Chinese residing in Russian territory was to be taken up.

Anti-Bolshevik military groups continued to use Xinjiang as a sanctuary, however, approximating the situation in Mongolia and Manchuria. Consequently, the now triumphant Bolshevik government in Turkestan put pressure on Xinjiang to suppress White activities. Since this was beyond the power of the Chinese, an agreement was reached on April 30, 1921, permitting Soviet forces to enter Xinjiang temporarily to strike at White Guard forces.[51] Units of the Red Army then entered Xinjiang, destroyed the bulk of the White forces, and then returned to Soviet territory. The Bolsheviks repeatedly cited this action as proof that they had no territorial ambitions within the region.

In Mongolia, of course, although some parts of the scenario were similar, as we have seen, matters were to take a different course—partly because Mongolia had a recent political legacy quite different from that of Xinjiang, and the Russians could easily be tempted to take advantage of it by supporting Mongol nationalism against Chinese nationalism. In Xinjiang anti-Chinese indigenous leadership or cohesion was lacking, despite the larger Uighur and Kazakh populations. In addition, Xinjiang—isolated, sparsely populated, and separated from Russian Turkestan by mountains and desert—was less of a security threat than the Mongolian-Manchurian region. That region fronted on Siberia, where Russia's vital artery to this enormously rich region, the trans-Siberian railway, was within easy range, and there was a history of Russo-Chinese competition over much of the territory. Moreover, the Japanese presence in Manchuria was formidable, in contrast to Xinjiang.

In any case, as the decade of the 1920s dawned, the new Soviet authorities were being pulled in one direction by the political and moral imperatives of a genuinely internationalist revolution devoted to Marxian principles, and in an opposite direction by historic policy concerns that stemmed from a sense of Russian national interest. And nowhere was this conflict more manifest than in the issue of the Chinese Eastern Railway.

As early as July 1918, Georgii Chicherin, the commissar for foreign affairs, had announced that the Soviet government was prepared to relinquish "the conquests of the czarist government in Manchuria."[52] The Chinese Eastern Railway, he said, was the property of the Chinese and Russian people, having been built with their money. Because the Russian people had contributed money to defray some of the railroad costs, they should be repaid, but the Chinese people were entitled to purchase the railroad outright, without waiting for the terms embodied in the 1896 agreement, which had been "violently imposed upon China."[53]

The next pronouncement on the CER, and one that was later to stir up great controversy, came in mid-1919 when a statement dated July 25 and issued in the name of the Council of People's Commissars was made public at a meeting of Chinese workers held in late August and was reported in *Pravda* on August 26. This statement, which came to be known as the First Karakhan Manifesto, after Leo Karakhan, the Soviet acting commissar for foreign affairs, had a dual aim: first, to provide concrete evidence of the new Soviet government's commitment to anti-imperialism, thereby lending credibility to the Bolshevik drive to increase Soviet influence among the colonial and semicolonial peoples; and second, to set forth the most attractive proposal possible to the Beijing (and South China) authorities, in the hope that it would persuade China to break away from the Allies and enter into relations with the Soviets. It must be remembered that the Karakhan pronouncement came less than three months after the May Fourth Movement and at a time when anti-imperialist agitation was still mounting—developments the Bolsheviks had noted with great interest. It was also a time of trauma for the Bolsheviks at home. The civil war was expanding, the Allies had intervened on the side of the Whites, and Lenin's government was in serious economic and political straits as well.

The July Manifesto called for negotiations between the Soviet and Chinese governments with the object of revoking the treaty of 1896, the 1901 protocol (pertaining to Boxer indemnities), and all agreements concluded between the czarist government and Japan from 1907 to 1916. The key passage with respect to the CER (as later published) read as follows: "The Soviet Government returns to the Chinese people, without demanding any kind of compensation, the Chinese Eastern Railway, as well as all the mining concessions, forestry, gold mines, and all other things which were seized from them by the Government of the Tsar, [the Government] of Kerensky, and the brigands Horvath, Semenov, Kolchak, [and] the Russian ex-generals, merchants, and capitalists."[54] It was also pledged that the Soviet government would relinquish its claims on further Boxer indemnities, abandon extraterritoriality, prohibit any interference on the part of its citizens in Chinese internal affairs, and "settle once and for all the cases of acts of violence and injustice [committed by] Russia, acting together with Japan and the Allies."[55]

As Whiting points out, it is curious that no reference was made to this declaration in any Soviet publication for a month, and in the accounts published in *Izvestiia* and *Pravda* in late August, there was no pledge to return the CER without compensation.* The Soviet historian and official, M. S. Kapitsa, using Foreign Affairs archives, has written that the sentence we have quoted was included in one early draft, but that this draft had not been submitted to the Soviet government for approval and was never an officially sanctioned document. Kapitsa acknowledges that Vladimir Vilenskii, who participated in the drafting of the Manifesto, did "mistakenly publish" the draft in a small booklet in 1919 without checking the text of the final Manifesto, and that this version was also transmitted from Irkutsk to Beijing at a later point, creating confusion.[56]

Recent research by Sow-Theng Leong, however, suggests that Kapitsa's

*Whiting, *Soviet Policies in China*, p. 30. The *Pravda* account is entitled "An Appeal of Soviet Russia to China" and opens with a description of the day-long meeting of some 500 Asians, mostly Chinese, at the House of the Union of Eastern Soviets. The Chinese present, presumably all laborers, divided themselves into groups according to the dialect they spoke; the largest group was from Shandong, and only a small number were from southern China, mainly Shanghai. Speeches by a Chinese and a Korean pledged an end to hostility between the two peoples and a united struggle against Japanese imperialism. There followed a discussion of the plight of unemployed Chinese workmen. Some 40,000 had returned home via Siberia, but that route was now blocked. The high point of the meeting came when Comrade Voznesenskii "made public the appeal/memoire of Soviet Russia to the Chinese people and the governments of North and South China which has been sent to China on July 25, 1919, and which will be disseminated in Chinese in dozens of copies" (*Pravda*, August 26, 1919, p. 1). The Manifesto followed, but with no specific mention of the CER.

explanation is less than adequate. It appears from the complex evidence now available that throughout this period Russian officials were divided over the question of how generous the Soviet terms on the CER should be, and that the shifting Bolshevik fortunes in the civil war probably played some role in determining the balance between the "idealists" and the advocates of "national interest."[57]

Actually, the Chinese did not hear of the First Karakhan Manifesto until late March 1920, a full eight months after its enunciation. In early 1920, when the Russian civil war was generally turning in their favor and the Western Allies were abandoning intervention, the Soviets made diplomatic overtures to Japan and China. A three-man mission composed of Vilenskii, Y. D. Yanson, and a man named Rudoi arrived in Irkutsk on February 14 with instructions to seek contacts with Japanese and Chinese officials.* Their purpose was to try to counter Japanese expansionism, if possible, and to break Chinese foreign policy away from Allied dominance. To the Japanese, the mission expressed a Soviet willingness to recognize Japan's special economic interests in the Russian Far East in exchange for peaceful relations. On March 2, however, Yanson sent the Karakhan Manifesto to the Chinese consulate in Irkutsk, requesting that it be forwarded to Beijing and that negotiations between the Soviet and Chinese governments be opened immediately. For some reason, this message did not reach Beijing until April 9, when the consul, Wei Bo, brought it back in person. But on March 26 Yanson himself, having received no response, telegraphed the text of the Manifesto and his own request to the Chinese government. A few days earlier, moreover, a Soviet official in Harbin had given the declaration to General Zhang Silin, and on March 31 Vilenskii provided Shao Hengjun, the Chinese consul in Vladivostok, with a copy. In all of these cases, the declaration contained the sentence promising Soviet return of the CER without a request for compensation.

The Chinese press had learned of the existence of the Karakhan Manifesto in late March, according to some accounts, from its publication in Vladivostok in the local Russian Communist Party newspaper. Xiang Qing has claimed that Grigorii Voitinskii and his party, who had arrived in Beijing in March, also had a copy and saw that it was distributed.[58] In any case, it is

*Leong, *Sino-Soviet Diplomatic Relations*, p. 138. Vilenskii, also known as Vladimir Siburyakov, had been an active revolutionary since 1903. He had served for four years at hard labor in Nerchinsk, after which he had settled in the Yakutsk Central Executive Committee of the Soviets of Siberia. During the Kolchak period, he had engaged in underground work. He later served in Beijing, and was an editor and writer for various journals, including *Izvestiia*, *Katorga i Ssylka* (Incarceration and Exile) and *Severnaia Aziia* (North Asia), as well as the author of various books on China, Japan, and Mongolia. He was expelled from the Communist Party in 1927 for deviation. (See Eudin and North, *Soviet Russia and the East*, p. 463.) Iakov Davidovich Yanson (also Ianson and Janson, with a Japanese pseudonym, Hayama) was a Latvian who had been involved in the revolutionary cause since 1905. He had been imprisoned and then exiled to Siberia in 1914. After the February Revolution, he became active in Irkutsk, serving as chairman of the regional Executive Committee of the Party's East Siberian branch and as representative of the People's Commissariat of Foreign Affairs in Irkutsk between 1918 and 1920, later appointed foreign minister of the Far Eastern Republic (1921–1922), member of trade delegations to the West, and the first Soviet trade representative in Japan (1925–1928), where he is said to have been a Comintern agent as well. (See Eudin and North, pp. 459–460.) No information is currently available about Rudoi.

clear that Soviet representatives were engaged in a concerted campaign to use the Manifesto as a means of wooing the Beijing government and, beyond that, the Chinese people.

As we have noted, the Chinese dilemma was acute. Nationalist pressures against the Japanese, especially from student-intellectual circles, were very strong, and a split had occurred between the Western Allies and Japan over intervention in Siberia, with some Western nations abandoning the White cause and in certain cases seeking ties with Moscow. These and other factors could be cited in arguing for a carefully timed, modest Chinese accommodation to the new Soviet government—a government that now seemed capable of surviving by certain Western European nations. On the other hand, because Japan was the only foreign military force of consequence nearby, the Beijing government did not want to become isolated from the West on an issue like policies toward Soviet Russia. It had to consider, in addition, the attitudes of various autonomous militarists, especially Zhang Zuolin. Moreover, it feared the influence of Bolshevism in China, its people now being riven with dissension, and it resented the fact that the Karakhan Manifesto had been addressed to the Canton government and the Chinese people at large as well as to itself.

For these reasons, when the cabinet first took up the matter in late March of 1920, it requested Consul Shao to ascertain the authenticity of the declaration. A few days later, in a meeting with Shao, Vilenskii assured him that the offers contained in the statement had been made by his government in all sincerity, and indicated that the condition for their fulfillment would be the removal from the CER zone of all White Russians in authority. When the cabinet convened on April 3, after weighing the pros and cons, the government decided to send an emissary to Vladivostok to meet secretly with Vilenskii; he was to promise that when other countries formally recognized the Soviet government, China would do likewise and would use the proposals contained in the Karakhan Manifesto as the basis for negotiations.[59]

Chinese uncertainties, however, were heightened when it became apparent that the Vladivostok government, headed by Medvedev, a Social Revolutionary, while working in concert with the central Soviet regime, did not accept the Karakhan Manifesto, at least with respect to certain sections. China's emissary, Fan Qiguang, met with Vilenskii in Vladivostok on May 22, and it soon became clear that China was not prepared to move toward recognition of the Soviet government at this time. In mid-June, Vilenskii abandoned his effort. Obtaining a tourist visa, he visited China for several weeks and later reported that in Shanghai and several other cities he had found that intellectuals like Chen and Li were leading student movements, but that there was not a single workers' cell and scarcely any proletariat organization or political effort.[60]

Several months later, on October 2, a Second Karakhan Manifesto (dated September 27) was presented to a Chinese mission that was visiting the Soviet capital. This mission was headed by Major General Zhang Silin and had originally been appointed in April by the Frontier Defense Army, a military unit theoretically under the presidency. Its purpose was supposedly to contact the Soviets in order to investigate the condition of Chinese nationals in Irkutsk. But Zhang, deciding that the authority of the Far Eastern Republic was too limited, took it upon himself to pursue his political mission in Moscow. His delegation arrived in the Soviet capital on September 5, where they were warmly welcomed by Chicherin and Karakhan. Zhang was later received by Lenin, who reportedly said to him that "the Chinese revolution will lead to revolution throughout the entire East, and will finally bring about the downfall of world imperialism."[61]

The revised declaration continued to use expansive language, speaking of the commitment of the Soviet government to nullifying all concessions, treaties, and territories claimed by czarist Russia "without compensation and forever."[62] Concerning the CER, however, the new Soviet proposal read: "The Russian and Chinese governments agree to conclude a special treaty with respect to the rules and regulations governing the use of the Chinese Eastern Railway for the needs of Soviet Russia. In the making of said treaty, the Far Eastern Republic shall also participate." At this point, all Soviet representatives vigorously denied that the Soviet government had ever promised to restore the CER to China without any conditions. According to Zhang Silin, Karakhan really was prepared to have the CER zone administered and policed by Chinese, but argued that since the railway had been built with funds supplied by "the Russian masses," the Russians deserved guaranteed rights of use and lower tariffs than other nations. The issue of compensation appears to have been left open.[63]

After establishing contact with Soviet officials at the highest level, Zhang and his group were denied permission to undertake negotiations and were ordered to return to China. A change of governments had again taken place at home, and in any case Zhang's mission had never been given direct approval by the Beijing Foreign Ministry. Thus, when Zhang returned to China toward the end of November, no progress in Soviet-Chinese relations had been achieved.

Meanwhile, another channel had been opened by means of Soviet overtures made through the Far Eastern Republic in Siberia. In May of 1920 a five-man delegation headed by Ignatius L. Yurin left Verkhne Udinsk bound for Beijing, bearing the label of a commercial and trade mission of the new Siberian state.* The delegation's purpose, however, as clearly set forth from the beginning, was to arrange for the establishment of a permanent diplomatic and consular staff in Beijing. When the mission arrived in Kiakhta on June 10, it asked Chinese officials at the frontier for permission to proceed to the Chinese capital. But Chen Lu, China's acting foreign minister, sent instructions that negotiations should take place on the border.

There were several reasons for Chen's decision. There had been no prior consultation between Verkhne Udinsk and Beijing, and the status of the Yurin group was not clear to the Chinese. Also, Prince Kudashev still enjoyed full recognition as the Russian representative in Beijing, and until this condition was altered, it was not feasible for Beijing to deal officially with FER representatives. Finally, the Beijing government had dispatched three

*Marc Kasanin (Mark Isaakovich Kazanin), who had earlier lived in Harbin, and who used both Chinese and English, was summoned to Verkhne Udinsk from a small town where he was living, and, after conversations with Krasnoshchokov and Yurin, was appointed second secretary of the mission. He described the first secretary, Gromov, as an old Bolshevik who had spent years in America. The others were Yurin's personal secretary, Pavel Khretinin, a young Siberian partisan who was the treasurer of the group, and Misha Gurianov, a cipher clerk from the War Ministry. After the group reached Kiakhta, a sixth member joined it briefly. His name was Negrebetskii, and his expertise in commercial matters was supposed to give the group credibility in the economic area, but he was soon dismissed as too "bourgeois." For a personal account of the Yurin mission, see Kasanin, *China in the Twenties*, pp. 31–32.

foreign presidential advisers—Lenox Simpson, John C. Ferguson, and George Padoux—to Siberia to prepare a report on the character and status of the various Siberian governments, and they had not yet returned. The Chinese did put together a delegation for talks at the border, but before it could be dispatched, the government was overthrown in the course of the Anfu-Zhili struggle.[64]

The Yurin mission protested the Beijing government's decision, and after some two months—during which various events favorable to Chinese-FER discussions had ensued—the mission was allowed to advance, and arrived in Beijing on August 26.* Less than a month later, on September 23, the Chinese government withdrew its recognition of Prince Kudashev and other representatives of the former Russian government.** This move was naturally greeted with enthusiasm by the Yurin mission, but Chinese authorities moved slowly and were obviously reluctant to open formal talks. Yurin was not able to meet Foreign Minister Yan Huiqing until December 7, when their meeting took place unofficially, in Yan's private residence. No official recognition was in the offing.

The central problem was that all of the foreign powers were becoming increasingly worried about two possibilities. First, it was possible that China would take advantage of the collapse of the czarist regime and the pledges of the Soviet government to advance its own claims, thereby challenging the network of privileges that every foreign power shared in some degree. Second, China might recognize the Lenin government, thereby accelerating antiforeignism in general and Bolshevism in particular within China. The second fear was frequently stated in the foreign press. One variation contained in an article in the *North China Herald* went as follows:

> There can be no doubt that the intelligent middle classes in North China regard the introduction into China of an adapted Bolshevism as the best immediate solution of this country's troubles. Bolshevism means something different to each individual who studies and preaches it, but to the merchants and educators who now constitute China's literate middle class, it means a popular rising which would drive all the militarist officials into the foreign concessions; which would put every Chinese province under the direct government of its provincial assembly, and would yield up to the people all the spoils of the militarists for free division. The land question would not enter into Chinese

*Kasanin gives an amusing description of the trip from Kiakhta to Beijing. To achieve status, the group traveled in a black Cadillac they acquired in Verkhne Udinsk. When they left Kiakhta, with flags flying and a cavalry escort, Yurin stood up in the car to acknowledge the shouts of the crowd lining the streets, and when others tried to stand, he shoved them down. Getting the Cadillac to Beijing proved an arduous task. On one occasion it had to be pulled across a river by oxen, and it completed the last leg of the journey on a railway flat-car (Kasanin, *China in the Twenties*, pp. 33–43).

**As early as February 26, 1920, the Chinese cabinet had accepted the recommendations of Lenox Simpson, adviser to President Xu, that ties with the old Russian diplomats be broken. But no action was taken until after the overthrow of the Anfu government, when the new cabinet under Premier Jin Yunpeng (with Yan Huiqing as foreign minister) concluded that the Soviet government would continue in power, and decided to deal with the Yurin mission and break relations with Kudachev. Even so, they approached the matter cautiously. When a Ussuri Cossack under arrest disappeared, and was later found hiding on the Russian consulate premises, it was used as an excuse for severing ties with the czarist group. (Leong, *Sino-Soviet Diplomatic Relations*, pp. 116–121.)

> Bolshevism, and the very large number of middle-class intellectuals who are now advocating a Red rule in China anticipate no more than the overthrow of their parasitical official class. . . . However short-sighted they may be, they believe in the power of the movement and one hears everywhere in Peking the prophecy that within six months, Bolshevism will drive the Japanese from the mainland of Asia; that Korea will be free; and that Port Arthur and Dalny (Dairen) will be restored to China.[65]

Whether this was an accurate analysis of "middle-class" Chinese views on Bolshevism may be doubted, but there can be no question that many foreigners residing in China (and their legations) watched the rise of a new Chinese nationalism with apprehension. Visions of a Chinese alignment with Soviet Russia and the reemergence of a virulent xenophobia like that witnessed during the Boxer uprising were widespread.* Yet neither the Western powers nor Japan were prepared to match Soviet pledges to abandon earlier concessions.

Thus, as 1920 came to an end, the new Soviet government had failed to overcome the obstacles to official recognition by the Chinese government. Beijing wanted to reassert its rights in many vital areas: Mongolia, the Chinese Eastern Railway and Manchuria, Xinjiang, concessions, and extraterritoriality. It saw the opportunities implicit in Soviet overtures concerning these issues, and through unofficial or local contacts it moved as far as it dared, meanwhile using such military and political strength as it had to substitute Chinese for Russian authority in the old czarist enclaves. But the perilous state of the Chinese polity, together with the need to take Allied and particularly Japanese pressure seriously, precluded boldness. Every Beijing government of this era found itself confronted on the one hand by a rising Chinese nationalism, of which the May Fourth Movement was the most prominent symbol, and on the other hand by the reality of a powerful Japan, unleashed from Western restraints by the events of World War I and its aftermath. China's weaknesses and disunity made it unable to offer an independent answer to Japanese pressure, despite student demands. It therefore decided to proceed cautiously and with due regard for the views of the major Western powers, particularly the United States, in the hope that they would act as a restraining influence on Tokyo, despite signs to the contrary.

BOLSHEVIK COMINTERN EMISSARIES AND THE BUILDING OF A CHINESE SOCIALIST MOVEMENT

Recognizing that various pressures and inhibitions were likely to obstruct official recognition by the Beijing government, and having scant respect for that government in any case, Soviet authorities had determined from an early point to establish contacts with any Chinese of political promise, whatever their status or relationship to Beijing, both in the name of Soviet Russia and through the newly organized Communist International.

*One dissent to this view, though written from a strategic perspective, was voiced at this time from a most extraordinary source. On February 1, 1920, in a Vladivostok dispatch to the secretary of the navy, the commander in chief of the U.S. Asiatic Fleet wrote: "Revolutionary Siberia may prove to be an ally to the United States in the Far East . . . [and] an important feature in checking Japan. . . . All Russia wants now is to get back her territory, to be free from foreign intervention" (*NAMP/RDSRIAC*, 893.00/3314).

Two broad approaches were used. At first, contacts were almost exclusively with Chinese who were already in Russia, since about 150,000 of them had come there during World War I to serve as construction workers, miners, and manual laborers; by the time of the October Revolution, many had already returned home, but among those remaining, a trade union was organized, with a membership said to be from fifty to sixty thousand.[66] As we have seen, the leaders of this union were the first invitees to Bolshevik-sponsored international conferences.

With the advent of civil war, conditions rapidly deteriorated, and many Chinese workers, finding themselves without employment or the means of returning home, became destitute. It is not surprising, therefore, that several thousand of them were recruited as soldiers, and fought with both the Red and the White armies.* There is little evidence, however, that those who served as workers or soldiers with the Communist forces played any significant role in introducing Marxism-Leninism into China, or even in creating the early Chinese labor movement. Being illiterate and probably none too happy with their experiences in Russia, they disappeared from sight on their return to China. More important, as we shall see, were several educated Chinese who, as students in Russia, had become attracted to Bolshevik doctrines and policies. They could serve as the first bridges between the Bolshevik Revolution and those Chinese intellectuals at home who were prepared to be receptive to its message.

Yet the main channel of communication was between Bolshevik spokesmen or representatives and key figures within China. Interestingly, one of the first of such contacts was initiated not by the Soviets but by Sun Yat-sen. In the summer of 1918, after he had left Canton bitterly disillusioned and, following a brief sojourn in Japan, had arrived in Shanghai (June 25), Sun sent a telegram to Lenin in the name of the Chinese Revolutionary Party. According to the version of this telegram contained in the Sun Yat-sen memorial museum in Zhongshan University, its brief message read as follows: "The Chinese Revolutionary Party expresses great respect for the difficult and determined struggle being conducted by your nation's revolutionary party, and beyond this, looks forward to unity and a common struggle between the Chinese and Soviet revolutionary parties."[67]

A Soviet response, somewhat belated, was dispatched on August 1, when Georgii Chicherin, then commissar for foreign affairs, sent Sun a long, eulogistic message.[68] Addressing Sun as "respected leader," and praising him for having led the Chinese working masses against the northern Chinese capitalist class, as well as against the foreign capitalists and imperialists, Chicherin thanked him for his message, and indicated that although the

* By early 1919, accounts were reaching China of varying numbers of Chinese fighting with Red or White armies. An article in the *North China Herald* quoted a prominent Russian manufacturer who had escaped from Moscow as stating that Chinese were being used as street patrols there; he added that the Chinese serving in Bolshevik military ranks were probably coolies recruited in Manchuria a few years earlier to work in the Don Basin coal mines. He also said that good wages had attracted "entire battalions of natives from Shantung," some of them drawn from outlaw bands, who were fighting with the White Guards; and that according to their Russian commanders, they were rendering a very good account of themselves when called upon to fight (January 18, 1919, pp. 144–145). The commander of the U.S. Asiatic Fleet reported from Vladivostok on February 1, 1920, that there were about 30,000 Chinese soldiers in the Red Army. (*NAMP/RDSRIAC*, 893.00/3314, Vladivostok, U.S. Asiatic Fleet, from the Commander in Chief to the Secretary of the Navy.)

Russian and foreign capitalists were using "the hired men of Czechoslovakia" to cut the Soviet people off from the proletariat of South China, with their lackies spreading lies about the revolution, the worker-peasant government continued to exist and held high the banners of proletarian victory. "Our victory is your victory," Chicherin concluded; "let us form close cooperation among our forces in the great struggle on behalf of the common interests of the world's proletarian class. . . . Long live the alliance of the proletarian classes of the two countries."

Sun was later to assert that he never received Chicherin's message. His first direct contact with an individual having some connection with the new Soviet government appears to have come approximately a year and a half later, when he met with a General Potapoff, who was described by K. J. McEuen, then police commissioner of the International Shanghai Municipal Council, as "a well-known Bolshevik" and who, according to Council records, stayed in Shanghai from December 17, 1919, to April 22, 1920.*

The precise date and number of meetings between Potapoff and Sun are not known, but we have an account of one conversation from George Sokolsky. According to Sokolsky, Sun asked "Popoff" whether Moscow would assist him in his desire to crush the Guangxi militarists. "Popoff" in turn asked Sun why he did not first attack Little Xu (General Xu Shuzheng) and Duan Qirui, the "pro-Japanese elements," warning that Sun's effort to align himself with the Anfu clique would boomerang, since men like Duan would use him and then destroy him. Sun reportedly responded by saying that he had to take care of the southern militarists first, after which he could handle the North, and that the Anfu group could not destroy him, because his power was greater than theirs.[69]

The Shanghai police records indicating that Potapoff traveled to Zhangzhou at the end of April to meet General Chen Jiongming appear to be cor-

*The Shanghai report also indicated that another Russian, V. A. Stophany (Stofanii?), and a Chinese called "Loh Sik Kya," later associated with General Chen, had started a school to teach Esperanto in February 1920, and that "Stophany" was also associated with a Russian newspaper, *Shanghai Life*, which was reported to be the pivot of Bolshevik activities among the some 1,000 Russians resident in the city. The list of Chinese radicals provided in McEuen's report (which was solicited by the U.S. consulate on orders from Washington) suggests that the Shanghai police found it hard to distinguish "Bolshevik adherents" from other radicals or progressives. Thus, the famed anarchist Wu Zhihui was listed, together with Liang Pingxian, also an anarchist sympathizer closely associated with General Chen, and others ranging from social democrats to syndicalists. And there is no mention of Chen Duxiu, who was at this point the most active among the Chinese proto-Communists, nor of others associated with Chen in his current organization-building efforts. (See No. 479, American Consulate General, Shanghai, November 17, 1920, enclosing letter from K. J. McEuen dated November 11, 1920.)

In this same period, a "Confidential Memorandum on Conditions in China," dated May 18, 1920, was prepared for the U.S. consulate in Shanghai by George E. Sokolsky, a young American journalist, who identified himself as manager of the China Bureau of Public Information, and who stated that he had recently accepted the position of adviser to the Military Government (the Sun rump "government" in Shanghai) with special jurisdiction over foreign affairs. In this memorandum, Sokolsky refers to Sun's contact with "Mr. Popoff, the Bolshevik representative to China" (*NAMP/RDSRIAC*, 893.00/3376, report from Cunningham to Tenney, May 26, 1920). It seems very likely that Potapoff and Popoff were the same person, although Sokolsky spoke of two Russians, a "General Potapoff" and a "Colonel Popoff," the latter having come to China about the time of the May Fourth Movement. (See Wilbur, *Sun Yat-sen*, pp. 115–116 and p. 326 n. 6.) The confusion is compounded by the fact that in his *Memoirs* Horvath refers to a Consul General Popov in Harbin, whom he said remained strongly anti-Bolshevik during this period.

rect. Chen, it will be recalled, had made his headquarters in this Fujian city since mid-1918 and, associating himself with Sun, was in the process of conducting a broadly gauged reform program which he hoped would serve as a model for other regions. He had long had ties with Chinese radicalism. He had been a member of the Tongmeng Hui in his student days, and was later affiliated with the anarchist movement—indeed, at one point he had been a member of Shifu's assassination group. He trained his soldiers to develop ethical-political values and insisted on strict military discipline. Under his direction, road building, municipal improvements, a new educational program, and cultural development had begun. More than eighty students were sent to France with his support, including Peng Pai, who was later to become a famous Communist peasant leader. In his organ *Minxing bao* (Star of Fujian), developments in Russia were occasionally praised; radical literature, particularly of an anarchist type, flourished for a time in Fujian; and Chen himself contributed funds for Sun's Shanghai journal *Jianshe* (Reconstruction), which was being edited by Liao Zhongkai, Hu Hanmin, and Sun.[70] During this period, Chen served as the sole military arm of Sun's revolutionary movement, and was soon to assist him in returning to Canton in the fall of 1920 after a victorious military campaign in Guangdong. It is not surprising that the Bolsheviks sought to communicate with Chen at an early point.*

From several sources other than the Shanghai police, we learn that in late April 1920 a Russian emissary went to Zhangzhou to visit Chen.** According to one source, "Lu-po" was willing to aid Chen financially, but Chen said that a revolutionary movement should be self-reliant and declined the offer; another account indicates greater interest in such aid on Chen's part.† At some point during this period, Chen is reported to have written to Lenin to express sympathy with the Russian Revolution, and after his return to Canton, he not only summoned Sun but also gathered a number of

*The U.S. consular reports from Amoy during this period speak of extensive "Bolshevik propaganda" being disseminated in the Zhangzhou schools and in the city, but the samples provided indicate that most of the radical literature was anarchist and included articles from the old Paris *New Century* and Shifu's writings, among other items. For example, see *NAMP/RDSRIAC*, 893.00/3213, Beijing, April 26, 1920, from Tenney to Secretary of State, enclosing Dispatch No. 306 dated April 10, 1920, from the American consul, Amoy.

**Wu Xiangxiang asserts that the man was known as General Lu-po, and that he arrived in Zhangzhou about April 29, which would mesh well with the Shanghai records. He notes, however, that Liang (Haiyu Guke) recalled that his name sounded as if it began with a V, and therefore Wu guesses that it might have been Voitinskii. But Liang in his own account writes that when inquiries were made later about what happened to V, it was discovered that he had died on his way back to Moscow. Haiyu Guke, "An Unofficial Record of Liberation," *Ziyou ren*, December 26, 1951, p. 4. Liang's account of the talks between Chen and V (Potapoff/Popoff) is interesting. He said that Chen and the group around him expressed respect for the Russian Revolution, but did not approve of policies following the revolution, indicating that Chinese socialists prized their freedom, and were not prepared to be subject to the control of others. V (Potapoff) responded that Russia was not unwilling to offer freedom, but the danger of a counterrevolution still existed, precluding laxness at present. Here we encounter the anarchist-Marxist controversy that had been under way in Russia for several years and was commencing in China.

†Wu Xiangxiang, "A Preliminary Study," in *Zhongguo xiandai shi congkan* (see n. 70). Liang, on the contrary, writing that V offered Soviet assistance, asserts that Chen did want help in obtaining military supplies so that he could control Guangdong and Guangxi. He does not indicate that the offer was rejected, and suggests that had V lived, developments might have taken a different turn.

revolutionaries, including Chen Duxiu, who became the first head of the Guangdong Educational Association. However, Chen Jiongming's basic ideological leanings remained anarchist, and, in any case, practical military and political considerations were shortly to take over, as he began a struggle to consolidate his power in South China. Disputes over both military strategy and political policies were eventually to cause a split between Chen and Sun, as we noted earlier. For all of these reasons, Soviet interest in Chen faded.

The Soviet favorite of the early period was neither Sun nor Chen, but General Wu Peifu. The attraction to Wu was understandable—and shared by a number of American and British officials. The general was about forty-five years of age in 1920, and was regarded as progressive, honest, and strongly opposed to the Japanese, being a Chinese patriot.* He was thus in Soviet terms a logical contender for the label "bourgeois democrat," someone with whom the "proletariat" could potentially unite. It will be recalled that Liu Shaozhou praised Wu in brief remarks at the Second Comintern Congress in late July 1920. A Chinese laborer with no political standing almost certainly could not have made these public remarks before such a body had they not been approved in advance by the Comintern's Far Eastern Bureau. And there is abundant later evidence that individuals like Vilenskii and Grigorii Voitinskii regarded Wu as the most promising "bourgeois democrat" in China—a man with whom the socialists could work.**

This faith was not entirely misplaced. Wu was never a socialist, let alone a Marxist, but he was strongly committed to parliamentarism and basic reform, and showed a broad tolerance for "progressive ideas." Moreover, his chief political adviser, Bei Jianwu, had been a schoolmate of Li Dazhao and the two were close friends. Using this connection, Voitinskii was able to come into personal contact with Wu and, according to one source, influenced him to appoint certain radicals to administrative posts in the key railway systems under his control.[71] In any case, Wu later permitted union activities among railway workers, thereby enabling the Chinese Communists to obtain their first meaningful association with a sizable group of laborers. This development ended in disaster for many of those centrally involved, and embittered the Communists permanently against Wu. Even before the latter episode, however, Soviet-Comintern hopes with respect to Wu had dimmed when it was discovered that on the international front his tilt was irrevocably toward the United States and Great Britain, not toward Soviet Russia.

*A contemporary American perspective on Wu was provided by Major Wallace Philoon, a U.S. professional military officer who traveled with Wu's troops for a time in the fall of 1920. According to Philoon, Wu was very democratic, loved by his soldiers, outspoken against the Japanese, and prepared to fight against those corrupt Chinese officials "controlled by Japan." Philoon reported that Wu said that when the military struggle against Japan began, China would furnish the troops, but America, he hoped, would furnish the funds and naval support. For another highly favorable American evaluation of Wu, see a report by Commander C. Hutchins prepared on December 3, 1920, after a meeting with the Chinese general and enclosed in a communication from Crane to the Secretary of State, *NAMP/RDSRIAC*, 893.00/3771, Beijing, January 8, 1921.

**On October 9, 1920, in an article in *Izvestiia*, Vilenskii praised Wu, indicating that he was a bourgeois democrat with whom the Soviets could work. Other sources, including Henk Sneevliet (Maring), were to report that Voitinskii and the Far Eastern Bureau believed that Wu offered the best chance for united front activities. (See Xiang Qing, "The Comintern and the Chinese Revolution," pp. 16–18.)

There were several points of considerable interest in the initial Soviet efforts to make contact with influential Chinese political-military figures outside the Beijing government. First, the Soviets faced the same problem that confronted the Western powers and Japan. Given the socioeconomic and political atmosphere in China, it was exceedingly difficult to find an individual of promise who had both talent and power. Moreover, no one seemed to remain of the same political disposition for very long; everyone was fluid, or to use a harsher term, opportunistic. Soviet evaluations of Sun Yat-sen during this period did not differ significantly from those of a number of foreign observers (and many Chinese). Sun was seen as mercurial, weak in administrative and organizational skills, idealistic, and lacking in sound judgment. Thus, although the Russians did not completely write him off and treated him with deference in their communications, they did not consider him their most promising prospect. Yet neither Chen Jiongming nor Wu Peifu, the initial favorite, proved to be viable for Soviet purposes. And there would be others of similar type, among them Feng Yuxiang. Ultimately, events conspired to bring Sun and the Russians together, although the marriage was never one of complete trust or confidence on either side.

Meanwhile, the Chinese Communist movement was emerging, guided at each step by Russian instructors. Preliminary activities had begun in 1919, centering on small clusters of students and intellectuals, with Peking University a focal point.[72] One young man who served as a catalyst at the beginning was Zhang Ximan. Zhang had studied at the School of Far Eastern Languages in Vladivostok between 1911 and 1914, where he took courses in politics and economics and naturally learned the Russian language. According to his memoirs, he also had substantial contact with certain Russian student activists whom he describes as Nihilists.[73] He was in northeast China at the time of the October Revolution, but managed to return to Vladivostok in 1918, eager to learn as much as possible about the Bolsheviks. There he met various revolutionaries, collected Communist documents, and acquired knowledge of the essentials of the Soviet system. According to Zhang, while in Vladivostok he wrote letters to Wan Fuhai, a revolutionary elder, and Cai Yuanpei, the chancellor of Peking University, urging them to take the leadership in creating a society to study socialism, so that Chinese intellectuals might come abreast of current developments in Russia.[74]

He also reports that in early 1919, prior to the First Comintern Congress held in March, he returned secretly to Shanghai, where he met with Sun and urged him to model his party after that of the Russian Communists, applying their techniques of organization and mass mobilization. He further suggested that Sun send a representative to the forthcoming meeting of the Communist International. Sun could not be persuaded, and Zhang returned to Vladivostok.* In July, however, after the events of May 4, he came back to China, going to Beijing. Somewhat later, Zhang's first proposal was realized. Over one hundred progressive students and intellectuals from various areas organized the Shehuizhuyi yanjiuhui (Society for the Study of Socialism), with branches in various major centers. The Society, according to

*Zhang states that Sun's unwillingness to accept his ideas was due to the "stubbornness" of Hu Hanmin and others around Sun, to the "anti-Russian propaganda being spread by imperialists," to uncertainties regarding the strength of the Soviet government, and to the influence of Japan's Amur River Society (Kokuryūkai) upon Sun (Zhang Ximan, *Lishi huiyi*, pp. 86–87).

72. *Zhou Enlai in Nankai Middle School, fourth year, with American teacher, Albert P. Ludwig*

Zhang, was restricted to studying means whereby socialist thought could be propagated; it refrained from engaging in open propaganda, hoping not to provoke military intervention. Cai, though he wanted to be supportive, dared not take a leading role, for he was under surveillance as a result of the May Fourth incident and its aftermath. Li Dazhao was an active member, as were Chen Duxiu, Zhang Guotao, and many others, among whom Zhang mentions both Mao Zedong and Zhou Enlai. It is possible that Mao and Zhou were members of branch associations, but Mao was in Changsha when the society was founded (he returned to Beijing briefly from February to April of 1920). Zhou, who had returned from Japan in June of 1919, was engaged in student nationalist activities in Tianjin, but there is no evidence of his involvement with the socialist movement at this point.

However, Zhou Enlai's subsequent role in the politics of modern China was to be so prominent as to demand consideration of his early life at this point. He was born on March 5, 1898, in Huaian, a small town in Jiangsu province. He came from a family of officials, but in recent times the family fortunes had been in decline. His father, a minor functionary, earned little and had been posted in another province for years. Zhou was adopted by an aunt when he was one year old, but the family was reunited when they went to live with a maternal grandfather in Huaiyin in 1904. There, Zhou began his education in the classical manner, with private lessons in his grandfather's house. Both his natural mother and his adopted mother died when Zhou was nine, and the family returned to Huaian. In the summer of 1910 Zhou accompanied an uncle to Manchuria; he stayed for three years in Shenyang, continuing his primary school education.

In the fall of 1913 Zhou passed the examinations for entry into Nankai

73. *Zhou as Nankai student, April 1917*

Middle School in Tianjin. Tuition charges were waived because of his lack of funds and his high examination scores. Zhou soon began to take an active interest in political writings, both Chinese and foreign. He acquired a rudimentary knowledge of English, and in his second year helped organize one of the typical student study groups of the period—this one called the Study and Friendship Society (March 1914). Like most of his fellow students, Zhou acquired a strong nationalist consciousness as a result of the events of this era, a consciousness he expressed in poetry and speeches. He was a good public speaker, enjoyed writing, and also took part in at least one dramatic performance, playing the female lead.

In September of 1917 Zhou went to Japan, where he remained until June of 1919. Studying in a preparatory school in the Kanda district of Tokyo, Zhou learned some Japanese and is reported to have made his first contact with Marxism through the writings of Kawakami Hajime, but he does not appear to have advanced his higher education significantly. He was not in China at the time of the May Fourth incident, but on his return to Tianjin a month later, he began to participate actively in the newly organized Student Union and served as one of the editors of its daily newspaper, the *Tianjin Students' Union Bulletin*.

In an official biography, it is recorded that Zhou explained Marxist theory in simple terms to printing-plant workers, but one must be skeptical. It is clear, however, that he plunged into student activism on behalf of the nationalist goals epitomized by the May Fourth Movement, participating in petition drives and protest marches, both in Tianjin and Beijing. And on September 16, 1919, he took part in the organization of a new student group, the Awakening Society, comprising some two dozen young men and women. The society voiced reformist and nationalist goals very much in line with the mainstream student movements of the time.

At this point, Zhou enrolled in a university class that had just been set up at the Nankai school, but according to his own account he spent little time in the classroom, being ever more actively involved in the political movement with a number of others, including his wife-to-be, Deng Yingchao. On January 29, 1920, Zhou and certain fellow activists were arrested and were not released until April 7. Throughout this period Zhou's commitments appear to have been largely if not wholly nationalist, although he may well have acquired an interest in Marxism through *New Youth* and other publications. Li Dazhao, moreover, is said to have talked with Awakening Society members and other student representatives in Tianjin in the summer of 1920 and to have made suggestions concerning their activities.

In November, Zhou and some fellow students left for France as part of the work-study program. Soon, as we shall note, he was to devote his principal energies to political activities there, quickly gravitating to the Communist movement.[75] It seems likely that prior to his departure from China, Zhou had already had some exposure to the new socialist trends. It is important to emphasize, however, that many creeds competed for support. Thus, the Society for the Study of Socialism, reflecting the diverse philosophic currents to be found among the Chinese avant-garde, quickly divided into factions. Zhang records that societies dedicated to the study of guild socialism, syndicalism, and anarchism soon appeared, each with different leaders and members. Therefore, it was natural that in March 1920, Li Dazhao and a few others initiated a small study group that eventually took the name

74. Members of the New China Association, a patriotic, anti-imperialist association of Chinese students in Japan, December 1918. Zhou Enlai was one member.

Makesi xueshuo yanjiuhui (Society for the Study of Marxism), with a parallel organization, the Society for the Study of Russia, also emerging.* In the fall of 1920, moreover, a new Russian Department was inaugurated at Peking University, fulfilling another of Zhang Ximan's hopes.**

Several Russians were in contact with a few of the young Chinese radicals during this period. According to the later account of A. A. Muller, he and a friend, N. Bortman, met Li Dazhao and some of his students in 1919 and urged them to organize the Tianjin dock and textile workers. When they left China in January 1920, such activities had begun, he reported.[76] More important was the role of Sergei Polevoi. A student of the Chinese classics, Polevoi had come to China from Russia earlier, seeking to learn the vernacular language. At the time of the October Revolution, he was teaching at

*Actually, the Society for the Study of Marxism was not formally and openly established until October 1921, but in the announcement setting forth the purposes and membership of the association, it was stated that the study society had first been initiated in March 1920, and now had nineteen members, with 120 yuan collected for the purchase of books. See Office of School History, Peking University, comp., "The Society for the Study of Marxism of the University of Peking," *Jindai shi ziliao* (Contemporary Historical Materials), April 1955, pp. 161–173.

**According to Zhang, Cai did not agree to the creation of a Russian Department until the fall of 1920. In order to get students, it was decided to admit those who were on the waiting list for entry to the university if they were prepared to become first-year students in the new department. Almost all of those in this category (70 to 80 persons) took the opportunity, but since they were not required to remain in this department, some two-thirds ultimately left Russian studies, and only a few actually remained by the time of graduation. There were other problems. No one was prepared to head the department, and finally the dean, Gu Mengyu, was assigned this additional task. Faculty were recruited from among individuals attached to the Russian embassy in Beijing, and presumably they were persons who were apolitical or not hostile to the new order. (Zhang Ximan, *Lishi huiyi*, pp. 3–5.)

75. *In September 1919 Zhou Enlai and others organized a revolutionary association called Juewu She (Awakening Society). This picture was taken in 1920, with some of the members. From the left, front row: Cheng Zhidu, Xue Hanyue, Zheng Xueqing, Zhou Zhilian, Deng Yingchao, Liu Qingyang, Li Zhenyin; back row: Chen Xiaocen, Pan Shilun, Ma Jun, Li Xijin, Guo Longzhen, Hu Weixian, and Zhou Enlai*

Peking University, and through some channel, he was appointed cultural representative of the Comintern. This enabled him to issue entry papers to Chinese youths who wanted to go to Russia. He was also active in making initial contacts with various Chinese intellectuals on behalf of the Bolshevik cause. According to Liang Binxian, Polevoi was the individual who, writing in Esperanto, communicated with him and others associated with the South China anarchist movement in the spring of 1920; he introduced himself as a socialist who hoped to aid in bringing the free socialists (anarchists) and Russian socialists together.[77] Polevoi, being at the same institution, had become acquainted at some point with both Li Dazhao and Chen Duxiu, and it was he who introduced Voitinksii to Li.*

As we have noted, certain members of the Russian community in Shanghai also identified themselves with the new Soviet government and sought to support its cause.[78] One problem, as is suggested by the case of Potapoff (Popoff), is to establish both the personal identity of such individuals and the way in which they were affiliated with or recognized by either the Soviet government or the Comintern. Some Chinese sources speak of Moscow's having sent an individual named Stolmichuskii (from the Chinese transliteration) to Shanghai prior to the arrival of Voitinskii, but there is no record of anyone with such a name, unless the reference is a garbled one to Vilenskii (Siburyakov) or "Stophany" (Stofanii?). It is known that a few Russian supporters of the Bolsheviks were seeking to influence opinion, mainly within the Shanghai Russian colony, by means of journalistic efforts, lectures, and pamphlets.[79] Only with the arrival of the Voitinskii mission, how-

* According to Zhang Ximan, Polevoi reported expenses to the Comintern in connection with student transportation, costs, and other items which in fact were never paid, pocketing the money that he received as supposed compensation. When his superiors discovered irregularities and took steps to recall him to Russia for investigation, he renounced his Russian citizenship and emigrated to the United States. (Zhang Ximan, *Lishi huiyi*, p. 10.)

76. Zhou Enlai in France, with other students, February 1921 (Zhou in center back)

ever, did a bona fide representative of the Comintern dedicate himself and his team to organizational efforts within the Chinese community over a protracted period of time.

Grigorii Naumovich Voitinskii (Zarkhin) was only twenty-seven years old when he arrived in China in March 1920, but he had already had an eventful career.[80] Born in Nevel in 1893, Voitinskii migrated to the United States in 1913 for economic reasons. He remained there until the spring of 1918, and had joined the American Socialist Party in 1915. After the October Revolution he returned to Russia and went directly to Siberia, where he joined the Russian Communist Party in 1918. Participating in the struggle in the Omsk region against the Kolchak forces, Voitinskii was captured in May 1919 and imprisoned, first in Vladivostok, then in Sakhalin. But in a January 1920 prison uprising, he escaped, and shortly thereafter became affiliated with the Comintern's Eastern Secretariat in Irkutsk. In this capacity, he was sent to China, where he arrived with his wife, a secretary named I. K. Mamaev, and a Chinese interpreter, Yang Mingzhai.*

* Precisely when Voitinskii arrived in China has long been a matter of uncertainty. Many earlier works use the date May 1920, but the evidence now available strongly points toward March. As we noted earlier, the Voitinskii group brought with them the First Karakhan Manifesto and had it published in Chinese newspapers in early April. It is also interesting to note that on April 3 the *North China Herald* carried the following: "It is understood that recently an authorized Bolshevik emissary from Siberia arrived in Shanghai, and he is believed to have made the statement that the local Bolsheviks were merely free lancers" ("Bolsheviks in Shanghai," p. 23. See also Xiang Qing, "The Comintern and the Chinese Revolution," pp. 92–116).

The small group went first to Beijing, where, with the help of Polevoi, they met Li Dazhao and some of his student followers. The records concerning this phase of Voitinskii's activities are sparse, but one may presume that encouragement was given for organizational activities, and information was exchanged about the situation in China and Russia. Beijing, however, was not the most logical place for Voitinskii's efforts, and the group moved on to Shanghai in April.[81]

When they arrived, they immediately sought out Chen Duxiu, as Li had suggested, and discovered that under his aegis a very small band of intellectuals had constituted themselves a Marxist group.* Voitinskii conceived his task to be that of giving this group a firmer structure, motivating them to make contact with genuine proletarians through publications geared to that purpose, and encouraging them to help set up labor unions. Since the Communist movement was certain to have its greatest appeal to young intellectuals, moreover, it was essential to establish a Socialist Youth League and to use it as a recruiting vehicle for the party itself. All of these activities were pursued. By May, Chen and his fellow intellectuals had been organized into what resembled a Communist cell, and by mid-year they claimed to have some seventy members. In late July a Socialist Youth League was formally inaugurated, and soon its organ, *Xianqu* (The Pioneer), appeared with an initial printing of 5,000 copies. It is reported that one of Voitinskii's early contributions was to give two thousand yuan so that a printing operation could get under way.[82] Somewhat later, two publications attuned to workers were begun, and unionization efforts got under way, with attention directed first toward mechanics, then toward printers and textile workers.

Shanghai was the center of Voitinskii's efforts and the efforts of the embryonic Chinese Communist movement, but similar activities were undertaken in other cities, sometimes with direct assistance from the Voitinskii group. For obvious reasons, Beijing and Canton were of cardinal importance if Communism was to be a national movement. In Beijing a small Communist cell was organized in September, and pursuant to Voitinskii's urgings, a weekly newspaper addressed to the workers was launched.** Night courses for workers at one of the stations of the Beijing–Hankou railway were also started, along with efforts to launch unions.

In Canton three Cantonese who had been schoolmates at Peking Univer-

*Among the Communist documents seized in the 1927 Beijing raid on the Soviet legation was "A Brief History of the Chinese Communist Party." These documents have been edited and published by C. Martin Wilbur and Julie Lien-ying How, *Documents on Communism, Nationalism, and Soviet Advisers in China, 1918–1927*. They report that according to the Japanese author Otsuka Reizō, the "Brief History" was drafted by Chen Duxiu before being subsequently written in final form by a Russian. In that document it is reported that at the beginning of 1920 Chen and six others had organized a Marxist group. The most important figure in the group other than Chen was Dai Jitao, who had already acquired a strong interest in Marxism. Dai was to remain active in the embryonic Communist movement until the First Party Congress, but his associations with Sun and the Guomindang took priority. Later, convinced that Marxism would never work in China, he became one of the most powerful anti-Communist theorists. Actually, of the original seven cell members, four left the group for various reasons.

**The initial Beijing Communist group consisted of eight persons, six of whom were anarchists! The anarchists soon withdrew, leaving Li and Zhang Guotao as the two survivors. New members were gradually acquired, but the Beijing cell remained very small in its early months, with about ten comrades (Wilbur and How, *Documents on Communism*, p. 52).

sity—Chen Gongbo, Tan Pingshan, and Dan Zhitang—played the leading role in launching the movement.[83] On the eve of General Chen Jiongming's seizure of power, they had begun a newspaper, *Guangdong qunbao* (Guangdong Masses News). With General Chen's victory in October of 1920, and the arrival of Chen Duxiu as head of the new Guangdong Educational Committee, conditions were ripe for political activism. According to Chen Gongbo, two socialists came to Canton at this point, posing as merchants; Liang reports that one was a Russian (Minno) and the other an American Communist, Percy, who served as interpreter. Through Qu Shengbai, a prominent anarchist, these two met Chen Gongbo and his colleagues. Although they knew practically nothing about socialism, the three former schoolmates agreed to organize a Guangdong Communist Party as well as a Socialist Youth League. Chen Duxiu, of course, influenced this decision; Chen Gongbo was head of the Propaganda and Speech Department of Chen's Educational Committee, as well as a faculty member of the local teachers college.

Chen Gongbo recalls that it was not difficult to recruit intellectuals, although most of the anarchist members soon departed. The problem lay in getting any workers to join, since Canton did not have what might be called modern industrial workers. The young intellectuals concentrated on machinists and seamen, with rather slim results. Chen also recollects an amusing incident that illustrates the problems of giving international communism an identity in China. Shanghai (presumably Voitinskii) insisted that the Canton cell conduct a memorial parade to commemorate the deaths of the German Communists Rosa Luxemburg and Karl Liebnecht. But when the parade was held, with pictures of the Communist martyrs carried through the streets, the onlookers thought that a missionary and his wife had passed away.[84]

Meanwhile, similar small-scale organizational activities on behalf of the Communist movement were taking place in Tianjin, Wuhan, and Changsha, among other places. In Shanghai, under Voitinskii's guidance, a School of Foreign Languages had been opened, specifically to train students in the Russian language and to prepare them in other ways for study in Moscow. About sixty students were enrolled by the end of 1920, most of them (like Liu Shaoqi) members of the Socialist Youth League.

By the autumn of 1920, each of the Communist groups in Shanghai, Beijing, and Canton had a labor journal: *Laodong jie* (Labor World) in Shanghai, *Laodongren* (The Worker) in Beijing, and *Laodong sheng* (The Voice of Labor) in Canton. The Foreword to the first issue of *Laodongren* suggests the general approach being taken.[85] After asserting that workers—not presidents, militarists, country gentlemen, or bosses—were the most useful and most noble citizens, the writer deplored the bitterly hard life forced upon them. This was a universal phenomenon, but foreign workers were not as miserable as Chinese workers, and their political consciousness was higher. The first step for the Chinese workers was to seek higher wages, shorter working hours, and improved working conditions. But the basic problem was the unequal distribution of goods produced by labor, and to solve this problem a fundamental reform of society was required. This reform would be the second step. In Europe and America the first step had been taken and the second was about to commence, but in China even the first step was not in sight. To cause workers to think about their immediate problems and to help in their organizational efforts were described as the purposes of this journal.

Although the ideas presented here were expressed rather simply, one must doubt whether such journals could have had any influence on the Chinese working class of this period, except for the tiniest segment of literate workers—most of them in skilled occupations. In November 1920 there appeared another type of journal, *Gongchandang* (literally, The Communist Party), subtitled in English *The Communist*. Its six issues, published over nine months, set forth the central principles of the new movement in relatively uncomplicated fashion. The journal was primarily dedicated to the task of reaching and influencing the intellectual community, especially youths like those being recruited into the Socialist Youth League. All articles and editorials were written under a pseudonym or carried no author's name, but various sources indicate that the chief editor-writer was Chen Duxiu. What role Voitinskii played in making certain that the Comintern position was understood and supported cannot be fully ascertained, but according to the Soviet scholar V. I. Glunin, Voitinskii himself wrote several of the articles.

Four basic themes dominated *Gongchandang* writings. First, it was necessary to define contemporary China in economic and, more precisely, in class terms, and also to assess China's developmental status in relation to that of the West. In the journal's opening statement, the latter issue was addressed: Whereas capitalism in Europe and America had reached the point of destruction, it was said, capitalism in China was only beginning to develop and display its evils.[86] The question occupying greater attention, however, related to the class nature of Chinese society. Marxists obviously had to combat the widely held thesis that in essence China was a classless society, characterized by minimal economic and social differences and high socioeconomic mobility. *Gongchandang* argued that this view was deeply flawed. One analysis identified four classes: the officials (with their monarchist antecedents); the militarists (presently bathing China in blood); the gentry and other "middle class" elements; and the "proletariat," which included urban workers, farmers, and ordinary soldiers.[87]

Although greatest homage was paid to the concept of an organized proletariat in the Western (Soviet) sense, *Gongchandang* writers devoted much more attention to China's farmers, acknowledging that they formed the great majority of the population and the bulk of China's proletariat. Predictably, they saw pervasive inequality in the Chinese countryside among four classes: the big landlords, who did not cultivate their land; the owner-tillers; those who owned some land, but not enough to provide for their family needs, so that it was necessary for them to rent an additional portion; and the "lumpenproletariat," who "had no place to put a needle and thread" and depended solely on their labor as tenants or day laborers.[88] Since the third and fourth categories were the largest, argued the writer, life for most farmers was very harsh. Nor was there a proper and equitable distribution of production between tenants and landlords. The owners fixed an amount of grain to be delivered regardless of the size of the harvest, and they enforced the collection of it.[89]

The Chinese farmer's life was no less burdensome than that of the Russian farmer before the 1917 Revolution, and the suppressed resentment was already great, the author continued. The massive famine in the North was now adding to the misery, with millions scheduled to die. The time was not far off when an enraged peasantry would explode, as was suggested by the recent events at Pingjiang.*

The industrial workers suffered conditions much worse than those of their European, American, and Japanese counterparts, because China was still in the first stages of the industrial revolution. With a huge labor surplus, it was not easy to organize trade unions, but it was essential to do so if the struggle against the capitalist class was to be effectively carried out. It was particularly important to note that the Chinese worker was exploited not only by Chinese capitalists but also by international capitalism. The foreign capitalists were bringing cheap manufactured goods into China, ruining the domestic handicraft industries and thereby adding to the workers' woes. The unwholesome alliance between international capitalism and Chinese militarists also governed the domestic political scene, enabling the militarists to make provinces like Hunan and Hebei run red with blood.

A second theme was the necessity of pursuing Marxist techniques in advancing a social revolution. The fundamental task was to unite workers, peasants, and soldiers in an alliance strong enough to overthrow the capitalists; it was necessary to seize power by conducting class warfare, and then to found a workers' state by imposing a dictatorship of the proletariat.** An important part of this task was to unionize urban workers, since the proletarian class had to be the vanguard of the mass movement, as in the Petrograd revolution of 1917 and in the Japanese rice riots of August 1918.[90] Interestingly, in this same article, criticism was directed at the May Fourth Movement: although it had initially possessed great strength, "it had gone in the wrong direction"—presumably because of its failure to recruit the masses and its concentration on purely nationalist themes.[91]

If proletarian leadership was essential, however, it was equally important to lead the peasants toward class consciousness. They formed the great majority of the Chinese population, and were thus destined to play an important role in the coming revolution.[92] Once their class consciousness had been elevated, they would engage in class struggle, thereby providing the Chinese social revolution with a reasonable chance of success. It was cru-

* In the midst of the many problems in Hunan to which we have earlier referred, a revolt spearheaded by unpaid soldiers, reportedly with some peasant involvement, took place in 1920 in Pingjiang, eastern Hunan. Rumors that "Bolshevik propaganda" had influenced the uprising were fed by stories that some soldiers refused to salute their officers, forced them to walk with the men instead of riding in sedan chairs as was the custom, and in other respects showed radical indoctrination. (See *NAMP/RDSRIAC*, 893.00/3710, November 27, 1920, Meinhardt to the Secretary, "Political Conditions in Hunan.") Whatever the facts, the Pingjiang uprising was subsequently hailed by the Chinese Communists as a harbinger of things to come.

** See Ji-sheng, "To the Workers, Soldiers and Peasants," *Gongchandang*, May 7, 1921, pp. 4–13. In the article by Jiang-Chun on April 7, three methods of developing a social revolution were outlined: the parliamentary method, working through the labor movement, and "direct action." According to the author, parliamentary bodies were always controlled by the capitalist class, hence were incapable of making basic reforms. There were various types of labor movements, from reformist to revolutionary, and their chief weapon was the general strike, but in China, given the weakness of the industrial workers, this was not feasible. Thus "direct action" was the only effective method available. "Direct action" required that after an intensive organization of unions, workers must ally themselves with other proletarian elements to create a broad front against the capitalist class ("The Commercial Rights of a Social Revolution," pp. 2–3).

cial, therefore, to explode the myths that the Chinese farmer was happy, that harmony prevailed in the countryside, and that land ownership was widely distributed. Otherwise, the peasantry would remain sunk in apathy and indifference.

One had to accept the state as a necessary if temporary instrument of basic social renovation. Nationalism, on balance, was bad, and internationalism was critical to socialist success; but the state apparatus had to be maintained during the crucial early phases of socialism, both for economic and for political-security reasons.[93]

In this as in other respects, the *Gongchandang* writers made it clear that China's model had to be that of Soviet Russia. If the coming Chinese revolution were merely political and not socioeconomic as well, then politics, law, education, the military structure, and indeed the entire social and economic system would remain tied to the old capitalist order.[94] The essential need was thus to replace capitalist dictatorship with proletarian dictatorship, to centralize the power of the working class during the revolution itself and the first phase of the postrevolutionary era.

In explicating the Marxist (Leninist) requirements, *Gongchandang* authors took up a third theme, the necessity of an unrelenting attack on both liberalism and anarchism, the two principal foes. What the liberals called democratic or parliamentary politics was no more than a system established by capitalists for their own class interests and bore no relationship to the interests of the working class. The parliamentary system corrupted true revolutionary movements—witness what had happened to the German Social Democratic Party in the course of the recent war.[95] This did not mean that one should ignore or boycott parliament, as was advocated by the anarchists. The instruments of the bourgeoisie should be used whenever they could serve the interests of the proletariat, but parliamentarism and the system of elections surrounding it should elicit neither trust nor exclusive reliance, as was advocated by the social democrats.

In China, one writer said, some had argued for provincial self-rule, but that was simply a peg upon which to hang gentry rule. The idea that the gentry could oust all corrupt officials and evil militarists and make themselves the representatives of the capitalist middle class was an impossible dream. In their relations with the common people, the gentry were indistinguishable from the militarists; as the old proverb had it, the tiger in front of the mountain is the same as the tiger in back of the mountain—he will eat people. The Chinese middle class, unlike the middle class in Western nations, was not capable of conducting a bourgeois-democratic revolution; they could only exploit, oppress, and make themselves attractive to foreign capitalism.[96] Thus, middle-class democratic politics under their aegis could never be achieved.

The attack on the anarchists was hardly less severe, despite some occasional kind words. The anarchist party was a friend of the Communists, but not a comrade. It was a friend because it also wanted to overthrow capitalism; but it was not a comrade, because it lacked a method of accomplishing its goal.[97] There were many Chinese adherents to anarchism, one writer acknowledged, but their energies were not being put to good use. The fundamental problem was that the anarchists were too optimistic about human nature and too pessimistic about politics. Mankind was not intrinsically good, as the anachists seemed to think. Throughout human history, men had fought each other—invading, expelling, killing. And a few evil men could defeat the purposes of a great multitude unless they were controlled. Thus, a police and security system was needed to deal with the enemies of communism. Otherwise, counterrevolution could destroy all the gains and make all the sacrifices futile.

The anarchists believed that individualism—and a society with no centralized program or structure—could advance justice and freedom. But the real result of anarchist policies would be inequality, injustice, and chaos. Again, mankind was not perfect—some people were lazy, others covetous. Unless there were centralized programs and plans for a national allocation of resources, great inequities would occur. Communism, of course, could not guarantee that there would be no lazy people, but it could guarantee that everyone would be working for their daily food, and that under the proper use of authority, justice and humanity could be advanced.* Heretofore, the two main streams of socialism had been those of Marx and Bakunin; but now that an increasing number of people were beginning to understand the weaknesses of anarchism and the strengths of communism, the tide was running in the direction of Marx.

A final theme running through *Gongchandang* articles was perhaps the most interesting, in light of subsequent events: it concerned the applicability of "bourgeois democracy" and communism to China, hence the proper nature and timing of China's revolution. As we have seen, *Gongchandang* writers were sharply critical of the Chinese middle class and its political capacities. But would China nevertheless have to go through a bourgeois-democratic phase? On this critical question, *Gongchandang* writers displayed a certain vagueness. According to socialist principles, asserted one author, a social revolution will come about naturally when the capitalist system has reached a given stage. But human action can have a critical effect in hastening the process. The capitalist systems in Britain and America were ten times more developed than the system in Russia, as were the trade unions. Why did the social revolution not occur first in these two countries instead of in Russia? The answer lay in the effective power and policies of the Russian revolutionary party. Therefore, "in China, we need not be held back by the restraints of theory, but can endeavor to work toward the realization of revolution."[98] Using various urban centers as our base, the author continued, we should unite the workers, peasants, soldiers, and others belonging to the proletarian class to form one big organization, and then engage in large-scale movements to seize local political power. Through the aggregation of such power, we can gain full control over our economy and society. Direct action, he asserted, was the only effective way to advance a social revolution. A necessary supplement was the full use of propaganda, open and secret, to educate the proletariat to the fact that the propertied classes were their enemies.

In another piece, the author noted that the common people of France

* "Why We Advocate Communism," *Gongchandang*, May 7, 1921, pp. 23–30. In conclusion, the author (almost certainly Chen Duxiu) argues as follows. Our people are hungry. Do we want to hasten to save ourselves, or do we want to dream about the perfect utopia represented by anarchism, which cannot save us now? Communism is like a bowl of rough rice set before the people. Anarchism is like a bowl of delicacies several hundred miles away (pp. 29–30).

had stormed the Bastille with their bare hands, without weapons, and yet achieved success. We can use the same means, and at once, he argued. Why follow the wrong road? If the gentry were to seize power at this point, it would be much more difficult to turn the situation around, and their efforts to expel the militarists would in any case fail. The case was clear: what China needed was a proletarian revolution.[99] The model was available in the form of the Soviet experience. In Russia the workers had been victorious, and during three years of socialism countless hardships had been overcome. Even many who were once skeptical had become convinced that the revolution in Russia was succeeding.

Several of the themes set forth in *Gongchandang*—notably the impossibility of a true bourgeois-democratic revolution in China, and the possibility of mobilizing the "proletariat" very soon for a successful revolutionary thrust—followed M. N. Roy's criticisms of Lenin's doctrine that a bourgeois-democratic stage was necessary for revolution in colonial countries. The coming effort of the Comintern and its representatives in China to commit the Chinese Communists to policies of alignment with the Guomindang and the pursuit of bourgeois democracy, therefore, were destined from the outset to meet opposition. On balance, however, *Gongchandang* articles expressed staunch adherence to Marxism-Leninism in its current form. The small band of Communist intellectuals who ran the journal thought of themselves as members of an international movement, and were prepared to accept the guidance of its official representatives. From the beginning, of course, certain individuals associated with the Communist cause refused to adopt this attitude and ended their affiliation, usually in the name of nationalism.

Nonetheless, by early 1921, an outpost of the Communist International had been established in China, and a tiny group of intellectuals in the major urban centers had made a commitment to communism. The great bulk of the Chinese intellectual community, it is worth repeating, held to other political faiths. In this regard, John Dewey's observations about the status of Bolshevism within Chinese intellectual circles at the end of 1920 are of interest because no foreigner had enjoyed greater contact with this group over the previous eighteen months than he. In a report to the American legation in Beijing, he made the following comments, which we shall paraphrase:

> I have seen no direct evidence of Bolshevism in China. I have come into contact with teachers, writers, and students who are sometimes called Bolsheviks and who are, in fact, quite radical in their social and economic ideas, being opposed to old institutions, especially the family system, and disgusted with politics. They have decided that the Revolution of 1911 was a failure, and they want intellectual change. Such views are particularly strong among the younger teachers, the older ones being rather conservative.
>
> Almost all students are "socialists," and some call themselves Communists and think that the Russian Revolution is a very fine thing. But while this may seem Bolshevistic, it has not been inspired from Russia. No doubt there are some Bolshevik propagandists in China, but they have nothing to do with the radical temper in the country. It is stimulated by the corruption and inefficiency of the government, and the pro-Japanese character

> of the former cabinet. Much is silly and superficial, but is a good sign for the future.
>
> There is no discontented proletariat in China, and the farmers who form 90 percent of the population are highly conservative. In Changsha, I was invited to attend a meeting called to organize a branch of a labor association, but there was not a single day-laborer at the meeting, the attendees being mainly merchants with some students. The students are too theoretical to engage successfully in practical movements. Their influence in politics is now slight in contrast to two years ago.[100]

At the time Professor Dewey wrote this report, his views were not far off the mark, though he underestimated the impact of the Russian Revolution on the young intellectual radicals. Nevertheless, several significant events would have to occur before the Communist movement could be considered a formidable factor in Chinese society. The first of these events, however—Sun's decision to align his movement with the fledgling Communists and, more important, to accept Soviet guidance in restructuring the Guomindang party and its military forces—was only a few years away.*

POLITICIZATION AMONG THE OVERSEAS CHINESE STUDENTS

As we have seen, the first major wave of Chinese students to go abroad for study began in about 1900 and reached a peak some seven or eight years later. China's internal problems and then the coming of the First World War slowed the student exodus, even as the latter event led to the exportation of Chinese labor. Indeed, the dispatch of unskilled labor in massive quantities was the primary contribution of China to the Allied war effort, and the largest number of workers went to Russia and France. It will be remembered that Li Shizeng and others, taking advantage of this situation, had organized the Qingong Jianxue Hui (Association for Diligent Work and Frugal Study) in mid-1915, with the idea of helping prospective students find part-time work. For various reasons, however, the flow of students to France did not begin until the war had ended. Nevertheless, most of the students who headed overseas after 1918 did go to Europe, and primarily to France.[101]

* For a somewhat different view of Bolshevism in China, rendered extremely interesting by later developments, see a letter initialed NTJ, written on the letterhead of the Division of Far Eastern Affairs, U.S. Department of State, dated January 21, 1921, and addressed to Bullard MacMurray (*NAMP/RDSRIAC*, 893.00/3710, Meinhardt to the Secretary of State). After asserting that he agreed heartily with the thesis that neither the Chinese nation nor the Chinese people were in much danger from Bolshevism, the writer qualified his statement with the following observation: "There exists in China today a comparatively large class which we call coolies but which corresponds in all respects to the class in Europe which Marx called 'the laboring proletariat.' It is quite true that this class in China is not an industrial 'proletariat' in the sense used by Marx. It is, however, composed of the laboring element in China, 'the hewers of wood and drawers of water,' comprising first, the tenant farmer (who is to a certain extent as fixed to the soil as was the serf of Russia), the boatman, the porter, and others of their type." The writer went on to assert that whereas manual labor for this class had been plentiful some fifteen years earlier, with railways being built and other developments taking place, these very gains had produced changes in trade methods and routes, thereby throwing surplus coolie labor onto the country. Thus, those aspiring to political power could recruit "from the drifting proletariat, bodies of men whom they have armed, uniformed, fed and housed, who are only too glad under the circumstances to march and fight at their bidding."

Study in Tokyo had limited appeal in these years of strong anti-Japanese sentiment, and the United States was considered too expensive and lacking in support facilities.

With language training under way in Beijing and several other places, work-study students began to go to France in groups of 30 to 50 during the summer of 1919, and the number per ship significantly increased in early 1920, sometimes reaching 200. By late 1921 there were some 2,000 Chinese students in France. More than 1,500 of them were work-study students; the others were supported by government funds or through private, usually family, sources.[102] Meanwhile, another organization, the Sino-French Educational Association, had established offices in both China and France to advance cultural and particularly educational relations. Still a third organization, the Work-Study Mutual Assistance Group, was established in Beijing in 1919 by Wang Guangqi, and branches were soon opened in other cities. Its aim was to enable poor students to go to Europe, with the idea that once there they would form cooperative groups to run various enterprises, sharing the profits.[103]

As we indicated, the bulk of the work-study students were from Sichuan, Hunan, and Guangdong, and the large majority came from families of very limited means. In most cases their capacity to speak or read French was at first feeble (even among those with some previous training in China). Li Shizeng therefore arranged to have most new arrivals sent to small French communities for further language training and education at roughly the high school level, combined with some paying work. Three communities provided facilities for many students: Montargis, Melun, and Fontainebleau.[104]

Toward the end of 1919, a Chinese-language weekly called *LuOu zhoukan* (Weekly Journal of Students in Europe), with the French subtitle *Journal Chinois Hebdomadaire*, began publication in Paris. From its articles we can learn something about the thoughts and problems of the students and their counselors.[105] In the opening statement of the first issue, the purposes of the journal were set forth. In addition to providing news of China for Chinese living in Europe, the editors had three other goals: to report on the activities of labor and intellectual organizations, commenting on current events in "a fair, balanced manner"; to publish works of Western scholars in condensed form; and to work for all overseas Chinese, not merely those in Europe.[106]

In the course of the next year, four general subjects were repeatedly covered in this journal. The first, naturally enough, was the "diligent work and frugal study movement" itself—its purposes, values, and problems. Readers were assured that the central purpose of the movement was not merely to enable students without funds to further their education; indeed, to emphasize work simply as a means of supporting study was wrong. The central purpose of the program was to cultivate both the mind and the body. A well-rounded personality could not be constructed if one were committed too heavily to either work or study, nor would such a commitment serve the needs of China. Strong bodies combined with active, educated minds were a requirement if the Chinese nation were to survive.[107]

Further, through work, one could come to appreciate the value of labor and begin to bridge the gap between the worker and the intellectual. In this process, moreover, one could acquire a sense of the importance of mutual assistance, of placing the collectivity ahead of individual gain. A new morality would emerge.

More than one contributor acknowledged that to combine study and work in a foreign environment tested both the character and the stamina of every youth. One lament was that many students actively disliked physical labor; the traditional scholar's disdain for soiling his hands remained.[108] Others had come in weakened physical condition and were unable to work. And there were those who were unwilling to save the money they earned, squandering it on a wild life in an environment in which they fancied themselves anonymous.[109] Then, when they were destitute, they demanded assistance, refusing to take any responsibility for their plight.

Concern over the problems of the work-study program merged with a second general subject, the need to create a new culture and morality to which the youth of China could dedicate themselves. In many articles dealing with this theme, one finds strong echoes of the earlier student essays published in the Tokyo student journals. In one case, even the author was the same: Wang Jingwei contributed an article in the first issue, noting the concern being voiced about the imminent collapse of China and the extinction of the Chinese race.[110] And there were numerous essays that sought to analyze the cultural and personal defects of the Chinese people in general, or Chinese students in particular.[111] In reciting these shortcomings, one author emphasized the fact that Chinese lacked an "active, courageous attitude," being prepared to take things for granted without attempting to make any changes. This basic timidity, he argued, could be changed only if students, acting in concert, could form a powerful organization of their own, a structure that would enable each member to give the others courage through mutual assistance and collective action.[112] In another article the same author deplored the fact that in all national societies of the Far East the minority controlled the majority, and the masses followed their leaders simply to avoid trouble. Nothing was brought before public tribunals to be judged by the people.[113]

Several of the essays called for a thorough investigation of one's past life-style, conduct, and writings in a manner startlingly similar to the call for self-criticism of a later day.* And in the appeal for a new morality, the family once again came in for trenchant criticism. Because the Chinese people found comfort only in their familial environment, they were not prepared to have any public consciousness. Society was regarded as evil, and a negative attitude was taken toward the public at large.[114] Yet despite the journal's extensive criticism of China, some of its contributors, writing in a vein parallel to that of Liang Qichao, Zhang Junmai, and other "neo-traditionalists," warned against blindly following the West. One of them, Hua Lin, asserted that life under the European economic system was restrictive, mechanical, and monotonous; and Wang Guangqi argued that the Chinese could not follow the European concept of mutual assistance, because it was based on material gain, not morality.[115] While there might be basic agreement on the need for a new culture to guide China, there was no consensus on the precise ingredients that should go into that new culture.

Given the strong emphasis on physical labor in the work-study program, it is not surprising that a third topic of interest revolved around the worker and the labor movement. It was admitted that most students knew very little

* See, for example, You Gong, "Self-Examination and Self-Realization," *LuOu zhoukan*, May 8, 1920, p. 1. Said the author, "In order to examine myself fundamentally, I must search into all of my writings, my personal conduct and my life-style."

about the Chinese working class. Articles concerning the labor movement were published in various journals, but most of them were addressed to an audience of intellectuals by authors who were trying to display their knowledge of sophisticated themes, and such essays did little to bring the two classes together.[116] Meanwhile, it was charged, one of the stratagems of the capitalists and politicians was to prevent the worker from obtaining an education, thereby perpetuating their own power and wealth. The worker's greatest need was not for money, since he required little; nor for honor, since work was honorable; nor for power, since that would be obtained through unions. His greatest need was for knowledge.[117] Throughout history the better educated had ruled the less educated, and so the working class had been deprived of power. But if the intellectuals and workers could learn to understand each other by combining study and work, the overthrow of capitalism and the creation of a just society would become possible.[118]

As these latter remarks suggest, the final category of subjects with which *LuOu zhoukan* dealt were those of an overt political-ideological nature. The central thrust was anticapitalist and revolutionary, with strong anarchist preferences, as befitted a movement sponsored by Li Shizeng and members of the earlier Paris group. Li himself set the tone with an article in the second issue which combined Francophile sentiments with a clear commitment to anarchism. Writing on the differences and similarities between German and French intellectuals, he defined the Germans as authoritarian and selfish, like Nietzsche, and the French as having libertarian and fraternal values, like Jauré. The German sociologist Marx had proposed state centralism and a proletarian dictatorship, Li remarked, whereas the Frenchman Proudhon had advocated decentralization and confederation. The German intellectuals were "explosive," but Germany had now collapsed, leaving the road open to libertarian values.[119]

Wang Guangqi ended one of his articles by asserting that mutual aid, the goal toward which all should strive, could not be realized by peaceful means; a bloody revolution would be necessary.[120] As in the earlier *New Century* writings, support for anarchism was supplemented by a vigorous defense of science and an equally unyielding attack on religion and nationalism.[121] Science, one author proclaimed, required that truth be discovered through experimentation, and the current revolution was aimed at disconnecting science and art from religion and politics, thereby revealing "truth, kindness, and beauty."[122] In a humanistic society, there would be no religion or government. Through syndicates, cooperatives, and workers' councils, individuals could enjoy a collective life, working hard for the entire society and sharing equally in productive gains.

The strong emphasis on morality, characteristic of all Chinese humanistic writings, was accompanied by a new interest in organization, a result of Western learning. One author combined these interests as follows: A revolution without moral foundations would be senseless, but a capacity for organization was also crucial, and the lack of this capacity was a primary deficiency of the Chinese people. They were not inferior to others in intelligence and ability, but they had no organizational skills, and without this attribute it was futile to debate the respective merits of democracy, socialism, and anarchism.[123]

While the anarchist flavor of most articles in *LuOu zhoukan* was unmistakable, a certain eclecticism was present, together with a considerable degree of confusion about political distinctions. This can be seen clearly in an essay entitled "The Three Stages of Socialism."[124] The author defined the first stage as that of seeking to return to the ancient, simple communalism of the past. The second stage consisted of recognizing that restoration of such an order was impossible, and of making the commitment to "scientific" or "pragmatic" socialism. This stage reflected a willingness to base governance on the masses, but it required the retention of a bureaucracy over them; its character was reflected in the policies of the German Social Democratic Party. The third stage was that of "utopian socialism," which the Russian movement had reached to some degree. If one aspired to this course, however, it would be necessary to work hard in preparing for it, by educating and propagandizing the Chinese people.

LuOu zhoukan provides a basis for understanding the values and concepts that were dominant in the work-study movement in 1919 and 1920, but it cannot capture the growing crisis that was to plunge many students into discontent and strife. For a sense of this we must turn to other sources, including memoirs and interviews. One can easily recognize, of course, the potential for disaster that existed in the circumstances surrounding the work-study project. First, over 1,500 work-study students had been hastily recruited, usually by haphazard methods. Very few of the students chosen had adequate linguistic training or general educational preparation.[125] Most of them were extremely young, ranging in age between eighteen and twenty-two. Almost none had any experience in dealing with foreigners; they were not products of missionary schools. Every aspect of their new experience was therefore totally strange. Nor, with very few exceptions, were they accustomed to manual labor, let alone dock and construction work, or work in an automobile factory like Renault. And even when they proved to be quick learners, many found the tasks physically beyond them.[126]

Furthermore, this was hardly a propitious time to seek employment in France. The war was over, but the destruction and dislocations it had produced lingered on. Many factories were in the process of being reconverted to peacetime production, and large numbers of demobilized French soldiers were seeking work. Generally, only the most menial tasks were available to the students, types of unskilled labor that usually affronted their dignity. Nor were all Frenchmen kind.[127] Language problems and lack of money made it difficult for them to develop close acquaintance with French students, and in loneliness and adversity they naturally tended to stick together.

For many if not most work-study students, however, the truly critical problem was money. Unlike the government-supported students and those with private means, they had come with virtually no funds (despite rules that directed otherwise), and the organizations that had recruited them or pledged assistance lacked the structure and the resources to underwrite a large number of indigent individuals. Hope and expectation gave way to bewilderment and confusion, and then to anger and "direct action." It should be emphasized that a majority of the students *did* find and hold jobs, and remained aloof from the struggle against their sponsors or from broader political activism.* But a sizable minority vented their anger in protests and rallies, and many of these individuals were easily attracted to the new form of political radicalism known as communism.

*At the height of the political agitation over funds and jobs, only about one-fifth of the approximately 2,000 students were directly involved, although there were undoubtedly many additional sympathizers.

77. *Cai Yuanpei in later life (circa 1924)*

The serious trouble erupted in early 1921. At that point, a number of students in desperate financial straits had come to realize that the Association for Diligent Work and Frugal Study would not be able to give them adequate assistance, despite the efforts of Li.[128] They pinned their hopes on the Sino-French Educational Association, but on January 12, Cai Yuanpei, who had come to Europe, made an announcement to the effect that the Educational Association was disassociating itself from the "diligent work and frugal study" students. The Association took the position that it had not selected these students and could not be financially responsible for them.

Various meetings between Cai and the students were held, and angry words were exchanged. It was finally decided that funds from the Chinese government would be sought, and a meeting with legation officials was held at the end of January, after which a cable was sent to Beijing in the name of the Chinese minister to France, Chen Lu. Chen previously had made it clear that the legation lacked the money to run its own operations properly and could not possibly provide assistance.

Within a month a similar message came from the Beijing government. In its cable the government suggested that the legation make arrangements to send unemployed students without funds back to China. This both angered and frightened the students, and on February 27 a protest near the Chinese legation was organized, with about four hundred students participating. The students demanded a meeting with Chen Lu, and the minister appeared. The discussion, which took place in a nearby park, broke up amid violence, and Chen retreated into the legation quarters under police protection.* From this point on, recriminations flew back and forth, culminating in a new crisis in the fall of 1921 over the establishment of a Sino-French University at Lyons, where a number of Chinese radical students who had attempted to occupy the quarters were forcibly removed and later deported from the country.

All of these developments were naturally conducive to the rapid politicization of the more dissident students. Certain students, to be sure, had begun their political pilgrimage to the Left even before leaving China. Some had belonged to the Xinmin Xuehui (New People's Study Association), for example, as we shall note later in assessing the important role of one of its leaders, Cai Hesen. And there were a few others, including Zhou Enlai, who had been active in radical nationalist movements or socialist study groups at home. But they were the exceptions. For the most part, those who joined the Communist movement in Europe had arrived there as political innocents.**

The incubator for Chinese radicalism in France was a small bookstore in Paris operated by the two sons of Chen Duxiu, Chen Yannian and Chen Qiaonian, who had arrived in France with one of the early groups in 1919. Their bookstore carried radical literature, both in Chinese and in French, and stocked such classics as the Communist Manifesto, the constitution of the Russian Communist Party, and a host of similar documents.[129] Since it also was virtually the only outlet for Chinese publications like *Xin qingnian* (New Youth), Chinese students gravitated to the store. Chen Yannian, the more politically active of the two brothers, recruited Zhao Shiyang, a bright student from Sichuan, and established a close relation with Cai Hesen and the Montargis branch of the Xinmin Xuehui group. Wang Ruofei, studying

*According to He Jianggong, when the students first arrived at the entrance to the legation, the staff bolted the doors. The students then cut the telephone lines and poured alcohol on the door, setting it afire. The door was opened at this point, and negotiations began. (He Jianggong, *Qingong jianxue shenghuo huiyi*, p. 122.). Zhou's account of the incident is very scanty (Zhou Enlai, "A Major Incident," pp. 31–32).

**Ren Zhuoxuan, for example, who was to become one of the leading student Communists, recalled that when he first arrived in France, his political attitudes were purely nationalist and included a commitment to a militarily strong China and a penchant for heroes. A combination of personal hardships in connection with the work-study program and observations of France caused him to gravitate toward communism. (Robert A. Scalapino interview, December 7, 1973.)

78. Members of the Society for the Study of Marxism, established in March 1920. From the left, first row: 2d, Fan Hongji; 4th, Luo Zhanglong; 5th, He Mengxiong; 7th, Miao Boying; second row: 6th, Deng Zhongxia

at Melun, was also brought into the circle at an early point. By the summer of 1920 a Socialist Youth organization had been created in Paris, with over one hundred Chinese students—most of them work-study students—listed as members. Many of them—notably Zhou Enlai, Li Fuchun, Li Lisan, Li Weihan, Xu Teli, and Nie Yongzhen—later had long careers in the Chinese Communist movement. This helps to explain Mao's subsequent remark that the Communist Party of China was largely the work of the French and the Hunan groups.[130]

The precise connections between these young Chinese radicals and European socialists, including Comintern representatives, are difficult to establish. Li Huang, who later became a leader in the Young China Party and a strong opponent of the Communists, recalls that he attended meetings in 1920 at the home of Henri Barbusse, a well-known French novelist whose sympathies were with the Left, and that Comintern views were set forth there.[131] He has also claimed that Comintern representatives were already in touch with Chinese student radicals at about that time—initially through a Chinese named Wang, who was about fifty, and later through a Russian representative of the Third International.[132] Other anti-Communists like Liu He also insist that such contacts did exist, and that Comintern funds were dispensed to help students meet expenses, to support publications, and to engage in recruitment.[133] Proof from other sources is lacking, but it would be surprising if the Comintern had made no effort at all to tap such a promising source of support as the dissident Chinese students.

There are indications, however, that these contacts, if they existed, were restricted. For example, Ren Zhuoxuan, who played a prominent role in

79. Meeting of members of the Xinmin Xuehui (New Youth Society) in Montargis, France, July 1920, where Cai Hesen advocated establishment of a Chinese Communist Party

the early Chinese Communist movement in France, and subsequently in Moscow and China, has asserted that he had no contact with Russian or Western European Communists in Paris.[134] In general, moreover, language problems prevented more than slight contact with French Communists, and we know of no Chinese students who joined the French Communist Party.

Nonetheless, by late 1920 and early 1921, many Chinese students, mostly in the work-study category, had shown an interest in the international Communist movement or had affiliated themselves with it. Ren Zhuoxuan has estimated that there were some three hundred in these categories at the peak, whereas seventy to eighty students were affiliated with the Guomindang and a smaller number were active anarchists. In 1923, when the anti-communist Chinese Youth Party was formally organized in France, it was able to recruit over a hundred members.

If these figures are accurate, by early 1921 there were many more Chinese Communists or proto-Communists in Europe (mainly in France) than existed in China. Nonetheless, Bolshevism had secured a beachhead on Chinese soil. Its doctrines and, more important, its promising techniques for successful revolution had made an impression. With various kinds of support from the Comintern, and under personal and national conditions that served to radicalize a growing portion of the Chinese student-intellectual community, a new movement flying red banners had been launched at home and abroad.

12

ON THE HORIZON: YOUNG CHIANG AND MAO

As the third decade of the twentieth century opened, no one could have foreseen that Chiang Kai-shek and Mao Zedong, two young men from south-central China, would play crucial roles in shaping the destiny of their country for the next half-century—and beyond. Looking back over their careers, however, we can see that certain personal qualities combined with a particular sociopolitical environment to make them eligible for leadership. If we can discover why those qualities and that environment could interact effectively, we can gain an insight into the basic nature of China between the Sino-Japanese War and the end of World War I.

THE EARLY CAREER OF CHIANG KAI-SHEK

Chiang Kai-shek* was born on October 31, 1887, in the hamlet of Xikou, Fenghua district, Zhejiang province.[1] His ancestors had left North China to settle in Fenghua district in the thirteenth century. The region in which the Chiang family lived had great scenic beauty; green rice fields, misty mountains, swift-running streams, and a small lake were present to inspire the artist and the poet. Yet despite its rural charms, Fenghua was not isolated. Only forty kilometers away was Ningbo, one of China's major commercial ports and a window to the outside world.

The Chiang family traced its ancestry to the third son of the Duke of Zhou, but the ancestral tablets indicated a lengthy succession of farmers, identical to the backgrounds of millions of other Chinese families. Chiang's grandfather had broken this cycle by entering trade and developing a prosperous salt business. The Taiping Rebellion seriously affected Fenghua, and the Chiang family fortunes declined sharply, but Chiang's father managed to rebuild the business, and the family was considered well-to-do financially at the time of Chiang's birth. At that point, his father was forty-four and his mother twenty-four. It was the father's third marriage, his first two wives having died young. When Chiang was nine, his father passed away, leaving a

*Chiang's birth-name, given to him by his grandfather, was Chiang Jui-yuan (Jiang Ruiyuan). He was named Chiang Chung-cheng (Zhongzheng) by his mother, and later took the name Chieh-shih (Jieshi)—pronounced Kai-shek in Cantonese.

widow of thirty-three to raise Chiang, a daughter, and two stepchildren. (Two other children born of the third marriage had died at an early age.) According to varous records and Chiang's own later account, his mother was strong-willed and determined, a devout Buddhist, a vegetarian, and a strict disciplinarian.[2] He appears to have scarcely known his father.*

Although the Chiang family was not impoverished after the father's death, it seems to have had some financial problems; Chiang later said that local officials were partly to blame for these, having treated the family unfairly because it had no influence in the community. Young Chiang began his schooling at the age of five and in the traditional manner. A private tutor instructed him in a family school, and the first major task was to memorize the four great Confucian classics.** Later, other traditional literature was studied, and the students practiced writing eight-legged essays. All of this was in preparation for the civil service examinations; but when Chiang took the examination in 1902 at the age of fourteen, he failed and made no further attempt to become an official through this route.

It will be recalled that in the years immediately after the Boxer uprising, various reforms, including educational reforms, were under way. In 1903, shortly after he had failed the examination, young Chiang left home for the first time to attend the Fenglu School in the district township. Here instruction was available in mathematics and in English as well as in traditional subjects. But he was apparently dissatisfied with conditions at the school, and led a student protest that nearly resulted in his expulsion.† Chiang, incidentally, was now married, having been formally wed to a local girl in 1902 through his mother's arrangements when he was about fourteen years old.

Most accounts say that the turning point in young Chiang's life came in 1905 when he transferred to the Jianjin School in Ningbo. There he came under the strong influence of a particular teacher, Gu Qinglian.[3] Gu introduced his pupil to more classical works, but also encouraged him to read Sun Zi's famous study on war, thereby stimulating him to become interested in a military education. Gu supported military self-strengthening for China and was apparently also a sympathizer with Sun Yat-sen and his movement, since Chiang recalls having first heard of Sun from his teacher. Gu persuaded Chiang that "if one sought to learn military science, one had to seek new learning, and if one sought to protect the nation, one must study abroad."[4]

Chiang decided that he wanted modern military training, and that Japan was the appropriate place to get it. In January 1906 he entered a middle school in Fenghua to study the Japanese language, and four months later, in April, he left for Tokyo.‡ Here a major disappointment awaited him. He

* In his various writings, Chiang hardly mentions his father. He was clearly devoted to his mother, and in his eulogy to her, he implied that married life had been difficult for her. He also expresses strong affection for his paternal grandfather, who gave him a great deal of attention when he was still a rather frail child. See Loh, *The Early Chiang Kai-shek*, pp. 5–13.

** Chiang's first tutor was Ren Jiemei; others were Jiang Jinfan and Mao Sicheng.

† Mao Sicheng suggests that Chiang was a moody, rebellious child whose periods of quiet were broken by sudden outbursts of unruliness. His friends noted that he was stubborn and fiercely determined to carry through on any course he set for himself. In his later years Chiang himself frequently acknowledged that he had a volcanic temper. (See Mao, *Minguo shiwu nian*, p. 0016, and Qin, *Zongtong Chiang-gong* 1:10.)

‡ As his first act of defiance against the Manchu, Chiang cut off his queue and sent it home, much to the distress of his mother and other villagers. Mao Sicheng says this hap-

discovered that as a private student he could not attend a Japanese military academy; only those officially sponsored by the Chinese government were granted this privilege. Hence, he had to content himself with enrollment in the Tokyo Qinghua School where he continued his study of Japanese. When he returned home after six months, he had made his first contact with the revolutionary movement by forming a friendship with Chen Qimei, a fellow Zhejiang compatriot ten years his senior who was already active in Sun's Tongmeng Hui. Chiang's ties with Chen were to have vitally important consequences for his later career, although he did not join the Tongmeng Hui at this time.[5]

Shortly after returning to Zhejiang, Chiang learned that competitive examinations were soon to be held in various provincial capitals to select cadets for the newly created Short-Course National Army School, the predecessor of the Baoding Military Academy. He passed the examination and entered the school in the summer of 1907. That winter he was selected as one of forty cadets qualified to pursue advanced military studies in Japan. Another youth chosen was Zhang Qun, a Sichuanese who was to become Chiang's lifelong friend and political associate.[6]

Thus, when Chiang returned to Japan early in 1908, he had achieved his first major goal. He and others were enrolled in the Shimbu Gakkō (Shimbu School), a special training institute established in 1903 to prepare Chinese cadets for regular Japanese military academies. Chiang remained in this school for nearly three years, mastering the essentials of Japanese military science and also developing a political commitment. Using an introduction from Chen Qimei, he joined the Tongmeng Hui shortly after his return and began to discuss political issues in regular secret meetings with various friends, mainly fellow provincials. Besides reading Japanese military manuals, he read the radical Chinese student journals being published in Tokyo, as well as Zou Rong's famous revolutionary pamphlet. At one point, Chiang participated in the publication of a military journal, *Wuxue zazhi* (Journal of Military Science). He also returned to China several times during vacation periods, a secret but confirmed revolutionary and a devoted follower of Chen Qimei. Chen, incidentally, had organized a clandestine organization in 1908 to promote revolution in Jiangsu and Zhejiang. Chiang attempted unsuccessfully to get one of Chen's key associates out of prison in the summer of 1911. Meanwhile, he had also become a father as a result of his first home leave; his son Chiang Ching-kuo was born in 1910.

According to some accounts, Chiang's initial meeting with Sun Yat-sen took place in 1910, before he graduated from Shimbu Gakkō. Whether this meeting actually occurred is a matter in dispute; but even if it did, it does not seem to have made a major impression on Chiang.* His revolutionary mentor during this period remained Chen Qimei.

Upon his graduation from Shimbu Gakkō in the winter of 1910, Chiang,

---

pened in 1905, when Chiang was eighteen; Qin says it was in 1906. See Mao, *Minguo shiwu*, p. 0018, and Qin, *Zongtong Chiang-gong* 1:14.

*Furuya asserts that the meeting took place in June (*Chiang Kai-shek*, p. 15). Qin's record indicates that it took place in the winter of 1910 (*Zongtong Chiang-gong*, p. 17), but as C. Martin Wilbur has pointed out to us, Sun was present in Japan only between June 10 and June 25 of that year. Both Wilbur and Pichon Loh doubt whether a meeting took place at this time, since it is not mentioned in such standard sources as Luo Jialun, *Guofu nianpu chugao*, or Mao Sicheng, *Minguo shiwu nian yiqian zhi Chiang Kai-shek xiansheng*. (Wilbur, private letter; and Loh, *The Early Chiang Kai-shek*, pp. 19–20. For a discussion of when Chiang and Sun first met, see Loh, p. 124, n. 47.)

along with some fifty other Chinese students, was assigned to the 19th Field Artillery Regiment, 13th Division, Imperial Japanese Army, stationed at Takada (now Joetsu), Niigata prefecture. His rank was private second-class, and like all enlisted men in the Japanese army, he underwent rigorous training. Summer and winter, reveille was at five A.M., and after a quick wash (ice-water in the winter), the soldiers turned to various tasks, such as grooming the horses used to pull the heavy guns. Meals consisted of one bowl of rice topped with three slices of dried turnip and sometimes a small piece of salted fish.[7] Chiang did not impress his Japanese commander with any particular brilliance, but the commander was later to remark favorably on Chiang's character, particularly his deep respect for those who taught him.*

Fighting the Enemy

When the Wuchang revolt broke out in October 1911, Chiang was still in Takada, but he immediately received a cable from Chen requesting that he return to China. With some difficulty, he and two friends, including Zhang Qun, left the regiment. They went to the Zhejiang Tongmeng Hui office in Tokyo to obtain passage money, changed into civilian clothes to avoid being arrested by Japanese police for desertion, and sailed for Shanghai with many others on October 30. Upon his arrival, Chiang immediately contacted Chen, and then began recruiting men for a Dare-to-Die Corps. Leading about one hundred volunteers, Chiang attacked imperial forces in Hangzhou on November 4, at the same time that Chen was commanding the revolutionary assault on Shanghai. Victorious in the struggle for Hangzhou, Chiang returned to Shanghai shortly thereafter, where Chen, now military governor of the metropolitan area, made him a regiment commander.

Chiang occupied this post for about four months, but in March 1912 he suddenly resigned his command and left for Japan. According to several accounts, Chiang's departure was prompted by his involvement in the death of Tao Chengzhang, an influential leader of the regional Guangfu Hui and a rival of Chen Qimei.[8] Reportedly, Tao was plotting the assassination of Chen; in any case, Chiang among others decided that Tao had to go, and he was killed. According to at least one account, Chiang himself shot Tao.** Chiang therefore left the area to avoid embarrassing Chen.

In Japan once again, Chiang began a study of German, having decided to go to Germany to pursue advanced military studies. In this period he first gave a public indication of his views on political and military matters, in a foreword and five articles written for *Junsheng zazhi* (The Military Voice Magazine), a journal he edited in the latter part of 1912.[9] Chiang's writings show us a young man generally in the mainstream of youthful Chinese na-

*General Nagaoka Gaishi, then commanding general of the 13th Division, later described Chiang as one whose "outward appearance did not reveal innate ability, and there was nothing to indicate that he would ever rise to the heights that he subsequently attained." But Nagaoka was touched by the fact that Chiang treated him with deep respect in later years and once presented him with a scroll containing four characters, "Bu fu shi jiao" ("Never do anything contrary to the precepts of your teacher").

**Loh, in *The Early Chiang*, p. 27, quotes Deng Wenyi, *Chiangzhuxi*, p. 16, as follows: "The Chairman, angry beyond control, yanked out his pistol and killed [T'ao] with one shot." For more subdued versions, which merely implicated Chiang in the assassination, see Mao, *Minguo shiwu nian*, pp. 0026–0027 and Qin, *Zongtong Chiang-gong* 1:18.

80. *Chiang Kai-shek in 1911*

tionalists. He was deeply concerned about imperialist inroads in China, especially those emanating from the Russians, the Japanese, and the British (in Tibet). He regarded China's main task after the 1911 Revolution, now that "internal problems have been solved," as dealing with the external threat by developing a strong, centralized state and a powerful military force. Denouncing regional armies as a threat to unity, Chiang argued for regional military districts under centralized control. His views on political matters were somewhat vague, but in general he appeared to look favorably on some form of enlightened authoritarian rule that would promote national unity while avoiding both Bonapartism and anarchism.[10] On military tactics Chiang was more specific. To combat the Japanese, China should prepare for a protracted war that would deplete Japan's manpower and financial resources. To defeat the Russians, China should launch an attack on Russian Central Asia.

Chiang's "first retirement" from the Chinese political and military arena ended in mid-1913. He had returned home once, toward the end of 1912, but apparently made no effort to contact Chen. However, when the Second Revolution broke out in the summer of 1913, Chiang immediately rejoined Chen in Shanghai. Serving as staff officer, he drew up a plan to capture the arsenal in Shanghai, but the effort failed, like most other rebel attempts. After the Second Revolution collapsed (Shanghai fell to Yuan's forces on September 1), Chiang, along with hundreds of other Guomindang supporters, returned to Japan after some weeks of concealment.

In the fall of 1913, Sun had begun to organize his new party, the Gemingdang, and according to the records, Chiang was the one hundred and second individual to become a member, having joined the new party in Shanghai. In December, Sun received Chiang alone for the first time, and thereafter relations between the two men appear to have become closer.[11]

During 1914 Sun sent Chiang on at least two secret trips to China to explore the possibilities of reopening military operations against the Yuan government. The purpose of the first, in the spring, was to examine the prospects for an uprising in Shanghai. Chiang found them unpromising; indeed, several of his men were arrested and shot, and he himself barely escaped. Later in the year he was sent to Heilongjiang to investigate reports that Manchuria offered excellent opportunities for rebellion. Once again, Chiang's investigation found the prospects dim. Meanwhile, he was using his second exile in Japan to advance his education. He read many military treatises and studied the writings of Wang Yangming, Zeng Guofan, and Hu Linyi. Chiang later credited these three individuals, and particularly Zeng, with providing the foundations for his political views.[12]

In the fall of 1915, Chiang became personally involved in another assassination plot. The Gemingdang leaders had decided that Zheng Rucheng, the key military official in Shanghai and a man responsible for the deaths of many revolutionaries, had to be eliminated. Sun consulted with Chen, who had come to Tokyo secretly from Shanghai. Chen later returned to China and then summoned Chiang. Together they planned the assassination, although neither participated directly. On November 10 Zheng was shot in his automobile while en route to a reception at the Japanese consulate in Shanghai. A month later Chen, Chiang, and their followers made another attempt to seize the Shanghai arsenal and failed miserably. Twenty of their men were killed and approximately one hundred were wounded. Chiang remained in China, and in the spring of 1916 he led an attack on a Yangtze

81. *Chiang at the time of the "Second Revolution,"* 1913

fortress between Nanjing and Shanghai; the fort was taken, but a mutiny broke out among the revolutionaries, and Chiang was forced to flee to Shanghai.

Chen Qimei and most other revolutionaries made their headquarters in the Shanghai French Concession, thereby reducing the risk of capture by government forces. On May 18, however, using a renegade from the revolutionary ranks as the central figure, government agents were able to assassinate Chen. Chiang was devastated. He wrote in his eulogy, "Henceforth, who in this world will know me as intimately and love me as generously as you, sir?"[13]

Gravitation to Sun

With Chen gone, Chiang's allegiance shifted to Sun. He remained in the revolutionary underground in China, and in June 1916 Sun sent him to serve as chief of staff to Ju Zheng, the head of the revolutionaries' Northeast Army in Shandong. By the time he arrived, however, the death of Yuan had changed the political climate, and Ju's army was in disarray.[14] Nevertheless, with politics at the national level becoming increasingly chaotic, new opportunities arose for Sun's forces. In July 1917, after the abortive monarchical coup by Zhang Xun in Beijing, Sun and his key lieutenants returned to Guangdong, where they set up a rival government in Canton, with the support or at least the acquiescence of General Lu Rongting (and General Tang Jiyao).

After a brief period in Beijing observing events, Chiang settled down in Shanghai. He was said to be responsible for party and military affairs on behalf of the Gemingdang in the Southeast, Shanghai serving as headquarters. He also drafted two military plans. The first was for a northern expedition against the Beijing government, initially breaking enemy strength in Central China by taking Wuchang and then Nanjing. The second, of more modest proportions, aimed at securing Fujian and Zhejiang provinces for the revolutionaries.[15]

Chiang left Shanghai for Guangdong on March 2, 1918, having been summoned by Sun, who wanted resolute military action at this point. On March 15 Chiang was named head of the Field Operations Department under General Chen Jiongming, the commander in chief of the Guangdong Army. Six months later, he was made commander of the 2nd Detachment, composed of about a thousand men. Shortly thereafter he was involved in heavy fighting in Fujian under Chen's command, in a campaign to oust Li Houji, the military governor of the province and a Duan follower. In one engagement in December, Chiang's forces suffered a serious defeat and he asked to be relieved of command, but Chen, it is reported, insisted that he remain. He did so, and continued in the service of the Guangdong Army until July 1919, after a two-month leave earlier in the year.

It is clear from his personal account that Chiang had been growing progressively more dissatisfied and was in a period of personal turmoil. Continuous problems with his fellow officers in Chen's army had cropped up. He frequently complained of "factionalism," of cliques that conspired against him. One reason for this might have been that most of these officers were Cantonese, whereas Chiang was a native of Zhejiang. But Chiang himself was having emotional and physical difficulties, and in mid-1919 he therefore wrote a firm letter of resignation, although he appears to have remained in Fujian until the fall.*

From this point until the end of 1921, Chiang's actions and behavior were often erratic. He spent much of the time in Shanghai and Zhejiang, although at the urging of Sun and other Guomindang leaders he made several brief trips to Fujian and Guangdong, always retreating after a few days or weeks. On October 23, 1919, Chiang sailed for Japan again, carrying

*Loh, *The Early Chiang*, p. 101. In his letter of July 9, Chiang said he was suffering from gastric problems and insomnia, and that he was mentally exhausted. He also complained that other officers were discriminating against him. From *Chiang Zongtong yanlun huibian* 24:82–87, cited by Furuya. See also Mao, *Minguo shiwu*, pp. 0074–0082.

82. *Chiang with Sun supporter Yamada Junsaburo, Shanghai, 1915*

with him various letters of introduction from Sun. While there, he visited many of Sun's old Genyōsha friends, including Toyama Mitsuru. A cable from General Chen Jiongming urged him to return to Fujian, but he declined, returning instead to Shanghai in November. Little is known about his activities thereafter, but according to the few accounts available, he consorted with such friends as Dai Jitao and Zhang Jingjiang, conferred on occasion with Sun and other party figures like Liao Zhongkai, and read widely.

During this period, we should recall, Dai had become keenly interested in Marxism, and it is quite likely that he urged Chiang to turn his thinking in this direction. Besides reading the avant-garde journals—*Xin qingnian*, *Xin chao*, and *Dongfang zazhi*—and thereby becoming acquainted with Ibsen, Tolstoy, Dewey, and Marx, Chiang took up the study of Russian. He even expressed a strong interest in going to the Soviet Union. On learning of this, Sun offered Chiang three options in the fall of 1920: go to Russia for study; go to Sichuan, which Chiang continued to believe was a key to revolutionary victory; or go to Guangdong, still the revolutionary heartland for Sun and his lieutenants.

Chiang decided not to go to the Soviet Union, because of reservations about his prospective companions, it was said, and initially opted for Sichuan. Under heavy pressure from others, however, he finally agreed to go to Guangdong, and departed from Shanghai on September 30. Once again Chiang found the Canton atmosphere stifling, and his views incompatible with those of Chen Jiongming. By November he was back in Shanghai, and from there he went on to his home in Zhejiang, where, despite the entreaties of Sun and others, he remained until late December. It is clear that throughout this period Chiang was undergoing great emotional turmoil and was quarreling with even his close friends.*

Chiang had long pushed for a northern expedition. Indeed, this plan had been the chief bone of contention between himself and Chen Jiongming, even though it had bound Sun to him. Once again, in January 1921, he outlined to Sun a plan for striking at Sichuan and simultaneously mounting a maritime expedition from Guangdong to Jinwangdao on the Hebei coast.[16] He continued to express doubts about Chen and the viability of the Guangdong government, but when it appeared that Chen had finally consented to a Guangxi expedition as the first step in a broader military campaign, he once again returned to Canton, in early February 1921. He remained for only a week, however. To his bitter disappointment, he found that there had been no real agreement for such an expedition, and over the next few months he vigorously criticized Chen in messages to friends. Once again, in April, Sun persuaded Chiang to return by telling him that mobilization or-

*Pichon Loh has introduced various letters—especially exchanges between Chiang and Dai Jitao in late 1920 and early 1921—which are most revealing. Chiang had quarreled bitterly with Dai at one point, and his letters suggest a man torn between remorse and truculence, defensiveness and belligerence. He was harsh in his judgment, blunt in his words, and passages in some letters suggest a great inner struggle. Clearly, Chiang was going through a difficult emotional period. (See Loh, *The Early Chiang*, pp. 32–52, and Mao, *Minguo shiwu*, pp. 0103–0104.) A number of family problems were related to Chiang's tension. His mother, to whom he had always been powerfully drawn, fell ill and then died in June 1921; six months later Chiang decided to separate from his wife and also from his concubine; and he worried about giving proper guidance to his two young sons. His own health was also a problem. Between 1919 and 1921, he suffered from an eye ailment, typhoid fever, and nervous disorders.

ders for an expedition had been issued. After only four days in Canton, however, Chiang supposedly had a dream that boded ill for his mother's health, and he promptly left. In fact, she died on June 14, and Chiang went into mourning.

Only in mid-August did Chiang agree to return to Canton, and because of various interruptions he did not actually arrive in the city until September 13. After talking with Sun and others, he went to Nanning to consult with Chen. The meeting was a disaster. Chiang left in a rage and shortly thereafter returned to Shanghai. Finally, at the end of 1921 Chiang returned once more to the South, and spent some four months with Sun, who had by now established a headquarters in Guilin for what came to be known as the First Northern Expedition. By this time, however, relations between Sun and Chen were deteriorating, and since the expedition was a central issue, the plans once again came to nothing. As the Sun-Chen dispute grew more serious, Chiang supported Sun unflinchingly, and this loyalty was to bring him from relative obscurity to a position of power within the Guomindang in a remarkably short period of time.

In reflecting upon Chiang's early life, one is impressed by five factors. First, Chiang's familial circumstances helped to shape both his character and his subsequent career. He came from a rural but middle-class background, which permitted him to have a classical education and then move into the larger world in successive stages. His village was close enough to Ningbo to enable the first moves to be made without much difficulty. Personally, Chiang was influenced by his deep affection for his mother and by the lack of a meaningful relationship with his father. For these and other reasons, he was a rebellious as well as a strong-willed youth. He was prone to periods of great emotional strain marked by quarrelsomeness, suspicion of others, and a sense of being forsaken, of standing alone against the world. In most of these respects, incidentally, we shall find parallels in Mao's early life and personality.

Second, Chiang's character displayed courage, determination amounting to stubbornness, and absolute loyalty to those with whom he had formed a special attachment. There is no evidence that he was gifted intellectually, though he was not unintelligent. In any case, despite his interest in certain classics—and some of the new radical literature—he did not aspire to be an intellectual. He wanted to be a military man, and to this end he devoted his energies with a single-mindedness born of deep commitment. Chiang clearly enjoyed action, both as a planner and on the battlefield. From his men, he insisted upon all the qualities demanded by the Japanese military commanders he greatly admired: discipline, bravery, and a willingness to accept sacrifice. He himself did not shrink from hardship and danger, and he expected others to behave likewise. Though he was never particularly interested in money or luxury, power fascinated him. And he was not squeamish in dispatching opponents. If a man was an enemy, Chiang was quite willing to see him killed. In this, he was no different from many other revolutionaries, including his later rival, Mao Zedong.

Third, Chiang's political commitments were basically quite simple. He was first and last a nationalist, a strong believer in the Han race, in Han culture, and in the need for a powerful China. Throughout his life, his values were shaped primarily by the combination of the Chinese classics and his early Japanese military training. He was not against modernization, but he was not attuned to Westernization, except in certain facets of the military field. He was, in short, intensely Chinese. It should also be said that to a great degree he derived his political commitments from his personal associations, rather than vice versa. His ties to Chen Qimei and then to Sun Yat-sen remained paramount to him during their lifetimes. There was a period when Dai Jitao pulled him leftward, but Dai was to change, and so was Chiang.

Fourth, despite Chiang's strength of character, intense determination, and military ability, the course of his career was shaped by events beyond his influence. To be sure, that was true of almost all Chinese leaders during this era, given the circumstances of their nation. In Chiang's case, the first accident was his personal survival. As an underground revolutionary and later as field commander actively engaged, Chiang repeatedly ran very high risks. Many men in his category were killed at an early age. Beyond this, Chiang made himself dependent upon the fate of other men—first Chen Qimei, and ultimately Sun Yat-sen. Had Sun's movement failed, Chiang almost certainly would have disappeared into obscurity.

Finally, even in these early years, one can see the seeds of Chiang's lifelong dilemma: his relations with Japan and the Japanese. Although he was to some degree anti-Western, Chiang had a deep respect for Japan and had many Japanese friends. He spoke the language and greatly admired most aspects of Japanese culture. He found in Japan the order and discipline, the efficiency and purposeful use of power that he cherished for China. Yet at the same time, Chiang was a firm patriot. He recognized the Japanese proclivity for expansionism, and he resented it, like other young Chinese nationalists. The dilemma could only grow as he moved toward power.

THE EARLY YEARS OF MAO ZEDONG

Mao Zedong was born on December 26, 1893, in an east Hunan village, into a peasant family of modest means but upwardly mobile prospects.[17] In each of these separate but related facts lies a significance that goes far beyond Mao. His birth date coincided with the beginning of a tempestuous, explosive era for China and the world. The central issue for China in the decades of Mao's adolescence and young manhood was not whether to change but what to change. And that issue was presented with such intensity and complexity that it could not help but divide China's intellectual and political elites. In three decades, the challenges confronting China—domestically and internationally—were so extensive that no one could have been expected to provide satisfactory answers to all of them. This is one reason why these decades produced no heroes and no institutions of lasting worth. What they did produce—and it is a fact often overlooked—were generational cleavages that were more significant than class cleavages. If they held to their ideas for even a decade, individuals who were at first thought radical and daring were labeled conservative and timid, as each successive generation of Chinese youth reached for the latest distillation of what was new and hopeful. This generational cleavage, occurring in a society that has long venerated age, still provokes great trauma. Even today, another generation of Chinese youth is viewing its Communist elders with a combination of

83. *Mao Zedong in 1919* ▶

cynicism and patriotic hope. The opposite side of the coin was a pervasive lack of consistency in ideas, whether in the inner structure of a given set of arguments or in the broad philosophic position held over time. Indeed, rapid *shifts*, especially by young Chinese intellectuals, were the rule, not the exception, as each successive wave of theory struck China's shores, and world-shaking events occurred with dizzying frequency.

Mao was born in Hunan, south-central China, and Hunan hardly seems an obvious cradle for progressives or revolutionaries. It had a long history of xenophobia and exclusiveness; it was one of the last provinces to be opened to foreigners; and it harbored a powerful coterie of conservative gentry—men of local eminence, accustomed to a considerable measure of effective self-rule, who saw the Western barbarian and all his works as anathema. But first impressions can deceive: the province of Hunan also had a legacy of boldness and pragmatic innovation on the intellectual-political front. During his Changsha school days, Mao and his mentor studied the early Qing philosopher, Wang Fuzhi, a fervent Han patriot who also ardently supported the theory that the state could only be justified as an institution that served the people.[18] Mao's early social and political beliefs were also shaped by enlightened conservatives from Hunan—men like the famous statesman Zeng Guofan, who had been born of poor peasant parents in Xiangxiang township, very close to Mao's village of Shaoshan. The Hunan official-scholar community had begun to espouse reform after the Sino-Japanese War, and in 1897 and 1898 a vigorous education and political modernizing movement began. Its center was the newly created Changsha School of Current Affairs.[19] The young Liang Qichao, already strongly influenced by Kang Youwei and currently the editor of a Shanghai journal dedicated to introducing "fresh ideas," was brought to serve as head of the faculty, it will be recalled. These events occurred just before Mao began his schooling, but their subsequent influence on him was powerful. Mao himself later said that Kang Youwei and Liang Qichao were two of his first role models.

Furthermore, important portions of Hunan were not isolated. In traditional and early modern times, China's highways were waterways. On Hunan's northern border lay Lake Dongting, fed by four large rivers that ran through the province from south to north and served as primary arteries of trade and communications. The lake itself emptied into the Yangtze, one of China's great waterways leading to the sea. The largest of the rivers that fed this lake was called the Xiang, an ancient name for Hunan and also a name adopted by Mao for his first journal. About thirty miles from Mao's village, the Xiang ran through the city of Xiangtan, an important distribution center for trade between Hunan and Canton, and from there it ran northward through Changsha, the capital of the province, about sixty miles from Mao's birthplace. The village of Shaoshan itself was nestled in a partly mountainous area, neither one of the most richly endowed nor one of the poorest sites. The villagers made their livelihood on rice, vegetables, pigs, and poultry—which was typical of the South China countryside.

These facts are important because millions of Chinese born during this and subsequent years resided in regions too remote to be touched by the stimuli that were now flowing into China from abroad. In their secluded hamlets and villages, they continued to live and think as their ancestors had. They knew nothing, or very little, about the events that were shaking Beijing and other major centers. Thus, they were unavailable for political leadership, or even for political participation—except of the most traditional type, which was banditry.

In a different sense, this was also true of the millions who lived in China's great metropolitan centers, as we noted earlier. To be sure, they were close to the ferment in political and intellectual circles. But—curiously perhaps—the major cities provided a weak base for sustained political mobilization or the creation of leaders. Despite its ancient roots, the essential characteristics of the city remained foreign to Chinese culture. Familial-clan ties still ran to ancestral homes in the countryside. Anomie derived from separateness—despite the existence of guilds, intellectual study circles, and (later on) trade unions—permeated the urban atmosphere. Within the great cities a sense of broader community, a consciousness of issues, and an aggregation of interests could exist only in embryonic form in China's preindustrial era.

The large majority of China's early modern leaders came from what one might call a "sub-urban" environment. They were born and raised in a largely rural setting, which connected them closely with the major traditions of Chinese culture. Yet their native place was not so distant from a center of learning and communication as to make it impossible for them to see the trends and, taking advantage of their abilities and good fortune, to move with them. As we have seen, Chiang Kai-shek, Kang Youwei, Liang Qichao, Sun Yat-sen, Yuan Shikai, Mao Zedong, and countless others fell into this category.

Beyond this, was there really a "Hunan personality," a set of traits connected with this subculture which, if not universal, were sufficiently prevalent to permit generalization? The question must be approached with the greatest caution, for most generalizations of this type are spurious, distorted, or oversimplified. Yet the Chinese themselves have long believed in the existence of regional characteristics and have shown no hesitation in recording them. Thus, Hunanese have been described as distinguished for their inflexibility and courage, for their bravado and clanishness. The extensive banditry in the region, moreover, led to the saying that "the bandits are as thick as the hairs on your head."[20] Can those qualities of stubbornness, bravery, and xenophobia—coexisting uneasily with Mao's universalistic creed and commitment to modernization—be ascribed in some degree to the subculture from which he came? Or as the data relating to Chiang suggest, did such qualities exist in Chinese from various subcultures within the society?

Finally, one comes to Mao's immediate family. Here our information comes almost exclusively from Mao himself, in the form of his famous recital to Edgar Snow. Mao described his father as a self-made man, who had begun life as a poor peasant and was compelled to go into military service for a time because of debts. When he reentered civilian life he gradually accumulated enough money to buy land, and he eventually acquired the status of rich peasant and small businessman, operating a transport service in addition to his farm. Like many self-made men, Mao's father appears to have lived for work, and he expected the same from his family. His story, of course, was not untypical. Few Chinese rural families remained in precisely the same socioeconomic status through many generations. Mobility, paradoxically, was a key to China's stability in traditional times. Family fortunes rose and fell, with a corresponding effect on the members. Luck, acumen, and hard work raised the status of some households. Others were generally resigned to their fate, and took solace in the thought that fortune would shine on them in the next life.

In his reminiscences, Mao stressed his incompatibility with his father, and certain crises in their relationship were obviously etched deeply in his mind. Various scholars have seen in Mao's hatred of his father and love of his mother the psychological underpinnings of his character and subsequent leadership style. Unquestionably, Mao's familial relations had an influence on his personality and his career. The problem is how to weigh this factor with others. Many sons have a competitive or conflictual relationship with their fathers or a special relation with their mothers, but the results vary in later life. What causes submissiveness in one case and rebellious expressions in another, and how do these figure in the range of outcomes, from deep withdrawal to the quest for dominance?

The social and economic condition of Mao's family was at least as important as his psychological experience. By the time he reached adolescence, Mao, like Chiang, was a member of a comfortably well-off family, measured by prevailing standards. This fact alone enabled him to complete a secondary-school education, thereby putting him in a very special category among men of his generation. Had his family remained poor peasants, such a development would have been much more unlikely. To be sure, in talking about his school days in Xiangxiang and Changsha, Mao spoke of his poverty in comparison with "the rich men's sons" who were his classmates. Yet the fact remains that he felt no compunction about writing home for money when he wanted to continue his schooling in Changsha. No poor peasant's son would have dreamed of doing that.

This is not to suggest that Mao lived a luxurious or wasteful life on family money. It appears that he received only meager economic assistance from home, and from all accounts, including those of his schoolmates, he lived very modestly. He cared little about material comforts. He was frequently disheveled, often sloppy; he took no interest in fine food; and perhaps he did not bathe as often as he should have. He spent most of his money, when he had any, on books, journals, and newspapers. Like some other men destined to become leaders, his interests were focused on "more serious matters"—organization and programs leading to the acquisition of power. A compulsive reader from his early years, Mao had the capacity to reject the trivial and the irrelevant and to focus on what was important to him. This attribute was more significant than all others: concentration—the ability to focus single-mindedly on one's principal talent and primary goal—is a key to achievement in all fields.

To summarize, the circumstances surrounding Mao's birth made him eligible for political leadership along with thousands, but separate from millions. He was born at the right time if his predilections were toward iconoclasm and the continuous quest for new ideas. He came from a region which made it possible for him to appraise his times and come abreast of them, but which also ensured that he would remain close to Chinese culture, retaining always his very strong "Chineseness."

In some respects, the juxtaposition of two elements derived from this background symbolized Mao's life: on the one hand, commitment to modernization, defined in scientific and technological (hence Western) terms, and to the search for a genuine internationalism based on a universally valid doctrine; on the other hand, a strong quotient of peasant culture with its bent toward exclusiveness, xenophobia, and localism. In broader terms, of course, Mao's dilemma was that of China itself: self-reliance versus a turning out; a narrow, traditional, Sinocentrism rooted in feelings of racial superiority versus a willingness to interact freely with other cultures and nations, and to move toward an internationalism buttressed by modern values and institutions. Paralleling this conflict was another one at the personal or philosophic level: the constant battle within Mao between humanism, a concern for the liberation of all men, and a drive to regulate, control, and even suppress individual rights on behalf of collective goals, combined with an enormous ego that could lead him to acts of great cruelty against those whom he saw as enemies or challengers. Finally, Mao was born into a family and a community that enabled him to become part of the educated elite of his country, but *not* a member of the top intellectual elite—a condition of major importance in his subsequent attitudes toward the intelligentsia. Mao could be considered a "petit intellectual," not in the sense of his innate abilities, which were very considerable, but in the sense of his "class status" within the Chinese intellectual community, a fact which he bore with continuous resentment.

Education: Formal and Informal

Mao's formal education followed a pattern that was common for the educated youth of his era. He attended schools for approximately twelve years, with certain periods of work or informal study interspersed with classroom attendance. He was twenty-five years old when he finally completed his higher-school education at the Hunan First Normal School in the summer of 1918.

He began primary schooling at the age of eight in his native village and continued it until he was thirteen. In those years Mao was instructed in the Confucian classics by a stern taskmaster, and if we may accept his own account, he found the required studies boring and generally unintelligible, at least as interpreted by his teacher.[21] It remains important, however, that Mao's initial training was a classical one. Furthermore, according to one account, before his next experience in school, Mao went to an old scholar's home for further instruction in Confucianism and history.[22] Between the ages of thirteen and sixteen, Mao worked on the family homestead and read extensively in his leisure time. His avid commitment to books and his interest in further schooling undoubtedly reflected a subconscious competition with, and a quest for respect from, his father. The elder Mao had had only two years of schooling, and Mao's mother was illiterate. Thus, Mao recalls that he quickly became the family "scholar."[23]

At sixteen, Mao left home for the first time, to enter the Dongshan higher primary school in Xiangxiang county, about twenty-five kilometers from Shaoshan. Although he remained there for only a year, Mao's first formal introduction to "Western learning" came at this point; the Dongshan school was considered relatively "modern," and provided courses in foreign history, geography, and languages. But Mao soon wanted something more than Dongshan had to offer. In the spring of 1911, he went to the capital of Changsha, passed the entrance examinations for middle school, and began his studies there. In less than half a year, however, he left school to join the army during the 1911 Revolution. His military career at this point was brief and undistinguished. He ended up in a Changsha unit and apparently saw no action.

There followed a period of indecision and searching, in which Mao considered various possibilities—police school, a trade school that taught soap-making, law school, a commercial course. For one reason or another, he rejected all these possibilities and entered the First Provincial Middle School. Once again, however, he found himself dissatisfied with the school's curriculum and regulations and soon dropped out to undertake a program of "self-education." He visited the Hunan Provincial Library regularly, and according to his own account read widely from works that had been translated into Chinese by Yan Fu and others: Adam Smith, Darwin, John Stuart Mill, Spencer, and Rousseau, along with an eclectic assortment of poetry, romance, history, and geography.[24] However, Mao's father had said that he would provide no financial support unless his son were formally enrolled in school, and this may have been one reason why the young man decided to enter normal school in the spring of 1913. In the fall of that year, his school was amalgamated with the First Normal School, and he was to remain there as a student for five years.

Our concern is not with the details of Mao's school life, but rather with the successive influences that shaped his thought and actions, as well as personal traits bearing political significance that emerged during these years. In our opinion, Mao's first intellectual experience was the most important one in his life. His initial classical training, interwoven into his early environment and reinforced at crucial stages during his higher education, continued to be the single most powerful influence on his ideas and his actions, despite the Western-derived knowledge he later acquired.

When Mao entered Changsha Normal School at the age of nineteen, his formal education had been primarily in the classics. In his efforts at self-education, moreover, he had been limited to Chinese-language materials. Under this condition, new ideas—even profoundly novel ones—could be grasped, but to some degree they would always be cast in a Chinese mold. To put it differently, new "facts" and even new concepts might be derived from translated Western sources, but it is less clear whether a new intellectual *process* or *method* could be so derived. The process of formulating and building upon ideas derives from a combination of language and culture; and as many have noted, the differences between Chinese and Western languages are profound, including differences of an intellectual nature. Mao's modification of Marxism is only a specific instance of a general phenomenon of transcendent importance to modern China. Among the influences that have widened and differentiated the spectrum of modern Chinese intellectuals, that of linguistic capacity (together with foreign educational and cultural experience) must certainly be considered vital.

Mao's intimate relation to traditional Chinese thought did not end when he first came into contact with "fresh ideas" derived from other sources. At First Normal School, for instance, he mastered the classical style of writing well enough to impress one of his traditionalist instructors. Of greater importance, during this same period Mao came under the strong influence of Professor Yang Changji, whose daughter he was later to marry. Yang's students called him "Mr. Confucius" because of his moral rectitude and his penchant for lecturing to them on ethical matters.[25]

Yang was ideally qualified to present certain elements of Western philosophy in a way that connected them with classical Chinese writings. He had been educated as a neo-Confucian and retained his basic commitment to key Confucian doctrines throughout his life. But he had also spent some years in study abroad, first in Japan and later in Great Britain and Germany, and his major interest was in philosophy. He returned embued with Kantian idealism, and well acquainted with the work of T. H. Green, Friedrich Paulsen, and Henri Bergson. Each of these philosophers, in his own way, had been centrally concerned with the relation of the individual to the collectivity, with the challenge of relating the individual spirit and will to societal requirements in ways that would permit the highest moral attainments for man. The same issue of social man and a similar ethical imperative were at the root of Confucian concerns.

It is not surprising, therefore, that Yang was able to find a synthesis between his earlier and his later education, and that he was able to project certain avant-garde themes into Chinese intellectual circles. In his essay in *Xin qingnian* (New Youth), one can see the main threads of his value-policy orientation. He believed in the cultivation of the individual in all of his attributes—intellectual, physical, and moral—and through this process, the liberation of the individual mind and will on behalf of creativity. This creativity in turn would be conducive to national redemption, to the sort of total strength that would enable China to be reborn and then to survive in a dangerous and highly competitive world.[26] This outlook, of course, was the dominant one in Chinese intellectual circles during this period, and was expressed by many who had not had Yang's educational opportunities; but few were as well qualified as he to unite neo-Confucianism with the idealism of the neo-Kantian and neo-Hegelian schools.

One hardly need look further for the source of Mao's heroic struggle, over the decades ahead, to reconcile two opposing impulses—a commitment to individual self-fulfillment and a belief in the ultimate primacy of the *societal* good. Both were exemplified in the sources to which Yang directed his students. In a sense, of course, this dilemma is a universal one, discovered and rediscovered in all philosophic quests, regardless of the culture or the age. But it is also true that when a particular man assigns a weight to each opposing commitment, he reveals his own philosophic and cultural proclivities. And in this sense, Mao was Yang's natural disciple, as a student and a leader of men.

To be sure, Mao himself was later to claim that although he was strongly influenced by idealism during his Normal School days, he later abandoned it for the "more valid, more satisfying" materialism that lay beneath "scientific socialism." That this was a half-truth at best, Mao could not have been expected to understand. Yet it might be noted, among other things, that there was a gap of twenty years between Mao's educational experiences of the 1913–1918 period and his serious perusal of Marxism as philosophy. Not until 1936–1937 did Mao have the opportunity for relatively intensive reading in Marxist literature (as opposed to fragments and secondary summaries or assessments). By this time he was a mature revolutionary with many years of guerrilla experience.

Under Yang's guidance Mao had examined such neo-Confucianists as Wang Fuzhi, the seventeenth-century Hunanese scholar and Han patriot, which provided yet another stimulus to his awakening nationalism. Yang also introduced him to the work of Friedrich Paulsen, the German neo-Kantian. On his copy of the Chinese translation of Paulsen, Mao took copious notes. Yet it is difficult to know how thoroughly he was able to absorb the more formidable intellectual complexities of neo-Kantian thought, or indeed of other branches of Western thought. Many of his notes suggest that he usually grasped Western concepts by comparing them to ideas with which he was familiar from his classical studies.* Certainly, little of the strenuous intellectualism of the Western philosophers to whom he was being introduced at this time comes through in Mao's early writings. His first published essays, on the contrary, were characterized by a sustained simplicity of style and thought.

The great Chinese classical novels provided a stimulus at least equal to that of philosophic works in equipping Mao with a foundation for values and life-style. In such works as *Shuihu zhuan* (Water Margin) and *San guo yanyi* (Romance of the Three Kingdoms), action predominated over theory, and individuals triumphed or were crushed in the battle between justice and injustice, supineness and rebellion. Heroes and villains were larger than life. These actions, however, were set entirely within a classical frame of reference, and Confucian values projected themselves throughout. There were other sources, too, that suggested concepts of individual heroism. As a youth, Mao read accounts of Washington, Napoleon, Catherine and Peter of Russia, Wellington, Gladstone, Rousseau, Montesquieu, and Lincoln. Here was a mix of activists and thinkers that symbolized the forces competing for primacy within young Mao. And clearly the activists predominated.

A somewhat different turn in Mao's intellectual evolution began with his reading of Zheng Guanying's work, *Shengshi weiyan* (Words of Warning to an Affluent Age), first published in 1893. (Zheng, as we noted earlier, was a Cantonese compradore who had influenced Sun Yat-sen—and perhaps been influenced by him as well.) Mao reportedly read Zheng's book sometime after he completed lower primary school and before he entered the Dongshan school. It brought him into contact with specific formulas for changing old China—methods of modernization derived largely from Western science and technology.

It was a short but significant step from Zheng to Kang Youwei and Liang Qichao, a step which Mao took in Dongshan, when he pored over several works sent to him by his cousin. The effect was powerful. "I worshipped Kang and Liang," he later recounted.[27] In these men, reform—even radical reform—and neo-Confucianism were united. And Mao appears to have kept his faith in Kang and Liang somewhat longer than many students. If his later recollections are correct, his first effort at political expression came in the spring of 1913, when he posted a big-character poster on his Changsha middle-school wall urging that Sun be recalled from Japan to become president of a new government, with Kang as premier and Liang as minister of foreign affairs.[28]

Slightly earlier, when he first reached Changsha, Mao had come into contact for the first time with *Minli bao*, the Tongmeng Hui, and Sun, thereby being introduced to the mainstream of the revolutionary movement of the period. Yet as a provincial, and one only recently arrived in the

*According to Li Rui, Mao wrote more than twelve thousand words in the margin of his copy of Paulsen's work. The sample Li gives cannot be considered inspired. See Li Jui (Li Rui), *The Early Revolutionary Activities of Comrade Mao Tse-tung*, pp. 36–40.

Hunan capital, he could not have been expected to be abreast of the newest ideas and movements that preoccupied his more advanced peers.

At about this time Mao made his initial acquaintance with socialism by reading newspaper articles and pamphlets written by Jiang Kanghu. Socialist ideas had a very limited influence on Mao at this point, however. Far more significant were the writings contained in *New Youth* to which his teacher Yang Changji now introduced him. His new models became Hu Shi and Chen Duxiu—who along with Li Dazhao quickly replaced Kang, a man still vainly seeking to restore monarchism, and Liang, whose affiliation with the Beijing government had tarnished his reputation with young progressives.

Despite an initial tardiness, Mao's political commitments had developed in a quite orthodox manner by the eve of the May Fourth Movement, and were the same as those of hundreds of other young Chinese intellectuals. As he later described his position: "At this time my mind was a curious mixture of ideas of liberalism, democratic reformism, and Utopian Socialism. I had somewhat vague passions about 'nineteenth-century democracy,' Utopianism, and old-fashioned liberalism, and I was definitely anti-militarist and anti-imperialist."[29] This statement is true, but again not fully reflective of the complex facts. At this point Mao was above all a nationalist, committed to whatever could strengthen China.

There can be no doubt that after the Revolution of 1911 the deplorable circumstances into which China was brought and the flood-tide of revolutionary new ideas entering the country—principally liberal, but often anarchist and anarcho-syndicalist—soon influenced Mao and other young intellectuals. Indeed, it was in this period that Western influence on Mao, and on China, reached its peak. (We distinguish Bolshevism—or Marxism in its Russian form—from Westernism.)

Mao now espoused certain views strongly associated with China's youthful avant-garde, such as fierce rejection of Confucianism and all other "outmoded" ideas. Yet his experiences and his life-style—especially the strong quotient of provincialism that clung to him—tended to distance him, both personally and intellectually, from his more strongly Westernized compatriots. His aloofness toward such individuals was instinctive. Subconsciously, Mao measured Chineseness as well as political views in assessing his compatibility with others.

Thus, Mao's liberalism, however sincerely embraced for the moment, was likely to have an ephemeral quality, as indeed proved to be the case. In no sense, however, did this mean that his concern for the individual vanished. As we have suggested, the struggle within Mao (and others) over individual versus collective rights was lifelong and was never resolved intellectually. Yet this struggle did not have to flow from Western liberalism, any more than the Chinese commitment to work and the accumulation of capital had to stem from the Protestant ethic. The deepest roots of Mao's lifelong political dilemma were indigenous, not Western.

Two other factors revealed themselves during the course of his formal education which are of importance in understanding his personality and later career. First, while obviously a very intelligent young man, Mao's abilities and interests were not evenly distributed. He accepted science and technology as important to the creation of a new China, but he could summon up no personal interest in them; in school, he avoided science and mathematics or did poorly in them. His talents and his interests were to be found in the humanities—in literature, history, and philosophy. In this, incidentally, he was more like a traditional Chinese scholar than a member of any new scientific-technological elite. And like Li and Chen, he eventually came to Marxism not through science but by walking the humanist path.

Second, it is a point of more than passing interest that very early in life Mao had become a devotee of physical fitness. To quote Li Rui, Mao and his friends advocated "a civilized spirit, a barbarian body."[30] He did regular morning exercises, swam throughout the year, and took cold showers and long walks. On several occasions he walked for weeks at a time through the countryside. In striking contrast to the cult of physical fitness in our own time, Mao's commitment had strongly political connotations. Since the early twentieth century, as we have noted, Chinese progressives had been deploring the tradition of the white-faced, short-of-breath scholar, who symbolized for them the weakness of the nation and its inability to ward off foreign intrusion. Mao's increasingly nationalistic sentiments and his impatience with many of the aspects of the formal educational system of his time combined to make him highly receptive to such themes.*

It should not be surprising, therefore, that his first published article, written when he was twenty-three and still a student at the First Normal School, was entitled "A Study of Physical Education" and was printed in the April 1917 issue of *New Youth.*[31] In his opening sentences, Mao clearly defined the political implications of physical fitness: "Our nation is wanting in strength. The military spirit has not been encouraged. The physical condition of the population deteriorates daily. This is an extremely disturbing phenomenon."[32] From weak bodies, he asserted, came cowardice and thus an inability to achieve one's goals in the face of enemy challenge. Self-preservation, he continued, was a natural instinct, and after "the advent of the sages" people had begun to live more regularly, paying attention to matters affecting their health.[33] In modern times Germany had set the pace, and Japan had *bushido,* Mao asserted, implying that these were two countries to emulate in matters relating to physical culture. He then argued that development of the body was a primary not a secondary obligation because the body was the receptacle housing both knowledge and morality.

There followed a strong attack on the current Chinese educational system, undoubtedly based on Mao's own frustrations. "In the educational system of our country," he wrote, "required courses are as thick as the hairs on a cow. Even an adult with a tough, strong body cannot stand it, let alone those who have not reached adulthood, or those who are weak."[34] Then his anger rose. Educators seemed determined to design a curriculum that would exhaust students. They trampled on their bodies and ruined their lives. And if the students did not accept the regulations, they would be punished. The most intelligent students, moreover, were induced by honeyed words and powerful rewards to tackle additional lessons and books.

Throughout his essay Mao referred to China's major philosophers, but not always with approbation. Indeed, he launched a mildly worded but

*These themes appeared in the numerous articles in the Chinese student journals published in Tokyo, some of which are cited in chapter 4, and in the article by Chen Duxiu entitled "The New Youth" (*Xin qingnian,* September 1, 1916, pp. 1–4), which almost certainly inspired Mao's first published article.

penetrating attack on the concepts of tranquility, contemplation, and non-action which lay at the heart of the teachings of Zhu Xi, Lao Zi, and the Buddhists. The disciples of these philosophers might boast of the effectiveness of such methods, Mao asserted, but in his own opinion there was only change and movement in the world. He then went on to argue that the world's greatest thinkers—men like Confucius, Buddha, Jesus, and Mohammed—had for the most part lived very active lives and lived to ripe old age, except for Jesus, "who had the misfortune to die unjustly." In these passages one can sense an attribute of Mao's that can scarcely be exaggerated. However much he might aspire to be accepted as a philosopher in later years, and however much time he might spend in the study or at his desk writing, he was essentially an activist. Mobilizing, campaigning, fighting "the enemy"—these were the pursuits that gave Mao a sense of fulfillment, an awareness that he was using his considerable political talents to the utmost. In time, this requirement for the man was to become a requirement for the nation.

In the central section of his essay on physical education, Mao argued that a strong body was essential to a strong mind, and that when the body was perfect, knowledge was perfect. But it soon become clear that he had more than pure knowledge in mind. "The principal aim of physical education," he wrote, "is military heroism." The virtues of courage, boldness, and tenacity were essential to defeating one's enemies and building a nation. The future of China would ultimately depend on creating individuals who combined physical strength and a firm will.[35]

As his essay drew to a close, Mao did not hesitate to mention Confucian and Taoist classics again, but to his own purposes. Behind the old adage that the good man did not become a soldier, he said, lay a fear or a contempt for exercise and the active life. But exercise built character as well as bodily strength. To be effective, exercise required perseverance, concentration, and a type of primitive vigor—precisely the attributes required for a reinvigorated Chinese race.

The relatively martial, strongly nationalistic themes of this essay were characteristic of the times, especially in the writings and thought of the younger generation of Chinese intellectuals. As we have seen, journals and newspapers were filled with calls for a strong China capable of meeting the twin threats of foreign imperialism and domestic chaos. Such a China required men of physical strength, courage, and determination. Repeatedly, it was proclaimed that the time for action had come.

Organize, Unite, Struggle!

Very shortly after his essay appeared in print, Mao had the opportunity to put his words into practice, at least on a small scale. In the autumn of 1917 he became director of the education and study section of his school's Student Union, and among his duties was that of directing student physical training. According to his recent biographers, he made many suggestions for improving physical education, including the introduction of ping-pong![36]

This assignment, which lasted until the summer of 1918, illustrates a much more fundamental fact about Mao's aptitudes and preferences. From an early point in his career as First Normal School student, he had shown a ceaseless dedication to organizational activities. Indeed, during the years between 1915 and 1920, this aspect of his life overshadowed all others, including the pursuit of a higher education.

Not only did he play an extremely active role in the Student Union during these years, serving as secretary for four semesters before assuming the post of education-study director. In early 1915 he tried to organize a group of "patriotic" students who might be prepared to discuss means of saving China—an effort, which, according to his later account, drew three and one-half responses.* In that year also he is said to have taken an active role in the movement against Yuan Shikai's plan to become emperor; near the end of the year he participated in a student strike against tuition increases, and wrote a handbill attacking the principal. In 1916 he helped to organize Changsha students and citizens in order to protect the city against the depredations of retreating troops (Hunan was now entering its era of greatest torment, when rival military forces repeatedly used the province as a battleground). In the fall of 1917 he organized a night school for workers.**

Most accounts of Mao's ventures during these years are exaggerated and distorted by political bias.† Nevertheless, they do illustrate his mounting commitment to activist politics. In this connection, moreover, certain traits now began to appear which proved of critical importance to his future career. As we have seen, Mao's first love intellectually lay in the fields of philosophy, history, and literature—fields susceptible to conceptualization and even to grand theory (to which, in a part of himself, he was powerfully attracted). In his organizational activities, however, Mao was very much a "nuts and bolts" man, deeply concerned about those matters of detail which

*Mao's recollection of this episode, as recounted by Edgar Snow, is interesting: "Feeling expansive and the need for a few intimate companions, I one day inserted an advertisement in a Changsha paper, inviting young men interested in patriotic work to make contact with me. I specified youths who were hardened and determined, and ready to make sacrifices for their country. To this advertisement I received three and one-half replies. One was from Liu Chiang-lung, who later was to join the Communist Party and afterward to betray it. Two others were from young men who later were to become ultra-reactionaries. The 'half' reply came from a noncommital youth named Li Li-san. Li listened to all I had to say, and then went away without making any definite proposals himself, and our friendship never developed" (Snow, *Red Star*, p. 144). Of course, Mao was speaking after Li had been virtually purged from the CCP and was living in exile in Moscow.

**Li Rui provides some details. According to the *First Normal School Record* of 1918, Mao gave four reasons why the night school should be established: power in modern society rested with the majority of uneducated citizens; universal education had yielded good results in Europe and America; a night school would provide valuable teacher-training for the advanced students of the First Normal School; and it could help bridge the gap between the community and the school. The first notices posted drew no registrants, and a wider distribution drew only nine. But by house-to-house canvassing and passing out handbills in person, the students finally signed up 120 persons. Classes began on November 9, 1917, and the curriculum consisted of Chinese language, arithmetic, and "general knowledge." The school apparently operated—with a dwindling enrollment—until the summer of 1918, when Mao and others graduated. (Li, *The Early Revolutionary Activities*, pp. 59–64; *Mao Zedong tongzhi*, pp. 71–76.)

†Despite certain recent revisionist trends, studies on Mao produced in the People's Republic of China to date must be used with great caution; they generally portray Mao as the initiator or leader of every activity in which he was involved, and omit anything that might reflect adversely on his judgment or character. Notwithstanding occasional vagueness and inaccuracies in dates, names, and places, Mao's own recollections given to Snow remain the most balanced and generally accurate account of his early life.

can cumulatively determine whether an organization will be effective: finances, communications, regularity of meetings, agendas, and procedures.[37] It was through paying close attention to such matters and exhibiting great tenacity and singleness of purpose that Mao gradually assumed primary responsibility or leadership in certain situations. Rarely did he begin at the top of an association with which he became affiliated—either in this or in later periods. He *climbed* there, and in addition to his other talents, his extraordinary ability to judge the strengths and weaknesses of co-workers was a powerful asset for him until many years later, when the weaknesses of advanced age blurred this and other visions—just as he had predicted.

Mao's organizational talents came into play in connection with the first important organization in which he was centrally involved, the Xinmin Xuehui (New People's Study Association). As we previously noted, this group was formally organized on April 18, 1919, by some thirteen individuals gathered at the home of Cai Hesen, a man who was later of special importance in guiding Mao's final steps into Communism. The association's primary purpose was to study and act upon the new ideas that were now flooding China. Its inspiration came from *New Youth* and that triumvirate of writers so influential during these years—Chen Duxiu, Li Dazhao, and Hu Shi. Mao helped draft the association's constitution, and as one of its secretaries he handled recruitment and organizational matters. His friend Xiao Xisheng (Siao-yu) was elected general secretary. In time, the Xinmin Xuehui acquired seventy to eighty members, including an active group of women. And when Xiao later went to France as a student, Mao inherited the key position within the association in Changsha.

As we have indicated, Mao himself was at one time quite interested in going to France as a student. Shortly after his graduation from First Normal School in June 1918, he received a letter from his old mentor, Yang Changji, who was now teaching at Peking University, informing him that a program to recruit work-study students to go to France had been reestablished, and that it offered opportunities for Hunanese who might wish to pursue their education abroad. This information was channeled to Xinmin Xuehui members and others. In several groups, a number of students journeyed to Beijing. Mao traveled there with some twenty-five others in mid-August. At twenty-four years of age, he was making his first trip outside Hunan.

Three schools were set up to give those students who intended to go to France preliminary language training and supplementary lectures.[38] It is not clear whether Mao actually enrolled in this program, and if he did, how long he remained in it. It would appear, however, that at an early point he took a different path. Why did he drop out? His own explanation, given some eighteen years later to Edgar Snow, is vague and not wholly convincing: "I felt that I did not know enough about my own country, and that my time could be more profitably spent in China. . . . I had other plans."[39]

One might guess that the real reasons had to do with Mao's great difficulty with foreign languages, and beyond this, an apprehension (or sense of inadequacy) about foreign ways which never left him. In certain respects Mao was shrewd and even highly sophisticated, but one could not describe his lifestyle as cosmopolitan. More than most of his fellow Hunanese students, he seemed to dread the thought of reducing the Chinese element in his life. Had he been committed to science and technology, of course, he would have been much more strongly motivated to go abroad. But that was not the case.

Consequently, he turned his energies to other opportunities, primarily involving activities on the Peking University campus. First, through an introduction from Professor Yang, he obtained a job in the university library, and thus was placed under Li Dazhao, the head of the library—which brings us to a delicate matter. Although Mao later reported that he joined several campus organizations, among them the Philosophical Society and the Journalist Research Society, and also audited some courses, he said he found himself regarded as a country bumpkin in China's most sophisticated city. As he put it to Snow, "My office was so low that people avoided me. One of my tasks was to register the names of people who came to read newspapers, but to most of them I did not exist as a human being. . . . They had no time to listen to an assistant librarian speaking [a] southern dialect."[40] In this connection, Mao mentions several individuals, including Luo Jialun, then a famous student leader, but he does not refer to any professors. At a later point in his recital to Snow, moreover, he acknowledges Li Dazhao as one of "the brilliant intellectual leaders of China," and claims that he "rapidly moved toward Marxism" under Li's guidance.[41]

It is interesting, however, that when he recalled for Snow the individuals from the *New Youth* group who were most influential in his ideas, Mao cites Chen and Hu but not Li. And as we shall see, in an article written shortly after his Beijing sojourn, Li is rather conspicuously omitted from a list of those contributing to major reform in China. It seems likely that along with his real indebtedness to Li for "fresh ideas" (Mao was in Beijing at the time Li's articles hailing the masses and the Bolshevik Revolution were first published), this young Hunanese could not help resenting the limited attention he probably got from this busy and important man. Li's inner circle of students at this time did not include Mao, which was only natural, given his status. Mao was never one to take slights (real or fancied) lightly, as his later interaction with the Russians would demonstrate.

Whatever his inner feelings, Mao now came into brief but meaningful contact with writings that supported or described anarchism and Marxism. And he makes it clear that like many of his contemporaries (including Li), he was most strongly influenced by Kropotkin and Tolstoy. Anarchism was a powerful force within the small Chinese radical community during these years, and it gave ground only very stubbornly to the new Marxist tides.

In March 1919 Mao left Beijing to accompany some students to Shanghai, where they began their voyage to France. He returned to Hunan in April, on the eve of the May Fourth Movement, and was soon deeply involved in organizational activities. The dramatic events occurring in Beijing naturally provided an enormous stimulus for him. On May 7 the first student demonstration against Versailles and the Japanese took place in Changsha, and was broken up by the military governor, Zhang Jingyao. By the end of the month Mao was taking a prominent role in reconstructing the United Association of Hunan Students. Various tactics were employed or discussed—a boycott, a general strike, agitation calculated to involve the populace at large. Midsummer saw the creation of the Hunan Union of All Circles, an umbrella organization that would unite groups from various walks of life—and the need for such unity would soon become a central theme of the new journal edited by Mao.

The Xiang River Review

During this period, Mao served as editor of the Hunan Student Union's *Xiang jiang pinglun* (*Xiang River Review*). The first issue came out on July 14, 1919, and a total of four issues and one "extra" issue were printed (the fifth was confiscated at the press before distribution).[42] This journal presented Mao's most important solo performance to date, and was a venture that brought him some national recognition—a partial compensation for the indifference shown a lowly librarian at Beida only a few months earlier.

In his "Opening Declaration" inaugurating the new journal, however, Mao showed no particular originality of thought; instead he gave ample evidence of having absorbed ideas—and modes of expression—that were characteristic of the Peking University luminaries. The call for a world revolution is rising, he asserted. The movement on behalf of human liberation is advancing rapidly and there is no way to hold it back. We must now ask questions we have never dared to raise, and consider methods we have never dared to use. The greatest problem confronting the world is that of food; the strongest force, that of the united masses. In our search for answers, nothing is to be feared—not heaven, ghosts, dead ancestors, bureaucrats, militarists, or capitalists. Since the Renaissance and the liberation of man's mind, Mao continued, deciding how man should live had become the problem of greatest importance. Reforms had been made in many areas: in religion, they brought freedom of conscience; in literature, they allowed popular, modern, and lively works to replace rigid and aristocratic classical writings; in politics, there was a shift from dictatorial regimes to representative systems, with a movement from restricted to universal suffrage; in society, there had been a transition from the dark order dominated by the few to a bright order that encouraged the free development of all; in learning, the principle of popular education had taken root; in the economy, the trend had been toward equality of distribution and favorable treatment for labor; in ideology, experimentalism (pragmatism) had arisen; and in the international sphere, there was now the League of Nations. Taken collectively, these reforms amounted to a movement away from coercion and toward freedom, and the force that was basic to resisting coercion was *pingminzhuyi*—the principle of the common man.

Despite the inclusion of "capitalists" in his list of generally unsavory elements that were not to be feared, and his vague hint that a new economic order (socialism?) might be coming, Mao placed himself squarely in the liberal camp in the statements that followed. He took his stand with vernacular literature, parliamentarism, maximum civil liberties, unionism, public education, the philosophy of John Dewey as explicated by Hu Shi, and internationalism as embodied in the League of Nations (not the Third International, which had held its First Congress in early March).

Furthermore, Mao committed himself quite straightforwardly to political moderation. There was no longer a place for power politics in any sphere of life, he insisted. The choice was between coercive power and freedom, and the only principle to pursue in overthrowing power was that of the common man (populism). Democracy was the wave of the future. There were of course two methods of overturning power—a moderate way and a radical way. The moderate way requires us to admit that those who practice power politics are individuals of our own kind, and that their abuses are mistakes committed unconsciously, because they too are victims of the thought and values of the old society. If we adopt the radical approach, continued Mao, and seek to overthrow power with power, the result will be self-defeating, as is demonstrated by the war recently waged between rival factions in Europe and the current struggle between North and South in China.

Thus, Mao concluded, we should undertake a sincere and thorough search for the truth, unrestrained by old legacies and superstitions. In human affairs, we should focus on reaching unity with the masses, and we should direct a "campaign of sincere advice" at those who hold power, making appeals for bread, freedom, and equality, which if heeded could lead to a bloodless revolution. "We advocate neither the creation of great chaos nor a futile, ineffective revolution by bombs, a bloody revolution."[43] The most immediate sign of power politics in the international sphere was the expansionist action of Japan, but here the student-merchant-workers' strikes and boycotts had achieved good results.

In these passages, one can easily detect the themes being propagated at the time by John Dewey and Hu Shi, yet with more than a touch of the messages of Li Dazhao and Chen Duxiu, together with the suggestion that some of the central appeals of the Russian Revolution might be harnessed to a bloodless revolution, one produced by political pressure rather than bombs. Mao's message was an eclectic one, absorbing and seeking to synthesize ideas from a variety of sources.

Mao approached the end of his essay with a critical and rather gloomy appraisal of the status of intellectual life and political consciousness among his fellow Hunanese. The people who live along the Xiang River, he remarked, know nothing of developments in the outer world and remain unorganized as a community; they simply perpetuate their narrow-minded, shortsighted existence. Long-term friendships are rare, for individuals understand only competition motivated by self-interest. A certain process of education occurred when tidal waves rolled in from the outside world, but even then a handful of bureaucratic educators had managed to treat students like prisoners and turn schools into jails. And when some good students went abroad for an education, they were given no chance to use what they had learned. Educational leaders seemed unable to tolerate differences of opinion. Reform was essential if the many capable youth were to make use of the new knowledge and technology available, but no one seemed capable of undertaking improvements. Meanwhile, provincialism remained strong, as was suggested by the popular slogan "Hunan food for Hunanese only."

Yet Mao managed to end on an upbeat note, returning to his initial theme. Great waves were pounding against Hunan, bringing new ideas with them. To accept these meant life; to oppose them, death. Discovering how to assimilate these new ideas, how to disseminate them, how to study them and put them into practice were the tasks to which the *Xiang River Review* had dedicated itself.

In an article entitled "On Events in the West," the young editor then presented information about strikes by French, British, Italian, German, and Hungarian workers protesting rising living costs, limits on unionization rights (among the British police), and food shortages.[44] In the United States, the journal reported, 60,000 Chicago telegraph workers and operators had planned to strike in opposition to President Wilson's position at the Paris Peace Conference, but the strike did not materialize. All in all, the selections, in addition to betraying a certain anarchist influence, indicated that Mao saw Western politics as being in turmoil.

"On Events in the East" contained a long account of Chen Duxiu's arrest the previous month.[45] Quoting from a dispatch put out by the "Sino-American press," Mao's journal reported that the leaflet Chen had been distributing outlined six demands: abolition of secret treaties between China and Japan; dismissal of key Beijing officials and their expulsion from the capital; disbandment of the army headquarters, the firing of the commander of the Beijing garrison, and their replacement with a Beijing security force organized by merchants and other citizens; facilitation of peace between North and South; and absolute freedom of speech, the press, and assembly for the people. The leaflet, according to this account, stated that it was hoped that these demands would be achieved peacefully, but if the government ignored "the people's will," the citizens of Beijing would have "to resort to direct action aiming at a radical transformation."

In a commentary, Mao wrote, "We cannot see anything wrong with the leaflet." He recounted Chen's reported treatment at the hands of the police, and the efforts of students and others, including the Shanghai Industrial Association, to free him. "We consider Mr. Chen a star in the world of thought," he wrote, adding that the most dangerous thing in China at the moment was not military weakness, or the lack of financial resources, or civil strife, but emptiness and corruption in people's thought. The overwhelming majority of the Chinese people were dominated by superstition and had no confidence in themselves. This was the result of underdeveloped scientific thinking. The Republic, meanwhile, had become only a facade for dictatorship, and the situation was growing progressively worse. Chen had been imprisoned for his belief in science and democracy, but his arrest could only brighten his image as the champion of new ideas and elicit the admiration of the people. In a burst of youthful bravado, Mao said he doubted whether the government would dare execute Chen, but if it did, his spirit would only become more powerful than ever. "I wish Mr. Chen a long life! I wish a long life to Mr. Chen's resolute, high spirit!" he added.

In commenting on certain international developments, Mao provided interesting evidence of his current attitudes toward Russia and America.[46] Employing the ironic approach often used by Chinese intellectuals, he noted that both the Afghan incursion into India and the recent agitation on behalf of independence in Korea were being blamed on the "Russian radical party." Now there is a real radical party, he said, and added, echoing Li Dazhao's comments in a recent issue of *Meizhou pinglun*, "we should study it and find out what it is all about."

Turning to Versailles, Mao spoke in disparaging tones. Poland had been restored as a nation in the name of self-determination, but the real purpose was only to keep Germany down. The Arabs were dividing up the former Turkish empire under the guise of self-determination. The Jews were seeking to build a nation in Palestinian territory, but they were being rebuffed because this had little to do with Allied aims. The Siberian government (under Kolchak), however, had been recognized only because it had attacked the Russian radicals; Japan had taken the lead in backing this move because it harbored the intention of invading Siberia. Korea, on the other hand, had long demanded independence, and many had died for that cause, but the peace conference had simply ignored Korean pleas.

Mao then made some remarks about Woodrow Wilson that were virtually identical to those previously expressed by Li Dazhao. The Paris Peace Conference, he said, was nothing but an occasion for dividing up territories and obtaining reparations, and Wilson had hardly been able to speak his mind, surrounded as he was by robbers like Clemenceau, Lloyd George, Orlando, and others. Reuters had reported that Wilson had finally agreed with Clemenceau not to allow Germany to be admitted to the League of Nations. "When I read the words 'finally agreed,' I was deeply upset and felt greatly disturbed for him for a long time," Mao wrote. "Poor Wilson!"

There followed a highly unfavorable sketch of life in the United States. Bombs had exploded in eight American cities, it was reported, and anarchists were creating havoc everywhere. Posters had been put up proclaiming "Class war is here" and asserting that the struggle would not end until international labor had won a total victory. Congressmen, "who get votes on the basis of how much money they put into elections," had denounced the terrorists and advocated severe punishment. But, said Mao, I have a word of warning: "When doomsday comes, if you want to survive, have some rice to eat and clothes to wear, then you had better change your opinion thoroughly [literally, "wash your brain thoroughly"], take off your tall hats and formal attire, and with the common citizens of your country go to work in a factory or on a farm." Then, after quoting an attack on monopoly by Samuel Gompers (the "chief of the American Labor Party"), Mao concluded that the United States was the first nation in which monopoly had come to dominate all business, and that it had also originated the evil trust system, under which the misery of millions supported the enjoyments of a few, and the plight of the common people grew steadily worse as commerce and industry expanded. It was good, Mao commented, that someone (Gompers) had said "no" to monopoly; when millions joined in that assertion, the real liberation of mankind would arrive.[47]

Here we see an interesting phenomenon and one that was by no means unique to Mao. Like many Chinese intellectuals of this era and earlier, Mao seemed to feel that conditions in the West—and notably in the United States—were worse than those in China and required more radical solutions. Influenced by news reports from Europe and America, at a time of growing disillusion about the Versailles settlement, Mao was prepared to believe the worst about Western political and economic conditions. Thus, he might advocate parliamentary reforms and a bloodless revolution for China, but for the West it was presumably too late for such measures.

The second issue of the *Review* opened with the first installment of the most important essay it was to publish—Mao's "The Great Union of the Masses."[48] Its central theme was stated immediately: when a nation or a people were besieged, the basic response required was to form a great union of the masses. In the past, union had been the instrument of rulers, aristocrats, and capitalists. It had also taken the form of alliances between nations, parliaments within states, and trusts in the business world. But recently, as conditions of life had deteriorated, such ties had become obsolete, and reform and resistance were now inevitable, hence the need for a great union of the masses. The more powerful unity of the French people had defeated the united aristocrats and permitted the accomplishment of major reforms. The same thing had happened in other countries, such as Russia, Hungary, and

Austria, and Germany was now also moving toward far-reaching social alterations. Soon, drastic changes would spread to the entire world.

Why was a great union of the masses so powerful? The answer lay in numbers, said Mao. The aristocrats, capitalists, and rulers might exploit the masses by using their knowledge, money, and military forces; they owned the land and the factories, paid low wages, and used armies to defend their interests. But the ordinary people had come to understand the ways of the rulers, their eyes had been opened to prevailing inequities, and they knew that soldiers were hired mostly from the masses and could not be relied upon to obey orders to fire on their own kin. How significant it was, he added, that hundreds of thousands of Russians had replaced their aristocracy with a red flag. The common man now knew that the secret of power lay in unity, and he had begun to form great unions. After such unions had been formed, there were two courses. One, the radical course advocated by Marx, was to treat them as they had treated us. The other, a moderate course, stressed the morality of mutual aid advocated by Kropotkin, and the desirability of accommodating the capitalists if they were willing to cooperate with the masses. As we have seen, Mao had already stated his personal choice between these options in the inauguration of the *Review*: he favored the moderate course. Here, however, he concluded merely by asserting that if the Chinese people wanted to break the historic bondage that kept them from getting things done, they must organize themselves into a great union, as people had done in other countries.

In the second installment of his essay (in the *Review's* third issue), Mao began by stating that a great union should stem from many small unions, each formed on the basis of occupational or social interests.[49] In outlining the most logical groups, he provided a picture of his recent experience and concerns. He dealt first with the peasants, thereby acknowledging their importance as the largest contingent among China's common people. His remarks were relatively brief and covered the central issues in a straightforward, unemotional manner: only those who actually cultivated the land could accurately express peasant interests and deal with such questions as the treatment of tenants by landlords, rents, taxes, and the availability of food. Next he dealt with the workers, and again his remarks were general in nature: the workers should organize themselves to resolve such issues as wages, working hours, bonuses, and recreation. When he came to his third category, students, Mao showed deep personal concern and went to greater lengths in describing their problems: wretched facilities that damaged their health, backward pedagogical methods, and arrogant, unfeeling teachers.* His recommendation, which he had previously followed on his own, was for students to form small groups that could pursue self-directed study.

Mao then considered the plight of three other groups—women, primary-

* If we are students, Mao wrote, we are probably having a hard time under old-fashioned teachers, who treat us like prisoners and slaves and keep us reading books until we all become near-sighted and ruin our health; the laboratories have little equipment, we are forced to write compositions in an antiquated style, the libraries are empty, the sports fields are filthy, and patriotism is a forbidden sentiment at a time when the country faces ruin. We have suffered enough at their hands, Mao fumed, and now we must seek salvation by organizing ourselves into a union for self-education. Then, if anything happens, we can march against them in a fury. ("The Great Union of the Masses," *Xiang jiang pinglun*, no. 3, p. 1.)

school teachers, and policemen. Mao's deep concern about the status of women was not new; it may have stemmed partly from his strong affection for his mother (instead of his father), and it could have been stimulated by the essays of Jiang Kanghu and others. Women were bound to a bitter life, he wrote, separated from the public and society, and in some cases confined to houses of prostitution where they were visited by all sorts of rascals. They were deprived of the right to love, even as the virtues of "virginity" and "fidelity" were publicly praised. If they were students, they were taught only how to be good wives and mothers, and told not to make trouble. "O God of Liberty, where are you?" he exclaimed, speaking in the voice of oppressed women. Primary-school teachers, another group with which Mao was well acquainted, were overworked, had no time for recreation or further study, and often went hungry because of low wages—wages that were further reduced when certain headmasters kept a portion for themselves. If we are in this group, Mao complained, we are like a phonograph record repeating what we were taught in school, frequently separated from our wives and families and living like slaves. If we are policemen, he continued, we also need a union for our physical and mental health. In Japan people say that beggars, primary-school teachers, and policemen are the most miserable groups in society, "and we share that view." Rickshaw men also needed unions, working as they did for long hours at low wages. Other logical workers' unions would serve railroad workers, miners, telegraph operators, telephone workers, workers in shipbuilding, metallurgy, and textiles, streetcar drivers, and construction workers. These unions in turn should be joined together in a larger federation.

The third and concluding installment of the essay appeared in the fourth issue of the *Xiang River Review*.[50] At the outset, Mao explained that he would investigate a large question: did the Chinese people have the consciousness, the motives, and the abilities needed to build unions into successful and federated associations? He began by exploring the nature of the 1911 Revolution.

On the surface, he said, the Revolution had seemed to stem from a union of the masses, but in reality this was not the case. It had grown out of the initiative of the returned students, the activities of the secret societies, and the revolt of certain New Army soldiers. Speaking for the masses, Mao said, "We agreed with their course, but we did not take part in it." But the people had learned something: the almighty emperor could be overthrown, and a revolutionary democracy could be built. After the 1911 Revolution, China had been beset with problems. A new emperor had risen and fallen; a war between North and South had erupted; and various bureaucrats, militarists, and politicians had done grievous harm. But with the World War, the masses all over the globe had arisen. In Russia the aristocrats had been vanquished and the wealthy class driven out; the workers and peasants had united to set up a new government, and the Red Army had defeated its foes, to the astonishment of the world. Popular movements were emerging elsewhere in Europe, and in Asia as well. In China the May Fourth Movement had spread over the entire nation. "We are awakening!" Mao concluded. The consciousness needed for forming a great union of the masses therefore existed in China.

Did the necessary motivation and experience exist? In search of an answer, Mao reviewed organizational efforts in China since the late Qing era.

He discussed the recent history of political organizations, revolutionary and moderate, and the formation of the national and provincial assemblies. Private interest groups in particular—educational associations, chambers of commerce, and peasant unions—had proved stable and solid, he wrote, as had units in other fields, such as alumni associations, student federations, newspaper associations, and various guilds and institutes. Organizations of this sort, he asserted, owed their existence to open politics and freedom of political expression; they could never have emerged under dictatorial rule. And they represented precisely the type of small union he had described earlier. Furthermore, the motive to form a larger federation had been enhanced by a growing awareness of the foreign threat to the nation. Such groups as the National Federation of Education, the National Chamber of Commerce, and the guild federations in Shanghai, Canton, and elsewhere were strengthened by it. The National Federation of Students, remarked Mao, was a particularly strong force for counteracting power politics at home and abroad. Although some of these associations could be entered and even manipulated by aristocrats or politicians, in general they were vehicles of great potential for the masses, and the need to establish them should be apparent by now.

Finally, did the people have the ability needed to form associations that would succeed? There were problems, Mao acknowledged. In the past, many foolish things had been done, many weaknesses revealed. Businessmen did not know how to set up cooperatives, and workers did not understand how to establish a labor party. Scholars kept their learning to themselves and did not join in group studies. Government in China was a mess. The post office and the salt gabelle, both run by foreigners, were in better shape than Chinese-operated ventures. Two Chinese shipping companies were losing money, and when one compared the railways managed by foreigners with those managed by Chinese, the difference was clear. We Chinese, lamented Mao, seem unable to manage anything—a school, a family, even ourselves.

The real problem, however, was not an absence of innate ability but a lack of experience. The Chinese nation had long been under a single ruler, and the people had been treated like slaves—forbidden to have any ideas, display any talent, or develop any organizational skills. But now times have changed, and liberation was everywhere on the horizon—in politics, in the economy, in ideology, in education. The gates of hell had been flung open, and the people could now see the blue skies. Mao finished with a burst of patriotic fervor. The Chinese people were a great people. The deeper their oppression, the stronger their reaction would be. The longer the restraints had lasted, the more quickly they would be shaken off. "I dare say that the Chinese nation will have a bright future, brighter than that of any other nation. We shall have our great union of the masses ahead of all others. We must make every effort to undertake this advance. The bright world to which we look forward lies just ahead!"

Many insights into Mao's current views may be gathered from his writings in the *Xiang River Review*. For us, five observations seem particularly important. First, Mao had a near-mystical faith in the common man, and the buoyant optimism so characteristic of the revolutionary personality. The Chinese masses might still be ignorant, stubbornly provincial, and lacking in self-esteem (as Mao had acknowledged), but in the larger pattern of politics preordained for the future, their liberation was assured, and the great union of the masses would overcome all obstacles—obliterating the militarists, removing the menace of foreign imperialism, and realizing the potential that lay within Chinese society. In imagining the leap from present to future conditions, Mao (like many contemporary "progressives") relied heavily on global trends to sweep China along. Mobilization of the common man had occurred in France, and recently in Russia, and was bound to occur in China in the years ahead.

Second, Mao's principal political ideas during this period were derived chiefly from essays and editorials by others, in *New Youth* and *Meizhou pinglun*. For example, the idea that self-government could be promoted by a union of the citizenry, federated up to the provincial level, had been set forth explicitly in the first issue of *Meizhou pinglun*.[51] In particular, Li Dazhao's writings constituted a primary source. It was under the stimulus of Li that Mao became attracted to the Bolshevik Revolution. He came to see it as a successful assertion of political supremacy by the common man, in a social setting where the common man had been dominated by a "feudal" aristocracy which had thrived under an antiquated monarchical structure. Russia thus set a course to which China could legitimately aspire with new hope.

But, as in the case of Li, this view did not lead Mao immediately to Marxism. There were two other bodies of political thought and practice that continued to lay claim to his allegiance. One was anarchism. At various points in his *Xiang River Review* writings, Mao makes clear his sympathy with mutual aid (as opposed to class struggle), which he defined as the "moderate" approach. In this, he was thinking of Kropotkin, not of the other radical and incendiary branches of the anarchism movement. But although anarchism retained a substantial appeal for him, Mao had by no means abandoned liberalism. Indeed, in his opening statement in the *Xiang River Review*, he took his stand squarely with parliamentarism, pragmatism, and a bloodless revolution to be conducted by investigating and then exposing the "facts." In these respects, Mao was inspired less by Li than by Hu Shi and Deweyism.* In short, Mao was not yet wedded to any single ideological line. Furthermore, he did not seem uncomfortable with his eclecticism, partly because he made no sharp distinction between the anarchism of Kropotkin and the liberalism of Dewey, but saw both as based on principles of humanism and freedom and as essentially nonviolent in method. To this important matter, we shall return.

*During the time he was editing the *Xiang River Review*, Mao also organized a Society for the Study of Problems (Wenti Yanjiu Hui), and sent its charter to individuals and groups throughout China. (See *Makesizhuyi yanjiu cankao ziliao* (*MYCZ*), February 1981, pp. 23–26.) In the charter, 140 specific problems were outlined as worthy of study. This new organization, it should be noted, was created by Mao at precisely the same time that Hu Shi was engaged in debate with Li Dazhao in *Meizhou pinglun* over the issue of whether one should engage in concrete research on specific problems or advance broad, generalized theories ("isms"). Li Rui argues that Mao really stood on Li's side in this argument, because he took the position that problems and "isms" are inseparable (Li, *The Early Revolutionary Activities*, p. 117). But this view is untenable. Mao could not possibly have chosen the name he did for his organization without realizing its implications. In fact, he was seeking to put Hu Shi's views (and Dewey's) into action. It was not surprising, therefore, that *Meizhou pinglun*, now under the editorship of Hu, praised the *Xiang River Review* for its contributions to Chinese politics.

Third, Mao evaluated events in the West and in China very differently. When discussing the West, Mao saw capitalism as evil incarnate, spreading oppression and misery in its wake. Only the aroused Western masses obtained his approval, and he assessed the United States—which some of his compatriots considered the most advanced nation in the world—as the worst example of man's inhumanity to man, as a country where monopolies and trusts were relentlessly crushing the common people. Despite his sympathy for Wilson, therefore, Mao came closest to a doctrine of class struggle when he was analyzing the West; in this he resembled Liang Qichao before him. When he turned to China, however, he had no complaints against the Chinese bourgeoisie. On the contrary, he praised their organizational efforts and saw them as a part of "the masses," particularly in their fight against foreign dominance. Indeed, Mao's early exposition of China's problems was in no sense based on a class analysis. He described the people as pitted against the politicians, the militarists, and the bureaucrats. But he did not dwell extensively upon injustices suffered by peasants or workers. He devoted greater attention to the injustices suffered by students, women, and primary-school teachers. Such views, it should be emphasized, had less in common with Marxism than with other "progressive" or "revolutionary" writings of the period. In a sense, Mao and some of his contemporaries unconsciously anticipated the Leninist strategy of using the bourgeoisie as an essential force in the completion of the nationalist-democratic revolution. At this time, however, their formulations had none of the theoretical apparatus necessary to make them compatible with Marxism-Leninism.*

Fourth, Mao was intensely committed to matters of organization. His proposal for creating small unions and then bringing them into a larger federation was doubtless drawn from his own organizational work with the Hunan Student Union and the more broadly based Hunan Union of All Circles. Indeed, the Union of All Circles, officially established on July 9, 1919, resembled quite closely the sort of provincial-level federation of diverse occupations and social categories that Mao was expounding. Thus, his personal activities meshed well with the guidance offered him by such sources as *Meizhou pinglun*. But it was characteristic of Mao to be concerned about identifying the particular types of workers or occupational groups that might be available for organizational purposes—a matter of "detail" not likely to have troubled such Beida intellectuals as Li.

Fifth, and finally, Mao was above all a Chinese nationalist. He was determined to believe that the Chinese were truly a great people (perhaps *the* greatest people), and that the Chinese nation was capable of enjoying a brighter future than any other country in the world. He saw no reason why the Chinese people, once they were mobilized, could not achieve a compre-

* An article from the May 4, 1919, issue of *Meizhou pinglun*, however, went further than any essay we have seen in foreshadowing Leninist themes while still retaining a uniquely Chinese perspective. Its author, Yi Hu, argued that the Chinese bourgeoisie could not lead the Chinese democratic revolution, and so that task had to fall to the workers and peasants; their principal targets had to be the literati and officials who had survived the Revolution of 1911, sometimes acting as aristocrats, sometimes as bourgeoisie. Why the workers and peasants? Because, the author responded, all others want to be literati-officials themselves. After the old-style bourgeois revolution has been completed, he continued, China will have its social revolution—which will be much easier to accomplish than in Russia "because we do not have big capitalists" (Yi Hu, "The Crimes of the Chinese Literati and Official Class," *Meizhou pinglun*, May 4, 1919, p. 20).

hensive unity more quickly and thoroughly than anyone else, despite all their current deficiencies. As we have seen, despair and hope, shame and pride were contrapuntal themes in many of the student-intellectual writings of this era. In individuals like Mao, pride won out in the end, however dark the immediate horizon might seem. The inner confidence of belonging to a superior civilization and a supremely talented people could not be eradicated.

Another subject of particular interest discussed in the *Xiang River Review* was educational reform in China. The organization of a new institute in Changsha gave Mao the opportunity to comment further on Chinese educational trends, past and present.[52] Paying homage to the reform efforts of Tan Sitong, another one of Mao's first role models, and to the activities of "such famous scholars as Liang Qichao and Mai Menghua" in running the Changsha School of Current Affairs, Mao defined the "dominant idea" of the earlier period as one of "conceit"—a belief that China should master Western methods only in order to take revenge in kind, to defeat imperialism with its own weapons. This attitude toward acquiring knowledge was unrealistic, and it prevented both students and teachers from undertaking the practical studies needed to get at the facts. China was supposed to be superior to the West in ethics, and the West was supposed to excel only at making military weapons, and anyone who failed to acknowledge these "facts" was accused of being "pro-Western," a stigma that would remain for life.

Now twenty years had passed, reported Mao, and the situation had changed considerably, but it was still not possible to replace the old values and the old learning completely. Why? The primary problem was the lack of a central pattern of thought, a unifying theme. This in turn was due to the absence of a real institute or university in Hunan. Also, too few people went abroad for study in the West, and among those who did, many returned only to plunge into making money, often in a field unrelated to their special knowledge. Those who had gone to Japan, Mao continued, had been drawn into the political movement led by Huang Xing (not Sun), and given the confused state of political developments, they had found little time for study. Meanwhile, since the 1911 Revolution, most schoolteachers had been of low quality.

Now there were currently some pioneers in the reform movement nationally, covering a wide range of fields from politics to religion and art, continued Mao. Who were the leaders? Mao mentioned five: Cai Yuanpei, Jiang Kanghu, Wu Jingheng, Liu Shifu, and Chen Duxiu.[53] This was a strange list. Li Dazhao, Sun Yat-sen, and Hu Shi were not included; Wu (better known as Wu Zhihui) and Liu were prominent anarchists; Cai had also once held strong anarchist views; Jiang had been one of the earliest public exponents of socialism, though he was currently in bad repute. One cannot escape the impression that in compiling this list Mao revealed certain personal feelings along with his political proclivities. There are several indirect indications that he did not think highly of Sun Yat-sen at this point, either as a political leader or as a reformer. The omission of Li Dazhao is more surprising, since Mao owed so much to Li's ideas and certainly Li was in the forefront of the "progressive" movement. Perhaps, as we suggested earlier, Mao was unhappy that Li, an enormously busy man, had not included him in his circle of privileged students during Mao's brief stay in

Beijing. He may have held a similar resentment against Hu Shi, who had a reputation for being curt with students and rather arrogant. In any case, Mao's current eclecticism was indicated by the persons he did list. It was clear, of course, that he did not belong to the ranks of the neo-traditionalists, whose movement—now being led by Liang Qichao, Liang Shuming, and Zhang Junmai—was gaining momentum in certain quarters. But he did express respect for such diverse individuals as Jiang Kanghu, Cai Yuanpei, Chen Duxiu, and John Dewey, and for the Russian Revolution as well. When he wrote that no "central pattern of thought" had emerged in China, he might have been acknowledging his own uncertainties.

Mao had concluded his article on the new Changsha Institute with an attack on Confucianism and praise for the fact that the institute was dedicated to disseminating the latest ideas and literary achievements. English classes would help those who wanted to read English books so as to go directly to the source of Western learning. And lectures on such subjects as the Wrong View of Life and Death in China, How to Conduct Oneself, Education and the Ordinary Chinese, and the Adoption of Dewey's Pedagogy were all very much to the point—good subjects for discussion. Moreover, Mao added, the lectures and discussions should be open to the public so that everyone could come and listen.

The latter issues of *Xiang River Review* contained several letters from Hunanese work-study students living in France. The first letter published, dated May 17, was written by a student who had just arrived. On the whole, it was cheerful in tone, though the writer stressed the need to be extremely careful with one's money.[54] A more interesting letter, also written by a recent arrival, commented on the problem of educating the Chinese laborers who had come to France during the war.[55] We had intended to set up a school for them, the correspondent wrote, but the project had thus far failed. The students would continue in the effort, but those interested in helping workers should know the characteristics of these laborers: they were old and had deep prejudices; some were completely illiterate; most were not interested in learning or curious about world affairs; most spent their free time gambling and visiting whorehouses, and so night schools were difficult to establish. This evaluation left little grounds for optimism.

Toward an Independent Hunan

When the *Xiang River Review* was suppressed in early August of 1919, Mao took up the editorship of the journal *Xin Hunan* (New Hunan), another weekly run by students, commencing with its seventh issue. He announced that he intended to introduce "social criticism, ideological reconstruction, recent learning, and the discussion of problems."[56] But after its tenth issue, *Xin Hunan* was also closed, and Mao found an outlet for his views in the Changsha newspaper *Dagong bao*. Among his articles were some stirring pieces in support of women's rights, several of them occasioned by the suicide of an unwilling bride.[57]

As the fall began, Mao plunged into the movement to oust Zhang Jingyao, the Anfu faction militarist whose troops controlled a portion of the province and who had been appointed military governor by Duan. In December a general strike of Changsha students in vocational middle and higher schools was proclaimed. Precisely what role Mao played in this strike is unclear, but Li Rui records that he convened a meeting of the New People's Study Association and other organizations to discuss further measures in the movement to oust Zhang.[58]

In the same month a revealing article by Mao was published in the *Hunan jiaoyu yuekan* (Hunan Educational Monthly) entitled "The Work of a Student." In it Mao spoke of an earlier plan he had devised to establish a work-study program for Hunan, to be located on Mount Yuelun. When he had returned to the province in April, Mao wrote, he had conceived of the idea of establishing a "new village," with a school devoted to the general study of socialism and dedicated to the goal of creating a new educational program, a new family structure, and a new society. He then set forth in detail the regimen he had in mind. Each day was to be divided into five parts: sleep for eight hours, and four hours each for recreation, self-directed study, lectures, and work. Work was to consist of agricultural labor—raising vegetables, cultivating crops, and caring for domestic animals. All would be aimed at production.

At this point, Mao reiterated precisely the theme set forth by Li Dazhao in his articles entitled "Youth and the Rural Villages," published in *Chen bao* (Morning News) in February 1919. After graduation, students loved to stay in the city and hated the thought of returning to the countryside. But if they would go to the villages, assist in the political education of the peasantry, and participate in elections there, genuine representative politics could take root.[59]

The purpose of education, Mao asserted, was to train an individual to be independent and have a sound personality, but the Chinese family and society sought to sacrifice the individual for the whole. Hence family and society had to be restructured in order to build a new culture and a new life. In addition to the new education, his model village would ultimately include public nurseries, facilities for the poor, banks, farms, industries, cooperatives, and parks and museums.

The symbol of political revolution, Mao continued, was France; the symbol of social revolution was Russia. Paris was a model of beauty, Berlin of cleanliness. But his goal for China was more modest. Borrowing again from Li's essays, he wrote that in order to spread socialism, Russian youth had gone to the countryside to live with the peasants. He then added that the new village movement had also appealed to Japanese youth, and that the work-study movement was taking hold in such different places as the Philippines, the United States, and France. In concluding, Mao reverted to his central theme: work in the countryside could help the student build a new and productive life, both physically and spiritually.

It is fascinating to realize that young Mao's first serious attention to the issue of tutoring the peasantry, and the role of the student in this process, derived so fully from Li Dazhao's thinking on this same issue, expressed some eight or nine months earlier. And one cannot help seeing in Mao's unrealized utopian plans an image of monumental things to come, including the commune system and the "down to the countryside movement" of later years.

Meanwhile, the Hunan student activists continued their campaign to oust Zhang Jingyao, with Mao playing an important role. A decision was made to send delegations to various centers in China to mobilize support. Wu Peifu, the progressive military leader sympathetic to the Hunanese cause, was also asked for assistance. Mao left with fellow delegates in January 1920 for Hankou, and in February he reached Beijing—his second visit to the capital. He stayed until April, reading works dealing with socialism and Marxism, and developing "especially close ties" with Li Dazhao and Deng Zhongxia.* He was reported to be involved in the decision to set up an organization "along the lines of a self-study university" to explore Marxism-Leninism thoroughly. (Possibly this was the Society for the Study of Marxism, which was established shortly thereafter.) In his letters to Changsha comrades he also suggested the desirability of organizing a group to travel to the Soviet Union.**

In April he went to Shanghai. There he met with certain Xinmin Xuehui members who were preparing to leave for France, and he also had contacts with Chen Duxiu, who was then in the process of organizing the Communist group with Voitinskii's assistance. Later, Mao was to say that Chen's influence on him was very great at this point, and that they discussed, among other things, the Hunan self-government movement that was then being mounted.† Mao was able to return safely to Hunan in the summer, for Zhang Jingyao's forces had been driven out of the province in late June by Wu Peifu. Shortly thereafter, he plunged into political activities of several types, but gave his greatest attention to the drive for a self-governing Hunan.

Just as Mao returned to Hunan, the Hunan Gaizao Cucheng Hui (Association for the Promotion of Hunan Reconstruction) was formed. Its basic objectives were not self-evident, because different participants had somewhat different goals in mind. The new association's declaration, published on July 6, 1920, began with the assertion that "the militarists of North and South have successfully taken advantage of the situation to persecute us, to occupy Hunan as their own territory and tie up the people's wealth in their sacks." It was therefore essential to abolish rule by militarists and establish the rule of the people. By Hunanese self-determination, the document's authors continued, we do not mean tribalism or localism; we simply mean that the people of Hunan should take responsibility for their own development. The declaration ended with praise for Tan Yankai (currently governor) and Zhao Yanwu (another Hunan military commander). They were hailed as local heroes for their role in expelling Zhang Jingyao, and they were urged never again to "invite the tiger" into the house, and to adhere to democracy, to cleanse themselves of militarist, bureaucratic, and gentry airs, and to take their lead from the opinion of the thirty million Hunanese citizens.[60]

* Mao told Edgar Snow that during this period he read *The Communist Manifesto*, Kautsky's *Class Struggle*, and Thomas Kirkup's *History of Socialism* (Snow, *Red Star*, p. 158). Wakeman, in *History and Will*, pp. 216–219, gives an analysis of Kirkup's survey.

** Mao wrote several letters to Xinmin Xuehui colleagues while he was in Beijing. (These letters, taken from *Xinmin Xuehui huiyuan tongxin ji*, vol. 1, are reprinted in *MYCZ*, February 1981, pp. 22–25.) His plan for going to Russia was mentioned in his letter to Dao Yi dated February 1920. In a second letter to Zhou Shizhao, dated March 14, Mao mentioned having a conversation with Hu Shi and then discoursed briefly on the two mainstreams in world civilization, the Eastern and the Western—without showing a trace of Marxist influence. There followed this assertion: "Frankly, I do not have clear ideas regarding a theory or set of basic principles." At this point, Mao was still searching for an ideology or coherent set of political beliefs.

† Zhang Guotao, who arrived in Shanghai in mid-July 1920, after Mao had returned to Hunan, has written: "Chen was greatly impressed by Mao's talent; he was going to write to Mao to explain his plans, seek his endorsement, and ask him to organize a [Communist] nucleus in Hunan" (Chang Kuo-t'ao, *The Rise of the Communist Party* 1:105).

There was a strong link between the Hunan self-government movement of this period and earlier proposals dating from the first decade of the century, including those developed within Sun Yat-sen's revolutionary movement. At various points, student-intellectual writers in the journals published in Tokyo and elsewhere had suggested that their particular province should pioneer in revolutionary change and self-government, thereby serving as a model for other provinces. It is difficult to discern the extent to which these themes reflected a primary desire for independence—a separatist movement—and the degree to which they reflected the feeling that establishing "model provinces" was the most practical way to generate a new China, building the larger edifice step by step. Probably the mix of the two sentiments varied from individual to individual and depended also upon the immediate circumstances, namely, the degree of order or chaos traceable to the larger entity known as China.

Certainly, in the case of Sun Yat-sen and his close followers, it was the second view that prevailed. Sun's movement had embraced the idea that several developmental stages would follow the revolution. In the first, there would be martial law and military rule; in the second, local self-government would develop, and presumably be accompanied by a process of "demilitarization." When this second stage was under way (or completed) in a sufficient number of provinces, China as a whole could proceed to constitutional democratic government.

What were Mao's views on Hunanese self-determination at this point? In June, even before he had returned to Changsha, Mao had written some articles for the Shanghai newspaper *Shishi xinbao* (Daily News) in which he expressed his opinions in a preliminary way.[61] The main thrust of these articles was that while the ouster of Zhang Jingyao was critical, Hunan's citizens should take the further step of abolishing the military governorship, getting rid of the provincial military forces, reconstructing education, and developing an industrial base. The goal was to be democracy for Hunan, but that would take at least twenty years. The preparations just listed, however, should be undertaken now. If Hunan were first, other provinces could follow.

At the beginning of September, after a stay of three weeks in his native village, Mao returned to Changsha and immediately plunged into the self-determination movement. Fortunately, we now have two sources for his writings of this period, and we can analyze his views with reasonable accuracy.[62] By the fall of 1920 two issues faced the movement: how should self-government for Hunan be organized and led, and to what extent should Hunan be truly independent?

In addressing the first issue, Governor Tan Yankai had taken the lead by appointing a small group of gentry officials to recommend legislation that would establish self-government. However, individuals like Long Jiangong, then chief editor of the Changsha *Dagong bao*, strongly objected to this procedure, arguing that Hunan's future ought not to be determined by a small group of officials. They insisted that a Hunan People's Congress or Constitutional Conference should be convened, based on the widest possible representation.

In confronting the second issue, Wang Wuwei and others had made it clear that they did not want to see self-government used to promote provincial separatism. Hunan should not apply its own "Monroe Doctrine," Wang asserted, meaning a policy of seeking to exclude all non-Hunanese. There was a natural evolution in politics from tribalism to nationhood, and from nationhood to universal order. One must not use self-government to destroy nationhood and thereby sink back into tribalism, "even though certain Hunanese persist in this attitude."[63]

One of Wang's targets was Long, who introduced the term "Monroeism" into the debate, and another was Mao, whose first article for *Dagong bao* on this issue, published on September 6, was entitled "Absolutely Favoring 'Hunan Monroeism.'"[64] Mao began by strongly endorsing Long's plea for popular participation in the self-government movement. Then, accepting Long's definition of "Monroeism" as not interfering in other people's business and not allowing them to interfere in ours, Mao acknowledged that in the past the Hunanese had violated this precept—and that as a consequence they had been conquered three times in the past nine years. "Monroeism," he wrote, was entirely appropriate and favored by a clear majority of Hunanese, but since the minority that opposed it might manipulate the results of any election, the ballot boxes should be carefully guarded.

Ten days later, Mao began a series of articles that argued for an interpretation of self-government which amounted to *temporary independence*. His first article, published on September 13, was entitled "The Fundamental Issue Relating to the Problem of Hunan Reconstruction—A Hunan Republic."[65] He began by boldly stating that he was opposed to a "Great Republic of China," but favored a "Republic of Hunan." It was foolish, he wrote, to say that nations in the future must be big. Such a view had led to an expanding imperialism and the suppression of weak states. Certain Western nations had achieved an ephemeral success, but China had been denied even this. Han relations with the national minorities were terrible. Chaos reigned in the eighteen provinces: there were three governments and three national assemblies and more than twenty military governors. The common people were being killed daily, and China's foreign debt was huge. The Chinese government might be called a republic, but few Chinese knew what a republic was; at least 390 million of China's 400 million people were illiterate. The Chinese government had proven incapable of effectively operating railways, postal services, or shipping. Hunan, like various other provinces, had been repeatedly conquered by others. All this, Mao wrote, was the crime of empire—the crime of the fallacy that nations must be big.[66] Because a national constitution for China could not be achieved for many years to come, each province should begin work now to achieve self-government. "Since there are currently twenty-two provinces, three special districts, and two autonomous regions, making a total of twenty-seven units, China would benefit from splitting into twenty-seven nations."[67] If the Hunanese people did not have the determination and courage to establish Hunan as an independent nation, there was absolutely no hope.

The following day, Mao continued his exposition in an essay entitled "Hunan Has Been Troubled by China, as Proven by History and the Current Situation."[68] After a detailed recital of the wrongs suffered by Hunan at the hands of the imperialists, and the recent invasions, Mao drew the basic lesson: when a small entity obeys a big entity—in this case, when Hunan takes orders on everything from the center—only bad results follow. If Hunan could have achieved independence in 1907, a new Hunan could have been created, and that would also have been true after 1911. "There is no government in China," Mao asserted; "all is chaos," and this situation would last for seven or eight years, with further splits and greater chaos occurring. The militarists would become more violent, and politics would become more corrupt. All this could be changed only by a movement of the people of each province to overthrow the militarists and bureaucrats and to replace them with systems of popular self-government. The Hunanese would struggle for self-government. The citizens of Guangdong and Sichuan would do the same. "Then, after another ten or twenty years, there would be another uprising like that of the Blue Turban Army, and that would produce a general revolution."[69] With this prescient remark, Mao moved toward his conclusion and ended on an optimistic note: "Hunanese, our mission is truly important, our chances for success very bright. We must strive to found a Republic of Hunan with new ideals and a new life, making Hunan the first of twenty-seven nations."

From these writings it is easy to see why Wang could criticize Mao as a supporter of "tribalism" and "Monroeism." Given the intensely nationalist sentiments of an all-China nature which Mao had advanced only a few months earlier, the strong language and new themes are startling. But despite this apparently sharp turn from views he had expressed in the previous year, in none of his writings did Mao abandon the goal of eventually achieving a *federated, democratic* China.*

Unquestionably, Mao, like many others, was now being influenced by the accelerating chaos into which China was falling and by the seeming hopelessness of any near-term solutions at the national level. It is also quite possible, however, that he was at least equally influenced by the new views on autonomy, nationalism, and internationalism emanating from the Soviet Union. The Soviet system was being heralded by its leaders as one which linked self-governing states together in a federation, from which they could secede if they chose, and which had the ultimate goal of replacing national boundaries with a truly international political order. Such a theme was being advanced in China in more subdued form by Li and Chen, as we noted earlier. Yet it is curious that Mao would evoke the imagery of "Monroeism" and, with his colleagues, would assemble such august liberals as Cai and John Dewey to support the self-government movement.** It would appear that uncertainties and confusion in Mao's political views lingered on.

It is striking that only a decade later Mao was deeply involved in the

* In an article entitled "Total Autonomy versus Half Autonomy," published in *Dagong bao* on October 3, 1920, Mao summarized his position on the question of nationhood. Criticizing the proposal for organizing an All-China Federation, Mao argued that there was, at this point, nothing with which to unite; that was why Hunanese should aim at constructing a fully autonomous state—which, after all, had been the procedure followed in the United States and Germany prior to federation. After many independent states had been formed, federation would be natural, but he doubted whether that could be accomplished within twenty years. He was therefore opposed to the concept of a national (All-China) assembly or a national constitution, and also to North-South negotiations. There should be a separation between the South and the North, he argued, and beyond that, each province should be autonomous (*MYCZ*, pp. 20–21. See also an article of October 7, 1920, entitled "A Warning to the Three Hundred Thousand People of Changsha Concerning Hunan Autonomy," ibid., p. 21).

** On November 1, 1920, a major conference on constitutionalism and self-government was held in Changsha. In addition to Cai Yuanpei and John Dewey, a broad array of distinguished Chinese intellectuals and journalists participated; among them were Wu Zhihui, Zhou Zhenlin, and Bao Daoping. (See Wang Wuwei, *Hunan zizhi*, pp. 69–71, and McDonald, *The Urban Origins*, pp. 46–47.)

Jiangxi Soviet Republic, an attempt to create a wholly independent government that could serve as a model for other regions, and ultimately for all of China. The Chinese Communists, moreover, were to debate the tactics and strategy of revolution at great length, focusing on such questions as whether the movement could afford to shift its main base of operations from urban centers to rural areas, and whether it should concentrate on building a successful movement in one or two provinces, waiting until times were more propitious to project it on a national scale. As it turned out, of course, these debates were settled by the objective circumstances in which they found themselves.

In any case, on the eve of the establishment of the Chinese Communist Party, Mao was already involved in the paradox that was to run through his life and the lives of others of his faith. He was dedicated to the cultivation of the individual, to local self-government, and to the type of populism that he equated with democracy and socialism. Yet he was also dedicated to *organized* man, to collective man, in forms that would ultimately sustain a unified, powerful China; and organization on this scale was certain to be centralized, bureaucratized, and autocratic, no matter what links between localities and the center were devised.

The Seeds of Communism

Despite his involvement in the Hunan self-government movement, Mao found time to engage in a number of other political activities after his return to Changsha in September 1920. In these activities, all aimed at the creation of a socialist movement in his province, he was frequently guided by prior developments in Shanghai and Beijing. It will be recalled that he had been in Beijing as recently as April and had left Shanghai only in early July. He was thus fully aware of the political activities that were taking place in these two cities under the aegis of Li and Chen.

Mao's first step in the direction of creating a Hunan Communist group was to open a Cultural Book Society in September, shortly after his return to Changsha. This was a useful strategy, of course, because it provided a means of obtaining and disseminating socialist literature, thereby building through propaganda the necessary base for later political activities.* In the same month, Mao had become principal of the primary school attached to the First Normal School, a post that gave him a regular income and further access to Changsha's educational circles. With a few close friends, he had also created the Eluosi Yanjiu Hui (Society for the Study of Russia). At a meeting on September 16, Jiang Yanhong was made chairman, Mao secretary, and Peng Huang treasurer. Four resolutions were passed, which approved plans for "independent study" by the members; the collection of materials pertaining to Russia; the publication of certain works; and preparations for trips to the Soviet Union, as well as a request that Russians in Shanghai come to Changsha to teach the Russian language.[70]

The previous month, in August, the Socialist Youth League had been set

*The Cultural Book Store formally opened in September with a selection of approximately 200 books, 40 magazines, and 3 newspapers—which was all Mao could do, given the meager finances available to him. Interestingly, however, Mao had obtained support from several prominent educators in Changsha, and even from the Chamber of Commerce, and no less a personage than Governor Tan was asked to provide the calligraphy for the society's sign (Li Rui, *The Early Revolutionary Activities*, pp. 152–153).

up in Shanghai. Mao did not receive its constitution and bylaws until October, but when he did he immediately began to canvass the key schools for members, and a Changsha branch of the League was soon established with thirty-eight initial recruits. He had also begun to renew his interest in the labor movement. A union-organizing effort spearheaded by two young anarchists, Huang Ai and Pang Renquan, was already under way, and it would be some time before the Communists were able to take the lead in this field. But in an article published in December 1920, Mao indicated that he and his colleagues were involved in organizing the Hunan working class.

As we have emphasized, Mao's activities on behalf of the embryonic Communist movement were stimulated by Chen and Li, especially Chen. Shanghai had become the fountainhead of Chinese Communism, and when *Gongchandang* began to be published in November, another major source of information and instruction for the Changsha converts became available. At the same time, one can hardly overestimate the influence on Mao that came from another source—his old schoolmates and colleagues now in France, particularly Cai Hesen. Fortunately, some of the letters exchanged between Mao and Cai have been preserved. We do not have the letters Mao wrote to Xiao Xisheng on April 1 and 4, 1920, while he was still out of Hunan, but we can infer their principal contents from the later replies by Cai, Xiao, and others. Mao had indicated that he intended to return to Changsha, teach primary school, and devote his spare time to organizing a work-study and mutual-aid association, strengthening the Xinmin Xuehui, and preparing for study in Russia.

In his first letter to Mao, dated May 28, 1920, Cai commended Mao for his plans and then said that since he had been in France for only five months, he was still "deaf and dumb" in the French language—but not blind, because with the aid of a dictionary, he was gaining ground in reading French newspapers.[71] Through them he was beginning to see the course of Western political developments, including the momentous happenings in Germany. He planned to stay in France for five years, devoting his first year to learning the French language and acquiring an understanding of the Socialist Party, syndicalism, and the international Communist movement.*

In August, Mao received a second letter from France, this one written by Xiao.[72] In it Xiao reported on the meeting that had been held at Montargis, near Paris, between July 5 and 10. Fourteen persons had attended, most of them relatives or old friends and original members of the Xinmin Xuehui. Part of the time had been devoted to assessing the personal strengths and weaknesses of those in attendance (and some absentees), in an effort to help each person improve his or her character. The more important activity, however, had been a discussion about whether to organize a Communist party. Cai had proposed that such a party be organized, based on the principle of the dictatorship of the proletariat and committed to reforming both China and the world simultaneously. Xiao, arguing that the happiness of the majority should not be sought at the sacrifice of the minority, argued for another route: the projection of a more gradual, milder revolution through

*Cai also wrote that he had borrowed funds from the Sino-French Association and would continue to do so for several months before going to work. Costs were low, he reported, and there were about a thousand work-study students in France, but "good members are in a minority." It would be premature to try to organize them now, or to open a branch of the Xinmin Xuehui, he concluded.

education, using syndicates and cooperatives as primary instruments. Cai favored Marx's way, Xiao espoused the way of Proudhon, and others had their own ideas.

Although there were differences of opinion on basic principles, it was agreed that the new party should be kept secret; and that if it proved necessary, in order to preserve its secrecy the party should come into being as a separate entity, with Xinmin Xuehui members joining it, assuming they agreed. But too many indifferent individuals should not be invited, lest the movement be diluted. In recruiting members, the goal should be one thousand (or at least five hundred) individuals familiar with foreign languages; another one thousand teachers, especially primary-school instructors; at least one thousand workers, peasants, and "some businessmen." A budget of $100,000 was to be used for publications, school activities, and other associational expenses.

Activities in China should be concentrated in Changsha and Shanghai; recruiters should be sent to Japan, Germany, England, and the United States, and intensive recruiting should be undertaken in France. In France, special attention should be devoted to the institution now being established at Lyon especially for Chinese students, and to expanding the work-study clubs. As for Russia, Mao and He (He Shuhen) should go, and some key people should also be sent to southern Asia. Cai, reported Xiao, was making great progress in reading French; and besides having a rough understanding of the political situation, he had collected several hundred books and pamphlets from various political parties. The responsibility for reading these had been distributed among the members. Cai was to read the *Communist Party Monthly* and a "Commentary on Events in Russia." Others would read publications from the Second and the Third International, works on women's rights, cooperatives, social policies, and so on.

The primary task, Xiao wrote, was to expand what had been a small elitist study group into a dynamic organization committed to action as well as study. Most Xinmin Xuehui members had been primary-school teachers and therefore had good connections with China's educated class; the association also had many women comrades, and was unique in this respect. But it had been weak and immature organizationally, and a majority of its members had been relatively passive. This had to be changed.

Xiao had started his letter in late July and completed it in early August, according to his final words. It must have reached Mao at about the same time as a second letter from Cai dated August 13, which was a long account of exceptional interest.[73] Cai opened by saying that because the situation in Hunan was peaceful, he assumed that Mao had returned to the province. Then, after mentioning the meeting held at Montargis the previous month, he began to discuss "the situation in the world revolutionary movement," and indicated immediately what he considered the key factor: the *one* place where the proletarian revolution had succeeded was Russia. It had failed in Central Europe and the Balkans, and the struggle that lay ahead would be directed against "the five powers," presumably the United States, Great Britain, France, Italy, and Japan.

Cai then asserted that once the concept of class had been realized, the colonies and oppressed nations, including China, would be led to Bolshevism. There were four powerful weapons for a proletarian revolution, he said: first, the party, which had to be led by a vanguard; second, a strong revolutionary army and impregnable revolutionary mass organizations, to which would later be added revolutionary economic units of production; third, economic organizations in the form of cooperatives structured for revolution, which would later become consumer organizations; fourth, political organizations in the form of soviets (councils), to be created after the proletarian revolution.

Cai went on to discuss methods whereby the global revolution could be advanced. He said the international Communist Party with its headquarters in Russia was the heart of the new international movement, and that international unionism was a promising means of advancing the revolution, citing the pledge of the international miners' union to order a strike in France and Great Britain if the Allies attacked Russia.

These themes, Cai said, together with conditions in the Soviet Union after the revolution, had been the subject of his recent research. He hoped to finish his writing by the end of the year, but his conclusions were already prepared. "I have found that socialism is really the prescription for the world, even for China." The socialist mission was to destroy the capitalist economic system, using class warfare and a proletarian dictatorship. Briefly put, class warfare was a political struggle, aimed at destroying such middle-class weapons as parliament and in their place erecting instruments for the proletariat in the form of soviets, organs in which only the working class could participate—hence the concept of a proletarian dictatorship.

There were two reasons why the nonpropertied class had to exercise dictatorship, Cai wrote. First, the economic system could not be reformed so long as property belonged to the bourgeois rather than to society as a whole. Second, unless the proletarian class controlled political power, the revolution could not be protected, and the defeated class would rise again. Thus, continued Cai, I do not think that anarchism is feasible at present. The contest is between two classes—the proletariat and the bourgeoisie—and if in the aftermath of the revolution the proletariat establishes a firm dictatorship, no one can defeat it, as the case of Russia demonstrates.

At this point, Cai expressed the strong conviction that a renovation of China required the application of socialism, and he outlined the need for what he called "the four powerful instruments." First, we should organize a Chinese Communist Party, he asserted, because it is the initiator, the propagandist, the vanguard, and the fighting front of the revolutionary movement. And it should be organized now. I predict, he went on, that China will have a February Revolution and a Kerensky type of government within three to five years, and it will be headed by an old militarist, politician, or businessman. Your task, he told Mao, is to prepare for China's October Revolution.

In order to lay the foundations for a Chinese Communist Party, Cai said, some comrades should go to work in capitalist factories, whereas others should enter governmental institutions and become legislators in parliament, thereby participating in the current organs of the middle class. I learned this method, Cai reported, from the Bolsheviks. This was what they did after the February Revolution; even Lenin participated in the Kerensky government. This was why the October Revolution succeeded.

Cai then reported on his own plans. I am organizing a group that will go to work in Russia within two years, he wrote, and through the members of various progressive organizations, I intend to attract 10,000 youth to work there permanently. If we can obtain agreement, Cai continued, we will form a Chinese Communist party here. Then he recounted for Mao the formation of the Third International in Moscow in March 1919 and urged that someone be sent to Japan, since cooperation between the Chinese and the Japanese proletariat would guarantee revolutionary success. But "everything depends upon Russia," he wrote. Russia could keep Japan from interfering in the Chinese revolution, just as she had kept Poland from interfering in Russia.

Cai ended his long letter with an assessment of the Chinese scene. If China took the Russian Revolution as a model, the antirevolutionary forces would be larger than they had been in Russia, because although there were fewer capitalists and landowners in China, there were more people who had between one hundred and two hundred thousand dollars. I do not agree, Cai continued, that there are no classes in China. Workers and peasants have no knowledge at all, but once they have achieved class consciousness, the political atmosphere in China will be as favorable as it has been in Europe. In Russia, he noted, there were only 10,000 Communists at the time of the October Revolution, whereas now there are 600,000. The organization of a Chinese Communist Party should take place in secret, and "rascals"—industrialists and the bourgeoisie—should be excluded. In closing, Cai urged Mao to remember two things: that the dictatorship of the proletariat is essential, and that the international class movement cannot be based on patriotism (nationalism).

A second long letter from Cai followed, dated September 16.[74] He began by discussing the basic ideological division in the modern world—the division between idealism and materialism. Idealism was the instrument of the bourgeoisie; it was supported by such revisionists as Kautsky and Bernstein, and its "masterpieces" were bourgeois democracy and Wilson's Fourteen Points. The theoretical differences between idealism and materialism could be illustrated in concrete terms by comparing the Russian Revolution with the German social democratic movement. The Russian Revolution was based on materialism, took class struggle and the proletarian dictatorship as its methods, and made its goal that of creating a classless society and a true international order by abolishing the nation-state. The German social democrats had taken their stand with bourgeois democracy and revisionism, had agreed to ally with an imperialist government and the bourgeoisie, and to pursue the goal of a government of workers *and* capitalists. The result was the extension of capitalist politics, conflict, economic bankruptcy, and the suppression of the working class.

Cai then attacked anarcho-syndicalism, asserting that it was unable to go beyond dealing with such economic concerns as wages and prices. The Russian system, on the other hand, enabled the soviets to deal with *all* issues, including production and distribution, and was therefore the only system capable of providing real liberation for the workers. But in order for the system to work, the proletariat had to seize political power by exercising a class dictatorship.

There followed a long and detailed discussion of the Third International, which Cai describes as "the most thorough, the most meaningful international institution for the proletariat," in contrast to the League of Nations. After reviewing developments in the socialist-communist movement in several countries, he offered a careful description of what had caused the split between Bolsheviks and Mensheviks, how the current Russian Communist Party was organized, and how it functioned to govern the society. He discussed the recruitment, training, and responsibilities of party members, and emphasized the need for iron discipline, so that party members would serve as both leaders and models for the society at large. He described the organizational structure of the party and the functions of its various departments. In Russia, he said, there is absolutely no individual action, because all actions and policies are supervised and controlled by the Central Committee of the Communist Party. For this reason, the problems caused by parliaments in other countries do not arise under the Bolsheviks.

In the concluding section of his letter, Cai turned to China. China's problems cannot be resolved under current conditions, he argued, and so a socialist revolution is inevitable. If we do not organize for this revolution now, there will only be greater bloodshed and fear in the future. But with a strong, effective organization, this fate can be avoided. In organizing, the key is union with the people, and this requires a comprehensive understanding of the role of propaganda in all its forms. To propagandize effectively, one must first demand freedom of speech, the press, and association, along with the abolition of security regulations, police suppression, and other restraints on liberty. Party members must be chosen very carefully and then distributed to key parts of the society. A powerful organ should be openly published, and an open Communist Party bravely created. At the same time, it was important that certain parts of the party engage in underground work and thoroughly investigate conditions in each province. And it was also essential that there be a censorship division within the party, to make certain that erroneous theories or positions contradicting Communism were not published.

Cai ended by repeating that the key to Leninism was the necessity of a proletarian dictatorship. Leninists, he said, did not disagree with the anarchists and anarcho-syndicalists about ultimate goals. After Communism had been fully established, when classes had disappeared, there would be no further need for the state. But this goal could not be reached except through class struggle and a proletarian dictatorship. I think it is essential, he concluded, to follow the Russian method. Without political power, how can one reform society? Without a proletarian dictatorship, capitalism and war will reemerge, the working class will suffer greater disasters, the victorious bourgeoisie will acquire more indemnities and colonies, and the international power-structure represented by the League of Nations will become more consolidated. The next capitalist war will focus on China. Hence we must organize.

In responding to the letters of Cai and Xiao, Mao wrote several letters in which he set forth his thoughts very clearly. The first letter preserved is dated December 1, 1920, and is addressed to Cai Hesen, Xiao Xisheng, and other members of the Xinmin Xuehui.[75] Here Mao at last seemed to have reached a consistent political position: he would take his stand with internationalism against nationalism and with Marxism against anarchism. He began by noting with approval the July 1920 meeting at Montargis, adding that he agreed completely with the principle that the purpose of the new party should be to reform China *and* the world. Most individuals, he continued, had given up patriotism and now thought of themselves as members of humankind. They did not wish to restrict themselves to nation, family, or religion, but sought the common good—socialism. Truly international socialism had to be without a patriotic color. Thus, Mao said, we should help the Russians complete their socialist revolution, we should advance the cause of independence in southern Asia, and we should help Mongolia, Xinjiang, and Qinghai achieve autonomy.

As for the methods of achieving socialism, Mao wrote, the differences between Cai and Xiao were significant. He said that although he agreed theoretically with members Xiao and Li (Heseng), he could not regard their approach as practical. He then reported that he had recently attended Bertrand Russell's lecture in Changsha. Russell had stated that he favored communism but that he was opposed to a proletarian-peasant dictatorship. Mao said that in a spirited debate with friends afterwards, he had opposed Russell's position as being impractical, like the views of Xiao.

Mao then outlined the reasons why a peaceful, gradual revolution based on popular education would not succeed. His central theme was that education under the old order would always be in the hands of the capitalists. They had the money; the educational administrators would be their tools; the schools and the press would be controlled by them by means of their legislatures and governmental structures. Consequently, pursuing the educational route would only mean that "fewer and fewer individuals will believe in communism." In any case, despots, imperialists, and militarists never gave up power voluntarily. They had to be resisted by a greater force. In sum, the belief that one should avoid revolution or war, though splendid as a theory, would not work in practice. The Russian Revolution was the only practical way; all other methods were impossible. Curiously, Mao then sought to harness demography to his political position with a pessimistic Malthusian argument: the birth rate was going up and the death rate declining, and this would end in disaster for many people. Thus, although absolute freedom in the form of anarchism and democracy sounded good, it could not be realized.

The first letter ended with references to eighteen points raised by Cai and Xiao regarding the organization, membership, and activities of the new party. In general, Mao accepted all the suggestions that had been advanced—although in talking about the period of preparation for revolution, he said that five years should be added to Xiao's projection of readiness by 1936, making the date 1941. (It seems clear that few of these young men expected an early or easy victory of the revolution.) Mao also agreed that it was most important to focus the party's work on France, Russia, southern Asia, and Hunan (other parts of China were not mentioned).

Using Cai's guidelines, Mao was now prepared to push forward on the home front. A three-day meeting of the Changsha Xinmin Xuehui began on January 1, 1921.[76] Its purpose, as stipulated in the minutes, was to discuss three questions: What should be the goals of the association? What methods should it use to reach those goals? And when and how do we start? On the first day, Mao led off the discussion by reporting on the Montargis meeting, outlining the key themes and the central topic of debate. He remarked that the same division of opinion expressed at Montargis existed within China; Chen Duxiu, for example, favored revolutionary transformation, and Liang Qichao favored gradual reform. Mao made it clear that he stood with Chen. He also defended the idea of reforming both China *and* the world; to the suggestion that the world was too large to be a suitable target, he responded that one could not consider China in isolation. The method, morever, had to be the one adopted by Russia. All other approaches had failed.

On the second day, Mao urged that the new association be a secret one, but not inactive. He also reported on the methods adopted by the French group for self-improvement and study, and advocated a careful selection of topics for research and a time-schedule to ensure results. The session concluded with a discussion of qualifications for membership, registration procedures, and how the charter of the Xinmin Xuehui should be revised. It was decided that members should be "pure, sincere, and eager to improve their character"—qualities that would not have been uppermost in the minds of European radicals. Mao's position on all issues apparently carried the day among the small group convened. The vote on the basic goal was as follows: 10 votes for reforming China and the world; 5 votes for reforming the world; 2 votes for promoting the evolution of society through education (Xiao's position); and 2 abstentions (for a total of 19). With respect to method, Mao had advanced five alternatives for discussion: advocacy of social policies; social democracy; radical communism (Lenin's position); moderate communism (Russell's views); and anarchism. In the ensuing discussion Mao was not reticent about expressing his own position. To advocate social policies, he remarked, was not really a *method* of effecting changes; it was only a way of trying to solve specific problems. Social democracy used legislatures as an instrument of reform, but legislatures always protected the propertied class. Anarchism was impossible to achieve, as was moderate communism, which relied extensively on individual free will. Radical communism that depended on the peasants and the workers, however, could be achieved by a class dictatorship, and it was therefore the most suitable method. Again, Mao's position carried. Of those present, 12 voted to support Bolshevism, 2 voted for social democracy, 1 voted for moderate communism, and 3 abstained.[77] The third and final day of the conference was devoted to a discussion of organizational matters, including the methods of undertaking research and self-training.

At another associational meeting less than two weeks later, on January 16, there was a discussion of each individual's personal plans, and Mao's report is most interesting.[78] He began by saying that he regarded common sense as very important, and he intended to be practical about his plans until he reached thirty years of age (note his borrowing from Xiao). He also planned to make up his deficiencies in mathematics, physics, and chemistry. But his real interest was in philosophy and writing, and he hoped to study the techniques and theories of education. A year ago he had announced that he wanted to spend two years in Hunan and then go to Russia, and he was sticking to that plan. In the meantime, he intended to expand the Cultural Bookstore. He ended with a lament that it had proven very difficult to study and work at the same time, and the past half year had been wasted. From now on, he pledged, he would devote two hours a day to reading books and newspapers. Later in the meeting, Mao spoke in a more personal vein. The activities he enjoyed most were teaching and writing (as a journalist), and he would like to pursue one or the other as an occupation. But since it was hard to find such work, he thought he might turn to some kind of manual labor, such as weaving socks or making bread. Such work was easily learned and would enable one to make a living anywhere in the world. Besides, he favored the simple life and objected to luxury.[79]

Five days after this meeting, on January 21, Mao wrote a second, very short letter to Cai; in it he agreed that materialism was the philosophical foundation of the party and repeated his opposition to anarchism. The anarcho-syndicalists, he asserted, did not understand—or pretended not to understand—that there were no intrinsic differences between a national political organization and factory-level political organizations. Without acquiring *national* political power, Mao asserted, a revolution could not be undertaken, protected, and advanced. The ideas expressed in your letter, he told Cai, "were so correct that I did not object to a single word."[80]

This correspondence clarifies several matters of major importance. It shows that Mao had taken his stand with Marxism, not because he had gained a thorough understanding of Marxist or Marxist-Leninist theory (except as derived from Cai's descriptions), but because he had accepted the argument made by Cai (and others) that the Russians had discovered the only successful road to revolution, and that revolution was necessary for China and the world. In the process of reaching this position, Mao had discarded his earlier partial commitments to anarchism and liberalism; he had become convinced that the freedom and democracy they promised, however desirable in theoretical terms, were utopian dreams so far as China and the world were concerned. The need was for power to oppose power. It was necessary to forcefully remove the propertied class and establish a proletarian-peasant dictatorship, for only in that way could radical change be instituted and protected. Besides accepting Cai's central arguments on this matter, Mao had made an intellectual commitment to internationalism over nationalism. Patriotism, he had proclaimed, was passé. The revolutionary's commitment had to be a global one, directed toward all humankind.

It is apparent that Cai's letters had a great effect on Mao. Whatever guidance Mao may have been receiving from Chen, Cai's messages from France were a model of clarity and comprehensiveness, and raised all the points critical to a basic understanding of Leninism in theory and action: the class struggle; the proletarian dictatorship; socialist internationalism under the Third International; the defects of "bourgeois democracy," revisionism, and anarcho-syndicalism; and the operational character of the Russian party and state. In addition, they offered detailed instructions about how to create and develop a Communist Party in China—instructions that Mao later followed in full. Cai's letters were influential, not merely because they came from an old and trusted friend, but also because they came from a man who now had close contact with the latest currents of the "new socialism."

With Chen becoming active in Shanghai (complemented by Li in Beijing) and Cai prepared to lead the movement overseas, Mao now committed himself to the revolutionary cause with confidence and enthusiasm. A concatenation of events had made 1920 a year of decision for him—and he was not to turn back.

AN OVERVIEW

The personal traits and early careers of Chiang Kai-shek and Mao Zedong can tell us much about the larger issues confronting China in the early twentieth century. In virtually every sense, each was a child of the times, though born to certain advantages not available to the millions. Both had strength of character, were schooled to hardship and discipline, and possessed a fierce determination to prevail. Neither was especially attracted to money or luxurious living. What attracted them was power—the power to change the helpless and hopeless society in which they lived. And in their pursuit of power, they had similar advantages: their families had some resources to support upward mobility, and they grew up in regions that enabled conversance with the outside world.

Unquestionably, Mao had the more powerful mind and the greater intellectual curiosity. He was in contact with the higher Chinese intellectual circles of the times, and he was acquainted with the basic elements of liberalism, anarchism, and Marxism—the prevailing ideological currents flowing from the West. To a certain extent, moreover, Mao always aspired to be an intellectual, to be accepted as the equal of the men he admired—Chen Duxiu, Cai Yuanpei, and, more begrudgingly, Li Dazhao and Hu Shi. Chiang, on the other hand, clearly did not aspire to be an intellectual, nor did he have the requisite skills. He was a youth of few words, spoken or written. His ambition was to become a great military tactician and field commander so that he could right the wrongs done to China by the Manchu, the foreign powers, and the enemies of Sun Yat-sen.

Despite this significant difference, Chiang and Mao shared certain intellectual-ideological dispositions. One basic similarity was that their early classical training retained a powerful hold on them throughout life. In Chiang's case, the reasons for this are readily apparent. After his early schooling in the classics, he went directly into military training programs; he received virtually no civilian higher education of a formal type. On the whole, the doctrines which he acquired through Japanese military training meshed well with his Confucian upbringing. His contact with Western ideas was limited, and came largely through intermediaries to whom he was personally devoted—Chen Qimei, Sun Yat-sen, and Dai Jitao. He accepted their political views largely because he accepted them as friends and moral exemplars.

The case of Mao is far more complex, but in the end perhaps more instructive. This youthful Hunanese went through an educational-ideological progression not unusual for the students of his era. Yet there were factors that set him apart from many others who were later to become prominent. The values inculcated by his classical education were challenged repeatedly by powerful iconoclasts with whom he had close intellectual contact, by the extraordinary events affecting his country, and by Mao himself, when he lashed out in rage against the humiliation of China's recent past—and yet they survived. There were many reasons for that survival, but the most fundamental one lay in the intellectual perspective established by culture, language, and experience—a perspective somewhat narrower and more sharply focused than that of his more Westernized peers. To some degree, every idea and action was sooner or later strained through the Chinese mesh that encased Mao's world, as tightly in most respects as a similar mesh encased the world of Chiang. In life-style, intellectual method, and values, both men remained deeply Chinese.

In Mao's case, however, the enduring influence of Chinese classical thought, and his continuing commitment to a distinctively Chinese mode of intellectualism, did not prevent him from sampling Western philosophy and politics. He began by admiring the great reformers of the late Qing era, and developed a respect for science and technology. Then a heightened sense of nationalism, and a growing realization of the need for fundamental change, led him to the prevailing philosophic by-products of advanced Westernism—liberalism and anarchism. He had reached this point—the zenith of his "Westernization"—by 1919.

Mao's more or less simultaneous attraction to liberalism and anarchism can be explained. First, the anarchism he admired was derived primarily from Kropotkin, not Bakunin; it did not rest on violence and destruction. Second, his brand of liberalism pertained to politics, not economics. He was committed to parliamentarism, pragmatism, and political freedom. But like John Dewey and Hu Shi, who influenced him in this respect, he was no supporter of laissez-faire economics or Western-style capitalism. On the contrary, like Liang Qichao before him, he regarded much of the West as a negative example, even during his liberal phase. It was the concept of *freedom*—the liberation of the individual spirit—that unified liberalism and anarchism in Mao's mind.

Mao's liberal period did not last long, as we have seen. In part, this was because he had come to admire its key concepts relatively late, at a time when many of his idealistic compatriots saw the long shadow of Versailles casting doubt on the fundamental morality of the West. For them, as for Mao, politics was intrinsically a moral matter. In Mao's case, however, there was an additional factor: for him, the West remained very distant and very foreign. He had no personal or emotional commitments, no deep career investments in it. Retreat from the predominant Western model was therefore not painful.

Nevertheless, his brief infatuation with liberalism reinforced within Mao a dilemma that had deep roots in Chinese as well as Western tradition. Could freedom be individual, or must it be societal? Did the liberation of individual men await the liberation of whole societies, or the world? Was authoritarianism a necessary first step toward human freedom? His own background and his society's cultural traditions, as well as the utter failure of parliamentary democracy to function in China, combined to lead him away from individualism, even while he was proclaiming his commitment to democracy and freedom. As a hope was kindled that the liberation of a whole society or a nation might lead to the liberation of its nuclear units, the moral gap between means and ends grew wider. The paradox that unfolded would not be resolved in the twentieth century.

In Chiang's case, this dilemma, if it existed at all, was less acute. His training and contacts, being more uniform, sustained his belief that the community or group was more important than the individual, and the cause of the nation more important than the benefits that might be derived from an emphasis on pluralism or individual rights. First and foremost, young Chiang was a nationalist. Like Sun Yat-sen, the man he served, he was passionately dedicated to the creation of a strong and unified China. All other commitments were subordinate to that one. If parliamentary methods could be effective, as Sun currently preached, Chiang could accept them. But whatever the method, unity and strength had to be the supreme goals.

Again, Mao's views were more complex and less consistent. Perhaps his greatest oscillations during this period pertained to nationalism. From the time of the 1911 Revolution until the opening of the May Fourth Movement he was a dedicated Han nationalist. By mid-1919, however, he was denouncing the "imperialism" of the Chinese central government and arguing the case for a Hunan nation. It is true that he saw the independent development of Hunan (and of the other twenty-six units making up China) as a preparatory step toward a greater unity, a continent-wide revolution that would permanently eliminate militarists, bureaucrats, and other leeches, and thus clear the way for the establishment of populist government. But his espousal of separatism threw him sharply out of step with the accelerating nationalist cadence of this period.

Less than a year later, Mao was attacking nationalism from precisely the opposite direction. In moving toward Leninism and following Cai Hesen, he had shifted to an internationalist position: patriotism was outdated, and the salvation of China was intimately connected with the salvation of the world. It can be argued, of course, that this position in fact recommitted Mao to a nationalist course, because what he saw in global revolution was a way to improve China's precarious situation. Perhaps his internationalism was always relatively superficial, a mask behind which he continued to see China as the center of the world. Or perhaps as he entered old age, his earliest psychological and political instincts reasserted themselves in a renewed commitment to Chinese tradition, on the one hand, and to Chinese nationalism, on the other.

In the largest sense, both Chiang and Mao were political as well as cultural nationalists, despite Mao's waverings and greater difficulties in coming to terms with nationalism. And this was only natural, considering the abuses heaped upon China and the Chinese during this era, and the strong sense of cultural superiority shared by almost all educated Chinese.

At least equally important is the fact that both men were by temperament activists, and came to regard practice—in the military as well as the purely political realm—as their forte. In this respect, Mao's attitudes are particularly fascinating. Throughout his lifetime he expressed deep suspicion, and sometimes hatred, toward the Chinese intellectual community—understandably, for he was a proud man, and he did not belong to the intellectual elite of his society when he had no college or university credentials to offer. As an intellectual, he was a self-made man working outside the establishment. He stated at the age of twenty-seven that he aspired to no more exalted role than that of a primary-school teacher or a journalist. But was this true? Did not a much greater ambition burn within him? Did he not yearn to be a *leader*—whether in politics or philosophy? Certainly Mao wanted to study and learn. He was committed to self-education, and he sought the guidance of fellow students and teachers, including some of the mighty; he owed a sizable debt to Chen Duxiu, Li Dazhao, and Hu Shi. Yet, however much time Mao might spend at his study, one part of him—and, we would argue, the larger part by a considerable measure—was activist by nature. He had enormous political talent, and showed great skill in mobilization, exhortation, and organization even during his youth. Mao sensed that his greater talents lay here, not in the preparation of learned treatises, and this was a central reason for his enduring love-hate relations with intellectualism, and for his constant insistence that theory must be wedded to practice.

For Chiang, intellectuals were a more remote group. He respected some of them—teachers who had instructed him, activist intellectuals in the movement for which he fought, military theorists whose works he had read. But as a class, intellectuals made him uneasy. He was comfortable with action, and felt no need for a study group. He was prepared to welcome intellectuals who were willing to join the cause for which he provided a portion of the military muscle, and he was equally prepared to eliminate those who opposed him. Paradoxically, Mao came to share this disposition later on. It is also ironic that the ultimate test for both men came on the battlefield, although each had had wide political experience when that test came.

In another curious result of their early careers, it was Chiang and not Mao who worked more closely with the Chinese peasant. The great bulk of the troops Chiang commanded came from peasant stock, especially after the Second Revolution of 1913. Chiang felt that he understood the Chinese peasant. If one treated him fairly and firmly—applying traditional Confucian principles and sharing gains and setbacks—he would respond with loyalty, selflessness, and dedication. He saw the peasant, not as the member of a class, but as Chinese.

Mao's personal identification during this period, despite his own rural background, was less with the peasantry than with the student class. He approached the problems of students and primary-school teachers with an emotional intensity derived from personal experience. His treatment of workers and peasants, while clearly sympathetic, revealed a certain remoteness. He understood intellectually that they *were* the masses, however, and that their participation was crucial to the success of the politics to which he subscribed. Hence he assigned students and teachers a key role in their tutelage and political mobilization. He himself took an early interest in educating and organizing workers, and following Li's pioneer injunction, he urged that students dedicate themselves to uplifting the peasantry. Before he became acquainted with Leninist doctrines, Mao, like others of similar commitment, was prepared to acknowledge the importance of the peasant to any mass movement in Chinese society, and his utopian plans for a work-study program in Hunan envisioned wedding students to agricultural labor, thereby cementing a crucial union.

On the issue of modernization, or more particularly the uses of science and technology, Chiang and Mao had similar attitudes. Chiang naturally developed a strong commitment to technology as an instrument of military modernization, a cause to which he was fully dedicated, but neither his training nor his personal bent caused him to have any deep interest in science. His basic values came primarily from the traditions of Chinese humanism as expressed in the classics he had studied in his earliest years. And although Mao emphasized the importance of science to China's future and to the general progress of mankind, and in later years made a great point of displaying some scientific knowledge, he did not have much personal interest in this field. And when he approached Marxism, or more precisely Leninism, he came by way of the humanist path, in the same manner as Li Dazhao and Chen Duxiu. In truth, the priorities of early-twentieth-century China continued to tilt against science despite all the verbal homage paid to the scientific method.

Finally, for both Chiang and Mao politics was highly personalized. Chiang, in good military tradition, always accepted the authority of his superiors; if grievances mounted to an unbearable level, he would resign. His commitments to Chen Qimei, and then Sun, were absolute. In this respect, Chiang was very much in the mainstream of Chinese politics, past and present. Mao also had certain personal attachments, and in his later years these seemed to become increasingly important. Very early in his career, however, it became apparent that he was unable or unwilling to make a full and permanent commitment to another individual, or indeed to accept the concept of inferior status within a hierarchical structure. This became the basis for a deep contradiction that plagued Mao throughout his life. He was vitally interested in organizational matters, and always gave them a very high priority. Yet his anarchistic-egoistic streak led him to reject allegiance to others, to play with concepts of maximum autonomy, and to display a tendency toward personal aloofness.

By 1920 Mao had already espoused Bolshevism, not as a philosophic truth but as a successful method of revolution. Leninism appealed to the activist rebel in him, a rebel eager to find a way of conducting a revolution that would change China fundamentally and permanently, as the Revolution of 1911 had not done. The Russian Revolution had toppled militarism, monarchism, and bureaucratism—precisely the evils from which China suffered. If Russia—with all its handicaps—could accomplish this, was there not hope for China?

By the same year, Chiang had cast his lot with Sun Yat-sen. Sun's future did not look bright at the moment, but men like Chiang might make a difference. The Guomindang desperately needed both military and political strength. In the Bolshevik party and the Soviet system, new models were available. The West and Japan had apparently given up on Sun—the man and his chances—but the Soviet leaders, despite their doubts, might be prepared to risk helping him. It fitted not only their ideological commitments to a bourgeois revolution for China, but also their sense of the need for an Asian connection that would serve Soviet national interests.

Thus, as China entered the new decade, Chiang and Mao were being drawn together politically by forces beyond the influence of either. Such were the times.

13

SOURCES OF THE CHINESE REVOLUTION

THE OPENING stages of modern China's revolutionary process were shaped by the interaction of five central factors derived from human, institutional, cultural, spatial, and temporal conditions. Having introduced them separately in earlier chapters, we may now bring them together to form a conceptual framework within which to view the first phase of the continuing Chinese revolution.

The first factor was the human element—more specifically, the character and capacities of the political actors on center stage during the crucial decades from the mid-nineteenth century onward. Most Western social scientists, in contrast to their Chinese counterparts, have been reluctant to treat the human element in Chinese politics seriously. They have preferred to concentrate on impersonal, structural factors, seeking rational explanations for historical events in the socioeconomic system or in official policies. But as Chinese observers have long recognized, the governance of their country has always contained a strong personal element. In China, the ordinary subject rarely concerned himself with political institutions in the abstract. Even the monarchy, surrounded as it was by a religious or supernatural aura, engendered reverence from the commoner primarily through its living representative, the emperor. Other "great men," moreover, strengthened the loyalties of the citizenry by underwriting the legitimacy of those in supreme authority, thus assuring themselves of a place in the ancestral tablets of their family. At a broader level, written history was constructed largely of eulogies to the victorious; losers were either ignored or vilified in official accounts. The folk literature, too, focused on heroes, although they might be antitypes, Robin Hoods who championed the cause of the little man. In any case, despite its extensive bureaucratization, traditional Chinese politics was always closely connected with the personal qualities of individual leaders—a fact reinforced by the prevailing Confucian ideology, which dictated that the true source of good government lay not in the law but in the actions of wise and virtuous men.

The specific ways in which the human element influenced the revolutionary process were determined by several conditions. At a time when Chinese national consciousness was being aroused by various assaults and challenges from the West, the Qing dynasty was Manchu, not Han. Because it was vulnerable to the rising tide of Han nationalism, the monarchy in China, unlike its counterparts in Japan or Thailand, was not readily available as a major rallying point in the process of nation-building.

An additional complication lay in the fact that the era of heightening turmoil connected with China's growing contact with the external world coincided with the declining vigor of the Qing monarchy. A uniform problem with bestowing power upon a given family or clan in perpetuity lies in the impossibility of excellence continuously reproducing itself within a single genetic strain. A succession of Qian Longs is highly improbable. The empress dowager Cixi had certain qualities that made her an effective traditional ruler, but these did not include breadth of vision. She was unable to come abreast of the era in which she lived with sufficient understanding or the proper timing. And aside from Cixi, the throne in the late nineteenth century was occupied by mediocrities or weak figures, of whom Guangxu is the most pathetic example. At the end, the Qing emperor was an infant, and the real ruler a faceless regent.

Of equal importance, the personal deficiencies of the monarchy were paralleled by weakness in the top echelons of the bureaucracy. The generations of Zeng Guofan or Li Hongzhang and Zhang Zhidong did not reproduce themselves. In the time of China's greatest need—in the two decades preceding the Revolution of 1911—no distinguished new leaders appeared to assume command. Young reformers like Kang Youwei and Liang Qichao tried to fill the vacuum, but they lacked the political experience and institutional support to succeed. A more conservative modernizer like Yuan Shikai—a conceivable counterpart to early Meiji leaders such as Itō Hirobumi—was effectively excluded from power in the final years of Qing rule. And so China teetered on the edge of disintegration, threatened with dismemberment, virtually without leaders.

Of course, one must consider the context in which this situation arose. To a certain degree—and the exact degree will always be debatable—leadership is a product of the times. If the inherent talents of an individual or a generation are to flourish, a rough balance between challenge and coherence must prevail. The challenges must not be so overwhelming as to prevent a coherent response—unless the goal is revolution. In modern China, it had become clear that the status quo no longer sufficed. But whereas most internal circumstances—including the nation's deep-rooted political culture—dictated moderation and gradualism, the pressures generated by the outside world, both "positive" and "negative," were conducive to forms of political radicalism that Chinese society could not satisfactorily assimilate.

At least one generation of potential Chinese leaders was virtually destroyed by this situation. It had been possible for the generation represented by Zhang Zhidong to advocate modernization within the traditional political framework, trusting that that framework would be modified over time and brought somewhat closer to the Japanese model. By the time the next generation should have been prepared to move forward, however, coherence in the training, values, and goals of the political elite had been severely damaged. On the one hand, those brought up under the traditional system to become successful degree-holders and officials found their status challenged, their values under siege, and their capacity to deal with their own society and the external world sharply limited. Some of them responded by accepting the necessity for reforms, but many others clung desperately to the old order and became progressively embittered by the compromises being made. Meanwhile, a younger generation—also largely from well-to-do agrarian and gentry backgrounds—claimed a right to authority by virtue of their "modern training," whether obtained at home or abroad. But they, too, were seriously divided on such issues as reform versus revolution, and in any case, sufficient adherence to seniority remained to keep them generally in subordinate roles. Under these conditions, it was virtually impossible for a broadly acceptable leadership to emerge.

This fragmentation of the traditional political elite paved the way for the 1911 Revolution and enormously complicated the postrevolutionary era. The divisions deepened and proliferated in the years immediately after 1911. Very few who engaged in political activity achieved either success or widespread approval; all seemed bound together by a thread of failure. On every hand, reputations were tarnished and careers ruined. It was an era that seemed to breed knaves and fools, but not heroes. And with no accepted leadership, China could only lurch from crisis to crisis, in continuing danger of further domestic upheaveal.

The crisis of leadership, the human factor, was closely related to an institutional factor, which may be broadly defined as the issue of a political model. The traditional political structure and the ideology accompanying it had served China far better than most forms of traditionalism in other societies; indeed, it had been exported over the centuries to many neighboring peoples, making China the hub of a greater Sinic world in Asia. This traditional political order was based on an ingenious mix of public and private governance.

In the public structure of governance, power rested on a balance between the prerogatives of the throne and those of the ruling bureaucracy. The absolute power of the reigning monarch was modified by elaborate rituals and Confucian rescripts that defined the proper conduct of the good ruler—and only the good ruler was legitimate. Positions in the bureaucracy were open only to the literati, and according to traditional values, this ensured the recruitment of properly educated men, thus strengthening the legitimacy of the system. The private structure of governance, which operated with particular effectiveness at the provincial and local levels, was intimately related to the familial-clan structure of Chinese society and to the role of its unique gentry class, who served as a bridge between public and private rule. The average citizen was more immediately, more intensely, and more consistently affected by the actions of private "governors" than by those of public officials. The continuity and stability of private government at the local level enabled the society to survive chaos with its basic political culture intact. In its capacity to transcend problems of scale and local variation, it was a system built to endure.

When China's traditional institutional structure began to collapse under the impact of Westernism in all of its facets, there seemed to be only one alternative model for building a new order. That model was Western-style democracy, and a choice could be made only between two of its variants—constitutional monarchy and republican government. Constitutional monarchy was certainly better suited to China's political culture and stage of development. But because China's monarchy was alien and its bureaucracy anchored to conservative values, it became increasingly difficult to chart a course from absolutism to constitutional monarchy. And the other course, toward parliamentary republicanism, required radically different skills of political navigation, as well as calm seas. Neither could be found in China between 1911 and 1920, and so the Chinese government ran aground on the same rocks that later shattered many new nations launched after World War II. There is no need to repeat here the litany of shortcomings, abuses, and crimes associated with the Chinese attempt at democracy during these years.

One might argue, as certain Chinese intellectuals and politicians have argued, that these were only the growing pains of a young nation, and that in time parliamentary democracy could have become Sinicized in a manner acceptable to the Chinese people and serviceable in terms of Chinese national interests. But if this were possible, it could have occurred only under different conditions. The political unity of the national elite would have been especially important, such as was possible in India after 1945, a legacy of British tutelage. But China began its republican period deeply divided as a people and as a nation, and that division only seemed to grow deeper with the passage of time. Adding to the problem were the intense foreign pressures, especially from Japan. Thus, an increasing number of the elite—particularly within the intellectual and military communities, but not excluding the industrial-commercial class—came to doubt the feasibility of liberalism for China.

In their search for a viable political model, therefore, some Chinese turned back to their own tradition in one form or another. A much smaller number of them gravitated toward the New Democracy pledged by Bolshevism. The Communists used all the appealing words—democracy, freedom, and development—while pursuing methods that guaranteed order, unity, and concentration upon economic and social modernization. Freedom in its liberal form appeared to be a force for disintegration at a time when China needed unity. "Freedom" in its Bolshevik form—which rested on the right, and indeed the duty, to believe in "truth" and the obligation of the "proletariat" (represented by the intellectuals) to tutor the people—was much closer to the values of traditional China.

Although there was much confusion among the Chinese intelligentsia—as elsewhere—about the precise nature of Bolshevism, and particularly about its relation to anarchism, the critical fact was not theoretical but practical: the Soviet Union was emerging as an alternative to the economic and political model represented by the United States, and it was an alternative seemingly unburdened with imperialist associations. A strong majority of Chinese intellectuals, and many political figures as well, continued to commit themselves to parliamentarism and a politically open society, but doubts were growing. The endless crises over political institutionalization were one more indication that the Chinese revolution was far from over as World War I came to a close.

This brings us to the cultural factor. We have already touched upon certain aspects of Chinese culture that affected the human and institutional attributes of the political order. We may now point briefly to some other broad dimensions of the cultural legacy that influenced the forms which China's modern revolution took.

There can be no question that the capacity of Chinese society to reach a very high level of agricultural productivity by means of relatively sophisticated premodern technology had a powerful role in shaping and sustaining the traditional order. The great army of cultivators generally upheld traditionalism and looked with deep suspicion upon all who sought to change their way of life—indeed, upon all interlopers from outside. And why not? The Chinese farmer had perfected his technology far beyond that of most traditional societies and had even reduced (though not eliminated) his dependence on the weather. Who could offer more—at least until the modern age was well advanced? He had also created, out of the rules and rituals governing familial and clan relations, a social order in microcosm, which was supported in its values by a combination of Confucian, Taoist, and Buddhist precepts.

In its social and philosophic dimensions, then, classical Chinese society was no less advanced than in its economic aspects. The political order, taking its basic shape from the familial model, was further legitimized because the right to govern was equated with both morality and wisdom—and wisdom, it was thought, was tested through the famed examination system. Anyone could aspire to the status of scholar-bureaucrat. Family fortunes were not externally fixed, but varied from generation to generation, a condition encouraged by the system of equal inheritance. And belief that the social order did not support a system of permanent privilege for a few was reinforced by the Buddhist doctrine of karma. Thus the ethical foundations of Chinese culture were truly formidable.

The socioeconomic system under which this culture operated had little in common with the feudalism of medieval Europe, where great lords exerted independent authority over vast tracts of land and governed sizable communities of serfs, retainers, knights, artisans, and merchants. China departed from anything resembling such a system at a very early point in its history. Landholding was private, and for the most part small-scale. The landlord, the owner-cultivator, and the tenant existed in a continuum, and individuals were constantly moving into and out of each category.

Strict rules, to be sure, governed owner-tenant relations, and violations on either side could lead to acrimony. Recurrent riots in the towns and in the countryside were testimony to the fact that in the face of natural disaster, perceived injustice, or the breakdown of governmental responsibility, the citizenry was not always passive. But at most times and in most places, landlord-tenant relations—and on a broader level, gentry-commoner relations—were marked by harmony, sweetened by a considerable element of paternalism and a strong sense of community. This sense of community was reinforced by unique factors of dialect, food, dress, and other conditions that create a cohesive subculture. A localism that cut across social and economic lines was one of the truly powerful forces in the vast continent called China—as successive generations of leaders (and rebels) were to discover. Political recruitment, indeed, could not succeed unless it paid homage to this fact.

Another aspect of Chinese culture that had a great influence on political life was the remarkable degree to which the political system welded officialdom and the intelligentsia into a single class. By hyphenating the terms "literati-official" and "scholar-bureaucrat" we acknowledge the fact that the great majority of intellectuals focused their energies on achieving success in the examinations and then holding office. There was no separate religious institution—like the Christian church in the West—to compete for intellectual talent or to challenge the state for both moral and secular supremacy, thereby laying the foundations for political modernization. The Chinese intellectual might periodically retire from politics, voluntarily or otherwise, to engage in the pursuits available to an educated individual. But in career terms, he was wedded to the state.

Hence, in considering the nature and the timing of change in modern China, one can hardly overestimate the role of the intellectual as conservative. While the Chinese literati became acquainted with Western thought and institutions at least as early as the Japanese samurai-intellectuals, their unwillingness to accept more than certain technological aspects of the "new learning" served to delay or abort all serious efforts at reform until a very late hour. And even then, as we have seen, the intellectuals as a group were deeply divided over the value of Western learning.

Thus, with the voice of the intellectuals a cacophony of confusion, the commercial and embryonic industrial class still in a phase of development that demanded mercantilism instead of liberalism, and the rural classes either apolitical or deeply conservative with respect to basic values, it is no wonder that cohesion was impossible.

To fill this vacuum, two types of leaders, both largely alien to traditional China, were logical entrants: the foreign-educated man and the new military man. These types, of course, were not mutually exclusive; they sometimes worked in coalition, and were occasionally fused in a single individual. It was thus entirely logical that Sun Yat-sen and Yuan Shikai, in their differences and their compatibilities, came to symbolize the China of their times. Yet both failed: Sun because he lacked the necessary organizational talent, and because he advanced a program that went far beyond the current capacities of his society to realize it; Yuan because the obstacles confronting any leader seeking to combine traditionalism with Western-style liberalism were awesome, and because he allowed himself to be lured into steps leading to the unreachable past, and thereby fell into a political trap. Nevertheless, it was in the hands of men who combined some of the qualities of Sun and Yuan that China's immediate future lay. That is why Chiang Kai-shek and Mao Zedong assume an importance that transcends their personal destinies. They symbolized the path of the future in a way that men like Kang Youwei and Liang Qichao, for all their brilliance, could not.

Chinese culture, in sum, presented sizable obstacles to any successful adaptation of the prevailing Western model. It did not dictate the emergence of specific political programs, institutions, or leaders. What it did provide was an environment—physical, intellectual, and institutional—that established a steeply graded table of probability for the tempo and the basic character of China's political evolution.

A fourth factor that cast a pervasive influence over China's revolutionary process was that of scale. China's vast size, though capable of being accommodated by the loose imperial system which evolved in ancient times (and representing a very rough parallel in the Roman Empire), defied the organizational and structural requirements of the European-style nation-state. Had China undergone the process of political subdivision that occurred in modern Europe, and emerged as a set of independent states, it is likely that competitive experiments in economic and political development would have born fruit. This possibility did not go unnoticed in China. As we have seen, the concepts of provincial self-governance or independence strongly attracted certain Chinese activists, including the young Mao Zedong.

It might be argued, of course, that in terms of scale China resembled two other continental societies, the United States and Russia. That may be true in the most general sense, but the differences were greater than the similarities and more significant. Unlike China, the United States acquired a great amount of territory within a short time; its total population was not large; and its political and cultural heartland was confined to one region, the northeast, so that modernization could spread freely to outlying regions, unfettered by a feudal tradition. Peripheral areas could be easily assimilated as their economic and political capacities increased. And if the whole of America was open to new development, the American West, especially, was virgin territory, where the sparse indigenous population was quickly overrun by the flow of immigrants and the extension of a dynamic new culture.

Russia was more similar to China, except that the population of China was vastly larger. Despite profound cultural differences, the political evolution of the two empires had much in common. Both societies entered the stream of modernization quite late, against a background of ambivalence toward the influence of foreign cultures. Russia's political system was more centralized, for various reasons, but in certain respects it was also more pluralized, with a powerful if state-aligned church and a quasi-independent intelligentsia. It was not accidental, therefore, that Chinese leaders and intellectuals watched Russia as a model for reform (after 1905) or as a harbinger of the revolution that lay ahead for their own society.

It is true that within the Chinese empire, "inner China"—the densely populated, intensively cultivated region occupied predominantly by Han—was considerably smaller in area than the peripheral regions, where great expanses of land inhospitable to intensive agriculture were sparsely populated, and non-Han peoples were often in the majority. But inner China alone was the most populous area of the modern world under a single government, and its physical proportions, from north to south, dwarfed those of the European states. Evidence accumulated over the past few centuries suggests that there is an optimal size for rapid or successful modernization, whether its goals are measured in economic or in political terms. The country with the best chance of success will have a population between ten and sixty million, at least to begin with, and a territory small enough to be conveniently traversed within a brief time by the current means of transport. On both counts, nineteenth-century China was far too large, and the significance of this fact for the modern Chinese revolution can hardly be exaggerated.

Finally, we must consider the temporal factor—the timing of China's emergence into the modern world, as it related both to indigenous conditions and to the prevailing global environment. In the nineteenth-century West, the tempo of change was steadily accelerating. In the emergence of a modern nation—or, more accurately, of its modern elite—a difference of fifty or even twenty-five years could have a great effect on subsequent developments. China began its sustained interaction with the West in the 1830s, and by the 1860s and 1870s Western contacts and influences were significant for at least a small elite. Indeed, by the 1870s the influence of the West upon China, though confined to a few enclaves, was greater than it was upon Japan. Over the next half-century, however, Japan steadily increased its interaction with the outside world and progressively modified its economy, its political institutions, and many aspects of its culture; but China took only the most tentative steps in this direction, and these steps were often followed by retreats. In part, this was a result of problems of scale. But it was also a result of self-satisfaction and arrogance among the literati-officials who controlled the destiny of their country.

Thus by the 1890s, when the encroachment of the "advanced" world could no longer be avoided or repelled, the time left for adjustment had been appreciably shortened, and the foreign stimuli were both diverse and corrosive. These circumstances could only exacerbate existing divisions within the political and intellectual elites. The Chinese avant-garde, aware that time was running out, sought to encompass Mill and Marx at the same time, searching for a political philosophy that could be tailored to fit China's current requirements. Little wonder that confusion abounded, and that the ideas and programs of one decade seemed anachronistic in the next.

Timing dictated that China would continue to be gripped by a deep ambivalence toward the West throughout its struggle to find a new path. On the one hand, the dazzling array of Western accomplishments suddenly thrust before the Chinese, ranging from the material to the philosophic, eventually demanded respect, even awe. Yet the raw power of the West (and Japan) during this, the heyday of imperialism, together with the supreme self-satisfaction and arrogance with which Western leaders viewed the world, made Sino-Western harmony virtually impossible. The clash over concepts, such as suzerainty versus sovereignty, and the superiority of the Central Kingdom in its world versus the equality of nation-states under Western-developed international law, ensured successive crises. And in each crisis, the lesser power would have to bend.

In political terms, it was almost certain that a sizable portion of the elite in China would come to accept democracy as the wave of the future. Yet in the second decade of the twentieth century, precisely the time when China was wrestling with the problem of instituting parliamentary democracy, a challenge to that model of government was emerging within the West itself, in the form of Leninism. Already, and without external prompting, certain Chinese intellectuals had begun to espouse a theory of tutelage—the concept that a liberated and literate elite should train the masses for political participation so that democracy could ultimately be realized. But as we have noted, the quickening tempo of Chinese world politics in the first decades of the twentieth century allowed no time for experiments in gradualism. Instead, artificial republicanism and real militarism came to dominate the scene.

The militarism of this period was also changing with the times. Since political consensus was not possible, it was natural for political goals to be pursued through a resort to force, and increasingly with modern weapons obtained from Western and Japanese sources. It must not be forgotten that many "warlords" attached as much importance to their political activities as to their military exploits. Some, to be sure, seemed to have no objective beyond holding power and enriching themselves. But a larger number had developed certain political ideals or values in response to the contemporary era, and some of them tried to express these values in concrete programs, on a provincial or a regional basis. Indeed, military governance—good, bad, and indifferent—tended to divide China into certain natural units, and had this situation persisted over time, it might have resulted in the stabilization of separate polities. Under the prevailing chaotic circumstances, however, few of the political entities created by military power during this period had stability or continuity. In some cases, moreover—because of allegiance to Beijing or the southern government, or because of the existence of a loose coalition that cut across several provinces—individual military leaders rejected independence in theory even though they frequently pursued it in practice.

In the quest for a stronger unity, one that would provide a defense against foreign threats, Great Han nationalism prevailed over the calls for provincial autonomy or independence. It was inevitable that centralization required some form of concentrated power, possibly one uniting a military class with Leninist doctrines, whereas decentralization was associated with popular rule. This was to be one of the great issues of the Chinese revolution, an issue not yet resolved.

One final characteristic of China's revolutionary process warrants special notice—a characteristic that derives from the combination of culture and timing. To move away from a culture as rich and pervasive as that of China, to alter substantially or break with processes of thought, behavior patterns, and a way of life was possible only over time—and as the socioeconomic foundations of the society itself underwent change. It could not be accomplished in a few decades. Consequently, each high tide in the revolution was followed by a powerful ebb tide of traditionalism, which wore down or subverted most of those who tried to struggle against it. One after another, the rebels were drawn back toward the fold.

Thus, Hong Xiuquan and his Taiping movement ended much as all traditional dynasties had ended. The reformers of 1898 launched a new era, but they later raised a series of doubts about "Westernization" and came to hold positions not inaccurately defined as neo-traditionalist. And the Revolution of 1911 fell back under the pull of traditionalism, epitomized by recurrent efforts to restore monarchism and Confucianism. Even Sun Yat-sen, the very model of the iconoclastic rebel against Chinese tradition, retreated after the failure of the Second Revolution of 1913 and tried to rebuild his movement along the more traditional lines of the secret society and highly personalized allegiance.

This pattern would be repeated in later years, as the Nationalists and then the Communists, after initial periods of idol-smashing, were pulled back toward values and policies honored in the past. Thus Chiang Kai-shek returned to Confucianism, and Mao died an emperor. Even in the Deng Xiaoping era, another "New Life" movement based on traditional moral values was launched. Successive political revolutions have taken place, but China's social revolution is still in its early stages, and more political upheavals may attend its further progress.

Whatever lay ahead, the Chinese revolution had just begun as the 1920s got under way, despite the cataclysmic events of the previous twenty years. Thus, the traditional political culture of this ancient society was certain to constrain and shape much that sought to be new.

NOTES

ABBREVIATIONS USED IN THE NOTES

HB	*Heng bao*
LZ	*LuOu zhoukan*
MB	*Min bao*
MLB	*Minli bao*
MP	*Meizhou pinglun*
MYCZ	*Makesizhuyi yanjiu cankao ziliao*
NAMP/RDSRIAC	*National Archives Microfilm Publication: Records of the Department of State Relating to Internal Affairs of China,* 1919–1929
NCH	*North China Herald*
QYB	*Qingyi bao*
QZ	*Qingnian zazhi*
SB	*Su bao*
TYB	*Tienyi bao*
XJP	*Xiang Jiang pinglun*
XMCB	*Xinmin congbao*
XQ	*Xin qingnian*
XS	*Xin shiji*

CHAPTER ONE

1. Wallerstein's neo-Marxist thesis can be set forth briefly as follows: historically, there have been two basic economic systems, aggregative in nature, an early "mini-system" based on "a complete division of labor and a single cultural framework," now defunct, and a "world system," defined as "a unit with a single division of labor and multiple cultural systems." The world system with a common political structure was the "world empire," based on a redistributive economy. It too is presently defunct. Dominating the scene today is the "capitalist world-economy," with its essential features the class conflict between the bourgeoisie and the proletariat on an international scale, and its key feature production for sale (trade) with the aim maximum profit. Capitalism, argues Wallerstein, was from the beginning "an affair of the world economy and not of nation-states."

The "capitalist world economy" is three-tiered, being composed of core, semi-peripheral, and peripheral elements, with the semiperiphery an essential element providing both flexibility (interaction with and movement toward the other entities) and political stability in systemic terms (a cushioning effect, preventing sharp clashes between top and bottom). To date, there have been four stages in the evolution of the world economy, with the present stage characterized by core societies possessing a complex variety of economic activities and strong governments, capable of appropriating the surplus of the entire world economy through a combination of commercialized agriculture and industrialization; the semiperipheral societies based on a middle position in terms of export products, wage levels, and profit margins, trading in both directions, and with the state showing strong interest in market control; and the peripheral societies, monocultural with cash crop estates, slave labor, and weak states.

Since it is not possible for the simultaneous "development" of the three tiers, class struggle at the world level unfolds in the conflict that ensues, and in broader terms, classes, ethnic groups, political institutions, and all other elements take their form and roles from their station in the "capitalist world economy." This includes socialist states, since they cannot avoid being a part of the system—until the advent of a socialist world government. The latter development is an article of faith for Wallerstein, the only issue being that of timing. Indeed, having set forth his conviction that social science can never be value-free, Wallerstein expresses his own values frequently and at length on a wide range of subjects. He is favorably inclined toward recent "liberation movements" such as those that have taken place in Vietnam, Cuba, and Angola; toward Maoism as he understands it (viewed from the mid-1970s); and he quotes Kim Il-sŏng on socialist doctrine approvingly. He is sharply critical of modernization theory, liberalism (and liberals)—indeed, of all non-Marxists—although he uses such individuals as Weber and Tillich when passages from their writings suit his purposes.

The weaknesses and errors of the Wallerstein thesis are multiple. Despite homage paid to social and political factors as dependent but complex variables and the collection of elaborate historical data, all must be fitted onto the Procrustean bed of Marxism writ global. There is a single independent variable—the economic. This type of reductionism distorts reality and casts radically different societies into Wallerstein's three tiers, although he himself seems aware at times of the dubious fit of his categories. From an empirical standpoint, the knowledgeable reader is treated to one shock after another: Vietnam as a semiperipheral entity together with China, Zaire, South Africa, and Canada, as one example. Such categorizations rule out meaningful comparisons and render prediction impossible. Moreover, in making a sharp distinction between the states that in Wallerstein's opinion have undergone "great social revolutions"—e.g., the Soviet Union, China, and Vietnam and those which are to be denominated "bourgeois capitalist," including the United States and Japan—he not only minimizes the intricate mix of the old and the new coexisting in the former, but fails to see the truly revolutionary character of the latter created by the accelerating socioeconomic change that has altered the lives of the masses far more radically—for both good and ill—than in societies where the pace of change has not kept up with revolutionary rhetoric. For Wallerstein's themes, see his *The Modern World-System: Capitalist Agriculture and the Origins of the European World-Economy in the Sixteenth Century* (New York: Academic Press, 1974) and *The Capitalist World-Economy: Essays by Immanuel Wallerstein* (Cambridge: Cambridge University Press, 1979).

2. These criteria, with some amendments and additions, have been taken from an earlier essay by the senior author, "Environmental and Foreign Contributions—Japan," pp. 64–90 in Robert E. Ward and Dankwart A. Rustow, eds., *Political Modernization in Japan and Turkey* (see pp. 65–66).

3. For salient literature on modernization, in addition to the work noted above, see Gabriel Almond and Barry Powell, *Comparative Politics: A Development Approach*; Robert Bates, *Rural Responses to Industrialization*; Leonard Binder, et al.,

Crises and Sequences in Political Development; S. N. Eisenstadt, *Modernization: Protest and Change*; Peter Evans, *Dependent Development: The Alliance of Multinational, State, and Local Capital in Brazil*; Jason Finkle and Richard Gable, eds., *Political Development and Social Change*; Bert Hoselitz and Wilbert Moore, eds., *Industrialization and Society*; Samuel P. Huntington, *Political Order in Changing Societies*; Daniel Lerner, *The Passing of Traditional Society*; Joel Migdal, *Peasants, Politics and Revolution: Pressures Toward Political and Social Change in the Third World*; Lucian Pye, *Aspects of Political Development*; Lucian Pye and Sidney Verba, eds., *Political Culture and Political Development*; Everett M. Roger, *Modernization Among Peasants*; Norman Uphoff and Warren Ilchman, eds., *The Political Economy of Development*; Claude Welch, comp., *Political Modernization*.

4. The literature dealing with Confucian thought and institutions is vast. In Chinese, for discussions of Confucianism, see Du Shousu, *Zhongguo sixiang tongshi*; *Kongzi zhexue taolun ji*; Zhen Daji, *Kongzi xueshui*; Zhen Jianfu, *Kongzi xueshui xinlun*; and *Zhongguo zhexueshi wenji*.

In English, see Etienne Balazs, *Chinese Civilization and Bureaucracy*; Wing-tsit Chan, tr., *A Source Book in Chinese Philosophy*; Carsun Chang (Chang, Chia-sen), *The Development of Neo-Confucian Thought*; Confucius, *The Analects*; Herrlee G. Creel, *Chinese Thought from Confucius to Mao Tse-Tung*; W. Theodore de Bary, Wing-tsit Chan, and Burton Watson, eds., *Sources of Chinese Tradition*; Sebastian de Grazia, ed., *Masters of Chinese Political Thought*; Werner Eichhorn, *Chinese Civilization*; John K. Fairbank, *The Chinese World Order*; idem (ed.), *Chinese Thought and Institutions*; Fung Yu-lan, *A History of Chinese Philosophy*, tr. Derk Bodde; Marcel Granet, *Chinese Civilization*, tr. Kathleen E. Innes and Mabel R. Brailsford; *Han Fei Tsu, The Complete Works: A Classic of Chinese Political Science*, tr. and annotated by Arthur Waley; E. R. Hughes, tr., *Chinese Philosophy in Ancient Times*; James Legge, tr., *The Chinese Classics*; Joseph R. Levenson, *Confucian China and Its Modern Fate*; Liang, Ch'i-ch'ao, *Intellectual Trends in the Ch'ing Period*; Frederick W. Mote, *Intellectual Foundations of China*; Edwin O. Reischauer, John K. Fairbank and Albert Craig, *A History of East Asian Civilization*; Burton Watson, tr., *Basic Writings of Mo Tzu, Hsün Tzu and Han Fei Tzu*; Max Weber, *The Religion of China: Confucianism and Taoism*, tr. Hans Gerth; and Arthur F. Wright and Denis Twitchett; *Confucian Personalities*.

5. Studies of the traditional bureaucracy in Chinese include Deng Siyu, *Zhongguo kaoshi zhidushi*; Fu Zongmao, *Qingdai dufu zhidu*; Xu Daolin, *Zhongguo fazhi shilunlue*; Yan Gengwang, *Zhongguo difang xingzheng zhidushi juan shang: Qin-Han difang xingzheng zhidu*; and Zhang Jinjian, *Zhongguo wenguan zhidushi*.

In English, see Etienne Balazs, *Chinese Civilization*; Chung-li Chang, *The Chinese Gentry*; Ch'ü, T'ung-tsu, *Law and Society in Traditional China*; idem, *Local Government in China Under the Ch'ing*; Ho, Ping-ti, *The Ladder of Success in Imperial China*; Hsiao Kung-ch'üan, *Rural China: Imperial Control in the Nineteenth Century*; Hsieh, Pao Chao, *The Government of China (1644–1911)*; Immanuel C. Y. Hsu, *The Rise of Modern China*; E. A. Kracke, Jr., *Civil Service in Early Sung China—960–1067*; Thomas A. Metzger, *The Internal Organization of Ch'ing Bureaucracy—Legal, Normative and Communication Aspects*; and David S. Nivison and Arthur F. Wright, eds., *Confucianism in Action*.

6. Ho Ping-ti, in his later work cited above, argues that in Ming-Qing times, the *shengyuan*, or lowest degree holders, while regarded legally and in status terms as the leading group among commoners, in the final analysis belonged to the latter category rather than the gentry class. See Ho, *Success in Imperial China*, pp. 34ff.

7. See Philip A. Kuhn, *Rebellion and Its Enemies in Late Imperial China: Mili-*

tarization and Social Structure, 1796–1864, pp. 3–4; also Ch'u T'ung-tsu, *Local Government,* 169–192.

8. For important works in Chinese on the traditional military, see Ling Tian, *Xian-Tong Guizhou junshi shi;* Luo Ergang, "The Origin of Personal Armies in the Late Qing Period," *Zhongguo shehui jingji shi jikan;* Luo Ergang, *Xiangjun xinzhi; Luying bingzhi;* Wang Ermin, *Huaijun zhi;* and Wang Kaijun, *Xiangjun zhi.*

In English, in addition to Kuhn, cited above, see Chiang Siang-tse, *The Nien Rebellion;* Hsiao Ch'i-ch'ing, *The Military Establishment of the Yuan Dynasty;* Frank A. Kierman, Jr., ed., *Chinese Ways in Warfare;* Ralph Powell, *The Rise of Chinese Military Power, 1895–1912;* Stanley Spector, *Li Hung-chang and the Huai Army;* Frederic Wakeman, Jr., *Strangers at the Gate: Social Disorder in South China,* 1839–1861; and the literature on the Taiping cited below.

9. In addition to the works already cited, insights into the classical Chinese intellectual tradition can be gained from Arthur F. Wright, ed., *Studies in Chinese Thought.*

10. At this point, the literature on the Taiping Rebellion is voluminous. It exists in various languages, ranges from eyewitness accounts to very recent studies, and is reflective of diverse ideological perspectives. For important non-Marxist works in Chinese, see Cheng Yansheng, *Taiping tianguo shiliao;* Fan Wenlan, *Taiping tianguo geming yundong;* Jian Youwen, *Taipingjun Guangxi shouyi shi;* Luo Ergang, *Taiping tianguo shigang;* and Xie Xingyao, *Taiping tianguo di shehui zhengzhi sixiang.* For Marxist documentary collections and interpretations, see Luo Ergang, *Taiping tianguoshi shigao;* Mao Jiaju, Fang Jiguang, and Dang Guanghua, *Taiping tianguo xingwangshi;* Mo Anshi, *Taiping tianguo; Renmin ribao,* editorial, January 11, 1951; Xiang Da et al., comp., *Zhongguo jindaishi ziliao congkan: Taiping tianguo;* and *Zhongguo jindai lishi yanjiu gangyao.*

For early foreign accounts, some of them by observers, see Lindsay Brine, *The Taiping Rebellion in China—A Narrative of Its Rise and Progress, Based Upon Original Documents and Information Obtained in China;* A. Egmont Hake, *Events in the Taiping Rebellion—Being Reprints of Mss. Copied by General Gordon, C.B.;* Lin-he (Augustus F. Lindley), *Ti-Ping T'ien Kwoh—The History of the Ti-ping Revolution;* Thomas T. Meadows, *The Chinese and Their Rebellions, Viewed in Connection with Their National Philosophy, Ethics, Legislation and Administration;* and Samuel Wells Williams, *The Middle Kingdom.*

For more recent analyses of special value, see Eugene P. Boardman, *Christian Influence Upon the Ideology of the Taiping Rebellion,* 1851–1864; J. C. Cheng, *Chinese Sources for the Taiping Rebellion,* 1850–1864; Jen Yu-wen, *The Taiping Revolutionary Movement;* Franz Michael and Chung-li Chang, *The Taiping Rebellion: History and Documents;* Vincent Y. C. Shih, *The Taiping Ideology: Its Sources, Interpretations, and Influences;* and Ssu-yu Teng, *The Taiping Rebellion and the Western Powers.*

11. Cited in Shih, *Taiping Ideology,* 493–494.

12. Ibid., 494–495.

13. For a translation of the *Renmin ribao* editorial of January 11, 1951, in which these views are put forth, see ibid., 453–457. One of the most recent "traditional Marxist" interpretations is to be found in the work compiled by members of the history departments of Fudan and Shanghai Teachers' Universities, entitled *The Taiping Revolution* (in both Chinese and English), English edition (Beijing: Foreign Languages Press, 1976). Defining the Taiping uprising as the "first great high tide of the revolution in the history of modern China" (168), the authors assert that Hong Xiuquan, in addition to being "the earliest of the progressive Chinese who looked to

the West for truth," advanced programs to give land to the tillers and a blueprint for a capitalist society (171). But "feudal power combined with the aggressive strength of the foreign capitalists" to provide formidable opposition, and the Taiping movement, being "a peasant revolutionary movement," could not benefit from "the leadership of the Chinese working class and its Party" (173).

14. In this section, we have drawn heavily on the work of Jen Yu-wen, Franz Michael, Vincent Shih, and Ssu-yu Teng, and wish to acknowledge our indebtedness to their scholarship. The interpretations that follow are, of course, our responsibility.

15. J. L. Cranmer-Byng, *An Embassy to China*, 239.

16. Philip Kuhn, *Rebellion and Its Enemies*.

17. In April 1852, Hong Rengan, temporarily in Hong Kong, presented an account of Hong Xiuquan's life, including details concerning his "vision," to the Rev. Theodore Hamberg. Hamberg published Rengan's account under the title *The Visions of Hung-Siu-Tsheun, and Origin of the Kwang-si Insurrection* (Hong Kong: *China Mail* Office, 1854). This has been duplicated by the Chinese Materials Center, Inc., San Francisco, 1975, and in that form, used by us. A Taiping account under the title *Taiping Tianri* is used by Rudolf Wagner, *Reenacting the Heavenly Vision*.

18. See Jen, *Revolutionary Movement*, 52ff.

19. See Michael, *History and Documents* 1:88–92; Jen, *Revolutionary Movement*, 45–49.

20. Ibid., 61–65.

21. Ibid., 73.

22. See Laai Yi-faai, "The Part Played by the Pirates of Kwangtung and Kwangsi Provinces in the Taiping Insurrection," Ph.D. dissertation, University of California, Berkeley, 1950.

23. For details, see Teng, *The Taiping Rebellion*, 115–116; Shih, *The Taiping Ideology*, 60–73.

24. Shih presents a very detailed and highly useful account of Taiping ideology; see ibid., 141–390. For a recent stimulating analysis using primary sources, see Rudolf Wagner, *Reenacting the Heavenly Vision*.

25. Jen, *The Taiping Revolutionary Movement*, 144.

26. Ibid.

27. For one earlier study of Zeng Guofan, useful for some of the data contained despite its eulogistic quality, see William James Hail, *Tseng Kuo-fan and the Taiping Rebellion*. See also Kenneth E. Folsom, *Friends, Guests and Colleagues: The Mu-fu System in the Late Ch'ing Period*, especially 58–96, and Zeng's biography by S. Y. Teng in Arthur W. Hummel, *Eminent Chinese of the Ch'ing Period* 2:751–756. For a succinct, analytical account of Zeng's role in the Taiping Rebellion, see Frederic Wakeman, Jr., *The Fall of Imperial China*, 168–174. In Chinese, one should consult *Zeng Wenzheng gong shoushi riji*; *Zeng Wenzheng gong quanji*; Li Fangchen, *Zhongguo jindai shi*; and Luo Ergang, *Xiangjun xinzhi*.

28. For a detailed account, see Jen, *The Taiping Revolutionary Movement*, 287–320.

29. Two recent works dealing with the Ever Victorious Army are Richard J. Smith, *Mercenaries and Mandarins: The Ever-Victorious Army in Nineteenth Century China*, and Robert Rantoul, *Frederick Townsend Ward*. An earlier study of continuing value dealing with Ward is Holger Cahill, *A Yankee Adventurer*; see also Jonathan Spence, *To Change China: Western Advisers in China, 1620–1960*; Earl Swisher, *China's Management of the American Barbarians*; and Stephen Uhalley,

Jr.,' "The Foreign Relations of the Taiping Revolution," Ph.D. dissertation, University of California, Berkeley, 1967.

30. For Taiping relations with the Western powers in the initial years after their occupation of Nanjing, see, in addition to Uhalley, Teng, *The Taiping Rebellion*, 206–230.

31. U.S. Congress, *House Executive Documents*, 33rd Congress, 1st Session, 203–209, as quoted as ibid., 223.

32. In Chinese, see *Li Wenzhang gong quanji*. In English, see J. O. P. Bland, *Li Hung-chang*; and Stanley Spector, *Li Hung-chang and the Huai Army*.

33. Spector's study covers this subject in excellent fashion.

34. In addition to the recent fine work of Richard J. Smith, cited above, a number of studies have focused on Gordon through the years, among them Bernard Allen, *Gordon in China*; Demetriu Boulger, *The Life of Gordon*; also, the Gordon Papers located in the manuscript division of the British Museum are available. A dissertation on Burgevine is that of Robert H. Detrick, "Henry Andrea Burgevine in China: A Biography" Ph.D. dissertation, Indiana University, 1968.

35. For example, see Zhang Yiwen's article "Problems of Strategy Concerning the Battles of the Late Taiping Period." Zhang stresses two military errors: the failure to attack Zeng Guofan's headquarters during the second western expedition in the fall of 1860, assaulting Wuhan instead; and Li Xiucheng's decision to launch a campaign against Shanghai after the withdrawal of forces from Wuzhang. He also underlines the growing corruption characterizing Taiping politics, the lack of a unified command center, the increasingly poor quality of Taiping military commanders, and the growth of localism and insubordination, all cited as factors affecting Taiping military performance. A final theme in Zhang's essay is that the Taiping placed too much reliance on the advice of foreigners (157–161).

On the issue of making Nanjing the capital, see Mo Haijian, "The Taiping Decision to Establish the Capital at Nanjing Was a Major Strategic Mistake." Mo argues that even if the Taiping had refrained from engaging in their disastrous northern expedition later, they could not have maintained themselves by concentrating solely on a southern base. Ultimately, he asserts, the Qing forces would have overwhelmed them, since South China was vital to the Manchu from an economic standpoint, and the main body of Qing military forces would not have been damaged. At the same time, he claims that of the three principal enemies of the Taiping—"the Qing banner troops, the armed landlord class and the foreign forces"—the second group was the most formidable, thereby holding to the centrality of a class conflict analysis.

A contrary view regarding the issue of the capital is advanced in the edited work by Mao, Fang, and Dang, *Taiping Tianguo xingwangshi*, who assert that this decision was not critical to Taiping fortunes. The basic causes of failure, according to these scholars, were the Taiping inability to create an effective coalition of forces, military errors in various campaigns, the failure to carry through their original socioeconomic policies rigorously, the fratricide at Nanjing, and the mishandling of relations with the major powers.

36. For a discussion of how to classify the Taiping Rebellion, see the papers by Mo Anshi, Zhong Renwei and Fang Xiao, Yuan Segao, Zhang Lianji, and Sun Gefu listed in the bibliography. All of these scholars take the basic position outlined above, using Marxist-Leninist theory to sustain their views. Zhong and Fang argue that in a feudal society, the productive relationship involves both peasants and landlords, hence it is possible for the peasants to build a political position antagonistic to the landowner even though it will be temporary. Within that position, conflicting properties of revolution and feudalism will exist, with the latter ultimately prevailing.

Yuan asserts that the Taiping revolutionary movement represented one of the great peasant wars in Chinese history, but since the peasants did not represent a new productive force, they could not create a scientific revolutionary theory and were forced to rely on religious superstition. Thus, in the end, the feudal system survived. Sun advances a similar thesis, arguing that as Lenin noted, a revolutionary movement can obtain temporary support from the peasantry, but this will ultimately disappear if, as in the case of the Taiping revolution, it is the sole source of assistance. The peasant leaders will become progressively "feudalized" or "corrupted." Zhang asserts that the Taiping represented a movement fundamentally based upon peasant power, but since it occurred after the Opium War, it had certain properties of a bourgeois-democratic as well as peasant revolution.

37. Fang Yang asserts that "the original purpose of Western missionaries was to use religion to anesthetize the Chinese so as to open the road for Western capitalist aggression, politically, economically, and culturally." He goes on, however, to say that the Christian God was altered by Hong to become a symbol for the struggle against feudalism and imperialism. Under a mystic, religious cloak was concealed a revolutionary essence.

38. This is the view of Liu Shenyi. See also the paper by Lu Lianzhang. Even Huang Zhenhei acknowledges that by emphasizing monotheism and ultimately maneuvering to become the Chinese Emperor-God himself, Hong constructed a "strong and lengthy string" attaching the royalist-inclined peasants to him, thereby using religion for revolutionary purposes.

39. This is most noteworthy in Zhang Lianji's essay. Zhang asserts that Hong himself advocated such economic innovations as the use of more modern means of transport, the establishment of banks, the development of mining, and a modern postal system—all ideas garnered from his contacts with foreigners.

40. Duan Yunzhang, in his rebuttal of Du Renguo's negative evaluation of Western influences on the Taiping, argues that since the movement drew extensively upon individuals from regions within China where contact with Westerners had been greatest, it was natural that Hong and others would look favorably on Western innovations, including modern weaponry and new military strategies.

41. Authors like Liu Shenyi challenge the authenticity of the supposed Taiping commitment to doctrines of equality, agrarian socialism, and other radical concepts set forth in the initial stages of the uprising. Liu argues that despite the emphasis on equality before God, the Taiping always classified people into two distinct categories, civilians and officials, with the peasants at the lowest level and the highest power belonging to the Heavenly King, thus sustaining a pyramidal social structure. He notes that taxes and payment for food were instituted, notwithstanding the pledge of a communal system, and that the socialist land program was never transferred from paper to reality. In addition, while certain forms of equality were given women to take advantage of their labor power, Liu asserts, there was no sexual equality, and monogamy applied only to commoners, not to kings.

Several writers, including Zhen Renzhun and Zhang Yin, also regard Taiping policies toward the intellectual class as seriously flawed. Zhen argues that Hong, Feng, and Shi were themselves intellectuals, and that they sought the services of the literati, respecting their education and knowledge. The obstacles, however, lay not merely in the Taiping religious creed, but related to this, also in the restructuring of the examination system, with questions on the Bible replacing the old questions on Confucian texts, both angering and intimidating the classically trained intellectuals. The fact that Hong's armies in the early period destroyed Confucian temples and burned classics also created problems. Further, many of the intellectuals were basically antiforeign, and they regarded the Taiping as too accepting of the missionary and other foreigners.

42. For this theme, among others, see Zhu Zhixin. Both Dang Shangyi and Ma Qingchong take the position that despite its inner contradictions and retreat from the initial goals, the Taiping movement remained a peasant revolution to the end, never abandoning the effort to destroy the old order. In this connection, Dang presents an analysis containing fascinating if unarticulated parallels to the Communist era. The Taiping, he argues, represented a temporary dictatorship of workers and peasants deeply antagonistic to the feudal landowner class and Qing power. But without the principles of democracy and equality, he adds, any dictatorship will become increasingly more despotic, "regardless of who is at the head or what is its organizational structure." The Taiping revolution, he continues, was not the same as earlier peasant rebellions nor did it sustain the feudal system of the past two thousand years. Its uniqueness—and the basic cause for its failure—he maintains, lay in the contradiction between the values implicit in a peasant dictatorship (that dictatorship constituting the national system) and the feudal despotic order under which the peasants had to operate (constituting the socioeconomic and political structure).

CHAPTER TWO

1. For Chinese-language materials on the Tongzhi period, see Chen Tao, ed., *Tongzhi zhongxing jingwai zouji yuebian*; the papers of Li Hongzhang and Zeng Guofan; the diaries of Weng Tonghe; and Fan Wenlan, *Zhongguo jindai shi*, ch. 5. A valuable work in English on this period is Mary Clabaugh Wright, *The Last Stand of Chinese Conservatism: The T'ung Chih Restoration, 1862–1874*. Professor Wright's work provides an invariably stimulating, often brilliant interpretation of the era which has been of great service to us. Although we are compelled to diverge from some of her interpretations, we nevertheless regard this study as one of the truly interesting works produced on nineteenth-century China by an American scholar.

A series of stimulating essays on nineteenth-century reform efforts are to be found in the work edited by Paul A. Cohen and John E. Schrecker, *Reform in Nineteenth Century China*. On the Tongzhi Restoration in particular, see Saundra Sturdevant, "Imperialism, Sovereignty, and Self-strengthening—A Reassessment of the 1870s," and Kwang-Ching Liu, "Politics, Intellectual Outlook and Reform: The T'ung-wen kuan Controversy of 1867." In *The Cambridge History of China*, ed. John K. Fairbank, see Kwang-Ching Liu, "The Ch'ing Restoration" (10:409–490), and Ting-Yee Kuo and Kwang-Ching Liu, "Self-strengthening: The Pursuit of Western Technology" (10:491–542). For a general study encompassing the Tongzhi reforms, see Frederic Wakeman, Jr., *The Fall of Imperial China*, 163ff.

2. On the One Hundred Days' Reform in Chinese, see Kang Youwei, *Zibian nianpu*, 15a–29b; Kang Tongjia, *Kang Youwei yu wuxu bianfa*; Liang Qichao, *Wuxu zhengbianji*; Tang Zhijun, *Wuxu bianfa jianshi*; Zhang Pengyuan, *Liang Qichao yu Qingji geming*, and *Liang Qichao yu ninguo zhengzhi*. In English, see Paul A. Cohen, *Between Tradition and Modernity: Wang T'ao and Reform in Late Ch'ing China*; Frederic Wakeman, Jr., *History and Will*, especially 115–152; Lloyd Eastman, "Political Reformism in China Before the Sino-Japanese War"; Richard Howard, Introduction, "The Chinese Reform Movement of the 1890s: A Symposium"; and Kung-chuan Hsiao, *A Modern China and a New World: K'ang Youwei, Reformer and Utopian, 1858–1927*, 196ff., an outstanding study, compulsory

for all students of this era. See also Wolfgang Franke, *Die staatspolitischen Reformsversuche K'ang Yu-weis und seiner Schule.*

3. For details, see Susan Mann Jones and Philip A. Kuhn, "Dynastic decline and the roots of rebellion," in John K. Fairbank, ed., *The Cambridge History of China* 10:116–119.

4. A detailed account can be found in K. C. Liu, "The Ch'ing Restoration," 419–422.

5. For details, see John K. Fairbank, *Trade and Diplomacy* and "The Creation of the Treaty System"; Frederic Wakeman, Jr., *Strangers at the Gate*; Immanuel C. Y. Hsu, *China's Entrance into the Family of Nations*; and the works of John F. Cady, W. C. Costin, J. Y. Wong, Jack J. Gerson, Ssu-yu Teng and John K. Fairbank, Douglas Hurd, Alexander Michie, Henri Cordier, and R. K. I. Quested.

6. For a discussion of the reform leaders, see Mary Wright, *The Last Stand*, 70–79, and K. C. Liu, "The Ch'ing Restoration," 415ff.

7. In addition to works previously cited on the Nian rebellion, see Perry, ed., *Chinese Perspectives on the Nien Rebellion*, and Kuhn, "The Taiping Rebellion," *Cambridge History of China*, 10:310–316.

8. Feng Guifen, "Sheng zeli yi," *Jiaobinlu kangyi*, ch. 1, 14b–16b, as quoted in Wright, *The Last Stand*, 66. See also James Polachek, "Gentry Hegemony—Soochow in the T'ung-chih Restoration," in Frederic Wakeman, Jr., and Carolyn Grant, eds., *Conflict and Control in Late Imperial China*, 211–256, and Wakeman's introduction, 1–25.

9. For a discussion of developments regarding foreign-language and science training, see Martin, *A Cycle of Cathay*, 293–327; Knight Biggerstaff, *The Earliest Modern Government Schools in China*; and Ting-Yee Kuo and Kwang-Ching Liu, "Self-strengthening," 525–532.

10. The temporary cessation of military assaults by external powers as an important factor in enabling reform efforts is very well developed by Wright in *The Last Stand*, 21–42. See also the excellent account by Masataka Banno, *China and the West*, especially 237–246. Details relating to Great Britain are to be found in John F. Cady, *The Roots of French Imperialism in Eastern Asia*, W. C. Costin, *Great Britain and China*, and Stanley Lane-Poole, *Sir Henry Parkes in China*.

11. Wright, *The Last Stand*, 300ff.

12. J. O. P. Bland and E. Backhouse have written a dramatic account of Cixi and her times, entitled *China Under the Empress Dowager*. Unfortunately, the work must be discounted despite the fact that the two British authors were Beijing residents during this era and had numerous political contacts. First, J. J. L. Duyvendak and more recently Hugh Trevor-Roper (*Hermit of Peking*) have revealed that Backhouse was not only extremely eccentric but thoroughly dishonest in matters scholarly, although Trevor-Roper's account exonerates Bland, a reputable journalist. The so-called diary of the Manchu official, Jingshan, supposedly found by Backhouse and figuring prominently in the Bland-Backhouse book, is almost certainly bogus, casting doubt upon the entire work. For a recent study seeking to redress the balance in assessing Cixi, see "The Image of the Empress Dowager Tz'u-hsi," by Sue Fawn Chung based upon a revision of her doctoral dissertation, "The Much Maligned Empress Dowager: A Revisionist Study of the Empress Dowager Tz'u-hsi."

13. For one analysis of the North and South parties of this period, see Fan Wenlan, *Zhongguo jindai shi*, 297–315.

14. For important Chinese sources, see Kang's own writings: his complete works, cited earlier, and *Kang Nanhai wenji*. In Western languages, in addition to Kung-ch'uan Hsiao's major study, see Hidemi Onogawa, "K'ang Yu-wei's Idea of Reform";

Ho Ping-ti, "Weng T'ung-ho and the 'One Hundred Days of Reform'"; Richard C. Howard, "K'ang Yu-wei (1858–1927): His Intellectual Background and Early Thought"; Hsiao Kung-ch'uan, "The Case for Constitutional Monarchy: K'ang Yu-wei's Plan for the Democratization of China"; "Economic Modernization: K'ang Yu-wei's Ideas in Historical Perspective"; "The Philosophical Thought of K'ang Yu-wei: An Attempt at a New Synthesis"; "Weng T'ung-ho and the Reform Movement of 1898"; William F. Hummel, "K'ang Yu-wei, Historical Critic and Social Philosopher, 1858–1927"; K'ang Yu-wei, *Ta T'ung Shu: The One-World Philosophy of K'ang Yu-wei*; Kao Chung Ju (Bernard), *Le mouvement intellectuel en Chine et son rôle dans la revolution chinoise (entre 1898 et 1937)*; Lo Jung-pang, ed., *K'ang Yu-wei: A Biography and a Symposium*; Ma Te-chih, "Le mouvement reformiste et les événements de la cour de Pékin en 1898"; James R. Pusey, "K'ang Yu-wei and Pao-chiao: Confucian Reform and Reformation"; Tikhvinsky, S. L., *Dvizhenie za reformy v Kitae v Kontse XIX veka Kan Iu-wei.*

15. For excellent studies of Liang Qichao in Chinese, see the two works by Zhang Pengyuan cited previously. In Western languages, see three stimulating, diverse works: Joseph R. Levenson, *Liang Ch'i-ch'ao and the Mind of Modern China*; Hao Chang, *Liang Ch'i-ch'ao and Intellectual Transition in China*; and Philip C. Huang, *Liang Ch'i-ch'ao and Modern Chinese Liberalism.*

16. For studies of Yuan Shikai in Chinese, see Lin Mingde, *Yuan Shikai yu Chaoxian*; Liu Fenghan, *Xinjian lujun*; Bai Jiao, *Yuan Shikai yu Zhonghua minguo*; Li Chunyi, *Yuan Shikai zhuan.* In Western languages, consult the major sources: Jerome Ch'en, *Yuan Shih-K'ai*; Ernest Young, *The Presidency of Yuan Shih-k'ai: Liberalism and Dictatorship in Early Republican China*; and Stephen R. MacKinnon, *Power and Politics in Late Imperial China: Yuan Shi-kai in Beijing and Tianjin, 1901–1908.*

17. For the precise terms of the Jiaozhou agreement, see *Qing mo duiwai jiaoshe tiaoyueji* 2:400–401. General studies of this era stressing Western intrusions and Chinese foreign policy include the following in Chinese: Liu Yan, *Zhongguo waijiao shi*, especially the first fourteen chapters; and Ding Minnan, et al., *Diguo chuyi qinhua shi.* In Western languages, see H. B. Morse and Harley F. MacNair, *Far Eastern International Relations*; C. Y. Hsu, *China's Entrance into the Family of Nations*; and John E. Schrecker, *Imperialism and Chinese Nationalism: Germany in Shantung.*

18. For the March 1898 Agreement, see *Qing mo duiwai jiaoshe tiaoyueji* 2: 403–407.

19. See Simon Kuznets, *Economic Growth and Structure*; and *Toward a Theory of Economic Growth with Reflections on the Economic Growth of Modern Nations.*

20. For a thoughtful exposition of this position, see E. Sydney Crawcour, "The Tokugawa Heritage," in William W. Lockwood, ed., *The State and Economic Enterprise in Japan*, 17–44.

21. William W. Lockwood, "Prospectus and Summary," in ibid., 4.

22. For work in the field of Japanese economic history to which we are indebted, we would underline all of the essays in the Lockwood volume cited above, and in addition: Ohkawa Kazushi, et al., *The Growth Rate of the Japanese Economy Since 1878*; Marius B. Jansen, ed., *Changing Japanese Attitudes Toward Modernization*; Henry Rosovsky, *Capital Formation in Japan, 1868–1940*; Ohkawa Kazushi and Henry Rosovsky, *A Century of Growth*; G. C. Allen and Audrey G. Donnithorne, *Western Enterprise in Far Eastern Economic Development*; William W. Lockwood, *The Economic Development of Japan: Growth and Structural Change, 1868–1940*; and Thomas C. Smith, *The Agrarian Origins of Modern Japan.*

23. The following section is indebted to these works: In Chinese, Fu Zhufu, *Zhongguo jingjishi luncong*; Gong Jun, *Zhongguo xin gongye fajiangshi dagang*; Li Guoqi, *Zhongguo zaoqi di tielu jingying*; Qian Gongbo, *Zhongguo jingji fazhanshi*; and Zhang Nan and Wang Renzhi, eds., *Xinhai geming qianshinian jian shilun xuanji*. In English, Wellington K. K. Chan, *Merchants, Mandarins and Modern Enterprise in Late Ch'ing China*; Mark Elvin, *The Pattern of the Chinese Past*; Albert Feuerwerker, *China's Early Industrialization: Sheng Hsuan-huai (1844–1916) and Mandarin Enterprise*; Hao, Yen-p'ing, *The Compradore in Nineteenth Century China: Bridge Between East and West*; Hou Chi-ming, *Foreign Investment and Economic Development in China: 1840–1937*; Thomas L. Kennedy, *The Arms of Kiangnan*; G. William Skinner, ed., *The City in Late Imperial China*; W. E. Willmott, ed., *Economic Organization in Chinese Society*.

24. In addition to Skinner's works already cited, the early studies of Qiao Qiming, Yang Qingkun (C. K. Yang), and Yang Mouchun (Martin Yang) have contributed greatly to an understanding of the socioeconomic context of traditional Chinese politics.

25. Skinner, "Marketing and Social Structure in Rural China," Part II, 228.

26. Ibid., 227–228.

27. One of the more recent works attempting to argue the case for the dominance of the external variable is that of Frances V. Moulder, *Japan, China, and the Modern World Economy*. Moulder, following the work of Immanuel Wallerstein, has sought to explain the differences between Chinese and Japanese economic development by contrasting the degree to which the two societies were incorporated into the world economy, beginning in the nineteenth century. Using this perspective, she argues that the relative autonomy of Japan in contrast to China's extensive incorporation into the global capitalist-imperialist order had a major influence in shaping the economic and political capacities of the two states. China's incorporation resulted in its underdevelopment, she asserts, whereas Japanese autonomy made possible its transformation into a strong nation with a powerful capitalist economy. Like all reductionist theories, this explanation is unsatisfactory. In minimizing the "pre-modern" differences between the two societies, especially in political organization and social structure, and ignoring the critical factor of scale, she slights the key variables. The diverse initiatives taken by indigenous Japanese and Chinese elites in responding to the Western influence reflected the cultural-political-economic proclivities within their respective societies, and as we have noted, the Western influence varied *primarily* in accordance with those proclivities while affecting them *secondarily*.

The ideological underpinnings of the Moulder study are clearly expressed in two passages in the preface: "The lessons of Japan and China for these nations (late developing societies) would seem to be that if national industrialization is to occur, revolutionary Communist movements will be necessary to bring it about" (as in the case of South Korea, Taiwan and Singapore?); and "Although we are often told that Japan and the other industrial capitalist nations are *developed*, this term obfuscates the reality for millions in the industrialized capitalist world: an inferior, deteriorating, and ever insecure living standard and a legal-political framework that hinders efforts of the people to organize for fundamental improvement. Which is more 'developed' today, the People's Republic of China or Japan?" (Preface, ix).

28. See an admirable study by E-tu (Zen) Sun, *Chinese Railways and British Interests, 1898–1911*.

29. Key recent sources such as the work of Paul A. Cohen have already been cited. An earlier standard Western source is Kenneth S. Latourette, *A History of*

Christian Missions in China. See also Columba Cary-Elwes, *China and the Cross: A Survey of Missionary History*; and F. Sutherland, *China Crises: A Missionary Study Book*.

For additional interpretations relating to Western missionaries reflecting a variety of viewpoints, see Irwin T. Hyatt, *Our Ordered Lives Confess: Three Nineteenth Century American Missionaries in East Shantung*; Daniel W. Fisher, *Calvin Wilson Mateer, Forty-Five Years a Missionary in Shantung Province, China: A Biography*; Lovelace S. Foster, *Fifty Years in China: An Eventful Memoir of the Life of Tarleton Perry Crawford, D.D.*; John K. Fairbank, *The Missionary Enterprise in China and America*; Alice H. Gregg, *China and Educational Autonomy: The Changing Role of the Protestant Educational Missionary in China, 1807–1937*; D. McGillivray, ed., *A Century of Protestant Missions in China, 1807–1907*.

30. See Frederic Wakeman, Jr., "The Canton Trade and the Opium War," ch. 4 in *Cambridge History of China*, vol. 10, Part 1, ed. John K. Fairbank.

31. Memorials to the throne of this general period depicting these attitudes toward Westerners can be found in *Yihe Tuan dangan shiliao*.

32. The report is to be found in *NCH*, December 31, 1899, 1229.

33. "An Account from North Kiangsu," *NCH*, January 9, 1899, 17. It was in the same dispatch that the writer added the "Catholic problem" noted earlier.

34. Chiang Monlin, *Tides From the West: A Chinese Autobiography*, 11.

35. For this imperial decree, see *Wuxu bianfa* 2:7–8.

36. For background material, we are much indebted to four scholars: in Chinese, Luo Ergang, "Qingji bing wei jiangyou di qiyuan," and *Xiangjun xinzhi* (A New Treatise on the Hunan Army); *Luying bingzhi*; and Wang Ermin, *Huaijun zhi*; and two Americans, Ralph L. Powell's pioneer work, *The Rise of Chinese Military Power, 1895–1912*, and Philip A. Kuhn, *Rebellion and Its Enemies*. Other works of importance in Western languages include John Rawlinson, *China's Struggle for Naval Development: 1839–1895*; Stephen MacKinnon, "The Peiyang Army, Yuan Shi-k'ai and the Origins of Modern Chinese Warlordism," and his larger work, *Power and Politics in Late Imperial China*, previously cited. In Chinese, see Wen Gongzhi, *Zuijin sanshi nian Zhongguo junshi shi*. This is a reprint of a study first published in 1929. See especially the first three chapters in Section I.

37. Luo argues that indeed the Banner forces were shown to be ineffective as early as the White Lotus Rebellion, at the end of the eighteenth century, with the Green Standard's decline coming somewhat later, although thoroughly revealed at the time of the Opium War ("Qingji bing," 237–240).

38. Reported in *NCH*, February 27, 1899, 336.

39. For a discussion of this question, see Franz Michael's insightful introduction to the work by Stanley Spector, "Regionalism in Nineteenth-Century China," xxi–xliii.

40. "The Real Chinese Problem, III," *NCH*, August 19, 1904, 402–403.

41. Richard, *Forty-five Years*, 223–224.

42. For details, see the well-researched work of Charlton M. Lewis, *Prologue to the Chinese Revolution: The Transformation of Ideas and Institutions in Hunan Province, 1891–1907*, 41–68. In addition, see W. E. Soothill, *Timothy Richard of China*. For the works published by missionary presses during this period, see John Fryer, *The Educational Directory for China*, and *Report of the Society for the Diffusion of Christian and General Knowledge*. Latourette in his *Christian Missions*, and Biggerstaff in *The Earliest Modern Government Schools*, provide detailed accounts of early educational developments in mission schools.

43. See Lewis, *Prologue*, 44–45; also see a stimulating, provocative monograph by Joseph Esherick, *Reform and Revolution in China*, 13–19.

44. For the Qingxue Hui's principles, written at the time of its establishment by Kang Youwei and Liang Qichao, see the section in *Wuxu bianfa* 4:373–394.

45. For the details, see Kung-ch'uan Hsiao, *K'ang Yu-wei*, 193ff. The full memorials in Chinese can be found in *Wuxu bianfa* 2:123–306. We have drawn extensively from the latter collection.

46. The emergence of publications directing attention to overseas events; the creation of discussion groups, formal and informal; the gradual introduction of foreign matters into school curriculum; and the rising tendency of individuals from the gentry and merchant communities to voice their opinions on questions of foreign policy, especially in settings like the treaty ports—all provided the indispensable background to the reform efforts.

47. See Kung-ch'uan Hsiao, "Weng T'ung-ho and the Reform Movement of 1898," 166–179; He Bingti (Ho Ping-ti), "Zhang Yinhuan shizhi," in Bao Zunpeng et al., *Zhongguo jindai shi luncong* 7:108–109. He (Ho) takes the position that Zhang Yinhuan as close friend and confidant to the emperor was the individual primarily responsible for Kang's introduction to the emperor. It should be noted that most of the above individuals were punished in one manner or another after the September coup, since all were involved with Kang in relatively intimate fashion.

The only official reference to Kang comes in the following imperial instructions: "On 13th June, we received a memorial from Xu Zhijing, Recorder of the Hanlin Academy, recommending to our favorable notice Kang Youwei, 3rd Class Secretary of the Board of Works and Zhang Yuanji, 3rd Class Secretary of the Board of Punishments as being men of deep learning and exceptional abilities and progressive ideas. Let the two be presented to us in special audience on the 16th. As for *Zhuren* Liang Qichao, who has been recommended in the same manner, we hereby command the Zongli Yamen to find out where he is at present and report to us." Quoted in *NCH*, September 5, 1898, 439.

48. For the imperial decrees relating to educational reform and the examinations, see the decrees of 11 June, 4 July, 22 August, and 11 September, 1898, in *Wuxu bianfa* 2:17–84.

49. For the imperial decree of June 11, see *Wuxu bianfa* 2:17–19.

50. Many accounts of the September 1898 coup have been written. In Chinese, see Tang Zhijin, *Wuxu bianfa luncong*, and *Wuxu bianfa jian shi*; Liang Qichao, *Wuxu zhengbian ji*. See also the accounts in *Wuxu bianfa*, vol. 2. In English, see Jerome Ch'en, *Yuan Shih-k'ai*; Li Chien-nung, *The Political History of China, 1840–1928*, edited and translated by Ssu-yu Teng and Jeremy Ingalls; Timothy Richard, *Forty-five Years*, 264–268; Meribeth E. Cameron, *The Reform Movement in China, 1898–1912*, 47–50; and Hao Chang, "Intellectual Change and the Reform Movement, 1890–1898."

51. For works in Western languages on secret societies, see Jean Chesneaux, ed., *Popular Movements and Secret Societies in China: 1840–1950*; Jean Chesneaux, *Secret Societies in China in the Nineteenth and Twentieth Centuries*; Benoit Favre, *Les Sociétés secretes en Chine*; Rev. F. H. James, "Secret Societies in Shantung"; W. H. Pickering, "Chinese Secret Societies and Their Origin"; D. H. Porter, "Secret Societies in Shantung." Japanese scholars have done extensive and highly important work on the Chinese secret societies. See Hirayama Shū (Hirayama Amane), *Chūgoku himitsu shakai shi*; Inaba Seiichi, "Shindai no himitsu kessha"; Sakai Tadao, "Gendai Chūgoku ni okeru himitsu kessha"; Suemitsu Takayoshi, *Shina no himitsu kessha to jizen kessha*.

52. On the Yihe Tuan, in Chinese, see Dai Xuanxi, *Yihe Tuan yuanjiu*, and *Yihe Tuan*. The most recent PRC scholarship on the Yihe Tuan is to be found in the papers prepared for a special conference on this subject held in Jinan, Shan-

dong, November 14–20, 1980, attended by some two hundred Chinese scholars and ten foreign scholars. We are much indebted to Professor David Buck for loaning us copies of papers presented.

In Western languages, see Jerome Ch'en, "The Nature and Characteristics of the Boxer Movement: A Morphological Study"; Peter Fleming, *The Siege at Peking*; Robert C. Forsyth, comp. and ed., *The China Martyrs of 1900*; L. R. Marchant, *The Siege of the Peking Legations—A Diary—Lancelot Giles*; Victor Purcell, *The Boxer Uprising: A Background Study*; Chester C. Tan, *The Boxer Catastrophe*. A lengthy discussion of the shift of name to Yihe Tuan and its implications is contained in Purcell, *Boxer Uprising*, 183ff.

53. For details, see Purcell, *Boxer Uprising*, 223–234.

54. See Chester C. Tan, *The Boxer Catastrophe*, 70–75.

55. For details, see Purcell, *Boxer Uprising*, 240–262.

56. For example, the June 6 decree was highly conciliatory. Both the Chinese Christians and the Yihe Tuan "are equally sons of the country and will receive the same treatment from the Court. . . . Yihe Tuan members have now organized into groups and the bad elements among them have destroyed churches and railroads, the latter belonging to the state and the former to the missionaries and the Chinese Christians. How could they so irresponsibly destroy such, causing difficulties for the state?" The decree continued that "if there were seditious elements, the Yihe Tuan should surrender the leaders to be punished according to the law." For the June decrees, see *Yihe Tuan dangan shiliao* 1:118–207.

57. According to the July 1 decree, "Since the coming of the foreign missionaries, there had been incidents between the people and the Christians . . . violence had resulted. But Christians too are sons of the country and they are not without good followers; however, they are being deceived by corrupt teachings while being protected by the missionaries . . . and they blindly followed superstitions and refused to repent." The decree continued by calling upon "Christians to awaken to their wrongdoings and repent." They would be allowed to begin life anew, without regard to their past. Finally, "Since hostilities between China and the foreign powers have begun, all foreign missionaries must be expelled and returned to their countries." For the July 1 decree, see ibid., 214–215.

58. See, for example, Compilation Group for the History of Modern China, ibid., 82ff.

59. Ibid., 124.

60. Ding Mingnan, "Some Opinions Evoked by the Summary of Reports: Answering Comrade Wang Zhizhong," *Guangming ribao*, August 19, 1980, 4.

61. In the paper by Song Qinglan and Guo Dasong, "On the Origins of the Yihe Tuan," the authors assert that there was no direct linkage between the Boxers and the White Lotus sect. Whereas the White Lotus had as their central objective the overthrow of the Qing and the restoration of the Ming, they assert, the Yihe Tuan theme became "Uphold the Qing and eliminate the foreign devils." Sentiment in favor of Ming restoration, they contend, no longer had mass appeal. Rather, the Yihe Tuan represented an organization of the "broad peasant masses," with the fresh objective of fighting imperialism. Li Shiyu, however, in his paper, "Another Inquiry into the Origins of the Yihe Tuan," takes the view that the Boxers began as a grass-roots movement which over time drew into its membership many religious elements, among them the White Lotus. He cites as an example of the White Lotus influence the adoption of the Eight Diagrams for the Yihe Tuan military organization, and asserts that the White Lotus involvement added great strength to the new movement.

62. Wang Nufeng and Dang Dexin, in their paper, "On the Question of the

Anti-feudalism of the Yihe Tuan," argue that the Boxers took an antifeudalist position, although not in a complete manner. They assert that Yihe Tuan roots were in the White Lotus, "a North China peasant-mass, antifeudal, secret organization," and that the antifeudal character of such movements lay in their basic opposition to officialdom. They acknowledge that when the Boxers accepted the slogan "Uphold the Qing, eliminate the foreign devils," the antifeudal dimension of the movement was weakened, whereas the anti-imperialist dimension was strengthened, and they blame the former development on the limitations of a peasant-based leadership.

Dong Qing and Da Song in their paper, "On the Question of Whether the Yihe Tuan was Antifeudal," insist that because the Boxers sought to protect the Qing, they cannot be considered antifeudal. Nor were they so considered by the Qing court. Individuals like Yuan Shikai who opposed the Boxers did so without the sanction of the court, according to them. Those who argue that the movement was antifeudal, they submit, dare not admit that one could be anti-imperialist but pro-Qing because the Qing government itself had a side that was anti-imperialist. Thus, at root, the Yihe Tuan represented an anti-imperialist, pro-Qing movement.

Wu Yannan in his paper, "The Yihe Tuan Movement and the Awakening of the Chinese People," expresses the prevailing Marxist interpretation when he asserts that the Boxers represented an anti-imperialist, patriotic movement, spontaneously organized with the peasants as its main force, "which dealt a setback to the imperialist partition of China." The Yihe Tuan thus made a contribution to China's revolutionary development, serving to awaken the Chinese people. The weaknesses of the movement—its adherence to primitive superstition and promonarchist views—reflected the limitations of the peasant class from which it had sprung.

Another article, by Ye Fengmei, "An Historical Analysis of the Yihe Tuan Movement," advances the thesis that the movement "put a stop to the imperialist division of China," and had a deep influence on the Chinese people. The lesson to be derived from the movement, however, is that a revolution must have a clear revolutionary program. This the peasant class lacked.

Liu Qinwu's paper, "A Preliminary Discussion of the Historical Role of the Yihe Tuan Movement," sets forth the view that the Boxers emerged as a response to the imperialist invasion of China, and such resulting ills as increased taxation, the destruction of local handicrafts, and the activities of the missionaries. The peasant masses, however, were politically immature. Seeing only the immediate suffering—not the broader nature of imperialism—their antiforeignism contained an element of blindness. This did not mean that the Boxers were wholly backward, but signified the fact that a purely peasant movement could not achieve victory over imperialism and feudalism. Nonetheless, by raising the consciousness of the Chinese people and weakening the Manchu—exposing "their oppression of the people internally and their surrenderism to the powers externally"—the Boxers prepared the way for the 1911 Revolution.

63. See, for example, Wu Siou, "A Preliminary Investigation into the Yihe Tuan Cry, 'Uphold the Qing, Eliminate the Foreign Devils'," 53. Among other papers of interest in this respect are Shao Hongya and Han Min, "The Anti-Church Struggle in Shanxi During the Yihe Tuan Movement Era," and Li Kongchun, "Several Questions Concerning the Tianjin Yihe Tuan Movement."

64. For a translation of a Kang-Liang manifesto first published in Japan, see *NCH*, October 10, 1900, 774. An earlier pamphlet, smuggled into China, was carried in translations in the *NCH* issues of April 18, April 25, and May 2, 1900.

65. For a report, including lengthy excerpts from the speeches, see *NCH*, May 8, 1901, 904.

66. Ibid.

67. Martins's comments are also to be found in ibid., 885. In addition, see W. A. P. Martin, *A Cycle of Cathay.*

CHAPTER THREE

1. Liang got the money to start this journal from Chinese merchants resident in Japan. In addition to his journalistic activities, he took up teaching again, gathering some of his old Hunan students and tutoring them in his house. Later, a school was organized in Tokyo, in 1899, known as the Gaodeng Dadong Xuexiao (The Great Harmony Higher School), with Liang serving as principal. See Hao Chang, *Intellectual Transition,* 133–134. In the opening issue of *Qingyi bao* (henceforth *QYB*), Liang provided the English title, *The China Discussion,* but this is neither good English nor an accurate translation. For a discourse on the term *qingyi,* see Lloyd E. Eastman, *Throne and Mandarins,* 16–29.

2. *Xinmin congbao* (henceforth *XMCB*) has been translated variously. Recent authors have tended to use the term "new citizen" for *xinmin,* and from the very first articles contained in the journal, one can infer that Liang has this concept in mind on occasion. However, the literal translation of *xinmin* is "new people," and at the time, there was no Chinese ideographic equivalent for the Western term "citizen." Later, Liang and others introduced two new compounds into their writings, both in usage in Japanese works: first, *guomin,* literally, "nationals," and later, *gongmin* a term that should be translated as "citizen." To retain the literal meaning of these terms is to convey the groping toward appropriate terminology for Western political themes that characterized this era. So far as we can determine, the term *gongmin* was first introduced in a major article by Minyi (Hu Hanmin), "The Self-Government of Citizens," *XMCB,* April 8, 1902, 37–46. At a later point, Liang himself used the term *shimin* (literally, city-person or burgher), but he put after it the word "citizen" in English, explaining that there was no term for the latter word in Chinese. See A New Man of China, "On New People," Part 24, "On Political Capacity," *XMCB,* June 28, 1904, 8. Bernal uses the title *The Renovation of the People,* and while that is more elegant, it seems to us somewhat inflated from the original Chinese.

3. "Preface," *QYB,* December 23, 1898, 1a–2a (1:3–6). Citations of *Qingyi bao* are from the 12-volume reprinted edition published by the Zhengwen Publishing Co., Taibei, 1967. In addition to providing the original data in terms of dates and page numbers, we have also provided in parentheses the location in the Taibei edition of items cited.

4. For a discussion of Liang's early contacts with Japanese Pan-Asianists, see Phillip C. Huang, *Liang Ch'i-ch'ao,* 47–53.

5. Mai Menghua, "Whether or Not China Is to Die Is to Be Decided Today," *QYB,* February 11, 1900, 1a–4b (5:2465–2472).

6. One Who Sips Ice (Yinbingzi, a favorite pseudonym of Liang), "Worry about Country and Love of Country," *XMCB,* February 8, 1902, 1. Liang went on to state that if China could be independent, it would not be concerned as to whether Europeans were either scorpions or gods.

7. Shangxinren (Mai Menghua), "On Slaves," *QYB,* January 11, 1901, 1a–4b (9:4417–4424).

8. Mai Menghua, "Whether or Not China Will Die," 3a.

9. *QYB,* December 23, 1898, 1a–1b. Later, Liang's optimism waned on occasion, as we shall note, and indeed, his gradual shift toward deeper pessimism served to precipitate and reinforce shifts in his basic political ideas. For an early indication

of the shift, see his "An Historical Discussion of China in the Past Ten Years," beginning in *QYB* on April 29, 1901, and continuing through July 6, 1901. Here, Liang described China's condition as equivalent to that of a person suffering from consumption and refusing to admit that he was ill. Good physicians existed, but unless their talents were utilized, it would soon be too late.

10. See A New Man of China, "Foreign Capital Investments in China," *XMCB*, September 10, 1904, (no. 53, 6–8).

11. Shangxinren (Mai Menghua), continuing "On the Boxer Rebellion," *QYB*, June 1, 1900, 1a–4a (6:3051–3055); and "On the Responsibility of Regional Officials," by the same author, *QYB*, July 17, 1900, 1a–4b (7:3299–3306). For Liang's own comments, see "Commemorative Words for the One-Hundredth Issue of This Newspaper and a Discussion of the Duty and Experience of This Newspaper," *QYB*, December 22, 1901, 1a–8a (12:6287–6301). Liang blamed the uprising on the empress dowager, asserting that her anger (against the reformers of 1898) finally turned to madness, and she started awarding bandits as if they were righteous individuals and permitted the killing of foreign ministers. Then, asserted Liang, the "tigerish allies" from ten countries attacked "sheep-like China," and within fifty days "the sacred capital" had fallen. Never in several thousand years had China's humiliation been so extreme. Later, however, some articles in *XMCB* were to suggest that while events such as the Boxer Rebellion accomplished nothing except to advance misery at the time, their longer-range effect was to stimulate the reform movement. See Guan Yun, "External and Internal Actions," *XMCB*, April 19, 1905, 1–8.

12. Liang Qichao, "How Should the Foreign Powers Deal with China Today?" *QYB*, August 5, 1900, 3a–4b (7:3427–3430), and August 25, 1900, 3a–4b (7:3553–3556). If the situation were mishandled, asserted Liang, China would become a huge battlefield for the next twenty years, where the blood of whites and yellows would mingle.

13. See Mai Menghua, "China After the Peace Treaty," *QYB*, February 19, 1901, 1a–3b (9:4481–4486), and March 1, 1901, 1a–4b (9:4543–4550).

14. Liang Qichao, "A New Way for National Extinction," *QYB*, July 6, 1901, 1a–5b (10:5399–5408); July 26, 1901, 1a–4b (11:5461–5466); and August 24, 1907, 1a–4a (11:5643–5649). Liang remarked that Russia had conquered Poland, not because of Russian adroitness, but because the Polish aristocracy had invited the Russians into the country. Similar developments were taking place in China. Regional officials in southeastern China were signing agreements with various foreign powers for assistance. This was tantamount to handing the Yangtze region over to foreign states, especially the British.

15. A New Man of China, "On the Tendency Toward Competition Among Races," *XMCB*, February 23, 1902, 29–42.

16. Ibid., 37–39.

17. One Who Sips Ice, "Travels on the New Continent," *XMCB*, January 27, 1903, 1–6. Yet in this same essay Liang noted that the United States faced definite problems—such as assimilating its diverse immigrants effectively—and might ultimately suffer the fate of the Roman Empire.

18. One Who Sips Ice, "Boycotting the United States' Ban on Chinese Labor and Sino-U.S. Relations," *XMCB*, May 4, 1905, 1–7. For an account of the problems of Chinese immigrants in South Africa, see "The Tragedy of Chinese Immigrants in South Africa," *XMCB*, June 28, 1904, 105.

19. "Commentary on German Control of the Qingdao-Jinan Railroad," *XMCB*, June 28, 1904, 2.

20. A New Man of China, "Foreign Capital Investments in China." *XMCB*, Part 1, 1–22, and Part 2, no. 53, 1–13.

For another article decrying the "subjugation of China" through foreign control of railways, see A New Man of China, "The Transfer of Railroad Rights," *XMCB*, September 10, 1904, 1–5.

21. "A Commentary on the British-Tibetan Treaty," *XMCB*, Oct. 9, 1904, 3.

22. "The Influence of the Russian Revolution," *XMCB*, January 6, 1905, 25–35; February 4, 1905, 47–54.

23. "The Future of Manchuria," *XMCB*, March 20, 1904, 1–22. For additional evidence of Liang's concern about Japanese expansionism, see Yinbing (Liang), "Japan's Korea: A Reference Point for My Country's Police Authority," *XMCB*, January 6, 1905, 76–79.

24. "On Extraterritorial Rights and the Thought Processes of the Chinese People," *XMCB*, March 6, 1905, 1–4.

25. One particularly trenchant essay illustrative of these themes was that by Guan Yun cited in n. 11. Asserted the author: "Since demands by foreign powers upon China can never be satiated, the best thing to do is not to yield to any of them. We can cope with their demands by doing the things they want to do. For example, if they want to build railways in China, we should build the railways ourselves" (p. 7). The thesis of self-reliance, in fact, had been enunciated in the earliest reformer essays. For example, see Feng Chiqiang, "On Independence," *QYB*, August 25, 1900, 3a–5b (7:3739–3744), and Liang Qichao, "Preserving China," *QYB*, December 23, 1899, 4a–4b (5:2141–2142).

26. This theme was presented in many of Liang's essays, but for its most extended treatment, see One Who Sips Ice, "On the Advantages and Disadvantages of Racial and Political Revolutions," *XMCB*, March 9, 1906, 31–36.

27. For details, see Hao Chang, *Liang Ch'i-ch'ao*, 121–131; and Huang, *Liang Ch'i-ch'ao*, 24–35. As we noted earlier, Liang's "early Beijing period," from mid-1895 to the spring of 1896, had given him considerable visibility as a publicist and reformer, even though he was a mere twenty-two years of age. In addition to assisting Kang in the promotion of the Qiangxue Hui, he served as editor and chief writer for that society's short-lived organ, *Zhongwai gongbao*. It was also during this period that Liang had intimate contact with several American missionaries, including Timothy Richard. Liang's first efforts to grapple with the revolutionary ideas of the West derive from these months.

A second period commenced when Liang went to Shanghai in early 1896 to launch *Shiwu bao* with Wang Kangnian and Huang Cunxian, a promising official of progressive bent. Until late 1897, Liang operated in the milieu of the Chinese city closest to the external world, a city sprinkled with young intellectuals eager to revitalize their society by borrowing from the West. The passionate and highly intelligent Tan Sitong, soon to be martyred in the aftermath of the 1898 reform fiasco, became one of his close friends, and there were other young reformers attracted to *Shiwu bao*. During this period also, Liang came under the influence of Yan Fu, as we have seen, which opened another channel to Westernism.

A third period began toward the end of 1897, when Liang moved briefly to Hunan, serving as lecturer in the newly created Academy of Current Affairs. This was a part of a larger reform effort, as we have noted, sponsored by Chen Baozhen, the progressive governor of the province. At this point, Liang was already prepared to espouse concepts of democracy and parliamentarism, and to give vent to some of the sharpest anti-Manchu sentiments of his career. After a serious illness in the spring of 1898, Liang returned to Beijing in time to participate in the reform efforts. In the brief span of three years, Liang had encompassed a range of contacts and experiences belying his youthfulness and setting the stage for the views expressed during his lengthy exile.

28. Liang Qichao, "On Patriotism," *QYB*, February 20, 1899, 1a–3b (1:327–332), and March 2, 1899, 1a–3a (1:391–395).

29. "On New People," *XMCB*, February 8, 1902, 1–4.

30. A New Man of China, "Hungarian Patriot Kossuth," *XMCB*, March 24, 1902, 1–13.

31. "On New People," *XMCB*, February 8, 1902, 9.

32. Ibid.

33. "On Patriotism." This theme was to be reiterated and amplified in Liang's "A Historical Discussion of China in the Past Ten Years" (n. 9 above). We cannot deny, stated Liang, that our spirit of patriotism is more feeble than that of the West or Japan, and this is a source of weakness. He went on to assert that the problem lay in three conceptual deficiencies. First, the Chinese had never been able to distinguish between the state (*guojia*) and the world (*tianxia*), hence they had never recognized their society as a state. For centuries, the Chinese had referred to their country as *tianxia* (literally, "[all] under heaven"), relegating everything else to barbarism. In the West, where a multistate system existed, love of country (through a comparison/contrast with others) naturally emerged. Another factor lay in the inability of the Chinese to distinguish between the state and dynasty. It was strange but true that the Chinese themselves never referred to *China* but only to various dynastic names. The Chinese were prepared to follow even people of another race if they assumed power, treating them as sovereigns. Finally, the Chinese made no differentiation between the state and its nationals (*guomin*). In the West, it was commonly recognized that rulers and officials were public servants of the nationals. Hence the commitment of the people to the state was strong. But in China it was precisely the reverse.

34. A New Man of China, "On Nationalism," *XMCB*, March 24, 1902, 1–12.

35. See Shangxinren (Mai Menghua), "On Slaves" (n. 7 above).

36. Fen Fansheng, "On Military Nationals," *XMCB*, February 8, 1902, 1–10; continued on March 10, 1–8.

37. Ibid., part 1 (7).

38. Ibid., part 2 (8).

39. Ibid., part 1 (6).

40. A New Man of China, "On New People," part 4: "On Nationalism," *XMCB*, March 24, 1902, 1–21; and "On Changes and Varieties of Nationalism," *XMCB*, June 20, 1902, 19–33.

41. See "On New People," *XMCB*, March 10, 1902, 107ff.

42. For details, see Feng Ziyou, *Zhongguo minguo* 1:76–79, and Lewis, *Prologue*, 93–109.

43. An account of the complex relations between Liang and Sun during this period can be found in various sources. In Chinese, see Feng Ziyou, *Geming yishi* 1:47–50; Luo Jialun, *Guofu nianpu chugao* 1:111; Zhang Pengyuan, *Liang Qichao yu Qingji geming*; and Chen Shaobai, *Xingzhonghui geming shiyao*. In Japanese, see Miyazaki Torazō, *Sanjū-sannen no yume*, now available in English translation, Etō Shinkichi and Marius B. Jansen, trans., *My Thirty-three Years' Dream*. A detailed presentation is to be found in Yen-p'ing Hao, "The Abortive Cooperation Between Reformers and Revolutionaries," 93–95, and Harold Z. Schiffrin, *Sun*

Yat-sen and the Origins of the Chinese Revolution, 163–165 and 184–189. See also Hao Chang, *Intellectual Transition*, 134–140, and Huang, *Chinese Liberalism*, 91–96.

44. Despite the available documentation, it has been difficult to fix precisely Liang's political attitudes and actions in the years 1899–1900. Generally, scholars have emphasized the degree to which Liang veered toward revolution and republicanism in this period, and his near-break with Kang. Certain letters and personal accounts appear to give substance to this interpretation. In his work, *Intellectual Trends in the Qing period*, first published in Chinese in 1921 and translated later by Immanuel C. Y. Hsu, Liang presents a picture of himself which most scholars accept without question. He writes in a curious third-person, seemingly detached fashion about his activities and views—long after the Revolution of 1911 and the end of the monarchy were faits accomplis. Liang portrays himself as having "daily espoused the revolutionary and republican cause against the Manchu arousing Kang's strong disapproval (during an unspecified period) (102). He continues by asserting that even after he had become "somewhat displeased" by the work of the revolutionaries, his conservative and progressive instincts "frequently fought each other within himself" so that his views of one day often contradicted those of an earlier day (102–103).

When matched against the evidence of the period, however, this account raises problems of credibility in our opinion. At a minimum, it is too dramatic, causing one to suspect that he was writing with an eye to his current and future audiences. It is true that Liang hoped to effect some type of union with the Sun group. But as we shall indicate, a careful reading of *Qingyi bao* provides no contemporary evidence to support the thesis that Liang had swung over to a support of republicanism—the cardinal difference between the Bao Huang Hui (The Society to Protect the Emperor) and the Sun forces at this point. Neither Kang nor Liang opposed the use of violence to restore the emperor, as we have noted.

45. Liang Qichao, "Political Reform Must be Predicated On Equality Between the Han and the Manchu," *QYB*, December 23, 1898, 1a–4b (1:7–12); and January 2, 1899, 1a–3b (1:67–72).

46. See Kang Youwei, "Mister Nanhai on Revolution," *XMCB*, September 16, 1902, 59–69.

47. Ibid., 59.

48. Ibid., 64.

49. A New Man of China, "A Study of Revolutions in Chinese History," *XMCB*, February 14, 1904, 1–17.

50. A New Man of China, "On Political Capability," *XMCB*, February 4, 1905, 1–10.

51. One Who Sips Ice, "On the Advantages and Disadvantages of Racial and Political Revolutions" (n. 26 above).

52. Ibid., 15–17.

53. You Ze, "On Political Parties in China, Present and Future," *XMCB*, November 30, 1906, 1–22.

54. Liang Qichao, "On Constitutional Government," *QYB*, June 7, 1901, 1a–5b (10:5163–5172).

55. Ibid., 10.

56. A New Man of China, "On Legislative Power," *XMCB*, February 23, 1902, 1–10.

57. A New Man of China, "The Relation Between Geography and Civilization," *XMCB*, Feb. 23, 1902, 53–57.

58. A New Man of China, "On Government's and People's Rights and Their Limits," *XMCB*, March 10, 1902, 25–32.

59. Liang Qichao, "On Religious Reform in China," *QYB*, June 28, 1899, 9a–13b (3:1237–1248), and July 8, 1899, 4a–5b (3:1311–1314).

60. Liang Qichao, "The Two Great Founding Philosophers of Contemporary Civilization and Their Writings," *XMCB*, February 8, 1902, 1–7.

61. A New Man of China, "On the Idea of Rights," *XMCB*, April 22, 1902, 1–15.

62. A New Man of China, "A Short History of Economics," *XMCB*, May 8, 1902, 1–18.

63. A New Man of China, "On Progress," *XMCB*, June 20, 1902, 1–8.

64. A New Man of China, "On the Cultivation of Military Strength," ibid., 8.

65. One Who Sips Ice, "Travels on the New Continent," *XMCB*, January 27, 1903, Appendix 1–6.

66. A New Man of China, "On Political Capacity," *XMCB*, June 28, 1904, 1–12.

67. Guan Yun, "Recent Theories of Majoritarianism and How to View Them," *XMCB*, June 28, 1904, 39–48.

68. A New Man of China, "On Russian Anarchism," *XMCB*, November 2, 1903, 59–75.

69. See "Alas! Constitutionalism in Russia," *XMCB*, September 10, 1904, 1–8; A New Man of China, "The Influence of the Russian Revolution," *XMCB*, January 6, 1905, 25–35; and One Who Sips Ice, "A Continued Discussion of Russia's Constitutional Problem," ibid., 73–76.

70. One Who Sips Ice, "On Enlightened Absolutism," *XMCB*, January 25 (1–24), February 8 (1–16), February 23 (1–50), and March 25 (1–10), 1906.

71. *XMCB*, February 8, 1906, 9–10.

72. Ibid., 10–11.

73. *XMCB*, February 23, 1906, 25–26.

74. Ibid., 44.

75. Can Liang's attitude toward the need for a stage of "enlightened absolutism" be reconciled with his earlier attitudes? If one takes Huang Keqiang in the novel *The Future of New China* to be Liang, there is little difficulty. One must point out, however, that in that same period, Liang had leveled a strong criticism against *Chinese-style* absolutism in an essay entitled "On Absolutism Which Has a Hundred Harms to the Ruler But Not a Single Benefit," *XMCB*, November 30, 1902, 15–33. In this essay, Liang emphasized the thesis that absolutism was even more harmful to the ruler than to the people since many of the court intrigues and estrangements between monarch and people that had perennially existed could be eliminated only through constitutionalism. Moreover, since absolutism was doomed, how the court handled the issue of constitutional reform would determine whether China could evolve into a Japan or an England (constitutional monarchy) or become another France or United States (republic). If we understand Liang's "enlightened absolutism" to represent tutelage preparatory to constitutionalism, this essay is not in contradiction to his later views, although the thrust is clearly different.

76. *XMCB*, February 23, 1906, 45.

77. Xianyou Zi, "On Power," *QYB*, May 24, 1900, 1a–4b (6:2861–2868). In the following section, we have drawn heavily on an earlier article, Robert A. Scalapino and Harold Schiffrin, "Early Socialist Currents in the Chinese Revolutionary Movement: Sun Yat-sen versus Liang Qichao." Certain sentences and paragraphs have been taken verbatim from this article, or transferred with minimal change.

For details of the first introduction of socialist concepts into China, see Li Yu-ning, *The Introduction of Socialism into China*, and Martin Bernal, *Chinese Socialism to 1907*. Both authors make the linkage between Kang's ideas concerning an era of "great harmony," the progression of mankind toward a utopian world of peace and justice, and the socialist currents that were now circulating in the West. Bernal speculates that since Kang apparently began using the concept "great harmony" in about 1891, he may have come to the idea through acquaintance with the synopsis of Edward Bellamy's *Looking Backward* which had been published in translation in *The Review of the Times*, the S. D. K. missionary publication earlier noted (22–30).

For a detailed account of the first introduction of Western events involving socialists, anarchists, and nihilists, see Bernal, 32ff. These came through brief articles in *The Review of the Times* and its predecessor, *The Globe Magazine*, and necessitated the creation of new compounds to identify the Western political groups. By 1899, Marx along with other socialists had been introduced through this channel, by means of a translation of portions of Benjamin Kidd's *Social Evolution* (p. 37). By this time, of course, the reformers were in Japan where they had available to them a much wider range of Japanese materials on socialism, including many translations of Western works, and it is clear that from 1899 on, this source provided the principal stimuli. Bernal indicates that it was in 1903 that "an explosion of information on socialism available in Chinese" occurred, in the main through translations of Japanese works published by the Bookshop for the Diffusion of Knowledge in Shanghai, an outlet established in 1901 with money raised by Liang from Chinese merchants in Japan (94ff.). See also Li Yu-ning, 12–21.

78. A New Man of China, "On Liberty," *XMCB*, May 22, 1902, 1–8.

79. Liang Qichao, "On the Influence of Scholarly Writings on the World," *XMCB*, February 8, 1902, 1–10. In this same article, Liang mentions the writings of Saint Simon and August Comte.

80. A New Man of China, "The Influence of the Russian Revolution," *XMCB*, January 6, 1905, 1–8.

81. One Who Sips Ice, "On Enlightened Absolutism," *XMCB*, February 23, 1906, 1–50.

82. One Who Sips Ice, "Miscellaneous Answers to a Certain Paper: Is a Social Revolution Necessary in Present-day China?" *XMCB*, September 3, 1906, 5–52.

83. Ibid., 9.

84. Ibid., 44.

85. Ibid., 47.

86. Ibid., 48.

87. Ibid., 49–50.

88. For various accounts of the Japanese socialist movement of this period and its influence, in Japanese, see Arahata Kanson, *Heiminsha jidai: Nihon shakaishugi undō no yōran*; Itoya Toshio, *Nihon shakaishugi no reimei*; Nishikawa Fumiko, "Meiji shakai undō no omoide," in *Rōdō undōshi kenkyū*; Okamoto Hiroshi, *Nihon shakaishugi seitō ronshi josetsu*; Ota Masao, *Meiji shakaishugi seitō shi*; Watanabe Haruo, *Nihon Marukusushugi undō no reimei*; and Watanabe Toru and Asukai Masamichi, eds., *Nihon shakaishugi undō shiron*.

In English, see Hyman Kublin, *Asian Revolutionary: The Life of Katayama Sen*; F. G. Notehelfer, *Kōtoku Shūshi: Portrait of a Japanese Radical*; Robert A. Scalapino, *Democracy and the Party Movement in Prewar Japan*; Irwin Scheiner, *Christians, Converts and Social Protest in Meiji Japan*; and George M. Wilson, *Radical Nationalist in Japan: Kita Ikki, 1883–1937*.

89. Wu Zhongyao, "A Discussion of Socialism," *XMCB*, October 18, 1906, 35–56.

90. One Who Sips Ice, "A Further Refutation of a Certain Paper's Land Nationalization Doctrine," *XMCB*, May 1907, 1–57. This long essay was in answer to *Min bao*, March 6, 1907, 1–19, and was spread over three issues, April, May, and June 1907.

91. *XMCB*, June 1907, 20–21.

92. *XMCB*, May 1907, 56.

93. See Minyi, "Responding to Him Who Challenged the Principles of People's Livelihood," *Min bao*, March 6, 1907, 1–112.

CHAPTER FOUR

1. The competition to claim Sun has steadily escalated between the Nationalists and the Communists in recent years. For Chinese works of a documentary nature, historical studies of an earlier vintage, and studies from a Nationalist perspective, see Feng Ziyou, *Zhonghua minguo kaiguo qian geming shi*; Feng Ziyou, *Geming yishi*; Luo Jialun, *Guofu nianpu*; Luo Jialun, ed. and comp., *Geming wenxian*; Luo Gang, *Le bian guofu nianpu jiumiu*, ed. Luo Jialun; Guomindang, eds., *Guofu quanji*; Zou Lu, *Zhongguo Guomindang shigao*; Huang Jilu, ed., *Yanjiu Zhongshan xiansheng di shiliao yu shixue*; Committee for the Compilation of Materials on the Party History, Luo Jialun and Huang Jilu, eds., *Guofu nianpu zengding ben*; and Chen Pengren, *Sun Zhongshan xiansheng yu Riben youren*.

Materials dealing with Sun Yat-sen published in the PRC recently include: Chinese People's Political Consultative Conference, Guangdong Committee et al., *Sun Zhongshan shiliao quanji*; Chinese People's Political Consultative Conference, Guangdong Committee, *Sun Zhongshan yu Xinhai geming shiliao quanji*; Guangdong Committee, Historical Research Division, et al., *Jinian Sun Zhongshan xiansheng*; Guangdong Social Science Research Institute, Historical Research Division, et al., *Sun Zhongshan nianpu*; Li Zehou, "An Outline of the Thought of the Revolutionary Faction of the Bourgeoisie at the Beginning of the Twentieth Century," and "On Sun Yat-sen's Thought"; Shang Mingxuan, *Sun Zhongshan zhuan*; Shao Zhuanli, *Sun Zhongshan*; Zhang Kaiyuan and Lin Zhangbing, eds., *Xinhai geming shi*; Wei Yingdao and Wu Yennan, *Xinhai geming shi*, vol. 2. In addition, writings on Sun can also be found in current periodical literature; see, for example, *Zhongshan daxue xuebao*, no. 4, 1979.

In English, the most authoritative and carefully researched work on Sun's early career is Harold Z. Schiffrin, *Sun Yat-sen and the Origins of the Chinese Revolution*, previously cited. This study ends with the formation of the Tongmeng Hui in 1905. Schiffrin has also prepared a general study of Sun for the nonspecialist, drawn mainly from his earlier research, *Sun Yat-sen: Reluctant Revolutionary*. An indispensable companion to Schiffrin's monograph is the excellent study by C. Martin Wilbur, *Sun Yat-sen: Frustrated Patriot*, which is built around certain critical topics, particularly Sun's quest for foreign assistance, and focuses extensively upon his career after 1905.

Scholars also remain indebted to two earlier works, Paul Linebarger, *Sun Yat-sen, and the Chinese Republic*; and Lyon Sharman, *Sun Yat-sen: His Life and Its Meaning*, first published in 1934, which still conveys a vivid portrayal of Sun. This work was reissued by Stanford University Press in 1968 with a discerning introduction by Lyman P. Van Slyke. An account by a leading Soviet scholar is S. L. Tikhvinsky, *Sun Yat-sen: On the Occasion of the Centenary of his Birth (1866–1966)*; see also his "Sun Yat-sen and Problems of Solidarity of the Peoples of Asia." In addition, see Marius B. Jansen, *The Japanese and Sun Yat-sen*, for a model monographic study of Sun's relation with the Japanese.

Sun's own "autobiography," *Memoirs of a Chinese Revolutionary: A Programme of National Reconstruction for China*, is deeply disappointing. The greater part of the work is devoted to an effort to prove one of Sun's primary theses, namely, "that action is easy, but knowledge is difficult." This section is followed by an exposition of Sun's ambitious plan for China's industrialization, and the memoirs are contained in a single chapter. Perhaps this is just as well, inasmuch as they are inaccurate as well as incomplete. In Japanese, see Miyazaki Torazō (Tōten), *Sanjūsannen no yume*. This has recently been translated into English by Eto Shinkichi and Marius Jansen with an introduction, *My Thirty-three Years' Dream*. Our citations are from the Japanese edition.

2. For details, see Zhong Guanyi, *Wo zai xiaweiyi de qishijiu nian*; Schiffrin, *Origins*, 14–17; Feng, *Geming yishi* 2:2.

3. For the section in Miyazaki discussing Sun's emerging revolutionary ideas, see 79–87. See also Luo Jialun, *Guofu nianpu* 1:36–53, and Chen Shaobai, *Xingzhong Hui geming shiyao*, 4–10. The latter work was first published in 1935.

4. Schiffrin, *Origins*, 27–29. For further details of this episode, see Chen Shaobai, *Xingzhong Hui*, 12–14.

5. Schiffrin, *Origins*, 38.

6. Sun Yat-sen, "Letter to Li Hongzhang Setting Forth a Grand Plan to Save the Country," June 1894, in *Guofu quanji*, 5:1–12.

7. See Luo Jialun, *Guofu nianpu* 1:62.

8. Ibid.

9. Schiffrin, *Origins*, 73–77; Zhang and Lin, *Xinhai geming shi*, 95.

10. Chen Shaobai, *Xingzhong Hui*, 16.

11. Ibid., 17–19. Chen asserts that it was he who rebutted the argument of Zheng Shiliang that Yang should be killed, and Sun agreed with him.

12. Feng Ziyou, *Zhonghua minguo*, 14–30.

13. Schiffrin, *Origins*, 70–77.

14. Chen Shaobai, *Xingzhong Hui*, 17–22; Schiffrin, *Origins*, 77–87.

15. Ibid., 13.

16. See Sun Yat-sen, *Kidnapped in London*, 28–39.

17. Chen Shaobai, *Xingzhong Hui*, 26–27.

18. Sun Yat-sen, "The Philosophy of Sun Wen," in *Guofu quanji* 2:84.

19. Miyazaki, *Sanjūsannen*, 110–114. Miyazaki's account of his relations with Sun covers only the period between September 1897 and the fall of 1900 when he and Sun were forced to witness yet another revolutionary failure, that at Huizhou (Waichow). Having been written and published very shortly thereafter, however, his memoirs were fresh and his account of certain episodes extraordinarily detailed, as in the case of this first meeting.

20. See Miyazaki, *Sanjūsannen*, 144–147; also Jansen, *The Japanese*, 68–74.

21. Chen Shaobai, *Xingzhong Hui*, 79–83; Feng Ziyou, *Geming yishi* 1:75, and Miyazaki, *Sanjūsannen*, 154–158.

22. Ibid., 209–222.

23. Luo, *Guofu nianpu* 1:165–166.

24. Feng Ziyou, "Summary of the Affairs of Qin Lishan," in *Geming yishi* 1:85–92.

25. For a recent analysis of one of these journals—*Hubei xuesheng kai* (Hubei Student's World)—from a Marxist perspective, see Huang Guohua, "The Hubei Student's World: the First Journal of Students in Japan Named after a Province at

the End of the Qing Dynasty." *Hubei xuesheng kai*, the first issue of which was published in January 1903 and continued for eight issues (with the sixth issue, the name was changed to *Han sheng* [The Voice of Han]), is defined by Huang as the organ of "the revolutionary faction of the bourgeoisie," exposing the trickery of constitutional monarchy, propagandizing for democratic rights, and focusing on the need for a new national education as well as the importance of borrowing from Western science and technology to develop Chinese industry and agriculture. The weaknesses, according to Huang, stemmed from its representation of the propertied class. Thus, it was "unable to advance powerful anti-imperialist or antifeudal positions," nor "to escape Great Han chauvinism." Its appeal, moreover, "was directed primarily to intellectuals, not to the masses" (37).

26. This section borrows extensively from an earlier study by Robert A. Scalapino, "Prelude to Marxism: The Chinese Student Movement in Japan, 1900–1910." For other studies, see Sanetō Keishū, *Chūgokujin ni Nihon ryūgaku shi*; "The Chinese Students in Japan," *Kakumei hyōron* (Revolutionary Review), September 5, 1906, 1; Roger F. Hackett, "Chinese Students in Japan, 1900–1910."

27. Feisheng, "On National Spirit," *Zhejiang zhao* (The Zhejiang Current), April 1903, 1–12.

28. See, for example, the "Opening Statement" in *Hubei xuesheng jie* (The Hubei Student World), January 1903, 1–16; also "On Nationalism," *Zhejiang zhao*, January 1903, 19–27.

29. For an interesting synthesis between pessimism and optimism, see "The Relation Between Education and Self-Government," *Hubei xuesheng jie*, April 1903, 15–23.

30. See Zhongkan, "On Self-Government," *Zhejiang zhao*, July 1903, 1–10.

31. See Sixian, "Disputing the *Xinmin congbao*'s Discussion of a Nonracial Revolution," *Fu bao*, May 25, 1906, no pagination; "The Dangerous State of the Han People's Freedom to Assemble and Speak," *Zhongguo ribao* (China News), March 9 and 11, 1907, 2.

32. Xiaozi, "To Correct the Falseness of the Han Thieves, Kang and Liang," *Dajiang* (The Great River), nos. 2–3, 8–13.

33. "The National Heritage," *Han sheng*, June 1904, 2. See also Feisheng, "On National Spirit" (n. 27 above).

34. See the Student News section, *Hubei xuesheng jie*, May 1903.

35. "Agitation Against Closing Student Associations," *Fu bao*, April 25, 1906, 34–35.

36. "Opening Proclamation," *Zhejiang zhao*, January 1903, 1–6.

37. "The Connection Between Military Matters and the State," *Hubei xuesheng jie*, April 1903, 49–62.

38. "The Citizen's Education," *Hubei xuesheng jie*, March 1903, 13–20; see also "Fundamental Laws," *Jiangsu*, no. 2: 15–22.

39. "The Rise and Decline of the Chinese Race," *Jiangsu*, no. 4, 1–8.

40. "Concerning the Future of China and the Welfare of Our People," *Hubei xuesheng jie*, March 1903, 1–12.

41. "Opening Statement," *Fu bao*, April 15, 1906, 1–2.

42. "An Argument for a Family Revolution," *Jiangsu*, no. 7, 13–22; and Yijiu, "The Education of the Anglo-Saxon Race," ibid., 41–43.

43. "The Relations Between Education and Self-Government" (n. 29 above).

44. "The Problem of Jiangsu Morality," *Jiangsu*, no. 7, 11–12; and Zongshi, "On the Responsibility of Yunnanese," *Yunnan*, 1907, no pagination.

45. "An Open Letter to the Honorable Elders of Our Country," *Yunnan*, 1907.

46. "The Problem of Jiangsu Morality," 10–11; "Causes for the Lack of Development of Chinese Industry," *Hubei xuesheng jie,* March 1903, 31–38.

47. "Opening Statement," *Hubei xuesheng jie,* January 1903, 1–16.

48. "Opening Statement of the Yunnan Journal," *Yunnan,* August 28, 1906, 1–9.

49. For one such advocacy, see "Concerning Local Self-Rule in China," *Han sheng,* June 1904, 1–8.

50. See "On Sending Shanxi Students to Japan," *You bao* (Window News), no. 2, 115.

51. "An Open Letter to the Honorable Elders of Our Country" (n. 45 above), is one of the few articles making any reference to the training of officials.

52. "Greeting Fellow Students," *Hubei xuesheng jie,* May, 1903, 1–16.

53. "The New Spirit of Citizens," *Jiangsu,* no. 5: 1–9.

54. Wei Zhong, "Opening Statement of *Twentieth Century China,*" in *Ershi shiji zhi Zhina,* May 1, 1905, 1–14.

55. See, for example, Yeguang, "Should China Aspire to Constitutionalism Today?" *Fu bao,* April 25, 1906, no pagination.

56. Feng Ziyou, "The 1903 Tokyo Youth Association," in *Geming yishi* 1: 102–104.

57. Feng Ziyou, "The Youth Association and the Resist Russia Military Corps," in *Geming yishi* 1:104–107.

58. For the details of Huang's early life from which this account is primarily drawn, see the thorough research of Chun-tu Hsueh, *Huang Hsing,* 1–12.

59. Feng Ziyou, "The Tokyo Association for National Military Education," in *Geming yishi* 1:109–112.

60. Ibid.

61. See *NCH,* May 7, 1903, 885.

62. *Su bao* (henceforth *SB*), July 1, 1903.

63. *SB,* May 8, 1903.

64. Ibid.

65. *SB,* May 13, 1903.

66. On May 27, *Su bao* reprinted Zhang Binglin's "An Introduction to Zou's work," and on June 9 it carried a favorable review.

67. Zou's essay *Geming jun* has been reprinted a number of times. Our edition was published in Shanghai in 1958. For a brief analysis, see the fine monograph by Michael Gasster, *Chinese Intellectuals and the Revolution of* 1911, 37–42.

68. See *SB,* May 30, 1903.

69. Ibid.

70. *SB,* May 22, 1903.

71. *SB,* June 9, 1903.

72. *SB,* July 1, 1903.

73. *SB,* June 7, 1903.

74. *SB,* June 1, 1903.

75. A detailed account of the trials is carried in *NCH.* See in particular the issue of July 17, 1903.

76. See Zhang Xingyan, *Su bao anji shi*; and "Su Bao an," in *Xinhai geming,* 1:329–500.

77. "Huaxing Hui" (The Society for the Revival of China) in *Xinhai geming,* 1:501–512; and Hsueh, *Huang Hsing,* 13–25.

78. See n. 77.

79. See "Students in Europe and the Tongmeng Hui," in Feng Ziyou, *Geming*

yishi, 2nd ed., 2:132–141. For more details, see Luo, *Geming wenxian* 64: 533–541.

80. Song's diary, *Wo zhi lishi*, first published in Hunan, 1920, and republished in Taibei in 1962, is an extremely valuable source for this period. A collection of Song's writings between 1902 and 1913 is contained in *Song Jiaoren ji*.

81. Song, *Wo zhi lishi*, 70. See also Wei and Wu, *Xinhai geming shi*, 1:18–20. According to them, the initial structure of the Tongmeng Hui, as a union of individuals who previously belonged to other groups, some with strong provincial ties, paved the way for factionalization from the outset. For a fine monographic account of Song's revolutionary career, see K. S. Liew, *Struggle for Democracy: Sung Chiao-jen and the 1911 Revolution*. In Chinese, see Fang Zuhua, *Song Jiaoren chuan*.

82. *Geming wenxian* 2:65–66. Chun-tu Hsueh has an excellent account of the activities surrounding the formation of the Tongmeng Hui in his *Huang Hsing*, 40–48, drawing upon various Chinese sources. We have consulted some of the same sources.

83. See Hsueh, *Huang Hsing*, 44. For the official Guomindang records, see Zhongguo Guomindang, Historical Commission, "Historical Data on the Tongmeng Hui's Revolution," *Geming wenxian* 65.

84. See *Min bao* (henceforth *MB*), Number 1, November 26, 1905.

85. For a well-researched study of the influence of the Russian revolutionary movement on Chinese radicals, see Donald C. Price, *Russia and the Roots of the Chinese Revolution, 1896–1911*.

86. Sun Yat-sen, "Preface to Min Bao," *MB*, no. 1, 1–2.

87. A brief biography of Wang Jingwei in English is to be found in Howard L. Boorman and Richard C. Howard, eds., *Biographical Dictionary of Republican China* 3:369–370.

88. Wang Jingwei, "(Creating) Nationals from (Diverse) Races," *MB*, no. 1, 9.

89. *MB*, no. 1, 30. The general analysis of the running debate between the Sun and Liang forces to be found in Gasster, *Chinese Intellectuals*, 68ff., has great merit.

90. Oushan, "Regarding the Manchu Desire to Establish a Constitutional Monarchy and Why They Cannot Do So," *MB*, no. 1, 31–40 (see 39). In this essay, the themes of hatred and revenge were especially pronounced. For the Han, the author asserted, the humiliations and sufferings of the past had not yet been avenged; hence, constitutionalism under the Manchu would be nothing more than a scrap of paper, completely impossible to apply effectively (34).

91. "Si Wang," for example, used an argument found also in earlier student and reformer journals: long before Westerners had acquired an advanced civilization, the Chinese had reached a zenith of cultural development. The absence of racial competition, however, caused a decline. Fortunately, contact with the West was now causing China to awaken slowly from its long sleep. See Si Wang, "Regarding Reformation Leading to a Democratic Government as More Suitable for China," *MB*, no. 1, 44.

92. Hu's own account of his early life can be found in Hu Hanmin, *Zizhuan* (Autobiography), in *Geming wenxian* 3:372–422. See also Boorman and Howard, eds., *Biographical Dictionary* 2:159–166.

93. Hu Hanmin, "The Six Principles of Min Bao," *MB*, April 5, 1906, 7–22. Hu's division of the six principles—and specific tasks—of Tongmeng Hui adherents were these: the removal of a bad government; the construction of a republican system; the nationalization of land; contributions to world peace; friendship between the Chinese and the Japanese people; and efforts to obtain the support of other na-

tions for China's revolution. The first three tasks, it will be noted, constituted the core of the Sun program (with some ambiguity regarding land policy, which we shall have occasion to discuss soon). The latter three tasks comprised efforts both to protect the revolution from external interference and to introduce China into a new relationship with the outside world.

94. "Sanminzhuyi (The Three People's Principles) and China's National Future," a speech by Sun Yat-sen on the first anniversary of *Min bao*, Tokyo, December 2, 1906, in *MB*, no. 10, December 20, 1906, 3–16. See also an anonymous article entitled "On the Anniversary Meeting of the Chinese Revolutionaries," in *Kakumei hyōron* (Review of Revolutions), January 1, 1907, 3–5. According to the author, the meeting was held in the Kanda district of Tokyo on the evening of December 2, 1906, with some 5,000 persons in attendance. The gist of Sun's speech is produced in this Japanese journal. See also Song, *Wo zhi lishi*, 206–7.

Wei and Wu in *Xinhai geming shi* argue that Sun's nationalism flowed from two sources, the traditional anti-Manchu rebelliousness "of the peasant class," and Western bourgeois nationalism. The latter force predominated, according to them, with anti-Manchu slogans of the traditional type primarily advanced as tools to win support from the secret societies and some gentry. But the models actually being followed were those of the American and French revolutions (1:38). This was true of Sun himself, and of *some* of his followers, but the situation was by no means as clear-cut as Wei and Wu suggest. The simple appeal to racism (anti-Manchuism) had enormous emotional effect upon many of Sun's young followers and represented the central driving force motivating them toward revolution, whatever additional political and ideological baggage they were prepared to carry. Gradually, it is true, they made stronger commitments to other facets of political modernization. But one must not underestimate the strength of simple anti-Manchu sentiments—as Sun's progressive victories over Kang-Liang for student support prove. Wei and Wu fault Sun's nationalism for being unable to "articulate explicitly anti-imperialism" (1:42–44). In point of fact, Sun hoped to secure Western and Japanese services on a much larger scale in the economic modernization and political integration of China, believing that the Western influence need not necessarily be a negative one.

95. *MB*, no. 10, December 20, 1906, 3–16.

96. In addition to the *Min bao* articles already cited, see those by Wang Jingwei, "Those Who Wish the Manchu to Establish Constitutional Government, Listen to This," April 5, 1906, 1–18; Zhuan Zhen, "Refutation of the *Legal News* Discussion of the Manchu Establishment of a Constitution," April 5, 1906, 1–8 (new pagination for each article); and Wang Jingwei, "The Manchu Creation of a Constitution and the National Revolution," *Minbao*, November 25, 1906, 1–22.

97. As one example, see Ji Sang (Wang Yuzao), "Regarding Revolution as the Prelude to China's Establishment of a Constitution," *MB*, January 22, 1906, 1–10 (see 1, 4, 6).

98. Ji Sang, "A Reply to the *Xinmin congbao*'s Questions," *MB*, November 15, 1906, 1–10.

99. See Wang Jingwei, "Refuting *Xinmin congbao*'s Arguments Against Revolution," *MB*, April 28, 1906, 1–37 (see 17–18). Said Wang: I think that the popularization of nationalism and racial consciousness can reduce the people who are against revolution to the Manchu and their lackies. . . . When the revolution starts, everyone will respond to it favorably . . . everywhere, uprisings based upon the same principles will occur.

100. Wang Jingwei, "Refuting the Thesis that Revolution Would Lead to Internal Disorder," *MB*, November 15, 1906, 1–24. In this same article, Wang admitted

that revolution necessarily involved violence, but argued that without revolution the people would die under Manchu oppression or because of starvation. Thus, a single act of violence could prevent the type of "long-term violence" that would be far more costly in the end.

101. Wang Jingwei, "Refuting *Xinmin congbao*'s Arguments Against Revolution," 20–28.

102. Po Man (Wang Jingwei), "Suggestions on Revolution," *MB*, April 5, 1906, 1–11.

103. Wang Jingwei, "The Manchu Creation of a Constitution and the National Revolution," *MB*, October 8, 1906, 1–22.

104. Sun, "Preface to Min Bao," 2–3.

105. Sun, "Sanminzhuyi and the Chinese National Future," 3–16.

106. For Henry George's theories, see his most famous work, *Progress and Poverty: An Inquiry into the Cause of Industrial Depressions and of Increase of Want with Increase of Wealth—The Remedy*, first published in 1879 in New York. For various accounts of George's life and work, all of them sympathetic, see Henry George, Jr., *The Life of Henry George*; Albert Jay Nock, *Henry George: An Essay*; Anna George de Mille, *Henry George: Citizen of the World*; and Steven B. Cord, *Henry George: Dreamer or Realist?*

107. Miyazaki's discussion of socialism was generally accurate, although some of his categories or designations were puzzling. He defined the primary purpose of socialism as that of redistributing land and capital back to society, to be regulated by the government. The means of production were to be owned by society as a whole, with strict limitations on private holdings. Miyazaki then remarked that the principles advanced by "Karl Merks and Engel" [*sic*] had become very popular in Europe. The type of socialism having the most extreme ideals was communism, Miyazaki continued, suggesting that he did not put Marx and Engels in that category. Christian socialism represented another subdivision, with its stress on ethics and religion. There were also "moderates" who placed more emphasis on direct action rather than parliamentarism, and Miyazaki listed Hyndman, Jaures, Bebel, Debs, and De Leon in these ranks.

Anarchism, according to Miyazaki, was divided into three main branches: philosophic, Christian, and revolutionary or destructive anarchism. Adherents to the latter branch took their doctrines from Bakunin, and were also known as communist anarchists, or Nihilists. All anarchists aimed at the total destruction of the old order and the creation of a new society based on human equality and complete freedom.

Equalization of land was based on the principle that land was given by nature, not created by man. Since all production came from the land directly or indirectly, every individual should have the right to share in that production, and once that right was equalized, everyone became an independent, free entrepreneur, thus enabling a new and just society. There were two major branches within the movement to equalize land, according to Miyazaki, one advocating public ownership of land by the method of making landlords sell back their land to local organizations, through which the land would be redistributed. The leader of this movement was Alfred Wallace, with its center in Great Britain. The other school proposed a single tax on the unearned increment, namely, the increasing value of land due to economic development. This school was headed by Henry George.

The translator of Miyazaki's essay presented his own critique of each school in the final sections of this article. All three major branches of the social revolutionary movement aimed at the creation of equality, liberty, brotherhood, and humanity, he noted. All emphasized *minshengzhuyi* and attacked the inequality between rich and poor. The problem with socialism was that in its stress on economic equality, it belittled freedom. Anarchism, on the other hand, in its extreme emphasis on individual freedom, was unrealistic and, in the end, likely to lead to a loss of the goal toward which it aimed. The author then made it clear that his own preference was for land equalization, although here too he saw problems. The approach of Alfred Wallace, that of turning land over to local groups might preclude the right of land use by individuals. On the other hand, the George proposal did not guarantee the equal distribution of land. He left the precise form of land equalization which he would adopt unclear, suggesting his ambivalence concerning full nationalization and a tax on land value. See Member of *Min bao*, "Types of European and American Social Revolutionary Movements and a Discussion of Them," *MB*, April 28, 1906, 1–11. We are indebted to Martin Bernal (in *Chinese Socialism*, 112) for pointing out that the author of the bulk of the *Min bao* article just cited was Miyazaki Tamizō. It should be noted, however, that the final critique was not that of Miyazaki and left the issue of the best form of land equalization unsettled.

108. (Hu) Hanmin, "The Six Principles of *Min bao*," 12 (n. 93 above).

109. Xian Jie (Zhu Zhixin), "Discussing from a Socialist Viewpoint Railway Nationalization and Chinese Government or Private Management of Railways," *MB*, April 28, 1906, 1–12.

110. Xian Jie (Zhu Zhixin), "Why a Social Revolution Should be Carried Out Simultaneously with a Political Revolution," *MB*, June 26, 1906, 43–66.

111. Ibid.

112. For a discussion of this article, see chapter 3, pp. 141–144.

113. Minyi (Hu Hanmin), "To Those Who Challenge *minshengzhuyi*," *MB*, March 6, 1907, 45–156.

114. Ibid., 120–121.

115. Yinbing, "Again Refuting the Land Nationalization Theory of a Certain Journal," *XMCB*, April 1907, 1–34; May 1907, 1–57; and June 1907, 1–22. For our earlier discussion, see chapter 3, pp. 144–145.

116. *XMCB*, May 1907, 20–21.

117. Xian Jie (Zhu Zhixin), "Land Nationalization and Finance," *MB*, July 5, 1907, 1–34, and September 25, 1907, 1–40. The subtitle of this article is "Again Refuting *Xinmin congbao*'s Questioning of the Land Nationalization Policy."

118. Taiqiu, "To Criticize the Mistakes of *Xinmin congbao*'s Rebuttal of Land Nationalization," *MB*, October 25, 1907, 61–85.

119. Liu Guanghan, "Grieving for the Peasant," *MB*, July 5, 1907, 19–34.

120. "The Declaration of the Chinese Tongmeng Hui Military Government," 1905, *Guofu quanji* 4:59–62. Also to be found in Zhongguo Guomindang Historical Commission, *Geming wenxian* 65:35–37.

121. Lewis provides a detailed account of the Ping-Liu-Li Uprising; see *Prologue*, 175–196.

122. Sun, *Memoirs of a Chinese Revolutionary*, 206–207. Sun asserts, however, that these incidents provided the first sacrifices, some comrades being executed or imprisoned after the defeat, and he counts this as the third revolutionary defeat (following those in 1895 and 1900). Huang made an effort to reach the revolutionaries arriving in Guangdong in January 1907, but the situation was too dangerous and he returned. See Hsueh, *Huang Hsing*, 61. For a contemporary account by a British missionary who may have been an eye-witness, see *NCH*, May 31, 1907, pp. 522–523. He reported that several hundred armed men had operated in Pingxian, his area, with banners of "varied wonderous description," most of which proclaimed "Down with the Qing—Restore the Ming." The latter fact revealed the ten-

uous connection with the Tokyo-based radicals. The fact that Ma Juyi, martyred after the Changsha plot was uncovered, had come from Liling district undoubtedly stimulated the Gelao Hui in this area to seek revenge.

123. For the materials that follow, we are indebted to an article by Lin Wei-hung, "Activities of Woman Revolutionists in the Tung Meng Hui Period (1905–1912)." Lin's research, together with the Chinese sources to which he led us, provides the basis for this section. See the Chinese-language writings of Chen Dongyuan, Ke Gongzhen, Tan Sheying, and Wang (Qiu) Canzhi cited in the bibliography.

124. Yan Bin, "Notice of the Founding of the Association of Chinese Women Students in Japan," *Geming wenxian*, 66:389–393. The notice appeared originally in *Zhongguo xinnujie zazhi* 2:75–82.

125. Qiu Jin is regarded as the most prominent woman revolutionary prior to the Revolution of 1911. See Zhou Shusan, "Women Revolutionary Comrades Before the Founding of the Republic," *Geming wenxian* 66:427–434. For additional biographical data on Qiu, see Zhen Qubing, "A Biography of the Woman Hero, Qiu Jin," in Chai Degeng, *Xinhai geming* 3:184–186, and Feng Ziyou, "The Woman Hero, Qiu Jin," *Geming yishi* 2:177–182.

126. Qiu Jin, "Opening Statement of the *Chinese Women's Journal*," *Geming wenxian* 66:266–268. Actually, two versions of this statement exist, one written in the vernacular style, the other written in classical form. The *Geming wenxian* version, written in the vernacular, is taken from a reprint of the statement found in *Xin shiji* (The New Century), the Paris-based anarchist journal, dated August 31, 1907. A classical style version may be found in *Xinhai geming* 3:182–183. For a sample of Qiu's other writings, see *Geming wenxian* 1:133–140. Her appeals, highly nationalist in tone, include proposals for the organization of a revolutionary army.

127. *NCH*, August 9, 1907, 321.

128. *NCH*, August 16, 1907, 381.

129. For details of this event, in Chinese, see *Guofu nianpu* 1:245–251; *Zhongguo Tongmeng Hui geming shiliao*, 1–65; Hu Hanmin, "Autobiography," 22–24 (394–396). In English, see Hsueh, *Huang Hsing*, 65–66. See also the extensive study by Jeffrey G. Barlow, *Sun Yat-sen and the French*, 1900–1908, 72–74; and Sun, *Memoirs*, 208–209.

130. For the statement addressed to the British authorities in June 1900, see Feng Ziyou, *Zhonghua minguo kaiguo qian geming shi* 1:60–63.

131. See Luo Jialun, ed., *Guofu nianpu* 1:301–306; and Wilbur, *Frustrated Patriot*, 67–73.

132. For an account of Sun's relations with the Japanese, we have relied heavily on Miyazaki for the early period, and for the later period, *Geming yishi* and Jansen.

133. For details, see Kim Munholland, "The French Connection That Failed: France and Sun Yat-sen, 1900–1908," and Barlow, *Sun Yat-sen and the French, 1900–1908*, especially 52ff.

134. Karl Mannheim, *Ideology and Utopia: An Introduction to the Sociology of Knowledge*.

135. For a stimulating effort to make this distinction and apply it to post-1949 China, see Franz Schurmann, *Ideology and Organization in Communist China*.

CHAPTER FIVE

1. We are indebted to several studies of Western anarchism for providing us with an interpretive overview: James Jolle, *The Anarchists*; and especially George Woodcock, *Anarchism: A History of Libertarian Ideas and Movements*. We have also

consulted the major writings of Proudhon, Kropotkin, and Tolstoy pertinent to the Chinese anarchist movement.

2. Shijieshe (Le Monde), ed., *LuOu jiaoyu yundong*, 49. This is an extremely valuable source for the study of the Chinese student movement in France, particularly the anarchist-sponsored work-study movement.

3. For an excellent brief biography of Li Hongzao, see the account written by Fang Chaoying in Arthur Hummel, ed., *Eminent Chinese of the Ch'ing Period*, 471–472.

4. A full account of Wu's life is given in Zhang Wenbo, *Zhilao xianhua*. For details that pertain to Wu's relations with Sun Yat-sen, see a series of articles by Yang Kailing, "The Father of Our Country and Mr. Wu Zhihui," published in the magazine *Sanminzhuyi banyuekan*, nos. 1–4, (May 15–June 15, 1953). In English, see Howard Boorman and Richard Howard, eds., *Biographical Dictionary of Republican China* 3:416–419.

5. Zhang Wenbo, *Zhilao xianhua*, 24.

6. *LuOu jiaoyu yundong*, 16. For the results of Li's research on soya beans, see Li Youyong (Li Shizeng), *Le Soya Essay Culture: Ses Usages Alimentaires, Thérapeutiques, Agricoles et Industriels.*

7. A complete collection of *Xin shiji*, together with some of the pamphlets published by the Paris group, was reprinted in four volumes in Shanghai in 1947. All citations from XS are from this edition.

8. Robert A. Scalapino interview with Li Shizeng, Taibei, July 16, 1959.

9. For a discussion of this point, see Woodcock, *Anarchism*, 213–217. In Kropotkin's own writings, see *The Conquest of Bread*, 9–14; *The Place of Anarchism in Socialistic Evolution*, 1–19; *An Appeal to the Young*, 1–20.

10. Zhang Ji, *Zhang Puquan xiansheng quanji*, 229–235.

11. For two accounts of Liu, see Cai Yuanpei, "A Brief Account of the Activities of Liu Shenshu" in *Liu Shenshu yishu*, 1–3, and Wu Zhihui, "Tidbits," *XS*, no. 109: 13–14.

12. In his writings for *Min bao*, Liu used the pen name Wei Yi. See *MB* (1907), May 5, 1–16; June 8, 23–28 and 39–111; July 5, 19–34 and 35–62; and December 25, 1–26.

13. *TYB*, October 1907.

14. *TYB*, November 1907.

15. "A Letter with Answers," *XS*, July 27, 1907, 1 (answers by Li Shizeng).

16. "A Letter to *Xin shiji* from a Certain Individual, with Answers," *XS*, August 10, 1907, 2–3 (answers by Li).

17. Shen Shu (Liu Guanghan), "A View of the Equality of Anarchism," *TYB*, August 10, 1907, 81–90.

18. Ibid.

19. "A Letter with Answers."

20. Ibid.

21. Ibid.

22. Shen Shu (Liu Guanghan), "The Current Situation in Asia," *TYB*, November 1907, 345–368.

23. Ibid., 367.

24. "A Letter to *Xin shiji* from a Certain Individual, with Answers," 3.

25. "A Discussion with a Friend Concerning *Xin shiji*," *XS*, July 6, 1907, 1–2.

26. "Anarchism Can Be Steadfastly Matched Against the Sense of Responsibility of the Revolutionary Party," *XS*, August 1, 1908, 10–13.

27. "National Extinction," *XS*, May 23, 1908, 1–2.

28. "An Extended Discussion . . . ," XS, July 27, 1907, 3.
29. "A Letter to *Xin shiji* from a Certain Individual, with Answers," 3.
30. Wu Zhihui, "Degrees," XS, June 29, 1907, 1.
31. Wu Zhihui, "Answering the Writings of a Certain Gentleman," XS, April 11, 1908, 2–3.
32. "This Is Known as a Chinese Sage," XS, June 22, 1907, 3.
33. Chu Minyi, "Looking at the Past," XS, November 30, 1907, 2.
34. Ibid.
35. Shen Shu, "The Current Situation in Asia," *TB*, November 1907, 350.
36. He Zhen and Shen Shu, "The Relationship Between Racist Revolution and Anarchist Revolution," *TB*, October 1907, 135–144.
37. Shen Shu, "Socialism in the Western Han Dynasty," *TYB*, August 1907, 91–94.
38. "Communism in China," *HB*, May 8, 1908, 1.
39. Shen Shu, "A View on the Equality of Anarchism," *TB*, August 10, 1907.
40. Shen Shu, "On Human Equality," *TB*, July 1907, 24–36.
41. Li Shizeng, "On Knowledge," XS, August 3, 1907, 2.
42. "On Anarchism" (continued), XS, August 3, 1907, 4.
43. "Hurried Thoughts at the Advent of *Xin shiji*," XS, June 22, 1907, 1.
44. "On Anarchism" (continued), XS, February 15, 1908, 3–4.
45. "A Rejection of *Xin shiji* Writings on Revolution" (with answers by Li Shizeng), XS, July 20, 1907, 1–2.
46. "On the Uselessness of Jumping into the Ocean," XS, July 27, 1907, 2.
47. "General Revolution," XS, October 12, 1907, 2–3.
48. Li Shizeng and Chu Minyi (?), *La révolution*, Paris, 1907 (8-page pamphlet); republished Shanghai, 1947.
49. "Go and Join Ranks with the Secret Societies," XS, April 11, 1908, 1–2 (authorship unknown).
50. Ibid., 2.
51. "Communism in China" (n. 38 above), 1.
52. Chu Minyi, "Rejecting *Shi bao's* 'Why China Cannot Now Promote Communism'," XS, November 7, 1908, 7–14.
53. "A Comparison of the Three Principles of Nationalism, Democracy and Socialism," XS, July 27, 1907, 1.
54. Ibid.
55. See, for example, Si Wang, "On Democratic Governmental Reform as More Suitable for China," *MB*, November 25, 1905, 47.
56. Ye Xiasheng, "Explaining the Anarchist Party and the Revolutionary Party," *MB*, September 5, 1906, 111–123.
57. See *TYB*, January 1908, 461–468, and February 1908, 511–529.
58. Our account is drawn primarily from our earlier work on Chinese anarchism.
59. Feng Ziyou, "The Master of the *Xin shiji*, Zhang Jingjiang," *Geming yishi* 2:227–230.
60. Ibid., 229.
61. For a discussion of the manifesto, see "Advice," XS, November 13, 1909, 4–11.
62. "On Government," *MB*, October 25, 1907, 87–97.
63. Wu's open letters to Zhang appear in XS, January 4, 1908, 1; April 25, 1908, 4; and September 5, 1908, 13–14. See also, "Advice."
64. Lin Yutang, *History of the Press and Public Opinion in China*, 102.
65. For an analysis of Zhang and Liu, together with a description of their activi-

ties during this era, see Wei and Wu, *Xinhai geming shi*, 159–160, and Li Zehou, *Ershi shiji zhi Zhina*, 305–308.

66. "Meeting of the Overseas Students to Oppose a Supervisor," *XS*, June 22, 1907, 3–4.

67. Ibid.

68. "Record of the Supervisor's Speech at the Association of Overseas Students in France," *XS*, June 6, 1908, 2–3.

69. Cai Yuanpei, "A Brief Account of the Activities of Liu Shenshu," 1–3.

70. A brief biography of Shifu appears at the beginning of his collective works, *Shifu wencun*. In addition, see his biography in the anarchist publication, *Geming xiangu*. We have also had access to a manuscript written by Mo Jipeng, *Recalling Shifu*. Mo was a close friend of Shifu, and had first-hand information on many of his activities after 1910. For a sketch of Shifu in English, see H. E. Shaw, "A Chinese Revolutionist," *Mother Earth* 10 (October 1915): 284–285.

71. *Shifu wencun*. Chen Jiongming joined this group, according to Mo (*Recalling Shifu*, 14a).

72. Ibid., 18a.

CHAPTER SIX

1. Among the works that have stimulated us, we would cite Hannah Arendt, *On Revolution*; David V. J. Bell, *Resistance and Revolution*; Crane Brinton, *Anatomy of Revolution*; Peter Calvert, *Revolution*; Ortega Y. Gasset, *The Revolt of the Masses*; Ted Robert Gurr, *Why Men Rebel*; Mark N. Hagopian, *The Phenomenon of Revolution*; Chalmers Johnson, *Revolutionary Change*, rev. ed.; Carl Leiden and Karl M. Schmitt, *The Politics of Violence: Revolution in the Modern World*; Clifford T. Paynton and Robert Blackey, eds., *Why Revolution?*; and Theda Skocpol, *States and Social Revolutions*.

2. For details, see Cameron, *The Reform Movement in China, 1896–1912*, 71–72. Her account is taken from E. T. Williams, "Report on Recent Educational Reforms in China," in *United States Foreign Relations*, 1905, enclosure in no. 180, and *China Year Book*, 1912, 315–319. Approximately one year earlier, in February 1903, Yuan Shikai and Zhang Zhidong had petitioned the throne along similar lines, but violent conservative opposition had caused the memorial to be shelved. MacKinnon, *Power and Politics in Late Imperial China*, 144.

3. *China Year Book*, 1912, 322–324. Also see *NCH*, March 3, 1911, 497–498.

4. *NCH*, July 12, 1907, 81.

5. The work of Ralph Powell, cited earlier, has been of major assistance; the section on military reform also owes much to the recent research of Stephen R. MacKinnon, previously cited, and Edmund S. K. Fung, *The Military Dimension of the Chinese Revolution*. For the details on the Zhang-Liu memorials, see Powell, *The Rise of Chinese Military Power*, 132.

6. MacKinnon, *Power and Politics in Late Imperial China*, 93–94; and Fung, *The Military Dimension of the Chinese Revolution*, 72–73.

7. MacKinnon, *Power and Politics in Late Imperial China*, 110. For an excellent account of the financing of the Beiyang Army, see 103–114.

8. For details of the Commission report, see Powell, *Military Power*, 173–180. For the imperial decree and the military reorganization, see *Guangxu zhengyao* (Important Political Events of the Guangxu Reign), Shen Dongsheng, Dong Yuan, and Dong Run, eds., 25:37a and 38a–41a.

9. MacKinnon argues that in seeking to build the Beiyang Army as a modern professional force, Yuan sacrificed some of the close personal ties with his officers characteristic of the old Huai and Xiang armies, and thereby reduced the element of personal loyalty (*Power and Politics in Late Imperial China*, 117ff.). He points out that officers were drawn from gentry, merchant, and rich peasant families, and not a small number were recruited from those who had previously trained in Japan, some of the latter being imbued with revolutionary sentiments. Fung makes a similar point, asserting that the Beiyang Army supported Yuan not out of personal loyalty but because of the widespread feeling that he was the only man capable of creating a government strong enough to ward off foreign aggression (*The Military Dimension of the Chinese Revolution*, 11). Unquestionably, these points are well taken, but they must be regarded in relative terms. Many of the senior Beiyang officers (for example, Feng Guoshang, Cao Kun, Wang Shizhen, and Duan Qirui) were repeatedly chosen or approved for important posts by Yuan in subsequent years, and, for the most part, remained close to him personally until Yuan's monarchical fiasco posed such a stark threat to their careers that a number of old associates abandoned ship.

10. Powell, *The Rise of Chinese Military Power*, 297–298.

11. Fung is somewhat more positive in his evaluations of reform efforts during these years. He acknowledges that Zhili and Hubei led the way, but notes that officers who had graduated from military schools were being assigned to various provinces, with serious efforts having been made to recruit more promising officer candidates through various promises and emoluments, including liberal pay. Significantly, the military reforms stressed local recruitment of soldiers for divisions stationed in the province rather than the use of non-natives, thereby increasing their localist quotient. But at this level, also, greater care in selection was emphasized. Yet Fung points out the continuing influence of the past, the lack of provincial support, and the serious financial problems that collectively plagued reform efforts, and concludes by asserting, "With the possible exception of the Beiyang divisions, the national army existed more on paper than in reality" (*The Military Dimension of the Chinese Revolution*, 61).

12. See *NCH*, July 7, 1905, 24.

13. Ibid.

14. For details, see *Guangxu zhengyao* 27:51a and 63a.

15. For the imperial edict, see *NCH*, December 1, 1905, 487. In Chinese, see *Guangxu zhengyao* 27:76b.

16. For a further exploration of constitutional reform efforts in English, see Cameron, *The Reform Movement in China*, 100–125. In Chinese for the reports of the commission, see *Guangxu zhengyao* 27:92a–92b, and 28:1a–2b, 10a–11b, 17a–17b, and 28a–30a.

17. A full translation of the edict is contained in various sources. See *Papers Relating to the Foreign Relations of the United States*, 1906, Part I, 349–350. The imperial edict of August 26, 1906, ordering the creation of a committee to consider the recommendations of the high commissioners recently returned from overseas is on p. 349.

18. Ibid., 350.

19. For the edict of September 2, see ibid., 352.

20. For the imperial edict ordering the reorganization of Manchuria, dated April 20, 1907, see ibid., 178–179. The July 7 edict on provincial reorganization is on pp. 184–189.

21. The regulations for Tianjin self-government are set forth in ibid., 189–190.

22. See the interesting report on efforts to equalize Manchu and Han from Minister Rockhill to the secretary of state, accompanied by a memorial from the Manchu governor-general Duanfang in ibid., 192–193.

23. Ibid., 196, for this edict.

24. Ibid., 197. For details relating to the Guangdong provincial assembly, see Edward J. M. Rhoads, *China's Republican Revolution: The Case of Kwangtung, 1895–1913*, 153–179.

25. Ibid., 198.

26. For the edict, see *Guangxu zhengyao* 29:65a–66a.

27. Ibid., 65b.

28. See *Guangxu zhengyao* 29:55a–58a.

29. See *Guangxu zhengyao* 30:18a–20a.

30. Ibid.

31. See *Guangxu zhengyao* 30:18a–20a.

32. Ibid., 36b–42b.

33. Ibid.

34. Ibid.

35. Ibid.

36. Ibid.

37. See *Xuantong zhengji*, compiled by Liu Jiayetang, 1:2a.

38. *Xuantong zhengji* 6:18b–19a.

39. For the regulations, see *Xuantong zhengji* 13:7b–14b. A summary history of the national constitutional assembly can be found in Huang Hongshou's *Qingshi jishi benwei*, 577–580. For a collection of documents and essays on the constitutional movement, see Chai Degeng et al., *Xinhai geming* 4:1–164.

40. See, for example, the account in *Qingshi jishi benwei*. See also Zhang Pengyuan, *Lixianpai yu Xinhai geming*.

41. *Xuantong zhengji* 18:1b.

42. Ibid. 18:15a.

43. Ibid. 23:14a–14b.

44. See George Beckmann, *The Making of the Meiji Constitution*, 1–11.

45. See Michael T. Florinsky, *The End of the Russian Empire*, especially chap. 5.

46. Perkins, *Agricultural Development in China*, 85–110; Myers, *The Chinese Peasant Economy*, 234–240.

47. Yeh-Chien Wang, *Land Taxation in Imperial China, 1750–1911*, 128.

48. Wang, *Land Taxation in Imperial China*, 121. Note Wang's further remarks: ". . . it is obvious that for three decades from 1875 to 1906 the landowners' burden decreased a great deal owing to rising prices; only in the last few years of the dynasty did the tax increase outrun prices in this particular district" (126, speaking of Tingchou district, Zhili province). Summarizing his conclusions, Wang stated, "In retrospect, the greatest defect of the Ch'ing land tax administration was rather its inability to capture increased income as the economy grew. Moreover, its decentralized nature deprived the imperial government of a controlling hand over the management of the country's largest source of public revenue. Consequently, the land tax in China played a diminishing part in government financing in the late Ch'ing just as the public expenditure was increasing. Should the land tax, like its counterpart in Meiji Japan, have played the crucial role in the fiscal system of late Ch'ing, not only the financial condition then but also the political development of modern China might have been decisively different" (131).

49. Perkins et al., *Agricultural Development in China*, 154.

50. *NCH*, September 9, 1911, 626–627.

51. For a detailed account of the Changsha riot, including its background in the current economic crisis in central China, see Esherick, *Reform and Revolution in China*, 125–142. See also Arthur L. Rosenbaum, "Gentry Power and the Changsha Rice Riot of 1910." In Chinese, see Ding Yuanying, "The 'Rice Theft' Incident of the Changsha People in 1910," from *Zhongguo kexueyuan lishi yanjiu suo jikan*, 45–55.

52. Wei and Wu, *Xinhai geming shi* 2:314–322. The Chinese literature on "mass uprisings," and especially on peasant conditions and activities in the late Qing period is extensive, as might be expected. For representative works, see *Zhongguo fengjian shehui nongmin zhanzheng wenti taolun ji*; and Li Zhuren, *Xinhai geming qian di chunzhong douzheng*.

For a stimulating English-language study which seeks to quantify data relating to popular uprisings in nineteenth-century China, see C. K. Yang, "Some Preliminary Statistical Patterns of Mass Actions in Nineteenth-Century China," 174–210. Yang indicates at the outset that his data has not yet been fully processed and that it also contains various limitations. There are some problems, moreover, of definition and categorization. Nevertheless, the principal theses are highly suggestive, and tend to be summarized as follows: (1) The great peak of incidents came in the 1846–1875 period, which encompassed both the Taiping and the Nian rebellions, and the Qing empire never fully recovered from these assaults (178). (2) Most mass actions were short- or middle-term incidents terminating without subsequent development—but the continued outbreak of brief incidents testified to the persistence of the causes generating them (179). (3) Most incidents were confined to a single *xian* reflective of the small-group nature of local community organizations. (4) The largest numerical concentration of incidents was on the North China plain—the center of national political power and a region plagued with natural disasters (but reporting may also have been most complete in this region), followed quite closely by Central China (Anhui, Jiangxi, Hubei, and Hunan) (181–186). (5) Subdivisional capitals led all other sites for mass-action incidents—places where local government came into close touch with the life of the common people—yet the sizable number of incidents in Beijing and provincial capitals poses many questions, according to Yang, about the governability of nineteenth-century China (187). (6) The motivations were political in many cases, but traditional rather than renovationist (192). (7) The participants in antigovernmental activities were very diverse in socioeconomic classification. For example, while the gentry and the landlords were predominantly engaged in actions supportive of the prevailing political order, representatives of such groups could also be found involved in antigovernment incidents, not infrequently in leadership roles (199–200). A far less satisfactory study, with some very questionable generalizations based on limited data, is that of Jean Chesneaux, *Peasant Revolts in China: 1840–1949*.

53. For additional facts, see Rhoads, *China's Republican Revolution*, 80ff. In Chinese, consult Luo Jialun, ed., *Guofu nianpu* 1:297–299, for a detailed account of this episode.

54. An extensive description of the various revolutionary societies and groups organized with the participation of military men in Hubei prior to the Wuchang uprising is contained in Fung, *The Military Dimension of the Chinese Revolution*, 114–144. Fung, it should be noted, regards the Hubei army as atypical in the large number of revolutionaries within it. For the activities of the Guangfu Hui, especially its connection with the uprisings in Jiangsu and Zhejiang, see Zhang Yufa, "The Restoration Society and the Revolution of 1911."

55. For a collection of Chinese documents on relations with Russia during the final years of the Qing, see *Qing Xuantong zhao waijiao shiliao*.

56. Chun-tu Hsueh, *Huang Hsing and the Chinese Revolution*, 79–83.

57. Zhang Guogan, ed., *Xinhai geming shiliao* 1:43–63.

58. Ibid., 26–42.

59. For detailed accounts of the Wuchang uprisings in Chinese, see ibid., 1–194; the Hubei and Wuhan Committees, the Chinese People's Political Consultative Conference, the Modern History Institute, the Chinese Academy of Social Sciences, et al., *Wuchang qiyi dangan ziliao*; Modern Chinese History Teaching and Research, History Department, Wuhan University, compiler, *Xinhai geming zai Hubei shiliao xuanji*; Editorial Committee, Documents on the 50th Anniversary of the Founding of the Republic of China, *Wuchang shouyi*. For accounts of the revolutionary activities by a number of participants, see Hubei Committee, Chinese People's Political Consultative Conference, *Xinhai shouyi huiyi lu*. For an account of the revolutionary movement and activities in Guangdong, see Guangdong Committee, Chinese People's Political Consultative Conference, *Guangdong xinhai geming shiliao*.

In English, see Esherick, *Reform and Revolution in China*, 177ff., for a well-researched study of the Revolution in Hunan and Hubei. A more recent account stressing the importance of the uprising in Wuchang as the indispensable trigger of the 1911 Revolution is to be found in Fung, *The Military Dimension of the Chinese Revolution*, 202ff.

60. This theme is set forth most forcefully in Esherick, *Reform and Revolution in China*, and MacDonald, *The Urban Origins of Rural Revolution*. It takes shape in a different form in the recent writings of PRC scholars on the Xinhai Revolution.

61. Such interpretations, for example, are set forth in Wei and Wu, *Xinhai geming shi*, vol. 2; and Zhu Zongzhen, "When Did the Revolution of 1911 Come to an End?" in *Jindai shi yanjiu*. See also from the papers delivered at the 1981 Wuhan Conference on the Xinhai Revolution those from Li Shiyue, "The Evolution of Modern China and the Xinhai Revolution"; Li Shu, "Reexamining Several Issues Concerning the Xinhai Revolution"; and Kong Li, Lin Jinshi, Chen Zaizheng, and Guo Liang, "The Overseas Chinese and the Xinhai Revolution."

62. It should be noted that the paper presented by the French scholar, Marie-Claire Bergere, entitled "The Bourgeois Class and the Revolution of 1911," takes a different position from that of the PRC scholars noted in n. 61. She argues that although the Xinhai Revolution manifested the dynamic role of the bourgeois class in the social and economic life of China during this era and profoundly affected the fate of that class, it cannot be classified as a bourgeois revolution. Even in Shanghai, asserts Bergere, the role of the merchants was supplementary.

63. For a discussion of the varied antecedents of the Chinese merchant-entrepreneurial class, see Li Shu, "Reexamining Several Issues," 35–36. Li engages in an interesting criticism of the Japanese Marxist scholar, Yokoyama Ei. Yokoyama's central thesis is that modern China witnessed the emergence of two types of challenges to the traditional order. The one response, coming from the masses, and primarily the peasants, was epitomized by the anti-imperialist, antifeudal struggles commencing with the Taiping, thence to the Yihe Tuan, and culminating in the May Fourth Movement. The other, to be characterized as a bourgeois struggle encumbered with semicolonial and semifeudal overtones was typified by the Westernization movement, with its hallmark the 1898 reform effort and the Xinhai Revolution. Yokoyama argues that the Xinhai Revolution was not a genuine revolution, inasmuch as the Chinese bourgeoisie, its progenitors, evolved under the direction of the capitalist, imperialist powers.

In challenging this thesis, Li argues that the "old political forces," composed of peasants, handicraft-workers, and laborers, were tied to the traditional feudal economy, whereas the "new political forces," made up of the bourgeoisie and the petit bourgeoisie, were identified with the new capitalist economy; and while the latter group were weak and "prone to compromise with imperialism and feudalism," their status dictated that they lead "the old democratic revolution" (the bourgeois democratic revolution) with peasant support, fighting for national independence, political democracy, and the development of capitalism (4–6). In the end, however, he acknowledges that it was essentially the "petit bourgeois intellectuals" as represented by the Tongmeng Hui that provided the Xinhai Revolution with its successes.

64. For accounts of the role of the Wuhan and Guangdong merchant communities, see Pi Minxiao, "Chambers of Commerce and Business Groups in Wuhan During the Wuchang Uprising," and Jiao Re, "The Guangdong Businessmen and the Xinhai Revolution."

65. Note, for example, Zhao Shiyuan, "The Second Revolution and the Revolution of 1911."

66. Wu and Wei, *Xinhai geming shi* 2:292–295.

67. As was noted earlier, a detailed account of these uprisings is to be found in ibid., 314–374.

68. Cai Shaoqing, "On the Relation of the Xinhai Revolution with the Secret Societies."

69. Ibid., 12.

70. Theda Skocpol, *States and Social Revolutions: A Comparative Analysis of France, Russia and China*.

71. Ibid., 99.

72. Of the various studies of revolution, we have found Crane Brinton's classic study first published nearly forty years ago, and Chalmers Johnson's more recent work, revised in 1982, of greatest stimulation, and in our ideas we owe a substantial debt to these two individuals, although we have also advanced some theses not completely in line with their views.

73. Eric Hoffer in his brilliant essays entitled *The True Believer* delineated with exceptional clarity the characteristics of the hard-core supporters of any movement.

CHAPTER SEVEN

1. See George T. Yu, *Party Politics in Republican China*. We have borrowed extensively from this earlier work by one of the authors, in the sections that follow, and have not always regarded it as necessary to cite this source. See also Chun-Tu Hsueh, *Huang Hsing*, 119–130, who provides a detailed account of the political maneuverings of the period, from which we have drawn liberally. For three Chinese sources covering this general era from a Guomindang perspective, each of them documentary in character, see "Historical Sources of the Guomindang During the Early Years of the Republic," Zhongguo Guomindang Historical Commission, *Geming wenxian*, vol. 41; Bao Zunpeng, et al. eds., *Zhongguo jindai shi luncong*; and *Xinhai geming*. PRC historians are beginning to subject this period to extensive research, and we shall subsequently have occasion to refer to a number of specialized essays and monographs produced by them.

2. The text of Sun's cable is in *Minli bao* (*MLB*), November 17, 1911, 1.

3. This information is carried in *MLB*, December 26, 1911, 5, but most individuals were not identified.

4. On December 28, 1911, a reporter of the *China Press* of Shanghai conducted interviews with both Sun and Lea. When Lea was asked how he could serve as chief

of staff of the Revolutionary Army when he was an American citizen, he reportedly said only that "this has been arranged," and that a number of American as well as British generals were coming to help. Queried as to whether he expected to direct all military operations of the Revolutionary Army including those of General Li Yuanhong, Lea stated, "No. I don't expect to interfere with General Li's operations. Of course, a chief of staff is simply the means of transmitting orders from the president to the army." For the interview, see *National Archives Microfilm Publication: Records of the Department of State Relating to Internal Affairs of China*, 1910–1929 (*NAMP/RDSRIAC*), 893.00/1008, the *China Press*, Shanghai, December 28, 1911, "Interviews with Sun Yat Sen and 'General' Homer Lea."

5. The *New York Times*, November 2, 1912. For additional details on Lea, see Wilbur, *Sun Yat-sen*, 311, n. 5.

6. This telegram is contained in *NAMP/RDSRIAC*, 893.00/801, dated December 21, 1911.

7. Hu Hanmin, "Autobiography," in *Geming wenxian* 3:53–56.

8. A contemporary account of the ceremonies can be found in *MLB*, January 3, 1912, 2. See also "Historical Materials on the Period of the Founding of the Republic of China," *Geming wenxian* 1:1–96. For a detailed account in English, see the dispatch from Nanking published in the *North China Daily News*, January 2, 1912, "President Sun Yat-sen—The Inauguration Ceremony," an enclosure in *NAMP/RDSRIAC*, 893.00/1047, "Revolutionary Movement at Nanking—January 1 to 8, 1912," January 8, 1912.

9. A letter of Father Hugh Scallan dated November 25, 1911, written from Xianfu, Shaanxi, in ibid., 893.00/892. Extensive slaughter of Manchu was also reported from Taiyuan, the capital of Shanxi, with some 2,000 killed. See ibid., 893.00/790, Williams to the Secretary of State, November 9, 1911; and 893.00/942, "Statement of Swedish Refugees from Southwestern Shanxi," and "Statement of Mr. K. McCoy Regarding the Troubles in Shanxi Province."

10. For example, for accounts of Manchu killing of Han and destruction of property in Fujian, see *MLB*, November 1 and 21, 1911, 1 and 4.

11. *NAMP/RDSRIAC*, 893.00/790, Williams to the Secretary of State, November 9, 1911.

12. Ibid., 893.00/650, telegram of November 10, 1911, Williams to Knox and Knox to American Legation.

13. See a report of Yuan's conversation of January 3 with the American minister, W. G. Calhoun, contained in a telegram of January 3, 1912 to the Secretary of State, ibid., 893.00/881.

14. One of Yuan's staff called on Calhoun on December 23, informing him that on Yuan's request he was reporting that the head of state was very much disappointed in Tang and would never consent to a republic or the acceptance of the presidency (*NAMP/RDSRIAC*, 893.00/895, December 24 telegram from American legation, Beijing, to the Secretary of State).

15. For an account of the agreement, see *MLB*, December 30, 1911, 5. An English text of the agreement is carried in *NCH*, January 6, 1912. A detailed, well-documented study of the North-South negotiations taking place during this period and the ensuing accords can be found in Huang Jiudian, *Minguo yuannian nanbei zhengfu heyi zhi yenjiu*.

16. For the exchange between Yuan and Wu, see *MLB*, January 5, 1912, 2. A telegram from Yuan to Sun inquiring about the meaning of the founding of the Republic and Sun's response are in *MLB*, January 6, 1912, 2.

17. For the December 6 edict, see *Xuantong zhengji* 16:41:21a–22a and 25b.

18. In a telegram from Calhoun to the Secretary of State dated January 19, 1912, Washington was notified that Yuan had drafted the imperial edict whereby the emperor abdicated and consented to the reorganization of republican government with Yuan serving as plentipotentiary. Calhoun reported that Yuan expected to conduct the government from Tianjin (*NAMP/RDSRIAC*, 893.00/937). For contemporary accounts from the republican viewpoint, see various articles in *MLB*, January 1912.

19. Sun's telegrams to Yuan are to be found in *Guofu quanji* 4:157–158, 162–163. See also Sun's wire to Wu Tingfang on the terms of the Manchu abdication, in *MLB*, January 23, 1912, 2.

20. For accounts of the northern military disturbances in the republican press, see *MLB*, March 2–9, 1911, various pages. Observations by American diplomats and military men on the scene are to be found in *NAMP/RDSRIAC*, 893.00/1215, Calhoun to the Secretary of State, March 1, 1912, and 893.00/1238, April 6, 1912, containing dispatch 685-JBM-V, U.S. Asiatic Fleet CIC, J. B. Murdock to the Secretary of Navy, March 6, 1912. In the latter account, reference is made to republican suspicions concerning Yuan's involvement. See also Jerome Ch'en, *Yuan Shih-k'ai*, 107–108.

21. For full terms of the National Assembly regarding Yuan's assumption of office, see *MLB*, March 8, 1912, 3.

22. Ernest Young has a detailed analysis of Yuan's appointees in his well-crafted monograph, *The Presidency of Yuan Shih-k'ai*, pp. 50ff.

23. Taken from the dispatch of W. G. Calhoun, American Minister, Peking, to Secretary to State in *NAMP/RDSRIAC*, 893.00/1338, May 21, 1912.

24. An American observer noted that while there was a strong prejudice against the alien Manchu dynasty among Chinese, "outside of Canton and perhaps Fuzhou, the merchants, farmers, and laboring classes generally are indifferent to the form of government as long as they are permitted to pursue their advocation in peace" (ibid., 893.00/1156, American Legation, Peking, to the Secretary of State, February 13, 1912).

25. *MLB*, January 22, 1912, 2, and February 24, 1912, 3.

26. For the full text of the constitution, see *MLB*, March 6, 1912, 2; March 8, 1912, 2. For other details, including the program and election of officials, see *MLB* issues of March 5, 6, and 9; also, *Geming wenxian* 3:63ff.

27. The elements involved in the union were the Minshe, the Minguo Gong Hui (National People's Association), Guomin Jiejin Hui (National People's Progressive Society), the Tongyidang (Unification Party), and the Guomindang (Nationalist Party)—the last-named not to be confused with the later Guomindang. See Yang Youzhun, *Zhongguo zhengdang shi*, 56–57.

28. A brief account of the Tongyi Gonghedang as well as a history of the early years of the republic by one of its leaders is Gu Zhongxiu, *Zhonghua minguo kaiguo shi*. This work was first published in 1914.

29. Yang, *Zhongguo zhengdang shi*, 55, and Xie Bin, *Minguo zhengdang shi*, 45–47.

30. The full text of the Guomindang manifesto may be found in *MLB*, August 14, 1912, 3, and in Zou Lu, *Zhongguo Guomindang shigao* 1:126–128.

31. For the full text of Sun's speech, see *Guofu quanji* 3:51–53.

32. Yu Youren, "Answer to a Certain Person," *MLB*, September 13, 1912, 2.

33. A report of this speech is carried in *MLB*, August 30, 1912, 3. For the text, see *Guofu quanji* 3:53–54.

34. The document is reprinted in Zhang Pufan and Zeng Xianyi, *Zhongguo*

xianfa shilue, 299–303. For an English version, see Mingchen Joshua Bau, *Modern Democracy in China*, 394–400.

35. The sketches that follow are drawn from these sources: in Chinese, Wu Xiangxiang, *Minguo bairen zhuan*; Liu Shaotang, ed., *Minguo renwu xiao zhuan*; and Fei Xingjian, *Dangdai mingren zhuan*. This is a reprint of a work originally published in Shanghai in 1926. In English, see the monumental dictionary compiled under the editorship of Howard Boorman and Richard Howard, *Biographical Dictionary of Republican China*.

36. Fei, *Dangdai mingren*, 21–23; Liu, *Minguo renwu* 1:128–130; Boorman and Howard, eds., *Biographical Dictionary* 3:232–236.

37. Fei, *Dangdai mingren*, 29–32; Liu, *Minguo renwu* 1:113–114; Boorman and Howard, eds., *Biographical Dictionary* 3:330–335.

38. Fei, *Dangdai mingren*, 30.

39. Ibid., 23–24.

40. Ibid., 25–27; Liu, *Minguo renwu* 2:249–251; Boorman and Howard eds., *Biographical Dictionary* 2:112–116.

41. Fei, *Dangdai mingren*, 28–29, Liu, *Minguo renwu* 1:195–196; Boorman and Howard, eds., *Biographical Dictionary* 2:441–444.

42. Fei, *Dangdai mingren*, 38–39; Liu, *Minguo renwu* 2:84–85.

43. Fei, *Dangdai mingren*, 37–38; Liu, *Minguo renwu* 1:247–249; Wu, *Minguo bairen* 1:13–50; Boorman and Howard, eds., *Biographical Dictionary* 3: 295–299.

44. Fei, *Dangdai mingren*, 39–40; Liu, *Minguo renwu* 1:21–22; Boorman and Howard, eds., *Biographical Dictionary* 3:376–378.

45. In addition to Song's autobiography, see Liu, *Minguo renwu* 1:66–67; Wu, *Minguo bairen* 1:381–385; Boorman and Howard, eds., *Biographical Dictionary* 3:192–195.

46. Liu, *Minguo renwu* 1:186–187; Tan Huisheng, ed., *Minguo weiren zhuanji*, 75–91.

47. Hsueh, *Huang Hsing*, 137–138.

48. Young, *The Presidency of Yuan Shih-k'ai*, 85–86.

49. For Li's telegram, see *NCH*, April 20, 1912, 183.

50. Sun's statement was made to Charles D. Tenney, American consul general, Nanjing, on February 15, 1912. Sun further indicated that about 150,000 of these soldiers were Cantonese (*NAMP/RDSRIAC*, 893.00/1213, February 16, 1912, Tenney to Calhoun). In October, the British consul in Changsha asserted that he believed that the republican government in Hunan had enrolled some 200,000 men at the high point in that province alone, but that formal disbanding of "really organized units" had begun in June, at which time there were about 40,000 soldiers in the region (ibid., 893.00/1493, October 8, 1912, Greene to Calhoun). The governor of Shandong reported in November that his most important problem was the disbanding of 40,000 to 50,000 troops in the province, 10,000 being ample for the preservation of order (ibid., 893.00/1512, November 12, 1912, Arnold to the Secretary of State). Canton, on the other hand, had more or less successfully disbanded its ex-pirate republican soldiers as early as March and April, 1912.

51. For an account, including documents, of events associated with the foreign loan to Yuan, see *Geming wenxian* 42–43:315–486. As was to be expected, Yuan kept close personal touch with the Western ministers to Beijing, seeking to persuade them that foreign financial support was imperative. His entreaties were not without effect. In early December, Sir John Jordan recommended to the manager of the Hong Kong bank that he resume negotiations with Beijing, promising the support of the British legation. The French chargé d'affaires also favored this course of action,

as did the Germans. Cables went out to home offices and governments, seeking authorization to advance Yuan 3 million taels to tide him over the period of negotiations. The American minister, Calhoun, urged the support of the State Department for this loan, asserting that otherwise Yuan would fail and anarchy loomed ahead (*NAMP/RDSRIAC*, 893.00/745, telegram, December 6, 1911, Calhoun to the Secretary of State).

A few days later, Calhoun reiterated his support for a loan, asserting that it would not be spent for active military operations, but would be used solely to preserve the status quo during the peace negotiations, and could be administered under foreign supervision if necessary. However, cognizant of the growing controversy within British circles (British interests in Shanghai strongly objected to a loan at this time, fearing revolutionary retaliation), Calhoun now qualified his earlier recommendation with the assertion that the United States should not take the lead in this matter, but should follow British leadership—and admitted that the British now seemed to equivocate.

It was soon reported that Yuan's own representative in Shanghai, Tang Shaoyi, opposed a foreign loan while the conflict continued, and throughout this period Washington continued to reiterate its adherence to "strict neutrality." Thus, Calhoun reported on December 24 that he had discouraged a representative of Salomon of New York when he had indicated that he was discussing a loan of one million pounds with the Board of Finance (ibid., 893.00/806, telegram, December 24, 1911, Calhoun to the Secretary of State).

Meanwhile, Yuan and his emissaries were urging support, insisting that dire consequences would flow from failure to act. In mid-December, the Board of Finance reported that it had only 400,000 taels on hand, and would need 1.3 million taels to meet the payrolls due in a few days. And in an interview with U.S. official Tenney at the end of December, Yuan told Tenney that he had a mere 1.1 million taels in his treasury, and that if no assistance were received, he could not maintain order in the North, widespread pillage from discontented troops being likely. Two million taels per month were required, he asserted, and with 10 million taels, he could hold out for some time. In the course of his remarks, he bitterly criticized what he termed British duplicity, saying that initially the British had encouraged him and intimated support, but now they refused aid while Shanghai British interests were actively aiding the revolutionaries.

Once again, Calhoun recommended aid to Yuan, indicating his view that if support had been given earlier, Yuan could have ended the revolution, and that continued neutrality could only encourage disorder, leading to the necessity for intervention of some sort at a later point. See ibid., 893.00/832, telegram, December 28, 1911, Calhoun to the Secretary of State. Washington did not completely rule out Calhoun's recommendation, but insisted that any action had to be based on a unanimous decision of the major powers, and in subsequent statements indicated its continued adherence to "strict neutrality," asserting that it looked with "disfavor" upon loans by its nationals unless they would have a "neutral effect." On January 2, Yuan received gold bullion worth 3 million taels, silver, from the empress dowager, and reported that he would be able to carry on.

52. For the Straight letter, dated February 4, 1912, see ibid., 893.00/1191.

53. *NCH*, February 10, 1912, 368.

54. See *Geming wenxian* 42–43:315–486.

55. For the text of this and other decrees, see Xu Youpeng, *Yuan dazongtong shudu huibien*.

56. See Bai Jiao, *Yuan Shikai yu Zhonghua minguo*. This work was first published in 1936 and is an important source on Yuan's role during the early repub-

lican years, containing many original documents and contemporary newspaper accounts.

57. On two occasions Sun set forth his ideas in speeches before welcoming meetings during his visit to the North in the early fall of 1912. See *Guofu quanji* 3:73–78 and 82–83; and also *NCH*, September 21, 1912, 831, and September 28, 1912, 873–874.

58. See Zou Lu's essay in Bao Zunpeng et al., eds., *Zhongguo jindai shi luncong*, 81–95.

59. Song's program contained directives on two levels: the governmental structure and the broad policies to be pursued. Regarding the former, Song outlined five principles: (1) a unitary state rather than a federal state; (2) a responsible cabinet system; (3) provincial governors, initially elected locally, but eventually appointed by the national government; (4) provinces to have certain autonomous rights, with provincial legislatures possessing the power to act on local matters; (5) the premier to be elected by the House of Representatives. Despite the 4th principle, Song clearly remained wedded to his conviction that the national interest would be best served by a substantial degree of centralization, more than was palatable to many Guomindang members.

A ten-point program accompanied Song's statement of principles: (1) military reorganization; (2) the creation of two basic administrative units below the national government, namely, province and locality, with the province serving as the primary unit below the national level; (3) the appointment of provincial officers by the national government; (4) financial reform; (5) the development of natural resources; (6) promotion of local self-government; (7) state-owned communications; (8) the promotion of education; (9) a coordinated judicial system; (10) a quest for foreign allies, but care in the solicitation of foreign loans. For Song's proposals, see *MLB*, April 2, 1913, 2; April 3, 3; April 4, 2; April 5, 3; April 6, 3; and April 7, 3. It should be noted that these were not published until after Song's death.

60. The text of the decree is contained in Bai Jiao, *Yuan Shikai yu Zhonghua minguo*, 153–155. In English, see *NCH*, March 29, 1913, 937.

61. Extensive accounts of the Song murder trial can be found in various sources. In Chinese, see the news reports in *Minli bao* during March and April 1912 and the summary accounts in the *Geming wenxian*, vols. 42–43. In English, see *NCH*, April 12, 1913, 184–189; May 3, 1913, 315–347; May 10, 1913, 415–416.

62. See *NCH*, April 12, 1913, 127.

63. For a discussion of the merger of the three parties and contemporary party politics, see Li Shougong, *Minchu zhi guohui*, 90–93.

64. Bashford immediately reported his conversation to the American consul general, Amos Wilder, and it was transmitted to Beijing. See *NAMP/RDSRIAC*, 893.00/1683, May 6, 1913.

65. For the Wilder report that includes the Bashford-Sun conversation, see *NAMP/RDSRIAC*, 893.00/1683, May 6, 1913.

66. The second Wilder report of this period, dated May 7, 1913, is contained in ibid., 893.00/1702. Wilder also noted that a number of foreigners had been counseling Sun, including Dr. Timothy Richard.

67. See *Guofu quanji*, 3:281–290 for the speech.

68. See *China Republican*, March 28, 1913, 13.

69. *MLB*, March 26, 1913, 10.

70. This telegram is contained in *Guofu quanji* 4:229–230. In English, see *NCH*, September 6, 1913, 736.

71. *Guofu quanji* 4:183–184.

72. *Central China Post,* June 24, 1913, 1.

73. For details, see *Geming wenxian* 6:30–40. It will be recalled that prior to the Revolution of 1911, a four-power consortium of foreign bankers had existed, consisting of American, British, German, and French institutions. After the establishment of the Republic in 1912, Russian and Japanese banking interests joined the group, causing it to be known as the Six Power or Sextuple Banking Consortium, and it was with this group that the Yuan administration negotiated. On March 13, 1913, however, President Wilson withdrew sanction for American participation, leaving the group representative of five powers.

74. See *NAMP/RDSRIAC,* 893.00/1799, May 13, 1913, Williams to the Secretary of State.

75. See ibid., 893.00/1680, May 28, 1913, telegram Williams to the Secretary of State.

76. For the presidential mandate, see Bai Jiao, *Yuan Shikai yu Zhonghua minguo,* 58–59. In English, see *NCH,* August 9, 1913, 414.

77. The Guomindang committee's response is contained in *NCH,* August 9, 1913, 446.

78. For an outline of Xiong's program, see *NCH,* August 30, 1913, 662.

79. Liang's plan is presented in its main elements in *NCH,* November 15, 1913, 530–531.

80. For a "popular" treatment of the Confucian revitalization movement, see Sun Kefu et al., *Yuan Shikai zun Kong fubi chouju.* For a report on the September 3 meeting, see *NCH,* September 6, 1913, 744. During this period the press also carried accounts of the formation of various societies to promote Confucianism as a state religion, and in Canton a celebration of Confucius's birthday in September received major support from the local government.

81. An English text of this mandate, issued on November 26, is carried in *NCH,* December 6, 1913, 747.

82. Kang arrived in Canton on December 12, and after being presented with scrolls of condolence, was given a guard of 200 soldiers and a gunboat to accompany him as he conveyed the remains of his mother for interment in her native village. See *NCH,* December 27, 1913, 985.

83. The document entitled *Zhonghua minguo xianfa caoan* (Draft Constitution of the Republic of China) was approved by the constitutional committee on October 31. For the draft, see Zhang Pufan and Zeng Xianyi, *Zhongguo xianfa shilue.* An account relating to events surrounding the drafting of the Temple of Heaven Constitution can be found also in Luo Zhiyuan, *Zhongguo xianfa shi,* 92–98.

84. *NCH,* November 1, 1913, 365.

85. The Goodnow draft constitution together with explanatory notes written by Goodnow is to be found in Bau, *Modern Democracy,* Appendix V, 424–439.

86. Li Shougong, *Minchu zhi guohui,* 126; *NCH,* October 11, 1913, 85. (The latter source states that 733 of 868 members were present for Yuan's election.)

87. For Yuan's inaugural address, see Bai Jiao, *Yuan Shikai yu Zhonghua minguo,* 62–68. In English, see *Peking Gazette,* October 1, 1913, clipping in *NAMP/RDSRIAC,* 893.00/2004, October 11, 1913.

88. For these orders, see Bai Jiao, *Yuan Shikai yu Zhonghua minguo,* 79–96. In English, see *NCH,* November 8, 1913, 446–447.

89. For details, see Shuhsi Hsu, *China and Her Political Entity,* 352.

90. Sterling interview with Kozakoff, Chief of the Far Eastern Affairs Department, Russian Foreign Office, January 11, 1912, in NAMP/RDSRIAC, 893.00/1000, St. Petersburg, January 13, 1912, Sterling to the Secretary of State. See also

the official statement of the Russian Ministry of Foreign Affairs on the Mongolian question contained in this dispatch.

91. For a report on the Mongolian reforms, see *NCH*, April 20, 1912, 183–184.

92. *NCH*, July 27, 1912, 268.

93. For an English translation of the Russo-Chinese Agreement of November 5, see *NCH*, November 15, 532.

94. *NAMP/RDSRIAC*, 893.00/1244, Calhoun to the Secretary of State, March 15, 1912.

95. Two works in English, written from different perspectives, are most useful in providing data and documents relating to Tibet during this period: Tieh-Tseng Li, *Tibet Today and Yesterday*; and H. E. Richardson, *A Short History of Tibet*.

96. For earlier Russian activities relating to Tibet, see Richardson, *Short History of Tibet*, 78–82. For a more skeptical account of the Russian threat and British motives, see Li, *Tibet*, 84–85; but Li also cites evidence of Russian interest in Tibet (119ff.).

97. The Anglo-Russian Convention of 1907 is reproduced in Richardson, *Short History of Tibet*, 258–260.

98. For the British protest and an American analysis of the current situation, see *NAMP/RDSRIAC*, 893.00/1434, telegram, Beijing, August 29, 1912, and 893.00/1435, telegram, Beijing, August 31, 1912, Calhoun to the Secretary of State.

99. See Li, *Tibet*, 133.

100. For the full text of the Simla draft, see Richardson, *Short History of Tibet*, Appendix 16, 268–272.

101. Ibid., 118.

102. For example, see the letter of Austin P. Brown, self-styled Real Estate, Railroad and Corporate Financier, to Secretary of State Bryan, dated March 14, 1913, and also a letter from the San Francisco Labor Union Council, *NAMP/RDSRIAC*, 893.00/1634, along with scores of others contained in this file.

103. This letter was carried in the *North China Daily News*, Shanghai, November 15, 1911, and the clipping is to be found in *NAMP/RDSRIAC*, 893.00/793, November 20, 1911, Wilder to the Secretary.

104. Ibid.

105. For various responses, see *NAMP/RDSRIAC*, 893.00/1406, 1406B, 1407, 1413, 1414, and 1420, all dated July and August 1912.

106. "American Views of China," *NCH*, April 12, 1913, 182.

107. Ibid., 183.

CHAPTER EIGHT

1. Edward Friedman in his monograph *Backward Toward Revolution* has dealt at some length with White Wolf and his movement. See pp. 122–128ff.

2. See "China's Attitude to the War," Beijing, September 4, 1914, in *NCH*, September 12, 1914, 841.

3. For the full text of the demands in English, see "The Sino-Japanese Negotiations of 1915."

4. For a detailed discussion of the monarchical movement in English, see Ernest P. Young, *The Presidency of Yuan Shih-K'ai*, 210–240. In Chinese, see Bai Jiao, *Yuan Shikai yu zhonghua minguo*, 97–391.

5. The rebel manifesto is carried in *NCH*, January 8, 1916, 20–21.

6. This section draws heavily upon George T. Yu, *Party Politics in Republican China*, 117–147.

7. For the full text of the oath, see Zou Lu, *Zhongguo Guomindang shigao* 1:159–160.

8. Sun claimed 400 to 500 members in a letter to Deng Zeru of April 8, 1914. See *Geming wenxian* 5:579–580. Other sources, however, assert that by the spring of 1914 less than 200 had joined Sun's movement. See Zhu Zheng, *Zhu Zhuosheng xiansheng quanji* 1:155; and Feng Ziyou in *Geming wenxian* 5:628. For further details on the organizational efforts, see Zou Lu, 1:271. The majority of Sun's followers now came from the provinces of Hubei, Hunan, Anhui, and Jiangxi, with some from Zhejiang, Guangdong, Sichuan, Fujian, and Jiangsu. As usual, the revolutionary roots were strongest in central and south China.

9. See Zhang Ji, *Zhang Puquan xiansheng quanji*, 241.

10. For the full text of the manifesto, see Zou Lu, *Zhongguo Guomindang shigao* 1:18.

11. The translation of the letter used here is to be found in Lo Hui-min, ed., *The Correspondence of G. E. Morrison*, 2:324–328. See also Wilbur, *Sun Yat-sen*, 80, 316 n.26.

12. Feng Ziyou in *Geming wenxian* 5:65.

13. For information about Huang's arrival and subsequent activities, see *Chungsai Yat-po* (East West Daily), San Francisco, July 16, July 27, 1914; *San Francisco Chronicle*, July 31, 1914; Deng Jiayen, ed., *Zhongguo Guomindang kenqin dahui shimoji*.

14. Feng Ziyou, in *Geming wenxian* 5:640.

15. For Sun's initial declaration issued from Shanghai on May 9, 1916, see *Guofu quanji* 4:16–19.

16. For a Guomindang account of this period, see *Geming wenxian*, vol. 49. A detailed account of the history and politics of the Beiyang military may be found in Tao Juyin, *Beiyang junfa tongzhi shiqi shihua*; and Dian Buyi et al., *Beiyang junfa shihua*. In English, see Li Chien-nung, *The Political History of China*, 1840–1928; and Ch'ien Tuan-sheng, *The Government and Politics of China*, in addition to the works of Fung, Gillin, Jansen, MacKinnon, Powell, and Sheridan.

17. For a detailed account of Beijing's financial problems and its efforts to secure funds, internal and external, see Nathan, *Peking Politics*, 74ff.

18. See *United States Foreign Relations* (1915), 108–111.

19. The politics of this era is well described in Tao Juyin, *Beiyang junfa tongzhi shiqi shihua*, vol. 4. For a detailed account from an official American perspective, see NAMP/RDSRIAC, 893.00/2838, Beijing, April 30, 1918, Reinsch to the Secretary.

20. Nathan, *Peking Politics*, 98–101.

21. For a thorough discussion of the Anfu Club in English, see Nathan, *Peking Politics*, 106–111. In Chinese, see Yang Youzhun, *Zhongguo Zhengdang shi*, 106–110.

22. Nathan, *Peking Politics*, 103–105.

23. Tao Juyin, *Beiyang junfa tongzhi shiqi shihua* 4:167–171.

24. For this report, see NAMP/RDSRIAC, 893.00/2417, April 3, 1916, Changsha, Johnson to Reinsch.

25. See Hsi-Sheng Ch'i, *Warlord Politics in China*, esp. 18–32.

26. See NAMP/RDSRIAC, 893.00/2879, Changsha, July 17, 1918, Johnson to MacMurray.

27. See Russell Fifield, *Woodrow Wilson and the Far East: The Diplomacy of the Shantung Question*, 84.

28. See Nathan, *Peking Politics*, 138ff.

29. For details, see *NCH*, April 19, 1919, 149.

30. Chow Tse-tung has provided massive data on the May Fourth Movement in his study *The May Fourth Movement*, and his account has been most useful to us. Joseph T. Chen has written a detailed account of the movement in Shanghai, which is also very helpful. See Chen, *The May Fourth Movement in Shanghai*. In Chinese, see *Wusi aiguo yundong*. This is chiefly a compilation of works which had earlier appeared in *Modern Historical Materials* (Beijing) from 1954 through 1965. For a collection of essays by participants in the movement, see *Wusi yundong huiyi lu*.

31. For details, see *Wusi yundong huiyi lu* and *Wusi aiguo yundong*, vol. 1. In English, see Chow, *The May Fourth Movement*, 100–104.

32. For a detailed account of the demonstrations and meetings held by various groups in China and abroad on May 7, see Liu Likai, "A Daily Record of Major Events of the Patriotic Movement from May 4 to June 3," in *Wusi aiguo yundong* 2:489–490; personal accounts can be found in Xiao San et al., *Qingnian yundong huixi bu*.

33. For the text of the Canton parliament telegram, see Chow, *The May Fourth Movement*, 126–127.

34. Ibid., 127.

35. Ibid., 140–141.

36. See Chen, *The May Fourth Movement in Shanghai*, 46–51.

37. For details, see *NAMP/RDSRIAC*, 893.00/3875, April 23, 1921, "Visit of Military Inspector Chang Tso-lin to Tientsin and Peking," Pontius (Mukden CG) to the Secretary.

38. See ibid., 893.00/3907, May 9, 1921; 3922, May 18, 1921; and "China's Military Oppressors," *Peking and Tientsin Times*, May 26, 1921.

39. The description that follows is drawn mainly from U.S. consular and legation reports, and from various accounts carried in the Chinese and foreign press of this period.

40. Sun's proposals were first published in English in 1922 under the title *The International Development of China*.

41. For details, see *NAMP/RDSRIAC*, 893.00/3868, April 20, 1921, "Political Conditions in the Canton Consular District," Price to the Secretary. The American vice-consul in Canton, Ernest B. Price, while acknowledging divisions of opinion among Canton politicians on the advisability of electing Sun president at this time, defended the actions taken, asserting that although it might be questionable whether one could consider it proper to accept the acts of some 222 legislators out of an original 1,000, a quorum could not possibly have been rounded up, and those assembled were members of the only legally elected parliament in China. Further, it was better to have a government functioning by the will of those remaining than to have no legal government whatsoever.

42. See chapter 11.

43. For terms of the Kiakhta Agreement, see Gerard M. Friters, *Outer Mongolia and Its International Position*, 175ff.; and Ma Hot'ien, *Chinese Agent in Mongolia*, 81.

44. See an article by David Fraser, "The Mongolian Situation," *NCH*, June 28, 1919, 833–835. An account of the Mongolian situation during these years can be found in Robert A. Rupen, *Mongols of the Twentieth Century*, Part I, ch. 5.

45. Details can be found in various reports from Albert Pontius, American consul in Mukden, and from U.S. legation reports to Washington. See *NAMP/RDSRIAC*, 893.00 series, numbers 3814 (March 5, 1921); 3816 (February 24, 1921); 3848 (March 15, 1921); 3850 (March 21, 1921); 3853 (March 28, 1921); and 3961 (June 6, 1921).

CHAPTER NINE

1. For a sample of such writings, see Feng Chengzhun, "The Party System in England and France," *Dongfang zazhi* (Eastern Miscellany) 8, no. 7 (1911): 18–21; "The Relationship Between the State and Law," a translation of an article by a Japanese author, Nomura Sōji, ibid., no. 8 (1911): 1–13; "A Comparison of the American and Canadian Constitutions," a translation from an American source, ibid., no. 10 (1911).

2. Gao Lao, translated excerpts from Kōtoku Shūsui, *Shakaishugi shinzui*, in *Dongfang zazhi* 8, no. 11 (1912): 9–12, and no. 12 (1912): 5–10.

3. Ouyang Fucun (pseudonym), "Socialism," *Dongfang zazhi*, 8, no. 12 (1912): 1–5.

4. Ibid., 5.

5. Editorial, "On World Citizens," *MLB*, October 15, 1910, 1.

6. Ibid.

7. For example, see the *Minli bao* editorial of October 25, 1910, "What Is Socialism? No One Is Selfish," 1.

8. Data on Jiang Kanghu can be found in *Jiang Kanghu boshi yenjiang lu*. See also Wu Xiangxiang (ed.), *Zhongguo xiandai shi congkan* 2:51–95, and Boorman and Howard (eds.), *Biographical Dictionary* 1:338–344.

9. *MLB*, January 12, 1912, 8.

10. Letter from a reader, *MLB*, April 4, 1912, 2.

11. Editor's column, *MLB*, April 6, 1912, 2.

12. *MLB*, August 2, 1912, 8.

13. See Jiang Kanghu, "Declaration of the Chinese Socialist Party," *MLB*, November 3, 1912, 12.

14. For Jiang's proclamation, see Jiang Kanghu, "The Commitments of Members of the Chinese Socialist Party," in *MLB*, November 17, 19, 21, 22, 23, 26, 1912, all on p. 8.

15. *MLB*, November 20, 1912, 8.

16. *MLB*, November 26, 1912, 8.

17. Jiang's letter to Yuan is in *MLB*, December 10, 1912, 8.

18. Ibid.

19. The texts of these messages are contained in *MLB*, April 29, 8; May 5, 10; and May 16, 1913, 8.

20. *MLB*, May 2, 1913, 4.

21. *MLB*, May 5, 1913, 8.

22. *MLB*, May 10, 1913, 8.

23. *MLB*, June 13, 1913, 8.

24. His speech is reproduced as "The Principle of People's Livelihood and the Social Revolution," *Guofu quanji* 3:20–26.

25. Ibid., 21.

26. Ibid., 25.

27. For the *Minli bao* version, see "Mr. Sun's Speech on Socialism," *MLB*, October 15, 16, 18, 19, 21, and 23, 1912, all on p. 2. The speeches as reproduced in his Collected Works are entitled "A Critique of Socialism and Its Factions," a speech to the Chinese Socialist Party, Shanghai, October 15–17, 1912, *Guofu quanji* 6:12–32. The *MLB* coverage is briefer, and omits the last lecture. An abbreviated version of Sun's lectures is also to be found in *International Socialist Review* 13, no. 4:320. For further comment on these lectures, see J. Tsang Ly, "Dr. Sun and China," 14, no. 3 (September 1913): 173–176.

28. *International Socialist Review*, 13.

29. *MLB*, October 15, 1912, 2. Also *Guofu quanji* 6:14.
30. *Guofu quanji* 6:15. *MLB*, October 16, 1912, 2.
31. *Guofu quanji* 6:16.
32. Ibid., 21.
33. Ibid., 22.
34. Ibid., 27.
35. Ibid., 30.
36. "Covenant of the Jinde Hui," *MLB*, February 26, 1912, 2.
37. Ibid.
38. Ibid.
39. Ibid.
40. Materials on Shifu include Mo Jipeng, "Recalling Shifu," privately circulated, hand-written manuscript in Chinese; *Shifu wencun*; and the anarchist publication, *Geming pinglun minzhong xianfeng*. In English, see the sketch by H. E. Shaw, "A Chinese Revolutionist," *Mother Earth* 10 (October 1915): 284–285.
41. *MLB*, March 2, 1912, 3.
42. *MLB*, March 6, 1912, 3.
43. *MLB*, April 21, 1912, 2.
44. "Declaration," *Huiminglu*, August 20, 1913, 1–2.
45. Ibid., 2.
46. "A Simple Explanation of Anarchism," ibid., 2–8.
47. Ibid.
48. "Explaining the term 'Anarchist-Communism'," *Min sheng*, April 11, 1914, 1–5.
49. Ibid.
50. "The Aims and Methods of the Anarchist-Communist Party," *Min sheng*, July 18, 1914, 6–9.
51. "First Letter of Shifu to Wu Zhihui," ibid., August 27, 1913, 9–10.
52. "Wu Zhihui's Reply," ibid., 10.
53. "Shifu's Letter to Zhang Ji," ibid., 10–11.
54. See especially "The Socialism of Sun Yat-sen and Jiang Kanghu," ibid., April 18, 1914, 1–7, and "Jiang Kanghu's 'Anarchism'," ibid., July 4 and 11, 1914, 6–7; 5–7.
55. "The Socialism of Sun Yat-sen and Jiang Kanghu," ibid., 1–7.
56. Ibid.
57. "Argument Against Jiang Kanghu," *Min sheng*, June 13, 1914, 159–167, continued on June 20, 171–177. See also "The Anarchism of Jiang Kanghu," ibid., July 4, 1914, 6–7, continued on July 11, 5–7.
58. See Shifu's "In Answer to Luowu," ibid., April 25, 1914, 9–11; and his "On the Socialist Party," ibid., May 9, 1914, 1–6.
59. Wu Zhihui, "Remembering Mr. Shifu," in *Wu Zhihui quanji* 8:115–117.
60. For one valuable contemporary account of the French work-study movement, see a book written in Chinese and published in Paris: Shijieshe, ed., *LuOu jiaoyu yundong*. Note especially the section entitled "Reasons for Leaning Towards a French Education," 63–65. Recent studies on the French work-study movement include: Zhang Yunhou et al., *LiuFa qingong jianxue yundong*, vol. 1; Chinese Communist Party Study Group, Qinghua University, ed., *FuFa Qingong jianxue yundong shiliao*, Series 1 and 2. These works consist of contemporary letters from participants in the program, newspaper accounts, letters, and other reports on the movement.
61. *LuOu jiaoyu yundong*, 63.
62. Ibid., 65.

63. Wu Zhihui, "Writing My Thoughts on the Frugal Study Society in the East, July 13, 1913," in *Wu Zhihui xiansheng quanji* 2:199–201. This volume, incidentally, has a number of important essays on the work-study movement, written in 1912 and 1913.

64. *Lu-Ou jiaoyu yundong*, 50–55.

65. Ibid., 50.

66. Ibid., 56.

67. Shu Xincheng, *Jindai Zhongguo linxue shi*, 8.

68. He Jianggong, *Qingong jianxue*, 1–59. See also the account by Xuesheng, "Origins of the Diligent Work and Frugal Study in France," in *FuFa Qingong jianxue yundong shiliao*, Series 2, 1:47–52.

CHAPTER TEN

1. For Chen's early career, in Chinese, see *Chen Duxiu shian zizhuan*. In English, see Boorman and Howard, *Biographical Dictionary* 1:240–248; Thomas C. T. Kuo, *Chen Tu-hsiu (1879–1942) and the Chinese Communist Movement*; Richard C. Kagan, *The Chinese Trotskyist Movement and Ch'en Tu-hsiu: Culture, Revolution and Policy*.

2. Li Dazhao's early career is sketched briefly in *Li Dazhao xuanji*, 1–3; *Li Dazhao zhuan*; Li Xinghua, "Remembering My Father, Li Dazhao," *Zhongguo qingnian*, 8 (April 16, 1959): 19–25. In English, see the fine work by Maurice Meisner; Boorman and Howard, eds., *Biographical Dictionary* 2:329–333; Huang Sung-k'ang, *Li Ta-chao and the Impact of Marxism on Modern Chinese Thinking*.

3. The early life of Hu Shi is treated in Chinese in *Hu Shi liuxue riji*, 4 vols.; Hu Shi, *Sishi zishu: Zhuishi Hu Shizhi xiansheng zhuanji*; Li Ao, *Hu Shi pingzhuan*. In English, in addition to the well-researched and objective study by Jerome B. Grieder, *Hu Shih and the Chinese Renaissance*, see "Dr. Hu Shih's Personal Reminiscences," interviews compiled and edited by Te-kong Tong, 1958, typescript in the archive of the Oral History Project, Columbia University (and the Chinese translation, *Hu Shi koushu zhizhuan*); and Vincent Shih, "A Talk with Hu Shih," *China Quarterly*, April–June, 1962, 149–165.

4. See Chen's opening message, "To Respectfully Alert Our Youth," *Qingnian zazhi* (hereafter QZ) 1 (September 15, 1915): 1–6; also Chen Duxiu, "Today's Educational Guidelines," QZ 1 (October 15, 1915), 3–4, and Chen Duxiu, "To Refute Kang Youwei's Letter to the President and Premier," *Xin qingnian* (hereafter XQ) 2 (October 1, 1916): 1–4.

5. Chen Duxiu, "Today's Educational Guidelines," 4.

6. Chen Duxiu, "To Respectfully Alert Our Youth," 5–6.

7. Chen Duxiu, "The French People and Modern Civilization," QZ 1 (September 15, 1915): 1–4.

8. Chen Duxiu, "The True Meaning of Man's Life," XQ 4 (February 15, 1918): 90–93.

9. Chen Duxiu, "Again, On the Problem of Confucianism," XQ 2 (January 1, 1917): 1–4.

10. Chen, "To Refute Kang Youwei's Letter . . . ," 4.

11. Chen Duxiu, "The Confucian Way and Modern Life," XQ 2 (December 1, 1916): 1–7.

12. Ibid., 6–7.

13. Chen Duxiu, "The Constitution and Confucianism," XQ 2 (November 1, 1916): 1–5; see also Chen, "The Confucian Way . . . ," 2–3.

14. Chen Duxiu, "The Difference between Eastern and Western People in Their

Basic Thinking," *XQ* 1 (December 15, 1915): 1–4; see also Chen Duxiu, "Resistance," *XQ* 1 (November 15, 1915): 1–5.

15. Chen, "The Difference . . . ," 3.

16. The fullest exposition of Chen's homage to the French is found in his essay "The French People and Modern Civilization" (n. 7 above).

17. Ibid., 3.

18. Chen Duxiu, "Our Final Awakening and Enlightenment," *XQ* 1 (February 15, 1916): 1–4.

19. Ibid., 2.

20. Chen Duxiu, "The New Youth," *XQ* 2 (September 1, 1916): 1–4.

21. Chen Duxiu, "My Patriotism," *XQ* 2 (October 1, 1916): 1–5.

22. Chen Duxiu, "Diplomacy with Germany," *XQ* 3 (March 1, 1917): 1–4.

23. Chen Duxiu, "The Russian Revolution and the Awareness of Our Compatriots," *XQ* 3 (April 1, 1917): 1–3.

24. Chang Naizhi, "A Record of Mr. Chen Duxiu's Lecture," *XQ* 3 (May 1, 1917): 1–2.

25. See, for example, Chen's "Miscellaneous Feelings about the Current Situation," *XQ* 3 (June 1, 1917): 1–4.

26. Ibid., 3.

27. Ibid.

28. See Chen Duxiu, "The Political Problems of Today's China," *XQ* 5 (July 15, 1918): 1–4.

29. Chen Duxiu, "The Von Ketteler Monument," *XQ* 5 (October 15, 1918): 449–458.

30. Chen Duxiu, "A Defense of Charges Against This Journal," *XQ* 6 (January 15, 1919): 10–11.

31. Chen Duxiu, "How Should We Be?" *XQ* 6 (April 15, 1919): 447–449.

32. Chen Duxiu, "The Problem of Virtue and Marx's Materialist Concept of History," *XQ* 6 (May 1919): 500–505.

33. Chen Duxiu, "The Foundation of Practicing People's Rule," *XQ* 7 (December 1, 1919): 13–21.

34. A full set of the thirty-seven issues of *Meizhou pinglun* (hereafter *MP*), reprinted, is available at Peking University Library, and also in several American libraries, including the East Asiatic Library, University of California, Berkeley. Generally, the articles contained in the six-page newsprint publication were brief, with the authors writing under a pseudonym. Li Dazhao contributed some fifty-five articles and a few editorials. Chen wrote most of the editorials and large numbers of articles until his arrest in June 1919.

35. *MP*, December 22, 1918, 1.

36. *MP*, May 4, 1919, 1.

37. *MP*, May 4, 1919, 1.

38. *MP*, June 15, 1919 (1–4), for a translation of Dewey's lecture "The Development of Popular Politics in the United States"; and in the succeeding issue (June 22, 1919, 1–4), his lecture "Trends in Modern Education."

39. *MP*, December 22, 1918, 1.

40. See, for example, "Sharing Rice and Sharing Jobs," *MP*, December 22, 1918, 1; Cai Yuanpei, "The Sacredness of Labor," reprinted from *Peking University Monthly*, in ibid., 4, and an article on labor education by Li Dazhao, *MP*, February 16, 1919, 3.

41. *MP*, March 9, 1919, 1.

42. *MP*, December 22, 1918, 1.

43. "Concerning the National Defense Army," *MP*, January 5, 1919, 2.
44. *MP*, January 5, 1919, 1.
45. *MP*, January 12, 1919, 1.
46. *MP*, January 26, 1919, 1.
47. *MP*, February 23, 1919, 1.
48. August Bebel's essay on the differences between utopian and modern socialism was published in translation in *MP* on March 30, 1919 (2), and in the following issue of April 6 an excerpt of the *Communist Manifesto* with commentary was published (3).
49. *MP*, April 27, 1919, 1.
50. *MP*, May 4, 1919, 1.
51. See Li Dazhao, "Youthful Spring," *XQ* 2 (September 1, 1916): 1–11. This article was actually written in Japan in the spring of 1916.
52. Ibid.
53. Li Dazhao, "Youth and Old Men," *XQ* 3 (April 1, 1917): 1–4.
54. Li Dazhao, "Now," *XQ* 4 (May 15, 1918): 446–449.
55. Li Dazhao, "The Triumph of Bolshevism," *XQ* 5 (October 15, 1918): 442–448. This essay was actually delivered initially as a speech at a rally in Tiananmen on November 11, 1918, celebrating the armistice.
56. Li Dazhao, "The Triumph of Bolshevism," 448.
57. Li Dazhao, "The Triumph of the Common People," *XQ* 5 (October 15, 1918): 436–438.
58. Li Dazhao, "The Problem of Women After the War," *XQ* 6 (February 15, 1919): 141–147.
59. We are indebted to Maurice Meisner's earlier research for uncovering these articles contained in Li's selected writings. Meisner has also done an excellent job of highlighting the major themes contained therein. See his study, *Li Ta-chao and the Origins of Chinese Marxism*, 71–89. For the articles themselves, see *Li Dazhao xuanji*, 146–150.
60. Li Dazhao, "My View of Marxism," Part 1, *XQ* 6 (May 1919): 521–537; Part 2, *XQ* 6 (November 1, 1919): 612–624.
61. Gu Zhaoxiong, "The Theory of Marxism," *XQ* 6 (November 1, 1919): 450–465.
62. Ibid., 465.
63. Ling Shuang, "A Critique of Marxism," *XQ* 6 (November 1, 1919): 466–469.
64. Ibid., 467.
65. Angelo S. Rappoport, "The Foundations of Russian Revolutionary Philosophy," *XQ* 6 (November 1, 1919): 470–478.
66. Ibid., 473.
67. Yuan Quan, "Marx's Materialist Historiography," (an essay taken from *Chen bao*), *XQ* 6 (May 1919): 5. In the introduction, Yuan asserts that the essay was written by Kawakami, with his contribution only that of translation.
68. Li Dazhao, "My View of Marxism," Part 1, 534–535.
69. Ibid., 536. Schwartz noted this point very accurately. See his *Chinese Communism and the Rise of Mao*, 16–17.
70. Li Dazhao, "My View of Marxism," Part 2.
71. For Hu's initial article, see *Jianshe*, October 1, 1919, 513–543, and November 1, 1919, 33–69. For his critique of Li, see *Jianshe*, December 1, 1919, 945–989. For a general analysis of the journal *Jianshe*, see Corinna Hana, *Sun Yatsen's Parteiorgan Chien-she (1919–1920)*.

72. Chang (Li Dazhao), "Dangerous Thought and Freedom of Speech," *MP*, June 1, 1919, 3.

73. Chang (Li), "Life in Prison," *MP*, June 29, 1919, 4.

74. Shou Chang (Li), "The World and I," *MP*, July 6, 1919, 4.

75. Shou Chang (Li), "The Class Struggle and Mutual Aid," *MP*, July 6, 1919, 2.

76. Li Dazhao, *MP*, August 1919.

77. Li Dazhao, "Material Change and Moral Change," *XQ*, December 1, 1919.

78. Li Dazhao, "An Economic Interpretation of the Cause of Change in Modern Chinese Ideology," *XQ* 7 (January 1, 1920): 47–54.

79. Shou Chang (Li), "From a Vertical to a Horizontal Structure," *Jiefang yu gaizao* (Liberation and Reform) 2 (January 15, 1920), in *Li Dazhao xuanji*, 303–304.

80. Gu Song (Li), "The Victory of the Intellectual Class," *Xinshenghuo* (New Life), January 25, 1920, in *Li Dazhao xuanji*, 308.

81. Li Dazhao, "An Economic Interpretation . . . ," 302.

82. Li Dazhao, "Greater Pan-Asianism and the New Pan-Asianism," *Guomin* (The Citizen) 1 (February 1919): 1–3.

83. Ming Ming (Li), "The Doctrine of a Strong Nation," *MP*, March 16, 1919, 2.

84. *Li Dazhao zhuan*, 51–80.

85. Chang (Li), "Secret Diplomacy and the Robbers' World," *MP*, May 18, 1919, 2.

86. Ibid.

87. See, for example, Shou Chang (Li), "The Real Liberation," *MP*, July 13, 1919, 3.

88. "A Talk on the Occasion of the First Anniversary of 'National Magazine'," October 12, 1919, published in *Guomin zazhi* (National Magazine) 2 (November 1919), contained in *Li Dazhao xuanji*, 255.

89. "On New Asianism Again—A Response to Mr. Gao Chengyuan," 2 (December 12, 1919), contained in *Li Dazhao xuanji*, 278–282.

90. Gu Song (Li), "A Pair of Brotherly Countries," *New Life*, February 8, 1920, in ibid., 310.

91. Li Dazhao, "The Promising Asian Youth Movement," *Young China* 2 (August 15, 1920), in ibid., 327–329.

92. Shou Chang (Li), "The Present and Future," *Chen bao* (Morning News), March 28, 1919, in ibid., 164–165.

93. Gu Song (Li), "National Day Under Civil Rule," *New Life*, October 12, 1919, in ibid., 245.

94. Gu Song (Li), "Offical Posts on Sale: Tramping upon One's Personality," *New Life*, November 9, 1919, in ibid., 249.

95. Gu Song (Li), "Security Risks," *New Life*, November 9, 1919, in ibid., 251.

96. Gu Song (Li), "Who Has 'Strength'?" *New Life*, November 9, 1919, in ibid., 248.

97. Li Shouzhang, "For a Free Convening of a National Assembly," *Morning News*, August 17, 1920, in ibid., 330–332.

98. Gu Song (Li), "A Driving Force for Change," *New Life*, October 17, 1920, in ibid., 333.

99. For Dewey's central themes, see his work *Essays in Experimental Logic*; *Experiences and Nature*; and two collections edited by Joseph Ratner, *Characters and Events: Popular Essays in Social and Political Philosophy*, 2 vols.; and *Intelligence*

in the Modern World: John Dewey's Philosophy. See also Paul Schilpp, ed., *The Philosophy of John Dewey*, 2d ed., and George Dykhuizen, *The Life and Mind of John Dewey*.

100. For details, see Grieder, *Hu Shih and the Chinese Renaissance*, 61–62. Hu's views were set forth in an article entitled "A Plea for Patriotic Sanity: An Open Letter to All Chinese Students," published in the *Chinese Students Monthly*, 10 (April 1915): 425–426.

101. See Grieder, *Hu Shih and the Chinese Renaissance*, 66–70.

102. For Chen's remarks, see XQ 1 (December 15, 1915): 2.

103. Hu Shi, "Tentative Proposals for Literary Reform," XQ 2 (January 1917): 1–11.

104. Chen Duxiu, "On the Literary Revolution," XQ 2 (February 1917): 1–4.

105. Hu Shi, "A Constructive View of the Literary Revolution," XQ 4 (April 1918): 289–306.

106. Ibid.

107. Ibid.

108. See XQ 4 (June 1918), and especially the article by Hu entitled, "Ibsenism," 489–507.

109. Ibid.

110. "Introducing My Own Thought," *Hu Shi wencun* 4:607–624.

111. Ibid.

112. Hu Shi, "Study Problems More, Discuss Isms Less," *MP*, July 20, 1919, 1.

113. Ibid.

114. Hu Shi, "The Meaning of the New Thought Tide," XQ 7 (December 1919): 5–12.

115. Ibid. This translation is virtually the same as that presented by Grieder, *Hu Shih and the Chinese Renaissance*, 126.

116. Jane Dewey, "Biography of John Dewey," in Paul Schilpp, *Philosophy of John Dewey*, 40.

117. Barry Keenan, *The Dewey Experiment in China: Educational Reform and Political Power in the Early Republic*, 30.

118. For widely varying evaluations of Dewey's lectures among Chinese writers, both at the time and subsequently, see Chen Qitian, *Zuijin sanshi nian Zhongguo jiaoyu shi*; Chen Huqin, *Pipan Duwei fandong jiaoyu xue dizhexue jichu*; Zheng Zonghai, "The Educational Principles of Mr. Dewey"; Jiang Menglin, "Dewey's Ethics"; Qui Youzhen, *Guofu, Duwei, Makesi*; Xu Wenqiang, "Dewey's Conception of Education"; and Tao Xingzhi, "Introducing Professor Dewey's Educational Theory." In English, in addition to Kennan, see Thomas Berry, "Dewey's Influence in China," in John Blewitt, ed., *John Dewey: His Thought and Influence*; Albert Borowitz, "Chiang Monlin: Theory and Practice of Chinese Education, 1917–1930"; C. F. Remer, "John Dewey in China"; and Nancy Sizer, "John Dewey's Ideas in China, 1919 to 1921."

119. For Dewey's trip and lectures, in addition to Clapton and Ou, see also John and Alice Dewey, *Letters from China and Japan*.

120. See Dewey's lecture "Science and Knowing," in Clapton and Ou, *John Dewey: Lectures in China*, 245–251.

121. Clapton and Ou, *John Dewey*, 121.

122. See Kennan, *The Dewey Experiment in China*, 33.

123. Chen Duxiu, "The Basis for the Realization of Democracy," XQ 7 (December 1919): 13–21.

124. For the *Manifesto*, see ibid., 1–4. Analyses are to be found in Chow Tse-tsung, *The May Fourth Movement*, 174–176, and Grieder, *Hu Shih and the Chinese Renaissance*, 183–184.

125. *XQ*, December 1, 1919, 121–134.

126. For some insightful essays on the general topic of "conservatism" during this period, see the work edited by Charlotte Furth, *The Limits of Change: Essays on Conservative Alternatives in Republican China*.

127. See chapter 3, pp. 134–135.

128. Liang's original account was contained in articles published in *Shishi xinbao* (Current News), in Shanghai. These have been republished as *Ouyou xinying lu jielu*.

129. Guy S. Alitto has written a stimulating work on Liang entitled *The Last Confucian: Liang Shu-ming and the Chinese Dilemma of Modernity*.

130. For accounts of Zhang Junmai's views during this period, see Grieder, *Hu Shih and the Chinese Renaissance*, 145–150, and Alitto, *The Last Confucian*, 77–81. The senior author was privileged to have various conversations with Zhang in the late 1950s when he was in the San Francisco area. Zhang's exposition of his views can be found in *Mingri zhi Zhongguo wenhua*.

131. See Grieder, *Hu Shih and the Chinese Renaissance*, 161. Grieder's section on Hu's response to the neo-traditionalists is excellent (see 150–169). For a fine study of one of Hu's fellow liberals, see Charlotte Furth, *Ting Wen-chiang: Science and China's New Culture*.

CHAPTER ELEVEN

1. "The War in China," first published in December 1900, *Iskra*, 1, contained in *Collected Works* 4:372–377, and republished in V. I. Lenin, *The National Liberation Movement in the East*, 3d rev. ed., 21–26.

2. See the Resolution reportedly written by Lenin for the Sixth (Prague) All-Russia Conference of the R.S.D.R.P., in *National Liberation Movement*, 54–55.

3. Ibid., 56–62. This article was originally published in *Nevskaya zvezda* (The Neva Star) 17 (July 15, 1912). For another interpretation, see the excellent pioneer study by Allen S. Whiting, *Soviet Policies in China, 1917–1924*, 12–17.

4. Lenin, *National Liberation Movement*, 59–60.

5. Ibid., 60–62.

6. From *Pravda* (Truth), November 8, 1912, signed T., in ibid., 65–66.

7. "Struggle of the Parties in China," (originally published in *Pravda*, May 3, 1913), ibid., 75–77.

8. See Stephen F. Cohen, *Bukharin and the Bolshevik Revolution—A Political Biography, 1888–1938*, 5. This is not only a highly perceptive account of Bukharin, but contains many insights into the Russian Revolution as a whole.

9. For the April Theses, see Vladimir Ilich Lenin, *The April Conference*.

10. For Lenin's early views, no source is better than his *State and Revolution*.

11. See Eudin and North, *Soviet Russia and the East*, 77–78.

12. See *Zhizn Natsionalnoster* 36:44, 79; also Lenin, *Collected Works* 30, "Address to the Second All-Russian Congress of Communist Organizations of the Peoples of the East, November 22, 1919," 151–162. For Stalin's message, see Document 28, Eudin and North, *Soviet Russia and the East*, 163–164.

13. The Second Congress has been explored in a variety of sources. See Whiting, *Soviet Policies in China*, 42–48; also Eudin and North, *Soviet Russia and the East*, 44 and 63–71. The full proceedings are available in English: The Second Congress of the Communist International: *Proceedings of Petrograd Session of July*

17th and of Moscow Sessions of July 19th–August 7th, Moscow, 1920 (hereafter Second Congress *Proceedings*). See also Degras, *The Communist International* 1:109–183.

14. For data on Roy and his activities during this period, see John P. Haithcox, *Communism and Nationalism in India, M. N. Roy and the Comintern Policy,* 1920–1939, and Robert C. North and Xenia J. Eudin, *M. N. Roy's Mission to China: The Communist-Kuomintang Split of* 1927. An earlier study of Indian communism containing materials on Roy is that of Marshall Windmiller and Gene D. Overstreet, *Communism in India.*

15. Second Congress *Proceedings*, 573–575. See also Eudin and North, *Soviet Russia and the East*, 63–65.

16. Second Congress *Proceedings*, 576–579, and Eudin and North, *Soviet Russia and the East*, 65–67.

17. Eudin and North, 67.

18. Lenin, *Collected Works* 31:240–245. See also Eudin and North, *Soviet Russia and the East*, 68–70.

19. Eudin and North, 69.

20. See Xiang Qing, "The Comintern and the Chinese Revolution During the Period of the Founding of the Chinese Communist Party," in *Jindai shi yanjiu* (Research on Modern History) 4 (1980): 92–116. According to Xiang, an association initially called the Federation of Overseas Chinese in Russia had been formed by some of the thousands of Chinese who had come to Russia during World War I as laborers. Later the association was renamed the Federation of Chinese Workers in Russia, and Liu and Chang as leaders of the organization were invited by the Soviet Commissariat of Foreign Affairs to attend the First Congress. Liu spoke on March 5, the day before the Congress ended, but no record of his remarks is available. For his own recollection, see Liu Zeying (Shaozhou), "A Memoir on Meeting the Great Lenin," in *Renmin ribao* (People's Daily), April 21, 1960, 3. Lenin met with the two Chinese while the Congress was in session.

21. For a brief but well-documented account of the Baku Conference by a Soviet scholar, see G. Z. Sorkin, *Pervyi syezd narodov vostoka.*

22. Figures relating to the number of delegates vary. Both in the stenographic records of the conference and in the Conference Manifesto the number listed was 1,891 delegates in attendance. Sorkin says that there were 2,050 people present, yet his breakdown of the official record totals only 1,926: 1,071 delegates were listed as Communist Party members, 334 as sympathizers, and an additional 31 members of the Communist Youth League and 11 members of the Communist Bund. Of the others, 467 were reported to have no party affiliation, 9 from the Persian Revolutionary Party, and 1 each were listed as a "social revolutionary," a "left social revolutionary," and an anarchist. (See Sorkin, 21–23.)

23. The largest number of delegates, according to Sorkin, came from Azerbaijan (469), followed by the mountain people of the northern Caucasus (461), Turkestan (322), Persia (202), Georgia (137), Armenia (131), Turkey (105), Kirgizia (85), Afghanistan (40), the Tartar region (20), India (14), Bukhara (14), Kiva (14), Bashkiria (13), Crimea (8), Kalmyk Republic (8), and China (7), (Ibid., 21–22.)

24. Sorkin, 21.

25. Excerpts of the key speeches, taken from *Pervyi syezd narodov vostoka, Baku, 1–8 1920 g. stenograficheskie otchety*, are presented by Eudin and North, *Soviet Russia and the East*, 165–172.

26. See Sorkin, *Pervyi syezd narodov vostoka*, 24–27; Eudin and North, *Soviet Russia and the East*, 80–81.

27. For the Zinoviev speech, see *Narody vostoka* (Peoples of the East), 15–20.

28. For the Radek speech, see ibid., October 1920, 21–26.

29. For these speeches, see ibid., 27–44, and for Pavlovich, also Eudin and North, *Soviet Russia and the East*, 168–169. Another report on the agrarian question was given by P. E. Skachko. See *Narody vostoka*, 35–41.

30. Indeed, Bela Kun's report was entitled "On Soviet Construction in the East." See *Narody vostoka*, 42–44.

31. For the September 6 Theses, see Eudin and North, *Soviet Russia and the East*, 169–170.

32. Ibid., 170–171.

33. Sorkin, *Pervyi syezd narodov vostoka*, 39–40.

34. Ibid., 42–44.

35. Eudin and North, *Soviet Russia and the East*, 82.

36. Ibid., 84, quoting from I. I. Genkin, "Konets Ungerna i nachalo novoi Mongolii," *Severnaia Aziia* 2, no. 20 (1928): 81.

37. For English-language materials, see C. E. Bechhofer-Roberts, *In Denikin's Russia and the Caucasus, 1919–1920*; J. F. Bradley, *Allied Intervention in Russia, 1917–1920*, and *Civil War in Russia, 1917–1920*; G. A. Brinkley, *The Volunteer Army and Allied Intervention in South Russia*; E. H. Carr, *The Bolshevik Revolution, 1917–1923*, 3 vols.; W. H. Chamberlin, *The Russian Revolution, 1917–1921*, 2 vols.; A. I. Denikin, *The White Army*, trans. Catherine Zveginstev; P. Fleming, *The Fate of Admiral Kolchak*; D. J. Footman, *Civil War in Russia*; W. S. Graves, *America's Siberian Adventure, 1918–1920*; George F. Kennan, *Soviet-American Relations, 1917–1920* (vol. 1, *Russia Leaves the War*; vol. 2, *The Decision to Intervene*); James Morley, *The Japanese Thrust into Siberia, 1918*; G. Stewart, *The White Armies of Russia*; Richard H. Ullman, *Anglo-Soviet Relations, 1917–1921* (vol. 1, *Intervention and the War*; vol. 2, *Britain and the Russian Civil War*); B. M. Unterberger, *America's Siberian Expedition*; E. Varneck and H. H. Fisher, eds., *The Testimony of Kolchak and Other Siberian Materials*; D. Fedotoff White, *Survival Through War and Revolution in Russia*; P. N. Wrangel, *The Memoirs of General Wrangel*.

38. E. H. Carr, *The Bolshevik Revolution* 1:110.

39. A well-documented, two-volume study of the Russian civil war is Peter Kenez, *Civil War in South Russia, 1918: The First Year of the Volunteer Army*, and *Civil War in South Russia, 1919–1920: The Defeat of the Whites*.

40. For details, see George Kennan, *The Decision to Intervene*, 381–452, and James Morley, *The Japanese Thrust into Siberia*, 260–313.

41. Morley, *The Japanese Thrust into Siberia*, 308–309, and Hosoya Chihiro, *Siberia shuppei no shiteki kenkyū*.

42. For Horvath's discussion of the Ufa Conference, see his *Memoirs*, chap. 15, 10–13.

43. For a discussion of the Japanese campaign and various battles, see Hosoya, *Siberia shuppei no shiteki kenkyū*, 159–236.

44. For a well-researched Soviet study of the Far Eastern Republic, see M. A. Persits, *Dalnevostochnaia Respublika i Kitai*.

45. Persits, 45–62; Allen Whiting, *Soviet Policies in China, 1917–1924*, 27–28; and Sow-Theng Leong, *Sino-Soviet Diplomatic Relations, 1917–1926*, 29–32. The latter two works are indispensable English sources for early Soviet-Chinese relations. Whiting's pioneer study remains a valuable interpretation. Leong, using Chinese, Japanese, and Russian sources, has provided additional data, making certain revisions of earlier held theses. For two very good Chinese sources, see Wang Yujin, *Zhong-Su waijiao di xumo*, and Modern History Institute, Academia Sinica, ed., *Zhong-Su quanxi shiliao*.

46. Leong has a chapter devoted to the Harbin Soviet (16–35), and his research has brought to our attention a useful Japanese study, Seki Hiroharu, *Gendai higashi Ajia kokusai kankyō no tanjō*, which contains detailed data relating to the Bolsheviks in Harbin and the Chinese Eastern Railway zone. For journalistic accounts written by correspondents in Harbin at the time, see the articles in the *North China Herald* between 1917 and 1920. See also the Horvath *Memoirs*, chaps. 9–11.

47. Taking his figures from an official Japanese source, Seki asserts that between 1916 and 1918 the Chinese population went from 45, 481 to 94,000; the Russian increase was from 34,115 to 60,200, with the Japanese population going from 2,006 to 2,768. Presumably, the turmoil following the Russian Revolution had caused this influx into the city. (Seki, *Gendai higashi Ajia*, 40–41).

48. An account of this election is to be found in *NCH*, December 1, 1917, in a dispatch "From Our Correspondent" in Harbin, dated November 19, 523. In his *Memoirs*, Horvath indignantly refers to the election as determined by many voters unknown in the region; see chapter IX, 17–20.

49. Leong, *Sino-Soviet Diplomatic Relations*, 26–27. For a contemporary account, see *NCH*, January 5, 1918, "Affairs at Harbin," 11, 22–23.

50. For a detailed Soviet study of early Bolshevik-Chinese relations in Xinjiang, see B. P. Gurevich, "Vzaimnootnosheniia Sovetskikh Respublik s provintsiei Siatsyan v 1918–1921 gg., published in *Sovetskoe Kitaevedenie* 2 (1958): 96–105. A brief English-language survey of Central Asia by a Soviet author, including sections on the 1918–1920 civil war in the region, is Devendra Kanshik, *Central Asia in Modern Times: A History from the Early 19th Century*.

51. Gurevich, "Vzaimnootnosheniia," 104–105.

52. The Chicherin speech is reproduced in full in *Izvestiia*, July 5, 1918, 7; Whiting, *Soviet Policies in China*, 38–39; Leong, *Sino-Soviet Diplomatic Relations*, 34–35.

53. Whiting, *Soviet Policies in China*, 28.

54. An English translation of the First Karakhan Manifesto is in *China Year Book*, 1924, 868. For one Chinese account in English, see Aitchen K. Wu, *China and the Soviet Union: A Study of Sino-Soviet Relations*, 134–137. Wu had formerly been Chinese consul general in Vladivostok. Whiting and Leong both present detailed accounts: Whiting, *Soviet Policies in China*, 29 ff., and Leong, *Sino-Soviet Diplomatic Relations*, 130–161. For a Soviet view, see Mikhail Stepanovich Kapitsa, *Sovetsko-Kitaiskie otnosheniia*, 32–35. A scholarly Chinese analysis is contained in Wang Yujin, *Zhong-Su waijiao di xumo*, 47–50.

55. *China Year Book*, 1924, 868.

56. Kapitsa, *Sovetsko-Kitaiskie otnosheniia*, 35–36. The work cited by Whiting and Kapitsa is V. Vilenskii [Siburyakov], *Kitai i Sovetskaia Rossiaia: Iz voprosov nashii ialnevotstochnoi politiki* (China and Soviet Russia: Questions of Our Far Eastern Policy), Far East Series No. 2 (Moscow: The State Publishing House, 1919). This pamphlet is in the Hoover Institution, Stanford University. The key passage from the Vilenskii work regarding the Chinese Eastern Railway reads: "The Soviet Government is returning to the Chinese people without any compensation the Chinese Eastern Railway and all mining, forest, gold and other concessions that were expropriated during the rule of the Czarist government" (15).

57. Leong, *Sino-Soviet Diplomatic Relations*, 141–149.

58. Xiang Qing, "The Comintern and the Chinese Revolution During the Period of the Founding of the Chinese Communist Party," 92–93; and Robert A. Scalapino discussion with Xiang, Beijing, April 20, 1981.

59. Leong, *Sino-Soviet Diplomatic Relations*, 142–144.

60. Ibid., 147.

61. Wang, *Zhong-Su waijiao di xumo*, 71, and Eudin and North, *Soviet Russia and the East*, 129.

62. Wu, *China and the Soviet Union*, 137–139. See also Whiting, *Soviet Policies in China*, 148–150, and Leong, *Sino-Soviet Diplomatic Relations*, 147–148.

63. Leong, *Sino-Soviet Diplomatic Relations*, 148.

64. Ibid., 152–153.

65. *NCH*, "China's Interests in Siberia," January 31, 1920, 286.

66. Kapitsa states that of the 150,000, about 40,000 returned to China before the Allied intervention in Siberia, and that others followed later. He reports that in April 1918 a conference of the Chinese trade unionists was held in Petrograd, at which time the organization was given a "revolutionary character." An appeal was issued to the Chinese people, which read in part: "The Chinese workers in Russia find themselves by the will of fate in the vanguard of the global revolution. They must remember that the fate of the revolution in China is closely tied to the fate of the Russian revolution. Only in close union with the Russian working class is the victory of the revolution in oppressed China possible" (Kapitsa, *Sovetsko-Kitaiskie otnosheniia*, 30–31).

67. "Sun's Telegraphic Greetings to Lenin on the Victory of the Russian October Socialist Revolution," Sun Yat-sen Museum, Zhongshan University, Canton. Whether this version is authentic and complete cannot be determined, but it resembles the quotations from other sources. See Wilbur, *Sun Yat-sen*, 114 and 325 n. 2.

68. "Message of Georgii Chicherin, Commissar for Foreign Affairs, to Sun Yat-sen," ibid. The message is also to be found in *Izvestiia*, 53, March 9, 1919, 1.

69. Sokolsky Memorandum, *NAMP/RDSRIAC* 893.00/3376.

70. For details, see "A Preliminary Study of the Relationship between Chen Jiongming and the Narkomindel and the Chinese Communist Party," in Wu Xiangxiang, ed., *Zhongguo xindai shi congkan* 2:97–118, and Haiyu Guke (Liang Binxian), "An Unofficial Record of Liberation," in *Ziyou ren* 76 (November 24, 1951), 4th installment, 4. (Liang, active in the anarchist movement and close to General Chen Jiongming, presented his memoirs in this journal in fourteen installments.)

71. Yun Nong, "Origins of the Chinese Communist Party," *Dangdai minzhu* 7–14 (July 16, 1957), part 1: 13–16.

72. Ibid., 16.

73. See Zhang Ximan, *Lishi huiyi*. This book consists of a collection of essays by Zhang, all of them having previously appeared in journals and newspapers. It is an extremely valuable source since no one else duplicates Zhang's experiences.

74. Ibid., 100–101.

75. This account has been drawn largely from a work by Hu Hua, *Qinshao nian shiji de Zhou Enlai tongzhi*. It has been translated into English under the title *The Early Life of Zhou Enlai* (Beijing: Foreign Languages Press, 1980).

76. Dov Bing, "Sneevliet and the Early Years of the CCP," *China Quarterly* 48 (October/December 1971): 677–697, and Dov Bing, "Reply," *China Quarterly* 56 (October/December 1973): 751–761.

77. Haiyu Guke (Liang Binxian), "An Unofficial Record of Liberation."

78. A Soviet source of considerable usefulness on early Comintern activities in China is R. A. Ulyanovsky, ed., *The Comintern and the East*. This work, translated from the Russian edition, contains a number of interesting essays, including one by V. I. Glunin entitled "The Comintern and the Rise of the Communist Movement in China, 1920–1927," 280–344.

79. A report of activities on behalf of Moscow on the part of a small Russian group in Tianjin was made by the American consul, dated December 16, 1920, but the only sizable pro-Bolshevik movement among Russians living in China was in Harbin. Throughout 1920, American consular reports indicated that the Bolsheviks were active there, and that some of their literature was directed toward the Chinese. This literature, however, related primarily to the need to oust Horvath and other czarist-era officials from the region. (See *NAMP/RDSRIAC*, 893.00 B/1, No. 800, Douglas Jenkins to Charles D. Tenney, January 12, 1920.)

80. For an informative account of Voitinskii by a Soviet scholar, see V. I. Glunin, "Grigorii Voitinskii (1893–1953)."

81. According to Glunin, the Comintern made the decision to use Shanghai as its primary base in China because it was a major intellectual *and* industrial center; it was most accessible to the outside world; and imperialist contradictions were most manifest here. ("Grigorii Voitinskii," 70.)

82. Haiyu Guke, "An Unofficial Record." Also Wilbur and How, *Documents on Communism*, 52.

83. The best source for the early Canton Communist movement is an essay of Chen Gongbo. His essays and articles, written between 1935 and 1944, are contained in a work entitled *Hanfengji*. The pertinent article is "Myself and the Communist Party," written in 1943; 191–267.

84. Ibid., 204.

85. Foreword in *Laodongren*, October 3, 1920, reproduced in *Zhonggongdang shi cankao ziliao*, 221–223.

86. "Opening Statement," *Gongchandang*, November 7, 1920, 1. See also Jiang-chun, "The Commercial Rights of a Social Revolution," *Gongchandang*, November 7, 1920, 2–9.

87. See "The Self-Government Movement and the Social Revolution," *Gongchandang*, April 7, 1921, 7–10.

88. Fragment, ibid., 3–7. This article starts in mid-sentence, with the comment that page two was censored by the Shanghai French police. Thus no title is available. At the end, the date of December 23, 1920, is given, indicating the time at which the article presumably was completed.

89. Ibid., 4–5.

90. "The Commercial Rights of a Social Revolution," 5–7.

91. Fragment, 3.

92. "Opening Statement," *Gongchandang*, November 7, 1920, 1.

93. "Opening Statement," *Gongchandang*, December 7, 1920, 1.

94. Editorial, *Gongchandang*, April 7, 1921, 1.

95. Jiang-chun, "Commercial Rights," 6–7.

96. "The Self-Government Movement," 8–9.

97. Jiang-chun, "An Explanation of Anarchism," *Gongchandang*, May 7, 1921, 14–23.

98. Jiang-chun, "Commercial Rights," 9.

99. "The Self-Government Movement," 9–10.

100. *NAMP/RDSRIAC*, Roll 71, 893.00B, "Bolshevism in China," a report to Colonel Drysdale, U.S. Legation, Beijing, dated December 1, 1920.

101. A basic source for an examination of the Chinese overseas students in France is Qinghua University Faculty Research Unit on the History of the Chinese Communist Party, *FuFa qingong jianxue yundong shiliao*, 3 vols.

102. Figures on the number of work-study students vary somewhat, but in an article entitled "The Final Fate of Work-Study Students in France," Zhou, writing

from France at the end of 1921, presents a very detailed breakdown, according to which there were 1,579 work-study students in France at that point, of whom 378 came from Sichuan, 346 from Hunan, 251 from Guangdong, and 147 from Hebei. Three other provinces—Fujian, Zhejiang, and Jiangxi—currently had more than fifty students in France (*FuFa qingong*, 1:43). It is to be noted that most of the students came from south and central China. Zhou also presented figures which indicated that only 599 of these students were actually in school at the time, with the great bulk of these (522) being in ordinary high schools. The others—nearly 1,000—"had not settled down," mainly because of financial difficulties. Over 200 were working in factories, but many had been unable or unwilling to find employment, according to Zhou (55).

103. The nature and purposes of the organization were set forth by Wang in an article entitled "The Work-Study Mutual Aid Group and the Diligent Work-Frugal Study Associations," *LuOu zhoukan* (henceforth *LZ*), June 3, 1920, 1–2.

104. For details, see *My Memoirs* by Li Huang, vol. 1, deposited in the Columbia University Oral History Collection. Robert A. Scalapino had an interview with Li Huang in Hong Kong on December 19, 1973, from which additional data was obtained. Two other individuals were most helpful in the course of our research, namely, Liu He (Scalapino interview, Taibei, August 28, 1976) and Ren Zhouxuan (Scalapino interview, Taibei, December 7, 1973). In addition, we were able to read the interview conducted by Joseph Miller with Peng Shuzhi, August 11–13, 1966, near Paris.

105. We are indebted to Alberta Tang of the Institute of Oriental Studies in Paris for making available to us on microfilm the existing copies of *LuOu zhoukan* from the library collection. The initial issue was published on November 15, 1919, with the final issue known to us, no. 52, published on November 6, 1920.

106. Dai Xuan, "Preface," *LZ*, November 15, 1919, 1.

107. Xiao-yai, "What is Diligent Work-Frugal Study?" *LZ*, March 27, 1920, 1.

108. Fei Feizi, "The Reasons for Becoming Diligent Work-Frugal Study Students," *LZ*, November 6, 1920, 3.

109. Yuan Shu, "An Atmosphere of Study," *LZ*, December 13, 1919, 1.

110. Jingwei, "The Responsibility of the Overseas Chinese in Europe," *LZ*, November 15, 1919, 1.

111. See, for example, Dai Xuan, "The Self-Consciousness of Students Studying Abroad," *LZ*, January 10, 1920, 1; continued January 17, 1920, 1; and by the same author, "Training for the 'Public'," *LZ*, February 28, 1920, 1; "Public Trial," *LZ*, March 6, 1920, 1; and Hua Lin, "The Dangers to an Atmosphere of Study," *LZ*, May 22, 1920, 1.

112. Dai Xuan, "The Self-Consciousness of Students," *LZ*, January 17, 1920, 1.

113. Dai Xuan, "Public Trial," *LZ*, March 6, 1920, 1.

114. Hua Lin, "The Dangers to an Atmosphere of Study," *LZ*, May 22, 1920, 1.

115. Hua Lin, "The Academic World," *LZ*, July 31, 1920, 1, and Wang Guangqi, "Division of Labor and Mutual Assistance," *LZ*, October 2, 1920, 1.

116. Xing Hou, "The Focus of the Cultural Movement Should Be Transferred to the Labor Movement," *LZ*, September 11 (4), 18 (3–4), and 25 (3–4), 1920. See also Dong Shiji, "The Relationship Between Diligent Work-Frugal Study Students and the Chinese Workers' Association," *LZ*, November 6, 1920, 4.

117. You Gong, "What are the Necessities Requested by the Laborer of Today?" *LZ*, December 6, 1919, 1.

118. You Gong, "The Culture Movement and the Labor Movement," *LZ*, June 26, 1920, 1.

119. Shizeng, "Differences and Similarities Between German and French Intellectuals," *LZ*, November 22, 1919, 1.

120. Wang Guangqi, "The Work-Study Mutual Aid Group and the Diligent Work-Frugal Study Association," *LZ*, June 12, 1920, 1–2.

121. Hua Lin, "The Idea and Method of the Work-Study Program," *LZ*, September 18, 1920, 1.

122. Hua Lin, "What is the Scientific Method?" *LZ*, April 3 and 10, 1920.

123. Dai Xuan, "A Discussion of Organization," *LZ*, July 17, 1920, 1.

124. You Gong, "The Three Stages of Socialism," *LZ*, May 15, 1920, 1.

125. Robert A. Scalapino interviews with Li Huang, Liu He, and Ren Zhuoxuan. See also Zhou Enlai's article, "A Major Incident Among the Diligent Work-Frugal Study Students in France," first published in the Tianjin *Yishi bao*, May 5–19, 1921, reproduced in *FuFa qingong jianxue yundong shiliao* 1:3–36. Interestingly, Zhou is very critical, not only of the preparation, but also of the behavior and attitude of some of the students after their arrival in France, and, in general, takes a moderate position in this lengthy account.

126. For an account of the hardships, see He Jianggong, *Qingong jianxue shenghuo huiyi*, 86–89, 92–97.

127. Ibid., 89.

128. For details, see Zhou Enlai, "A Major Incident." Another account is given by He, *Qingong Jianxue*, 100–122, from an activist perspective. Later recollections are also provided by Liu He and Li Huang in the interviews and *Memoirs* cited.

129. Li Huang, *Memoirs* 1:144–146.

130. Scalapino interview with Ren Zhuoxuan, December 7, 1973.

131. Li Huang, *Memoirs* 1:148–150.

132. Ibid., 152–155.

133. Scalapino interview with Liu He, August 28, 1976.

134. Scalapino interview with Ren Zhuoxuan, December 7, 1973.

CHAPTER TWELVE

1. Various Chinese and English sources on Chiang's life are available. In Chinese, see Cheng Ou, *Chiang zhuxi zhuan*; Li Dongfang, *Chiang-gong Kai-shek xuzhuan*; Mao Sicheng, comp., *Minguo shiwu nian yiqian zhi Chiang Kai-shek xiansheng*; Qin Xiaoyi, chief compiler, *Zongtong Chiang-gong dashi zhangbian chugao*, 8 vols.; and Wu Yizhou, *Chiang zongtong di yisheng*.

English-language sources include Boorman and Howard, eds., *Biographical Dictionary of Republican China*, 1:319–338; Emily Hahn, *Chiang Kai-shek: An Unauthorized Biography*; Paul M. A. Linebarger, *The China of Chiang Kai-shek: A Political Study*; Pichon P. Y. Loh, *The Early Chiang Kai-shek*; Robert Payne, *Chiang Kai-shek*; Hollington K. Tong, *Chiang Kai-shek*; and "President Chiang Kai-shek: A Chronological Table," in *Tribute to President Chiang Kai-shek, Collection of Writings to Commemorate the 3rd Anniversary of His Passing*, 87–125.

In Japanese, a massive collection of materials was serialized in the newspaper *Sankei shimbun* under the title *Sho Kai-seki hiroku*, from August 15, 1974, to the end of 1976, and was subsequently put out in fifteen bound volumes. An abridged edition of this work prepared by Keiji Furuya has been translated by Chun-ming Chang under the title *Chiang Kai-shek: His Life and Times*.

2. For an account by Chiang of his mother, written in 1921, see Qin, *Zongtong Chiang-gong* 1:42–45. See also, Li, *Chiang-gong Jieshi xuzhuan*, 9–19, and Furuya, *Chiang*, 7.

3. Li, *Chiang-gong Kai-shek xuzhuan*, 17; Furuya, *Chiang*, 9–10, citing Chiang Kai-shek, "Baoguo you siqin" (My Duty to My Country and My Memory of My Mother), 31 October 1936.

4. Qin, *Zongtong Chiang-gong* 1:11; Mao, *Minguo shiwu*, 0017.

5. Qin, *Zongtong Chiang-gong* 1:15; Mao, *Minguo shiwu*, 0022.

6. Furuya, *Chiang*, 13.

7. Chiang was to recount his life as a private in the Japanese army in "Dui qingnian yuanzhengzhun duiwu shibing xunci." From this and another speech of 1944, Furuya has reproduced extensive quotations (*Chiang*, 16–17). See also Li, *Chiang-gong Jieshi xuzhuan*, 24–25.

8. Qin, *Zongtong Chiang-gong* 1:18; Mao, *Minguo shiwu*, 0026–0027; and Loh, *The Early Chiang Kai-shek*, 26–27.

9. Qin, *Zongtong Chiang-gong* 1:18; Mao, *Minguo shiwu*, 0027–0028; and Loh, *The Early Chiang Kai-shek*, 53–56.

10. *The Early Chiang Kai-shek*, 54.

11. Qin, *Zongtong Chiang-gong* 1:20; Furuya, *Chiang*, 56.

12. Qin, *Zongtong Chiang-gong* 1:22–23; Mao, *Minguo shiwu*, 0033–0034.

13. Qin, *Zongtong Chiang-gong* 1:22–23; Mao, *Minguo shiwu*, 0037–0034.

14. Qin, *Zongtong Chiang-gong* 1:23; Mao, *Minguo shiwu*, 0038.

15. Qin, *Zongtong Chiang-gong* 1:25; Mao, *Minguo shiwu*, 0041–0047.

16. The section which follows owes much to Loh, *The Early Chiang Kai-shek*, 32ff. See also Qin, *Zongtong Chiang-gong* 1:40–50.

17. The principal Chinese sources for Mao's early life are Li Rui, *Mao Zedong tongzhi di chuqi geming huodong*; the first edition has been translated by Anthony W. Sariti and edited by James C. Hsiung with the English title *The Early Revolutionary Activities of Comrade Mao-Tse-tung*; and Xin Jiang Pinglun editorial department, *Mao Zedong tongzhi di qingshaonian shidai*.

In English, the classic work remains Edgar Snow's *Red Star Over China*, since Mao's revelations and interpretations of his youth still constitute the primary data for this period, and later authors, Chinese as well as foreign, have relied heavily upon this account. The two general biographies of Mao of greatest worth are Jerome Ch'en, *Mao and the Chinese Revolution*, and Stuart Schram, *Mao Tse-tung*. The latter work, perceptive in itself, has been supplemented by Schram's other writings, especially *The Political Thought of Mao Tse-tung*. Several specialized works by individuals who knew Mao in his early years include that by his schoolmate, later a staunch opponent of communism, Siao-yu, *Mao Tse-tung and I Were Beggars*, and the eulogistic work by Siao-yu's pro-Communist brother, Hsiao San, *Mao Tse-tung, His Childhood and Youth*.

In addition to Schram's writings, three major studies dealing with the evolution of Mao's political commitments are the classic work by Benjamin I. Schwartz, *Chinese Communism and the Rise of Mao*; Frederic Wakeman, Jr., *History and Will: Philosophical Perspectives of Mao Tse-tung's Thought*; and Brantley Womack, *The Foundations of Mao Zedong's Political Thought, 1917–1935*. Two scholars have written sophisticated studies stressing the psychological-cultural factors bearing upon Mao: Lucian W. Pye, *The Spirit of Chinese Politics*, and *The Man in the Leader*; and Richard H. Solomon, *Mao's Revolution and the Chinese Political Culture*.

For appraisals concentrating more on Mao's later role as theorist and political leader from varied points of view, but with relevance to his early years, see Richard Baum, *Prelude to Revolution: Mao, the Party, and the Peasant Question, 1962–1966*; Arthur A. Cohen, *The Communism of Mao Tse-tung*; C. P. Fitzgerald, *Mao*

Tse-tung and China; James C. Hsiung, ed., *The Logic of "Maoism": Critiques and Explication*; Institute of Philosophy and the Institute of the Far East, U.S.S.R. Academy of Sciences, *A Critique of Mao Tse-tung's Theoretical Conceptions*; Stanley Karnow, *Mao and China: From Revolution to Revolution*; Franz Michael, *Mao and the Perpetual Revolution*; Edward Rice, *Mao's Way*; John Starr, *Continuing the Revolution: The Political Thought of Mao*; O. Vladimirov and V. Ryazantsev, *Mao Tse-tung—A Political Portrait*; and Dick Wilson, ed., *Mao Tse-tung in the Scales of History*. Finally, one should naturally consult Mao's collected works. In English, see Mao Tse-tung, *Selected Works*, 4 vols.

The section on Mao which follows was first published in abridged form in Robert A. Scalapino, "The Evolution of a Young Revolutionary—Mao Zedong in 1919–1921," *Journal of Asian Studies* 42, no. 1 (November 1982).

18. Arthur Hummel, *Eminent Chinese of the Ch'ing Period* 2:817–819.

19. See three stimulating works previously cited: Charlton M. Lewis, *Prologue to the Chinese Revolution—The Transformation of Ideas and Institutions in Hunan Province, 1891–1907*; Joseph W. Esherick, *Reform and Revolution in China: The 1911 Revolution in Hunan and Hubei*; and Angus W. McDonald, Jr., *The Urban Origins of Rural Revolution—Elites and the Masses in Hunan Province, China, 1911–1927*.

20. Siao-yu, *Mao Tse-tung and I Were Beggars*, 3.

21. Snow, *Red Star*, 127, 129–130.

22. *Mao Zedong tongzhi*, 11–12.

23. Snow, *Red Star*, 120.

24. Ibid., 141–142.

25. Siao-yu, *Mao Tse-tung and I Were Beggars*, 45–49.

26. See Yang Changji, "On Regulating One's Life," XQ, December 1, 1916 (1–8); January 1, 1917 (1–8). For an excellent analysis of Yang's basic theses and his influence on Mao, see Wakeman, *History and Will*, 157ff.

27. Snow, *Red Star*, 134–135.

28. Ibid., 136.

29. Ibid., 146.

30. Li, *The Early Revolutionary Activities*, 30. See also Siao-yu, *Mao Tse-tung and I Were Beggars*, 103ff.

31. See "Twenty-eight Stroke Student," "A Study of Physical Education," XQ, April 1, 1917, 145–155. This article has been translated in its entirety into French by Stuart Schram with a commentary: *Mao Ze-dong, Une étude de l'éducation physique* and extensive excerpts in English appear in his *The Political Thought of Mao Tse-tung*, 152–160.

32. "Twenty-eight Stroke Student," 145; Schram, *The Political Thought*, 152–153.

33. "Twenty-eight Stroke Student," 146.

34. Ibid., 147; Schram, *The Political Thought*, 154.

35. "Twenty-eight Stroke Student," 148; Schram, *The Political Thought*, 157–158.

36. *Mao Zedong tongzhi*, 55.

37. For an illustration of this in connection with the workers' night school, see Li Rui's account drawn from the *Night School Record* in *The Early Revolutionary Activities*, 63–64.

38. For details, see He Jianggong, *Qingong jianxue shenghuo huiyi*, 1–59.

39. Snow, *Red Star*, 148.

40. Ibid.

41. Snow, *Red Star*, 154.

42. We were able to use the five available issues of *Xiang jiang pinglun* while in Beijing in early 1981. The four regular issues are dated July 14, 21, 28, and August 4, 1919, and the one special issue is dated July 21. It is reported that the news-sheet which was printed on tabloid-size newspaper, four pages per issue, started with 2,000 copies, and later increased to 5,000. The English title of the news-sheet was *Shian Kian Weekly Review*. The fifth regular issue, printed later in August, was confiscated at the press. The journal's name, in addition to reflecting a traditional name for Hunan, borrowed from that of Changsha's first "moderate" journal, the *Xiangxue bao* (The Hunan Learning News), published in 1897. See Lewis, *Prologue*, 43. The principal contents have been reproduced in *Makesizhuyi yanjiu cankao ziliao* (*MYCZ*), February 1981, 1–22. A complete translation of the *Xiang jiang pinglun* articles is also now available in Italian together with a commentary. See Giorgio Mantici, *Mao Zedong Pensiere del fiume Xiang*. Our citations are from the originals.

43. *XJP*, July 14, 1919, 1.

44. Ibid., 1–2.

45. Ibid., 2–3.

46. Ibid., 3.

47. Ibid.

48. This essay has been translated under the title, "The Great Union of the Popular Masses," by Stuart Schram in the *China Quarterly* 49 (January/March 1972): 76–87. Schram used the text then available in volume 1 of *Zhongguo gongchandang dangshi shiliao ji*, which proves to be a faithful reproduction of the original. He accompanies his translation with a commentary (88–105) which is a stimulating interpretation of the main themes, but our emphases and interpretations differ on certain points, as a comparison of our analyses will indicate.

49. *XJP*, July 28, 1919, 1.

50. *XJP*, August 4, 1919, 1–2.

51. In addition to articles by Li Dazhao and others cited earlier, see Ron Yu, "The Reform of International Society," *MP*, December 22, 1918, 1–2. The basic theme here, while presented in abbreviated form, is similar to that which Mao expounded in his extended essay.

52. (Mao) Zedong, "Notes on Xiang Jiang Events," *XJP* special issue, July 21, 1919, 1–2.

53. "Founding and Proceedings," ibid., 1–2.

54. Ibid., 2.

55. Zhisun, "Correspondence from France," *XJP*, July 28, 1919, 3–4.

56. *Xin qingnian* provided a commentary to the new contents of *Xin Hunan* under Mao which is reproduced in Li Rui, *The Early Revolutionary Activities*, 118.

57. In addition to Mao's *Dagong bao* contributions, which are reproduced in *MYCZ*, 27–36, see the article by Roxanne Witke, "Mao Tse-tung, Women and Suicide in the May Fourth Era," *China Quarterly* 31:128–147.

58. Li Rui, *The Early Revolutionary Activities*, 129.

59. For a discussion of Li's articles by us and by Meisner, see chapter 9.

60. Li, *The Early Revolutionary Activities*, 137–138.

61. *MYCZ*, 13.

62. Scholars are greatly indebted to Angus W. McDonald for his discovery in Japan of the work compiled by Wang Wuwei, *Hunan zizhi yundong shi* (History of the Hunan Self-Government Movement), Part I, published in Shanghai, De-

cember 1920. McDonald has set forth his interpretation of this movement in his work, *The Urban Origins of Rural Revolution* (37–47). He has also translated four articles by Mao contained in the Wang volume, together with a commentary, in the *China Quarterly* 68 (December 1976): 751–777. Our interpretations are somewhat different, but we have profited from McDonald's extensive studies. Some additional Mao writings pertaining to the movement have now been republished in *MYCZ*, February 1981, 12–21, including articles written in Shanghai prior to his return and articles published afterward, in Changsha.

63. Wang, *Hunan zizhi yundong shi*, 4.

64. *MYCZ*, 18.

65. Wang, *Hunan zizhi yundong shi*, 145–146; McDonald, "The Fundamental Issue," *China Quarterly* 68:767–769.

66. Wang, 145; McDonald, 768.

67. Wang, 145; McDonald, 769.

68. Wang, 146–148; McDonald, 769–771.

69. Wang, 148; McDonald, 771.

70. For details, see "Symposium on Russia in Hunan," *Minkuo ribao* (Republican News), September 23, 1920, in *Zhonggongdangshi cankao ziliao* 1:214–225.

71. *MYCZ*, Supplement, 5–7.

72. *MYCZ*, 10–14.

73. *MYCZ*, 7–10.

74. *MYCZ*, Supplement, 15–19.

75. *MYCZ*, 2–5.

76. *MYCZ*, 19–31.

77. *MYCZ*, 24.

78. *MYCZ*, 27.

79. *MYCZ*, 31.

80. *MYCZ*, 15.

BIBLIOGRAPHY

Alitto, Guy S. *The Last Confucian: Liang Shu-ming and the Chinese Dilemma of Modernity*. Berkeley: University of California Press, 1979.

Allen, Bernard. *Gordon in China*. London: Macmillan, 1933.

Allen, George C., and Donnithorne, Audrey G. *Western Enterprise in Far Eastern Economic Development*. London: Jarrold and Sons, 1962.

Almond, Gabriel, and Powell, Barry. *Comparative Politics: A Developmental Approach*. Boston: Little, Brown, 1966.

Altman, Albert A., and Schiffrin, Harold Z. "Sun Yat-sen and the Japanese: 1914–16." *Modern Asian Studies* 6, no. 4 (1972): 385–400.

Arahata Kanson. *Heiminsha jidai: Nihon shakaishugi undō no yōran* (The Era of the Commoner Association: Origins of the Japanese Socialist Movement). Tokyo: Chūō Koronsha, 1973.

Arendt, Hannah. *On Revolution*. New York: Viking Press, 1963.

Bai Jiao. *Yuan Shikai yu Zhonghua Minguo* (Yuan Shikai and the Republic of China). Reprinted in *Yuan Shikai shiliao huikan xubian*, edited by Shen Yunlong. Vol. 14. Taibei: Wenhai Chubanshe. Reprint Taibei: Wenxing, 1962.

Baker, Hugh D. R. "Extended Kinship in the Traditional City." In *The City in Late Imperial China*, ed. G. William Skinner. 1977.

Balazs, Etienne. *Chinese Civilization and Bureaucracy*. With an introduction by Arthur F. Wright, ed. New Haven: Yale University Press, 1964.

Banno, Masataka. *China and the West, 1858–1861: The Origins of the Tsungli Yamen*. Cambridge: Harvard University Press, 1964.

Bao Zunpeng et al., eds. *Zhongguo jindai shi luncong* (A Collection of Discussions on Modern Chinese History). Taibei: Zhengzhong, 1957.

Barlow, Jeffrey G. *Sun Yat-sen and the French, 1900–1908*. Berkeley: Institute of East Asian Studies, University of California, 1979.

Bates, Robert. *Rural Responses to Industrialization*. New Haven: Yale University Press, 1976.

Bau, Joshua Mingchen. *Modern Democracy in China*. Shanghai: Commercial Press, 1923.

Baum, Richard. *Prelude to Revolution: Mao, the Party, and the Peasant Question, 1962–1966*. New York: Columbia University Press, 1975.

Bays, Daniel H. *China Enters the Twentieth Century: Chang Chih-tung and the Issues of a New Age, 1895–1909*. Ann Arbor: University of Michigan Press, 1978.

Bechhofer-Roberts, C. E. *In Denikin's Russia and the Caucasus, 1919–1920*. London: W. Collins' Sons and Co., 1921.

Beckmann, George. *The Making of the Meiji Constitution*. Lawrence: University of Kansas Press, 1957.

Bell, David V. J. *Resistance and Revolution*. Boston: Houghton Mifflin, 1973.
Bergere, Marie-Claire. "The Bourgeois Class and the Revolution of 1911." Paper, Wuhan Conference on the Xinhai Revolution, 1981.
Bernal, Martin. *Chinese Socialism to 1907*. Ithaca: Cornell University Press, 1976.
Bernstein, Gail. *Japanese Marxist: A Portrait of Kawakami Hajime, 1879–1946*. Cambridge: Harvard University Press, 1976.
Berry, Thomas. "Dewey's Influence in China." In *John Dewey: His Thought and Influence*, edited by John Blewitt. New York: Fordham University Press, 1960.
Biggerstaff, Knight. *The Earliest Modern Government Schools in China*. Ithaca: Cornell University Press, 1961.
Binder, Leonard, et al. *Crises and Sequences in Political Development*. Princeton: Princeton University Press, 1971.
Bland, John O. P. *Li Hung-chang*. New York: Constable, 1917.
Bland, John O. P., and Backhouse, E. *China Under the Empress Dowager*. London: William Heinemann, 1910.
Boardman, Eugene P. *Christian Influence Upon the Ideology of the Taiping Rebellion, 1851–1864*. Madison: University of Wisconsin Press, 1952.
Boorman, Howard L., and Howard, Richard C., eds. *Biographical Dictionary of Republican China*. 3 vols. New York: Columbia University Press, 1967–1971.
Borowitz, Albert. "Chiang Monlin: Theory and Practice of Chinese Education, 1917–1930." In *Harvard Papers on China* 8 (1954).
Boulger, Demetriu. *The Life of Gordon*. London: T. Fisher Unwin, 1896.
Bradley, John F. *Allied Intervention in Russia, 1917–1920*. London: Seidenfeld and Nicolson, 1968.
Bradley, John Francis Nejez. *Civil War in Russia, 1917–1920*. London and Sydney: B. T. Batsford, 1975.
Brine, Lindsay. *The Taiping Rebellion in China: A Narrative of Its Rise and Progress, Based Upon Original Documents and Information Obtained in China*. London: John Murray, 1862.
Brinkley, George A. *The Volunteer Army and Allied Intervention in South Russia*. Notre Dame: Notre Dame Press, 1966.
Brinton, Crane. *Anatomy of Revolution*. Englewood Cliffs, N.J.: Prentice-Hall, 1938.
Cady, John F. *The Roots of French Imperialism in Eastern Asia*. Ithaca: Cornell University Press, 1954.
Cahill, Holger. *A Yankee Adventurer*. New York: Macaulay, 1930.
Cai Shaoqing. "On the Relation of the Xinhai Revolution with the Secret Societies." Paper, Wuhan Conference on the Xinhai Revolution, 1981.
Cai Yuanpei. "A Brief Account of the Activities of Liu Shenshu." In *Liu Shenshu yishu* (Posthumous Writings of Liu Shenshu). Taibei: 1936.
Calvert, Peter. *Revolution*. New York: Praeger, 1970.
Cameron, Meribeth E. *The Reform Movement in China, 1896–1912*. Reprint. New York: Octagon Books, 1963.
Carr, Edward H. *The Bolshevik Revolution, 1917–1923*. 3 vols. London: Macmillan, 1950–52.
Cary-Elwes, Columba. *China and the Cross: A Survey of Missionary History*. New York: P. J. Kennedy, 1956.
Central China Post. 1913–1914.
Chai Degeng et al., comps. *Xinhai geming* (The Revolution of 1911). 8 vols. Shanghai: Renmin chubanshe, 1957.

Chamberlin, William H. *The Russian Revolution, 1917–1921*. 2 vols. New York: Macmillan, 1935.

Chan, F. Gilbert. "Socialism and Single Tax: Liao Chung-k'ai in Kwangtung (1912–1913)." In *Symposium on the History of the Republic of China* 2:327–346.

Chan, Wellington K. K. *Merchants, Mandarins and Modern Enterprise in Late Ch'ing China*. Cambridge: East Asian Research Center, Harvard University, 1977.

Chan, Wing-tsit, tr. *A Source Book in Chinese Philosophy*. Princeton: Princeton University Press, 1963.

Chang, Carsun (Chang Jia-sen). *The Development of Neo-Confucian Thought*. New York: Bookman Associates, 1957.

Chang, Chung-li. *The Chinese Gentry*. Seattle: University of Washington Press, 1955.

Chang, Hao. *Liang Ch'i-ch'ao and Intellectual Transition in China, 1890–1907*. Cambridge: Harvard University Press, 1971.

———. "Intellectual Change and the Reform Movement, 1890–1898." In John K. Fairbank and Kuang-Ching Liu, eds., *The Cambridge History of China* 11:274–338.

Chang, Kuo-t'ao. *The Rise of the Chinese Communist Party, 1921–1927. Vol. One of the Autobiography of Chang Kuo-t'ao*. Lawrence: University of Kansas Press, 1971.

Chang, Yufa. "The Restoration Society and the Revolution of 1911." In *Symposium on the History of the Republic of China* 1:324–356.

Chen, Chi-yun. "Liang Ch'i-ch'ao's Missionary Education: A Case Study of Missionary Influence on the Reformers." In *Harvard Papers on China* 16 (1962): 66–125.

Chen Dongyuan. *Zhongguo funu shenghuo shi* (History of Chinese Women's Life). 3d ed. Taibei: Commercial Press, 1970.

Chen Duxiu. *Chen Duxiu shian zizhuan* (Autobiography of Chen Duxiu). Taibei: Zhuanji, 1967.

Chen Gongbo. "Myself and the Communist Party (1943)." In Chen Gongbo, *Hanfengji* (Collection of the Cold Wind). 2d ed. Pp. 191–267. Shanghai, 1943.

Chen Huqin. *Pipan Duwei fandong jiaoyu xue dizhexue jichu* (A Criticism of the Philosophic Foundations of Dewey's Reactionary Educational Thought). Shanghai: Xin zhishi chubanshe, 1956.

Ch'en, Jerome. *Mao and the Chinese Revolution*. London: Oxford University Press, 1965.

———. "The Nature and Characteristics of the Boxer Movement: A Morphological Study." *Bulletin of the School of Oriental and African Studies* 23, no. 2 (1960).

———. *Yuan Shih-k'ai*. 2d ed. Stanford: Stanford University Press, 1972.

Chen, Joseph T. *The May Fourth Movement in Shanghai*. Leiden: E. J. Brill, 1971.

Chen Pengren. *Sun Zhongshan xiansheng yu Riben youren* (Mr. Sun Yat-sen and His Japanese Friends). Taibei: Dabin Book Co., 1973.

Chen Qitian. *Zuijin sanshi nian Zhongguo jiaoyu shi* (A History of Chinese Education during the Last Thirty Years). Taibei: Wenxing shudian, 1962.

Chen Shaobai. *Xingzhong Hui geming shiyao*. (Outline of the Revolutionary History of the Xingzhong Hui). Nanjing: 1935. Reprinted. Taibei: Zhongyang wenwu kungying she, 1956.

Chen Tao, ed. *Tongzhi zhongxing jingwai zouji yuebian* (Compilation of Tongzhi Restoration Memorials). Taibei: Wenhai, 1966. Reprint of 1875 edition.

Chen, Yu-ching. "The Overseas Chinese in [the] United States and National Revolution." In *Symposium on the History of the Republic of China*, 1:408–426.

Cheng, J. C. *Chinese Sources for the Taiping Rebellion, 1850–1864*. Hong Kong: Hong Kong University Press, 1963.

Cheng Ou. *Chiang zhuxi zhuan* (A Biography of Chairman Chiang). Shanghai (?): Zhengyi chubanshe, 1947.

Cheng, Shelley Hsien. *The T'ung Meng Hui: Its Organization, Leadership and Finances, 1905–1912*. Ann Arbor: University Microfilms, 1962.

Cheng Yansheng. *Taiping tianguo shiliao* (A Historical Compilation of the Taiping). 3 vols. Beijing: Beijing daxue chubanbu, 1926.

Chesneaux, Jean. *Peasant Revolts in China: 1840–1949*. London: Thames and Hudson, 1973.

Chesneaux, Jean, ed. *Popular Movements and Secret Societies in China, 1840–1950*. Stanford: Stanford University Press, 1972.

———. *Secret Societies in China in the Nineteenth and Twentieth Centuries*. Ann Arbor: University of Michigan Press, 1971.

Ch'i, Hsi-sheng. *Warlord Politics in China, 1916–1918*. Stanford: Stanford University Press, 1976.

Chiang, Monlin. *Tides from the West: A Chinese Autobiography*. New Haven: Yale Univesity Press, 1947.

Chiang, Siang-tse. *The Nien Rebellion*. Seattle: University of Washington Press, 1945.

Chiang Zongtong yanlun huibian (Collected Works of President Chiang). Taibei, 1956.

Chicherin, Georgi, Commissar for Foreign Affairs, Message to Sun Yat-sen. Canton: Sun Yat-sen Museum, Zhongshan University.

Ch'ien, Tuan-sheng. *The Government and Politics of China*. Cambridge: Harvard University Press, 1960.

The China Press. 1911.

China Republican. 1913.

China Year Book, 1912–1939. Shanghai: North China Daily News and Herald.

Chinese People's Political Consultative Conference, Guangdong Committee, et al. *Sun Zhongshan shiliao quanji* (Special Collection of Historical Materials on Sun Yat-sen). Guangzhou: Renmin chubanshe, 1979.

———. *Sun Zhongshan yu Xinhai geming shiliao quanji* (Special Collection of Historical Materials on Sun Yat-sen and the 1911 Revolution). Guangzhou: Guangzhou chubanshe, 1981.

Chow Tse-tsung (Chou, Ts'e-tsung). *The May Fourth Movement: Intellectual Revolution in Modern China*. Cambridge: Harvard University Press, 1960.

Chow, Yung-teh. *Social Mobility in China: Status Careers Among the Gentry in a Chinese Community*. New York: Atherton Press, 1966.

Ch'ü, T'ung-tsu. *Law and Society in Traditional China*. Paris and The Hague: Mouton, 1961.

———. *Local Government in China Under the Ch'ing*. Cambridge: Harvard University Press, 1962.

Chung, Sue Fawn. "The Much Maligned Empress Dowager: A Revisionist Study of the Empress Dowager Tz'u-hsi." Ph.D. dissertation, University of California, Berkeley, 1975.

Chung-sai yat-po (The East-West Daily). San Francisco, 1914.
Clapton, Robert W., and Ou, Tsuin-Chen, eds. and trans. *John Dewey: Lectures in China, 1919–1920.* Honolulu: University of Hawaii Press, 1973.
Clarke, Prescott, and Gregory, J. S., eds. *Western Reports on the Taiping: A Selection of Documents.* Honolulu: University of Hawaii Press, 1982.
Cohen, Arthur A. *The Communism of Mao Tse-tung.* Chicago: University of Chicago Press, 1964.
Cohen, Paul A. *Between Tradition and Modernity: Wang T'ao and Reform in Late Ch'ing China.* Cambridge: Harvard University Press, 1974.
———. *China and Christianity: The Missionary Movement and the Growth of Chinese Anti-Foreignism, 1860–1870.* Cambridge: Harvard University Press, 1963.
Cohen, Paul A., and Schrecker, John E., eds., *Reform in Nineteenth Century China.* Cambridge: East Asian Research Center, Harvard University, 1976.
Cohen, Stephen F. *Bukharin and the Bolshevik Revolution: A Political Biography, 1888–1938.* Oxford and New York: Oxford University Press, 1971.
Cole, James H. *The People versus the Taipings: Bao Lisheng's Righteous Army of Dongan.* Berkeley: Institute of East Asian Studies, University of California, 1982.
Confucius. *The Analects.* Translated and annotated by Arthur Waley. London: G. Allen and Unwin, 1956.
Cord, Steven B. *Henry George: Dreamer or Realist?* Philadelphia: University of Pennsylvania Press, 1965.
Cordier, Henri. *L'Expedition de Chine de 1857–1858, Histoire Diplomatique.* Paris: 1905.
Costin, W. C. *Great Britain and China, 1833–1860.* London: Oxford University Press, 1937.
Cranmer-Byng, J. L. (ed. and with notes). *An Embassy to China: Being the Journal kept by Lord Macartney during His Embassy to the Emperor Ch'ien-lung, 1793–1794.* Hamden, Conn.: Archon Books, 1963.
Crawcour, E. Sydney. "The Tokugawa Heritage." In *The State and Economic Enterprise in Japan,* edited by William W. Lockwood. Princeton: Princeton University Press, 1965. Pp. 17–44.
Creel, Herrlee G. *Chinese Thought from Confucius to Mao Tse-Tung.* Chicago: University of Chicago Press, 1953.
Dai Xuanxi, *Yihe Tuan* (The Yihe Tuan). 4 vols. Shanghai: Zhonghua, 1957.
———. *Yihe Tuan yuanjiu* (A Study of the Yihe Tuan). Taibei: Shangwu, 1953.
Dang Shangyi. "On the National and Political Systems of the Taiping." Paper, Taiping Conference, People's Republic of China, 1981.
de Bary, W. Theodore; Chan, Wing-tsit; and Watson, Burton, eds. *Sources of Chinese Tradition.* 2 vols. New York: Columbia University Press, 1964.
Degras, Jane. *The Communist International: Documents, 1919–1943.* Vol. 1, 1919–1922. London: Frank Cass and Co., 1960.
De Mille, Anna George. *Henry George: Citizen of the World.* Chapel Hill: University of North Carolina Press, 1951.
Deng Jiayen, ed. *Zhongguo Guomindang kenqin dahui shimoji* (Record of the Convention of the Chinese Nationalist League in the U.S.A.). San Francisco, 1915.
Deng Siyu. *Zhongguo kaoshi zhidushi* (A History of China's Examination System). Taibei: Xuesheng shuyi, 1967.
Denikin, Anton I. *The White Army.* Translated by Catherine Zveginstev. London: J. Cape and Co., 1930.

Detrick, Robert H. "Henry Andrea Burgevine in China: A Biography." Ph.D. dissertation, Indiana University, 1968.

Dewey, Jane. "Biography of John Dewey." In *Philosophy of John Dewey*. 2d ed. New York: Tudor, 1951.

Dewey, John. "Classical Individualism and Free Enterprise." In *John Dewey: Lectures in China, 1919–1920*, ed. and trans. Robert W. Clapton and Tsuin-Chen Ou.

———. *Essays in Experimental Logic*. Chicago: University of Chicago Press, 1916.

———. *Experience and Nature*. Chicago and London: Open Court, 1925.

———. "Science and Knowing." In Clapton and Ou, *John Dewey: Lectures in China, 1919–1920*.

Dewey, John, and Dewey, Alice. *Letters from China and Japan*. New York: E. P. Dutton, 1920.

Dian Buyi et al. *Beiyang junfa shihua* (Historical Records on the Beiyang Militarists). 6 vols. Taibei: Chinqui, 1967.

Ding Minnan et al. *Diguo zhuyi qinhua shi* (History of the Imperialist Invasion of China). Beijing: Renmin chubanshe, 1961.

Ding Wenjiang. *Liang Rengong xiansheng nianpu changbian chugao* (A Draft of a Comprehensive Biography of Mr. Liang Qichao). Taibei: World Book Company, 1958.

Ding Yuanying. "The 'Rice Theft' Incident of the Changsha People in 1910." *Zhongguo kexueyuan lishi yanjiu suo disan suo jikan* (Journal of the 3d Section of the Historical Research Institute, Chinese Academy of Science). No. 1. Reprinted in *Lidai nongmin qiyi luncong* (A Collection of Treatises on Successive Peasant Uprisings in History). 2 vols. Hong Kong: Great Eastern Publishers, 1978.

Dong Qing and Da Song. "On the Question of Whether the Yihe Tuan was Antifeudal." Paper, Jinan Conference on the Yihe Tuan, 1980.

Dongfang zazhi (Eastern Miscellany).

Dore, Ronald P. *Education in Tokugawa Japan*. London: Routledge and Kegan Paul, 1965.

Dov, Bing. "Reply." *The China Quarterly* 56 (Oct.–Dec. 1973): 751–761.

———. "Sneevliet and the Early Years of the CCP." *The China Quarterly* 48 (Oct.–Dec. 1971): 677–697.

Du Shousu. *Zhongguo sixiang tongshi* (A Comprehensive History of Chinese Thought). 3 vols. Shanghai: Shenghuo, Dushu, Xinshi, 1949.

Duan Yunzhang. "Was It Possible for Hong Xiuquan to Seek Truth from Western Countries?" Paper, Taiping Conference, People's Republic of China, 1981.

Duiker, William J. *Ts'ai Yuan-p'ei: Educator of Modern China*. University Park: The Pennsylvania State University Press, 1977.

Dykhuizen, George. *The Life and Mind of John Dewey*. Carbondale: Southern Illinois University Press, 1973.

Eastman, Lloyd E. "Political Reformism in China Before the Sino-Japanese War." *Journal of Asian Studies* 27 (August 1968): 695–710.

———. *Throne and Mandarins: China's Search for a Policy During the Sino-French Controversy, 1880–1885*. Cambridge: Harvard University Press, 1967.

"Economic Modernization: K'ang You-wei's Ideas in Historical Perspective." *Monumenta Sinica* 21 (1962): 129–193.

Eichhorn, Werner. *Chinese Civilization*. New York: Praeger, 1969.
Eisenstadt, S. N. *Modernization: Protest and Change*. Englewood Cliffs, N.J.: Prentice-Hall, 1966.
Elvin, Mark. "The Administration of Shanghai." In *The Chinese City Between Two Worlds*, ed. Mark Elvin and G. William Skinner.
———. "Making Progress Pay: A Basic Problem in China's Early Economic Modernization." In *Symposium on the History of the Republic of China* 3.
———. "Market Towns and Waterways: The County of Shang-hai from 1480 to 1910." In *The City in Late Imperial China*, ed. G. William Skinner.
———. *The Pattern of the Chinese Past*. Stanford: Stanford University Press, 1973.
Elvin, Mark, and Skinner, G. William. *The Chinese City Between Two Worlds*. Stanford: Stanford University Press, 1974.
Ershi shiji zhi Zhina (Twentieth Century China). Song Jiaoren, ed. Tokyo, 1905.
Esherick, Joseph W. *Reform and Revolution in China: The 1911 Revolution in Hunan and Hubei*. Berkeley: University of California Press, 1976.
Eto, Shinkichi, and Jansen, Marius, trans. *My Thirty-three Years' Dream*, by Miyazaki Torazō. With an introduction by Eto Shinkichi and Marius Jansen. Princeton: Princeton University Press, 1982.
Eudin, Xenia Joukoff, and North, Robert C. *Soviet Russia and the East, 1920–1927: A Documentary Survey*. Stanford: Stanford University Press, 1957.
Evans, Peter. *Dependent Development: The Alliance of Multinational, State, and Local Capital in Brazil*. Princeton: Princeton University Press, 1979.
Fairbank, John K. *The Chinese World Order*. Cambridge: Harvard University Press, 1968.
———. *The Missionary Enterprise in China and America*. Cambridge: Harvard University Press, 1974.
———. "Patterns Behind the Tientsin Massacre." *Harvard Journal of Asiatic Studies* 20 (1957): 480–511.
———. *Trade and Diplomacy on the China Coast, 1842–1854*. Cambridge: Harvard University Press, 1953.
Fairbank, John K., ed. *The Cambridge History of China*. Vol. 10: *Late Ch'ing, 1800–1911, Part 1*. Cambridge: Cambridge University Press, 1978.
———. *Chinese Thought and Institutions*. Chicago: University of Chicago Press, 1957.
Fairbank, John K., and Liu, Kwang-Ching, eds. *The Cambridge History of China*. Vol. 11: *Late Ching, 1800–1911, Part 2*. Cambridge: Cambridge University Press, 1982.
Fan Wenlan. *Taiping tianguo geming yundong* (The Taiping Revolutionary Movement). Rev. ed. Shenyang: Dongbe renmin chubanshe, 1951.
———. *Zhongguo jindai shi* (Modern History of China). Beijing: Renmin, 1961. Ch. 5.
Fang, Yang. "On the Historical Impact of Taiping Religious Philosophy." Paper, Taiping Conference, People's Republic of China, 1981.
Fang Zuhua. *Song Jiaoren zhuan* (Biography of Song Jiaoren). Taibei: Jindai Zhongguo, 1980.
Favre, Benoit. *Les Sociétés secretes en Chine*. Paris: G. P. Maison neuve, 1933.
Fay, Peter Ward. *The Opium War: 1840–1842*. Chapel Hill: University of North Carolina Press, 1975.
Fei, Hsiao-t'ung. *China's Gentry: Essays in Rural-Urban Relations*. Chicago: University of Chicago Press, 1955.

Fei Xingjian. *Dangdai mingren zhuan* (Biography of Famous Contemporaries). Hong Kong: Zhongshan, 1973.

Feng Ziyou. *Geming yishi* (Reminiscences of the Revolution). 5 vols. Changsha, 1939.

———. *Zhonghua minguo kaiguo qian geming shi* (A History of the Revolution Prior to the Founding of the Chinese Republic). 3 vols. n.p., 1944.

Feuerwerker, Albert. *China's Early Industrialization: Sheng Hsuan-huai (1844–1916) and Mandarin Enterprise*. Cambridge: Harvard University Press, 1958.

Feuerwerker, Albert; Murphey, Rhoads; and Wright, Mary C. *Approaches to Modern Chinese History*. Berkeley: University of California Press, 1967.

Fifield, Russell. *Woodrow Wilson and the Far East: The Diplomacy of the Shantung Question*. Hamden, Conn.: Archon Books, 1952.

Finkle, Jason, and Gable, Richard, eds. *Political Development and Social Change*. New York: Wiley, 1966.

Fisher, Daniel W. *Calvin Wilson Mateer, Forty-five Years a Missionary in Shantung Province, China: A Biography*. Philadelphia: The Westminster Press, 1911.

Fitzgerald, C. P. *Mao Tse-tung and China*. London: Hodder and Stoughton, 1976.

Fleming, Peter. *The Fate of Admiral Kolchak*. London: Hart-Davis, 1963.

———. *The Siege at Peking*. New York: Harper, 1959.

Florinsky, Michael T. *The End of the Russian Empire*. New York: Oxford University Press, 1931.

Folsom, Kenneth E. *Friends, Guests and Colleagues: The Mu-fu System in the Late Ch'ing Period*. Berkeley: University of California Press, 1968.

Footman, David J. *Civil War in Russia*. New York: Praeger, 1961.

Forsyth, Robert C., comp. and ed. *The China Martyrs of* 1900. London: The Religious Tract Society, 1904.

Foster, Lovelace S. *Fifty Years in China: An Eventful Memoir of the Life of Tarleton Perry Crawford, D.D.* Nashville: Bayless-Pullen Co., 1909.

Franke, Wolfgang. *Die staatspolitischen Reformsversuche K'ang Yu-weis und seiner Schule*. n.p.: 1935?

Friedman, Edward. *Backward Toward Revolution: The Chinese Revolutionary Party*. Berkeley: University of California Press, 1974.

Friters, Gerard M. *Outer Mongolia and Its International Position*. Baltimore: Johns Hopkins Press, 1949.

Fryer, John. *The Educational Directory for China*. Shanghai: Presbyterian Mission Press, 1895.

———. *Report of the Society for the Diffusion of Christian and General Knowledge*. n.p., 1900.

Fu Zhufu. *Zhongguo jingjishi luncong* (Discussions on Chinese Economic History). Beijing: Shenghuo, 1980.

Fu Zongmao. *Qingdai dufu zhidu* (The Institution of the Governor-General and the Governor in the Qing Dynasty). Taibei: National Zhengji University, 1963.

Fung, Edmond S. K. *The Military Dimension of the Chinese Revolution*. Vancouver: University of British Columbia Press, 1980.

Fung, Yu-lan. *A History of Chinese Philosophy*. Translated by Derk Bodde. Princeton: Princeton University Press, 1955.

Furth, Charlotte. *Ting Wen-chiang: Science and China's New Culture*. Cambridge: Harvard University Press, 1970.

Furth, Charlotte, ed. *The Limits of Change: Essays on Conservative Alternatives in Republican China*. Cambridge: Harvard University Press, 1976.

Furuya, Keiji. *Chiang Kai-shek: His Life and Times*. New York: St. John's University Press, 1981.

Gasster, Michael. *Chinese Intellectuals and the Revolution of 1911*. Seattle: University of Washington Press, 1969.

Geming pinglun minzhong xianfeng (The Vanguard of the Revolution). Shanghai: Geming pinglunshe, 1928.

Geming wenxian. See Zhongguo Guomindang Historical Commission, *Geming wenxian*.

George, Henry. *Progress and Poverty: An Inquiry into the Cause of Industrial Depressions and the Increase of Want with Increase of Wealth—The Remedy*. New York: Appleton, 1879.

George, Henry, Jr. *The Life of Henry George*. New York: Doubleday and McClure, 1900.

Gerson, Jack L. *Horatio Nelson Lay and Sino-British Relations, 1854–1864*. Cambridge: Harvard University Press, 1976.

Giles, Lancelot. *The Siege of the Peking Legations: A Diary*. Edited with an introduction, "Chinese Anti-Foreignism and the Boxer Uprising," by Leslie Ronald Marchant. Nedlands, Western Australia: University of Western Australia Press, 1970.

Gillin, Donald G. *Warlord: Yen Hsi-shan in Shansi Province, 1911–1949*. Princeton: Princeton University Press, 1967.

Glunin, V. I. "The Comintern and the Rise of the Communist Movement in China, 1920–1927." In *The Comintern and the East*, edited by R. A. Ulyanovsky. Pp. 280–344. Moscow: Progress Publishers, 1979.

———. "Grigorii Voitinskii (1893–1953)." In *Vidnie Sovietskie Kommunisty-Uchastniki Kitaiskoi Revoliutsii* (Distinguished Soviet Communist Participants in the Chinese Revolution). Pp. 66–88. Moscow: Nauka, 1970.

Golas, Peter J. "Early Ch'ing Guilds." In *The City in Late Imperial China*, ed. G. William Skinner.

Gong Jun. *Zhongguo xin gongye fajiangshi dagang* (An Outline History of Modern Chinese Industrial Development). Shanghai, 1933.

Granet, Marcel. *Chinese Civilization*. Translated by Kathleen E. Innes and Mabel R. Brailsford. New York: Knopf, 1930.

Graves, W. S. *America's Siberian Adventure, 1918–1920*. New York: J. Cape and H. Smith, 1931.

Grazia, Sebastian de, ed. *Masters of Chinese Political Thought*. New York: Viking Press, 1973.

Gregg, Alice H. *China and Educational Autonomy: The Changing Role of the Protestant Educational Missionary in China, 1807–1937*. Syracuse: Syracuse University Press, 1946.

Grieder, Jerome B. *Hu Shih and the Chinese Renaissance*. Cambridge: Harvard University Press, 1970.

———. *Intellectuals and the State in Modern China*. New York: The Free Press, 1981.

Grimm, Tilemann. "Academies and Urban Systems in Kwangtung." In *The City in Late Imperial China*, ed. G. William Skinner.

Gu Zhaoxiong. "The Theory of Marxism." *Xin qingnian* 6 (November 1, 1919): 450–465.

Gu Zhongxiu. *Zhonghua minguo kaiguo shi* (A History of the Founding of the Chinese Republic). 1914. Reprint. Taibei: Wenxing, 1962.

Guangdong Committee. Chinese People's Political Consultative Conference. *Guangdong xinhai geming shiliao* (Historical Materials on the 1911 Revolution in Guangdong). Guangdong: Renmin, 1981.

Guangdong Social Science Committee, Historical Research Division, et al. *Jinian Sun Zhongshan xiansheng* (In Memory of Mr. Sun Zhongshan). Beijing: Wenwu, 1981.

Guangdong Social Science Research Institute. Historical Research Division. *Sun Zhongshan nianpu* (A Chronological Biography of Sun Zhongshan). Beijing: Zhonghua, 1980.

Guofu quanji (Collected Works of the Father of the Country). Guomindang, eds. 2 vols. Rev. ed. Taibei: Zhongyang wenwu kungqing she, 1957.

Gurevich, B. P. "Vzaimnootnosheniia Sovetskikh Respublik s provintsiei Siatsyan v 1918–1921. gg." (The Relations of the Soviet Republics with Sinkiang Province in 1918–1921). In *Sovetskoe Kitaevedenie* (Soviet Sinology) 2 (1958): 96–105.

Gurr, Ted Robert. *Why Men Rebel.* Princeton: Princeton University Press, 1971.

Hackett, Roger F. "Chinese Students in Japan, 1900–1910." In *Harvard Papers on China* 3 (May 1949).

Hagopian, Mark N. *The Phenomenon of Revolution.* New York: Dodd, Mead and Co., 1974.

Hahn, Emily. *Chiang Kai-shek: An Unauthorized Biography.* New York: Doubleday and Co., 1955.

Hail, William James. *Tseng Kuo-fan and the Taiping Rebellion.* New Haven: Yale University Press, 1927.

Haithcox, John P. *Communism and Nationalism in India: M. N. Roy and the Comintern Policy, 1920–1939.* Princeton: Princeton University Press, 1971.

Hake, A. Egmont. *Events in the Taiping Rebellion: Being Reprints of Mss. Copied by General Gordon, C.B.* London: W. H. Allen, 1891.

Hamberg, Theodore, Rev. *The Visions of Hung-Siu-Tshuen, and the Origin of the Kwang-si Insurrection.* Hong Kong: China Mail Office, 1854. Reprint. San Francisco: Chinese Materials Center, Inc., 1975.

Han Fei Tsu, The Complete Works: A Classic of Chinese Political Science. Translated and annotated by Arthur Waley. London: G. Allen and Unwin, 1938.

Hana, Corinna. *Sun Yat-sen's Parteiorgan Chien-she (1919–1920).* Munchener Ostasiatische Studien, Band 14. Weisbaden: Herausgegeben von Wolfgang Bauer und Herbert Franke, 1978.

Hao, Yen-p'ing. "The Abortive Cooperation Between Reformers and Revolutionaries." In *Harvard Papers on China* 15 (December 1961).

———. *The Compradore in Nineteenth Century China: Bridge Between East and West.* Cambridge: Harvard University Press, 1970.

Hao, Yen-p'ing, and Wang, Erh-min, "Changing Chinese Views of Western Relations, 1840–1895." In John K. Fairbank and Kwang-ching Liu, eds., *The Cambridge History of China,* vol. 11, part 2.

Hart, Sir Robert. *These from the Land of Sinim: Essays on the Chinese Question.* London: Chapman and Hall, 1901.

He Jianggong. *Qingong jianxue shenghuo huiyi* (Memoirs of Studying and Working in France). Beijing: Renmin, 1958. This work has been translated into Japanese by Kawata Teiichi and Mori Tokihiko, and was published by Iwanami (Tokyo) in 1976.

Heng bao (Equity). 1908.

Hirayama Shū (Hirayama Amane). *Chūgoku himitsu shakai shi* (History of Secret Societies in China). Shanghai, 1912.

Ho, Ping-ti. *The Ladder of Success in Imperial China.* New York: Columbia University Press, 1962.

———. "Weng T'ung-ho and the 'One Hundred Days Reform.'" *Far Eastern Quarterly* 11 (February 1951): 125–135.

Horvath, Dmitrii L. *The Memoirs of Lt. General Dmitrii L. Horvath.* Retained in the archives of the Hoover Institution, Stanford University.

Hoselitz, Bert, and Moore, Wilbert, eds. *Industrialization and Society.* Paris: UNESCO, Mouton, 1968.

Hosoya Chihiro. *Siberia shuppei no shiteki kenkyū* (An Historical Study of the Siberian Expedition). Tokyo: Yuhikaku, 1955.

Hou, Chi-ming. *Foreign Investment and Economic Development in China: 1840–1937.* Cambridge: Harvard University Press, 1965.

Howard, Richard C. Introduction to "The Chinese Reform Movement of the 1890s: A Symposium." *Journal of Asian Studies* 29 (November 1969): 7–14.

———. "K'ang Yu-wei (1858–1927): His Intellectual Background and Early Thought." In *Confucian Personalities,* edited by Arthur F. Wright and Denis Twitchett. Stanford: Stanford University Press, 1962.

Hsiao, Ch'i-ch'ing. *The Military Establishment of the Yuan Dynasty.* Cambridge: Fairbank Center for Research, Harvard University, 1978.

Hsiao, Kung-ch'üan. "The Case for Constitutional Monarchy: K'ang Yu-wei's Plan for the Democratization of China." *Monumenta Sinica* 24 (1965): 1–83.

———. *A Modern China and a New World: K'ang Yu-wei, Reformer and Utopian, 1858–1927.* Seattle: University of Washington Press, 1975.

———. "The Philosophical Thought of K'ang Yu-wei: An Attempt at a New Synthesis." *Monumenta Sinica* 21 (1962): 129–193.

———. *Rural China: Imperial Control in the Nineteenth Century.* Seattle: University of Washington Press, 1960.

———. "Weng T'ung-ho and the Reform Movement of 1898." *Tsing Hua Journal of Chinese Studies,* new series, 1 (April 1957): 111–245.

Hsiao, San. *Mao Tse-tung, His Childhood and Youth.* Bombay, 1953.

Hsieh, Pao Chao. *The Government of China (1644–1911).* Baltimore: Johns Hopkins University Press, 1925.

Hsieh, Winston. "The Crowd in the Revolution of 1911: The People's Armies from a Silk-Producing Region in the Canton Delta, A Case Study." In *Symposium on the History of the Republic of China* 1:231–247.

———. "Peasant Insurrection and the Marketing Hierarchy in the Canton Delta, 1911." In *The Chinese City Between Two Worlds,* ed. Mark Elvin and G. William Skinner.

Hsiung, James C., ed. *The Logic of "Maoism": Critiques and Explication.* New York: Praeger, 1974.

Hsu, Immanuel C. Y. *China's Entrance into the Family of Nations: The Diplomatic Phase, 1858–1880.* Cambridge: Harvard University Press, 1960.

———. "Late Ch'ing Foreign Relations, 1866–1905." In John K. Fairbank and Kwang-ching Liu, eds., *The Cambridge History of China*, vol. 11, part 2, 70–141.
———. *The Rise of Modern China*. New York: Oxford University Press, 3d ed., 1983.
Hsu, Shuhsi. *China and Her Political Entity*. London: Oxford University Press, 1926.
Hsueh, Chun-tu. *Huang Hsing and the Chinese Revolution*. Stanford: Stanford University Press, 1961.
Hu Hanmin. "Zizhuan" (Autobiography). In *Geming wenxian*. Vol. 3. Taibei: Zhongyang wenwu, 1953.
Hu Hua. *Qinshao nian shiji de Zhou Enlai tongzhi* (The Early Life of Comrade Zhou Enlai). Beijing: Zhongguo qingnian chubanshe, 1977. Translated into English as *The Early Life of Zhou Enlai*. Beijing: Foreign Language Press, 1980.
Hu Sheng. *Cong yapian zhanzheng dao wu si yundong* (From the Opium War to the May Fourth Movement). 2 vols. Beijing: Renmin, 1981.
Hu Shi. *Sishi zishu* (A Self-Account at Forty). Taibei: Yuandong gongsi, 1959.
Hu Shi koushu zizhuan (Hu Shi's Oral Autobiography). Taibei: Zhuanji, 1981.
Hu Shi liuxue riji (Hu Shi's Diary as an Overseas Student). 4 vols. Taibei: Commercial Press, 1980.
Hu Shi wencun (Collected Essays of Hu Shi). 4 vols. Taibei: Yundong, 1953.
Huang Dianzhu. "Missionaries at the Taiping (Court)." Paper, Taiping Conference, People's Republic of China, 1981.
Huang Guohua. "The Hubei Student's World: The First Journal of Students in Japan Named after a Province at the End of the Qing Dynasty." In *Lishi jiaoxue* (Historical Studies) 4 (1980): 33–38.
Huang Hongshou. *Qingshi jishi benwei* (Essential Record of Qing History). Taibei: Sanmin, 1959.
Huang Jilu, ed. *Yanjiu Zhongshan xiansheng di shiliao yu shixue* (Historical Documents and Studies on Sun Yat-sen). In *Minguo shi yanjiu congshu* (A Collection of Historical Documents on the Republic). Vol. 2. Taibei: Zhongyang wenwu kungying she, 1975.
Huang Jiudian. *Minguo yuannian nanbei zhengfu heyi zhi yenjiu* (Research on the Peace Negotiations between the North and South Governments During the First Year of the Republic). Taibei, 1975.
Huang, Philip C. *Liang Ch'i-ch'ao and Modern Chinese Liberalism*. Seattle: University of Washington Press, 1972.
Huang, Sung-k'ang. *Li Ta-chao and the Impact of Marxism on Modern Chinese Thinking*. Paris: Mouton, 1965.
Huang Zhenhei. "Hong's Self-Divination and the Rise and Fall of the Taiping." Paper, Taiping Conference, People's Republic of China, 1981.
"Huaxing Hui" (The Society for the Revival of China). In Chai Degeng et al., *Xinhai geming* 1:501–512. Shanghai: Renmin chubanshe, 1957.
Hubei Committee, Chinese People's Political Consultative Conference. *Xinhai shouyi huiyi lu* (Reminiscences of the First Uprising of the 1911 Revolution). 4 vols. Hubei: Renmin, 1957–1981.
Hubei and Wuhan Committees, the Chinese People's Political Consultative Conference, the Modern History Institute, the Chinese Academy of Social Sciences, et al. *Wuchang qiyi dangan ziliao* (Compilation of

Records of the Wuchang Uprising). Vol. I. Wuhan: Hubei Renmin, 1981.
Hubei xuesheng jie. 1903. Eight issues published; became *Han sheng* (The Voice of Han).
Hughes, Ernest Richard, tr. *Chinese Philosophy in Ancient Times*. 2d ed., rev. New York: Dutton, 1942.
———. *The Invasion of China by the Western World*. London: Adam and Charles Black, 1937.
Huiminglu (Voice of the Crowing Cock). Canton, August 1912 to July 1914. Various articles and editorials.
Hummel, Arthur, ed. *Eminent Chinese of the Ch'ing Period*. 2 vols. Washington, D.C.: U.S. Government Printing Office, 1943–1944.
Hummel, William F. "K'ang Yu-wei, Historical Critic and Social Philosopher, 1858–1927." *Pacific Historical Review* 4 (1935): 343–355.
Hunan Province Annals Compilation Committee, ed. *Hunan sheng zhi, Hunan jinbainian dashi jishu* (Annals of Hunan Province, Brief Record of Important Events of Hunan in the Last Hundred Years). Vol. 1. 2d ed., rev. Changsha: Hunan Renmin, 1979.
Hunan Xuesheng. "Origins of the Diligent Work and Frugal Study in France." In *FuFa qingong jianxue yundong shiliao*. Series 2. Vol. 1. Beijing: Beijing chubanshe, 1980.
Huntington, Samuel P. *Political Order in Changing Societies*. New Haven: Yale University Press, 1968.
Hurd, Douglas. *The Arrow War: An Anglo-Chinese Confusion, 1856–1860*. New York: The Macmillan Co., 1967.
Hyatt, Irwin T. *Our Ordered Lives Confess: Three Nineteenth Century American Missionaries in East Shantung*. Cambridge: Harvard University Press, 1976.
Inaba Seiichi. "Shindai no himitsu kessha" (The Secret Societies in the Qing Period). In *Shibun* (Historical Materials) 5 (October 1952): 12–24.
Institute of Philosophy and the Institute of the Far East, U.S.S.R. Academy of Sciences. *A Critique of Mao Tse-tung's Theoretical Conceptions*. Moscow: Progress Publishers, 1972.
Itoya, Toshio. *Nihon shakaishugi no reimei* (The Dawn of Japanese Socialism). Tokyo: Shin Nihon Shuppansha, 1972.
Izvestiia. 1918–1919.
James, F. H., Rev. "Secret Societies in Shantung." In *Records of the 1890 Missionary Conference*. Shanghai, 1890.
Jansen, Marius B., ed. *Changing Japanese Attitudes Toward Modernization*. Princeton: Princeton University Press, 1964.
———. *The Japanese and Sun Yat-sen*. Cambridge: Harvard University Press, 1954.
Jen, Yu-wen. *The Taiping Revolutionary Movement*. New Haven: Yale University Press, 1973.
Jian Youwen. *Taipingjun Guangxi shouyi shi* (A History of the Guangxi Taiping Military). Chonqing: Shangwu yinshuguan, 1944.
Jiang Kanghu. "On Social Revolution" [speech]. In *Zhongguo xiandai shi congkan* 3.
Jiang Kanghu boshi yenjiang lu (Collected Speeches of Doctor Jiang Kanghu). Shanghai: Nanfang daxue, 1923–1924.

Jiang Menglin. "Dewey's Ethics." *Xin jiaoyu* (New Education) 1 (April 1919): 255–262.
Jiang Yihua, ed. *Shehuizhuyi xueshuo zai Zhongguo di chubu chuanbo* (The Initial Spread of Socialist Theories in China). Shanghai: Fudan University Press, 1984.
———. "The Principle of People's Livelihood and the Social Revolution." In *Zhongguo xindai shi congkan* 3.
Jiao Re. "The Guangdong Businessmen and the Xinhai Revolution." Paper, Wuhan Conference on the Xinhai Revolution, 1981.
Jindai lishi shiliao (Modern Historical Materials). Beijing, 1954–1965.
Johnson, Chalmers A. *Revolutionary Change.* Rev. ed. Boston: Little, Brown, 1982.
Jolle, James. *The Anarchists.* London: Eyre and Spottiswoode, 1964.
———. *The Second International, 1889–1914.* New York, 1956.
Kagan, Richard C. *The Chinese Trotskyist Movement and Chen Tu-hsiu: Culture, Revolution and Policy.* With an appended translation of Chen Duxiu's autobiography. Ph.D. dissertation on microfilm. Ann Arbor: University Microfilms, 1970.
Kang Tongjia. *Kang Youwei yu wuxu bianfa* (Kang Youwei and the 1898 Coup). Taibei: Wenhai, 1973.
Kang Youwei. *Ta T'ung Shu* (The One-World Philosophy of K'ang Yu-wei). Translated by Laurence G. Thompson. London: Allen and Unwin, 1958.
———. *Zibian nianpu* (Self-edited Chronological History). n.p., 1898.
Kang Youwei and Liang Qichao. "Qiangxue Hui's Principles." In *Wuxu bianfa* (The Reform Movement of 1898) 4:373–394.
"Kang's Memorials to the Emperor, 1888–1898." In *Wuxu bianfa* 2:123–306. n.p., n.d.
Kanshik, Devendra. *Central Asia in Modern Times: A History from the Early 19th Century.* Moscow: Progress Publishers, 1970.
Kao, Chung Ju (Bernard). *Le mouvement intellectuel en Chine et son rôle dans la révolution Chinoise (entre 1898 et 1937).* Aix-en-Provence: Saint-Thomas, 1957.
Kapitsa, Mikhail Stepanovich. *Sovetsko-Kitaiskie otnosheniia* (Soviet-Chinese Relations). Moscow: Gosudarstvennoe Izdatelstvo Politicheskoi Literatury, 1958.
Karnow, Stanley. *Mao and China: From Revolution to Revolution.* London: Macmillan, 1973.
Kasanin, Marc (Mark Isaakovich Kazanin). *China in the Twenties.* Moscow: Central Department of Oriental Literature, 1973.
Ke Gongzhen. *Zhongguo xinwen shi* (A History of Chinese Journalism). 2d ed. Taibei: Xuezhen Book Co., 1964.
Keenan, Barry. *The Dewey Experiment in China: Educational Reform and Political Power in the Early Republic.* Cambridge: Council on East Asian Studies, Harvard University, 1977.
Kennan, George F. *Soviet-American Relations, 1917–1920.* 2 vols. Vol. 1: *Russia Leaves the War* (1956). Vol. 2: *The Decision to Intervene* (1958). Princeton: Princeton University Press.
Kennedy, Thomas L. *The Arms of Kiangnan: Modernization in the Chinese Ordnance Industry, 1860–1895.* Boulder, Colo.: Westview Press, 1978.
Kenez, Peter. *Civil War in South Russia, 1918: The First Year of the Volunteer Army.* Berkeley: University of California Press, 1971.

———. *Civil War in South Russia, 1919–1920: The Defeat of the Whites*. Berkeley: University of California Press, 1977.

Kierman, Frank A., Jr., ed. *Chinese Ways in Warfare*. Cambridge: East Asian Research Center, Harvard University, 1974.

King, Wunsz. *China at the Paris Peace Conference in 1919*. Jamaica, N.Y.: St. John's University Press, 1961.

Kong Li, Lin Jinshi, Chen Zaizheng, and Guo Liang. "The Overseas Chinese and the Xinhai Revolution." Paper, Wuhan Conference on the Xinhai Revolution, 1981.

Kongzi zhexue taolun ji (Discussions on the Philosophy of Confucius). Beijing: Zonghua, 1963.

Koo, Dr. V. K. Wellington, *Papers* and *Personal Reminiscence*. Unpublished materials, Butler Library, Columbia University, New York.

Kracke, Edward A., Jr. *Civil Service in Early Sung China, 960–1067*. Cambridge: Harvard University Press, 1953.

Kropotkin, Peter A. *An Appeal to the Young*. New York: The Resistance Press, 1948.

———. *The Conquest of Bread*. New York: G. P. Putnam's Sons, 1907.

———. *The Place of Anarchism in Socialistic Evolution*. London: W. Reeves, 1886.

Kublin, Hyman. *Asian Revolutionary: The Life of Katayama Sen*. Princeton: Princeton University Press, 1964.

Kuhn, Philip A. *Rebellion and Its Enemies in Late Imperial China: Militarization and Social Structure, 1796–1864*. Cambridge: Harvard University Press, 1970.

Kuo, Thomas C. T. *Chen Tu-hsiu (1879–1942) and the Chinese Communist Movement*. South Orange, N.J.: Seton Hall Press, 1975.

Kuznets, Simon. *Economic Growth and Structure*. New York: Norton, 1965.

———. *Toward a Theory of Economic Growth with Reflections on the Economic Growth of Modern Nations*. New York: Norton, 1968.

Laai, Yi-faai. "The Part Played by the Pirates of Kwangtung and Kwangsi Provinces in the Taiping Insurrection." Ph.D. dissertation, University of California, Berkeley, 1950.

Lane-Poole, Stanley. *Sir Harry Parkes in China*. London: Macmillan, 1894.

Latourette, Kenneth Scott. *A History of Christian Missions in China*. New York: Macmillan Co., 1929.

Legge, James, tr. *The Chinese Classics*. 5 vols. Reprinted. Hong Kong: Hong Kong University Press, 1960.

Leiden, Carl and Schmitt, Karl M. *The Politics of Violence: Revolution in the Modern World*. Englewood Cliffs, N.J.: Prentice-Hall, 1968.

Lenin, Vladimir Ilich. *The April Conference*. New York: International Publishers, 1932.

———. *Collected Works*. 45 vols. Moscow: Progress Publishers, 1970–1975.

———. *The National Liberation Movement in the East*. 3d rev. ed. Moscow: Progress Publishers, 1969.

———. *State and Revolution*. New York: International Publishers, 1932.

Leong, Sow-Theng. *Sino-Soviet Diplomatic Relations, 1917–1926*. Canberra: Australia National University Press, 1976.

Lerner, Daniel. *The Passing of Traditional Society*. Glencoe, Ill.: Free Press, 1958.

Levenson, Joseph R. *Confucian China and Its Modern Fate*. 3 vols. Berkeley: University of California Press, 1964–1965.

———. *Liang Ch'i-ch'ao and the Mind of Modern China*. Cambridge: Harvard University Press, 1953.
Lewis, Charlton M. *Prologue to the Chinese Revolution: The Transformation of Ideas and Institutions in Hunan Province, 1891–1907*. Cambridge: East Asian Research Center, Harvard University, 1976.
Li Ao. *Hu Shi pingzhuan* (A Critical Biography of Hu Shi). Taibei: Wenxing, 1964.
Li, Chien-nung. *The Political History of China, 1840–1928*. Edited and translated by Ssu-yu Teng and Jeremy Ingalls. Princeton: Van Nostrand, 1956.
Li Chunyi. *Yuan Shikai zhuan* (Biography of Yuan Shikai). Beijing: Zhonghua, 1980.
Li Dazhao xuanji (Collected Writings of Li Dazhao). Beijing: Renmin chubanshe, 1962.
Li Dazhao zhuan (Biography of Li Dazhao). Beijing: Renmin chubanshe, 1979.
Li Dongfang. *Chiang-gong Kaishek xuzhuan* (A Preliminary Biography of the Honorable Chiang Kai-shek). Rev. ed. Taibei: Lianjing chubanshe, 1976.
Li Fangchen. *Zhongguo jindai shi* (Modern History of China). Taibei: Wuzhou chubanshe, 1960.
Li Guoqi. *Zhongguo zaoqi di tielu jingying* (Early Railroad Management in China). Taibei: Zhongyang yanjiu yuan jindai yanjiushou, 1961.
Li Hongzhang. *Li Wenzheng gong quanji* (Complete Papers of Li Hongzhang). Shanghai: Commercial press, photo reprint of reprint of Nanjing 1908 edition. Taipei: Wenhai reproduction, 1962.
Li Huang. *My Memoirs*. Vol. 1. Deposited in the Columbia University Oral History Collection.
Li Rui. *Mao Zedong tongzhi di chuqi geming huodong* (The Early Revolutionary Activities of Comrade Mao Tse-tung). Beijing: Renmin chubanshe, 1957. Rev. ed., 1980. First edition translated by Anthony W. Sariti and edited by James C. Hsiung. White Plains, N.Y.: M. E. Sharpe, 1977.
Li Shiyu. "Another Inquiry into the Origins of the Yihe Tuan." Paper, Jinan Conference on the Yihe Tuan, 1980.
———. "The Evolution of Modern China and the Xinhai Revolution." Paper, Wuhan Conference on the Xinhai Revolution, 1981.
Li, Shizeng and Chu, Minyi. *La Revolution*. Paris, 1907. Reprinted. Shanghai, 1947.
Li Shougong. *Minchu zhi guohui* (Parliament During the Early Years of the Republic). Taibei: Taiwan Shangwu, 1963.
Li Shu. "Reexamining Several Issues Concerning the Xinhai Revolution." Paper, Wuhan Conference on the Xinhai Revolution, 1981.
Li, Tieh-Tseng. *Tibet: Today and Yesterday*. New York: Bookman, 1960.
Li, Youyong (Li, Shizeng). *Le Soja Essay Culture: Ses Usages Alimentaires, Thérapeutiques, Agricoles et Industriels*. Paris: Shijieshe, 1912.
Li, Yu-ning. *The Introduction of Socialism into China*. New York: Columbia University Press, 1971.
Li, Yu-ning, ed. *The First Emperor of China*. White Plains, N.Y.: International Arts and Sciences Press, 1975.
Li Zehou. "On Sun Yat-sen's Thought." In *Zhongguo jindai shi sixiang shilun* (Essays on the History of Modern Chinese Thought). Beijing: Renmin chubanshe, July 1979. Pp. 312–381.
———. "An Outline of the Thought of the Revolutionary Faction of the Bourgeoisie at the Beginning of the Twentieth Century." In *Zhongguo jindai shi sixiang shilun*. Pp. 1–311.

Li Zhuren, *Xinhai geming qian di chunzhong douzheng* (Struggles of the Masses Before the Xinhai Revolution). Beijing: Tonggu duwu chubanshe, 1957.

Liang, Ch'i-ch'ao. *Intellectual Trends in the Ch'ing Period*. Translated by Immanuel C. Y. Hsu. Cambridge: Harvard University Press, 1959.

Liang Qichao. *Ouyou xinying lu jielu* (Reflections on a European Trip). Taibei: Taiwan Zhonghua, 1960.

———. "Record of the 1898 Political Reforms." In *Wuxu bianfa* 1:249–328. n.p., n.d.

———. *Wuxu zhengbian ji* (An Account of the 1898 Reform Movement). Reprint of 1936 edition. Taibei: Taiwan Zhonghua shufu, 1965.

Liew, Kit S. *Struggle for Democracy: Sung Chiao-jen and the 1911 Revolution*. Berkeley: University of California Press, 1971.

Lin Mingde. *Yuan Shikai yu Chaoxian* (Yuan Shikai and Korea). Taibei: Zhongyang yanjiuyuan jindai yanjiushou, 1970.

Lin, Wei-hung. "Activities of Woman Revolutionists in the Tung Meng Hui Period." *China Forum* 2 (July 1975): 245–299.

Lin, Yutang. *History of the Press and Public Opinion in China*. Shanghai: Kelly and Walsh, Ltd., 1936.

Lin Zhangbing, ed., *Xinhai geming* (The 1911 Revolution). 3 vols. Beijing, 1981.

Linebarger, Paul M. A. *The China of Chiang Kai-shek: A Political Study*. Boston: World Peace Foundation, 1941.

———. *Sun Yat-sen and the Chinese Republic*. New York: The Century Co., 1925.

Ling Tian. *Xian-Tong Guizhou junshi shi* (A History of Military Affairs in Guizhou During the Xianfeng and Tong-zhi Periods). Taibei: Wenhai chubanshe, 1967.

Lin-he (Augustus F. Lindley). *Ti-Ping T'ien Kwoh—The History of the Ti-ping Revolution*. 2 vols. London: Day and Son, 1866.

Liu Danian et al. *The 1911 Revolution—A Retrospective After 70 Years*. Beijing: New World Press, 1983.

Liu Fenghan. *Xinjian lujun* (The Newly Created Army). Taibei: Zhongyang yanjiuyuan jindai yanjiushou, 1967.

Liu Jiayetang, comp. *Xuantong zhengji* (Political Records of the Xuantong Reign). Vols. 1–23. Beijing: Liaohai, 1934.

Liu, Kwang-Ching. "The Limits of Regional Power in the Late Ch'ing Period: A Reappraisal." In *The Tsing Hua Journal of Chinese Studies*. July 1974. Chinese, pp. 176–207; English, pp. 207–223.

———. "Politics, Intellectual Outlook and Reform: The T'ung-wen kuan Controversy of 1867." In Paul A. Cohen and John E. Schrecker, eds. *Reform in Nineteenth Century China*.

Liu Likai. "A Daily Record of Major Events of the Patriotic Movement from May 4 to June 3." In *Wusi aiguo yundong* (The May Fourth Patriotic Movement) 2:489–490. Beijing: The Chinese Social Science Publishing House, 1979.

Liu Qinwu. "A Preliminary Discussion of the Historical Role of the Yihe Tuan Movement." Paper, Jinan Conference on the Yihe Tuan, 1980.

Liu Shaotang, ed. *Minguo renwu xiao zhuan* (Brief Biographies of Republican Personalities). 5 vols. Taibei: Zhuanji wenxue, 1972.

Liu Shenyi. "Questions Regarding the Quality of Democracy in Taiping Thought Relating to the 'Equality of the Big Four.'" Paper, Taiping Conference, People's Republic of China, 1981.

Liu, Tai. "The Railroad Storming Szechuan: A Study of Its Intellectual Background and Development." In *Symposium on the History of the Republic of China* 1:249–266.

Liu Yan. *Zhongguo waijiao shi* (A History of China's Foreign Relations). Taibei: Sanmin, 1962.

Liu Yue. "Several Issues Regarding Research on Modern Chinese History." *Shehui kexue zhanxian* (Social Science Front) 3, no. 2 (10) (1980): 174–181.

Lo, Hui-min, ed. *The Correspondence of G. E. Morrison*. 2 vols. Cambridge: Cambridge University Press, 1978.

Lo, Jung-pang, ed. *K'ang Yu-wei: A Biography and a Symposium*. Tucson: University of Arizona Press, 1967.

Lockwood, William W. *The Economic Development of Japan: Growth and Structural Change, 1868–1940*. Princeton: Princeton University Press, 1954.

Lockwood, William W., "Prospectus and Summary." In Lockwood, William W., ed. *The State and Economic Enterprise in Japan*. Princeton: Princeton University Press, 1965. P. 4.

Loh, Pichon P. Y. *The Early Chiang Kai-shek*. New York: Columbia University Press, 1971.

Lu Lianzhang. "On Hong Xiuquan's Anti-Confucian Thought." Paper, Taiping Conference, People's Republic of China, 1981.

Luo Ergang. "Qingji bing wei jiangyou di qiyuan" (The Origin of Personal Armies in the Late Qing Period). *Zhongguo shehui jingji shi jikan* (Journal of Chinese Social and Economic History) 5, no. 2 (1937): 235–250.

———. *Taiping tianguo shigang* (An Outline History of the Taiping). Shanghai: Shangwu Yinshuguan, 1937.

———. *Taiping tianguoshi shigao* (A Draft History of the Taiping). Beijing: Kaiming shudian, 1951.

———. *Xiangjun xinzhi* (A New Account of the Hunan Army). Changsha: Commercial Press, 1939.

———. *Xiangjun xinshi* (A New Treatise on the Hunan Army). Taibei: Yangmingshan zhuang, 1951.

Luo Gang. *Lie bian guofu nianpu jiumiu* (Correcting the Errors in the Chronological Biography of Sun Yat-sen). Edited by Luo Jialun. Taibei: Guomin tushu chubanshe, 1962.

Luo Jialun. *Guofu nianpu chugao* (A Preliminary Chronological Biography of the Father of the Country). 2 vols. Rev. ed. Taibei: Zhongguo Guomindang zhongyang weiyuan hui shiliao bianzhi weiyuanhui, 1965.

———. *Heixue baoyu dao mingxia* (From the Black Snow and Violent Rain to the Bright Dawn). 1943. Reprint. Taibei: Xuetian, 1970.

Luo Jialun, ed. and comp. *Geming wenxian* (Documents on the Revolution). Vols. 1–5. Taibei: Zhongyang wenwu kungying she, 1973.

Luo Jialun and Huang Jilu, eds. *Guofu nianpu zengding ben* (A Chronological Biography of the Father of the Country). 3d ed. 2 vols. Taibei: Zhongguo Guomindang, Party History Commission, 1969.

Luo Xianglin. *Guofu zhi daxue shidai* (Sun Yat-sen's University Days). Chongqing: Duli chubanshe, 1945.

Luo Yuanken. *Qingji jiaoan shihao* (Historical Materials on Missionary Incidents in the Later Qing). Vol. 1. Beijing: Gugong bowu yuan, 1948.

———. *Zhongguo jinbainian shi* (History of China During the Past One Hundred Years). Vol. 1. Shanghai: Commercial Press, 1933.

Luo Zhiyuan. *Zhongguo xianfa shi* (A History of Constitutionalism in China). Taibei: Taibei Shangwu, 1967.

LuOu zhoukan (Weekly Journal of Students in Europe). November 15, 1919, to November 6, 1920(?).

Luying bingzhi (A Treatise on the Army of the Green Standard). Chongqing: Shangwu yinshuguan, 1945.

Ly, J. Tsang. "Dr. Sun and China." *International Socialist Review* 14 (September 1913): 173–176.

Ma, Ho-t'ien. *Chinese Agent in Mongolia*. Baltimore: Johns Hopkins Press, 1949.

Ma Qingchong. "Viewpoints on Several Questions Relating to the Nature of Taiping Political Power." Paper, Taiping Conference, People's Republic of China, 1981.

Ma, Te-chih. "Le mouvement reformiste et les événements de la cour de Pékin en 1898." Ph.D. dissertation, l'Université de Lyon, 1934.

McDonald, Angus W., Jr., trans. "Four Articles by Mao Taken from *Hunan zizhi yundong shi* (History of the Hunan Self-Government Movement) Part I, compiled by Wang Wuwei." *China Quarterly* 68 (December 1976): 751–777.

———. *The Urban Origins of Rural Revolution: Elites and the Masses in Hunan Province, China, 1911–1927*. Berkeley: University of California Press, 1978.

McGillivray, Donald, ed. *A Century of Protestant Missions in China, 1807–1907*. Shanghai, 1907.

MacKinnon, Stephen R. "The Peiyang Army, Yuan Shi-k'ai and the Origins of Modern Chinese Warlordism." *Journal of Asian Studies* 32 (May 1973): 405–423.

———. *Power and Politics in Late Imperial China: Yuan Shi-kai in Beijing and Tianjin, 1901–1908*. Berkeley: University of California Press, 1980.

Makesizhuyi yanjiu cankao ziliao (Research Materials for the Study of Marxism). February 1981.

Mannheim, Karl. *Ideology and Utopia: An Introduction to the Sociology of Knowledge*. Translated by Louis Wirth and Edward Shils. New York: Harcourt, Brace, 1946.

Mantici, Giorgio. *Mao Zedong Pensiere del fiume Xiang*. Roma: Editori Riunti, 1981.

Mao Jiaju, Fang Jiguang, and Dang Guanghua. *Taiping tianguo xingwangshi* (The History of the Rise and Fall of the Taiping). Shanghai: Renmin chubanshe, 1980.

Mao Sicheng, comp. *Minguo shiwu nian yiqian zhi Chiang Kai-shek xiansheng* (Mr. Chiang Kai-shek Before the Fifteenth Year of the Republic (1926)). Hong Kong: Longmen chubanshe, 1965. Reprint of 1936 edition.

Mao Tse-tung. *Selected Works*. 4 vols. Beijing: Foreign Languages Press, 1961–1965.

Marchant, L. R. *The Siege of the Peking Legations—A Diary—Lancelot Giles*. Nedlands: University of Western Australia Press, 1970.

Marcuse, Herbert. *Counterrevolution and Revolt*. Boston: Beacon Press, 1972.

Martin, William Alexander Parsons. *A Cycle of Cathay*. New York: Fleming H. Revell, 1896.

———. *The Siege in Peking: China Against the World*. New York: Fleming H. Revell, 1900.

Meadows, Thomas T. *The Chinese and Their Rebellions, Viewed in Connection with Their National Philosophy, Ethics, Legislation and Administration*. London: Smith Elder, 1856.

Meisner, Maurice. *Li Ta-chao and the Origins of Chinese Marxism*. New York: Cambridge: Harvard University Press, 1967–1968.
Meizhou pinglun (Weekly Review). 1918–1919. 37 issues. Reprint. In East Asiatic Library, University of California, Berkeley; Peking University Library.
Meng, S. M. *The Tsungli Yamen: Its Organization and Functions*. Cambridge: East Asian Research Center, Harvard University Press, 1970.
Metzger, Thomas A. *The Internal Organization of Ch'ing Bureaucracy: Legal, Normative and Communication Aspects*. Cambridge: Harvard Studies in East Asian Law, 1973.
Michael, Franz. *Mao and the Perpetual Revolution*. Woodbury, N.Y.: Barron's, 1977.
Michael, Franz, and Chang, Chung-li. *The Taiping Rebellion: History and Documents*. 3 vols. Seattle: University of Washington Press, 1966.
Michie, Alexander. *The Englishman in China During the Victorian Era, as Illustrated in the Career of Sir Arthur Rutherford Alcock*. 2 vols. London: 1900.
Migdal, Joel. *Peasants, Politics and Revolution: Pressures Toward Political and Social Change in the Third World*. Princeton: Princeton University Press, 1974.
Min bao. November 1905 to February 1910. Irregular publication.
Minli bao (People's Independence). Shanghai, October 11, 1910–June 20, 1913. Various articles and editorials.
Miyazaki Torazō. *Sanjūsannen no yume* (A Dream of Thirty-three Years). Tokyo: Kokkō shobō, 1902.
Mo Anshi. "Can the Taiping Movement Be Called a Revolution and a Peasant Revolution?" Paper, Taiping Conference, People's Republic of China, 1981.
———. *Taiping tianguo* (The Taiping). Shanghai: Renmin chubanshe, 1959.
Mo Haijian. "The Taiping Decision to Establish the Capital at Dianjing (Nanjing) Was a Major Strategic Mistake." *Lishi jiaoxue* (Historical Teaching) 3 (1981): 13–17.
Mo Jipeng. "Recalling Shifu." Macao, c. 1961. Manuscript.
Modern Chinese History Teaching and Research, History Department, Wuhan University, comp. *Xinhai geming zai Hubei shiliao xuanji* (Collective Historical Sources of the 1911 Revolution in Hubei). Hubei: Renmin, 1981.
Morgan, W. P. *Triad Societies in Hong Kong*. Hong Kong: Government Press, 1960.
Morley, James P. *The Japanese Thrust into Siberia, 1918*. New York: Columbia University Press, 1957.
Morse, Hosea B., and MacNair, Harley F. *Far Eastern International Relations*. Boston: Houghton Mifflin, 1933.
Mote, Frederick W. *Intellectual Foundations of China*. New York: Alfred A. Knopf, 1971.
———. "The Transformation of Nanking, 1350–1400." In *The City in Late Imperial China*, ed. G. William Skinner.
Moulder, Frances V. *Japan, China, and the Modern World Economy*. Cambridge: Cambridge University Press, 1977.
Munholland, Kim. "The French Connection that Failed: France and Sun-Yat-sen, 1900–1908." *Journal of Asian Studies* 32 (November 1972): 77–95.
Murphey, Rhoads. "The Treaty Ports and China's Modernization." In *The Chinese City Between Two Worlds*, ed. Mark Elvin and G. William Skinner.

Myers, Ramon H. *The Chinese Peasant Economy: Agricultural Development in Hopei and Shantung, 1890–1949*. Taibei: Rainbow-Bridge Book Co., 1970.
———. "Trends in Agriculture: 1911–1949." In *Cambridge History of China* 11, ed. John K. Fairbank and Liu, Kwang-Ching.
Nathan, Andrew. *Peking Politics, 1918–1923: Factionalism and the Failure of Constitutionalism*. Berkeley: University of California Press, 1976.
National Archives Microfilm Publication: Records of the Department of State Relating to Internal Affairs of China, 1910–1929. Nos. 893.000 001/338–893.00/3771.
New York Times. November 2, 1912.
Nishikawa Fumiko. "Meiji shakai undō no omoide (Thoughts on the Meiji Socialist Movement)." In *Rōdō undōshi kenkyū* (Studies on the History of the Labor Movement). September 1958, 11.
Nivison, David S., and Wright, Arthur F., eds. *Confucianism in Action*. Stanford: Stanford University Press, 1959.
Nock, Albert Jay. *Henry George: An Essay*. New York: William Morrow and Co., 1939.
North, Robert C., and Eudin, Xenia J. *M. N. Roy's Mission to China: The Communist-Kuomintang Split of 1927*. Berkeley: University of California Press, 1963.
North China Daily News. 1911–1912.
North China Herald. April 18, 1898–April 3, 1920.
Notehelfer, F. G. *Kōtoku Shūsui: Portrait of a Japanese Radical*. Cambridge: Harvard University Press, 1971.
Office of School History, Peking University, comp. "The Society for the Study of Marxism of the University of Peking." *Jindai shi ziliao* (Contemporary Historical Materials). April 1955, 161–173.
Ohkawa Kazushi and Rosovsky, Henry. *A Century of Growth*. Stanford: Stanford University Press, 1973.
Ohkawa Kazushi et al. *The Growth Rate of the Japanese Economy Since 1878*. Tokyo: Kinokuniya, 1957.
Okamoto Hiroshi. *Nihon shakaishugi seitō ronshi josetsu* (An Introduction to the History of Japanese Socialist Parties). Kyoto: Horitsu Bunkasha, 1968.
Onogawa Hidemi. "K'ang You-wei's Idea of Reform." *Studies on Modern China* 2 (1958): 112–113.
Ortega y Gasset, Jose. *The Revolt of the Masses*. New York: W. W. Norton and Co., 1932.
Ota Masao. *Meiji shakaishugi seitō shi* (A History of Meiji Socialist Parties). Kyoto: Mineba Shobo, 1971.
Papers Relating to the Foreign Relations of the United States, 1906. Part I. Washington, D.C.: U.S. Government Printing Office, 1909.
Papers Relating to the Foreign Relations of the United States, 1907. Part I. Washington, D.C.: U.S. Government Printing Office, 1910.
Payne, Robert. *Chiang Kai-shek*. New York: Weybright and Talley, 1969.
Paynton, Clifford T., and Blackey, Robert, eds. *Why Revolution?* Cambridge, Mass.: Schenkman, 1971.
The Peking Leader. 1918–1919.
Peng, Tse-chou. "Dr. Sun Yat-sen and China Development Company." In *Symposium on the History of the Republic of China* 1:196–222.
Perkins, Dwight H.; Wang, Yeh-Chien; Hsiao, Kuo-ying Wang; and Su, Yung-

Ming. *Agricultural Development in China, 1368–1968*. Chicago: Aldine Publishing Co., 1969.
Perry, Elizabeth, ed. *Chinese Perspectives on the Nien Rebellion*. New York: M. E. Sharpe, 1981.
Persits, Moisei Aronovich. *Dalnevostochnaia Respubliki i Kitai* (The Far Eastern Republic and China). Moscow: Publishing House of Oriental Literature, 1962.
Pi Minxiao. "Chambers of Commerce and Business Groups in Wuhan During the Wuhan Uprising." Paper, Wuhan Conference on the Xinhai Revolution, 1981.
Pickering, W. H. "Chinese Secret Societies and Their Origin." *Journal of the Royal Asiatic Society* (Straits Branch) 1 (1878).
Porter, D. H. "Secret Societies in Shantung." *Chinese Recorder* 17 (1886).
Powell, Ralph L. *The Rise of Chinese Military Power, 1895–1912*. Princeton: Princeton University Press, 1955.
Pravda. 1918–1919.
"President Chiang Kai-shek: A Chronological Table." In *Tribute to President Chiang Kai-shek, Collection of Writings to Commemorate the Third Anniversary of His Passing*. Taibei: Guomindang, 1978. Pp. 87–125.
Price, Donald C. *Russia and the Roots of the Chinese Revolution, 1896–1911*. Cambridge: Harvard University Press, 1974.
Purcell, Victor. *The Boxer Uprising: A Background Study*. London: Cambridge University Press, 1963.
Pusey, James R. "K'ang Yu-wei and Pao-chiao: Confucian Reform and Reformation." East Asian Research Center. *Harvard Papers on China* 20 (December 1966): 144–176.
Pye, Lucian W. *Aspects of Political Development*. Boston: Little, Brown, 1966.
———. *The Man in the Leader*. New York: Basic Books, 1976.
———. *The Spirit of Chinese Politics*. Cambridge: MIT Press, 1968.
Pye, Lucian W., and Verba, Sidney, eds. *Political Culture and Political Development*. Princeton: Princeton University Press, 1965.
Qian Gongbo. *Zhongguo jingji fazhanshi* (A History of Chinese Economic Development). Taibei: Wenjing, 1974.
Qin Xiaoyi, chief compiler. *Zongtong Chiang-gong dashi zhangbian chugao* (Preliminary Draft of Important Affairs Based Upon Various Sources and Arranged Chronologically Relating to President Chiang). 4 vols. Taibei: Guomindang, 1978.
Qing mo duiwai jiaoshe tiaoyueji (Collection of Treaties Negotiated in the Late Qing Period). 2 vols. Taibei: Guofeng, 1963.
Qing Xuantong zhao waijiao shiliao (Documents on the Foreign Relations of the Qing Xuantong Reign). Beijing: Wang Xiyin, 1933.
Qinghua University Faculty Research Unit on the History of the Chinese Communist Party, ed. *FuFa qingong jianxue yundong shiliao* (Documents on the Diligent Work-Frugal Study Movement for Going to France). 3 vols. Beijing: Beijing chubanshe, 1979–1981.
Qingji jiaoan shiliao (Historical Materials on Missionary Incidents in the Late Qing). Vol. 1. Beijing: Gugong bowu yuan, 1948.
Qingnian zazhi (Youth Magazine). September 15, 1915, to September 1916. Renamed and published as *Xin qingnian* (New Youth).
Qingyi bao (Journal of Dispassionate Opinion). Edited by Liang Qichao. Reprinted in 12 volumes. Taibei: Zhengwen Publishing Co., 1967.

Quested, R. K. I. *The Expansion of Russia in East Asia, 1857–1860*. Kuala Lumpur: The University of Malaysia, 1968.
Qui Youzhen. *Guofu, Duwei, Makesi* (The Father of the Nation, Dewey, and Marx). Taibei: Youshi shudian, 1965.
Rankin, Mary Backus. "'Public Opinion' and Political Power: Qingyi in Late Nineteenth Century China." *Journal of Asian Studies* 41 (May 1982): 453–477.
Rantoul, Robert. *Frederick Townsend Ward*. Salem: The Essex Institute, 1980.
Ratner, Joseph, ed. *Characters and Events: Popular Essays in Social and Political Philosophy*. 2 vols. New York: Henry Holt, 1929.
Ratner, Joseph, ed. *Intelligence in the Modern World: John Dewey's Philosophy*. New York: Modern Library, 1939.
Rawlinson, John. *China's Struggle for Naval Development: 1839–1895*. Cambridge: Harvard University Press, 1967.
Rawski, Evelyn Sakakida. *Education and Popular Literacy in Ch'ing China*. Michigan Studies on China. Ann Arbor: University of Michigan Press, 1979.
Reischauer, Edwin O.; Fairbank, John K.; and Craig, Albert. *A History of East Asian Civilization*. Boston: Houghton Mifflin, 1960.
Remer, C. F. "John Dewey in China." *Millard's Review* 13 (July 1920): 266–268.
Rhoads, Edward J. M. *China's Republican Revolution: The Case of Kwangtung, 1895–1913*. Cambridge: Harvard University Press, 1975.
———. "Merchant Associations in Canton, 1895–1911." In *The Chinese City Between Two Worlds*, ed. Mark Elvin and G. William Skinner.
Rice, Edward. *Mao's Way*. Berkeley: University of California Press, 1972.
Richard, Timothy. *Forty-five Years*. New York: Frederick Stokes Co., 1916.
Richardson, Hugh Edward. *A Short History of Tibet*. New York: E. P. Dutton, 1962.
Roger, Everett M. *Modernization Among Peasants*. New York: Holt, Rinehart and Winston, 1969.
Rosenbaum, Arthur L. "Gentry Power and the Changsha Rice Riot of 1910." *Journal of Asian Studies* 34 (May 1975): 3, 689–715.
Rosovsky, Henry. *Capital Formation in Japan, 1868–1940*. New York: Free Press, 1961.
Rozman, Gilbert, ed. *The Modernization of China*. New York: Free Press, 1981.
Rupen, Robert A. *Mongols of the Twentieth Century*. Part 1. Bloomington: Indiana University Press, 1964.
Sakai Tadao. "Gendai Chūgoku ni okeru himitsu kessha" (Secret Societies in Contemporary China). In *Kindai Chūgoku kenkyū* (Modern Chinese Studies), 1948.
Sanetō Keishū. *Chūgokujin ni Nihon ryūgaku shi* (A History of Chinese Students in Japan). Tokyo: 1960.
Sankei shimbun. August 15, 1974–[December] 1976.
Scalapino, Robert A. *Democracy and the Party Movement in Prewar Japan*. Berkeley: University of California Press. Second edition, 1967.
———. "The Evolution of a Young Revolutionary: Mao Zedong in 1919–1921." *Journal of Asian Studies* 42 (November 1982).
———. "Prelude to Marxism: The Chinese Student Movement in Japan, 1900–1910." In *Approaches to Modern Chinese History*, ed. A. Feuerwerker, R. Murphey, and M. C. Wright. Pp. 190–215.
Scalapino, Robert A., ed. *Elites in the People's Republic of China*. Seattle: University of Washington Press, 1972.

Scalapino, Robert A., and Schiffrin, Harold Z. "Early Socialist Currents in the Chinese Revolutionary Movement: Sun Yat Sen versus Liang Ch'i-ch'ao." *Journal of Asian Studies* 18 (May 1959): 321–342.
Scalapino, Robert A., and Yu, George T. *The Chinese Anarchist Movement*. Berkeley: Institute of International Studies, University of California, 1961.
Scheiner, Irwin. *Christians, Converts and Social Protest in Meiji Japan*. Berkeley: University of California Press, 1970.
Schiffrin, Harold Z. *Sun Yat-sen and the Origins of the Chinese Revolution*. Berkeley: University of California Press, 1970.
———. *Sun Yat-sen: Reluctant Revolutionary*. Boston: Little, Brown, 1980.
Schilpp, Paul, ed. *The Philosophy of John Dewey*. 2d ed. New York: Tudor, 1951.
Schram, Stuart. *Mao Tse-tung*. Middlesex, Eng.: Penguin, 1966.
———. *The Political Thought of Mao Tse-tung*. Rev. and enl. ed. New York: Praeger, 1969.
Schram, Stuart, trans. "The Great Union of the Popular Masses." *China Quarterly* 49 (Jan.–Mar. 1972): 76–87.
———, trans. with commentary. *Mao Zedong, Une étude de l'éducation physique*. Paris: Mouton, 1962.
Schrecker, John E. *Imperialism and Chinese Nationalism: Germany in Shantung*. Cambridge: Harvard University Press, 1971.
Schurmann, Franz. *Ideology and Organization in Communist China*, 2d ed. Berkeley: Univesity of California Press, 1968.
Schwartz, Benjamin I. *Chinese Communism and the Rise of Mao*. Cambridge: Harvard University Press, 1958.
———. *In Search of Wealth and Power: Yen Fu and the West*. Cambridge: Harvard University Press, 1964.
The Second Congress of the Communist International. *Proceedings of Petrograd Session of July 17th and of Moscow Sessions of July 19th–August 7th, Moscow, 1920*.
Seki Hiroharu. *Gendai higashi Ajia kokusai kankyō no tanjō* (The Birth of an International Settlement in Modern East Asia). Tokyo: Fukumura Shupan Kabushiki Kaisha, 1969.
Shang Mingxuan. *Sun Zhongshan zhuan* (Biography of Sun Yat-sen). 2d ed. Beijing: Beijing chubanshe, 1981.
Shao, Zhuanli. *Sun Zhongshan* (Sun Yat-sen). Shanghai: Renmin chubanshe, 1980.
Sharman, Lyon. *Sun Yat-sen: His Life and Its Meaning*. 1934. Reprint. Stanford: Stanford University Press, 1968.
Shaw, H. E. "A Chinese Revolutionist." *Mother Earth* 10:8 (1915): 284–285.
Shen Dongsheng, Dong Yuan, and Dong Run, eds. *Guangxu zhengyao* (Important Political Events of the Guangxu Era). 30 vols. Shanghai, 1909.
Shen Maoyuan. "Several Questions Concerning Hong Xiuquan's Thought During His Earlier Period." Paper, Taiping Conference, People's Republic of China, 1981.
Sheridan, James E. *Chinese Warlord: The Career of Feng Yu-hsiang*. Stanford: Stanford University Press, 1966.
Shiba, Yoshinobu. "Ningpo and Its Hinterland." In *The City in Late Imperial China*, ed. G. William Skinner.
Shifu wencun (Collected Works of Shifu). Canton: Gexin shudian, 1928.
Shih, Vincent Y. C. *The Taiping Ideology: Its Sources, Interpretations, and Influences*. Seattle: University of Washington Press, 1967.

———. "A Talk with Hu Shih." *China Quarterly* (Apr.–June 1962): 149–165.
Shijieshe (Le Monde), ed. *LuOu jiaoyu yundong* (The Educational Movement in Europe). Tours, France: Shijieshe, 1916.
Shu Xincheng. *Jindai Zhongguo liuxue shi* (A History of Students Abroad in Modern China). Shanghai: Shangwu, 1933.
Siao-yu. *Mao Tse-tung and I Were Beggars*. New York: Collier Books, 1973.
"The Sino-Japanese Negotiations of 1915." In *Carnegie Endowment for International Peace, Division of International Law*. Pamphlet 45. Washington, 1921. Pp. 10–19.
Sizer, Nancy. "John Dewey's Ideas in China, 1919 to 1921." *Comparative Education Review* 10 (October 1966): 390–404.
Skachko, P. E. "Report on the Agrarian Question." *Narody vostoka* (Peoples of the East), October 1920, pp. 15–20.
Skinner, G. William. "Cities and the Hierarchy of Local Systems." In *The City in Late Imperial China*, ed. G. William Skinner.
———. "Marketing and Social Structure in Rural China." Part I. *Journal of Asian Studies* 24, no. 1 (1964).
———. "Marketing and Social Structure in Rural China." Part II. *Journal of Asian Studies* 24, no. 2 (1965).
———. "Regional Urbanization in Nineteenth Century China." In *The City in Late Imperial China*, ed. G. William Skinner.
Skinner, G. William, ed. *The City in Late Imperial China*. Stanford: Stanford University Press, 1977.
Skocpol, Theda. *States and Social Revolutions: A Comparative Analysis of France, Russia and China*. Cambridge: Cambridge University Press, 1979.
Smith, Richard J. *Mercenaries and Mandarins: The Ever-Victorious Army in Nineteenth Century China*. Millwood, N.Y.: KTO Press, 1978.
Smith, Thomas C. *The Agrarian Origins of Modern Japan*. Stanford: Stanford University Press, 1959.
Snow, Edgar. *Red Star Over China*. London: Victor Gollancz, 1937.
Solomon, Richard H. *Mao's Revolution and the Chinese Political Culture*. Berkeley: University of California Press, 1971.
Song Jiaoren. *Wo zhi lishi* (My Diary). Hunan, 1920. Reprint. Taibei: Wenxing, 1962.
Song Jiaoren ji (Collected Works of Song Jiaoren). 2 vols. Beijing: Zhonghua, 1981.
Song Qinglan and Guo Dasong. "On the Origins of the Yihe Tuan." Paper, Jinan Conference on the Yihe Tuan, 1980.
Soothill, W. E. *Timothy Richard of China*. London: Seeley, Service and Co., Ltd., 1926.
Sorkin, Grigorii Zakharovich. *Pervyi syezd narodov vostoka* (The First Congress of the Peoples of the East). Moscow: Oriental Literature Publishing House, 1961.
Spector, Stanley. *Li Hung-chang and the Huai Army*. Seattle: University of Washington Press, 1964.
Spence, Jonathan D. *To Change China: Western Advisers in China, 1620–1960*. Boston: Little, Brown, 1969.
———. *The Gate of Heavenly Peace: The Chinese and Their Revolution, 1895–1980*. New York: Penguin Books, 1981.
Stalin, Iosif. "Document No. 7," and "Document No. 8." In *Soviet Russia and the East, 1920–1927: A Documentary Survey*, by Xenia Joukoff Eudin and Robert C. North. Stanford: Stanford University Press, 1957.

Starr, John Bryan. *Continuing the Revolution: The Political Thought of Mao.* Princeton: Princeton University Press, 1979.

Stewart, George. *The White Armies of Russia.* New York: Macmillan, 1933.

Sturdevant, Saundra. "Imperialism, Sovereignty, and Self-strengthening—A Reassessment of the 1870s." In *Reform in Nineteenth Century China*, ed. Paul A. Cohen and John E. Schrecker.

Su bao. May 1, 1903 to July 1, 1903.

Suemitsu Takayoshi. *Shina no himitsu kessha to jizen kessha* (Secret Societies and Philanthropic Societies in China). Tokyo: Manchu and Mongol Publishers, 1932.

Sun, E-tu (Zen). *Chinese Railways and British Interests, 1898–1911.* New York: Columbia University King's Crown Press, 1954.

Sun Kefu. "A Discussion of the Political Power of the Taiping." Paper, Taiping Conference, People's Republic of China, 1981.

Sun Kefu et al. *Yuan Shikai zunKong fubi chouju* (Yuan Shi-kai's Disgraceful Ploy to Revitalize Confucianism and Restore the Monarchy). Beijing: Zhonghua, 1975.

Sun Yat-sen. "Equalization of Land Rights" and "Further Comments on the Equalization of Land Rights." In *Zhongguo xiandai shi congkan* 3.

———. *The International Development of China.* London: 1922. Taibei: China Culture Service, 1953.

———. *Kidnapped in London: Being the Story of My Capture by, Detention at, and Release from the Chinese Legation.* London: J. W. Arrowsmith, 1897. Photographic reprint, London: China Society, 1969.

———. *Memoirs of a Chinese Revolutionary: A Programme of National Reconstruction for China.* London: Hutchinson and Co., 1919.

———. "Resolving the Question of the People's Livelihood." In *Zhongguo xiandai shi congkan* 3. Ed. Wu Xiangxiang.

Sutherland, F. *China Crises: A Missionary Study Book.* Kansas City, Mo.: Nazarene Publishing Co., 1946.

Swisher, Earl. *China's Management of the American Barbarians.* New Haven: Yale University Press, 1950.

"Symposium on Russia in Hunan." *Minkuo ribao* (People's Daily News), September 23, 1920. In *Zhong gongdang shi zangao shiliao* 1:214–225.

Symposium on the History of the Republic of China. Compilation Committee of the Symposium on the History of the Republic of China. 5 vols. 1: Revolution of 1911. 2: Early Period of the Republic. 3: Northern Expedition and Period of Political Tutelage. 4: War of Resistance Against Japan. 5: National Reconstruction Years. Taibei: China Cultural Service, 1981.

The Taiping Revolution. English edition. Beijing: Foreign Languages Press, 1976.

Tan, Chester C. *The Boxer Catastrophe.* New York: Columbia University Press, 1955.

Tan Huisheng, ed. *Minguo weiren zhuanji* (Biographies of Great Persons of the Republic). Beijing: Gaoxiong, 1976.

Tan Sheying. *Fuyun sishi nian* (Forty Years of the Women's Movement). Taibei: n.d.

Tang, Anthony M. "China's Agricultural Legacy." *Economic Development and Cultural Change* 28 (1979): 1–22.

T'ang, Leang-Li. *The Inner History of the Chinese Revolution.* London: George Routledge and Sons, 1930.

Tang Zhijin. *Wuxu bianfa jianshi* (A Brief History of the 1898 Reform Movement). Beijing: Zhonghua, 1960.

———. *Wuxu bianfa luncong* (Collected Essays on the 1898 Reform Movement). Hong Kong: Congwen, 1973.

Tao, Hsi-sheng. "The Role and Significance of the May Fourth Movement." In *Symposium on the History of the Republic of China* 2:208–251.

Tao Juyin. *Beiyang junfa tongzhi shiqi shihua* (Historical Record of the Period of Rule by the Beiyang Militarists). 6 vols. Beijing: Shenghuo, 1957.

Tao, Xingzhi. "Introducing Professor Dewey's Educational Theory." *Xin zhongguo* (New China) 1 (July 15, 1919): 271–272.

Teng, Ssu-yu. *The Taiping Rebellion and the Western Powers*. Oxford: Oxford University Press, 1971.

———. "Ts'ai Yuan-p'ei's Revolutionary Activities." In *Symposium on the History of the Republic of China* 1:304–320.

Teng, Ssu-yu, and Fairbank, John K. with Sun, E-tu Zen; Fang, Chaoying, and others. *China's Response to the West: A Documentary Survey, 1839–1923*. New York: Atheneum Press, 1965.

Tienyi bao (Natural Justice Journal). 1907–1908.

Tikhvinsky, Sergei Leonodovich. *Dvizhenie za reformy v Kitae v Kontse XIX veka Kan Iu-wei*. (The Reform Movement in China in the Late 19th Century: Kang Youwei). Moscow: Izadatelstvo vastochnoi literatury, 1959.

———. "Sun Yat-sen and Problems of Solidarity of the Peoples of Asia." In *Papers of the 26th International Congress of Orientalists*. Moscow, 1963.

———. *Sun Yat-sen: On the Occasion of the Centenary of His Birth (1866–1966)*. Moscow: Novosto Press, 1966.

Tong, Hollington K. *Chiang Kai-shek*. Taibei: China Publishing Co., 1953.

Tong, Te-kong, comp. and ed. "Dr. Hu Shih's Personal Reminiscences." Oral History Project, Columbia University, New York, 1958.

Totten, George O. *The Social Democratic Movement in Prewar Japan*. New Haven: Yale University Press, 1966.

Trevor-Roper, Hugh. *Hermit of Peking: The Hidden Life of Sir Edmund Backhouse*. New York: Alfred A. Knopf, 1977.

U.S. Congress. *House Executive Documents*. 33rd Congress, 1st Session. Washington, D.C.: U.S. Government Printing Office, 1854.

Uhalley, Stephen, Jr. "The Foreign Relations of the Taiping Revolution." Ph.D. dissertation, University of California, Berkeley, 1967.

Ullman, Richard H. *Anglo-Soviet Relations, 1917–1921*. 2 vols. Vol. 1: *Intervention and War*. Vol. 2: *Britain and the Russian Civil War*. Princeton: Princeton University Press, 1961, 1968.

Ulyanovsky, Rostislav Aleksandrovich, ed. *The Comintern and the East*. Moscow: Progress Publishers, 1979.

United States Foreign Relations. Washington, D.C.: U.S. Government Printing Office, 1915.

Unterberger, Betty M. *America's Siberian Expedition*. Durham, N.C.: Duke University Press, 1956.

Uphoff, Norman, and Ilchman, Warren, eds. *The Political Economy of Development*. Berkeley: University of California Press, 1972.

Van Der Sprenkle, Sybille. "Urban Social Control." In *The City in Late Imperial China*, ed. G. William Skinner.

Varneck, Elena, and Fisher, H., eds. *The Testimony of Kolchak and Other Siberian Materials*. Stanford: Stanford University Press, 1935.

Vilenskii, V. (Siburyakov). *Kitai i Sovetskaia Rossiaia: Iz voprosov nashii Ialnevostochnoi politiki* (China and Soviet Russia: Questions of Our Far Eastern Policy). Far East Series No. 2. Moscow: The State Publishing House, 1919.

Vladimirov, Oleg Evgenevich, and Ryazantsev, V. *Mao Tse-tung: A Political Portrait.* Moscow: Progress Publishers, 1976.

Wagner, Rudolf G. *Reenacting the Heavenly Vision: The Role of Religion in the Taiping Rebellion.* Berkeley: Institute of East Asian Studies, 1983.

Wakeman, Frederic, Jr. "The Canton Trade and the Opium War." In *Cambridge History of China,* vol. 10, ed. John K. Fairbank.

———. *The Fall of Imperial China.* New York: The Free Press, 1975.

———. *History and Will: Philosophical Perspectives of Mao Tse-Tung's Thought.* Berkeley: University of California Press, 1973.

———. *Strangers at the Gate: Social Disorder in South China, 1839–1861.* Berkeley: University of California Press, 1966.

Wakeman, Frederic, Jr., and Grant, Carolyn, eds. *Conflict and Control in Late Imperial China.* Berkeley: University of California Press, 1975.

Wang (Qiu) Canzhi. *Qiu Jin nuxia yeji* (Collected Works of Qiu Jin, the Heroine). Taibei: Zhonghua Book Co., 1958.

Wang Ermin. *Huaijun zhi* (An Analysis of the Huai Army). Taibei: Shangwu yinshuguan, 1967.

Wang Kaijun. *Xiangjun zhi* (A Treatise on the Xiang Army). Taibei: Chengwen chubanshe, 1958.

Wang Nufeng and Dang Dexin. "On the Question of the Antifeudalism of the Yihe Tuan." Paper, Jinan Conference on the Yihe Tuan, 1980.

Wang Wuwei. *Hunan zizhi yundong shi* (History of the Hunan Self-Government Movement) Part I. Shanghai, 1920.

Wang, Yeh-Chien. *Land Taxation in Imperial China, 1750–1911.* Cambridge: Harvard University Press, 1973.

Wang Yujin. *Zhong-Su waijiao di xumo* (The First Phase of Sino-Soviet Diplomacy). Taibei: Modern History Institute, Academia Sinica, 1973.

Ward, Robert E., and Rustow, Dankwart A., eds. *Political Modernization in Japan and Turkey.* Princeton: Princeton University Press, 1964.

Watanabe Haruo. *Nihon Marukusushugi undō no reimei* (The Dawn of the Japanese Marxist Movement). Tokyo: Aoki Shobo, 1957.

Watanabe Toru and Asukai Masamichi, eds. *Nihon shakaishugi undō shiron* (An Historical Analysis of Japanese Socialist Movements). Tokyo: Shanichi shobo, 1973.

Watson, Burton, tr. *Basic Writings of Mo Tzu, Hsun Tzu and Han Fei Tzu.* New York: Columbia University Press, 1967.

Watt, John R. "The Yamen and Urban Revolution." In *The City in Late Imperial China,* ed. G. William Skinner.

Weber, Max. *The Religion of China: Confucianism and Taoism.* Translated by Hans Gerth. Glencoe, Ill.: Free Press, 1951.

Wei Yingdao and Wu Yennan. *Xinhai geming shi* (A History of the 1911 Revolution). 2 vols. Beijing: Renmin chubanshe, 1980.

Welch, Claude, comp. *Political Modernization.* Belmont, Calif.: Wadsworth, 1967.

Wen Gongzhi. *Zuijin sanshi nian Zhongguo junshi shi* (A Military History of China During the Last Thirty Years). 2 vols. Shanghai: Taipingyang, 1936.

Weng Tonghe. *Weng Wenkong kong riji* (Weng Tonghe's Diaries). Shanghai: Commercial Press, 1925.
White, D. Fedotoff. *Survival Through War and Revolution in Russia.* London: Oxford University Press, 1939.
Whiting, Allen S. *Soviet Policies in China, 1917–1924.* New York: Columbia University Press, 1954.
Wilbur, C. Martin. *Sun Yat-sen: Frustrated Patriot.* New York: Columbia University Press, 1976.
Wilbur, C. Martin, and How, Julie Lien-ying, eds. *Documents on Communism, Nationalism, and Soviet Advisers in China, 1918–1927: Papers Seized in the 1927 Peking Raid.* New York: Columbia University Press, 1956.
Williams, E. T. "Report on Recent Educational Reforms in China," in *United States Foreign Relations, 1905.* Enclosure in No. 180 and in *China Year Book* (1912): 315–319.
Williams, Samuel Wells. *The Middle Kingdom.* 2 vols. London: Wiley and Putnam, 1948.
Willmot, W. E., ed. *Economic Organization in Chinese Society.* Stanford: Stanford University Press, 1972.
Wilson, Dick, ed. *Mao Tse-tung in the Scales of History.* Cambridge: Cambridge University Press, 1977.
Wilson, George M. *Radical Nationalist in Japan: Kita Ikki, 1883–1937.* Cambridge: Harvard University Press, 1969.
Windmiller, Marshall, and Overstreet, Gene D. *Communism in India.* Berkeley: University of California Press, 1959.
Witke, Roxanne. "Mao Tse-tung, Women and Suicide in the May Fourth Era." *China Quarterly* 31:128–147.
Wittfogel, Karl. *Oriental Despotism.* New Haven: Yale University Press, 1957.
Womack, Brantley. *The Foundations of Mao Zedong's Political Thought, 1917–1935.* Honolulu: University of Hawaii Press, 1982.
Wong, J. Y. *Yeh Ming-ch'en: Viceroy of Liang Kuang (1852–58).* Cambridge: Cambridge University Press, 1976.
Wong, Young-tsu. "Chang Pinglin and Republican China." In *Symposium on the History of the Republic of China* 2:149–189.
Woodcock, George. *Anarchism: A History of Libertarian Ideas and Movements.* Cleveland: World Publishing Co., 1961.
Wou, Odoric Y. K. *Militarism in Modern China: The Career of Wu P'ei-fu, 1916–1939.* Folkestone, England: Dawson, 1978.
Wrangel, Peter Nicholaievich. *The Memoirs of General Wrangel.* New York: Duffield and Co., 1930.
Wright, Arthur F., ed. *Studies in Chinese Thought.* Chicago: University of Chicago Press, 1953.
Wright, Arthur F., and Twitchett, Denis. *Confucian Personalities.* Stanford: Stanford University Press, 1962.
Wright, Mary Clabaugh. *The Last Stand of Chinese Conservatism: The T'ung Chih Restoration, 1862–1874.* Stanford: Stanford University Press, 1957.
Wu, Aitchen K. *China and the Soviet Union: A Study of Sino-Soviet Relations.* New York: John Day, 1950.
Wu Xiangxiang. "Jiang Kanghu and the Chinese Socialist Party." In *Zhongguo xiandai shi congkan* 2.
———. *Minguo bairen zhuan* (One Hundred Biographies of Men and Women of the Republic). 4 vols. Taibei: Zhuanji wenxue, 1971.

———. "A Preliminary Study of the Relationship Between Chen Jiongming and the Narkomindel and the Chinese Communist Party." In *Zhongguo xiandai shi congkan* (Collected Works on the Modern History of China), vol. 2.
———. *Sun Yixian xiansheng zhuan* (Biography of Mr. Sun Yixian [Sun Yatsen]). 2 vols. Taibei: Yuandong, 1982.
Wu Yannan. "The Yihe Tuan Movement and the Awakening of the Chinese People." Paper, Jinan Conference on the Yihe Tuan, 1980.
Wu Yizhou. *Jiang zongtong di yisheng* (President Chiang's Lifetime). Taibei: Zhongzheng chubanshe, 1975.
Wu Zhihui xiansheng quanji (Complete Works of Mr. Wu Zhihui). 18 vols. Edited by Luo Jialun and Huang Jilu, Guomindang Committee to Compile the Party History. Taibei: Zhongyang wenwu, 1969.
Wuchang shouyi (Wuchang, the First Revolutionary Uprising). 2 vols. Taibei: Editorial Committee, Documents on the 50th Anniversary of the Founding of the Republic of China, 1961.
Wusi aiguo yundong (The May Fourth Patriotic Movement). 2 vols. Beijing: The Chinese Social Sciences Publishing House, 1979.
Wusi yundong huiyi lu (Memoirs of the May Fourth Movement). Beijing: Zhonghua, 1959.
Wuxu bianfa (The Reform Movement of 1898). Compiled by the Chinese Historical Association. 4 vols. Shanghai: Shenzhou guoquanshe, 1953.
Xia Liangzai. "A Preliminary Discussion of the Chinese Socialist Party During the Early Republic Years." In *Lishi jiaoxue* (History Teaching) 4 (April 1980): 39–43.
Xiang Da et al., comp. *Zhongguo jindaishi ziliao congkan* (Documentary Collection on Modern Chinese History). Part 2: *Taiping tianguo* (The Taiping). Shanghai: Shenzhou guo chuban, 1952.
———. *Zhongguo jindai lishi yanjiu gangyao* (An Outline of a Study of Modern Chinese History). Shanghai: Shangwu, 1946.
Xiang Qing. "The Comintern and the Chinese Revolution During the Period of the Founding of the Chinese Communist Party." *Jindai shi yanjiu* (Research on Modern History) 4 (1980): 92–116.
Xiang Jiang pinglun (Shian Kian Weekly Review). 1919.
Xiangjun xinzhi (A New Treatise on the Hunan Army). Taibei: Yangmingshan Zhuang, 1951. Reprint of Changsha edition, 1955.
Xiao Dehou. "On the Decision of the Taiping Army to Stay in Yanan." Paper, Taiping Conference, People's Republic of China, 1981.
Xiao Gongchuan et al. *Shehuizhuyi* (Socialism). Taibei: Shibao, 1980.
Xiao San et al. *Qingnian yundong huixi bu* (Recollections of the Youth Movement). Vol. 2. Beijing: Zhongguo qingnian, 1979.
Xie Bin. *Minguo zhengdang shi* (A History of Political Parties of the Chinese Republic). Shanghai: Xuezhu yanjiu hui, 1928.
Xie Xingyao. *Taiping tianguo di shehui zhengzhi sixiang* (The Social and Political Thought of the Taiping). Shanghai: Shangwu yinshuguan, 1935.
Xin Jiang Pinglun editorial department. *Mao Zedong tongzhi qingshaonian shidai* (The Period of Comrade Mao Zedong's Youth). Beijing: Zhongguo qingnian chubanshe, 1979.
Xin qingnian (New Youth). September 15, 1915, to May 1, 1920.
Xin shiji (The New Century). Reprinted. 4 vols. Shanghai, 1947.
Xinhai geming yantaohui lunwenji (Collected Papers of the Conference to Discuss the 1911 Revolution). Taibei: Academia Sinica, 1983.

Xinmin congbao (The New People's Journal). February 8, 1902, to November 20, 1907.

Xu Daolin. *Zhongguo fazhi shilunlue* (An Outline History of China's Legal Institutions). Taibei: Zhengzhong, 1953.

Xu Wenqiang. "Dewey's Conception of Education." *Xin xuebao* (New Learning) 1 (January 1920): 9–17.

Xu Youpeng. *Yuan dazongtong shudu huibian* (Collected Writings and Documents of President Yuan). 1914. Reprint. Taibei: Wenxing, 1962.

Xuantong zhengji (Political Events of the Xuantong Era), 16 vols., Shenyang liaohai shushe, 1934.

Yan Gengwang. *Zhongguo difang xingzheng zhidushi juan shang: Qin-Han difang xingzheng zhidu* (A History of Regional and Local Administration in China, Part One: The Qin and Han Periods). 2 vols. Taibei: Academia Sinica, The Institute of History and Philology, 1961.

Yang, C. K. *A North China Local Market Economy*. New York: Institute of Pacific Relations, 1944.

———. "Some Preliminary Statistical Patterns of Mass Actions in Nineteenth-Century China." In *Conflict and Control in Late Imperial China*, ed. Frederic Wakeman, Jr., and Carolyn Grant.

Yang, Martin. *A Chinese Village: T'ai-tou, Shantung Province*. New York: Columbia University Press, 1945.

Yang Youzhun. *Jindai Zhongguo lifa shi* (A Legislative History of Modern China). 1935. Reprint. Taibei: Taiwan Commercial Press, 1966.

———. *Zhongguo zhengdang shi* (A History of Chinese Political Parties). 2d ed. Shanghai: Shangwu, n.d.

Ye Fengmei. "An Historical Analysis of the Yihe Tuan Movement." Paper, Jinan Conference on the Yihe Tuan, 1980.

Yi Ho Tuan Movement of 1900. Peking: Foreign Language Press, 1976.

Yihe Tuan dangan shiliao (Documentary Files on the Yihe Tuan [Boxers]). 2 vols. Beijing: Zhonghua, 1959.

Young, Ernest P. *The Presidency of Yuan Shih-k'ai: Liberalism and Dictatorship in Early Republican China*. Ann Arbor: University of Michigan Press, 1977.

Yu, George T. *Party Politics in Republican China: The Kuomintang, 1912–1924*. Berkeley: University of California Press, 1966.

Yuan Segao. "The Taiping Revolutionary Movement and Hong's Philosophy." Paper, Taiping Conference, People's Republic of China, 1981.

Zeng Guofan. *Zeng Wenzheng gong (Guofan) quanji* (Complete Papers of Zeng Guofan). Amplified version, 1876 et seq. 40 vols. Reproduction. Taibei: Wenhai, 1974.

Zeng Wenzheng gong shoushi riji (Zeng Guofan's Diary). 6 vols. Taibei: Xuesheng shuju, 1965.

Zhang Guogan, ed. *Xinhai geming shiliao* (Historical Sources on the Xinhai Revolution). 2 vols. Shanghai: Longmen lianhei sheju, 1958.

Zhang Ji. *Zhang Puquan xiansheng quanji* (The Collected Works of Mr. Zhang Puquan). Taibei: Zhongyang wenhua, 1951.

Zhang Jinjian. *Zhongguo wenguan zhidushi* (A History of China's Civil Service). Taibei: Zhonghua wenhua chuban shiye weiyuan hui, 1955.

Zhang Junmai. *Mingri zhi Zhongguo wenhua* (The Chinese Culture of Tomorrow). Shanghai: Commercial Press, 1936.

Zhang Kaiyuan and Lin Zhangbing, eds. *Xinhai geming shi* (A History of the 1911 Revolution). 3 vols. Beijing: Renmin chubanshe, 1981.

Zhang Lianji. "A Great Peasant Revolution: On the Properties of the Taiping." Paper, Taiping Conference, People's Republic of China, 1981.
Zhang Nan and Wang Renzhi, eds. *Xinhai geming qianshinian jian shilun xuanji* (Selected Essays During the Decade Prior to the Xinhai Revolution). 4 vols. Beijing: Shenghuo, 1960–1962.
Zhang Pengyuan. *Liang Qichao yu minguo zhengzhi* (Liang Qichao and National Politics). Taibei: Shihuo sheban, 1978.
———. *Liang Qichao yu Qingji geming* (Liang Qichao and the Late Qing Revolution). Nankang, Taiwan: Modern History Institute, Academia Sinica, 1964.
———. *Lixianpai yu Xinhai geming* (The Constitutionalist Faction and the 1911 Revolution). Taibei: Institute of Modern History, Academia Sinica, 1969.
———. *Zhongguo xiandaihua di quyu yanjiu: Hunan sheng 1860–1911* (Modernization in China: A Regional Study of Social and Economic Change in Hunan Province, 1860–1911). Taibei: Academia Sinica, 1983.
Zhang Pufan and Zeng Xianyi. *Zhongguo xianfa shilue* (A General History of Constitutionalism in China). Beijing: Beijing chubanshe, 1979.
Zhang Wenbo. *Zhilao xianhua* (Chit-chat about Old Zhi). Taibei: Zhongyang wenwu, 1952.
Zhang Ximan. *Lishi huiyi* (Historical Reflections). Shanghai, 1949.
Zhang Xingyan. *Su bao anji shi* (An Account of the *Su bao* Case). Taibei: Zhongguo Guomindang, Party History Commission, 1968.
Zhang, Yin. "On Taiping Policy Regarding Intellectuals." Paper, Taiping Conference, People's Republic of China, 1981.
Zhang Yiwen. "Problems of Strategy Concerning the Battles of the Late Taiping Period," *Zhongguo shehuikexue* (Chinese Social Science) 3 (1981): 149–164.
Zhang Yufa. "The Restoration Society and the Revolution of 1911." Paper, Taibei Conference on the 1911 Revolution, 1981.
———. *Zhongguo xiandaihua di quyu yanjiu: Shandong sheng 1860–1916* (Modernization in China: A Regional Study of Social and Economic Change in Shandong Province, 1860–1916). Taibei: Academia Sinica, 1982.
Zhang Yufa and Li Youning, eds. *Zhongguo funu shi lunwenji* (Collection of Discussions on Chinese Women). Taibei: Shangwu, 1981.
Zhang Yunhou et al. *LiuFa qingong jianxue yundong* (The French Diligent Work and Frugal Study Movement). Vol. 1. Shanghai: Renmin, 1980.
Zhang Zhonghe. "Fubi xiangzhi" (Detailed Record of the Restoration of the Monarchy). In *Jindai Zhongguo shiliao congkan* (Library of Historical Materials on Modern China), edited by Shen Yunlong. Vol. 90. Taibei: Wenhai, n.d.
Zhao Qiming. "Jiangning xian-Shunhua-zhen xiancun shehuigu zhi yenjiu" (A Study of the Rural Community of Shunhua Township, Jiangning xian). In *Jinling daxue, nongling congkan* (Agriculture-Forestry Series, Jinling University), no. 31. Nanking: May 1926.
Zhao Shiyuan. "The Second Revolution and the Revolution of 1911." Paper, Wuhan Conference on the Xinhai Revolution, 1981.
Zhen Daji. *Kongzi xueshui* (Confucian Theory). Taibei: Zhengzhong, 1964.
Zhen Huaxin. "On the Development of Hong's Anti-Qing Revolutionary Thought." Paper, Taiping Conference, People's Republic of China, 1981.
Zhen Jianfu. *Kongzi xueshui xinlun* (New Discussions of Confucian Theory). Taibei: Wenyuan, 1967.

Zhen Renzhun. "How Did Taiping Political Power Treat the Intellectuals?" Paper, Taiping Conference, People's Republic of China, 1981.

Zhen Renwei and Fang Xiao. "On the Nature of Taiping Political Power." Paper, Taiping Conference, People's Republic of China, 1981.

Zhen Sanjing, ed. *Qingong jianxue yundong* (The Diligent Work and Frugal Study Movement). Taibei: Zhengzhong, 1981.

Zheng Zonghai. "The Educational Principles of Mr. Dewey." *Xin jiaoyu* (New Education) 1 (March 1919): 129–139.

Zhong Guanyi. *Wo zai xiaweiyi de qishijiu nian* (My Seventy-Nine Years in Hawaii). Hong Kong: 1960.

Zhong Renwei and Fang Xiao. "On the Nature of Taiping Political Power." Paper, Taiping Conference, People's Republic of China, 1981.

Zhong Wendian. *Taipingjun zai Yongan* (The Taiping Army at Yongan). Beijing: Shanlian shudian, 1962.

Zhonggongdang shi cankao ziliao (References for the History of the Chinese Communist Party). 4 vols. Beijing: Renmin chubanshe, 1979.

Zhongguo fengjian shehui nongmin zhanzheng wenti taolun ji (Collected Essays on Peasant War Questions in Chinese Feudal Society). Beijing: Shenhuo, 1962.

Zhongguo Guomindang Historical Commission. *Geming wenxian.* 67 vols., Taibei, 1953–.

Zhongguo jindai lishi yanjiu sangyao (An Outline of A Study of Modern Chinese History). Shanghai: Shangwu, 1946.

Zhongguo xinnujie zazhi (Journal of the New Women of China). Tokyo: 1906–1907. Reprint. Taibei: Shiwen, 1977.

Zhongguo xiandai shi congkan (Collected Works on Contemporary Chinese History). Edited by Wu Xiangxiang. 3 vols. Taibei: Zhengzhong, 1960.

Zhongguo zhexueshi wenji (Collected Essays on the History of Chinese Philosophy). Chilin: Renmin, 1979.

Zhongshan daxue xuebao (Journal of Sun Yat-sen University, Social Science Edition). No. 4, 1979.

Zhong-Su guanxi shiliao (Historical Materials on Sino-Soviet Relations). Taibei: Modern History Institute, Academia Sinica, 1968.

Zhou Enlai. "A Major Incident Among the Diligent Work-Frugal Study Students in France." First published in the Tianjin *Yishi bao,* May 15–19, 1921. Reproduced in *FuFa qingong jianxue yundong shiliao* 1:3–36.

Zhu Zheng. *Zhu Zhuosheng xiansheng quanji* (The Collected Works of Mr. Zhu Zhuosheng). 2 vols. Taibei: n.d.

Zhu Zhixin. "Hong and the Emperor God." Paper, Taiping Conference, People's Republic of China, 1981.

Zhu Zongzhen. "When Did the Revolution of 1911 Come to an End?" In *Jindai shi yanjiu* (Research on Contemporary History). Beijing: Xinhua, 1979.

Zou Lu. *Zhongguo Guomindang shigao* (Draft History of the Guomindang). 2 vols. Chongqing: Shangwu, 1944.

Zou Rong. *Geming jun* (The Revolutionary Army). Reprint. Shanghai: Zhonghua, 1958.

Zuishi Hu Shizhi xiansheng zhuanji (Memorial Essays in Honor of Mr. Hu Shizhi). Tainan: Changuang chubanshe, 1962.

INDEX

Designer: Randall Goodall
Compositor: G&S Typesetters, Inc.
Text: 11/12 Electra
Display: Benguiat
Printer: Malloy Lithographing, Inc.
Binder: John H. Dekker & Sons